David R. Anderson • Dennis J. Sweeney
Thomas A. Williams • Mik Wisniewski

AN INTRODUCTION TO MANAGEMENT SCIENCE

QUANTITATIVE APPROACHES TO DECISION MAKING

second edition

CENGAGE Learning

Australia • Brazil • Japan • Korea • Mexico • Singapore • Spain • United Kingdom • United States

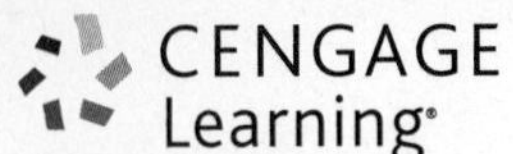

An Introduction to Management Science: Quantitative Approaches to Decision Making, 2nd Edition

Anderson, Sweeney, Williams and Wisniewski

Publisher: Andrew Ashwin

Development Editor: Felix Rowe

Senior Production Editor: Alison Burt

Editorial Assistant: Jenny Grene

Senior Manufacturing Buyer: Eyvett Davis

Typesetter: Integra Software Services PVT. LTD

Cover design: Adam Renvoize

Text design: Design Deluxe

For product information and technology assistance,
contact **emea.info@cengage.com.**

For permission to use material from this text or product,
and for permission queries,
email **emea.permissions@cengage.com.**

British Library Cataloguing-in-Publication Data
A catalogue record for this book is available from the British Library.

ISBN: 978-1-4080-8840-1

Cengage Learning EMEA
Cheriton House, North Way, Andover, Hampshire, SP10 5BE
United Kingdom

Cengage Learning products are represented in Canada by
Nelson
Education Ltd.

For your lifelong learning solutions, visit **www.cengage.co.uk**

Purchase your next print book, e-book or e-chapter at
www.cengagebrain.com

Printed by Croatia By Zrinsky d.d.
1 2 3 4 5 6 7 8 9 10 – 16 15 14

Brief contents

Contents

11 Queuing Models 451

12 Simulation 489

ONLINE CHAPTERS

About the authors

David R. Anderson

David R. Anderson is Professor of Quantitative Analysis in the College of Business Administration at the University of Cincinnati. Born in Grand Forks, North Dakota, he earned his B.S., M.S., and Ph.D. degrees from Purdue University. Professor Anderson has served as Head of the Department of Quantitative Analysis and Operations Management and as Associate Dean of the College of Business Administration.

Professor Anderson has co-authored many textbooks in the areas of statistics, management science, linear programming and production and operations management. He is an active consultant in the field of sampling and statistical methods.

Dennis J. Sweeney

Dennis J. Sweeney is Professor of Quantitative Analysis and Founder of the Center for Productivity Improvement at the University of Cincinnati. Born in Des Moines, lowa, he earned a B.S.B.A. degree from Drake University and his MBA and DBA degrees from Indiana University, where he was an NDEA Fellow.

Professor Sweeney has published more than thirty articles and monographs in the area of management science and statistics. The National Science Foundation, IBM, Procter & Gamble, Federated Department Stores, Kroger and Cincinnati Gas & Electric have funded his research, which has been published in *Management Science, Operations Research, Mathematical Programming, Decision Sciences* and other journals.

Professor Sweeney has co-authored many textbooks in the areas of statistics, management science, linear programming and production and operations management.

Thomas A. Williams

Thomas A. Williams is Professor of Management Science in the College of Business at Rochester Institute of Technology. Born in Elmira, New York, he earned his B.S. degree at Clarkson University. He did his graduate work at Rensselaer Polytechnic Institute, where he received his M.S. and Ph.D. degrees.

Professor Williams is the co-author of many textbooks in the areas of management science, statistics, production and operations management and mathematics. He has been a consultant for numerous *Fortune* 500 companies and has worked on projects ranging from the use of data analysis to the development of large-scale regression models.

Mik Wisniewski

Mik has over 40 years' management science experience. His teaching at undergraduate and postgraduate levels focuses on the practical application to management decision making. He has taught at many different universities and colleges in the UK, across Europe, African and the Middle East. He has extensive consultancy experience with clients including Shell, KPMG, PriceWaterhouseCoopers,

Scottish & Newcastle, British Energy and ScottishPower. He has worked with a large number of government agencies in the UK and globally including health, housing, police, local and central government and utilities. He has degrees from Loughborough University and Birmingham University in the UK and is also an Elected Fellow of the Operational Research Society and an Elected Fellow of the Royal Statistical Society. He is the author of over a dozen academic texts on management science, business and analysis and optimization.

Preface

Welcome to the second Europe, Middle East and Africa Edition of *An Introduction to Management Science* by Anderson, Sweeney, Williams and Wisniewski.

The first edition of this text was based on the best-selling US version and deliberately set out to adapt and tailor the US version for a non-US university audience. The content was adapted to better suit university teaching of quantitative management science in the UK, across Europe, Africa and the Middle East; the focus was given a more global and international feel and cases and examples were internationalized.

The first edition has been extremely successful in its target markets and this edition has further tailored and adapted the content to give broad international appeal.

A quick tour of the text

An Introduction to Management Science continues to be very much applications oriented and to use the problem-scenario approach that has proved to be very popular and successful. This approach means that we describe a typical business scenario or problem faced by many organizations and managers. This might relate to allocating staff to tasks or projects; determining production over the next planning period; deciding on the best use of a limited budget; forecasting sales over the coming time period and so on. We explore and explain how particular management science techniques and models can be used to help managers and decision makers decide what to do in that particular scenario or situation. This approach means that students not only develop a good technical understanding of a particular technique or model but also understand how it contributes to the decision-making process.

In this new edition we have taken advantage of the Internet and world-wide web to make some chapters available online. The chapters that remain in the textbook itself cover the topics most commonly-covered on undergraduate and postgraduate management science programmes. Chapters available online cover topics which, although useful and important, are less frequently included.

Chapter 1 provides an overall introduction to the text; the origins and developments in management science are outlined; there are detailed examples of areas in business and management where management science is frequently applied; there is a detailed discussion of the wider management science methodology and a section on the modelling process itself.

Chapters 2–6 cover the core topic of *Linear Programming (LP)*. The technique is introduced and graphical solution methods developed. This is followed by the development of sensitivity analysis. The Simplex method is then introduced for large scale problem solution and full coverage of simplex based sensitivity is covered. There is a full chapter on applications of LP grouped around five main areas of business application.

Chapter 7 extends the coverage of optimization to look at techniques related to *transshipment, assignment and transportation* problems. Solution methods for each class of problem are given. Chapter 8 introduces the *network* model and examines the *shortest route* problem, the *minimal spanning tree* problem and the *maximal flow* problem. Chapter 9 introduces *project scheduling* and *project management* problems. There is full coverage of PERT/CPM and a short section explaining the use of Gantt charts in project management and expands the section on crashing a project. There is also an appendix discussing activity on arrow networks in some detail.

Chapters 10 and 11 look at two common types of business model. Chapter 10 looks at *inventory* (or stock control) models whilst Chapter 11 looks at *queuing* models. The relevance of both types of model to business decision making is examined and solution techniques developed. Chapter 12 introduces *simulation* modelling and shows how such models can be used alongside the other models developed in the text.

Chapters 13 and 14 look at the area of decision analysis and decision making. Chapter 13 looks at the principles of *decision analysis* and introduces decision trees, expected value and utility. Chapter 14 looks at the topic of *multicriteria decision making* with coverage of goal programming, scoring models and the analytic hierarchy process (AHP) approach.

The textbook closes with discussion of management science in practice, considering some of the practical issues faced when implementing management science techniques for real.

In addition there are four slightly more specialized chapters available on the accompanying online platform. These take exactly the same format and structure as chapters included in the text.

Chapter 15 introduces *integral linear programming* both as an extension to linear programming and as a model in its own right. The chapter looks at the branch and bound solution method in detail. Chapter 16 looks at business *forecasting* techniques and models. Time series models are introduced as well as trend projection models and there is coverage of regression modelling also. Chapter 17 looks at the topic of *dynamic programming* with coverage of the shortest route problem and the knapsack problem. Finally, Chapter 18 introduces *Markov models* which can be useful where we wish to examine behaviour or performance over successive periods of time.

The online platform contains an array of additional resources to aid learning. See the 'Digital Resources' page for further details.

Acknowledgements

The publishers and author team would like to thank the following academics for their helpful advice in contributing to the development research underpinning both the first and second Europe, Middle East and Africa Editions of *An Introduction to Management Science* and reviewing draft chapter material:

Husain A. Al-Omani	GTSC (Saudi Arabia)
Phil Ansell	Newcastle University (UK)
Julia Bennell	University of Southampton (UK)
James M. Freeman	University of Manchester (UK)
Paul Hudson	Queen's University Belfast (UK)
Yuan Ju	University of York (UK)
Cesarettin Koc	Dubai Women's College (Dubai)
Petroula Mavrikiou	Frederick University (Cyprus)
Gilberto Montibeller	London School of Economics (UK)
Max Moullin	Sheffield Hallam University (UK)
David Newlands	IESEG School of Management (France)
Mustafa Ozbayrak	Brunel University (UK)
Peter Stoney	Liverpool University Management School (UK)

Key Features of the Text

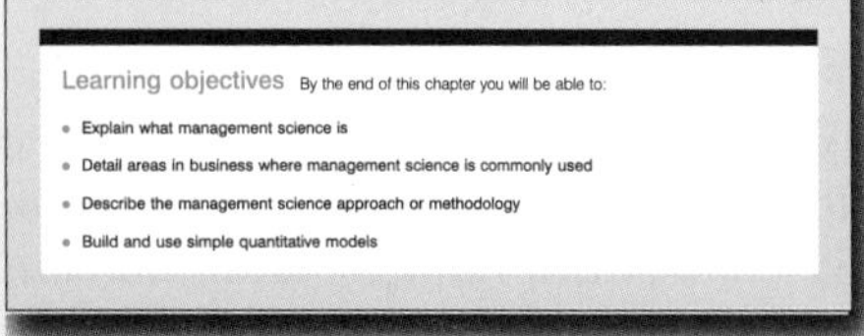

Learning objectives By the end of this chapter you will be able to:

- Explain what management science is
- Detail areas in business where management science is commonly used
- Describe the management science approach or methodology
- Build and use simple quantitative models

Learning objectives are set out at the start of each chapter and summarize what the reader should have learned on completion of that chapter. They also serve to highlight what the chapter covers and help the reader review and check knowledge and understanding.

MANAGEMENT SCIENCE IN ACTION

Scoring Model at Ford Motor Company

Ford Motor Company needed benchmark data in order to set performance targets for future and current model automobiles. A detailed proposal was developed and sent to five suppliers. Three suppliers were considered acceptable for the project.

Because the three suppliers had different capabilities in terms of teardown analysis and testing, Ford developed three project alternatives:

Alternative 1: Supplier C does the entire project alone.

Alternative 2: Supplier A does the testing portion of the project and works with Supplier B to complete the remaining parts of the project.

Alternative 3: Supplier A does the testing portion of the project and works with Supplier C to complete the remaining parts of the project.

For routine projects, selecting the lowest cost alternative might be appropriate. However, because this project involved many nonroutine tasks, Ford incorporated four criteria into the decision process.

The four criteria selected by Ford are as follows: nication; and past Ford experience. In total, 17 subcriteria were considered. A team-consensus weighting process was used to develop percentage weights for the subcriteria. The weights assigned to the skill-level subcriteria were 40 per cent for project manager leadership; 20 per cent for team structure organization; 20 per cent for team players' communication; and 20 per cent for past Ford experience.

Team members visited all the suppliers and individually rated them for each subcriterion using a 1–10 scale (1-worst, 10-best). Then, in a team meeting, consensus ratings were developed. For Alternative 1, the consensus ratings developed for the skill-level subcriteria were 8 for project manager leadership; 8 for team structure organization; 7 for team players' communication; and 8 for past Ford experience. Because the weights assigned to the skill-level subcriteria are 40 per cent, 20 per cent, 20 per cent, and 20 per cent, the rating for Alternative 1 corresponding to the skill-level criterion is

$$\text{Rating} = .4(8) + .2(8) + .2(7) + .2(8) = 7.8$$

Management Science in Action case studies show actual applications of the techniques and models covered in each chapter.

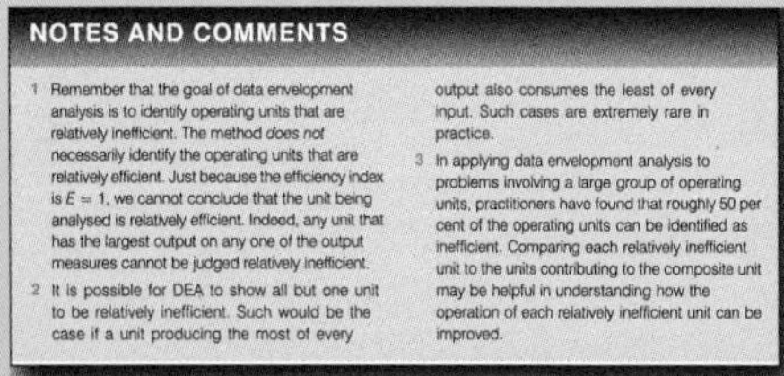

Summary

This chapter has introduced a model commonly used in management science, that of linear programming (LP). LP models are used in many different situations, for many different types of problem and across many different types of business organization.

- LP is an optimization model, where we seek to determine an optimal solution to some problem subject to a number of constraints.
- LP problems can be formulated with an objective function which could be for maximization or for minimization. Constraints in an LP problem place some restriction on what we are able to do in our search for an optimal solution and LP constraints can take one of three forms: $\leq$, $\geq$, or $=$.
- Both the objective function and all constraints must take a linear form mathematically.
- The simplest form of an LP problem involves two decision variables and can be solved graphically.
- At the optimal solution some constraints will be binding and some non-binding. A binding constraint is exactly satisfied at the optimal solution. A non-binding constraint will have slack, or surplus, associated with it.

Summaries are given at the end of each chapter to recap on key points.

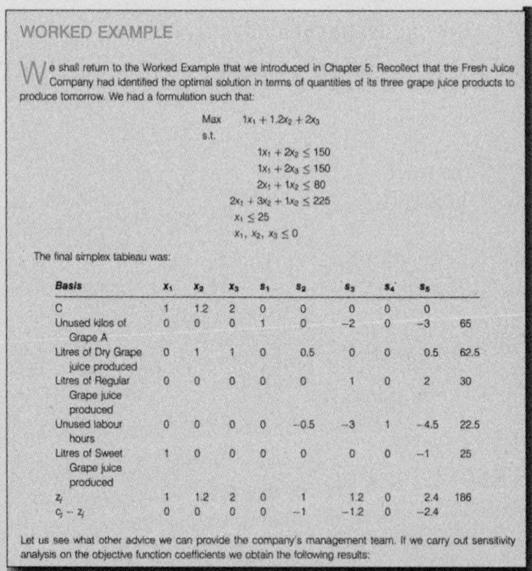

WORKED EXAMPLE

We shall return to the Worked Example that we introduced in Chapter 5. Recollect that the Fresh Juice Company had identified the optimal solution in terms of quantities of its three grape juice products to produce tomorrow. We had a formulation such that:

$$
\begin{aligned}
\text{Max} \quad & 1x_1 + 1.2x_2 + 2x_3 \\
\text{s.t.} \quad & \\
& 1x_1 + 2x_2 \leq 150 \\
& 1x_1 + 2x_3 \leq 150 \\
& 2x_1 + 1x_2 \leq 80 \\
& 2x_1 + 3x_2 + 1x_2 \leq 225 \\
& x_1 \leq 25 \\
& x_1, x_2, x_3 \leq 0
\end{aligned}
$$

The final simplex tableau was:

Basis	x_1	x_2	x_3	s_1	s_2	s_3	s_4	s_5	
C	1	1.2	2	0	0	0	0	0	
Unused kilos of Grape A	0	0	0	1	0	−2	0	−3	65
Litres of Dry Grape juice produced	0	1	1	0	0.5	0	0	0.5	62.5
Litres of Regular Grape juice produced	0	0	0	0	0	1	0	2	30
Unused labour hours	0	0	0	0	−0.5	−3	1	−4.5	22.5
Litres of Sweet Grape juice produced	1	0	0	0	0	0	0	−1	25
z_j	1	1.2	2	0	1	1.2	0	2.4	186
$c_j - z_j$	0	0	0	0	−1	−1.2	0	−2.4	

Let us see what other advice we can provide the company's management team. If we carry out sensitivity analysis on the objective function coefficients we obtain the following results:

NOTES AND COMMENTS

1 Remember that the goal of data envelopment analysis is to identify operating units that are relatively inefficient. The method *does not* necessarily identify the operating units that are relatively efficient. Just because the efficiency index is $E = 1$, we cannot conclude that the unit being analysed is relatively efficient. Indeed, any unit that has the largest output on any one of the output measures cannot be judged relatively inefficient.

2 It is possible for DEA to show all but one unit to be relatively inefficient. Such would be the case if a unit producing the most of every output also consumes the least of every input. Such cases are extremely rare in practice.

3 In applying data envelopment analysis to problems involving a large group of operating units, practitioners have found that roughly 50 per cent of the operating units can be identified as inefficient. Comparing each relatively inefficient unit to the units contributing to the composite unit may be helpful in understanding how the operation of each relatively inefficient unit can be improved.

Worked Examples are shown at the end of each chapter walking you through a detailed problem step-by-step, showing how a solution to the problem can be obtained using the techniques and models in that chapter.

Notes and Comments provide extra context and explanatory notes to help the reader's understanding.

Problems

1 The RMC Corporation blends three raw materials to produce two products: a fuel additive and a solvent base. Each ton of fuel additive is a mixture of 0.4 ton of material 1 and 0.6 ton of material 3. A ton of solvent base is a mixture of 0.5 ton of material 1, 0.2 ton of material 2, and 0.3 ton of material 3. RMC's production is constrained by a limited availability of the three raw materials. For the current production period, RMC has the following quantities of each raw material: material 1, 20 tons; material 2, 5 tons; material 3, 21 tons. Management wants to achieve the following P_1 priority level goals.

Problems given at the end of each chapter provide an opportunity to test your knowledge and understanding of that chapter. Some problems test you ability to develop and solve a particular model. Others are more complex requiring you to interpret and explain results in a business context.

Appendix 1.2 The Management Scientist Software

Developments in computer technology play a major role in making management science techniques available to decision makers. A software package called *The Management Scientist* Version 6.0 is available for Windows 95 through to Windows XP operating systems.[1] This software can be used to solve problems in the text as well as small-scale problems encountered in practice. Using The Management Scientist will provide an understanding and appreciation of the role of the computer in applying management science to decision problems.

The Management Scientist contains 12 modules, or programs, that will enable you to solve problems in the following areas:

Chapters 2–6	Linear programming
Chapter 7	Transportation and assignment
Chapter 8	Integer linear programming
Chapter 9	Shortest route and minimal spanning tree
Chapter 10	PERT/CPM

The **Management Scientist Software** Version 6.0 accompanies this text. The software allows you to formulate and solve many of the models introduced in the text.

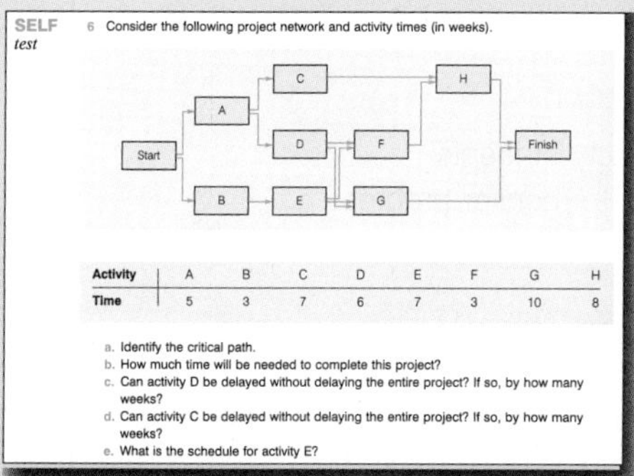

SELF *test* 6 Consider the following project network and activity times (in weeks).

Activity	A	B	C	D	E	F	G	H
Time	5	3	7	6	7	3	10	8

a. Identify the critical path.
b. How much time will be needed to complete this project?
c. Can activity D be delayed without delaying the entire project? If so, by how many weeks?
d. Can activity C be delayed without delaying the entire project? If so, by how many weeks?
e. What is the schedule for activity E?

Self test problems are linked to specific parts of each chapter and allow you to check your knowledge and understanding of that chapter on an incremental basis. Problems marked with the self test icon are located in Appendix D at the back of the book.

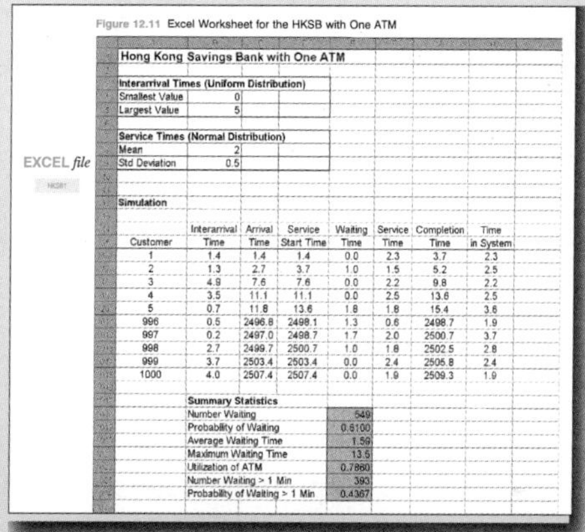

Figure 12.11 Excel Worksheet for the HKSB with One ATM

EXCEL *file* HKSB1

Hong Kong Savings Bank with One ATM

Interarrival Times (Uniform Distribution)	
Smallest Value	0
Largest Value	5

Service Times (Normal Distribution)	
Mean	2
Std Deviation	0.5

Simulation

Customer	Interarrival Time	Arrival Time	Service Start Time	Waiting Time	Service Time	Completion Time	Time in System
1	1.4	1.4	1.4	0.0	2.3	3.7	2.3
2	1.3	2.7	3.7	1.0	1.5	5.2	2.5
3	4.9	7.6	7.6	0.0	2.2	9.8	2.2
4	3.5	11.1	11.1	0.0	2.5	13.6	2.5
5	0.7	11.8	13.6	1.8	1.8	15.4	3.6
996	0.5	2496.8	2498.1	1.3	0.6	2498.7	1.9
997	0.2	2497.0	2498.7	1.7	2.0	2500.7	3.7
998	2.7	2499.7	2500.7	1.0	1.8	2502.5	2.8
999	3.7	2503.4	2503.4	0.0	2.4	2505.8	2.4
1000	4.0	2507.4	2507.4	0.0	1.9	2509.3	1.9

Summary Statistics	
Number Waiting	549
Probability of Waiting	0.6100
Average Waiting Time	1.59
Maximum Waiting Time	13.5
Utilization of ATM	0.7860
Number Waiting > 1 Min	393
Probability of Waiting > 1 Min	0.4367

Excel, and other spreadsheets, have a key role to play in management science. Output from Excel is used frequently throughout the text to illustrate solutions. Appendices to chapters provide a step-by-step explanation of how to solve particular models using Excel.

CASE PROBLEM R.C. Coleman

R.C. Coleman distributes a variety of food products that are sold through grocery store and supermarket outlets. The company receives orders directly from the individual outlets, with a typical order requesting the delivery of several cases of anywhere from 20 to 50 different products. Under the company's current warehouse operation, warehouse clerks dispatch order-picking personnel to fill each order and have the goods moved to the warehouse shipping area. Because of the high labour costs and relatively low productivity of hand order-picking, management has decided to automate the warehouse operation by installing a computer-controlled order-picking system, along with a conveyor system for moving goods from storage to the warehouse shipping area.

R.C. Coleman's director of material management has been named the project manager in charge of the automated warehouse system. After consulting with members of the engineering staff and warehouse management personnel, the director compiled a list of activities associated with the project. The optimistic, most probable and pessimistic times (in weeks) have also been provided for each activity.

Case Problems are given at the end of most chapters. These are more complex problems relating to the techniques and models introduced in that chapter. A management report is typically required to be written. The Case Problems are well suited for group work.

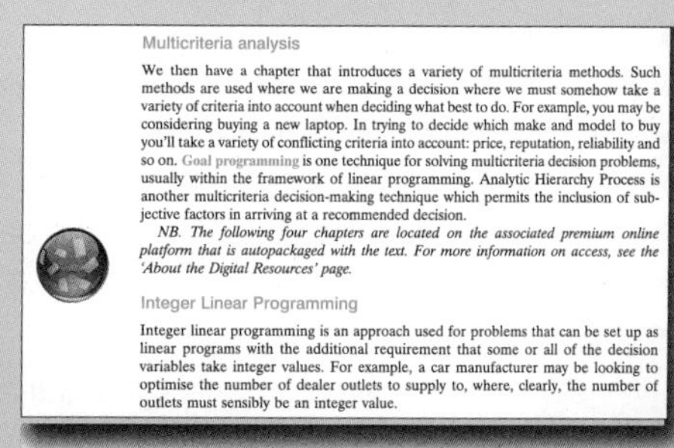

Multicriteria analysis

We then have a chapter that introduces a variety of multicriteria methods. Such methods are used where we are making a decision where we must somehow take a variety of criteria into account when deciding what best to do. For example, you may be considering buying a new laptop. In trying to decide which make and model to buy you'll take a variety of conflicting criteria into account: price, reputation, reliability and so on. Goal programming is one technique for solving multicriteria decision problems, usually within the framework of linear programming. Analytic Hierarchy Process is another multicriteria decision-making technique which permits the inclusion of subjective factors in arriving at a recommended decision.

NB. The following four chapters are located on the associated premium online platform that is autopackaged with the text. For more information on access, see the 'About the Digital Resources' page.

Integer Linear Programming

Integer linear programming is an approach used for problems that can be set up as linear programs with the additional requirement that some or all of the decision variables take integer values. For example, a car manufacturer may be looking to optimise the number of dealer outlets to supply to, where, clearly, the number of outlets must sensibly be an integer value.

Online Supplements This edition comes with an array of additional online materials. See the 'Digital Resources' page for more details and information on how to access them.

DIGITAL RESOURCES

Dedicated Instructor Resources

To discover the dedicated instructor online support resources accompanying this textbook, instructors should register here for access: **http://login.cengage.com**

Resources include:

- Solutions Manual
- Testbank
- PowerPoint slides

Instructor access

Instructors can access the online student platform by registering at **http://login.cengage.com** or by speaking to their local Cengage Learning EMEA representative.

Instructor resources

Instructors can use the integrated Engagement Tracker to track students' preparation and engagement. The tracking tool can be used to monitor progress of the class as a whole, or for individual students.

Student access

Log In & Learn In 4 Easy Steps

1. To register a product using the access code printed on the inside front-cover of the book please go to: **http://login.cengagebrain.com**
2. Register as a new user or log in as an existing user if you already have an account with Cengage Learning or CengageBrain.com
3. Follow the online prompts
4. If your instructor has provided you with a course key, you will be prompted to enter this after opening your digital purchase from your CengageBrain account homepage

Student resources

The platform offers a range of interactive learning tools tailored to the second edition of *An Introduction to Management Science* including:

- Four additional online chapters
- More problems, exercises, and answer section
- Datasets referred to throughout the text
- Interactive eBook
- The Management Scientist 6.0 software package
- Glossary, flashcards, crossword puzzles and more

Look out for this symbol throughout the text to denote accompanying digital resources.

Chapter 1

Introduction

Learning objectives

By the end of this chapter you will be able to:

- Explain what management science is
- Detail areas in business where management science is commonly used
- Describe the management science approach or methodology
- Build and use simple quantitative models

1.1 Introduction to Management Science

Air New Zealand; Amazon; American Airlines; AT&T; Boeing; BMW; British Airways; Citibank; Dell; Delta Airlines; Eastman Kodak; Federal Express; Ford; GE Capital; Hanshin Expressway, Japan; an Indian tea producer; IBM; Kellogg; NASA; National Car Rental; Nokia; Procter & Gamble; Renault; UPS; Vancouver Airport.

At first sight it's not obvious what connects these organizations together. They're from different countries; some are private sector, some public sector; some operate internationally, some domestically; they're in different industrial and commercial sectors; they're of different sizes. However, they do have one thing in common – they all successfully use management science to help run their organization.

Management science (MS) has been defined as ***helping people make better decisions***. Clearly, decision-making is at the heart of a manager's role in any organization. Some of these decisions will be strategic and long-term: which new products and services to develop; which markets to expand into and which to withdraw from. Some will be short-term and operational: how many checkouts to open at the supermarket over the weekend; which members of staff to allocate to a new project. Get the decisions right and the organization continues to succeed. Get the decisions wrong and the organization may fail and disappear. Managers in just about any organization round the world will almost certainly tell you that life has never been tougher. There's increasingly fierce competition – in the public sector as well as private sector; customers require more and more but want to pay less; technological changes continue to gather speed; financial pressures mean that costs and productivity are constantly under scrutiny. Organizations are under pressure to do things better, do them faster and do them for less in terms of costs. Making the right decisions under such pressures isn't easy and it's no surprise that many organizations have turned to management science to help.

In today's harsh business environment organizations and managers are looking for structured, logical and evidence-based ways of making decisions rather than relying solely on intuition, personal experience and gut-feel. Management Science (also known as Operational Research) applies advanced analytical methods to business decision problems. ***Management*** emphasizes that we're interested in helping manage the organization better – that MS is very much focussed on the practical, real world. ***Science*** means that we're interested in rigorous, analytical and systematic ways of managing the organization better.

Does it Work?

Well, lots of organizations – like those above – think so. And there's plenty of evidence to show that MS really makes a difference. Some examples:

- The UK telecoms company BT used MS in the way it planned the work of its repair engineers, saving around £125 million a year.
- British Airways used MS to review its spare parts policies for its aircraft fleet and identified £21 million of savings.
- Motorola applied MS to its procurement strategy. During the first 18 months of implementation, Motorola saved US$600 million, or approximately 4 per cent, on US$16 billion of parts purchases
- Ford used MS to optimize the way it designs and tests new vehicle prototypes, saving over £150 million
- A leading UK bank, LloydsTSB, used MS to design the seating configuration in its call centres eliminating the need to build, and pay for, additional capacity

MANAGEMENT SCIENCE IN ACTION

Revenue Management at American Airlines*

One of the great success stories in management science involves the work done by the operations research (OR) group at American Airlines. In 1982, Thomas M. Cook joined a group of 12 operations research analysts at American Airlines. Under Cook's guidance, the OR group quickly grew to a staff of 75 professionals who developed models and conducted studies to support senior management decision making. Today the OR group is called Sabre and employs 10 000 professionals worldwide. One of the most significant applications developed by the OR group came about because of the deregulation of the airline industry in the late 1970s. As a result of deregulation, a number of low-cost airlines were able to move into the market by selling seats at a fraction of the price charged by established carriers such as American Airlines. Facing the question of how to compete, the OR group suggested offering different fare classes (discount and full fare) and in the process created a new area of management science referred to as yield or revenue management. The OR group used forecasting and optimization techniques to determine how many seats to sell at a discount and how many seats to hold for full fare. Although the initial implementation was relatively crude, the group continued to improve the forecasting and optimization models that drive the system and to obtain better data. Tom Cook counts at least four basic generations of revenue management during his tenure. Each produced in excess of US$100 million in incremental profitability over its predecessor. This revenue management system at American Airlines generates nearly $1 billion annually in incremental revenue. Today, virtually every airline uses some sort of revenue management system. The cruise, hotel and car rental industries also now apply revenue management methods, a further tribute to the pioneering efforts of the OR group at American Airlines.

*Based on Peter Horner, 'The Sabre Story', OR/MS Today (June 2000).

- Samsung used MS to cut the time taken to produce microchips, increasing sales revenue by around £500 million.
- A UK hospital used MS to develop a computerized appointments system that cut patient waiting times by 50 per cent.
- Peugeot applied MS to its production line in its car body shops where bottlenecks were occurring. MS improved production with minimal capital investment and no compromise in quality contributing US$130 million to revenue in one year alone.
- Air New Zealand wanted to improve the way it scheduled staff allocation and rostering. Applying MS methods enabled the company to save NZ$15 million per year as well as implement staff rosters that built in staff preferences
- Procter and Gamble, the consumer products multinational, used MS to review its approach to buying billions of US$ of supplies. Over a two year period this generated financial savings of over US$300 million.

Source: Operational Research Society and the Institute for Operations Research and the Management Sciences (INFORMS)

And to achieve these results organizations need people who understand the subject – ***management scientists*** – and this is why this textbook has been written. The aim of this text is to provide you with a number of the technical skills that a management scientist needs and also to provide you with a conceptual understanding as to where and how management science can successfully be used. To help with this, and to reinforce the practice of management science, we will be using *Management Science in Action* case studies throughout the text. Each case outlines a real application of management science in practice. The first of these, Revenue Management at American Airlines, describes one of the most significant applications of management science in the airline industry.

1.2 Where Did MS Come From?

Patrick Blackett (1897–1974) – later Baron Blackett – was one of the leading figures in the UK in the early years of operational research during Word War II and after. With a background in physics (for which he was awarded the Nobel Prize), his declared aim was to find numbers on which to base decisions, not emotion.

At this stage you may be wondering; where did MS come from, how did it develop? It is generally accepted that management science as a recognized subject has its origins in the United Kingdom around the time of the Second World War (1939–1945). The UK's very survival was threatened by its military enemies and the UK government established a number of multidisciplinary groups to apply scientific methods to its military planning and activities. Such groups consisted of scientists from a variety of backgrounds: mathematics, statistics, engineering, physics, electronics, psychology as well as military personnel and were tasked with researching into more effective military operational activities (hence the name *operational research*). These groups made significant contributions to the UK's war efforts including: improvements in the early-warning radar system which was critical to victory in the Battle of Britain; the organization of antisubmarine warfare; determination of optimum naval convoy sizes; the accuracy of bombing; the organization of civilian defence systems. The fact that these teams were multidisciplinary but also scientifically trained contributed significantly to their success. Their scientific training and thinking meant they were used to challenging existing ideas, they were used to querying assumptions made by others, they saw experimentation as a routine part of their analysis, they applied logic to problem solving and decision making, they collected and analyzed data to support their thinking and their conclusions. The fact that members of the team had different backgrounds, expertise and experience meant that not only could they challenge each other's thinking but they could also combine different approaches and thinking together for the first time. With the entry of the USA into the Second World War following Pearl Harbor, and given the obvious success of operational research in the UK, a number of similar groups were also established throughout the US military (usually known as *operations* research groups).

In 1948 the Operational Research Club of Great Britain was established as a way of bringing together those with an interest in seeing OR introduced into industry, commerce and government. The Club became the OR Society in 1953.

After the war, operational research continued to develop in the military and in defence-related industries on both sides of the Atlantic. In the US, there was considerable academic development of management science partially financed by the US military, particularly in the areas of mathematical techniques. In the UK, however, operational research took on a new role contributing to the programme of economic reconstruction and economic and social reform pursued by the new Labour Government at the end of the war. The challenges faced by industry and government in the UK at the time were major. There were issues relating to the move back to a peacetime economy and the huge transition that this would require; there were issues relating to the management and development of the newly nationalized industrial organizations in industries such as coal, steel, gas, electricity, transport; there was the huge demobilization of workers moving away from supporting the war effort and back into peacetime employment. Partly as a result, and partly because of the perceived success of operational research in the military, a number of large operational research groups were established in these industries and in government. Around this time also, academic programmes in management science began to be introduced and the first dedicated textbooks started to appear.

The first Masters and Ph.D academic programmes in OR were established in 1951 at the Case Institute of Technology, Cleveland Ohio.

Since then management science teams and management science techniques have spread into a wide variety of industrial and commercial companies, central government, local government, health and social care, across many different countries. This development was in part facilitated by the huge explosion in computing facilities and computer power. In the twenty-first-century management science techniques are now a standard part of popular computer software, such as Excel, and management science techniques are routinely taught across university business and management programmes. Many countries now have their own professional society for management scientists with the International Federation of Operational Research Societies (IFORS) acting as an umbrella organization comprising the national management science societies of over forty five countries with a total combined membership of over 25 000. Welcome to the club!

IFORS was founded in 1959

1.3 Management Science Applications

At this stage it will be worthwhile providing an overview of some of the decision areas where MS is applied. Later on in the chapter, we shall examine the more common management science techniques that are applied across these application areas and that we shall be developing in detail through the text.

Assignment

Assignment problems arise in business where someone has to *assign* resources or assets (like people, vehicles, aeroplanes) to specific tasks and where we want to do this to minimize the costs involved or to maximize the return or profit we earn. A simple example of this situation arises when an ambulance depot has a given number of emergency ambulances available throughout the day. Based on past experience it expects a number of emergency calls throughout the day to which it has to respond swiftly. Each of its ambulances has a dedicated crew but the crews have differing expertise and experience. The depot has to decide which individual ambulance to assign to each emergency call. It may try to do this to minimize the time taken to reach the location or to minimize the travel distance covered, or to send the 'best' crew to each type of emergency call. Whilst assignment problems often look simple, in real life they can be extremely complex and difficult to get right. Examples of assignment problems include: assigning referees to World Cup soccer matches; assigning students to classes; assigning airline crews to aircraft; assigning surgical teams to patients; assigning construction equipment to different construction projects. Management science has developed special techniques to help formulate and solve such assignment problems.

Data Mining

Largely because of the technology now available, many organizations are collecting large volumes of data about sales, customers, spending patterns, lifestyles and the like. Think about what happens when you use your credit card to buy groceries at the supermarket. The supermarket knows what you've bought (and can track trends in your purchases over time); the supermarket's suppliers know which products are selling and which are not; your bank knows your spending profile across the year. Used smartly, this data can allow organizations to understand better what is happening and to tailor and adapt their strategies, products and services accordingly. The supermarket can send you details of special offers on the items you normally buy (or perhaps on the ones that you don't buy); your bank knows when you might need a loan. Data mining is concerned with sifting through large amounts of data and identifying and analyzing relevant information. Historically, its use has been concentrated on business intelligence and in the financial sector, although its use is rapidly expanding across other business sectors. Data mining goes beyond routine descriptive or quantitative analysis through the application of sophisticated techniques and algorithms.

Financial Decision Making

MS plays a considerable role in financial decision making and the finance sector is a major user of MS techniques. Think about your credit card again. Someone at your bank or finance company had to decide what credit limit to give you when you took out the card. Too little and you might use a card from another bank. Too much and you may get into debt and be unable to pay them back the money they've effectively let you spend. Areas where MS is routinely used include credit scoring – where an individual's or an organization's ability to repay credit or loans is assessed quantitatively so that the lender can assess the risks involved in the loan; capital and investment budgeting – where an organization must decide on the appropriate capital or investment projects it will fund; portfolio management – where a suitable mix of investments must be determined.

Forecasting

It seems self evident that business organizations need to undertake effective forecasting of key business variables. Forecasting future sales for a retail organization; forecasting air traffic volumes for a busy airport; forecasting demand for medical care at a new hospital. Getting such forecasts right typically involves analyzing the situation both quantitatively and qualitatively and a number of MS techniques are usefully applied in forecasting situations.

Logistics

Logistics management is typically concerned with managing an organization's supply chain efficiently and effectively. All organization's need to manage the supply of resources that they need to produce goods and services – all the way from having a new factory built, to the supply of machinery to run the factory, to the power needed to run the machinery, to the paper clips that will be used in the factory office. In an increasingly global and competitive economy, good logistics management can make the difference between business success and failure. MS is routinely used to help organizations make logistical decisions.

Marketing

The area of marketing is another that makes extensive use of MS. Managers frequently have to make decisions regarding their organization's marketing strategy – the mixture of different marketing media that will be used to promote goods or services. The decision problem is that different media will incur different costs and will reach different audiences with varying degrees of effectiveness. The problem for the manager is deciding what a suitable marketing strategy looks like.

Networks

A network is typically defined as an interconnected group or system of things. The things might be roads or railways in terms of a transportation network; or computers in a computer network; or telephones in a telecoms network. Planning and managing such networks is a critical task if the network is to function effectively – we've probably all been stuck in a traffic jam at some time where the road network couldn't handle the traffic volumes or we've called through to a call centre to be put on hold because the phone network couldn't cope with demand. MS techniques are applied to examine network flows – how quickly and efficiently things flow, or move, through the network.

Optimization

Organizations are frequently looking for the best, or optimal, solution to a decision problem they have. How do we maximize profit from our sales? How do we minimize production costs? What is the optimum size for our workforce? In the search for such an optimum solution, organizations will not have a totally free hand in deciding what to do. Typically they will face certain restrictions or constraints on what they are able to do. An organization seeking to maximize profit from sales may face constraints in terms of its production capacity, or the finite demand for its products. A company seeking to minimize production costs may be locked into long-term supply contracts with some of its customers and is constrained to meet these contract requirements. An organization looking to determine the optimum size of its workforce may have certain health and safety requirements to meet. MS has developed a number of different techniques for dealing with such optimization problems.

Project Planning and Management

All organizations need to be able to plan and manage projects effectively. The project may be relatively small involving few resources and capable of being completed fairly quickly – organizing the move of a team from one part of the office to another – or it may be large and complex with a large budget and requiring considerable time and effort – planning the 2016 Rio de Janeiro Olympics. Once again, MS has developed techniques to allow for the efficient and effective planning and management of projects.

Queuing

We've all been in one at some time – a queue. It may have been a queue at a supermarket while we're waiting at the checkout; or a queue of cars at a traffic signal; or a queue of print jobs at the network printer. Queues are frustrating for those affected but are also difficult to manage cost-effectively. Putting extra staff on the supermarket checkout may well reduce the time customers spend queuing but this will also increase the supermarket's operating costs, so some compromise will be needed. MS uses queuing theory to examine the impact of management decisions on queues.

Simulation

It's not usual in business and management to be able to experiment before making a major decision. For example, we may be considering a major alteration to our production lines to boost productivity. We may be thinking about altering an airline's global flight timetable to increase competitiveness and market share. We may be thinking about redeploying police patrol vehicles to help tackle crime. It's unlikely that we would in practice be able to experiment and try different solutions to see what happened, although most managers would like to be able to do so, to assess the likely consequences of alternative decisions. However, whilst we can't experiment in the real world we can experiment using computer modelling known as simulation. Computer simulation involves running virtual experiments so that the consequences of alternative decisions can be analyzed.

MANAGEMENT SCIENCE IN ACTION

Workforce Scheduling For British Telecommunications PLC

British Telecommunications (BT) are leading providers of telecommunications services in the UK. BT employs over 50 000 field engineers to maintain telecoms networks, repair faults and provide a variety of services to customers. Managing the workforce effectively is critical to efficiency, profitability, customer service, service quality and to staff morale and motivation. Workforce scheduling is essentially about making sure the right field engineer goes to the right customer at the right time with the right equipment. However, BT faced a very complex task. The skills and experience of engineers varied considerably; their geographical location was effectively fixed; scheduling had to incorporate individual engineer constraints such as breaks and holidays; the difficulty of predicting in advance how much time some jobs would take. The Operational Research department at BT developed Work Manager, an information system that automates work management and field communications. Rolled out in 1997 and reaching 20 000 engineers in 1998, this was saving BT US$150 million a year on operational costs by 2000. When deployed over the targeted workforce of 40 000 people, the system was projected to save an estimated US$250 million a year.

Based on David Lesaint, Christos Voudoris, Noder Azarmi 'Dynamic Workforce Scheduling for British Telecommunications plc', Interfaces 30, no. 1 (Jan/Feb 2000): 45–56

Transportation

Transportation problems involve, predictably enough, situations where items have to be transported in an efficient and effective way. This might involve transporting manufactured products, such as smartphones, from where they're made to where they're sold. It might involve transporting medical supplies, such as blood and plasma, from where they're collected to where they're needed. It might involve transporting food and emergency supplies from donor countries to the site of a natural disaster such as an earthquake or cyclone. MS has developed techniques to help managers make appropriate decisions about transportation problems.

We've tried to show in this section that MS isn't just a collection of specialized techniques only of interest to the MS specialist but rather that MS has a role to play in many organizations where managers face such decisions. Throughout the text, we'll deliberately be introducing MS techniques in a business and management context. That is we'll be looking at a typical business decision problem and then seeing how MS can help managers make better decisions.

1.4 The MS Approach

Not surprisingly, given the emphasis on a *scientific* approach to management, management scientists try to follow a logical, systematic and analytical method when looking at a decision problem. This approach (or methodology) is summarized in Figure 1.1 and follows a sequence of: *Problem Recognition; Problem Structuring and Definition; Modelling and Analysis; Solution and Recommendations; Implementation*. (Note: different management scientists have their own versions of this methodology. However, most of these are similar in content.)

We shall use a simple scenario to show how the methodology is applied. The President of the College where you are studying has heard that you're studying management

Figure 1.1 The MS approach

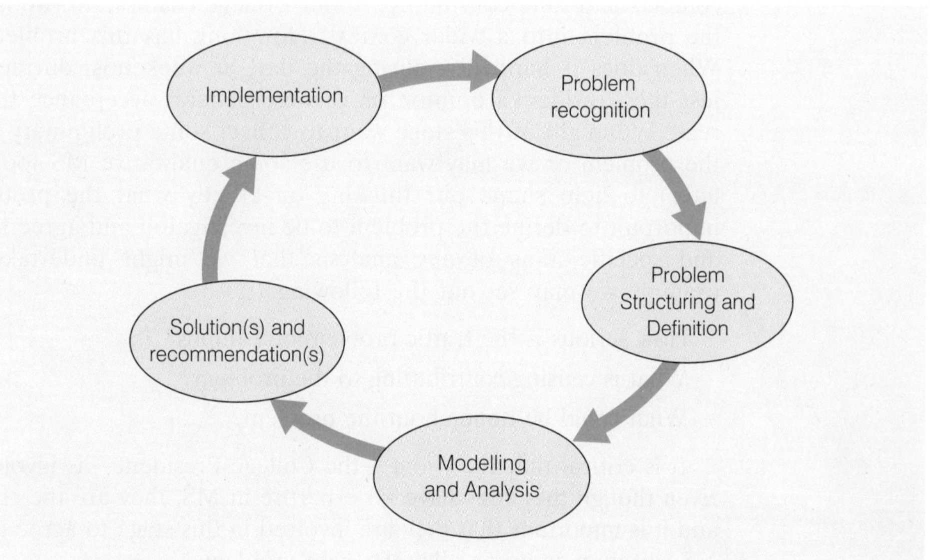

'scientifically' and has asked for your help. The President has become increasingly concerned about traffic congestion on campus and in the nearby community that neighbours the College. There seem to be an increasing number of cars using the campus, parking is becoming increasingly difficult especially at peak periods, there has been a spill-over effect on the local community with more cars parked off-campus making it difficult for local residents to go about their business or to park themselves. The President has asked for your help in terms of what to do about the problem.

Problem Recognition

The first step is clearly to realize that a problem exists that requires a decision. This may seem obvious – and the College President has already done this – but in a wider management context it implies that an organization has systems in place for undertaking monitoring and observation so that problem situations are identified at an early a stage as possible. This implies that an organization has robust performance monitoring and measurement systems in place at both the operational, day-to-day level and at the strategic, long-term level. It is also worth noting that such observations will typically be undertaken by the manager in an organization – like the College President – rather than the management scientist.

We have used the word 'problem' here which is standard MS terminology. Whilst MS is typically focussed on helping solve problems – as in the case of the College traffic levels – it is also extensively used in situations to help evaluate opportunities. The College may be thinking, for example, of introducing a specialist MS degree programme and wants to know which type of publicity and marketing to use – the Internet? TV and radio? Social media? Business press?

Problem Structuring and Definition

The next stage of the MS approach is to structure the problem. This is about ensuring that the problem is properly understood, it is placed in context and that a clear definition of the problem to be investigated is agreed. This stage is critically important to effective MS. Improper, or inappropriate, structuring and definition of the problem may result in inappropriate analysis and inappropriate solutions being identified and in the real world this problem structuring phase can be difficult, complex and time-consuming. In our College example we would need first to put the problem into a wider context. How long has this problem been going on? When does it happen – during the day, at weekends, during semester? Is this just the President's opinion or is there general acceptance that the problem is real? We might at this stage want to collect some preliminary data to help scope the problem or we may want to use some qualitative MS tools (that we discuss later) to help shape our thinking on exactly what the problem is. It is then important to define the problem to be investigated and agree the overall purpose and specific aims of any analysis that we might undertake. In the College example we may set out the following:

How serious is the traffic problem on campus?

What is causing/contributing to the problem?

What could be done about the problem?

It is critical that the client – the College President – is involved in this process. Even though they may have no expertise in MS, they are the client for the project and it is important that they are involved in this stage to agree the problem so that MS can then go on to solve the right problem.

Modelling and Analysis

Once we have an understanding of the wider problem context and the specific aims of the project we can begin our analysis of the problem. Such analysis is likely to be a combination of two types: quantitative analysis and qualitative analysis. These are sometimes referred to as hard MS and soft MS respectively and a good management scientist will need to develop skills in both. **Soft MS** relies on a range of primarily qualitative approaches to decision making and focuses on the people making a decision rather than on the decision problem itself. The role of the management scientist in such a situation is primarily in facilitating a critical, but open, discussion of differing viewpoints and perceptions of the decision problem. Soft MS relies on verbal problem descriptions and makes extensive use of diagrams and pictorial presentations. Such soft methods help the decision makers to develop a shared understanding of the problem they face and to agree on a consensus course of action to which they are committed. **Hard MS**, on the other hand, tends to focus primarily on the decision problem and applies mathematical and statistical techniques to finding a solution to the problem. In this text we are concerned primarily with quantitative analysis, hard MS, and through the text we shall be introducing a variety of techniques that are commonly used – typically referred to as **models**. A manager can increase their decision-making effectiveness by learning more about quantitative methodology and models and by better understanding their contribution to the decision-making process. A manager who is knowledgeable in quantitative decision-making models is in a much better position to compare and evaluate both the qualitative and quantitative sources of recommendations and ultimately to combine the two sources in order to make the best possible decision. The skills of the quantitative approach can be learned only by studying the assumptions and methods of management science. In the case of the College traffic problem we may end up analyzing the situation in a number of different ways:

- Undertaking a quantitative analysis of past and current traffic flows on campus.
- Producing quantitative forecasts of likely future traffic flows.
- Determining the optimum amount of traffic that the campus can handle.
- Analyzing the effect of alternative traffic schemes on campus.

Solutions and Recommendations

Once the problem analysis is complete through the use of an appropriate MS model, we should be in a position to offer a solution – or sometimes alternative solutions – for the problem. However, it is important to realize that such solutions must be placed in the wider problem context. MS is rarely able to offer a definitive solution to a manager in the form: *this is what you should do*. Rather the application of MS generates additional information about the problem – and often this information is available only through the application of MS – which the manager must evaluate alongside other information they will have about the problem. In the case of the College, through appropriate application of MS we may be able to offer potential solutions to the President for consideration. However, these solutions will need to be placed in the wider problem context – what budget is available for any changes to road layouts, for example; what would staff and student reaction be to such changes? And so on.

Implementation

Finally, we come to implementation of the solution. Again, this is likely to be a managerial action rather than that of the management scientist. However, the management scientist has an important role to play here. Successful implementation of results is of critical importance to the management scientist as well as the manager. If the results of the analysis and solution process are not correctly implemented, the entire effort may be of no value. It doesn't take too many unsuccessful implementations before the management scientist is out of work. Because implementation often requires people to do things differently, it often meets with resistance. People want to know, '*What's wrong with the way we've been doing it*?' and so on. One of the most effective ways to ensure successful implementation is to include users throughout the modelling process. A user who feels a part of identifying the problem and developing the solution is much more likely to enthusiastically implement the results. The success rate for implementing the results of a management science project is much greater for those projects characterized by extensive user involvement.

And of course that brings us back full circle in Figure 1.1 to Problem Recognition! It will be necessary to set up some observation system so that the solution that has been implemented is monitored and evaluated so that we will know whether the problem has been resolved or whether further analysis and work is needed.

It is also worth commenting that in practice the management science methodology outlined, will not be as neat, logical or as easy as it appears in Figure 1.1. In practice many management science problems are messy and will require an iterative approach where we move back and forth across the different stages of the methodology. We may develop an agreed problem structure and definition but when we move on to the Modelling and Analysis stage we realize our problem definition was inappropriate and needs revisiting. We may develop what we believe to be an appropriate model and make recommendations only to find that the recommendations cannot realistically be implemented because of factors our model did not take into account. Figure 1.2 is a more realistic picture of the methodology we're likely to have to follow in real life indicating that we may have to jump around the approach a lot, go back to earlier stages, redefine the problem and so on. It looks a mess, doesn't it? And that's deliberate because a lot of MS in the real world is messy (ask any management scientist). We start by recognizing that there's some problem. We do some problem structuring and then some modelling and analysis. It may be at that stage we realize we haven't actually structured and defined the problem properly so have to go back a step. Eventually when we've got the analysis right we present recommendations to the client who tells us they are not realistic or practical so may have to go back to the drawing board again.

Figure 1.2 Revised MS approach

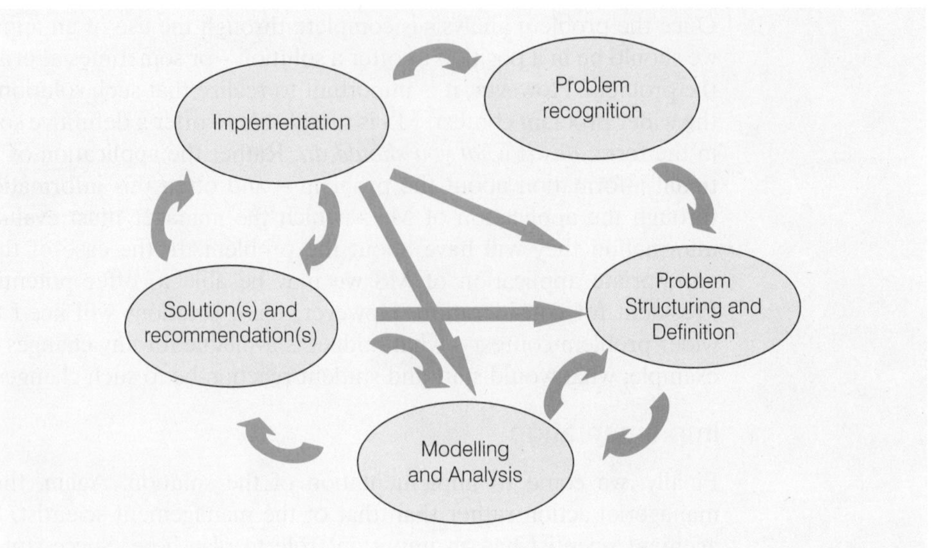

1.5 Models

Management science makes considerable use of models. Models are representations of real objects or situations and can be presented in various forms. For example, Airbus may make a scale model of an aeroplane that they're thinking of producing. VW may make a model of a new vehicle prototype. The model aeroplane and vehicle are examples of models that are physical replicas of real objects. In modelling terminology, physical replicas are referred to as **iconic models**. Another classification of models – the type we will primarily be studying – includes representations of a problem by a system of symbols and quantitative relationships or expressions. Such models are referred to as **mathematical models** and are a critical part of any quantitative approach to decision making. For example, the total profit from the sale of a product can be determined by multiplying the profit per unit by the quantity sold. If we let x represent the number of units sold and P the total profit, then, with a profit of €10 per unit, the following mathematical model defines the total profit earned by selling x units:

$$P = 10x \qquad \textbf{(1.1)}$$

The symbols P and x are known as variables – their exact numerical value can vary, it is not predetermined or fixed. The variable P, profit, is known as a dependent variable since its value depends on x, the number of units sold. x is referred to as an independent variable since its value in this equation is not dependent on another variable. The whole equation is referred to as a functional relationship. We are relating profit, P, to the number of units sold, x, and we are saying that profit is a *function* of sales. The value of €10 in equation (1.1) is known as a **parameter**. Parameters are known, constant values. Unlike variables their value does not change. The values for parameters in a model are usually obtained from observed data. In this case the data is likely to be readily available and reliable and accurate, after all, we know the price we're selling the product for. In other cases, however, the value of a parameter may have to be estimated using the best available data and may be less reliable. Consider a different model, for example, where we are relating the number of

MANAGEMENT SCIENCE IN ACTION

Quantitative Analysis At Merrill Lynch*

Merrill Lynch, a brokerage and financial services firm with more than 56 000 employees in 45 countries, serves its client base through two business units. The Merrill Lynch Corporate and Institutional Client Group serves more than 7 000 corporations, institutions and governments. The Merrill Lynch Private Client Group (MLPC) serves approximately four million households, as well as 225 000 small to mid-sized businesses and regional financial institutions, through more than 14 000 financial consultants in 600-plus branch offices. The management science group, established in 1986, has been part of MLPC since 1991. The mission of this group is to provide high-end quantitative analysis to support strategic management decisions and to enhance the financial consultant–client relationship. The group has successfully implemented models and developed systems for asset allocation, financial planning, marketing information technology, database marketing and portfolio performance measurement. Although technical expertise and objectivity are clearly important factors in any analytical group, the group attributes much of its success to communications skills, teamwork and consulting skills. Each project begins with face-to-face meetings with the client. A proposal is then prepared to outline the background of the problem, the objectives of the project, the approach, the required resources, the time schedule and the implementation issues. At this stage, analysts focus on developing solutions that provide significant value and are easily implemented. As the work progresses, frequent meetings keep the clients up-to-date. Because people with different skills, perspectives and motivations must work together for a common goal, teamwork is essential. The group's members take classes in team approaches, facilitation and conflict resolution. They possess a broad range of multifunctional and multidisciplinary capabilities and are motivated to provide solutions that focus on the goals of the firm. This approach to problem solving and the implementation of quantitative analysis has been a hallmark of the group. The impact and success of the group translates into hard dollars and repeat business. The group recently received the annual Edelman award given by the Institute for Operations Research and the Management Sciences for effective use of management science for organizational success. As Launny Stevens, Merrill Lynch Vice Chairman commented, '*Operational Research allowed us to seize the initiative in the marketplace. We have moved forward like a bullet train and it is our competitors that are scrambling not to get run over*'.

*Based on Russ Labe, Raj Nigam, and Steve Spence, 'Management Science at Merrill Lynch Private Client Group', Interfaces 29, no. 2 (March/April 1999): 1–14. and The Guide to Operational Research, http://www.theorsociety.com/Science_of_Better/htdocs/prospect/or_executive_guide.pdf

items sold to the price charged. In this case we know that if we increase the price of the product it will affect sales but we may not know for certain the exact numerical effect – the exact value of the parameter. Here, we would have to estimate the parameter value and recognize that this may affect the reliability of the model results – the model can only be as accurate as the data used in its construction. Understandably this is why so much effort goes into data collection in management science.

The purpose, or value, of any model is that it enables us to make inferences about the real situation by studying and analyzing the model which in turn can help us make decisions. For example, an aeroplane designer might test an iconic model of a new aeroplane in a wind tunnel to learn about the potential flying characteristics of the full-size aeroplane. Similarly, a mathematical model may be used to make inferences about how much profit will be earned if a specified quantity of a particular product is sold. According to the mathematical model of Equation (1.1), we would expect selling three hundred units of the product ($x = 300$) would provide a profit of $P = 10(300) = €3000$.

In general, experimenting with models requires less time and is less expensive than experimenting with the real object or situation. A model aeroplane is certainly quicker and less expensive to build and study than the full-size aeroplane. Similarly, the mathematical model in Equation (1.1) allows a quick identification of profit expectations without actually requiring the manager to produce and sell 300 units. Models also have the advantage of reducing the risk associated with experimenting with the real situation. In particular, bad designs or bad decisions that cause the model aeroplane to crash or a mathematical model to project a €10 000 loss can be avoided in the real situation. The value of model-based conclusions and decisions is dependent on how well the model represents the real situation. The more closely the model aeroplane represents the real aeroplane the more accurate the conclusions and predictions will be. Similarly, the more closely the mathematical model represents the company's true profit-volume relationship, the more accurate the profit projections will be.

Obviously our model in equation (1.1) is quite simple and basic – it consists of only one equation after all. To illustrate some additional aspects of MS models we'll expand the situation. Let us assume that management have agreed, during the problem structuring and definition phase, that their problem is to maximize the company's profit, P. However, they have also identified certain factors that must be taken into account when seeking to maximize profit. One critical requirement relates to the fact that each unit of the item produced by the company takes five hours of production time and that each day there are only 40 hours of production time available given the existing workforce. We can show the company's objective mathematically as:

$$\text{Maximize } P = 10x$$

And we refer to this as the **objective function**. We can also show the production limitation as:

$$5x \leq 40$$

where $5x$ shows the amount of production time need to produce x units and 40 shows the total available production time. The symbol shows that the amount of production time needed must be less than, or equal to, the 40 hours maximum that is available. We refer to this expression as a **constraint**. We also have a 'common sense' requirement that:

$$x \geq 0$$

that is, that production cannot be negative. Clearly, this makes sense from a business perspective and whilst it may seem unnecessary to be this explicit it is important to specify such requirements mathematically to ensure our model represents business reality as closely as possible. We then have a complete model for the production situation:

$$\text{Maximize } P = 10x$$

Subject to:

$$5x \leq 40$$

$$x \geq 0$$

This model can now be used to help management. Clearly, the decision relates to the value of x which will maximize profit, P, but also meets the specified constraint requirements. x is often referred to as the **decision variable** – the variable about which we need to take some decision typically in the context of what numerical value it should take.

MANAGEMENT SCIENCE IN ACTION

Models in Federal Express*

Today, Federal Express (FedEx), is an acknowledged leader in delivery services worldwide with an annual revenue of over $30 billion and around ¼ million employees and contractors. It has the largest civil aviation fleet in the world. Its founder and CEO, Frederick W. Smith acknowledges the role that models and management science have played in the company's success. Indeed, if it hadn't been for this FedEx might not be here today! Smith started FedEx in 1973 offering an overnight package delivery service between 11 cities in the south and southeast of the US. The innovative service operated on a hub-and-spoke system (named after an old fashioned wagon wheel, where the hub is the centre part of the wheel and the spokes radiate out from the centre to the edge of the wheel). Smith's idea was to use a fleet of aeroplanes to transport all packages from their origin, to a central hub facility (in Memphis). Then all the packages would be sorted and flown back out across the spokes to the city of destination. Many people commented at the time that this was a crazy idea and would never work. They were almost right. FedEx had acquired a fleet of 22 executive jets to use as cargo planes and the service started in March 1973 between 11 cities. It was hardly an auspicious start – only six packages needed delivery and the next couple of days proved no better. The company stopped its air delivery service. Fortunately Smith brought in colleagues who had an analytical and modelling background. An initial model was developed looking at improving the origin-destination network that had originally been set up across 11 cities by taking a more analytical approach looking at the types of business in each city (FedEx's potential customers), competition, likely market share. As a result a new 26 city network was proposed and two months later, in April 1973, FedEx reopened its air delivery service to great success. Additional models were developed not long after, helping the business grow and succeed: a flight scheduling and resourcing model and a financial planning model allowing FedEx to assess the financial implications of alternative routes and flying schedules. Unsurprisingly, CEO Fred Smith has become a strong supporter of management science modelling.

**Source*: FedEx website and on *Absolutely, Positively Operations Research: the Federal Express Story*, R.O. Mason, J.L. McKenney, W. Carlson and D. Copeland in Interfaces 27:2 March-April 1997 pp 17–36

1.6 Models of Cost, Revenue and Profit

Some of the most basic quantitative models arising in business and economic applications are those involving the relationship between a volume variable – such as production volume or sales volume – and cost, revenue and profit. Through the use of these models, a manager can determine the projected cost, revenue, and/or profit associated with an established production quantity or a forecasted sales volume. Financial planning, production planning, sales quotas and other areas of decision making can benefit from such cost, revenue and profit models.

Cost and Volume Models

The cost of manufacturing or producing a product is a function of the volume produced. This cost can usually be defined as a sum of two costs: fixed cost and variable cost. Fixed cost is the portion of the total cost that does not depend on the production volume: this cost remains the same no matter how much is produced. Variable cost, on the other hand, is the portion of the total cost that is dependent on and varies with the production volume. To illustrate how cost and volume models can be developed, we will consider a manufacturing problem faced by Nowlin Plastics in Shanghai. Nowlin Plastics produces a variety of compact disc (CD) storage cases. Nowlin's bestselling product is the CD-50, a slim, plastic CD/DVD holder with a specially designed lining that protects the optical surface of the disc. The holders are sold in units of 50 cases. Several products are produced on the same manufacturing line, and a setup cost is incurred each time a changeover is made for a new product. Suppose that the setup cost for the CD-50 is €3000. This setup cost is a fixed cost that is incurred regardless of the number of units eventually produced. In addition, suppose that labour and material costs are €2 for each unit produced. The cost-volume model for producing x units of the CD-50 can be written as:

$$C(x) = 3000 + 2x \quad \textbf{(1.2)}$$

where

$$x = \text{production volume in units}$$
$$C(x) = \text{total cost of producing x units}$$

Once a production volume is determined, the model in Equation (1.2) can be used to calculate the total production cost. For example, management have an order for 1200 units (x = 1200) and using equation (1.2) we can see that this would result in a total cost of C(1200) = 3000 + 2(1200) = €5400.

Marginal cost is defined as the rate of change of the total cost with respect to production volume. That is, it is the cost increase associated with a one-unit increase in the production volume. In the cost model of Equation (1.3), we see that the total cost C(x) will increase by €2 for each unit increase in the production volume. Thus, the marginal cost is €2. With more complex total cost models, marginal cost may depend on the production volume. In such cases, we could have marginal cost increasing or decreasing with the production volume x.

Revenue and Volume Models

Management of Nowlin Plastics will also want information on the projected revenue associated with selling a specified number of units – a model of the relationship between revenue and volume is also needed. Each case of CD-50 units sells for €5. The model for total revenue can now be written as:

$$R(x) = 5x \quad \textbf{(1.3)}$$

where

$$x = \text{sales volume in units}$$
$$R(x) = \text{total revenue from selling x units}$$

Marginal revenue is defined as the rate of change of total revenue with respect to sales volume. That is, it is the increase in total revenue resulting from a one-unit increase in sales volume. In the model of Equation (1.3), we see that the marginal revenue is €5. In this case, marginal revenue is constant and does not vary with the sales volume. With more complex models, we may find that marginal revenue increases or decreases as the sales volume x increases.

Profit and Volume Models

One of the most important criteria for management decision making in the private sector is profit. Managers need to be able to know the profit implications of their decisions. If we assume that we will only produce what can be sold, the production volume and sales volume will be equal. We can combine Equations (1.2) and (1.3) to develop a profit-volume model that will determine the total profit associated with a specified production-sales volume. Total profit, denoted P(x), is total revenue minus total cost; therefore, the following model provides the total profit associated with producing and selling x units:

$$\begin{aligned} P(x) &= R(x) - C(x) \\ &= 5x - (3000 + 2x) = -3000 + 3x \end{aligned} \quad \textbf{(1.4)}$$

Breakeven Analysis

Using Equation (1.4), we can now determine the total profit associated with any production volume x. For example, suppose that a demand forecast indicates that 500 units of the product can be sold. The decision to produce and sell the 500 units results in a projected profit of:

$$P(500) = -3000 + 3(500) = -1500$$

In other words, a loss of €1500 is predicted. If sales are expected to be 500 units, the manager may decide against producing the product. However, a demand forecast of 1800 units would show a projected profit of:

$$P(1800) = -3000 + 3(1800) = 2400$$

or €2400. This profit may be enough to justify proceeding with the production and sale of the product. We see that a volume of 500 units will yield a loss, whereas a volume of 1800 provides a profit. The volume that results in total revenue equalling total cost (providing €0 profit) is called the **breakeven point**. If the breakeven point is known, a manager can quickly infer that a volume above the breakeven point will result in a profit, while a volume below the breakeven point will result in a loss. Thus, the breakeven point for a product provides valuable information for a manager who must make a yes/no decision concerning production of the product. Let us now return to the Nowlin Plastics example and show how the total profit model in Equation (1.4) can be used to compute the breakeven point. The breakeven point can be found by setting the total profit expression equal to zero and solving for the production volume.

Using equation (1.4), we have:

$$\begin{aligned} P(x) &= -3000 + 3x \\ 0 &= -3000 + 3x \\ 3000 &= 3x \\ x &= 1000 \end{aligned}$$

With this information, we know that production and sales of the product must be greater than 1000 units before a profit can be expected. The graphs of the total cost model, the total revenue model, and the location of the breakeven point are shown in Figure 1.3.

Figure 1.3 Graph of the Breakeven Analysis for Nowlin Plastics

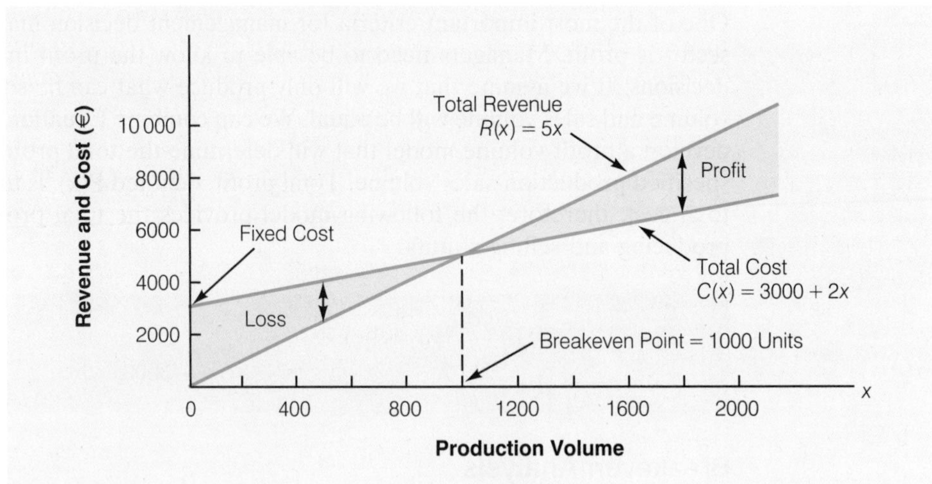

MANAGEMENT SCIENCE IN ACTION

A Spreadsheet Tool for Catholic Relief Services*

Catholic Relief Services (CRS) is a not-for-profit organization that supports development activities and humanitarian relief efforts across the world operating with around 4000 field staff in almost 100 different countries. Its work is both short-term – responding with emergency programmes to natural and man-made disasters – and longer-term – supporting development programmes in agriculture, education and health. Its annual budget is around US$500 million with around half of this going on emergency aid and support. Each year managers in CRS have to decide how best to allocate the available funding to different projects in different countries. Some of these projects are already in place and need continuing funding and support and yet each year requests for new projects have to be considered. Not only do managers have to take into account the available funding but also try to ensure this funding is being used to best effect in the context of the CRS mission and objectives. At the time there was little in the way of analysis that was used to help managers and CRS decide that it needed a simple-to-use tool that would help managers make more effective budget allocation decisions. A budget allocation model was developed with a spreadsheet tool. The spreadsheet model allocates available funds in order to have maximum impact but at the same time to be consistent with CRS mission objectives and priorities. Managers are able to influence the allocation, for example by setting limits to what each country could practically cope with. Management have responded positively to the current model and spreadsheet tool partly because it is simple to use and partly because they were involved in shaping the model so have an understanding as to how the spreadsheet tool works and can have trust and confidence in its results.

*Based on Investment Analysis and Budget Allocation at Catholic Relief Services, I. Gamvros, R. Nidel and S. Raghavan, Interfaces Vol. 36, No. 5, September-October 2006, pp 400–406

1.7 The Modelling Process

As we have discussed, one of the features that distinguishes management science from other management disciplines is the extensive use of models – both qualitative and quantitative. Throughout the text we shall be introducing a number of the more common quantitative models used in management science. However, it must be appreciated that such models and the process of creating suitable models is part of the wider management science methodology that we discussed in Section 1.4. Management science models are not plug-and-play solutions to management problems (although some organizations do see, and use, them this way.) That is, it is not simply a situation of choosing a model, plugging it into the problem and finding a solution. Rather, model building in management science is both a science and an art. The *science* comes from knowing what models are available, how they are typically constructed and used and what their limitations are. The *art* relates to the process of adapting the model to the business problem being examined – making the model fit the problem situation as well as it can and also appreciating where some of this fit is less good. It must be remembered that any model is a simplified version of reality – we are not trying to capture the problem situation in all its complexity but rather simplify the problem down to its key elements so that we can more easily make sense of it and better analyze it.

The modelling process typically consists of a number of iterative stages. Initial model selection involves the management scientist identifying which model, or models, seem best suited for the problem. This typically follows the Problem Structuring stage of the overall methodology outlined earlier in Figure 1.2. Obviously, this assumes that the management scientist is aware of the different models available. Clearly, this is one of the purposes of this text – to help you become aware of the different quantitative models available. However, for the management science practitioner, this stage is less obvious than it first appears. Management Science, like all other academic disciplines, is constantly changing with new models and techniques being developed. It is also worth realizing that in practice more than one model may be used. For example, in order to build and use a revenue model we might first need to build a forecasting model to forecast consumer reaction to price and volume changes. Following initial model selection we then typically get involved in data collection as the next stage. This will involve searching for and collecting the data needed by the model we have decided to use. Different models have different data requirements and to some extent the availability of appropriate data may restrict the choice of model. As we shall see, some models require a lot of accurate and reliable data – they're often referred to as data-hungry models. If this isn't available, the management scientist may have to choose another model which has fewer data requirements (or set out to collect the data that the first-choice model needs if time and budget permit). Assuming appropriate data is available, the next stage is model construction – building an appropriate model for the problem. Once again, in practice, this is more difficult than it seems. Any model is a simplified version of reality – in other words there are certain aspects of the problem that we conveniently push to one side in order to build a simpler picture of the problem situation we face. This often requires the modeller to make certain assumptions and these assumptions can make all the difference between a good model and a bad one. Sometimes these assumptions may be explicitly stated. In other cases they may be implied. If we return to the Nowlin breakeven model that we built in Section 1.5 there are no explicit assumptions stated. However, there are certain assumptions implied in the model. These include:

- We assume that the data used – such as fixed cost and variable cost – is known for certain, is accurate and is fixed and constant.
- We assume that customers will continue to buy the product at €5 no matter how many we sell and no matter what our competitors might do.

Such assumptions may be necessary to allow us to build a suitable model but they may not always be reliable assumptions – or rather they may be reliable only under certain limited conditions. The assumptions made may affect the reliability and usefulness of the model. This is another reason why the client/decision-maker should also be involved in the modelling process – they may know better than the management scientist which assumptions are realistic and which less so. Model testing or model validation is typically the next stage. This is where we use the model and the data to analyze/solve the problem and try to assess whether the model is a reasonable one for the problem situation. In part this is about assessing whether the output we get from the model appears sensible given the problem context. Finally, if we are satisfied the model has been validated then we can proceed to model use – starting to use the model to assist the decision-maker. Again, it is worth emphasizing that in practice the modelling process – like the rest of the management science methodology – is messy, iterative, time-consuming and typically frustrating with a lot of trial-and-error often taking place before a satisfactory outcome has been realized.

1.8 Management Science Models and Techniques

In this section we give a brief overview of the MS techniques and models covered in this text and on the complementary online platform. Don't be put off by the fact that some may seem very technical. We'll see later how these techniques work and how they can be used effectively in decision-making.

Linear Programming

We start the text by looking in detail at one of the classic MS techniques – that of linear programming (LP). LP is a problem-solving approach developed for situations where we require to determine an optimum solution and where we face certain limitations or constraints on what we are able to do. We may seek to maximize profit, minimize costs, minimize travel time, maximize sales but subject to various constraints imposed on the problem. The term *programming* refers not to the need for computer programming but to the fact that technique comprises a set of logical steps to determine the optimal solution to an LP problem. The term *linear* indicates that the problem can be set out using linear (straight-line) relationships between the variables.

Transportation and Assignment

We next look at a specialized group of techniques that are applied to transportation and assignment problems. These are common application areas where items have to be transported between locations or where resources have to be assigned to particular tasks. Because of their relatively specialized focus, a number of solution techniques have been developed for these types of problem.

Network Models

Specialized solution procedures exist for problems involving some sort of network (such as roads or routes) enabling us to quickly and effectively solve problems in such areas as transportation system design, information system design and project scheduling.

Project Management

In many situations, managers are responsible for planning, scheduling and controlling projects that consist of numerous separate jobs or tasks performed by a variety of departments, individuals and so forth. The PERT (Programme Evaluation and Review Technique) and CPM (Critical Path Method) techniques help managers carry out their project scheduling responsibilities.

Inventory Models

Having the right levels of inventory, or stock, is critical for many organizations. Too much inventory makes costs escalate. Too little inventory and sales and production may suffer. Inventory models are used by managers faced with the dual problems of maintaining sufficient inventories, or stock, to meet demand for goods and, at the same time, incurring the lowest possible inventory costs.

Queuing Models

Waiting-line or queuing models have been developed to help managers understand and make better decisions concerning the operation of situations involving queues. Using mathematical models we shall see how queuing situations can be analyzed to predict factors such as the time a customer may have to wait in a queue before service, the likely size of queues that may build up and the effect on queues of changing the service process.

Simulation

Simulation is a computer-based technique used to model the operation of a system or process so that experimentation can be conducted to evaluate the consequences of alternative decisions. This technique employs computer programs to model the operation and perform simulation computations.

Decision Analysis

Decision analysis is a formal approach to decision making and can be used to determine optimal strategies in situations where there are several decision alternatives and where the outcomes or consequences of these decisions are uncertain.

Multicriteria analysis

We then have a chapter that introduces a variety of multicriteria methods. Such methods are used where we are making a decision where we must somehow take a variety of criteria into account when deciding what best to do. For example, you may be considering buying a new laptop. In trying to decide which make and model to buy you'll take a variety of conflicting criteria into account: price, reputation, reliability and so on. **Goal programming** is one technique for solving multicriteria decision problems, usually within the framework of linear programming. **Analytic Hierarchy Process** is another multicriteria decision-making technique which permits the inclusion of subjective factors in arriving at a recommended decision.

The following four chapters are located on the associated premium online platform that is autopackaged with the text. For more information on access, see the 'Digital Resources' page at the front of the book.

Integer Linear Programming

Integer linear programming is an approach used for problems that can be set up as linear programmes with the additional requirement that some or all of the decision variables take integer values. For example, a car manufacturer may be looking to optimize the number of dealer outlets to supply to, where, clearly, the number of outlets must sensibly be an integer value.

Forecasting

We then look at a variety of forecasting techniques that can be used to predict future aspects of a business operation. We look at **time series models** which analyze the movement of a business variable over time; we look at methods of

trend projection where we forecast the future trend in some variable; we look at **regression analysis** which focuses on trying to quantitatively explain and predict the movement in a variable; and we introduce a number of qualitative approaches to forecasting.

Dynamic Programming

In this next online chapter, we look at dynamic programming which is an approach that allows us to break up a large problem in such a fashion that once all the smaller problems have been solved, we are left with an optimal solution to the large problem. As with linear programming, the *programming* term indicates a logical series of stages in our solution method.

Markov Process Models

Finally, in this last online chapter we look at Markov process models, which are useful in studying the evolution of processes of systems over repeated trials. For example, Markov processes have been used to describe the probability that a machine, functioning in one period, will break down in another period.

Summary

- This text focuses on the quantitative techniques and models that are commonly used in management science.
- The primary purpose of such techniques and models is providing information that will help people make better decisions than they otherwise could have done.
- Management science is used successfully in many business organizations and makes a substantial contribution to improved performance at both the operational and strategic levels.
- One of the distinguishing features of management science is its extensive use of models – both qualitative and quantitative – to help decision-making. Knowledge of the quantitative management science models that are available and their appropriate use is critical to a successful management scientist. Equally important is a knowledge of the modelling process and where this fits into the wider methodology adopted by management scientists.
- As we progress through the text, we shall be developing your knowledge and understanding of the more common quantitative management science models; we shall help you understand where their use is appropriate through examples, case studies and *Management Science in Action* examples; we shall develop your skills in modelling and we will help you become a better management scientist!

WORKED EXAMPLE

At the end of each chapter we shall introduce a detailed business problem and show how the problem can be analyzed using MS techniques introduced in that chapter. You should read the example and then develop your own solution to the problem before going on to read our suggestions.

In this chapter we introduced the scenario that the President of your College had approached you seeking help with the problem of increased traffic congestion on campus. Some initial survey work suggests that during semesters around 5000 cars per weekday arrive on campus although most do not stay all day. Following some initial consultation, one option now under consideration relates to the construction of an additional short-term car park on some spare land next to the campus. Initial analysis has concluded that the car park could be constructed for a one-off cost of €2 million. To pay for the construction the College is able to take a 20-year loan from the local bank (run by one of the College's alumni). Under the terms of the loan, the College would pay off the amount at a rate of €250 000 per year for 20 years. It is estimated that the car park would cost a further €150 000 per year to operate and maintain regardless of how many cars used it. Students and staff using the car park during semester would be charged €1 for two hours parking. Outside of semester, parking would be free. Initial market research suggests that each car using the car park would stay on average for five hours. Semesters typically cover 25 weeks each year and during semester the car park would be open from 7.00 a.m. until 10.00 p.m. To offset pollution and carbon emissions, the College will contribute €0.25 for each car using the car park to a carbon offset scheme which will use the money for additional tree planting. You have been asked about how many cars would need to use the car park for it to breakeven.

The President is also looking for any other advice that you can offer.

Solution

Well, where to start?

It's a typical, messy management science problem. There's some data, we've been given a task which is fairly specific (work out breakeven for the car park) but we've also been given a fairly open-ended remit in terms of any other advice we can offer. Clearly, in terms of Figure 1.2 we're effectively at the Modelling and Analysis stage so let's do what we can. We've been asked to determine the number of cars needed to use the proposed car park for it to breakeven. Let's collect together the data we have and build a basic breakeven model. The College will incur two fixed costs if it goes ahead with the project. There's the annual repayment to the bank of €250 000 and there's the annual operating cost of €150 000. Both these costs remain constant, or fixed, no matter how many cars use the car park. There's also a variable cost of €0.25 to the carbon offset scheme for each car using the car park. On the revenue side the College will get €1 for every two hours of parking during semester time with cars on average staying for five hours. This equates to a revenue per car per stay of €2.50. If we let x be the number of cars using the car park over a year (the decision variable) we then have:

$$\text{Cost} = 400\,000 + 0.25x$$

$$\text{Revenue} = 2.50X$$

Breakeven occurs when cost = revenue so we have:

$$400\,000 + 0.25x = 2.50x$$

And solving for x gives $x = 177{,}777.8$. For reporting purposes in practice we'd probably show this as 177 800 or even 180 000. So, with the information given, 180 000 cars a year would need to pay to use the car park for the project to breakeven. However, we can also provide some additional information that might help the President. Under the proposal only cars using the car park during semester would be charged. Semesters last 25 weeks so on average, we'd need around 7200 cars per week (180 000 divided by 25) to breakeven. This also equates to 1440 cars per day (assuming the College operates five days per week). Clearly, at this stage we'd need to go back to the President and ask whether the 1440 cars per day looked a realistic target. After all, we have no information on the size of the College, the number of students attending per day, how many students travel by car and so on. We can also go one stage further and speculate about the required size of the car park. With 1440 cars required per day to breakeven, we know from the information given that each car stays an average of five hours. That gives a total of 7200 hours of parking each day (1440 x 5). The car park is open 15 hours each day (from 7.00 a.m. until 10.00 p.m.) so dividing the total parking hours (7200) by the hours available (15) the car park would require a minimum of 480 parking places. This is based on the assumption that parking would be evenly spread through the 15 hours the car park is open. This is an unrealistic assumption but the only one we can make on the information currently available. So, we'd need to advise the President that it looks like the car park will need to be able to accommodate around 500 cars for breakeven. To summarize we can now inform the President that, based on the information available:

- The proposed car park will need around 180 000 cars a year paying an average of €2.50 per stay to break even.
- This equates to around 1440 cars per day during semester.

- The car park will need a minimum of 500 parking spaces.

We've had to make a number of assumptions to get to this stage and, in practice, it would be worthwhile checking with the client that these were appropriate and realistic. Amongst the assumptions we've had to make are:

- The annual repayment amount of €250 000 is fixed over the next 20 years.
- The annual operating cost is €150 000 is also fixed over the next 20 years.
- The car park charges and the carbon offset charge will remain the same over the next 20 years.
- The carbon offset contribution of €0.25 only applies to those cars paying for car parking during semester.

Clearly, if the President felt that some, or all, of these assumptions were unrealistic then we could change the model accordingly. For example, we could build year-on-year increases into the operating costs figure and the car park charge to build in likely inflation. In practice, we'd probably want to build a simple spreadsheet model so the President could do some what-if analysis – analyzing the impact on breakeven if some aspects of the problem are assumed to change.

And recollecting that we've been asked to get involved in this project at the Modelling and Analysis stage, we might suggest to the President that it may be worth going back a stage and spending some time structuring and defining the problem. After all, we're starting from a position that it's already been decided that a new car park is the solution to the problem. Well, maybe it is and maybe it isn't. Have other factors been considered? Have other possible options been considered and evaluated? For example, are we sure the problem is one of too many cars? Or is too few people in most cars? Then perhaps promoting a car-sharing scheme might be more cost-effective? Is it poor public transport links to the College? If so, discussions with local transport companies might prove productive. And if it is a problem with too many cars, maybe we should look for other solution options. How about reducing the need for students to be on campus so often perhaps making library material available online could cut down on traffic volume. Perhaps for some classes running them as virtual classes through the Internet rather than face-to-face classes may also cut down on traffic and may even increase student numbers! That's good MS!

Problems

1 List and discuss the different stages of the management science approach.

SELF *test*

2 Discuss the different roles played by the qualitative and quantitative approaches to managerial decision making. Why is it important for a manager or decision maker to have a good understanding of both of these approaches to decision making?

3 A firm has just completed a new plant that will produce more than 500 different products, using more than 50 different production lines and machines. The production scheduling decisions are critical in that sales will be lost if customer demands are not met on time. If no individual in the firm has experience with this production operation, and if new production schedules must be generated each week, why should the firm consider a quantitative approach to the production scheduling problem? Why will qualitative analysis also be necessary?

SELF *test*

4 What are the advantages of analyzing and experimenting with a model as opposed to a real object or situation?

5 Suppose that a manager has a choice between the following two mathematical models of a given situation: (a) a relatively simple model that is a reasonable approximation

of the real situation, and (b) a thorough and complex model that is the most accurate mathematical representation of the real situation possible. Why might the model described in part (a) be preferred by the manager?

SELF *test*

6 Suppose you are going on a weekend trip to a city that is d kilometres away. Develop a model that determines your round-trip fuel costs. What assumptions or approximations are necessary? Are these assumptions or approximations acceptable to you?

7 A food store in Glasgow specializes in selling organic produce to local restaurants. In the summer it buys fresh raspberries (a Scottish delicacy) from two authorized organic farms in Tayside – the McGregor Farm and the Campbell Farm. Raspberries are supplied ready for sale in cartons containing ½ kilo. The McGregor Farm charges the food store £0.20 per carton and can supply no more than 4000 cartons a week during the short growing season. The Campbell Farm charges £0.25 per carton and can supply no more than 3000 cartons a week. The food store anticipates being able to sell cartons at £0.75.

Let x to represent the number of cartons each week shipped from the McGregor Farm and y to represent the number of cartons each week shipped from the Campbell Farm.

a. Write a mathematical expression to show the total number of cartons received each week by the Glasgow food store.
b. Write a mathematical expression to show the total cost of cartons received each week.
c. Write a mathematical expression to show the total profit made by the food store each week from selling cartons to local restaurants.
d. The food store anticipates that local restaurants will buy no more than 5000 cartons a week. Write this mathematically as a constraint.
e. Write mathematically the supply constraint for each farm.
f. Assuming the food store wants to maximize profit from selling raspberries, write out the full mathematical model.
g. What key assumptions have you had to make for f?

SELF *test*

8 For most products, higher prices result in a decreased demand, whereas lower prices result in an increased demand. Let:

$$d = \text{annual demand for a product in units}$$
$$p = \text{price per unit}$$

Assume that a firm accepts the following price-demand relationship as being realistic:

$$d = 800 - 10p$$

where p must be between €20 and €70.

a. How many units can the firm sell at the €20 per-unit price? At the €70 per-unit price?
b. Show the mathematical model for the total revenue (TR), which is the annual demand multiplied by the unit price.
c. Based on other considerations, the firm's management will only consider price alternatives of €30, €40 and €50. Use your model from part (b) to determine the price alternative that will maximize the total revenue.
d. What are the expected annual demand and the total revenue corresponding to your recommended price?

9 The O'Neill Shoe Manufacturing Company in Ireland will produce a special-style shoe if the order size is large enough to provide a reasonable profit. For each special-style order, the company incurs a fixed cost of €1000 for the production setup. The variable cost is €30 per pair, and each pair sells for €40.

a. Let x indicate the number of pairs of shoes produced. Develop a mathematical model for the total cost of producing x pairs of shoes.
b. Let P indicate the total profit. Develop a mathematical model for the total profit realized from an order for x pairs of shoes.
c. How large must the shoe order be before O'Neill will break even?

SELF *test*

10 Micromedia is a small computer training company based in South Africa. The company organizes training workshops for local employees who want to improve their skills in word processing, spreadsheets and so on. Micromedia is currently planning a two-day workshop on the use of Microsoft Excel in quantitative business modelling. The company intends to charge a fee per participant of 3000 Rand. The company estimates that it will cost around 48 000 Rand to run the workshop. This cost includes conference room, tutor fees, marketing. In addition the company rents PCs for its workshops from a local IT company at 300 Rand per day per PC.

a. Develop a model for the total cost to put on the seminar. Let x represent the number of participants who enrol in the workshop.
b. Develop a model for the total profit if x participants enrol in the workshop.
c. Micromedia has forecasted an enrolment of 30 participants for the workshop. How much profit will be earned if their forecast is accurate?
d. Calculate the breakeven point.

11 Naser Publishing Company is considering publishing a DVD on spreadsheet applications for business. The fixed cost of preparation, design and production setup is estimated to be €80 000. Variable production and material costs are estimated to be €3 per DVD. Demand over the life of the DVD is estimated to be 4000 copies. The publisher plans to sell the DVD to college and university bookstores for €20 each.

a. What is the breakeven point?
b. What profit or loss can be anticipated with a demand of 4000 copies?
c. With a demand of 4000 copies, what is the minimum price per copy that the publisher must charge to break even?
d. If the publisher believes that the price per DVD could be increased to €25.95 and not affect the anticipated demand of 4000 DVDs, what action would you recommend? What profit or loss can be anticipated?

SELF *test*

12 Preliminary plans are under way for the construction of a new stadium for a football team in Italy. Officials have questioned the number and profitability of the luxury corporate boxes planned for the upper deck of the stadium. Corporations and selected individuals may buy the boxes for €100 000 each. The fixed construction cost for the upper-deck area is estimated to be €1 500 000, with a variable cost of €50 000 for each box constructed.

a. What is the breakeven point for the number of luxury boxes in the new stadium?
b. Preliminary drawings for the stadium show that space is available for the construction of up to 50 luxury boxes. Promoters indicate that buyers are available and that all 50 could be sold if constructed. What is your recommendation concerning the construction of luxury boxes? What profit is anticipated?

CASE PROBLEM Uhuru Craft Cooperative, Tanzania

The Uhuru Craft Cooperative in Tanzania was established a few years ago by a number of aid agencies in an attempt to help the local economy diversify and increase income levels of the local community. The community itself is largely subsistence-based, has very low income levels, low levels of education, poor quality housing. The Cooperative brings together local craftworkers – wood carvers, potters, weavers and so on, to produce a variety of craft products using traditional techniques. These products are then sold on to FairTade retail companies across Europe for re-sale to consumers. The local craftworkers are paid immediately by the Cooperative and do not have to worry about marketing, sales, transportation of their products as all of this is taken care of by the Cooperative. The Cooperative operates on a commercial basis but any profit made by the Cooperative is ploughed back into the project or into the local community. The Cooperative also organizes training for local young people so they can develop their own craft skills. The project has proved both popular and successful to such an extent that expansion is now under consideration and the Cooperative is looking for your help. The Cooperative is keen to bring more women into the scheme and is considering investing in an additional workshop where local women will be able to produce traditional children's dolls. The initial investment will be around €25 000 for a new building and for sewing equipment that the local women will use. It's estimated that it will cost around €10 per item to produce, market and ship the dolls to Europe. One FairTrade company has already expressed an interest in buying the product indicating it would be prepared to pay around €30 per item. A second option under consideration is to buy second hand sewing equipment which will reduce the initial investment to €17 500. However, this will push up the cost per item to €12.

Managerial Report

Prepare a report for the Cooperative Manager. Your report should include:

1 Information about the breakeven sales volume if new sewing equipment is purchased.
2 Information about the breakeven sales volume if second hand sewing equipment is purchased.
3 Any other advice you can give that would help the Cooperative decide what to do.

Appendix 1.1 Using Excel for Breakeven Analysis

We introduced the Nowlin Plastics production example to illustrate how quantitative models can be used to help a manager determine the projected cost, revenue and/or profit associated with an established production quantity or a forecasted sales volume. We now introduce spreadsheet applications by showing how to use Microsoft Excel to perform a quantitative analysis of the Nowlin Plastics example.

Refer to the worksheet shown in Figure 1.4. We begin by entering the problem data into the top portion of the worksheet. The value of 3000 in cell B3 is the setup cost, the value of 2 in cell B5 is the variable labour and material costs per unit and the value of 5 in cell B7 is the selling price per unit. In general, whenever we perform a quantitative analysis using Excel, we will enter the problem data in the top portion of the worksheet and reserve the bottom portion for model development. The label 'Models' in cell A10 helps to provide a visual reminder of this convention.

Cell B12 in the models portion of the worksheet contains the proposed production volume in units. Because the values for total cost, total revenue and total profit depend upon the value of this decision variable, we have placed a border around cell B12 and screened the cell for emphasis. Based upon the value in cell B12, the cell formulas in cells B14, B16 and B18 are used to compute values for total cost, total revenue and total profit (loss), respectively. First, recall that the value of total cost is

Figure 1.4 Formula Worksheet for the Nowlin Plastics Production Example

	A	B	C
1	**Nowlin Plastics**		
2			
3	**Fixed Cost**	3000	
4			
5	**Variable Cost Per Unit**	2	
6			
7	**Selling Price Per Unit**	5	
8			
9			
10	**Models**		
11			
12	**Production Volume**	800	
13			
14	**Total Cost**	=B3+B5*B12	
15			
16	**Total Revenue**	=B7*B12	
17			
18	**Total Profit (Loss)**	=B16-B14	
19			

EXCEL *file*

NOWLIN

the sum of the fixed cost (cell B3) and the total variable cost. The total variable cost – the product of the variable cost per unit (cell B5) and the production volume (cell B12) – is given by B5*B12. So, to compute the value of total cost we entered the formula = B3+B5*B12 in cell B14. Next, total revenue is the product of the selling price per unit (cell B7) and the number of units produced (cell B12), which is entered in cell B16 as the formula = B7*B12. Finally, the total profit (or loss) is the difference between the total revenue (cell B16) and the total cost (cell B14). Thus, in cell B18 we have entered the formula = B16–B14. The worksheet shown in Figure 1.4 shows the formulas used to make these computations; we refer to it as a formula worksheet.

To examine the effect of selecting a particular value for the production volume, we entered a value of 800 in cell B12. The worksheet shown in Figure 1.5 shows the values obtained by the formulae; a production volume of 800 units results in a total cost of €4600, a total revenue of €4000, and a loss of €600. To examine the effect of other production volumes, we only need to enter a different value into cell B12. To examine the effect of different costs and selling prices, we simply enter the appropriate values in the data portion of the worksheet; the results will be displayed in the model section of the worksheet.

In Section 1.6 we illustrated breakeven analysis. Let us now see how Excel's Goal Seek tool can be used to determine the breakeven point for the Nowlin Plastics production example.

Determining the Breakeven Point Using Excel's Goal Seek Tool

The breakeven point is the production volume that results in total revenue equal to total cost and hence a profit of €0. One way to determine the breakeven point is to use a trial-and-error approach. For example, in Figure 1.5 we saw that a trial production volume of 800 units resulted in a loss of €600. Because this trial solution resulted in a loss, a production volume of 800 units cannot be the breakeven point. We could continue to experiment with other production volumes by simply entering different values into cell B12 and observing the resulting profit or loss in cell B18. A better approach is to use Excel's Goal Seek tool to determine the breakeven point.

Figure 1.5 Solution Using a Production Volume of 800 Units for the Nowlin Plastics Production Example

	A	B	C
1	**Nowlin Plastics**		
2			
3	**Fixed Cost**	€3 000	
4			
5	**Variable Cost Per Unit**	€2	
6			
7	**Selling Price Per Unit**	€5	
8			
9			
10	**Models**		
11			
12	**Production Volume**	800	
13			
14	**Total Cost**	€4 600	
15			
16	**Total Revenue**	€4 000	
17			
18	**Total Profit (Loss)**	-€600	
19			

Excel's Goal Seek tool allows the user to determine the value for an input cell that will cause the value of a related output cell to equal some specified value (called the *goal*). In the case of breakeven analysis, the 'goal' is to set Total Profit to zero by 'seeking' an appropriate value for Production Volume. Goal Seek will allow us to find the value of production volume that will set Nowlin Plastics' total profit to zero. The following steps describe how to use Goal Seek to find the breakeven point for Nowlin Plastics:

Step 1. Select the **Tools** menu

Step 2. Choose the **Goal Seek** option

Step 3. When the **Goal Seek** dialog box appears:
Enter B18 in the **Set cell** box
Enter 0 in the **To value** box
Enter B12 in the **By changing cell** box
Click **OK**

The completed Goal Seek dialogue box is shown in Figure 1.6, and the worksheet obtained after selecting **OK** is shown in Figure 1.7. The Total Profit in cell B18 is zero, and the Production Volume in cell B12 has been set to the breakeven point of 1000.

Figure 1.6 Goal Seek Dialogue Box for the Nowlin Plastics Production Example

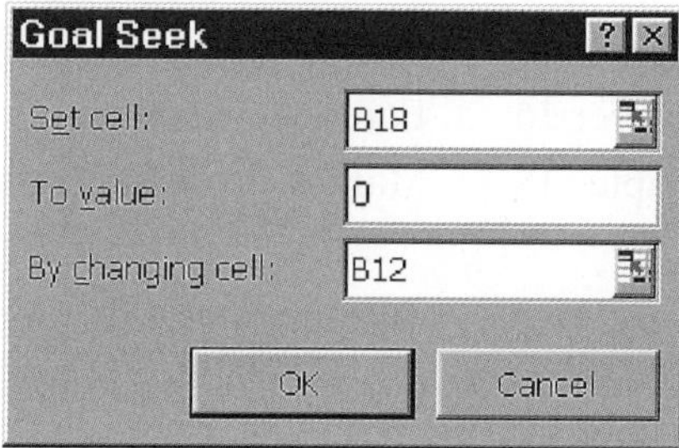

Figure 1.7 Breakeven Point Found Using Excel's Goal Seek Tool for the Nowlin Plastics Production Example

	A	B	C
1	**Nowlin Plastics**		
2			
3	**Fixed Cost**	€3 000	
4			
5	**Variable Cost Per Unit**	€2	
6			
7	**Selling Price Per Unit**	€5	
8			
9			
10	**Models**		
11			
12	**Production Volume**	1000	
13			
14	**Total Cost**	5 000	
15			
16	**Total Revenue**	5 000	
17			
18	**Total Profit (Loss)**	0	
19			

Appendix 1.2 The Management Scientist Software

Developments in computer technology play a major role in making management science techniques available to decision makers. A software package called *The Management Scientist* Version 6.0 for most Windows operating systems is provided on the online plaform accompanying this text.[1] This software can be used to solve problems in the text as well as small-scale problems encountered in practice. Using The Management Scientist will provide an understanding and appreciation of the role of the computer in applying management science to decision problems.

The Management Scientist contains 12 modules, or programmes, that will enable you to solve problems in the following areas:

Chapters 2–6	Linear programming
Chapter 7	Transportation and assignment
Chapter 8	Shortest route and minimal spanning tree
Chapter 9	PERT/CPM
Chapter 10	Inventory models
Chapter 11	Waiting line models
Chapter 13	Decision analysis
Chapter 15	Integer linear programming (online)
Chapter 16	Forecasting (online)
Chapter 18	Markov processes (online)

[1]Version 6.0 has been designed to run optimally on computers with screen resolutions of 1024×768 or higher. Computers with lower screen resolutions can still run Version 6.0. Scroll bars appear when necessary for working with large problems. See the 'Digital Resources' page in the front of the book for details on accessing the online platform.

Figure 1.8 Module Selection Screen for the Management Scientist Version 6.0

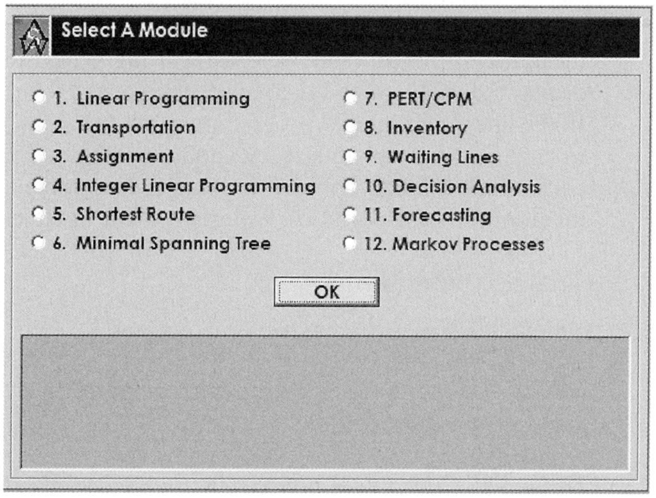

Select A Module

1. Linear Programming
2. Transportation
3. Assignment
4. Integer Linear Programming
5. Shortest Route
6. Minimal Spanning Tree
7. PERT/CPM
8. Inventory
9. Waiting Lines
10. Decision Analysis
11. Forecasting
12. Markov Processes

OK

Use of The Management Scientist with the text is optional. Occasionally, we insert a figure in the text that shows the output The Management Scientist provides for a problem. However, familiarity with the use of the software is not necessary to understand the figure and the text material. The remainder of this appendix provides an overview of the features and the use of the software.

Selecting a Module

After starting The Management Scientist, you will encounter the module selection screen as shown in Figure 1.8. The choices provide access to the 12 modules. Simply click the desired module and select OK to load the requested module into the computer's memory.

The File Menu

After a module is loaded, you will need to click the File menu to begin working with a problem. The File menu provides the following options.

New Select this option to begin a new problem. Dialogue boxes and input templates will guide you through the data input process.

Open Select this option to retrieve a problem that has been previously saved. When the problem is selected it will be displayed on the screen for you to verify as the problem you want to solve.

Save Once a new problem has been entered, you may want to save it for future use or modification. The Save option will guide you through the naming and saving process. If you create a folder named Problems, the Open and Save options will take you automatically to the Problems folder.

Change Modules This option returns control to the screen in Figure 1.8 and another module may be selected.

Exit This option will exit The Management Scientist.

The Edit Menu

After a new problem has been solved, you may want to make one or more modifications to the problem before resolving. The Edit menu provides the option to display the problem and then make revisions in the problem before solving or saving. In the linear and integer programming modules, the Edit menu also includes options to change the problem size by adding or deleting variables and adding or deleting constraints. Similar options to change the problem size are provided in the Edit menu of the transportation and assignment modules.

The Solution Menu

The Solution menu provides three options.

Solve This option solves the current problem and displays the solution on the screen.

Print Once the solution is on the screen, the Print option sends the solution to a printer.

Save As Text File Once the solution is on the screen, the Save As Text File option enables the solution to be saved as a text file. The text file can be accessed later by a word processor so that the solution output may be displayed as part of a solution report.

Advice About Data Input

Any time a new problem is selected, the appropriate module will provide dialogue boxes and forms for describing the features of the problem and for entering data. When using The Management Scientist, you may find the following data input suggestions helpful.

1. Do not enter commas (,) with your input data. For example, the value 104,000 should be entered with the six digits: 104000.
2. Do not enter the dollar sign ($) for profit or cost data. For example, a cost of $20.00 should be entered as 20.
3. Do not enter the percent sign (%) if percentage is requested. For example, 25% should be entered as 25, not 25% or .25.
4. Occasionally, a model may be formulated with fractional values such as $^1/_4$, $^2/_3$, $^5/_6$, and so on. The data input for The Management Scientist must be in decimal form. The fraction $^1/_4$ can be entered as .25. However, fractions such as $^2/_3$ and $^5/_6$ have repeating decimal forms. In these cases, we recommend the convention of rounding to five places such as .66667 and .83333.
5. Finally, we recommend that in general you attempt to scale extremely large input data so that smaller numbers may be input and operated on by the computer. For example, costs such as $2 500 000 may be scaled to 2.5 with the understanding that the data used in the problem reflect millions of dollars.

Chapter 2

An Introduction to Linear Programming

Learning objectives

By the end of this chapter you will be able to:

- Formulate a linear programme
- Solve a two variable linear programming problem
- Interpret the computer solution to a linear programming problem

We saw in Chapter 1 that management science makes extensive use of mathematical models. One of the first types of model to be developed – and since used extensively – is that of ***linear programming***. In fact, linear programming (LP) is sufficiently important to management science that we shall be spending the next five chapters looking at LP and its developments. Linear programming is a management science technique used in many countries and by many different types of organization – manufacturing companies, service organizations, government agencies, not-for-profit organizations. Delta Airlines facing a decision problem in deciding which type of aircraft in its fleet should be allocated to different flight routes; health care planners in Rome planning the home care service provided to patients with AIDS; the Arabian Light Metals Company in Kuwait trying to decide on the mixture of aluminium-based products to manufacture; London Underground trying to decide on crew rostering for its services. Managers are often in a situation where they are looking to make the best decision possible but where the options they face limit – or *constraint* – what they are actually able to do. In such situations, LP can often prove a very useful model to apply. To illustrate some of the properties that all LP problems have in common, let us consider the following typical applications:

George B. Dantzig (1914–2005) is the American mathematician generally credited with suggesting linear programming in 1947, although it was independently suggested some years earlier by Soviet economist and mathematician Leonid Kantorovich.

1. A manufacturer of mobile phones is looking at the production schedule for the next few months and trying to decide how many of each phone model to manufacture in order to meet demand forecasts for different sales regions. Clearly, the production schedule will need to ensure that enough phones are produced to meet projected demand in each sales region but at the same time *minimize* production costs.
2. A financial analyst must select an investment portfolio for a high-value client from a variety of investment alternatives. The analyst would like to establish the portfolio that *maximizes* the return on investment. At the same time, though, the analyst also has to satisfy certain client requirements in terms of the mix of investments and the risk associated with each.
3. A marketing manager wants to determine how best to allocate a fixed advertising budget among alternative advertising media such as Internet, television, newspaper and magazine. The manager would like to determine the media mix that *maximizes* advertising effectiveness but within the budget constraint faced.
4. A regional health centre collects and stores blood donations that are used in the region's hospitals. The transportation manger has to ensure that each hospital receives the supply of blood it needs to treat patients and at the same time *minimize* the time taken to transport blood supplies from the centre to the various hospitals.

In this chapter we shall introduce the basic concepts of linear programming and see how to formulate and solve linear programming problems. In subsequent chapters we shall expand on the basic model.

These examples are only a few of the situations in which linear programming has been used successfully, but they illustrate the diversity of linear programming applications. A close scrutiny reveals one basic property they all have in common. In each example, we were concerned with *maximizing* or *minimizing* some quantity. In example 1, the manufacturer wanted to minimize costs; in example 2, the financial analyst wanted to maximize return on investment; in example 3, the marketing manager wanted to maximize advertising effectiveness; and in example 4, the company wanted to minimize total transportation time. *In all linear programming problems, the maximization or minimization of some quantity is the objective.*

Linear programming was initially referred to as 'programming in a linear structure'. In 1948 Tjalling Koopmans suggested to George Dantzig that the name was much too long; Koopmans suggested shortening it to linear programming. George Dantzig agreed and the field we now know as linear programming was named.

All linear programming problems also have a second property: restrictions or **constraints** that limit the degree to which the objective can be pursued. In example 1, the manufacturer is restricted by constraints requiring product demand to be satisfied and

MANAGEMENT SCIENCE IN ACTION

The Kellogg Company

The Kellogg Company is the world's largest producer of cereals and has an international brand awareness. Like many companies Kellogg is faced with a variety of routine, inter-connected decisions about its cereal production. It produces hundreds of different products, with new products frequently introduced as consumer demand and preferences change. Its products are produced at a number of different production plants and the company has a number of operational decisions to take to ensure profitability. What quantities of each product should be produced over the next planning period? How much of each product should be produced at each plant? Which plants should supply which customers and sales outlets? How much should we produce for stocks/inventory and how much for sales? The company has been developing and using since the late 1980s in-house planning systems which are structured around a large scale, multi-period linear programming model (KPS). The model is used to help with decision making at both the operational and strategic levels. The operational version of the KPS is used on a weekly basis to help management take decisions on production, packaging, inventory and distribution. The KPS is also used on a longer term basis to help develop plans relating to plant development, capacity expansion and plant location. It is estimated that savings of around $4.5 million a year have already been realized from using the model and that when completed annual savings of around $35–40 million will be achieved.

Based on Gerald Brown, Joseph Keegan, Brian Vigus and Kevin Wood, 'The Kellogg Company Optimizes Production, Inventory and Distribution', *Interfaces* 31 6 (Nov/Dec 2001): 1–15.

Dantzig's contribution to LP was recognized by the Mathematical Programming Society through the Dantzig Award, given every three years since 1982 to one or two people who have made a significant impact in the field of mathematical programming.

by the constraints limiting production capacity. The financial analyst's portfolio problem is constrained by the total amount of investment funds available and the maximum amounts that can be invested in each stock or bond. The marketing manager's media selection decision is constrained by a fixed advertising budget and the availability of the various media. In the transportation problem, the minimum-time shipping schedule is constrained by the supply of blood available and the demand from hospitals. *Thus, constraints are another general feature of every linear programming problem.*

2.1 A Maximization Problem

GulfGolf is a small family-run company in the United Arab Emirates. It manufactures golfing equipment aimed at the increasing demand, primarily from tourists coming for golfing holidays in the Gulf region. The company has decided to manufacture two new products: a medium-priced golf bag and a more up-market, expensive golf bag. The company's products are priced in US$ given its international customer base. The company's distributor is enthusiastic about the new product line and has agreed to buy all the golf bags the company produces over the next three months.

After a thorough investigation of the steps involved in manufacturing a golf bag, management determined that each golf bag produced will require the following four operations:

1. Cutting and dyeing the material needed.
2. Sewing.
3. Finishing (inserting umbrella holder, club separators, etc.).
4. Inspection and packaging.

Table 2.1 Production Requirements Per Golf Bag

	Production Time (hours)	
Department	**Standard Bag**	**Deluxe Bag**
Cutting and Dyeing	$^{7}/_{10}$	1
Sewing	$^{1}/_{2}$	$^{5}/_{6}$
Finishing	1	$^{2}/_{3}$
Inspection and Packaging	$^{1}/_{10}$	$^{1}/_{4}$

The director of manufacturing analyzed each of the operations and concluded that if the company produces a medium-priced standard model, each bag will require $^{7}/_{10}$ hours in the cutting and dyeing department, $^{1}/_{2}$ hour in the sewing department, one hour in the finishing department, and $^{1}/_{10}$ hour in the inspection and packaging department. The more expensive deluxe model will require one hour for cutting and dyeing, $^{5}/_{6}$ hour for sewing, $^{2}/_{3}$ hour for finishing, and $^{1}/_{4}$ hour for inspection and packaging. This production information is summarized in Table 2.1.

Production is constrained by the limited number of hours available in each department. After studying departmental workload projections, the director of manufacturing estimates that 630 hours for cutting and dyeing, 600 hours for sewing, 708 hours for finishing and 135 hours for inspection and packaging will be available for the production of golf bags during the next three months.

The accounting department analyzed the production data, assigned all relevant variable costs and arrived at prices for both bags that will result in a profit contribution[1] of $10 for every standard bag and $9 for every deluxe bag produced.

It is important to understand that we are maximizing profit contribution, not profit. Overhead and other shared costs must be deducted before arriving at a profit figure.

It is fairly clear what the decision problem is that the company faces: how many of the two types of golf bag should it manufacture in order to maximize profit contribution? What is less clear is the answer to the problem. This is where LP can help and we will work through a number of stages. First, that of **problem formulation**, where we produce a mathematical statement of the LP problem. Then that of **problem solution**, where we find the answer to the decision problem we are looking at. Finally, that of **interpretation**, where we consider what the company should do.

Problem Formulation

Problem formulation or **modelling** is the process of translating the verbal statement of a problem into a mathematical statement. Formulating models is an art that can only be mastered with practise and experience. But even though every problem has some unique features, most problems also have common features. As a result, *some* general guidelines for model formulation can be helpful, especially for beginners. We will illustrate these general guidelines by developing a mathematical model for the GulfGolf problem.

Understand the Problem Thoroughly We selected the GulfGolf problem to introduce linear programming because it is easy to understand. However, more complex problems will require much more thinking in order to identify the items that need to be included in the model. In such cases, read the problem description quickly to get a feel for what is involved. Taking notes will help you focus on the key issues and facts.

[1]From an accounting perspective, profit contribution is more correctly described as the contribution margin per bag; for example, overhead and other shared costs have not been allocated.

Describe the Objective The objective here is to maximize the total contribution to profit.

Describe Each Constraint Four constraints relate to the number of hours of manufacturing time available; they restrict the number of standard bags and the number of deluxe bags that can be produced.

Constraint 1 Number of hours of cutting and dyeing time used must be less than or equal to the number of hours of cutting and dyeing time available.

Constraint 2 Number of hours of sewing time used must be less than or equal to the number of hours of sewing time available.

Constraint 3 Number of hours of finishing time used must be less than or equal to the number of hours of finishing time available.

Constraint 4 Number of hours of inspection and packaging time used must be less than or equal to the number of hours of inspection and packaging time available.

Define the Decision Variables A decision variable is one where management can control its value and therefore decide what value the variable should take. The controllable values for GulfGolf are (1) the number of standard bags produced, and (2) the number of deluxe bags produced. Let:

$$S = \text{number of standard bags}$$
$$D = \text{number of deluxe bags}$$

In linear programming terminology, S and D are referred to as the **decision variables**.

Write the Objective in Terms of the Decision Variables The company's profit contribution comes from two sources: (1) the profit contribution made by producing S standard bags, and (2) the profit contribution made by producing D deluxe bags. If the company makes \$10 for every standard bag, the company will make \$10S if S standard bags are produced. Also, if the company makes \$9 for every deluxe bag, the company will make \$9D if D deluxe bags are produced. So, we have:

$$\text{Total Profit Contribution} = 10S + 9D$$

Because the objective – maximize total profit contribution – is a function of the decision variables S and D, we refer to $10S + 9D$ as the *objective function*. Using 'Max' as an abbreviation for maximize, we write GulfGolf's objective as follows:

$$\text{Max } 10S + 9D$$

Write the Constraints in Terms of the Decision Variables
Constraint 1:

$$\begin{pmatrix}\text{Hours of cutting and} \\ \text{dyeing time used}\end{pmatrix} \leq \begin{pmatrix}\text{Hours of cutting and} \\ \text{dyeing time available}\end{pmatrix}$$

Every standard bag GulfGolf produces will use $^{7}/_{10}$ hour cutting and dyeing time; therefore, the total number of hours of cutting and dyeing time used in the manufacture of S standard bags is $^{7}/_{10}S$. In addition, because every deluxe bag produced uses one hour of cutting and dyeing time, the production of D deluxe bags will use $1D$ hours of cutting and dyeing time. So, the total cutting and dyeing time required for the production of S standard bags and D deluxe bags is given by:

The units of measurement on the left-hand side of the constraint must match the units of measurement on the right-hand side.

$$\text{Total hours of cutting and dyeing time used} = {}^{7}/_{10}\, S + 1D$$

The director of manufacturing stated that GulfGolf has at most 630 hours of cutting and dyeing time available. Therefore, the production combination we select must satisfy the requirement:

$$\tfrac{7}{10}S + 1D \leq 630 \tag{2.1}$$

Constraint 2:

$$\begin{pmatrix}\text{Hours of sewing}\\ \text{time used}\end{pmatrix} \leq \begin{pmatrix}\text{Hours of sewing}\\ \text{time available}\end{pmatrix}$$

From Table 2.1 we see that every standard bag manufactured will require $^1\!/_2$ hour for sewing, and every deluxe bag will require $^5\!/_6$ hour for sewing. Because 600 hours of sewing time are available, it follows that:

$$\tfrac{1}{2}S + \tfrac{5}{6}D \leq 600 \tag{2.2}$$

Constraint 3:

$$\begin{pmatrix}\text{Hours of finishing}\\ \text{time used}\end{pmatrix} \leq \begin{pmatrix}\text{Hours of finishing}\\ \text{time available}\end{pmatrix}$$

Every standard bag manufactured will require one hour for finishing, and every deluxe bag will require $^2\!/_3$ hour for finishing. With 708 hours of finishing time available, it follows that:

$$1S + \tfrac{2}{3}D \leq 708 \tag{2.3}$$

Constraint 4:

$$\begin{pmatrix}\text{Hours of inspection and}\\ \text{packaging time used}\end{pmatrix} \leq \begin{pmatrix}\text{Hours of inspection and}\\ \text{packaging time available}\end{pmatrix}$$

Every standard bag manufactured will require $^1\!/_{10}$ hour for inspection and packaging, and every deluxe bag will require $^1\!/_4$ hour for inspection and packaging. Because 135 hours of inspection and packaging time are available, it follows that:

$$\tfrac{1}{10}S + \tfrac{1}{4}D \leq 135 \tag{2.4}$$

We have now specified the mathematical relationships for the constraints associated with the four departments. Have we forgotten any other constraints? Can the company produce a negative number of standard or deluxe bags? Clearly, the answer is *no*. So, to prevent the decision variables S and D from having negative values, two constraints,

$$S \geq 0 \quad \text{and} \quad D \geq 0 \tag{2.5}$$

must be added. These constraints ensure that the solution to the problem will contain nonnegative values for the decision variables and are referred to as the **nonnegativity constraints**. Nonnegativity constraints are a general feature of all linear programming problems and may be written in the abbreviated form:

$$S,\ D \geq 0$$

Mathematical Statement of the GulfGolf Problem

Try Problem 13 to test your ability to formulate a mathematical model for a maximization linear programming problem with less-than-or-equal-to constraints.

The mathematical statement or mathematical formulation of the GulfGolf problem is now complete. We succeeded in translating the objective and constraints of the problem into a set of mathematical relationships referred to as a **mathematical model**. The complete mathematical model for the problem is then:

$$\begin{array}{lll} \text{Max} & 10S + 9D & \\ \text{subject to (s.t.)} & & \\ & \tfrac{7}{10}S + 1D \leq 630 & \text{Cutting and dyeing} \\ & \tfrac{1}{2}S + \tfrac{5}{6}D \leq 600 & \text{Sewing} \\ & 1S + \tfrac{2}{3}D \leq 708 & \text{Finishing} \\ & \tfrac{7}{10}S + \tfrac{1}{4}D \leq 135 & \text{Inspection and packaging} \\ & S,\ D \geq 0 & \end{array}$$

However, because we shall be carrying out a variety of mathematical operations using these data it will be useful to show the formulation in decimal notation rather than fractional, giving:

$$\begin{array}{ll} \text{Max} & 10S + 9D \\ \text{s.t.} & \\ & 0.7S + 1D \leq 630 \\ & 0.5S + 0.8333D \leq 600 \\ & 1S + 0.6667D \leq 708 \\ & 0.1S + 0.25D \leq 135 \\ & S, D \geq 0 \end{array} \quad \textbf{(2.6)}$$

Our job now is to find the product mix (i.e., the combination of S and D) that satisfies all the constraints and, at the same time, yields the maximum possible value for the objective function. Once these values are calculated, we will have found the optimal solution to the problem.

This mathematical model of the problem is a **linear programming model**, or **linear programme**. The problem has the objective and constraints that, as we said earlier, are common properties of all *linear* programmes. But what is the special feature of this mathematical model that makes it a linear programme? The special feature that makes it a linear programme is that the objective function and all constraint functions (the left-hand sides of the constraint inequalities) are linear functions of the decision variables.

Try Problem 1 to test your ability to recognize the types of mathematical relationships that can be found in a linear programme.

Mathematical functions in which each variable appears in a separate term and is raised to the first power are called **linear functions**. The objective function ($10S + 9D$) is linear because each decision variable appears in a separate term and has an exponent of 1. The amount of production time required in the cutting and dyeing department ($0.7S + 1D$) is also a linear function of the decision variables for the same reason. Similarly, the functions on the left-hand side of all the constraint inequalities (the constraint functions) are linear functions. Thus, the mathematical formulation of this problem is referred to as a linear programme.

Linear *programming* has nothing to do with computer programming. The use of the word *programming* here means 'choosing a course of action'. Linear programming involves choosing a course of action when the mathematical model of the problem contains only linear functions.

NOTES AND COMMENTS

1 The three key assumptions necessary for a linear programming model to be appropriate are proportionality, additivity and divisibility. *Proportionality* means that the contribution to the objective function and the amount of resources used in each constraint are proportional to the value of each decision variable. *Additivity* means that the value of the objective function and the total resources used can be found by summing the objective function contribution and the resources used for all decision variables. *Divisibility* means that the decision variables are continuous. The divisibility assumption plus the nonnegativity constraints mean that decision variables can take on any value greater than or equal to zero.

2 Management scientists formulate and solve a variety of mathematical models that contain an objective function and a set of constraints. Models of this type are referred to as *mathematical programming models*. Linear programming models are one type of mathematical programming model in that the objective function and all constraint functions are linear.

2.2 Graphical Solution Procedure

Kellogg's KPS LP model has around 100 000 constraints and 700 000 variables.

A linear programming problem involving only two decision variables can be solved using a graphical solution procedure. Clearly, in the real world LP problems will have many more decision variables (and constraints) and cannot be solved graphically (we will see how bigger problems are solved in later chapters). However, the graphical solution introduces some important principles of LP solution that we need to understand. Let us begin the graphical solution procedure by developing a graph that displays the possible solutions (S and D values) for the GulfGolf problem. The graph (Figure 2.1) will have values of S on the horizontal axis and values of D on the vertical axis (it wouldn't matter if we put these the other way around). Any point on the graph can be identified by the S and D values, which indicate the position of the point along the horizontal and vertical axes, respectively. Because every point (S, D) corresponds to a possible solution, every point on the graph is called a *solution point*. The solution point where $S = 0$ and $D = 0$ is referred to as the origin. Because S and D must be nonnegative, the graph in Figure 2.1 only displays solutions where $S \geq 0$ and $D \geq 0$.

Earlier, we saw that the inequality representing the cutting and dyeing constraint is:

$$0.7S + 1D \leq 630$$

To show all solution points that satisfy this relationship, we start by graphing the solution points satisfying the constraint as an equality. That is, the points where $0.7S + 1D = 630$. Because the graph of this equation is a line, it can be obtained by identifying any two points that satisfy the equation and then drawing a line through those points. Setting $S = 0$ and solving for D, we see that the point ($S = 0, D = 630$) satisfies the equation. To find a second point satisfying this equation, we set $D = 0$ and solve for S. By doing so, we obtain $0.7S + 1(0) = 630$, or $S = 900$. Thus, a second point satisfying the equation is ($S = 900$, $D = 0$). Given these two points, we can now graph the line corresponding to the equation. This line, which will be called the cutting and dyeing *constraint line*, is shown in Figure 2.2. We label this line 'C & D' to indicate that it represents the cutting and dyeing constraint line.

Figure 2.1 Solution Points for the Two-Variable GulfGolf Problem

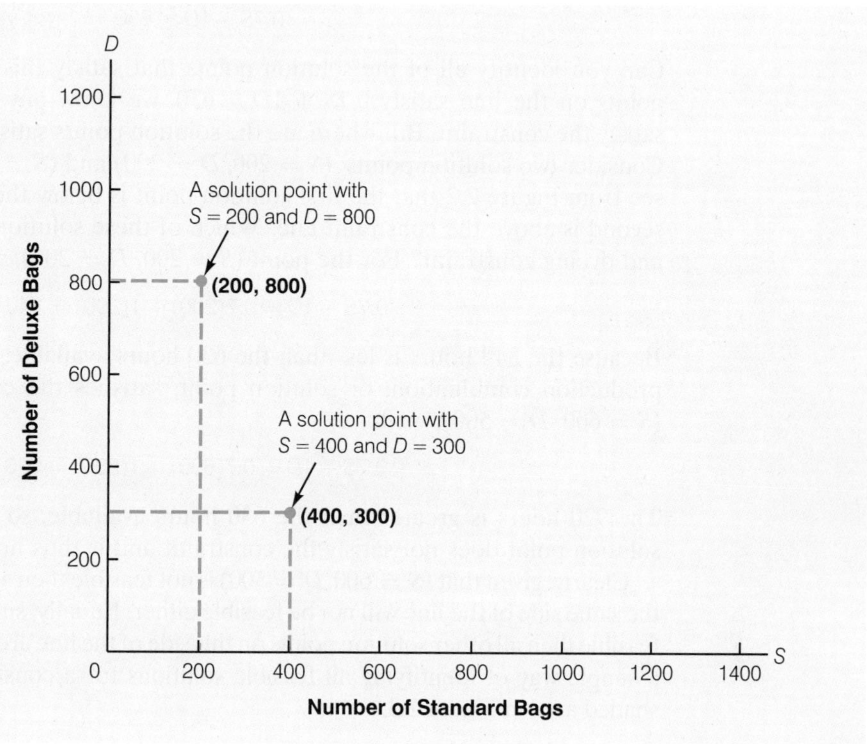

Figure 2.2 The Cutting and Dyeing Constraint Line

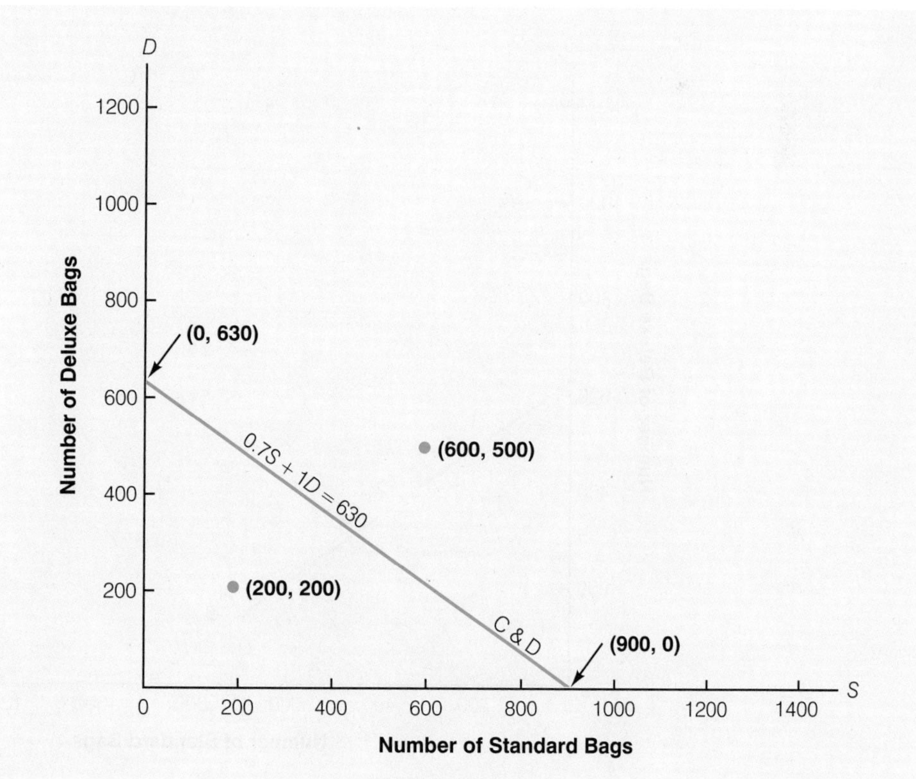

Recall that the inequality representing the cutting and dyeing constraint is:

$$0.7S + 1D \leq 630$$

Can you identify all of the solution points that satisfy this constraint? Because all points on the line satisfy $0.7S + 1D = 630$, we know any point on this line must satisfy the constraint. But where are the solution points satisfying $0.7S + 1D < 630$? Consider two solution points: ($S = 200, D = 200$) and ($S = 600, D = 500$). You can see from Figure 2.2 that the first solution point is below the constraint line and the second is above the constraint line. Which of these solutions will satisfy the cutting and dyeing constraint? For the point ($S = 200, D = 200$), we see that:

$$0.7S + 1D = 0.7(200) + 1(200) = 340$$

Because the 340 hours is less than the 630 hours available, the ($S = 200, D = 200$) production combination, or solution point, satisfies the constraint. For the point ($S = 600, D = 500$), we have:

$$0.7S + 1D = 0.7(600) + 1(500) = 920$$

The 920 hours is greater than the 630 hours available, so the ($S = 600, D = 500$) solution point does not satisfy the constraint and is thus not feasible.

Clearly, given that ($S = 600, D = 500$) is not feasible then all other solution points on the same side of the line will not be feasible either. Equally, since ($S = 200, D = 200$) is feasible then all other solution points on this side of the line are also feasible. So, we have a simple way of identifying all feasible solutions for a constraint, as shown with the shaded area in Figure 2.3.

Figure 2.3 Feasible Solutions for the Cutting and Dyeing Constraint, Represented by the Shaded Region

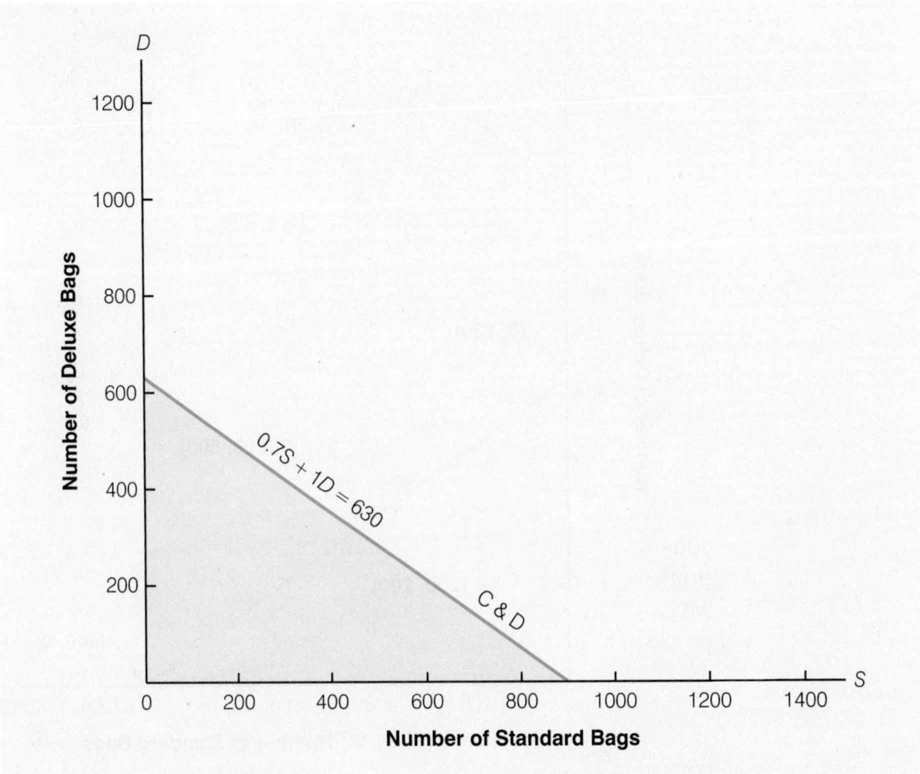

Figure 2.4 Feasible Solutions for the Sewing, Finishing, and Inspection and Packaging Constraints, Represented by the Shaded Regions

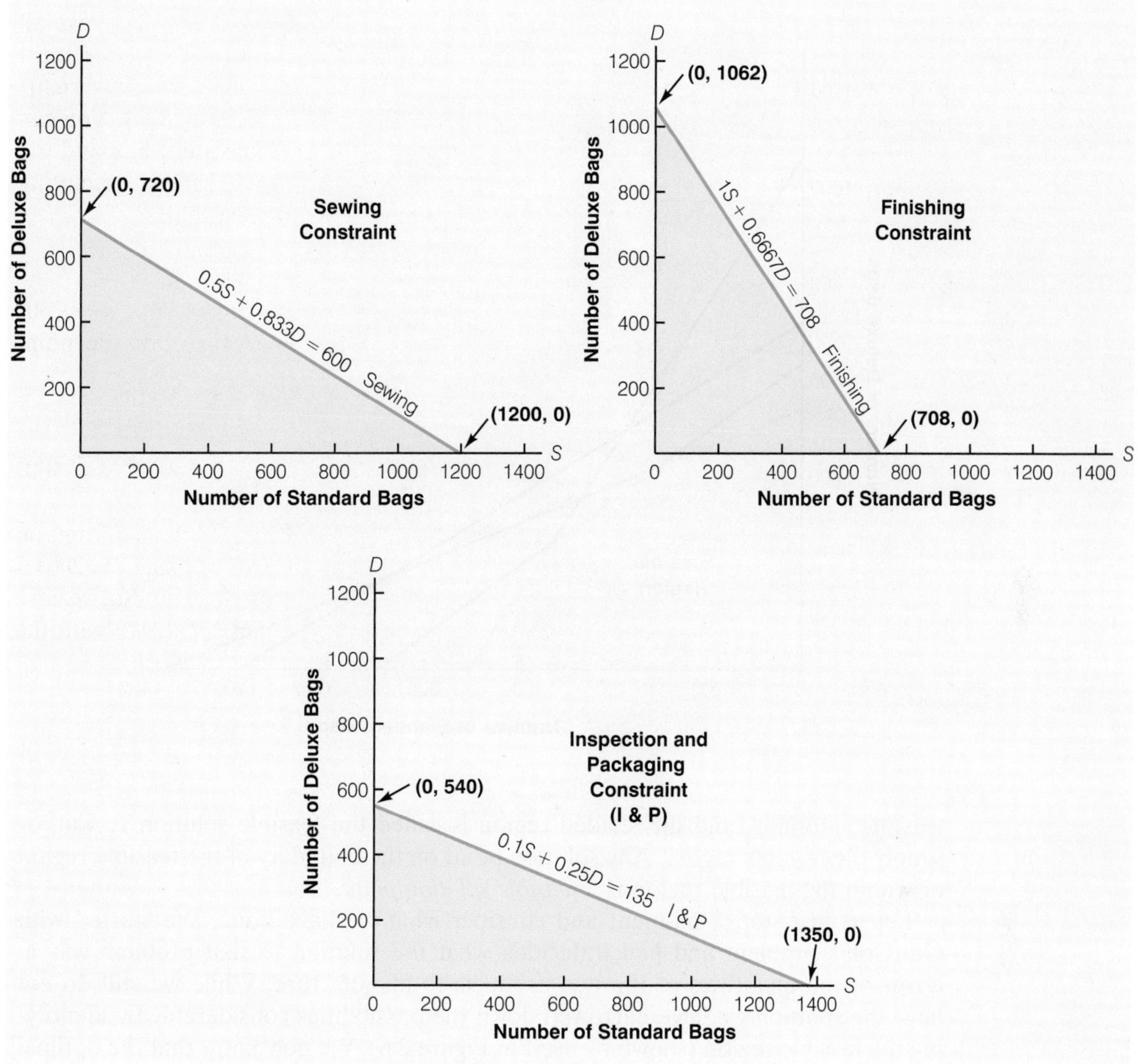

We can do the same for each of the other three constraints. The solutions that are feasible for each of these constraints are shown in Figure 2.4. We would normally draw all the constraints on a single graph but here we have drawn them separately to help you understand the principles more easily.

Four separate graphs now show the feasible solution points for each of the four constraints. In a linear programming problem, we need to identify the solution points that satisfy *all* the constraints *simultaneously*. To find these solution points, we can draw all four constraints on one graph and observe the region containing the points that satisfy all the constraints simultaneously.

Try Problem 6 to test your ability to find the feasible region given several constraints.

The graphs in Figures 2.3 and 2.4 can be superimposed to obtain one graph with all four constraints. This combined-constraint graph is shown in Figure 2.5. The shaded region in this figure includes every solution point that satisfies *all* the constraints simultaneously. Solutions that satisfy all the constraints are termed

Figure 2.5 Combined-Constraint Graph Showing the Feasible Region for the GulfGolf Problem

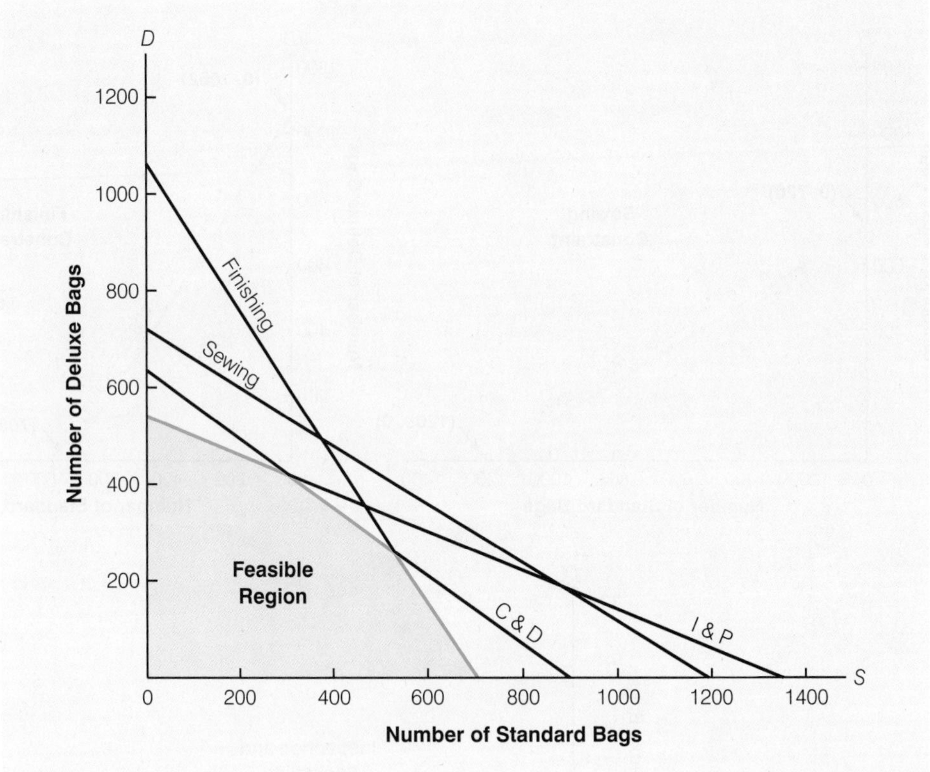

feasible solutions, and the shaded region is called the feasible solution region, or simply the feasible region. Any solution point on the boundary of the feasible region or within the feasible region is a *feasible solution point*.

Let us just stop a moment and consider what we have done. We started with GulfGolf's problem and had little idea what the solution to that problem was in terms of the quantities of the two products to manufacture. While we still do not have the solution we have narrowed down the possibilities considerably by identifying the feasible region (shown by itself in Figure 2.6). We now know that the optimal solution must be somewhere within this feasible region. But exactly where?

One approach to finding the optimal solution would be to calculate the objective function for each feasible solution; the optimal solution would then be the one with the largest value. The difficulty with this approach is that there are a huge number of feasible solutions so this trial-and-error procedure cannot be used to identify the optimal solution.

It's often useful to choose an arbitrary value which is a multiple of the two objective function coefficients (here 10×9). This makes some of the subsequent calculations easier.

So, rather than trying to calculate the profit contribution for every feasible solution, we select one arbitrary value for profit contribution and identify all the feasible solutions (S, D) that yield this selected value. For example, what feasible solutions provide a profit contribution of \$1800? (Note that the value of \$1800 is an arbitrary one. We could just as easily have chosen \$100, \$5000 or \$2348.97. However, when we choose an arbitrary value it helps to have one that is convenient for the arithmetic calculations we will be carrying out.) These solutions are given by the values of S and D in the feasible region that will make the objective function:

$$10S + 9D = 1800$$

Figure 2.6 Feasible Region for the GulfGolf Problem

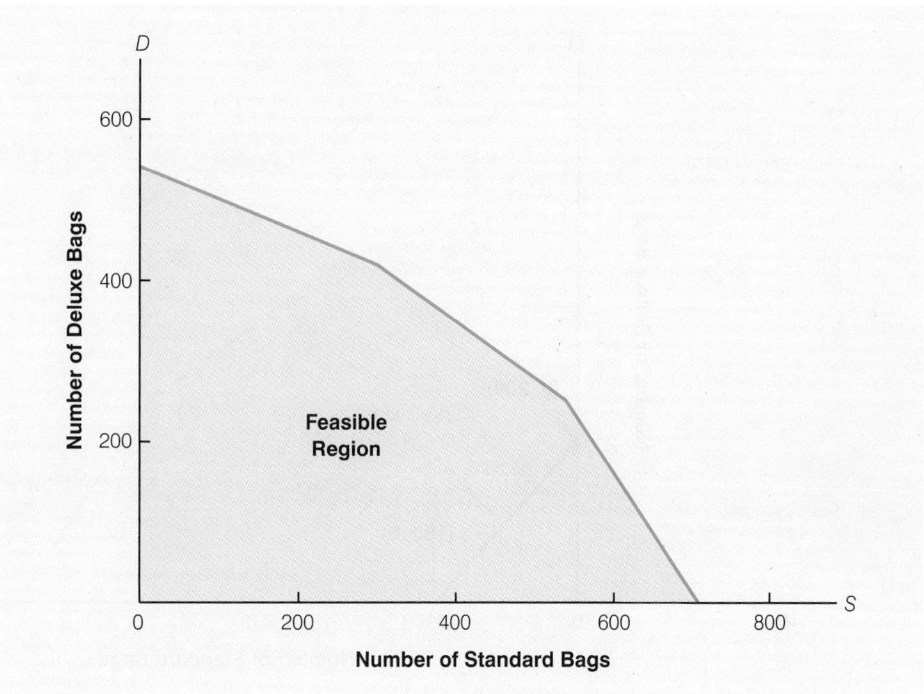

This expression is simply the equation of a line. So, all feasible solution points (S, D) yielding a profit contribution of $1800 must be on this line. We learned earlier in this section how to graph a constraint line. The procedure for graphing the profit or objective function line is the same. Letting $S = 0$, we see that D must be 200; so, the solution point $(S = 0, D = 200)$ is on the line. Similarly, by letting $D = 0$, we see that the solution point $(S = 180, D = 0)$ is also on the line. Drawing the line through these two points identifies all the solutions that have a profit contribution of $1800. A graph of this profit line is presented in Figure 2.7.

However, as we know, the $1800 profit contribution was an arbitrary choice. Remember also, that as we have a maximization LP problem we are seeking the maximum possible profit. So let us also consider profit contributions of $3600 and $5400. Repeating what we did for $1800 we can draw these profit lines on the graph also, as shown in Figure 2.8.

Can you graph the profit line for a linear programme? Try Problem 5.

Look at Figure 2.8, and see what general observations you can make about the profit lines already drawn. Note the following: (1) the profit lines are *parallel* to each other, and (2) higher profit lines are obtained as we move farther from the origin.

Because the profit lines are parallel and higher profit lines are farther from the origin, we can obtain solutions that give increasingly larger values for the objective function by continuing to move the profit line farther from the origin in such a fashion that it remains parallel to the other profit lines. However, at some point we will find that any further outward movement will place the profit line completely outside the feasible region. Because solutions outside the feasible region are unacceptable, the point in the feasible region that lies on the highest profit line is the optimal solution to the linear programme.

You should now be able to identify the optimal solution point for this problem. Use a ruler or the edge of a piece of paper, and move the profit line as far from the

Figure 2.7 $1800 Profit Line for the GulfGolf Problem

Figure 2.8 Selected Profit Lines for the GulfGolf Problem

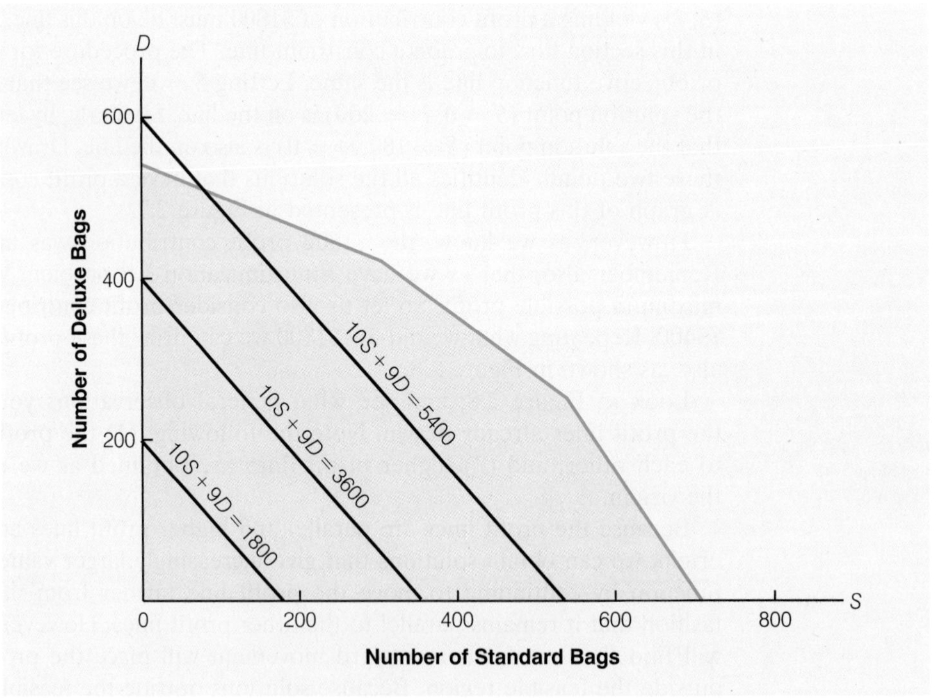

origin as you can. What is the last point in the feasible region that you reach? This point, which is the optimal solution, is shown graphically in Figure 2.9.

Figure 2.9 Optimal Solution for the GulfGolf Problem

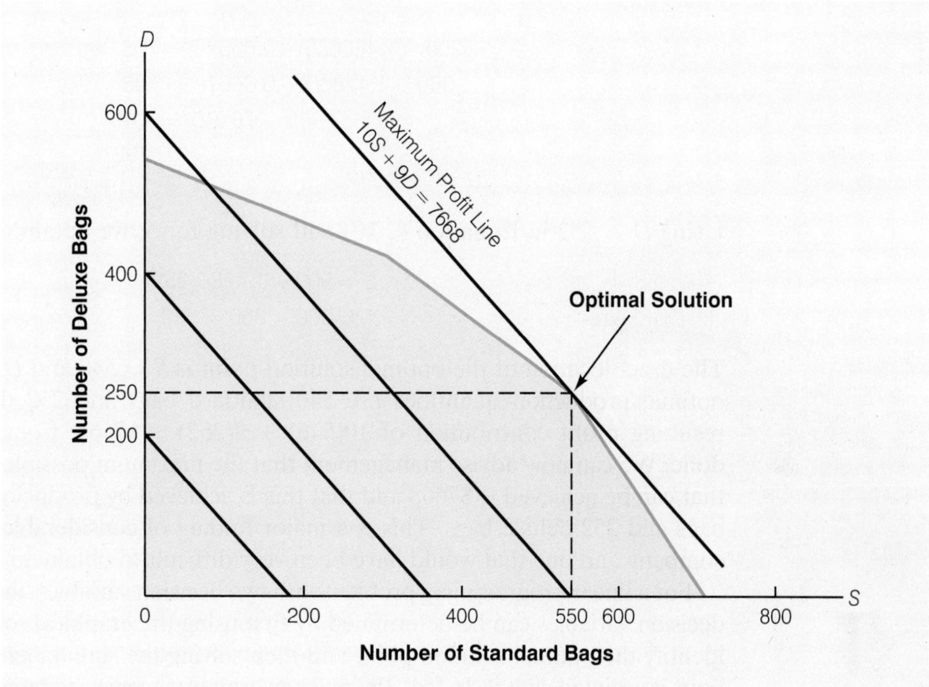

The optimal values of the decision variables are the S and D values at the optimal solution. Depending on the accuracy of the graph, you may or may not be able to determine the *exact* S and D values. Referring to the graph in Figure 2.9, the best we can do is conclude that the optimal production combination consists of approximately 550 standard bags (S) and approximately 250 deluxe bags (D).

A closer inspection of Figures 2.5 and 2.8 shows that the optimal solution point is at the intersection of the cutting and dyeing and the finishing constraint lines. That is, the optimal solution point is on both the cutting and dyeing constraint line:

$$0.7S + 1D = 630 \tag{2.7}$$

and the finishing constraint line:

$$1S + 0.6667D = 708 \tag{2.8}$$

Thus, the optimal values of the decision variables S and D must satisfy both Equations (2.7) and (2.8) simultaneously. Using Equation (2.7) and solving for S gives:

$$0.7S = 630 - 1D$$

or

$$S = 900 - 1.4286D \tag{2.9}$$

Substituting this expression for S into Equation (2.8) and solving for D provides the following:

$$1(900 - 1.4286D) + 0.6667D = 708$$
$$900 - 1.4286D + 0.6667D = 708$$
$$-.7619D = -192$$
$$D = \frac{192}{.7619} = 252$$

Using $D = 252$ in Equation (2.10) and solving for S, we obtain:

$$S = 900 - 1.4286(252)$$
$$= 900 - 360 = 540$$

Although the optimal solution to the GulfGolf problem consists of integer values for the decision variables, this result will not always be the case.

The exact location of the optimal solution point is $S = 540$ and $D = 252$. Hence, the optimal production quantities are 540 standard bags and 252 deluxe bags, with a resulting profit contribution of 10(540) + 9(252) = \$7668. Consider what we have done. We can now advise management that the maximum possible profit contribution that can be achieved is \$7668 and that this is achieved by producing 540 standard golf bags and 252 deluxe bags. This is a major finding of considerable importance to the company and one that would have been very difficult to obtain any other way.

For a linear programming problem with two decision variables, the exact values of the decision variables can be determined by first using the graphical solution procedure to identify the optimal solution point and then solving the simultaneous constraint equations associated with it. In fact, the two constraints we have used to confirm the optimal solution are referred to as **binding constraints**. Effectively at the optimal solution it is these two constraints that *bind* the solution – they prevent a higher value for the objective function. It is easy to see why. For the cutting and dyeing constraint we had:

$$0.7S + 1D = 630$$

That is, at the optimal solution point of $S = 540$ and $D = 252$ and in order to produce this quantity of the two products, all of the 630 hours of cutting and dyeing time available is required. Further production of S and D is not possible as we have used all the available cutting and dyeing time. Similarly for the Finishing constraint this is also binding, hence we need all the available finishing time to be able to produce the optimal quantities of S and D. However, our other two constraints, for Sewing and for Inspection and Packaging are non-binding. **Non-binding constraints** do not directly affect the optimal solution. We shall see later that important management information can be obtained through understanding binding and non-binding constraints for an LP solution.

A Note on Graphing Lines

Try Problem 7 to test your ability to use the graphical solution procedure to identify the optimal solution and find the exact values of the decision variables at the optimal solution.

An important aspect of the graphical method is the ability to graph lines showing the constraints and the objective function of the linear programme. The procedure we used for graphing the equation of a line is to find any two points satisfying the equation and then draw the line through the two points. For the GulfGolf constraints, the two points were easily found by first setting $S = 0$ and solving the constraint equation for D. Then we set $D = 0$ and solved for S. For the cutting and dyeing constraint line:

$$0.7S + 1D = 630$$

this procedure identified the two points ($S = 0$, $D = 630$) and ($S = 900$, $D = 0$). The cutting and dyeing constraint line was then graphed by drawing a line through these two points.

All constraints and objective function lines in two-variable linear programmes can be graphed if two points on the line can be identified. However, finding the two points on the line is not always as easy as shown in the GulfGolf problem. For example, suppose a company manufactures two models of a small handheld computer: the Assistant (A) and the Professional (P). Management needs 50 units of the Professional model for its own salesforce, and expects sales of the Professional to be at most one-half of the sales of the Assistant. A constraint enforcing this requirement is:

$$P - 50 \leq 0.5A$$

or

$$2P - 100 \leq A$$

or

$$2P - A \leq 100$$

Using the equality form and setting $P = 0$, we find the point ($P = 0$, $A = -100$) is on the constraint line. Setting $A = 0$, we find a second point ($P = 50$, $A = 0$) on the constraint line. If we have drawn only the nonnegative ($P \geq 0$, $A \geq 0$) portion of the graph, the first point ($P = 0$, $A = -100$) cannot be plotted because $A = -100$ is not on the graph. Whenever we have two points on the line, but one or both of the points cannot be plotted in the nonnegative portion of the graph, the simplest approach is to enlarge the graph. In this example, the point ($P = 0$, $A = -100$) can be plotted by extending the graph to include the negative A axis. Once both points satisfying the constraint equation have been located, the line can be drawn. The constraint line and the feasible solutions for the constraint $2P - A \leq 100$ are shown in Figure 2.10.

Figure 2.10 Feasible Solutions for the Constraint $2P - A \leq 100$

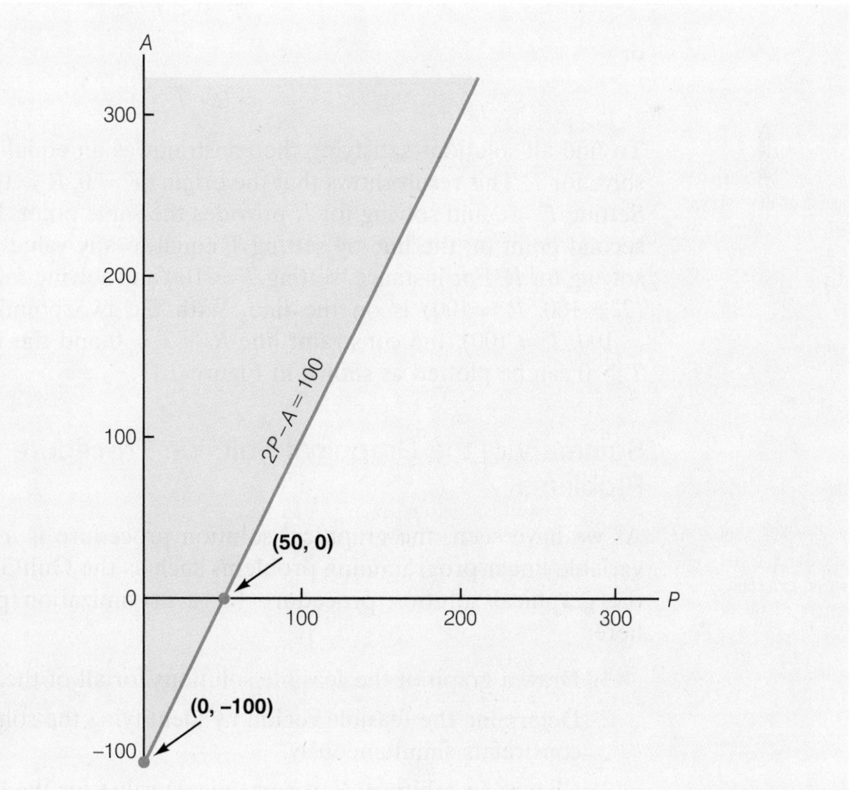

Figure 2.11 Feasible Solutions for the Constraint $R - T \geq 0$

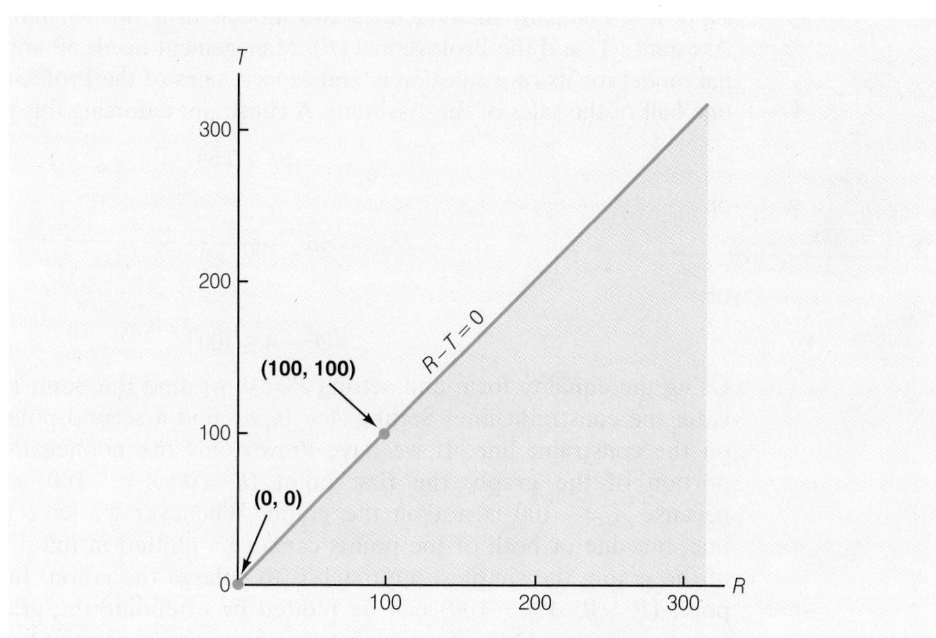

As another example, consider a problem involving two decision variables, R and T. Suppose that the number of units of R produced had to be at least equal to the number of units of T produced. A constraint enforcing this requirement is:

$$R \geq T$$

or

$$R - T \geq 0$$

Can you graph a constraint line when the origin is on the constraint line? Try Problem 4.

To find all solutions satisfying the constraint as an equality, we first set $R = 0$ and solve for T. This result shows that the origin ($T = 0, R = 0$) is on the constraint line. Setting $T = 0$ and solving for R provides the same point. However, we can obtain a second point on the line by setting T equal to any value other than zero and then solving for R. For instance, setting $T = 100$ and solving for R, we find that the point ($T = 100$, $R = 100$) is on the line. With the two points ($R = 0$, $T = 0$) and ($R = 100$, $T = 100$), the constraint line $R - T = 0$ and the feasible solutions for $R - T \geq 0$ can be plotted as shown in Figure 2.11.

Summary of the Graphical Solution Procedure for Maximization Problems

For additional practise in using the graphical solution procedure, try Problem 13 a-d.

As we have seen, the graphical solution procedure is a method for solving two-variable linear programming problems such as the GulfGolf problem. The steps of the graphical solution procedure for a maximization problem are summarized here:

1. Draw a graph of the feasible solutions for all of the constraints.
2. Determine the feasible region by identifying the solutions that satisfy all the constraints simultaneously.
3. Choose an arbitrary (but convenient) value for the objective function.

4 Draw a line on the graph showing the values of the decision variables that will give this value for the objective function.

5 Using a ruler or straightedge, move the objective function line as far from the origin as possible until any further movement would take the line out of the feasible region altogether.

6 The feasible solution on this objective function line is the optimal solution.

7 Confirm the solution point mathematically using simultaneous equations.

One of the convenient things about LP is that we literally have a programme of steps to follow that are the same for every maximization problem.

Slack Variables

In addition to the optimal solution and its associated profit contribution, GulfGolf management will want information about the production time requirements for each production operation. How many hours do we actually need to produce the optimal solution quantities? We can determine this information by substituting the optimal solution values ($S = 540$, $D = 252$) into the constraints of the linear programme.

Constraint	Hours Required for $S = 540$ and $D = 252$	Hours Available	Unused Hours
Cutting and dyeing	$\frac{7}{10}(540) + 1(252) = 630$	630	0
Sewing	$\frac{1}{2}(540) + \frac{5}{6}(252) = 480$	600	120
Finishing	$1(540) + \frac{2}{3}(252) = 708$	708	0
Inspection and packaging	$\frac{1}{10}(540) + \frac{1}{4}(252) = 117$	135	18

The complete solution tells management that the production of 540 standard bags and 252 deluxe bags will require all available cutting and dyeing time (630 hours) and all available finishing time (708 hours), while $600 - 480 = 120$ hours of sewing time and $135 - 117 = 18$ hours of inspection and packaging time will remain unused. The 120 hours of unused sewing time and 18 hours of unused inspection and packaging time are referred to as *slack* for the two departments. In linear programming terminology, any unused capacity for a $\leq$ constraint is referred to as the *slack* associated with the constraint.

Can you identify the slack associated with a constraint? Try Problem 13(e).

Earlier, we introduced the distinction between binding and non-binding constraints. By definition, for constraints taking the form $\leq$, a binding constraint will have a slack value of zero at the optimal solution point since by definition for a binding constraint, both sides of the constraint will be equal. For a non-binding constraint taking the form $\leq$, however, the slack value will be positive since, again, by definition, for a non-binding constraint the left-hand side of the constraint will be less than the right-hand side. Looking at the slack values (unused hours) in the table above we can confirm directly that cutting and dyeing is a binding constraint as is finishing whilst the other two constraints are non-binding.

Often variables, called **slack variables**, are added to the formulation of a linear programming problem to represent the slack, or idle capacity. Unused capacity makes no contribution to profit; thus, slack variables have coefficients of zero in the objective function. After the addition of four slack variables, denoted S_1, S_2, S_3 and S_4, the mathematical model of the GulfGolf problem becomes:

$$\begin{aligned}
\text{Max} \quad & 10S + 9D + 0S_1 + 0S_2 + 0S_3 + 0S_4 \\
\text{s.t.} \quad & \\
& \tfrac{7}{10}S + 1D + 1S_1 = 630 \\
& \tfrac{1}{2}S + \tfrac{5}{6}D + 1S_2 = 600 \\
& 1S + \tfrac{2}{3}D + 1S_3 = 708 \\
& \tfrac{1}{10}S + \tfrac{1}{4}D + 1S_4 = 135 \\
& S,\ D,\ S_1,\ S_2,\ S_3,\ S_4 \geq 0
\end{aligned}$$

Can you write a linear programme in standard form? Try Problem 11.

Whenever a linear programme is written in a form with all constraints expressed as equalities, it is said to be written in **standard form**.

Referring to the standard form of the GulfGolf problem, we see that at the optimal solution ($S = 540$ and $D = 252$), the values for the slack variables are:

Constraint	Value of Slack Variable
Cutting and dyeing	$S_1 = 0$
Sewing	$S_2 = 120$
Finishing	$S_3 = 0$
Inspection and packaging	$S_4 = 18$

Could we have used the graphical solution to provide some of this information? The answer is yes. By finding the optimal solution point on Figure 2.5, we can see that the cutting and dyeing and the finishing constraints restrict, or *bind*, the feasible region at this point. Thus, this solution requires the use of all available time for these two operations. In other words, the graph shows us that the cutting and dyeing and the finishing departments will have zero slack. On the other hand, the sewing and the inspection and packaging constraints are not binding the feasible region at the optimal solution, which means we can expect some unused time or slack for these two operations.

As a final comment on the graphical analysis of this problem, look at the sewing capacity constraint as shown in Figure 2.5. Note, in particular, that this constraint did not affect the feasible region. That is, the feasible region would be the same whether the sewing capacity constraint were included or not, which tells us that there is enough sewing time available to accommodate any production level that can be achieved by the other three departments. The sewing constraint does not affect the feasible region and thus cannot affect the optimal solution; it is called a **redundant constraint**.

NOTES AND COMMENTS

1 In the standard-form representation of a linear programming model, the objective function coefficients for slack variables are zero. This zero coefficient implies that slack variables, which represent unused resources, do not affect the value of the objective function. However, in some applications, unused resources can be sold and contribute to profit. In such cases, the corresponding slack variables become decision variables representing the amount of unused resources to be sold. For each of these variables, a nonzero coefficient in the objective function would reflect the profit associated with selling a unit of the corresponding resource.

2 Redundant constraints do not affect the feasible region; as a result, they can be removed from a linear programming model without affecting the optimal solution. However, if the linear programming model is

to be re-solved later, changes in some of the data might make a previously redundant constraint a binding constraint. Thus, we recommend keeping all constraints in the linear programming model even though at some point in time one or more of the constraints may be redundant.

2.3 Extreme Points and the Optimal Solution

Suppose that the profit contribution for the company's standard golf bag is reduced from \$10 to \$5 per bag, while the profit contribution for the deluxe golf bag and all the constraints remain unchanged. The complete linear programming model of this new problem is identical to the mathematical model in Section 2.1, except for the revised objective function:

$$\text{Max} \quad 5S + 9D$$

How does this change in the objective function affect the optimal solution to the problem? Figure 2.12 shows the graphical solution of this new problem with the revised objective function. Note that without any change in the constraints, the feasible region does not change. However, the profit lines have been altered to reflect the new objective function.

By moving the profit line in a parallel manner toward higher profit values, we find the optimal solution as shown in Figure 2.12. The values of the decision variables at this point are $S = 300$ and $D = 420$. The reduced profit contribution for the standard bag caused a change in the optimal solution. In fact, as you may have suspected, we are cutting back the production of the lower-profit standard bags and increasing the production of the higher-profit deluxe bags.

Figure 2.12 Optimal Solution for the GulfGolf Problem with an Objective Function of $5S + 9D$

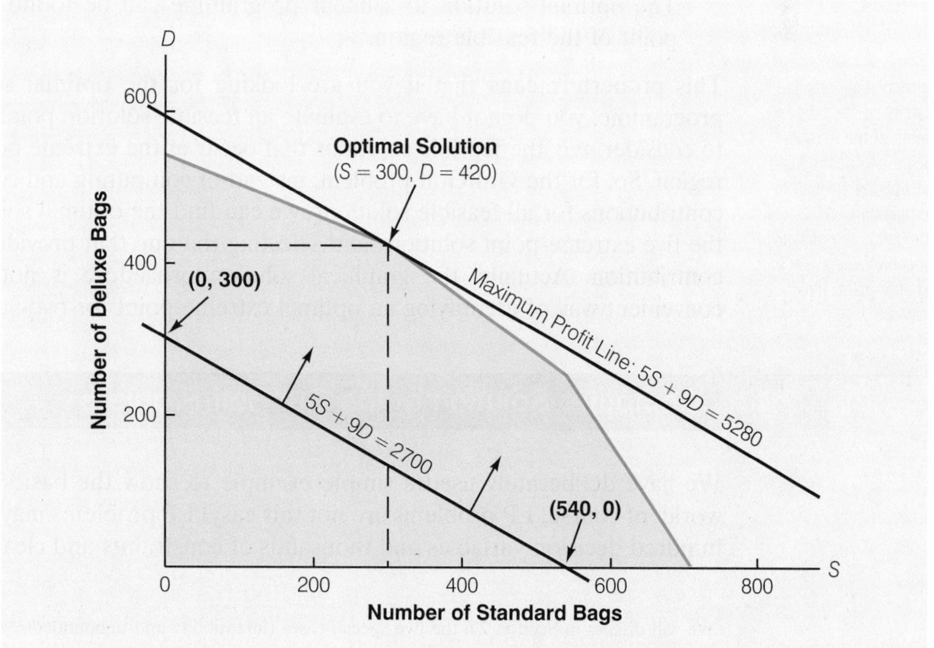

Figure 2.13 The Five Extreme Points of the Feasible Region for the GulfGolf Problem

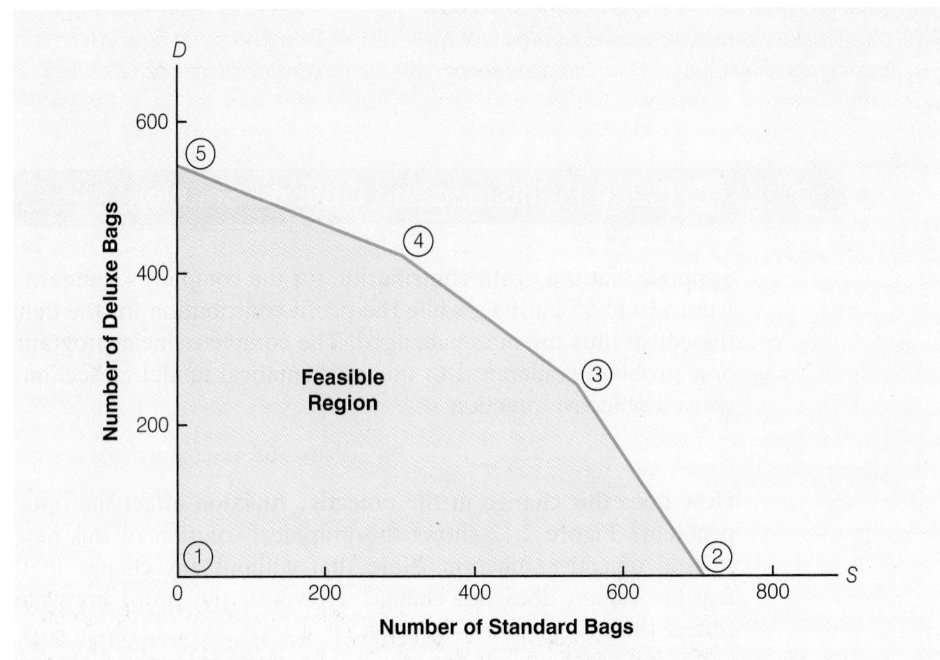

What observations can you make about the location of the optimal solutions in the two linear programming problems solved thus far? Look closely at the graphical solutions in Figures 2.9 and 2.12. Notice that the optimal solutions occur at one of the vertices or 'corners' of the feasible region. In linear programming terminology, these vertices are referred to as the **extreme points** of the feasible region. The GulfGolf feasible region has five vertices, or five extreme points (see Figure 2.13). We can now formally state our observation about the location of optimal solutions as follows:

> The optimal solution to a linear programme can be found at an extreme point of the feasible region.[2]

For additional practise in identifying the extreme points of the feasible region and determining the optimal solution by computing and comparing the objective function value at each extreme point, try Problem 9.

This property means that if you are looking for the optimal solution to a linear programme, you do not have to evaluate all feasible solution points. In fact, you have to consider *only* the feasible solutions that occur at the extreme points of the feasible region. So, for the GulfGolf problem, instead of computing and comparing the profit contributions for all feasible solutions, we can find the optimal solution by evaluating the five extreme-point solutions and selecting the one that provides the largest profit contribution. Actually, the graphical solution procedure is nothing more than a convenient way of identifying an optimal extreme point for two-variable problems.

2.4 Computer Solution of the GulfGolf Problem

We have deliberately used a simple example to show the basics of LP. In the real world, of course, LP problems are not this easy! LP problems may easily have several hundred decision variables and thousands of constraints and clearly these cannot be

[2]We will discuss in Section 2.6 the two special cases (infeasibility and unboundedness) in linear programming that have no optimal solution, and for which this statement does not apply.

In January 1952 the first successful computer solution of a linear programming problem was performed on the SEAC (Standards Eastern Automatic Computer). The SEAC, the first digital computer built by the National Bureau of Standards under US Air Force sponsorship, had a 512-word memory and magnetic tape for external storage.

In 2005, a survey reviewed around 50 different LP computer programs. *OR/MS Today*, June 2013, Linear Programming Software Survey.

solved graphically but have to be solved through an appropriate computer package. Computer programs designed to solve linear programming problems are now widely available. Most companies and universities have access to these. After a short period of familiarization with the specific features of the package, users are able to solve linear programming problems with few difficulties. Most large linear programmes can be solved with just a few minutes of computer time; small linear programmes usually require only a few seconds.

More recently, with the virtual explosion of software for personal computers, a large number of user-friendly computer programs that can solve linear programmes became available. These programs, developed by academicians and small software companies, are almost all easy to use. Most of these programs are designed to solve smaller linear programmes (a few hundred variables). But, some can be used to solve problems involving thousands of variables and constraints. Linear programming solvers are now part of many spreadsheet packages. In Appendixes 2.1 and 2.2 we show how to solve LP problems with Microsoft Excel and with the Management Scientist software package developed by the authors of this text.

Interpretation of Computer Output

Figure 2.14 shows the Excel Solver spreadsheet for the GulfGolf problem. The top part of the spreadsheet (Rows 4 to 9) shows the problem information – the coefficients and values for each constraint and the objective function. The bottom part of the spreadsheet shows information about the optimal solution.

Figure 2.14 Excel Solution for the GulfGolf Problem

EXCEL *file*

GULFGOLF

	A	B	C	D	E
1	**Gulf Golf**				
2					
3		**Production Time**			
4	**Operation**	**Standard**	**Deluxe**	**Time Available**	
5	Cutting and Dyeing	0.7	1	630	
6	Sewing	0.5	0.83333	600	
7	Finishing	1	0.66667	708	
8	Inspection and Packaging	0.1	0.25	135	
9	**Profit Per Bag**	10	9		
10					
11					
12	**Model**				
13					
14		**Decision Variables**			
15		**Standard**	**Deluxe**		
16	**Bags Produced**	539.99842	252.00110		
17					
18	**Maximize Total Profit**	7668			
19					
20	**Constraints**	**Hours Used (LHS)**		**Hours Available (RHS)**	
21	Cutting and Dyeing	630	<=	630	
22	Sewing	479.99929	<=	600	
23	Finishing	708	<=	708	
24	Inspection and Packaging	117.00012	<=	135	
25					

MANAGEMENT SCIENCE IN ACTION

Optimizing production planning at Jan de Wit Company, Brazil

You might be forgiven for thinking initially that mathematical linear programming and the genteel business of growing lily flowers in Brazil couldn't be further apart from each other. And you couldn't be more wrong! Johannes de Wit is owner and general manager of the Jan de Wit company in Brazil. The company is Brazil's largest producer of Oriental and Asian lily flowers in a domestic market with an annual value of over US$1 billion. Johannes credits the introduction of linear programming into the business with helping:

- increase company revenue by 26 per cent;
- reduce costs as a percentage of sales by around 3 percentage points;
- increase the return on owner's equity by over 7 percentage points;
- increase the quality of lily production.

Try telling him that LP and lilies don't mix.

Production planning in such a business is not a trivial task. The bulbs from which the flowers grow are imported from Holland, although a bulb will take two years before it is sufficiently mature to produce flowers. The company imports around 3.5 million bulbs a year in over 50 different varieties. The company also faces very seasonal demand with peaks at specific dates, such as Mother's Day, Easter, All Soul's Day and Christmas and to complicate this further the varieties and colours in demand vary for each peak period. Depending on the variety, the bulb size, and the time of planting the production cycle can vary from six to 16 weeks. To succeed, Jan de Wit Company must plant the right bulbs during the right week. An LP optimization model was developed to maximize total contribution margin. Considerable effort was taken to involve the company's top management in the modelling process and to ensure that the computer model used was as user-friendly as possible for the non-MS staff in the company.

Based on J. V. Caixeta-Filho, J. M. van Swaay-Neto and A. de Pa'dua Wagemaker, 'Optimization of the Production Planning and Trade of Lily Flowers at Jan de Wit Company', *Interfaces* 32 (Jan–Feb, 2002): 35–46.

First we note in Row 18 Maximize Total Profit at 7668, which is the value of the objective function at the optimal solution. Just above, Row 16, we see Bags Produced with 539.99842 for Standard bags and 252.00110 for Deluxe bags. After rounding, this confirms our graphical solution of 540 and 252 bags respectively. The last section, Constraints, shows the left-hand side (LHS) value for each constraint at the optimal solution against the RHS value in the initial problem formulation. So, for the cutting and dyeing constraint, we see that initially we have 630 hours available (RHS) and at the optimal solution calculated we are using 630 hours (LHS). We know, therefore that this constraint is binding.

It is worth noting that Excel Solver produces additional output in the form of optional reports. We shall see later how to use the information that these reports contain.

NOTES AND COMMENTS

Linear programming solvers are now a standard feature of most spreadsheet packages. Excel, Lotus 1- 2-3 and Quattro Pro all come with built-in solvers capable of solving optimization problems, including linear programmes. The solver in each of these spreadsheet packages was developed by Frontline Systems and provides a similar user interface. In Appendix 2.1 we show how spreadsheets can be used to solve linear programmes by using Excel to solve the GulfGolf problem.

2.5 A Minimization Problem

So far, we have looked at problems where we want to *maximize* the objective function. LP problems where we seek to *minimize* the objective function are just as common. M&D Chemicals is based in Germany and manufactures a variety of chemical products that are sold to other companies who produce bath soaps and shower gels. Based on an analysis of current inventory levels and potential demand for the coming week, M&D's management specified that the combined production for products A and B must total at least 350 litres. Separately, a major customer's order for 125 litres of product A must also be satisfied. Product A requires two hours of processing time per litre and product B requires one hour of processing time per litre. For the coming week, 600 hours of processing time are available. M&D's objective is to satisfy these requirements at a minimum total production cost. Production costs are €2 per litre for product A and €3 per litre for product B.

To find the minimum-cost production schedule, we will formulate the M&D Chemicals problem as a linear programme. Following a procedure similar to the one used for the GulfGolf problem, we first define the decision variables and the objective function for the problem. Let:

$$A = \text{number of litres of product A}$$
$$B = \text{number of litres of product B}$$

With production costs at €2 per litre for product A and €3 per litre for product B, the objective function that corresponds to the minimization of the total production cost can be written as:

$$\text{Min} \quad 2A + 3B$$

Next consider the constraints placed on the M&D Chemicals problem. To satisfy the major customer's demand for 125 litres of product A, we know *A* must be at least 125. Thus, we write the constraint:

$$1A \geq 125$$

For the combined production for both products, which must total at least 350 litres, we can write the constraint:

$$1A + 1B \geq 350$$

Finally, for the limitation of 600 hours on available processing time, we add the constraint:

$$2A + 1B \leq 600$$

After adding the nonnegativity constraints ($A, B \geq 0$), we arrive at the following linear programme for the M&D Chemicals problem:

$$\begin{aligned} \text{Min} \quad & 2A + 3B \\ \text{s.t.} \quad & \\ 1A &\geq 125 \quad \text{Demand for product A} \\ 1A + 1B &\geq 350 \quad \text{Total production} \\ 2A + 1B &\leq 600 \quad \text{Processing time} \\ A, B &\geq 0 \end{aligned}$$

Because the linear programming model has only two decision variables, the graphical solution procedure can be used to find the optimal production quantities. The

Figure 2.15 The Feasible Region for the M&D Chemicals Problem

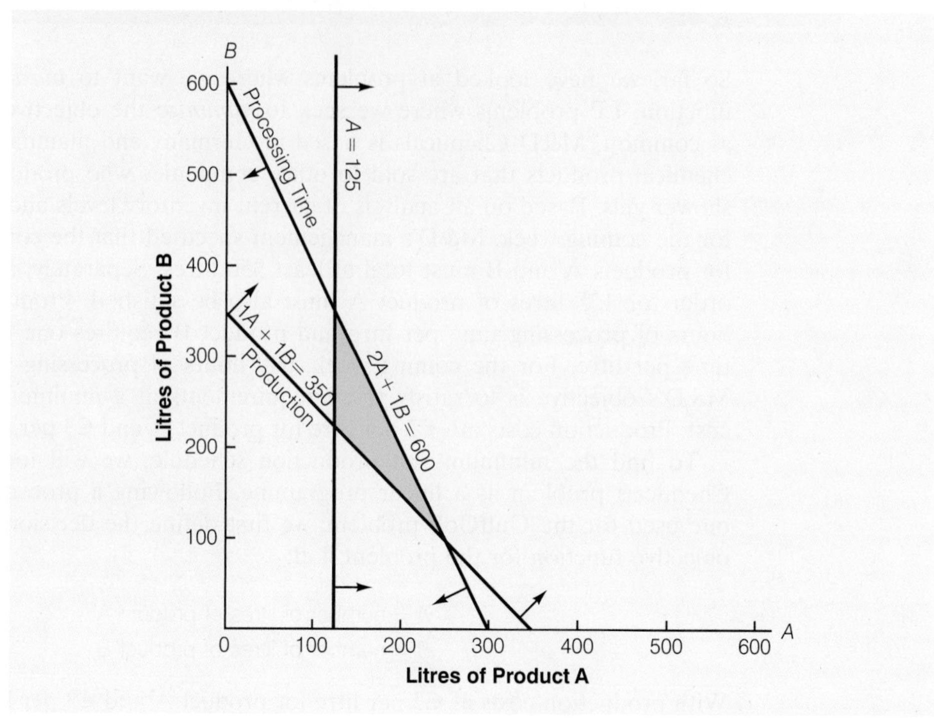

graphical solution procedure for this problem, just as in the GulfGolf problem, requires us to first graph the constraint lines to find the feasible region. By graphing each constraint line separately and then checking points on either side of the constraint line, the feasible solutions for each constraint can be identified. By combining the feasible solutions for each constraint on the same graph, we obtain the feasible region shown in Figure 2.15.

To find the minimum-cost solution, we now draw the objective function line corresponding to a particular total cost value. For example, we might start by drawing the line $2A + 3B = 1200$. This line is shown in Figure 2.16. Clearly some points in the feasible region would provide a total cost of €1200. To find the values of A and B that provide smaller total cost values, we move the objective function line in a lower left direction until, if we moved it any farther, it would be entirely outside the feasible region. Note that the objective function line $2A + 3B = 800$ intersects the feasible region at the extreme point $A = 250$ and $B = 100$. This extreme point provides the minimum-cost solution with an objective function value of 800. From Figures 2.15 and 2.16, we can see that the total production constraint and the processing time constraint are binding. Just as in every linear programming problem, the optimal solution occurs at an extreme point of the feasible region.

Summary of the Graphical Solution Procedure for Minimization Problems

Can you use the graphical solution procedure to determine the optimal solution for a minimization problem? Try problem 8

The steps of the graphical solution procedure for a minimization problem are summarized here:

1 Prepare a graph of the feasible solutions for each of the constraints.

2 Determine the feasible region by identifying the solutions that satisfy all the constraints simultaneously.

Figure 2.16 Graphical Solution for the M&D Chemicals Problem

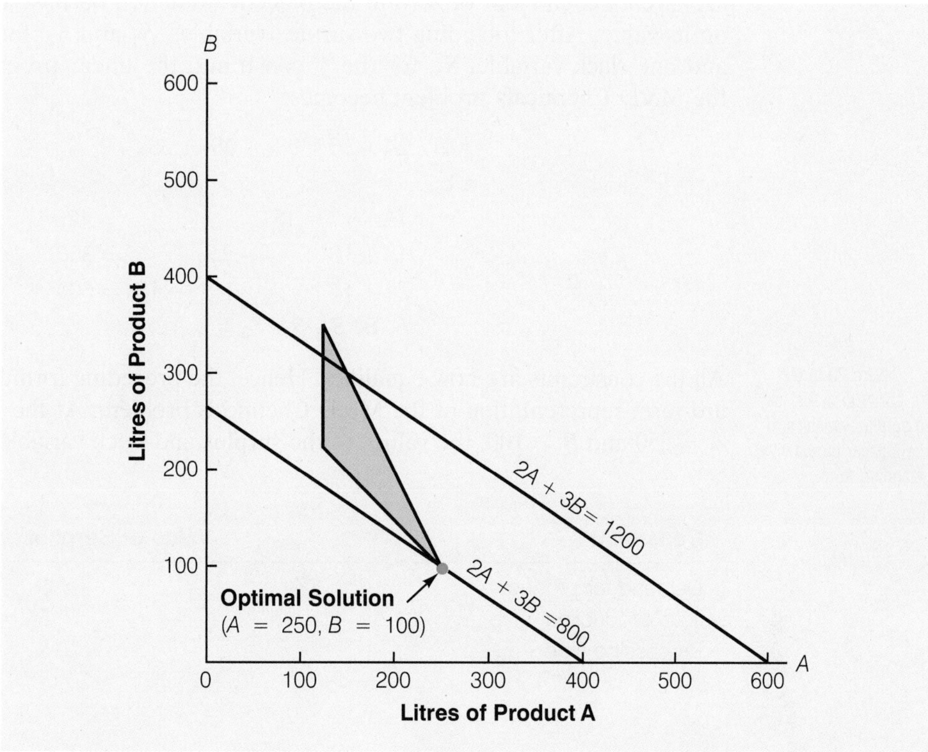

3 Choose an arbitrary (but convenient) value for the objective function.
4 Draw a line on the graph showing the values of the decision variables that will give this value for the objective function.
5 Using a ruler or straightedge, move the objective function line as close to the origin as possible until any further movement would take the line out of the feasible region altogether.
6 The feasible solution on this objective function line is the optimal solution.
7 Confirm the solution point mathematically using simultaneous equations.

You may have noticed that this is exactly the same procedure as for a maximization problem except for the direction we push the objective function. For a maximization problem we push the objective function as far away from the origin as possible. For a minimization problem we push the objective function line as close to the origin as possible.

Surplus Variables

The optimal solution to the M&D Chemicals problem shows that the desired total production of $A + B = 350$ litres has been achieved by using all available processing time of $2A + 1B = 2(250) + 1(100) = 600$ hours. In addition, note that the constraint requiring that product A demand be met has been satisfied with $A = 250$ litres. In fact, the production of product A exceeds its minimum level by $250 - 125 = 125$ litres. This excess production for product A is referred to as *surplus*. In linear programming terminology, any excess quantity corresponding to a $\geq$ constraint is referred to as surplus.

Recall that with a $\leq$ constraint, a slack variable can be added to the left-hand side of the inequality to convert the constraint to equality form. With a $\geq$ constraint, a **surplus variable** can be subtracted from the left-hand side of the inequality to convert the constraint to equality form. Just as with slack variables, surplus variables are given a coefficient of zero in the objective function because they have no effect on its value. After including two surplus variables, S_1 and S_2, for the $\geq$ constraints and one slack variable, S_3, for the $\leq$ constraint, the linear programming model of the M&D Chemicals problem becomes:

$$\begin{aligned}
\text{Min} \quad & 2A + 3B + 0S_1 + 0S_2 + 0S_3 \\
\text{s.t.} \quad & \\
& 1A \qquad - 1S_1 \qquad\qquad\qquad = 125 \\
& 1A + 1B \qquad\quad - 1S_2 \qquad\quad = 350 \\
& 2A + 1B \qquad\qquad\qquad + 1S_3 = 600 \\
& A,\ B,\ S_1,\ S_2,\ S_3 \geq 0
\end{aligned}$$

Try Problem 20 to test your ability to use slack and surplus variables to write a linear programme in standard form.

All the constraints are now equalities. Hence, the preceding formulation is the standard-form representation of the M&D Chemicals problem. At the optimal solution of $A = 250$ and $B = 100$, the values of the surplus and slack variables are as follows:

Constraint	Value of Surplus or Slack Variables
Demand for product A	$S_1 = 125$
Total production	$S_2 = 0$
Processing time	$S_3 = 0$

Refer to Figures 2.15 and 2.16. Note that the zero surplus and slack variables are associated with the constraints that are binding at the optimal solution – that is, the total production and processing time constraints. The surplus of 125 units is associated with the nonbinding constraint on the demand for product A.

In the GulfGolf problem all the constraints were of the $\leq$ type, and in the M&D Chemicals problem the constraints were a mixture of $\geq$ and $\leq$ types. The number and types of constraints encountered in a particular linear programming problem depend on the specific conditions existing in the problem. Linear programming problems may have some $\leq$ constraints, some $\geq$ constraints, and some $=$ constraints. For an equality constraint, feasible solutions must lie directly on the constraint line.

Try Problem 21 to practice solving a linear programme with all three constraint forms.

An example of a linear programme with two decision variables, G and H, and all three constraint forms is given here:

$$\begin{aligned}
\text{Min} \quad & 2G + 2H \\
\text{s.t.} \quad & \\
& 1G + 3H \leq 12 \\
& 3G + 1H \geq 13 \\
& 1G - 1H = 3 \\
& G,\ H \geq 0
\end{aligned}$$

The standard-form representation of this problem is:

$$\begin{aligned}
\text{Min} \quad & 2G + 2H + 0S_1 + 0S_2 \\
\text{s.t.} \quad & \\
& 1G + 3H + 1S_1 \qquad\quad = 12 \\
& 3G + 1H \qquad\quad - 1S_2 = 13 \\
& 1G - 1H \qquad\qquad\qquad = 3 \\
& G,\ H,\ S_1,\ S_2 \geq 0
\end{aligned}$$

The standard form requires a slack variable for the $\leq$ constraint and a surplus variable for the $\geq$ constraint. However, neither a slack nor a surplus variable is required for the third constraint since it is already in equality form.

When solving linear programmes graphically, it is not necessary to write the problem in its standard form. Nevertheless, you should be able to calculate the values of the slack and surplus variables and understand what they mean, because the values of slack and surplus variables are included in the computer solution of linear programmes and have an important management use. In Chapter 5 we will introduce an algebraic solution procedure, the simplex method, which can be used to find optimal extreme-point solutions for linear programming problems with as many as several thousand decision variables. The mathematical steps of the simplex method involve solving simultaneous equations that represent the constraints of the linear programme. Thus, in setting up a linear programme for solution by the simplex method, we must have one linear equation for each constraint in the problem; therefore, the problem must be in its standard form.

A final point: the standard form of the linear programming problem is equivalent to the original formulation of the problem. That is, the optimal solution to any linear programming problem is the same as the optimal solution to the standard form of the problem. The standard form has not changed the basic problem; it has only changed how we write the constraints for the problem.

Computer Solution of the M&D Chemicals Problem

The solution obtained using Excel Solver is presented in Figure 2.17. The computer output shows that the minimum-cost solution yields an objective function value of €800. The values of the decision variables show that 250 litres of product A and 100 litres of product B provide the minimum-cost solution.

From the **Constraints** section of the solution, we can see that constraint 2 and 3 are binding whilst constraint 1 has a surplus of 125 units.

EXCEL *file*

M&D

Figure 2.17 Excel solution for M&D Chemicals

Target Cell (Min)

Name	Original Value	Final Value
Minimize Cost Product A	0	800

Adjustable Cells

Name	Original Value	Final Value
Litres produced Product A	0	250
Litres produced Product B	0	100

Constraints

Name	Cell Value	Status	Slack
Demand for product A (LHS)	250	Not Binding	125
Total production (LHS)	350	Binding	0
Processing time (LHS)	600	Binding	0

2.6 Special Cases

In this section we discuss three special situations that can arise when we attempt to solve linear programming problems.

Alternative Optimal Solutions

From the discussion of the graphical solution procedure, we know that optimal solutions are found at the extreme points of the feasible region. Now let us consider the special case in which the optimal objective function line coincides with one of the binding constraint lines on the boundary of the feasible region. We will see that this situation can lead to the case of **alternative optimal solutions**; in such cases, more than one solution provides the optimal value for the objective function.

To illustrate the case of alternative optimal solutions, we return to the GulfGolf problem. However, let us assume that the profit for the standard golf bag (S) has been decreased to \$6.30. The revised objective function becomes $6.3S + 9D$. The graphical solution of this problem is shown in Figure 2.18. Note that the optimal solution still occurs at an extreme point. In fact, it occurs at two extreme points: extreme point ④ ($S = 300$, $D = 420$) and extreme point ③ ($S = 540$, $D = 252$).

The objective function values at these two extreme points are identical; that is,

$$6.3S + 9D = 6.3(300) + 9(420) = 5670$$

and

$$6.3S + 9D = 6.3(540) + 9(252) = 5670$$

Furthermore, any point on the line connecting the two optimal extreme points also provides an optimal solution. For example, the solution point ($S = 420$, $D = 336$),

Figure 2.18 GulfGolf Problem with an Objective Function of 6.3S + 9D (Alternative Optimal Solutions)

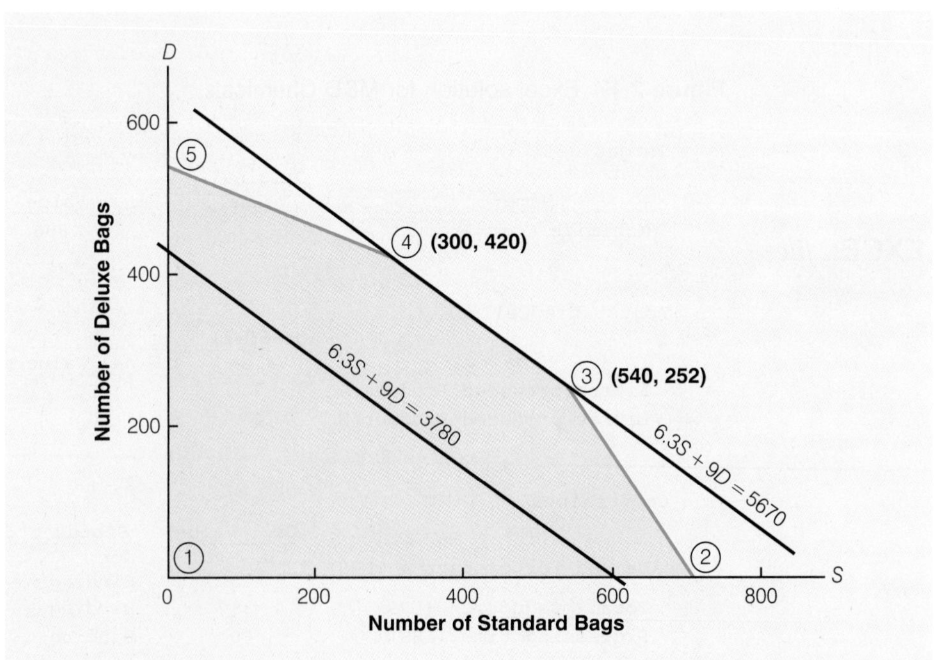

which is halfway between the two extreme points, also provides the optimal objective function value of:

$$6.3S + 9D = 6.3(420) + 9(336) = 5670$$

A linear programming problem with alternative optimal solutions is generally a good situation for the manager or decision maker. It means that several combinations of the decision variables are optimal and that the manager can select the most desirable optimal solution. Unfortunately, determining whether a problem has alternative optimal solutions is not a simple matter.

Infeasibility

Problems with no feasible solution do arise in practice, most often because management's expectations are too high or because too many constraints have been placed on the problem.

Infeasibility means that no solution to the linear programming problem satisfies all the constraints, including the nonnegativity conditions. Graphically, infeasibility means that a feasible region does not exist; that is, no points satisfy all the constraints and the nonnegativity conditions simultaneously. To illustrate this situation, let us look again at the problem faced by GulfGolf.

A large hotel chain in the region which offers golfing holidays has approached the company and is interested in placing an order for golf bags. It is thinking of buying at least 500 of the standard bags and at least 360 of the deluxe bags. These would now represent two additional constraints for the original formulation and can be graphed as usual. The graph of the solution region may now be constructed to reflect these new requirements (see Figure 2.19). The shaded area in the lower left-hand portion of the graph depicts those points satisfying the departmental constraints on the availability of time. The shaded area in the upper right-hand portion depicts those points satisfying the minimum production requirements of 500 standard and 360 deluxe bags. But no points satisfy both sets of constraints. Thus, we see that if management imposes these

Figure 2.19 No Feasible Region for the GulfGolf Problem with Minimum Requirements of 500 Standard and 360 Deluxe Bags

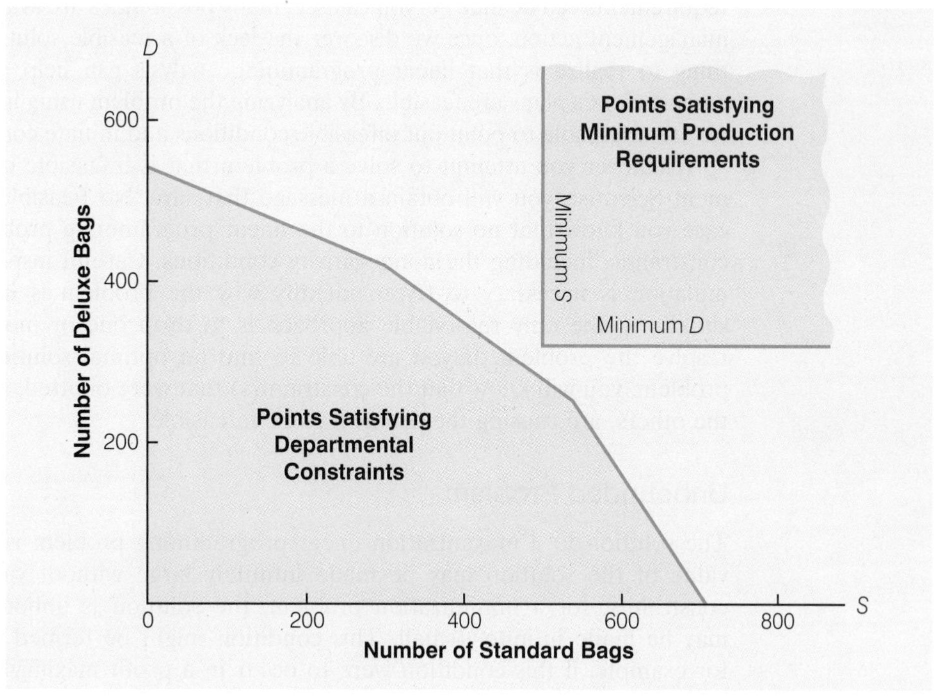

Table 2.2 Resources Needed to Manufacture 500 Standard Bags and 360 Deluxe Bags

Operation	Minimum Required Resources (hours)	Available Resources (hours)	Additional Resources Needed (hours)
Cutting and dyeing	0.7(500) + 1(360) = 710	630	80
Sewing	0.5(500) + 0.8333(360) = 550	600	None
Finishing	1(500) + 0.6667(360) = 740	708	32
Inspection and packaging	0.1(500) + 0.25(360) = 140	135	5

minimum production requirements, no feasible region exists for the problem. Attractive though a large order from the hotel chain might be, production of these quantities is simply not feasible given the production time available to the company.

How should we interpret infeasibility in terms of this current problem? First, we should tell management that given the resources available (i.e., production time for cutting and dyeing, sewing, finishing and inspection and packaging), it is not possible to make 500 standard bags and 360 deluxe bags. Moreover, we can tell management exactly how much of each resource must be expended to make it possible to manufacture 500 standard and 360 deluxe bags. Table 2.2 shows the minimum amounts of resources that must be available, the amounts currently available and additional amounts that would be required to accomplish this level of production. Thus, we need 80 more hours for cutting and dyeing, 32 more hours for finishing and five more hours for inspection and packaging to meet management's minimum production requirements.

If, after reviewing this information, management still wants to manufacture 500 standard and 360 deluxe bags, additional resources must be provided. Perhaps by hiring another person to work in the cutting and dyeing department, transferring a person from elsewhere in the plant to work part-time in the finishing department or having the sewing people help out periodically with the inspection and packaging, the resource requirements can be met. As you can see, many possibilities are available for corrective management action, once we discover the lack of a feasible solution. The important thing to realize is that linear programming analysis can help determine whether management's plans are feasible. By analyzing the problem using linear programming, we are often able to point out infeasible conditions and initiate corrective action.

Whenever you attempt to solve a problem that is infeasible using The Management Scientist, you will obtain a message that says 'No Feasible Solution'. In this case you know that no solution to the linear programming problem will satisfy all constraints, including the nonnegativity conditions. Careful inspection of your formulation is necessary to try to identify why the problem is infeasible. In some situations, the only reasonable approach is to drop one or more constraints and resolve the problem. If you are able to find an optimal solution for this revised problem, you will know that the constraint(s) that were omitted, in conjunction with the others, are causing the problem to be infeasible.

Unbounded Problems

The solution to a maximization linear programming problem is **unbounded** if the value of the solution may be made infinitely large without violating any of the constraints; for a minimization problem, the solution is unbounded if the value may be made infinitely small. This condition might be termed *managerial utopia*; for example, if this condition were to occur in a profit maximization problem, the manager could achieve an unlimited profit.

However, in linear programming models of real problems, the occurrence of an unbounded solution probably means that the problem has been improperly formulated. We know it is not possible to increase profits indefinitely. Therefore, we must conclude that if a profit maximization problem results in an unbounded solution, the mathematical model doesn't represent the real-world problem sufficiently. Usually, what has happened is that a constraint has been omitted during problem formulation.

As an illustration, consider the following linear programme with two decision variables, X and Y:

$$\text{Max} \quad 20X + 10Y$$

s.t.

$$1X \geq 2$$
$$1Y \leq 5$$
$$X, Y \geq 0$$

In Figure 2.20 we have graphed the feasible region associated with this problem. Note that we can only indicate part of the feasible region since the feasible region extends indefinitely in the direction of the X axis. Looking at the objective function lines in Figure 2.20, we see that the solution to this problem may be made as large as we desire. That is, no matter what solution we pick, we will always be able to reach some feasible solution with a larger value. Thus, we say that the solution to this linear programme is *unbounded*.

Whenever you attempt to solve a problem that is unbounded using The Management Scientist, you will obtain a message that says, 'Problem is Unbounded'.

Figure 2.20 Example of an Unbounded Problem

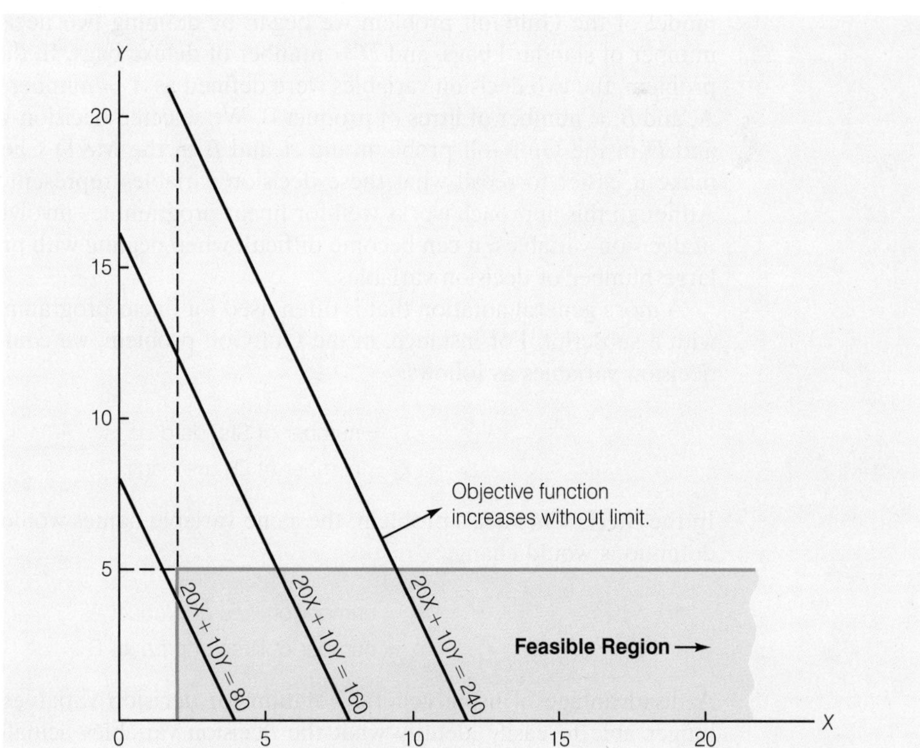

Can you recognize whether a linear programme involves alternative optimal solutions, infeasibility or is unbounded? Try Problems 17 and 18

Because unbounded solutions cannot occur in real problems, the first thing you should do is to review your model to determine whether you have incorrectly formulated the problem. In many cases, this error is the result of inadvertently omitting a constraint during problem formulation.

NOTES AND COMMENTS

1 Infeasibility is independent of the objective function. It exists because the constraints are so restrictive that there is no feasible region for the linear programming model. Thus, when you encounter infeasibility, making changes in the coefficients of the objective function will not help; the problem will remain infeasible.

2 The occurrence of an unbounded solution is often the result of a missing constraint. However, a change in the objective function may cause a previously unbounded problem to become bounded with an optimal solution. For example, the graph in Figure 2.20 shows an unbounded solution for the objective function Max $20X + 10Y$. However, changing the objective function to Max $- 20X - 10Y$ will provide the optimal solution $X = 2$ and $Y = 0$ even though no changes have been made in the constraints.

2.7 General Linear Programming Notation

In this chapter we showed how to formulate linear programming models for the GulfGolf and M&D Chemicals problems. To formulate a linear programming model of the GulfGolf problem we began by defining two decision variables: $S =$ number of standard bags, and $D =$ number of deluxe bags. In the M&D Chemicals problem, the two decision variables were defined as $A =$ number of litres of product A, and $B =$ number of litres of product B. We selected decision-variable names of S and D in the GulfGolf problem and A and B in the M&D Chemicals problem to make it easier to recall what these decision variables represented in the problem. Although this approach works well for linear programmes involving a small number of decision variables, it can become difficult when dealing with problems involving a large number of decision variables.

A more general notation that is often used for linear programmes uses the letter x with a subscript. For instance, in the GulfGolf problem, we could have defined the decision variables as follows:

$$x_1 = \text{number of Standard bags}$$
$$x_2 = \text{number of Deluxe bags}$$

In the M&D Chemicals problem, the same variable names would be used, but their definitions would change:

$$x_1 = \text{number of litres of product A}$$
$$x_2 = \text{number of litres of product B}$$

A disadvantage of using general notation for decision variables is that we are no longer able to easily identify what the decision variables actually represent in the mathematical model. However, the advantage of general notation is that formulating a mathematical model for a problem that involves a large number of decision variables is much easier. For instance, for a linear programming model with three decision variables, we would use variable names of x_1, x_2 and x_3; for a problem with four decision variables, we would use variable names of x_1, x_2, x_3 and x_4 and so on. Clearly, if a problem involved 1000 decision variables, trying to identify 1000 unique names would be difficult. However, using the general linear programming notation, the decision variables would be defined as $x_1, x_2, x_3, \ldots, x_{1000}$.

To illustrate the graphical solution procedure for a linear programme written using general linear programming notation, consider the following mathematical model for a maximization problem involving two decision variables:

$$\begin{aligned} &\text{Max} \quad 3x_1 + 2x_2 \\ &\text{s.t.} \\ &\qquad 2x_1 + 2x_2 \leq 8 \\ &\qquad 1x_1 + 0.5x_2 \leq 3 \\ &\qquad x_1, x_2 \geq 0 \end{aligned}$$

We must first develop a graph that displays the possible solutions (x_1 and x_2 values) for the problem. The usual convention is to plot values of x_1 along the horizontal axis and values of x_2 along the vertical axis. Figure 2.21 shows the graphical solution for this two-variable problem. Note that for this problem the optimal solution is $x_1 = 2$ and $x_2 = 2$, with an objective function value of 10.

Using general linear programming notation, we can write the standard form of the preceding linear programme as follows:

$$\begin{aligned} &\text{Max} \quad 3x_1 + 2x_2 + 0S_1 + 0S_2 \\ &\text{s.t.} \\ &\qquad 2x_1 + 2x_2 + 1S_1 \qquad\quad = 8 \\ &\qquad 1x_1 + 0.5x_2 \qquad\quad + 1S_2 = 3 \\ &\qquad x_1, x_2, S_1, S_2 \geq 0 \end{aligned}$$

Thus, at the optimal solution $x_1 = 2$ and $x_2 = 2$; the values of the slack variables are $s_1 = s_2 = 0$.

Summary

This chapter has introduced a model commonly used in management science, that of linear programming (LP). LP models are used in many different situations, for many different types of problem and across many different types of business organization.

- LP is an optimization model, where we seek to determine an optimal solution to some problem subject to a number of constraints.
- LP problems can be formulated with an objective function which could be for maximization or for minimization. Constraints in an LP problem place some restriction on what we are able to do in our search for an optimal solution and LP constraints can take one of three forms: $\leq$, $\geq$, or $=$.
- Both the objective function and all constraints must take a linear form mathematically.
- The simplest form of an LP problem involves two decision variables and can be solved graphically.
- At the optimal solution some constraints will be binding and some non-binding. A binding constraint is exactly satisfied at the optimal solution. A non-binding constraint will have slack, or surplus, associated with it.

Figure 2.21 Graphical Solution of a Two-Variable Linear Programme with General Notation

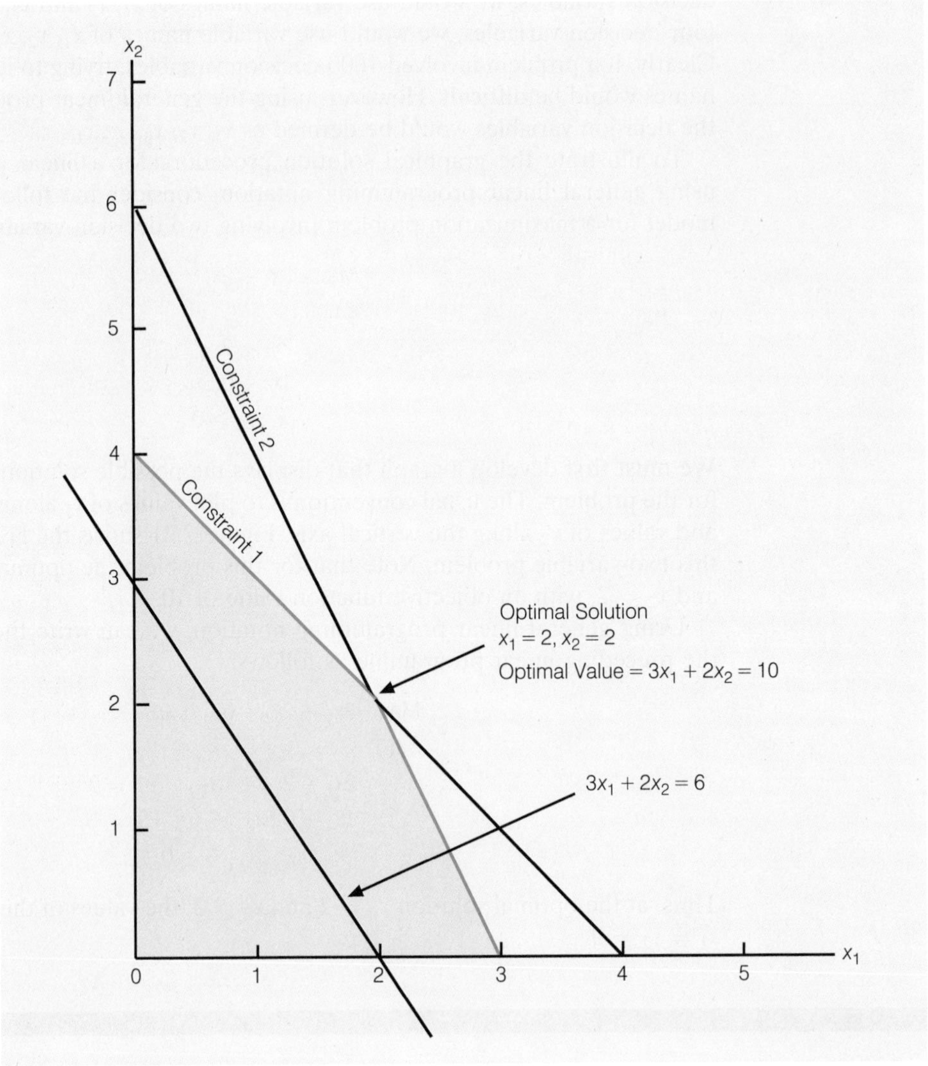

WORKED EXAMPLE

Blair & Rosen PLC (B&R), is a UK based brokerage firm that specializes in building investment portfolios designed to meet the specific needs of its clients who are mostly private individuals wishing to invest their savings in stocks and shares. One client who contacted B&R recently has a maximum of £500 000 to invest. B&R's investment advisor has decided to recommend a portfolio consisting of two investment funds: an Internet fund, where the companies are all active in Internet businesses of one kind or another, and a Blue Chip fund which is more conservative and traditional. The Internet fund has a projected annual return over the next few years of 12 per cent, while the Blue Chip fund has a projected annual return of 9 per cent. The investment advisor has decided that at most £350 000 of the client's funds should be invested in the Internet fund. B&R services include a risk rating for each investment alternative. The Internet fund, which is the more risky of the two investment alternatives, has a risk rating of 6 for every thousand £s invested. The Blue Chip fund has a risk rating of 4 per thousand £s invested. So, for example, if £10 000 is invested in each of the two investment funds, B&R's risk rating for the portfolio would be 6(10) + 4(10) = 100. Finally, B&R has developed a questionnaire to measure each client's risk tolerance. Based on the responses, each client is classified as a conservative, moderate or aggressive investor. The questionnaire results have classified the current client as a moderate investor. B&R recommends that a client who is a moderate investor limit his or her portfolio to a maximum risk rating of 240. You have been asked to help the B&R investment advisor.

a. What is the recommended investment portfolio for this client?
b. What is the annual return for the portfolio?
c. A second client, also with £500 000 to invest, has been classified as an aggressive investor. B&R recommends that the maximum portfolio risk rating for an aggressive investor is 320. What is the recommended investment portfolio for this aggressive investor? Explain what happens to the portfolio under the aggressive investor strategy.

Solution

Let us formulate the LP problem for the first investor. We will let X equal the investment made in the Internet fund and Y the investment made in the Blue Chip fund. X and Y will then be our decision variables. It seems reasonable to assume that the client will want to maximize the return on their investment so we will need a Maximization objective function. We would then have a formulation:

$$\text{Max} \quad 0.12X + 0.09Y$$

$$\begin{aligned} \text{s.t.} \quad X + Y &\leq 500000 \\ X &\leq 350000 \\ 0.0006X + 0.0004Y &\leq 240 \\ X, Y &\geq 0 \end{aligned}$$

Note: we have shown the annual returns in the objective function in percentage terms (0.12, and .09) so that the solution will show the actual annual return in £s directly. You could have formulated the OF as $12X + 9Y$ as well.

We have not drawn a graph of this problem (although you might want to to get some extra practise) but simply used Excel. The output is shown in Exhibit 2.1.

Target Cell (Max)

Name	Original Value	Final Value
Values OF	0	51 000

Adjustable Cells

Name	Original Value	Final Value
Value X	0	200 000
Value Y	0	300 000

Constraints

Name	Cell Value	Status	Slack
LHS	500 000	Binding	0
LHS	200 000	Not Binding	150 000
LHS	240	Binding	0

We see that *X* takes an optimal value of £200 000 and *Y* of £300 000 with the objective function taking a value of £54 000. Putting this back into the context of the problem we can inform the investment advisor that, based on the information given, their client can obtain a maximum annual return of £54 000 by investing £200 000 in the Internet fund and £300 000 in the Blue Chip fund. We see further from the Excel output that the first and third constraints are binding but the second constraint is not. The first constraint related to the maximum available funding of £500 000. All of this is being invested at the optimal solution (slack is zero). Similarly, for the third constraint. This relates to the maximum risk rating of 240. With the recommended investment mix, this rating is exactly met – in other words we are at the upper limit of the client's risk tolerance with this investment mix. On the other hand, the second constraint is non-binding with a slack of £150 000. This relates to the advisor's requirement that no more than £350 000 be invested in the Internet fund.

For the advisor's second client we have a similar problem but we now change the maximum risk rating to 320. The Excel solution is shown in Exhibit 2.2.

Target Cell (Max)

Name	Original Value	Final Value
Values OF	0	55 000

Adjustable Cells

Name	Original Value	Final Value
Value X	0	350 000
Value Y	0	150 000

Constraints

Name	Cell Value	Status	Slack
LHS	500 000	Binding	0
LHS	350 000	Binding	0
LHS	270	Not Binding	50

We now have an optimal solution of £350 000 invested in the Internet fund with the remainder of £150 000 in the Blue Chip fund generating an annual return of £55 500. The first constraint is binding (we are investing all the available amount) as is the second (we are investing the maximum into the Internet fund). The third constraint is non-binding – we are well below the client's maximum risk rating (the slack value is shown as 50 but it is difficult to interpret this given the complexity of the actual constraint).

On comparison with client 1 we see that client 2's portfolio has invested more in the higher-return – but also higher-risk – Internet fund. Client 1 was prevented from investing more than £200 000 in this fund because of the risk rating constraint which was binding for this client.

We might also want to point out to the investment advisor that the model results are only as good as the data that we used, particularly the projected annual returns for the two types of fund.

MANAGEMENT SCIENCE IN ACTION

Using Linear Programming for Traffic Control

The Hanshin Expressway was the first urban toll expressway in Osaka, Japan. Although in 1964 its length was only 2.3 kilometres, today it is a large-scale urban expressway network of 200 kilometres. The Hanshin Expressway provides service for the Hanshin (Osaka-Kobe) area, the second-most populated area in Japan. An average of 828 000 vehicles use the expressway each day, with daily traffic sometimes exceeding one million vehicles. In 1990, the Hanshin Expressway Public Corporation started using an automated traffic control system in order to maximize the number of vehicles flowing into the expressway network.

The automated traffic control system relies on two control methods: (1) limiting the number of cars that enter the expressway at each entrance ramp; and (2) providing drivers with up-to-date and accurate traffic information, including expected travel times and information about accidents. The approach used to limit the number of vehicles depends upon whether the expressway is in a normal or steady state of operation, or whether some type of unusual event, such as an accident or a breakdown, has occurred.

In the first phase of the steady-state case, the Hanshin system uses a linear programming model to maximize the total number of vehicles entering the system, while preventing traffic congestion and adverse effects on surrounding road networks. The data that drive the linear programming model are collected from detectors installed every 500 metres along the expressway and at all entrance and exit ramps. Every five minutes the real-time data collected from the detectors are used to update the model coefficients, and a new linear programme computes the maximum number of vehicles the expressway can accommodate.

The automated traffic control system has been successful. According to surveys, traffic control decreased the length of congested portions of the expressway by 30 per cent and the duration by 20 per cent. It proved to be extremely cost effective, and drivers consider it an indispensable service.

Based on T. Yoshino, T. Sasaki and T. Hasegawa, 'The Traffic-Control System on the Hanshin Expressway' *Interfaces* (January/February 1995): 94–108.

The *Management Science in Action*, Using Linear Programming for Traffic Control, provides just one of many examples of the widespread use of linear programming. In the next two chapters we will see many more applications of linear programming.

Problems

SELF *test*

1 Which of the following mathematical relationships could be found in a linear programming model, and which could not? For the relationships that are unacceptable for linear programmes, state why.

a. $-1x_1 + 2x_2 - 1x_3 \leq 70$
b. $2x_1 - 2x_3 = 50$
c. $1x_1 - 2x^2_2 + 4x_3 \leq 10$
d. $\sqrt[3]{x_1} + 2x_2 - 1x_3 \geq 15$
e. $1x_1 + 1x_2 + 1x_3 = 6$
f. $2x_1 + 5x_2 + 1x_1x_2 \leq 25$

SELF *test*

2 Find the feasible solution points for the following constraints:

a. $4x_1 + 2x_2 \leq 16$
b. $4x_1 + 2x_2 \geq 16$
c. $4x_1 + 2x_2 = 16$

3 Show a separate graph of the constraint lines and feasible solutions for each of the following constraints:

a. $3x_1 + 2x_2 \leq 18$
b. $12x_1 + 8x_2 \geq 480$
c. $5x_1 + 10x_2 = 200$

SELF *test*

4 Show a separate graph of the constraint lines and feasible solutions for each of the following constraints:

a. $x_1 \geq 0.25\ (x_1 + x_2)$
b. $x_2 \leq 0.10\ (x_1 + x_2)$
c. $x_1 \leq 0.50\ (x_1 + x_2)$

SELF *test*

5 Three objective functions for linear programming problems are $7x_1 + 10x_2$, $6x_1 + 4x_2$ and $-4x_1 + 7x_2$. Determine the slope of each objective function. Show the graph of each for objective function values equal to 420.

SELF *test*

6 Identify the feasible region for the following set of constraints:

$$\begin{aligned} \tfrac{1}{2}x_1 + \tfrac{1}{4}x_2 &\geq 30 \\ 1x_1 + 5x_2 &\geq 250 \\ \tfrac{1}{4}x_1 + \tfrac{1}{2}x_2 &\leq 50 \\ x_1,\ x_2 &\geq 0 \end{aligned}$$

SELF *test*

7 For the linear programme:

$$\begin{aligned} \text{Max}\quad & 2x_1 + 3x_2 \\ \text{s.t.}\quad & \\ & 1x_1 + 2x_2 \leq 6 \\ & 5x_1 + 3x_2 \leq 15 \\ & x_1,\ x_2 \geq 0 \end{aligned}$$

find the optimal solution using the graphical solution procedure. What is the value of the objective function at the optimal solution?

SELF *test*

8 Consider the following linear programme:

$$\begin{aligned} \text{Min}\quad & 3x_1 + 4x_2 \\ \text{s.t.}\quad & \\ & 1x_1 + 3x_2 \geq 6 \\ & 1x_1 + 1x_2 \geq 4 \\ & x_1,\ x_2 \geq 0 \end{aligned}$$

Identify the feasible region and find the optimal solution using the graphical solution procedure. What is the value of the objective function?

SELF *test*

9 Consider the following linear programme:

$$\begin{aligned} \text{Max}\quad & 1x_1 + 2x_2 \\ \text{s.t.}\quad & \\ & 1x_1 \qquad\quad \leq 5 \\ & \qquad\quad 1x_2 \leq 4 \\ & 2x_1 + 2x_2 = 12 \\ & x_1,\ x_2 \geq 0 \end{aligned}$$

a. Show the feasible region.
b. What are the extreme points of the feasible region?
c. Find the optimal solution using the graphical procedure.

10 Refer to the GulfGolf problem described in Section 2.1. Suppose that management encounters each of the following situations:

a. The accounting department revises its estimate of the profit contribution for the deluxe bag to $18 per bag.
b. A new low-cost material is available for the standard bag, and the profit contribution per standard bag can be increased to $20 per bag. (Assume the profit contribution of the deluxe bag is the original $9 value.)
c. New sewing equipment is available that would increase the sewing operation capacity to 750 hours. (Assume $10S + 9D$ is the appropriate objective function.)

If each of these conditions is encountered separately, what are the optimal solution and the total profit contribution for each situation?

SELF *test*

11 Write the following linear programme in standard form:

$$\begin{aligned} \text{Max} \quad & 5x_1 + 2x_2 + 8x_3 \\ \text{s.t.} \quad & \\ & 1x_1 + 2x_2 + \tfrac{1}{2}x_3 \leq 420 \\ & 2x_1 + 3x_2 - 1x_3 \leq 610 \\ & 6x_1 - 1x_2 + 3x_3 \leq 125 \\ & x_1,\ x_2,\ x_3 \geq 0 \end{aligned}$$

SELF *test*

12 RMC, Inc., is a small firm that produces a variety of chemical products. In a particular production process, three raw materials are blended (mixed together) to produce two products: a fuel additive and a solvent base. Each kilo of fuel additive is a mixture of 0.4 kilos of material 1 and 0.6 kilos of material 3. A kilo of solvent base is a mixture of 0.5 kilos of material 1, 0.2 kilos of material 2 and 0.3 kilos of material 3. After deducting relevant costs, the profit contribution is €40 for every kilo of fuel additive produced and €30 for every kilo of solvent base produced.

RMC's production is constrained by a limited availability of the three raw materials. For the current production period, RMC has available the following quantities of each raw material:

Raw Material	Amount Available for Production
Material 1	20 kilos
Material 2	5 kilos
Material 3	21 kilos

Assuming that RMC is interested in maximizing the total profit contribution, answer the following:

a. What is the linear programming model for this problem?
b. Find the optimal solution using the graphical solution procedure. How many kilos of each product should be produced, and what is the projected total profit contribution?
c. Is there any unused material? If so, how much?
d. Are there any redundant constraints? If so, which ones?

SELF *test*

13 GulfGolf also make two different types of golfing gloves: a regular model and a professional model. The firm has 900 hours of production time available in its cutting and sewing department, 300 hours available in its finishing department and 100 hours available in its packaging and shipping department. The production time requirements and the profit contribution per glove are given in the following table.

	Production Time (hours)			
Model	**Cutting and Sewing**	**Finishing**	**Packaging and Shipping**	**Profit/ Glove**
Regular model	1	0.5	0.125	\$5
Professional's model	1.5	0.3333	0.25	\$8

Assuming that the company is interested in maximizing the total profit contribution, answer the following:

a. What is the linear programming model for this problem?
b. How many gloves of each model should GulfGolf manufacture?
c. What is the total profit contribution the company can earn with the listed production quantities?
d. How many hours of production time will be scheduled in each department?
e. What is the slack time in each department?

14 A local health clinic is keen to raise awareness and understanding of AIDS/HIV in the local community and has managed to attract some funding for local advertising. The clinic would like to determine the best way to allocate a monthly advertising budget of €1000 between newspaper advertising and radio advertising. Management has decided that at least 25 per cent of the budget must be spent on each type of media, and that the amount of money spent on local newspaper advertising must be at least twice the amount spent on radio advertising. A marketing consultant has developed an index that measures audience exposure per euro of advertising on a scale from 0 to 100, with higher values implying greater audience exposure. If the value of the index for local newspaper advertising is 50 and the value of the index for spot radio advertising is 80, how should the clinic allocate its advertising budget in order to maximize the value of total audience exposure?

a. Formulate a linear programming model that can be used to determine how the clinic should allocate its advertising budget in order to maximize the value of total audience exposure.
b. Find the optimal solution using the graphical solution procedure.

SELF *test*

15 Miguel's Mexican produces various Mexican food products and sells them to Western Foods, a chain of grocery stores located in Europe. Miguel's makes two salsa products: Western Foods Salsa and Mexico City Salsa. Essentially, the two products have different blends of whole tomatoes, tomato sauce and tomato paste. The Western Foods Salsa is a blend of 50 per cent whole tomatoes, 30 per cent tomato sauce and 20 per cent tomato paste. The Mexico City Salsa, which has a thicker and chunkier consistency, consists of 70 per cent whole tomatoes, 10 per cent tomato sauce and 20 per cent tomato paste. Each jar of salsa produced weighs 280gms. For the current production period Miguel's can purchase up to 280 kilos of whole tomatoes, 130 kilos of tomato sauce and 100 kilos of tomato paste; the price per kilo for these ingredients is €0.96, €0.64 and €0.56, respectively. The cost of the spices and the other ingredients is approximately €0.10 per jar. Miguel's buys empty glass jars for €0.02

each, and labelling and filling costs are estimated to be €0.03 for each jar of salsa produced. Miguel's contract with Western Foods results in sales revenue of €1.64 for each jar of Western Foods Salsa and €1.93 for each jar of Mexico City Salsa.

a. Develop a linear programming model that will enable Miguel's to determine the mix of salsa products that will maximize the total profit contribution.
b. Find the optimal solution.

SELF *test*

16 As part of a quality improvement initiative, government employees complete a three-day training programme on teamwork and a two-day training programme on problem solving. The manager of quality improvement requested that at least eight training programmes on teamwork and at least ten training programmes on problem solving be offered during the next six months. In addition, senior-level management specified that at least 25 training programmes must be offered during this period. A consultant is used to teach the training programmes. During the next six months, the consultant has 84 days of training time available. Each training programme on teamwork costs €10 000 and each training programme on problem solving costs €8000.

a. Formulate a linear programming model that can be used to determine the number of training programmes on teaming and the number of training programmes on problem solving that should be offered in order to minimize total cost.
b. Graph the feasible region.
c. Determine the coordinates of each extreme point.
d. Solve for the minimum-cost solution.

SELF *test*

17 Does the following linear programme involve infeasibility, unbounded and/or alternative optimal solutions? Explain.

$$\begin{aligned} \text{Max} \quad & 4x_1 + 8x_2 \\ \text{s.t.} \quad & \\ & 2x_1 + 2x_2 \leq 10 \\ & -1x_1 + 1x_2 \geq 8 \\ & x_1, x_2 \geq 0 \end{aligned}$$

SELF *test*

18 Does the following linear programme involve infeasibility, unbounded and/or alternative optimal solution? Explain.

$$\begin{aligned} \text{Max} \quad & 1x_1 + 1x_2 \\ \text{s.t.} \quad & \\ & 8x_1 + 6x_2 \geq 24 \\ & 4x_1 + 6x_2 \geq -12 \\ & 2x_2 \geq 4 \\ & x_1, x_2 \geq 0 \end{aligned}$$

19 Management of High Tech Services (HTS) would like to develop a model that will help allocate their technicians' time between service calls to regular contract customers and new customers. A maximum of 80 hours of technician time is available over the two-week planning period. To satisfy cash flow requirements, at least €800 in revenue (per technician) must be generated during the two-week period. Technician time for regular customers generates €25 per hour. However, technician time for new customers only generates an average of €8 per hour because in many cases a new customer contact does not provide billable services. To ensure that new customer contacts are being maintained, the technician time spent on new customer contacts must be at least 60 per cent of the time spent on regular customer contacts. Given these revenue and policy requirements, HTS would like to determine how to allocate technician time

between regular customers and new customers so that the total number of customers contacted during the two-week period will be maximized. Technicians require an average of 50 minutes for each regular customer contact and one hour for each new customer contact.

a. Develop a linear programming model that will enable HTS to allocate technician time between regular customers and new customers.
b. Find the optimal solution.

SELF *test*

20 For the linear programme

$$\begin{aligned} \text{Min} \quad & 6x_1 + 4x_2 \\ \text{s.t.} \quad & \\ & 2x_1 + 1x_2 \geq 12 \\ & 1x_1 + 1x_2 \geq 10 \\ & 1x_2 \leq 4 \\ & x_1, x_2 \geq 0 \end{aligned}$$

a. Write the linear programme in standard form.
b. Find the optimal solution using the graphical solution procedure.
c. What are the values of the slack and surplus variables?

SELF *test*

21 Consider the following linear programme:

$$\begin{aligned} \text{Min} \quad & 2x_1 + 2x_2 \\ \text{s.t.} \quad & \\ & 1x_1 + 3x_2 \leq 12 \\ & 3x_1 + 1x_2 \geq 13 \\ & 1x_1 - 1x_2 = 3 \\ & x_1, x_2 \geq 0 \end{aligned}$$

a. show the feasible region.
b. what are the extreme points of the feasible region?
c. Find the optimal solution using the graphical solution procedure.

CASE PROBLEM 1 Workload Balancing

Digital Imaging (DI) produces photo printers for both the professional and consumer markets. The DI consumer division recently introduced two photo printers that provide colour prints rivalling those produced by a professional processing lab. The DI-910 model can produce a 10cm × 15cm borderless print in approximately 37 seconds. The more sophisticated and faster DI-950 can even produce a 35cm × 50cm borderless print. Financial projections show profit contributions of \$42 for each DI-910 and \$87 for each DI-950.

The printers are assembled, tested and packaged at DI's plant located in Shanghai. This plant is highly automated and uses two manufacturing lines to produce the printers. Line 1 performs the assembly operation with times of three minutes per DI-910 printer and six minutes per DI-950 printer. Line 2 performs both the testing and packaging operations. Times are four minutes per DI-910 printer and two minutes per DI-950 printer. The shorter time for the DI-950 printer is a result of its faster print speed. Both manufacturing lines are in operation one eight-hour shift per day.

Managerial Report

Perform an analysis for Digital Imaging in order to determine how many units of each printer to produce. Prepare a report to DI's president presenting your findings and recommendations. Include (but do not limit your discussion to) a consideration of the following:

1 The recommended number of units of each printer to produce to maximize the total contribution to profit for an eight-hour shift. What reasons might management have for not implementing your recommendation?
2 Suppose that management also states that the number of DI-910 printers produced must be at least as great as the number of DI-950 units produced. Assuming that the objective is to maximize the total contribution to profit for an eight-hour shift, how many units of each printer should be produced?
3 Does the solution you developed in part (2) balance the total time spent on line 1 and the total time spent on line 2? Why might this balance or lack of it be a concern to management?
4 Management requested an expansion of the model in part (2) that would provide a better balance between the total time on line 1 and the total time on line 2. Management wants to limit the difference between the total time on line 1 and the total time on line 2 to 30 minutes or less. If the objective is still to maximize the total contribution to profit, how many units of each printer should be produced? What effect does this workload balancing have on total profit in part (2)?
5 Suppose that in part (1) management specified the objective of maximizing the total number of printers produced each shift rather than total profit contribution. With this objective, how many units of each printer should be produced per shift? What effect does this objective have on total profit and workload balancing?

For each solution that you develop include a copy of your linear programming model and graphical solution in the appendix to your report.

CASE PROBLEM 2 Production Strategy

Better Fitness, Inc. (BFI), manufactures exercise equipment at its plant in Munich, Germany. It recently designed two universal weight machines for the home exercise market. Both machines use BFI-patented technology that provides the user with an extremely wide range of motion capability for each type of exercise performed. Until now, such capabilities have been available only on expensive weight machines used primarily by physical therapists.

At a recent trade show, demonstrations of the machines resulted in significant dealer interest. In fact, the number of orders that BFI received at the trade show far exceeded its manufacturing capabilities for the current production period. As a result, management decided to begin production of the two machines. The two machines, which BFI named the BodyPlus 100 and the BodyPlus 200, require different amounts of resources to produce.

The BodyPlus 100 consists of a frame unit, a press station and a pec-dec station. Each frame produced uses four hours of machining and welding time and two hours of painting and finishing time. Each press station requires two hours of machining and welding time and one hour of painting and finishing time, and each pec-dec station uses two hours of machining and welding time and two hours of painting and finishing time. In addition, two hours are spent assembling, testing and packaging each BodyPlus 100. The raw material costs are €450 for each frame, €300 for each press station and €250 for each pec-dec station; packaging costs are estimated to be €50 per unit.

The BodyPlus 200 consists of a frame unit, a press station, a pec-dec station and a leg-press station. Each frame produced uses five hours of machining and welding time and four hours of painting and finishing time. Each press station requires three hours machining and welding time and two hours of painting and finishing time, each pec-dec station uses two hours of machining and welding time and two hours of painting and finishing time, and each leg-press station requires two hours of machining and welding time and two hours of painting and finishing time. In addition, two hours are spent assembling, testing and packaging each BodyPlus 200. The raw material costs are €650 for each frame, €400 for each press station, €250 for each pec-dec station and €200 for each leg-press station; packaging costs are estimated to be €75 per unit.

For the next production period, management estimates that 600 hours of machining and welding time, 450 hours of painting and finishing time and 140 hours of assembly, testing and packaging time will be available. Current labour costs are €20 per hour for machining and welding time, €15 per hour for painting and finishing time and €12 per hour for assembly, testing and packaging time. The market in which the two machines must compete suggests a retail price of €2400 for the BodyPlus 100 and €3500 for the BodyPlus 200, although some flexibility may be available to BFI because of the unique capabilities of the new machines. Authorized BFI dealers can purchase machines for 70 per cent of the suggested retail price.

BFI's president believes that the unique capabilities of the BodyPlus 200 can help position BFI as one of the leaders in high-end exercise equipment. Consequently, he has stated that the number of units of the BodyPlus 200 produced must be at least 25 per cent of the total production.

Managerial Report

Analyze the production problem at Better Fitness, Inc., and prepare a report for BFI's president presenting your findings and recommendations. Include (but do not limit your discussion to) a consideration of the following items:

1. What is the recommended number of BodyPlus 100 and BodyPlus 200 machines to produce?
2. How does the requirement that the number of units of the BodyPlus 200 produced be at least 25 per cent of the total production affect profits?
3. Where should efforts be expended in order to increase profits?

Include a copy of your linear programming model and graphical solution in an appendix to your report.

CASE PROBLEM 3 Blending

A local healthfood cooperative runs a community café and produces two vegetarian burgers. The large burger makes a profit of 85 cents per unit sold and the standard burger 55 cents. Each burger is made from three basic ingredients as shown below. The café reckons it never sells more than a total of 100 burgers in any one day (unsold burgers have to be thrown away for health reasons) but that it typically sells at least 30 of the standard burgers every day and 25 of the large.

	Vegetable mix	Soybean mix	Crumb mix
Large burger	30 grams	150 grams	20 grams
Standard burger	30 grams	100 grams	20 grams
Availability	4 kilograms	10 kilograms	1.5 kilograms

Managerial Report

1. Provide a full explanation of the problem formulation for management (who have never heard of LP).
2. Provide management with advice as to what to do to maximize profit in this situation.
3. Advise management of the limitations of this analysis.

Provide model details and relevant computer output in a report appendix.

Appendix 2.1 Solving Linear Programmes With Excel

In this appendix, we will use an Excel worksheet to solve the GulfGolf linear programming problem. We will enter the problem data for the problem in the top part of the worksheet and develop the linear programming model in the bottom part of the worksheet.

Formulation

Whenever we formulate a worksheet model of a linear programme, we perform the following steps:

Step 1. Enter the problem data in the top part of the worksheet.

Step 2. Specify cell locations for the decision variables.

Step 3. Select a cell and enter a formula for computing the value of the objective function.

Step 4. Select a cell and enter a formula for computing the left-hand side of each constraint.

Step 5. Select a cell and enter a formula for computing the right-hand side of each constraint.

The formula worksheet that we developed for the GulfGolf problem using these five steps is shown in Figure 2.22. Note that the worksheet consists of two sections: a data section and a model section. The four components of the model are screened, and the cells reserved for the decision variables are enclosed in a boldface box. Figure 2.22 is called a formula worksheet because it displays the formulas that we have entered and not the values computed from those formulas. In a moment we will see how Excel's Solver is used to find the optimal solution to the problem. But first, let's review each of the preceding steps as they apply to the problem.

Figure 2.22 Formula Worksheet for the GulfGolf Problem

	A	B	C	D	E
1	**Gulf Golf**				
2					
3		**Production Time**			
4	**Operation**	**Standard**	**Deluxe**	**Time Available**	
5	Cutting and Dyeing	0.7	1	630	
6	Sewing	0.5	0.83333	600	
7	Finishing	1	0.66667	708	
8	Inspection and Packaging	0.1	0.25	135	
9	**Profit Per Bag**	10	9		
10					
11					
12	**Model**				
13					
14		**Decision Variables**			
15		**Standard**	**Deluxe**		
16	**Bags Produced**				
17					
18	**Maximize Total Profit**	=B9*B16+C9*C16			
19					
20	**Constraints**	**Hours Used (LHS)**		**Hours Available (RHS)**	
21	Cutting and Dyeing	=B5*B16+C5*C16	<=	=D5	
22	Sewing	=B6*B16+C6*C16	<=	=D6	
23	Finishing	=B7*B16+C7*C16	<=	=D7	
24	Inspection and Packaging	=B8*B16+C8*C16	<=	=D8	
25					

Step 1. Enter the problem data in the top part of the worksheet.
Cells B5:C8 show the production requirements per unit for each product.
Cells B9:C9 show the profit contribution per unit for the two products.
Cells D5:D8 show the number of hours available in each department.

Step 2. Specify cell locations for the decision variables.
Cell B16 will contain the number of standard bags produced, and cell C16 will contain the number of deluxe bags produced.

Step 3. Select a cell and enter a formula for computing the value of the objective function.
Cell B18: =B9*B16 + C9*C16

Step 4. Select a cell and enter a formula for computing the left-hand side of each constraint.
With four constraints, we have:
Cell B21:=B5*B16 + C5*C16
Cell B22:=B6*B16 + C6*C16
Cell B23:=B7*B16 + C7*C16
Cell B24:=B8*B16 + C8*C16

Step 5. Select a cell and enter a formula for computing the right-hand side of each constraint.
With four constraints, we have:
Cell D21:=D5
Cell D22:=D6
Cell D23:=D7
Cell D24:=D8

Note that descriptive labels make the model section of the worksheet easier to read and understand. For example, we added 'Standard', 'Deluxe' and 'Bags Produced' in rows 15 and 16 so that the values of the decision variables appearing in cells B16 and C16 can be easily interpreted. In addition, we entered 'Maximize Total Profit' in cell A18 to indicate that the value of the objective function appearing in cell B18 is the maximum profit contribution. In the constraint section of the worksheet we added the constraint names as well as the '<=' symbols to show the relationship that exists between the left-hand side and the right-hand side of each constraint. Although these descriptive labels are not necessary to use Excel Solver to find a solution to the GulfGolf problem, the labels make it easier for the user to understand and interpret the optimal solution.

Excel Solution

The standard Excel Solver developed by Frontline Systems can be used to solve all of the linear programming problems presented in this text. However, a more powerful version referred to as Premium Solver for Education is available. When first started, Premium Solver looks and behaves exactly like the standard Excel Solver. But, when the 'Premium' button in the main Solver Parameters dialogue box is selected, this version provides a variety of new features, including an online user's guide. The Premium Solver for Education has the same problem size limits as the standard Excel Solver: 200 decision variables and 100 constraints. We recommend that you install the new version and use the 'Premium' mode option when developing and solving spreadsheet models of linear programmes.

The following steps describe how Frontline Systems' Premium Solver for Education can be used to obtain the optimal solution to the GulfGolf problem.

Step 1. Select the **Tools** menu.

Step 2. Select the **Solver** option.

Step 3. When the **Solver Parameters** dialogue box appears (see Figure 2.23):
Enter B18 into the **Set Cell** box
Select the **Equal To: Max** option
Enter B16:C16 into the **By Changing Variable Cells** box
Select **Add**

Step 4. When the **Add Constraint** dialogue box appears:
Enter B21:B24 in the **Cell Reference** box
Select <=
Enter D21:D24 into the **Constraint** box
Click **OK**

Step 5. When the **Solver Parameters** dialogue box reappears:
Choose **Options**

Step 6. When the **Solver Options** dialogue box appears:
Select **Assume Non-Negative**
Click **OK**

Step 7. When the **Solver Parameters** dialogue box appears:
Choose **Solve**

Step 8. When the **Solver Results** dialogue box appears:
Select **Keep Solver Solution**
Click **OK**

If the Standard button and Standard Simplex LP option do not appear, click the Premium button and select the Standard Simplex LP option.

Figure 2.23 shows the completed Solver Parameters dialogue box, and Figure 2.24 shows the optimal solution in the worksheet. Note that after rounding, the optimal solution of 540 standard bags and 252 deluxe bags is the same as we obtained using the graphical solution procedure. In addition to the output information shown in Figure 2.24, Solver has an option to provide sensitivity analysis information. We discuss sensitivity analysis in Chapter 3.

In Step 6 we selected the Assume Non-Negative option in the Solver Options dialogue box to avoid having to enter nonnegativity constraints for the decision variables. In general, whenever we want to solve a linear programming model in which the decision variables are all restricted to be nonnegative, we will select this option. In addition, in Step 4 we entered all four less-than-or-equal-to constraints simultaneously by entering B21:B24 into the Cell Reference box, selecting <=, and entering D21:D24 into the Constraint box. Alternatively, we could have entered the four constraints one at a time.

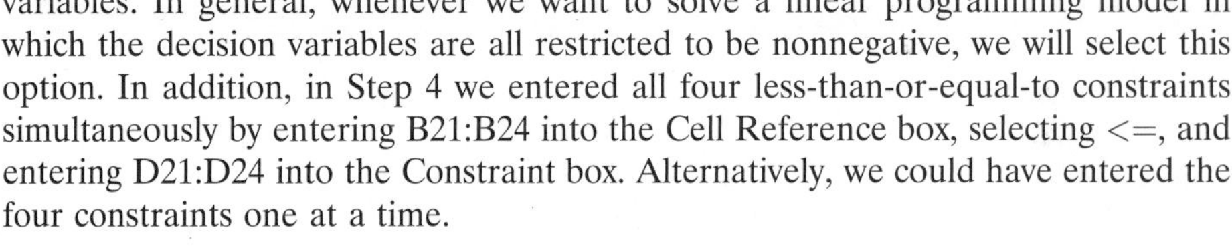

Figure 2.23 Solver Parameters Dialogue Box for the GulfGolf Problem

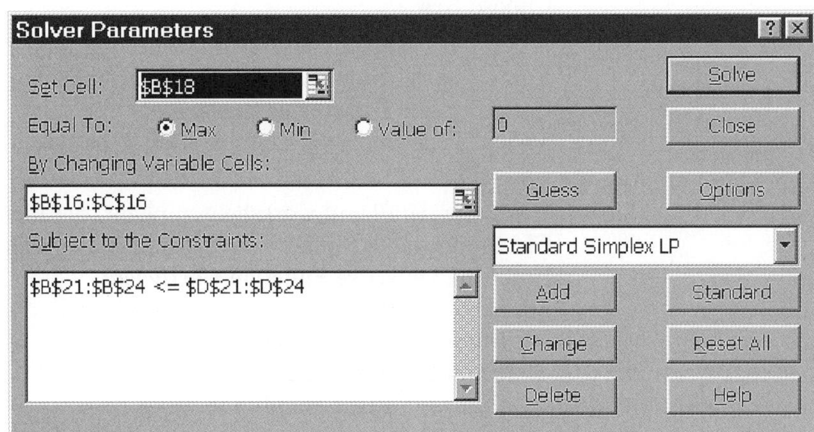

Figure 2.24 Excel Solution for the GulfGolf Problem

EXCEL *file*

GULFGOLF

	A	B	C	D	E
1	Gulf Golf				
2					
3		Production Time			
4	Operation	Standard	Deluxe	Time Available	
5	Cutting and Dyeing	0.7	1	630	
6	Sewing	0.5	0.83333	600	
7	Finishing	1	0.66667	708	
8	Inspection and Packaging	0.1	0.25	135	
9	Profit Per Bag	10	9		
10					
11					
12	Model				
13					
14		Decision Variables			
15		Standard	Deluxe		
16	Bags Produced	539.99842	252.00110		
17					
18	Maximize Total Profit	7668			
19					
20	Constraints	Hours Used (LHS)		Hours Available (RHS)	
21	Cutting and Dyeing	630	<=	630	
22	Sewing	479.99929	<=	600	
23	Finishing	708	<=	708	
24	Inspection and Packaging	117.00012	<=	135	
25					

Appendix 2.2 Solving Linear Programmes With the Management Scientist

In this appendix we describe how The Management Scientist software package can be used to solve the GulfGolf linear programming problem. After starting The Management Scientist, execute the following steps.

Step 1. Select the **Linear Programming** module

Step 2. Select the **File** menu
Choose **New**

Step 3. When the **Problem Features** dialogue box appears:
Enter 2 in the **Number of Decision Variables** box
Enter 4 in the **Number of Constraints** box
Select Maximize in the **Optimization Type** box
Click **OK**

Step 4. When the data input worksheet appears (see Figure 2.26):
Change **Variable Names** from X1 and X2 to S and D, respectively.
Enter the **Objective Function Coefficients**
For each constraint:
Enter the **Coefficients**
Enter the **Relation** (<, =, >)
Enter the **Right-Hand-Side** value

Step 5. Select the **Solution** menu
Choose **Solve**

The Management Scientist interprets the $<$ symbol as $\leq$ and the $>$ symbol as $\geq$.

The user entries in the data input worksheet are shown in Figure 2.26. The output from The Management Scientist is shown in Figure 2.25. When entering the problem data, zero coefficients do not have to be entered. The original problem can be edited or changed by selecting the **Edit** menu. Finally, printed output can be obtained by selecting the **Solution** menu and then selecting the **Print** option.

The Management Scientist output is shown in Figure 2.25. First, note the number 7667.99417, which appears to the right of Objective Function Value. Rounding this value, we can conclude that the optimal solution to this problem will provide a profit of \$7668. Directly below the objective function value, we find the values of the decision variables at the optimal solution. After rounding we have $S = 540$ standard bags and $D = 252$ deluxe bags as the optimal production quantities. The information in the Reduced Costs column indicates how much the objective function coefficient of each decision variable would have to improve before it would be possible for that variable to assume a positive value in the optimal solution. If a decision variable is already positive in the optimal solution, its reduced cost is zero. For the GulfGolf problem, the optimal solution is $S = 540$ and $D = 252$. Both variables already have positive values; therefore, their corresponding reduced costs are zero. In Chapter 3 we will interpret the reduced cost for a decision variable that does not have a positive value in the optimal solution.

Immediately following the optimal S and D values and the reduced cost information, the computer output provides information about the status of the constraints. Recall that the GulfGolf problem had four less-than-or-equal-to constraints corresponding to the hours available in each of four production departments. The

Figure 2.25 The Management Scientist Solution for the GulfGolf Problem

EXCEL *file*

GULFGOLF

```
Objective Function Value =                7667.99417

    Variable              Value              Reduced Costs
 --------------    ----------------       ------------------
        S              539.99842                0.00000
        D              252.00110                0.00000

   Constraint          Slack/Surplus          Dual Prices
 --------------    ----------------       ------------------
        1                0.00000                4.37496
        2              120.00071                0.00000
        3                0.00000                6.93753
        4               17.99988                0.00000

OBJECTIVE COEFFICIENT RANGES

   Variable     Lower Limit     Current Value     Upper Limit
 ------------  -------------   ---------------   -------------
       S          6.30000         10.00000          13.49993
       D          6.66670          9.00000          14.28571

RIGHT HAND SIDE RANGES

  Constraint    Lower Limit     Current Value     Upper Limit
 ------------  -------------   ---------------   --------------
       1         495.60000        630.00000          682.36316
       2         479.99929        600.00000     No Upper Limit
       3         580.00140        708.00000          900.00000
       4         117.00012        135.00000     No Upper Limit
```

Figure 2.26 Data Input Worksheet for the GulfGolf Problem

Optimization Type: Max				
	Objective Function			
Variable Names:	S	D		
Coefficients:	10	9		
	Constraints			
Subject To:	S	D	Relation(<,=,>)	Right-Hand-Side
Constraint 1	0.7	1	<	630
Constraint 2	0.5	0.83333	<	600
Constraint 3	1	0.66667	<	708
Constraint 4	0.1	0.25	<	135

information shown in the Slack/Surplus column provides the value of the slack variable for each of the departments. The rest of the output can be used to determine how a change in a coefficient of the objective function or a change in the right-hand side value of a constraint will affect the optimal solution. We will discuss the use of this information in Chapter 3 when we study the topic of sensitivity analysis.

Chapter 3

Linear Programming: Sensitivity Analysis and Interpretation of Solution

Learning objectives

By the end of this chapter you will be able to:

- Explain the importance of sensitivity analysis in linear programming
- Undertake graphical sensitivity analysis
- Undertake sensitivity analysis using computer output
- Explain the management implications of sensitivity analysis

In Chapter 2 we saw how to formulate and then solve an LP problem. This provides management with the optimal solution to their decision problem. However, it is highly unlikely that this will be enough by itself for management, given that the business environment for most organizations is both constantly changing and increasingly uncertain and unpredictable. Management are likely to say 'OK, so that's the optimal solution *now*. But suppose things change? Suppose our costs change? Suppose demand for the products changes? Suppose our workforce are willing to work overtime? What should we do then to ensure an optimal solution?'. Such questions are often referred to as *what-if* questions. Clearly, if some part of an LP decision problem changes then we could re-formulate the problem taking into account such changes and then re-solve the problem. However, this is time-consuming and costly, especially in the real world where LP problems are large. Fortunately we don't always need to do this. We can make use of **sensitivity analysis**. Sensitivity analysis is a study of how changes in the numerical coefficients of a linear programme affect the current, optimal solution. We conduct this analysis from the information we already have about the optimal solution without having to re-formulate and re-solve the problem. This is a particularly powerful feature of LP and one which makes it attractive to many decision makers.

Because sensitivity analysis is concerned with how these changes affect the optimal solution, the analysis does not begin until the optimal solution to the original linear programming problem has been obtained. For that reason, sensitivity analysis is often referred to as *postoptimality analysis*.

Our approach to sensitivity analysis parallels the approach used to introduce linear programming in Chapter 2. We begin by showing how a graphical method can be used to perform sensitivity analysis for linear programming problems with two decision variables. Then, we show how computer packages, like Excel provide sensitivity analysis information.

Finally, we extend the discussion of problem formulation started in Chapter 2 by formulating and solving three larger linear programming problems. In discussing the solution for each of these problems, we focus on managerial interpretation of the optimal solution and sensitivity analysis information.

3.1 Introduction to Sensitivity Analysis

Sensitivity analysis is important to decision makers because real-world problems exist in a changing environment. Prices of raw materials change, product demand changes, companies purchase new machinery, stock prices fluctuate, employee turnover occurs and so on. If a linear programming model has been used in such an environment, we can expect some of the coefficients to change over time. We will then want to determine how these changes affect the optimal solution to the original linear programming problem. Sensitivity analysis provides us with the information needed to respond to such changes without requiring the complete solution of a revised linear programme.

Remember the GulfGolf problem in Chapter 2:

$$
\begin{aligned}
&\text{Max} \quad 10S + 9D \\
&\text{s.t} \\
&\qquad 0.7S + 1D \le 630 \quad \text{Cutting and dyeing} \\
&\qquad 0.5S + 0.8333D \le 600 \quad \text{Sewing} \\
&\qquad 1S + 0.6667D \le 708 \quad \text{Finishing} \\
&\qquad 0.1S + 0.25D \le 135 \quad \text{Inspection and packaging} \\
&\qquad S, D \ge 0
\end{aligned}
$$

MANAGEMENT SCIENCE IN ACTION

Assigning Products to Worldwide Facilities at Eastman Kodak

One of the major planning issues at Eastman Kodak involves the determination of what products should be manufactured at Kodak's facilities located throughout the world. The assignment of products to facilities is called the 'world load'. In determining the world load, Kodak faces a number of interesting trade-offs. For instance, not all manufacturing facilities are equally efficient for all products, and the margins by which some facilities are better varies from product to product. In addition to manufacturing costs, the transportation costs and the effects of customs duty and duty drawbacks can significantly affect the allocation decision.

To assist in determining the world load, Kodak developed a linear programming model that accounts for the physical nature of the distribution problem and the various costs (manufacturing, transportation and duties) involved. The model's objective is to minimize the total cost subject to constraints such as satisfying demand and capacity constraints for each facility.

The linear programming model is a static representation of the problem situation, and the real world is always changing. Thus, the linear programming model must be used in a dynamic way. For instance, when demand expectations change, the model can be used to determine the effect the change will have on the world load. Suppose that the currency of country A rises compared to the currency of country B. How should the world load be modified? In addition to using the linear programming model in a 'how-to-react' mode, the model is useful in a more active mode by considering questions such as the following: Is it worthwhile for facility F to spend *d* dollars to lower the unit manufacturing cost of product P from *x* to *y*? The linear programming model helps Kodak evaluate the overall effect of possible changes at any facility.

In the final analysis, managers recognize that they cannot use the model by simply turning it on, reading the results and executing the solution. The model's recommendation combined with managerial judgement provide the final decision.

Based on information provided by Greg Sampson of Eastman Kodak.

The optimal solution, $S = 540$ standard bags and $D = 252$ deluxe bags, was based on profit contribution figures of \$10 per standard bag and \$9 per deluxe bag. We are now told by the Sales Dept. that, because of increased competition they have reduced prices and the profit contribution for the standard bag has fallen from \$10 to \$8.50. Sensitivity analysis can be used to determine whether the production schedule calling for 540 standard bags and 252 deluxe bags is still best. If it is, solving a modified linear programming problem with $8.50S + 9D$ as the new objective function will not be necessary.

Sensitivity analysis can also be used to determine which coefficients in a linear programming model are crucial. For example, the Accounting Department has indicated that the \$9 profit contribution for the deluxe bag is only a best estimate and could be lower. The problem for management is that 252 deluxe bags are currently being produced, based on the \$9 profit contribution estimate. If the profit contribution is actually lower should they stop producing the deluxe bag and switch production to the standard bag instead? Sensitivity analysis can be used to calculate how much lower the \$9 profit contribution would need to be for the deluxe bag not to be profitable enough to produce.

Another aspect of sensitivity analysis concerns changes in the right-hand side values of the constraints. Recall that in the GulfGolf problem the optimal solution used all available time in the cutting and dyeing department and the finishing department. What would happen to the optimal solution and total profit contribution if the company could obtain additional quantities of either of these resources? Sensitivity analysis can help determine how much each additional hour of production time is worth and how many hours can be added before diminishing returns set in.

3.2 Graphical Sensitivity Analysis

For linear programming problems with two decision variables, graphical solution methods can be used to perform sensitivity analysis on the objective function coefficients and the right-hand side values for the constraints.

Objective Function Coefficients

Let us consider how changes in the objective function coefficients might affect the optimal solution to the GulfGolf problem. The current contribution to profit is $10 per unit for the standard bag and $9 per unit for the deluxe bag. It seems obvious that an increase in the profit contribution for one of the bags might lead management to increase production of that bag, and a decrease in the profit contribution for one of the bags might lead management to decrease production of that bag. It is not obvious, however, how much the profit contribution would have to change before management would want to change the production quantities.

The current optimal solution to this problem calls for producing 540 standard golf bags and 252 deluxe golf bags. The **range of optimality** for each objective function coefficient provides the range of values over which the current solution will remain optimal. In other words, it will show a lower value and an upper value and between these values the current optimal solution will remain as the optimal solution. Managerial attention needs to be focused on those objective function coefficients that have a narrow range of optimality and coefficients near the end points of the range. With these coefficients, a small change can mean modifying the optimal solution. Let us now calculate the ranges of optimality for this problem.

Figure 3.1 shows the graphical solution. A careful inspection of this graph shows that as long as the slope of the objective function line is between the slope of line A (which coincides with the cutting and dyeing constraint line) and the slope of line B (which coincides with the finishing constraint line), extreme point ③ with $S = 540$ and $D = 252$ will be optimal. Changing an objective function coefficient for S or D will cause the slope of the objective function line to change. In Figure 3.1 we see that such changes cause the objective function line to rotate around extreme point ③. However, as long as the objective function line stays within the shaded region, extreme point ③ will remain optimal.

Rotating the objective function line *anticlockwise* causes the slope to become less negative, and the slope increases. When the objective function line rotates anticlockwise (slope increased) enough to coincide with line A, we obtain alternative optimal solutions between extreme points ③ and ④. Any further anticlockwise rotation of the objective function line will cause extreme point ③ to be nonoptimal. Hence, the slope of line A provides an upper limit for the slope of the objective function line.

The slope of the objective function line is negative; hence, rotating the objective function line clockwise makes the line steeper even though the slope is getting smaller (more negative).

Rotating the objective function line *clockwise* causes the slope to become more negative, and the slope decreases. When the objective function line rotates clockwise (slope decreases) enough to coincide with line B, we obtain alternative optimal solutions between extreme points ③ and ②. Any further clockwise rotation of the objective function line will cause extreme point ③ to be nonoptimal. Hence, the slope of line B provides a lower limit for the slope of the objective function line.

Figure 3.1 Graphical Solution of GulfGolf Problem with Slope of Objective Function Line Between Slopes of Lines A and B; Extreme Point ③ Is Optimal

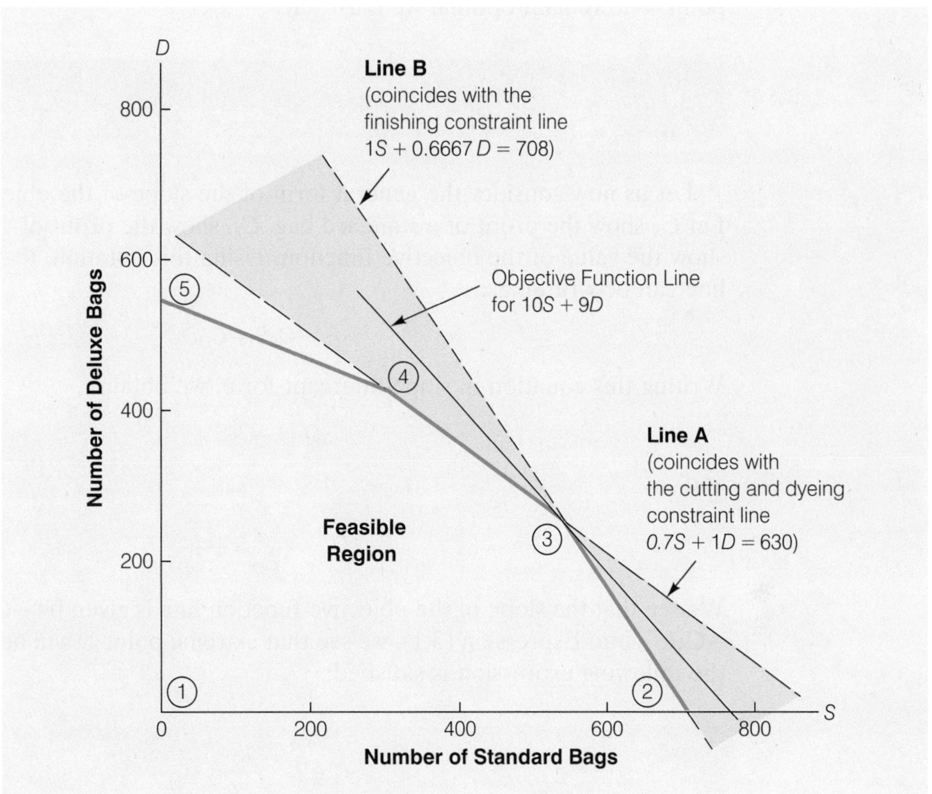

Thus, extreme point ③ will be the optimal solution as long as:

$$\text{Slope of line B} \leq \text{slope of the objective function line} \leq \text{slope of line A}$$

In Figure 3.1 we see that the equation for line A, the cutting and dyeing constraint line, is:

$$0.7S + 1D = 630$$

By solving this equation for D, we can write the equation for line A in its slope-intercept form, which yields:

$$D = \underset{\substack{\uparrow \\ \text{Slope of} \\ \text{line A}}}{-0.7S} + \underset{\substack{\uparrow \\ \text{Intercept of} \\ \text{line A on} \\ D \text{ axis}}}{630}$$

Thus, the slope for line A is −0.7, and its intercept on the D axis is 630.

The equation for line B in Figure 3.1 is:

$$1S + 0.6667D = 708$$

Solving for D provides the slope-intercept form for line B. Doing so yields:

$$0.6667D = -\,1S + 708$$
$$D = -\,1.5S + 1062$$

Thus the slope of line B is -1.5 and its intercept on the D axis is 1062.

Now that the slope of lines A and B have been calculated, we see that for extreme point ③ to remain optimal we must have:

$$-1.5 \leq \text{slope of objective function} \leq -0.7 \tag{3.1}$$

Let us now consider the general form of the slope of the objective function line. Let C_S show the profit of a standard bag, C_D show the profit of a deluxe bag, and P show the value of the objective function. Using this notation, the objective function line can be written as:

$$P = C_S S + C_D D$$

Writing this equation in slope-intercept form, we obtain:

$$C_D D = -C_S S + P$$

and

$$D = -\frac{C_S}{C_D} S + \frac{P}{C_D}$$

We see that the slope of the objective function line is given by $-C_S/C_D$. Substituting $-C_S/C_D$ into Expression (3.1), we see that extreme point ③ will be optimal as long as the following expression is satisfied:

$$-1.5 \leq -\frac{C_S}{C_D} \leq -0.7 \tag{3.2}$$

To calculate the range of optimality for the standard-bag profit contribution, we hold the profit contribution for the deluxe bag fixed at its initial value $C_D = 9$. Doing so in expression (3.2), we obtain:

$$-1.5 \leq -\frac{C_S}{9} \leq -0.7$$

From the left-hand inequality, we have:

$$-1.5 \leq -\frac{C_S}{9} \quad \text{or} \quad 1.5 \geq \frac{C_S}{9}$$

Thus,

$$13.5 \geq C_S \quad \text{or} \quad C_S \leq 13.5$$

From the right-hand inequality, we have:

$$-\frac{C_S}{9} \leq -0.7 \quad \text{or} \quad \frac{C_S}{9} \geq 0.7$$

Thus,

$$C_S \geq 6.3$$

Can you calculate the range of optimality using the graphical solution procedure? Try Problem 3.

Combining the calculated limits for C_S provides the following range of optimality for the standard-bag profit contribution:

$$6.3 \leq C_S \leq 13.5$$

In the original problem for GulfGolf, the standard bag had a profit contribution of \$10. The resulting optimal solution was 540 standard bags and 252 deluxe bags. The range of optimality for C_S tells management that, with other coefficients unchanged, the profit contribution for the standard bag can vary between \$6.30 and \$13.50 and the production quantities of 540 standard bags and 252 deluxe bags will remain optimal. Note, however, that even though the production quantities will not change, the total profit contribution (the value of objective function) will change due to the change in profit contribution per standard bag.

These calculations can be repeated, holding the profit contribution for standard bags constant at $C_S = 10$. In this case, the range of optimality for the deluxe-bag profit contribution can be determined. Check to see that this range is $6.67 \leq C_D \leq 14.29$.

In cases where the rotation of the objective function line about an optimal extreme point causes the objective function line to become *vertical*, there will either be no upper limit or no lower limit for the slope as it appears in the form of expression (3.2). To show how this special situation can occur, suppose that the objective function for the GulfGolf problem is $18C_S + 9C_D$. In this case, extreme point ② in Figure 3.2 provides the optimal solution. Rotating the objective function line anticlockwise around extreme point ② provides an upper limit for the slope when the objective function line coincides with line B. We showed previously that the slope of line B is -1.5, so the upper limit for the slope of the objective function line must be -1.5. However, rotating the objective function line clockwise results in the slope becoming more and more negative, approaching a value of minus

Figure 3.2 Graphical Solution of GulfGolf Problem with an Objective Function of $18S + 9D$; Optimal Solution At Extreme Point ②

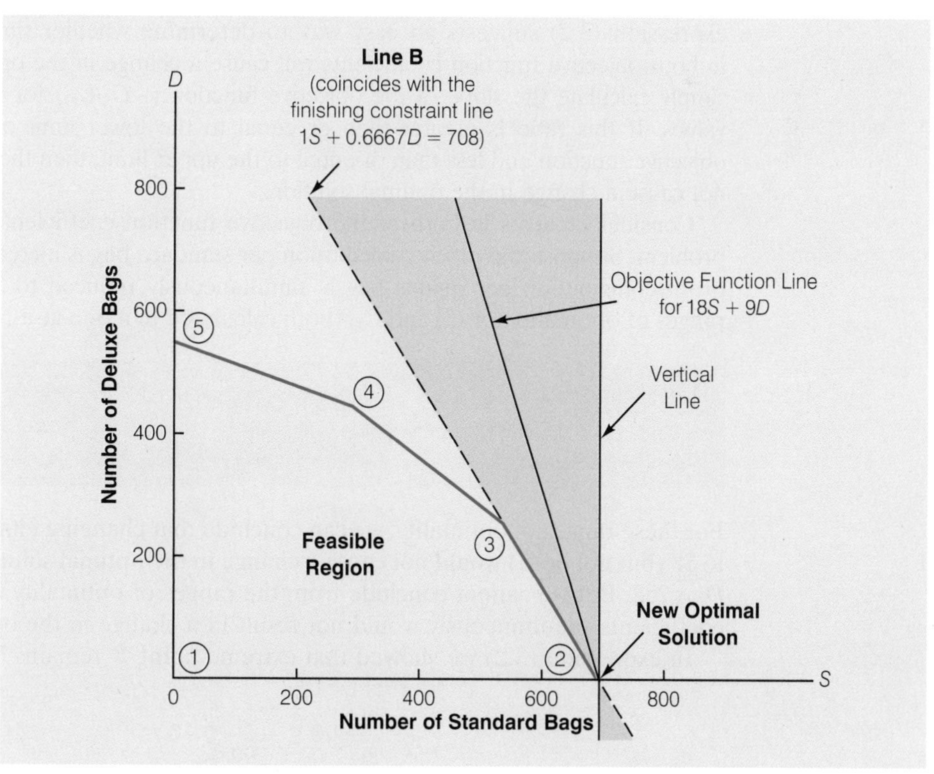

infinity as the objective function line becomes vertical; in this case, the slope of the objective function has no lower limit. Using the upper limit of -1.5, we can write:

$$-\frac{C_S}{C_D} \leq -1.5$$

Slope of the objective function line

Following the previous procedure of holding C_D constant at its original value, $C_D = 9$, we have:

$$-\frac{C_S}{9} \leq -1.5 \quad \text{or} \quad \frac{C_S}{9} \geq 1.5$$

Solving for C_S provides the following result:

$$C_S \geq 13.5$$

In reviewing Figure 3.2 we note that extreme point ② remains optimal for all values of C_S above 13.5. Thus, we obtain the following range of optimality for C_S at extreme point ②:

$$13.5 \leq C_S < \infty$$

That is, the current solution will remain optimal as long as C_s is at least 13.5. Once above this value, C_s can increase indefinitely (to infinity, or ∞) and the optimal solution will remain unchanged.

Simultaneous Changes

The range of optimality for objective function coefficients is only applicable for changes made to one coefficient at a time. All other coefficients are assumed to be fixed at their initial values. If two or more objective function coefficients are changed simultaneously, further analysis is necessary to determine whether the optimal solution will change. However, when solving two-variable problems graphically, expression (3.2) suggests an easy way to determine whether simultaneous changes in both objective function coefficients will cause a change in the optimal solution. We simply calculate the slope of the objective function ($-C_S/C_D$) for the new coefficient values. If this ratio is greater than or equal to the lower limit on the slope of the objective function and less than or equal to the upper limit, then the changes made will not cause a change in the optimal solution.

Consider changes in both of the objective function coefficients for the GulfGolf problem. Suppose the profit contribution per standard bag is increased to \$13 and the profit contribution per deluxe bag is simultaneously reduced to \$8. Recall that the ranges of optimality for C_S and C_D (both calculated in a one-at-a-time manner) are:

$$6.3 \leq C_S \leq 13.5 \quad \textbf{(3.3)}$$

$$6.67 \leq C_D \leq 14.29 \quad \textbf{(3.4)}$$

For these ranges of optimality, we can conclude that changing either C_S to \$13 or C_D to \$8 (but not both) would not cause a change in the optimal solution of $S = 540$ and $D = 252$. But we cannot conclude from the ranges of optimality that changing both coefficients simultaneously would not result in a change in the optimal solution.

In expression (3.2) we showed that extreme point ③ remains optimal as long as:

$$-1.5 \leq -\frac{C_S}{C_D} \leq -0.7$$

If C_S is changed to 13 and simultaneously C_D is changed to 8, the new objective function slope will be given by:

$$-\frac{C_S}{C_D} = -\frac{13}{8} = -1.625$$

Because this value is less than the lower limit of −1.5, the current solution of $S = 540$ and $D = 252$ will no longer be optimal. By re-solving the problem with $C_S = 13$ and $C_D = 8$ we will find that extreme point ② is the new optimal solution.

Looking at the ranges of optimality, we concluded that changing either C_S to \$13 or C_D to \$8 (but not both) would not cause a change in the optimal solution. But in recalculating the slope of the objective function with simultaneous changes for both C_S and C_D, we saw that the optimal solution did change. This result emphasizes the fact that a range of optimality, by itself, can only be used to draw a conclusion about changes made to *one objective function coefficient at a time*.

Right-Hand Sides

Let us now consider how a change in the right-hand side of a constraint may affect the feasible region and perhaps cause a change in the optimal solution to the problem. To illustrate this aspect of sensitivity analysis, let us consider what happens if an additional ten hours of production time become available in the cutting and dyeing department of GulfGolf. The right-hand side of the cutting and dyeing constraint is changed from 630 to 640, and the constraint is rewritten as:

$$0.7S + 1D \leq 640$$

By obtaining an additional ten hours of cutting and dyeing time, we expand the feasible region for the problem, as shown in Figure 3.3. With an enlarged feasible region, we now want to determine whether one of the new feasible solutions provides an improvement in the value of the objective function. Application of the graphical solution procedure to the problem with the enlarged feasible region shows that the extreme point with $S = 527.5$ and $D = 270.75$ now provides the optimal solution. The new value for the objective function is 10(527.5) + 9(270.75) = \$7711.75, with an increase in profit of \$7711.75 – \$7668.00 = \$43.75. Thus, the increased profit occurs at a rate of \$43.75/10 hours = \$4.375 per hour added.

Although we used a graphical approach here to undertake sensitivity analysis on the cutting and dyeing constraint, it is actually easier to use the relevant equations. We know that for the GulfGolf problem, the optimal solution is at the intersection of the cutting and dyeing constraint line and the finishing constraint line. So, we have (as in Chapter 2):

$$0.7S + 1D = 630 \quad \textbf{(3.5)}$$

$$1S + 0.6667D = 708 \quad \textbf{(3.6)}$$

at the current optimal solution. If we now want to do a sensitivity analysis on the cutting and dyeing constraint (3.5) we can re-write the equation as:

$$0.7S + 1D = 631 \quad \textbf{(3.7)}$$

Figure 3.3 Effect of a Ten-Unit Change in the Right-Hand Side of the Cutting And Dyeing Constraint

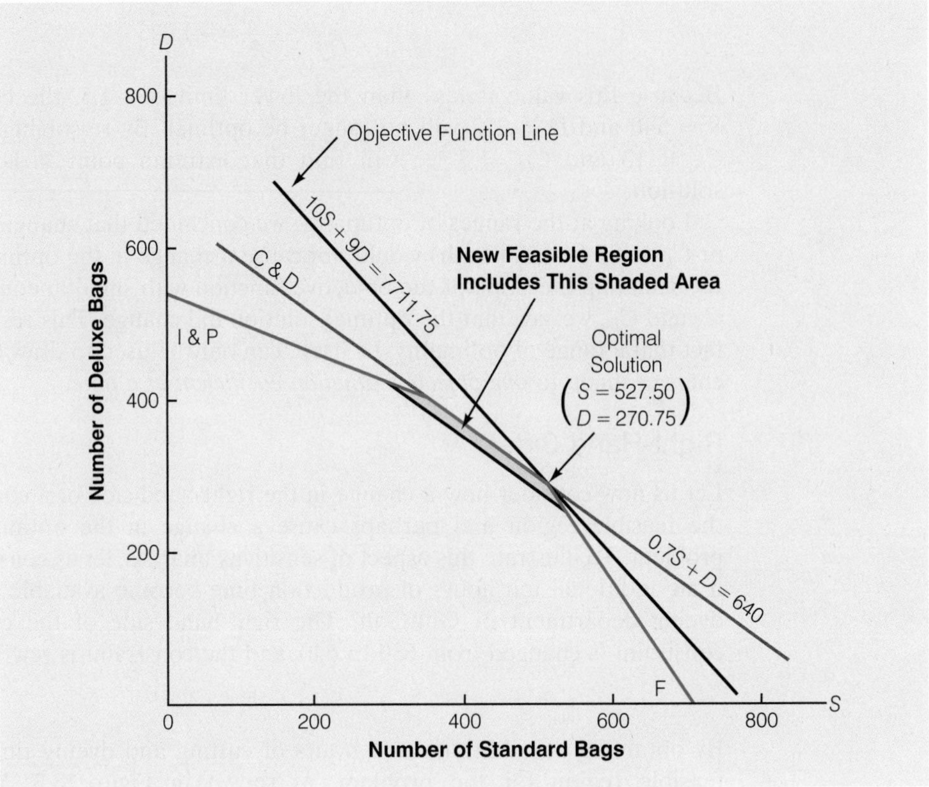

That is, allowing a marginal (one unit) change in the constraint. We can now solve Equations. 3.7 and 3.6 to find the new optimal solution which is:

$$S = 538.75$$

$$D = 253.875$$

$$\text{Profit contribution} = \$7672.375$$

Confirming that if we increase the cutting and dyeing constraint by one hour then profit contribution increases by $4.375. However, we can now undertake the same analysis on the other constraints, again seeing how a marginal increase in the right-hand side of a constraint changes the value of the objective function. If we look at a marginal change in the finishing constraint we have:

$$0.7S + 1D = 630$$

$$1S + 0.6667D = 709$$

which gives a new solution of:

$$S = 541.875$$

$$D = 250.6875$$

$$\text{Profit contribution} = 7674.9375$$

In the case of the finishing constraint, there is an increase in profit contribution of $6.9375 for a marginal increase in finishing hours. But what about the other two constraints: Sewing and inspection and packaging? Looking at equations (3.5) and (3.6) we can see that increasing the time available to sewing and to inspection and packaging will not affect these two equations (which relate, after all to cutting and dyeing and to finishing). This implies that a marginal increase in sewing time and a marginal increase in inspection and packaging time will have no effect on the optimal solution and no effect on profit contribution.

What do we make of this? Recollect that these two constraints were non-binding and had slack time associated with them. That is, at the current optimal solution there is unused sewing time and also unused inspection and packaging time. So, given we are not currently using all the existing available time for each of these constraints, adding further time to capacity will have no effect on production and so no effect on profit contribution.

The change in the value of the optimal solution per unit increase in the right-hand side of a constraint is called the **dual price**. Here, the dual price for the cutting and dyeing constraint is \$4.375; in other words, if we increase the right-hand side of the cutting and dyeing constraint by one unit, the value of the objective function will improve by \$4.375. Conversely, if the right-hand side of the cutting and dyeing constraint were to decrease by one unit, the objective function would get worse by \$4.375. The dual price can generally be used to determine what will happen to the value of the objective function when we make a one-unit change in the right-hand side of a constraint. The dual price has a number of other names – **dual value**, **shadow price**, **opportunity cost** are all used. Whichever name we use, it provides management with important information. It tells management the change in the objective function value for a marginal (one unit) change in the right-hand side value of a constraint. In the case of the cutting and dying constraint, the dual price is \$4.375. So, if we could persuade our workforce to work one extra hour on cutting and dyeing, this will allow additional production that will increase the total profit contribution by \$4.375. The dual price also allows management to place a value on such additional time. One of our workers may come along and say they are prepared to put an extra hour's work into cutting and dyeing but they expect a bonus payment for doing so. How much of a bonus should management be prepared to pay? The answer is given by the dual price. Given that the value to the company of this extra hour is \$4.375 then clearly management should be prepared to offer a maximum bonus which is just less than this. In other words, management can place a value on the acquisition of scarce resources.

Can you calculate and interpret the dual price for a constraint? Try Problem 4.

We caution here that the value of the dual price may be applicable only for small changes in the right-hand side. As more and more resources are obtained and the right-hand side value continues to increase, other constraints will become binding and limit the change in the value of the objective function. For example, in the problem for GulfGolf we would eventually reach a point where more cutting and dyeing time would be of no value; it would occur at the point where the cutting and dyeing constraint becomes nonbinding. At this point, the dual price would equal zero. In the next section we will show how to determine the range of values for a right-hand side over which the dual price will accurately predict the improvement in the objective function.

To illustrate the correct interpretation of dual prices for a minimization problem, suppose we had solved a problem involving the minimization of total cost and that the value of the optimal solution was \$100. Furthermore, suppose that the dual price for a particular constraint was −\$10. The *negative dual price* tells us that the objective function *will not improve* if the value of the right-hand side is increased by one unit. Thus, if the right-hand side of this constraint is increased by one unit, the value of the objective function will get worse by the amount of \$10. Becoming worse in a minimization problem means an increase in the total cost. In this case, the value of the objective function will become \$110 if the right-hand side is increased by one unit. Conversely, a decrease in the right-hand side of one unit will decrease the total cost by \$10.

MANAGEMENT SCIENCE IN ACTION

Evaluating Options for the Provision of School Meals in Chile

The National School Assistance and Scholarship Board (JUNAEB) in Chile is a public sector agency tasked with responsibility for a variety of public welfare programmes aimed at encouraging better student performance and academic attainment, reducing pupil absenteeism, truancy and drop out rates. Chile is a developing country with a population of over 15 million and sees education as a key element of its development strategy. The country has around 14 000 primary and secondary level schools but with over 90 per cent of this provided, or supported, by the government. Unsurprisingly, there are high levels of poverty – 30 per cent of children are estimated to live below the official poverty level – with subsequent effects on children's education. JUNAEB is responsible for ensuring the provision of free school meals across Chile and has an annual budget of around US$140m to feed around 1.2 million school children. JUNAEB contracts out the actual catering service provision to private sector companies. This is done through a rolling cycle of three-year contracts covering one-third of schools each time. Private companies are invited to bid for the catering contracts through an auction process, where JUNAEB specifies the quantity and quality of services to be provided in each geographical area. JUNAEB uses a number of criteria to assess the bids received, including an assessment of the overall quality of the firm bidding; the nutritional requirements of the specified meals; quality standards; operating conditions. JUNAEB seeks to identify the combination of bids that will minimize cost but at the same time satisfy the various constraints required. In the late 1990s JUNAEB developed an LP model to help with the decision problem. Sensitivity analysis is carried out on the optimal solution routinely. Examples include:

- looking at the effect on total cost (the objective function) of changing the quality of meals to be provided;
- assessing the effects on the solution of changing the specified nutritional content of meals;
- evaluating the effect of assigning more contracts to those firms which have better overall performance ratings. In this case, JUNAEB concluded that contracts could be awarded to firms so that firms were 40 per cent better qualified than those in the original solution. This added only 4 per cent to the original objective function cost.

The LP model is rated as highly successful and the sensitivity analysis particularly so, allowing different scenarios to be easily explored and evaluated. The model is estimated to have improved the price/quality ration of school meals with annual savings of about $40 million – the cost of feeding 30 000 schoolchildren.

Based on Rafael Epstein, Lysette Henriquez, Jaime Catalan, Gabriel Y. Weintraub and Cristian Martinez, 'A Combinational Auction Improves School Meals in Chile' *Interfaces* 32 6 (Nov/Dec 2002): 1–14.

NOTES AND COMMENTS

1 If two objective function coefficients change simultaneously, both may move outside their respective ranges of optimality and not affect the optimal solution. For instance, in a two-variable linear programme, the slope of the objective function will not change at all if both coefficients are changed by the same percentage.

2 Some texts associate the term *shadow price* with each constraint. The concept of a shadow price is closely related to the concept of a dual price. The shadow price associated with a constraint is the *change* in the value of the optimal solution per unit increase in the right-hand side of the constraint. In general, the dual price and the shadow price are the *same* for all *maximization* linear programmes. In *minimization* linear programmes, the shadow price is the *negative* of the corresponding dual price.

3.3 Sensitivity Analysis: Computer Solution

In Section 2.4 we showed how computer packages can be used to solve the GulfGolf linear programme. Let us demonstrate the use of The Management Scientist in performing sensitivity analysis by considering the solution to the GulfGolf linear programme shown in Figure 3.4.

Interpretation of Computer Output

In Appendix 2.2 we discussed the Management Scientist output in the top portion of Figure 3.4. So, after rounding, we see that the optimal solution is $S = 540$ standard bags and $D = 252$ deluxe bags; the value of the optimal solution is $7668. The **Reduced Costs** indicate how much the objective function coefficient of each decision variable would have to improve before that variable could assume a positive value in the optimal solution. For the GulfGolf problem, both variables already have positive values, and so their corresponding reduced costs are zero. In Section 3.4 we will interpret the reduced cost for a decision variable that does not have a positive value in the optimal solution.

Immediately following the optimal S and D values and the reduced cost information, the computer output provides information about the constraints. Recall that the problem had four less-than-or-equal-to constraints corresponding to the hours

Figure 3.4 The Management Scientist Solution for the GulfGolf Problem

```
Objective Function Value =     7667.99463

     Variable              Value              Reduced Costs
  --------------    ---------------    -----------------
         S                539.99841              0.00000
         D                252.00113              0.00000

    Constraint         Slack/Surplus          Dual Prices
  --------------    ---------------    -----------------
         1                  0.00000              4.37496
         2                120.00070              0.00000
         3                  0.00000              6.93753
         4                 17.99988              0.00000

OBJECTIVE COEFFICIENT RANGES

  Variable      Lower Limit     Current Value     Upper Limit
 ------------ ---------------- ---------------- ----------------
      S            6.30000         10.00000          13.49993
      D            6.66670          9.00000          14.28572

RIGHT HAND SIDE RANGES

  Constraint     Lower Limit     Current Value     Upper Limit
 ------------ ---------------- ---------------- ----------------
      1          495.59998        630.00000         682.36316
      2          479.99930        600.00000    No Upper Limit
      3          580.00146        708.00000         900.00000
      4          117.00012        135.00000    No Upper Limit
```

EXCEL *file*

GulfGolf

available in each of four production departments. The information shown in the Slack/Surplus column provides the value of the slack variable for each of the departments. This information (after rounding) is summarized here:

Constraint Number	Constraint Name	Slack
1	Cutting and dyeing	0
2	Sewing	120
3	Finishing	0
4	Inspection and packaging	18

From this information, we see that the binding constraints (the cutting and dyeing and the finishing constraints) have zero slack at the optimal solution. The sewing department has 120 hours of slack, or unused capacity, and the inspection and packaging department has 18 hours of slack or unused capacity.

The Dual Prices column contains information about the marginal value of each of the four resources at the optimal solution. In Section 3.2 we defined the *dual price* as follows:

> The dual price associated with a constraint is the change in the value of the solution per unit change in the right-hand side of the constraint.

Try Problem 10 to test your ability to use computer output to determine the optimal solution and to interpret the values of the dual prices.

So, the nonzero dual prices of 4.37496 for constraint 1 (cutting and dyeing constraint) and 6.93753 for constraint 3 (finishing constraint) tell us that an additional hour of cutting and dyeing time increases the value of the optimal solution by $4.37 and an additional hour of finishing time increases the value of the optimal solution by $6.94. So, if the cutting and dyeing time were increased from 630 to 631 hours, with all other coefficients in the problem remaining the same, the company's profit would be increased by $4.37 from $7668 to $7668 + $4.37 = $7672.37. A similar interpretation for the finishing constraint implies that an increase from 708 to 709 hours of available finishing time, with all other coefficients in the problem remaining the same, would increase the company's profit to $7668 + $6.94 = $7674.94. Because the sewing and the inspection and packaging constraints both have slack or unused capacity available, the dual prices of zero show that additional hours of these two resources will not improve the value of the objective function. The output confirms the calculations we did earlier.

Referring again to the computer output in Figure 3.4, we see that after providing the constraint information on slack/surplus variables and dual prices, the solution provides ranges for the objective function coefficients and the right-hand sides of the constraints.

Considering the information provided under the computer output heading labelled OBJECTIVE COEFFICIENT RANGES, we see that variable S, which has a current profit coefficient of 10, has the following *range of optimality* for C_S:

$$6.30 \leq C_S \leq 13.49993$$

So, as long as the profit contribution associated with the standard bag is between $6.30 and $13.50, the production of $S = 540$ standard bags and $D = 252$ deluxe bags will remain the optimal solution. Note that the range of optimality is the same as obtained by performing graphical sensitivity analysis for C_S in Section 3.2.

Using the objective function coefficient range information for deluxe bags, we see the following range of optimality:

$$6.6667 \leq C_D \leq 14.8572$$

This result tells us that as long as the profit contribution associated with the deluxe bag is between \$6.67 and \$14.29, the production of $S = 540$ standard bags and $D = 252$ deluxe bags will remain the optimal solution.

Try Problem 11 to test your ability to use computer output to determine the ranges of optimality and the ranges of feasibility.

The final section of the computer output (RIGHT HAND SIDE RANGES) provides the limits within which the dual prices are applicable. As long as the constraint right-hand side is between the lower and upper limit values, the associated dual price gives the improvement in the value of the optimal solution per unit increase in the right-hand side. For example, let us consider the cutting and dyeing constraint with a current right-hand-side value of 630. Because the dual price for this constraint is \$4.37, we can conclude that additional hours will increase the objective function by \$4.37 per hour. It is also true that a reduction in the hours available will reduce the value of the objective function by \$4.37 per hour. From the range information given, we see that the dual price of \$4.37 is valid for increases up to 682.36316 and decreases down to 495.59998. A similar interpretation for the finishing constraint's right-hand side (constraint 3) shows that the dual price of \$6.94 is applicable for increases up to 900 hours and decreases down to 580.00146 hours.

As mentioned, the right-hand side ranges provide limits within which the dual prices are applicable. For changes outside the range, the problem must be resolved to find the new optimal solution and the new dual price. We shall call the range over which the dual price is applicable the **range of feasibility**. The ranges of feasibility for the GulfGolf problem are summarized here:

Constraint	Min RHS	Max RHS
Cutting and dyeing	495.6	682.4
Sewing	480.0	No upper limit
Finishing	580.0	900.0
Inspection and packaging	117.0	No upper limit

As long as the values of the right-hand sides are within these ranges, the dual prices shown on the computer output will not change. Right-hand side values outside these limits will result in changes in the dual price information.

Simultaneous Changes

The sensitivity analysis information in computer output is based on the assumption that only one objective function coefficient changes; it is assumed that all other coefficients will remain as stated in the original problem. In many cases, however, we may be interested in what would happen if two or more coefficients are changed simultaneously. As we will demonstrate, some analysis of simultaneous changes is possible with the help of the **100 per cent rule**.[1] We begin by showing how the 100 per cent rule applies to simultaneous changes in the objective function coefficients.

[1]See S. P. Bradley, A. C. Hax, and T. L. Magnanti, *Applied Mathematical Programming* (Reading, MA: Addison-Wesley, 1977).

Suppose that in the GulfGolf problem the accounting department concluded that the original profit contributions of \$10 and \$9 for the standard and deluxe bags, respectively, were incorrectly calculated; the correct values should have been \$11.50 and \$8.25. To determine what effect, if any, these simultaneous changes have on the optimal solution, we need to first define the terms *allowable increase* and *allowable decrease*. For an objective function coefficient, the allowable increase is the maximum amount the coefficient may increase without exceeding the upper limit of the range of optimality; the allowable decrease is the maximum amount the coefficient may decrease without dropping below the lower limit of the range of optimality.

From Figure 3.4 we see that the upper limit for the objective function coefficient of S is 13.49993; so, the allowable increase is 3.49993 (13.49993 – 10). In terms of percentage change, the increase of \$1.50 in the objective function coefficient (from 10 to 11.50) for the standard bags is (1.50/3.49993)(100) = 42.86 per cent of the allowable increase. Given the lower limit of 6.66670 for D, the allowable decrease for D is 2.33330 (9 – 6.66670). In terms of percentage change, the decrease of \$0.75 in the objective function coefficient (from 9 to 8.25) for the deluxe bags is (0.75/2.33330)(100) = 32.14 per cent of the allowable decrease. The sum of the percentage change of the allowable increase (42.86 per cent) and the percentage change of the allowable decrease (32.14 per cent) is 75.00 per cent.

Let us now state the 100 per cent rule as it applies to simultaneous changes in the objective function coefficients.

100 Per cent Rule for Objective Function Coefficients

For all objective function coefficients that are changed, sum the percentages of the allowable increases and the allowable decreases represented by the changes. If the sum of the percentage changes does not exceed 100 per cent the optimal solution will not change.

So, because the sum of the two percentage changes in the objective function coefficients for the problem is 75 per cent, these simultaneous changes will not affect the optimal solution. Note, however, that although the optimal solution is still S = 539.99841 and D = 252.00113, the value of the optimal solution will change because the profit contribution for the standard bags has increased to \$11.50 and the profit contribution of the deluxe bags has decreased to \$8.25.

The 100 per cent rule does not, however, say that the optimal solution will change if the sum of the percentage changes exceeds 100 per cent. It is possible that the optimal solution will not change even though the sum of the percentage changes exceeds 100 per cent. When the 100 per cent rule is not satisfied, we must re-solve the problem to determine what affect such changes will have on the optimal solution.

A similar version of the 100 per cent rule also applies to simultaneous changes in the constraint right-hand sides.

100 Per cent Rule for Constraint Right-Hand Sides

For all right-hand sides that are changed, sum the percentages of allowable increases and allowable decreases. If the sum of percentages does not exceed 100 per cent, then the dual values will not change.

Let us illustrate the 100 per cent rule for constraint right-hand sides by considering simultaneous changes in the right-hand sides for the GulfGolf problem. Suppose, for instance, that in this problem we could obtain 20 additional hours of cutting and dyeing time and 100 additional hours of finishing time. The allowable increase for cutting and dyeing time is 682.36316 – 630.0 = 52.36316, and the allowable increase for finishing time is 900.0 – 708.0 = 192.0 (see Figure 3.4).

The 20 additional hours of cutting and dyeing time are (20/52.36316)(100) = 38.19 per cent of the allowable increase in the constraint's right-hand side. The 100 additional hours of finishing time are (100/192)(100) = 52.08 per cent of the allowable increase in the finishing time constraint's right-hand side. The sum of the percentage changes is 38.19 per cent + 52.08 per cent = 90.27 per cent. The sum of the percentage changes does not exceed 100 per cent; therefore, we can conclude that the dual prices are applicable and that the objective function will improve by (20)(4.37) + (100)(6.94) = 781.40.

Interpretation of Computer Output – A Second Example

In Appendix 2.3 we saw how Excel Solver can be used to solve an LP formulation. We will now see how it can be used to carry out sensitivity analysis. We will use the example of the M&D Chemicals problem introduced in Section 2.5. M&D's objective was to find the minimum-cost production schedule for products A and B. The linear programming model for this problem is restated as follows, where A = number of litres of product A and B = number of litres of product B.

$$\begin{aligned} \text{Min} \quad & 2A + 3B \\ \text{s.t} \quad & \\ & 1A \geq 125 \quad \text{Demand for product A} \\ & 1A + 1B \geq 350 \quad \text{Total production} \\ & 2A + 1B \leq 600 \quad \text{Processing time} \\ & A,\ B \geq 0 \end{aligned}$$

The Excel formulation is shown in Figure 3.5. When Excel Solver finds the optimal solution to an LP problem, the Solver Results dialogue box (see Figure 3.6) appears on the screen. This provides an option for different types of report on the problem. The Answer report provides details of the optimal solution.

Figure 3.5 Excel Formulation for the M&D Chemicals Problem

	A	B	C	D	E	F
1	**M& D Chemicals**					
4			**Product A**	**Product B**		**RHS**
5	**Customer demand for A**		1		>=	125
6	**Combined production**		1	1	>=	350
7	**Processing time**		2	1	<=	600
9	**Cost per litre**		2	3		
12	**Litres produced**		0	0		
14	**Minimise total cost**		0			
17	**Constraints**			**LHS**		**RHS**
18	**Customer demand for A**			0	>=	125
19	**Combined production**			0	>=	350
20	**Processing time**			0	<=	600

Solver Parameters
Set Target Cell: $C$14
Equal To: Max Min Value of: 0
By Changing Cells:
$C$12:$D$12
Subject to the Constraints:
$D$18 >= $F$18
$D$19 >= $F$19
$D$20 <= $F$20
Solve Close Guess Options Add Change Delete Reset All Help

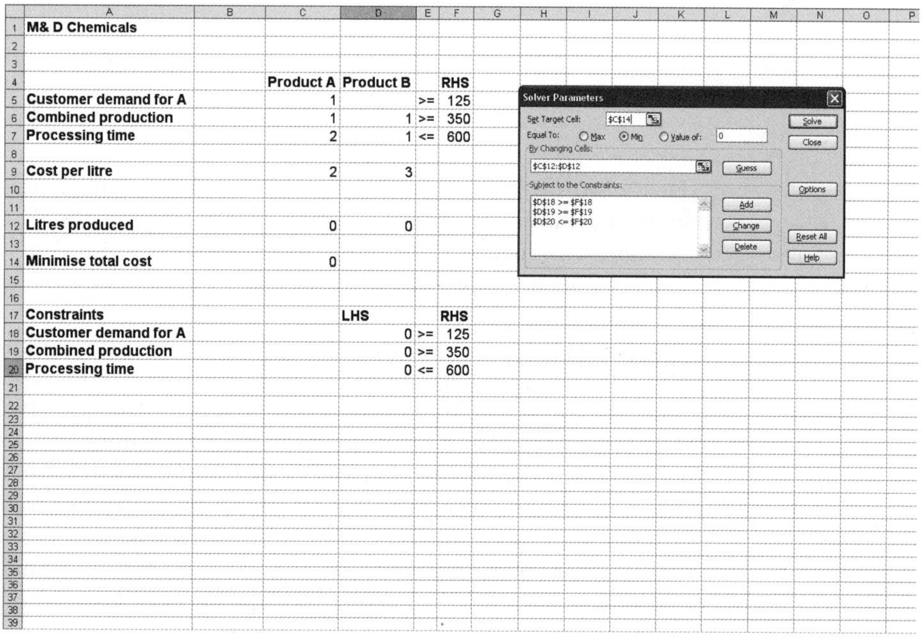

Figure 3.6 Excel Solver Results Dialogue Box

Solver Results

Solver found a solution. All constraints and optimality conditions are satisfied.

Reports

Answer
Sensitivity
Limits

Keep Solver Solution

Restore Original Values

OK | Cancel | Save Scenario... | Help

Figure 3.7 Excel Solver Answer Report for the M&D Chemicals Problem

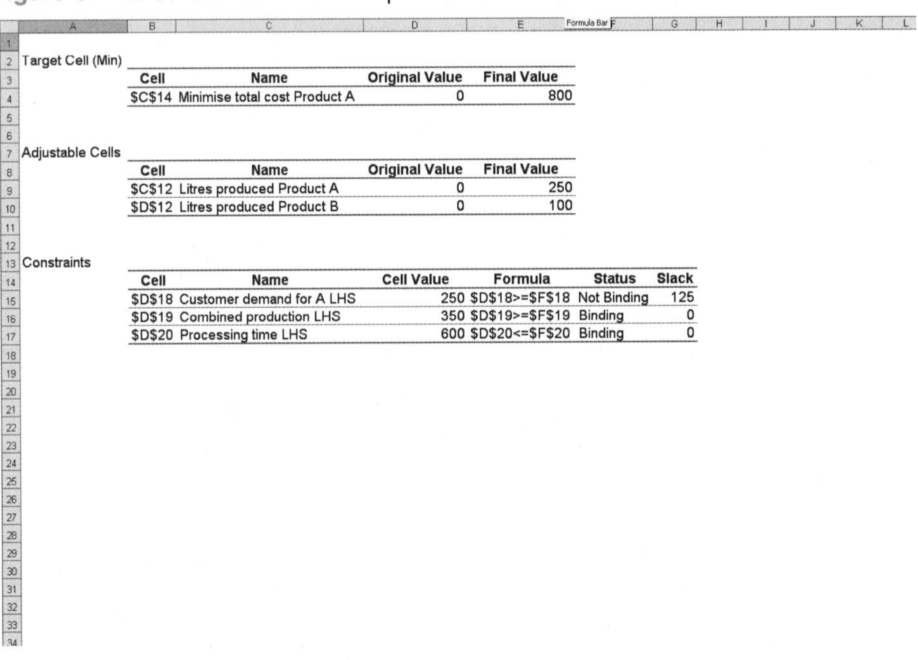

Target Cell (Min)

Cell	Name	Original Value	Final Value
$C$14	Minimise total cost Product A	0	800

Adjustable Cells

Cell	Name	Original Value	Final Value
$C$12	Litres produced Product A	0	250
$D$12	Litres produced Product B	0	100

Constraints

Cell	Name	Cell Value	Formula	Status	Slack
$D$18	Customer demand for A LHS	250	$D$18>=$F$18	Not Binding	125
$D$19	Combined production LHS	350	$D$19>=$F$19	Binding	0
$D$20	Processing time LHS	600	$D$20<=$F$20	Binding	0

The Sensitivity report provides sensitivity analysis on the optimal solution. Any combination of reports can be selected before clicking OK. Excel Solver will then create an additional worksheet for each report selected. The Answer report for the M&D Chemicals problem is shown in Figure 3.7 and the Sensitivity report in Figure 3.8.

The Answer report provides basic information on the optimal solution (clearly what appears in the cells labelled 'Cell' and 'Name' will depend on how we set up our original Excel spreadsheet formulation). The Target Cell relates to the objective function that we set up. Here we are reminded that this is a minimization problem (Min) and that the final (optimal) value for the objective function is 800. In our problem this gives a cost minimization solution of €800. The Adjustable Cells section of the report relates to the decision variables, here the quantities of the two products A and B. We see that their final (optimal value) is 250 and 100 (litres) respectively. Finally in the Answer report we have the

Figure 3.8 Excel Solver Sensitivity Report for the M&D Chemicals Problem

Adjustable Cells

Cell	Name	Final Value	Reduced Cost	Objective Coefficient	Allowable Increase	Allowable Decrease
$C$12	Litres produced Product A	250	0	2	1	1E+30
$D$12	Litres produced Product B	100	0	3	1E+30	1

Constraints

Cell	Name	Final Value	Shadow Price	Constraint R.H. Side	Allowable Increase	Allowable Decrease
$D$18	Customer demand for A LHS	250	0	125	125	1E+30
$D$19	Combined production LHS	350	4	350	125	50
$D$20	Processing time LHS	600	-1	600	100	125

Constraints section. This shows each of the constraints in the formulation. The Cell Value shows the LHS value of each constraint for the optimal values of A and B. So, in constraint 2 for example, the optimal values for A and B of 250 and 100 respectively give a LHS of 600 ($2 \times 250 + 1 \times 100$). Solver informs us that this constraint is Binding.

Next, let us look at the Sensitivity report in Figure 3.8. In the Adjustable Cells section of the Sensitivity Report, the column labelled Final Value contains the optimal values of the decision variables, with the optimal solution 250 litres of A and 100 litres of B. Next, let us look at the values in the Reduced Cost column. In Excel, the value of a nonzero reduced cost indicates how much the value of the objective function would change[2] if the corresponding variable were increased by one unit. For the M&D problem, the reduced costs for both decision variables are zero; they are at their optimal values. We shall see later that in large problems some decision variables will have reduced cost values which are nonzero. To the right of the Reduced Cost column, we find three columns labelled Objective Coefficient, Allowable Increase and Allowable Decrease. For the A decision variable, the (current) objective function coefficient value is 2, the allowable increase is 1 and the allowable decrease is shown as 1E + 30. The allowable increase/decrease shows the range of optimality for this objective function coefficient. Note that the term 1E + 30 is Excel's way of showing ∞. For B, the allowable increase in infinite whilst the allowable decrease is 1.

Turning to the Constraints section of the report, the Final Value shows the RHS value of each constraint for the optimal solution. So, for constraint 1 ($1A \geq 125$) with the optimal value of A at 250, 1A is obviously 250 also. The Shadow Price

[2]This definition of reduced cost is slightly different from (but equivalent to) the one in the glossary. Excel's solution algorithm permits variables in solution at their upper bound to have a nonzero reduced cost.

shows, as usual, the change in the objective function for a change in the RHS of each constraint while the Allowable Increase and Allowable Decrease show how much the RHS of each constraint can change and the current solution still remain as the optimal solution.

So, let's pull this together into a brief report for management.

The company can minimize its cost by producing 250 litres of A and 100 litres of B. Cost will be €800. The cost per litre of A (currently €2 per litre) could rise by as much as €1 and the optimal combination of A and B would not change (although the actual total cost clearly would). The unit cost of A could decrease indefinitely and again the optimal combination would not change. For product B, the equivalent changes are an infinite increase and a decrease of €1.

Turning to the constraints, we must produce a minimum of 125 litres of A and we do so in fact producing a further 125 litres. For the second constraint, we were required to limit total production to no more than 350 litres in total. We have kept within this limit. The shadow price tells us that if we change this constraint – for example allowing a unit increase in production to 351 – then total costs will increase by €4 for each unit change in the RHS. This would apply for changes in the RHS up to 475 litres and as low as 300 litres. Finally, looking at constraint 3, we only had 600 hours of production time available. With the optimal combination of A and B we are using all of these 600 hours. In fact, we know that if we could obtain additional hours then we could actually reduce total costs (the shows price is negative). An extra production hour would allow us to reduce total cost by €1, up to a maximum of an additional 100 hours of production time.

Try problem 14 to test your ability to interpret the computer output for a minimization problem.

Cautionary Note on the Interpretation of Dual Prices

As stated previously, the dual price is the change in the value of the optimal solution per unit change in the right-hand side of a constraint. When the right-hand side of the constraint represents the amount of a resource available, the associated dual price is often interpreted as the maximum amount one should be willing to pay for one additional unit of the resource. However, such an interpretation is not always correct. To see why, we need to understand the difference between sunk and relevant costs. A **sunk cost** is one that is not affected by the decision made. It will be incurred no matter what values the decision variables assume. A **relevant cost** is one that depends on the decision made. The amount of a relevant cost will vary depending on the values of the decision variables.

Let us reconsider the GulfGolf problem. The amount of cutting and dyeing time available is 630 hours. The cost of the time available is a sunk cost if it must be paid regardless of the number of standard and deluxe golf bags produced. It would be a relevant cost if the company only had to pay for the number of hours of cutting and dyeing time actually used to produce golf bags. All relevant costs should be reflected in the objective function of a linear programme. Sunk costs should not be reflected in the objective function. For GulfGolf we have been assuming that the company must pay its employees' wages regardless of whether their time on the job is completely utilized. Therefore, the cost of the labour-hours resource for the company is a sunk cost and has not been reflected in the objective function.

When the cost of a resource is *sunk*, the dual price can be interpreted as the maximum amount the company should be willing to pay for one additional unit of the resource. When the cost of a resource used is relevant, the dual price can be interpreted as the amount by which the value of the resource exceeds its cost. So, when the resource cost is relevant, the dual price can be interpreted as the maximum premium over the normal cost that the company should be willing to pay for one unit of the resource.

Only relevant costs should be included in the objective function.

NOTES AND COMMENTS

1 Computer software packages for solving linear programmes are readily available. Most of these provide as a minimum the optimal solution, dual or shadow price information, the range of optimality for the objective function coefficients and the range of feasibility for the right-hand sides. The labels used for the ranges of optimality and feasibility may vary, but the meaning is the same as what we have described here.

2 Whenever one of the right-hand sides is at an end point of its range of feasibility, the dual and shadow prices only provide one-sided information. In this case, they only predict the change in the optimal value of the objective function for changes toward the interior of the range.

3 A condition called *degeneracy* can cause a subtle difference in how we interpret changes in the objective function coefficients beyond the end points of the range of optimality. Degeneracy occurs when the dual price equals zero for one of the binding constraints. Degeneracy does not affect the interpretation of changes toward the interior of the range of optimality. However, when degeneracy is present, changes beyond the end points of the range do not necessarily mean a different solution will be optimal. From a practical point of view, changes beyond the end points of the range of optimality necessitate re-solving the problem.

4 The 100 per cent rule permits an analysis of multiple changes in the right-hand sides or multiple changes in the objective function coefficients. But the 100 per cent rule cannot be applied to changes in both objective function coefficients *and* right-hand sides at the same time. In order to consider simultaneous changes for *both* right-hand side values and objective function coefficients, the problem must be re-solved.

5 Managers are frequently called on to provide an economic justification for new technology. Often the new technology is developed, or purchased, in order to conserve resources. The dual price can be helpful in such cases because it can be used to determine the savings attributable to the new technology by showing the savings per unit of resource conserved.

3.4 More than Two Decision Variables

The graphical solution procedure is useful only for linear programmes involving two decision variables. Computer software packages are designed to handle linear programmes involving large numbers of variables and constraints. In this section we discuss the formulation and computer solution for two linear programmes with three decision variables. In doing so, we will show how to interpret the reduced-cost portion of the computer output and will also illustrate the interpretation of dual prices for constraints that involve percentages.

The Modified GulfGolf Problem

The original GulfGolf problem is restated as follows:

$$\begin{array}{lrll}
\text{Max} & 10S + 9D & & \\
\text{s.t.} & & & \\
& 0.7S + 1D & \leq 630 & \text{Cutting and dyeing} \\
& 0.5S + 0.83333D & \leq 600 & \text{Sewing} \\
& 1S + 0.66667D & \leq 708 & \text{Finishing} \\
& 0.1S + 0.25D & \leq 135 & \text{Inspection and packaging} \\
& S, D \geq 0 & &
\end{array}$$

Recall that S is the number of standard golf bags produced and D is the number of deluxe golf bags produced. Suppose that management is also considering producing a lightweight model designed specifically for women golfers. The design department estimates that each new lightweight model will require 0.8 hours for cutting and dyeing, one hour for sewing, one hour for finishing and 0.25 hours for inspection and packaging. Because of the unique capabilities designed into the new model, management feels they will realize a profit contribution of $12.85 for each lightweight model produced during the current production period.

Let us consider the modifications in the original linear programming model that are needed to incorporate the effect of this additional decision variable. We will let L denote the number of lightweight bags produced. After adding L to the objective function and to each of the four constraints, we obtain the following linear programme for the modified problem:

$$\begin{array}{lrll}
\text{Max} & 10S + 9D + 12.85L & & \\
\text{s.t.} & & & \\
& 0.7S + 1D + 0.8L & \leq 630 & \text{Cutting and dyeing} \\
& 0.5S + 0.83333D + 1L & \leq 600 & \text{Sewing} \\
& 1S + 0.66667D + 1L & \leq 708 & \text{Finishing} \\
& 0.1S + 0.25D + 0.25L & \leq 135 & \text{Inspection and packaging} \\
& S, D, L \geq 0 & &
\end{array}$$

Figure 3.9 shows the solution to the modified problem using Excel Solver, using both the Answer report and the Sensitivity report. We see that the optimal solution calls for the production of 280 standard bags, 0 deluxe bags and 428 of the new lightweight bags; the value of the optimal solution after rounding is $8299.80.

Let us now look at the information contained in the Reduced Costs column. Recall that the reduced costs indicate how much each objective function coefficient would have to improve before the corresponding decision variable could assume a positive value in the optimal solution. As the computer output shows, the reduced costs for S and L are zero because the corresponding decision variables already have positive values in the optimal solution. The reduced cost of 1.15003 for decision variable D tells us that the profit contribution for the deluxe bag would have to increase to at least $9 + $1.15003 = $10.15003 before D *could* assume a positive value in the optimal solution.[3] In other words, unless the profit

[3]In the case of degeneracy, a variable may not assume a positive value in the optimal solution even when the improvement in the profit contribution exceeds the value of the reduced cost. Our definition of reduced costs, stated as '... could assume a positive value...,' provides for such special cases. More advanced texts on mathematical programming discuss these special types of situations.

Figure 3.9 Excel Solution for the Modified GulfGolf Problem

Name	Original Value	Final Value
Maximize Total Profit Standard	0	8299.8

Name	Original Value	Final Value
Bags produced Standard	0	280
Bags produced Deluxe	0	0
Bags produced Lightweight	0	428

Name	Cell Value	Status	Slack
Cutting and Dyeing Hours Used (LHS)	538.4	Not Binding	91.6
Sewing Hours Used (LHS)	568	Not Binding	32
Finishing Hours Used (LHS)	708	Binding	0
Inspection and Packaging Hours Used(LHS)	135	Binding	0

Adjustable Cells

Name	Final Value	Reduced Cost	Objective Coefficient	Allowable Increase	Allowable Decrease
Bags produced Standard	280	0	10	2.070069297	4.86
Bags produced Deluxe	0	-1.150026998	9.000000002	1.150026998	1E+30
Bags produced Lightweight	428	0	12.85	12.15	0.940932891

Constraints

Name	Final Value	Shadow Price	Constraint R.H. Side	Allowable Increase	Allowable Decrease
Cutting and Dyeing Hours Used (LHS)	538.4	0	630	1E+30	91.6
Sewing Hours Used (LHS)	568	0	600	1E+30	32
Finishing Hours Used (LHS)	708	8.1	708	144.6315789	168
Inspection and Packaging Hours Used (LHS)	135	19	135	9.6	64.2

EXCEL *file*

contribution for D increases by at least \$1.15 the value of D will remain at zero in the optimal solution.

Suppose we increase the coefficient of D by \$1.1500 and then re-solve the problem. Figure 3.10 shows the new solution. We note that D has now entered the solution (although the value of the objective function remains unchanged indicating an alternative optimal solution) and all three variables have a reduced cost coefficient of 0.

Returning to Figure 3.9 we note that the shadow prices for constraints 3 and 4 are 8.1 and 19, respectively, indicating that these two constraints are binding in the optimal solution. So, each additional hour in the finishing department would increase the value of the optimal solution by \$8.10 and each additional hour in the inspection and packaging department would increase the value of the optimal solution by \$19.00. Because of a slack of 91.6 hours in the cutting and dyeing department and 32 hours in the sewing department (see Figure 3.9), management might want to consider the possibility of redeploying these unused hours in the finishing or inspection and packaging departments. For example, it may be that

Figure 3.10 Excel Solution for the Modified GulfGolf Problem with the Coefficient of D increased by $1.15004

Name	Original Value	Final Value
Maximize Total Profit Standard	0	8299.8

Name	Original Value	Final Value
Bags produced Standard	0	403.7831816
Bags produced Deluxe	0	222.811955
Bags produced Lightweight	0	155.6747724

Name	Cell Value	Status	Slack
Cutting and Dyeing Hours Used (LHS)	630	Binding	0
Sewing Hours Used (LHS)	543.2422496	Not Binding	56.75775038
Finishing Hours Used (LHS)	708	Binding	0
Inspection and Packaging Hours Used (LHS)	135	Binding	0

Adjustable Cells

Name	Final Value	Reduced Cost	Objective Coefficient	Allowable Increase	Allowable Decrease
Bags produced Standard	403.7831816	0	10	2.510712954	2.34002E-05
Bags produced Deluxe	222.811955	0	10.15004	5.257854737	1.3E-05
Bags produced Lightweight	155.6747724	0	12.85	1.06364E-05	2.196870893

Constraints

Name	Final Value	Shadow Price	Constraint R.H. Side	Allowable Increase	Allowable Decrease
Cutting and Dyeing Hours Used (LHS)	630	3.16218E-05	630	52.36315884	91.6
Sewing Hours Used (LHS)	543.2422496	0	600	1E+30	56.75775038
Finishing Hours Used (LHS)	708	8.099979973	708	144.6315789	127.9986
Inspection and Packaging Hours Used (LHS)	135	18.99997892	135	16.1540957	17.99988187

some of the employees in the cutting and dyeing department could be used to perform certain operations in either the finishing department or the inspection and packaging department. In the future, management may want to explore the possibility of cross-training employees so that unused capacity in one department could be shifted to other departments.

Suppose that after reviewing the solution shown in Figure 3.9, management insist that they will not consider any solution that does not include the production of some deluxe bags. Management then decides to add the requirement that the number of deluxe bags produced must be at least 30 per cent of the number of standard bags produced. Writing this requirement using the decision variables S and D, we obtain:

$$D \geq 0.3S$$

or

$$-0.3S + D \geq 0$$

Adding this new constraint to the modified linear programme and re-solving the problem, we obtain the optimal solution shown in Figure 3.11.

Let us consider the interpretation of the dual price for constraint 5, the requirement that the number of deluxe bags produced must be at least 30 per cent of the number of standard bags produced. The dual price of -1.38 indicates that a one-unit increase in the right-hand side of the constraint will lower profits by \$1.38. So, what the dual price of -1.38 is really telling us is what will happen to the value of the optimal solution if the constraint is changed to:

$$D \geq 0.3S + 1$$

The correct interpretation of the dual price of -1.38 can now be stated as follows: If we are forced to produce one deluxe bag over and above the minimum 30 per cent requirement, total profits will decrease by \$1.38. Conversely, if we relax the minimum 30 per cent requirement by one bag ($D \geq 0.3S - 1$), total profits will increase by \$1.38. So, we are able to tell management that their insistence on having the number of deluxe bags at least 30 per cent of the number of standard bags is costing the company money – profit is adversely affected.

The dual price for similar percentage (or ratio) constraints will not directly provide answers to questions concerning a percentage increase or decrease in the right-hand side of the constraint. For example, we might wonder what would happen to the value of the optimal solution if the number of deluxe bags has to be at least 31 per cent of the number of standard bags. To answer such a question, we would re-solve the problem using the constraint $-0.31S + D \geq 0$.

Because percentage (or ratio) constraints frequently occur in linear programming models, let us consider another example. For instance, suppose that management states that the number of lightweight bags produced may not exceed 20 per cent of the total golf bag production. If the total production of golf bags is $S + D + L$, we can write this constraint as:

$$L \leq 0.2(S + D + L)$$

$$L \leq 0.2S + 0.2D + 0.2L$$

$$-0.2S - 0.2D + 0.8L \leq 0$$

The solution obtained for the model that incorporates both the effects of this new percentage requirement and the previous requirement ($-0.3S + D \geq 0$) is shown in Figure 3.12. After rounding, the dual price corresponding to the new constraint (constraint 6) is 0.89. So, every additional lightweight bag we are allowed to produce over the current 20 per cent limit will increase the value of the objective function by \$0.89; moreover, the right-hand side range for this constraint shows that this interpretation is valid for increases of up to 156 units.

The Kenya Cattle Company Problem

To provide additional practise in formulating and interpreting the computer solution for linear programmes involving more than two decision variables, we consider a minimization problem involving three decision variables. Kenya Cattle Company (KCC), located in Kenya, East Africa, has been experimenting with a special diet for its cattle. The feed components available for the diet are a standard feed product, a vitamin-enriched product and a new vitamin and mineral feed additive. The

Figure 3.11 Excel Solution for the Modified GulfGolf Problem with the 30 per cent Deluxe Bag Requirement

Target Cell (Max)

Name	Original Value	Final Value
Maximize Total Profit Standard	0	8183.87751

Adjustable Cells

Name	Original Value	Final Value
Bags produced Standard	0	335.999328
Bags produced Deluxe	0	100.7997984
Bags produced Lightweight	0	304.8004704

Constraints

Name	Cell Value	Status	Slack
Cutting and Dyeing Hours Used (LHS)	579.8397043	Not Binding	50.16029568
Sewing Hours Used (LHS)	556.7996304	Not Binding	43.2003696
Finishing Hours Used (LHS)	708	Binding	0
Inspection and Packaging Hours Used (LHS)	135	Binding	0
Minimum production of Deluxe	0	Binding	0

Adjustable Cells

Name	Final Value	Reduced Cost	Objective Coefficient	Allowable Increase	Allowable Decrease
Bags produced Standard	335.999328	0	10	2.070069301	3.705
Bags produced Deluxe	100.7997984	0	9	1.150027	12.35
Bags produced Lightweight	304.8004704	0	12.85	5.292857143	0.940932893

Constraints

Name	Final Value	Shadow Price	Constraint R.H. Side	Allowable Increase	Allowable Decrease
Cutting and Dyeing Hours Used (LHS)	579.8397043	0	630	1E+30	50.16029568
Sewing Hours Used (LHS)	556.7996304	0	600	1E+30	43.2003696
Finishing Hours Used (LHS)	708	7.40998518	708	57.00045	168
Inspection and Packaging Hours Used (LHS)	135	21.76005928	135	12.00007333	31.75008604
Minimum production of Deluxe	0	-1.38002964	0	101.6770005	84

nutritional values in units per kilo and the costs for the three feed components are summarized in Table 3.1; for example, each kilo of the standard feed component contains 0.8 units of ingredient A, 1 unit of ingredient B and 0.1 units of ingredient C. The minimum daily diet requirements for each cow are three units of ingredient A, six units of ingredient B and four units of ingredient C. In addition, to control the weight of the cattle, the total daily feed for a cow should not exceed six kilos. KCC would like to determine the minimum-cost mix that will satisfy the daily diet requirements.

Figure 3.12 The Management Scientist Solution for the Modified GulfGolf Problem Incorporating the 20 per cent Lightweightbag Requirement and the 30 per cent Deluxe Bag Requirement

Target Cell (Max)

Name	Original Value	Final Value
Maximize Total Profit Standard	0	8044.255497

Adjustable Cells

Name	Original Value	Final Value
Bags produced Standard	0	403.4473181
Bags produced Deluxe	0	222.2073946
Bags produced Lightweight	0	156.4136782

Constraints

Name	Cell Value	Status	Slack
Cutting and Dyeing Hours Used (LHS)	629.7514598	Not Binding	0.248540212
Sewing Hours Used (LHS)	543.3094253	Not Binding	56.69057465
Finishing Hours Used (LHS)	708	Binding	0
Inspection and Packaging Hours Used(LHS)	135	Binding	0
Minimum production of Deluxe Hours Used (LHS)	101.1731992	Not Binding	101.1731992
Lightweight bags requirement Hours Used (LHS)	0	Binding	0

Adjustable Cells

Name	Final Value	Reduced Cost	Objective Coefficient	Allowable Increase	Allowable Decrease
Bags produced Standard	403.4473181	0	10	2.070069301	6.862
Bags produced Deluxe	222.2073946	0	9	1.1500271	2.5232981
Bags produced Lightweight	156.4136782	0	12.85	E + 30	0.940932893

Constraints

Name	Final Value	Shadow Price	Constraint R.H. Side	Allowable Increase	Allowable Decrease
Cutting and Dyeing Hours Used(LHS)	629.7514598	0	630	1E+30	0.248540212
Sewing Hours Used(LHS)	543.3094253	0	600	1E+30	56.69057465
Finishing Hours Used(LHS)	708	8.87329575	708	0.696391304	311.99856
Inspection and Packaging Hours Used(LHS)	135	13.05157115	135	0.088983729	16.0328649
Minimum production of Deluxe Hours Used(LHS)	101.1731992	0	0	101.1731992	1E+30
Lightweight bags requirement Hours Used (LHS)	0	0.892264327	0	156.480551	0.779209407

Formulation of the KCC Problem

To formulate a linear programming model for the KCC problem, we introduce the following three decision variables:

Table 3.1 Nutritional Value and Cost Data for the KCC Problem

Feed Component	Standard	Enriched	Additive
Ingredient A	0.8	0.2	0.0
Ingredient B	1.0	1.5	3.0
Ingredient C	0.1	0.6	2.0
Cost per kilo (Kenyan shillings)	25	50	300

S = number of kilos of the standard product

E = number of kilos of the enriched product

A = number of kilos of the vitamin and mineral feed additive

Using the data in Table 3.1, the objective function for minimizing the total cost associated with the daily feed can be written as follows:

$$\min 25S + 50E + 300A$$

For a minimum daily requirement for ingredient A of three units, we obtain the constraint:

$$0.8S + 0.2E \geq 3$$

The constraint for ingredient B is:

$$1.0S + 1.5E + 3.0A \geq 6$$

and the constraint for ingredient C is:

$$0.1S + 0.6E + 2.0A \geq 4$$

Finally, the constraint that restricts the mix to at most six kilos is:

$$S + E + A \leq 6$$

Combining all the constraints with the nonnegativity requirements enables us to write the complete linear programming model for the problem as follows:

$$\begin{aligned}
\text{Min} \quad & 25S + 50E + 300A \\
\text{s.t} \quad & \\
& 0.8S + 0.2E \geq 3 && \text{Ingredient A} \\
& 1.0S + 1.5E + 3.0A \geq 6 && \text{Ingredient B} \\
& 0.1S + 0.6E + 2.0A \geq 4 && \text{Ingredient C} \\
& S + E + A \leq 6 && \text{Weight} \\
& S, E, A \geq 0
\end{aligned}$$

Computer Solution and Interpretation for the KCC Problem

The output obtained using The Management Scientist to solve the KCC problem is shown in Figure 3.13. After rounding, we see that the optimal solution calls for a daily diet consisting of 3.51 kilos of the standard product, 0.95 kilos of the enriched product and 1.54 kilos of the vitamin and mineral feed additive. Thus, with feed component costs of 25 sh., 50 sh. and 300 sh., the total cost of the optimal diet is:

$$\begin{aligned}
3.51 \text{ kilos @ 25 sh per kilo} &= 85 \text{ sh} \\
0.95 \text{ kilos @ 50 sh per kilo} &= 47 \text{ sh} \\
1.54 \text{ kilos @ 300 sh per kilo} &= \underline{462 \text{ sh}} \\
\text{Total cost} &= 597 \text{ sh}
\end{aligned}$$

Figure 3.13 The Management Scientist Solution for the KCC Problem

```
Objective Function Value =              597.297

    Variable              Value              Reduced Costs
 --------------      ---------------      ----------------
           S              3.514                   0.000
           E              0.946                   0.000
           A              1.541                   0.000

   Constraint          Slack/Surplus          Dual Prices
 --------------      ---------------      ----------------
           1              0.000                -121.622
           2              3.554                   0.000
           3              0.000                -195.946
           4              0.000                   91.92

OBJECTIVE COEFFICIENT RANGES

Variable        Lower Limit      Current Value     Upper Limit
------------  ---------------  ---------------  ---------------
S                   -39.286             25.00   No Upper Limit
E            No Lower Limit             50.00            92.50
A                   152.174            300.00   No Upper Limit

RIGHT HAND SIDE RANGES

Constraint      Lower Limit      Current Value     Upper Limit
------------  ---------------  ---------------  ---------------
1                     1.143             3.000            3.368
2            No Lower Limit             6.000            9.554
3                     2.100             4.000            4.875
4                     5.562             6.000            8.478
```

EXCEL *file*

KCC

Note that after rounding, this result is the same as the objective function value in the computer output (Figure 3.13).

Looking at the Slack/Surplus section of the computer output, we find a value of 3.554 for constraint 2. Because constraint 2 is a greater-than-or-equal-to constraint, 3.554 is the surplus; the optimal solution exceeds the minimum daily diet requirement for ingredient B (six units) by 3.554 units. Because the surplus values for constraints 1 and 3 are both zero, we see that the optimal diet just meets the minimum requirements for ingredients A and C; moreover, a slack value of zero for constraint 4 shows that the optimal solution provides a total daily feed weight of six kilos.

The dual price (after rounding) for the ingredient A constraint (constraint 1) is −121.62. To interpret this value properly, we first look at the sign; it is negative, and so we know that increasing the right-hand side of constraint 1 will cause the solution value to worsen. In a minimization problem, 'worsen' means that the total daily cost will increase, and therefore, a one-unit increase in the right-hand side of constraint 1 will increase the total cost of the daily diet by 121.62 sh. Conversely, it is also correct to conclude that a decrease of one unit in the right-hand side will decrease the total cost by the same amount. Looking at the RIGHT HAND SIDE RANGES section of the computer output, we see that these interpretations are valid as long as the right-hand side is between 1.143 and 3.368.

MANAGEMENT SCIENCE IN ACTION

The Nutricia Dairy and Drinks Group, Hungary

Since the early 1990s, much of what used to be called Eastern Europe has been undergoing major economic, political and social transformation moving from the old Soviet Union command economy into market economies. This has meant major efforts to improve performance and economic efficiency. The Nutricia Dairy and Drinks group (NDDG) started acquiring dairy companies in Hungary in 1995 and has been using linear programming to help it improve efficiency and also to undertake scenario planning using sensitivity analysis.

The overall structure of NDDG's business is as follows. Its nine plants are supplied with raw milk by over 400 farmers throughout Hungary. The plants produce a range of dairy and dairy-related products – over 300 different products in total. Some products are produced at individual plants. Other products are semi-finished at one plant and then shipped to another plant to be turned into fully finished products. The plant output is sent to 17 distribution centres which in turn supply over 17 000 shops. NDDG had identified a number of major costs in its operations. First, milk collection costs incurred in collecting from individual farms (which range from supplying only 20 000 litres a year to those supplying around 11 million litres) to central collection points; transportation costs involved in shipping the milk from the central collection points to the plants; production costs; inter-plant costs incurred when semi-finished products are shipped from one plant to another; transportation costs to the distribution centres; warehousing costs involved in storing products at the distribution centres. NDDG developed an LP model to minimize total costs but was particularly interested in using the model to undertake scenario planning – looking at a variety of strategic options for rationalizing the supply side of the business. The sensitivity findings include the following:

- A change in production costs of up to 10 per cent had no impact on the optimal solution.
- An increase of 5 per cent in milk transportation costs would make the opening of three new plants cost-effective.
- Changes in inter-plant costs had no effect on the optimal solution.

Based on FHE. Wouda, P van beck, JGAJ. van der Vorst and H. Tacke, 'An application of mixed-integer linear programming models on the redesign of the supply network of Nutricia Dairy and Drinks Group in Hungary', *OR Spectrum* 24/4 (Nov. 2002): 449–465.

Suppose that management is willing to reconsider their position regarding the maximum weight of the daily diet. The dual price of 91.92 for constraint 4 shows that a one-unit increase in the right-hand side of constraint 4 will reduce total cost by 91.92 sh. The RIGHT HAND SIDE RANGES section of the output shows that this interpretation is valid for increases in the right-hand side up to a maximum of 8.478 kilos. Thus, the effect of increasing the right-hand side of constraint 4 from six to eight kilos is a decrease in the total daily cost of 2×91.92 or 183.84 sh. Keep in mind that if this change were made, the feasible region would change, and we would obtain a new optimal solution.

The OBJECTIVE COEFFICIENT RANGES section of the computer output shows a lower limit of -39.29 for S. Clearly, in a real problem, the objective function coefficient of S (the cost of the standard product) cannot take on a negative value. So, from a practical point of view, we can think of the lower limit for the objective function coefficient of S as being zero. We can thus conclude that no matter how much the cost of the standard mix were to decrease, the optimal solution would not change. Even if KCC could obtain the standard product for free, the optimal solution would still specify a daily diet of 3.51 kilos of the standard product, 0.95 kilos of the enriched product and 1.54 kilos of the vitamin and mineral feed additive. However, any decrease in the per-unit cost of the standard feed would result in a decrease in the total cost for the optimal daily diet.

Note that the objective function coefficient values for S and A have no upper limit. Even if the cost of A were to increase, for example, from 300 sh. to 1300 sh. per kilo, the optimal solution would not change; the total cost of the solution, however, would increase by 1000 sh. (the amount of the increase) times 1.541 or 1541 sh. You must always keep in mind that the interpretations we have made using the sensitivity analysis information in the computer output are only appropriate if all other coefficients in the problem do not change. To consider simultaneous changes we must use the 100 per cent rule or re-solve the problem after making the changes.

3.5 The Taiwan Electronic Communications (TEC) Problem

So far, we have looked mostly at basic, two-variable LP problems so that we can focus easily on the general principles of formulation and solution. In the next chapter we will illustrate how more complex situations can be modelled with LP and highlight common types of LP models. An ability to formulate, solve and then interpret more complex problems is critical and we shall introduce a slightly more complex problem to provide additional practise.

The Taiwan Electronic Communications (TEC) company is based in Taiwan and has an international reputation for manufacturing communication equipment for use by both business and individuals. Its latest product is an encrypted portable radio system that allows for secure radio communications between users with a range of up to 25 kilometres. The company intends to target the new product at four specific markets:

1 oil rigs;
2 agriculture and forestry;
3 retail sales through local distributors;
4 Internet sales through its own website.

Because the product is new, the company has decided on an initial, limited production to test market the product.

Because of differing distribution and promotional costs, the profitability of the product will vary with the target market. In addition, the advertising cost and the personal sales effort required will vary with the target market. Table 3.2 summarizes the contribution to profit, advertising cost and personal sales effort data. The firm has set the advertising budget at \$5000, and a maximum of 1800 hours of salesforce time is available for allocation to the sales effort. Management also decided to produce 600 units for the current production period. Finally, an ongoing contract with a chain of retail stores requires that at least 150 units be available for retail sales.

Table 3.2 Profit, Advertising Cost, and Personal Sales Time Data for the TEC Problem

Target Market	Profit per Unit Sold (\$)	Advertising Cost per Unit Sold (\$)	Personal Sales Effort per Unit Sold (hours)
Oil rigs	90	10	2
Agriculture and Forestry	84	8	3
Retail stores	70	9	3
Internet Sales	60	15	None

TEC is now faced with the problem of establishing a strategy that will provide for the distribution of the radios in such a way that overall profitability of the new radio production will be maximized. Decisions must be made as to how many units should be allocated to each of the four distribution channels, as well as how to allocate the advertising budget and salesforce effort to each of the four distribution channels.

Problem Formulation

For the objective function, we can write:

Objective function: Maximize profit

Four constraints appear necessary for this problem. They are necessary because of (1) a limited advertising budget, (2) limited salesforce availability, (3) a production requirement and (4) a retail stores distribution requirement.

Constraint 1 Advertising expenditures $\leq$ Budget

Constraint 2 Sales time used $\leq$ Time available

Constraint 3 Radios produced $=$ Management requirement

Constraint 4 Retail sales $\geq$ Contract requirement

These expressions provide descriptions of the objective function and the constraints. We are now ready to define the decision variables that will represent the decisions the manager must make.

For the TEC problem, we introduce the following four decision variables:

A = the number of units produced for the oil rigs market

B = the number of units produced for the agriculture and forestry market

C = the number of units produced for retail sales

D = the number of units produced for Internet sales

Using the data in Table 3.2, the objective function for maximizing the total contribution to profit associated with the radios can be written as follows:

$$\text{Max } 90A + 84B + 70C + 60D$$

Let us now develop a mathematical statement of the constraints for the problem. Because the advertising budget is set at \$5000, the constraint that limits the amount of advertising expenditure can be written as follows:

$$10A + 8B + 9C + 15D \leq 5000$$

Similarly, because the sales time is limited to 1800 hours, we obtain the constraint:

$$2A + 3B + 3C \leq 1800$$

Management's decision to produce exactly 600 units during the current production period is expressed as:

$$A + B + C + D = 600$$

Finally, to account for the fact that the number of units distributed by the national chain of retail stores must be at least 150, we add the constraint:

$$C \geq 150$$

Combining all of the constraints with the nonnegativity requirements enables us to write the complete linear programming model for the TEC problem as follows:

$$
\begin{aligned}
\text{Max} \quad & 90A + 84B + 70C + 60D \\
\text{s.t} \quad & \\
& 10A + 8B + 9C + 15D \leq 5000 \quad \text{Advertising budget} \\
& 2A + 3B + 3C \leq 1800 \quad \text{Salesforce availability} \\
& A + B + C + D = 600 \quad \text{Production level} \\
& C \geq 150 \quad \text{Retail stores requirement} \\
& A, B, C, D \geq 0
\end{aligned}
$$

Computer Solution and Interpretation

EXCEL ***file***

TEC

A portion of the output obtained using Excel to solve the TEC problem is shown in Figure 3.14. The Objective Function Value section shows that the optimal solution to

Figure 3.14 A Portion of the Excel Computer Output for the TEC Problem

Target Cell (Max)

Name	Original Value	Final Value
Obj Function	0	48450

Adjustable Cells

Name	Original Value	Final Value
A	0	25
B	0	425
C	0	150
D	0	0

Constraints

Name	Cell Value	Status	Slack
Advertising	5000	Binding	0
Salesforce	1775	Not Binding	25
Production	600	Binding	0
Retail	150	Binding	0

Adjustable Cells

Name	Final Value	Reduced Cost	Objective Coefficient	Allowable Increase	Allowable Decrease
A	25	0	90	1E+30	6
B	425	0	84	6	34
C	150	0	70	17	1E+30
D	0	45	60	45	1E+30

Constraints

Name	Final Value	Shadow Price	Constraint R.H. Side	Allowable Increase	Allowable Decrease
Advertising	5000	3	5000	850	50
Salesforce	1775	0	1800	1E+30	25
Production	600	60	600	3.571428571	85
Retail	150	-17	150	50	150

the problem will provide a maximum profit of $48 450. The optimal values of the decision variables are given by $A = 25$, $B = 425$, $C = 150$ and $D = 0$. Thus, the optimal strategy is to concentrate on agriculture and forestry with $B = 425$ units. In addition, the firm should allocate 25 units to the oil rig market ($A = 25$) and meet its 150-unit commitment to the national retail chain store ($C = 150$). With $D = 0$, the optimal solution indicates that the firm should not use the Internet market.

Looking at the four constraints, we see that those for advertising, the production level and the retail stores requirement are binding. We are using all the available advertising budget; we are matching the required production level of 600 units in total; and we are meeting the minimum requirement for supplying retail stores, although for this last constraint there is no surplus either. The constraint relating to salesforce availability, however, is non-binding and has a slack value of 25. That is, we do not require all the available salesforce time; 25 hours of the available 1800 hours is unused. Looking now at the sensitivity information output, we see that for the reduced cost for the four decision variables, three are zero and one nonzero, that for variable D at 45. Recall that reduced costs indicate by how much each objective function coefficient would have to change before the corresponding decision variable took a positive value in the optimal solution. Fairly obviously, the first three decision variables, A, B, C, have zero reduced costs since they are already taking positive values in the solution. For variable D, however, we see a reduced cost value of 45. Recollect that variable D indicates the number of radios sold through the Internet. At the optimal solution, this is set to zero – none of our sales will be through this channel. Effectively, since we are seeking to maximize profit, we are being told that D is not sufficiently profitable at $60 per unit, other things being equal. The reduced costs figure of $45 for D tells us how much more profitable D needs to be to take a nonzero value. Radios sold through the Internet would need to make $105 ($60 + $45) profit per unit sold to be viable. Let us also look at the other sensitivity information about the objective function. We can summarize the range of optimality for each of the objective function coefficients as follows:

A	$84 \leq C_A \leq$ No upper limit
B	$50 \leq C_b \leq 90$
C	No lower limit $< C_c \leq 87$
D	No lower limit $< C_d \leq 105$

So, we see that the current solution will remain optimal as long as the objective function coefficients remain in the given ranges of optimality. For radios sold to oil rigs, A, the profit per unit can fall to $84 and A will still remain in the solution. For radios sold to agriculture and forestry, the profit contribution could be between $50 and $90 and B remains in the solution. For radios sold through local distributors, C, there is no lower limit but an upper limit of $87 per unit. For D, the figures confirm the reduced cost value that we discussed earlier.

Let us now look at the sensitivity information for the four constraints. We already know that three constraints are binding. Looking at the shadow price for each constraint and the allowable increase/decrease we can provide the following management information. The advertising budget of $5000 is all spent at the optimal solution. The shadow price of $3 indicates that for each extra dollar spent on advertising over and above the current budget of $5000 total profit will increase by $3. This will be valid up to an increase of $850. After that we cannot tell from the sensitivity information what will happen to profit. To do so, we would need to reformulate and re-solve the problem. Other things being equal, then, management should give serious consideration to increasing the advertising budget to $5850. Our second constraint, that relating to salesforce availability is non-binding (and has a shadow price of zero). Increasing the salesforce availability beyond its current maximum of 1800 hours will add nothing to profit, given that we are not using all the 1800 hours anyway. In fact, we can advise management that they can reduce availability by 25 hours without affecting current maximum profit. The third constraint was the production constraint imposed by management. Given that this was a strict equality constraint then it is no surprise to see it as a binding constraint (without this constraint being met the problem would not have a solution at all). It has a shadow price of \$60 implying that a relaxation of this constraint by 1 (i.e., to 601) would increase profit by \$60. However, we also see from the allowable increase that only a small increase would be permissible in any event (of 3.57 units). Finally, we have the retail stores constraint, requiring us to provide at least 150 units to retail stores. This constraint is also binding, and as we noted earlier, the surplus associated with this variable (since it takes the form $\geq$) is also zero. In other words, the 150 unit requirement is being met in the current optimal solution but only just. This implies that this requirement, whilst being met, is actually having an adverse effect on potential profit. This is confirmed if we look at the constraint's shadow price. Here it is −\$17, a negative value. Recollect the meaning of a shadow price. It shows the change in the objective function if we allow a marginal increase in the right-hand side. In other words if we set this constraint equal to 151 then the shadow price

MANAGEMENT SCIENCE IN ACTION

Tea Production and Distribution in India

In India, one of the largest tea producers in the world, approximately \$1 billion of tea packets and loose tea are sold. Duncan Industries Limited (DIL), the third largest producer of tea in the Indian tea market, sells about \$37.5 million of tea, almost all of which is sold in packets.

DIL has 16 tea gardens, three blending units, six packing units and 22 depots. Tea from the gardens is sent to blending units, which then mix various grades of tea to produce blends such as Sargam, Double Diamond and Runglee Rungliot. The blended tea is transported to packing units, where it is placed in packets of different sizes and shapes to produce about 120 different product lines. For example, one line is Sargam tea packed in 500-gram cartons, another line is Double Diamond packed in 100-gram pouches and so on. The tea is then shipped to the depots that supply 11 500 distributors through whom the needs of approximately 325 000 retailers are satisfied.

For the coming month, sales managers provide estimates of the demand for each line of tea at each depot. Using these estimates, a team of senior managers would determine the amounts of loose tea of each blend to ship to each packing unit, the quantity of each line of tea to be packed at each packing unit, and the amounts of packed tea of each line to be transported from each packing unit to the various depots. This process requires two to three days each month and often results in stockouts of lines in demand at specific depots.

Consequently, a linear programming model involving approximately 7000 decision variables and 1500 constraints was developed to minimize the company's freight cost while satisfying demand, supply and all operational constraints. The model was tested on past data and showed that stockouts could be prevented at little or no additional cost. Moreover, the model was able to provide management with the ability to perform various what-if types of exercises, convincing them of the potential benefits of using management science techniques to support the decision-making process.

Based on Nilotpal Chakravarti, 'Tea Company Steeped in OR', *OR/MS Today* (April 2000).

indicates that total profit will *fall* by $17. In other words, relaxing this constraint (say to 149 units) will actually be beneficial to profit. Management may, therefore, wish to re-consider their commitment to selling through retail stores.

It is worth re-emphasizing the importance of *sensitivity analysis*, or *post-optimality analysis*. The information provided through such analysis allows us to answer a considerable number of what-if questions about the current problem and its optimal solution without further calculation or solution. If we know what we are doing, we can provide management with information about the effects of changes in any of the objective function coefficients and on changes in the right-hand side of each of the problem constraints. This allows management to consider the effects of any assumptions built into the existing model and to consider management actions that may lead to an ever better solution to the problem under consideration.

Again, the sensitivity analysis or post-optimality analysis provided by computer software packages for linear programming problems considers only *one change at a time*, with all other coefficients of the problem remaining as originally specified. As mentioned earlier, simultaneous changes can sometimes be analyzed without re-solving the problem, provided that the cumulative changes are not large enough to violate the 100 per cent rule.

Finally, recall that the complete solution to the TEC problem requested information not only on the number of units to be sold to each target market, but also on the allocation of the advertising budget and the salesforce effort to each market channel. For the optimal solution of $A = 25$, $B = 425$, $C = 150$ and $D = 0$, we can simply evaluate each term in a given constraint to determine how much of the constraint resource is allocated to each market. For example, the advertising budget constraint of:

$$10A + 8B + 9C + 15D \geq 5000$$

shows that $10A = 10(25) = \$250$, $8B = 8(425) = \$3400$, $9C = 9(150) = \$1350$ and $15D = 15(0) = \$0$. Thus, the advertising budget allocations are, respectively, $250, $3400, $1350 and $0 for each of the four markets. Making similar calculations for the salesforce constraint results in the managerial summary of the optimal solution as shown in Table 3.3.

Table 3.3 Profit-Maximizing Strategy for the Problem

Target Market	Volume	Advertising Allocation, $	Salesforce Allocation (hours)
Oil rigs	25	250	50
Agriculture and Forestry	425	3 400	1 275
Retail Sales	150	1 350	450
Internet Sales	0	0	0
Total	600	5 000	1 775
Projected total profit= $48 450			

Summary

- This chapter has introduced and developed sensitivity analysis as a standard part of the LP solution and analysis. Sensitivity analysis, or post-optimality analysis, is concerned with showing how changes in the formulation parameters will affect the optimal solution.
- Sensitivity analysis can be undertaken on the objective function coefficients and on the right-hand side values of the constraints.
- Computer output from LP solutions provides the sensitivity information that we can use.
- Sensitivity analysis provides useful information to management allowing them to undertake what-if analysis without the need for re-formulation and re-solution of the original problem.

WORKED EXAMPLE

Vollmer Manufacturing in Germany produces a variety of components used in refrigerators. The components are produced for a variety of refrigeration companies such as Neff, Bosch, Hotpoint. The company is in the process of planning its next batch of production. Three particular components are being planned: BFX1, AHS15 and CTY45. Each of the three components goes through a two-part production process using automated machinery and systems: a shaping process and a grinding process. Each component requires a differing amount of time on the two processes, shown below in minutes per component:

Component	Shaping	Grinding
BFX1	6	4
AHS15	4	5
CTY45	4	2

For the next production period, there will be an anticipated 120 hours available for the shaping process and an anticipated 11 hours for the grinding. The three components have profit contribution, respectively, of €8, €6 and €9. Based on previous production and sales, the company expects to sell no more than 200 units of CTY45, although expected sales for the other two components could reach 1000 units each. In addition, the company already has an order for 600 units of BFX1.

What advice can you give the company?

Solution

Well, let us start by formulating the LP problem. We have effectively got three decision variables – how many of each of the three components should we make. We only have information about profit, so it will be a profit maximization problem. We obviously have constraints relating to the two production processes and there are also constraints about sales of the three components. If we rename the components as B, A and C for simplicity we would then have a formulation of:

Max $8B + 6A + 9C$

s.t

$6B + 4A + 4C \leq 7200$ (Shaping constraint converted to minutes)

$4B + 5A + 2C \leq 6600$ (Grinding constraint converted to minutes)

$C \leq 200$ (maximum sales of CTY45)

$B \leq 1000$ (maximum sales of BFX1)

$A \leq 1000$ (maximum sales of AHS15)

$B \geq 600$ (existing order for BFX1)

$A, B, C \geq 0$

The Excel output for the problem is shown below. From the first part of the output we can advise management on the optimum production mix for the next production period. This is:

BFX1	600 units
AHS15	700 units
CTY45	200 units

This production mix will generate a profit contribution of €10 800. However we can go further and provide information from the binding/non-binding constraints. We can advise management that the profit contribution is being prevented from increasing further by the available amount of Shaping time; the maximum sales of CTY45; and the existing order for BFX1. If management wish to increase profit contribution further then these three areas should be examined further. Looking at Shaping time first, the company currently has an anticipated 7200 minutes available (120 hours). All of this is needed for the optimum production mix. We can advise management that any shortfall in the anticipated time availability of 120 hours will affect production and hence profit. The *Shadow price* of €1.50 tells us that each minute shortfall will reduce profit contribution by €1.50. Conversely, if management can somehow increase the amount of available shaping time beyond 120 hours this will allow us to produce more and increase profit contribution by €1.50 for each extra minute of Shaping time we can obtain. Looking at the *Available increase* information, we can advise management that it would be worthwhile trying to increase the available shaping time by an extra four hours (240 minutes). After this point, we are no longer sure from the existing sensitivity analysis what would happen to the optimum solution.

If we look at the second binding constraint, maximum sales of CTY45, we are producing the maximum quantity permitted at the optimum solution. Again, the *Shadow price* of €3 indicated the opportunity cost of this constraint. Other things being equal, if we were allowed to relax this constraint (i.e., produce more than 200 units) then profit contribution would increase by €3 for each extra unit of CTY45 produced. We also see from the *Allowable increase* that we could profitably produce an extra 700 units. Clearly, we do not know from the information given why this constraint is there. It may be that Sales and Marketing in the company have advised that realistically we cannot sell more than 200 units. However, the sensitivity information allows management to consider the consequences of this. Our third binding constraint related to the requirement to produce at least 600 units of BFX1 because of an existing order. In this case the *Shadow price* is negative, at −€1. This indicates that any increase in this constraint will actually cost us money and decrease profit contribution for each extra unit above the 600 that we produce. Conversely, if we could relax this constraint and produce less than 600 units in the next period then profit contribution would increase. Again, it may be that management are unable to alter this constraint, we may already have signed a contract with the customer. Again, however, the sensitivity analysis information allows management to see the consequences of this and maybe to consider alternatives. Could we persuade the customer to delay the order? We could even offer a financial incentive for them to do this, up to €1 for each unit we didn't produce for them.

Is there anything else we can tell management? Well, we can advise that we do not actually need all the available grinding time, since five hours (300 minutes) remains unused at the optimum production mix. We can also inform them if there is any uncertainty about the product profit contributions (of €8, €6 and €9) we can advise on the effects of this. For example, that BFX1's profit contribution could increase from €8 up to €9 without affecting the optimum production mix; and that its profit contribution could effectively fall to zero and still not affect the optimum solution. The latter point may need further explaining. Even if BFX1 has a zero profit contribution we would still have to produce a minimum of 600 units because of the relevant constraint.

Target Cell (Max)

Name	Original Value	Final Value
Obj. Function	0	10800

Adjustable Cells

Name	Original Value	Final Value
Units B	0	600
Units A	0	700
Units C	0	200

Constraints

Cell	Name	Cell Value	Status	Slack
Shaping time	<=	7200	Binding	0
Grinding time	<=	6300	Not Binding	300
Max sales of C	<=	200	Binding	0
Max sales of B	<=	600	Not Binding	400
Max sales of A	<=	700	Not Binding	300
Min sales of B	>=	600	Binding	0

Adjustable Cells

Name	Final Value	Reduced Cost	Objective Coefficient	Allowable Increase	Allowable Decrease
Units B	600	0	8	1	1E + 30
Units A	700	0	6	3	0.666666667
Units C	200	0	9	1E + 30	3

Constraints

Cell	Name	Final Value	Shadow Price	Constraint R.H. Side	Allowable Increase	Allowable Decrease
Shaping time	<=	7200	1.5	7200	240	2800
Grinding time	<=	6300	0	6600	1E + 30	300
Max sales of C	<=	200	3	200	700	100
Max sales of B	<=	600	0	1000	1E + 30	400
Max sales of A	<=	700	0	1000	1E + 30	300
Min sales of B	>=	600	-1	600	400	85.71428571

Problems

1 Recall the RMC problem (Chapter 2, Problem 12). Letting:

F = kilos of fuel additive

S = kilos of solvent base

leads to the formulation:

$$\begin{aligned} \text{Max} \quad & 40F + 30S \\ \text{s.t} \quad & \\ & {}^{2}/_{5}F + {}^{1}/_{2}S \leq 20 \quad \text{Material 1} \\ & {}^{1}/_{2}S \leq 5 \quad \text{Material 2} \\ & {}^{3}/_{5}F + {}^{3}/_{10}S \leq 21 \quad \text{Material 3} \\ & F, S \geq 0 \end{aligned}$$

Use the graphical sensitivity analysis approach to determine the range of optimality for the objective function coefficients.

SELF *test*

2 For Problem 1 use the graphical sensitivity approach to determine what happens if an additional three kilos of material 3 become available. What is the corresponding dual price for the constraint?

SELF *test*

3 Consider the following linear programme:

$$\begin{aligned} \text{Max} \quad & 2x_1 + 3x_2 \\ \text{s.t} \quad & \\ & x_1 + x_2 \leq 10 \\ & 2x_1 + x_2 \geq 4 \\ & x_1 + 3x_2 \leq 24 \\ & 2x_1 + x_2 \leq 16 \\ & x_1, x_2 \geq 0 \end{aligned}$$

a. Solve this problem using the graphical solution procedure.
b. Calculate the range of optimality for the objective function coefficient of x_1.
c. Calculate the range of optimality for the objective function coefficient of x_2.
d. Suppose the objective function coefficient of x_1 is increased from 2 to 2.5. What is the new optimal solution?
e. Suppose the objective function coefficient of x_2 is decreased from 3 to 1. What is the new optimal solution?

SELF *test*

4 Refer to Problem 3. Calculate the dual prices for constraints 1 and 2 and interpret them.

5 Consider the following linear programme:

$$\begin{aligned} \text{Min} \quad & x_1 + x_2 \\ \text{s.t} \quad & \\ & x_1 + 2x_2 \geq 7 \\ & 2x_1 + x_2 \geq 5 \\ & x_1 + 6x_2 \geq 11 \\ & x_1, x_2 \geq 0 \end{aligned}$$

a. Solve this problem using the graphical solution procedure.
b. Calculate the range of optimality for the objective function coefficient of x_1.
c. Calculate the range of optimality for the objective function coefficient of x_2.
d. Suppose the objective function coefficient of x_1 is increased to 1.5. Find the new optimal solution.
e. Suppose the objective function coefficient of x_2 is decreased to one-third. Find the new optimal solution.

SELF *test*

6 Refer to Problem 5. Calculate and interpret the dual prices for the constraints.

7 Refer again to Problem 3.

a. Suppose the objective function coefficient of x_1 is increased to 3 and the objective function coefficient of x_2 is increased to 4. Find the new optimal solution.
b. Suppose the objective function coefficient of x_1 is increased to 3 and the objective function coefficient of x_2 is decreased to 2. Find the new optimal solution.

SELF *test*

8 Recall the GulfGolf glove problem (Chapter 2, Problem 13). Letting:

$$R = \text{number of regular gloves}$$

$$P = \text{number of professional gloves}$$

leads to the following formulation:

$$\begin{aligned} \text{Max} \quad & 5R + 8P \\ \text{s.t} \quad & \\ & R + \tfrac{3}{2}P \leq 900 \quad \text{Cutting and dyeing} \\ & \tfrac{1}{2}R + \tfrac{1}{3}P \leq 300 \quad \text{Finishing} \\ & \tfrac{1}{8}R + \tfrac{1}{4}P \leq 100 \quad \text{packaging and shipping} \\ & R, P \geq 0 \end{aligned}$$

The computer solution obtained using The Management Scientist is shown in Figure 3.15.

a. What is the optimal solution, and what is the value of the total profit contribution?
b. Which constraints are binding?
c. What are the dual prices for the resources? Interpret each.
d. If overtime can be scheduled in one of the departments, where would you recommend doing so?

9 Refer to the computer solution in Figure 3.15 (see Problem 8).

a. Calculate the ranges of optimality for the objective function coefficients.
b. Interpret the ranges in part (a).
c. Interpret the range of feasibility for the right-hand sides.
d. How much will the value of the optimal solution improve if 20 extra hours of packaging and shipping time are made available?

SELF *test*

10 Investment Advisors, Inc., is a brokerage firm that manages stock portfolios for a number of clients. A particular portfolio consists of U shares of United Oil and H shares of Huber Steel. The annual return for United Oil is €3 per share and the annual return for Huber Steel is €5 per share. United Oil sells for €25 per share and Huber Steel sells for €50 per share. The portfolio has €80 000 to be invested. The portfolio risk index (0.50 per share of United Oil and 0.25 per share of Huber Steel) has a maximum of 700. In addition, the portfolio is limited to a maximum of 1000 shares of United Oil. The linear programming formation that will maximize the total annual return of the portfolio is as follows:

$$\begin{aligned} \text{Max} \quad & 3U + 5H \qquad \text{Maximize total annual return} \\ \text{s.t} \quad & \\ & 25U + 50H \leq 80,000 \quad \text{Funds available} \\ & 0.50U + 0.25H \leq 700 \quad \text{Risk maximum} \\ & 1U \leq 1000 \quad \text{United Oil maximum} \\ & U, H \geq 0 \end{aligned}$$

Figure 3.15 The Management Scientist Solution for the GulfGolf Glove Problem

Name	Original Value	Final Value
Maximize Total Profit	0	3700

Name	Original Value	Final Value
Units produced Regular	0	500
Units produced Professional	0	150

Name	Cell Value	Status	Slack
Cutting and Sewing Hours Used(LHS)	725	Not Binding	175
Finishing Hours Used(LHS)	300	Binding	0
Packaging and shipping Hours Used(LHS)	100	Binding	0

Adjustable Cells

Name	Final Value	Reduced Cost	Objective Coefficient	Allowable Increase	Allowable Decrease
Units produced Regular	500	0	5	7	1
Units produced Professional	150	0	8	2	4.666666667

Constraints

Name	Final Value	Shadow Price	Constraint R.H. Side	Allowable Increase	Allowable Decrease
Cutting and Sewing Hours Used(LHS)	725	0	900	1E+30	175
Finishing Hours Used(LHS)	300	3	300	100	166.6666667
Packaging and shipping Hours Used(LHS)	100	28	100	35	25

The computer solution of this problem is shown in Figure 3.16.

a. What is the optimal solution, and what is the value of the total annual return?
b. Which constraints are binding? What is your interpretation of these constraints in terms of the problem?
c. What are the dual prices for the constraints? Interpret each.
d. Would it be beneficial to increase the maximum amount invested in United Oil? Why or why not?

SELF *test*

11 Refer to Figure 3.16, which shows the computer solution of Problem 10.

a. How much would the estimated per-share return for United Oil have to increase before it would be beneficial to increase the investment in this stock?
b. How much would the estimated per-share return for Huber Steel have to decrease before it would be beneficial to reduce the investment in this stock?
c. How much would the total annual return be reduced if the United Oil maximum were reduced to 900 shares?

Figure 3.16 Excel Solution for the Investment Advisors Problem

Name	Original Value	Final Value
Maximize Total Profit United Oil	0	8400

Name	Original Value	Final Value
Optimum values United Oil	0	800
Optimum values Huber Steel	0	1200

Name	Cell Value	Status	Slack
Funds available LHS	80000	Binding	0
Risk maximum LHS	700	Binding	0
United Oil maximum LHS	800		200

Adjustable Cells

Name	Final Value	Reduced Cost	Objective Coefficient	Allowable Increase	Allowable Decrease
Optimum values United Oil	800	0	3	7	0.5
Optimum values Huber Steel	1200	0	5	1	3.5

Constraints

Name	Final Value	Shadow Price	Constraint R.H. Side	Allowable Increase	Allowable Decrease
Funds available LHS	80000	0.093333333	80000	60000	15000
Risk maximum LHS	700	1.333333333	700	75	300
United Oil maximum LHS	800	0	1000	1E+30	200

SELF *test*

12 Recall the Miguel's problem in Chapter 2, Problem 15. Letting:

W = jars of Western Foods Salsa
M = jars of Mexico City Salsa

leads to the formulation:

$$\text{Max} \quad 1W + 1.25M$$
s.t

$$\begin{aligned} 104W + 196M &\leq 280000 && \text{Whole tomatoes} \\ 84W + 28M &\leq 130000 && \text{Tomato sauce} \\ 56W + 56M &\leq 100000 && \text{Tomato paste} \\ W, M &\geq 0 \end{aligned}$$

The solution is shown in Figure 3.17.

a. What is the optimal solution, and what are the optimal production quantities?
b. Specify the range of optimality for the objective function coefficients.
c. What are the dual prices for each constraint? Interpret each.
d. Identify the range of feasibility for each of the right-hand-side values.

Figure 3.17 Excel Solution for the Salsa Problem

Name	Original Value	Final Value
Maximize total profit	0	1919.642857

Adjustable Cells

Name	Original Value	Final Value
Units produced W	0	1250
Units produced M	0	535.7142857

Constraints

Name	Cell Value	Status	Slack
Whole tomatoes grams used (LHS)	280000	Binding	0
Tomato sauce grams used (LHS)	120000	Not Binding	10000
Tomato paste grams used (LHS)	100000	Binding	0

Adjustable Cells

Name	Final Value	Reduced Cost	Objective Coefficient	Allowable Increase	Allowable Decrease
Units produced W	1250	0	1	0.25	0.107142857
Units produced M	535.7142857	0	1.25	0.15	0.25

Constraints

Name	Final Value	Shadow Price	Constraint R.H. Side	Allowable Increase	Allowable Decrease
Whole tomatoes grams used (LHS)	280000	0.004464286	280000	70000	10000
Tomato sauce grams used (LHS)	120000	0	130000	1E+30	10000
Tomato paste grams used (LHS)	100000	0.006696429	100000	2500	20000

13 Quality Air Conditioning manufactures three home air conditioners: an economy model, a standard model and a deluxe model. The profits per unit are €63, €95 and €135, respectively. The production requirements per unit are as follows:

	Number of Fans	Number of Cooling Coils	Manufacturing Time (hours)
Economy	1	1	8
Standard	1	2	12
Deluxe	1	4	14

For the coming production period, the company has 200 fan motors, 320 coolling coils and 2400 hours of manufacturing time available. How many economy models (*E*), standard models (*S*) and deluxe models (*D*) should the company produce in order to maximize profit? The linear programming model for the problem is as follows:

Figure 3.18 Solution for the Quality Air Conditioning Problem

```
Objective Function Value =          16440.000

   Variable              Value               Reduced Costs
 --------------    ---------------         ----------------
            E               80.000                    0.000
            S              120.000                    0.000
            D                0.000                   24.000

  Constraint          Slack/Surplus             Dual Prices
 --------------    ---------------         ----------------
            1                0.000                   31.000
            2                0.000                   32.000
            3              320.000                    0.000

OBJECTIVE COEFFICIENT RANGES

 Variable      Lower Limit      Current Value     Upper Limit
------------ --------------- ---------------- ---------------
     E             47.500            63.000           75.000
     S             87.000            95.000          126.000
     D     No Lower Limit           135.000          159.000

RIGHT HAND SIDE RANGES

 Constraint      Lower Limit      Current Value     Upper Limit
------------ --------------- ---------------- ---------------
     1            160.000           200.000          280.000
     2            200.000           320.000          400.000
     3           2080.000          2400.000   No Upper Limit
```

$$\begin{aligned} \text{Max} \quad & 63E + 95S + 135D \\ \text{s.t} \quad & \\ & 1E + 1S + 1D \le 200 \quad \text{Fan motors} \\ & 1E + 2S + 4D \le 320 \quad \text{Cooling coils} \\ & 8E + 12S + 14D \le 2400 \quad \text{Manufacturing time} \\ & E, S, D \ge 0 \end{aligned}$$

The computer solution is shown in Figure 3.18.

a. What is the optimal solution, and what is the value of the objective function?
b. Which constraints are binding?
c. Which constraint shows extra capacity? How much?
d. If the profit for the deluxe model were increased to €150 per unit, would the optimal solution change? Use the information in Figure 3.19 to answer this question.

SELF *test*

14 Refer to the computer solution of Problem 13 in Figure 3.18.

a. Identify the range of optimality for each objective function coefficient.
b. Suppose the profit for the economy model is increased by €6 per unit, the profit for the standard model is decreased by €2 per unit, and the profit for the deluxe model is increased by €4 per unit. What will the new optimal solution be?

c. Identify the range of feasibility for the right-hand side values.

d. If the number of fan motors available for production is increased by 100, will the dual price for that constraint change? Explain.

15 Digital Controls, Inc. (DCI), manufactures two models of a radar speed device used by police to monitor the speed of automobiles. Model A has an accuracy of plus or minus one km per hour, whereas the smaller model B has an accuracy of plus or minus three km per hour. For the next week, the company has orders for 100 units of model A and 150 units of model B. Although DCI purchases all the electronic components used in both models, the plastic cases for both models are manufactured at a DCI plant in China. Each model A case requires four minutes of injection-moulding time and six minutes of assembly time. Each model B case requires three minutes of injection-moulding time and eight minutes of assembly time. For next week, the plant has 600 minutes of injection-moulding time available and 1080 minutes of assembly time available. The manufacturing cost is €10 per case for model A and €6 per case for model B. Depending upon demand and the time available at the plant, DCI occasionally purchases cases for one or both models from an outside supplier in order to fill customer orders that could not be filled otherwise. The purchase cost is €14 for each model A case and €9 for each model B case. Management wants to develop a minimum-cost plan that will determine how many cases of each model should be produced at the plant and how many cases of each model should be purchased. The following decision variables were used to formulate a linear programming model for this problem:

$$AM = \text{number of cases of model A manufactured}$$

$$BM = \text{number of cases of model B manufactured}$$

$$AP = \text{number of cases of model A purchased}$$

$$BP = \text{number of cases of model B purchased}$$

The linear programming model that can be used to solve this problem is as follows:

$$\begin{aligned}
\text{Min} \quad & 10AM + 6BM + 14AP + 9BP \\
\text{s.t} \quad & \\
& 1AM + 1AP = 100 \quad \text{Demand for model A} \\
& 1BM + IBP = 150 \quad \text{Demand for model B} \\
& 4AM + 3BM \leq 600 \quad \text{Injection-moldingtime} \\
& 6AM + 8BM \leq 1080 \quad \text{Assembly time} \\
& AM, BM, AP, BP \geq 0
\end{aligned}$$

The computer solution developed is shown in Figure 3.19.

a. What is the optimal solution, and what is the optimal value of the objective function?

b. Which constraints are binding?

c. What are the dual prices? Interpret each.

d. If you could change the right-hand side of one constraint by one unit, which one would you choose? Why?

SELF *test*

16 Refer to the computer solution of Problem 15 in Figure 3.19.

a. Interpret the ranges of optimality for the objective function coefficients.

b. Suppose that the manufacturing cost increases to €11.20 per case for model A. What is the new optimal solution?

Figure 3.19 Solution for the Digital Controls, Inc. Problem

```
Objective Function Value =        2170.000

   Variable              Value              Reduced Costs
 --------------    ---------------    -----------------
        AM              100.000                 0.000
        BM               60.000                 0.000
        AP                0.000                 1.750
        BP               90.000                 0.000

  Constraint          Slack/Surplus          Dual Prices
 --------------    ---------------    -----------------
        1                 0.000               -12.250
        2                 0.000                -9.000
        3                20.000                 0.000
        4                 0.000                 0.375

OBJECTIVE COEFFICIENT RANGES

  Variable      Lower Limit     Current Value    Upper Limit
------------  ---------------  ---------------  ---------------
    AM        No Lower Limit          10.000           11.750
    BM                 3.667           6.000            9.000
    AP                12.250          14.000   No Upper Limit
    BP                 6.000           9.000           11.333

RIGHT HAND SIDE RANGES

 Constraint     Lower Limit     Current Value    Upper Limit
------------  ---------------  ---------------  ---------------
    1                  0.000         100.000          111.429
    2                 60.000         150.000   No Upper Limit
    3                580.000         600.000   No Upper Limit
    4                600.000        1080.000         1133.333
```

c. Suppose that the manufacturing cost increases to €11.20 per case for model A and the manufacturing cost for model B decreases to €5 per unit. Would the optimal solution change? Use the 100 per cent rule and discuss.

17 Tucker Inc. produces high-quality suits and sport coats for men. Each suit requires 1.2 hours of cutting time and 0.7 hours of sewing time, uses six metres of material, and provides a profit contribution of €190. Each sport coat requires 0.8 hours of cutting time and 0.6 hours of sewing time, uses four metres of material, and provides a profit contribution of €150. For the coming week, 200 hours of cutting time, 180 hours of sewing time and 1200 metres of fabric are available. Additional cutting and sewing time can be obtained by scheduling overtime for these operations. Each hour of overtime for the cutting operation increases the hourly cost by €15, and each hour of overtime for the sewing operation increases the hourly cost by €10. A maximum of 100 hours of overtime can be scheduled. Marketing requirements specify a minimum production of 100 suits and 75 sport coats.

S = number of suits produced

SC = number of sport coats produced

D_1 = hours of overtime for the cutting operation

D_2 = hours of overtime for the sewing operation

Figure 3.20 Solution For The Tucker Inc. Problem

```
Objective Function Value =          40900.000

    Variable               Value              Reduced Costs
 --------------      ---------------       ------------------
      S                  100.000                  0.000
      SC                 150.000                  0.000
      D1                  40.000                  0.000
      D2                   0.000                 10.000

   Constraint          Slack/Surplus           Dual Prices
 --------------      ---------------       ------------------
       1                   0.000                 15.000
       2                  20.000                  0.000
       3                   0.000                 34.500
       4                  60.000                  0.000
       5                   0.000                -35.000
       6                  75.000                  0.000

OBJECTIVE COEFFICIENT RANGES

 Variable      Lower Limit      Current Value     Upper Limit
------------ --------------- --------------- ---------------
    S        No Lower Limit         190.000         225.000
    SC              126.667         150.000  No Upper Limit
    D1             -187.500         -15.000           0.000
    D2       No Lower Limit         -10.000           0.000

RIGHT HAND SIDE RANGES

 Constraint    Lower Limit      Current Value     Upper Limit
------------ --------------- --------------- ---------------
     1              140.000         200.000         240.000
     2              160.000         180.000  No Upper Limit
     3             1000.000        1200.000        1333.333
     4               40.000         100.000  No Upper Limit
     5                0.000         100.000         150.000
     6       No Lower Limit          75.000         150.000
```

The computer solution is shown in Figure 3.20.

a. What is the optimal solution, and what is the total profit? What is the plan for the use of overtime?
b. A price increase for suits is being considered that would result in a profit contribution of €210 per suit. If this price increase is undertaken, how will the optimal solution change?
c. Discuss the need for additional material during the coming week. If a rush order for material can be placed at the usual price plus an extra €8 per metre for handling, would you recommend the company consider placing a rush order for material? What is the maximum price Tucker would be willing to pay for an additional metre of material? How many additional metres of material should Tucker consider ordering?
d. Suppose the minimum production requirement for suits is lowered to 75. Would this help or hurt profit? Explain.

18 Round Tree Manor is a hotel that has two types of rooms with three rental classes: Super Saver, Deluxe and Business. The profit per night for each type of room and rental class is as follows:

		Rental Class		
		Super Saver	**Deluxe**	**Business**
Room	**Type I**	£30	£35	—
	Type II	£20	£30	£40

Type I rooms do not have Internet access and are not available for the Business rental class.

Round Tree's management makes a forecast of the demand by rental class for each night in the future. A linear programming model developed to maximize profit is used to determine how many reservations to accept for each rental class. The demand forecast for a particular night is 130 rentals in the Super Saver class, 60 rentals in the Deluxe class and 50 rentals in the Business class. Round Tree has 100 Type I rooms and 120 Type II rooms.

a. Use linear programming to determine how many reservations to accept in each rental class and how the reservations should be allocated to room types. Is the demand by any rental class not satisfied? Explain.
b. How many reservations can be accommodated in each rental class?
c. Management is considering offering a free breakfast to anyone upgrading from a Super Saver reservation to Deluxe class. If the cost of the breakfast to Round Tree is £5, should this incentive be offered?
d. With a little work, an unused office area could be converted to a rental room. If the conversion cost is the same for both types of rooms, would you recommend converting the office to a Type I or a Type II room? Why?
e. Could the linear programming model be modified to plan for the allocation of rental demand for the next night? What information would be needed and how would the model change?

19 Abu Dhabi Savings Bank (ADSB) has $1 million in new funds that must be allocated to home loans, personal loans and automobile loans. The annual rates of return for the three types of loans are 7 per cent for home loans, 12 per cent for personal loans and 9 per cent for automobile loans. The bank's planning committee decided that at least 40 per cent of the new funds must be allocated to home loans. In addition, the planning committee specified that the amount allocated to personal loans cannot exceed 60 per cent of the amount allocated to automobile loans.

a. Formulate a linear programming model that can be used to determine the amount of funds ADSB should allocate to each type of loan in order to maximize the total annual return for the new funds.
b. How much should be allocated to each type of loan? What is the total annual return? What is the annual percentage return?
c. If the interest rate on home loans increased to 9 per cent, would the amount allocated to each type of loan change? Explain.
d. Suppose the total amount of new funds available was increased by $10 000. What effect would this change have on the total annual return? Explain.
e. Assume that ADSB has the original $1 million in new funds available and that the planning committee agreed to relax by 1 per cent the requirement that at least 40 per cent of the new funds must be allocated to home loans. How much would the annual return change? How much would the annual percentage return change?

SELF *test*

20 The programme manager for Channel 10 would like to determine the best way to allocate the time for the 11:00–11:30 evening news broadcast. Specifically, she would like to determine the number of minutes of broadcast time to devote to local news, national news, weather and sports. Over the 30-minute broadcast, ten minutes are set aside for advertising. The station's broadcast policy states that at least 15 per cent of the time available should be devoted to local news coverage; the time devoted to local news or national news must be at least 50 per cent of the total broadcast time; the time devoted to the weather segment must be less than or equal to the time devoted to the sports segment; the time devoted to the sports segment should be no longer than the total time spent on the local and national news; and at least 20 per cent of the hould be devoted to the weather segment. The production costs per minute are €300 for local news, €200 for national news, €100 for weather and €100 for sports.

a. Formulate and solve a linear programme that can determine how the 20 available minutes should be used to minimize the total cost of producing the programme.
b. Interpret the dual price for the constraint corresponding to the available time. What advice would you give the station manager given this dual price?
c. Interpret the dual price for the constraint corresponding to the requirement that at least 15 per cent of the available time should be devoted to local coverage. What advice would you give the station manager given this dual price?
d. Interpret the dual price for the constraint corresponding to the requirement that the time devoted to the local and the national news must be at least 50 per cent of the total broadcast time. What advice would you give the station manager given this dual price?
e. Interpret the dual price for the constraint corresponding to the requirement that the time devoted to the weather segment must be less than or equal to the time devoted to the sports segment. What advice would you give the station manager given this dual price?

CASE PROBLEM 1 Product Mix

TJ's, Inc., makes three nut mixes for sale to grocery chains located in India. The three mixes, referred to as the Regular Mix, the Deluxe Mix and the Holiday Mix, are made by mixing different percentages of five types of nuts.

In preparation for the next production period, TJ's has just purchased the following shipments of nuts at the prices shown:

Type of Nut	Shipment Amount (kilos)	Cost per Shipment ($)
Almond	6 000	7 500
Brazil	7 500	7 125
Filbert	7 500	6 750
Pecan	6 000	7 200
Walnut	7 500	7 875

The Regular Mix consists of 15 per cent almonds, 25 per cent Brazil nuts, 25 per cent filberts, 10 per cent pecans and 25 per cent walnuts. The Deluxe Mix consists of 20 per cent of each type of nut, and the Holiday Mix consists of 25 per cent almonds, 15 per cent Brazil nuts, 15 per cent filberts, 25 per cent pecans and 20 per cent walnuts.

TJ's accountant analyzed the cost of packaging materials, sales price per kilo and so forth, and determined that the profit contribution per kilo is €1.65 for the Regular Mix, €2.00 for the Deluxe Mix and €2.25 for the Holiday Mix. These figures do not include the cost of specific types of nuts in the different mixes because that cost can vary greatly in the commodity markets.

Customer orders already received are summarized here:

Type of Mix	Orders (Kilos)
Regular	10 000
Deluxe	3 000
Holiday	5 000

Because demand is running high, it is expected that TJ's will receive many more orders than can be satisfied.

TJ's is committed to using the available nuts to maximize profit; nuts not used will be given to a local charity. Even if it is not profitable to do so, TJ's president indicated that the orders already received must be satisfied.

Managerial Report

Perform an analysis of TJ's product-mix problem, and prepare a report for TJ's president that summarizes your findings. Be sure to include information and analysis on the following:

1. The cost per kilo of the nuts included in the Regular, Deluxe and Holiday mixes.
2. The optimal product mix and the total profit contribution.
3. Recommendations regarding how the total profit contribution can be increased if additional quantities of nuts can be purchased.
4. A recommendation as to whether TJ's should purchase an additional 1000 kilos of almonds for €1000 from a supplier who overbought.
5. Recommendations on how profit contribution could be increased (if at all) if TJ's does not satisfy all existing orders.

CASE PROBLEM 2 Investment Strategy

J. D. Williams, Inc., is an investment advisory firm that manages more than €120 million in funds for its numerous clients. The company uses an asset allocation model that recommends the portion of each client's portfolio to be invested in a growth stock fund, an income fund and a money market fund. To maintain diversity in each client's portfolio, the firm places limits on the percentage of each portfolio that may be invested in each of the three funds. General guidelines indicate that the amount invested in the growth fund must be between 20 per cent and 40 per cent of the total portfolio value. Similar percentages for the other two funds stipulate that between 20 per cent and 50 per cent of the total portfolio value must be in the income fund and at least 30 per cent of the total portfolio value must be in the money market fund.

In addition, the company attempts to assess the risk tolerance of each client and adjust the portfolio to meet the needs of the individual investor. For example, Williams just contracted with a new client who has €800 000 to invest. Based on an evaluation of the client's risk tolerance, Williams assigned a maximum risk index of 0.05 for the client. The firm's risk indicators show the risk of the growth fund at 0.10, the income fund at 0.07, and the money market fund at 0.01. An overall portfolio risk index is computed as a weighted average of the risk rating for the three funds where the weights are the fraction of the client's portfolio invested in each of the funds.

Additionally, Williams is currently forecasting annual yields of 18 per cent for the growth fund, 12.5 per cent for the income fund and 7.5 per cent for the money market fund. Based on the information provided, how should the new client be advised to allocate the €800 000 among the growth, income and money market funds? Develop a linear programming model that will provide the maximum yield for the portfolio. Use your model to develop a managerial report.

Managerial Report

1. Recommend how much of the €800 000 should be invested in each of the three funds. What is the annual yield you anticipate for the investment recommendation?
2. Assume that the client's risk index could be increased to 0.055. How much would the yield increase and how would the investment recommendation change?
3. Refer again to the original situation where the client's risk index was assessed to be 0.05. How would your investment recommendation change if the annual yield for the growth fund were revised downward to 16 per cent or even to 14 per cent?
4. Assume that the client expressed some concern about having too much money in the growth fund. How would the original recommendation change if the amount invested in the growth fund is not allowed to exceed the amount invested in the income fund?
5. The asset allocation model you developed may be useful in modifying the portfolios for all of the firm's clients whenever the anticipated yields for the three funds are periodically revised. What is your recommendation as to whether use of this model is possible?

CASE PROBLEM 3 Truck Leasing Strategy

The Transportation Ministry is undertaking construction work relating to the excavation and site preparation of a new rest area on a major highway. The Ministry estimated that it would take four months to perform the work and that ten, 12, 14 and eight trucks would be needed in months one to four, respectively.

The Ministry currently has 20 trucks of the type needed to perform the work on the new project. These trucks were obtained last year when the Ministry signed a long-term lease with a truck leasing company. Although most of these trucks are currently being used on existing jobs, the Ministry estimates that one truck will be available for use on the new project in month 1, two trucks will be available in month 2, three trucks will be available in month 3 and one truck will be available in month 4. Thus, to complete the project, the Ministry will have to lease additional trucks.

The long-term leasing contract the Ministry has incurs a monthly cost of €600 per truck. The Ministry pays its truck drivers €20 an hour, and daily fuel costs are approximately €100 per truck. All maintenance costs are paid by the leasing company. For planning purposes the Ministry estimates that each truck used on the new project will be operating eight hours a day, five days a week for approximately four weeks each month.

The Ministry does not believe that current business conditions justify committing to additional long-term leases. In discussing the short-term leasing possibilities with the leasing company, the Ministry learned that they can obtain short-term leases of one-four months. Short-term leases differ from long-term leases in that the short-term leasing plans include the cost of both a truck and a driver. Maintenance costs for short-term leases also are paid by the leasing company. The following costs for each of the four months cover the lease of a truck and driver:

Length of Lease	Cost per Month (€)
1	4 000
2	3 700
3	3 225
4	3 040

The Ministry would like to acquire a lease that would minimize the cost of meeting the monthly trucking requirements for the new project, but the Ministry also takes great pride in the fact that they have never laid off employees. The Ministry is committed to maintaining the ministry no lay off policy; that is, the Ministry will use its own drivers even if costs are higher.

Managerial Report

Perform an analysis of the Ministry's leasing problem and prepare a report that summarizes your findings. Be sure to include information on and analysis of the following items:

1. the optimal leasing plan;
2. the costs associated with the optimal leasing plan;
3. the cost for the Ministry to maintain its current policy of no layoffs.

Chapter 4

Linear Programming Applications

Learning objectives

By the end of this chapter you will be able to:

- Recognize common application areas for LP
- Formulate complex LP problems
- Interpret the solutions to common LP problems

In the previous chapters linear programming was introduced and a method of determining the solution to such a simple problem provided. In subsequent chapters we shall examine a more rigorous and general purpose solution method and discuss the management information that can be obtained from the application of the technique. Before doing so, however, it is worthwhile examining a variety of typical applications of LP. This will serve two purposes. The first is that it will provide an overview of the tremendous diversity of business applications to which the technique has been applied. LP has turned out to be one of the most successful quantitative models in decision making. Applications have been reported in almost every industry and sector. The second is that it will provide further insight into the process of LP problem formulation. In previous chapters it was apparent that an LP problem typically falls into three parts: problem formulation, solution and interpretation. The solution of an LP problem is generally straightforward, particularly when a suitable computer package is used, and the interpretation of that solution is equally straightforward, at least to a management scientist familiar with the technique. Both these stages, however, are totally dependent upon the correct and appropriate formulation of the problem.

This chapter focuses on a number of detailed examples of typical management applications. Over time, LP applications have come to be classed or categorized by their type and we shall look at examples in each category. The purpose of such categorization is primarily to help the management scientist at the problem formulation stage. By looking at other examples of the same type of LP problem, it may be easier and quicker to come up with an appropriate problem formulation.

4.1 The Process of Problem Formulation

In Section 2.1 we provided some general guidelines for modelling linear programming problems. You may want to review Section 2.1 before proceeding with the linear programming applications in this chapter.

The process of formulating an LP application requires the management scientist to be able to 'translate' the business problem under investigation into a form suitable for solution by the technique. Over the years such formulation has developed into almost an art form and it is only fair to point out that it is this stage that will provide most difficulty in virtually every LP application. The methods of solution and interpretation are, fortunately, fairly similar no matter what the problem. The formulation, however, is likely to be almost unique to the problem under consideration. Fortunately, many problems do fall into general application categories that provide some guidance to the practitioner on the basic formulation approach to be adopted. It is also worthwhile pointing out that there is no magic formula that can be provided to ease the burden of this process. The development of appropriate LP formulation skills only comes with time and practise and the more examples and case studies you are able to access the quicker these skills will be developed. However, adopting a logical and consistent process when attempting to formulate a problem can be a big help. Naturally, like all such processes, it will not conform exactly to every problem that is examined but it does provide a useful general framework and is detailed below:

1. Provide a detailed verbal description of the problem under consideration, ensuring that related information is unambiguous and sufficiently precise. It is essential that we have a clear and adequate understanding of the problem under investigation before we seek to apply the technique itself. In practice, the management scientist may find themselves going back to the client several times to clarify some aspect of the problem that is not clear or to check on some of the data provided.

2 Determine the overall objective that appears to be relevant. It will usually be clear whether the objective relates to maximization or minimization, to cost or profit and so on. An adequate understanding of the overall objective can be of considerable assistance in unravelling other aspects of the problem.

3 Determine the factors (constraints) that appear to restrict in some way the attainment of the objective identified in the previous stage.

These three stages together will provide a detailed verbal exposition of the complete problem under investigation. The next step is to put the verbal description into a suitable mathematical framework.

4 Define the decision variables that are relevant to the problem and ensure that their units of measurement are explicitly stated. Failure to do so may well lead to difficulty in formulating appropriate constraints and in interpreting the solution results.

5 Using these decision variables, formulate an objective function. It is clear that this function should incorporate all of the decision variables. If it does not, then it signifies either a lack of information or an incorrect choice of decision variables.

6 For each of the factors identified in Stage 3, formulate a suitable mathematical constraint. Again, each constraint must include at least some of the decision variables and, again, the units of measurement of each constraint should be explicit.

7 Lastly, check the entire formulation to ensure linearity of all variables and constraints.

It should not be concluded, on the basis of this process, that problem formulation will be as simple and straightforward as this. It will typically involve considerable backtracking (the methodology structure discussed in Chapter 1 is clearly appropriate to this process). You may consider initially that you have identified the appropriate decision variables but are then unable to formulate a particular constraint involving these variables. This failure suggests that a full reconsideration of the problem is necessary. Equally you may complete the formulation only to find that there is no apparent solution to the problem as formulated. Typically this may imply an incorrect formulation. It is equally important that once an optimal solution has been found, you need to 'translate' the solution back into the original, verbal, problem to ensure that the mathematical solution is appropriate for the original problem. A frequent mistake made by many students is to produce a formulation (often lacking some critical constraint) to solve the problem and then simply to assume that because they have a solution then their formulation must be correct. Only if the mathematical solution can be tied in with the original problem are we in a position to assume that our problem formulation is the correct one.

To illustrate the process and to provide examples of some of the more common areas of LP applications to business problems we shall now look at a number of problems and their formulation in detail. These problems have been categorized in terms of their general area of applicability but it must be stressed that the divisions between such categories are arbitrary and serve only as a general guide. In the real world practical applications of the technique will not fall neatly into one particular category, although it is frequently useful to undertake such categorization to help focus on an appropriate overall structure to the formulation.

MANAGEMENT SCIENCE IN ACTION

A Marketing Planning Model at Marathon Oil Company

Marathon Oil Company has four refineries within the United States, operates 50 light products terminals and has product demand at more than 95 locations. The Supply and Transportation Division faces the problem of determining which refinery should supply which terminal and, at the same time, determining which products should be transported via pipeline, barge or tanker to minimize cost. Product demand must be satisfied, and the supply capability of each refinery must not be exceeded. To help solve this difficult problem, Marathon Oil developed a marketing planning model.

The marketing planning model is a large-scale linear programming model that takes into account sales not only at Marathon product terminals but also at all exchange locations. An exchange contract is an agreement with other oil product marketers that involves exchanging or trading Marathon's products for theirs at different locations. All pipelines, barges and tankers within Marathon's marketing area are also represented in the linear programming model. The objective of the model is to minimize the cost of meeting a given demand structure, taking into account sales price, pipeline tariffs, exchange contract costs, product demand, terminal operating costs, refining costs and product purchases.

The marketing planning model is used to solve a wide variety of planning problems that vary from evaluating gasoline blending economics to analyzing the economics of a new terminal or pipeline. With daily sales of about ten million gallons of refined light product, a saving of even one-thousandth of a cent per gallon can result in significant long-term savings. At the same time, what may appear to be a saving in one area, such as refining or transportation, may actually add to overall costs when the effects are fully realized throughout the system. The marketing planning model allows a simultaneous examination of this total effect.

Based on information provided by Robert W. Wernert at Marathon Oil Company, Findlay, Ohio.

4.2 Production Management Applications

We have already introduced and examined in detail applications that fall into this general category (the GulfGolf problem in the previous chapters for example). Typically such problems involve a range of available resources each of which is available in only limited quantities. Demand for these resources typically arises from the production of items, and the solution to the problem provides the 'ideal' product mix in the sense that it optimizes the use of the available resources in the context of some defined objective, typically expressed in terms of profit, of revenue or of cost. This is one of the classic areas of LP applications. Given that in most business organizations some resources will be in short supply and that such resources face competing demands, then LP is an obvious method of determining an optimum allocation of such scarce resources. However, production management applications can go further than the standard 'how much of each product shall we make' problem. In this section we shall look at production management applications looking at make-or-buy decisions, production scheduling and workforce planning.

Make-or-Buy Decisions

We illustrate the use of a linear programming model to determine how much of each of several component parts a company should manufacture and how much it should purchase from an outside supplier. Such a decision is referred to as a make-or-buy decision.

The Janders Company markets various business and engineering products across Europe. Currently, Janders is preparing to introduce two new PDAs (Personal Digital Assistant): one for the business market called the Financial Manager and one for the engineering market called the Technician. Each PDA has three components: a base, an electronic cartridge and a faceplate or top. The same base is used for both products, but the cartridges and tops are different. All components can be manufactured by the company or purchased from outside suppliers. The manufacturing costs and purchase prices for the components are summarized in Table 4.1.

Company forecasters indicate that 3000 Financial Manager PDAs and 2000 Technician PDAs will be needed for the next production period. However, manufacturing capacity is limited. The company has 200 hours of regular manufacturing time and 50 hours of overtime that can be scheduled for the calculators. Overtime involves a premium at the additional cost of €9 per hour. Table 4.2 shows manufacturing times (in minutes) for the components.

Let us apply our formulation process outlined in Section 4.1. We already have a description of the problem. Given that we have information on costs, then it seems likely that a suitable objective will be to minimize production costs for the two products. A number of constraints become apparent: we must produce enough of the two types of PDA to meet forecasted demand; there is limited regular manufacturing time; there is limited overtime. The decision variables are then the quantities of the five components that we either manufacture ourselves or that we buy in from our suppliers and we show these as follows:

BM = number of bases manufactured
BP = number of bases purchased
FCM = number of Financial cartridges manufactured
FCP = number of Financial cartridges purchased
TCM = number of Technician cartridges manufactured
TCP = number of Technician cartridges purchased
FTM = number of Financial tops manufactured
FTP = number of Financial tops purchased
TTM = number of Technician tops manufactured
TTP = number of Technician tops purchased

One additional decision variable is needed to determine the hours of overtime that must be scheduled:

OT = number of hours of overtime to be scheduled

The objective function is to minimize the total cost, including manufacturing costs, purchase costs and overtime costs. Using the cost-per-unit data in Table 4.1 and

Table 4.1 Manufacturing Costs and Purchase Prices for Janders PDA Components

	Cost per Unit, €	
Component	**Manufacture (regular time)**	**Purchase**
Base	€0.50	€0.60
Financial cartridge	€3.75	€4.00
Technician cartridge	€3.30	€3.90
Financial top	€0.60	€0.65
Technician top	€0.75	€0.78

Table 4.2 Manufacturing Times in Minutes Per Unit for Janders PDA Components

Component	Manufacturing Time
Base	1.0
Financial cartridge	3.0
Technician cartridge	2.5
Financial top	1.0
Technician top	1.5

the overtime premium cost rate of €9 per hour, we can write the objective function as:

$$\text{Min} \quad 0.5BM + 0.6BP + 3.75FCM + 4FCP + 3.3TCM + 3.9TCP + 0.6FTM$$
$$+ 0.65FTP + 0.75TTM + 0.78TTP + 9OT$$

The first five constraints specify the number of each component needed to satisfy the demand for 3000 Financial Manager PDAs and 2000 Technician PDAs. A total of 5000 base components are needed, with the number of other components depending on the demand for the particular calculator. The five demand constraints are:

$$\begin{aligned} BM + BP &= 5000 \quad \text{Bases} \\ FCM + FCP &= 3000 \quad \text{Financial cartridges} \\ TCM + TCP &= 2000 \quad \text{Technician cartridges} \\ FTM + FTP &= 3000 \quad \text{Financial tops} \\ TTM + TTP &= 2000 \quad \text{Technician tops} \end{aligned}$$

Two constraints are needed to guarantee that manufacturing capacities for regular time and overtime cannot be exceeded. The first constraint limits overtime capacity to 50 hours, or:

$$OT \leq 50$$

The same units of measurement must be used for both the left-hand side and right-hand side of the constraint. In this case, minutes are used.

The second constraint states that the total manufacturing time required for all components must be less than or equal to the total manufacturing capacity, including regular time plus overtime. The manufacturing times for the components are expressed in minutes, so we state the total manufacturing capacity constraint in minutes, with the 200 hours of regular time capacity becoming $60(200) = 12\,000$ minutes. The actual overtime required is unknown at this point, so we write the overtime as $60OT$ minutes. Using the manufacturing times from Table 4.2, we have:

$$BM + 3FCM + 2.5TCM + FTM + 1.5TTM \leq 12000 + 60OT$$

Moving the decision variable for overtime to the left-hand side of the constraint provides the manufacturing capacity constraint:

$$BM + 3FCM + 2.5TCM + FTM + 1.5TTM - 60OT \leq 12000$$

The complete formulation of the Janders make-or-buy problem with all decision variables greater than or equal to zero is then:

$$\begin{aligned}\text{Min}\quad & 0.5BM + 0.6BP + 3.75FCM + 4FCP + 3.3TCM + 3.9TCP \\ & +0.6FTM + 0.65FTP + 0.75TTM + 0.78TTP + 9OT\end{aligned}$$

s.t.

$$\begin{array}{lr l}
BM + BP = & 5000 & \text{Bases} \\
FCM + FCP = & 3000 & \text{Financial cartridges} \\
TCM + TCP = & 2000 & \text{Technician cartridges} \\
FTM + FTP = & 3000 & \text{Financial tops} \\
TTM + TTP = & 2000 & \text{Technician tops} \\
OT \leq & 50 & \text{Overtime hours} \\
BM + 3FCM + 2.5TCM + FTM + 1.5TTM - 60OT \leq & 12000 & \text{Manufacturing capacity}
\end{array}$$

The optimal solution to this 11-variable, 7-constraint linear program is shown in Figure 4.1. If we pull the decision variable values together, we see that we have the following, in terms of number of units:

Component	Manufactured	Purchased	Total
Bases	5 000		5 000
Financial cartridges	666.7	2 333.3	3 000
Technician cartridges	2 000		2 000
Financial tops		3 000	3 000
Technician tops	2 000		2 000

To minimize cost the company should manufacture all the bases, technician cartridges and technician tops itself. All the financial tops should be bought in from suppliers. Production of financial cartridges should be split with the company manufacturing 667 (we round the solution) and buying in the remaining 2333. We shall not carry out a full sensitivity analysis since our main interest in this chapter is on formulation, but we shall highlight a few of the findings and you should complete the rest of the analysis yourself.

We note that we are not using any of the 50 hours available as overtime. Examination of the reduced costs value of €4 indicates that overtime costs would have to fall by €4 per hour (to €5) for them to be financially viable. We can also assess the effect of any price changes by our suppliers. For example, we are currently purchasing zero bases from our suppliers. Examination of the allowable decrease shows that we would continue to do this as long as the bought-in cost was higher than €0.583 (0.60 – 0.017). In other words if our supplier continues to charge at least €0.583 for bases we would continue to manufacture in-house, other things being equal.

Production Scheduling

One of the most important applications of linear programming deals with multiperiod planning such as production scheduling. The solution to a production scheduling problem enables the manager to establish an efficient low-cost production schedule for one or more products over several time periods (weeks or months). Essentially, a production scheduling problem can be viewed as a product-mix problem for each of several periods in the future. The manager must determine the production levels that will allow the company to meet product demand requirements, given limitations on production capacity, workforce capacity and storage space, while minimizing total production costs or maximizing profit.

Figure 4.1 The Excel Solution for the Janders Make-or-Buy Problem

TARGET CELL (MIN)

Name	Original Value	Final Value
Objective Function	0	24443.33333

ADJUSTABLE CELLS

Name	Original Value	Final Value
BM	0	5000
BP	0	0
FCM	0	666.6666667
FCP	0	2333.333333
TCM	0	2000
TCP	0	0
FTM	0	0
FTP	0	3000
TTM	0	0
TTP	0	2000
OT	0	0

CONSTRAINTS

Name	Cell Value	Status	Slack
Bases	5000	Not Binding	0
Financial cartridges	3000	Not Binding	0
Technician cartridges	2000	Not Binding	0
Financial tops	3000	Not Binding	0
Technician tops	2000	Not Binding	0
Overtime	0	Not Binding	50
Manf capacity	12000	Binding	0

ADJUSTABLE CELLS

Name	Final Value	Reduced Cost	Objective Coefficient	Allowable Increase	Allowable Decrease
BM	5000	0	0.5	0.016666667	1E+30
BP	0	0.016666667	0.6	1E+30	0.016666667
FCM	666.6666667	0	3.75	0.1	0.05
FCP	2333.333333	0	4	0.05	0.1
TCM	2000	0	3.3	0.391666667	1E+30
TCP	0	0.391666667	3.9	1E+30	0.391666667
FTM	0	0.033333333	0.6	1E+30	0.033333333
FTP	3000	0	0.65	0.033333333	1E+30
TTM	0	0.095	0.75	1E+30	0.095
TTP	2000	0	0.78	0.095	1E+30
OT	0	4	9	1E+30	4

EXCEL *file*

Janders

CONSTRAINTS

Name	Final Value	Shadow Price	Constraint R.H. Side	Allowable Increase	Allowable Decrease
Bases	5000	0.583333333	5000	2000	5000
Financial cartridges	3000	4	3000	1E+30	2333.333333
Technician cartridges	2000	3.508333333	2000	800	2000
Financial tops	3000	0.65	3000	1E+30	3000
Technician tops	2000	0.78	2000	1E+30	2000
Overtime	0	0	50	1E+30	50
Manf capacity	12000	-0.083333333	12000	7000	2000

One advantage of using linear programming for production scheduling problems is that they recur. A production schedule must be established for the current month, then again for the next month, for the month after that and so on. When looking at the problem each month, the production manager will find that, although demand for the products has changed, production times, production capacities, storage space limitations and so on are roughly the same. So, the production manager is basically re-solving the same problem handled in previous months, and a general linear programming model of the production scheduling procedure may be frequently applied. Once the model has been formulated, the manager can simply supply the data – demand, capacities and so on – for the given production period and use the linear programming model repeatedly to develop the production schedule.

Let us consider the case of the Bollinger Electronics Company, which produces two different electronic components for a major aeroplane engine manufacturer. The aeroplane engine manufacturer notifies the Bollinger sales office each quarter of its monthly requirements for components for each of the next three months. The monthly requirements for the components may vary considerably, depending on the type of engine the aeroplane engine manufacturer is producing. The order shown in Table 4.3 has just been received for the next three-month period.

After the order is processed, a demand statement is sent to the production department. The production department must then develop a three-month production plan for the components. In arriving at the desired schedule, the production manager will want to identify the following:

1 Production cost.
2 Inventory, or stock, holding cost.
3 Change-in-production-level costs.

Production cost will be the actual cost of producing the components. *Inventory, or stock, holding cost* will measure the cost of holding finished components in stock until they are shipped to the customer. It may be, for example, in April, that we decide to produce more than the customer needs in that month. Surplus production would then need to be stored until May or even June. *Change-in-production-level* costs refer to costs incurred when production levels are changed from one period to another. Increasing production, for example, may need extra staff, extra supplies; decreasing production may mean laying off staff temporarily and cancelling supplies that have been ordered. Such short-term actions may cost the company money.

In the remainder of this section, we show how to formulate a linear programming model of the production and inventory process for Bollinger Electronics to minimize the total cost.

To develop the model, we let x_{im} denote the production volume in units for product i in month m. Here $i = 1, 2,$ and $m = 1, 2, 3$; $i = 1$ refers to component 322A, $i = 2$ refers to component 802B, $m = 1$ refers to April, $m = 2$ refers to May and $m = 3$ refers to June. The purpose of the double subscript is to provide a more descriptive notation. We could simply use x_6 to represent the number of units of product 2 produced in month 3, but x_{23} is more descriptive, identifying directly the product and month represented by the variable.

Component 322A costs €20 per unit produced and component 802B costs €10 per unit produced, so the total production cost part of the objective function is:

$$\text{Total production cost} = 20x_{11} + 20x_{12} + 20x_{13} + 10x_{21} + 10x_{22} + 10x_{23}$$

Because the production cost per unit is the same each month, we don't need to include the production costs in the objective function; that is, regardless of the production schedule selected, the total production cost will remain the same. In other words, production costs are not relevant costs for the production scheduling decision under consideration. In cases in which the production cost per unit is expected to change each month, the variable production costs per unit per month must be included in the objective function. The solution for the Bollinger Electronics problem will be the same whether these costs are included, therefore we include them so that the value of the linear programming objective function will include all the costs associated with the problem.

To incorporate the relevant inventory holding costs into the model, we let s_{im} denote the inventory level for product i at the end of month m. Bollinger determined that on a monthly basis inventory holding costs are 1.5 per cent of the cost of the product; that is, (0.015)(€20) = €0.30 per unit for component 322A and (0.015)(€10) = €0.15 per unit for component 802B. A common assumption made in using the linear programming approach to production scheduling is that monthly ending inventories are an acceptable approximation to the average inventory levels throughout the month. Making this assumption, we write the inventory holding cost portion of the objective function as:

$$\text{Inventory holding cost} = 0.30s_{11} + 0.30s_{12} + 0.30s_{13} + 0.15s_{21} + 0.15s_{22} + 0.15s_{23}$$

To incorporate the costs of fluctuations in production levels from month to month, we need to define two additional variables:

$$I_m = \text{increase in the total production level necessary during month } m$$
$$D_m = \text{decrease in the total production level necessary during month } m$$

Table 4.3 Three-Month Demand Schedule for Bollinger Electronics Company

Component	April	May	June
322A	1 000	3 000	5 000
802B	1 000	500	3 000

After estimating the effects of employee layoffs, turnovers, reassignment training costs and other costs associated with fluctuating production levels, Bollinger estimates that the cost associated with increasing the production level for any month is €0.50 per unit increase. A similar cost associated with decreasing the production level for any month is €0.20 per unit. Thus, we write the third portion of the objective function as:

$$\begin{aligned}\text{Change-in-production-level costs} = {} & 0.5I_1 + 0.50I_2 + 0.50I_3 \\ & + 0.20D_1 + 0.20D_2 + 0.20D_3\end{aligned}$$

Note that the cost associated with changes in production level is a function of the change in the total number of units produced in month m compared to the total number of units produced in month $m - 1$. In other production scheduling applications, fluctuations in production level might be measured in terms of machine hours or labour-hours required rather than in terms of the total number of units produced.

Combining all three costs, the complete objective function becomes:

$$\begin{aligned}\text{Min} \quad & 20x_{11} + 20x_{12} + 20x_{13} + 10x_{21} + 10x_{22} + 10x_{23} + 0.30s_{11} \\ & + 0.30s_{12} + 0.30s_{13} + 0.15s_{21} + 0.50s_{22} + 0.15s_{23} + 0.50I_1 \\ & + 0.50I_2 + 0.50I_3 + 0.20D_1 + 0.20D_3 + 0.20D_3\end{aligned}$$

We now consider the constraints. First, we must guarantee that the schedule meets customer demand. Because the units shipped can come from the current month's production or from inventory carried over from previous months, the demand requirement takes the form:

$$\begin{pmatrix}\text{Ending} \\ \text{inventory} \\ \text{from previous} \\ \text{month}\end{pmatrix} + \begin{pmatrix}\text{Current} \\ \text{production}\end{pmatrix} - \begin{pmatrix}\text{Ending} \\ \text{inventory} \\ \text{for this} \\ \text{month}\end{pmatrix} = \begin{pmatrix}\text{This month's} \\ \text{demand}\end{pmatrix}$$

Suppose that the inventories at the beginning of the three-month scheduling period were 500 units for component 322A and 200 units for component 802B. The demand for both products in the first month (April) was 1000 units, so the constraints for meeting demand in the first month become:

$$\begin{aligned}500 + x_{11} - s_{11} &= 1000 \\ 200 + x_{21} - s_{21} &= 1000\end{aligned}$$

Moving the constants to the right-hand side, we have:

$$\begin{aligned}x_{11} - s_{11} &= 500 \\ x_{21} - s_{21} &= 800\end{aligned}$$

Similarly, we need demand constraints for both products in the second and third months. We write them as follows.

Month 2

$$\begin{aligned}s_{11} + x_{12} - s_{12} &= 3000 \\ s_{21} + x_{22} - s_{22} &= 500\end{aligned}$$

Month 3

$$\begin{aligned}s_{12} + x_{13} - s_{13} &= 5000 \\ s_{22} + x_{23} - s_{23} &= 3000\end{aligned}$$

Table 4.4 Machine, Labour and Storage Capacities for Bollinger Electronics

Month	Machine Capacity (hours)	Labour Capacity (hours)	Storage Capacity (square metres)
April	400	300	10 000
May	500	300	10 000
June	600	300	10 000

If the company specifies a minimum inventory level at the end of the three-month period of at least 400 units of component 322A and at least 200 units of component 802B, we can add the constraints:

$$s_{13} \geq 400$$
$$s_{23} \geq 200$$

Suppose that we have the additional information on machine, labour and storage capacity shown in Table 4.4. Machine, labour and storage space requirements are given in Table 4.5. To reflect these limitations, the following constraints are necessary.

Machine Capacity

$$0.10x_{11} + 0.08x_{21} \leq 400 \quad \text{Month 1}$$
$$0.10x_{12} + 0.08x_{22} \leq 500 \quad \text{Month 2}$$
$$0.10x_{13} + 0.08x_{23} \leq 600 \quad \text{Month 3}$$

Labour Capacity

$$0.05x_{11} + 0.07x_{21} \leq 300 \quad \text{Month 1}$$
$$0.05x_{12} + 0.07x_{22} \leq 300 \quad \text{Month 2}$$
$$0.05x_{13} + 0.07x_{23} \leq 300 \quad \text{Month 3}$$

Storage Capacity

$$2s_{11} + 3s_{21} \leq 10000 \quad \text{Month 1}$$
$$2s_{12} + 3s_{22} \leq 10000 \quad \text{Month 2}$$
$$2s_{13} + 3s_{23} \leq 10000 \quad \text{Month 3}$$

One final set of constraints must be added to guarantee that I_m and D_m will reflect the increase or decrease in the total production level for month m. Suppose that the production levels for March, the month before the start of the current production scheduling period, had been 1500 units of component 322A and 1000 units of component 802B for a total production level of 1500 + 1000 = 2500 units.

Table 4.5 Machine, Labour and Storage Requirements for Components 322A and 802B

Component	Machine (hours/unit)	Labour (hours/unit)	Storage (square metres/unit)
322A	0.10	0.05	2
802B	0.08	0.07	3

We can find the amount of the change in production for April from the relationship:

$$\text{April production} - \text{March production} = \text{Change}$$

Using the April production variables, x_{11} and x_{21}, and the March production of 2500 units, we have:

$$(x_{11} + x_{21}) - 2500 = \text{Change}$$

Note that the change can be positive or negative. A positive change reflects an increase in the total production level, and a negative change reflects a decrease in the total production level. We can use the increase in production for April, I_1, and the decrease in production for April, D_1, to specify the constraint for the change in total production for the month of April:

$$(x_{11} + x_{21}) - 2500 = I_1 - D_1$$

Of course, we cannot have an increase in production and a decrease in production during the same one-month period; thus, either, I_1 or D_1 will be zero. If April requires 3000 units of production, $I_1 = 500$ and $D_1 = 0$. If April requires 2200 units of production, $I_1 = 0$ and $D_1 = 300$. This approach of denoting the change in production level as the difference between two nonnegative variables, I_1 and D_1, permits both positive and negative changes in the total production level. If a single variable (say, c_m) had been used to represent the change in production level, only positive changes would be possible because of the nonnegativity requirement.

Using the same approach in May and June (always subtracting the previous month's total production from the current month's total production), we obtain the constraints for the second and third months of the production scheduling period:

$$(x_{12} + x_{22}) - (x_{11} + x_{21}) = I_2 - D_2$$
$$(x_{13} + x_{23}) - (x_{12} + x_{22}) = I_3 - D_3$$

Placing the variables on the left-hand side and the constants on the right-hand side yields the complete set of what are commonly referred to as production-smoothing constraints:

$$\begin{aligned} x_{11} + x_{21} \qquad\qquad\qquad\qquad\qquad & - I_1 + D_1 = 2500 \\ -x_{11} - x_{21} + x_{12} + x_{22} \qquad\qquad\quad & - I_2 + D_2 = 0 \\ - x_{12} - x_{22} + x_{13} + x_{23} & - I_3 + D_3 = 0 \end{aligned}$$

Problem 14 involves a production scheduling application with labour-smoothing constraints.

The initially rather small, two-product, three-month scheduling problem has now developed into an 18-variable, 20-constraint linear programming problem. Note that in this problem we were concerned only with one type of machine process, one type of labour and one type of storage area. Actual production scheduling problems usually involve several machine types, several labour grades and/or several storage areas, requiring large-scale linear programmes. For instance, a problem involving 100 products over a 12-month period could have more than 1000 variables and constraints.

The full model formulation is then:

$$\text{Min } 20x_{11} + 20x_{12} + 20x_{13} + 10x_{21} + 10x_{22} + 10x_{23} + 0.3s_{11} + 0.3s_{12} + 0.3s_{13} + 0.15s_{21} + 0.5s_{22} + 0.15s_{23} + 0.5I_1 + 0.5I_2 + 0.5I_3 + 0.2D_1 + 0.2D_2 + 0.2D_3$$

s.t.

$$x_{11} - s_{11} = 500$$
$$x_{21} - s_{21} = 800$$
$$s_{11} + x_{12} - s_{12} = 3000$$
$$s_{21} + x_{22} - s_{22} = 500$$
$$s_{12} + x_{23} - s_{13} = 5000$$

$$s_{22} + x_{23} - s_{23} = 3000$$
$$s_{13} \geq 400$$
$$s_{23} > 200$$
$$0.1x_{11} + 0.08x_{21} \leq 400$$
$$0.1x_{12} + 0.08x_{22} \leq 500$$
$$0.1x_{13} + 0.08x_{23} \leq 600$$
$$0.05x_{11} + 0.07x_{21} \leq 300$$
$$0.05x_{12} + 0.07x_{22} \leq 300$$
$$0.05x_{13} + 0.07x_{23} < 300$$
$$2s_{11} + 3s_{21} \leq 10000$$
$$2s_{12} + 3s_{22} < 10000$$
$$2s_{13} + 3s_{23} \leq 10000$$
$$x_{11} + x_{21} - I_1 + D_1 = 2500$$
$$-x_{11} - x_{21} + x_{12} + x_{22} - I_2 + D_2 = 0$$
$$-x_{12} - x_{22} + x_{13} + x_{23} - I_3 + D_3 = 0$$
$$x_{11},\ x_{12},\ x_{13},\ x_{21},\ x_{22},\ x_{23},\ s_{11},\ s_{12},\ s_{13},\ s_{21}, s_{22},\ s_{23}, I_1,\ I_2, I_3,\ D_2,\ D_3 \geq 0$$

Linear programming models for production scheduling are often very large. Thousands of decision variables and constraints are necessary when the problem involves numerous products, machines and time periods. Data collection for large-scale models can be more time-consuming than either the formulation of the model or the development of the computer solution.

Figure 4.2 shows the optimal solution to the Bollinger Electronics production scheduling problem. Table 4.6 contains a portion of the managerial report based on the optimal solution.

Consider the monthly variation in the production and inventory schedule shown in Table 4.6. Recall that the inventory cost for component 802B is one-half the inventory cost for component 322A. Therefore, as might be expected, component 802B is produced heavily in the first month (April) and then held in inventory for the demand that will occur in future months. Component 322A tends to be produced when needed, and only small amounts are carried in inventory.

The costs of increasing and decreasing the total production volume tend to smooth the monthly variations. In fact, the minimum-cost schedule calls for a 500-unit increase in total production in April and a 2200-unit increase in total production in May. The May production level of 5200 units is then maintained during June.

The machine usage section of the report shows ample machine capacity in all three months. However, labour capacity is at full utilization (slack = 0 for constraint 13 in Figure 4.2) in the month of May. The dual price shows that an additional hour of labour capacity in May will improve the value of the optimal solution (lower cost) by approximately €1.11.

A linear programming model of a two-product, three-month production system can provide valuable information in terms of identifying a minimum-cost production schedule. In larger production systems, where the number of variables and constraints is too large to track manually, linear programming models can provide a significant advantage in developing cost-saving production schedules.

Workforce Assignment

Workforce assignment problems frequently occur when production managers must make decisions involving staffing requirements for a given planning period. Workforce assignments often have some flexibility, and at least some personnel can be assigned to more than one department or work centre. Such is the case when employees have been cross-trained on two or more jobs or, for instance, when sales personnel can be transferred between stores. In the following application, we show how linear programming can be used to determine not only an optimal product mix, but also an optimal workforce assignment.

Figure 4.2 The Management Scientist Solution for the Bollinger Electronics Problem

EXCEL *file*

BOLLINGER

```
Objective Function Value =           225295.000

      Variable              Value              Reduced Costs
   --------------      ---------------      -----------------
         X11                500.000                 0.000
         X12               3200.000                 0.000
         X13               5200.000                 0.000
         X21               2500.000                 0.000
         X22               2000.000                 0.000
         X23                  0.000                 0.128
         S11                  0.000                 0.172
         S12                200.000                 0.000
         S13                400.000                 0.000
         S21               1700.000                 0.000
         S22               3200.000                 0.000
         S23                200.000                 0.000
         I1                 500.000                 0.000
         I2                2200.000                 0.000
         I3                   0.000                 0.072
         D1                   0.000                 0.700
         D2                   0.000                 0.700
         D3                   0.000                 0.628

     Constraint          Slack/Surplus           Dual Prices
   --------------      ---------------      -----------------
          1                   0.000               -20.000
          2                   0.000               -10.000
          3                   0.000               -20.128
          4                   0.000               -10.150
          5                   0.000               -20.428
          6                   0.000               -10.300
          7                   0.000               -20.728
          8                   0.000               -10.450
          9                 150.000                 0.000
         10                  20.000                 0.000
         11                  80.000                 0.000
         12                 100.000                 0.000
         13                   0.000                 1.111
         14                  40.000                 0.000
         15                4900.000                 0.000
         16                   0.000                 0.000
         17                8600.000                 0.000
         18                   0.000                 0.500
         19                   0.000                 0.500
         20                   0.000                 0.428
```

McCormick Manufacturing Company produces two products with contributions to profit per unit of €10 and €9, respectively. The labour requirements per unit produced and the total hours of labour available from personnel assigned to each of four departments are shown in Table 4.7. Assuming that the number of hours

MANAGEMENT SCIENCE IN ACTION

Scheduling the Orange Harvest in Brazil

Brazil is the world's largest exporter of orange juice and the product is critically important both to the economy at the macroeconomic level and to the individual farmers at the microeconomic level. To remain competitive, the quality of the final product must be both consistent and high. However, this is not necessarily as easy as it might seem. Typically, the orange producers are small, independent farmers, over 20 000 in one area of Brazil alone, who sell their produce to the processing companies who then transform the oranges into orange juice. The quality and quantity of the finished product will depend on several factors: the variety of oranges grown; their juice yield; the ratio of juice to solids; their acidity. These factors in turn are heavily affected by the decision of when to harvest the orange crop. This project developed a linear programming model to investigate the effect of the orange harvesting schedule. The model took into account factors such as the productivity characteristics of orange orchards, the fruit characteristics and transportation distances from the orchards to the processing plant. The model used two alternative objective functions to allow different scenarios to be examined. The first maximized the total soluble solids achieved through processing; the second maximized the total quantity of oranges harvested. The project found that, using the model, profit contribution could be increased by around US$2.5 million in a season.

Based on J. V. Caixeta-Filho, 'Orange harvesting scheduling management', *Journal of the Operational Research Society* 57 (2006): 37–42.

available in each department is fixed, we can formulate McCormick's problem as a standard product-mix linear program with the following decision variables:

$$P_1 = \text{units of product 1}$$
$$P_2 = \text{units of product 2}$$

Table 4.6 Minimum Cost Production Schedule Information for the Bollinger Electronics Problem

Activity	April	May	June
Production			
Component 322A	500	3 200	5 200
Component 802B	2 500	2 000	0
Totals	3 000	5 200	5 200
Ending inventory			
Component 322A	0	200	400
Component 802B	1 700	3 200	200
Machine usage			
Scheduled hours	250	480	520
Slack capacity hours	150	20	80
Labour usage			
Scheduled hours	200	300	260
Slack capacity hours	100	0	40
Storage usage			
Scheduled storage	5 100	10 000	1 400
Slack capacity	4 900	0	8 600
Total production, inventory and production-smoothing cost = €225 295			

Table 4.7 Departmental Labour-Hours Per Unit and Total Hours Available for the McCormick Manufacturing Company

Department	Labour-Hours per Unit		Total Hours Available
	Product 1	Product 2	
1	0.65	0.95	6 500
2	0.45	0.85	6 000
3	1.00	0.70	7 000
4	0.15	0.30	1 400

The linear programme is:

$$
\begin{aligned}
\text{Max} \quad & 10P_1 + 9P_2 \\
\text{s.t.} \quad & \\
& 0.65P_1 + 0.95P_2 \leq 6500 \\
& 0.45P_1 + 0.85P_2 \leq 6000 \\
& 1.00P_1 + 0.70P_2 \leq 7000 \\
& 0.15P_1 + 0.30P_2 \leq 1400 \\
& P_1, P_2 \geq 0
\end{aligned}
$$

The optimal solution to the linear programming model is shown in Figure 4.3. After rounding, it calls for 5744 units of product 1, 1795 units of product 2 and a total profit of €73 590. With this optimal solution, departments 3 and 4 are operating at capacity, and departments 1 and 2 have a slack of approximately 1062 and 1890 hours, respectively. We would anticipate that the product mix would change and that the total profit would increase if the workforce assignment could be revised so that the slack, or unused hours, in departments 1 and 2 could be transferred to the departments currently working at capacity. However, the production manager may be uncertain as to how the workforce should be reallocated among the four departments. Let us expand the linear programming model to include decision variables that will help determine the optimal workforce assignment in addition to the profit-maximizing product mix.

However, the company are keen to improve productivity and are launching a training programme for their workforce. The cross-training programme will train a number of workers in each department to undertake the task of workers in other departments. This will provide the company with some labour flexibility. By taking advantage of the cross-training skills, a limited number of employees and labour-hours may be transferred from one department to another. For example, the cross-training permits transfers as shown in Table 4.8. Row 1 of this table shows that some employees assigned to department 1 have cross-training skills that permit them to be transferred to department 2 or 3. The right-hand column shows that, for the current production planning period, a maximum of 400 hours can be transferred from department 1. Similar cross-training transfer capabilities and capacities are shown for departments 2, 3 and 4.

When workforce assignments are flexible, we do not automatically know how many hours of labour should be assigned to or be transferred from each department. We need to add decision variables to the linear programming model to account for such changes.

Figure 4.3 The Excel Solution for the McCormick Manufacturing Company Problem with no Workforce Transfers Permitted

TARGET CELL (MAX)

Name	Original Value	Final Value
Objective function	0	73589.74359

ADJUSTABLE CELLS

Name	Original Value	Final Value
Units P1	0	5743.589744
Units P2	0	1794.871795

CONSTRAINTS

Name	Cell Value	Status	Slack
Dept. 1	5438.461538	Not Binding	1061.538462
Dept. 2	4110.25641	Not Binding	1889.74359
Dept. 3	7000	Binding	0
Dept. 4	1400	Binding	0

ADJUSTABLE CELLS

Name	Final Value	Reduced Cost	Objective Coefficient	Allowable Increase	Allowable Decrease
Units P1	5743.589744	0	10	2.857142857	5.5
Units P2	1794.871795	0	9	11	2

CONSTRAINTS

Name	Final Value	Shadow Price	Constraint R.H. Side	Allowable Increase	Allowable Decrease
Dept. 1	5438.461538	0	6500	1E+30	1061.538462
Dept. 2	4110.25641	0	6000	1E+30	1889.74359
Dept. 3	7000	8.461538462	7000	2333.333333	3733.333333
Dept. 4	1400	10.25641026	1400	418.1818182	350

EXCEL *file*

McCormick

b_i = the labour-hours allocated to department i for $i = 1, 2, 3,$ and 4

t_{ij} = the labour-hours transferred from department i to department j

The right-hand sides are now treated as decision variables.

With the addition of decision variables b_1, b_2, b_3 and b_4, we write the capacity restrictions for the four departments as follows:

$$0.65P_1 + 0.95P_2 \leq b_1$$
$$0.45P_1 + 0.85P_2 \leq b_2$$
$$1.00P_1 + 0.70P_2 \leq b_3$$
$$0.15P_1 + 0.30P_2 \leq b_4$$

Since b_1, b_2, b_3 and b_4 are now decision variables, we follow the standard practice of placing these variables on the left side of the inequalities, and the first four constraints of the linear programming model become:

Table 4.8 Cross-Training Ability and Capacity Information

From Department	Cross-Training Transfers Permitted to Department 1	2	3	4	Maximum Hours Transferable
1	—	yes	yes	—	400
2	—	—	yes	yes	800
3	—	—	—	yes	100
4	yes	yes	—	—	200

$$\begin{aligned}
0.65P_1 + 0.95P_2 - b_1 \qquad\qquad\qquad &\leq 0\\
0.45P_1 + 0.86P_2 \qquad - b_2 \qquad\qquad &\leq 0\\
1.00P_1 + 0.70P_2 \qquad\qquad - b_3 \qquad &\leq 0\\
0.15P_1 + 0.30P_2 \qquad\qquad\qquad - b_4 &\leq 0
\end{aligned}$$

The labour-hours ultimately allocated to each department must be determined by a series of labour balance equations, or constraints, that include the number of hours initially assigned to each department plus the number of hours transferred into the department minus the number of hours transferred out of the department. Using department 1 as an example, we determine the workforce allocation as follows:

$$b_1 = \begin{pmatrix}\text{Hours}\\\text{initially in}\\\text{department 1}\end{pmatrix} + \begin{pmatrix}\text{Hours}\\\text{transferred into}\\\text{department 1}\end{pmatrix} - \begin{pmatrix}\text{Hours}\\\text{transferred out of}\\\text{department 1}\end{pmatrix}$$

Table 4.7 shows 6500 hours initially assigned to department 1. We use the transfer decision variables t_{i1} to denote transfers into department 1 and t_{1j} to denote transfers from department 1. Table 4.8 shows that the cross-training capabilities involving department 1 are restricted to transfers from department 4 (variable t_{41}) and transfers to either department 2 or department 3 (variables t_{12} and t_{13}). Thus, we can express the total workforce allocation for department 1 as:

$$b_1 = 6500 + t_{41} - t_{12} - t_{13}$$

Moving the decision variables for the workforce transfers to the left-hand side, we have the labour balance equation or constraint:

$$b_1 - t_{41} + t_{12} + t_{13} = 6500$$

This form of constraint will be needed for each of the four departments. Thus, the following labour balance constraints for departments 2, 3 and 4 would be added to the model.

$$\begin{aligned}
b_2 - t_{12} - t_{42} + t_{23} + t_{24} &= 6000\\
b_3 - t_{13} - t_{23} + t_{34} &= 7000\\
b_4 - t_{24} - t_{34} + t_{41} + t_{42} &= 1400
\end{aligned}$$

Finally, Table 4.8 shows the number of hours that may be transferred from each department is limited, indicating that a transfer capacity constraint must be added for each of the four departments. The additional constraints are:

$$\begin{aligned} t_{12} + t_{13} &\le 400 \\ t_{23} + t_{24} &\le 800 \\ t_{34} \quad &\le 100 \\ t_{41} + t_{42} &\le 200 \end{aligned}$$

The complete linear programming model has two product decision variables (P_1 and P_2), four department workforce assignment variables (b_1, b_2, b_3 and b_4), seven transfer variables (t_{12}, t_{13}, t_{23}, t_{24}, t_{34}, t_{41} and t_{42}) and 12 constraints. The full formulation is then:

$$\text{Max} \quad 10P_1 + 9P_2 + 0b_1 + 0b_2 + 0b_3 + 0b_4 + 0t_{12} + 0t_{13} + 0t_{23} + 0t_{24} + 0t_{34} + 0t_{41} + 0t_{42}$$

s.t.

$$\begin{aligned} 0.65P_1 + 0.95P_2 - b_1 &\le 0 \\ 0.45P_1 + 0.85P_2 - b_2 &\le 0 \\ P_1 + 0.7P_2 - b_3 &\le 0 \\ 0.15P_1 + 0.3P_2 - b_4 &\le 0 \\ b_1 + t_{12} + t_{13} - t_{41} &= 6500 \\ b_2 - t_{12} + t_{23} + t_{24} - t_{42} &= 6000 \\ b_3 - t_{13} - t_{23} + t_{34} &= 7000 \\ b_4 - t_{24} - t_{34} + t_{41} + t_{42} &= 1400 \\ t_{12} + t_{13} &\le 400 \\ t_{23} + t_{24} &\le 800 \\ t_{34} &\le 100 \\ t_{41} + t_{42} &\le 200 \end{aligned}$$

$$P_1,\ P_2,\ b_1,\ b_2,\ b_3,\ b_4,\ t_{12},\ t_{13},\ t_{23},\ t_{24},\ t_{34},\ t_{41},\ t_{42} \ge 0$$

Notice that the objective function shows all the decision variables even though only two of them have non-zero coefficients, since it is only production of P_1 and P_2 that contribute financially to profit. Figure 4.4 shows the optimal solution to the problem.

McCormick's profit can be increased by €84 011 – €73 590 = €10 421 by taking advantage of cross-training and workforce transfers. The optimal product mix of 6825 units of product 1 and 1751 units of product 2 can be achieved if $t_{13} = 400$ hours are transferred from department 1 to department 3; $t_{23} = 651$ hours are transferred from department 2 to department 3; and $t_{24} = 149$ hours are transferred from department 2 to department 4. The resulting workforce assignments for departments 1–4 would provide 6100, 5200, 8051 and 1549 hours, respectively.

Variations in the workforce assignment model could be used in situations such as allocating raw material resources to products, allocating machine time to products and allocating salesforce time to stores or sales territories.

If a manager has the flexibility to assign personnel to different departments, reduced workforce idle time, improved workforce utilization and improved profit should result. The linear programming model in this section automatically assigns employees and labour-hours to the departments in the most profitable manner.

4.3 Blending, Diet and Feed-Mix Problems

A large category of LP applications fall into the area generally known as *blending,* or *diet* or *feed-mix* problems. Typically such problems revolve around the requirement to mix together a variety of ingredients in order to produce some final product in such a way that the final product meets certain specified criteria. Applications of blending problems range from the oil industry where crude oils have to be blended with other ingredients to make a variety of petrols and related fuels, through the

MANAGEMENT SCIENCE IN ACTION

Pilot Staffing and Training at Continental Airlines

Making sure that you have the right staff with the right skills in the right place at the right time is critical for any organization. For large organizations workforce planning and scheduling is not a trivial task and typically takes time and resources to get right. No wonder that organizations are keen to better planning and scheduling methods available through the application of MS models. Continental Airlines did just that and has saved an estimated US$10 million a year as a result. The airline operates a complex global flight schedule with over 1100 flights each day utilizing around 350 aircraft of different types. Amongst its 44 000 employees it has around 4500 pilots based at its four main crew locations. Clearly on a routine basis the company has to make sure its pilots are matched properly to flights and to aircraft but this is a complex task involving a number of factors: the start and end points of the flight; the flight duration; the type of aircraft; the training and experience of the pilot. On top of this, staff preferences also need to be taken into account – the type of aircraft the pilot prefers to fly; the type of flight schedule they prefer; holiday and family commitments and so on. The company developed a decision support system, CrewResourceSolver, that comprised four inter-connected models. The Staffing model looked at current staff availability, expected staff demand, new staff recruitment and staff losses to identify staff shortage and surpluses. The Vacation model analyzed the vacation periods available to pilots to avoid staff shortages at peak demand periods. The Planning Optimization model matched pilot availability with the airline's operational requirements. Finally, the Training Optimization model developed a staff training plan for pilots undertaking training and development, for example to qualify to fly a different type of aeroplane. The integrated modelling approach has not only cut costs and saved time but has also allowed the staff planners to examine alternative options and led to a change in the way the airline plans its pilot staffing and training. Darryal Chadler, Director of Crew Resources and Administration at Continental commented '*Solver provides the opportunity to run numerous scenarios to select the optimal plan that will meet the airline's flying requirement. . . . The system will be an invaluable tool that will help us maintain pilot productivity as we manage our business in the future*'.

Based on G. Yu, J. Pachon, B. Thengvall, D. Chandler and A. Wilson, 'Optimizing Pilot Planning and Training for Continental Airlines', *Interfaces* 34 4 (2004): 253–64.

chemical industry producing drugs, medicines, fertilizers, etc., to the food industry where different foodstuffs have to be mixed together to produce some food item or a balanced meal.

The blending problem was first applied to the Philadelphia Refinery of Gulf Oil in the 1950s

The Delta Oil Company (DOC) operates in Nigeria and runs an oil refinery that blends three different petroleum components into two different fuels. The fuels are sold on to fuel companies around the world depending on demand and worldwide fuel prices. The company calculates its costs and profits using the US$. The company is trying to plan its daily production. Currently DOC estimates it can sell its regular fuel at $1 per litre and its premium fuel at $1.08 per litre. The cost of the three petroleum components that it uses are shown in Table 4.9, together with available quantities.

Product specifications for the regular and premium fuels restrict the amounts of each component that can be used in each gasoline product. Table 4.10 lists the product specifications. Current commitments to customers require DOC to produce at least 10 000 litres of regular fuel each day.

The DOC blending problem is to determine how many litres of each component should be used in the regular blend and how many should be used in the premium blend. The optimal blending solution should maximize the firm's profit, subject to the constraints on the available petroleum supplies shown in Table 4.9, the product specifications shown in Table 4.10, and the required 10 000 litres of regular fuel.

Figure 4.4 Excel Solution for the McCormick Manufacturing Company Problem

TARGET CELL (MAX)

Name	Original Value	Final Value
Objective function	0	84011.29944

ADJUSTABLE CELLS

Name	Original Value	Final Value
P1	0	6824.858757
P2	0	1751.412429
b1	0	6100
b2	0	4559.887006
b3	0	8050.847458
b4	0	1549.152542
t12	0	0
t13	0	400
t23	0	650.8474576
t24	0	149.1525424
t34	0	0
t41	0	0
t42	0	0

CONSTRAINTS

Name	Cell Value	Status	Slack
Dept. 1	1.81899E-12	Binding	0
Dept. 2	0	Binding	0
Dept. 3	1.81899E-12	Binding	0
Dept. 4	-2.27374E-13	Binding	0
Balance 1	6500	Binding	0
Balance 2	5359.887006	Not Binding	640.1129944
Balance 3	7000	Binding	0
Balance 4	1400	Binding	0
Transfer 1	400	Binding	0
Transfer 2	800	Binding	0
Transfer 3	0	Not Binding	100
Transfer 4	0	Not Binding	200

We define the decision variables as:

x_{ij} = litres of component i used in fuel j,
where $i = 1, 2,$ or 3 for components 1, 2, or 3,
and $j = r$ if regular or $j = p$ if premium

The six decision variables are:

x_{1r} = litres of component 1 in regular fuel
x_{2r} = litres of component 2 in regular fuel
x_{3r} = litres of component 3 in regular fuel
x_{1p} = litres of component 1 in premium fuel
x_{2p} = litres of component 2 in premium fuel
x_{3p} = litres of component 3 in premium fuel

Figure 4.4 (continued)

ADJUSTABLE CELLS

Name	Final Value	Reduced Cost	Objective Coefficient	Allowable Increase	Allowable Decrease
P1	6824.858757	0	10	0.35	1.692307692
P2	1751.412429	0	9	1.833333333	0.304347826
b1	6100	0	0	7.457627119	0.790960452
b2	4559.887006	0	0	0	0.663507109
b3	8050.847458	0	0	1.794871795	4.782608696
b4	1549.152542	0	0	7.373737374	1.794871795
t12	0	-8.248587571	0	8.248587571	1E+30
t13	400	0	0	1E+30	7.457627119
t23	650.8474576	0	0	0	4.782608696
t24	149.1525424	0	0	4.782608696	0
t34	0	0	0	0	1E+30
t41	0	-7.457627119	0	7.457627119	1E+30
t42	0	-8.248587571	0	8.248587571	1E+30

CONSTRAINTS

Name	Final Value	Shadow Price	Constraint R.H. Side	Allowable Increase	Allowable Decrease
Dept. 1	1.81899E-12	0.790960452	0	536.9668246	338.4615385
Dept. 2	0	0	0	4559.887006	640.1129944
Dept. 3	1.81899E-12	8.248587571	0	1192.307692	2266
Dept. 4	-2.27374E-13	8.248587571	0	133.3333333	581.8181818
Balance 1	6500	0.790960452	6500	536.9668246	338.4615385
Balance 2	5359.887006	0	6000	1E+30	640.1129944
Balance 3	7000	8.248587571	7000	1192.307692	2266
Balance 4	1400	8.248587571	1400	133.3333333	581.8181818
Transfer 1	400	7.457627119	400	266.6666667	400
Transfer 2	800	8.248587571	800	892.1259843	581.8181818
Transfer 3	0	0	100	1E+30	100
Transfer 4	0	0	200	1E+30	200

EXCEL *file*

McCormick

The total number of litres of each type of fuel produced is the sum of the number of litres produced using each of the three petroleum components.

Total litres Produced

$$\text{Regular fuel} = x_{1r} + x_{2r} + x_{3r}$$
$$\text{Premium fuel} = x_{1p} + x_{2p} + x_{3p}$$

The total litres of each petroleum component are calculated in a similar fashion.

Total Petroleum Component Use

$$\text{Component 1} = x_{1r} + x_{1p}$$
$$\text{Component 2} = x_{2r} + x_{2p}$$
$$\text{Component 3} = x_{3r} + x_{3p}$$

Table 4.9 Petroleum Cost and Supply for the DOC Blending Problem

Petroleum Component	Cost/litre	Maximum Available
1	\$0.50	5 000 litres
2	\$0.60	10 000 litres
3	\$0.84	10 000 litres

Table 4.10 Product Specifications for the DOC Blending Problem

Product	Specifications
Regular fuel	At most 30% component 1
	At least 40% component 2
	At most 20% component 3
Premium fuel	At least 25% component 1
	At most 40% component 2
	At least 30% component 3

We develop the objective function of maximizing the profit contribution by identifying the difference between the total revenue from both fuels and the total cost of the three petroleum components. By multiplying the \$1.00 per litre price by the total litres of regular fuel, the \$1.08 per litre price by the total litres of premium fuel, and the component cost per litre figures in Table 4.9 by the total litres of each component used, we obtain the objective function:

$$\begin{aligned} \text{Max} \quad & 1.00(x_{1r} + x_{2r} + x_{3r}) + 1.08(x_{1p} + x_{2p} + x_{3p}) \\ & - 0.50(x_{1r} + x_{1p}) - 0.60(x_{2r} + x_{2p}) - 0.84(x_{3r} + x_{3p}) \end{aligned}$$

When we combine terms, the objective function becomes:

$$\text{Max} \quad 0.50x_{1r} + 0.40x_{2r} + 0.16x_{3r} + 0.58x_{1p} + 0.48x_{2p} + 0.24x_{3p}$$

The limitations on the availability of the three petroleum components are:

$$\begin{aligned} x_{1r} + x_{1p} &\leq 5\,000 \quad \text{Component 1} \\ x_{2r} + x_{2p} &\leq 10\,000 \quad \text{Component 2} \\ x_{3r} + x_{3p} &\leq 10\,000 \quad \text{Component 3} \end{aligned}$$

Six constraints are now required to meet the product specifications stated in Table 4.10. The first specification states that component 1 can account for no more than 30 per cent of the total litres of regular fuel produced. That is,

$$x_{1r} \leq 0.30(x_{1r} + x_{2r} + x_{3r})$$

Rewriting this constraint with the variables on the left-hand side and a constant on the right-hand side yields:

$$0.70x_{1r} - 0.30x_{2r} - 0.30x_{32} \leq 0$$

The second product specification listed in Table 4.10 becomes:

$$x_{2r} \geq 0.40(x_{1r} + x_{2r} + x_{3r})$$

and thus:

$$-0.40x_{1r} + 0.60x_{2r} - 0.40x_{3r} \geq 0$$

Similarly, we write the four remaining blending specifications listed in Table 4.10 as:

$$\begin{aligned}
-0.20x_{1r} - 0.20x_{2r} + 0.80x_{3r} &\leq 0 \\
+0.75x_{1p} - 0.25x_{2p} - 0.25x_{3p} &\geq 0 \\
-0.40x_{1p} + 0.60x_{2p} - 0.40x_{3p} &\leq 0 \\
-0.30x_{1p} - 0.30x_{2p} + 0.70x_{3p} &\geq 0
\end{aligned}$$

The constraint for at least 10 000 litres of regular fuel is:

$$x_{1r} + x_{2r} + x_{3r} \geq 10\,000$$

The complete linear programming model with six decision variables and ten constraints is then:

$$\begin{array}{ll}
\text{Max} & 0.50x_{1r} + 0.40x_{2r} + 0.16x_{3r} + 0.58x_{1p} + 0.48x_{2p} + 0.24x_{3p} \\
\text{s.t.} & \\
& x_{1r} + x_{1p} \leq 5\,000 \\
& x_{2r} + x_{2p} \leq 10\,000 \\
& x_{3r} + x_{3p} \leq 10\,000 \\
& 0.70x_{1r} - 0.30x_{2r} - 0.30x_{3r} \leq 0 \\
& -0.40x_{1r} + 0.60x_{2r} - 0.40x_{3r} \geq 0 \\
& -0.20x_{1r} - 0.20x_{2r} + 0.80x_{3r} \leq 0 \\
& 0.75x_{1p} - 0.25x_{2p} - 0.25x_{3p} \geq 0 \\
& -0.40x_{1p} + 0.60x_{2p} - 0.40x_{3p} \leq 0 \\
& -0.30x_{1p} - 0.30x_{2p} + 0.70x_{3p} \geq 0 \\
& x_{1r} + x_{2r} + x_{3r} \geq 10\,000 \\
& x_{1r}, x_{2r}, x_{3r}, x_{1p}, x_{2p}, x_{3p} \geq 0
\end{array}$$

Try Problem 11 as another example of a blending model.

The optimal solution to the DOC blending problem is shown in Figure 4.5. The optimal solution, which provides a daily profit of $9300, is summarized in Table 4.11. The optimal blending strategy shows that 10 000 litres of regular fuel should be produced. The regular fuel will be manufactured as a blend of 8000 litres of component 2 and 2000 litres of component 3. The 15 000 litres of premium fuel will be manufactured as a blend of 5000 litres of component 1, 2000 litres of component 2 and 8000 litres of component 3.

The interpretation of the slack and surplus variables associated with the product specification constraints (constraints 4–9) in Figure 4.5 needs some clarification. If the constraint is a $\leq$ constraint, the value of the slack variable can be interpreted as the litres of component use below the maximum amount of the component use specified by the constraint. For example, the slack of 3000.000 for constraint 4 shows that component 1 use is 3000 litres below the maximum amount of component 1 that could have been used in the production of 10 000 litres of regular fuel. If the product specification constraint is a $\geq$ constraint, a surplus variable shows the litres of component use above the minimum amount of component use specified by the blending constraint. For example, the surplus of 4000.000 for constraint 5 shows that component 2 use is 4000 litres above the minimum amount of component 2 that must be used in the production of 10 000 litres of regular fuel.

Figure 4.5 The Management Scientist Solution for the DOC Blending Problem

EXCEL *file*

DOC

```
Objective Function Value =            9300.000

      Variable              Value            Reduced Costs
    --------------     ---------------     -----------------
          X1R                 0.000                 0.000
          X2R              8000.000                 0.000
          X3R              2000.000                 0.000
          X1P              5000.000                 0.000
          X2P              2000.000                 0.000
          X3P              8000.000                 0.000

     Constraint          Slack/Surplus          Dual Prices
    --------------     ---------------     -----------------
            1                 0.000                 0.580
            2                 0.000                 0.480
            3                 0.000                 0.240
            4              3000.000                 0.000
            5              4000.000                 0.000
            6                 0.000                 0.000
            7              1250.000                 0.000
            8              4000.000                 0.000
            9              3500.000                 0.000
           10                 0.000                -0.080
```

Table 4.11 DOC Gasoline Blending Solution

	litres of Component (percentage)			
Fuel	**Component 1**	**Component 2**	**Component 3**	**Total**
Regular	0 (0%)	8 000 (80%)	2 000 (20%)	10 000
Premium	5 000 (33⅓%)	2 000 (13⅓%)	8 000 (53⅓%)	15 000

NOTES AND COMMENTS

A convenient way to define the decision variables in a blending problem is to use a matrix in which the rows correspond to the raw materials and the columns correspond to the final products. For example, in the DOC blending problem, we could define the decision variables as follows:

		Final Products	
		Regular Fuel	**Premium Fuel**
Raw Materials	**Component 1**	x_{1r}	x_{1p}
	Component 2	x_{2r}	x_{2p}
	Component 3	x_{3r}	x_{3p}

This approach has two advantages: (1) it provides a systematic way to define the decision variables for any blending problem; and (2) it provides a visual image of the decision variables in terms of how they are related to the raw materials, products and each other.

4.4 Marketing and Media Applications

Applications of linear programming in marketing are numerous. In this section we discuss applications in media selection and marketing research.

Media Selection

Media selection applications of linear programming are designed to help marketing managers allocate a fixed advertising budget to various advertising media. Potential media include newspapers, magazines, radio, television, Internet, SMS text messaging and direct mail. In these applications, the objective is to maximize reach, frequency and quality of exposure. Restrictions on the allowable allocation usually arise during consideration of company policy, contract requirements and media availability. In the application that follows, we illustrate how a media selection problem might be formulated and solved using a linear programming model.

The Lochside Development Corporation (LDC) is a joint public–private partnership venture based in Scotland. LDC's remit is to use private finance to fund housing and leisure construction projects that will boost tourism and increase economic growth and yet at the same time be environmentally friendly. One such project underway is to construct a small new community alongside a small loch (a lake in Scotland). Part of the development involves constructing homes, shops and leisure facilities for permanent residents. A second part involves constructing holiday homes and LDC is currently considering how best to market these. The primary market for these homes includes middle- and upper-income families within approximately 200 miles of the development. LDC have employed the advertising firm of Boone, Phillips and Jackson (BP&J) to design the promotional campaign.

After considering possible advertising media and the market to be covered, BP&J recommended that the first month's advertising be restricted to five media. At the end of the month, BP&J will then re-evaluate its strategy based on the month's results. BP&J collected data on the number of potential customers reached, the cost per advertisement, the maximum number of times each medium is available and the exposure quality rating for each of the five media. The quality rating is measured in terms of an exposure quality unit, a measure of the relative value of one advertisement in each of the media. This measure, based on BP&J's experience in the advertising business, takes into account factors such as audience demographics (age, income and education of the audience reached), image presented and quality of the advertisement. The information collected is presented in Table 4.12.

LDC provided BP&J with an advertising budget of £30 000 for the first month's campaign. In addition, LDC imposed the following restrictions on how BP&J may allocate these funds: at least ten television commercials must be used, at least 50 000 potential customers must be reached and no more than £18 000 may be spent on television advertisements. What advertising media selection plan should be recommended?

The decision to be made is how many times to use each medium. We begin by defining the decision variables:

DTV = number of times daytime TV is used
ETV = number of times evening TV is used
DN = number of times daily newspaper is used
SN = number of times Sunday newspaper is used
R = number of times radio is used

Table 4.12 Advertising Media Alternatives for LDC

Advertising Media	Number of Potential Customers Reached	Cost (£)per Advertisement	Maximum Times Available per Month*	Exposure Quality Units
1. Daytime TV (1 min)	1 000	1 500	15	65
2. Evening TV (30 sec)	2 000	3 000	10	90
3. Daily newspaper (full page)	1 500	400	25	40
4. Sunday newspaper magazine (½ page colour)	2 500	1 000	4	60
5. Radio, 8:00 A.M. or 5:00 P.M. news (30 sec)	300	100	30	20

* The maximum number of times the medium is available is either the maximum number of times the advertising medium occurs (e.g., four Sundays per month or the maximum number of times BP&J recommends that the medium be used).

The data on quality of exposure in Table 4.12 show that each daytime TV (*DTV*) advertisement is rated at 65 exposure quality units. Thus, an advertising plan with *DTV* advertisements will provide a total of 65*DTV* exposure quality units. Continuing with the data in Table 4.12, we find evening TV (*ETV*) rated at 90 exposure quality units, daily newspaper (*DN*) rated at 40 exposure quality units, Sunday newspaper (*SN*) rated at 60 exposure quality units and radio (*R*) rated at 20 exposure quality units. With the objective of maximizing the total exposure quality units for the overall media selection plan, the objective function becomes:

$$\text{Max} \quad 65DTV + 90ETV + 40DN + 60SN + 20R \quad \text{Exposure quality}$$

We now formulate the constraints for the model from the information given:

$$\left.\begin{aligned} DTV &\le 15 \\ ETV &\le 10 \\ DN &\le 25 \\ SN &\le 4 \\ R &\le 30 \end{aligned}\right\}\text{Availability of media}$$

$$1500DTV + 3000ETV + 400DN + 1000SN + 100R \le 30\,000 \quad \text{Budget}$$

$$\left.\begin{aligned} DTV + ETV &\ge 10 \\ 1500DTV + 3000ETV &\le 18\,000 \end{aligned}\right\}\text{Television restrictions}$$

$$1000DTV + 2000ETV + 1500DN + 2500SN + 300R \ge 50\,000 \quad \text{Customers reached}$$

$$DTV,\ ETV,\ DN,\ SN,\ R \ge 0$$

Care must be taken to ensure the linear programming model accurately reflects the real problem. Always review your formulation thoroughly before attempting to solve the model.

Problem 1 provides practise at formulating a similar media selection model.

The optimal solution to this five-variable, nine-constraint linear programming model is shown in Figure 4.6; a summary is presented in Table 4.13.

The optimal solution calls for advertisements to be distributed among daytime TV, daily newspaper, Sunday newspaper and radio. The maximum number of exposure quality units is 2370, and the total number of customers reached is 61 500. The Reduced Costs column in Figure 4.1 indicates that the number of exposure quality units for evening TV would have to increase by at least 65 before this media alternative could appear in the optimal solution. Note that the budget constraint (constraint 6) has a dual price of 0.060. Therefore, a £1.00 increase in the advertising budget will lead to an increase of 0.06 exposure quality units. The dual price of –25.000 for constraint 7 indicates that reducing the number of television commercials by one will increase the exposure quality of the advertising plan by 25 units. Thus, LDC should consider reducing the requirement of having at least ten television commercials.

More complex media selection models may include considerations such as the reduced exposure quality value for repeat media usage, cost discounts for repeat media usage, audience overlap by different media and/or timing recommendations for the advertisements.

A possible shortcoming of this model is that, even if the exposure quality measure were not subject to error, it offers no guarantee that maximization of total exposure quality will lead to a maximization of profit or of sales (a common surrogate for profit). However, this issue is not a shortcoming of linear programming; rather, it is a shortcoming of the use of exposure quality as a criterion. If we could directly measure the effect of an advertisement on profit, we could use total profit as the objective to be maximized.

EXCEL *file*

LOCHSIDE

Figure 4.6 The Management Scientist Solution for the LDC Problem

```
Objective Function Value =        2370.000

  Variable           Value            Reduced Costs
 -------------- -------------- ----------------
      DTV            10.000              0.000
      ETV             0.000             65.000
      DN             25.000              0.000
      SN              2.000              0.000
      R              30.000              0.000

   Constraint    Slack/Surplus       Dual Prices
 -------------- -------------- ---------------
       1              5.000              0.000
       2             10.000              0.000
       3              0.000             16.000
       4              2.000              0.000
       5              0.000             14.000
       6              0.000              0.060
       7              0.000            -25.000
       8           3000.000              0.000
       9          11500.003              0.000
```


Table 4.13 Advertising Plan for LDC

Media	Frequency	Budget
Daytime TV	10	£15 000
Daily newspaper	25	10 000
Sunday newspaper	2	2 000
Radio	30	3 000
		£30 000

Exposure quality units = 2 370

Total customers reached = 61 500

NOTES AND COMMENTS

1 The media selection model required subjective evaluations of the exposure quality for the media alternatives. Marketing managers may have substantial data concerning exposure quality, but the final coefficients used in the objective function may also include considerations based primarily on managerial judgement. Judgement is an acceptable way of obtaining input for a linear programming model.

2 The media selection model presented in this section uses exposure quality as the objective function and places a constraint on the number of customers reached. An alternative formulation of this problem would be to use the number of customers reached as the objective function and add a constraint indicating the minimum total exposure quality required for the media plan.

Marketing Research

An organization conducts marketing research to learn about consumer characteristics, attitudes and preferences. Marketing research firms that specialize in providing such information often do the actual research for client organizations. Typical services offered by a marketing research firm include designing the study, conducting market surveys, analyzing the data collected and providing summary reports and recommendations for the client. In the research design phase, targets or quotas may be established for the number and types of respondents to be surveyed. The marketing research firm's objective is to conduct the survey so as to meet the client's needs at a minimum cost.

Market Survey International (MSI), specializes in evaluating consumer reaction to new products, services and advertising campaigns. The company has been approached by a government housing agency which is reviewing its strategic priorities. As part of this review, the agency is keen to obtain the views of citizens and has commissioned MSI to undertake some structured market research. MSI will conduct a total of 1000 personal interviews with a number of households across the country. To try to ensure a representative cross-section of respondents, interviews will take place during the day and also in the evenings. The agency has also provided further details of the interviews it requires:

1 Interview at least 400 households with children.
2 Interview at least 400 households without children.
3 The total number of households interviewed during the evening must be at least as great as the number of households interviewed during the day.
4 At least 40 per cent of the interviews for households with children must be conducted during the evening.
5 At least 60 per cent of the interviews for households without children must be conducted during the evening.

Because the interviews for households with children take additional interviewer time and because evening interviewers are paid more than daytime interviewers, the cost varies with the type of interview. Based on previous research studies, estimates of the interview costs are as follows:

Household	Interview Cost	
	Day	Evening
Children	€20	€25
No children	€18	€20

What is the household, time-of-day interview plan that will satisfy the contract requirements at a minimum total interviewing cost?

In formulating the linear programming model for the MSI problem, we utilize the following decision-variable notation:

$$DC = \text{the number of daytime interviews of households with children}$$
$$EC = \text{the number of evening interviews of households with children}$$
$$DNC = \text{the number of daytime interviews of households without children}$$
$$ENC = \text{the number of evening interviews of households without children}$$

We begin the linear programming model formulation by using the cost-per-interview data to develop the objective function:

$$\text{Min} \quad 20DC + 25EC + 18DNC + 20ENC$$

The constraint requiring a total of 1000 interviews is:

$$DC + EC + DNC + ENC = 1000$$

The five specifications concerning the types of interviews are as follows.

- Households with children:

$$DC + EC \geq 400$$

- Households without children:

$$DNC + ENC \geq 400$$

- At least as many evening interviews as day interviews:

$$EC + ENC \geq DC + DNC$$

The usual format for linear programming model formulation and computer input places all decision variables on the left side of the inequality and a constant (possibly zero) on the right side. Thus, we rewrite this constraint as:

$$-DC + EC - DNC + ENC \geq 0$$

- At least 40 per cent of interviews of households with children during the evening:

$$EC \geq 0.4(DC + EC) \quad \text{or} \quad -0.4DC + 0.6EC \geq 0$$

- At least 60 per cent of interviews of households without children during the evening:

$$ENC \geq 0.6(DNC + ENC) \quad \text{or} \quad -0.6DNC + 0.4ENC \geq 0$$

When we add the nonnegativity requirements, the four-variable and six-constraint linear programming model becomes:

$$
\begin{array}{llr}
\text{Min} & 20DC + 25EC + 18DNC + 20ENC & \\
\text{s.t.} & & \\
& DC + EC + DNC + ENC = 1000 & \text{Total interviews} \\
& DC + EC \geq 400 & \text{Households with children} \\
& DNC + ENC \geq 400 & \text{Households without children} \\
& -DC + EC - DNC + ENC \geq 0 & \text{Evening interviews} \\
& -0.4DC + 0.6EC \geq 0 & \text{Evening interviews in households with children} \\
& -0.6DNC + 0.4ENC \geq 0 & \text{Evening interviews in households without children} \\
& DC, EC, DNC, ENC \geq 0 &
\end{array}
$$

The optimal solution to this linear program is shown in Figure 4.7. The solution reveals that the minimum cost of €20 320 occurs with the following interview schedule.

	Number of Interviews		
Household	**Day**	**Evening**	**Totals**
Children	240	160	400
No children	240	360	600
Totals	480	520	1 000

Hence, 480 interviews will be scheduled during the day and 520 during the evening. Households with children will be covered by 400 interviews, and households without children will be covered by 600 interviews.

Selected sensitivity analysis information from Figure 4.7 shows a dual price of −19.2 for constraint 1. In other words, the value of the optimal solution will get worse (the total interviewing cost will increase) by €19.20 if the number of interviews is increased from 1000 to 1001. Thus, €19.20 is the incremental cost of obtaining additional interviews. It also is the savings that could be realized by reducing the number of interviews from 1000 to 999.

The surplus variable, with a value of 200, for constraint 3 shows that 200 more households without children will be interviewed than required. Similarly, the surplus variable, with a value of 40, for constraint 4 shows that the number of evening interviews exceeds the number of daytime interviews by 40. The zero values for the surplus variables in constraints 5 and 6 indicate that the more expensive evening interviews are being held at a minimum. Indeed, the dual price of five for constraint 5 indicates that if one more household (with children) than the minimum requirement must be interviewed during the evening, the total interviewing cost will go up by €5.00. Similarly, constraint 6 shows that requiring one more household (without children) to be interviewed during the evening will increase costs by €2.00.

4.5 Financial Applications

In finance, linear programming can be applied in problem situations involving capital budgeting, make-or-buy decisions, asset allocation, portfolio selection, financial planning and many more. In this section, we describe a portfolio selection problem and a problem involving funding of an early retirement programme.

Figure 4.7 Excel Solution for the Market Survey Problem

TARGET CELL (MIN)

Name	Original Value	Final Value
Objective function	0	20320

ADJUSTABLE CELLS

Name	Original Value	Final Value
DC	0	240
EC	0	160
DNC	0	240
ENC	0	360

CONSTRAINTS

Name	Cell Value	Status	Slack
Total interviews	1000	Not Binding	0
Households with children	400	Binding	0
Households without children	600	Not Binding	200
Evening interviews	40	Not Binding	40
Evening interviews in households with children	0	Binding	0
Evening interviews in households with children	0	Binding	0

ADJUSTABLE CELLS

Name	Final Value	Reduced Cost	Objective Coefficient	Allowable Increase	Allowable Decrease
DC	240	0	20	5	4.666666667
EC	160	0	25	1E+30	5
DNC	240	0	18	2	1E+30
ENC	360	0	20	4.666666667	2

CONSTRAINTS

Name	Final Value	Shadow Price	Constraint R.H. Side	Allowable Increase	Allowable Decrease
Total interviews	1000	19.2	1000	1E+30	200
Households with children	400	2.8	400	100	400
Households without children	600	0	400	200	1E+30
Evening interviews	40	0	0	40	1E+30
Evening interviews in households with children	0	5	0	240	20
Evening interviews in households with children	0	2	0	240	20

EXCEL *file*

MARKET

MANAGEMENT SCIENCE IN ACTION

A Marketing Resource Allocation Model At Reckitt And Coleman

Reckitt and Coleman is a world leader in the manufacture and marketing of household, toiletry, food and pharmaceutical products employing over 25 000 people worldwide and with its products sold in over 40 countries. In the late 1990s it decided to adopt a more analytical and objective approach to decisions relating to the allocation of marketing funds to its industrial cleaning products. The company operated seven geographical regions globally and the marketing Vice President requested a model to determine the amount of marketing funds to be spent on current business and on new business opportunities within each region. The model was expected to be modified and used as management visited each region as part of their marketing planning. An LP model was developed covering the seven geographic regions; three product groups for each region (surface cleaners, disinfectants, oven cleaners); up to five new business opportunities for each region; together with additional marketing information such as market size, alternative marketing costs and so on. Interestingly, the model was built with 11 alternative marketing objectives, such as sales volume growth, brand value share allowing management to explore and evaluate the impact of marketing spend in different ways. The model estimates the revenue derived from the cost of the marketing mix chosen (such as advertising and store displays) and incorporates both marketing and budgetary constraints. The benefits reported from use of the model included improved profitability, a faster response to unexpected or unpredicted market conditions, more consistency in marketing decisions and the ability to explore alternative scenarios in detail.

Based on R. J. Richardson, 'A Marketing Resource Allocation Model', *Journal of Business and Economic Studies* 10 1 (2004): 43–53.

Portfolio Selection

Portfolio selection problems involve situations in which a financial manager must select specific investments – for example, stocks and bonds – from a variety of investment alternatives. Managers of mutual funds, credit unions, insurance companies and banks frequently encounter this type of problem. The objective function for portfolio selection problems usually is maximization of expected return or minimization of risk. The constraints usually take the form of restrictions on the type of permissible investments, company policy, maximum permissible risk and so on. Problems of this type have been formulated and solved using a variety of mathematical programming techniques. In this section we formulate and solve a portfolio selection problem as a linear programme.

Consider the case of Welte Mutual located in Berlin. Welte just obtained €100 000 by converting industrial bonds to cash and is now looking for other investment opportunities for these funds. Based on Welte's current investments, the firm's top financial analyst recommends that all new investments be made in the oil industry, steel industry or in government bonds. Specifically, the analyst identified five investment opportunities and projected their annual rates of return. The investments and rates of return are shown in Table 4.14.

Management of Welte imposed the following investment guidelines:

1 Neither industry (oil or steel) should receive more than €50 000.

2 Government bonds should be at least 25 per cent of the steel industry investments.

3 The investment in Pacific Oil, the high-return but high-risk investment, cannot be more than 60 per cent of the total oil industry investment.

Table 4.14 Investment Opportunities for Welte Mutual Funds

Investment	Projected Rate of Return (%)
Atlantic Oil	7.3
Pacific Oil	10.3
Midwest Steel	6.4
Huber Steel	7.5
Government bonds	4.5

What portfolio recommendations – investments and amounts – should be made for the available €100 000? Given the objective of maximizing projected return subject to the budgetary and managerially imposed constraints, we can answer this question by formulating and solving a linear programming model of the problem. The solution will provide investment recommendations for the management of Welte Mutual Funds.

Let:

$$A = \text{euros invested in Atlantic Oil}$$
$$P = \text{euros invested in Pacific Oil}$$
$$M = \text{euros invested in Midwest Steel}$$
$$H = \text{euros invested in Huber Steel}$$
$$G = \text{euros invested in government bonds}$$

Using the projected rates of return shown in Table 4.14, we write the objective function for maximizing the total return for the portfolio as:

$$\text{Max} \quad 0.073A + 0.103P + 0.064M + 0.075H + 0.045G$$

The constraint specifying investment of the available €100 000 is:

$$A + P + M + H + G = 100\,000$$

The requirements that neither the oil nor the steel industry should receive more than €50 000 are:

$$A + P \leq 50\,000$$
$$M + H \leq 50\,000$$

The requirement that government bonds be at least 25 per cent of the steel industry investment is expressed as:

$$G \geq 0.25(M + H) \quad \text{or} \quad -0.25M - 0.25H + G \geq 0$$

Finally, the constraint that Pacific Oil cannot be more than 60 per cent of the total oil industry investment is:

$$P \leq 0.60(A + P) \text{ or } -0.60A + 0.40P \leq 0$$

By adding the nonnegativity restrictions, we obtain the complete linear programming model for the Welte Mutual investment problem:

$$\begin{aligned}
\text{Max} \quad & 0.073A + 0.103P + 0.064M + 0.075H + 0.045G \\
\text{s.t.} \quad & \\
& A + P + M + H + G = 100\,000 \quad \text{Available funds} \\
& A + P \leq 50\,000 \quad \text{Oil industry maximum} \\
& M + H \leq 50\,000 \quad \text{Steel industry maximum} \\
& -0.25M - 0.25H + G \geq 0 \quad \text{Government bonds minimum} \\
& -0.6A + 0.4P \leq 0 \quad \text{Pacific Oil restriction} \\
& A, P, M, H, G \geq 0
\end{aligned}$$

The optimal solution to this linear programme is shown in Figure 4.8. Table 4.15 shows how the funds are divided among the securities. Note that the optimal solution indicates that the portfolio should be diversified among all the investment opportunities except Midwest Steel. The projected annual return for this portfolio is €8000, which is an overall return of 8 per cent.

The optimal solution shows the dual price for constraint 3 is zero. The reason is that the steel industry maximum isn't a binding constraint; increases in the steel industry limit of €50 000 will not improve the value of the optimal solution. Indeed, the slack variable for this constraint shows that the current steel industry investment is €10 000 below its limit of €50 000. The dual prices for the other constraints are nonzero, indicating that these constraints are binding.

The dual price for the available funds constraint provides information on the rate of return from additional investment funds.

The dual price of 0.069 for constraint 1 shows that the value of the optimal solution can be increased by 0.069 if one more euro can be made available for the portfolio investment. If more funds can be obtained at a cost of less than 6.9 per cent, management should consider obtaining them. However, if a return in excess of 6.9 per cent can be obtained by investing funds elsewhere (other than in these five securities), management should question the wisdom of investing the entire €100 000 in this portfolio.

Similar interpretations can be given to the other dual prices. Note that the dual price for constraint 4 is negative at –0.024. This result indicates that increasing the value on the right-hand side of the constraint by one unit can be expected to worsen the value of the optimal solution by 0.024. In terms of the optimal portfolio, then, if

Figure 4.8 The Management Scientist Solution for the Welte Problem

EXCEL *file*

WELTE

```
Objective Function Value =          8000.000

     Variable                Value              Reduced Costs
  --------------       ---------------       -----------------
        A                 20000.000                   0.000
        P                 30000.000                   0.000
        M                     0.000                   0.011
        H                 40000.000                   0.000
        G                 10000.000                   0.000

    Constraint           Slack/Surplus          Dual Prices
  --------------       ---------------       -----------------
        1                     0.000                   0.069
        2                     0.000                   0.022
        3                 10000.000                   0.000
        4                     0.000                  -0.024
        5                     0.000                   0.030
```

Table 4.15 Optimal Portfolio Selection for Welte Mutual

Investment	Amount	Expected Annual return
Atlantic Oil	€20 000	€1 460
Pacific Oil	30 000	3 090
Huber Steel	40 000	3 000
Government bonds	10 000	450
Totals	€100 000	€8 000
Expected annual return of €8 000		
Overall rate of return = 8%		

Welte invests one more euro in government bonds (beyond the minimum requirement), the total return will decrease by €0.024. To see why this decrease occurs, note again from the dual price for constraint 1 that the marginal return on the funds invested in the portfolio is 6.9 per cent (the average return is 8 per cent). The rate of return on government bonds is 4.5 per cent. Thus, the cost of investing one more euro in government bonds is the difference between the marginal return on the portfolio and the marginal return on government bonds: 6.9 per cent − 4.5 per cent = 2.4 per cent.

Note that the optimal solution shows that Midwest Steel should not be included in the portfolio ($M = 0$). The associated reduced cost for M of 0.011 tells us that the objective function coefficient for Midwest Steel would have to increase by 0.011 before considering the Midwest Steel investment alternative would be advisable. With such an increase the Midwest Steel return would be 0.064 + 0.011 = 0.075, making this investment just as desirable as the currently used Huber Steel investment alternative.

Practise formulating a variation of the Welte problem by working Problem 7.

Finally, a simple modification of the Welte linear programming model permits determining the fraction of available funds invested in each security. That is, we divide each of the right-hand side values by 100 000. Then the optimal values for the variables will give the fraction of funds that should be invested in each security for a portfolio of any size.

NOTES AND COMMENTS

1 The optimal solution to the Welte Mutual Funds problem indicates that €20 000 is to be spent on the Atlantic Oil stock. If Atlantic Oil sells for €75 per share, we would have to purchase exactly 266⅔ shares in order to spend exactly €20 000. The difficulty of purchasing fractional shares is usually handled by purchasing the largest possible integer number of shares with the allotted funds (e.g., 266 shares of Atlantic Oil). This approach guarantees that the budget constraint will not be violated. This approach, of course, introduces the possibility that the solution will no longer be optimal, but the danger is slight if a large number of securities are involved. In cases where the analyst believes that the decision variables *must* have integer values, the problem must be formulated as an integer linear programming model. Integer linear programming is the topic of online Chapter 15.

2 Financial portfolio theory stresses obtaining a proper balance between risk and return. In the Welte problem, we explicitly considered return in the objective function. Risk is controlled by choosing constraints that ensure diversity among oil and steel stocks and a balance between government bonds and the steel industry investment.

Financial Planning

Linear programming has been used for a variety of financial planning applications. The *Management Science in Action*, Optimal Lease Structuring at GE Capital, describes how linear programming is used to optimize the structure of a leveraged lease.

Hewlitt Corporation established an early retirement programme as part of its corporate restructuring. The company has asked employees who are within a few years of normal retirement if they would be willing to take early retirement. Staff who do so will be given a special financial payment by the company for each year before they reach the normal retirement age. So, for example, someone who would normally retire at the age of 60 who decides to take early retirement at the age of 55 will get five years of financial payments from the company. The company obviously will achieve savings by not having to pay the employee a salary plus benefits during those five years. So, for example, the company has to find €430 000 in year 1 to pay staff who have taken early retirement; €210 000 in year 2 and so on. At the close of the voluntary sign-up period, 68 employees had elected early retirement. As a result of these early retirements, the company incurs the following obligations over the next eight years.

Year	1	2	3	4	5	6	7	8
Cash Requirement	430	210	222	231	240	195	225	255

The cash requirements (in thousands of euro) are due at the beginning of each year.

The corporate treasurer must determine how much money must be set aside today to meet the eight yearly financial obligations as they come due. The financing plan for the retirement programme includes investments in government bonds as well as savings. The investments in government bonds are limited to three choices:

Bond	Price, €	Rate (%)	Years to Maturity
1	1 150	8.875	5
2	1 000	5.500	6
3	1 350	11.750	7

The bonds have a nominal, face value of €1000. So, for example, if the company buys Bond 1 at €1150 per bond, then it will receive an interest payment of 8.875 per cent of €1000 from the government each year for the next five years, when Bond 1 matures. At maturity, the government buys the bond back at face value of €1000. For the purposes of planning, the treasurer assumed that any funds not invested in bonds will be placed in savings and earn interest at an annual rate of 4 per cent.

We define the decision variables as follows:

F = total euros required to meet the retirement plan's eight-year obligation

B_1 = units of bond 1 purchased at the beginning of year 1

B_2 = units of bond 2 purchased at the beginning of year 1

B_3 = units of bond 3 purchased at the beginning of year 1

S_i = amount placed in savings at the beginning of year i for $i = 1, \dots, 8$

So, the company has to decide how many of each of the three bonds to buy at the start of year 1 and how much additional savings will be needed each year for the next

MANAGEMENT SCIENCE IN ACTION

Optimal Lease Structuring at GE Capital

GE Capital is a $70 billion subsidiary of General Electric. As one of America's largest and most diverse financial services companies, GE Capital arranges leases in both domestic and international markets, including leases for telecommunications; data processing; construction; and fleets of cars, trucks and commercial aircraft. To help allocate and schedule the rental and debt payments of a leveraged lease, GE Capital analysts developed an optimization model, which is available as an optional component of the company's lease analysis proprietary software.

Leveraged leases are designed to provide financing for assets with economic lives of at least five years, which require large capital outlays. A leveraged lease represents an agreement among the lessor (the owner of the asset), the lessee (the user of the asset) and the lender who provides a non recourse loan of 50 per cent to 80 per cent of the lessor's purchase price. In a non recourse loan, the lenders cannot turn to the lessor for repayment in the event of default. As the lessor in such arrangements, GE Capital is able to claim ownership and realize income tax benefits such as depreciation and interest deductions. These deductions usually produce tax losses during the early years of the lease, which reduces the total tax liability. Approximately 85 per cent of all financial leases in the United States are leveraged leases.

In its simplest form, the leveraged lease structuring problem can be formulated as a linear programme. The linear programme models the after-tax cash flow for the lessor, taking into consideration rental receipts, borrowing and repaying of the loan and income taxes. Constraints are formulated to ensure compliance with IRS guidelines and to enable customizing of leases to meet lessee and lessor requirements. The objective function can be entered in a custom fashion or selected from a predefined list. Typically, the objective is to minimize the lessee's cost, expressed as the net present value of rental payments, or to maximize the lessor's after-tax yield.

GE Capital developed an optimization approach that could be applied to single-investor lease structuring. In a study with the department most involved with these transactions, the optimization approach yielded substantial benefits. The approach helped GE Capital win some single-investor transactions ranging in size from $1 million to $20 million.

Based on C.J. Litty, 'Optimal Lease Structuring at GE Capital', *Interfaces* (May/June 1994): 34–45.

eight years. The objective function is to minimize the total euros needed to meet the retirement plan's eight-year obligation, or:

$$\text{Min} \quad F$$

A key feature of this type of financial planning problem is that a constraint must be formulated for each year of the planning horizon. In general, each constraint takes the form:

$$\begin{pmatrix}\text{Funds available at}\\ \text{the beginning of the year}\end{pmatrix} - \begin{pmatrix}\text{Funds invested in bonds}\\ \text{and placed in savings}\end{pmatrix} = \begin{pmatrix}\text{Cash obligation for}\\ \text{the current year}\end{pmatrix}$$

The funds available at the beginning of year 1 are given by F. With a current price of €1150 for bond 1 and investments expressed in thousands of euro, the total investment for B_1 units of bond 1 would be $1.15B_1$. Similarly, the total investment in bonds 2 and 3 would be $1B_2$ and $1.35B_3$, respectively. The investment in savings for year 1 is

S_1. Using these results and the first-year obligation of 430, we obtain the constraint for year 1:

$$F - 1.15B_1 - 1B_2 - 1.35B_3 - S_1 = 430 \quad \text{Year 1}$$

Investments in bonds can take place only in this first year, and the bonds will be held until maturity.

We do not consider future investments in bonds because the future price of bonds depends on interest rates and cannot be known in advance.

The funds available at the beginning of year 2 include the investment returns of 8.875 per cent on the nominal value of bond 1, 5.5 per cent on the nominal value of bond 2, 11.75 per cent on the nominal value of bond 3, and 4 per cent on savings. The new amount to be invested in savings for year 2 is S_2. With an obligation of 210, the constraint for year 2 is:

$$0.08875B_1 + 0.055B_2 + 0.1175B_3 + 1.04S_1 - S_2 = 210 \quad \text{Year 2}$$

Similarly, the constraints for years 3 to 8 are:

$$0.08875B_1 + 0.055B_2 + 0.1175B_3 + 1.04S_2 - S_3 = 222 \quad \text{Year 3}$$
$$0.08875B_1 + 0.055B_2 + 0.1175B_3 + 1.04S_3 - S_4 = 231 \quad \text{Year 4}$$
$$0.08875B_1 + 0.055B_2 + 0.1175B_3 + 1.04S_4 - S_5 = 240 \quad \text{Year 5}$$
$$1.08875B_1 + 0.055B_2 + 0.1175B_3 + 1.04S_5 - S_6 = 195 \quad \text{Year 6}$$
$$1.055B_2 + 0.1175B_3 + 1.04S_6 - S_7 = 225 \quad \text{Year 7}$$
$$1.1175B_3 + 1.04S_7 - S_8 = 255 \quad \text{Year 8}$$

Note that the constraint for year 6 shows that funds available from bond 1 are $1.08875B_1$. The coefficient of 1.08875 reflects the fact that bond 1 matures at the end of year 5. As a result, the nominal value plus the interest from bond 1 during year 5 is available at the beginning of year 6. Also, because bond 1 matures in year 5 and becomes available for use at the beginning of year 6, the variable B_1 does not appear in the constraints for years 7 and 8. Note the similar interpretation for bond 2, which matures at the end of year 6 and has the nominal value plus interest available at the beginning of year 7. In addition, bond 3 matures at the end of year 7 and has the nominal value plus interest available at the beginning of year 8.

Finally, note that a variable S_8 appears in the constraint for year 8. The retirement fund obligation will be completed at the beginning of year 8, so we anticipate that S_8 will be zero and no funds will be put into savings. However, the formulation includes S_8 in the event that the bond income plus interest from the savings in year 7 exceed the 255 cash requirement for year 8. Thus, S_8 is a surplus variable that shows any funds remaining after the eight-year cash requirements have been satisfied.

The optimal solution to this 12-variable, 8-constraint linear programme is shown in Figure 4.9. With an objective function value of 1728.79385, the total investment required to meet the retirement plan's eight-year obligation is €1 728 794. Using the current prices of €1150, €1000 and €1350 for each of the bonds respectively, we can summarize the initial investments in the three bonds as follows:

Bond	Units Purchased	Investment Amount
1	$B_1 = 144.988$	€1 150(144.988) = €166 736
2	$B_2 = 187.856$	€1 000(187.856) = €187 856
3	$B_3 = 228.188$	€1 350(228.188) = €308 054

Figure 4.9 The Management Scientist Solution for the Hewlitt Corporation Cash Requirements Problem

EXCEL *file*

HEWLITT

Objective Function Value = 1728.79385

Variable	Value	Reduced Costs
F	1728.79385	0.00000
B1	144.98815	0.00000
B2	187.85585	0.00000
B3	228.18792	0.00000
S1	636.14794	0.00000
S2	501.60571	0.00000
S3	349.68179	0.00000
S4	182.68091	0.00000
S5	0.00000	0.06403
S6	0.00000	0.01261
S7	0.00000	0.02132
S8	0.00000	0.67084

Constraint	Slack/Surplus	Dual Prices
1	0.00000	-1.00000
2	0.00000	-0.96154
3	0.00000	-0.92456
4	0.00000	-0.88900
5	0.00000	-0.85480
6	0.00000	-0.76036
7	0.00000	-0.71899
8	0.00000	-0.67084

The solution also shows that €636 148 (see S_1) will be placed in savings at the beginning of the first year. By starting with €1,728 794, the company can make the specified bond and savings investments and have enough left over to meet the retirement programme's first-year cash requirement of €430 000.

The optimal solution in Figure 4.9 shows that the decision variables S_1, S_2, S_3 and S_4 are all greater than zero, indicating investments in savings are required in each of the first four years. However, interest from the bonds plus the bond maturity incomes will be sufficient to cover the retirement programme's cash requirements in years 5 through 8.

The dual prices have an interesting interpretation in this application. Each right-hand side value corresponds to the payment that must be made in that year. Note that the dual prices are negative, indicating that reducing the payment in any year would be beneficial because the total funds required for the retirement programme's obligation would be less. Also note that the dual prices show that reductions are more beneficial in the early years, with decreasing benefits in subsequent years. As a result, Hewlitt would benefit by reducing cash requirements in the early years even if it had to make equivalently larger cash payments in later years.

In this application, the dual price can be thought of as the negative of the present value of each euro in the cash requirement. For example, each euro that must be paid in year 8 has a present value of €0.67084.

NOTES AND COMMENTS

1 The optimal solution for the Hewlitt Corporation problem shows fractional numbers of government bonds at 144.988, 187.856 and 228.188 units, respectively. However, fractional bond units usually are not available. If we were conservative and rounded up to 145, 188 and 229 units, respectively, the total funds required for the eight-year retirement programme obligation would be approximately €1254 more than the total funds indicated by the objective function. Because of the magnitude of the funds involved, rounding up probably would provide a workable solution. If an optimal integer solution were required, the methods of integer linear programming covered in Chapter 15 would have to be used.

2 We implicitly assumed that interest from the government bonds is paid annually. Investments such as treasury notes actually provide interest payments every six months. In such cases, the model can be reformulated with six-month periods, with interest and/or cash payments occurring every six months.

Revenue Management

Revenue management involves managing the short-term demand for a fixed perishable inventory in order to maximize the revenue potential for an organization. The methodology, originally developed for American Airlines, was first used to determine how many airline flight seats to sell at an early reservation discount fare and how many airline flight seats to sell at a full fare. By making the optimal decision for the number of discount-fare seats and the number of full-fare seats on each flight, the airline is able to increase its average number of passengers per flight and maximize the total revenue generated by the combined sale of discount-fare and full-fare seats. Today, all major airlines use some form of revenue management.

Given the success of revenue management in the airline industry, it was not long before other industries began using revenue management. Models have been expanded to include pricing strategies, overbooking policies, short-term supply decisions and the management of nonperishable assets. Application areas now include hotels, apartment rentals, car rentals, cruise lines and golf courses. The *Management Science in Action*, Revenue Management at National Car Rental, discusses how National Car Rental implemented revenue management.

The development of a revenue management system can be expensive and time-consuming, but the potential payoffs can be substantial. For instance, the revenue management system used at American Airlines generates nearly $1 billion in annual incremental revenue. To illustrate the fundamentals of revenue management, we will use a linear programming model to develop a revenue management plan for Leisure Air. The company is based in Scotland and, in the winter months, offers a service aimed at holidaymakers going on a skiing/snowboarding holiday in Switzerland and Austria. The company offers a daily flight from Glasgow to Salzburg and from Edinburgh to Geneva using two Boeing 737-400 aeroplanes each with a 132 seat capacity. Both flights stopover briefly in Amsterdam. The return flights are available later the same day.

Figure 4.10 illustrates the logistics of the Leisure Air problem situation. To keep the size of the problem manageable and understandable we shall look only at the outbound leg of the flights.

Leisure Air uses two fare classes: a discount-fare Q class and a full-fare Y class. Reservations using the discount-fare Q class must be made at least 14 days in

MANAGEMENT SCIENCE IN ACTION

Revenue Management at National Car Rental

During its recovery from a near liquidation in the mid-1990s, National Car Rental developed a revenue management system that uses linear programming and other analytical models to help manage rental car capacity, pricing and reservations. The goal of the revenue management system is to develop procedures that identify unrealized revenue opportunities, improve utilization and ultimately increase revenue for the company.

Management science models play a key role in revenue management at National. For instance, a linear programming model is used for length-of-rent control. An overbooking model identifies optimal overbooking levels subject to service level constraints, and a planned upgrade algorithm allows cars in a higher-priced class to be used to satisfy excess demand for cars in a lower-priced class.

Another model generates length-of-rent categories for each arrival day, which maximizes revenue. Pricing models are used to manage revenue by segmenting the market between business and leisure travel. For example, fares are adjusted to account for the fact that leisure travellers are willing to commit further in advance than business travellers and are willing to stay over a weekend.

The implementation of the revenue management system is credited with returning National Car Rental to profitability. In the first year of use, revenue management resulted in increased revenues of $56 million.

Based on M. K. Geraghty and Ernest Johnson, 'Revenue Management Saves National Car Rental', *Interfaces* 27, no. 1 (January/February 1997)107–127.

advance and are not changeable. Reservations using the full-fare Y class may be made anytime, with no penalty for changing the reservation at a later date. To determine the itinerary and fare alternatives that Leisure Air can offer its customers, we must consider not only the origin and the destination of each flight, but also the fare class. For instance, possible products include Glasgow to Amsterdam using Q class, Edinburgh to Salzburg using Q class, Amsterdam to Geneva using Y class and so on. Each product is referred to as an origin-destination-itinerary fare (ODIF). Leisure Air established fares and developed forecasts of customer demand for each of 16 ODIFs, as shown in Table 4.16.

Suppose that a customer calls the Leisure Air reservation office and requests a Q class seat from Glasgow to Geneva. Should Leisure Air accept the reservation? The difficulty in making this decision is that even though Leisure Air may have seats available, the company may not want to accept this reservation at the Q class fare of €268, especially if it is possible to sell the same reservation later at the Y class fare of €456. Thus, determining how many Q and Y class seats to make available are important decisions that Leisure Air must take in order to operate its reservation system.

To develop a linear programming model that can be used to determine how many seats Leisure Air should allocate to each fare class we need to define 16 decision variables, one for each origin-destination-itinerary fare alternative. The decision variables will relate to the number of seats to be sold and we shall use the ODIF codes in Table 4.16. So, for example, GAQ will refer to the number of seats sold at Q class between Glasgow and Amsterdam.

The objective is to maximize total revenue. Using the fares shown in Table 4.16, we can write the objective function for the linear programming model as follows:

$$\begin{aligned} \text{Max} \quad & 178GAQ + 268GSQ + 228GVQ + 380GAY + 456GSY + 560GVY \\ & + 199EAQ + 249ESQ + 349EVQ + 385EAY + 444ESY \\ & + 580EVY + 179ASQ + 380ASY + 224AVQ + 582AVY \end{aligned}$$

Figure 4.10 Logistics of the Leisure Air Problem

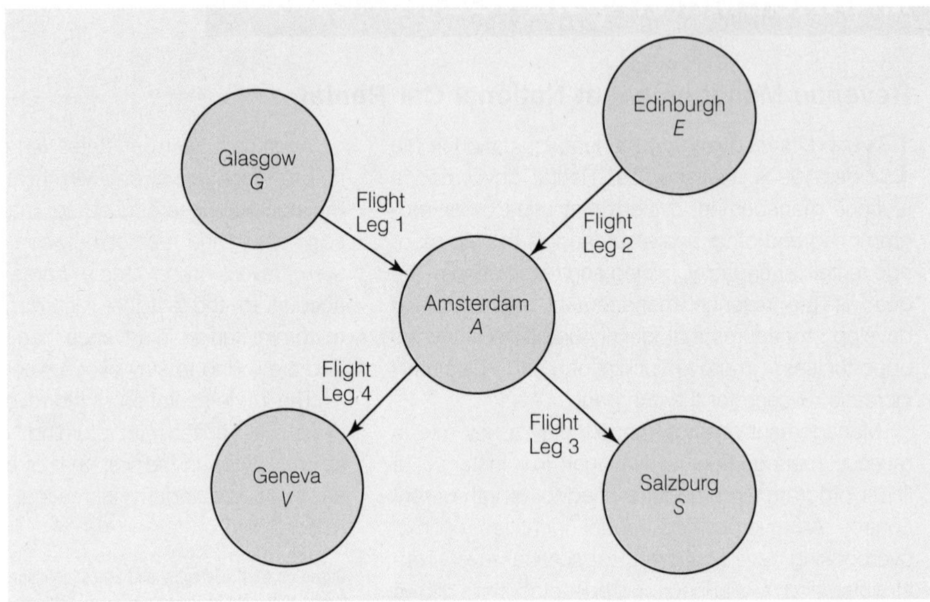

Next we must write the constraints. We need two types of constraints: capacity and demand. We begin with the capacity constraints.

Consider the Glasgow–Geneva flight leg in Figure 4.10. The Boeing 737–400 aeroplane has a 132-seat capacity. Three possible final destinations for passengers on this flight (Amsterdam, Salzburg or Geneva) and two fare classes (Q and Y) provide six ODIF alternatives: (1) Glasgow–Amsterdam Q class; (2) Glasgow–Salzburg Q class; (3) Glasgow–Salzburg Q class; (4) Glasgow–Amsterdam Y class; (5) Glasgow–Geneva Y class; and (6) Glasgow–Salzburg Y class. Thus, the number of seats allocated to the Glasgow–Amsterdam flight leg is $GAQ + GSQ + GVQ + GAY + GSY + GVY$. With the capacity of 132 seats, the capacity constraint is as follows:

$$GAQ + GSQ + GVQ + GAY + GSY + GVY \leq 132 \quad \text{Glasgow–Amsterdam}$$

The capacity constraints for the Edinburg–Amsterdam, Amsterdam–Geneva and Amsterdam–Salzburg flight legs are developed in a similar manner. These three constraints are as follows:

$$EAQ + ESQ + EVQ + EAY + ESY + EVY \leq 132 \quad \text{Edinburgh–Amsterdam}$$
$$GVQ + GVY + EVQ + EVY + AVQ + AVY \leq 132 \quad \text{Amsterdam–Geneva}$$
$$GSQ + GSY + ESQ + ESY + ASQ + ASY \leq 132 \quad \text{Amsterdam–Salzburg}$$

The demand constraints limit the number of seats for each ODIF based on the forecasted demand. Using the demand forecasts in Table 4.16, 16 demand constraints must be added to the model. The first four demand constraints are as follows:

$$GAQ \leq 33 \quad \text{Glasgow-Amsterdam Q class}$$
$$GSQ \leq 44 \quad \text{Glasgow-Geneva Q class}$$
$$GVQ \leq 45 \quad \text{Glasgow-Salzburg Q class}$$
$$GAY \leq 16 \quad \text{Glasgow-Amsterdam Y class}$$

The complete linear programming model with 16 decision variables, four capacity constraints and 16 demand constraints is as follows:

Table 4.16 Fare and Demand Data for 16 Leisure Air Origin-Destination-Itinerary Fares (ODIFS)

ODIF	Origin	Destination	Fare Class	ODIF Code	Fare, €	Forecasted Demand
1	Glasgow	Amsterdam	Q	GAQ	$178	33
2	Glasgow	Salzburg	Q	GSQ	268	44
3	Glasgow	Geneva	Q	GVQ	228	45
4	Glasgow	Amsterdam	Y	GAY	380	16
5	Glasgow	Salzburg	Y	GSY	456	6
6	Glasgow	Geneva	Y	GVY	560	11
7	Edinburgh	Amsterdam	Q	EAQ	199	26
8	Edinburgh	Salzburg	Q	ESQ	249	56
9	Edinburgh	Geneva	Q	EVQ	349	39
10	Edinburgh	Amsterdam	Y	EAY	385	15
11	Edinburgh	Salzburg	Y	ESY	444	7
12	Edinburgh	Geneva	Y	EVY	580	9
13	Amsterdam	Salzburg	Q	ASQ	179	64
14	Amsterdam	Salzburg	Y	ASY	380	8
15	Amsterdam	Geneva	Q	AVQ	224	46
16	Amsterdam	Geneva	Y	AVY	582	10

$$\text{Max } 178GAQ + 268GSQ + 228GVQ + 380GAY + 456GSY + 560GVY + 199EAQ + 249ESQ + 349EVQ + 385EAY + 444ESY + 580EVY + 179ASQ + 380ASY + 224AVQ + 582AVY$$

s.t.

$$\begin{aligned}
GAQ + GSQ + GVQ + GAY + GSY + GVY &\le 132 \\
EAQ + ESQ + EVQ + EAY + ESY + EVY &\le 132 \\
GVQ + GVY + EVQ + EVY + AVQ + AVY &\le 132 \\
GSQ + GSY + ESQ + ESY + ASQ + ASY &\le 132 \\
GAQ &\le 33 \\
GSQ &\le 44 \\
GVQ &\le 45 \\
GAY &\le 16 \\
GSY &\le 6 \\
GVY &\le 11 \\
EAQ &\le 26 \\
ESQ &\le 56 \\
EVQ &\le 39 \\
EAY &\le 15 \\
ESY &\le 7 \\
EVY &\le 9 \\
ASQ &\le 64 \\
ASY &\le 8 \\
AVQ &\le 46 \\
AVY &\le 10
\end{aligned}$$

$$GAQ, GSQ, GVQ, GAY, GSY, GVY, EAQ, ESQ, EVQ, EAY, ESY, EVY, ASQ, ASY, AVQ, AVY \ge 0$$

The optimal solution to the Leisure Air revenue management problem is shown in Figure 4.11. The value of the optimal solution is €103,103. The optimal solution shows that $GAQ = 33$, $GSQ = 44$, $GVQ = 22$, $GAY = 16$ and so on. Thus, to maximize revenue Leisure Air should allocate 33 Q class seats to Glasgow–Amsterdam, 44 Q class seats to Glasgow–Salzburg, 22 Q class seats to Glasgow–Geneva, 16 Y class seats to Glasgow–Amsterdam and so on.

Dual prices tell reservation agents the additional revenue associated with overbooking each ODIF.

Over time, reservations will come into the system and the number of remaining seats available for each ODIF will decrease. For example, the optimal solution allocated 44 Q class seats to Glasgow–Salzburg. Suppose that two weeks prior to the departure date, all 44 seats have been sold. Now, suppose that a new customer calls the Leisure Air reservation office and requests a Q class seat for the flight. Should Leisure Air accept the new reservation even though it exceeds the original 44-seat allocation? The dual price for the Glasgow–Salzburg Q class demand constraint will provide information that will help a Leisure Air reservation agent make this decision.

Constraint 6, $GSQ \leq 44$, restricts the number of Q class seats that can be allocated to Glasgow–Salzburg to 44 seats. In Figure 4.11 we see that the dual price for constraint 6 is €85. The dual price tells us that if one more Q class seat was available from Glasgow–Salzburg, revenue would improve by €85. This increase in revenue is referred to as the bid price for this origin-destination-itinerary fare. In general, the bid price for an ODIF tells a Leisure Air reservation agent the value of one additional reservation once a particular ODIF has been sold out.

By looking at the dual prices for the demand constraints in Figure 4.11, we see that the highest dual price (bid price) is €376 for constraint 8, $GAY \leq 16$. This constraint corresponds to the Glasgow–Amsterdam Y class itinerary. Thus, if all 16 seats allocated to this itinerary have been sold, accepting another reservation will provide additional revenue of €376. Given this revenue contribution, a reservation agent would most likely accept the additional reservation even if it resulted in an overbooking of the flight. Other dual prices for the demand constraints show a bid price of €358 for constraint 20 (AVY) and a bid price of €332 for constraint 10 (GVY). Thus, accepting additional reservations for the Amsterdam–Geneva Y class and the Glasgow–Geneva Y class itineraries is a good choice for increasing revenue.

A revenue management system like the one at Leisure Air must be flexible and adjust to the ever-changing reservation status. Conceptually, each time a reservation is accepted for an origin-destination-itinerary fare that is at its capacity, the linear programming model should be updated and re-solved to obtain new seat allocations along with the revised bid price information. In practice, updating the allocations on a real-time basis is not practical because of the large number of itineraries involved. However, the bid prices from a current solution and some simple decision rules enable reservation agents to make decisions that improve the revenue for the firm. Then, on a periodic basis such as once a day or once a week, the entire linear programming model can be updated and resolved to generate new seat allocations and revised bid price information.

4.6 Data Envelopment Analysis

Data envelopment analysis (DEA) is a specialist application of LP that analyzes the relative performance of a group of similar organizations. For example, we may have a company that operates with different business units across the world. We may want to compare the performance of the business unit in Asia with those in other parts of the world. We may have a large retail company that has stores located in different parts of the country. Again, we want to compare the performance of stores in relation to each other. We may have different university business schools running

Figure 4.11 The Excel Solution for the Leisure Air Revenue Management Problem

TARGET CELL (MAX)

Name	Original Value	Final Value
Objective function	0	103103

ADJUSTABLE CELLS

Name	Original Value	Final Value
GAQ	0	33
GSQ	0	44
GVQ	0	22
GAY	0	16
GSY	0	6
GVY	0	11
EAQ	0	26
ESQ	0	36
EVQ	0	39
EAY	0	15
ESY	0	7
EVY	0	9
ASQ	0	31
ASY	0	8
AVQ	0	41
AVY	0	10

CONSTRAINTS

Name	Cell Value	Status	Slack
1	132	Binding	0
2	132	Binding	0
3	132	Binding	0
4	132	Binding	0
5	33	Binding	0
6	44	Binding	0
7	22	Not Binding	23
8	16	Binding	0
9	6	Binding	0
10	11	Binding	0
11	26	Binding	0
12	36	Not Binding	20
13	39	Binding	0
14	15	Binding	0
15	7	Binding	0
16	9	Binding	0
17	31	Not Binding	33
18	8	Binding	0
19	41	Not Binding	5
20	10	Binding	0

ADJUSTABLE CELLS

Name	Final Value	Reduced Cost	Objective Coefficient	Allowable Increase	Allowable Decrease
GAQ	33	0	178	1E+30	174
GSQ	44	0	268	1E+30	85
GVQ	22	0	228	85	4
GAY	16	0	380	1E+30	376
GSY	6	0	456	1E+30	273
GVY	11	0	560	1E+30	332
EAQ	26	0	199	1E+30	129
ESQ	36	0	249	55	70
EVQ	39	0	349	1E+30	55
EAY	15	0	385	1E+30	315
ESY	7	0	444	1E+30	195
EVY	9	0	580	1E+30	286
ASQ	31	0	179	70	55
ASY	8	0	380	1E+30	201
AVQ	41	0	224	4	85
AVY	10	0	582	1E+30	358

CONSTRAINTS

Name	Final Value	Shadow Price	Constraint R.H. Side	Allowable Increase	Allowable Decrease
1	132	4	132	23	5
2	132	70	132	20	33
3	132	224	132	5	41
4	132	179	132	33	31
5	33	174	33	5	23
6	44	85	44	5	23
7	22	0	45	1E+30	23
8	16	376	16	5	16
9	6	273	6	5	6
10	11	332	11	22	11
11	26	129	26	33	20
12	36	0	56	1E+30	20
13	39	55	39	33	5
14	15	315	15	33	15
15	7	195	7	36	7
16	9	286	9	33	5
17	31	0	64	1E+30	33
18	8	201	8	31	8
19	41	0	46	1E+30	5
20	10	358	10	41	5

MBA programmes. We want to compare the performance of the different schools against each other. It is not immediately obvious why LP is relevant in this type of situation. After all, it does not look as if we will be trying to optimize anything. However, let us look at the information shown in Table 4.17 and see how LP can be applied. The data relate to four hospitals that provide health care in a particular

DEA was first proposed by Charnes, Cooper and Rhodes in 1978

region of the country: the General, the University, the County and the City hospitals. The data show a number of variables for each hospital:

- *Full time equivalent (FTE) staff*: the total number of full-time equivalent staff working in each hospital.
- *Supply costs*: the costs, in €000s, of running each hospital each year. Such costs will be made up of the cost of drugs and medicines as well as routine operational costs such as heating, maintenance, cleaning, etc.
- *Bed days available*: this measures the hospital's capacity to provide health care and measures the number of beds available multiplied by the number of days in the year each bed was available. For example, with ten beds available for, say, 350 days in the year we would have 3500 bed days available.
- *Number of in-patient days treatment provided*: an in-patient is someone admitted to hospital for health treatment. This variable measures the total number of days that in-patients were being treated at the hospital. For example, if we had 20 in-patients each staying five days in the hospital for treatment then the number of in-patient days provided would be 100.
- *Out-patients treated*: an out-patient is someone requiring medical treatment but who does not need to be admitted into the hospital. They can be treated at the hospital and leave the same day.
- *Nurses trained*: the number of people who have completed a formal nurse training programme at the hospital.
- *Paramedics trained*: the number of people who have completed a formal paramedic training programme at the hospital.

One aspect that hospital management is likely to be interested in is relative performance. How is an individual hospital performing in comparison with the others? Whilst there are a number of different ways we could approach such an investigation into efficiency the one we shall explore utilizes features of the basic LP model. We can actually view the information in the table as a set of **inputs** and a set of **outputs**. Simply, inputs are the resources going into a hospital so it can produce certain outputs. So, in the case of the hospitals, we have FTE staff, supply costs and available bed days as the inputs – the resources used by the hospitals. These resources are needed in order to produce outputs – here to provide treatment and care to patients in the form of in-patient days and out-patients treated; and to provide training to nurses and paramedics. Now, in terms of efficiency, other things being equal we would like to get the most outputs from the least inputs and we would be interested in seeing how the four hospitals are doing in terms of efficiency in relation to each other.

Table 4.17 Performance Data for the Four Hospitals

	Hospital			
Variable	**General**	**University**	**County**	**City**
FTE staff	285.2	162.3	275.7	210.4
Supply costs (€000s)	123.8	128.7	348.5	154.1
Bed days available (000s)	106.72	64.21	104.1	104.04
Number of in-patient days provided (000s)	48.14	34.62	36.72	33.16
Outpatients treated (000s)	43.1	27.11	45.98	56.46
Nurses trained	253	148	175	160
Paramedics trained	41	27	23	84

However, a simple examination of Table 4.17 suggests that such comparison is not going to be easy given that we have multiple inputs and multiple outputs. County hospital, for example, has a higher output of trained nurses than University hospital but a lower output of trained paramedics. And to make matters worse their inputs are different also! To progress, let us introduce a simple expression of efficiency:

$$\text{Efficiency} = \frac{\text{output}}{\text{input}}$$

That is, an organization will be more efficient the more output it produces in relation to its input. However, if we have multiple outputs and inputs, we must show this as some sort of average output to average input. Clearly, a simple average of outputs/inputs will not work given the varied units of measurement, so instead we have:

$$\text{Efficiency} = \frac{\text{weighted outputs}}{\text{weighted inputs}}$$

That is, an organization's efficiency is the ratio of its weighted outputs to its weighted inputs. Conventionally, efficiency is shown between 0 and 1 (or 0 to 100). However, we are still left with the problem of weights. How do we determine suitable weights? After all, different hospitals may place differing priorities on individual outputs and inputs. County hospital, for example, may decide to put more importance on out-patient treatments rather than paramedics trained while City hospital may put a higher weight on paramedics trained and less on in-patient days provided. DEA resolves this problem very simply. The DEA approach is to find the set of weights for hospital x that maximizes that particular hospital's efficiency score (and with the word *maximizes* we are back in LP territory once more). By definition, those weights will optimize hospital x's efficiency score. We then use those same weights to calculate the efficiency score for the other hospitals in the data set. Clearly those weights may not be the optimal weights for the other hospitals. However, by looking at the efficiency scores calculated, we can determine hospital x's efficiency relative to the other hospitals. For example, let us suppose that hospital x's efficiency score was 0.8 (on a scale from 0 to 1) whilst that for hospital y was 0.9 – calculated using the optimal weights for hospital x. We know that hospital x's weights are optimal for hospital x – this is the best efficiency score possible. And yet another hospital, using weights that may not be optimal for itself, has a higher efficiency. We would conclude that hospital x was relatively inefficient compared to hospital y. Hospital y is achieving more outputs and/or less input than hospital x.

So, we are looking to find a set of weights for hospital x that maximizes its efficiency score. That efficiency score will be relative to the efficiency scores of the other hospitals in the data set and all efficiency scores will be constrained to be between 0 and 1. We shall use as our decision variables, u_i and v_j, where u_i refer to the output weights and v_j refer to the input weights. In summary we will then have:

$$\text{Max.}\ \frac{\text{weighted outputs of hospital } x}{\text{weighted inputs of hospital } x}$$

s.t.

$$\frac{\text{weighted outputs of hospital 1}}{\text{weighted inputs of hospital 1}} \leq 1$$

$$\frac{\text{weighted outputs of hospital 2}}{\text{weighted inputs of hospital 2}} \leq 1$$

$$\frac{\text{weighted outputs of hospital 3}}{\text{weighted inputs of hospital 3}} \leq 1$$

$$\frac{\text{weighted outputs of hospital 4}}{\text{weighted inputs of hospital 4}} \leq 1$$

$$\text{weights} \geq 0$$

To see how this looks mathematically, let us examine County hospital's efficiency. We then have:

$$\text{Max}: \frac{36.72u_1 + 45.98u_2 + 175u_3 + 23u_4}{275.7v_1 + 348.5v_2 + 104.1v_3}$$

s.t.

$$\frac{48.14u_1 + 43.1u_2 + 253u_3 + 41u_4}{285.2v_1 + 123.8v_2 + 106.72v_3} \leq 1$$

$$\frac{34.62u_1 + 27.11u_2 + 148u_3 + 27u_4}{162.3v_1 + 128.7v_2 + 64.21v_3} \leq 1$$

$$\frac{36.72u_1 + 45.98u_2 + 175u_3 + 23u_4}{275.7v_1 + 348.5v_2 + 104.1v_3} \leq 1$$

$$\frac{33.16u_1 + 56.46u_2 + 160u_3 + 84u_4}{210.4v_1 + 154.1v_2 + 104.04v_3} \leq 1$$

$$u_1,\ u_2,\ u_3,\ u_4,\ v_1,\ v_2,\ v_3 \geq 0$$

The objective function is set to optimize the efficiency score by finding the most favourable values for the weights/decision variables. We then have a constraint for the efficiency score using the optimum weights for County for each of the four hospitals in the data set. Each constraint must be no greater than 1 given that we are assessing efficiency at between 0 and 1. Clearly the constraints are not in the standard linear format, but this is easily remedied. Transforming the first constraint, for example, we have:

$$\frac{48.14u_1 + 43.1u_2 + 253u_3 + 41u_4}{285.2v_1 + 123.8v_2 + 106.72v_3} \leq 1$$

$$48.14u_1 + 43.1u_2 + 253u_3 + 41u_4 \leq 285.2v_1 + 123.8v_2 + 106.72v_3$$

$$48.14u_1 + 43.1u_2 + 253u_3 + 41u_4 - 285.2v_1 - 123.8v_2 - 106.72v \leq 0$$

We can transform the other three constraints in the same way. Transforming the objective function, however, is less obvious. To do so we need to observe that when we are seeking to maximize a ratio, as in this case, it is the relative magnitude of the numerator and denominator that are of interest and not their individual values. We can therefore achieve the same by setting the denominator to some constant value and then maximize the numerator. Here we shall set the denominator, the weighted inputs, to take a value of 1. Our objective function then becomes:

$$\text{Max}:$$

$$36.72u_1 + 45.98u_2 + 175u_3 + 23u_4$$

But with an additional constraint that:

$$275.7v_1 + 348.5v_2 + 104.1v_3 = 1$$

The full formulation is then:

$$\begin{aligned}
&\text{Max}: \\
&36.72u_1 + 45.98u_2 + 175u_3 + 23u_4 \\
&\text{s.t.} \\
&275.7v_1 + 348.5v_2 + 104.1v_3 + 1 \\
&48.14u_1 + 43.1u_2 + 253u_3 + 41u_4 - 285.2v_1 - 123.8v_2 - 106.72v \leq 0 \\
&34.62u_1 + 27.11u_2 + 148u_3 + 27u_4 - 162.3v_1 - 128.7v_2 - 64.21v_3 \leq 0 \\
&36.72u_1 + 45.98u_2 + 175u_3 + 23u_4 - 275.7v_1 - 348.5v_2 - 104.1v_3 \leq 0 \\
&33.16u_1 + 56.46u_2 + 160u_3 + 84u_4 - 210.4v_1 - 154.1v_2 - 104.04v_3 \leq 0 \\
&u_1,\ u_2,\ u_3,\ u_4,\ v_1,\ v_2,\ v_3 \geq 0
\end{aligned}$$

The LP problem can now be solved in the usual way. Figure 4.12 shows the results. The objective function takes a value of 0.902. This is the efficiency score for County hospital. Given that this is less than 1 tells us that County hospital is relatively inefficient compared to at least one other hospital in the data set. Using the optimum weights for County hospital, we can calculate the efficiency scores for the other hospitals:

General hospital:	0.99
University hospital:	1.00
County hospital:	0.90
City hospital	1.00

The 'envelopment' part of DEA comes from the fact that the efficient units create an 'envelope' or frontier envelope, or frontier, around the data set.

In fact we see that all the other hospitals are more efficient than County with both University and City hospitals having maximum efficiency. This implies that County's efficiency can be improved – more outputs and/or less inputs are possible given the performance of the other hospitals. Advanced analysis of the DEA results (which is beyond this text) would also enable managers to set numerical targets in terms of what input/output quantities should be for County. We could now repeat the analysis for the other three hospitals in the data set to assess their relative efficiency. For example, we could re-formulate the problem to look at General hospital. The objective function would now use the numerical parameters for General hospital from Table 4.17 and the equality constraint would also use appropriate numerical parameters. Solving the new problem would give the optimum input/output weights for General hospital and again its own efficiency score.

Figure 4.12 Excel Solution for the Hospital DEA Problem

TARGET CELL (MAX)

Name	Original Value	Final Value
Objective function	0	0.901677796

ADJUSTABLE CELLS

Name	Original Value	Final Value
u1	0	0
u2	0	0.012377016
u3	0	0.001900472
u4	0	0
v1	0	0
v2	0	0
v3	0	0.009606148

CONSTRAINTS

Name	Cell Value	Status	Slack
Weight equality	-0.010899304	Not Binding	0.010899304
General	0	Binding	0
University	-0.098322204	Not Binding	0.098322204
County	0	Binding	0
City	1	Not Binding	0

DEA is a powerful application of linear programming and has been used to compare efficiency across many different types of organization such as schools, hospitals, banks, retail stores. It has proved so popular that it has its own specialist software packages and a number of dedicated websites.

NOTES AND COMMENTS

1 Remember that the goal of data envelopment analysis is to identify operating units that are relatively inefficient. The method *does not* necessarily identify the operating units that are relatively efficient. Just because the efficiency index is $E = 1$, we cannot conclude that the unit being analyzed is relatively efficient. Indeed, any unit that has the largest output on any one of the output measures cannot be judged relatively inefficient.

2 It is possible for DEA to show all but one unit to be relatively inefficient. Such would be the case if a unit producing the most of every output also consumes the least of every input. Such cases are extremely rare in practice.

3 In applying data envelopment analysis to problems involving a large group of operating units, practitioners have found that roughly 50 per cent of the operating units can be identified as inefficient. Comparing each relatively inefficient unit to the units contributing to the composite unit may be helpful in understanding how the operation of each relatively inefficient unit can be improved.

MANAGEMENT SCIENCE IN ACTION

Pupil transportation in North Carolina

Ensuring value for money for the taxpayer is a key expectation placed on every public sector organization. At the time of this project, North Carolina was spending around US$150 million every year on pupil transportation to and from school with around 13 000 school buses transporting almost 700 000 every day to 100 school districts. The Department of Public Instruction was tasked with reviewing the situation, specifically to ensure that school districts that operated efficiently were reimbursed in full for pupil transportation costs whilst those less efficient were reimbursed only as much as was seen to be fair and equitable. It was recognized that DEA had considerable potential to inform these decisions. The DEA model that was developed used two inputs: the number of buses used to transport pupils and total operating expenditure; and one output, the average number of pupils transported per day. However, the problem was complicated by the fact that school districts were very diverse in terms of their population base, demographic mix and school locations. As a result the initial efficiency scores resulting from the DEA solution were then adjusted to compensate for these different factors. There was then a programme over four years of phasing in the funding allocations to match the adjusted efficiency scores, with considerable effort going into convincing the decision makers that the new system was both fair and provided an incentive for the less efficient school districts to improve their performance over time and hence increase funding. The modelling project has resulted in school districts, including those with high efficiency scores, reviewing their transportation arrangements and seeking performance improvements. Among the improvements realized were:

- reduction in the number of buses needed;
- reduction in distance travelled;
- reduced operating costs;
- improved safety.

With total projected savings of around $130 million over a six-year period.

Based on T. R. Sexton, S. Sleeper and R. E. Taggart Jr, 'Improving pupil transportation in North Carolina', *Interfaces* 24 1 (1994): 87–103.

Summary

- This chapter has introduced a number of common areas of application of linear programming in business and management.
- The formulation stage of LP is typically one of the most difficult in the real world and one where practise, experience and awareness of other LP applications does make things much easier.
- LP applications in the same area often have similar characteristics and this can be helpful when formulating a new problem in the same area.
- Specialist software has been developed for a number of these application problem types, dedicated websites have been established to bring users together and in some cases academic journals and member societies created.

Problems

Note: The following problems have been designed to give you an understanding and appreciation of the broad range of problems that can be formulated as linear programmes. You should be able to formulate a linear programming model for each of the problems. However, you will need access to a linear programming computer package to develop the solutions and make the requested interpretations.

SELF *test*

1 The Uppsala Chamber of Commerce periodically sponsors public service seminars and programmes. Currently, promotional plans are under way for this year's programme. Advertising alternatives include television, Internet and newspaper. Audience estimates, costs and maximum media usage limitations are as shown.

Constraint	Television	Internet	Newspaper
Audience per advertisement	100 000	18 000	40 000
Cost per advertisement	€2 000	€300	€600
Maximum media usage	10	20	10

To ensure a balanced use of advertising media, Internet advertisements must not exceed 50 per cent of the total number of advertisements authorized. In addition, television should account for at least 10 per cent of the total number of advertisements authorized.

a. If the promotional budget is limited to €18 200, how many commercial messages should be run on each medium to maximize total audience contact? What is the allocation of the budget among the three media, and what is the total audience reached?
b. By how much would audience contact increase if an extra €100 were allocated to the promotional budget?

SELF *test*

2 The management of Hartman Company is trying to determine the amount of each of two products to produce over the coming planning period. The following information concerns labour availability, labour utilization and product profitability.

	Product (hours/unit)		
Department	1	2	Labour-Hours Available
A	1.00	0.35	100
B	0.30	0.20	36
C	0.20	0.50	50
Profit contribution/unit	€30.00	€15.00	

a. Develop a linear programming model of the Hartman Company problem. Solve the model to determine the optimal production quantities of products 1 and 2.
b. In calculating the profit contribution per unit, management doesn't deduct labour costs because they are considered fixed for the upcoming planning period. However, suppose that overtime can be scheduled in some of the departments. Which departments would you recommend scheduling for overtime? How much would you be willing to pay per hour of overtime in each department?

c. Suppose that ten, six and eight hours of overtime may be scheduled in departments A, B and C, respectively. The cost per hour of overtime is €18 in department A, €22.50 in department B and €12 in department C. Formulate a linear programming model that can be used to determine the optimal production quantities if overtime is made available. What are the optimal production quantities, and what is the revised total contribution to profit? How much overtime do you recommend using in each department? What is the increase in the total contribution to profit if overtime is used?

3 Hilltop Coffee manufactures a coffee product by blending three types of coffee beans. The cost per kilo and the available kilos of each bean are as follows:

Bean	Cost per kilo	Available kilos
1	€0.50	500
2	€0.70	600
3	€0.45	400

Consumer tests with coffee products were used to provide ratings on a scale of 0–100, with higher ratings indicating higher quality. Product quality standards for the blended coffee require a consumer rating for aroma to be at least 75 and a consumer rating for taste to be at least 80. The individual ratings of the aroma and taste for coffee made from 100 per cent of each bean are as follows.

Bean	Aroma Rating	Taste Rating
1	75	86
2	85	88
3	60	75

Assume that the aroma and taste attributes of the coffee blend will be a weighted average of the attributes of the beans used in the blend.

a. What is the minimum-cost blend that will meet the quality standards and provide 1000 kilos of the blended coffee product?
b. What is the cost per kilo for the coffee blend?
c. Determine the aroma and taste ratings for the coffee blend.
d. If additional coffee were to be produced, what would be the expected cost per kilo?

SELF *test*

4 Ajax Fuels is developing a new additive for aeroplane fuels. The additive is a mixture of three ingredients: A, B and C. For proper performance, the total amount of additive (amount of A + amount of B + amount of C) must be at least ten grams per litre of fuel. However, because of safety reasons, the amount of additive must not exceed 15 grams per litre of fuel. The mix or blend of the three ingredients is critical. At least one gram of ingredient A must be used for every gram of ingredient B. The amount of ingredient C must be at least one-half the amount of ingredient A. If the costs per gram for ingredients A, B and C are €0.10, €0.03 and €0.09, respectively, find the minimum-cost mixture of A, B and C for each litre of aeroplane fuel.

5 Kunz and Sons manufactures two products used in the heavy equipment industry. Both products require manufacturing operations in two departments. The following are the production time (in hours) and profit contribution figures for the two products.

		Labour-Hours	
Product	**Profit per Unit, €**	**Dept. A**	**Dept. B**
1	25	6	12
2	20	8	10

For the coming production period, Kunz has available a total of 900 hours of labour that can be allocated to either of the two departments. Find the production plan and labour allocation (hours assigned in each department) that will maximize the total contribution to profit.

SELF *test*

6 The North Somerset Police's Department schedules police officers for eight-hour shifts. The start times for the shifts are 8:00 A.M., noon, 4:00 P.M., 8:00 P.M., midnight and 4:00 A.M. An officer beginning a shift at one of these times works for the next eight hours. During normal weekday operations, the number of officers needed varies depending on the time of day. The department staffing guidelines require the following minimum number of officers on duty:

Time of Day	Minimum Officers on Duty
8:00 A.M.–Noon	5
Noon–4:00 P.M.	6
4:00 P.M.–8:00 P.M.	10
8:00 P.M.–Midnight	7
Midnight–4:00 A.M.	4
4:00 A.M.–8:00 A.M.	6

Determine the number of police officers that should be scheduled to begin the eight-hour shifts at each of the six times (8:00 A.M., noon, 4:00 P.M., 8:00 P.M., midnight and 4:00 A.M.) to minimize the total number of officers required. (*Hint*: Let x_1 = the number of officers beginning work at 8:00 A.M., x_2 = the number of officers beginning work at noon, and so on.)

SELF *test*

7 Reconsider the Welte Mutual Funds problem from Section 4.5. Define your decision variables as the fraction of funds invested in each security. Also, modify the constraints limiting investments in the oil and steel industries as follows: no more than 50 per cent of the total funds invested in stock (oil and steel) may be invested in the oil industry, and no more than 50 per cent of the funds invested in stock (oil and steel) may be invested in the steel industry.

a. Solve the revised linear programming model. What fraction of the portfolio should be invested in each type of security?
b. How much should be invested in each type of security?
c. What are the total earnings for the portfolio?
d. What is the marginal rate of return on the portfolio? That is, how much more could be earned by investing one more euro in the portfolio?

SELF *test*

8 A local hospital purchases two types of drug from three different suppliers. The suppliers have limited capacity, and no one supplier can meet all the hospital's needs. In addition, the suppliers charge different prices for the drugs. Price data (in price per unit) are as follows:

	Supplier		
Drug	**1**	**2**	**3**
A	€12	€13	€14
B	€10	€11	€10

Each supplier has a limited capacity in terms of the total number of units of each drug components it can supply. However, as long as the hospital provides sufficient advance orders, each supplier can devote its capacity to drug A, drug B or any combination of the two, if the total number of units ordered is within its capacity. Supplier capacities are as follows:

Supplier	1	2	3
Capacity	600	1000	800

If the hospital expects to need 1000 units of drug A and 800 units of drug B, what purchases do you recommend? That is, how many units of each drug should be ordered from each supplier? What is the total purchase cost for the drug?

9 The Atlantic Seafood Company (ASC) is a buyer and distributor of seafood products that are sold to restaurants and speciality seafood outlets throughout the Western Europe. ASC has a frozen storage facility in Lisbon that serves as the primary distribution point for all products. One of the ASC products is frozen large black tiger shrimp, which are sized at 16–20 pieces per pound. Each Saturday ASC can purchase more tiger shrimp or sell the tiger shrimp at the existing Lisbon warehouse market price. The ASC goal is to buy tiger shrimp at a low weekly price and sell it later at a higher price. ASC currently has 20 000 pounds of tiger shrimp in storage. Space is available to store a maximum of 100 000 pounds of tiger shrimp each week. In addition, ASC developed the following estimates of tiger shrimp prices for the next four weeks:

Week	**Price/lb.**
1	€6.00
2	€6.20
3	€6.65
4	€5.55

ASC would like to determine the optimal buying-storing-selling strategy for the next four weeks. The cost to store a pound of shrimp for one week is €0.15, and to account for unforeseen changes in supply or demand, management also indicated that 25 000 pounds of tiger shrimp must be in storage at the end of week 4. Determine the optimal buying-storing-selling strategy for ASC. What is the projected four-week profit?

SELF *test*

10 Romans Food Market, located in Italy, carries a variety of speciality foods from around the world. Two of the store's leading products use the Romans Food Market name: Romans Regular Coffee and Romans DeCaf Coffee. These coffees are blends of Brazilian Natural and Colombian Mild coffee beans, which are purchased from a distributor. Because Romans purchases large quantities, the coffee beans may be purchased on an as-needed basis for a price 10 per cent higher than the market price the distributor pays for the beans. The current market price is €0.47 per kilo for Brazilian Natural and €0.62 per kilo for Colombian Mild. The compositions of each coffee blend are as follows:

	Blend	
Bean	**Regular**	**DeCaf**
Brazilian Natural	75%	40%
Colombian Mild	25%	60%

Romans sells the Regular blend for €3.60 per kilo and the DeCaf blend for €4.40 per kilo. Romans would like to place an order for the Brazilian and Colombian coffee beans that will enable the production of 1000 kilos of Roman Regular coffee and 500 kilos of Roman DeCaf coffee. The production cost is €0.80 per kilo for the Regular blend. Because of the extra steps required to produce DeCaf, the production cost for the DeCaf blend is €1.05 per kilo. Packaging costs for both products are €0.25 per kilo. Formulate a linear programming model that can be used to determine the kilos of Brazilian Natural and Colombian Mild that will maximize the total contribution to profit. What is the optimal solution and what is the contribution to profit?

SELF *test*

11 Seastrand Oil Company produces two grades of fuel: regular and high octane. Both fuels are produced by blending two types of crude oil. Although both types of crude oil contain the two important ingredients required to produce both fuels, the percentage of important ingredients in each type of crude oil differs, as does the cost per litre. The percentage of ingredients A and B in each type of crude oil and the cost per fuel are shown.

Crude Oil	Cost	Ingredient A	Ingredient B
1	€0.10	20%	60%
2	€0.15	50%	30%

Crude oil 1
60% ingredient B

Each litre of regular fuel must contain at least 40 per cent of ingredient A, whereas each fuel of high octane can contain at most 50 per cent of ingredient B. Daily demand for regular and high-octane fuel is 800 000 and 500 000 litres, respectively. How many litres of each type of crude oil should be used in the two fuels to satisfy daily demand at a minimum cost?

12 Frandec Company manufactures, assembles and rebuilds material handling equipment used in warehouses and distribution centres. One product, called a Liftmaster, is assembled from four components: a frame, a motor, two supports and a metal strap.

Frandec's production schedule calls for 5000 Liftmasters to be made next month. Frandec purchases the motors from an outside supplier, but the frames, supports and straps may either be manufactured by the company or purchased from an outside supplier. Manufacturing and purchase costs per unit are shown.

Component	Manufacturing Cost	Purchase Cost
Frame	€38.00	€51.00
Support	€11.50	€15.00
Strap	€ 6.50	€ 7.50

Three departments are involved in the production of these components. The time (in minutes per unit) required to process each component in each department and the available capacity (in hours) for the three departments are as follows:

	Department		
Component	**Cutting**	**Milling**	**Shaping**
Frame	3.5	2.2	3.1
Support	1.3	1.7	2.6
Strap	0.8	—	1.7
Capacity (hours)	350	420	680

a. How many of each component should be manufactured and how many should be purchased?
b. What is the total cost of the manufacturing and purchasing plan?
c. How many hours of production time are used in each department?
d. How much should Frandec be willing to pay for an additional hour of time in the shaping department?
e. Another manufacturer has offered to sell frames to Frandec for €45 each. Could Frandec improve its position by pursuing this opportunity? Why or why not?

13 The Two-Rivers Oil Company near Pittsburgh transports gasoline to its distributors by truck. The company recently contracted to supply gasoline distributors in southern Ohio, and it has $600 000 available to spend on the necessary expansion of its fleet of gasoline tank trucks. Three models of gasoline tank trucks are available.

Truck Model	Capacity (gallons)	Purchase Cost	Monthly Operating Cost, Including Depreciation
Super Tanker	5 000	$67 000	$550
Regular Line	2 500	$55 000	$425
Econo-Tanker	1 000	$46 000	$350

The company estimates that the monthly demand for the region will be 550 000 gallons of gasoline. Because of the size and speed differences of the trucks, the number of deliveries or round trips possible per month for each truck model will vary. Trip capacities are estimated at 15 trips per month for the Super Tanker, 20 trips per month for the Regular Line and 25 trips per month for the Econo-Tanker. Based on maintenance and driver availability, the firm does not want to add more than 15 new vehicles to its fleet. In addition, the company has decided to purchase at least three of the new Econo-Tankers for use on short-run, low-demand routes. As a final constraint, the company does not want more than half the new models to be Super Tankers.

a. If the company wishes to satisfy the gasoline demand with a minimum monthly operating expense, how many models of each truck should be purchased?
b. If the company did not require at least three Econo-Tankers and did not limit the number of Super Tankers to at most half the new models, how many models of each truck should be purchased?

SELF *test*

14 The Silver Star Bicycle Company in India will be manufacturing both men's and women's models for its Easy-Pedal ten-speed bicycles during the next two months. Management wants to develop a production schedule indicating how many bicycles of each model should be produced in each month. Current demand forecasts call for 150 men's and 125 women's models to be shipped during the first month and 200 men's and 150 women's models to be shipped during the second month. Additional data are shown.

		Labour Requirements (hours)		
Model	**Production Costs Indian Rupees (Rs)**	**Manufacturing**	**Assembly**	**Current Inventory**
Men's	1 200	2.0	1.5	20
Women's	900	1.6	1.0	30

Last month the company used a total of 1000 hours of labour. The company's labour relations policy will not allow the combined total hours of labour (manufacturing plus assembly) to increase or decrease by more than 100 hours from month to month. In addition, the company charges monthly inventory at the rate of 2 per cent of the production cost based on the inventory levels at the end of the month. The company would like to have at least 25 units of each model in inventory at the end of the two months.

a. Establish a production schedule that minimizes production and inventory costs and satisfies the labour-smoothing, demand and inventory requirements. What inventories will be maintained and what are the monthly labour requirements?
b. If the company changed the constraints so that monthly labour increases and decreases could not exceed 50 hours, what would happen to the production schedule? How much will the cost increase? What would you recommend?

15 Filtron Corporation produces filtration containers used in water treatment systems. Although business has been growing, the demand each month varies considerably. As a result, the company utilizes a mix of part-time and full-time employees to meet production demands. Although this approach provides Filtron with great flexibility, it resulted in increased costs and morale problems among employees. For instance, if Filtron needs to increase production from one month to the next, additional part-time employees have to be hired and trained, and costs go up. If Filtron has to decrease production, the workforce has to be reduced and Filtron incurs additional costs in terms of unemployment benefits and decreased morale. Best estimates are that increasing the number of units produced from one month to the next will increase production costs by €1.25 per unit, and that decreasing the number of units produced will increase production costs by €1.00 per unit. In February Filtron produced 10 000 filtration containers but only sold 7500 units; 2500 units are currently in inventory. The sales

forecasts for March, April and May are for 12 000 units, 8 000 units and 15 000 units, respectively. In addition, Filtron has the capacity to store up to 3000 filtration containers at the end of any month. Management would like to determine the number of units to be produced in March, April and May that will minimize the total cost of the monthly production increases and decreases.

SELF *test*

16 Jansson Cabinets received a contract to produce loud speaker cabinets for a major hi-fi manufacturer. The contract calls for the production of 3300 bookshelf speakers and 4100 floor speakers over the next two months, with the following delivery schedule.

Model	Month 1	Month 2
Bookshelf	2 100	1 200
Floor	1 500	2 600

Jansson estimates that the production time for each bookshelf model is 0.7 hours and the production time for each floor model is one hour. The raw material costs are €10 for each bookshelf model and €12 for each floor model. Labour costs are €22 per hour using regular production time and €33 using overtime. Jansson has up to 2400 hours of regular production time available each month and up to 1000 additional hours of overtime available each month. If production for either cabinet exceeds demand in month 1, the cabinets can be stored at a cost of €5 per cabinet. For each product, determine the number of units that should be manufactured each month on regular time and on overtime to minimize total production and storage costs.

17 EZ-Windows manufactures replacement windows for the home renovation business. In January, the company produced 15 000 windows and ended the month with 9000 windows in inventory. EZ-Windows management team would like to develop a production schedule for the next three months. A smooth production schedule is obviously desirable because it maintains the current workforce and provides a similar month-to-month operation. However, given the sales forecasts, the production capacities and the storage capabilities as shown, the management team does not think a smooth production schedule with the same production quantity each month possible.

	February	March	April
Sales forecast	15 000	16 500	20 000
Production capacity	14 000	14 000	18 000
Storage capacity	6 000	6 000	6 000

The company's cost accounting department estimates that increasing production by one window from one month to the next will increase total costs by €1.00 for each unit increase in the production level. In addition, decreasing production by one unit from one month to the next will increase total costs by €0.65 for each unit decrease in the production level. Ignoring production and inventory carrying costs, formulate and solve a linear programming model that will minimize the cost of changing production levels while still satisfying the monthly sales forecasts.

SELF *test*

18 Western Family Restaurant offers a variety of low-cost meals and quick service. Other than management, the restaurant operates with two full-time employees who work eight hours per day. The rest of the employees are part-time employees who are scheduled for four-hour shifts during peak meal times. On Saturdays the restaurant is open from 11:00 A.M. to 10:00 P.M. Management wants to develop a schedule for part-time employees that will minimize labour costs and still provide excellent customer service. The average wage rate for the part-time employees is €7.60 per hour. The total number of full-time and part-time employees needed varies with the time of day as shown.

Time	Total Number of Employees Needed
11:00 A.M.–Noon	9
Noon–1:00 P.M.	9
1:00 P.M.–2:00 P.M.	9
2:00 P.M.–3:00 P.M.	3
3:00 P.M.–4:00 P.M.	3
4:00 P.M.–5:00 P.M.	3
5:00 P.M.–6:00 P.M.	6
6:00 P.M.–7:00 P.M.	12
7:00 P.M.–8:00 P.M.	12
8:00 P.M.–9:00 P.M.	7
9:00 P.M.–10:00 P.M.	7

One full-time employee comes on duty at 11:00 A.M., works four hours, takes an hour off, and returns for another four hours. The other full-time employee comes to work at 1:00 P.M. and works the same four-hours-on, one-hour-off, four-hours-on pattern.

a. Develop a minimum-cost schedule for part-time employees.
b. What is the total payroll for the part-time employees? How many part-time shifts are needed? Use the surplus variables to comment on the desirability of scheduling at least some of the part-time employees for three-hour shifts.
c. Assume that part-time employees can be assigned either a three-hour or four-hour shift. Develop a minimum-cost schedule for the part-time employees. How many part-time shifts are needed, and what is the cost savings compared to the previous schedule?

19 The Quick and Easy operates five fast-food restaurants in the UK. Input measures for the restaurants include weekly hours of operation, full-time equivalent staff and weekly supply expenses. Output measures of performance include average weekly contribution to profit, market share and annual growth rate. Data for the input and output measures are shown in the following tables.

	Input Measures		
Restaurant	Hours of Operation	FTE Staff	Supplies (£)
London	96	16	850
Manchester	110	22	1 400
Edinburgh	100	18	1 200
Bristol	125	25	1 500
Cardiff	120	24	1 600

	Output Measures		
Restaurant	Weekly Profit	Market Share (%)	Growth Rate (%)
London	£3 800	25	8.0
Manchester	£4 600	32	8.5
Edinburgh	£4 400	35	8.0
Bristol	£6 500	30	10.0
Cardiff	£6 000	28	9.0

a. Develop a linear programming model that can be used to evaluate the performance of the Manchester Quick and Easy restaurant.
b. Solve the model.
c. Is the Manchester Quick and Easy restaurant relatively inefficient? Discuss.
d. Where does the composite restaurant have more output than the Manchester restaurant? How much less of each input resource does the composite restaurant require when compared to the Manchester restaurant?
e. What other restaurants should be studied to find suggested ways for the Manchester restaurant to improve its efficiency?

SELF *test*

20 Reconsider the Leisure Air problem from Section 4.5. The demand forecasts shown in Table 4.16 represent Leisure Air's best estimates of demand. But, because demand cannot be forecasted perfectly, the number of seats actually sold for each origin-destination-itinerary fare (ODIF) may turn out to be smaller or larger than forecasted. Suppose that Leisure Air believes that economic conditions have improved and that their original forecast may be too low. To account for this possibility, Leisure Air is considering switching the Boeing 737–400 aeroplanes with Boeing 757–200 aeroplanes that Leisure Air has available in other markets. The Boeing 757–200 aeroplane has a seating capacity of 158.

a. Because of scheduling conflicts in other markets, suppose that Leisure Air is only able to obtain one Boeing 757–200. Should the larger plane be based in Glasgow or in Edinburgh? Explain.
b. Based upon your answer in part (a), determine a new allocation for the ODIFs. Briefly summarize the major differences between the new allocation using one Boeing 757–200 and the original allocation summarized in Figure 4.11.
c. Suppose that two Boeing 757–200 aeroplanes are available. Determine a new allocation for the ODIF's using the two larger aeroplanes. Briefly summarize the major differences between the new allocation using two Boeing 757–200 aeroplanes and the original allocation shown in Figure 4.11.
d. Consider the new solution obtained in part (b). Which ODIF has the highest bid price? What is the interpretation for this bid price?

CASE PROBLEM 1 Planning an Advertising Campaign

The Cossack Grill is an upscale restaurant located in St. Petersburg. To help plan an advertising campaign for the coming season, the restaurant's management team hired the advertising firm of Hartman & Jablinsky (HJ). The management team requested HJ's recommendation concerning how the advertising budget should be distributed across television, Internet and newspaper advertisements. The budget has been set at 279 000 Roubles.

In a meeting with the restaurant's management team, HJ consultants provided the following information about the industry exposure effectiveness rating per ad, their estimate of the number of potential new customers reached per ad and the cost for each ad.

Advertising Media	Exposure Rating per Ad	New Customers per Ad	Cost per Ad
Television	90	4 000	R10 000
Internet	25	2 000	R3 000
Newspaper	10	1 000	R1 000

The exposure rating is viewed as a measure of the value of the ad to both existing customers and potential new customers. It is a function of such things as image, message recall, visual and audio appeal and so on. As expected, the more expensive television advertisement has the highest exposure effectiveness rating along with the greatest potential for reaching new customers.

At this point, the HJ consultants pointed out that the data concerning exposure and reach were only applicable to the first few ads in each media. For television, HJ stated that the exposure rating of 90 and the 4000 new customers reached per ad were reliable for the first ten television ads. After ten ads, the benefit is expected to decline. For planning purposes, HJ recommended reducing the exposure rating to 55 and the estimate of the potential new customers reached to 1500 for any television ads beyond ten. For Internet ads, the preceding data are reliable up to a maximum of 15 ads. Beyond 15 ads, the exposure rating declines to 20 and the number of new customers reached declines to 1200 per ad. Similarly, for newspaper ads, the preceding data are reliable up to a maximum of 20; the exposure rating declines to five and the potential number of new customers reached declines to 800 for additional ads.

The restaurant's management team accepted maximizing the total exposure rating, across all media, as the objective of the advertising campaign. Because of management's concern with attracting new customers, management stated that the advertising campaign must reach at least 100 000 new customers. To balance the advertising campaign and make use of all advertising media, Flamingo's management team also adopted the following guidelines.

- Use at least twice as many Internet advertisements as television advertisements.
- Use no more than 20 television advertisements.
- The television budget should be at least R140 000.
- The Internet advertising budget is restricted to a maximum of R99 000.
- The newspaper budget is to be at least R30,000.

HJ agreed to work with these guidelines and provide a recommendation as to how the R279 000 advertising budget should be allocated among television, radio and newspaper advertising.

Managerial Report

Develop a model that can be used to determine the advertising budget allocation for the restaurant. Include a discussion of the following in your report.

1 A schedule showing the recommended number of television, Internet and newspaper advertisements and the budget allocation for each media. Show the total exposure and indicate the total number of potential new customers reached.

2 How would the total exposure change if an additional R10 000 were added to the advertising budget?

3 A discussion of the ranges for the objective function coefficients. What do the ranges indicate about how sensitive the recommended solution is to HJ's exposure rating coefficients?

4 After reviewing HJ's recommendation, the restaurant's management team asked how the recommendation would change if the objective of the advertising campaign was to maximize the number of potential new customers reached. Develop the media schedule under this objective.

5 Compare the recommendations from parts 1 and 4. What is your recommendation for the advertising campaign?

CASE PROBLEM 2 Phoenix Computer

Phoenix Computer manufactures and sells personal computers directly to customers. Orders are accepted by phone and through the company's website. Phoenix will be introducing several new laptop models over the next few months and management recognizes a need to develop technical support personnel to specialize in the new laptop systems. One option being considered is to hire new employees and put them through a three-month training programme. Another option is to put current customer service specialists through a two-month training programme on the new laptop models. Phoenix estimates that the need for laptop specialists will grow from 0 to 100 during the months of May through September as follows: May – 20; June – 30; July – 85; August – 85; and September – 100. After September, Phoenix expects that maintaining a staff of 100 laptop specialists will be sufficient.

The annual salary for a new employee is estimated to be €27 000 whether the person is hired to enter the training programme or to replace a current employee who is entering the training programme. The annual salary for the current Phoenix employees who are being considered for the training programme is approximately €36 000. The cost of the three-month training programme is €1500 per person, and the cost of the two-month training programme is €1000 per person. Note that the length of the training programme means that a lag will occur between the time when a new person is hired and the time a new laptop specialist is available. The number of current employees who will be available for training is limited. Phoenix estimates that the following numbers can be made available in the coming months: March – 15; April – 20; May – 0; June – 5; and July – 10. The training centre has the capacity to start new three-month and two-month training classes each month; however, the total number of students (new and current employees) that begin training each month cannot exceed 25.

Phoenix needs to determine the number of new employees that should begin the three-month training programme each month and the number of current employees that should begin the two-month training programme each month. The objective is to satisfy staffing needs during May through September at the lowest possible total cost; that is, minimize the incremental salary cost and the total training cost.

It is currently January, and Phoenix Computer would like to develop a plan for hiring new employees and determining the mix of new and current employees to place in the training programme.

Managerial Report

Perform an analysis of the Phoenix Computer problem and prepare a report that summarizes your findings. Be sure to include information on and analysis of the following items.

1 The incremental salary and training cost associated with hiring a new employee and training him/her to be a laptop specialist.
2 The incremental salary and training cost associated with putting a current employee through the training programme. (Don't forget that a replacement must be hired when the current employee enters the programme.)
3 Recommendations regarding the hiring and training plan that will minimize the salary and training costs over the February through August period as well as answers to these questions: What is the total cost of providing technical support for the new laptop models? How much higher will monthly payroll costs be in September than in January?

CASE PROBLEM 3 Textile Mill Scheduling

The Shimla Textile Mill* in India produces five different fabrics for European clothing manufacturers. Each fabric can be woven on one or more of the mill's 38 looms. The sales department's forecast of demand for the next month is shown in Table 4.18, along with data on the selling price per metre, variable cost per metre and purchase price per metre. Prices are in euros. The mill operates 24 hours a day and is scheduled for 30 days during the coming month.

*This case is based on the Calhoun Textile Mill Case by Jeffrey D. Camm, P.M. Dearing, and Suresh K. Tadisnia, 1987.

The mill has two types of looms: dobbie and regular. The dobbie looms are more versatile and can be used for all five fabrics. The regular looms can produce only three of the fabrics. The mill has a total of 38 looms: 8 are dobbie and 30 are regular. The rate of production for each fabric on each type of loom is given in Table 4.19. The time required to change over from producing one fabric to another is negligible and does not have to be considered.

The Mill satisfies all demand with either its own fabric or fabric purchased from another mill. Fabrics that cannot be woven at the Mill because of limited loom capacity will be purchased from another mill. The purchase price of each fabric is also shown in Table 4.18.

Managerial Report

Develop a model that can be used to schedule production for the Shimla Textile Mill, and at the same time, determine how many metres of each fabric must be purchased from another mill. Include a discussion and analysis of the following items in your report.

1 The final production schedule and loom assignments for each fabric.
2 The projected total contribution to profit.
3 A discussion of the value of additional loom time (The mill is considering purchasing a ninth dobbie loom. What is your estimate of the monthly profit contribution of this additional loom?).
4 A discussion of the objective coefficients ranges.
5 A discussion of how the objective of minimizing total costs would provide a different model than the objective of maximizing total profit contribution. (How would the interpretation of the objective coefficients ranges differ for these two models?).

Table 4.18 Monthly Demand, Selling Price, Variable Cost and Purchase Price Data for Shimla Textile Mill Fabrics

Fabric	Demand (metres)	Selling Price (€/metre)	Variable Cost (€/metre)	Purchase Price (€/metre)
1	16 500	0.99	0.66	0.80
2	22 000	0.86	0.55	0.70
3	62 000	1.10	0.49	0.60
4	7 500	1.24	0.51	0.70
5	62 000	0.70	0.50	0.70

Table 4.19 Loom Production Rates for the Shimla Textile Mill

	Loom Rate (metres/hour)	
Fabric	Dobbie	Regular
1	4.63	—
2	4.63	—
3	5.23	5.23
4	5.23	5.23
5	4.17	4.17

Note: Fabrics 1 and 2 can be manufactured only on the dobbie loom.

CASE PROBLEM 4 Workforce Scheduling

The Emergency Department at the local hospital provides emergency health care on an as-needed basis for people involved in accidents, having injuries, etc. Understandably, it is difficult to predict how busy the Department will be at any one time and, accordingly, it is also difficult to plan and schedule its workforce requirements, particularly for nurses qualified and experienced in working in such a department. Recently the hospital has started using WorkForce Unlimited, a company that specializes in providing temporary nursing staff to the health care sector. WorkForce Unlimited offered to provide temporary nurses under three contract options that differ in terms of the length of employment and the cost. The three options are summarized:

Option	Length of Employment	Cost
1	One month	€2 000
2	Two months	€4 800
3	Three months	€7 500

The longer contract periods are more expensive because WorkForce Unlimited experiences greater difficulty finding temporary nursing staff who are willing to commit to longer work assignments.

Over the next six months, the hospital projects the following needs for additional nurses in the Emergency Department.

Month	January	February	March	April	May	June
Nurses Needed	10	23	19	26	20	14

Each month, the hospital can hire as many temporary nurses as needed under each of the three options. For instance, if the hospital hires five nurses in January under Option 2, WorkForce Unlimited will supply the hospital with five temporary nurses who will work two months: January and February. For these nurses, the hospital will have to pay 5(€4800) = €24,000. Because of some negotiations under way, the hospital does not want to commit to any contractual obligations for temporary nurses that extend beyond June.

The hospital's health and safety programme requires each temporary nurse to receive training at the time of hire. The training programme is required even if the person worked for the hospital in the past. The hospital estimates that the cost of training is €875 each time a temporary nurse is hired. Thus, if a temporary nurse is hired for one month, the hospital will incur a training cost of €875, but will incur no additional training cost if the employee is on a two- or three-month contract.

Managerial Report

Develop a model that can be used to determine the number of temporary nurses the hospital should hire each month under each contract plan in order to meet the projected needs at a minimum total cost. Include the following items in your report:

1 A schedule that shows the number of temporary nurses that the hospital should hire each month for each contract option.

2 A summary table that shows the number of temporary nurses that the hospital should hire under each contract option, the associated contract cost for each option, and the associated training cost for each option. Provide summary totals showing the total number of temporary nurses hired, total contract costs and total training costs.

3 If the cost to train each temporary nurse could be reduced to €700 per month, what effect would this change have on the hiring plan? Explain. Discuss the implications that this effect on the hiring plan has for identifying methods for reducing training costs. How much of a reduction in training

costs would be required to change the hiring plan based on a training cost of €875 per temporary nurse?

4 Suppose that the hospital hired ten full-time nurses at the beginning of January in order to satisfy part of the requirements over the next six months. If the hospital can hire full-time nurses for €16.50 per hour, including fringe benefits, what effect would it have on total labour and training costs over the six-month period as compared to hiring only temporary nurses? Assume that full-time and temporary nurses both work approximately 160 hours per month. Provide a recommendation regarding the decision to hire additional full-time nurses.

CASE PROBLEM 5 Cinergy Coal Allocation*

Cinergy Corporation manufactures and distributes electricity for customers located in Indiana, Kentucky and Ohio. The company spends $725 to $750 million each year for the fuel needed to operate its coal-fired and gas-fired power plants; 92 per cent to 95 per cent of the fuel used is coal. Cinergy uses ten coal-burning generating plants: five located inland and five located on the Ohio River. Some plants have more than one generating unit. As the seventh-largest coal-burning utility in the United States, Cinergy uses 28–29 million tons of coal per year at a cost of approximately $2 million every day.

The company purchases coal using fixed-tonnage or variable-tonnage contracts from mines in Indiana (49 per cent), West Virginia (20 per cent), Ohio (12 per cent), Kentucky (11 per cent), Illinois (5 per cent) and Pennsylvania (3 per cent). The company must purchase all of the coal contracted for on fixed-tonnage contracts, but on variable-tonnage contracts it can purchase varying amounts up to the limit specified in the contract. The coal is shipped from the mines to Cinergy's generating facilities in Ohio, Kentucky and Indiana. The cost of coal varies from $19 to $35 per ton and transportation/delivery charges range from $1.50 to $5.00 per ton.

A model is used to determine the megawatt-hours (mWh)of electricity that each generating unit is expected to produce and to provide a measure of each generating unit's efficiency, referred to as the heat rate. The heat rate is the total BTUs required to produce one kilowatt-hour (kWh) of electrical power.

Coal Allocation Model

Cinergy uses a linear programming model, called the coal allocation model, to allocate coal to its generating facilities. The objective of the coal allocation model is to determine the lowest-cost method for purchasing and distributing coal to the generating units. The supply/availability of the coal is determined by the contracts with the various mines, and the demand for coal at the generating units is determined indirectly by the megawatt-hours of electricity each unit must produce.

The cost to process coal, called the add-on cost, depends upon the characteristics of the coal (moisture content, ash content, BTU content, sulfur content and grindability) and the efficiency of the generating unit. The add-on cost plus the transportation cost are added to the purchase cost of the coal to determine the total cost to purchase and use the coal.

Current Problem

Cinergy signed three fixed-tonnage contracts and four variable-tonnage contracts. The company would like to determine the least-cost way to allocate the coal available through these contracts to five generating units. The relevant data for the three fixed-tonnage contracts are as follows:

*The authors are indebted to Thomas Mason and David Bossee of Cinergy Corp. for their contribution to this case problem.

Supplier	Number of Tons Contracted For	Cost ($/ton)	BTUs/lb
RAG	350 000	22	13 000
Peabody Coal Sales	300 000	26	13 300
American Coal Sales	275 000	22	12 600

For example, the contract signed with RAG requires Cinergy to purchase 350 000 tons of coal at a price of $22 per ton; each pound of this particular coal provides 13 000 BTUs.

The data for the four variable-tonnage contracts follow:

Supplier	Number of Tons Available	Cost ($/ton)	BTUs/lb
Consol, Inc.	200 000	32	12 250
Cyprus Amax	175 000	35	12 000
Addington Mining	200 000	31	12 000
Waterloo	180 000	33	11 300

For example, the contract with Consol, Inc., enables Cinergy to purchase up to 200 000 tons of coal at a cost of $32 per ton; each pound of this coal provides 12 250 BTUs.

The number of megawatt-hours of electricity that each generating unit must produce and the heat rate provided are as follows:

Generating Unit	Electricity Produced (mWh)	Heat Rate (BTUs per kWh)
Miami Fort Unit 5	550 000	10 500
Miami Fort Unit 7	500 000	10 200
Beckjord Unit 1	650 000	10 100
East Bend Unit 2	750 000	10 000
Zimmer Unit 1	1 100 000	10 000

For example, Miami Fort Unit 5 must produce 550 000 megawatt-hours of electricity, and 10 500 BTUs are needed to produce each kilowatt-hour.

The transportation cost and the add-on cost in dollars per ton are shown here:

	Transportation Cost ($/ton)				
Supplier	Miami Fort Unit 5	Miami Fort Unit 7	Beckjord Unit 1	East Bend Unit 2	Zimmer Unit 1
RAG	5.00	5.00	4.75	5.00	4.75
Peabody	3.75	3.75	3.50	3.75	3.50
American	3.00	3.00	2.75	3.00	2.75
Consol	3.25	3.25	2.85	3.25	2.85
Cyprus	5.00	5.00	4.75	5.00	4.75
Addington	2.25	2.25	2.00	2.25	2.00
Waterloo	2.00	2.00	1.60	2.00	1.60

	Add-On Cost ($/ton)				
Supplier	**Miami Fort Unit 5**	**Miami Fort Unit 7**	**Beckjord Unit 1**	**East Bend Unit 2**	**Zimmer Unit 1**
RAG	10.00	10.00	10.00	5.00	6.00
Peabody	10.00	10.00	11.00	6.00	7.00
American	13.00	13.00	15.00	9.00	9.00
Consol	10.00	10.00	11.00	7.00	7.00
Cyprus	10.00	10.00	10.00	5.00	6.00
Addington	5.00	5.00	6.00	4.00	4.00
Waterloo	11.00	11.00	11.00	7.00	9.00

Managerial Report

Prepare a report that summarizes your recommendations regarding Cinergy's coal allocation problem. Be sure to include information and analysis for the following issues.

1 Determine how much coal to purchase from each of the mining companies and how it should be allocated to the generating units. What is the cost to purchase, deliver and process the coal?

2 Compute the average cost of coal in cents per million BTUs for each generating unit (a measure of the cost of fuel for the generating units).

3 Compute the average number of BTUs per pound of coal received at each generating unit (a measure of the energy efficiency of the coal received at each unit).

4 Suppose that Cinergy can purchase an additional 80 000 tons of coal from American Coal Sales as an 'all or nothing deal' for $30 per ton. Should Cinergy purchase the additional 80 000 tons of coal?

5 Suppose that Cinergy learns that the energy content of the coal from Cyprus Amax is actually 13 000 BTUs per pound. Should Cinergy revise its procurement plan?

6 Cinergy has learned from its trading group that Cinergy can sell 50 000 megawatt-hours of electricity over the grid (to other electricity suppliers) at a price of $30 per megawatt-hour. Should Cinergy sell the electricity? If so, which generating units should produce the additional electricity?

Appendix 4.1 Excel Solution of Hewlitt Corporation Financial Planning Problem

In Appendix 2.1 we showed how Excel could be used to solve linear programming problems. To illustrate the use of Excel in solving a more complex linear programming problems, we show the solution to the Hewlitt Corporation financial planning problem presented in Section 4.5.

The spreadsheet formulation and solution of the Hewlitt Corporation problem are shown in Figure 4.13. As described in Appendix 2.1, our practice is to put the data required for the problem in the top part of the spreadsheet and build the model in the bottom part of the spreadsheet. The model consists of a set of cells for the decision variables, a cell for the objective function, a set of cells for the left-hand-side

Figure 4.13 Excel Solution for the Hewlitt Corporation Problem

	A	B	C	D	E	F	G	H	I	J	K	L
1	**Hewlitt Corporation Cash Requirements**											
2												
3		**Cash**										
4	**Year**	**Rqmt.**				**Bond**						
5	1	430			1	2	3					
6	2	210		**Price (€1000)**	1.15	1	1.35					
7	3	222		**Rate**	0.08875	0.055	0.1175					
8	4	231		**Years to Maturity**	5	6	7					
9	5	240										
10	6	195		**Annual Savings Multiple**		1.04						
11	7	225										
12	8	255										
13												
14	**Model**											
15												
16	F	B1	B2	B3	S1	S2	S3	S4	S5	S6	S7	S8
17	1728.794	144.988	187.856	228.188	636.148	501.606	349.682	182.681	0	0	0	0
18												
19					**Cash Flow**		**Net Cash**		**Cash**			
20	**Min Funds**	1728.794		**Constraints**	In	Out	**Flow**		**Rqmt.**			
21				Year 1	1728.79	1298.79	430	=	430			
22				Year 2	711.606	501.606	210	=	210			
23				Year 3	571.682	349.682	222	=	222			
24				Year 4	413.681	182.681	231	=	231			
25				Year 5	240	0	240	=	240			
26				Year 6	195	0	195	=	195			
27				Year 7	225	0	225	=	225			
28				Year 8	255	0	255	=	255			
29												

functions and a set of cells for the right-hand sides of the constraints. The cells for each of these model components are screened; the cells for the decision variables are also enclosed by a boldface line. Descriptive labels are used to make the spreadsheet easy to read.

Formulation

The data and descriptive labels are contained in cells A1:G12. The screened cells in the bottom portion of the spreadsheet contain the key elements of the model required by the Excel Solver.

Decision Variables Cells A17:L17 are reserved for the decision variables. The optimal values rounded to three places, are shown to be F = 1728.794, B_1 = 144.988, B_2 = 187.856, B_3 = 228.188, S_1 = 636.148, S_2 = 501.606, S_3 = 349.682, S_4 = 182.681 and $S_5 = S_6 = S_7 = S_8 = 0$.

Objective Function The formula = A17 has been placed into cell B20 to reflect the total funds required. It is simply the value of the decision variable, *F*. The total funds required by the optimal solution is shown to be €1 728 794.

Left-Hand Sides The left-hand sides for the eight constraints represent the annual net cash flow. They are placed into cells G21:G28.
Cell G21 = E21 – F21 (Copy to G22:G28)

For this problem, some of the left-hand-side cells reference other cells that contain formulas. These referenced cells provide Hewlitt's cash flow in and cash flow out for each of the eight years.[1] The cells and their formulas are as follows:

Cell E21 = A17
Cell E22 = SUMPRODUCT($E$7 : $G$7, $B$17 : $D$17) + $F$10*E17
Cell E23 = SUMPRODUCT($E$7 : $G$7, $B$17 : $D$17) + $F$10*F17
Cell E24 = SUMPRODUCT($E$7 : $G$7, $B$17 : $D$17) + $F$10*G17
Cell E25 = SUMPRODUCT($E$7 : $G$7, $B$17 : $D$17) + $F$10*H17
Cell E26 = (1 + E7)*B17 + F7*C17 + G7*D17 + F10*I17
Cell E27 = (1 + F7)*C17 + G7*D17 + F10*J17
Cell E28 = (1 + G7)*D17 + F10*K17
Cell F21 = SUMPRODUCT(E6:G6,B17:D17) + E17
Cell F22 = F17
Cell F23 = G17
Cell F24 = H17
Cell F25 = I17
Cell F26 = J17
Cell F27 = K17
Cell F28 = L17

Right-Hand Sides The right-hand sides for the eight constraints represent the annual cash requirements. They are placed into cells I21:I28. Cell I21 = B5 (Copy to I22:I28)

Excel Solution

We are now ready to use the information in the spreadsheet to determine the optimal solution to the Hewlitt Corporation problem. The following steps describe how to use Excel to obtain the optimal solution.

Step 1. Select the **Tools** menu

Step 2. Select the **Solver** option

Step 3. When the **Solver Parameters** dialog box appears:
Enter B20 in the **Set Cell** box
Select the **Equal to: Min** option
Enter A17:L17 in the **By Changing Cells** box
Choose **Add**

Step 4. When the **Add Constraint** dialog box appears:
Enter G21:G28 in the **Cell Reference** box
Select =
Enter I21:I28 in the **Constraint** box
Click **OK**

Step 5. When the **Solver Parameters** dialog box appears:
Choose **Options**

Step 6. When the **Solver Options** dialog box appears:
Select **Assume Non-Negative**
Click **OK**

Step 7. When the **Solver Parameters** dialog box appears:
Choose **Solve**

[1]The cash flow in is the sum of the positive terms in each constraint equation in the mathematical model, and the cash flow out is the sum of the negative terms in each constraint equation.

Step 8. When the **Solver Results** dialog box appears:
Select **Keep Solver Solution**
Select **Sensitivity** in the **Reports** box
Click **OK**

The **Solver Parameters** dialogue box is shown in Figure 4.14. The optimal solution is shown in Figure 4.13; the accompanying sensitivity report is shown in Figure 4.15.

Figure 4.14 Solver Parameters Dialogue Box for the Hewlitt Corporation Problem

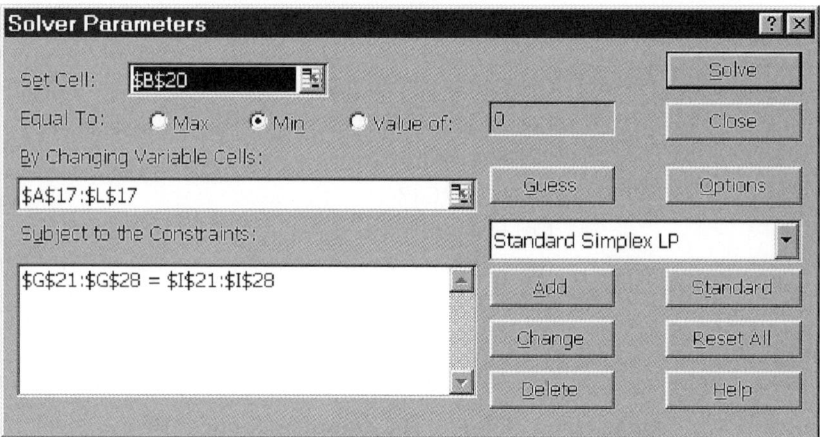

Figure 4.15 Excel's Sensitivity Report for the Hewlitt Corporation Problem

Adjustable Cells

Cell	Name	Final Value	Reduced Cost	Objective Coefficient	Allowable Increase	Allowable Decrease
$A$17	F	1728.793855	0	1	1E+30	1
$B$17	B1	144.9881496	0	0	0.067026339	0.013026775
$C$17	B2	187.8558478	0	0	0.012795531	0.020273774
$D$17	B3	228.1879195	0	0	0.022906851	0.749663022
$E$17	S1	636.1479438	0	0	0.109559907	0.05507386
$F$17	S2	501.605712	0	0	0.143307365	0.056948823
$G$17	S3	349.681791	0	0	0.210854199	0.059039182
$H$17	S4	182.680913	0	0	0.413598622	0.061382404
$I$17	S5	0	0.064025159	0	1E+30	0.064025159
$J$17	S6	0	0.012613604	0	1E+30	0.012613604
$K$17	S7	0	0.021318233	0	1E+30	0.021318233
$L$17	S8	0	0.670839393	0	1E+30	0.670839393

Constraints

Cell	Name	Final Value	Shadow Price	Constraint R.H. Side	Allowable Increase	Allowable Decrease
$G$21	Year 1 Flow	430	1	430	1E+30	1728.793855
$G$22	Year 2 Flow	210	0.961538462	210	1E+30	661.5938616
$G$23	Year 3 Flow	222	0.924556213	222	1E+30	521.6699405
$G$24	Year 4 Flow	231	0.888996359	231	1E+30	363.6690626
$G$25	Year 5 Flow	240	0.854804191	240	1E+30	189.9881496
$G$26	Year 6 Flow	195	0.760364454	195	2149.927647	157.8558478
$G$27	Year 7 Flow	225	0.718991202	225	3027.962172	198.1879195
$G$28	Year 8 Flow	255	0.670839393	255	1583.881915	255

Chapter 5

Linear Programming: The Simplex Method

Learning objectives

By the end of this chapter you will be able to:

- Formulate an LP problem using the Simplex method
- Calculate the Simplex tableau
- Find the optimum solution using the Simplex method
- Interpret the information in a Simplex tableau

MANAGEMENT SCIENCE IN ACTION

Fleet Assignment at Delta Air Lines

Delta Air Lines uses linear and integer programming in its Coldstart project to solve its fleet assignment problem. The problem is to match aircraft to flight legs and fill seats with paying passengers. Airline profitability depends on being able to assign the right size of aircraft to the right leg at the right time of day. An airline seat is a perishable commodity; once a flight takes off with an empty seat the profit potential of that seat is gone forever. Primary objectives of the fleet assignment model are to minimize operating costs and lost passenger revenue. Constraints are aircraft availability, balancing arrivals and departures at airports and maintenance requirements.

The successful implementation of the Coldstart model for assigning fleet types to flight legs shows the size of linear programmes that can be solved today. The typical size of the daily Coldstart model is about 60 000 variables and 40 000 constraints. The first step in solving the fleet assignment problem is to solve the model as a linear programme. The model developers report successfully solving these problems on a daily basis and contend that use of the Coldstart model will save Delta Air Lines $300 million over a three year period.

Based on R. Subramanian, R.P. Scheff, Jr., J.D. Quillinan, D.S. Wiper, and R.E. Marsten, 'Coldstart: Fleet Assignment at Delta Air Lines', *Interfaces* (January/February 1994): 104–120.

In Chapter 2 we saw how to solve simple, two variable LP problems using the graphical method. However, we also saw in Chapter 4 that LP problems are likely to be more complex than this, involving a large number of decision variables and constraints. The *Management Science in Action*, Fleet Management at Delta Airlines, illustrates an LP problem involving around 60 000 variables and 40 000 constraints. Clearly a graphical solution approach will not work so a mathematical method of finding the solution is needed. In this chapter we introduce the **Simplex method** which is the most widely used LP solution method and the basis for many LP computer software programs. The Simplex method provides a set of step-by-step instructions, known as an algorithm, for solving an LP problem of any size. In this chapter we look at how the Simplex method works and in the next chapter we see the sensitivity information that the Simplex method provides.

The Simplex method was developed by George Dantzig while working for the US Air Force. It was first published in 1949.

5.1 An Algebraic Overview of the Simplex Method

We will use a typical business problem to demonstrate the Simplex method. HighTech Industries imports electronic components that are used to assemble two different models of laptop computers. One model is called the Deskpro, and the other model is called the UltraPortable. HighTech's management is currently interested in developing a weekly production schedule for both products.

The Deskpro generates a profit contribution of €50 per unit, and the UltraPortable generates a profit contribution of €40 per unit. For next week's production, a maximum of 150 hours of assembly time can be made available. Each unit of the Deskpro requires three hours of assembly time, and each unit of the UltraPortable requires five hours of assembly time. In addition, HighTech currently has only 20 UltraPortable display components in inventory; so, no more than 20 units of the UltraPortable may be assembled. Finally, only 300 square metres of warehouse space can be made available for new production. Assembly of each Deskpro requires eight square metres of warehouse space; similarly, each UltraPortable requires five square metres.

To develop a linear programming model for the HighTech problem, we will use the following decision variables:

$$x_1 = \text{number of units of the Deskpro}$$
$$x_2 = \text{number of units of the UltraPortable}$$

The complete mathematical model for this problem is then:

$$\begin{aligned} \text{Max} \quad & 50x_1 + 40x_2 \\ \text{s.t.} \quad & \\ & 3x_1 + 5x_2 \leq 150 \quad \text{Assembly time} \\ & 1x_2 \leq 20 \quad \text{Portable display} \\ & 8x_1 + 5x_2 \leq 300 \quad \text{Warehouse capacity} \\ & x_1, x_2 \geq 0 \end{aligned}$$

Adding a slack variable to each of the constraints allows us to write the problem in standard form.

$$\text{Max} \quad 50x_1 + 40x_2 + 0s_1 + 0s_2 + 0s_3 \tag{5.1}$$

s.t.

$$3x_1 + 5x_2 + 1s_1 = 150 \tag{5.2}$$
$$1x_2 + 1s_2 = 20 \tag{5.3}$$
$$8x_1 + 5x_2 + 1s_3 = 300 \tag{5.4}$$
$$x_1, x_2, s_1, s_2, s_3 \geq 0 \tag{5.5}$$

The Simplex method was developed before computers were readily available. Dantzig tested the method on a diet problem. Using desk calculators it took 120 person days of time to find a solution. The method was judged a success!

Algebraic Properties of the Simplex Method

Constraint Equations (5.2) to (5.4) form a system of three simultaneous linear equations with five variables. Whenever a system of simultaneous linear equations has more variables than equations, we can expect an infinite number of solutions. The Simplex method can be viewed as an algebraic procedure for finding the best solution to such a system of equations. In our example, the best solution is the solution to Equations (5.2) to (5.4) that maximizes the objective function (5.1) and satisfies the nonnegativity conditions given by (5.5). This is the solution the Simplex method aims to find.

Determining a Basic Solution

For the HighTech Industries constraint equations, which have more variables (five) than equations (three), the Simplex method finds solutions for these equations by assigning zero values to two of the variables and then solving for the values of the remaining three variables. For example, if we set $x_2 = 0$ and $s_1 = 0$, the system of constraint equations becomes:

$$3x_1 = 150 \tag{5.6}$$
$$1s_2 = 20 \tag{5.7}$$
$$8x_1 + 1s_3 = 300 \tag{5.8}$$

Using Equation (5.6) to solve for x_1, we have:

$$3x_1 = 150$$

and hence $x_1 = 150/3 = 50$. Equation (5.7) provides $s_2 = 20$. Finally, substituting $x_1 = 50$ into Equation (5.8) results in:

$$8(50) + 1s_3 = 300$$

Solving for s_3, we obtain $s_3 = -100$.

So, we obtain the following solution to the three-equation, five-variable set of linear equations:

$$\begin{aligned} x_1 &= 50 \\ x_2 &= 0 \\ s_1 &= 0 \\ s_2 &= 20 \\ s_3 &= -100 \end{aligned}$$

A basic solution is obtained by setting two of the five variables equal to zero and solving the three equations simultaneously for the values of the other three variables. Mathematically, we are guaranteed a solution only if the resulting three equations are linearly independent. Fortunately, the Simplex method is designed to guarantee that a solution exists for the basic variables at each iteration.

This solution is referred to as a **basic solution**. To state a general procedure for determining a basic solution, we must consider a standard-form linear programming problem consisting of n variables and m linear equations, where n is greater than m.

Basic Solution

To determine a basic solution, set $n - m$ of the variables equal to zero, and solve the m linear constraint equations for the remaining m variables.[1]

In terms of the HighTech problem, a basic solution can be obtained by setting any two variables equal to zero and then solving the system of three linear equations for the remaining three variables. We shall refer to the $n - m$ variables set equal to zero as the **nonbasic variables** and the remaining m variables as the **basic variables**. So, in the preceding example, x_2 and s_1 are the nonbasic variables, and x_1, s_2, and s_3 are the basic variables.

Basic Feasible Solution

A basic solution can be either feasible or infeasible. A **basic feasible solution** is a basic solution that also satisfies the nonnegativity conditions. The basic solution found by setting x_2 and s_1 equal to zero and then solving for x_1, s_2 and s_3 is a basic infeasible solution because $s_3 = -100$ and negative values are not allowed in the formulation. However, suppose that we had chosen instead to make x_1 and x_2 nonbasic variables by setting $x_1 = 0$ and $x_2 = 0$. Solving for the corresponding basic solution is easy because with $x_1 = x_2 = 0$, the three constraint equations reduce to:

$$\begin{aligned} 1s_1 \qquad\qquad &= 150 \\ 1s_2 \qquad &= 20 \\ 1s_3 &= 300 \end{aligned}$$

The complete solution with $x_1 = 0$ and $x_2 = 0$ is then:

$$\begin{aligned} x_1 &= 0 \\ x_2 &= 0 \\ s_1 &= 150 \\ s_2 &= 20 \\ s_3 &= 300 \end{aligned}$$

This solution is a basic feasible solution because all of the variables satisfy the nonnegativity conditions.

The following graph shows all the constraint equations and basic solutions for the HighTech problem. Circled points ①–⑤ are basic feasible solutions; circled

[1] In some cases, a unique solution cannot be found for a system of m equations and n variables. However, these cases will never be encountered when using the Simplex method.

points ⑥–⑨ are basic solutions that are not feasible. The basic solution found by setting $x_2 = 0$ and $s_1 = 0$ corresponds to point ⑨; the basic feasible solution found by setting $x_1 = 0$ and $x_2 = 0$ corresponds to point ① in the feasible region.

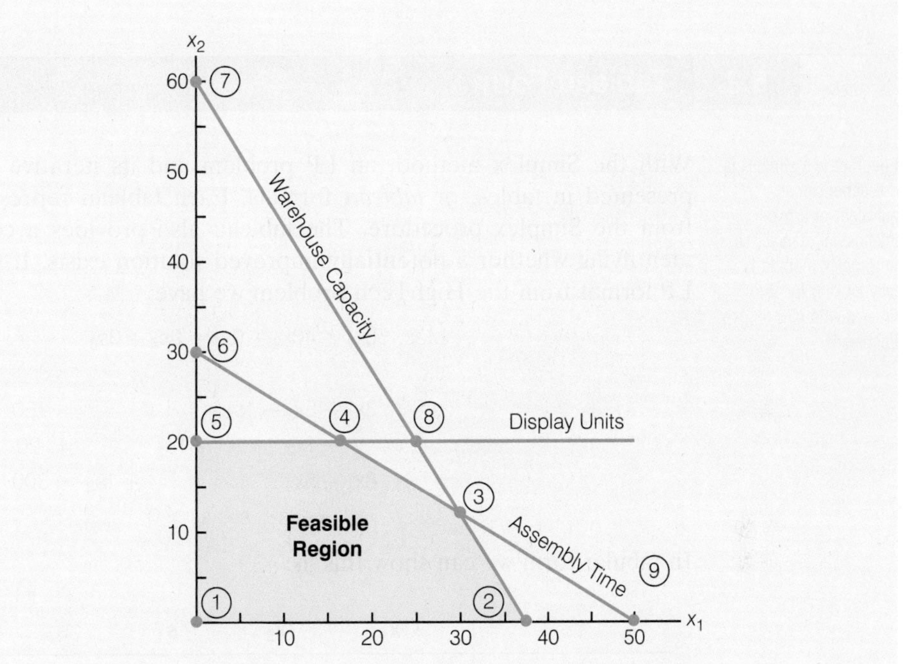

The graph in Figure 5.1 shows only the basic feasible solutions for the HighTech problem; note that each of these solutions is an extreme point of the feasible region. In Chapter 2 we showed that the optimal solution to a linear programming problem can be

Figure 5.1 Feasible Region and Extreme Points for the HighTech Industries Problem

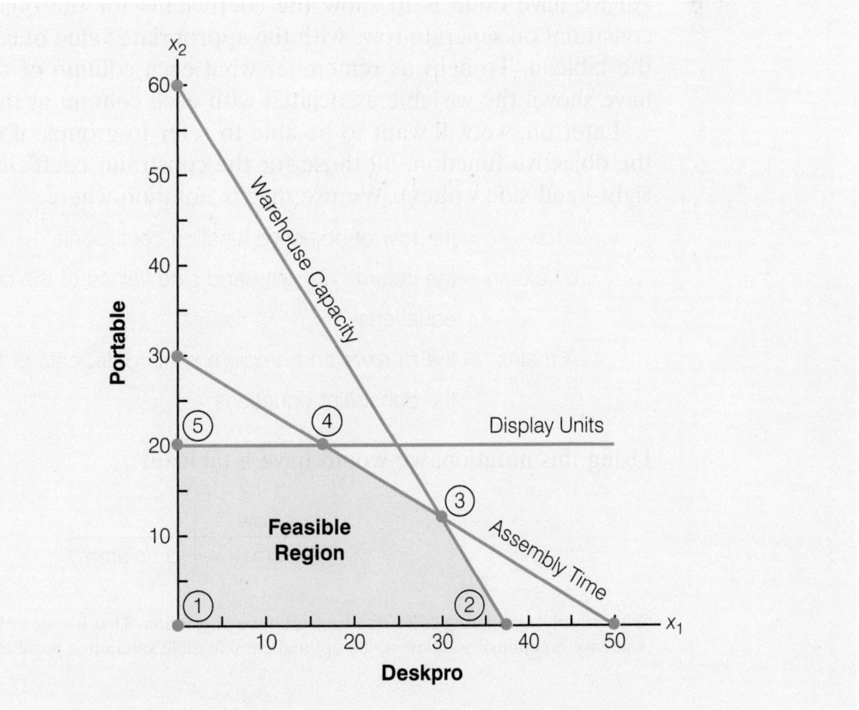

Can you find basic and basic feasible solutions to a system of equations at this point? Try Problem 1.

found at an extreme point. Because every extreme point corresponds to a basic feasible solution, we can now conclude that the HighTech problem does have an optimal basic feasible solution.[2] The Simplex method is an iterative procedure for moving from one basic feasible solution (extreme point) to another until the optimal solution is reached.

5.2 Tableau Form

In geometry, a simplex is an *n* dimensional equivalent of a two dimensional triangle, so the Simplex method is really looking for the corner points in *n* dimensions.

With the Simplex method, an LP problem and its iterative solutions are usually presented in tables, or *tableau* formats. Each tableau represents a basic solution from the Simplex procedure. The tableau also provides a convenient method of identifying whether a potentially improved solution exists. If we take our standard LP format from the HighTech problem we have:

$$\text{Max. } 50x_1 + 40x_2 + 0s_1 + 0s_2 + 0s_3$$

s.t.

$$\begin{aligned} 3x_1 + 5x_2 + 1s_1 \qquad\qquad &= 150 \\ 1x_2 \qquad + 1s_2 \qquad &= 20 \\ 8x_1 + 5x_2 \qquad\qquad + 1s_3 &= 300 \\ x_1,\ x_2,\ s_1,\ s_2,\ s_3 \geq 0 & \end{aligned}$$

In tabular form we can show this as:

	x_1	x_2	s_1	s_2	s_3	***Value***
Objective function	50	40	0	0	0	
Constraint 1	3	5	1	0	0	150
Constraint 2	0	1	0	1	0	20
Constraint 3	8	5	0	0	1	300

All we have done is to show the coefficients for the objective function and each constraint on separate rows with the appropriate value of each in the final column of the tableau. To help us remember what each column of the tableau relates to, we have shown the variable associated with each column at the top of the tableau.

Later on, we will want to be able to refer to groups of coefficients (all those for the objective function, all those for the constraint coefficients and all those for the right-hand side values). We use matrix notation where:

c row = the row of objective function coefficients

b column = the column of right-hand side values of the constraint equations

A matrix = the m rows and n columns of coefficients of the variables in the constraint equations

Using this notation, we would have a tableau:

c row	
A matrix	b column

[2]We are only considering cases that have an optimal solution. That is, cases of infeasibility and unboundedness will have no optimal solution, so no optimal basic feasible solution is possible.

Once we have the problem in tableau form, we then can obtain an initial Simplex tableau that shows a basic feasible solution and then use the Simplex procedure to search for improved solutions to this initial tableau. Given that the Simplex procedure is iterative, we keep searching for improved solutions until we can no longer find a better one. The current solution is then the optimal solution. To summarize, the following steps are appropriate:

Step 1. Formulate the problem.

Step 2. Set up the problem in the standard form using slack and surplus variables as appropriate.

Step 3. Set up the problem in tableau form.

Step 4. Set up the initial Simplex tableau.

Step 5. Search for improvements in the current solution shown in the tableau until no further improvement can be made.

5.3 Setting Up the Initial Simplex Tableau

Clearly, the tableau we have developed simply sets out the LP problem formulation. In order to proceed, we need to create a tableau that represents an initial basic, feasible solution. This will allow us to begin the Simplex procedure and search for the optimal solution. When an LP problem with all less-than-or-equal-to constraints is written in the standard form, it is easy to find a basic feasible solution. We simply set the decision variables equal to zero and solve for the values of the slack variables. For the HighTech problem, we then have: $x_1 = 0$, $x_2 = 0$, $s_1 = 150$, $s_2 = 20$ and $s_3 = 300$ as the initial basic feasible solution (the slack variables simply take the values of the right-hand side values of the constraints). Note that this solution puts us at Point 1 in Figure 5.1. We now need an initial Simplex tableau that corresponds to this point and to this basic, feasible, solution. This is not difficult to do. The initial Simplex tableau for the HighTech problem is shown below:

	x_1	x_2	s_1	s_2	s_3	***Value***
Basis	50	40	0	0	0	
s_1	3	5	1	0	0	150
s_2	0	1	0	1	0	20
s_3	8	5	0	0	1	300

To practise setting up the portion of the simplex tableau corresponding to the objective function and constraints at this point, try Problem 4.

We label the first column *Basis* to indicate the basic solution and we show the basic variables s_1, s_2, s_3. From the tableau we can determine the values for each of the basic variables: $s_1 = 150$, $s_2 = 20$, $s_3 = 300$. Non-basic variables – those not appearing in the Basis list – automatically take zero values. Here, we have x_1 and x_2 both equal to zero. Notice that for each basic variable, its corresponding column in the tableau has a 1 in the only non-zero position. Such columns are known as **unit columns** or **unit vectors**. Second, a row of the tableau is associated with each basic variable. This row has a 1 in the unit column corresponding to the basic variable. The value of each basic variable is then given by the b value in the

The simplex tableau is nothing more than a table that helps keep track of the simplex method calculations. Reconstructing the original problem can be accomplished from the initial simplex tableau.

row associated with the basic variable. In the tableau, row 2 is associated with basic variable s_1 because this row has a 1 in the unit column corresponding to s_1. So, the value of s_1 is given by the right-hand side value b_1: $s_1 = b_1 = 150$. In a similar fashion, $s_2 = b_2 = 20$, and $s_3 = b_3 = 300$.

If we study the standard-form representation of the HighTech constraint equations closely, we can identify two properties that make it possible to find an initial basic feasible solution. The first property requires that the following conditions be satisfied:

a. For each constraint equation, the coefficient of one of the m basic variables in that equation must be 1, and the coefficients for all the remaining basic variables in that equation must be 0.
b. The coefficient for each basic variable must be 1 in only one constraint equation.

When these conditions are satisfied, exactly one basic variable with a coefficient of 1 is associated with each constraint equation, and for each of the m constraint equations, it is a different basic variable. Thus, if the n–m non-basic variables are set equal to zero, the values of the basic variables are the values of the right-hand sides of the constraint equations.

Try Problem 5(a) for practise in setting up the complete initial simplex tableau for a problem with less-than-or-equal-to constraints.

The second property that enables us to find a basic feasible solution requires the values of the right-hand sides of the constraint equations to be nonnegative. This nonnegativity ensures that the basic solution obtained by setting the basic variables equal to the values of the right-hand sides will be feasible.

If a linear programming problem satisfies these two properties, it is said to be in tableau form.

5.4 Improving the Solution

Having found a basic feasible solution, the Simplex procedure now searches for an improved solution. The general principle is simple: will we get an improved, feasible solution if we add one of the non-basic variables to the current solution? In our HighTech problem, this would mean adding either variable x_1 or x_2 to the current solution (since these are the two non-basic variables). Effectively, this would mean letting either x_1 or x_2 take a nonzero value (or, in a business context, that we decide to produce some number of units of either the Deskpro model or the UltraPortable).

Referring to Figure 5.1, our initial solution puts us at Point 1 on the graph (the origin where both decision variables are zero). The Simplex procedure now determines whether a move to an *adjacent* corner point (either Point 5 or Point 2), would give an improved solution. (Note that Points 3 and 4 are not considered at this time since they are not adjacent to the current solution at Point 1.) However, if we were to introduce one of the non-basic variables into the solution then we would have to remove one of the existing basic variables – one of s_1, s_2 or s_3 would then take a zero value.

To help decide whether an improved solution is possible and determine which variables would be part of the solution and which would leave, we add some additional information to the Simplex tableau. To help with the Simplex calculations, we first add two more rows to the tableau.

	x_1	x_2	s_1	s_2	s_3	Value
Basis	50	40	0	0	0	0
s_1	3	5	1	0	0	150
s_2	0	1	0	1	0	20
s_3	8	5	0	0	1	300
z_j						
$c_j - z_j$						

The first row, labelled z_j, represents the decrease in the value of the objective function that will result if one unit of the variable corresponding to the jth column of the A matrix is brought into the basis. The second row, labelled $c_j - z_j$, represents the net change in the value of the objective function if one unit of the variable corresponding to the jth column of the A matrix is brought into the solution. We can refer to the $c_j - z_j$ row as the net evaluation row.

Let us first see how the entries in the z_j row are calculated. Suppose that we consider increasing the value of the non-basic variable x_1 by one unit – that is, from $x_1 = 0$ to $x_1 = 1$. Effectively we want x_1 to be one of our basic variables. In order to make this change, and at the same time continue to satisfy the constraint equations, the values of some of the other variables will have to be changed. As we will show, the Simplex method requires that the necessary changes be made to basic variables only. For example, in the first constraint we have:

$$3x_1 + 5x_2 + 1s_1 = 150$$

The current basic variable in this constraint equation is s_1. Assuming that x_2 remains a non-basic variable with a value of 0, then if x_1 is increased in value by 1, s_1 must be decreased by 3 for the constraint to be satisfied. Similarly, if we were to increase the value of x_1 by 1 (keeping $x_2 = 0$), we can see from the second and third equations that although s_2 would not change, s_3 would decrease by 8. By analyzing all the constraint equations, we see that the coefficients in the x_1 column indicate the amount of decrease in the current basic variables when the non-basic variable x_1 is increased from 0 to 1. In general, all the column coefficients can be interpreted in this way. For instance, if we make x_2 a basic variable with a value of 1, s_1 will decrease by 5, s_2 will decrease by 1 and s_3 will decrease by 5. This makes sense in the context of the HighTech problem. The tableau shows that we currently have 150 slack hours of assembly time (s_1), 20 unused display components (s_2) and 300 square metres of unused warehouse capacity (s_3). So, if we were to produce one unit of x_1 this would require three hours of assembly time, no display units as these as for the UltraPortable model, (x_2) and eight square metres of warehouse space.

To see how we now calculate the values for the z_j row, let us look at the x_1 column again. If x_1 were to increase by 1 (from 0 to 1) then we know that s_1 would need to decrease by 3, s_2 by 0 and s_3 by 8. Changing the values of the basic variables will also affect the objective function. To assess the effect we would need to look at the objective function coefficients for the current basic variables, shown in the c row of the tableau. Clearly, these are 0, 0 and 0 (since the slack variables add nothing to profitability). So, to calculate the change in the objective function, if we increase x_1 by 1 we would have:

$$z_1 = 0(3) + 0(0) + 0(8) = 0$$

Here we multiply the objective function coefficient of the relevant basic variable by the change in the value of that variable. This increases x_1 by 1. Clearly the net effect on the objective function is zero – reducing the value of s_1, s_2 and s_3 will have a zero effect on the objective function value. The comparable calculations for the other z_j values are then:

$$z_2 = 0(5) + 0(1) + 0(5) = 0$$
$$z_3 = 0(1) + 0(0) + 0(0) = 0$$
$$z_4 = 0(0) + 0(1) + 0(0) = 0$$
$$z_5 = 0(0) + 0(0) + 0(1) = 0$$

This then gives a tableau:

	x_1	x_2	s_1	s_2	s_3	*Value*
Basis	50	40	0	0	0	0
s_1	3	5	1	0	0	150
s_2	0	1	0	1	0	20
s_3	8	5	0	0	1	300
z_j	0	0	0	0	0	**0**
$c_j - z_j$						

In this tableau we also see a boldfaced 0 in the z_j row in the last column. This zero is the value of the objective function for the current basic feasible solution. It is calculated in the same way as the other z_j values by multiplying the objective function coefficients of the current basic variables by the values in the last column.

		x_1	x_2	s_1	s_2	s_3	*Value*
Basis	C_B	50	40	0	0	0	0
s_1	0	3	5	1	0	0	150
s_2	0	0	1	0	1	0	20
s_3	0	8	5	0	0	1	300
	z_j	0	0	0	0	0	**0**
	$c_j - z_j$						

The net evaluation row, $c_j - z_j$ is then simply the difference between the objective function coefficients shown in the c row and the z values we have just calculated. Adding these to the tableau we then have:

	x_1	x_2	s_1	s_2	s_3	**Value**
Basis	50	40	0	0	0	0
s_1	3	5	1	0	0	150
s_2	0	1	0	1	0	20
s_3	8	5	0	0	1	300
z_j	0	0	0	0	0	**0**
$c_j - z_j$	50	40	0	0	0	0

The interpretation of the coefficients in the net evaluation row is straightforward. If we take the value of 50, for example, relating to the x_1 column, this coefficient shows the net effect on the current objective function value of bringing one unit of x_1 into the current solution (making x_1 a basic variable and allocating it a value of 1). In other words, allowing one unit of x_1 to be produced will bring about a net change in profit of €50. Similarly, the coefficient of €40 for the x_2 column tells us that allowing x_2 to take a value of 1 in the solution would increase profit by this amount. We are now ready to see how the information in the table can be used to see if the current basic solution can be improved.

From the net evaluation row, we see that each unit of the Deskpro (x_1) introduced into the current basis would increase the value of the objective function by €50 and each unit of the UltraPortable (x_2) by €40. Because x_1 causes the largest per-unit increase, we choose it as the variable to bring into the basis. In other words, x_1 is set to enter the solution so that it will increase the objective function more than x_2. From Figure 5.1 we can also see the logic of this decision. From the current solution (Point 1), we can either move in the direction of Point 5 (introduce the UltraPortable, into the solution) or in the direction of Point 2 (introduce the Deskpro into the solution). Given that our objective is to maximize profit contribution, obviously it then makes sense to introduce the variable that makes the largest per unit profit contribution. This gives a simple decision rule:

> **Criterion for Entering a New Variable into the Basis**
> Look at the net evaluation row (c_j–z_j), and select the variable to enter the basis that will cause the largest per-unit improvement in the value of the objective function. In the case of a tie, follow the convention of selecting the variable to enter the basis that corresponds to the leftmost of the columns.

However, if a new variable is set to enter the solution (non-basic variables are set to become basic) then we must remove an existing variable from the solution (make an existing basic variable non-basic). Clearly, we have three choices in the HighTech problem: s_1, s_2, s_3 could all become non-basic. In discussing how to calculate the z_j values, we noted that each of the coefficients in the x_1 column indicates the amount of decrease in the corresponding basic variable that would result from increasing x_1 by one unit. Considering the first row, we see that every unit of the Deskpro produced will use three hours of assembly time, reducing s_1 by 3. In the current solution, $s_1 = 150$ and $x_1 = 0$. Considering this row only, the maximum possible value that x_1 could take can be calculated by solving:

$$3x_1 = 150 \text{ which gives } x_1 = 50$$

In other words, in relation only to s_1, the maximum value that x_1 could take if it came into the solution is 50 units. (Of course, this would mean that we were using all of the available assembly time to produce 50 units of x_1 – there would be no slack, $s_1 = 0$).

We can apply the same logic to s_2 and s_3 in turn. For s_2, introducing x_1 has no effect (a zero coefficient) but for s_3 the maximum value that x_1 could take would be:

$$8x_1 = 300 \text{ giving } x_1 = 37.5$$

This in turn would mean we were using all available warehouse space to store x_1, there would be no slack ($s_3 = 0$). If we now consider all three rows (constraints) simultaneously, we know that x_1 is set to enter the basic solution. The maximum possible increase in x_1 is given by the smallest, nonzero ratio calculation. Here, the maximum that x_1 can take at this stage in the procedure is a value of 37.5. At this level of production, s_3 would take a zero value – that is, s_3 would become a non-basic variable.

To determine which basic variable will become nonbasic, only the positive coefficients in the incoming column correspond to basic variables that will decrease in value when the new basic variable enters.

Criterion for Removing a Variable from the Current Basis (Minimum Ratio Test) Suppose the incoming basic variable corresponds to column j in the A portion of the simplex tableau. For each row i, compute the ratio b_i/a_{ij} for each a_{ij} greater than zero. The basic variable that will be removed from the basis corresponds to the minimum of these ratios. In case of a tie, we follow the convention of selecting the variable that corresponds to the uppermost of the tied rows.

So, we now know that x_1 is set to enter the solution as a basic variable, s_3 is set to leave the current solution and become non-basic and also that x_1 will take a value of 37.5 in the new solution. Clearly, if we are changing the basic solution, we will need to change the tableau to reflect the new solution. We look at how we do this next.

5.5 Calculating the Next Tableau

The way in which we transform the simplex tableau so that it still represents an equivalent system of constraint equations is to use the following elementary row operations.

Elementary Row Operations

1 Multiply any row (equation) by a nonzero number.

2 Replace any row (equation) by the result of adding or subtracting a multiple of another row (equation) to it.

The application of these elementary row operations to a system of simultaneous linear equations will not change the solution to the system of equations; however, the elementary row operations will change the coefficients of the variables and the values of the right-hand sides.

The purpose of these arithmetic operations is to transform the existing tableau into one that represents the new basic solution. We show the initial tableau below together with the ratio calculations we performed earlier.

Initial tableau

		x_1	x_2	s_1	s_2	s_3	*Value*	*Ratio (Value/x_1)*
Basis	C_b	50	40	0	0	0		
s_1	0	3	5	1	0	0	150	50
s_2	0	0	1	0	1	0	20	-
s_3	0	(8)	5	0	0	1	300	37.5
z_j		0	0	0	0	0	0	
$c_j - z_j$		50	40	0	0	0	0	

We know that x_1 is set to enter the new solution and that s_3 is set to leave. We refer to the x_1 column as the **pivot column**, the s_3 row as the **pivot row** and the coefficient at the intersection of the pivot row and column as the **pivot element** (here 8, shown circled). Looking at the pivot row we have:

$$8x_1 + 5x_2 + 1s_3 = 300$$

We know that in the improved solution, x_1 will enter the solution and that both x_2 and s_3 will be non-basic and take zero values. Given that, in the above equation we know that two of the variables will be zero, we can easily solve for the third, x_1, by dividing the entire row by 8, the pivot element:

$$\frac{8x_1}{8} + \frac{5x_2}{8} + \frac{1s_3}{8} = \frac{300}{8}$$

This gives:

$$1x_1 + 0.625x_2 + 0.125s_3 = 37.5$$

This row replaces the existing pivot row in the new tableau.

New tableau

		x_1	x_2	s_1	s_2	s_3	*Value*
Basis	C_b	50	40	0	0	0	
s_1	0						
s_2	0						
x_1	50	1	0.625	0	0	0.125	37.5
	z_j						
	$c_j - z_j$						

However, we also need to adjust the other rows in the Initial Tableau. To help understand the mathematics, let us explain what is happening in a business context. In the initial solution, HighTech were producing neither of the two products and consequently all their available resources were unused. Now, with the improved solution HighTech will be producing 37.5 units of x_1 and in doing so are using all the available warehouse space (hence $s_3 = 0$). But by producing 37.5 units of x_1, other available resources will also be needed. From the original problem formulation we know that each unit of x_1 required three hours of the available assembly time but that a number of available display components are only needed for x_2 (which we are not producing at this stage). So, we need to adjust the existing s_1 row to reflect the production of x_1 and we will not need to alter the s_2 row since this is unaffected by x_1 production. The new row we have just calculated, x_1, is a general expression for the number of units of x_1 produced. We know that each unit of x_1 produced will require three assembly hours. So, to calculate the total number of assembly hours required, we can multiply the entire x_1 row by 3:

x_1 row $\times$ 3:

$$3(1x_1 + 0.625x_2 + 0.125s_3) = 3(37.5)$$

or

$$3x_1 + 1.875x_2 + 0.375s_3 = 112.5$$

This expression indicates how many assembly hours will be needed for x_1. However, the s_1 row in the Initial tableau indicates how many assembly hours we have to begin with. So, to determine how many unused assembly hours (s_1) we will have in the new solution, we need to subtract the hours needed from the hours available, or:

Assembly hours available	$3x_1 + 5x_2 + 1s_1 + 0s_2 + 0s_3 = 150$
– assembly hours needed for x_1 production	$-(3x_1 + 1.875x_2 \quad + .375s_3 = 112.5)$
Giving s_1	$0x_1 + 3.125x_2 + 1s_1 + 0s_2 - 0.375s_3 = 37.5$

Our new tableau is then:

New tableau

		x_1	x_2	s_1	s_2	s_3	***Value***
Basis	C_b	50	40	0	0	0	
s_1	0	0	3.125	1	0	−0.375	37.5
s_2	0	0	1	0	1	0	20
x_1	50	1	0.625	0	0	0.125	37.5
z_j							1875
$c_j - z_j$							

The new solution is $s_1 = 37.5, s_2 = 20$ and $x_1 = 37.5$ (with x_2 and s_3 automatically set to zero since they are non-basic). We also can obtain the new value for the objective function:

$$0(37.5) + 0(20) + 50(37.5) = 1875$$

This is also shown in the new tableau. The calculations may look complex but they condense into a series of simple steps:

- Identify the pivot column showing the non-basic variable that is to enter the solution.
- Identify the pivot row that shows the basic variable that will leave the solution.
- Identify the pivot element at the intersection of the pivot row and column.
- Divide the existing pivot row by the pivot element.
- Adjust the other rows in the tableau in turn using the new pivot row and the appropriate coefficient from the pivot column.

Note also, that the new tableau satisfies the two required properties for tableau form that we set out in Section 5.2.

Interpreting the Results of an Iteration

In our example, the initial basic feasible solution was:

$$x_1 = 0$$
$$x_2 = 0$$
$$s_1 = 150$$
$$s_2 = 20$$
$$s_3 = 300$$

with a corresponding profit of €0. One iteration of the Simplex method moved us to another basic feasible solution with an objective function value of €1875. This new basic feasible solution is:

$$x_1 = 37.5$$
$$x_2 = 0$$
$$s_1 = 37.5$$
$$s_2 = 20$$
$$s_3 = 0$$

The first iteration moves us from the origin in Figure 5.2 to extreme point 2.

In Figure 5.2 we see that the initial basic feasible solution corresponds to extreme point ①. The first iteration moved us in the direction of the greatest increase per unit in profit – that is, along the x_1 axis. We moved away from extreme point ① in the x_1 direction until we could move no farther without violating one of the constraints. The tableau we obtained after one iteration provides the basic feasible solution corresponding to extreme point ②.

We note from Figure 5.2 that at extreme point ② the warehouse capacity constraint is binding with $s_3 = 0$ and that the other two constraints contain slack. From the simplex tableau, we see that the amount of slack for these two constraints is given by $s_1 = 37.5$ and $s_2 = 20$.

Moving Toward a Better Solution

To see whether a better basic feasible solution can be found, we need again to calculate the z_j and $c_j - z_j$ rows for the new simplex tableau. Recall that the elements in the z_j row are the sum of the products obtained by multiplying the elements in the c_B column of the simplex tableau by the corresponding elements in the columns of the A matrix. Thus, we obtain:

$$\begin{aligned}
z_1 &= 0(0) + 0(0) + 50(1) = 50\\
z_2 &= 0(31.25) + 0(1) + 50(0.625) = 31.25\\
z_3 &= 0(1) + 0(0) + 50(0) = 0\\
z_4 &= 0(0) + 0(1) + 50(0) = 0\\
z_5 &= (-0.375) + 0(0) + 50(0.125) = 6.25
\end{aligned}$$

Subtracting z_j from c_j to compute the new net evaluation row, we obtain the following simplex tableau:

		x_1	x_2	s_1	s_2	s_3	
Basis	c_B	50	40	0	0	0	
s_1	0	0	3.125	1	0	−0.375	**37.5**
s_2	0	0	1	0	1	0	**20**
x_1	50	1	0.625	0	0	0.125	**37.5**
z_j		50	31.25	0	0	6.25	**1 875**
$c_j - z_j$		0	8.75	0	0	−6.25	

Let us now analyze the $c_j - z_j$ row to see whether we can introduce a new variable into the basis and continue to improve the value of the objective function. Using the rule for determining which variable should enter the basis next, we select x_2 because it has the highest (and only) positive coefficient in the $c_j - z_j$ row. Referring to Figure 5.2 our current solution is at Point 2. The new solution introduces x_2 as a basic variable at Point 3. It is also worth noting for a moment the other nonzero coefficient in this

Figure 5.2 Feasible Region and Extreme Points for the HighTech Industries Problem

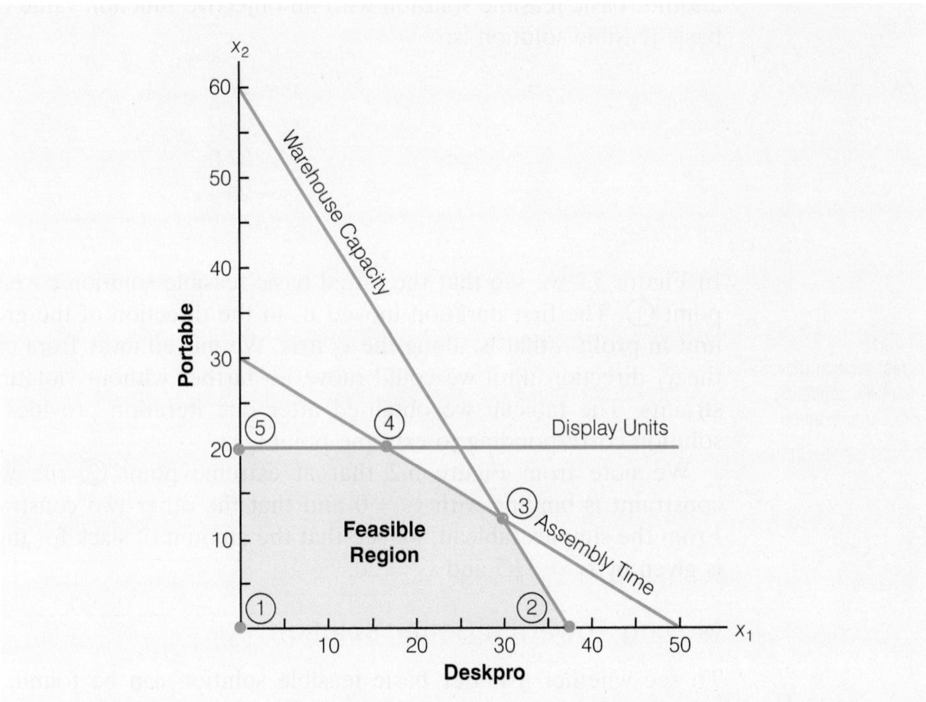

row – that for s_3 equals −6.25. One of the managerial benefits of the Simplex method is that virtually every part of the tableau can be used to help management understand the consequences of decisions. Here we see that s_3 takes a negative value of €6.25. The interpretation of this is straightforward; s_3 has just been taken out of the solution and is non-basic with a zero value. But this coefficient tells us that if we were to force s_3 back into the situation at this stage, it would have a negative impact on the objective function. In other words, if we insisted on having unused warehouse space (which is what s_3 measures), then each square metre of unused space will effectively cost HighTech €6.25 in lost profit contribution since the only way of freeing up warehouse space at this stage is to reduce production of x_1.

To determine which variable will be removed from the basis when x_2 enters, we must calculate for each row i the ratio b_i/a_{i2} (remember, though, that we should calculate this ratio only if a_{i2} is greater than zero); then we select the variable to leave the basis that corresponds to the minimum ratio. As before, we will show these ratios in an extra column of the simplex tableau:

		x_1	x_2	s_1	s_2	s_3		$\frac{b}{a_{i2}}$
Basis	c_B	50	40	0	0	0		
s_1	0	0	(3.125)	1	0	−0.375	**37.5**	$\frac{37.5}{3.125} = 12$
s_2	0	0	1	0	1	0	**20**	$\frac{20}{1} = 20$
x_1	50	1	0.625	0	0	0.125	**37.5**	$\frac{37.5}{0.625} = 60$
z_j		50	31.25	0	0	6.25	**1 875**	
$c_j - z_j$		0	8.75	0	0	−6.25		

With 12 as the minimum ratio, s_1 will leave the basis. The pivot element is $a_{12} = 3.125$, which is circled in the preceding tableau. The nonbasic variable x_2 must now be made a basic variable.

We can make this change by performing the following elementary row operations:

Step 1. Divide every element in row 1 (the pivot row) by 3.125 (the pivot element).

Step 2. Subtract the new row 1 (the new pivot row) from row 2.

Step 3. Multiply the new pivot row by 0.625, and subtract the result from row 3.

The new simplex tableau resulting from these row operations is as follows:

		x_1	x_2	s_1	s_2	s_3	
Basis	c_B	50	40	0	0	0	
x_2	40	0	1	0.32	0	−0.12	**12**
s_2	0	0	0	−0.32	1	0.12	**8**
x_1	50	1	0	−0.20	0	0.20	**30**
	z_j	50	40	2.8	0	5.20	**1 980**
	$c_j - z_j$	0	0	−2.8	0	−5.20	

Note that the values of the basic variables are $x_2 = 12$, $s_2 = 8$ and $x_1 = 30$, and the corresponding profit is 40(12) + 0(8) + 50(30) = 1980.

We must now determine whether to bring any other variable into the basis and thereby move to another basic feasible solution. Looking at the net evaluation row, we see that every element is zero or negative. Because $c_j - z_j$ is less than or equal to zero for both of the nonbasic variables s_1 and s_3, any attempt to bring a nonbasic variable into the basis at this point will result in a lowering of the current value of the objective function. Hence, this tableau represents the optimal solution. In general, the Simplex method uses the following criterion to determine when the optimal solution has been obtained:

Optimality Criterion
The optimal solution to a linear programming problem has been reached when all of the entries in the net evaluation row ($c_j - z_j$) are zero or negative. In such cases, the optimal solution is the current basic feasible solution.

Referring to Figure 5.2, we can see graphically the process that the Simplex method used to determine an optimal solution. The initial basic feasible solution corresponds to the origin ($x_1 = 0$, $x_2 = 0$, $s_1 = 150$, $s_2 = 20$, $s_3 = 300$). The first iteration caused x_1 to enter the basis and s_3 to leave. The second basic feasible solution corresponds to extreme point ② ($x_1 = 37.5$, $x_2 = 0$, $s_1 = 37.5$, $s_2 = 20$, $s_3 = 0$). At the next iteration, x_2 entered the basis and s_1 left. This iteration brought us to extreme point ③ and the optimal solution ($x_1 = 30$, $x_2 = 12$, $s_1 = 0$, $s_2 = 8$, $s_3 = 0$).

For the HighTech problem with only two decision variables, we had a choice of using the graphical or Simplex method. For problems with more than two variables, we shall always use the Simplex method.

Interpreting the Optimal Solution

Using the final simplex tableau, we find the optimal solution to the HighTech problem consists of the basic variables x_1, x_2 and s_2 and nonbasic variables s_1 and s_3 with:

$$\begin{aligned} x_1 &= 30 \\ x_2 &= 12 \\ s_1 &= 0 \\ s_2 &= 8 \\ s_3 &= 0 \end{aligned}$$

The value of the objective function is €1980. If management wants to maximize the total profit contribution, HighTech should produce 30 units of the Deskpro and 12 units of the UltraPortable. When $s_2 = 8$, management should note that there will be eight unused UltraPortable display units. Moreover, because $s_1 = 0$ and $s_3 = 0$, no slack is associated with the assembly time constraint and the warehouse capacity constraint; in other words, these constraints are both binding. Consequently, if it is possible to obtain additional assembly time and/or additional warehouse space, management should consider doing so.

The first computer-based simplex application was in 1951 when the US Air Force looked at the deployment and support of aircraft. The problem had 71 variables and 48 constraints. There were 73 simplex iterations needed to find the optimal solution and this took the computer 18 hours.

Figure 5.3 shows the computer solution to the HighTech problem using Excel. The optimal solution with $x_1 = 30$ and $x_2 = 12$ is shown to have an objective function value of €1980. The values of the slack variables complete the optimal solution with $s_1 = 0$, $s_2 = 8$ and $s_3 = 0$. The values in the Reduced Costs column are from the net evaluation row of the final simplex tableau. Note that the $c_j - z_j$ values in columns corresponding to x_1 and x_2 are both 0. The shadow prices are the z_j values for the three slack variables in the final simplex tableau. Referring to the final tableau, we see that the shadow price for constraint 1 is the z_j value corresponding to $s_1 = 2.8$. Similarly, the shadow price for constraint 2 is 0, and the dual price for constraint 3 = 5.2. The use of the Simplex method to calculate shadow (dual) prices will be discussed further when we cover sensitivity analysis in Chapter 6.

Summary of the Simplex Method

Let us now summarize the steps followed to solve a linear programme using the Simplex method. We assume that the problem has all less-than-or-equal-to constraints and involves maximization.

Step 1. Formulate a linear programming model of the problem.

Step 2. Add slack variables to each constraint to obtain standard form.

Step 3. Set up the initial simplex tableau.

Step 4. Choose the nonbasic variable with the largest entry in the net evaluation row to bring into the basis. This variable identifies the pivot column: the column associated with the incoming variable.

Step 5. Choose as the pivot row that row with the smallest ratio of b_i/a_{ij} for $a_{ij} > 0$ where j is the pivot column. This pivot row is the row of the variables leaving the basis when variable j enters.

Step 6. Perform the necessary elementary row operations.

a. Divide each element of the pivot row by the pivot element (the element in the pivot row and pivot column).

Figure 5.3 Excel Solution for the HighTech Industries Problem

Name	Original Value	Final Value
Maximize Total Profit	0	1980

Name	Original Value	Final Value
x1	0	30
x2	0	12

Name	Cell Value	Status	Slack
Assembly time used(LHS)	150	Binding	0
Display units used(LHS)	12	Not Binding	8
Warehouse space used (LHS)	300	Binding	0

ADJUSTABLE CELLS

Name	Final Value	Reduced Cost	Objective Coefficient	Allowable Increase	Allowable Decrease
x1	30	0	50	14	26
x2	12	0	40	43.33333333	8.75

CONSTRAINTS

Name	Final Value	Shadow Price	Constraint R.H. Side	Allowable Increase	Allowable Decrease
Assembly time used (LHS)	150	2.8	150	25	37.5
Display units used (LHS)	12	0	20	1E+3	8
Warehouse space used (LHS)	300	5.2	300	100	66.66666667

b. Obtain zeroes in all other positions of the pivot column by adding or subtracting an appropriate multiple of the new pivot row. Once the row operations have been completed, the value of the new basic feasible solution can be read from the *b* column of the tableau.

Step 7. Test for optimality. If $c_j - z_j \leq 0$ for all columns, the solution is optimal. If not, return to step 4.

To test your ability to solve a problem employing the Simplex method, try Problem 6.

The steps are basically the same for problems with equality and greater-than-or-equal-to constraints except that setting up the tableau form requires a little more work. We discuss what is involved in Section 5.6. The modification necessary for minimization problems is covered in Section 5.7.

NOTES AND COMMENTS

The entries in the net evaluation row provide the reduced costs that appear in the computer solution to a linear programme. Recall that in Chapter 3 we defined the reduced cost as the amount by which an objective function coefficient would have to improve before it would be possible for the corresponding variable to assume a positive value in the optimal solution. In general, the reduced costs are the absolute values of the entries in the net evaluation row.

5.6 Tableau Form: The General Case

This section explains how to get started with the Simplex method for problems with greater-than-or-equal-to and equality constraints.

When a linear programme contains all less-than-or-equal-to constraints with nonnegative right-hand side values, it is easy to set up the tableau form; we simply add a slack variable to each constraint. However, obtaining the tableau form is more complex if the linear programme contains greater-than-or-equal-to constraints, equality constraints and/or negative right-hand side values. In this section we describe how to develop tableau form for each of these situations and also how to solve linear programmes involving equality and greater-than-or-equal-to constraints using the Simplex method.

Greater-Than-or-Equal-to Constraints (≥)

Suppose that in the HighTech Industries problem, management wanted to ensure that the combined total production for both models would be at least 25 units. This requirement means that the following constraint must be added to the current linear programme:

$$1x_1 + 1x_2 \geq 25$$

Adding this constraint results in the following modified problem:

$$\begin{aligned}
\text{Max} \quad & 50x_1 + 40x_2 \\
\text{s.t.} \quad & \\
& 3x_1 + 5x_2 \leq 150 \quad \text{Assembly time} \\
& \phantom{3x_1 + {}} 1x_2 \leq 20 \quad \text{UltraPortable display} \\
& 8x_1 + 5x_2 \leq 300 \quad \text{Warehouse space} \\
& 1x_1 + 1x_2 \geq 25 \quad \text{Minimum total production} \\
& x_1,\ x_2 \geq 0
\end{aligned}$$

First, we use three slack variables and one surplus variable to write the problem in standard form. This provides the following:

$$\begin{aligned}
\text{Max} \quad & 50x_1 + 40x_2 + 0s_1 + 0s_2 + 0s_3 + 0s_4 \\
\text{s.t.} \quad & \\
& 3x_1 + 5x_2 + 1s_1 = 150 \qquad \textbf{(5.9)} \\
& 1x_2 + 1s_2 = 20 \qquad \textbf{(5.10)} \\
& 8x_1 + 5x_2 + 1s_3 = 300 \qquad \textbf{(5.11)} \\
& 1x_1 + 1x_2 - 1s_4 = 25 \qquad \textbf{(5.12)} \\
& x_1,\ x_2,\ s_1,\ s_2,\ s_3,\ s_4 \geq 0
\end{aligned}$$

Now let us consider how we obtain an initial basic feasible solution to start the Simplex method. Previously, we set $x_1 = 0$ and $x_2 = 0$ and selected the slack variables as the initial basic variables. The extension of this notion to the modified HighTech problem would suggest setting $x_1 = 0$ and $x_2 = 0$ and selecting the slack and surplus variables as the initial basic variables. Doing so results in the basic solution:

$$\begin{aligned} x_1 &= 0 \\ x_2 &= 0 \\ s_1 &= 150 \\ s_2 &= 20 \\ s_3 &= 300 \\ s_4 &= -25 \end{aligned}$$

Clearly this solution is not a basic feasible solution because $s_4 = -25$ violates the nonnegativity requirement. Here, with the Simplex method, we are trying to set x_1 and x_2 to zero. However, the minimum total production constraint we added requires that combined production must be at least 25 units and clearly we cannot set x_1 and x_2 to zero *and* meet the constraint requirement. The difficulty is that the standard form and the tableau form are not equivalent when the problem contains greater-than-or-equal-to constraints.

To set up the tableau form, we shall resort to a mathematical 'trick' that will enable us to find an initial basic feasible solution in terms of the slack variables s_1, s_2 and s_3 and a new variable we shall denote a_4. Variable a_4 really has nothing to do with the HighTech problem; it merely enables us to set up the tableau form and thus obtain an initial basic feasible solution. This new variable, which has been artificially created to start the Simplex method, is referred to as an **artificial variable**.

Artificial variables are appropriately named; they have no physical meaning in the real problem.

The notation for artificial variables is similar to the notation used to refer to the elements of the A matrix. To avoid any confusion between the two, recall that the elements of the A matrix (constraint coefficients) always have two subscripts, whereas artificial variables have only one subscript referring to the constraint.

With the addition of an artificial variable, we can convert the standard form of the problem into tableau form. We add artificial variable a_4 to constraint Equation (5.12) to obtain the following representation of the system of equations in tableau form:

$$\begin{aligned} 3x_1 + 5x_2 + 1s_1 \qquad\qquad\qquad\qquad &= 150 \\ 1x_2 \quad + 1s_2 \qquad\qquad\qquad &= 20 \\ 8x_1 + 5x_2 \qquad\qquad + 1s_3 \qquad\qquad &= 300 \\ 1x_1 + 1x_2 \qquad\qquad\qquad - 1s_4 + 1a_4 &= 25 \end{aligned}$$

Note that the subscript on the artificial variable identifies the constraint with which it is associated. Thus, a_4 is the artificial variable associated with the fourth constraint.

Because the variables s_1, s_2, s_3 and a_4 each appear in a different constraint with a coefficient of 1, and the right-hand side values are nonnegative, both requirements of the tableau form have now been satisfied. We can now obtain an initial basic feasible solution by setting $x_1 = x_2 = s_4 = 0$. The complete solution is:

$$\begin{aligned} x_1 &= 0 \\ x_2 &= 0 \\ s_1 &= 150 \\ s_2 &= 20 \\ s_3 &= 300 \\ s_4 &= 0 \\ a_4 &= 25 \end{aligned}$$

A basic feasible solution containing one or more artificial variables at positive values is not feasible for the real problem.

Is this solution feasible in terms of the real HighTech problem? No, it is not. It does not satisfy the constraint 4 combined total production requirement of 25 units. We must make an important distinction between a basic feasible solution for the tableau form and a feasible solution for the real problem. A basic feasible solution for the tableau form of a linear programming problem is not always a feasible solution for the real problem.

The reason for creating the tableau form is to obtain the initial basic feasible solution that is required to start the Simplex method. So, we see that whenever it is necessary to introduce artificial variables, the initial simplex solution will not in general be feasible for the real problem. This situation is not as difficult as it might seem, however, because the only time we must have a feasible solution for the real problem is at the last iteration of the Simplex method. So, devising a way to guarantee that any artificial variable would be eliminated from the basic feasible solution before the optimal solution is reached would eliminate the difficulty.

The way in which we guarantee that artificial variables will be eliminated before the optimal solution is reached is to assign each artificial variable a very large cost in the objective function. For example, in the modified HighTech problem, we could assign a very large negative number (such as -100 000) as the profit coefficient for artificial variable a_4. So, if this variable is in the basis, it will substantially reduce profits. As a result, this variable will be eliminated from the basis as soon as possible, which is precisely what we want to happen.

As an alternative to picking a large negative number such as $-100\,000$ for the profit coefficient, we will denote the profit coefficient of each artificial variable by $-M$. Here it is assumed that M represents a very large number – in other words, a number of large magnitude and hence, the letter M. This notation will make it easier to keep track of the elements of the simplex tableau that depend on the profit coefficients of the artificial variables. Using $-M$ as the profit coefficient for artificial variable a_4 in the modified HighTech problem, we can write the objective function for the tableau form of the problem as follows:

$$\text{Max} \quad 50x_1 + 40x_2 + 0s_1 + 0s_2 + 0s_3 + 0s_4 - Ma_4$$

The initial simplex tableau for the problem is shown here.

		x_1	x_2	s_1	s_2	s_3	s_4	a_4	
Basis	c_B	50	40	0	0	0	0	$-M$	
s_1	0	3	5	1	0	0	0	0	**150**
s_2	0	0	1	0	1	0	0	0	**20**
s_3	0	8	5	0	0	1	0	0	**300**
a_4	$-M$	①	1	0	0	0	−1	1	**25**
z_j		$-M$	$-M$	0	0	0	M	$-M$	**$-25M$**
$c_j - z_j$		$50 + M$	$40 + M$	0	0	0	$-M$	0	

This tableau corresponds to the solution $s_1 = 150$, $s_2 = 20$, $s_3 = 300$, $a_4 = 25$ and $x_1 = x_2 = s_4 = 0$. In terms of the simplex tableau, this solution is a basic feasible solution because all the variables are greater than or equal to zero, and $n - m = 7 - 4 = 3$ of the variables are equal to zero.

Since $c_1 - z_1 = 50 + M$ is the largest value in the net evaluation row, we see that x_1 will become a basic variable during the first iteration of the Simplex method. Further calculations with the Simplex method show that x_1 will replace a_4 in the basic solution. The following tableau is the result of the first iteration.

Result of Iteration 1

		x_1	x_2	s_1	s_2	s_3	s_4	a_4	
Basis	c_B	50	40	0	0	0	0	$-M$	
s_1	0	0	2	1	0	0	3	−3	**75**
s_2	0	0	1	0	1	0	0	0	**20**
s_3	0	0	−3	0	0	1	8	−8	**100**
x_1	50	1	1	0	0	0	−1	1	**25**
z_j		50	50	0	0	0	−50	50	**1 250**
c_j-z_j		0	−10	0	0	0	50	$-M-50$	

When the artificial variable $a_4 = 0$, we have a situation in which the basic feasible solution contained in the tableau is also a feasible solution to the real HighTech problem. In addition, because a_4 is an artificial variable that was added simply to obtain an initial basic feasible solution, we can now drop its associated column from the tableau. Indeed, whenever artificial variables are used, they can be dropped from the tableau as soon as they have been eliminated from the basic feasible solution. The artificial variable has served its purpose in providing us with a real, basic feasible solution and so is no longer needed.

When artificial variables are required to obtain an initial basic feasible solution, the iterations required to eliminate the artificial variables are referred to as **phase I** of the Simplex method. When all the artificial variables have been eliminated from the basis (in more complex problems of course there may be more than one $\geq$ constraint and so more than one artificial variable), phase I is complete, and a basic feasible solution to the real problem has been obtained. So, by dropping the column associated with a_4 from the current tableau, we obtain the following tableau at the end of phase I.

		x_1	x_2	s_1	s_2	s_3	s_4	
Basis	c_B	50	40	0	0	0	0	
s_1	0	0	2	1	0	0	3	**75**
s_2	0	0	1	0	1	0	0	**20**
s_3	0	0	−3	0	0	1	8	**100**
x_1	50	1	1	0	0	0	−1	**25**
z_j		50	50	0	0	0	−50	**1 250**
c_j-z_j		0	−10	0	0	0	50	

We are now ready to begin **phase II** of the Simplex method. This phase simply continues the Simplex method computations after all artificial variables have been removed. At the next iteration, variable s_4 with $c_j-z_j = 50$ is entered into the solution and variable s_3 is eliminated. The tableau after this iteration is:

		x_1	x_2	s_1	s_2	s_3	s_4	
Basis	c_B	50	40	0	0	0	0	
s_1	0	0	3.125	1	0	−0.375	0	**37.5**
s_2	0	0	1	0	1	0	0	**20**
s_4	0	0	−0.375	0	0	0.125	1	**12.5**
x_1	50	1	0.625	0	0	0.125	0	**37.5**
z_j		50	31.25	0	0	6.250	0	**1 875**
$c_j - z_j$		0	8.75	0	0	−6.250	0	

Another iteration is required. This time x_2 comes into the solution, and s_1 is eliminated. After performing this iteration, the following tableau shows that the optimal solution has been reached.

		x_1	x_2	s_1	s_2	s_3	s_4	
Basis	c_B	50	40	0	0	0	0	
x_2	40	0	1	0.320	0	−0.12	0	**12**
s_2	0	0	0	−0.320	1	0.12	0	**8**
s_4	0	0	0	0.12	0	0.08	1	**17**
x_1	50	1	0	−0.20	0	0.20	0	**30**
z_j		50	40	2.80	0	5.20	0	**1 980**
$c_j - z_j$		0	0	−2.80	0	−5.20	0	

It turns out that the optimal solution to the modified HighTech problem is the same as the solution for the original problem. However, the Simplex method required more iterations to reach this extreme point, because an extra iteration was needed to eliminate the artificial variable (a_4) in phase I.

Fortunately, once we obtain an initial tableau using artificial variables, we need not concern ourselves with whether the basic solution at a particular iteration is feasible for the real problem. We need only follow the rules for the Simplex method. If we reach the optimality criterion (all $c_j - z_j \leq 0$) and all the artificial variables have been eliminated from the solution, then we have found the optimal solution. On the other hand, if we reach the optimality criterion and one or more of the artificial variables remain in solution at a positive value, then there is no feasible solution to the problem. This special case will be discussed further in Section 5.8.

Equality Constraints

When an equality constraint occurs in a linear programming problem, we need to add an artificial variable to obtain tableau form and an initial basic feasible solution. For example, if constraint 1 is:

$$6x_1 + 4x_2 - 5x_3 = 30$$

we would simply add an artificial variable a_1 to create a basic feasible solution in the initial simplex tableau. With the artificial variable, the constraint equation becomes:

$$6x_1 + 4x_2 - 5x_3 + 1a_1 = 30$$

Now a_1 can be selected as the basic variable for this row, and its value is given by the right-hand side. Once we have created tableau form by adding an artificial variable to each equality constraint, the Simplex method proceeds exactly as before.

Eliminating Negative Right-Hand Side Values

One of the properties of the tableau form of a linear programme is that the values on the right-hand sides of the constraints have to be nonnegative. In formulating a linear programming problem, we may find one or more of the constraints have negative right-hand side values. To see how this situation might happen, suppose that the management of HighTech has specified that the number of units of the UltraPortable model, x_2, has to be less than or equal to the number of units of the Deskpro model, x_1, after setting aside five units of the Deskpro for internal company use. We could formulate this constraint as:

$$x_2 \leq x_1 - 5 \quad \textbf{(5.13)}$$

Subtracting x_1 from both sides of the inequality places both variables on the left-hand side of the inequality. So,

$$-x_1 + x_2 \leq -5 \quad \textbf{(5.14)}$$

Because this constraint has a negative right-hand side value, we can develop an equivalent constraint with a nonnegative right-hand side value by multiplying both sides of the constraint by -1. In doing so, we recognize that multiplying an inequality constraint by -1 changes the direction of the inequality.

So, to convert inequality (5.14) to an equivalent constraint with a nonnegative right-hand side value, we multiply by -1 to obtain:

$$x_1 - x_2 \geq 5 \quad \textbf{(5.15)}$$

We now have an acceptable nonnegative right-hand side value. Tableau form for this constraint can now be obtained by subtracting a surplus variable and adding an artificial variable.

For a greater-than-or-equal-to constraint, multiplying by -1 creates an equivalent less-than-or-equal-to constraint. For example, suppose we had the following greater-than-or-equal-to constraint:

$$6x_1 + 3x_2 - 4x_3 \geq -20$$

Multiplying by -1 to obtain an equivalent constraint with a nonnegative right-hand side value leads to the following less-than-or-equal-to constraint:

$$-6x_1 - 3x_2 + 4x_2 \leq 20$$

Tableau form can be created for this constraint by adding a slack variable.

For an equality constraint with a negative right-hand side value, we simply multiply by -1 to obtain an equivalent constraint with a nonnegative right-hand side value. An artificial variable can then be added to create the tableau form.

Summary of the Steps to Create Tableau Form

Step 1. If the original formulation of the linear programming problem contains one or more constraints with negative right-hand side values, multiply each of these constraints by -1. Multiplying by -1 will change the direction of the inequalities. This step will provide an equivalent linear programme with nonnegative right-hand side values.

Step 2. For $\leq$ constraints, add a slack variable to obtain an equality constraint. The coefficient of the slack variable in the objective function is assigned a value of zero. It provides the tableau form for the constraint, and the slack variable becomes one of the basic variables in the initial basic feasible solution.

Step 3. For $\geq$ constraints, subtract a surplus variable to obtain an equality constraint, and then add an artificial variable to obtain the tableau form. The coefficient of the surplus variable in the objective function is assigned a value of zero. The coefficient of the artificial variable in the objective function is assigned a value of $-M$. The artificial variable becomes one of the basic variables in the initial basic feasible solution.

Step 4. For equality constraints, add an artificial variable to obtain the tableau form. The coefficient of the artificial variable in the objective function is assigned a value of $-M$. The artificial variable becomes one of the basic variables in the initial basic feasible solution.

To obtain some practise in applying these steps, convert the following example problem into tableau form, and then set up the initial simplex tableau:

$$
\begin{aligned}
\text{Max} \quad & 6x_1 + 3x_2 + 4x_3 + 1x_4 \\
\text{s.t.} \quad & \\
& -2x_1 - 0.5x_2 + 1x_3 - 6x_4 = -60 \\
& 1x_1 + 1x_3 + 0.6667x_4 \leq 20 \\
& -1x_2 - 5x_3 \leq -50 \\
& x_1, x_2, x_3, x_4 \geq 0
\end{aligned}
$$

To eliminate the negative right-hand side values in constraints 1 and 3, we apply step 1. Multiplying both constraints by -1, we obtain the following equivalent linear programme:

$$
\begin{aligned}
\text{Max} \quad & 6x_1 + 3x_2 + 4x_3 + 1x_4 \\
\text{s.t.} \quad & \\
& 2x_1 + 0.5x_2 - 1x_3 + 6x_4 = 60 \\
& 1x_1 + 1x_3 + 0.6667x_4 \leq 20 \\
& 1x_2 + 5x_3 \leq 50 \\
& x_1, x_2, x_3, x_4 \geq 0
\end{aligned}
$$

Note that the direction of the $\leq$ inequality in constraint 3 has been reversed as a result of multiplying the constraint by -1. By applying step 4 for constraint 1, step 2 for constraint 2 and step 3 for constraint 3, we obtain the following tableau form:

$$
\begin{aligned}
\text{Max} \quad & 6x_1 + 3x_2 + 4x_3 + 1x_4 + 0s_2 + 0s_3 - Ma_1 - Ma_3 \\
\text{s.t.} \quad & \\
& 2x_1 + 0.5x_2 - 1x_3 + 6x_4 + 1a_1 = 60 \\
& 1x_1 + 1x_3 + 0.6667x_4 + 1s_2 = 20 \\
& 1x_2 + 5x_3 - 1s_3 + 1a_3 = 50 \\
& x_1, x_2, x_3, x_4, s_1, s_2, a_1, a_2 \geq 0
\end{aligned}
$$

The initial simplex tableau corresponding to this tableau form is:

		x_1	x_2	x_3	x_4	s_2	s_3	a_1	a_3	
Basis	c_B	6	3	4	1	0	0	$-M$	$-M$	
a_1	$-M$	2	0.5	-1	⑥	0	0	1	0	**60**
s_2	0	1	0	1	0.6667	1	0	0	0	**20**
a_3	$-M$	0	1	5	0	0	-1	0	1	**50**
	z_j	$-2M$	$-1.5M$	$-4M$	$-6M$	0	M	$-M$	$-M$	$-110M$
	$c_j - z_j$	$6 + 2M$	$3 + 1.5M$	$4 + 4M$	$1 + 6M$	0	$-M$	0	0	

For practise setting up tableau form and developing the initial simplex tableau for problems with any constraint form, try Problem 12.

Note that we have circled the pivot element indicating that x_4 will enter and a_1 will leave the basis at the first iteration.

NOTES AND COMMENTS

We have shown how to convert constraints with negative right-hand sides to equivalent constraints with positive right-hand sides. Actually, nothing is wrong with formulating a linear programme and including negative right-hand sides. But if you want to use the ordinary Simplex method to solve the linear programme, you must first alter the constraints to eliminate the negative right-hand sides.

5.7 Solving a Minimization Problem

We can use the Simplex method to solve a minimization problem in two ways. The first approach requires that we change the rule used to introduce a variable into the basis. Recall that in the maximization case, we select the variable with the largest positive $c_j - z_j$ as the variable to introduce next into the basis, because the value of $c_j - z_j$ tells us the amount the objective function will increase if one unit of the variable in column j is brought into the solution. To solve the minimization problem, we simply reverse this rule. That is, we select the variable with the most negative $c_j - z_j$ as the one to introduce next. Of course, this approach means the stopping rule for the optimal solution will also have to be changed. Using this approach to solve a minimization problem, we would stop when every value in the net evaluation row is zero or positive.

The second approach to solving a minimization problem is the one we shall employ in this book. It is based on the fact that any minimization problem can be converted to an equivalent maximization problem by multiplying the objective function by -1. Solving the resulting maximization problem will provide the optimal solution to the minimization problem.

In keeping with the general notation of this chapter, we are using x_1 and x_2 to represent units of product A and product B.

Let us illustrate this second approach by using the Simplex method to solve the M&D Chemicals problem introduced in Chapter 2. Recall that in this problem, management wanted to minimize the cost of producing two products subject to a demand constraint for product A, a minimum total production quantity requirement, and a constraint on available processing time. The mathematical statement of the M&D Chemicals problem is shown here.

$$
\begin{aligned}
&\text{Min} \quad 2x_1 + 3x_2 \\
&\text{s.t.} \\
&\qquad 1x_1 \qquad\quad\ \geq 125 \quad \text{Demand for product A} \\
&\qquad 1x_1 + 1x_2 \geq 350 \quad \text{Total production} \\
&\qquad 2x_1 + 1x_2 \leq 600 \quad \text{Processing time} \\
&\qquad x_1,\ x_2 \geq 0
\end{aligned}
$$

We convert a minimization problem to a maximization problem by multiplying the objective function by −1.

To solve this problem using the Simplex method, we first multiply the objective function by −1 to convert the minimization problem into the following equivalent maximization problem:

$$
\begin{aligned}
&\text{Max} \quad 2x_1 + 3x_2 \\
&\text{s.t.} \\
&\qquad 1x_1 \qquad\quad\ \geq 125 \quad \text{Demand for product A} \\
&\qquad 1x_1 + 1x_2 \geq 350 \quad \text{Total production} \\
&\qquad 2x_1 + 1x_2 \leq 600 \quad \text{Processing time} \\
&\qquad x_1,\ x_2 \geq 0
\end{aligned}
$$

The tableau form for this problem is as follows:

$$
\begin{aligned}
&\text{Max} \quad -2x_1 - 3x_2 + 0s_1 + 0s_2 + 0s_3 - Ma_1 - Ma_2 \\
&\text{s.t.} \\
&\qquad 1x_1 - 1s_1 + 1a_1 = 125 \\
&\qquad 1x_1 + 1x_2 - 1s_2 + 1a_2 = 350 \\
&\qquad 2x_1 + 1x_2 + 1s_3 = 600 \\
&\qquad x_1,\ x_2,\ s_1,\ s_2,\ s_3,\ a_1,\ a_2 \geq 0
\end{aligned}
$$

The initial simplex tableau is shown here:

		x_1	x_2	s_1	s_2	s_3	a_1	a_2	
Basis	c_B	−2	−3	0	0	0	−*M*	−*M*	
a_1	−*M*	①	0	−1	0	0	1	0	**125**
a_2	−*M*	1	1	0	−1	0	0	1	**350**
s_3	0	2	1	0	0	1	0	0	**600**
z_j		−2*M*	−*M*	*M*	*M*	0	−*M*	−*M*	**−475*M***
$c_j - z_j$		−2 + 2*M*	−3 + *M*	−*M*	−*M*	0	0	0	

At the first iteration, x_1 is brought into the basis and a_1 is removed. After dropping the a_1 column from the tableau, the result of the first iteration is as follows:

		x_1	x_2	s_1	s_2	s_3	a_2	
Basis	c_B	−2	−3	0	0	0	−*M*	
x_1	−2	1	0	−1	0	0	0	**125**
a_2	−*M*	0	1	1	−1	0	1	**225**
s_3	0	0	1	②	0	1	0	**350**
z_j		−2	−*M*	2 − *M*	*M*	0	−*M*	**−250 − 225*M***
$c_j - z_j$		0	−3 + *M*	−2 + *M*	−*M*	0	0	

Continuing with two more iterations of the Simplex method provides the following final tableau:

		x_1	x_2	s_1	s_2	s_3	
Basis	c_B	−2	−3	0	0	0	
x_1	−2	1	0	0	1	1	**250**
x_2	−3	0	1	0	−2	−1	**100**
s_1	0	0	0	1	1	1	**125**
z_j		−2	−3	0	4	1	**−800**
$c_j - z_j$		0	0	0	−4	−1	

The value of the objective function −800 must be multiplied by −1 to obtain the value of the objective function for the original minimization problem. Thus, the minimum total cost of the optimal solution is €800.

Try Problem 14 for practise solving a minimization problem with the Simplex method.

In the next section we discuss some important special cases that may occur when trying to solve any linear programming problem. We will only consider the case for maximization problems, recognizing that all minimization problems can be converted into an equivalent maximization problem by multiplying the objective function by −1.

5.8 Special Cases

In Chapter 2 we discussed how infeasibility, unboundedness and alternative optimal solutions could occur when solving linear programming problems using the graphical solution procedure. These special cases can also arise when using the Simplex method. In addition, a special case referred to as *degeneracy* can theoretically cause difficulties for the Simplex method. In this section we show how these special cases can be recognized and handled when the Simplex method is used.

Infeasibility

Infeasibility occurs whenever no solution to the linear programme can be found that satisfies all the constraints, including the nonnegativity constraints. Let us now see how infeasibility is recognized when the Simplex method is used.

In Section 5.6, when discussing artificial variables, we mentioned that infeasibility can be recognized when the optimality criterion indicates that an optimal solution has been obtained and one or more of the artificial variables remain in the solution at a positive value. As an illustration of this situation, let us consider another modification of the HighTech Industries problem. Suppose management imposed a minimum combined total production requirement of 50 units. The revised problem formulation is shown as follows.

$$
\begin{aligned}
\text{Max}\quad & 50x_1 + 40x_2 \\
\text{s.t.}\quad & \\
& 3x_1 + 5x_2 \le 150 \quad \text{Assembly time} \\
& 1x_2 \le 20 \quad \text{Ultraportable display} \\
& 8x_1 + 5x_2 \le 300 \quad \text{Warehouse space} \\
& 1x_1 + 1x_2 \ge 50 \quad \text{Minimum total production} \\
& x_1,\ x_2 \ge 0
\end{aligned}
$$

Two iterations of the Simplex method will provide the following tableau:

		x_1	x_2	s_1	s_2	s_3	s_4	a_4	
Basis	c_B	50	40	0	0	0	0	$-M$	
x_2	40	0	1	0.32	0	−0.12	0	0	**12**
s_2	0	0	0	−0.32	1	0.12	0	0	**8**
x_1	50	1	0	−0.20	0	0.20	0	0	**30**
a_4	$-M$	0	0	−0.12	0	−0.05	−1	1	**8**
	z_j	50	40	$2.8 + 0.12M$	0	$5.2 + 0.08M$	M	$-M$	**1 980 − 8*M***
	$c_j - z_j$	0	0	$-2.8 - 0.12M$	0	$-5.2 - 0.08M$	$-M$	0	

If an artificial variable is positive, the solution is not feasible for the real problem.

Note that $c_j - z_j \leq 0$ for all the variables; therefore, according to the optimality criterion, it should be the optimal solution. But this solution is *not feasible* for the modified HighTech problem because the artificial variable $a_4 = 8$ appears in the solution. The solution $x_1 = 30$ and $x_2 = 12$ results in a combined total production of 42 units instead of the constraint 4 requirement of at least 50 units. The fact that the artificial variable is in solution at a value of $a_4 = 8$ tells us that the final solution violates the fourth constraint ($1x_1 + 1x_2 \geq 50$) by eight units.

If management is interested in knowing which of the first three constraints is preventing us from satisfying the total production requirement, a partial answer can be obtained from the final tableau. Note that $s_2 = 8$, but that s_1 and s_3 are zero. This tells us that the assembly time and warehouse capacity constraints are binding. Because not enough assembly time and warehouse space are available, we cannot satisfy the minimum combined total production requirement.

The management implications here are that additional assembly time and/or warehouse space must be made available to satisfy the total production requirement. If more time and/or space cannot be made available, management will have to relax the total production requirement by at least eight units.

Try Problem 17 to practise recognizing when there is no feasible solution to a problem using the Simplex method.

In summary, a linear programme is infeasible if no solution satisfies all the constraints simultaneously. We *recognize infeasibility when one or more of the artificial variables remain in the final solution at a positive value*. In closing, we note that linear programming problems with all $\leq$ constraints and nonnegative right-hand sides will always have a feasible solution. Because it is not necessary to introduce artificial variables to set up the initial simplex tableau for these types of problems, the final solution cannot possibly contain an artificial variable.

Unbounded Problems

Usually a constraint has been overlooked if unboundedness occurs.

For maximization problems, we say that a linear programme is unbounded if the value of the solution may be made infinitely large without violating any constraints. So, when unboundedness occurs, we can generally look for an error in the formulation of the problem.

The coefficients in the column of the A matrix associated with the incoming variable indicate how much each of the current basic variables will decrease if one unit of the incoming variable is brought into solution. Suppose then, that for a particular linear programming problem, we reach a point where the rule for determining which variable should enter the basis results in the decision to enter variable x_2. Assume that for this variable, $c_2 - z_2 = 5$, and that all a_{i2} in column 2 are ≤ 0. So, each unit of x_2 brought into solution increases the objective function by five units.

Furthermore, because $a_{i2} \leq 0$ for all i, none of the current basic variables will be driven to zero, no matter how many units of x_2 we introduce. So, we can introduce an infinite amount of x_2 into solution and still maintain feasibility. Because each unit of x_2 increases the objective function by 5, we will have an unbounded solution. Hence, *the way we recognize the unbounded situation is that all the a_{ij} are less than or equal to zero in the column associated with the incoming variable.*

To illustrate this concept, let us consider the following example of an unbounded problem.

$$\begin{aligned} \text{Max} \quad & 20x_1 + 10x_2 \\ \text{s.t.} \quad & 1x_1 \geq 2 \\ & 1x_2 \leq 5 \\ & x_1, x_2 \geq 0 \end{aligned}$$

We subtract a surplus variable s_1 from the first constraint equation and add a slack variable s_2 to the second constraint equation to obtain the standard-form representation. We then add an artificial variable a_1 to the first constraint equation to obtain the tableau form. In the initial simplex tableau the basic variables are a_1 and s_2. After bringing in x_1 and removing a_1 at the first iteration, the tableau is as follows:

		x_1	x_2	s_1	s_2	
Basis	c_B	20	10	0	0	
x_1	20	1	0	−1	0	**2**
s_2	0	0	1	0	1	**5**
z_j		20	0	−20	0	**40**
$c_j - z_j$		0	10	20	0	

Because s_1 has the largest positive $c_j - z_j$, we know we can increase the value of the objective function most rapidly by bringing s_1 into the basis. But $a_{13} = -1$ and $a_{23} = 0$; hence, we cannot form the ratio b_i/a_{i3} for any $a_{i3} > 0$ because no values of a_{i3} are greater than zero. This result indicates that the solution to the linear programme is unbounded because each unit of s_1 that is brought into solution provides one extra unit of x_1 (since $a_{13} = -1$) and drives zero units of s_2 out of solution (since $a_{23} = 0$). Because s_1 is a surplus variable and can be interpreted as the amount of x_1 over the minimum amount required, the simplex tableau indicates we can introduce as much of s_1 as we desire without violating any constraints; the interpretation is that we can make as much as we want above the minimum amount of x_1 required. Because the objective function coefficient associated with x_1 is positive, there will be no upper bound on the value of the objective function.

In summary, a maximization linear programme is unbounded if it is possible to make the value of the optimal solution as large as desired without violating any of the constraints. When employing the Simplex method, an unbounded linear programme exists if *at some iteration, the Simplex method tells us to introduce variable j into the solution and all the a_{ij} are less than or equal to zero in the jth column.*

Try Problem 19 for another example of an unbounded problem.

We emphasize that the case of an unbounded solution will never occur in real cost minimization or profit maximization problems because it is not possible to reduce costs to minus infinity or to increase profits to plus infinity. So, if we encounter an unbounded solution to a linear programming problem, we should carefully reexamine the formulation of the problem to determine whether a formulation error has occurred.

Alternative Optimal Solutions

A linear programme with two or more optimal solutions is said to have alternative optimal solutions. When using the Simplex method, we cannot recognize that a linear programme has alternative optimal solutions until the final tableau is reached. Then if the linear programme has alternative optimal solutions, $c_j - z_j$ will equal zero for one or more non-basic variables.

To illustrate the case of alternative optimal solutions when using the Simplex method, consider changing the objective function for the HighTech problem from $50x_1 + 40x_2$ to $30x_1 + 50x_2$; in doing so, we obtain the revised linear programme:

$$\begin{aligned}
\text{Max} \quad & 30x_1 + 50x_2 \\
\text{s.t.} \quad & \\
& 3x_1 + 5x_2 \leq 150 \\
& 1x_2 \leq 20 \\
& 8x_1 + 5x_2 \leq 300 \\
& x_1, x_2 \geq 0
\end{aligned}$$

The final tableau for this problem is shown here:

		x_1	x_2	s_1	s_2	s_3	
Basis	c_B	30	50	0	0	0	
x_2	50	0	1	0	1	0	**20**
s_3	0	0	0	−2.6667	8.3333	1	**66.6667**
x_1	30	1	0	0.3333	−1.6667	0	**16.6667**
z_j		30	50	10	0	0	**1 500**
$c_j - z_j$		0	0	−10	0	0	

All values in the net evaluation row are less than or equal to zero, indicating that an optimal solution has been found. This solution is given by $x_1 = 16.6667$, $x_2 = 20$, $s_1 = 0$, $s_2 = 0$ and $s_3 = 66.6667$. The value of the objective function is 1500.

In looking at the net evaluation row in the optimal simplex tableau, we see that the $c_j - z_j$ value for non-basic variable s_2 is equal to zero. This indicates that the linear programme may have alternative optimal solutions. In other words, because the net evaluation row entry for s_2 is zero, we can introduce s_2 into the basis without changing the value of the solution. The tableau obtained after introducing s_2 follows:

		x_1	x_2	s_1	s_2	s_3	
Basis	c_B	30	50	0	0	0	
x_2	50	0	1	0.32	0	−0.12	**12**
s_3	0	0	0	−0.32	1	0.12	**8**
x_1	30	1	0	−0.20	0	0.20	**30**
z_j		30	50	10	0	0	**1 500**
$c_j - z_j$		0	0	−10	0	0	

Try Problem 18 for another example of alternative optimal solutions.

As shown, we have a different basic feasible solution: $x_1 = 30$, $x_2 = 12$, $s_1 = 0$, $s_2 = 8$ and $s_3 = 0$. However, this new solution is also optimal because $c_j - z_j \leq 0$ for all j. Another way to confirm that this solution is still optimal is to note that the value of the solution has remained equal to 1500.

In summary, *when using the Simplex method, we can recognize the possibility of alternative optimal solutions if* $c_j - z_j$ *equals zero for one or more of the non-basic variables in the final tableau.*

Degeneracy

A linear programme is said to be degenerate if one or more of the basic variables have a value of zero. **Degeneracy** does not cause any particular difficulties for the graphical solution procedure; however, degeneracy can theoretically cause difficulties when the Simplex method is used to solve a linear programming problem.

To see how a degenerate linear programme could occur, consider a change in the right-hand side value of the assembly time constraint for the HighTech problem. For example, what if the number of hours available had been 175 instead of 150? The modified linear programme is shown here.

$$\text{Max} \quad 50x_1 + 40x_2$$

s.t.

$$\begin{aligned} 3x_1 + 5x_2 &\leq 175 && \text{Assembly time increased to 175 hours} \\ 1x_2 &\leq 20 && \text{UltraPortable display} \\ 8x_1 + 5x_2 &\leq 300 && \text{Warehouse space} \\ x_1, x_2 &\geq 0 \end{aligned}$$

The simplex tableau after one iteration is as follows:

		x_1	x_2	s_1	s_2	s_3	
Basis	c_B	50	40	0	0	0	
s_1	0	0	3.125	1	0	−0.315	**62.5**
s_2	0	0	1	0	1	0	**20**
x_1	50	1	0.625	0	0	0.125	**37.5**
	z_j	50	31.25	0	0	6.25	**1 875**
	$c_j - z_j$	0	8.15	0	0	−6.25	

The entries in the net evaluation row indicate that x_2 should enter the basis. By calculating the appropriate ratios to determine the pivot row, we obtain:

$$\frac{b_1}{a_{12}} = \frac{62.5}{3.125} = 20$$

$$\frac{b_2}{a_{22}} = \frac{20}{1} = 20$$

$$\frac{b_3}{a_{32}} = \frac{37.5}{0.625} = 60$$

We see that the first and second rows tie, which indicates that we will have a degenerate basic feasible solution at the next iteration. Recall that in the case of a tie, we follow the convention of selecting the uppermost row as the pivot row. Here, it means that s_1 will leave the basis. But from the tie for the minimum ratio we see that the basic variable in row 2, s_2, will also be driven to zero. Because it does not leave the basis, we will have a basic variable with a value of zero after performing this iteration. The tableau after this iteration is as follows:

		x_1	x_2	s_1	s_2	s_3	
Basis	c_B	50	40	0	0	0	
x_2	40	0	1	0.32	0	−0.12	**20**
s_2	0	0	0	−0.32	1	0.12	**0**
x_1	50	1	0	−0.20	0	0.20	**25**
z_j		50	40	2.80	0	5.20	**2 050**
$c_j - z_j$		0	0	−2.80	0	−5.20	

As expected, we have a basic feasible solution with one of the basic variables, s_2, equal to zero. Whenever we have a tie in the minimum b_i/a_{ij} ratio, the next tableau will always have a basic variable equal to zero. Because we are at the optimal solution in the preceding case, we do not care that s_2 is in solution at a zero value. However, if degeneracy occurs at some iteration prior to reaching the optimal solution, it is theoretically possible for the Simplex method to cycle; that is, the procedure could possibly alternate between the same set of nonoptimal basic feasible solutions and never reach the optimal solution. Cycling has not proven to be a significant difficulty in practice. Therefore, we do not recommend introducing any special steps into the Simplex method to eliminate the possibility that degeneracy will occur. If while performing the iterations of the simplex algorithm a tie occurs for the minimum b_i/a_{ij} ratio, then we recommend simply selecting the upper row as the pivot row.

The Simplex method was chosen as one of the twentieth-century's top 20 algorithms

NOTES AND COMMENTS

1 We stated that infeasibility is recognized when the stopping rule is encountered but one or more artificial variables are in solution at a positive value. This requirement does not necessarily mean that all artificial variables must be non-basic to have a feasible solution. An artificial variable could be in solution at a zero value.

2 An unbounded feasible region must exist for a problem to be unbounded, but it does not guarantee that a problem will be unbounded. A minimization problem may be bounded whereas a maximization problem with the same feasible region is unbounded.

Summary

In this chapter we introduced the Simplex method as an algorithm for solving LP problems.

- The Simplex method follows a set of standard steps to find a basic, feasible solution and to search for an improved solution. The Simplex method stops when no improved solution is found.
- The Simplex method steps can be summarized as follows:

  Step 1: Formulate a linear programming model of the problem.

  Step 2: Define an equivalent linear programme by performing the following operations:

  a. Multiply each constraint with a negative right-hand side value by −1, and change the direction of the constraint inequality.

b. For a minimization problem, convert the problem to an equivalent maximization problem by multiplying the objective function by −1.

Step 3: Set up the standard form of the linear programme by adding appropriate slack and surplus variables.

Step 4: Set up the tableau form of the linear programme to obtain an initial basic feasible solution. All linear programmes must be set up this way before the initial simplex tableau can be obtained.

Step 5: Set up the initial simplex tableau to keep track of the calculations required by the Simplex method.

Step 6: Choose the non-basic variable with the largest $c_j - z_j$ to bring into the basis. The column associated with that variable is the pivot column.

Step 7: Choose as the pivot row that row with the smallest ratio of b_i/a_i for $a_{ij} > 0$
This ratio is used to determine which variable will leave the basis when variable j enters the basis. This ratio also indicates how many units of variable j can be introduced into solution before the basic variable in the ith row equals zero.

Step 8: Perform the necessary elementary row operations to convert the pivot column to a unit column.

a. Divide each element in the pivot row by the pivot element. The result is a new pivot row containing a 1 in the pivot column.

b. Obtain zeroes in all other positions of the pivot column by adding or subtracting an appropriate multiple of the new pivot row.

Step 9: Test for optimality. If $c_j - z_j \leq 0$ for all columns, we have the optimal solution.

If not, return to step 6.

- A number of special cases can occur involving: infeasibility, unbounded problems, alternative optimal solutions and degeneracy.

WORKED EXAMPLE

The Fresh Juice Company (FJC) is a small cooperative in South Africa that produces a range of locally produced fresh fruit juices for local retail stores. FJC is currently planning its next production of its grape juices for tomorrow. It produces three different grape juice products: Sweet Grape, Regular Grape and Dry Grape. Each of the products is produced by mixing two different types of local grape juice and natural flavourings. The relevant data for the three products are as follows:

	Sweet Grape	Regular Grape	Dry Grape	Availability
Profit contribution, Rand	1	1.2	2	
Grade A grapes - kilos	1	2		150 kilos
Grade B grapes - kilos	1		2	150 kilos
Natural flavourings - kilos	2	1		80 kilos
Labour hours	2	3	1	225 hours

So, for example, a litre of Sweet Grape will bring a profit contribution of 1R and require one kilo of Grade A grapes, one kilo of Grade B grapes, two kilos of natural flavourings and require two hours of labour. FJC has bought 150 kilos of each grade of grape, has 80 kilos of natural flavourings in stock and anticipates it will have 225 labour hours available for the next production batch. In addition it is contracted to supply at least 25 litres of Sweet Grape to a local café. How much of the three products should the company produce?

We cannot use the graphical method here as we have three decision variables so we shall use the Simplex. Following the steps set out earlier, using x_1, x_2 and x_3 as the decision variables for the quantities of the three products to be produced we have a formulation:

$$\text{Max } 1x_1 + 1.2x_2 + 2x_3$$

s.t.

$$\begin{aligned} 1x_1 + 2x_2 &\leq 150 \\ 1x_1 + 2x_3 &\leq 150 \\ 2x_1 + 1x_2 &\leq 80 \\ 2x_1 + 3x_2 + 1x_3 &\leq 225 \\ x_1 &\geq 25 \end{aligned}$$

$$x_1,\ x_2,\ x_3 \geq 0$$

Putting the problem into standard form we then have:

$$\text{Max } 1x_1 + 1.2x_2 + 2x_3 + 0s_1 + 0s_2 + 0s_3 + 0s_4$$

s.t.

$$\begin{aligned} 1x_1 + 2x_2 + 1s_1 &\leq 150 \\ 1x_1 + 2x_3 + 1s_2 &\leq 150 \\ 2x_1 + 1x_2 + 1s_3 &\leq 80 \\ 2x_1 + 3x_2 + 1x_3 + 1s_4 &\leq 225 \\ x_1 - 1s_5 &\geq 25 \end{aligned}$$

$$x_1,\ x_2,\ x_3,\ s_1,\ s_2,\ s_3,\ s_4 \geq 0$$

We note that we have one constraint which takes the form $\geq$ so we will require an artificial variable for this constraint and using the M method we then have:

$$\text{Max } 1x_1 + 1.2x_2 + 2x_3 + 0s_1 + 0s_2 + 0s_3 + 0s_4 - Ma_5$$

s.t.

$$\begin{aligned} 1x_1 + 2x_2 + 1s_1 &\leq 150 \\ 1x_1 + 2x_3 + 1s_2 &\leq 150 \\ 2x_1 + 1x_2 + 1s_3 &\leq 80 \\ 2x_1 + 3x_2 + 1x_3 + 1s_4 &\leq 225 \\ x_1 - 1s_5 + Ma_5 &\geq 25 \end{aligned}$$

$$x_1,\ x_2,\ x_3,\ s_1,\ s_2,\ s_3,\ s_4,\ s_5,\ a_5 \geq 0$$

This then gives an initial tableau:

		x_1	x_2	x_3	s_1	s_2	s_3	s_4	s_5	a_5	***Value***
Basis	c_B	1	1.2	2	0	0	0	0	0	–M	
s_1	0	1	2	0	1	0	0	0	0	0	**150**
s_2	0	1	0	2	0	1	0	0	0	0	**150**
s_3	0	2	1	0	0	0	1	0	0	0	**80**
s_4	0	2	3	1	0	0	0	1	0	0	**225**
a_5	–M	1	0	0	0	0	0	0	–1	1	**25**
z_j		–M	0	0	0	0	0	0	M	–M	**–25*M***
$c_j - z_j$		1+M	1.2	2	0	0	0	0	–M	0	

On inspection of the $c_j - z_j$ row, we see that three non-basic variables would improve the current basic solution: x_1, x_2 and x_3. However, because of the M value, we identify x_1 as the pivot column. Calculating the appropriate ratios (not shown here) indicates row a_5 as the pivot row and therefore the pivot element is 1 (the intersection of column x_1 and row a_5). So, a_5 is set to leave the solution and x_1 to enter. In the problem context this makes sense. We must produce at least 25 litres of x_1 no matter what else we do, so the Simplex method forces this solution as a first step. Completing the necessary arithmetic transformation on the initial table we have our next basic solution as:

		x_1	x_2	x_3	s_1	s_2	s_3	s_4	s_5	a_5	***Value***
Basis	c_B	1	1.2	2	0	0	0	0	0	–M	
s_1	0	0	2	0	1	0	0	0	1	–1	**125**
s_2	0	0	0	2	0	1	0	0	1	–1	**125**
s_3	0	0	1	0	0	0	1	0	2	–2	**0**
s_4	0	0	3	1	0	0	0	1	2	–2	**175**
x_1	1	1	0	0	0	0	0	0	–1	1	**25**
z_j		1	0	0	0	0	0	0	–1	1	**25**
$c_j - z_j$		0	1.2	2	0	0	0	0	0	–M–1	

For FJC this means they are producing 25 litres of Sweet Grape and nothing else to give a profit contribution of 25R. They still have 125 kilos each of Grade A and Grade B grapes unused, have 30 kilos of natural flavourings left and 175 hours of labour remain unused. Is there an even better solution? We note from the $c_j - z_j$ row that there are still positive values in this row so further improvement is possible. We also note that the artificial variable has been removed from the basis so phase I of the solution is complete. We can omit the a_5 column from further iterations.

The pivot column is x_3, we determine from the ratio calculations that the pivot row is s_2 so the pivot element is 2. Using this to transform the tableau in the usual way we have:

		x_1	x_2	x_3	s_1	s_2	s_3	s_4	s_5	***Value***
Basis	c_B	1	1.2	2	0	0	0	0	0	
s_1	0	0	2	0	1	0	0	0	1	**125**
x_3	2	0	0	1	0	0.5	0	0	0.5	**62.5**
s_3	0	0	1	0	0	0	1	0	2	**30**
s_4	0	0	3	0	0	–0.5	0	1	1.5	**112.5**
x_1	1	1	0	0	0	0	0	0	–1	**25**
z_j		1	0	2	0	1	0	0	0	**150**
$c_j - z_j$		0	1.2	0	0	–1	0	0	0	

We now have a solution for FJC where we are producing 25 litres of Sweet Grape, and 62.5 litres of Dry Grape to generate a profit contribution of 150R. There are 125 kilos of Grape A unused, 30 kilos of the natural flavourings and 112.5 hours of labour. We are using all the available supply of Grape B. Are further improvements possible? We have one positive value in the c_j–z_j row for x_2 so this is set to enter the basis and we calculate that s_3 will leave. Transforming the tableau we have:

		x_1	x_2	x_3	s_1	s_2	s_3	s_4	s_5	***Value***
Basis	c_B	1	1.2	2	0	0	0	0	0	
s_1	0	0	0	0	1	0	0	0	−3	**65**
x_3	2	0	0	1	0	0.5	0	0	0.5	**62.5**
x_2	12	0	1	0	0	0	1	0	2	**30**
s_4	0	0	0	0	0	−0.5	−3	1	−4.5	**22.5**
x_1	1	1	0	0	0	0	0	0	−1	**25**
	z_j	1	1.2	2	0	1	1.2	0	2.4	**186**
	$c_j - z_j$	0	0	0	0	−1	−1.2	0	−2.4	

This time we have the optimal solution given; there are no positive values in the c_j–z_j column. To generate a profit contribution of 186R from tomorrow's production FJC should produce 25 litres of Sweet Grape, 30 litres of Regular Grape and 62.5 litres of Dry Grape. It will still have 65 kilos of Grape A unused and 22.5 hours of labour.

Problems

SELF *test*

1 Consider the following system of linear equations:

$$3x_1 + x_2 = 6$$
$$2x_1 + 4x_2 + x_3 = 12$$

a. Find the basic solution with $x_1 = 0$.
b. Find the basic solution with $x_2 = 0$.
c. Find the basic solution with $x_3 = 0$.
d. Which of the preceding solutions would be basic feasible solutions for a linear programme?

SELF *test*

2 Consider the following linear programme:

$$\text{Max} \quad x_1 + 2x_2$$
s.t.
$$x_1 + 5x_2 \leq 10$$
$$2x_1 + 6x_2 \leq 16$$
$$x_1,\ x_2 \geq 0$$

a. Write the problem in standard form.
b. How many variables will be set equal to zero in a basic solution for this problem?
c. Find all the basic solutions, and indicate which are also feasible.
d. Find the optimal solution by computing the value of each basic feasible solution.

3 Consider the following linear programme:

$$\begin{aligned} \text{Max} \quad & 5x_1 + 9x_2 \\ \text{s.t.} \quad & \\ & 0.5x_1 + 1x_2 \leq 8 \\ & 1x_1 + 1x_2 \geq 10 \\ & 0.25x_1 + 1.5x_2 \geq 6 \\ & x_1, x_2 \geq 0 \end{aligned}$$

a. Write the problem in standard form.
b. How many variables will be set equal to zero in a basic solution for this problem? Explain.
c. Find the basic solution that corresponds to s_1 and s_2 equal to zero.
d. Find the basic solution that corresponds to x_1 and s_3 equal to zero.
e. Are your solutions for parts (c) and (d) basic feasible solutions? Extreme-point solutions? Explain.
f. Use the graphical approach to identify the solutions found in parts (c) and (d). Do the graphical results agree with your answer to part (e)? Explain.

SELF *test*

4 Consider the following linear programming problem:

$$\begin{aligned} \text{Max} \quad & 60x_1 + 90x_2 \\ \text{s.t.} \quad & \\ & 15x_1 + 45x_2 \leq 90 \\ & 5x_1 + 5x_2 \leq 20 \\ & x_1, x_2 \geq 0 \end{aligned}$$

a. Write the problem in standard form.
b. Develop the portion of the simplex tableau involving the objective function coefficients, the coefficients of the variables in the constraints and the constants for the right-hand sides.

SELF *test*

5 A partially completed initial simplex tableau is given:

		x_1	x_2	s_1	s_2	
Basis	c_B	5	9	0	0	
s_1	0	10	9	1	0	**90**
s_2	0	−5	3	0	1	**15**
z_j						
$c_j - z_j$						

a. Complete the initial tableau.
b. Which variable would be brought into solution at the first iteration?
c. Write the original linear programme.

SELF *test*

6 The following partial initial simplex tableau is given:

		x_1	x_2	x_3	s_1	s_2	s_3	
Basis	c_B	5	20	25	0	0	0	
		2	1	0	1	0	0	**40**
		0	2	1	0	1	0	**30**
		3	0	−0.5	0	0	1	**15**
z_j								
$c_j - z_j$								

a. Complete the initial tableau.
b. Write the problem in tableau form.
c. What is the initial basis? Does this basis correspond to the origin? Explain.
d. What is the value of the objective function at this initial solution?
e. For the next iteration, which variable should enter the basis, and which variable should leave the basis?
f. How many units of the entering variable will be in the next solution? Before making this first iteration, what do you think will be the value of the objective function after the first iteration?
g. Find the optimal solution using the Simplex method.

7 Solve the following linear programme using the graphical approach:

$$\begin{aligned} \text{Max} \quad & 4x_1 + 5x_2 \\ \text{s.t.} \quad & \\ & 2x_1 + 2x_2 \leq 20 \\ & 3x_1 + 7x_2 \leq 42 \\ & x_1,\ x_2 \geq 0 \end{aligned}$$

Put the linear programme in tableau form, and solve using the Simplex method. Show the sequence of extreme points generated by the Simplex method on your graph.

SELF *test*

8 Recall the problem for GulfGolf introduced in Section 2.1. The mathematical model for this problem is restated as follows:

$$\begin{aligned} \text{Max} \quad & 10x_1 + 9x_2 \\ \text{s.t.} \quad & \\ & 0.7x_1 + 1x_2 \leq 630 && \text{Cutting and sewing} \\ & 0.5x_1 + 0.8333x_2 \leq 600 && \text{Sewing} \\ & 1x_1 + 0.6667x_2 \leq 708 && \text{Finishing} \\ & 0.1x_1 + 0.25x_2 \leq 135 && \text{Inspection and packaging} \\ & x_1,\ x_2 \geq 0 \end{aligned}$$

where

$$x_1 = \text{number of standard bags produced}$$

$$x_2 = \text{number of deluxe bags produced}$$

a. Use the Simplex method to determine how many bags of each model GulfGolf should manufacture.
b. What is the profit GulfGolf can earn with these production quantities?
c. How many hours of production time will be scheduled for each operation?
d. What is the slack time in each operation?

9 Solve the RMC problem (Chapter 2, Problem 12) using the Simplex method. At each iteration, locate the basic feasible solution found by the Simplex method on the graph of the feasible region. The problem formulation is shown here:

$$\begin{aligned} \text{Max} \quad & 40x_1 + 30x_2 \\ \text{s.t.} \quad & \\ & 0.4x_1 + 0.5x_2 \leq 20 && \text{Material 1} \\ & 0.2x_2 \leq 5 && \text{Material 2} \\ & 0.6x_1 + 0.3x_2 \leq 21 && \text{Material 3} \\ & x_1,\ x_2 \geq 0 \end{aligned}$$

where

$$x_1 = \text{kilos of fuel additive produced}$$
$$x_2 = \text{kilos of solvent base produced}$$

SELF *test*

10 Suppose a company manufactures three products from two raw materials. The amount of raw material in each unit of each product is given.

Raw Material	Product A	Product B	Product C
I	7 kilos	6 kilos	3 kilos
II	5 kilos	4 kilos	2 kilos

If the company has available 100 kilos of material I and 200 kilos of material II, and if the profits for the three products are €20, €20 and €15, respectively, how much of each product should be produced to maximize profits?

11 Liva's Lumber manufactures three types of plywood. The following table summarizes the production hours per unit in each of three production operations and other data for the problem.

	Operations (hours)			
Plywood	I	II	III	Profit/Unit
Grade A	2	2	4	€40
Grade B	5	5	2	€30
Grade X	10	3	2	€20
Maximum time available	900	400	600	

How many units of each grade of plywood should be produced?

SELF *test*

12 Set up the tableau form for the following linear programme (do not attempt to solve):

$$\begin{aligned} \text{Max} \quad & 4x_1 + 2x_2 - 3x_3 + 5x_3 \\ \text{s.t.} \quad & \\ & 2x_1 - 1x_2 + 1x_3 + 2x_4 \geq 50 \\ & 3x_1 \qquad\quad - 1x_3 + 2x_4 \leq 80 \\ & 1x_1 + 1x_2 \qquad\quad + 1x_4 = 60 \\ & x_1,\ x_2,\ x_3,\ x_4 \geq 0 \end{aligned}$$

13 Set up the tableau form for the following linear programme (do not attempt to solve):

$$\begin{aligned} \text{Min} \quad & 4x_1 + 5x_2 + 3x_3 \\ \text{s.t.} \quad & \\ & 4x_1 \qquad\quad + 2x_3 \geq 20 \\ & \qquad\quad 1x_2 - 1x_3 \leq -8 \\ & 1x_1 - 2x_2 \qquad\quad = -5 \\ & 2x_1 + 1x_2 + 1x_3 \leq 12 \\ & x_1,\ x_2,\ x_3 \geq 0 \end{aligned}$$

SELF *test*

14 Solve the following linear programme:

$$\begin{aligned} \text{Min} \quad & 3x_1 + 4x_2 + 8x_3 \\ \text{s.t.} \quad & \\ & 4x_1 + 2x_2 \geq 12 \\ & 4x_2 + 8x_3 \geq 16 \\ & x_1,\ x_2,\ x_3 \geq 0 \end{aligned}$$

15 The Our-Bags-Don't-Break (OBDB) plastic bag company manufactures three plastic refuse bags for home use: a 20 litre garbage bag, a 30 litre garbage bag and a 33 litre leaf-and-grass bag. Using purchased plastic material, three operations are required to produce each end product: cutting, sealing and packaging. The production time required to process each type of bag in every operation and the maximum production time available for each operation are shown (note that the production time figures in this table are per box of each type of bag).

	Production Time (seconds/box)		
Type of Bag	Cutting	Sealing	Packaging
20 litre	2	2	3
30 litre	3	2	4
33 litre	3	3	5
Time available	2 hours	3 hours	4 hours

If OBDB's profit contribution is €0.10 for each box of 20 litre bags produced, €0.15 for each box of 30 litre bags and €0.20 for each box of 33 litre bags, what is the optimal product mix?

SELF *test*

16 Uforia Corporation sells two brands of perfume: Incentive and Temptation No. 1. Uforia sells exclusively through department stores and employs a three-person sales staff to call on its customers. The amount of time necessary for each sales representative to sell one case of each product varies with experience and ability. Data on the average time for each of Uforia's three sales representatives is presented here.

	Average Sales Time per Case (minutes)	
Salesperson	**Incentive**	**Temptation No. 1**
John	10	15
Brenda	15	10
Red	12	6

Each sales representative spends approximately 80 hours per month in the actual selling of these two products. Cases of Incentive and Temptation No. 1 sell at profits of €30 and €25, respectively. How many cases of each perfume should each person sell during the next month to maximize the firm's profits? (Hint: Let x_1 = number of cases of Incentive sold by John, x_2 = number of cases of Temptation No. 1 sold by John, x_3 = number of cases of Incentive sold by Brenda and so on.)

Note: In Problems 17–20, we provide examples of linear programmes that result in one or more of the following situations:

- Optimal solution.
- Infeasible solution.
- Unbounded solution.
- Alternative optimal solutions.
- Degenerate solution.

For each linear programme, determine the solution situation that exists, and indicate how you identified each situation using the Simplex method. For the problems with alternative optimal solutions, calculate at least two optimal solutions.

SELF *test* **17**

$$\begin{aligned} \text{Max} \quad & 4x_1 + 8x_2 \\ \text{s.t.} \quad & \\ & 2x_1 + 2x_2 \leq 10 \\ & -1x_1 + 1x_2 \geq 8 \\ & x_1, x_2 \geq 0 \end{aligned}$$

SELF *test* **18**

$$\begin{aligned} \text{Min} \quad & 3x_1 + 3x_2 \\ \text{s.t.} \quad & \\ & 2x_1 + 0.5x_2 \geq 10 \\ & 2x_1 \geq 4 \\ & 4x_1 + 4x_2 \geq 32 \\ & x_1, x_2 \geq 0 \end{aligned}$$

SELF *test* **19**

$$\begin{aligned} \text{Min} \quad & 1x_1 + 1x_2 \\ \text{s.t.} \quad & \\ & 8x_1 + 6x_2 \geq 24 \\ & 4x_1 + 6x_2 \geq -12 \\ & 2x_2 \geq 4 \\ & x_1, x_2 \geq 0 \end{aligned}$$

SELF *test* **20**

$$\begin{aligned} \text{Max} \quad & 2x_1 + 1x_2 + 1x_3 \\ \text{s.t.} \quad & \\ & 4x_1 + 2x_2 + 2x_3 \geq 4 \\ & 2x_1 + 4x_2 \leq 20 \\ & 4x_1 + 8x_2 + 2x_3 \leq 16 \\ & x_1, x_2, x_3 \geq 0 \end{aligned}$$

Chapter 6

Simplex-Based Sensitivity Analysis and Duality

Learning Objectives

By the end of this chapter you will be able to:

- Complete sensitivity analysis using the information in the simplex tableau
- Formulate the dual problem
- Interpret the dual problem and solution

In Chapter 3 we saw how simple sensitivity analysis could be applied to the optimal solution of an LP problem to examine how marginal changes in the problem might affect the current solution. In practice it is the sensitivity analysis information that may be of most value to management decision makers. In this chapter we look at sensitivity analysis in detail and show how the Simplex solution can be used to produce this information.

6.1 Sensitivity Analysis with the Simplex Tableau

The usual sensitivity analysis for linear programmes involves calculating ranges for the objective function coefficients and the right-hand side values, as well as the dual prices.

Objective Function Coefficients

Sensitivity analysis for an objective function coefficient involves placing a range on the coefficient's value. We call this range the **range of optimality**. As long as the actual value of the objective function coefficient is within the range of optimality, *the current basic feasible solution will remain optimal*. The range of optimality for a basic variable defines the objective function coefficient values for which that variable will remain part of the current optimal basic feasible solution. The range of optimality for a nonbasic variable defines the objective function coefficient values for which that variable will remain nonbasic.

In calculating the range of optimality for an objective function coefficient, all other coefficients in the problem are assumed to remain at their original values; in other words, *only one coefficient is allowed to change at a time*. To illustrate the process of computing ranges for objective function coefficients, recall the HighTech Industries problem introduced in Chapter 5. The linear programme for this problem is restated as follows:

$$\begin{aligned} \text{Max} \quad & 50x_1 + 40x_2 \\ \text{s.t.} \quad & \\ & 3x_1 + 5x_2 \leq 150 \quad \text{Assembly time} \\ & 1x_2 \leq 20 \quad \text{UltraPortable display} \\ & 8x_1 + 5x_2 \leq 300 \quad \text{Warehouse capacity} \\ & x_1,\ x_2 \geq 0 \end{aligned}$$

where

$$x_1 = \text{number of units of the Deskpro}$$
$$x_2 = \text{number of units of the UltraPortable}$$

The final tableau for the HighTech problem is as follows.

		x_1	x_2	s_1	s_2	s_3	
Basis	c_B	50	40	0	0	0	
x_2	40	0	1	0.32	0	−0.12	**12**
s_2	0	0	0	−0.32	1	0.12	**8**
x_1	50	1	0	−0.20	0	0.20	**30**
z_j		50	40	2.80	0	5.20	**1 980**
$c_j - z_j$		0	0	−2.80	0	−5.20	

Recall that when the Simplex method is used to solve a linear programme, an optimal solution is recognized when all entries in the net evaluation row ($c_j - z_j$) are ≤ 0. Because the preceding simplex tableau satisfies this criterion, the solution shown is optimal. However, if a change in one of the objective function coefficients were to cause one or more of the $c_j - z_j$ values to become positive, then the current solution would no longer be optimal; in such a case, one or more additional simplex iterations would be necessary to find the new optimal solution. *The range of optimality for an objective function coefficient is determined by those coefficient values that maintain for all values of j.*

$$c_j - z_j \leq 0 \tag{6.1}$$

Let us illustrate this approach by computing the range of optimality for c_1, the profit contribution per unit of the Deskpro. The value of c_1 is currently 50, the per-unit profit contribution in the objective function. Let us assume that x_1's profit contribution is now $50 + k$, where k is some number representing a change in x_1's profit contribution. The final simplex tableau is then given by (you may want to confirm this through your own calculations):

		x_1	x_2	s_1	s_2	s_3	**Value**
Basis	c_B	50+k	40	0	0	0	
x_2	40	0	1	0.32	0	−0.12	**12**
s_2	0	0	0	−0.32	1	0.12	**8**
x_1	50+k	1	0	−0.20	0	0.20	**30**
	z_j	50+k	40	2.8−0.2k	0	5.2+0.2k	**1 980+30k**
	$c_j - z_j$	0	0	−2.8+0.2k	0	−5.2−0.2k	

We can determine from this that the $c_j - z_j$ row has altered by subtracting k times the x_1 row from the original $c_j - z_j$ row. We know that this solution remains optimal as long as all $c_j - z_j \leq 0$. So, for the column for s_1 we must have:

$$-2.8 + 0.2k \leq 0$$

$$\text{or } 0.2k \leq 2.8$$

$$\text{or } k \leq 14$$

In other words, the current solution will remain optimal as long as x_1's profit contribution *increases* by no more than 14. Similarly for the s_3 column we have:

$$-5.2 - 0.2k \leq 0$$

$$\text{or } -0.2k \leq 5.2$$

$$\text{or } k \leq -26$$

In other words, the current solution will remain optimal as long as x_1's profit contribution *decreases* by no more than 14. Summarizing, we know that the current solution will remain optimal as long as x_1's profit contribution is in the range:

$$24 \leq c_1 \leq 64$$

To see how management of HighTech can make use of this sensitivity analysis information, suppose an increase in material costs reduces the profit contribution per unit for the Deskpro to €30. The range of optimality indicates that the current solution ($x_1 = 30$, $x_2 = 12$, $s_1 = 0$, $s_2 = 8$, $s_3 = 0$) is still optimal. To verify this solution, let us show the final simplex tableau after reducing the value of c_1 to 30.

We have simply set $c_1 = 30$ everywhere it appears in the previous tableau.

		x_1	x_2	s_1	s_2	s_3	
Basis	c_B	30	40	0	0	0	
x_2	40	0	1	0.32	0	−0.12	**12**
s_2	0	0	0	−0.32	1	0.12	**8**
x_1	30	1	0	−0.20	0	0.20	**30**
z_j		30	40	6.80	0	1.20	**1 380**
$c_j - z_j$		0	0	−6.80	0	−1.20	

Because $c_j - z_j \leq 0$ for all variables, the solution with $x_1 = 30, x_2 = 12, s_1 = 0, s_2 = 8$ and $s_3 = 0$ is still optimal. That is, the optimal solution with $c_1 = 30$ is the same as the optimal solution with $c_1 = 50$. Note, however, that the decrease in profit contribution per unit of the Deskpro has caused a reduction in total profit from €1980 to €1380.

What if the profit contribution per unit were reduced even further – say, to €20? Referring to the range of optimality for c_1 given by expression (6.4), we see that $c_1 = 20$ is outside the range; thus, we know that a change this large will cause a new basis to be optimal. To verify this new basis, we have modified the final simplex tableau by replacing c_1 by 20.

		x_1	x_2	s_1	s_2	s_3	
Basis	c_B	20	40	0	0	0	
x_2	40	0	1	0.32	0	−0.12	**12**
s_2	0	0	0	−0.32	1	0.12	**8**
x_1	20	1	0	−0.20	0	0.20	**30**
z_j		20	40	8.80	0	−0.80	**1 080**
$c_j - z_j$		0	0	−8.80	0	0.80	

At the endpoints of the range, the corresponding variable is a candidate for entering the basis if it is currently out, or for leaving the basis if it is currently in.

As expected, the current solution ($x_1 = 30, x_2 = 12, s_1 = 0, s_2 = 8$ and $s_3 = 0$) is no longer optimal because the entry in the s_3 column of the net evaluation row is greater than zero. This result implies that at least one more simplex iteration must be performed to reach the optimal solution. Continue to perform the simplex iterations in the previous tableau to verify that the new optimal solution will require the production of $16\frac{2}{3}$ units of the Deskpro and 20 units of the Ultra Portable.

The procedure we used to compute the range of optimality for c_1 can be used for any basic variable. In fact, we do not need to resort to the approach of adding k to the relevant objective function coefficient (we did this earlier to show how the range of optimality is determined). We can obtain the same information directly from the final tableau (which is why knowledge of the Simplex method is useful). The final tableau for the problem is shown again:

		x_1	x_2	s_1	s_2	s_3	**Value**
Basis	c_B	50	40	0	0	0	
x_2	40	0	1	0.32	0	−0.12	**12**
s_2	0	0	0	−0.32	1	0.12	**8**
x_1	50	1	0	−0.20	0	0.20	**30**
z_j		50	40	2.8	0	5.2	**1 980**
$c_j - z_j$		0	0	−2.8	0	−5.2	

To obtain the range of optimality for x_1 we take the $c_j - z_j$ row coefficients and divide by the x_1 row coefficients.

$c_j - z_j$	0	0	−2.8	0	−5.2
x_1	1	0	−0.20	0	0.20
$c_j - cz_j/x_1$	0	0	14	0	−26

The positive value of 14 indicates the maximum increase in x_1's objective function coefficient and the negative value of −26 indicates the maximum decrease, confirming our earlier, more laborious calculations. Let us repeat the calculations for the other basic variable, x_2.

$c_j - z_j$	0	0	−2.8	0	−5.2
x_2	0	1	0.32	0	−0.12
$c_j - cz_j/x_2$	0	0	−8.75	0	43.3

Interpretation is as before. The current solution will remain optimal as long as x_2's objective function coefficient is in the range 31.25–83.3 (40−8.75, 40+43.3).

The procedure for calculating the range of optimality for non-basic variables is as simple. Effectively, we want to calculate by how much a non-basic variable's objective function coefficient would need to change before it became basic. We could repeat the approach of adding k to a non-basic variable objective function coefficient (and you may wish to do this yourself to check your understanding). Looking again at the final simplex tableau for the HighTech problem we see that two variables are non-basic: s_1 and s_2. Let us look at s_1. We see this has a $c_j - z_j$ coefficient of −2.8. This indicates that s_1's objective function coefficient must increase by more than 2.8 in order for s_1 to enter the solution.

Can you compute the range of optimality for objective function coefficients by working with the final simplex tableau? Try Problem 1.

By using the range of optimality to determine whether a change in an objective function coefficient is large enough to cause a change in the optimal solution, we can often avoid the process of formulating and solving a modified linear programming problem.

Right-Hand Side Values

In many linear programming problems, we can interpret the right-hand side values (the 'b_i's) as the resources available. For instance, in the HighTech Industries problem, the right-hand side of constraint 1 represents the available assembly time, the right-hand side of constraint 2 represents the available Ultra Portable displays and the right-hand side of constraint 3 represents the available warehouse space. Dual prices provide information on the value of additional resources in these cases;

the ranges over which these dual prices are valid are given by the ranges for the right-hand side values.

Dual Prices In Chapter 3 we stated that the improvement in the value of the optimal solution per unit increase in a constraint's right-hand side value is called a **dual price**.[1] When the Simplex method is used to solve a linear programming problem, the values of the dual prices are easy to obtain. They are found in the z_j row of the final simplex tableau. To illustrate this point, the final tableau for the HighTech problem is again shown.

		x_1	x_2	s_1	s_2	s_3	
Basis	c_B	50	40	0	0	0	
x_2	40	0	1	0.32	0	−0.12	**12**
s_2	0	0	0	−0.32	1	0.12	**8**
x_1	50	1	0	−0.20	0	0.20	**30**
z_j		50	40	2.80	0	5.20	**1 980**
$c_j - z_j$		0	0	−2.80	0	−5.20	

The z_j values for the three slack variables are 2.80, 0 and 5.20, respectively. So, the dual prices for the assembly time constraint, UltraPortable display constraint and warehouse capacity constraint are, respectively, €2.80, €0.00 and €5.20. The dual price of €5.20 shows that more warehouse space will have the biggest positive impact on HighTech's profit.

To see why the z_j values for the slack variables in the final tableau are the dual prices, let us first consider the case for slack variables that are part of the optimal basic feasible solution. Each of these slack variables will have a z_j value of zero, implying a dual price of zero for the corresponding constraint. For example, consider slack variable s_2, a basic variable in the HighTech problem. Because $s_2 = 8$ in the optimal solution, HighTech will have eight UltraPortable display units unused. Consequently, how much would management of HighTech Industries be willing to pay to obtain additional UltraPortable display units? Clearly the answer is nothing because at the optimal solution HighTech has an excess of this particular component. Additional amounts of this resource are of no value to the company, and, consequently, the dual price for this constraint is zero. In general, if a slack variable is a basic variable in the optimal solution, the value of z_j – and hence, the dual price of the corresponding resource – is zero.

Consider now the nonbasic slack variables – for example, s_1. In the previous subsection we determined that the current solution will remain optimal as long as the objective function coefficient for s_1 (denoted c_{s_1}) stays in the following range:

$$c_{s_1} \leq 2.80$$

It implies that the variable s_1 should not be increased from its current value of zero unless it is worth more than €2.80 to do so. We can conclude then that €2.80 is the marginal value to HighTech of one hour of assembly time used in the production of Deskpro and UltraPortable computers. Thus, if additional time can be obtained,

[1]The closely related term *shadow price* is used by some authors. The shadow price is the same as the dual price for maximization problems; for minimization problems, the dual and shadow prices are equal in absolute value but have opposite signs. The Management Scientist provides dual prices as part of the computer output. Some software packages, such as Excel Solver, provide shadow prices.

HighTech should be willing to pay up to €2.80 per hour for it. A similar interpretation can be given to the z_j value for each of the non-basic slack variables.

With a greater-than-or-equal-to constraint, the value of the dual price will be less than or equal to zero because a one-unit increase in the value of the right-hand side cannot be helpful; a one-unit increase makes it more difficult to satisfy the constraint. For a maximization problem, then, the optimal value can be expected to decrease when the right-hand side of a greater-than-or-equal-to constraint is increased. The dual price gives the amount of the expected improvement – a negative number, since we expect a decrease. As a result, the dual price for a greater-than-or-equal-to constraint is given by the negative of the z_j entry for the corresponding surplus variable in the optimal simplex tableau.

Finally, it is possible to calculate dual prices for equality constraints. They are given by the z_j values for the corresponding artificial variables. We will not develop this case in detail here because we have recommended dropping each artificial variable column from the simplex tableau as soon as the corresponding artificial variable leaves the basis.

Try Problem 3, parts (a), (b) and (c), for practise in finding dual prices from the optimal simplex tableau.

To summarize, when the Simplex method is used to solve a linear programming problem, the dual prices for the constraints are contained in the final tableau. Table 6.1 summarizes the rules for determining the dual prices for the various constraint types in a maximization problem solved by the Simplex method.

Recall that we convert a minimization problem to a maximization problem by multiplying the objective function by -1 before using the Simplex method. Nevertheless, the dual price is given by the same z_j values because improvement for a minimization problem is a decrease in the optimal value.

To illustrate the approach for calculating dual prices for a minimization problem, recall the M&D Chemicals problem that we solved in Section 5.7 as an equivalent maximization problem by multiplying the objective function by -1. The linear programming model for this problem and the final tableau are restated as follows, with x_1 and x_2 representing manufacturing quantities of products A and B, respectively.

$$
\begin{aligned}
\text{Min} \quad & 2x_1 + 3x_2 \\
\text{s.t.} \quad & \\
& 1x_1 \geq 125 \quad \text{Demand for product A} \\
& 1x_1 + 1x_2 \geq 350 \quad \text{Total production} \\
& 2x_1 + 1x_2 \leq 600 \quad \text{Processing time} \\
& x_1,\ x_2 \geq 0
\end{aligned}
$$

		x_1	x_2	s_1	s_2	s_3	
Basis	c_B	−2	−3	0	0	0	
x_1	−2	1	0	0	1	1	**250**
x_2	−3	0	1	0	−2	−1	**100**
s_1	0	0	0	1	1	1	**125**
	z_j	−2	−3	0	4	1	**−800**
	$c_j - z_j$	0	0	0	−4	−1	

Following the rules in Table 6.1 for identifying the dual price for each constraint type, the dual prices for the constraints in the M&D Chemicals problem are given in Table 6.2. Constraint 1 is not binding, and its dual price is zero. The dual price for

Table 6.1 Tableau Location of Dual Price by Constraint Type

Constraint Type	Dual Price Given by
$\leq$	z_j value for the slack variable associated with the constraint
$\geq$	Negative of the z_j value for the surplus variable associated with the constraint
$=$	z_j value for the artificial variable associated with the constraint

Table 6.2 Dual Prices For M&D Chemicals Problem

Constraint	Constraint Type	Dual Price
Demand for product A	$\geq$	0
Total production	$\geq$	−4
Processing time	$\leq$	1

constraint 2 shows that the marginal cost of increasing the total production requirement is €4 per unit. Finally, the dual price of one for the third constraint shows that the per-unit value of additional processing time is €1.

Range of Feasibility As we have just seen, the z_j row in the final tableau can be used to determine the dual price and, as a result, predict the change in the value of the objective function corresponding to a unit change in a b_i. This interpretation is only valid, however, as long as the change in b_i is not large enough to make the current basic solution infeasible. Thus, we will be interested in calculating a range of values over which a particular b_i can vary without any of the current basic variables becoming infeasible (i.e., less than zero). This range of values will be referred to as the **range of feasibility**.

A change in b_i does not affect optimality ($c_j - z_j$ is unchanged), but it does affect feasibility. One of the current basic variables may become negative.

To demonstrate the effect of changing a b_i, consider increasing the amount of assembly time available in the HighTech problem from 150 to 160 hours. Will the current basis still yield a feasible solution? If so, given the dual price of €2.80 for the assembly time constraint, we can expect an increase in the value of the solution of $10(2.80) = 28$. The final tableau corresponding to an increase in the assembly time of 10 hours is shown here.

		x_1	x_2	s_1	s_2	s_3	
Basis	c_B	50	40	0	0	0	
x_2	40	0	1	0.32	0	−0.12	**15.2**
s_2	0	0	0	−0.32	1	0.12	**4.8**
x_1	50	1	0	−0.20	0	0.20	**28.0**
z_j		50	40	2.80	0	5.2	**2 008**
$c_j - z_j$		0	0	−2.80	0	−5.2	

The same basis, consisting of the basic variables x_2, s_2 and x_1, is feasible because all the basic variables are nonnegative. Note also that, just as we predicted using the dual price, the value of the optimal solution has increased by 10(€2.80) = €28, from €1980 to €2008.

You may wonder whether we had to re-solve the problem completely to find this new solution. The answer is no! The only changes in the final tableau (as compared with the final simplex tableau with $b_1 = 150$) are the differences in the values of the basic variables and the value of the objective function. That is, only the last column of the tableau changed. The entries in this new last column of the tableau were obtained by adding ten times the first four entries in the s_1 column to the last column in the previous tableau:

$$\text{New solution} = \underset{\substack{\text{Old}\\\text{solution}}}{\begin{bmatrix} 12 \\ 8 \\ 30 \\ \hline 1980 \end{bmatrix}} + \underset{\substack{\text{Change}\\\text{in } b_1}}{10} \underset{\substack{s_1\\\text{column}}}{\begin{bmatrix} 0.32 \\ -0.32 \\ -0.20 \\ \hline 2.80 \end{bmatrix}} = \underset{\substack{\text{New}\\\text{solution}}}{\begin{bmatrix} 15.2 \\ 4.8 \\ 28.0 \\ \hline 2008 \end{bmatrix}}$$

To practise finding the new solution after a change in a right-hand side without re-solving the problem when the same basis remains feasible, try Problem 3, parts (d) and (e).

Let us now consider why this procedure can be used to find the new solution. First, recall that each of the coefficients in the s_1 column indicates the amount of decrease in a basic variable that would result from increasing s_1 by one unit. In other words, these coefficients tell us how many units of each of the current basic variables will be driven out of solution if one unit of variable s_1 is brought into solution. Bringing one unit of s_1 into solution, however, is the same as reducing the availability of assembly time (decreasing b_1) by one unit; increasing b_1, the available assembly time, by one unit has just the opposite effect. Therefore, the entries in the s_1 column can also be interpreted as the changes in the values of the current basic variables corresponding to a one-unit increase in b_1.

The change in the value of the objective function corresponding to a one-unit increase in b_1 is given by the value of z_j in that column (the dual price). In the foregoing case, the availability of assembly time increased by ten units; thus, we multiplied the first four entries in the s_1 column by ten to obtain the change in the value of the basic variables and the optimal value.

How do we know when a change in b_1 is so large that the current basis will become infeasible? We shall first answer this question specifically for the HighTech Industries problem and then state the general procedure for less-than-or-equal-to constraints. The approach taken with greater-than-or-equal-to and equality constraints will then be discussed.

We begin by showing how to compute upper and lower bounds for the maximum amount that b_1 can be changed before the current optimal basis becomes infeasible. We have seen how to find the new basic feasible solution values given a ten-unit increase in b_1. In general, given a change in b_1 of Δb_1, the new values for the basic variables in the HighTech problem are given by:

$$\begin{bmatrix} x_2 \\ s_2 \\ x_1 \end{bmatrix} = \begin{bmatrix} 12 \\ 8 \\ 30 \end{bmatrix} + \Delta b_1 \begin{bmatrix} 0.32 \\ -0.32 \\ -0.20 \end{bmatrix} = \begin{bmatrix} 12 + 0.32\Delta b_1 \\ 8 - 0.32\Delta b_1 \\ 30 - 0.20\Delta b_1 \end{bmatrix} \tag{6.2}$$

As long as the new value of each basic variable remains nonnegative, the current basis will remain feasible and therefore optimal. We can keep the basic variables nonnegative by limiting the change in b_1 (i.e., Δb_1) so that we satisfy each of the following conditions:

$$12 + 0.32\Delta b_1 \geq 0 \tag{6.3}$$
$$8 - 0.32\Delta b_1 \geq 0 \tag{6.4}$$
$$30 - 0.20\Delta b_1 \geq 0 \tag{6.5}$$

The left-hand sides of these inequalities represent the new values of the basic variables after b_1 has been changed by Δb_1.

Solving for Δb_1 in inequalities (6.3), (6.4), and (6.5), we obtain:

$$\Delta b_1 \geq (3.125)(-12) = -37.5$$
$$\Delta b_1 \leq (-3.125)(-8) = 25$$
$$\Delta b_1 \leq (-5.0)(-30) = 150$$

Because all three inequalities must be satisfied, the most restrictive limits on b_1 must be satisfied for all the current basic variables to remain nonnegative. Therefore, Δb_1 must satisfy

$$-37.5 \leq \Delta b_1 \leq 25 \tag{6.6}$$

The initial amount of assembly time available was 150 hours. Therefore, $b_1 = 150 + \Delta b_1$, where b_1 is the amount of assembly time available. We add 150 to each of the three terms in expression (6.6) to obtain:

$$150 - 37.5 \leq 150 + \Delta b_1 \leq 150 + 25 \tag{6.7}$$

Replacing $150 + \Delta b_1$ with b_1, we obtain the range of feasibility for b_1:

$$112.5 \leq b_1 \leq 175$$

This range of feasibility for b_1 indicates that as long as the available assembly time is between 112.5 and 175 hours, the current optimal basis will remain feasible, which is why we call this range the range of feasibility.

Because the dual price for b_1 (assembly time) is 2.80, we know profit can be increased by €2.80 by obtaining an additional hour of assembly time. Suppose then that we increase b_1 by 25; that is, we increase b_1 to the upper limit of its range of feasibility, 175. The profit will increase to €1980 + (€2.80)25 = €2050, and the values of the optimal basic variables become:

$$x_2 = 12 + 25(0.32) = 20$$
$$s_2 = 8 + 25(-0.32) = 0$$
$$x_1 = 30 + 25(-0.20) = 25$$

What happened to the solution? The increased assembly time caused a revision in the optimal production plan. HighTech should produce more of the UltraPortable and less of the Deskpro. Overall, the profit will be increased by (€2.80)(25) = €70. Note that although the optimal solution changed, the basic variables that were optimal before are still optimal.

The procedure for determining the range of feasibility has been illustrated with the assembly time constraint. The procedure for calculating the range of feasibility for the right-hand side of any less-than-or-equal-to constraint is the same. The first step for a general constraint i is to calculate the range of values for b_i that satisfies the following inequalities.

$$\begin{bmatrix} \bar{b}_1 \\ \bar{b}_2 \\ \cdot \\ \cdot \\ \cdot \\ \bar{b}_m \end{bmatrix} + \Delta b_i \begin{bmatrix} \bar{a}_{1j} \\ \bar{a}_{2j} \\ \cdot \\ \cdot \\ \cdot \\ \bar{a}_{mj} \end{bmatrix} \geq \begin{bmatrix} 0 \\ 0 \\ \cdot \\ \cdot \\ \cdot \\ 0 \end{bmatrix} \tag{6.8}$$

Current solution (last column of the final simplex tableau)

Column of the final simplex tableau corresponding to the slack variable associated with constraint i

The inequalities are used to identify lower and upper limits on Δb_i. The range of feasibility can then be established by the maximum of the lower limits and the minimum of the upper limits.

Similar arguments can be used to develop a procedure for determining the range of feasibility for the right-hand side value of a greater-than-or-equal-to constraint. Essentially the procedure is the same, with the column corresponding to the surplus variable associated with the constraint playing the central role. For a general greater-than-or-equal-to constraint i, we first calculate the range of values for Δb_i that satisfy the inequalities shown in inequality (6.9).

$$\begin{bmatrix} \bar{b}_1 \\ \bar{b}_2 \\ \cdot \\ \cdot \\ \cdot \\ \bar{b}_m \end{bmatrix} - \Delta b_i \begin{bmatrix} \bar{a}_{1j} \\ \bar{a}_{2j} \\ \cdot \\ \cdot \\ \cdot \\ \bar{a}_{mj} \end{bmatrix} \geq \begin{bmatrix} 0 \\ 0 \\ \cdot \\ \cdot \\ \cdot \\ 0 \end{bmatrix} \tag{6.9}$$

Current solution (last column of the final simplex tableau)

Column of the final simplex tableau corresponding to the surplus variable associated with constraint i

Once again, these inequalities establish lower and upper limits on Δb_i. Given these limits, the range of feasibility is easily determined.

Try Problem 4 to make sure you can compute the range of feasibility by working with the final simplex tableau.

A range of feasibility for the right-hand side of an equality constraint can also be calculated. To do so for equality constraint i, one could use the column of the final simplex tableau corresponding to the artificial variable associated with constraint i in Equation (6.8). Because we have suggested dropping the artificial variable columns from the simplex tableau as soon as the artificial variable becomes non-basic, these columns will not be available in the final tableau. Thus, more involved calculations are required to compute a range of feasibility for equality constraints. Details may be found in more advanced texts.

Changes that force b_i outside its range of feasibility are normally accompanied by changes in the dual prices.

As long as the change in a right-hand side value is such that b_i stays within its range of feasibility, the same basis will remain feasible and optimal. Changes that force b_i outside its range of feasibility will force us to re-solve the problem to find the new optimal solution consisting of a different set of basic variables. (More advanced linear programming texts show how it can be done without completely re-solving the problem.) In any case, the calculation of the range of feasibility for each b_i is valuable management information and should be included as part of the management report on any linear programming project. The range of feasibility is typically made available as part of the computer solution to the problem.

Simultaneous Changes

In reviewing the procedures for developing the range of optimality and the range of feasibility, we note that only one coefficient at a time was permitted to vary. Our statements concerning changes within these ranges were made with the understanding that no other coefficients are permitted to change. However, sometimes we can make the same statements when either two or more objective function coefficients or two or more right-hand sides are varied simultaneously. When the simultaneous changes satisfy the 100 per cent rule, the same statements are applicable. The 100 per cent rule was explained in Chapter 3, but we will briefly review it here.

Let us define allowable increase as the amount a coefficient can be increased before reaching the upper limit of its range, and allowable decrease as the amount a coefficient can be decreased before reaching the lower limit of its range. Now suppose simultaneous changes are made in two or more objective function coefficients. For each coefficient changed, we compute the percentage of the allowable increase, or allowable decrease, represented by the change. If the sum of the percentages for all changes does not exceed 100 per cent, we say that the 100 per cent rule is satisfied and that the simultaneous changes will not cause a change in the optimal solution. However, just as with a single objective function coefficient change, the value of the solution will change because of the change in the coefficients.

Similarly, if two or more changes in constraint right-hand side values are made, we again compute the percentage of allowable increase or allowable decrease represented by each change. If the sum of the percentages for all changes does not exceed 100 per cent, we say that the 100 per cent rule is satisfied. The dual prices are then valid for determining the change in value of the objective function associated with the right-hand side changes.

NOTES AND COMMENTS

1 Sometimes, interpreting dual prices and choosing the appropriate sign can be confusing. It often helps to think of this process as follows. Relaxing a $\geq$ constraint means decreasing its right-hand side, and relaxing a $\leq$ constraint means increasing its right-hand side. Relaxing a constraint permits improvement in value; restricting a constraint (decreasing the right-hand side of a $\leq$ constraint or increasing the right-hand side of a $\geq$ constraint) has the opposite effect. In every case, the absolute value of the dual price gives the improvement in the optimal value associated with relaxing the constraint.

2 The Notes and Comments in Chapter 3 concerning sensitivity analysis are also applicable here. In particular, recall that the 100 per cent rule cannot be applied to simultaneous changes in the objective function *and* the right-hand sides; it applies only to simultaneous changes in one or the other. Also note that this rule *does not* mean that simultaneous changes that do not satisfy the rule will necessarily cause a change in the solution. For instance, any proportional change in *all* the objective function coefficients will leave the optimal solution unchanged, and any proportional change in *all* the right-hand sides will leave the dual prices unchanged.

6.2 Duality

Every linear programming problem has an associated linear programming problem called the **dual problem**. Referring to the original formulation of the linear programming problem as the **primal problem**, we will see how the primal can be converted into its corresponding dual. Then we will solve the dual linear programming problem and interpret the results. A fundamental property of the primal–dual relationship is that the optimal solution to either the primal or the dual problem also provides the optimal solution to the other. In cases where the primal and the dual problems differ in terms of computational difficulty, we can choose the easier problem to solve.

George B. Dantzig and Alex Orden presented their paper at a symposium in 1951 'A duality theorem based on the Simplex method'.

Let us return to the HighTech Industries problem. The original formulation – the primal problem – is as follows:

$$\begin{aligned}
\text{Max}\quad & 50x_1 + 40x_2 \\
\text{s.t.}\quad & \\
& 3x_1 + 5x_2 \leq 150 \quad \text{Assembly time} \\
& 1x_2 \leq 20 \quad \text{UltraPortable display} \\
& 8x_1 + 5x_2 \leq 300 \quad \text{Warehouse space} \\
& x_1,\ x_2 \geq 0
\end{aligned}$$

A maximization problem with all less-than-or-equal-to constraints and nonnegativity requirements for the variables is said to be in canonical form. For a maximization problem in canonical form, such as the HighTech Industries problem, the conversion to the associated dual linear programme is relatively easy. Let us state the dual of the HighTech problem and then identify the steps taken to make the primal–dual conversion. The HighTech dual problem is as follows:

$$\begin{aligned}
\text{Min}\quad & 150u_1 + 20u_2 + 300u_3 \\
\text{s.t.}\quad & \\
& 3u_1 \qquad\quad + 8u_3 \geq 50 \\
& 5u_1 + \ 1u_2 + 5u_3 \geq 40 \\
& u_1,\ u_2,\ u_3 \geq 0
\end{aligned}$$

This **canonical form for a minimization problem** is a minimization problem with all greater-than-or-equal-to constraints and nonnegativity requirements for the variables. So, the dual of a maximization problem in canonical form is a minimization problem in canonical form. The variables u_1, u_2 and u_3 are referred to as **dual variables**.

With the preceding example in mind, we make the following general statements about the *dual of a maximization problem in canonical form*.

1 The dual is a minimization problem in canonical form.

2 When the primal has n decision variables ($n = 2$ in the HighTech problem), the dual will have n constraints. The first constraint of the dual is associated with variable x_1 in the primal, the second constraint in the dual is associated with variable x_2 in the primal and so on.

3 When the primal has m constraints ($m = 3$ in the HighTech problem), the dual will have m decision variables. Dual variable u_1 is associated with the first primal constraint, dual variable u_2 is associated with the second primal constraint and so on.

4 The right-hand sides of the primal constraints become the objective function coefficients in the dual.

5 The objective function coefficients of the primal become the right-hand sides of the dual constraints.

6 The constraint coefficients of the ith primal variable become the coefficients in the ith constraint of the dual.

Try part (a) of Problem 12 for practise in finding the dual of a maximization problem in canonical form.

These six statements are the general requirements that must be satisfied when converting a maximization problem in canonical form to its associated dual: a minimization problem in canonical form. Even though these requirements may seem cumbersome at first, practise with a few simple problems will show that the primal–dual conversion process is relatively easy to implement.

We have formulated the HighTech dual linear programming problem, so let us now proceed to solve it. With three variables in the dual, we will use the Simplex method. After subtracting surplus variables s_1 and s_2 to obtain the standard form, adding artificial variables a_1 and a_2 to obtain the tableau form, and multiplying the objective function by -1 to convert the dual problem to an equivalent maximization problem, we arrive at the following initial tableau.

		u_1	u_2	u_3	s_1	s_2	a_1	a_2	
Basis	c_B	−150	−20	−300	0	0	$-M$	$-M$	
a_1	$-M$	3	0	⑧	−1	0	1	0	**50**
a_2	$-M$	5	1	5	0	−1	0	1	**40**
	z_j	$-8M$	$-M$	$-13M$	M	M	$-M$	$-M$	**$-90M$**
	$c_j - z_j$	$-150+8M$	$-20+M$	$-300+13M$	$-M$	$-M$	0	0	

At the first iteration, u_3 is brought into the basis, and a_1 is removed. At the second iteration, u_1 is brought into the basis, and a_2 is removed. At this point, the tableau appears as follows.

		u_1	u_2	u_3	s_1	s_2	
Basis	c_B	−150	−20	−300	0	0	
u_3	−300	0	−0.12	1	−0.20	0.12	**5.20**
u_1	−150	1	0.32	0	0.20	−0.32	**2.80**
	z_j	−150	−12	−300	30	12	**−1 980**
	$c_j - z_j$	0	−8	0	−30	−12	

Because all the entries in the net evaluation row are less than or equal to zero, the optimal solution has been reached; it is $u_1 = 2.80$, $u_2 = 0$, $u_3 = 5.20$, $s_1 = 0$ and $s_2 = 0$. We have been maximizing the negative of the dual objective function; therefore, the value of the objective function for the optimal dual solution must be $-(-1980) = 1980$.

The final tableau for the original HighTech Industries problem is shown here.

		x_1	x_2	s_1	s_2	s_3	
Basis	c_B	50	40	0	0	0	
x_2	40	0	1	0.32	0	−0.12	**12**
s_2	0	0	0	−0.32	1	0.12	**8**
x_1	50	1	0	−0.20	0	0.20	**30**
z_j		50	40	2.80	0	5.20	**1 980**
$c_j - z_j$		0	0	−2.80	0	−5.20	

The optimal solution to the primal problem is $x_1 = 30$, $x_2 = 12$, $s_1 = 0$, $s_2 = 8$ and $s_3 = 0$. The optimal value of the objective function is 1980.

What observation can we make about the relationship between the optimal value of the objective function in the primal and the optimal value in the dual for the HighTech problem? The optimal value of the objective function is the same (1980) for both. This relationship is true for all primal and dual linear programming problems and is stated as property 1.

Property 1
If the dual problem has an optimal solution, the primal problem has an optimal solution and vice versa. Furthermore, the values of the optimal solutions to the dual and primal problems are equal.

This property tells us that if we solved only the dual problem, we would know that HighTech could make a maximum of €1980.

Interpretation of the Dual Variables

Before making further observations about the relationship between the primal and the dual solutions, let us consider the meaning or interpretation of the dual variables u_1, u_2 and u_3. Remember that in setting up the dual problem, each dual variable is associated with one of the constraints in the primal. Specifically, u_1 is associated with the assembly time constraint, u_2 with the UltraPortable display constraint and u_3 with the warehouse space constraint.

To understand and interpret these dual variables, let us return to property 1 of the primal–dual relationship, which stated that the objective function values for the primal and dual problems must be equal. At the optimal solution, the primal objective function results in:

$$50x_1 + 40x_2 = 1980 \tag{6.10}$$

while the dual objective function is:

$$150u_1 + 20u_2 + 300u_3 = 1980 \tag{6.11}$$

Using Equation (6.10), let us restrict our interest to the interpretation of the primal objective function. With x_1 and x_2 as the number of units of the Deskpro and the UltraPortable that are assembled respectively, we have:

$$\begin{pmatrix}\text{value}\\\text{per unit of}\\\text{Deskpro}\end{pmatrix}\begin{pmatrix}\text{Number of}\\\text{units of}\\\text{Deskpro}\end{pmatrix}+\begin{pmatrix}\text{value}\\\text{per unit of}\\\text{UltraPortable}\end{pmatrix}\begin{pmatrix}\text{Number of}\\\text{units of}\\\text{UltraPortable}\end{pmatrix}=\begin{matrix}\text{Total}\\\text{value of}\\\text{production}\end{matrix}$$

From Equation (6.11), we see that the coefficients of the dual objective function (150, 20 and 300) can be interpreted as the number of units of resources available. Thus, because the primal and dual objective functions are equal at optimality, we have:

$$\begin{pmatrix}\text{Units of}\\\text{resource}\\1\end{pmatrix}u_1+\begin{pmatrix}\text{Units of}\\\text{resource}\\2\end{pmatrix}u_2+\begin{pmatrix}\text{Units of}\\\text{resource}\\3\end{pmatrix}u_3=\begin{matrix}\text{Total value}\\\text{of production}\end{matrix}$$

Thus, we see that the dual variables must carry the interpretations of being the value per unit of resource. For the HighTech problem,

$$\begin{aligned}u_1 &= \text{value per hour of assembly time}\\u_2 &= \text{value per unit of the UltraPortable display}\\u_3 &= \text{value per square metre of warehouse space}\end{aligned}$$

Have we attempted to identify the value of these resources previously? Recall that in Section 6.1, when we considered sensitivity analysis of the right-hand sides, we identified the value of an additional unit of each resource. These values were called dual prices and are helpful to the decision maker in determining whether additional units of the resources should be made available.

The analysis in Section 6.1 led to the following dual prices for the resources in the HighTech problem.

Resource	Value per Additional Unit (dual price)
Assembly time	€2.80
Portable display	€0.00
Warehouse space	€5.20

The dual variables are the shadow prices, but in a maximization problem, they also equal the dual prices. For a minimization problem, the dual prices are the negative of the dual variables.

Let us now return to the optimal solution for the HighTech dual problem. The values of the dual variables at the optimal solution are $u_1 = 2.80$, $u_2 = 0$ and $u_3 = 5.20$. For this maximization problem, the values of the dual variables and the dual prices are the same. For a minimization problem, the dual prices and the dual variables are the same in absolute value but have opposite signs. So, the optimal values of the dual variables identify the dual prices of each additional resource or input unit at the optimal solution.

In light of the preceding discussion, the following interpretation of the primal and dual problems can be made when the primal is a product-mix problem.

Primal Problem Given a per-unit value of each product, determine how much of each should be produced to maximize the value of the total production. Constraints require the amount of each resource used to be less than or equal to the amount available.

Dual Problem Given the availability of each resource, determine the per-unit value such that the total value of the resources used is minimized. Constraints require the resource value per unit to be greater than or equal to the value of each unit of output.

Using the Dual to Identify the Primal Solution

At the beginning of this section, we mentioned that an important feature of the primal–dual relationship is that when an optimal solution is reached, the value of the optimal solution for the primal problem is the same as the value of the optimal solution for the dual problem; see property 1. However, the question remains: if we solve only the dual problem, can we identify the optimal values for the primal variables?

Recall that in Section 6.1 we showed that when a primal problem is solved by the Simplex method, the optimal values of the primal variables appear in the right-most column of the final tableau, and the dual prices (values of the dual variables) are found in the z_j row. The final tableau of the dual problem provides the optimal values of the dual variables, and therefore the values of the primal variables should be found in the z_j row of the optimal dual tableau. This result is, in fact, the case and is formally stated as property 2.

> **Property 2**
> Given the simplex tableau corresponding to the optimal dual solution, the optimal values of the primal decision variables are given by the z_j entries for the surplus variables; furthermore, the optimal values of the primal slack variables are given by the negative of the $c_j - z_j$ entries for the u_j variables.

To test your ability to find the primal solution from the optimal simplex tableau for the dual and interpret the dual variables, try parts (b) and (c) of Problem 12.

This property enables us to use the final tableau for the dual of the HighTech problem to determine the optimal primal solution of $x_1 = 30$ units of the Deskpro and $x_2 = 12$ units of the UltraPortable. These optimal values of x_1 and x_2, as well as the values for all primal slack variables, are given in the z_j and $c_j - z_j$ rows of the final tableau of the dual problem, which is shown again here.

		u_1	u_2	u_3	s_1	s_2	
Basis	c_B	−150	−20	−300	0	0	
u_3	−300	0	−0.12	1	−0.20	0.12	**5.20**
u_1	−150	1	0.32	0	0.20	0.32	**2.80**
	z_j	−150	−12	−300	30	12	**−1 980**
	$c_j - z_j$	0	−8	0	−30	−12	

Finding the Dual of Any Primal Problem

The HighTech Industries primal problem provided a good introduction to the concept of duality because it was formulated as a maximization problem in canonical form. For this form of primal problem, we demonstrated that conversion to the dual problem is rather easy. If the primal problem is a minimization problem in canonical form, then the dual is a maximization problem in canonical form. Therefore, finding the dual of a minimization problem in canonical form is also easy. Consider the following linear programme in canonical form for a minimization problem:

$$\begin{aligned} \text{Min} \quad & 6x_1 + 2x_2 \\ \text{s.t.} \quad & \\ & 5x_1 - 1x_2 \geq 13 \\ & 3x_1 + 7x_2 \geq 9 \\ & x_1, x_2 \geq 0 \end{aligned}$$

The dual is the following maximization problem in canonical form:

$$\begin{aligned} \text{Max} \quad & 13u_1 + 9u_2 \\ \text{s.t.} \quad & \\ & 5u_1 + 3u_2 \leq 6 \\ & -1u_1 + 7u_2 \leq 2 \\ & u_1, u_2 \geq 0 \end{aligned}$$

Try Problem 13 for practise in finding the dual of a minimization problem in canonical form.

Although we could state a special set of rules for converting each type of primal problem into its associated dual, we believe it is easier to first convert any primal problem into an equivalent problem in canonical form. Then, we follow the procedures already established for finding the dual of a maximization or minimization problem in canonical form.

Let us illustrate the procedure for finding the dual of any linear programming problem by finding the dual of the following minimization problem:

$$\begin{aligned} \text{Min} \quad & 2x_1 - 3x_2 \\ \text{s.t.} \quad & \\ & 1x_1 + 2x_2 \leq 12 \\ & 4x_1 - 2x_2 \geq 3 \\ & 6x_1 - 1x_2 = 10 \\ & x_1, x_2 \geq 0 \end{aligned}$$

For this minimization problem, we obtain the canonical form by converting all constraints to greater-than-or-equal-to form. The necessary steps are as follows:

Step 1. Convert the first constraint to greater-than-or-equal-to form by multiplying both sides of the inequality by (-1). Doing so yields:

$$-x_1 - 2x_2 \geq -12$$

Step 2. Constraint 3 is an equality constraint. For an equality constraint, we first create two inequalities: one with $\leq$ form, the other with $\geq$ form. Doing so yields:

$$\begin{aligned} 6x_1 - 1x_2 &\geq 10 \\ 6x_1 - 1x_2 &\leq 10 \end{aligned}$$

Then, we multiply the $\leq$ constraint by (-1) to get two $\geq$ constraints.

$$\begin{aligned} 6x_1 - 1x_2 &\geq 10 \\ -6x_1 + 1x_2 &\geq -10 \end{aligned}$$

Now the original primal problem has been restated in the following equivalent form:

$$
\begin{aligned}
\text{Min} \quad & 2x_1 - 3x_2 \\
\text{s.t.} \quad & \\
& -1x_1 - 2x_2 \geq -12 \\
& 4x_1 - 2x_2 \geq 3 \\
& 6x_1 - 1x_2 \geq 10 \\
& -6x_1 + 1x_2 \geq -10 \\
& x_1,\ x_2 \geq 0
\end{aligned}
$$

With the primal problem now in canonical form for a minimization problem, we can easily convert to the dual problem using the primal–dual procedure presented earlier in this section. The dual becomes[2]:

$$
\begin{aligned}
\text{Max} \quad & -12u_1 + 3u_2 + 10u_3' - 10u_3'' \\
\text{s.t.} \quad & \\
& -1u_1 + 4u_2 + 6u_3' - 6u_3'' \leq 2 \\
& -2u_1 - 2u_2 - 1u_3' + 1u_3'' \leq -3 \\
& u_1,\ u_2,\ u_3',\ u_3'' \geq 0
\end{aligned}
$$

The equality constraint required two $\geq$ constraints, so we denoted the dual variables associated with these constraints as u'_3 and u''_3. This notation reminds us that u'_3 and u''_3 both refer to the third constraint in the initial primal problem. Because two dual variables are associated with an equality constraint, the interpretation of the dual variable must be modified slightly. The dual variable for the equality constraint $6x_1 - 1x_2 = 10$ is given by the value of $u'_3 - u''_3$ in the optimal solution to the dual. Hence, the dual variable for an equality constraint can be negative.

Can you write the dual of any linear programming problem? Try Problem 14.

Summary

In this chapter we have developed the simple sensitivity analysis introduced in Chapter 3 and also the dual problem.

- The information in the final simplex tableau provides the sensitivity analysis for the optimal solution.
- Sensitivity analysis can be carried out on the objective function coefficients and the right-hand side values of the constraints.
- It is important to remember that sensitivity analysis can normally only be carried out on one part of the problem at a time.
- The original LP problem can be converted into its associated dual LP problem.
- Solving either the primal or dual problem gives the solution to both.

[2]Note that the right-hand side of the second constraint is negative. Thus, we must multiply both sides of the constraint by -1 to obtain a positive value for the right-hand side before attempting to solve the problem with the Simplex method.

WORKED EXAMPLE

We shall return to the Worked Example that we introduced in Chapter 5. Recollect that the Fresh Juice Company had identified the optimal solution in terms of quantities of its three grape juice products to produce tomorrow. We had a formulation such that:

$$\text{Max} \quad 1x_1 + 1.2x_2 + 2x_3$$

s.t.

$$1x_1 + 2x_2 \leq 150$$
$$1x_1 + 2x_3 \leq 150$$
$$2x_1 + 1x_2 \leq 80$$
$$2x_1 + 3x_2 + 1x_2 \leq 225$$
$$x_1 \leq 25$$
$$x_1,\ x_2,\ x_3 \leq 0$$

The final simplex tableau was:

Basis	x_1	x_2	x_3	s_1	s_2	s_3	s_4	s_5	
C	1	1.2	2	0	0	0	0	0	
Unused kilos of Grape A	0	0	0	1	0	−2	0	−3	65
Litres of Dry Grape juice produced	0	1	1	0	0.5	0	0	0.5	62.5
Litres of Regular Grape juice produced	0	0	0	0	0	1	0	2	30
Unused labour hours	0	0	0	0	−0.5	−3	1	−4.5	22.5
Litres of Sweet Grape juice produced	1	0	0	0	0	0	0	−1	25
z_j	1	1.2	2	0	1	1.2	0	2.4	186
$c_j - z_j$	0	0	0	0	−1	−1.2	0	−2.4	

Let us see what other advice we can provide the company's management team. If we carry out sensitivity analysis on the objective function coefficients we obtain the following results:

	Current value	**Maximum increase**	**Maximum decrease**
x_1	1	2.4	∞
x_2	1.2	∞	1.2
x_3	2	∞	2

If we look at x_1 we see that there is an infinite allowable decrease. In other words, no matter how low the profit contribution of x_1 it will remain in the solution. In the context of the problem this is not surprising since we have a constraint forcing the company to produce 25 litres of x_1 no matter what. On the other hand, if the profit contribution of x_1 rises by more than 2.4, the current optimal solution will change. For x_2 and x_3 we see that there is an infinite increase allowed and a decrease in both cases that would take the profit contribution to zero. In other words, as long as the profit contribution for these two products is non-zero they will continue to be produced. If we now turn to sensitivity analysis on the constraints we see that the largest positive z_j value is associated with s_5 at 2.4. Recollect that s_5 is a surplus variable associated with a constraint of the type $\geq$ so we must see this as a negative value (Table 6.1). This indicates that if s_5 were to enter the solution, forcing production of x_1 above the minimum of 25 litres, then the optimal profit contribution would suffer and fall by R2.4. This implies that the current requirement to produce 25 litres of x_1 is adversely affecting profit contribution – if we didn't have this constraint the company would actually be able to increase total profit contribution. Finally, let us look at s_3 relating to the available supply of Natural Flavourings. This has a shadow price of 1.2 indicating that if we can increase supplies above the current limit of 80 kilos, profit contribution will increase by R1.2 for each extra kilo obtained. Examination of the s_3 column tells us that this will be achieved through increased production of Regular Grape, x_2. The analysis is valid up to an extra 30 kilos of Natural Flavouring. After that point we would need to re-formulate and re-solve the problem to assess the impact on the current optimal solution.

Problems

SELF *test*

1 Consider the following linear programming problem.

$$\begin{aligned} \text{Max} \quad & 5x_1 + 6x_2 + 4x_3 \\ \text{s.t.} \quad & \\ & 3x_1 + 4x_2 + 2x_3 \leq 120 \\ & x_1 + 2x_2 + x_3 \leq 50 \\ & x_1 + 2x_2 + 3x_3 \geq 30 \\ & x_1, x_2, x_3 \geq 0 \end{aligned}$$

The optimal simplex tableau is:

		x_1	x_2	x_3	s_1	s_2	s_3	
Basis	c_B	5	6	4	0	0	0	
s_3	0	0	4	0	−2	7	1	**80**
x_3	4	0	2	1	−1	3	0	**30**
x_1	5	1	0	0	1	−2	0	**20**
z_j		5	8	4	1	2	0	**220**
$c_j - z_j$		0	−2	0	−1	2–	0	

a. Calculate the range of optimality for c_1.
b. Calculate the range of optimality for c_2.
c. Calculate the range of optimality for c_{s_1}.

SELF *test*

2 For the HighTech problem, we found the range of optimality for c_1, the profit contribution per unit of the Deskpro. The final simplex tableau is given in Section 6.1. Find the following:

a. The range of optimality for c_2.
b. The range of optimality for c_{s_2}.
c. The range of optimality for c_{s_3}.
d. Suppose the per-unit profit contribution of the UltraPortable (c_2) dropped to €35. How would the optimal solution change? What is the new value for total profit?

SELF *test*

3 Refer to the problem formulation and optimal simplex tableau given in Problem 1.

a. Find the dual price for the first constraint.
b. Find the dual price for the second constraint.
c. Find the dual price for the third constraint.
d. Suppose the right-hand side of the first constraint is increased from 120 to 125. Find the new optimal solution and its value.
e. Suppose the right-hand side of the first constraint is decreased from 120 to 110. Find the new optimal solution and its value.

SELF *test*

4 Refer again to the problem formulation and optimal simplex tableau given in Problem 1.

a. Find the range of feasibility for b_1.
b. Find the range of feasibility for b_2.
c. Find the range of feasibility for b_3.

5 For the HighTech problem, we found the range of feasibility for b_1, the assembly time available (see Section 6.1).

a. Find the range of feasibility for b_2.
b. Find the range of feasibility for b_3.
c. How much will HighTech's profit increase if there is a 20-square-metre increase in the amount of warehouse space available (b_3)?

SELF *test*

6 Recall the GulfGolf problem introduced in Chapter 2. The linear programme for this problem is:

$$\begin{aligned}
\text{Max} \quad & 10x_1 + 9x_2 \\
\text{s.t.} \quad & \\
& 0.7x_1 + 1x_2 \leq 630 \quad \text{Cutting and dyeing time} \\
& 0.5x_1 + 0.8333x_2 \leq 600 \quad \text{Sewing time} \\
& 1x_1 + 0.6667x_2 \leq 708 \quad \text{Finishing time} \\
& 0.1x_1 + 0.25x_2 \leq 135 \quad \text{Inspection and packaging time} \\
& x_1, x_2 \geq 0
\end{aligned}$$

where:

x_1 = number of standard bags produced
x_2 = number of deluxe bags produced

The final simplex tableau is:

		x_1	x_2	s_1	s_2	s_3	s_4	
Basis	c_B	10	9	0	0	0	0	
x_2	9	0	1	1.875	0	1.3125	0	**252**
s_2	0	0	0	−0.9375	1	0.15625	0	**120**
x_1	10	1	0	−1.875	0	1.875	0	**540**
s_4	0	0	0	−0.34375	0	0.140625	1	**18**
	z_j	10	9	4.375	0	6.9315	0	**7 668**
	$c_j - z_j$	0	0	−4.375	0	−6.9375	0	

a. Calculate the range of optimality for the profit contribution of the standard bag.
b. Calculate the range of optimality for the profit contribution of the deluxe bag.

c. If the profit contribution per deluxe bag drops to €7 per unit, how will the optimal solution be affected?
d. What unit profit contribution would be necessary for the deluxe bag before the company would consider changing its current production plan?
e. If the profit contribution of the deluxe bags can be increased to €15 per unit, what is the optimal production plan? State what you think will happen before you compute the new optimal solution.

7 For Problem 6:

a. Calculate the range of feasibility for b_1 (cutting and dyeing capacity).
b. Calculate the range of feasibility for b_2 (sewing capacity).
c. Calculate the range of feasibility for b_3 (finishing capacity).
d. Calculate the range of feasibility for b_4 (inspection and packaging capacity).
e. Which of these four departments would you be interested in scheduling for overtime? Explain.

SELF *test*

8 a. Calculate the final simplex tableau for Problem 6 after increasing b_1 from 630 to $682^4/_{11}$.
b. Would the current basis be optimal if b_1 were increased further? If not, what would be the new optimal basis?

9 For Problem 6:

a. How much would profit increase if an additional 30 hours became available in the cutting and dyeing department (i.e., if b_1 were increased from 630 to 660)?
b. How much would profit decrease if 40 hours were removed from the sewing department?
c. How much would profit decrease if, because of an employee accident, only 570 hours instead of 630 were available in the cutting and dyeing department?

SELF *test*

10 The following are additional conditions encountered by GulfGolf (Problem 6).

a. Suppose because of some new machinery the company was able to make a small reduction in the amount of time it took to do the cutting and dyeing (constraint 1) for a standard bag. What effect would this reduction have on the objective function?
b. Management believes that by buying a new sewing machine, the sewing time for standard bags can be reduced from 0.5 to 0.3333 hour. Do you think this machine would be a good investment? Why?

11 Innis Investments manages funds for a number of companies and wealthy clients. For a new client, Innis has been authorized to invest up to 1.2 million in two investment funds: a stock fund and a money market fund. Each unit of the stock fund costs €50 and provides an annual rate of return of 10%; each unit of the money market fund costs €100 and provides an annual rate of return of 4%. The client wants to minimize risk subject to the requirement that the annual income from the investment be at least €60 000. According to Innis's risk measurement system, each unit invested in the stock fund has a risk index of 8, and each unit invested in the money market fund has a risk index of 3; the higher risk index associated with the stock fund simply indicates that it is the riskier investment. Innis's client also specified that at least €300,000 be invested in the money market fund. Letting:

$$x_1 = \text{units purchased in the stock fund}$$
$$x_2 = \text{units purchased in the money market fund}$$

leads to the following formulation:

$$\begin{array}{llr l}
\text{Min} & 8x_1 + 3x_2 & & \text{Total risk} \\
\text{s.t.} & & & \\
& 50x_1 + 100x_2 \leq & 1{,}200{,}000 & \text{Funds available} \\
& 5x_1 + 4x_2 \geq & 60{,}000 & \text{Annual income} \\
& 1x_2 \geq & 3{,}000 & \text{Minimum units in money market} \\
& x_1,\ x_2 \geq 0 & &
\end{array}$$

a. Solve this problem using the Simplex method.
b. The value of the optimal solution is a measure of the riskiness of the portfolio. What effect will increasing the annual income requirement have on the riskiness of the portfolio?
c. Find the range of feasibility for b_2.
d. How will the optimal solution and its value change if the annual income requirement is increased from €60 000 to €65 000?
e. How will the optimal solution and its value change if the risk measure for the stock fund is increased from 8 to 9?

SELF *test*

12 Suppose that in a product-mix problem x_1, x_2, x_3 and x_4 indicate the units of products 1, 2, 3 and 4, respectively, and we have:

$$\begin{aligned} \text{Max} \quad & 4x_1 + 6x_2 + 3x_3 + 1x_4 \\ \text{s.t.} \quad & \\ & 1.5x_1 + 2x_2 + 4x_3 + 3x_4 \leq 550 \quad \text{Machine A hours} \\ & 4x_1 + 1x_2 + 2x_3 + 1x_4 \leq 700 \quad \text{Machine B hours} \\ & 2x_1 + 3x_2 + 1x_3 + 2x_4 \leq 200 \quad \text{Machine C hours} \\ & x_1, x_2, x_3, x_4 \geq 0 \end{aligned}$$

a. Formulate the dual to this problem.
b. Solve the dual. Use the dual solution to show that the profit-maximizing product mix is $x_1 = 0$, $x_2 = 25$, $x_3 = 125$ and $x_4 = 0$.
c. Use the dual variables to identify the machine or machines that are producing at maximum capacity. If the manager can select one machine for additional production capacity, which machine should have priority? Why?

SELF *test*

13 Find the dual for the following linear programme:

$$\begin{aligned} \text{Min} \quad & 2800x_1 + 6000x_2 + 1200x_3 \\ \text{s.t.} \quad & \\ & 15x_1 + 15x_2 + 1x_3 \geq 5 \\ & 4x_1 + 8x_2 \geq 5 \\ & 12x_1 + 8x_3 \geq 24 \\ & x_1, x_2, x_3 \geq 0 \end{aligned}$$

SELF *test*

14 Write the following primal problem in canonical form, and find its dual.

$$\begin{aligned} \text{Max} \quad & 3x_1 + 1x_2 + 5x_3 + 3x_4 \\ \text{s.t.} \quad & \\ & 3x_1 + 1x_2 + 2x_3 = 30 \\ & 2x_1 + 1x_2 + 3x_3 + 1x_4 \geq 15 \\ & 2x_2 + 3x_4 \leq 25 \\ & x_1, x_2, x_3, x_4 \geq 0 \end{aligned}$$

15 Photo Chemicals produces two types of photograph-developing fluids at a cost of €1.00 per litre. Let:

$$x_1 = \text{litre of product 1}$$
$$x_2 = \text{litre of product 2}$$

Photo Chemicals management requires that at least 30 litres of product 1 and at least 20 litres of product 2 be produced. They also require that at least 80 kilos of a perishable raw material be used in production. A linear programming formulation of the problem is as follows:

$$
\begin{aligned}
\text{Min} \quad & 1x_1 + 1x_2 \\
\text{s.t.} \quad & \\
& 1x_1 \qquad\quad \geq 30 \quad \text{Minimum product 1} \\
& \qquad\quad 1x_2 \geq 20 \quad \text{Minimum product 2} \\
& 1x_1 + 2x_2 \geq 80 \quad \text{Minimum raw material} \\
& x_1, x_2 \geq 0
\end{aligned}
$$

a. Write the dual problem.

b. Solve the dual problem. Use the dual solution to show that the optimal production plan is $x_1 = 30$ and $x_2 = 25$.

c. The third constraint involves a management request that the current 80 kilos of a perishable raw material be used. However, after learning that the optimal solution calls for an excess production of five units of product 2, management is reconsidering the raw material requirement. Specifically, you have been asked to identify the cost effect if this constraint is relaxed. Use the dual variable to indicate the change in the cost if only 79 kilos of raw material have to be used.

SELF *test*

16 Consider the linear programme:

$$
\begin{aligned}
\text{Max} \quad & 3x_1 + 2x_2 \\
\text{s.t.} \quad & \\
& 1x_1 + 2x_2 \leq 8 \\
& 2x_1 + 1x_2 \leq 10 \\
& x_1, x_2 \geq 0
\end{aligned}
$$

a. Solve this problem using the Simplex method. Keep a record of the value of the objective function at each extreme point.

b. Formulate and solve the dual of this problem using the graphical procedure.

c. Compute the value of the dual objective function for each extreme-point solution of the dual problem.

d. Compare the values of the objective function for each primal and dual extreme-point solution.

e. Can a dual feasible solution yield a value less than a primal feasible solution? Can you state a result concerning bounds on the value of the primal solution provided by any feasible solution to the dual problem?

Chapter 7

Transportation, Assignment and Transshipment Problems

Learning Objectives

By the end of this chapter you will be able to:

- Formulate and solve transportation problems
- Formulate and solve assignment problems
- Formulate and solve transhipment problems
- Interpret and explain the management information provided in such solutions

We have spent the last few chapters looking in detail at linear programming. We have seen that LP can be applied to a wide variety of optimization problems. However, there are certain types of optimization problems that are worth looking at separately. In this chapter we will look at a particular group of optimization problems referred to as *network flow problems*. These typically relate to applications involving transportation, assignment and transshipment models. As we shall see, network flow problems are readily solved using LP. However, because of the special mathematical structure of network flow problems, special solution algorithms have been developed that we shall also consider.

7.1 Transportation Problem: A Network Model and a Linear Programming Formulation

The **transportation problem** arises frequently in planning for the distribution of goods and services from several supply locations to several demand locations. Typically, the quantity of goods available at each supply location (or origin) is limited, and the quantity of goods needed at each of several demand locations (or destinations) is known. The usual objective in a transportation problem is to minimize the cost of shipping goods from the origins to the destinations.

We'll illustrate by considering a transportation problem faced by Foster Electronics. Amongst other things, the company manufactures memory cards that are used in digital cameras. These are manufactured at three different plants: in the Czech Republic, in Brazil and in China. The production capacity for each plant over the next three-month planning period is shown below:

Origin	Plant	Three-Month Production Capacity (units)
1	Czech Republic	5 000
2	Brazil	6 000
3	China	2 500
		Total 13 500

The transportation problem was first formulated by F. L. Hitchcock in 1941 who also proposed a solution procedure similar to the general Simplex method. Independently T. C. Koopmans looked on the same problem in connection with his work as a member of the Joint Shipping Board. The problem is frequently referred to as the Hitchcock–Koopmans problem.

The firm distributes its products through four distribution centres located in Boston, Dubai, Singapore and London; the three-month forecast of demand for each of the distribution centres is as follows:

Destination	Distribution Centre	Three-Month Demand Forecast (units)
1	Boston	6 000
2	Dubai	4 000
3	Singapore	2 000
4	London	1 500
		Total 13 500

Management would like to determine how much of its production should be shipped from each manufacturing plant to each distribution centre. Figure 7.1 shows graphically the 12 distribution routes Foster can use. Such a graph is called a **network**; the circles are referred to as **nodes** and the lines connecting the nodes as **arcs**. Each origin or destination is represented by a node, and each possible shipping route is

Figure 7.1 The Network Representation of the Foster Electronics Transportation Problem

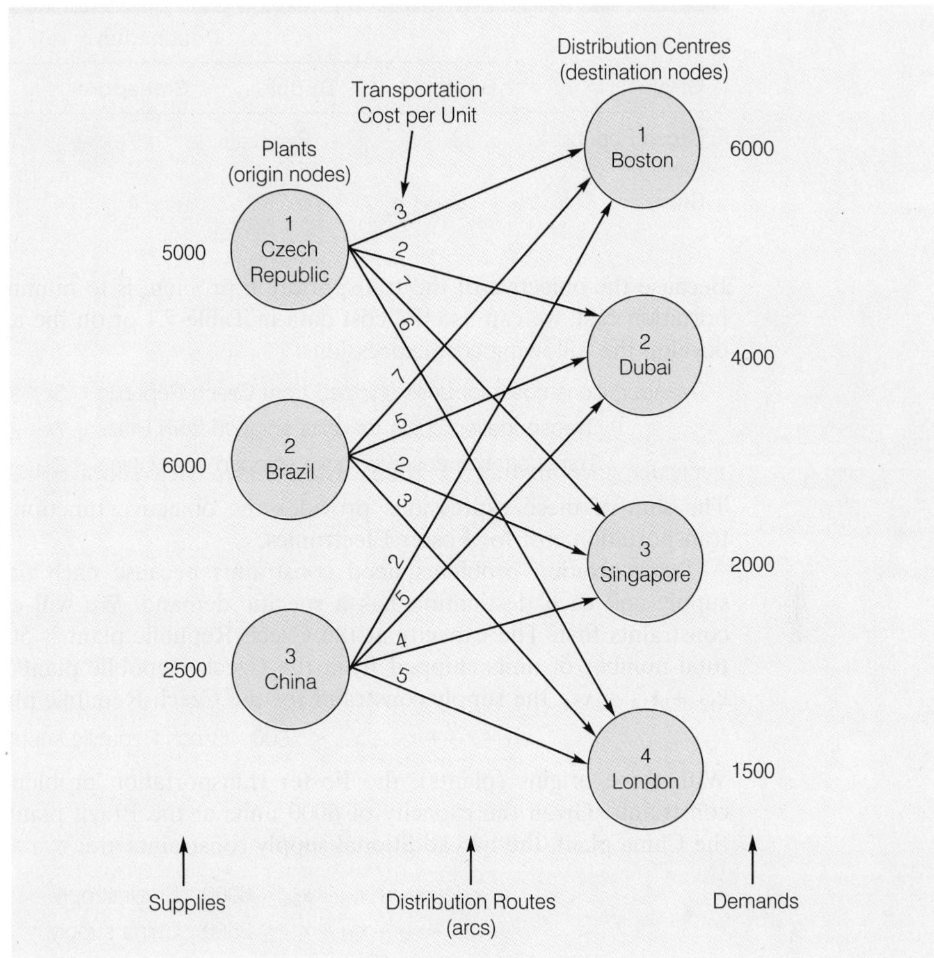

represented by an arc. The amount of the supply is written next to each origin node, and the amount of the demand is written next to each destination node. The goods shipped from the origins to the destinations represent the flow in the network. Note that the direction of flow (from origin to destination) is indicated by the arrows.

Try Problem 1 for practise in developing a network model of a transportation problem.

For Foster's transportation problem, the objective is to determine the routes to be used and the quantity to be shipped via each route that will provide the minimum total transportation cost. The cost for each unit shipped on each route is given in Table 7.1 and is shown on each arc in Figure 7.1.

Clearly, it looks as if we can develop an LP model for this problem – we have an objective function and we have a set of constraints. We will use double-subscripted decision variables, with x_{11} denoting the number of units shipped from origin 1 (Czech Republic) to destination 1 (Boston), x_{12} denoting the number of units shipped from origin 1 (Czech Republic) to destination 2 (Dubai) and so on. In general, the decision variables for a transportation problem having m origins and n destinations are written as follows:

The first subscript identifies the 'from' node of the corresponding arc and the second subscript identifies the 'to' node of the arc.

$$x_{ij} = \text{number of units shipped from origin } i \text{ to destination } j$$
$$\text{where } i = 1, 2, 3, \ldots, m, \text{and } j = 1, 2, \ldots, n$$

Table 7.1 Transportation Cost Per Unit for the Foster Electronics Transportation Problem (Euros)

	Destination			
Origin	**Boston**	**Dubai**	**Singapore**	**London**
Czech Republic	3	2	7	6
Brazil	7	5	2	3
China	2	5	4	5

Because the objective of the transportation problem is to minimize the total transportation cost, we can use the cost data in Table 7.1 or on the arcs in Figure 7.1 to develop the following cost expressions:

$$\text{Transportations costs for units shipped from Czech Republic} = 3x_{11} + 2x_{12} + 7x_{13} + 6x_{14}$$
$$\text{Transportation costs for units shipped from Brazil} = 7x_{21} + 5x_{22} + 2x_{23} + 3x_{24}$$
$$\text{Transportation costs for units shipped from China} = 2x_{31} + 5x_{32} + 4x_{33} + 5x_{34}$$

The sum of these expressions provides the objective function showing the total transportation cost for Foster Electronics.

Transportation problems need constraints because each origin has a limited supply and each destination has a specific demand. We will consider the supply constraints first. The capacity at the Czech Republic plant is 5000 units. With the total number of units shipped from the Czech Republic plant expressed as $x_{11} + x_{12} + x_{13} + x_{14}$, the supply constraint for the Czech Republic plant is:

$$x_{11} + x_{12} + x_{13} + x_{14} \leq 5000 \quad \text{Czech Republic supply}$$

With three origins (plants), the Foster transportation problem has three supply constraints. Given the capacity of 6000 units at the Brazil plant and 2500 units at the China plant, the two additional supply constraints are:

$$x_{21} + x_{22} + x_{23} + x_{24} \leq 6000 \quad \text{Brazil supply}$$
$$x_{31} + x_{32} + x_{33} + x_{34} \leq 2500 \quad \text{China supply}$$

To obtain a feasible solution, the total supply must be greater than or equal to the total demand.

With the four distribution centres as the destinations, four demand constraints are needed to ensure that destination demands will be satisfied:

$$x_{11} + x_{21} + x_{31} = 6000 \quad \text{Boston demand}$$
$$x_{12} + x_{22} + x_{32} = 4000 \quad \text{Dubai demand}$$
$$x_{13} + x_{23} + x_{33} = 2000 \quad \text{Singapore demand}$$
$$x_{14} + x_{24} + x_{34} = 1500 \quad \text{London demand}$$

Combining the objective function and constraints into one model provides a 12-variable, seven-constraint linear programming formulation of the Foster Electronics transportation problem:

$$\text{Min} \quad 3x_{11} + 2x_{12} + 7x_{13} + 6x_{14} + 7x_{21} + 5x_{22} + 2x_{23} + 3x_{24} + 2x_{31} + 5x_{32} + 4x_{33} + 5x_{34}$$

s.t.

$$\begin{aligned}
x_{11} + x_{12} + x_{13} + x_{14} &\leq 5000 \\
x_{21} + x_{22} + x_{23} + x_{24} &\leq 6000 \\
x_{31} + x_{32} + x_{33} + x_{34} &\leq 2500 \\
x_{11} + x_{21} + x_{31} &= 6000 \\
x_{12} + x_{22} + x_{32} &= 4000 \\
x_{13} + x_{23} + x_{33} &= 2000 \\
x_{14} + x_{24} + x_{34} &= 1500
\end{aligned}$$

$$x_{ij} \geq 0 \quad \text{for } i = 1, 2, 3;\ j = 1, 2, 3, 4$$

Figure 7.2 The Excel Solution for the Foster Electronics Transportation Problem

EXCEL *file*

FOSTER

```
Objective Function Value =              39500.000

      Variable            Value            Reduced Costs
   --------------    ---------------    ------------------
        X11              3500.000                 0.000
        X12              1500.000                 0.000
        X13                 0.000                 8.000
        X14                 0.000                 6.000
        X21                 0.000                 1.000
        X22              2500.000                 0.000
        X23              2000.000                 0.000
        X24              1500.000                 0.000
        X31              2500.000                 0.000
        X32                 0.000                 4.000
        X33                 0.000                 6.000
        X34                 0.000                 6.000
```

Table 7.2 Optimal Solution to the Foster Electronics Transportation Problem

Route				
From	**To**	**Units Shipped**	**Cost per Unit**	**Total Cost**
Czech Republic	Boston	3 500	€3	€10 500
Czech Republic	Dubai	1 500	€2	€ 3 000
Brazil	Dubai	2 500	€5	€12 500
Brazil	Singapore	2 000	€2	€ 4 000
Brazil	London	1 500	€3	€ 4 500
China	Boston	2 500	€2	€ 5 000
				€39 500

Comparing the linear programming formulation to the network in Figure 7.1 leads to several observations. All the information needed for the linear programming formulation is on the network. Each node requires one constraint and each arc requires one variable. The sum of the variables corresponding to arcs from an origin node must be less than or equal to the origin's supply, and the sum of the variables corresponding to the arcs into a destination node must be equal to the destination's demand.

Try Problem 2 to test your ability to formulate and solve a linear programming model of a transportation problem.

We solved the Foster Electronics problem with Excel. The computer solution (see Figure 7.2) shows that the minimum total transportation cost is €39 500. The values for the decision variables show the optimal amounts to ship over each route. For example, with $x_{11} = 3500$, 3500 units should be shipped from the Czech Republic to Boston, and with $x_{12} = 1500$, 1500 units should be shipped from Czech Republic to Dubai. Other values of the decision variables indicate the remaining shipping quantities and routes. Table 7.2 shows the minimum-cost transportation schedule, and Figure 7.3 summarizes the optimal solution on the network.

Problem Variations

The Foster Electronics problem illustrates use of the basic transportation model. Variations of the basic transportation model may involve one or more of the following situations:

Figure 7.3 Optimal Solution to The Foster Electronics Transportation Problem

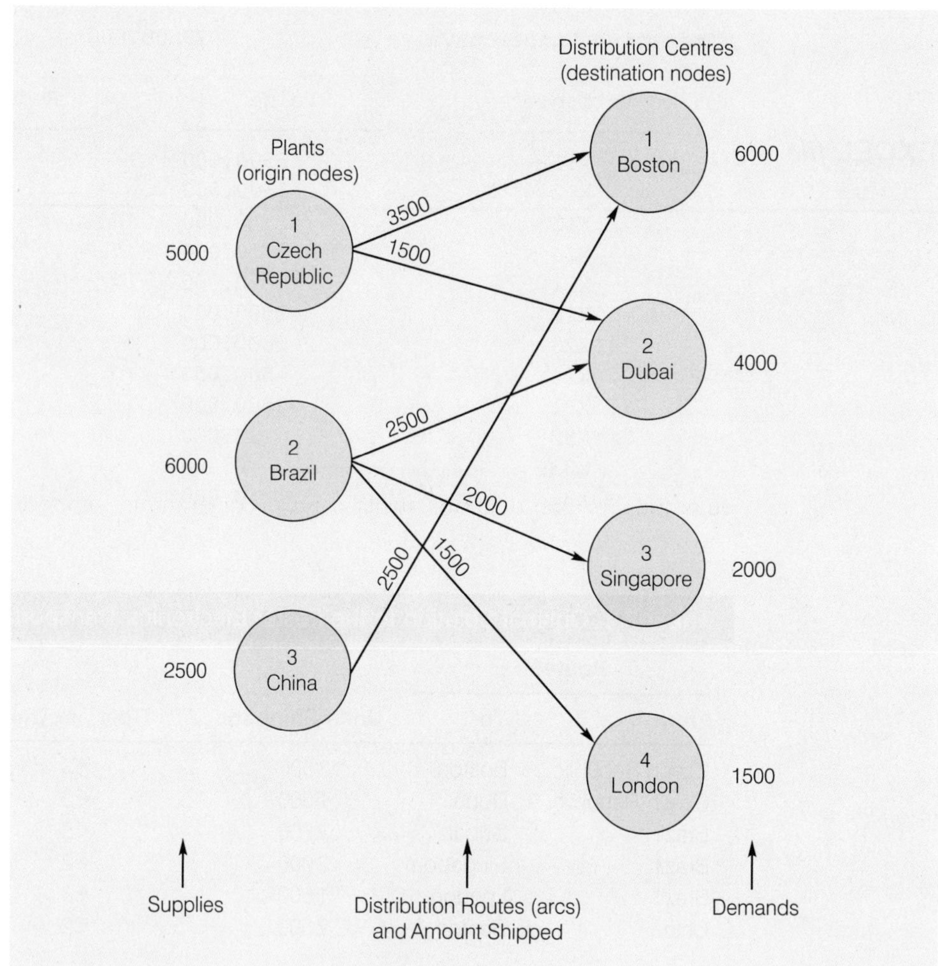

1 Total supply not equal to total demand.
2 Maximization objective function.
3 Route capacities or route minimums.
4 Unacceptable routes.

With slight modifications in the LP model, we can easily accommodate these situations.

Total Supply Not Equal to Total Demand Often *the total supply is not equal to the total demand*. If total supply exceeds total demand, no modification in the linear programming formulation is necessary. Excess supply will appear as slack in the linear programming solution. Slack for any particular origin can be interpreted as the unused supply or amount not shipped from the origin.

If total supply is less than total demand, the linear programming model of a transportation problem will not have a feasible solution. In this case, we modify the network representation by adding a *dummy origin* with a supply equal to the difference between the total demand and the total supply. With the addition of the dummy origin, and an arc from the dummy origin to each destination, the linear

Whenever total supply is less than total demand, the model does not determine how the unsatisfied demand is handled (e.g., backorders). The manager must handle this aspect of the problem.

programming model will have a feasible solution. A zero cost per unit is assigned to each arc leaving the dummy origin so that the value of the optimal solution for the revised problem will represent the shipping cost for the units actually shipped (no shipments actually will be made from the dummy origin). When the optimal solution is implemented, the destinations showing shipments being received from the dummy origin will be the destinations experiencing a shortfall or unsatisfied demand.

Try Problem 7 to test your ability to handle a case where demand is greater than supply with a maximization objective.

Maximization Objective Function In some transportation problems, the objective is to find a solution that maximizes profit or revenue. Using the values for profit or revenue per unit as coefficients in the objective function, we simply solve a maximization rather than a minimization linear programme. This change does not affect the constraints.

Route Capacities and/or Route Minimums The linear programming formulation of the transportation problem can also accommodate capacities and/or minimum quantities for one or more of the routes. For example, suppose that in the Foster Electronics problem the China–Boston route (origin 3 to destination 1) had a capacity of 1000 units because of limited space availability on its normal mode of transportation. With x_{31} denoting the amount shipped from China to Boston, the route capacity constraint for the China–Boston route would be:

$$x_{31} \leq 1000$$

Similarly, route minimums can be specified. For example,

$$x_{22} \geq 2000$$

would guarantee that a previously committed order for a Brazil–Dubai delivery of at least 2000 units would be maintained in the optimal solution.

Unacceptable Routes Finally, establishing a route from every origin to every destination may not be possible. This may happen, for example, because of safety or security concerns or because of physical barriers preventing certain routes from being used. To handle this situation, we simply drop the corresponding arc from the network and remove the corresponding variable from the linear programming formulation. For example, if the Czech Republic–Singapore route were unacceptable or unusable, the arc from Czech Republic to Singapore could be dropped in Figure 7.1, and x_{13} could be removed from the linear programming formulation. Solving the resulting 11-variable, seven-constraint model would provide the optimal solution while guaranteeing that the Czech Republic–Singapore route is not used.

A General Linear Programming Model of the Transportation Problem

1950 saw the first computer solution of a transportation problem.

To show the general linear programming model of the transportation problem, we use the notation:

$$\begin{aligned}
i &= \text{index for origins, } i = 1, 2, \ldots, m \\
j &= \text{index for destinations, } j = 1, 2, \ldots, n \\
x_{ij} &= \text{number of units shipped from origin } i \text{ to destination } j \\
c_{ij} &= \text{cost per unit of shipping from origin } i \text{ to destination } j \\
s_i &= \text{supply or capacity in units at origin } i \\
d_j &= \text{demand in units at destination } j
\end{aligned}$$

The general linear programming model of the m-origin, n-destination transportation problem is:

$$\text{Min} \quad \sum_{i=1}^{m}\sum_{j=1}^{n} c_{ij}x_{ij}$$

s.t.

$$\sum_{j=1}^{n} x_{ij} \leq s_i \quad i = 1, 2, \ldots, m \quad \text{Supply}$$

$$\sum_{i=1}^{m} x_{ij} = d_j \quad j = 1, 2, \ldots, n \quad \text{Demand}$$

$$x_{ij} \geq 0 \quad \text{for all } i \text{ and } j$$

As mentioned previously, we can add constraints of the form $x_{ij} \leq L_{ij}$ if the route from origin i to destination j has capacity L_{ij}. A transportation problem that includes constraints of this type is called a **capacitated transportation problem**. Similarly, we can add route minimum constraints of the form $x_{ij} \geq M_{ij}$ if the route from origin i to destination j must handle at least M_{ij} units.

NOTES AND COMMENTS

1 Transportation problems encountered in practice usually lead to large linear programmes. Transportation problems with 100 origins and 100 destinations are not unusual. Such a problem would involve (100)(100) = 10 000 variables.

2 To handle a situation in which some routes may be unacceptable, we stated that you could drop the corresponding arc from the network and remove the corresponding variable from the linear programming formulation. Another approach often used is to assign an extremely large objective function cost coefficient to any unacceptable arc. If the problem has already been formulated, another option is to add a constraint to the formulation that sets the variable you want to remove equal to zero.

3 The optimal solution to a transportation model will consist of integer values for the decision variables as long as all supply and demand values are integers. The reason is the special mathematical structure of the linear programming model. Each variable appears in exactly one supply and one demand constraint, and all coefficients in the constraint equations are 1s and 0s.

4 Although many transportation problems involve minimizing the cost of transporting goods between locations, many other applications of the transportation model exist.

7.2 Transportation Simplex Method: A Special-Purpose Solution Procedure

Solving transportation problems with a general-purpose linear programming code is fine for small to medium-sized problems. However, these problems often grow very large (a problem with 100 origins and 1000 destinations would have 100 000 variables), and more efficient solution procedures may be needed. The network structure of the transportation problem has enabled management scientists to develop special-purpose solution procedures that greatly simplify the calculations.

MANAGEMENT SCIENCE IN ACTION

UPS's optimization-based transportation planning system – VOLCANO

UPS is a major delivery company operating in over 200 countries and dealing with a huge volume of deliveries each day: over 13 million packages and eight million customers. One of its premium delivery services in the USA, next day air, utilizes the company's huge fleet of aircraft (over 250) to transport packages that have been dropped off by customers by early evening to their destinations by the following morning. Clearly, given the complexity of the delivery network and the huge volume of deliveries, decisions on transportation routes are critical to the company's success. In the case of the next day air service, UPS has a network with a central hub in Louisville, Kentucky six regional hubs in other key US locations and more than 100 airports. An optimization-based transportation planning system has been developed, called VOLCANO (the Volume, Location and Aircraft Network Optimizer) and UPS reckons to have saved over $90 million through using the optimization modeller with a further saving of $200 million over the next decade. UPS's Tome Weidemeyer commented 'VOLCANO will make UPS more competitive by ensuring we are running the most efficient network possible'.

Based on A. P. Armacost, C. Barnhart, K. A. Ware and A. M. Wilson 'UPS Optimizes its Air Network', *Interfaces* 34/1 (2004): 15–25.

In Section 7.1 we introduced the Foster Electronics transportation problem and showed how to formulate and solve it as a linear programme. The LP formulation involved 12 variables and seven constraints. In this section we describe a special-purpose solution procedure, called the transportation simplex method, that takes advantage of the network structure of the transportation problem and makes possible the solution of large transportation problems efficiently on a computer and small transportation problems by hand.

The transportation simplex method, like the simplex method for linear programmes, is a two-phase procedure; it involves first finding an initial feasible solution and then proceeding iteratively to make improvements in the solution until an optimal solution is reached. To summarize the data conveniently and to keep track of the calculations, we utilize a **transportation tableau**. The transportation tableau for the Foster Electronics problem is presented in Table 7.3.

Note that the 12 *cells* in the tableau correspond to the 12 arcs shown in Figure 7.1; that is, each cell corresponds to the route from one origin to one destination. So, each cell in the transportation tableau corresponds to a variable in the linear programming formulation. The entries in the right-hand margin of the tableau indicate the supply at each origin, and the entries in the bottom margin indicate the demand at each destination. Each row corresponds to a supply node, and each column corresponds to a demand node in the network model of the problem. The number of rows plus the number of columns equals the number of constraints in the linear programming formulation of the problem. The entries in the upper right-hand corner of each cell show the transportation cost per unit shipped over the corresponding route. Note also that for the Foster Electronics problem total supply equals total demand. The transportation simplex method can be applied only to a balanced problem (total supply = total demand); if a problem is not balanced, a dummy origin or dummy destination must be added. The use of dummy origins and destinations will be discussed later in this section.

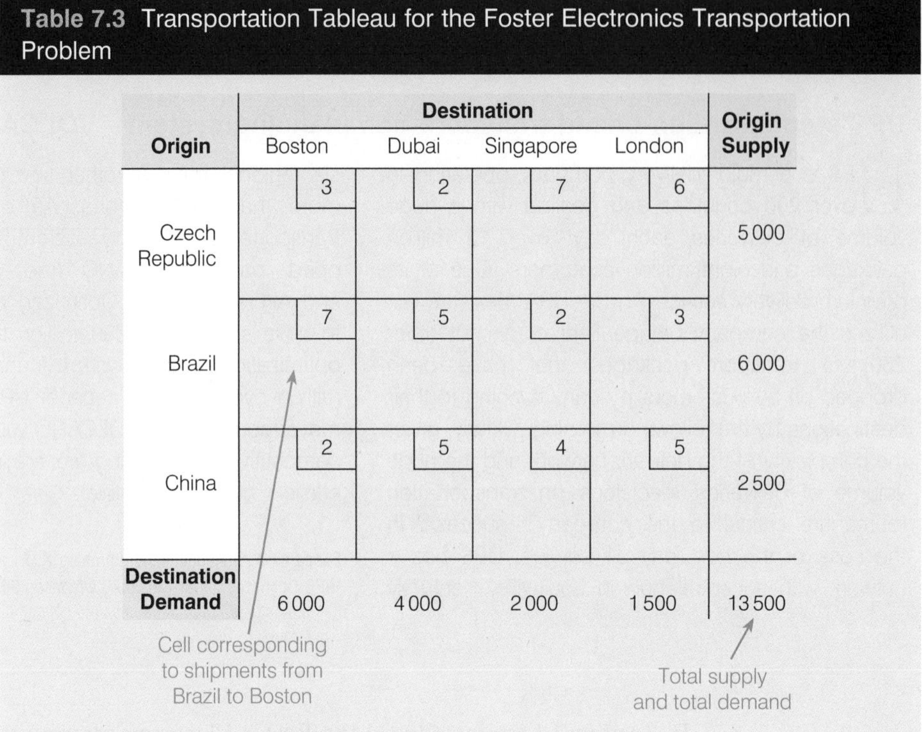

Table 7.3 Transportation Tableau for the Foster Electronics Transportation Problem

Origin	Destination: Boston	Dubai	Singapore	London	Origin Supply
Czech Republic	3	2	7	6	5000
Brazil	7	5	2	3	6000
China	2	5	4	5	2500
Destination Demand	6000	4000	2000	1500	13500

Phase I: Finding an Initial Feasible Solution

The first phase of the transportation Simplex method involves finding an initial feasible solution. Such a solution provides arc flows that satisfy each demand constraint without shipping more from any origin node than the supply available. The procedures most often used to find an initial feasible solution to a transportation problem are called heuristics. A **heuristic** is a commonsense procedure for quickly finding a solution to a problem.

Several heuristics have been developed to find an initial feasible solution to a transportation problem. Although some heuristics can find an initial feasible solution quickly, often the solution they find is not especially good in terms of minimizing total cost. Other heuristics may not find an initial feasible solution as quickly, but the solution they find is often good in terms of minimizing total cost. The heuristic we describe for finding an initial feasible solution to a transportation problem is called the **minimum cost method**. This heuristic strikes a compromise between finding a feasible solution quickly and finding a feasible solution that is close to the optimal solution.

We begin by allocating as much flow as possible to the minimum cost arc. In Table 7.3 we see that the Czech Republic–Dubai, Brazil–Singapore and China–London routes each qualify as the minimum cost arc because they each have a transportation cost of €2 per unit. When ties between arcs occur, we follow the convention of selecting the arc to which the most flow can be allocated. In this case it corresponds to shipping 4000 units from the Czech Republic to Dubai, so we write 4000 in the Czech Republic–Dubai cell of the transportation tableau. This selection reduces the available supply in the Czech Republic from 5000 to 1000; hence, we cross out the 5000-unit supply value and replace it with the reduced value of 1000. In addition, allocating 4000 units to this arc satisfies the demand at Dubai, so we reduce

Table 7.4 Transportation Tableau after One Iteration of the Minimum Cost Method

	Boston	Dubai	Singapore	London	**Supply**
Czech Republic	3	2 4 000	7	6	1 000 ~~5000~~
Brazil	7	5	2	3	6 000
China	2	5	4	5	2 500
Demand	6 000	~~4000~~ 0	2 000	1 500	

the Dubai demand to zero and eliminate the corresponding column from further consideration by drawing a line through it. The transportation tableau now appears as shown in Table 7.4.

Now we look at the reduced tableau consisting of all unlined cells to identify the next minimum cost arc. The routes between Brazil–Singapore and China–Boston tie with transportation cost of €2 per unit. More units of flow can be allocated to the China–Boston route, so we choose it for the next allocation. This step results in an allocation of 2500 units over the China–Boston route. To update the tableau, we reduce the Boston demand by 2500 units to 3500, reduce the China supply to zero, and eliminate this row from further consideration by lining through it. Continuing the process results next in an allocation of 2000 units over the Brazil–Singapore route and the elimination of the Singapore column because its demand goes to zero. The transportation tableau obtained after carrying out the second and third iterations is shown in Table 7.5.

We now have two arcs that qualify for the minimum cost arc with a value of 3: the Czech Republic–Boston and Brazil–London. We could allocate a flow of 1000 units to the Czech Republic–Boston route and a flow of 1500 to the Brazil–London route, so we allocate 1500 units to the Brazil–London route. Doing so results in a demand of zero at London and eliminates this column. The next minimum cost allocation is 1000 over the Czech Republic–Boston route. After we make these two allocations, the transportation tableau appears as shown in Table 7.6.

The only remaining unlined cell is Brazil–Boston. Allocating 2500 units to the corresponding arc uses up the remaining supply in Brazil and satisfies all the demand at Boston. The resulting tableau is shown in Table 7.7.

This solution is feasible because all the demand is satisfied and all the supply is used. The total transportation cost resulting from this initial feasible solution is calculated in Table 7.8. Phase I of the transportation Simplex method is now complete; we have an initial feasible solution. The total transportation cost associated with this solution is €42 000.

Table 7.5 Transportation Tableau after Three Iterations of the Minimum Cost Method

	Boston	Dubai	Singapore	London	**Supply**
Czech Republic	[3]	[2] 4 000	[7]	[6]	1 000 ~~5000~~
Brazil	[7]	[5]	[2] 2 000	[3]	4 000 ~~6000~~
~~China~~	[2] ~~2500~~	[5]	[4]	[5]	0 ~~2500~~
Demand	~~6000~~ 3 500	~~4000~~ 0	~~2000~~ 0	1 500	

Table 7.6 Transportation Tableau after Five Iterations of the Minimum Cost Method

	Boston	Dubai	Singapore	London	**Supply**
~~Czech Republic~~	[3] 1 000	[2] 4 000	[7]	[6]	0 ~~1000~~ ~~5000~~
Brazil	[7]	[5]	[2] 2 000	[3] 1 500	2 500 ~~4000~~ ~~6000~~
~~China~~	[2] 2 500	[5]	[4]	[5]	0 ~~2500~~
Demand	~~6000~~ ~~3500~~ 2 500	~~4000~~ 0	~~2000~~ 0	~~1500~~ 0	

Summary of the Minimum Cost Method Before applying phase II of the transportation Simplex method, let us summarize the steps for obtaining an initial feasible solution using the minimum cost method.

Step 1. Identify the cell in the transportation tableau with the lowest cost, and allocate as much flow as possible to this cell. In case of a tie, choose the cell corresponding to the arc over which the most units can be shipped. If ties still exist, choose any of the tied cells.

Step 2. Reduce the row supply and the column demand by the amount of flow allocated to the cell identified in step 1.

Table 7.7 Final Tableau Showing the Initial Feasible Solution Obtained Using the Minimum Cost Method

	Boston	Dubai	Singapore	London	**Supply**
Czech Republic	(3) 1 000	(2) 4 000	(7)	(6)	0 ~~1000~~ ~~5000~~
Brazil	(7) 2 500	(5)	(2) 2 000	(3) 1 500	0 ~~2500~~ ~~4000~~ ~~6000~~
China	(2) 2 500	(5)	(4)	(5)	0 ~~2500~~
Demand	~~6000~~ ~~3500~~ ~~2500~~ 0	~~4000~~ 0	~~2000~~ 0	~~1500~~ 0	

Table 7.8 Total Cost of the Initial Feasible Solution Obtained Using the Minimum Cost Method

Route				
From	**To**	**Units Shipped**	**Cost per Unit**	**Total Cost**
Czech Republic	Boston	1 000	€3	€ 3 000
Czech Republic	Dubai	4 000	€2	€ 8 000
Brazil	Boston	2 500	€7	€17 500
Brazil	Singapore	2 000	€2	€ 4 000
Brazil	London	1 500	€3	€ 4 500
China	Boston	2 500	€2	€ 5 000
				€42 000

Step 3. If *all* row supplies and column demands have been exhausted, then stop; the allocations made will provide an initial feasible solution. Otherwise, continue with step 4.

To test your ability to use the minimum cost method to find an initial feasible solution, try part (a) of Problem 15.

Step 4. If the row supply is now zero, eliminate the row from further consideration by drawing a line through it. If the column demand is now zero, eliminate the column by drawing a line through it.

Step 5. Continue with step 1 for all unlined rows and columns.

Phase II: Iterating to the Optimal Solution

Phase II of the transportation simplex method is a procedure for iterating from the initial feasible solution identified in phase I to the optimal solution. Recall that each cell in the transportation tableau corresponds to an arc (route) in the network model of the transportation problem. The first step at each iteration of phase II is to identify an incoming arc. The incoming arc is the currently unused route (unoccupied cell) where making a flow allocation will cause the largest per-unit reduction in total cost. Flow is then assigned to the incoming arc, and the amounts being shipped over all other arcs to which flow had previously been assigned (occupied cells) are adjusted as necessary to maintain a feasible solution. In the process of adjusting the flow assigned to the occupied cells, we identify and drop an outgoing arc from the solution. So, at each iteration in phase II, we bring a currently unused arc (unoccupied cell) into the solution, and remove an arc to which flow had previously been assigned (occupied cell) from the solution.

To show how phase II of the transportation Simplex method works, we must explain how to identify the incoming arc (cell), how to make the adjustments to the other occupied cells when flow is allocated to the incoming arc and how to identify the outgoing arc (cell). We first consider identifying the incoming arc.

As mentioned, the incoming arc is the one that will cause the largest reduction per unit in the total cost of the current solution. To identify this arc, we must compute for each unused arc the amount by which total cost will be reduced by shipping one unit over that arc. The *mo*dified *di*stribution or **MODI method** is a way to make this computation.

The MODI method requires that we define an index u_i for each row of the tableau and an index v_j for each column of the tableau. Calculating these row and column indexes requires that the cost coefficient for each occupied cell equal $u_i + v_j$. So, since c_{ij} is the cost per unit from origin i to destination j, $u_i + v_j = c_{ij}$ for each occupied cell. Let us return to the initial feasible solution which we found using the minimum cost method (see Table 7.9), and use the MODI method to identify the incoming arc.

Requiring that $u_i + v_j = c_{ij}$ for all the occupied cells in the initial feasible solution leads to a system of six equations and seven indexes, or variables:

Occupied Cell	$u_i + v_j = c_{ij}$
Czech Republic–Boston	$u_1 + v_1 = 3$
Czech Republic–Dubai	$u_1 + v_2 = 2$
Brazil–Boston	$u_2 + v_1 = 7$
Brazil–Singapore	$u_2 + v_3 = 2$
Brazil–London	$u_2 + v_4 = 3$
China–Boston	$u_3 + v_1 = 2$

With one more index (variable) than equation in this system, we can freely pick a value for one of the indexes and then solve for the others. We will always choose $u_1 = 0$ and then solve for the values of the other indexes. Setting $u_1 = 0$, we obtain:

$$0 + v_1 = 3$$
$$0 + v_2 = 2$$
$$u_2 + v_1 = 7$$
$$u_2 + v_3 = 2$$
$$u_2 + v_4 = 3$$
$$u_3 + v_1 = 2$$

Table 7.9 Initial Feasible Solution to the Foster Electronics Problem

	Boston	Dubai	Singapore	London	**Supply**
Czech Republic	[3] 1 000	[2] 4 000	[7]	[6]	5 000
Brazil	[7] 2 500	[5]	[2] 2 000	[3] 1 500	6 000
China	[2] 2 500	[5]	[4]	[5]	2 500
Demand	6 000	4 000	2 000	1 500	

Solving these equations leads to the following values for u_1, u_2, u_3, v_1, v_2, v_3 and v_4:

$$\begin{aligned} u_1 &= 0 & v_1 &= 3 \\ u_2 &= 4 & v_2 &= 2 \\ u_3 &= -1 & v_3 &= -2 \\ & & v_4 &= -1 \end{aligned}$$

Management scientists have shown that for each *unoccupied* cell, $e_{ij} = c_{ij} - u_i - v_j$ shows the change in total cost per unit that will be obtained by allocating one unit of flow to the corresponding arc. Thus, we will call e_{ij} the net evaluation index. Because of the way u_i and v_j are calculated the net evaluation index for each occupied cell equals zero.

Rewriting the tableau containing the initial feasible solution for the Foster Electronics problem and replacing the previous marginal information with the values of u_i and v_j, we obtain Table 7.10. We calculated the net evaluation index (e_{ij}) for each unoccupied cell, which is the circled number in the cell. So, shipping one unit over the route from origin 1 to destination 3 (Czech Republic–Singapore) will increase total cost by €9; shipping one unit from origin 1 to destination 4 (Czech Republic–London) will increase total cost by €7; shipping one unit from origin 2 to destination 2 (Brazil–Dubai) will decrease total cost by €1; and so on.

On the basis of the net evaluation indexes, the best arc in terms of cost reduction (a net evaluation index of −1) is associated with the Brazil–Dubai route (origin 2–destination 2); thus, the cell in row 2 and column 2 is chosen as the incoming cell. Total cost decreases by €1 for every unit of flow assigned to this arc. The question now is: How much flow should we assign to this arc? Because the total cost decreases by €1 per unit assigned, we want to allocate the maximum possible flow. To find that maximum, we must recognize that, to maintain feasibility, each unit of flow assigned to this arc will require adjustments in the flow over the other currently used arcs. The **stepping-stone method** can be used to determine the adjustments necessary and to identify an outgoing arc.

A. Charnes and W. W. Cooper published their article 'The Stepping Stone Method of Explaining Linear Programming Calculations in Transportation Problems' in the first publication of the *Management Science* journal in 1954.

The Stepping-Stone Method Suppose that we allocate one unit of flow to the incoming arc (the Brazil–Dubai route). To maintain feasibility – that is, not exceed the number of units to be shipped to Dubai – we would have to reduce the flow assigned to the Czech Republic–Dubai arc to 3999. But then we would have to

Table 7.10 Net Evaluation Indexes for the Initial Feasible Solution to the Foster Electronics Problem Calculated Using the MODI Method

u_i \ v_j	3	2	−2	−1
0	3 1 000	2 4 000	7 (9)	6 (7)
4	7 2 500	5 (−1)	2 2 000	3 1 500
−1	2 2 500	5 (4)	4 (7)	5 (7)

Table 7.11 Cycle of Adjustments in Occupied Cells Necessary to Maintain Feasibility When Shipping One Unit from Brazil to Dubai

	Boston	Dubai	Singapore	London	**Supply**
Czech Republic	3 1 001 ~~1000~~	2 3 999 ~~4000~~	7	6	5 000
Brazil	7 2 499 ~~2500~~	5 1	2 2 000	3 1 500	6 000
China	2 2 500	5	4	5	2 500
Demand	6 000	4 000	2 000	1500	

increase the flow on the Czech Republic–Boston arc to 1001 so that the total Czech Republic supply of 5000 units could be shipped. Finally, we would have to reduce the flow on the Brazil–Boston arc by 1 to satisfy the Boston demand exactly. Table 7.11 summarizes this cycle of adjustments.

The cycle of adjustments needed in making an allocation to the Brazil–Dubai cell required changes in four cells: the incoming cell (Brazil–Dubai) and three currently occupied cells. We can view these four cells as forming a stepping-stone path in the tableau, where the corners of the path are currently occupied cells. The idea behind the stepping-stone name is to view the tableau as a pond with the occupied cells as stones sticking up in it. To identify the stepping-stone path for an incoming cell, we start at the incoming cell and move horizontally and vertically using occupied cells as

Table 7.12 Stepping-Stone Path With The Brazil–Dubai Route as The Incoming Arc

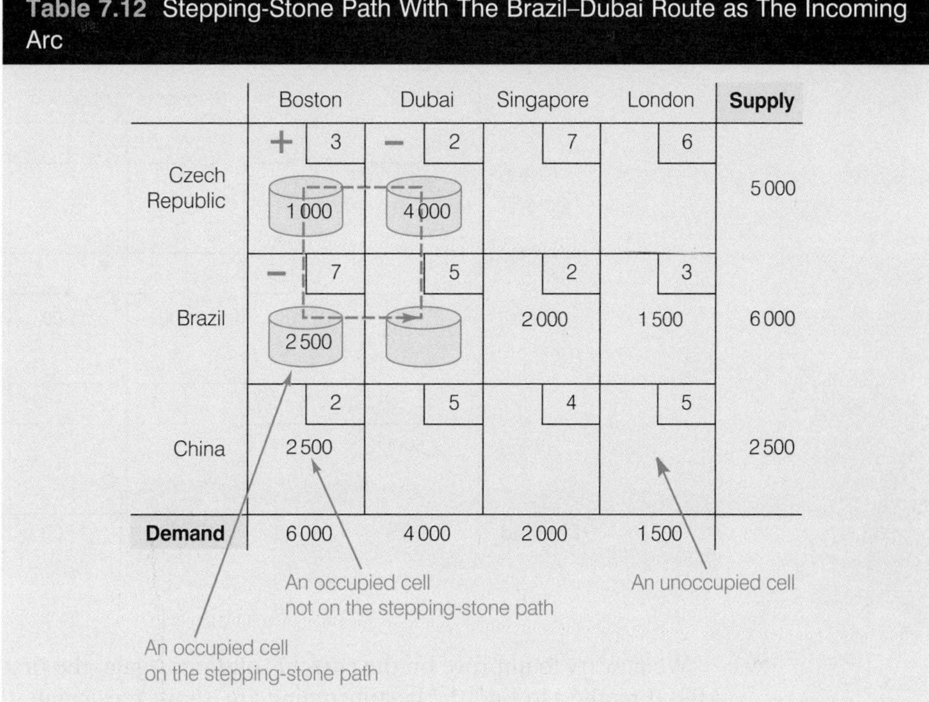

	Boston	Dubai	Singapore	London	**Supply**
Czech Republic	+ 3 1 000	− 2 4 000	7	6	5 000
Brazil	− 7 2 500	5	2 2 000	3 1 500	6 000
China	2 2 500	5	4	5	2 500
Demand	6 000	4 000	2 000	1 500	

the stones at the corners of the path; the objective is to step from stone to stone and return to the incoming cell where we started. To focus attention on which occupied cells are part of the stepping-stone path, we draw each occupied cell in the stepping-stone path as a cylinder, which should reinforce the image of these cells as stones sticking up in the pond. Table 7.12 depicts the stepping-stone path associated with the incoming arc of the Brazil–Dubai route.

In Table 7.12 we place a plus sign (+) or a minus sign (−) in each occupied cell on the stepping-stone path. A plus sign indicates that the allocation to that cell will increase by the same amount we allocate to the incoming cell. A minus sign indicates that the allocation to that cell will decrease by the amount allocated to the incoming cell. So, to determine the maximum amount that may be allocated to the incoming cell, we simply look to the cells on the stepping-stone path identified with a minus sign. Because no arc can have a negative flow, the minus-sign cell with the *smallest amount* allocated to it will determine the maximum amount that can be allocated to the incoming cell. After allocating this maximum amount to the incoming cell, we then make all the adjustments necessary on the stepping-stone path to maintain feasibility. The incoming cell becomes an occupied cell, and the outgoing cell is dropped from the current solution.

In the Foster Electronics problem, the Brazil–Boston and Czech Republic–Dubai cells are the ones where the allocation will decrease (the ones with a minus sign) as flow is allocated to the incoming arc (Brazil–Dubai). The 2500 units currently assigned to Brazil–Boston is less than the 4000 units assigned to Czech Republic–Dubai, so we identify Brazil–Boston as the outgoing arc. We then obtain the new solution by allocating 2500 units to the Brazil–Dubai arc, making the appropriate adjustments on the stepping-stone path and dropping Brazil–Boston from the solution (its allocation has been driven to zero). Table 7.13 shows the tableau associated with the new solution. Note that the only changes from the previous tableau are located on the stepping-stone path originating in the Brazil–Dubai cell.

Table 7.13 New Solution After One Iteration in Phase II of the Transportation Simplex Method

	Boston	Dubai	Singapore	London	**Supply**
Czech Republic	[3] 3 500	[2] 1 500	[7]	[6]	5 000
Brazil	[7]	[5] 2 500	[2] 2 000	[3] 1 500	6 000
China	[2] 2 500	[5]	[4]	[5]	2 500
Demand	6 000	4 000	2 000	1 500	

We now try to improve on the current solution. Again, the first step is to apply the MODI method to find the best incoming arc, so we recalculate the row and column indexes by requiring that $u_i + v_j = c_{ij}$ for all occupied cells. The values of u_i and v_j can easily be calculated directly on the tableau. Recall that we begin the MODI method by setting $u_1 = 0$. Thus, for the two occupied cells in row 1 of the table, $v_j = c_{1j}$; as a result, $v_1 = 3$ and $v_2 = 2$. Moving down the column associated with each newly calculated column index, we calculate the row index associated with each occupied cell in that column by subtracting v_j from c_{ij}. Doing so for the newly found column indexes, v_1 and v_2, we find that $u_3 = 2 - 3 = -1$ and that $u_2 = 5 - 2 = 3$. Next, we use these row indexes to calculate the column indexes for occupied cells in the associated rows, obtaining $v_3 = 2 - 3 = -1$ and $v_4 = 3 - 3 = 0$. Table 7.14 shows these new row and column indexes.

Also shown in Table 7.14 are the net changes (the circled numbers) in the value of the solution that will result from allocating one unit to each unoccupied cell. Recall that these are the net evaluation indexes given by $e_{ij} = c_{ij} - u_i - v_j$. Note that the net evaluation index for every unoccupied cell is now greater than or equal to zero. This condition shows that if current unoccupied cells are used, the cost will actually increase. Without an arc to which flow can be assigned to decrease the total cost, we have reached the optimal solution. Table 7.15 summarizes the optimal solution and shows its total cost. As expected, this solution is exactly the same as the one obtained using the linear programming solution approach (Figure 7.2).

Maintaining $m + n - 1$ Occupied Cells Recall that m represents the number of origins and n represents the number of destinations. A solution to a transportation problem that has less than $m + n - 1$ cells with positive allocations is said to be degenerate. The solution to the Foster Electronics problem is not degenerate; six cells are occupied and $m + n - 1 = 3 + 4 - 1 = 6$. The problem with **degeneracy** is that $m + n - 1$ occupied cells are required by the MODI method to compute all the row and column indexes. When degeneracy occurs, we must artificially create an occupied cell in order to compute the row and column indexes. Let us illustrate how degeneracy could occur and how to deal with it.

Table 7.14 MODI Evaluation of Each Cell in Solution

u_i \ v_j	3	2	−1	0
0	[3] 3 500	[2] 1 500	[7] ⑧	[6] ⑥
3	[7] ①	[5] 2 500	[2] 2 000	[3] 1 500
−1	[2] 2 500	[5] ④	[4] ⑥	[5] ⑥

Table 7.16 shows the initial feasible solution obtained using the minimum cost method for a transportation problem involving $m = 3$ origins and $n = 3$ destinations. To use the MODI method for this problem, we must have $m + n - 1 = 3 + 3 - 1 = 5$ occupied cells. Since the initial feasible solution has only four occupied cells, the solution is degenerate.

Suppose that we try to use the MODI method to calculate row and column indexes to begin phase II for this problem. Setting $u_1 = 0$ and calculating the column indexes for each occupied cell in row 1, we obtain $v_1 = 3$ and $v_2 = 6$ (see Table 7.16). Continuing, we then calculate the row indexes for all occupied cells in columns 1 and 2. Doing so gives $u_2 = 5 - 6 = -1$. At this point, we cannot calculate any more row and column indexes because no cells in columns 1 and 2 of row 3 and no cells in rows 1 or 2 of column 3 are occupied.

To calculate all the row and column indexes when fewer than $m + n - 1$ cells are occupied, we must create one or more 'artificially' occupied cells with a flow of zero. In Table 7.16 we must create one artificially occupied cell to have five occupied cells. Any currently unoccupied cell can be made an artificially occupied cell if doing so makes it possible to calculate the remaining row and column indexes. For instance, treating the cell in row 2 and column 3 of Table 7.16 as an

Table 7.15 Optimal Solution to the Foster Electronics Transportation Problem

Route				
From	**To**	**Units Shipped**	**Cost per Unit, €**	**Total Cost, €**
Czech Republic	Boston	3 500	3	10 500
Czech Republic	Dubai	1 500	2	3 000
Brazil	Dubai	2 500	5	12 500
Brazil	Singapore	2 000	2	4 000
Brazil	London	1 500	3	4 500
China	Boston	2 500	2	5 000
				39 500

Table 7.16 Transportation Tableau with a Degenerate Initial Feasible Solution

u_i \ v_j	3	6		Supply
0	[3] 35	[6] 25	[7]	60
−1	[8]	[5] 30	[7]	30
	[4]	[9]	[11] 30	30
Demand	35	55	30	

artificially occupied cell will enable us to calculate v_3 and u_3, but placing it in row 2 and column 1 will not.

As we previously stated, whenever an artificially occupied cell is created, we assign a flow of zero to the corresponding arc. Table 7.17 shows the results of creating an artificially occupied cell in row 2 and column 3 of Table 7.16. Creation of the artificially occupied cell results in five occupied cells, so we can now calculate the remaining row and column indexes. Using the row 2 index ($u_2 = -1$) and the artificially occupied cell in row 2, we calculate the column index for column 3; thus, $v_3 = c_{23} - u_2 = 7 - (-1) = 8$. Then, using the column 3 index ($v_3 = 8$) and the occupied cell in row 3 and column 3 of the tableau, we calculate the row 3 index:

Table 7.17 Transportation Tableau With An Artificial Cell in Row 2 and Column 3

u_i \ v_j	3	6	8	Supply
0	[3] 35	[6] 25	[7] (−1)	60
−1	[8] (6)	[5] 30	[7] 0 ← Artificially occupied cell	30
3	[4] (−2)	[9] (0)	[11] 30	30
Demand	35	55	30	

Table 7.18 Stepping-Stone Path for the Incoming Cell in Row 3 and Column 1

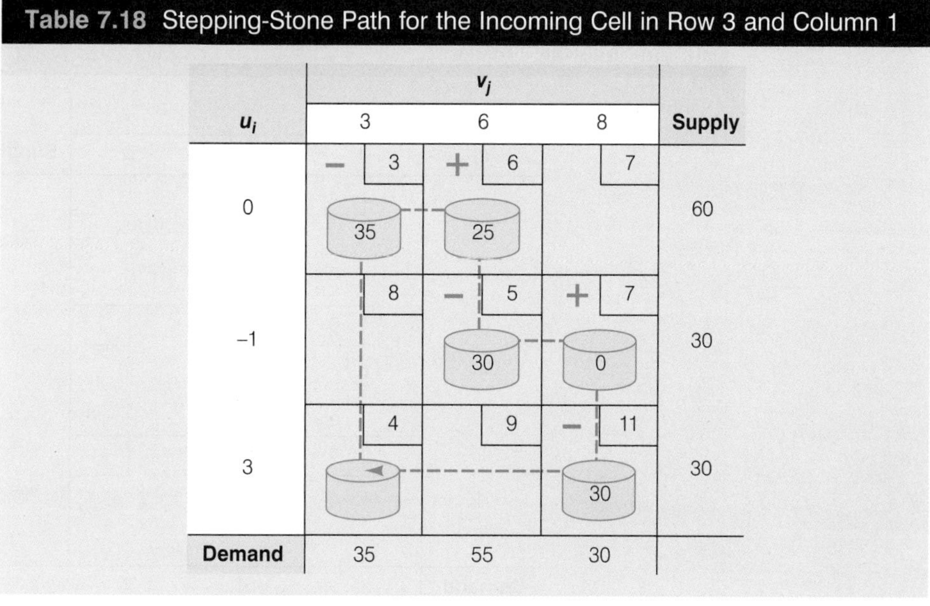

$u_3 = c_{33} - v_3 = 11 - 8 = 3$. Table 7.17 shows the complete set of row and column indexes and the net evaluation index for each unoccupied cell.

Reviewing the net evaluation indexes in Table 7.17, we identify the cell in row 3 and column 1 (net evaluation index = −2) as the incoming cell. The stepping-stone path and the adjustments necessary to maintain feasibility are shown in Table 7.18. Note that the stepping-stone path can be more complex than the simple one obtained for the incoming cell in the Foster Electronics problem. The path in Table 7.18 requires adjustments in all five occupied cells to maintain feasibility. Again, the plus-and minus-sign labels simply show where increases and decreases in the allocation will occur as units of flow are added to the incoming cell. The smallest flow in a decreasing cell is a tie between the cell in row 2 and column 2 and the cell in row 3 and column 3.

Because the smallest amount in a decreasing cell is 30, the allocation we make to the incoming cell is 30 units. However, when 30 units are allocated to the incoming cell and the appropriate adjustments are made to the occupied cells on the stepping-stone path, the allocation to two cells goes to zero (row 2, column 2 and row 3, column 3). We may choose either one as the outgoing cell, but not both. One will be treated as unoccupied; the other will become an artificially occupied cell with a flow of zero allocated to it. The reason we cannot let both become unoccupied cells is that doing so would lead to a degenerate solution, and as before, we could not use the MODI method to compute the row and column indexes for the next iteration. When ties occur in choosing the outgoing cell, we can choose any one of the tied cells as the artificially occupied cell and then use the MODI method to recalculate the row and column indexes. As long as no more than one cell is dropped at each iteration, the MODI method will work.

The solution obtained after allocating 30 units to the incoming cell in row 3 and column 1 and making the appropriate adjustments on the stepping-stone path leads to the tableau shown in Table 7.19. Note that we treated the cell in row 2 and column 2 as the artificially occupied cell. After calculating the new row and column indexes, we see that the cell in row 1 and column 3 will be the next incoming cell. Each unit allocated to this cell will further decrease the value of the solution by 1. The stepping-stone path associated with this incoming cell is shown in Table 7.20.

Table 7.19 New Row and Column Indexes Obtained after Allocating 30 Units to the Incoming Cell

	v_j			
u_i	3	6	8	**Supply**
0	[3] 5	[6] 55	[7] (−1)	60
−1	[8] (6)	[5] 0	[7] 30	30
1	[4] 30	[9] (2)	[11] (2)	30
Demand	35	55	30	

The cell in row 2 and column 3 is the outgoing cell; the tableau after this iteration is shown in Table 7.21. Note that we have found the optimal solution and that, even though several earlier iterations were degenerate, the final solution is not degenerate.

Summary of the Transportation Simplex Method

The transportation Simplex method is a special-purpose solution procedure applicable to any network model having the structure of the transportation problem. It is actually a clever implementation of the general Simplex method for linear

Table 7.20 Stepping-Stone Path Associated with the Incoming Cell in Row 1 and Column 3

	v_j			
u_i	3	6	8	**Supply**
0	[3] 5	− [6] 55	[7]	60
−1	[8]	+ [5] 0	− [7] 30	30
1	[4] 30	[9]	[11]	30
Demand	35	55	30	

Table 7.21 Optimal Solution to a Problem with a Degenerate Initial Feasible Solution

	v_j			
u_i	3	6	7	**Supply**
0	[3] 5	[6] 25	[7] 30	60
−1	[8] (6)	[5] 30	[7] (1)	30
1	[4] 30	[9] (2)	[11] (3)	30
Demand	35	55	30	

programming that takes advantage of the special mathematical structure of the transportation problem; but because of the special structure, the transportation Simplex method is hundreds of times faster than the general Simplex method.

Try part (b) of Problem 15 for practise using the transportation simplex method.

To apply the transportation Simplex method, you must have a transportation problem with total supply equal to total demand; so, for some problems you may need to add a dummy origin or dummy destination to put the problem in this form. The transportation Simplex method takes the problem in this form and applies a two-phase solution procedure. In phase I, apply the minimum cost method to find an initial feasible solution. In phase II, begin with the initial feasible solution and iterate until you reach an optimal solution. The steps of the transportation Simplex method for a minimization problem are summarized as follows.

Phase I Find an initial feasible solution using the minimum cost method.

Phase II

Step 1. If the initial feasible solution is degenerate with less than $m + n - 1$ occupied cells, add an artificially occupied cell or cells so that $m + n - 1$ occupied cells exist in locations that enable use of the MODI method.

Step 2. Use the MODI method to calculate row indexes, u_i, and column indexes, v_j.

Step 3. Calculate the net evaluation index $e_{ij} = c_{ij} - u_i - v_j$ for each unoccupied cell.

Step 4. If $e_{ij} \geq 0$ for all unoccupied cells, stop; you have reached the minimum cost solution. Otherwise, proceed to step 5.

Step 5. Identify the unoccupied cell with the smallest (most negative) net evaluation index and select it as the incoming cell.

Step 6. Find the stepping-stone path associated with the incoming cell. Label each cell on the stepping-stone path whose flow will increase with a plus sign and each cell whose flow will decrease with a minus sign.

Step 7. Choose as the outgoing cell the minus-sign cell on the stepping-stone path with the smallest flow. If there is a tie, choose any one of the tied cells. The tied cells that are not chosen will be artificially occupied with a flow of zero at the next iteration.

Step 8. Allocate to the incoming cell the amount of flow currently given to the out going cell; make the appropriate adjustments to all cells on the stepping-stone path, and continue with step 2.

Problem Variations

The following problem variations can be handled, with slight adaptations, by the transportation Simplex method:

1. total supply not equal to total demand;
2. maximization objective function;
3. unacceptable routes.

The case where the total supply is not equal to the total demand can be handled easily by the transportation Simplex method if we first introduce a dummy origin or a dummy destination. If total supply is greater than total demand, we introduce a **dummy destination** with demand equal to the excess of supply over demand. Similarly, if total demand is greater than total supply, we introduce a **dummy origin** with supply equal to the excess of demand over supply. In either case, the use of a dummy destination or a dummy origin will equalize total supply and total demand so that we can use the transportation Simplex method. When a dummy destination or origin is present, we assign cost coefficients of zero to every arc into a dummy destination and to every arc out of a dummy origin. The reason is that no shipments will actually be made from a dummy origin or to a dummy destination when the solution is implemented and thus a zero cost per unit is appropriate.

The transportation Simplex method can also be used to solve **maximization problems**. The only modification necessary involves the selection of an incoming cell. Instead of picking the cell with the smallest or most negative e_{ij} value, we pick that cell for which e_{ij} is largest. That is, we pick the cell that will cause the largest increase per unit in the objective function. If $e_{ij} \leq 0$ for all unoccupied cells, we stop; the maximization solution has been reached.

To handle **unacceptable routes** in a minimization problem, infeasible arcs must carry an extremely high cost, denoted M, to keep them out of the solution. Thus, if we have a route (arc) from an origin to a destination that for some reason cannot be used, we simply assign this arc a cost per unit of M, and it will not enter the solution. Unacceptable arcs would be assigned a profit per unit of $-M$ in a maximization problem.

NOTES AND COMMENTS

1. Research devoted to developing efficient special-purpose solution procedures for network problems has shown that the transportation Simplex method is one of the best. It is used in the transportation and assignment modules of The Management Scientist software package. A simple extension of this method also can be used to solve transshipment problems.
2. As we previously noted, each cell in the transportation tableau corresponds to an arc (route) in the network model of the problem and a variable in the linear programming formulation.

Phase II of the transportation Simplex method is thus the same as phase II of the Simplex method for linear programming. At each iteration, one variable is brought into solution and another variable is dropped from solution. The reason the method works so much better for transportation problems is that the special mathematical structure of the constraint equations means that only addition and subtraction operations are necessary. We can implement the entire procedure in a transportation tableau that has one row for each origin and one column for each destination. A simplex tableau for such a problem would require a row for each origin, a row for each destination and a column for each arc; thus, the simplex tableau would be much larger.

7.3 Assignment Problem: The Network Model and a Linear Programming Formulation

The assignment problem arises in a variety of decision-making situations; typical assignment problems involve assigning jobs to machines, people to tasks, sales personnel to sales territories, contracts to bidders and so on. A distinguishing feature of the assignment problem is that *one* person is assigned to *one and only one* task. Specifically, we look for the set of assignments that will optimize a stated objective, such as minimize cost, minimize time or maximize profit.

To illustrate the assignment problem, let us consider the case of Fowle Marketing Research, which has just received requests for market research studies from three new clients. The company faces the task of assigning a project leader (agent) to each client (task). Currently, three individuals are available for the project leader assignments. Fowle's management realizes, however, that the time required to complete each study will depend on the experience and ability of the project leader assigned. The three projects have approximately the same priority, and the company wants to assign project leaders to minimize the total number of days required to complete all three projects. If a project leader is to be assigned to one client only, what assignments should be made?

D. F. Votaw and Alex Orden presented their paper 'The personnel assignment problem' at a symposium in Washington DC in 1957 considered to be the first Mathematical Programming Symposium.

To answer the assignment question, Fowle's management must first consider all possible project leader–client assignments and then estimate the corresponding project completion times. With three project leaders and three clients, nine assignment alternatives are possible. The alternatives and the estimated project completion times in days are summarized in Table 7.22.

Figure 7.4 shows the network representation of Fowle's assignment problem. The nodes correspond to the project leaders and clients, and the arcs represent the possible assignments of project leaders to clients. The supply at each origin node and the demand at each destination node are 1; the cost of assigning a project leader to a client is the time it takes that project leader to complete the client's task. Note

Table 7.22 Estimated Project Completion Times (Days) for the Fowle Marketing Research Assignment Problem

	Client		
Project Leader	1	2	3
1. Terry	10	15	9
2. Karl	9	18	5
3. Mustafa	6	14	3

Figure 7.4 A Network Model of the Fowle Marketing Research Assignment Problem

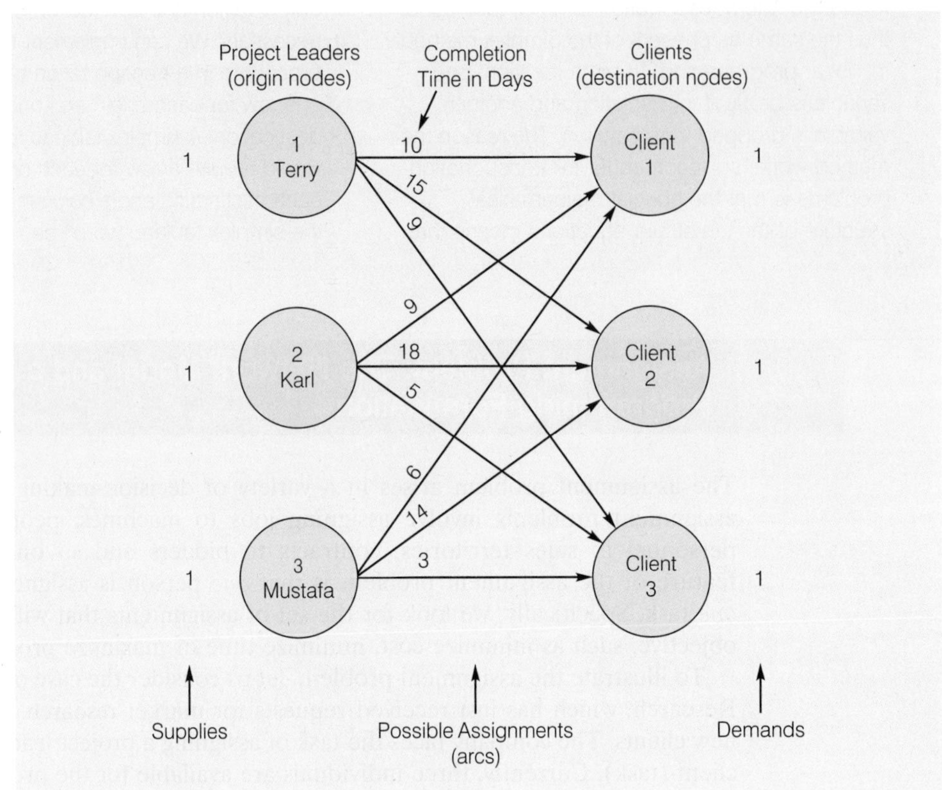

the similarity between the network models of the assignment problem (Figure 7.4) and the transportation problem (Figure 7.1). The assignment problem is a special case of the transportation problem in which all supply and demand values equal 1 and the amount shipped over each arc is either 0 or 1.

Try part (a) of Problem 9 for practise in developing a network model for an assignment problem.

Because the assignment problem is a special case of the transportation problem, a linear programming formulation can be developed. Again, we need a constraint for each node and a variable for each arc. As in the transportation problem, we use double-subscripted decision variables, with x_{11} denoting the assignment of project leader 1 (Terry) to client 1, x_{12} denoting the assignment of project leader 1 (Terry) to client 2 and so on. So, we define the decision variables for Fowle's assignment problem as:

$$x_{ij} = \begin{cases} 1 & \text{if project leader } i \text{ is assigned to client } j \\ 0 & \text{if otherwise} \end{cases}$$

where $i = 1, 2, 3;\ j = 1, 2, 3$

Using this notation and the completion time data in Table 7.22, we develop completion time expressions:

$$\begin{aligned} \text{Days required for Terry's assignment} &= 10x_{11} + 15x_{12} + 9x_{13} \\ \text{Days required for Karl's assignment} &= 9x_{21} + 18x_{22} + 5x_{23} \\ \text{Days required for Mustafa's assignment} &= 6x_{31} + 14x_{32} + 3x_{33} \end{aligned}$$

The sum of the completion times for the three project leaders will provide the total days required to complete the three assignments. Thus, the objective function is:

$$\text{Min} \quad 10x_{11} + 15x_{12} + 9x_{13} + 9x_{21} + 18x_{22} + 5x_{23} + 6x_{31} + 14x_{32} + 3x_{33}$$

The constraints for the assignment problem reflect the conditions that each project leader can be assigned to at most one client and that each client must have one assigned project leader. These constraints are written as follows:

Because the number of project leaders equals the number of clients, all the constraints could be written as equalities. But when the number of project leaders exceeds the number of clients, less-than-or-equal-to constraints must be used for the project leader constraints.

$$
\begin{aligned}
x_{11} + x_{12} + x_{13} &\le 1 \quad \text{Terry's assignment} \\
x_{21} + x_{22} + x_{23} &\le 1 \quad \text{Karl's assignment} \\
x_{31} + x_{32} + x_{33} &\le 1 \quad \text{Mustafa's assignment} \\
x_{11} + x_{21} + x_{31} &= 1 \quad \text{Client 1} \\
x_{12} + x_{22} + x_{32} &= 1 \quad \text{Client 2} \\
x_{13} + x_{23} + x_{33} &= 1 \quad \text{Client 3}
\end{aligned}
$$

Note that one constraint matches up with each node in Figure 7.4.

Combining the objective function and constraints into one model provides the following nine-variable, six-constraint linear programming model of the Fowle Marketing Research assignment problem.

$$
\begin{aligned}
\text{Min} \quad & 10x_{11} + 15x_{12} + 9x_{13} + 9x_{21} + 18x_{22} + 5x_{23} + 6x_{31} + 14x_{32} + 3x_{33} \\
\text{s.t.} \quad & \\
& x_{11} + x_{12} + x_{13} \le 1 \\
& x_{21} + x_{22} + x_{23} \le 1 \\
& x_{31} + x_{32} + x_{33} \le 1 \\
& x_{11} + x_{21} + x_{31} = 1 \\
& x_{12} + x_{22} + x_{32} = 1 \\
& x_{13} + x_{23} + x_{33} = 1 \\
& x_{ij} \ge 0 \quad \text{for } i = 1, 2, 3;\ j = 1, 2, 3
\end{aligned}
$$

Can you formulate and solve a linear programming model for an assignment problem? Try part (b) of Problem 9.

Figure 7.5 shows the computer solution for this model. Terry is assigned to client 2 ($x_{12} = 1$), Karl is assigned to client 3 ($x_{23} = 1$) and Mustafa is assigned to client 1 ($x_{31} = 1$). The total completion time required is 26 days. This solution is summarized in Table 7.23.

Problem Variations

Because the assignment problem can be viewed as a special case of the transportation problem, the problem variations that may arise in an assignment

Figure 7.5 The Excel Solution for the Fowle Marketing Research Assignment Problem

EXCEL *file* FOWLE

Objective Function Value = 26.000

Variable	Value	Reduced Costs
X11	0.000	0.000
X12	1.000	0.000
X13	0.000	3.000
X21	0.000	0.000
X22	0.000	4.000
X23	1.000	0.000
X31	1.000	0.000
X32	0.000	3.000
X33	0.000	1.000

Table 7.23 Optimal Project Leader Assignments for the Fowle Marketing Research Problem

Project Leader	Assigned Client	Days
Terry	2	15
Karl	3	5
Mustafa	1	6
		Total 26

problem parallel those for the transportation problem. Specifically, we can handle the following:

1 total number of people (supply) not equal to the total number of tasks (demand);

2 a maximization objective function;

3 unacceptable assignments.

The situation in which the number of people does not equal the number of tasks is analogous to total supply not equalling total demand in a transportation problem. If the number of people exceeds the number of tasks, the extra people simply remain unassigned in the linear programming model. If the number of tasks exceeds the number of people, the linear programming model will not have a feasible solution. In this situation, a simple modification is to add enough dummy people to equalize the number of people and the number of tasks. For instance, in the Fowle problem we might have had five clients (tasks) and only three project leaders. By adding two dummy project leaders, we can create a new assignment problem with the number of project leaders equal to the number of clients. The objective function coefficients for the assignment of dummy project leaders would be zero so that the value of the optimal solution would represent the total number of days required by the assignments actually made (no assignments will actually be made to the clients receiving dummy project leaders).

If the assignment alternatives are evaluated in terms of revenue or profit rather than time or cost, the linear programming formulation can be solved as a maximization rather than a minimization problem. In addition, if one or more assignments are unacceptable, the corresponding decision variable can be removed from the linear programming formulation. This scenario could happen, for example, if one person did not have the experience necessary for one or more of the tasks.

A General Linear Programming Model of the Assignment Problem

The general assignment problem involves m people and n tasks. If we let $x_{ij} = 1$ or 0 according to whether person i is assigned to task j, and if c_{ij} denotes the cost of assigning person i to task j, we can write the general assignment model as:

$$\text{Min} \quad \sum_{i=1}^{m}\sum_{j=1}^{n} c_{ij}x_{ij}$$

s.t.

$$\sum_{j=1}^{n} x_{ij} \leq 1 \qquad i = 1, 2, \ldots, m \quad \text{People}$$

$$\sum_{i=1}^{m} x_{ij} = 1 \qquad j = 1, 2, \ldots, n \quad \text{Tasks}$$

$$x_{ij} \geq 0 \qquad \text{for all } i \text{ and } j$$

Multiple Assignments

If some tasks require more than one person, the linear programming formulation can also accommodate the situation. Use the number of people required as the right-hand side of the appropriate task constraint.

At the beginning of this section, we indicated that a distinguishing feature of the assignment problem is that *one* person is assigned to *one and only one* task. In generalizations of the assignment problem where one person can be assigned to two or more tasks, the linear programming formulation of the problem can be easily modified. For example, let us assume that in the Fowle Marketing Research problem Terry could be assigned up to two clients; in this case, the constraint representing Terry's assignment would be $x_{11} + x_{12} + x_{13} \leq 2$. In general, if a_i denotes the upper limit for the number of tasks to which person i can be assigned, we write the people constraints as:

$$\sum_{j=1}^{n} x_{ij} \leq a_i \quad i = 1, 2, \ldots, m$$

Thus, we see that one advantage of formulating and solving assignment problems as linear programmes is that special cases such as the situation involving multiple assignments can be easily handled.

NOTES AND COMMENTS

1 As noted, the assignment model is a special case of the transportation model. We stated in the notes and comments at the end of the preceding section that the optimal solution to the transportation problem will consist of integer values for the decision variables as long as the supplies and demands are integers. For the assignment problem, all supplies and demands equal 1; so, the optimal solution must be integer valued and the integer values must be 0 or 1.

2 Combining the method for handling multiple assignments with the notion of a dummy person provides another means of dealing with situations when the number of tasks exceeds the number of people. That is, we add one dummy person, but provide the dummy person with the capability to handle multiple tasks. The number of tasks the dummy person can handle is equal to the difference between the number of tasks and the number of people.

3 The *Management Science in Action*, Heery International, describes how managers are assigned to construction projects. The application involves multiple assignments.

7.4 Assignment Problem: A Special-Purpose Solution Procedure

The Hungarian method was invented and published by Harold Kuhn, a US mathematician, in 1955. Kuhn gave the algorithm its name to reflect the fact that his work was largely based on the earlier works of two Hungarian mathematicians: Dénes König and Jenő Egerváry.

As mentioned previously, the assignment problem is a special case of the transportation problem. So, the transportation Simplex method can be used to solve the assignment problem. However, the assignment problem has an even more special structure: all supplies and demands equal 1. Because of this additional special structure, special-purpose solution procedures have been specifically designed to solve the assignment problem; one such procedure is called the **Hungarian method**. In this section we will show how the Hungarian method can be used to solve the Fowle Marketing Research problem.

Recall that the Fowle problem (see Section 7.3) involved assigning project leaders to clients; three project leaders were available and three research projects were to be

MANAGEMENT SCIENCE IN ACTION

Heery International

Heery International contracts with the State of Tennessee and others for a variety of construction projects including higher education facilities, hotels and park facilities. At any particular time, Heery typically has more than 100 ongoing projects. Each of these projects must be assigned a single manager. With seven managers available, it means that more than 700 = 7(100) assignments are possible. Assisted by an outside consultant, Heery International has developed a mathematical model for assigning construction managers to projects.

The assignment problem developed by Heery uses 0/1 decision variables for each manager/project pair, just as in the assignment problem discussed previously. The goal in assigning managers is to balance the workload among managers and, at the same time, to minimize travel cost from the manager's home to the construction site. Thus, an objective function coefficient for each possible assignment was developed that combined project intensity (a function of the size of the project budget) with the travel distance from the manager's home to the construction site. The objective function calls for minimizing the sum over all possible assignments of the product of these coefficients with the assignment variables.

With more construction projects than managers, it was necessary to consider a variation of the standard assignment problem involving multiple assignments. Of the two sets of constraints, one set enforces the requirement that each project receive one and only one manager. The other set of constraints limits the number of assignments each manager can accept by placing an upper bound on the total intensity that is acceptable over all projects assigned.

Heery International has implemented this assignment model with considerable success. According to Emory F. Redden, a Heery vice president, 'The optimization model... has been very helpful for assigning managers to projects.... We have been satisfied with the assignments chosen at the Nashville office.... We look forward to using the model in our Atlanta office and elsewhere in the Heery organization'.

Based on Larry J. LeBlanc, Dale Randels, Jr., and T.K. Swann, 'Heery International's Spreadsheet Optimization Model for Assigning Managers to Construction Projects', *Interfaces* (November/December 2000): 95–106.

completed for three clients. Fowle's assignment alternatives and estimated project completion times in days are restated in Table 7.24.

The Hungarian method involves what is called *matrix reduction*. Subtracting and adding appropriate values in the matrix yields an optimal solution to the assignment problem. Three major steps are associated with the procedure. Step 1 involves row and column reduction.

Step 1. Reduce the initial matrix by subtracting the smallest element in each row from every element in that row. Then, using this row-reduced matrix, subtract the smallest element in each column from every element in that column.

So, we first reduce the matrix in Table 7.24 by subtracting the minimum value in each row from each element in the row. With the minimum values of 9 for row 1, 5 for row 2 and 3 for row 3, the row-reduced matrix becomes:

	1	2	3
Terry	1	6	0
Karl	4	13	0
Mustafa	3	11	0

Table 7.24 Estimated Project Completion Times (Days) for the Fowle Assignment Problem

	Client		
Project Leader	**1**	**2**	**3**
Terry	10	15	9
Karl	9	18	5
Mustafa	6	14	3

The assignment problem represented by this reduced matrix is equivalent to the original assignment problem in the sense that the same solution will be optimal. To understand why, first note that the row 1 minimum element, 9, has been subtracted from every element in the first row. Terry must still be assigned to one of the clients, so the only change is that in this revised problem the time for any assignment will be nine days less. Similarly, Karl and Mustafa are shown with completion times requiring five and three fewer days, respectively.

Continuing with step 1 in the matrix reduction process, we now subtract the minimum element in each column of the row-reduced matrix from every element in the column. This operation also leads to an equivalent assignment problem; that is, the same solution will still be optimal, but the times required to complete each project are reduced. With the minimum values of 1 for column 1, 6 for column 2 and 0 for column 3, the reduced matrix becomes:

	1	2	3
Terry	0	0	0
Karl	3	7	0
Mustafa	2	5	0

The goal of the Hungarian method is to continue reducing the matrix until the value of one of the solutions is zero – that is, until an assignment of project leaders to clients can be made that, in terms of the reduced matrix, requires a total time expenditure of zero days. Then, as long as there are no negative elements in the matrix, the zero-valued solution will be optimal. The way in which we perform this further reduction and recognize when we have reached an optimal solution is described in the following two steps.

Step 2. Find the minimum number of straight lines that must be drawn through the rows and the columns of the current matrix so that all the zeros in the matrix will be covered. If the minimum number of straight lines is the same as the number of rows (or equivalently, columns), an optimal assignment with a value of zero can be made. If the minimum number of lines is less than the number of rows, go to step 3.

Applying step 2, we see that the minimum number of lines required to cover all the zeros is 2. So, we must continue to step 3.

	1	2	3	
Terry	0	0	0	Two straight lines will cover all the zeros (step 2)
Karl	3	7	0	
Mustafa	2	5	0	

Step 3. Subtract the value of the smallest unlined element from every unlined element, and add this same value to every element at the intersection of two lines. All other elements remain unchanged. Return to step 2, and continue until the minimum number of lines necessary to cover all the zeros in the matrix is equal to the number of rows.

The minimum unlined element is 2. In the preceding matrix we circled this element. Subtracting 2 from all unlined elements and adding 2 to the intersection element for Terry and client 3 produces the new matrix:

	1	2	3
Terry	0	0	2
Karl	1	5	0
Mustafa	0	3	0

Returning to step 2, we find that the minimum number of straight lines required to cover all the zeros in the current matrix is 3. The following matrix illustrates the step 2 calculations.

	1	2	3	
Terry	0	0	2	Three lines must be drawn to cover all zeros; therefore,
Karl	1	5	0	the optimal solution has been reached (the number of
Mustafa	0	3	0	lines is the same as the number of rows)

According to step 2, then, it must be possible to find an assignment with a value of zero. To do so we first locate any row or column that contains only one zero. If all have more than one zero, we choose the row or column with the fewest zeros. We draw a square around a zero in the chosen row or column, indicating an assignment, and eliminate that row and column from further consideration. Row 2 has only one zero in the Fowle problem, so we assign Karl to client 3 and eliminate row 2 and column 3 from further consideration. Mustafa must then be assigned to client 1 (the only remaining zero in row 3) and, finally, Terry to client 2. The solution to the Fowle problem, in terms of the reduced matrix, requires a time expenditure of zero days, as follows:

	1	2	3
Terry	0	[0]	2
Karl	1	5	[0]
Mustafa	[0]	3	0

We obtain the value of the optimal assignment by referring to the original assignment problem and summing the solution times associated with the optimal assignment – in this case, 15 for Terry to client 2, 5 for Karl to client 3 and 6 for Mustafa to client 1. So, we obtain the solution time of $15 + 5 + 6 = 26$ days.

Finding the Minimum Number of Lines

Sometimes it is not obvious how the lines should be drawn through rows and columns of the matrix in order to cover all the zeros with the smallest number of lines. In these cases, the following heuristic works well. Choose any row or column with a single zero. If it is a row, draw a line through the column the zero is in; if it is a column, draw a line through the row the zero is in. Continue in this fashion until you cover all the zeros.

Can you solve an assignment problem using the Hungarian method? Try Problem 19.

If you make the mistake of drawing too many lines to cover the zeros in the reduced matrix and thus conclude incorrectly that you have reached an optimal solution, you will be unable to identify a zero-value assignment. So, if you think you have reached the optimal solution, but cannot find a set of zero-value assignments, go back to the preceding step and check to see whether you can cover all the zeros with fewer lines.

Problem Variations

We now discuss how to handle the following problem variations with the Hungarian method:

1 number of people not equal to number of tasks;
2 maximization objective function;
3 unacceptable assignments.

Number of People Not Equal to Number of Tasks The Hungarian method requires that the number of rows (people) equal the number of columns (tasks). Suppose that in the Fowle problem four project leaders had been available for assignment to the three new clients (tasks). Fowle still faces the same basic problem, namely, which project leaders should be assigned to which clients to minimize the total days required. Table 7.25 shows the project completion time estimates with a fourth project leader.

We know how to apply the Hungarian method when the number of rows and the number of columns are equal. We can apply the same procedure if we can add a new client. If we do not have another client, we simply add a *dummy column*, or a dummy client. This dummy client is nonexistent, so the project leader assigned to the dummy client in the optimal assignment solution, in effect, will be the unassigned project leader.

Table 7.25 Estimated Project Completion Time (Days) for the Fowle Assignment Problem with Four Project Leaders

	Client		
Project Leader	**1**	**2**	**3**
Terry	10	15	9
Karl	9	18	5
Mustafa	6	14	3
Helen	8	16	6

Table 7.26 Estimated Project Completion Time (Days) for the Fowle Assignment Problem with a Dummy Client

	Client			Dummy client
Project Leader	**1**	**2**	**3**	**D**
Terry	10	15	9	0
Karl	9	18	5	0
Mustafa	6	14	3	0
Helen	8	16	6	0

What project completion time estimates should we show in this new dummy column? The dummy client assignment will not actually take place, which means that a zero project completion time for all project leaders seems logical. Table 7.26 shows the Fowle assignment problem with a dummy client, labelled D.

Note that if we had considered the case of four new clients and only three project leaders, we would have had to add a *dummy row* (dummy project leader) in order to apply the Hungarian method. The client receiving the dummy leader would not actually be assigned a project leader immediately and would have to wait until one becomes available. To obtain a problem form compatible with the solution algorithm, adding several dummy rows or dummy columns, but never both, may be necessary.

Maximization Objective To illustrate how maximization assignment problems can be handled, let us consider the problem facing management of Salisbury Discounts which has just leased a new store and is attempting to determine where various departments should be located within the store. The store manager has four locations that have not yet been assigned a department and is considering five departments that might occupy the four locations. The departments under consideration are shoes, toys, auto parts, housewares and DVDs. After a careful study of the layout of the remainder of the store, the store manager has made estimates of the expected daily profit for each department in each location. These estimates are presented in Table 7.27.

This assignment problem requires a maximization objective. However, the problem also involves more rows than columns. So, we must first add a dummy column, corresponding to a dummy or fictitious location, in order to apply the Hungarian

Table 7.27 Estimated Daily Profit (€1000s) for Each Department-Location Combination

	Location			
Department	**1**	**2**	**3**	**4**
Shoe	10	6	12	8
Toy	15	18	5	11
Auto parts	17	10	13	16
Housewares	14	12	13	10
DVDs	14	16	6	12

Table 7.28 Estimated Daily Profit (€1000s) for Each Department-Location Combination, Including a Dummy Location

	Location				
Department	**1**	**2**	**3**	**4**	**5** (Dummy location)
Shoe	10	6	12	8	0
Toy	15	18	5	11	0
Auto parts	17	10	13	16	0
Housewares	14	12	13	10	0
DVDs	14	16	6	12	0

method. After adding a dummy column, we obtain the 5 × 5 Salisbury Discounts, assignment problem shown in Table 7.28.

We can obtain an equivalent minimization assignment problem by converting all the elements in the matrix to **opportunity losses**. We do so by subtracting every element in each column from the largest element in the column. Finding the assignment that minimizes opportunity loss leads to the same solution that maximizes the value of the assignment in the original problem. So, any maximization assignment problem can be converted to a minimization problem by converting the assignment matrix to one in which the elements represent opportunity losses. Hence, we begin the solution to this maximization assignment problem by developing an assignment matrix in which each element represents the opportunity loss for not making the 'best' assignment. Table 7.29 presents the opportunity losses.

The opportunity loss from putting the shoe department in location 1 is €7000. That is, if we put the shoe department, instead of the best department (auto parts), in that location, we lose the opportunity to make an additional €7000 in profit. The opportunity loss associated with putting the toy department in location 2 is zero because it yields the highest profit in that location. What about the opportunity losses associated with the dummy column? The assignment of a department to this dummy location means that the department will not be assigned a store location in the optimal solution. All departments earn the same amount from this dummy location, zero, making the opportunity loss for each department zero.

Try Problem 20 for practise in using the Hungarian method for a maximization problem.

Using steps 1, 2 and 3 of the Hungarian method on Table 7.29 will minimize opportunity loss and determine the maximum profit assignment.

Table 7.29 Opportunity Loss (€1000s) for Each Department-Location Combination

	Location				
Department	**1**	**2**	**3**	**4**	**5** (Dummy location)
Shoe	7	12	1	8	0
Toy	2	0	8	5	0
Auto parts	0	8	0	0	0
Housewares	3	6	0	6	0
DVDs	3	2	7	4	0

Table 7.30 Estimated Profit for the Salisbury Department-Location Combinations

	Location				
Department	1	2	3	4	5
Shoe	10	6	12	8	0
Toy	15	$-M$	5	11	0
Auto parts	17	10	13	$-M$	0
Housewares	14	12	13	10	0
Video	14	16	6	12	0

Unacceptable Assignments As an illustration of how we can handle unacceptable assignments, suppose that in the Salisbury Discounts assignment problem the store manager believed that the toy department should not be considered for location 2 and that the auto parts department should not be considered for location 4. Essentially the store manager is saying that, based on other considerations, such as size of the area, adjacent departments and so on, these two assignments are unacceptable alternatives.

Using the same approach for the assignment problem as we did for the transportation problem, we define a value of M for unacceptable minimization assignments and a value of $-M$ for unacceptable maximization assignments, where M is an arbitrarily large value. In fact, we assume M to be so large that M plus or minus any value is still extremely large. So, an M-valued cell in an assignment matrix retains its M value throughout the matrix reduction calculations. An M-valued cell can never be zero, so it can never be an assignment in the final solution.

The Salisbury Discounts assignment problem with the two unacceptable assignments is shown in Table 7.30. When this assignment matrix is converted to an opportunity loss matrix, the $-M$ profit value will be changed to M.

7.5 Transshipment Problem: The Network Model and a Linear Programming Formulation

The **transshipment problem** is an extension of the transportation problem in which intermediate nodes, referred to as *transshipment nodes*, are added to account for locations such as warehouses. In this more general type of distribution problem, shipments may be made between any pair of the three general types of nodes: origin nodes, transshipment nodes and destination nodes. For example, the transshipment problem permits shipments of goods from origins to transshipment nodes and on to destinations, from one origin to another origin, from one transshipment location to another, from one destination location to another and directly from origins to destinations.

As was true for the transportation problem, the supply available at each origin is limited and the demand at each destination is specified. The objective in the transshipment problem is to determine how many units should be shipped over each arc in the network so that all destination demands are satisfied with the minimum possible transportation cost.

We shall use the following scenario. Ryan Pharmaceuticals manufactures specialist medical supplies and has facilities just outside Geneva and also in Stockholm. It is currently reviewing its supply activities to the UK's National Health Service (NHS). The

Table 7.31 Transportation Costs Per Unit for the Ryan Transshipment Problem, £s per unit

	Warehouse			
Plant	**London**	**Glasgow**		
Geneva	2	3		
Stockholm	3	1		
	Hospital			
Warehouse	**Edinburgh**	**Manchester**	**Southampton**	**Newcastle**
London	2	6	3	6
Glasgow	4	4	6	5

medical supplies that Ryan provides to the NHS are first transported to two regional warehouses, one in London and one in Glasgow. From there, supplies are then shipped as needed to specialist hospitals and clinics in Edinburgh, Manchester, Southampton and Newcastle. The transportation cost per unit for each distribution route is shown in Table 7.31. The key features of the problem are shown in the network model in Figure 7.6. Note that the supply at each origin and demand at each destination are shown in the left and right margins, respectively. Nodes 1 and 2 are the origin nodes; nodes 3 and 4 are the transshipment nodes; and nodes 5, 6, 7 and 8 are the destination nodes.

Try part (a) of Problem 11 for practise in developing a network representation of a transshipment problem.

As with the transportation and assignment problems, we can formulate a linear programming model of the transshipment problem from a network representation. Again, we need a constraint for each node and a variable for each arc. Let x_{ij} denote the number of units shipped from node i to node j. For example, x_{13} denotes the number of units shipped from the Geneva plant to the London warehouse, x_{14} denotes the number of units shipped from the Geneva plant to the Glasgow warehouse and so on. If the supply at the Geneva plant is 600 units, the amount shipped from the Geneva plant must be less than or equal to 600. Mathematically, we write this supply constraint as:

$$x_{13} + x_{14} \leq 600$$

Similarly, for the Stockholm plant we have:

$$x_{23} + x_{24} \leq 400$$

We now consider how to write the constraints corresponding to the two transshipment nodes. For node 3 (the London warehouse), we must guarantee that the number of units shipped out must equal the number of units shipped into the warehouse. Because:

$$\text{Number of units shipped out of node 3} = x_{35} + x_{36} + x_{37} + x_{38}$$

and

$$\text{Number of units shipped into node 3} = x_{13} + x_{23}$$

we obtain

$$x_{35} + x_{36} + x_{37} + x_{38} = x_{13} + x_{23}$$

Figure 7.6 Network Representation of The NHS Transshipment Problem

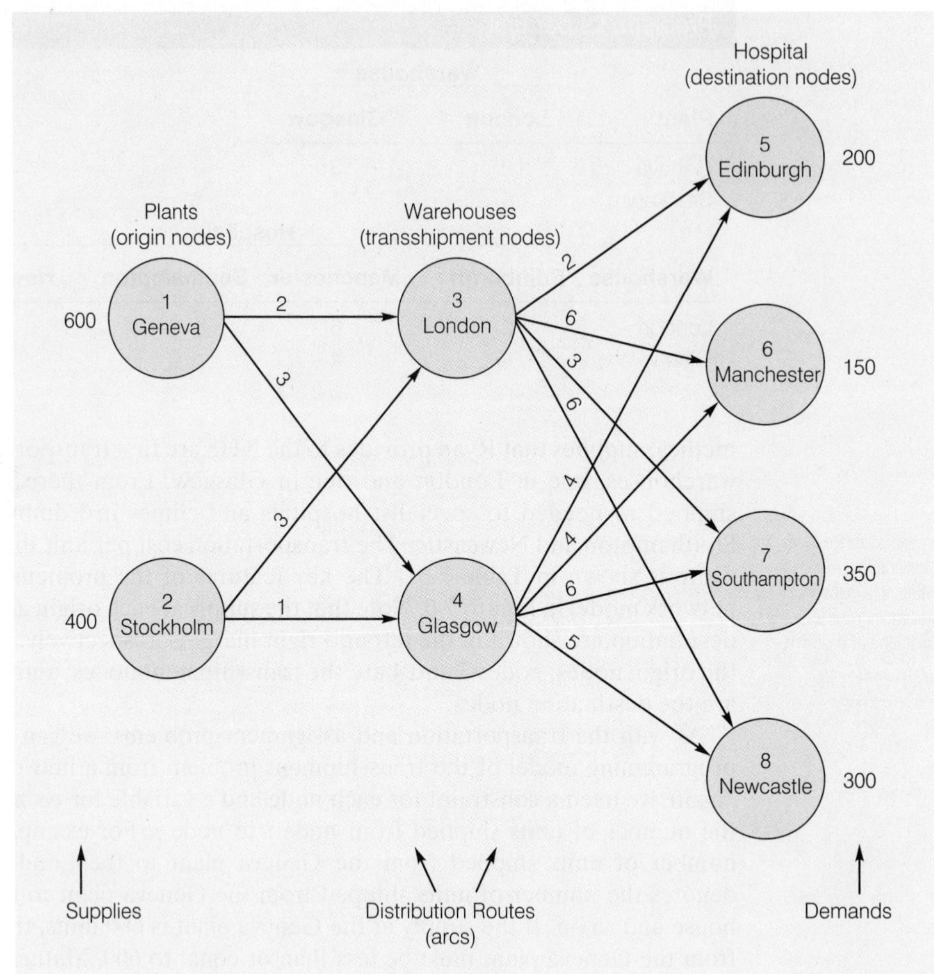

Placing all the variables on the left-hand side provides the constraint corresponding to node 3 as:

$$-x_{13} - x_{23} + x_{35} + x_{36} + x_{37} + x_{38} = 0$$

Similarly, the constraint corresponding to node 4 is:

$$-x_{14} - x_{24} + x_{45} + x_{46} + x_{47} + x_{48} = 0$$

To develop the constraints associated with the destination nodes, we recognize that for each node the amount shipped to the destination must equal the demand. For example, to satisfy the demand for 200 units at node 5 (the Edinburgh hospital), we write:

$$x_{35} + x_{45} = 200$$

Similarly, for nodes 6, 7 and 8, we have:

$$x_{36} + x_{46} = 150$$
$$x_{37} + x_{47} = 350$$
$$x_{38} + x_{48} = 300$$

Figure 7.7 Linear Programming Formulation of the NHS Transshipment Problem

$$\begin{aligned}
\text{Min } & 2x_{13} + 3x_{14} + 3x_{23} + 1x_{24} + 2x_{35} + 6x_{36} + 3x_{37} + 6x_{38} + 4x_{45} + 4x_{46} + 6x_{47} + 5x_{48} \\
\text{s.t.} & \\
& x_{13} + x_{14} \le 600 \\
& x_{23} + x_{24} \le 400 \\
& -x_{13} - x_{23} + x_{35} + x_{36} + x_{37} + x_{38} = 0 \\
& -x_{14} - x_{24} + x_{45} + x_{46} + x_{47} + x_{48} = 0 \\
& x_{35} + x_{45} = 200 \\
& x_{36} + x_{46} = 150 \\
& x_{37} + x_{47} = 350 \\
& x_{38} + x_{48} = 300 \\
& x_{ij} \ge 0 \text{ for all } i \text{ and } j
\end{aligned}$$

(First two constraints: Origin node constraints; next two: Transshipment node constraints; last four: Destination node constraints.)

Try part (b) of Problem 11 for practise in developing the linear programming model and solving a transshipment problem.

As usual, the objective function reflects the total shipping cost over the 12 shipping routes. Combining the objective function and constraints leads to a 12-variable, eight-constraint linear programming model of the NHS transshipment problem (see Figure 7.7). We used Excel to obtain the optimal solution. Figure 7.8 shows the computer output, and Table 7.32 summarizes the optimal solution.

As mentioned at the beginning of this section, in the transshipment problem arcs may connect any pair of nodes. All such shipping patterns are possible in a transshipment problem. We still require only one constraint per node, but the constraint must include a variable for every arc entering or leaving the node. For origin nodes, the sum of the shipments out minus the sum of the shipments in must be less than or equal to the origin supply. For destination nodes, the sum of the shipments in minus the sum of the shipments out must equal demand. For transshipment nodes, the sum of the shipments out must equal the sum of the shipments in, as before.

For an illustration of this more general type of transshipment problem, let us modify the NHS problem. Suppose that it is now possible to ship directly from Stockholm to Newcastle at £4 per unit and from Southampton to Newcastle at £1 per unit. The network model corresponding to this modified problem is shown in Figure 7.9, the linear programming formulation is shown in Figure 7.10 and the computer solution is shown in Figure 7.11.

Figure 7.8 Excel Solution for The NHS Transshipment Problem

EXCEL *file*

NHS

```
Objective Function Value =            5200.000

      Variable              Value              Reduced Costs
   --------------     ---------------     -----------------
        X13                550.000                 0.000
        X14                 50.000                 0.000
        X23                  0.000                 3.000
        X24                400.000                 0.000
        X35                200.000                 0.000
        X36                  0.000                 1.000
        X37                350.000                 0.000
        X38                  0.000                 0.000
        X45                  0.000                 3.000
        X46                150.000                 0.000
        X47                  0.000                 4.000
        X48                300.000                 0.000
```

Table 7.32 Optimal Solution to the NHS Transshipment Problem

Route				
From	**To**	**Units Shipped**	**Cost per Unit, £**	**Total Cost, £**
Geneva	London	550	2	1 100
Geneva	Glasgow	50	3	150
Stockholm	Glasgow	400	1	400
London	Edinburgh	200	2	400
London	Southampton	350	3	1 050
Glasgow	Manchester	150	4	600
Glasgow	Newcastle	300	5	1 500
				£5 200

In Figure 7.9 we added two new arcs to the network model. So, two new variables are necessary in the linear programming formulation. Figure 7.10 shows that the new variables x_{28} and x_{78} appear in the objective function and in the constraints corresponding to the nodes to which the new arcs are connected. Figure 7.11 shows that the value of the optimal solution has been reduced £600 by adding the two new shipping routes; $x_{28} = 250$ units are being shipped directly from Stockholm to Newcastle, and $x_{78} = 50$ units are being shipped from Stockholm to Newcastle.

Figure 7.9 Network Representation of The Modified NHS Transshipment Problem

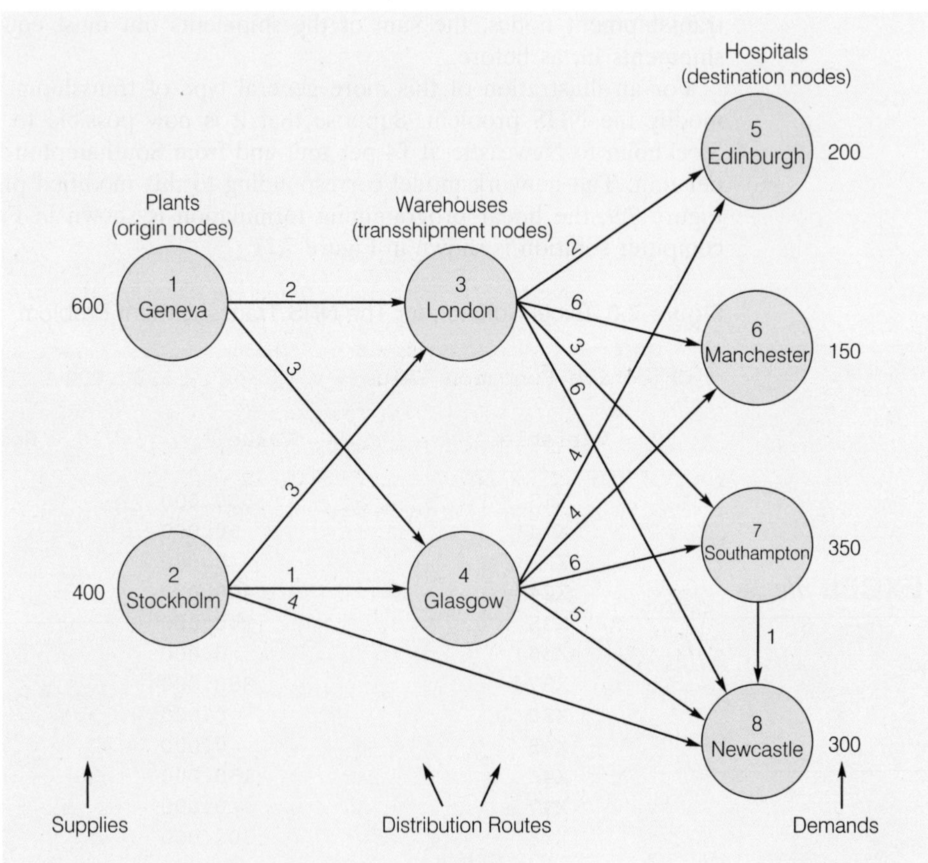

Figure 7.10 Linear Programming Formulation of The Modified NHS Transshipment Problem

$$
\begin{array}{llr}
\text{Min} & 2x_{13} + 3x_{14} + 3x_{23} + 1x_{24} + 2x_{35} + 6x_{36} + 3x_{37} + 6x_{38} + 4x_{45} + 4x_{46} + 6x_{47} + 5x_{48} + 4x_{28} + 1x_{78} & \\
\text{s.t.} & & \\
& x_{13} + x_{14} \le 600 & \text{Origin node constraints} \\
& x_{23} + x_{24} + x_{28} \le 400 & \\
& -x_{13} - x_{23} + x_{35} + x_{36} + x_{37} + x_{38} = 0 & \text{Transshipment node constraints} \\
& -x_{14} - x_{24} + x_{45} + x_{46} + x_{47} + x_{48} = 0 & \\
& x_{35} + x_{45} = 200 & \text{Destination node constraints} \\
& x_{36} + x_{46} = 150 & \\
& x_{37} + x_{47} - x_{78} = 350 & \\
& x_{38} + x_{48} + x_{28} + x_{78} = 300 & \\
& x_{ij} \ge 0 \text{ for all } i \text{ and } j &
\end{array}
$$

Problem Variations

As with transportation and assignment problems, transshipment problems may be formulated with several variations, including the following:

1. total supply not equal to total demand;
2. maximization objective function;
3. route capacities or route minimums;
4. unacceptable routes.

The linear programming model modifications required to accommodate these variations are identical to the modifications required for the transportation problem described in Section 7.1. When we add one or more constraints of the form $x_{ij} \le L_{ij}$ to show that the route from node i to node j has capacity L_{ij}, we refer to the transshipment problem as a capacitated transshipment problem.

Figure 7.11 The Excel Solution for the Modified NHS Transshipment Problem

Objective Function Value = 4600.000

Variable	Value	Reduced Costs
X13	600.000	0.000
X14	0.000	0.000
X23	0.000	3.000
X24	150.000	0.000
X35	200.000	0.000
X36	0.000	1.000
X37	400.000	0.000
X38	0.000	2.000
X45	0.000	3.000
X46	150.000	0.000
X47	0.000	4.000
X48	0.000	2.000
X28	250.000	0.000
X78	50.000	0.000

A General Linear Programming Model of the Transshipment Problem

The general linear programming model of the transshipment problem is:

$$\text{Min} \quad \sum_{\text{all arcs}} c_{ij}x_{ij}$$

s.t.

$$\sum_{\text{arcs out}} x_{ij} - \sum_{\text{arcs in}} x_{ij} \leq s_i \qquad \text{Origin nodes } i$$

$$\sum_{\text{arcs out}} x_{ij} - \sum_{\text{arcs in}} x_{ij} = 0 \qquad \text{Transshipment nodes}$$

$$\sum_{\text{arcs in}} x_{ij} - \sum_{\text{arcs out}} x_{ij} = d_j \qquad \text{Destination nodes } j$$

$$x_{ij} \geq 0 \text{ for all } i \text{ and } j$$

where

x_{ij} = number of units shipped from node i to node j
c_{ij} = cost per unit of shipping from node i to node j
s_i = supply at origin node i
d_j = demand at destination node j

NOTES AND COMMENTS

1 The *Management Science in Action*, Product Sourcing Heuristic at Procter & Gamble, describes how Procter & Gamble used a transshipment model to redesign its North American distribution system.

2 In more advanced treatments of linear programming and network flow problems, the capacitated transshipment problem is called the pure network flow problem. Efficient special-purpose solution procedures are available for network flow problems and their special cases.

3 In the general linear programming formulation of the transshipment problem, the constraints for the destination nodes are often written as:

$$\sum_{\text{arcs out}} x_{ij} - \sum_{\text{arcs in}} x_{ij} = -d_j$$

The advantage of writing the constraints this way is that the left-hand side of each constraint then represents the flow out of the node minus the flow in. But such constraints would then have to be multiplied by −1 to obtain nonnegative right-hand sides before the problem could be solved by many linear programming codes.

7.6 A Production and Inventory Application

The introduction to the transportation and transshipment problems in Sections 7.1 and 7.5 involved applications for the shipment of goods from several supply locations or origins to several demand sites or destinations. Although the shipment of goods is the subject of many transportation and transshipment problems, transportation and/or transshipment models can be developed for applications that have nothing to do with the physical shipment of goods from origins to destinations. In

MANAGEMENT SCIENCE IN ACTION

Product Sourcing Heuristic at Procter & Gamble

A few years ago Procter & Gamble (P&G) embarked on a major strategic planning initiative called the North American Product Sourcing Study. P&G wanted to consolidate its product sources and optimize its distribution system design throughout North America. A decision support system used to aid in this project was called the Product Sourcing Heuristic (PSH) and was based on a transshipment model much like the ones described in this chapter.

In a preprocessing phase, the many P&G products were aggregated into groups that shared the same technology and could be made at the same plant. The PSH employing the transshipment model was then used by product strategy teams responsible for developing product sourcing options for these product groups. The various plants that could produce the product group were the source nodes, the company's regional distribution centres were the transshipment nodes and P&G's customer zones were the destinations. Direct shipments to customer zones as well as shipments through distribution centres were employed.

The product strategy teams used the heuristic interactively to explore a variety of questions concerning product sourcing and distribution. For instance, the team might be interested in the impact of closing two of five plants and consolidating production in the three remaining plants. The Product Sourcing Heuristic would then delete the source nodes corresponding to the two closed plants, make any capacity modifications necessary to the sources corresponding to the remaining three plants and resolve the transshipment problem. The product strategy team could then examine the new solution, make some more modifications, solve again and so on.

The Product Sourcing Heuristic was viewed as a valuable decision support system by all who used it. When P&G implemented the results of the study, it realized annual savings in the $200 million range. The PSH proved so successful in North America that P&G used it in other markets around the world.

Based on information provided by Franz Dill and Tom Chorman of Procter & Gamble.

this section we show how to use a transshipment model to solve a production scheduling and inventory problem.

Contois Carpets is a small manufacturer of carpeting for home and office installations. Production capacity, demand, production cost per square metre and inventory holding cost per square metre for the next four quarters are shown in Table 7.33. Note that production capacity, demand and production costs vary by quarter, whereas the cost of carrying inventory from one quarter to the next is constant at €0.25 per square metre. Contois wants to determine how many square metres of carpeting to manufacture each quarter to minimize the total production and inventory cost for the four-quarter period.

We begin by developing a network representation of the problem. First, we create four nodes corresponding to the production in each quarter and four nodes corresponding to the demand in each quarter. Each production node is connected by an outgoing arc to the demand node for the same period. The flow on the arc represents the number of square metres of carpet manufactured for the period. For each demand node, an outgoing arc represents the amount of inventory (square metres of carpet) carried over to the demand node for the next period. Figure 7.12 shows the network model. Note that nodes 1–4 represent the production for each quarter and that nodes 5–8 represent the demand for each quarter. The quarterly production capacities are shown in the left margin, and the quarterly demands are shown in the right margin.

The fact that the network shows flows into and out of demand nodes is what makes the model a transshipment model.

Table 7.33 Production, Demand and Cost Estimates for Contois Carpets

Quarter	Production Capacity (square metres)	Demand (square metres)	Production Cost (€/ square metre)	Inventory Cost (€/ square metre)
1	600	400	2	0.25
2	300	500	5	0.25
3	500	400	3	0.25
4	400	400	3	0.25

Figure 7.12 Network Representation of the Contois Carpets Problem

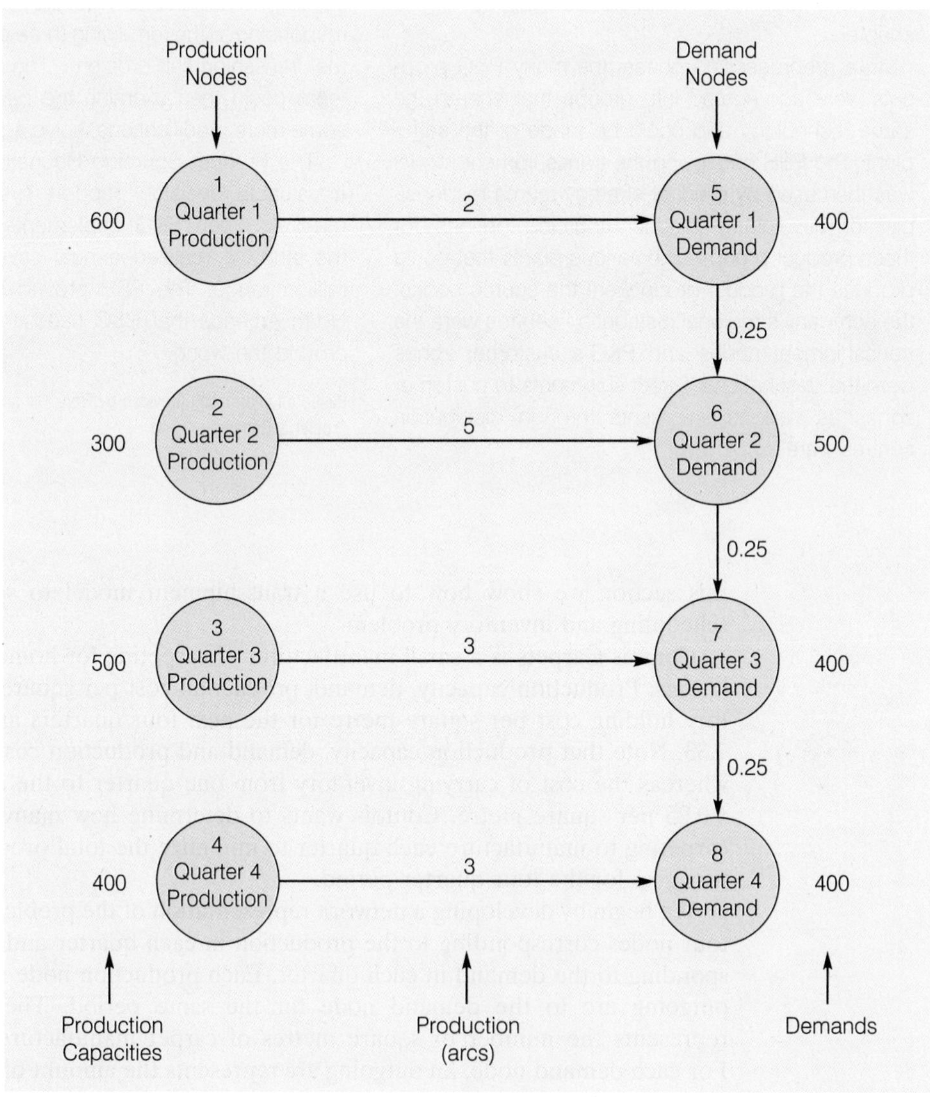

The objective is to determine a production scheduling and inventory policy that will minimize the total production and inventory cost for the four quarters. Constraints involve production capacity and demand in each quarter. As usual, a linear

programming model can be developed from the network by establishing a constraint for each node and a variable for each arc.

Let x_{15} denote the number of square metres of carpet manufactured in quarter 1. The capacity of the facility is 600 square metres in quarter 1, so the production capacity constraint is:

$$x_{15} \leq 600$$

Using similar decision variables, we obtain the production capacities for quarters 2–4:

$$\begin{aligned} x_{26} &\leq 300 \\ x_{37} &\leq 500 \\ x_{48} &\leq 400 \end{aligned}$$

We now consider the development of the constraints for each of the demand nodes. For node 5, one arc enters the node, which represents the number of square metres of carpet produced in quarter 1, and one arc leaves the node, which represents the number of square metres of carpet that will not be sold in quarter 1 and will be carried over for possible sale in quarter 2. In general, for each quarter the beginning inventory plus the production minus the ending inventory must equal demand. However, for quarter 1 there is no beginning inventory; thus, the constraint for node 5 is:

$$x_{15} - x_{56} = 400$$

The constraints associated with the demand nodes in quarters 2, 3 and 4 are:

$$\begin{aligned} x_{56} + x_{26} - x_{67} &= 500 \\ x_{67} + x_{37} - x_{78} &= 400 \\ x_{78} + x_{48} &= 400 \end{aligned}$$

Note that the constraint for node 8 (fourth-quarter demand) involves only two variables because no provision is made for holding inventory for a fifth quarter.

The objective is to minimize total production and inventory cost, so we write the objective function as:

$$\text{Min} \quad 2x_{15} + 5x_{26} + 3x_{37} + 3x_{48} + 0.25x_{56} + 0.25x_{67} + 0.25x_{78}$$

The complete linear programming formulation of the Contois Carpets problem is:

$$\begin{array}{llllllllll}
\text{Min} & 2x_{15} + 5x_{26} + 3x_{37} + 3x_{48} + 0.25x_{56} + 0.25x_{67} + 0.25x_{78} \\
\text{s.t.} \\
& x_{15} & & & & & & & \leq 600 \\
& & x_{26} & & & & & & \leq 300 \\
& & & x_{37} & & & & & \leq 500 \\
& & & & x_{48} & & & & \leq 400 \\
& x_{15} & & & & - x_{56} & & & = 400 \\
& & x_{26} & & & + x_{56} & - x_{67} & & = 500 \\
& & & x_{37} & & & + x_{67} & - x_{78} & = 400 \\
& & & & x_{48} & & & + x_{78} & = 400 \\
& x_{ij} \geq 0 \quad \text{for all } i \text{ and } j
\end{array}$$

Figure 7.13 Excel Solution for the Contois Carpets Problem

EXCEL *file*

Contois

```
Objective Function Value =                    5150.000

      Variable               Value          Reduced Costs
   --------------      ---------------     ----------------
         X15               600.000               0.000
         X26               300.000               0.000
         X37               400.000               0.000
         X48               400.000               0.000
         X56               200.000               0.000
         X67                 0.000               2.250
         X78                 0.000               0.000
```

We used Excel to solve the Contois Carpets problem. Figure 7.13 shows the results: Contois Carpets should manufacture 600 square metres of carpet in quarter 1, 300 square metres in quarter 2, 400 square metres in quarter 3 and 400 square metres in quarter 4. Note also that 200 square metres will be carried over from quarter 1 to quarter 2. The total production and inventory cost is €5150.

NOTES AND COMMENTS

1 Often the same problem can be modelled in different ways. In this section we modelled the Contois Carpets problem as a transshipment problem. It also can be modelled as a transportation problem. In Problem 18 at the end of the chapter, we ask you to develop such a model.

2 In the network model we developed for the transshipment problem, the amount leaving the starting node for an arc is always equal to the amount entering the ending node for that arc. An extension of such a network model is the case where a gain or a loss occurs as an arc is traversed. The amount entering the destination node may be greater or smaller than the amount leaving the origin node. For instance, if cash is the commodity flowing across an arc, the cash earns interest from one period to the next. Thus, the amount of cash entering the next period is greater than the amount leaving the previous period by the amount of interest earned. Networks with gains or losses are treated in more advanced texts on network flow programming.

Summary

- In this chapter we introduced transportation, assignment and transshipment problems.
- All three types of problems belong to the special category of linear programmes called *network flow problems*. The network model of a transportation problem consists of nodes representing a set of origins and a set of destinations. In the basic model, an arc is used to represent the route from each origin to each destination. Each origin has a supply and each destination has a demand. The problem is to determine the optimal amount to ship from each origin to each destination.

- The assignment model is a special case of the transportation model in which all supply and all demand values are equal to 1. We represent each agent as an origin node and each task as a destination node.
- The transshipment model is an extension of the transportation model to distribution problems involving transfer points referred to as transshipment nodes. In this more general model, we allow arcs between any pair of nodes. A variation of the transshipment problem allows for placing capacities on the arcs. This variation, called the capacitated transshipment problem, is also known in the network flow literature as the pure network problem.
- Each of these network flow problems can be modelled as a linear programme, and we solved each using a general-purpose linear programming computer package.
- However, many practical applications of network flow models lead to large problems for which general purpose linear programming codes are not efficient. The transportation Simplex method was presented as an efficient special purpose solution procedure for solving transportation problems. The procedure, and its extension to the transshipment problem, is hundreds of times faster than the general purpose Simplex method for large transportation and transshipment problems. The Hungarian method was presented as a special purpose solution procedure for assignment problems.

WORKED EXAMPLE

An international aid organization routinely transports aid donations to different parts of the world. It is currently reviewing its transportation arrangements from its depots in Europe to its distribution centres in Africa. The organization has three main European depots: Marseille, France; Portsmouth, UK; and Frankfurt, Germany. Aid donations such as clothing and medicines are sent to these depots where volunteers pack them into cases for transportation to the distribution centres. The organization estimates that the packing costs are €2.95 per case in Marseille, €3.10 in Portsmouth and €3.05 in Frankfurt. For the next planning period, the organization estimates that the Marseille depot can pack 400 cases per month, Portsmouth can pack 600 cases per month and Frankfurt 300 cases per month. There are three main regional distribution centres in Africa: Capetown, Dar es Salaam and Nairobi. Each of the distribution centres in Africa has limited capacity to receive the aid donations and then distribute them in their region so care must be taken not to send too many cases to any one centre. The organization has calculated that each centre can cope with up to 400 cases each month. The transportation costs vary depending which depot ships to which distribution centre and the costs are shown below:

Cost per case €

From/To	Capetown	Dar es Salaam	Nairobi
Marseille	1.45	1.60	1.40
Portsmouth	1.10	2.25	0.60
Frankfurt	1.20	1.20	1.80

The aid organization has asked for advice as to how it should organize its transportation of aid over the coming months. In addition, the organization is keen to ensure that all the donations from Marseille are used.

Solution

We have an obvious transportation problem where the organization is looking to minimize costs. The relevant costs are a combination of the packing costs and the transportation costs per case. For example the cost of using the Marseille–Capetown route is €2.95 + €1.45, or €4.40 per case. We also note that supply is greater than demand so we will need a dummy destination. Clearly, we could solve this problem in a number of ways. We shall use the MODI method. We shall also solve the problem initially without worrying that all of Marseille's cases are shipped out. Setting up the transportation tableau and using the minimum cost method to find an initial feasible solution we have:

Initial feasible solution: cases transported

From/To	Capetown	Dar es Salaam	Nairobi	Unused (Dummy)	Supply
Marseille	$200^{4.40}$	$100^{4.55}$	$0^{4.35}$	100	400
Portsmouth	$200^{4.20}$	$0^{5.35}$	$400^{3.70}$	0	600
Frankfurt	$0^{4.25}$	$300^{4.25}$	$0^{4.80}$	0	300
Capacity	400	400	400	100	1 300

The figures in the top right of each cell show the combined cost per case for each route. Because we have a dummy destination, technically their cost coefficients are zero and so we start by allocating cases to one of the dummy cells. So that you can check your own solution, the stages for this solution are:

- 100 cases for Marseille–Dummy. All three dummy cells have the same zero cost coefficient so we have made an arbitrary choice. The other two Dummy cells are set to zero.
- 400 cases for Portsmouth–Nairobi as this is now the least cost route.
- Marseille–Nairobi and Frankfurt–Nairobi cells are set to zero as the maximum capacity for Nairobi is now met.
- Next least cost route is Portsmouth–Capetown. Portsmouth is already shipping 400 cases to Nairobi so the remaining 200 cases are allocated to the Portsmouth–Capetown route. The Portsmouth–Dar es Salaam route is set to zero as Portsmouth has now allocated all its 600 cases.
- There are now two least cost cells: Frankfurt–Capetown and Frankfurt–Dar es Salaam. The latter has a higher capacity so is preferred and 300 units are allocated to this route. This is all the cases from Frankfurt so Frankfurt–Capetown is set to zero.
- This leaves Marseille–Capetown with 200 cases.

Total cost of this solution is €4930.

We now calculate the u and v values for the current solution, remembering that we must include the Dummy column which has cost coefficients of 0. Here we have:

$$u_1 + v_1 = 4.40$$
$$u_1 + v_2 = 4.55$$
$$u_1 + v_4 = 0$$
$$u_2 + v_1 = 4.20$$
$$u_2 + v_3 = 3.70$$
$$u_3 + v_2 = 4.25$$

Setting $u_1 = 0$ and solving for the remainder gives:

$$u_1 = 0$$
$$u_2 = -0.20$$
$$u_3 = -0.30$$
$$v_1 = 4.40$$
$$v_2 = 4.55$$
$$v_3 = 3.90$$
$$v_4 = 0$$

If we now calculate the net evaluation index for each unused route we have:

Route	Net evaluation index $c_{ij}-u_i-v_j$
Marseille-Nairobi	+0.45
Portsmouth-Dar-es-Salaam	+1.00
Portsmouth-Dummy	+0.20
Frankfurt-Capetown	+0.15
Frankfurt-Nairobi	+1.2
Frankfurt-Dummy	+0.30

By inspection we see that all the index values are positive, indicating that our first solution is also our optimal, least-cost solution. If we now examine the organization's desire to see all of Marseille's cases shipped out we see that currently this is not happening. There are 100 cases from Marseilles that are not used. Because we know that the current solution is optimal, we also know that insisting on all of Marseille's cases being shipped must increase costs. From the net evaluation index we know what this cost will be. If we force Marseille–Dummy to take a zero value then one of the other two cells in the Dummy column must be used instead. By inspection we see that the lowest cost cell is Portsmouth–Dummy at +0.20. So our new solution would be to ship only 500 units from Portsmouth. We can also track through the changes on the rest of the solution.

Marseille–Dummy	−100 cases
Portsmouth–Dummy	+100 cases
Portsmouth–Capetown	−100 cases (since this is the only stepping stone route for the Portsmouth row)
Marseille–Capetown	+100 cases

and a total increase in costs of €20.

Problems

Note: For some problems a variety of solution methods can be used. Where the solution method is not specified, you may use LP or the transportation or assignment modules of The Management Scientist or some other software package. Some problems are intended to be solved using the special purpose algorithms of Sections 7.2 and 7.4.

SELF *test*

1 A company imports goods at two ports: Lisbon and Le Havre. Shipments of one of its products are made to customers in Paris, Berlin, London and Milan. For the next planning period, the supplies at each port, customer demands and the shipping costs (€) per case from each port to each customer are as follows:

	Customers				
Port	Paris	Berlin	London	Milan	Port Supply
Lisbon	2	6	6	2	5000
Le Havre	1	2	5	7	3000
Demand	1400	3200	2000	1400.	

a. Develop a network model of the distribution system for this problem.

b. Solve the problem to determine the minimum cost shipping schedule.

SELF *test*

2 Consider the following network representation of a transportation problem:

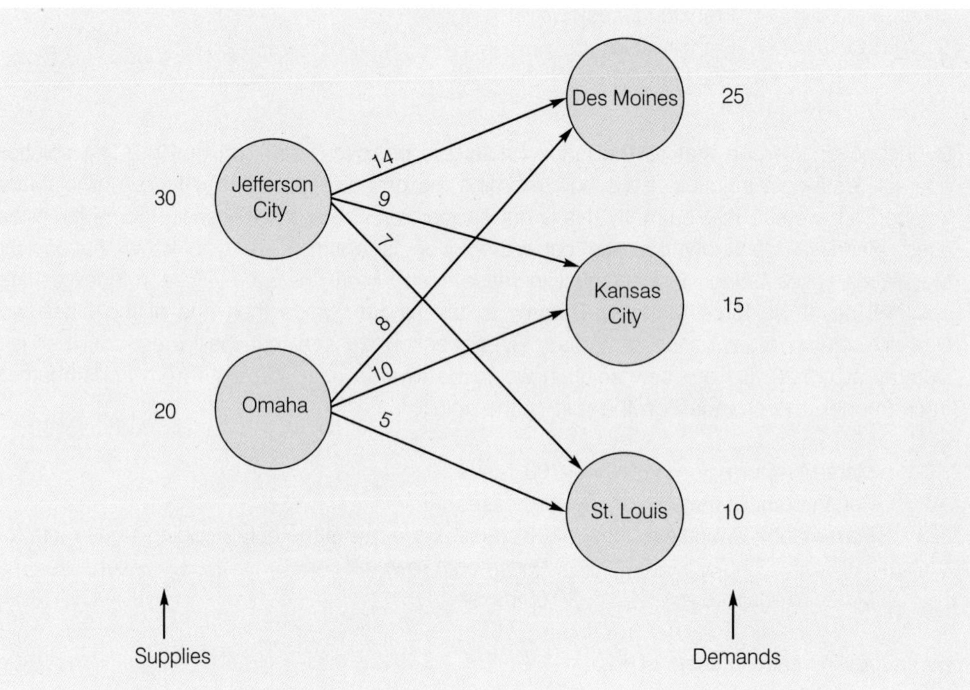

The supplies, demands and transportation costs per unit are shown on the network.

a. Develop a linear programming model for this problem; be sure to define the variables in your model.

b. Solve the linear programme to determine the optimal solution.

3 A product is produced at three plants and shipped to three warehouses (the transportation costs per unit are shown in the following table).

	Warehouse			
Plant	W_1	W_2	W_3	**Plant Capacity**
P_1	20	16	24	300
P_2	10	10	8	500
P_3	12	18	10	100
Warehouse demand	200	400	300	

a. Show a network representation of the problem.
b. Develop a linear programming model for minimizing transportation costs; solve this model to determine the minimum cost solution.
c. Suppose that the entries in the table represent profit per unit produced at plant *i* and sold to warehouse *j*. How does the model change from that in part (b)?

SELF *test*

4 Tri-County Utilities, Inc., supplies natural gas to customers in a three-county area. The company purchases natural gas from two companies: Southern Gas and Northwest Gas. Demand forecasts for the coming winter season are Hamilton County, 400 units; Butler County, 200 units; and Clermont County, 300 units. Contracts to provide the following quantities have been written: Southern Gas, 500 units; and Northwest Gas, 400 units. Distribution costs for the counties vary, depending upon the location of the suppliers. The distribution costs per unit (in €1000s) are as follows:

		To	
From	**Hamilton**	**Butler**	**Clermont**
Southern Gas	10	20	15
Northwest Gas	12	15	18

a. Develop a network representation of this problem.
b. Develop a linear programming model that can be used to determine the plan that will minimize total distribution costs.
c. Describe the distribution plan and show the total distribution cost.
d. Recent residential and industrial growth in Butler County has the potential for increasing demand by as much as 100 units. Which supplier should Tri-County contract with to supply the additional capacity?

5 Arnoff Enterprises manufactures the central processing unit (CPU) for a line of tablet computers. The CPUs are manufactured at three sites in China: Shanghai, Changchun and Nanchang and then shipped to warehouses in Singapore, Seattle, Lisbon, Sao Paulo and Dubai for further distribution. The following transportation tableau shows the number of CPUs available at each plant and the number of CPUs required by each warehouse. The shipping costs (dollars per unit) are also shown in each cell.

Plant	Warehouse: Singapore	Seattle	Lisbon	Sao Paulo	Dubai	CPUs Available
Shanghai	10	20	5	9	10	9 000
Changchun	2	10	8	30	6	4 000
Nanchang	1	20	7	10	4	8 000
CPUs Required	3 000	5 000	4 000	6 000	3 000	21 000

a. Develop a network representation of this problem.

b. Determine the amount that should be shipped from each plant to each warehouse to minimize the total shipping cost.

c. The Singapore warehouse has just increased its order by 1000 units, and Arnoff has authorized the Changchun plant to increase its production by 1000 units. Will this change lead to an increase or decrease in total shipping costs? Solve for the new optimal solution.

SELF *test*

6 Premier Consulting has two consultants, Avery and Baker, who can be scheduled to work for clients up to a maximum of 160 hours each over the next four weeks. A third consultant, Campbell, has some assignments already planned and is available for clients up to a maximum of 140 hours over the next four weeks. The company has four clients with projects in process. The estimated hourly requirements for each of the clients over the four-week period are:

Client	Hours
A	180
B	75
C	100
D	85

Hourly rates vary for the consultant–client combination and are based on several factors, including project type and the consultant's experience. The rates (dollars per hour) for each consultant–client combination are:

Consultant	Client A	Client B	Client C	Client D
Avery	100	125	115	100
Baker	120	135	115	120
Campbell	155	150	140	130

a. Develop a network representation of the problem.
b. Formulate the problem as a linear programme, with the optimal solution providing the hours each consultant should be scheduled for each client in order to maximize the consulting firm's billings. What is the schedule and what is the total billing?
c. New information shows that Avery doesn't have the experience to be scheduled for client B. If this consulting assignment is not permitted, what impact does it have on total billings? What is the revised schedule?

SELF *test*

7 Klein Chemicals, Inc., produces a special oil-based material that is currently in short supply. Four of Klein's customers have already placed orders that together exceed the combined capacity of Klein's two plants. Klein's management faces the problem of deciding how many units it should supply to each customer. Because the four customers are in different industries, different prices can be charged based on the various industry pricing structures. However, slightly different production costs at the two plants and varying transportation costs between the plants and customers make a 'sell to the highest bidder' strategy questionable. After considering price, production costs and transportation costs, Klein has established the following profit per unit for each plant–customer alternative.

	Customer			
Plant	D_1	D_2	D_3	D_4
Clifton Springs	€32	€34	€32	€40
Danville	€34	€30	€28	€38

The plant capacities and customer orders are as follows:

Plant Capacity (units)		Customer Orders (units)
Clifton Springs	5 000	D_1 2 000
		D_2 5 000
Danville	3 000	D_3 3 000
		D_4 2 000

How many units should each plant produce for each customer to maximize profits? Which customer demands will not be met?

SELF *test*

8 The Bahrain Manufacturing Company has orders for three similar products:

Product	Orders (units)
A	2 000
B	500
C	1 200

Three machines are available for the manufacturing operations. All three machines can produce all the products at the same production rate. However, due to varying defect percentages of each product on each machine, the unit costs of the products vary depending on the machine used. Machine capacities for the next week, and the unit costs, are as follows:

			Product		
Machine	**Capacity (units)**	**Machine**	**A**	**B**	**C**
1	1 500	1	€1.00	€1.20	€0.90
2	1 500	2	€1.30	€1.40	€1.20
3	1 000	3	€1.10	€1.00	€1.20

Formulate and solve a linear programming model that can be used to develop the minimum cost production schedule for the products and machines.

SELF *test*

9 Scott and Associates, Inc., is an accounting firm that has three new clients. Project leaders will be assigned to the three clients. Based on the different backgrounds and experiences of the leaders, the various leader–client assignments differ in terms of projected completion times. The possible assignments and the estimated completion times in days are:

	Client		
Project Leader	**1**	**2**	**3**
Jackson	10	16	32
Ellis	14	22	40
Smith	22	24	34

a. Develop a network representation of this problem.
b. Formulate the problem and solve. What is the total time required?

SELF *test*

10 Assume that in Problem 9 an additional employee is available for possible assignment. The following table shows the assignment alternatives and the estimated completion times.

	Client		
Project Leader	**1**	**2**	**3**
Jackson	10	16	32
Ellis	14	22	40
Smith	22	24	34
Burton	14	18	36

a. What is the optimal assignment?
b. How did the assignment change compared to the best assignment possible in Problem 9? Were any savings associated with considering Burton as one of the possible project leaders?
c. Which project leader remains unassigned?

SELF *test*

11 The distribution system for the Herman Company consists of three plants, two warehouses and four customers. Plant capacities and shipping costs (€) from each plant to each warehouse are:

	Warehouse		
Plant	**1**	**2**	**Capacity**
1	4	7	450
2	8	5	600
3	5	6	380

Customer demand and shipping costs per unit (in €) from each warehouse to each customer are:

	Customer			
Warehouse	**1**	**2**	**3**	**4**
1	6	4	8	4
2	3	6	7	7
Demand	300	300	300	400

a. Develop a network model of this problem.
b. Find the optimal shipping plan.
c. Suppose that shipments between the two warehouses are permitted at €2 per unit and that direct shipments can be made from plant 3 to customer 4 at a cost of €7 per unit. Find the optimal shipping plan.

SELF *test*

12 A rental car company has an imbalance of cars at seven of its locations. The following network shows the locations of concern (the nodes) and the cost to move a car between locations. A positive number by a node indicates an excess supply at the node, and a negative number indicates an excess demand.

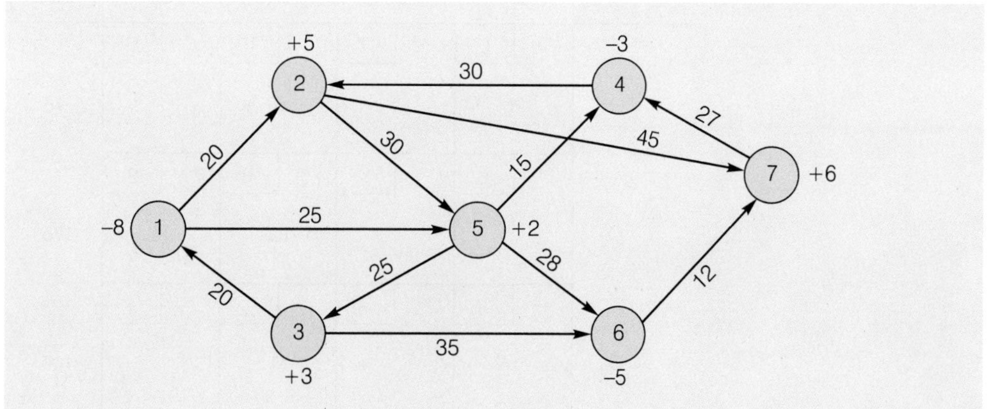

a. Develop a model for restoring the proper balance at the locations.
b. Solve the model formulated in part (a) to determine how the cars should be redistributed among the locations.

13 Naples Fishing Supply manufactures a variety of fishing equipment, which it sells throughout Europe. For the next three months, Naples estimates demand for a particular product at 150, 250 and 300 units, respectively. Naples can supply this demand by

producing on regular time or overtime. Because of other commitments and anticipated cost increases in month 3, the production capacities in units and the production costs per unit are as follows:

Production	Capacity (units)	Cost per Unit
Month 1 – Regular	275	€50
Month 1 – Overtime	100	80
Month 2 – Regular	200	50
Month 2 – Overtime	50	80
Month 3 – Regular	100	60
Month 3 – Overtime	50	100

Inventory may be carried from one month to the next, but the cost is €20 per unit per month. For example, regular production from month 1 used to meet demand in month 2 would cost Sanders €50 + €20 = €70 per unit. This same month 1 production used to meet demand in month 3 would cost Sanders €50 + 2(€20) = €90 per unit.

a. Develop a network representation of this production scheduling problem as a transportation problem. (*Hint*: Use six origin nodes; the supply for origin node 1 is the maximum that can be produced in month 1 on regular time, and so on.)
b. Develop a linear programming model that can be used to schedule regular and overtime production for each of the three months.
c. What is the production schedule, how many units are carried in inventory each month, and what is the total cost?
d. Is there any unused production capacity? If so, where?

Note: The remaining problems involve the use of the special purpose algorithms described in Sections 7.2 and 7.4 for solving transportation and assignment problems.

SELF *test*

14 Consider the following transportation tableau with four origins and four destinations.

Origin	Destination D_1	D_2	D_3	D_4	Supply
O_1	[5] 25	[7]	[10] 50	[5]	75
O_2	[6]	[5]	[8] 100	[2] 75	175
O_3	[6] 100	[6]	[12]	[7]	100
O_4	[8]	[5] 100	[14]	[4] 50	150
Demand	125	100	150	125	

a. Use the MODI method to determine whether this solution provides the minimum transportation cost. If it is not the minimum cost solution, find that solution. If it is the minimum cost solution, what is the total transportation cost?
b. Does an alternative optimal solution exist? Explain. If so, find the alternative optimal solution. What is the total transportation cost associated with this solution?

15 Consider the following minimum cost transportation problem.

Origin	Destination: Los Angeles	San Francisco	San Diego	Supply
San Jose	4	10	6	100
Las Vegas	8	16	6	300
Tucson	14	18	10	300
Demand	200	300	200	700

a. Use the minimum cost method to find an initial feasible solution.
b. Use the transportation Simplex method to find an optimal solution.
c. How would the optimal solution change if you must ship 100 units on the Tucson–San Diego route?
d. Because of road construction, the Las Vegas–San Diego route is now unacceptable. Resolve the initial problem.

16 Consider the following minimum cost transportation problem.

Origin	Destination: D_1	D_2	D_3	Supply
O_1	6	8	8	250
O_2	18	12	14	150
O_3	8	12	10	100
Demand	150	200	150	

a. Use the minimum cost method to find an initial feasible solution.
b. Use the transportation Simplex method to find an optimal solution.
c. Using your solution to part (b), identify an alternative optimal solution.

17 Use the per-unit cost changes for each unoccupied cell shown in Table 7.10 to do the following:

a. Consider the arc connecting Brazil and Dubai as a candidate for the incoming arc. Allocate 1 unit of flow, and make the necessary adjustments on the stepping-stone path to maintain feasibility. Compute the value of the new solution, and show that the change in value is exactly what has been indicated by the cost change per unit obtained using the MODI method.
b. Repeat part (a) for the arc connecting China and London.

SELF *test*

18 Refer again to the Contois Carpets problem for which the network representation is shown in Figure 7.12. This problem can also be formulated and solved as a transportation problem.

a. Develop a network representation of it as a transportation problem. (*Hint*: Eliminate the inventory arcs, and add arcs showing that quarterly production can be used to satisfy demand in the current quarter and all future quarters.)
b. Solve the problem using the transportation Simplex method.

SELF *test*

19 Refer to Problem 9. Using the Hungarian method, obtain the optimal solution.

SELF *test*

20 Use the Hungarian method to solve the Salisbury Discount, problem by using the profit data in Table 7.27.

CASE PROBLEM 1 Distribution System Design

A national charity organization operating throughout the UK provides support and advice to the elderly. One of their activities relates to home safety for the elderly whereby the charity will supply and install safety handles around the home. These handles are installed in bathrooms and by stairs and by other areas where the elderly person might need to support themselves safely. The charity started out its activities a few years ago operating only in parts of Scotland. However, this initiative has proved so successful that it has since been expanded to cover the whole of the UK.

Currently the charity buys sets of handles from two suppliers: one based in Sweden, the other in Germany and the handles are shipped to one of three regional distribution centres the charity has in Edinburgh, Leeds and Bristol. The cost of each set of handles from Sweden is €10.50 and €10 from Germany. The cost of shipping a set of handles from each of the two suppliers to each of the charity's distribution centres is shown in Table 7.34. Note that because of transport restrictions, it is not possible for the German supplier to ship to Edinburgh. The Swedish supplier can supply a maximum of 30 000 sets and the German supplier a maximum of 20 000.

The charity operates on a regional basis with nine regional zones across the UK. Table 7.35 shows the estimated annual demand in each zone for sets of handles over the next year (these are based on past demand and the workload capacity of the charity's staff in each zone). Each of the three distribution centres supplies some of the zones when they require sets for installation. The Edinburgh distribution centre currently supplies the Northeast, Northwest, Northern Ireland and Scotland; the Leeds centre supplies the Southeast, London and the Midlands; the Bristol centre supplies Wales and the Southwest. The current shipping cost per set of handles from each centre to each zone is shown in Table 7.36. Note that some zones cannot be supplied by some of the centres because of transport logistics constraints.

To determine how many sets to ship from each centre to each zone, the demand forecasts are aggregated and a transportation model is used to

Table 7.34 Shipping Cost Per Set from Suppliers to Distribution Centres (€)

	Distribution Centre		
Supplier	**Edinburgh**	**Leeds**	**Bristol**
Sweden	3.20	2.20	4.20
Germany	—	3.90	1.20

Table 7.35 Demand Forecast

Customer Zone	**Demand (sets)**
Northeast	6 300
Northwest	4 880
Northern Ireland	2 130
Scotland	1 210
Southeast	6 120
Midlands	4 830
London	2 750
Wales	8 580
Southwest	4 460

Table 7.36 Shipping Cost from the Distribution Centres to the Customer Zones (€)

	Customer Zone								
Distribution Centre	**Northeast**	**Northwest**	**Northern Ireland**	**Scotland**	**Southeast**	**Midlands**	**London**	**Wales**	**Southwest**
Edinburgh	0.3	2.1	3.1	4.4	6.0	—	—	—	—
Leeds	5.2	5.4	4.5	6.0	2.7	4.7	3.4	3.3	2.7
Bristol	—	—	—	—	5.4	3.3	2.4	2.1	2.5

minimize the total costs involved (supply costs and shipping costs to zones).

Managerial Report

Because of the rapid and unplanned growth of the initiative across the UK, the current distribution system is relatively unplanned. However, the charity's management now reckon it is time to look at the efficiency of the current system. You have been called in to undertake analysis and provide advice.

1 If the charity maintains its current supply and distribution strategy, what will its supply and distribution costs be for the coming year?

2 The company is willing to consider altering its current strategy so that any of the three distribution centres could supply any of the zones (where this is logistically feasible). Can costs be reduced? If so, by how much?

3 The charity is discussing with its Swedish and German suppliers the possibility of them supplying some of the zones directly. Under review are the possibilities of the German supplier shipping directly to Wales at a cost of €0.30 per set and to the Southeast at a cost of €0.70 per set. Similarly, the Swedish supplier is willing to ship directly to the Northwest at a cost of €3.50 per set. Would the charity reduce its costs by doing this?

Appendix 7.1 Excel Solution of Transportation, Assignment and Transshipment Problems

In this appendix we show how Excel Solver can be used to solve transportation, assignment and transshipment problems. We start with the Foster Electronics transportation problem (see Section 7.1).

Transportation Problem

The first step is to enter the data for the transportation costs, the origin supplies and the destination demands in the top portion of the worksheet. Then the linear programming model is developed in the bottom portion of the worksheet. As with all linear programmes the worksheet model has four key elements: the decision variables, the objective function, the constraint left-hand sides and the constraint right-hand sides. For a transportation problem, the decision variables are the amounts shipped from each origin to each destination; the objective function is the total transportation cost; the left-hand sides are the number of units shipped from each origin and the number of units shipped into each destination; and the right-hand sides are the origin supplies and the destination demands.

The formulation and solution of the Foster Electronics problem are shown in Figure 7.14. The data are in the top portion of the worksheet. The model appears in the bottom portion of the worksheet; the key elements are screened.

Formulation

The data and descriptive labels are contained in cells A1:F8. The transportation costs are in cells B5:E7. The origin supplies are in cells F5:F7, and the destination demands are in cells B8:E8. The key elements of the model required by the Excel

Figure 7.14 Excel Solution of the Foster Electronics Problem

EXCEL *file*

FOSTER

	A	B	C	D	E	F	G	H	I
1	**Foster Generators**								
2									
3			**Destination**						
4	**Origin**	Boston	Dubai	Singapore	London	**Supply**			
5	**Czech Republic**	3	2	7	6	5000			
6	**Brazil**	7	5	2	3	6000			
7	**China**	2	5	4	5	2500			
8	**Demand**	6000	4000	2000	1500				
9									
10									
11	**Model**								
12									
13		**Min Cost**	39500						
14									
15			**Destination**						
16	**Origin**	Boston	Dubai	Singapore	London	**Total**			
17	**Czech Republic**	3500	1500	0	0	5000	<=	5000	
18	**Brazil**	0	2500	2000	1500	6000	<=	6000	
19	**China**	2500	0	0	0	2500	<=	2500	
20	**Total**	6000	4000	2000	1500				
21		=	=	=	=				
22		6000	4000	2000	1500				
23									

Solver are the decision variables, the objective function, the constraint left-hand sides and the constraint right-hand sides. These cells are screened in the bottom portion of the worksheet.

Decision Variables — Cells B17:E19 are reserved for the decision variables. The optimal values are shown to be $x_{11} = 3500$, $x_{12} = 1500$, $x_{22} = 2500$, $x_{23} = 2000$, $x_{24} = 1500$ and $x_{41} = 2500$. All other decision variables equal zero indicating nothing will be shipped over the corresponding routes.

Objective Function — The formula = SUMPRODUCT(B5:E7,B17:E19) has been placed into cell C13 to compute the cost of the solution. The minimum cost solution is shown to have a value of €39 500.

Left-Hand Sides — Cells F17:F19 contain the left-hand sides for the supply constraints, and cells B20:E20 contain the left-hand sides for the demand constraints.

Cell F17 = SUM(B17:E17) (Copy to F18:F19)
Cell B20 = SUM(B17:B19) (Copy to C20:E20)

Right-Hand Sides — Cells H17:H19 contain the right-hand sides for the supply constraints, and cells B22:E22 contain the right-hand sides for the demand constraints.

Cell H17 = F5 (Copy to H18:H19)
Cell B22 = B8 (Copy to C22:E22)

Excel Solution

The solution shown in Figure 7.14 can be obtained by selecting **Solver** from the **Tools** menu, entering the proper values into the **Solver Parameters** dialogue box, selecting **Standard Simplex LP** and specifying the option **Assume Non-Negative**. Then click **Solve**. The information entered into the **Solver Parameters** dialogue box is shown in Figure 7.15.

Assignment Problem

The first step is to enter the data for the assignment costs in the top portion of the worksheet. Even though the assignment model is a special case of the transportation model, it is not necessary to enter values for origin supplies and destination demands because they are always equal to one.

Figure 7.15 Solver Parameters Dialogue Box for the Foster Electronics Problem

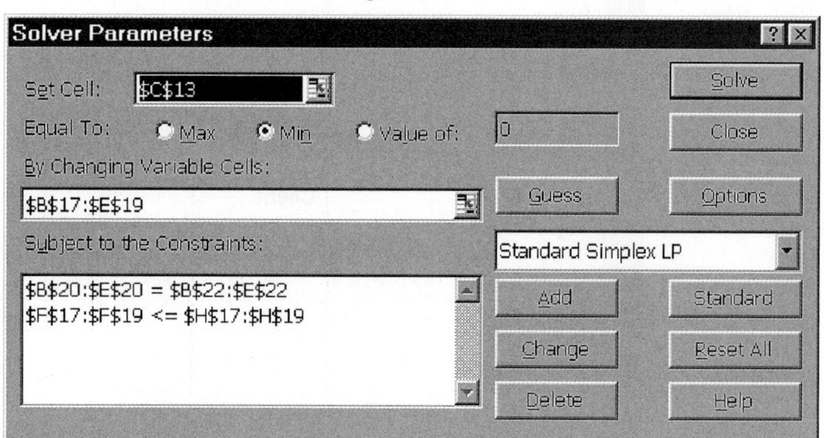

The linear programming model is developed in the bottom portion of the worksheet. As with all linear programmes the model has four key elements: the decision variables, the objective function, the constraint left-hand sides and the constraint right-hand sides. For an assignment problem the decision variables indicate whether a person is assigned to a task (with a 1 for yes or 0 for no); the objective function is the total cost of all assignments; the constraint left-hand sides are the number of tasks that are assigned to each person and the number of people that are assigned to each task; and the right-hand sides are the number of tasks each person can handle (1) and the number of people each task requires (1).

The worksheet formulation and solution for the Fowle Marketing Research Problem (see Section 7.3) are shown in Figure 7.16.

Formulation

The data and descriptive labels are contained in cells A1:D7. Note that we have not inserted supply and demand values because they are always equal to 1 in an assignment problem. The model appears in the bottom portion of the worksheet with the key elements screened.

Decision Variables: Cells B16:D18 are reserved for the decision variables. The optimal values are shown to be $x_{12} = 1, x_{23} = 1$, and $x_{31} = 1$ with all other variables = 0.

Objective Function: The formula =SUMPRODUCT(B5:D7,B16:D18) has been placed into cell C12 to compute the number of days required to complete all the jobs. The minimum time solution has a value of 26 days.

EXCEL *file*

FOWLE

Figure 7.16 Excel Solution Of The Fowle Marketing Research Problem

	A	B	C	D	E	F	G	H
1	**Fowle Marketing Research**							
2								
3			**Client**					
4	**Project Leader**	1	2	3				
5	Terry	10	15	9				
6	Karl	9	18	5				
7	Mustafa	6	14	3				
8								
9								
10	**Model**							
11								
12		**Min Time**	26					
13								
14			**Client**					
15	**Project Leader**	1	2	3	**Total**			
16	Terry	0	1	0	1	<=	1	
17	Karl	0	0	1	1	<=	1	
18	Mustafa	1	0	0	1	<=	1	
19	**Total**	1	1	1				
20		=	=	=				
21		1	1	1				
22								

Left-Hand Sides — Cells E16:E18 contain the left-hand sides of the constraints for the number of clients each project leader can handle. Cells B19:D19 contain the left-hand sides of the constraints requiring that each client must be assigned a project leader.

Cell E16 = SUM(B16:D16) (Copy to E17:E18)
Cell B19 = SUM(B16:B18) (Copy to C19:D19)

Right-Hand Sides — Cells G16:G18 contain the right-hand sides for the project leader constraints and cells B21:D21 contain the right-hand sides for the client constraints. All right-hand side cell values are 1.

Excel Solution

The solution shown in Figure 7.16 can be obtained by selecting **Solver** from the **Tools** menu, entering the proper values into the **Solver Parameters** dialogue box, selecting **Standard Simplex LP** and specifying the option **Assume Non-Negative**. Then click **Solve**. The information entered into the **Solver Parameters** dialogue box is shown in Figure 7.17.

Transshipment Problem

The worksheet model we present for the transshipment problem can be used for all the network flow problems (transportation, assignment and transshipment) in this chapter. We organize the worksheet into two sections: an arc section and a node section. Let us illustrate by showing the worksheet formulation and solution of the Ryan transshipment problem (see Section 7.5). Refer to Figure 7.18 as we describe the steps involved. The key elements are screened.

Formulation

The arc section uses cells A3:D16. For each arc, the start node and end node are identified in cells A5:B16. The arc costs are identified in cells C5:C16, and cells D5:D16 are reserved for the values of the decision variables (the amount shipped over the arcs).

Figure 7.17 Solver Parameters Dialogue Box For The Fowle Marketing Research Problem

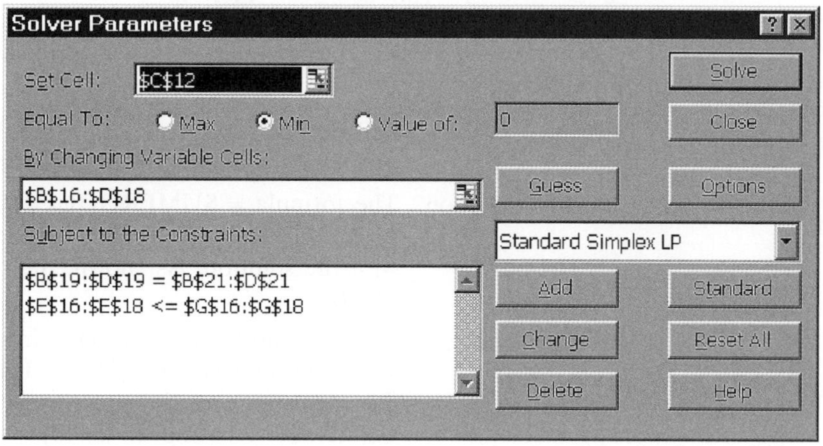

Solver Parameters
Set Cell: $C$12
Equal To: Max / Min / Value of: 0
By Changing Variable Cells: $B$16:$D$18
Subject to the Constraints:
$B$19:$D$19 = $B$21:$D$21
$E$16:$E$18 <= $G$16:$G$18
Standard Simplex LP
Solve | Close | Guess | Options | Add | Standard | Change | Reset All | Delete | Help

Figure 7.18 Excel Solution for the Ryan Problem

	A	B	C	D	E	F	G	H	I	J	K
1	**Ryan Transshipment**										
2											
3	**Arc**			**Units**							
4	Start Node	End Node	**Cost**	**Shipped**							
5	Geneva	London	2	550			**Units Shipped**		**Net**		
6	Geneva	Glosgow	3	50		**Node**	In	Out	**Shipments**		**Supply**
7	Stockholm	London	3	0		Geneva		600	600	<=	600
8	Stockholm	Glosgow	1	400		Stockholm		400	400	<=	400
9	London	Edinburgh	2	200		London	550	550	0	=	0
10	London	Manchester	6	0		Glosgow	450	450	0	=	0
11	London	Southampton	3	350		Edinburgh	200		-200	=	-200
12	London	New castle	6	0		Manchester	150		-150	=	-150
13	Glosgow	Edinburgh	4	0		Southampton	350		-350	=	-350
14	Glosgow	Manchester	4	150		New castle	300		-300	=	-300
15	Glosgow	Southampton	6	0							
16	Glosgow	New castle	5	300							
17											
18								**Total Cost**	5200		
19											

The node section uses cells F5:K14. Each of the nodes is identified in cells F7:F14. The following formulas are entered into cells G7:H14 to represent the flow out and the flow in for each node.

Units shipped in: Cell G9 = D5 + D7
Cell G10 = D6 + D8
Cell G11 = D9 + D13
Cell G12 = D10 + D14
Cell G13 = D11 + D15
Cell G14 = D12 + D16

Units shipped out: Cell H7 = SUM(D5:D6)
Cell H8 = SUM(D7:D8)
Cell H9 = SUM(D9:D12)
Cell H10 = SUM(D13:D16)

The net shipments in cells I7:I14 are the flows out minus the flows in for each node. For supply nodes, the flow out will exceed the flow in resulting in positive net shipments. For demand nodes, the flow out will be less than the flow in resulting in negative net shipments. The 'net'supply appears in cells K7:K14. Note that the net supply is negative for demand nodes.

As in previous worksheet formulations, we screened the key elements required by the Excel Solver.

Decision Variables: Cells D5:D16 are reserved for the decision variables. The optimal number of units to ship over each arc is shown.

Objective Function: The formula = SUMPRODUCT(C5:C16,D5:D16) is placed into cell I18 to show the total cost associated with the solution. As shown, the minimum total cost is $5200.

Left-Hand Sides: The left-hand sides of the constraints represent the net shipments for each node. Cells I7:I14 are reserved for these constraints.
Cell I7 =H7-G7 (Copy to I8:I14)

Right-Hand Sides	The right-hand sides of the constraints represent the supply at each node. Cells K7:K14 are reserved for these values. (Note the negative supply at the four demand nodes.)

Excel Solution

The solution can be obtained by selecting **Solver** from the **Tools** menu, entering the proper values into the **Solver Parameters** dialogue box, selecting **Standard Simplex LP** and specifying the option **Assume Non-Negative**. Then click **Solve**. The information entered into the **Solver Parameters** dialogue box is shown in Figure 7.19.

Figure 7.19 Solver Parameters Dialogue Box for the Ryan Problem

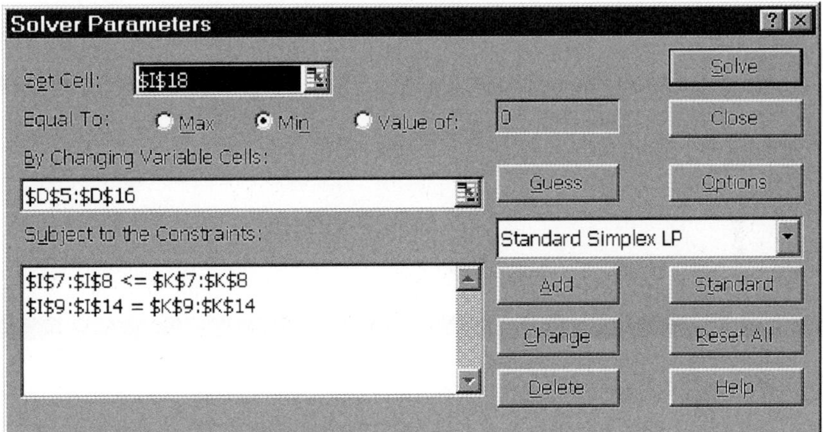

Chapter 8

Network Models

Learning Objectives

By the end of this chapter you will be able to formulate, solve and interpret in a business context a variety of network models including:

- Shortest-route networks
- Minimal spanning tree networks
- Maximal flow networks

MANAGEMENT SCIENCE IN ACTION

Optimizing Restoration Capacity At AT&T

AT&T is a global telecommunications company that provides long-distance voice and data, video, wireless, satellite and Internet services. The company uses state-of-the-art switching and transmission equipment to provide service to more than 80 million customers. In the continental United States, AT&T's transmission network consists of more than 40 000 miles of fibre-optic cable. On peak days AT&T handles as many as 290 million calls of various types.

Power outages, natural disasters, cable cuts and other events can disable a portion of the transmission network. When such events occur, spare capacity comprising the restoration network must be immediately employed so that service is not disrupted. Critical issues with respect to the restoration network are: How much capacity is necessary? Where should it be located? AT&T assembled a RestNet team to address these issues.

To optimize restoration capacity, the RestNet team developed a large-scale linear programming model. One subproblem in their model involves determining the shortest route connecting an origin and destination whenever a failure occurs in a span of the transmission network. Another subproblem solves a maximal flow problem to find the best restoration paths from each switch to a disaster recovery switch.

The RestNet team was successful, and their work is an example of how valuable management science methodology is to companies. According to C. Michael Armstrong, chair and CEO, 'Last year the work of the RestNet team allowed us to reduce capital spending by tens of millions of dollars'.

Based on Ken Ambs, Sebastian Cwilich, Mei Deng, David J. Houck, David F. Lynch and Dicky Yan, 'Optimizing Restoration Capacity in the AT&T Network', *Interfaces* (January/February 2000): 26–44.

Many managerial problems in areas such as transportation systems design, information systems design and project scheduling have been successfully solved with the aid of network models and network analysis techniques. In Chapter 7 we showed how *networks* consisting of nodes and arcs can be used to provide graphical representations of transportation, assignment and transshipment problems. In this chapter we present three additional network problems: the **shortest-route problem**, the **minimal spanning tree problem** and the **maximal flow problem**. In each case, we will show how a network model can be developed and solved in order to provide an optimal solution to the problem. The *Management Science in Action*, Optimizing Restoration Capacity at AT&T, notes that AT&T solved shortest-route and maximal flow problems in designing their transmission network.

8.1 Shortest-Route Problem

In this section we consider a network application in which the primary objective is to determine the **shortest route** or *path* between any pair of nodes in a network. We demonstrate the shortest-route problem by considering the situation facing the Government Development Agency (GDA) operating in Brunei, southeast Asia. The GDA has several economic development construction projects located throughout one region. The projects are designed to support local economic development in the area and consist of projects such as road-building, school construction and building medical clinics. Construction sites are sometimes located as far as 50km from GDA's main office. With multiple daily trips carrying personnel, equipment and supplies to and from the construction locations, the costs associated with

Figure 8.1 Road Network for the GDA Shortest-Route Problem

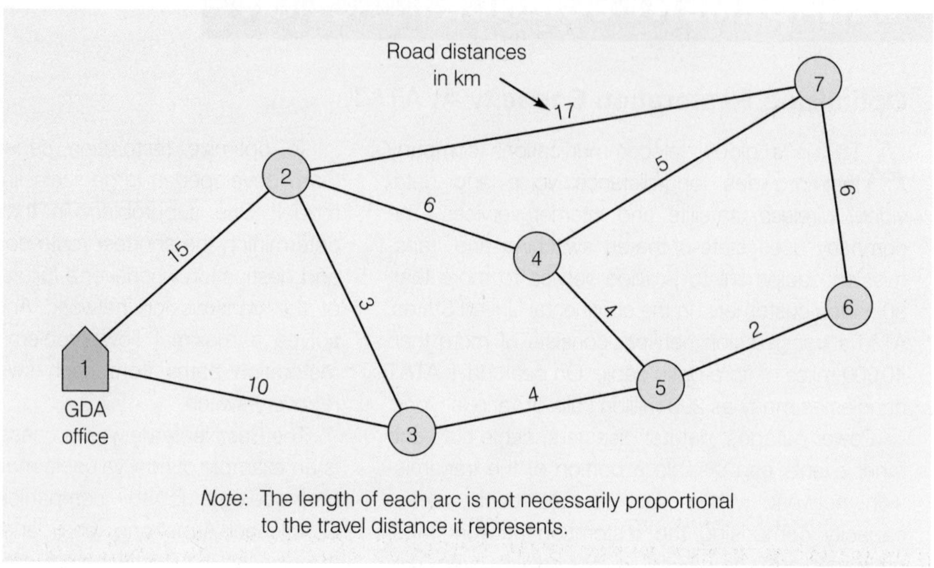

transportation activities are substantial particularly given that many of the trips are over very rough, undeveloped roads. For any given construction site, the travel alternatives between the site and the office can be described by a network of roads, streets and highways. The network shown in Figure 8.1 describes the travel alternatives to and from six of GDA's newest construction sites. The circles or *nodes* of the network correspond to the site locations. The roads, streets and highways appear as the *arcs* in the network. The distances between the sites are shown above the corresponding arcs. GDA would like to determine the routes or paths that will minimize the total travel distance from the office to each site.

A Shortest-Route Algorithm

To solve GDA's problem, we need to determine the shortest route from the GDA's office, node 1, to each of the other nodes in the network. The algorithm we present uses a labelling procedure to find the shortest distance from node 1 to each of the other nodes. As we perform the steps of the labelling procedure, we will identify a *label* consisting of two numbers enclosed in brackets for each node. The first number in the label for a particular node indicates the distance from node 1 to that node, while the second number indicates the preceding node on the route from node 1 to that node. We will show the label for each node directly above or below the node in the network. For example, a label for a particular node might appear as shown in Figure 8.2.

E. W. Dijkstre of the Netherlands proposed a solution algorithm for the shortest node problem in 1959

Figure 8.2 An Example of a Node Label

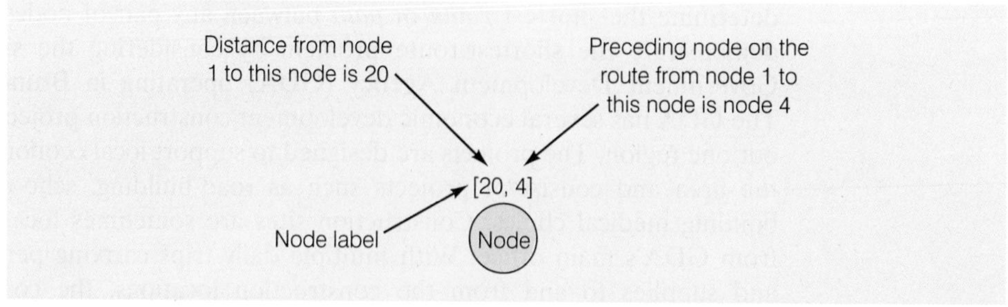

At any step of the labelling procedure, a node is said to be either labelled or unlabelled. A labelled node is any node for which we have identified a path from node 1 to that node, and an unlabelled node is any node for which a path has not yet been identified. A labelled node is also said to be either permanently or tentatively labelled. Whenever the algorithm has determined the *shortest* distance from node 1 to a particular node, the node is said to have a *permanent* label. If, however, the shortest distance from node 1 to a particular labelled node has not yet been determined, the node is said to have a *tentative* label. Now let us show how labels are calculated and how the labelling process can be used to determine the shortest route to each of the nodes in the network.

We begin the labelling process by giving node 1 the permanent label [0,S]. The 0 indicates that the distance from node 1 to itself is zero and the S identifies node 1 as the starting node. To distinguish between tentatively and permanently labelled nodes, we use dark shading for all permanently labelled nodes in the network. In addition, an arrow indicates the permanently labelled node being investigated at each step of the labelling algorithm. The initial identification of GDA's network is shown in Figure 8.3 when only node 1 is permanently labelled. The reason we distinguish between permanent and tentative labels is because we are adopting an iterative approach and will be comparing different nodes through the network in our search for the shortest node. Consider node 4, for example. To reach this node from node 1 there are several possibilities: node 1–2–4; 1–3–5–4; 1–2–7–4 and so on. We need to be able to distinguish between possible (tentative) nodes and those which are optimal (permanent).

To perform the first step or iteration of the labelling procedure, we must consider every node that can be reached directly from node 1; so, we look first at node 2 and then at node 3. We see that the direct distance from node 1 to node 2 is 15 km. So, node 2 can be tentatively labelled [15, 1], with the second number indicating that the preceding node on this route to node 2 is node 1. Next, we consider node 3 and find that the direct distance from node 1 to node 3 is 10km. So, the tentative label at node 3 is [10, 1]. Figure 8.4 shows the results so far with nodes 2 and 3 tentatively labelled.

Refer to Figure 8.4. We now consider all tentatively labelled nodes and identify the node with the smallest distance value in its label; so, node 3 with a travel distance of 10km is selected. Could we get to node 3 following a shorter route? Because any other route to node 3 would require passing through other nodes, and because the distance from node 1 to all other nodes is greater than or equal to ten, a shorter

Figure 8.3 Initial Network Identification for GDA's Shortest-Route Problem

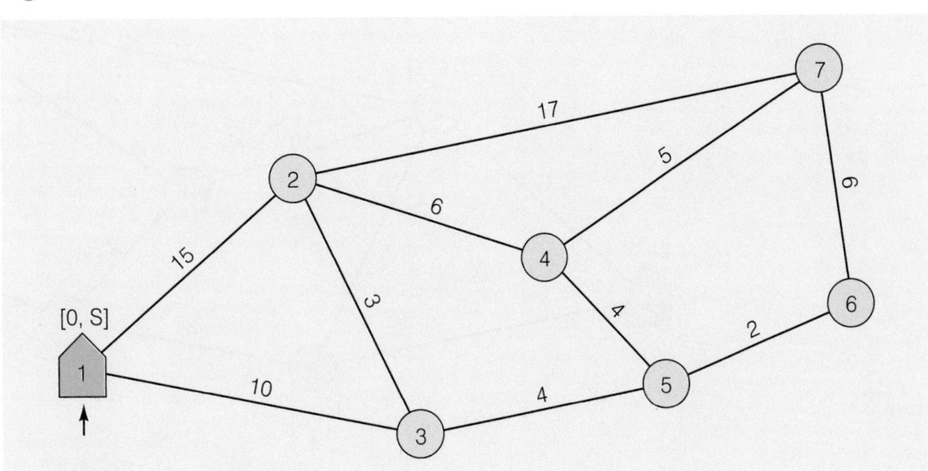

Figure 8.4 GDA's Network with Tentative Labels for Nodes 2 and 3

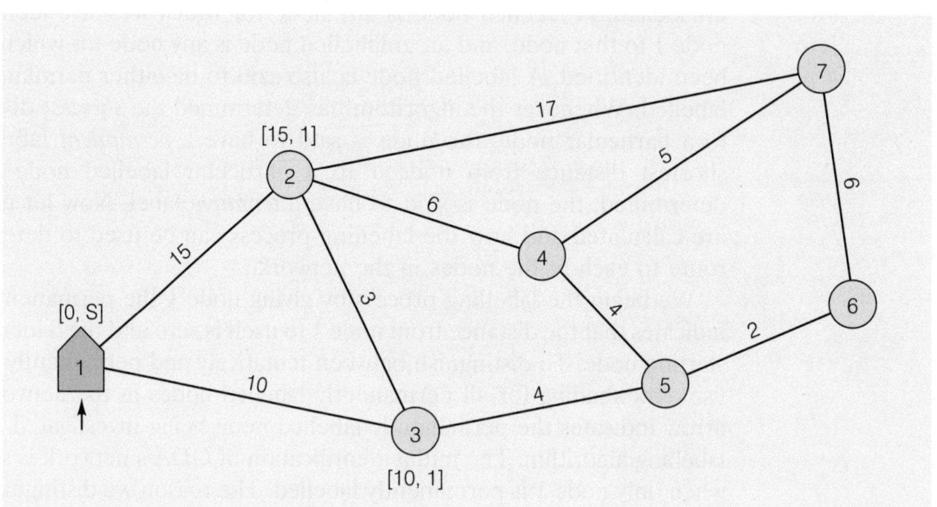

route to node 3 cannot be found. Accordingly, node 3 is permanently labelled with a distance of 10km. Dark shading indicates that node 3 is a permanently labelled node and the arrow indicates that node 3 will be used to start the next step of the labelling process; the result of these steps is shown in Figure 8.5.

We now proceed by considering all nodes that are not permanently labelled and that can be reached directly from node 3; these are nodes 2 and 5. Note that the direct distance is 3km from node 3 to node 2 and it is 4km from node 3 to node 5. Because node 3's permanent label indicates that the shortest distance to node 3 is 10km, we see that we can reach node 2 in 10 + 3 = 13km and node 5 in 10 + 4 = 14km. So, the tentative label at node 2 is revised to [13, 3] to indicate that we have now found a route from node 1 to node 2 that has a distance of 13kms and passes through node 3. The tentative label for node 5 is set to [14, 3]. Figure 8.6 shows the network calculations up to this point.

Figure 8.5 GDA's Network with Node 3 Identified as a Permanently Labelled Node

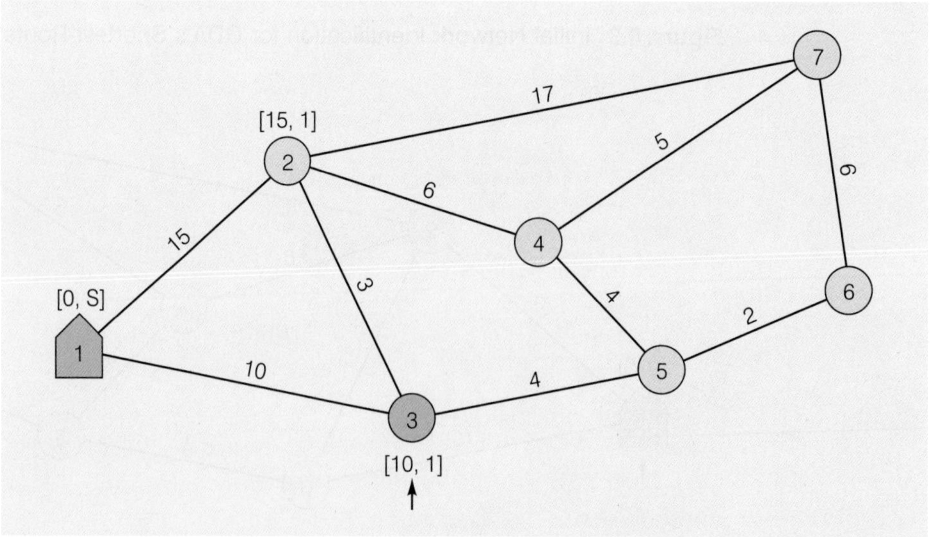

Figure 8.6 GDA's Network with New Tentative Labels for Nodes 2 and 5

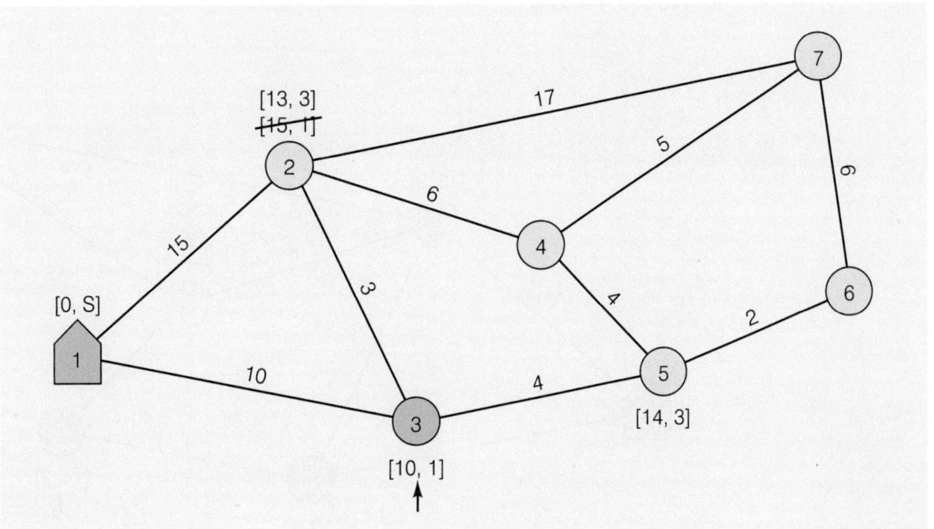

We next consider all tentatively labelled nodes in order to find the node with the smallest distance value in its label. From Figure 8.6 we see that this is node 2 with a distance of 13km. Node 2 is now permanently labelled because we know that it can be reached from node 1 in the shortest possible distance of 13km by going through node 3.

The next step or iteration begins at node 2, the most recently permanently labelled node. As before, we consider every non-permanently labelled node that can be reached directly from node 2; that is, nodes 4 and 7. Starting with the distance value of 13 in the permanent label at node 2 and adding the direct distance from node 2 to both nodes 4 and 7, we see that node 4 can be reached in 13 + 6 = 19km, while node 7 can be reached in 13 + 17 = 30km. So, the tentative labels at nodes 4 and 7 are as shown in Figure 8.7.

Figure 8.7 GDA's Network with a Permanent Label at Node 2 and New Tentative Labels for Nodes 4 and 7

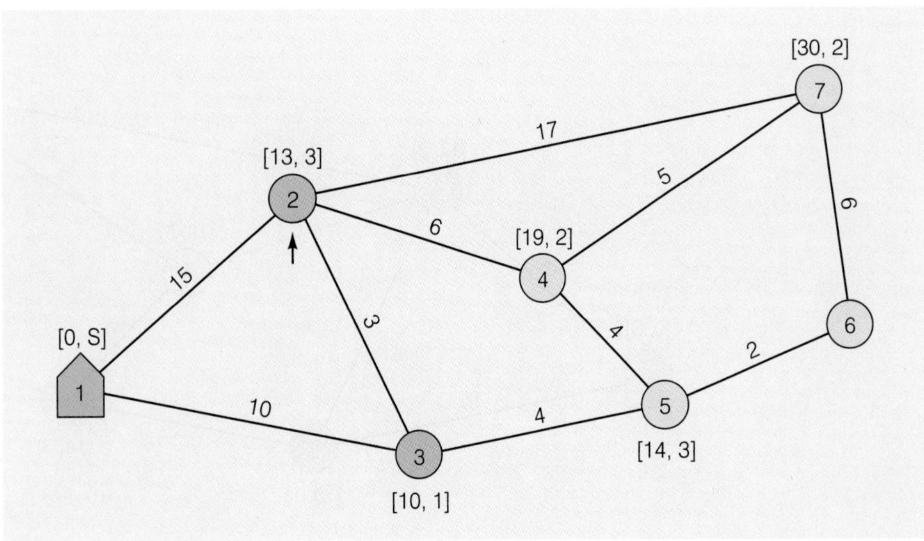

Figure 8.8 GDA's Network with a Permanent Label at Node 5 and New Tentative Labels for Nodes 4 and 6

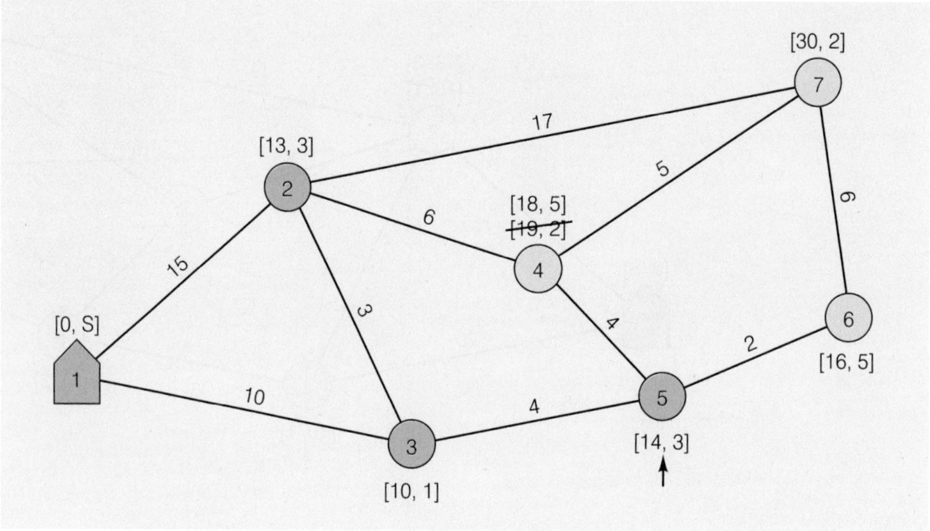

From the tentatively labelled nodes (nodes 4, 5 and 7), we select the node with the smallest distance value and declare that node permanently labelled. So node 5, with a distance of 14, becomes the new permanently labelled node. From node 5, then, we consider all non-permanently labelled nodes that can be reached directly from node 5. Thus, the tentative label on node 4 is revised, and node 6 is tentatively labelled. Figure 8.8 shows these.

The smallest distance is again identified for the remaining tentatively labelled nodes, and this results in node 6 being permanently labelled. From node 6 we can determine a new tentative label with a distance value of 22 for node 7. After this step, the network appears as shown in Figure 8.9.

Figure 8.9 GDA's Network with a Permanent Label at Node 6 and a New Tentative Label for Node 7

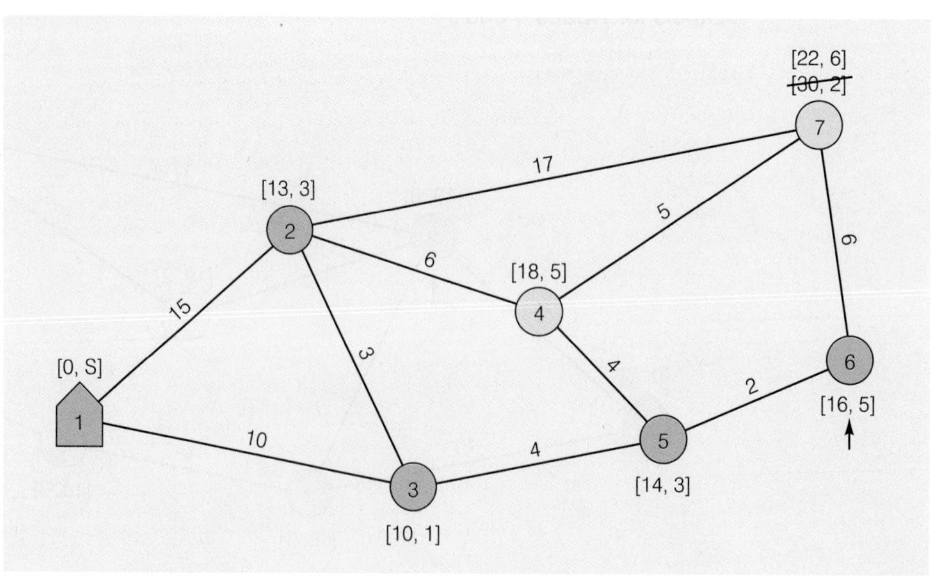

Figure 8.10 GDA's Network with a Permanent Label at Node 4

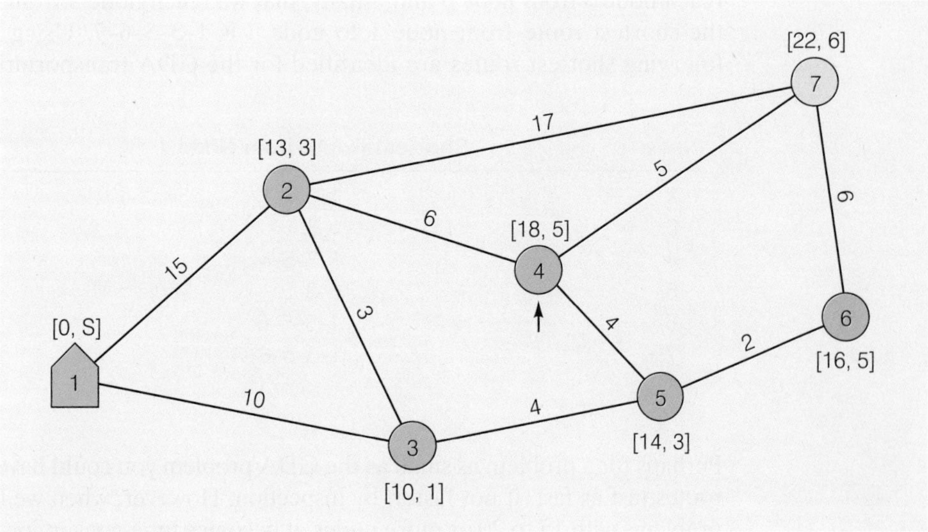

We now have only two remaining non-permanently labelled nodes. Because the distance value at node 4 is smaller than that at node 7, node 4 becomes the new permanently labelled node. Because node 7 is the only non-permanently labelled node that can be reached directly from node 4, we compare its distance value of 22 with the sum of the distance value at node 4 and the direct distance from node 4 to node 7, that is, 18 + 5 = 23. Because the [22, 6] tentative label at node 7 is smaller, it remains unchanged. Figure 8.10 shows the network at this point.

Because node 7 is the only remaining node with a tentative label, it is now permanently labelled. Figure 8.11 shows the final network with all nodes permanently labelled.

We can now use the information in the permanent labels to find the shortest route from node 1 to each node in the network. For example, node 7's permanent label tells us the shortest distance from node 1 to node 7 is 22km. To find the particular route that enables us to reach node 7 in 22km, we *start* at node 7 and work back to node 1. Node 7's label gives us the next direct link – node 6 – and node 6's label indicates

Figure 8.11 GDA's Network with All Nodes Permanently Labelled

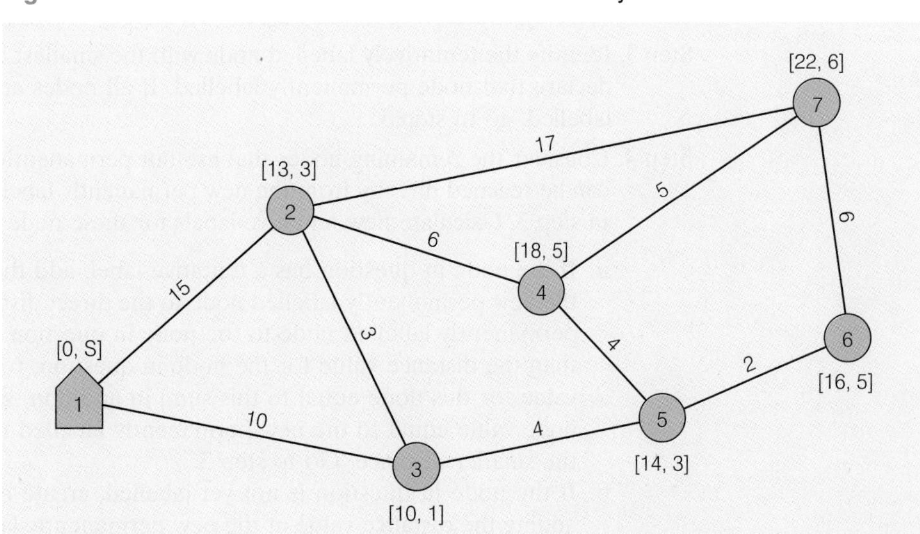

that node 5 is the next shortest-route link. Continuing this process, we note that we reach node 5 from node 3 and, finally, that we reach node 3 from node 1. Therefore, the shortest route from node 1 to node 7 is 1–3–5–6–7. Using this approach, the following shortest routes are identified for the GDA transportation network:

Node	Shortest Route from Node 1	Distance in km
2	1–3–2	13
3	1–3	10
4	1–3–5–4	18
5	1–3–5	14
6	1–3–5–6	16
7	1–3–5–6–7	22

Perhaps for a problem as small as the GDA problem you could have found the shortest routes just as fast, if not faster, by inspection. However, when we begin to investigate problems with 15 to 20 or more nodes, it becomes time-consuming to find the shortest routes by inspection. In fact, because of the increased number of alternate routes in a larger network, it is easy to miss one or more routes and come up with the wrong answer. So for larger problems a systematic procedure such as the preceding labelling procedure is required. Even with the labelling method, we find that as the networks grow in size, it becomes necessary to implement the algorithm on a computer.

As we summarize the shortest-route algorithm, think of a network consisting of N nodes. The following procedure can be used to find the shortest route from node 1 to each of the other nodes in the network.

Step 1. Assign node 1 the permanent label [0,S]. The 0 indicates that the distance from node 1 to itself is zero and the S indicates that node 1 is the starting node.

Step 2. Calculate tentative labels for the nodes that can be reached directly from node 1. The first number in each label is the direct distance from node 1 to the node in question; we refer to this portion of the label as the distance value. The second number in each label, which we refer to as the preceding node value, indicates the preceding node on the route from node 1 to the node in question; so, in this step the preceding node value is 1 because we are only considering nodes that can be directly reached from node 1.

Step 3. Identify the tentatively labelled node with the smallest distance value, and declare that node permanently labelled. If all nodes are permanently labelled, go to step 5.

Step 4. Consider the remaining nodes that are not permanently labelled and that can be reached directly from the new permanently labelled node identified in step 3. Calculate new tentative labels for these nodes as follows:

a. If the node in question has a tentative label, add the distance value at the new permanently labelled node to the direct distance from the new permanently labelled node to the node in question. If this sum is less than the distance value for the node in question, reset the distance value for this node equal to this sum; in addition, set the preceding node value equal to the new permanently labelled node that provided the smaller distance. Go to step 3.

b. If the node in question is not yet labelled, create a tentative label by adding the distance value at the new permanently labelled node to the direct distance from the new permanently labelled node to the node in question. The preceding node value is set equal to the new permanently labelled node. Go to step 3.

Step 5. The permanent labels identify both the shortest distance from node 1 to each node and the preceding node on the shortest route. The shortest route to a given node can be found by starting at the given node and moving backward to its preceding node. Continuing this backward movement through the network will provide the shortest route from node 1 to the node in question.

The shortest-route problem can also be formulated and solved as a transshipment problem. Simply set the supply at the start node and the demand at the end node equal to 1. However, unlike the labelling algorithm, this approach does not find the shortest route from the start node to every other node.

For practise in using the labelling algorithm to solve a shortest-route problem, try Problem 1.

This algorithm will determine the shortest distance from node 1 to each of the other nodes in the network. Note that N–1 iterations of the algorithm are required to find the shortest distance to all other nodes. If the shortest distance to every node is not needed, the algorithm can be stopped when those nodes of interest have been permanently labelled. The algorithm can also be easily modified to find the shortest distance from any node, say node k, to all other nodes in the network. To make such a change, we would merely begin by labelling node k with the permanent label [0,S]. Then by applying the steps of the algorithm, we can find the shortest route from node k to each of the other nodes in the network.

The Management Scientist software package can be used to solve small shortest-route problems. Input for the programme includes the number of nodes, the number of arcs and the length of each arc. The output shown in Figure 8.12 provides the shortest route from node 1 to node 7 for the GDA problem.

Figure 8.12 The Management Scientist Solution for the GDA Shortest-Route Problem

```
                 ****  NETWORK DESCRIPTION  ****

                     7 NODES AND 10 ARCS

     ARC    START NODE    END NODE    DISTANCE
     ---    ----------    --------    --------
      1         1            2           15
      2         1            3           10
      3         2            3            3
      4         2            4            6
      5         2            7           17
      6         3            5            4
      7         4            5            4
      8         4            7            5
      9         5            6            2
     10         6            7            6

     THE SHORTEST ROUTE FROM NODE 1 TO NODE 7
     ****************************************

     START NODE        END NODE        DISTANCE
     ----------        --------        --------
         1                3               10
         3                5                4
         5                6                2
         6                7                6

            TOTAL DISTANCE                22
```

NOTES AND COMMENTS

1 Many applications of the shortest-route algorithm involve criteria such as time or cost instead of distance. In these cases, the shortest-route algorithm provides the minimum-time or minimum-cost solution. However, since the shortest-route algorithm always identifies a minimum-value solution, it would not make sense to apply the algorithm to problems that involve a profit criterion.

2 In some applications, the value associated with an arc may be negative. For example, in situations where cost is the criterion, a negative arc value would denote a negative cost; in other words, a profit would be realized by traversing the arc. The shortest-route algorithm presented in this section can only be applied to networks with nonnegative arc values. More advanced texts discuss algorithms that can solve problems with negative arc values.

8.2 Minimal Spanning Tree Problem

In network terminology, the minimal spanning tree problem involves using the arcs of the network to reach *all* nodes of the network in such a fashion that the total length of all the arcs used is minimized. To better understand this problem, let us consider the communications system design problem encountered by a regional computer centre.

The Southwestern Regional Computer Centre must have special computer communications lines installed to connect five satellite users to a new central computer system. The telephone company will install the new communications network. However, the installation is an expensive operation. To reduce costs, the centre's management group wants the total length of the new communications lines to be as short as possible. Although the central computer could be connected directly to each user, it appears to be more economical to install a direct line to some users and let other users tap into the system by linking them with users already connected to the system. The determination of this minimal length communications system design is an example of the **minimal spanning tree** problem. The network for this problem with possible connection alternatives and distances is shown in Figure 8.13. An algorithm that can be used to solve this network model is explained in the following subsection.

Figure 8.13 Communications Network for the Regional Computer System

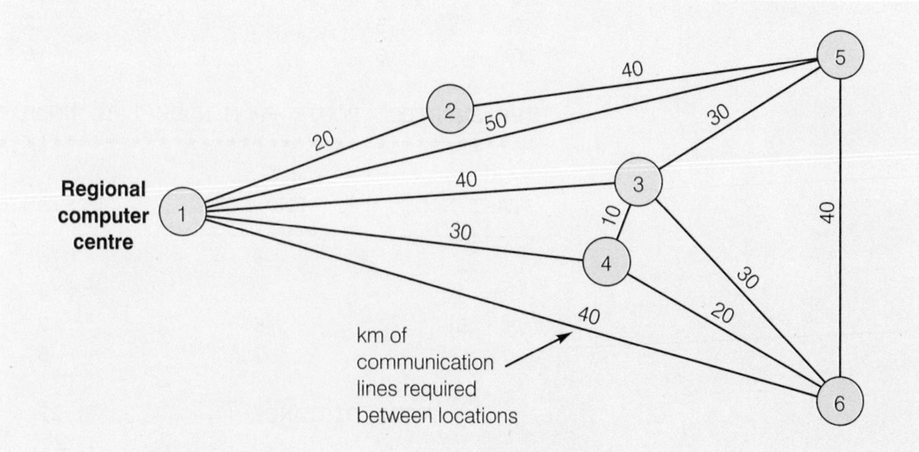

A Minimal Spanning Tree Algorithm

For a network consisting of N nodes, a spanning tree will consist of $N-1$ arcs.

A **spanning tree** for an N-node network is a set of N–1 arcs that connects every node to every other node. A minimal spanning tree provides this set of arcs at minimal total arc cost, distance or some other measure. The network algorithm that can be used to solve the minimal spanning tree problem is simple. The steps of the algorithm are as follows:

Step 1. Arbitrarily begin at any node and connect it to the closest node in terms of the criterion being used (e.g., time, cost or distance). The two nodes are referred to as *connected* nodes, and the remaining nodes are referred to as *unconnected* nodes.

Step 2. Identify the unconnected node that is closest to one of the connected nodes. Break ties arbitrarily if two or more nodes qualify as the closest node. Add this new node to the set of connected nodes. Repeat this step until all nodes have been connected.

This network algorithm is implemented by making the connection decisions directly on the network.

Dijkstre also published an algorithm for the spanning tree problem in 1956.

Referring to the communications network for the regional computer centre and arbitrarily beginning at node 1, we find the closest node is node 2 with a distance of 20. Using a bold line to connect nodes 1 and 2, step 1 of the algorithm provides the following result:

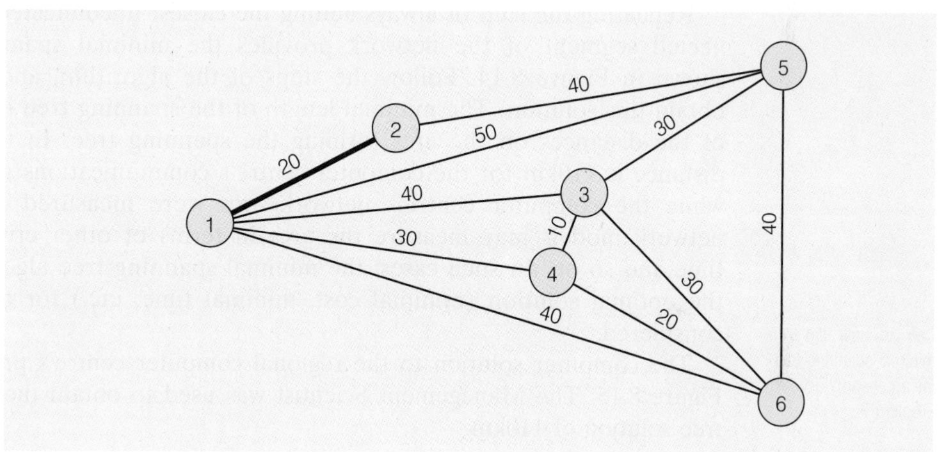

In step 2 of the algorithm, we find that the unconnected node closest to one of the connected nodes is node 4, with a distance of 30km from node 1. Adding node 4 to the set of connected nodes provides the following result:

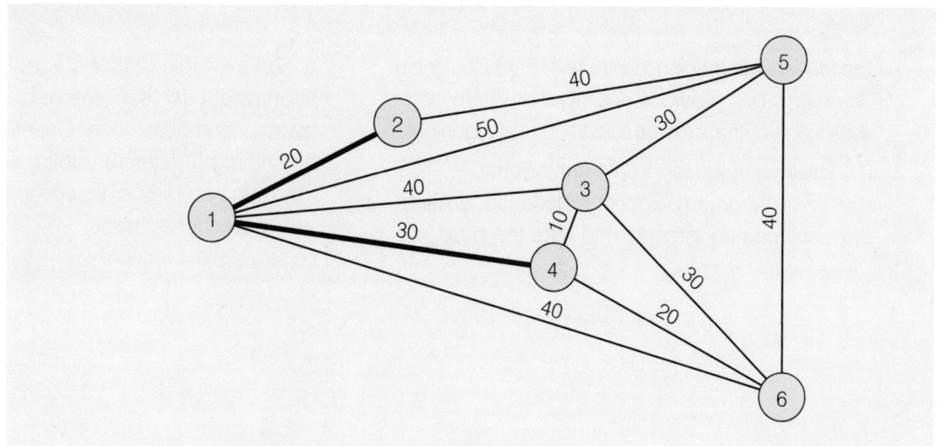

Figure 8.14 Minimal Spanning Tree Communications Network for the Regional Computer Centre

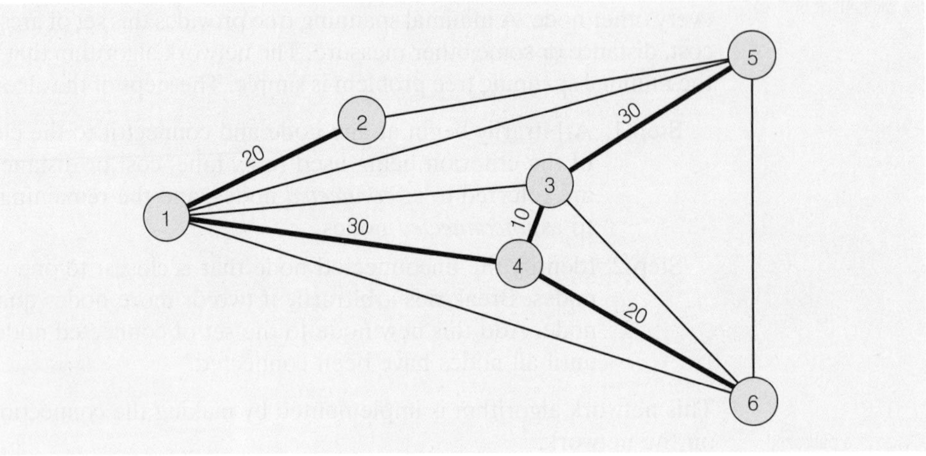

Repeating the step of always adding the closest unconnected node to the connected segment of the network provides the minimal spanning tree solution shown in Figure 8.14. Follow the steps of the algorithm, and see whether you obtain this solution. The minimal length of the spanning tree is given by the sum of the distances on the arcs forming the spanning tree. In this case, the total distance is 110km for the computer centre's communications network. Note that while the computer centre's network arcs were measured in distance, other network models may measure the arcs in terms of other criteria such as cost, time and so on. In such cases, the minimal spanning tree algorithm will identify the optimal solution (minimal cost, minimal time, etc.) for the criterion being considered.

Can you now find a minimal spanning tree for a network? Try Problem 7.

The computer solution to the regional computer centre's problem is shown in Figure 8.15. The Management Scientist was used to obtain the minimal spanning tree solution of 110km.

NOTES AND COMMENTS

1 The *Management Science in Action*, EDS Designs a Communication Network, describes an interesting application of the minimal spanning tree algorithm.

2 The minimal spanning tree algorithm is considered a *greedy algorithm* because at each stage we can be 'greedy' and take the best action available at that stage. Following this strategy at each successive stage will provide the overall optimal solution. Cases in which a greedy algorithm provides the optimal solution are rare. For many problems, however, greedy algorithms are excellent heuristics.

Figure 8.15 The Management Scientist Solution for the Regional Computer Centre Minimal Spanning Tree Problem

```
**** NETWORK DESCRIPTION ****

6 NODES AND 11 ARCS

ARC    START NODE    END NODE    DISTANCE
---    ----------    --------    --------
 1          1            2          20
 2          1            3          40
 3          1            4          30
 4          1            5          50
 5          1            6          40
 6          2            5          40
 7          3            4          10
 8          3            5          30
 9          3            6          30
10          4            6          20
11          5            6          40

MINIMAL SPANNING TREE
*********************

START NODE      END NODE      DISTANCE
----------      --------      --------
    1               2            20
    1               4            30
    4               3            10
    4               6            20
    3               5            30

      TOTAL LENGTH               110
```

8.3 Maximal Flow Problem

The objective in a **maximal flow** problem is to determine the maximum amount of flow (vehicles, messages, fluid, etc.) that can enter and exit a network system in a given period of time. In this problem, we attempt to transmit flow through all arcs of the network as efficiently as possible. The amount of flow is limited due to capacity restrictions on the various arcs of the network. For example, highway types limit vehicle flow in a transportation system, while pipe sizes limit oil flow in an oil distribution system. The maximum or upper limit on the flow in an arc is referred to as the **flow capacity** of the arc. Even though we do not specify capacities for the nodes, we do assume that the flow out of a node is equal to the flow into the node.

L. R. Ford and D. R. Fulkerson set out the procedure for solving the maximal flow problem in 1955.

As an example of the maximal flow problem, consider the road network system passing through Glasgow, Scotland. The vehicle flow travelling west to east reaches a level of 15 000 vehicles per hour at peak times. Due to a summer highway

MANAGEMENT SCIENCE IN ACTION

EDS Designs a Communication Network

EDS, headquartered in Plano, Texas, is a global leader in information technology services. The company provides hardware, software, communications and process solutions to many companies and governments around the world.

EDS designs communication systems and information networks for many of its customers. In one application, an EDS customer wanted to link together 64 locations for information flow and communications. Interactive transmission involving voice, video and digital data had to be accommodated in the information flow between the various sites. The customer's locations included approximately 50 offices and information centres in the continental United States; they ranged from Connecticut to Florida to Michigan to Texas to California. Additional locations existed in Canada, Mexico, Hawaii and Puerto Rico. A total of 64 locations formed the nodes of the information network.

EDS's task was to span the network by finding the most cost-effective way to link the 64 customer locations with each other and with existing EDS data centres. The arcs of the network represented communication links between pairs of nodes in the network. In cases where land communication lines were available, the arcs consisted of fibre-optic telephone lines. In other cases, the arcs represented satellite communication connections.

Using cost as the criterion, EDS developed the information network for the customer by solving a minimal spanning tree problem. The minimum cost network design made it possible for all customer locations to communicate with each other and with the existing EDS data centres.

The authors are indebted to Greg A. Dennis of EDS for providing this application.

maintenance programme, which calls for the temporary closing of lanes and lower speed limits, a network of alternate routes through Glasgow has been proposed by a transportation planning committee. The alternate routes include other main roads as well as city streets. Because of differences in speed limits and traffic patterns, flow capacities vary, depending on the particular streets and roads used. The proposed network with arc flow capacities is shown in Figure 8.16.

Figure 8.16 Network of Highway System and Flow Capacities (1000s/Hour) for Glasgow

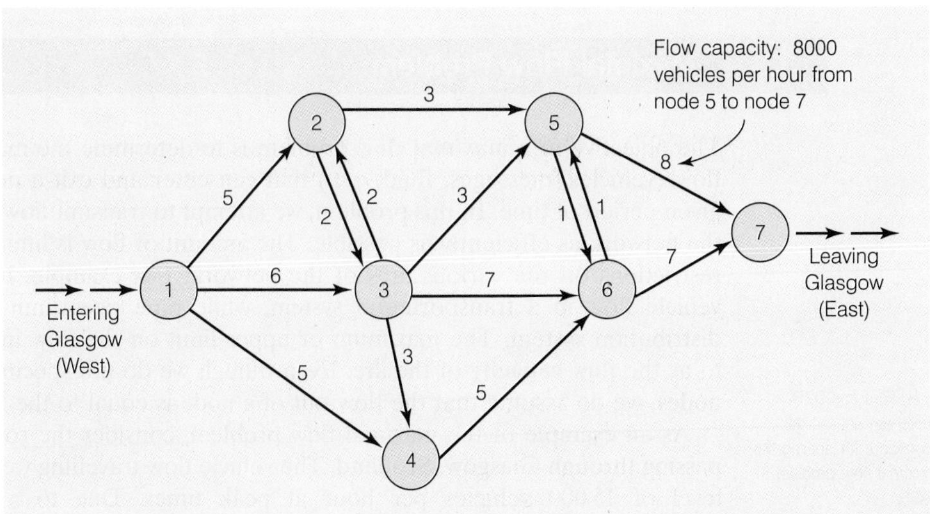

Figure 8.17 Flow Over Arc from Node 7 to Node 1 to Represent Total Flow Through the Glasgow System

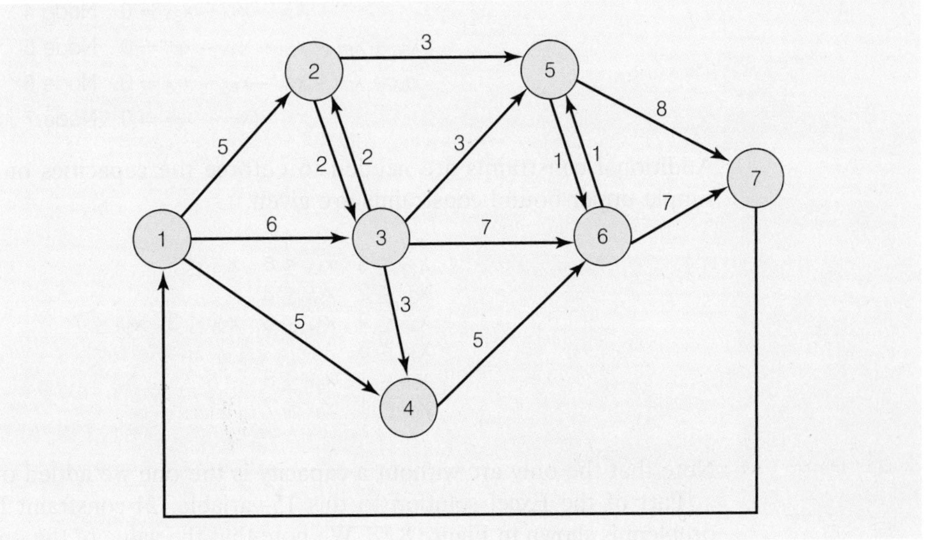

The direction of flow for each arc is indicated, and the arc capacity is shown next to each arc. Note that most of the streets are one-way. However, a two-way street can be found between nodes 2 and 3 and between nodes 5 and 6. In both cases, the capacity is the same in each direction.

We will show how to develop a capacitated transshipment model (see Chapter 7) for the maximal flow problem. First, we will add an arc from node 7 back to node 1 to represent the total flow through the highway system. Figure 8.17 shows the modified network. The newly added arc shows no capacity; indeed, we will want to maximize the flow over that arc. Maximizing the flow over the arc from node 7 to node 1 is equivalent to maximizing the number of cars that can get through the east–west road system passing through Glasgow.

As we did in Chapter 7 we define our decision variables as follows:

$$x_{ij} = \text{amount of traffic flow from node } i \text{ to node } j$$

The objective function that maximizes the flow over the road system is:

$$\text{Max } x_{71}$$

As with all transshipment problems, each arc generates a variable and each node generates a constraint. For each node, a conservation of flow constraint represents the requirement that the flow out must equal the flow in. Or, stated another way, the flow out minus the flow in must equal zero. For node 1, the flow out is $x_{12} + x_{13} + x_{14}$, and the flow in is x_{71}. Therefore, the constraint for node 1 is:

$$x_{12} + x_{13} + x_{14} - x_{71} = 0$$

The conservation of flow constraints for the other six nodes are developed in a similar fashion.

$$x_{23} + x_{25} - x_{12} - x_{32} = 0 \quad \text{Node 2}$$
$$x_{32} + x_{34} + x_{35} + x_{36} - x_{13} - x_{23} = 0 \quad \text{Node 3}$$
$$x_{46} - x_{14} - x_{34} = 0 \quad \text{Node 4}$$
$$x_{56} + x_{57} - x_{25} - x_{35} - x_{65} = 0 \quad \text{Node 5}$$
$$x_{65} + x_{67} - x_{36} - x_{46} - x_{56} = 0 \quad \text{Node 6}$$
$$x_{71} - x_{57} - x_{67} = 0 \quad \text{Node 7}$$

Additional constraints are needed to enforce the capacities on the arcs. These 14 simple upper-bound constraints are given.

$$x_{12} \leq 5 \quad x_{13} \leq 6 \quad x_{14} \leq 5$$
$$x_{23} \leq 2 \quad x_{25} \leq 3$$
$$x_{32} \leq 2 \quad x_{34} \leq 3 \quad x_{35} \leq 3 \quad x_{36} \leq 7$$
$$x_{46} \leq 5$$
$$x_{56} \leq 1 \quad x_{57} \leq 8$$
$$x_{65} \leq 1 \quad x_{67} \leq 7$$

Note that the only arc without a capacity is the one we added out of node 7.

Part of the Excel solution to this 15-variable, 21-constraint linear programming problem is shown in Figure 8.18. We note that the value of the optimal solution is 14. This result implies that the maximal flow over the road system is 14 000 vehicles. Figure 8.19 shows how the vehicle flow is routed through the original road network. We note, for instance, that 5000 vehicles per hour are routed between nodes 1 and 2, 2000 vehicles per hour are routed between nodes 2 and 3, and so on.

Try Problem 11 for practise in solving a maximal flow problem.

The results of the maximal flow analysis indicate that the planned road system will not handle the peak flow of 15 000 vehicles per hour. The transportation planners will have to expand the network, increase current arc flow capacities, or be prepared for serious traffic problems. If the network is extended or modified, another maximal flow analysis will determine the extent of any improved flow.

Figure 8.18 The Excel Solution to the Glasgow Road System Maximal Flow Problem

EXCEL *file*

ROAD SYSTEM

```
OPTIMAL SOLUTION

Objective Function Value = 14.000

       Variable               Value
    --------------       ---------------
         X12                      5.000
         X13                      6.000
         X14                      3.000
         X23                      2.000
         X25                      3.000
         X34                      0.000
         X35                      3.000
         X36                      5.000
         X32                      0.000
         X46                      3.000
         X56                      0.000
         X57                      7.000
         X65                      1.000
         X67                      7.000
         X71                     14.000
```

MANAGEMENT SCIENCE IN ACTION

Delivering frozen food products in Spain

The FRILAC company is based in Pamplona, Northern Spain and distributes frozen food products throughout the Navarre region by truck. The existing approach to scheduling deliveries of products to customers was judged to be time-consuming, occasionally inaccurate and expensive, so a project was established to look at improving the scheduling. A Decision Support System (DSS) was designed to allow scheduling to identify delivery routes that would minimize distance travelled as well as providing reports for vehicle drivers and estimating route delivery costs. However, a number of key constraints had to be incorporated into the model including the existing vehicle fleet size, the capacity of individual vehicles and the driving time available for each driver. The resulting network had around 50 nodes and 100 arcs with the arcs representing roads between delivery points. Attached to each arc was information on travel distance and average route speed. The model has delivered an estimated 10 per cent cost saving to the company as well as freeing up staff time, increasing productivity and reducing customer complaints.

Based on J. Faulin, P. Sarobe and J. Simal, 'The DSS LOGDIS optimizes delivery routes for FRILAC's frozen products', *Interfaces* 35/3 (2005): 202–214.

Figure 8.19 Maximal Flow Pattern for the Glasgow System Network

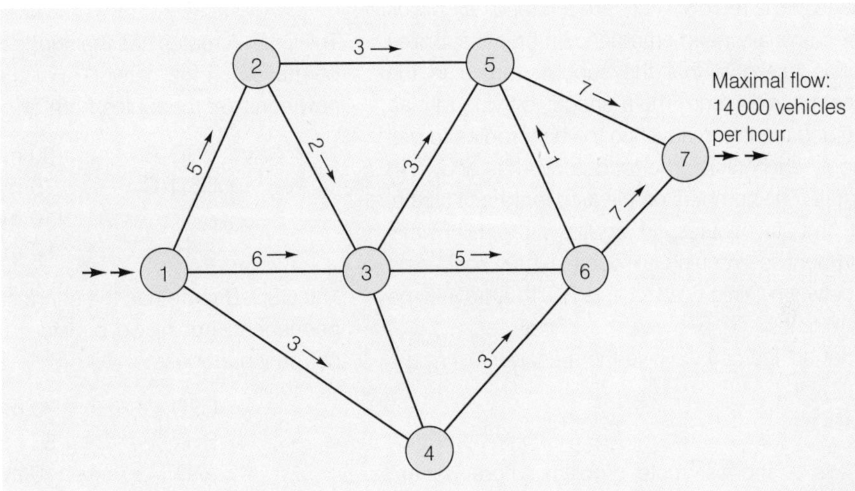

NOTES AND COMMENTS

1 The maximal flow problem of this section can also be solved with a slightly different formulation if the extra arc between nodes 7 and 1 is not used. The alternate approach is to maximize the flow into node 7 ($x_{57} + x_{67}$) and drop the conservation of flow constraints for nodes 1 and 7. However, the formulation used in this section is most common in practice.

2 Network models can be used to describe a variety of management science problems. Unfortunately, no one network solution algorithm can be used to solve every network problem. It is important to recognize the specific type of problem being modelled in order to select the correct specialized solution algorithm.

Summary

In this chapter we have introduced network models and shown how they can help with managerial decision making.

- Network models are concerned with the flow of an item through paths or routes.
- We introduced three types of network model: the shortest-route, the minimal spanning tree and the maximal flow.
- All three types of model have their own specialist solution algorithm which prove useful when the models become large and complex.

WORKED EXAMPLE

The transportation manager in the regional health service in Saudi Arabia is reviewing how she manages the transportation of emergency medical supplies to small community health clinics in different parts of the region. There are a total of six clinics that occasionally need emergency medical supplies and it is essential that the supplies arrive in the shortest possible time. The manager is trying to plan ahead and identify in advance the best routes to use to supply each clinic. The road network is shown in the figure. The numbers on the arcs represent typical travel time in minutes. In addition, the Highways Department is planning to open a new road next year between Clinic C and Clinic E with a travel time of 15 minutes.

What advice can we give the manager?

Solution

We have a shortest route problem where we are seeking the shortest route between the central supply depot (CSD) and each clinic.

The first iteration then looks at three routes:

CSD–A	50 minutes
CSD–B	60 minutes
CSD–C	70 minutes

The CSD–A routes has the shortest time so becomes permanent in the network. For the next iteration we now consider the routes from all permanent nodes:

CSD–B	60 minutes
CSD–C	70 minutes
A–D	110 minutes
A–B	80 minutes

The CSD–B route has the shortest time so becomes permanent. Again, we consider the routes from all permanent nodes:

CSD–C	70 minutes
B–C	80 minutes
A–D	110 minutes
B–D	80 minutes
B–E	90 minutes

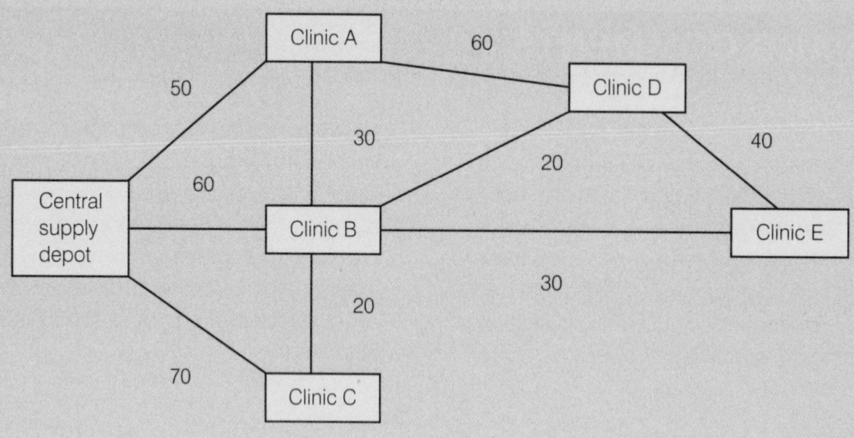

Route CSD–C now becomes permanent. The next iteration is then:

A–D	110 minutes
B–D	80 minutes
B–E	90 minutes

Route B–D is now permanent giving the next iteration:

D–E	120 minutes
B–D	90 minutes

with the B–D route the shortest option. We now have our solution. The supply routes from the Central supply depot to each clinic are:

CSD – Clinic A	50 minutes
CSD – Clinic B	60 minutes
CSD – Clinic C	70 minutes
CSD – Clinic D	80 minutes (via Clinic B)
CSD – Clinic E	90 minutes (via Clinic B)

We can also see by inspection of the network that when the new road is constructed there will be an arc (route) between Clinic C and Clinic E, with a travel time of 15 minutes. This will then be the preferred route to Clinic E with a total time from the central supply depot of 85 minutes compared with the current 90 minutes.

Problems

SELF *test* 1 Find the shortest route from node 1 to each of the other nodes in the transportation network shown.

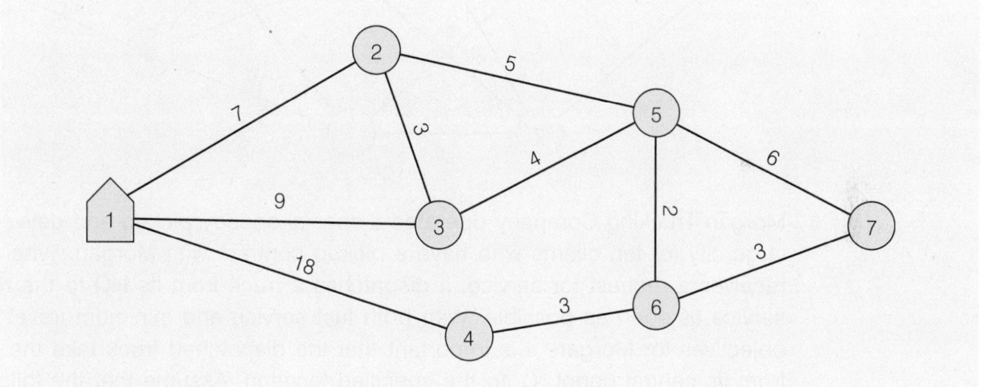

SELF *test* 2 For the GDA problem (see Figure 8.1), assume that node 7 is GDA's warehouse and supply centre. Several daily trips are commonly made from node 7 to the other nodes or construction sites. Using node 7 as the starting node, find the shortest route from this node to each of the other nodes in the network.

3 In the original GDA problem, we found the shortest distance from the office (node 1) to each of the other nodes or construction sites. Because some of the roads are highways and others are country tracks, the shortest-distance routes between the office and the construction sites may not necessarily provide the quickest or shortest-time routes. Shown here is the road network with travel time values rather than distance values. Find the shortest route from GDA's office to each of the construction sites if the objective is to minimize travel time rather than distance.

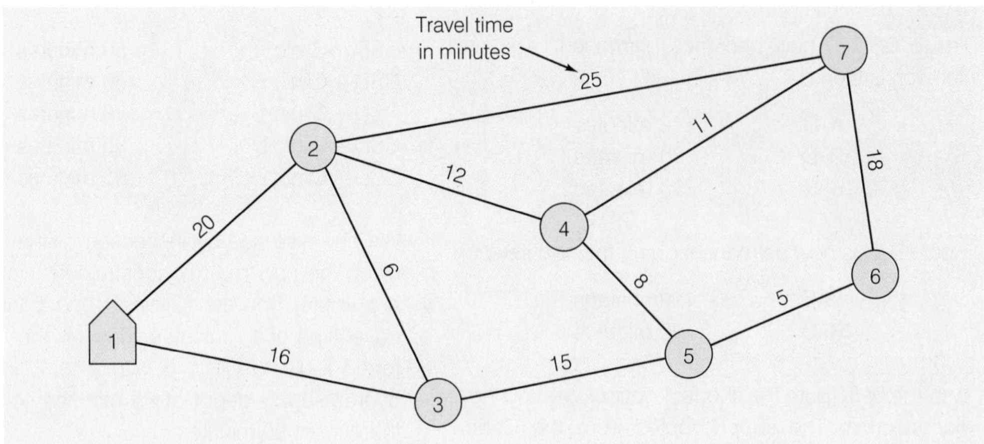

SELF *test*

4 Find the shortest route between nodes 1 and 10 in the following network:

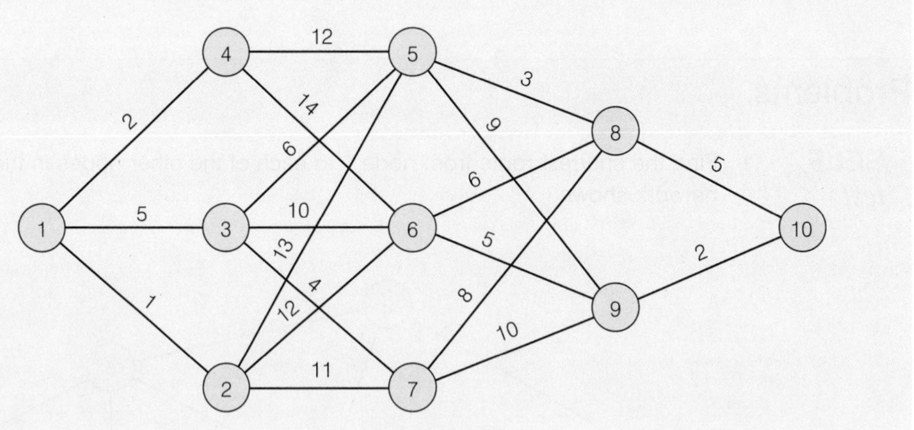

5 Morgan Trucking Company operates a special speedy pickup and delivery service in a large city for ten clients who have a pickup contract with Morgan. When Morgan receives a request for service, it dispatches a truck from its HQ to the requesting service as soon as possible. With both fast service and minimum travel costs as objectives for Morgan, it is important that the dispatched truck take the shortest route from its central depot, C, to the specified location. Assume that the following network (not drawn to scale) with distances given in km represents the highway network for this problem. Find the shortest-route distances from 'C' to all ten clients.

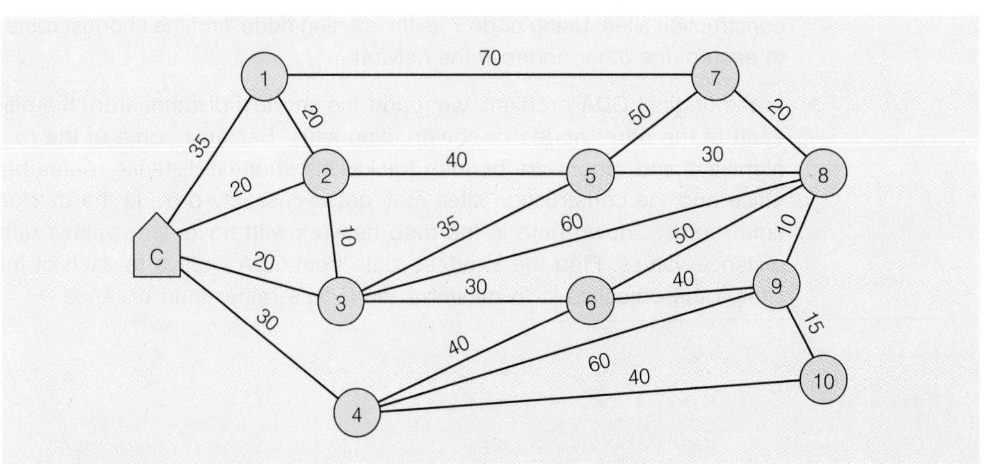

SELF *test* 6 Cairo City Cab Company identified ten primary pickup and drop locations for cab drivers. In an effort to minimize travel time and improve customer service and the utilization of the company's fleet of cabs, management would like the cab drivers to take the shortest route between locations whenever possible. Using the following network of roads and streets, what is the route a driver beginning at location 1 should take to reach location 10? The travel times in minutes are shown on the arcs of the network.

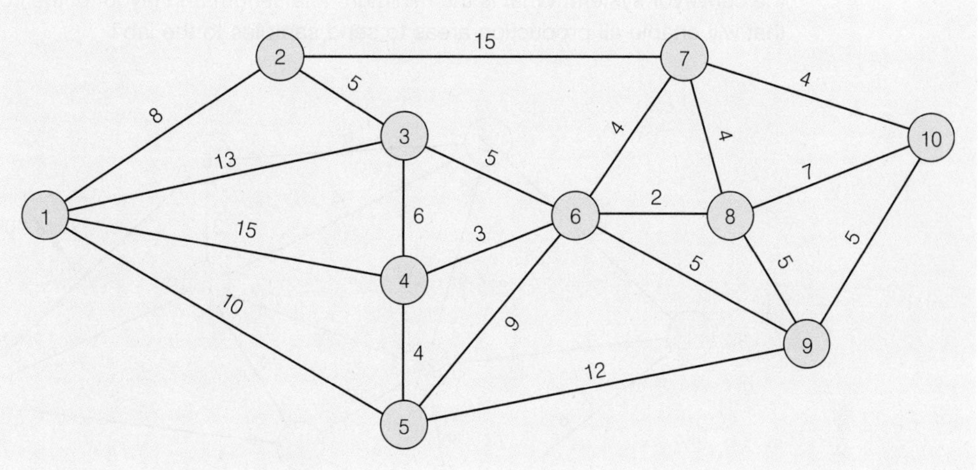

SELF *test* 7 The City of Copenhagen recently purchased land for a new country park, and park planners identified the ideal locations for the lodge, cabins, picnic groves, boat dock and scenic points of interest. These locations are represented by the nodes of the following network. The arcs of the network represent possible road connections in the park. If the state park designers want to minimize the total road miles that must be constructed in the park and still permit access to all facilities (nodes), which road connections should be constructed?

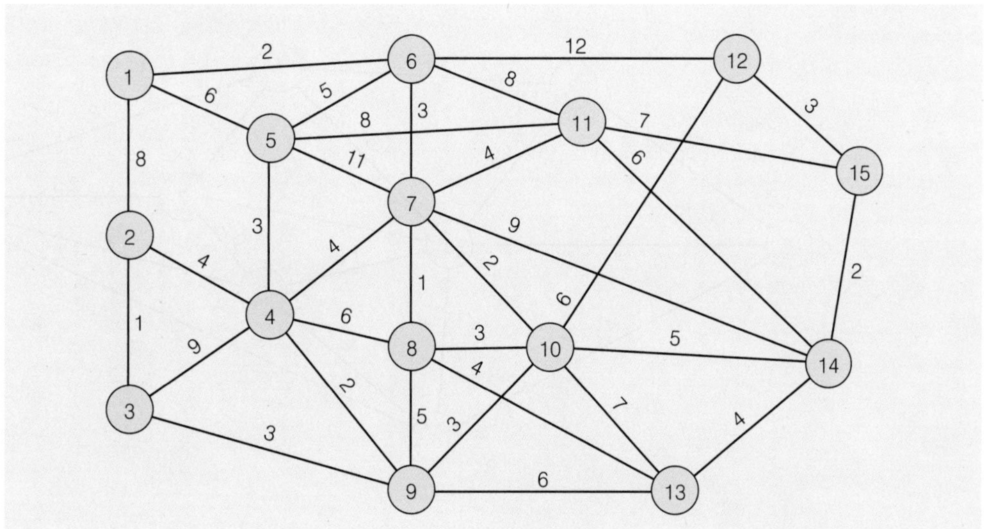

SELF *test*

8 In a large soap products plant, quality control inspectors take samples of various products from the different production areas and deliver them to the lab for analysis. The inspection process is slow, and the inspectors spend substantial time transporting samples from the production areas to the lab. The company is considering installing a pneumatic tube conveyor system that could transport the samples between the production areas and the lab. The following network shows the location of the lab and the production areas (nodes) where the samples must be collected. The arcs are the alternatives being considered for the conveyor system. What is the minimum total length and layout of the conveyor system that will enable all production areas to send samples to the lab?

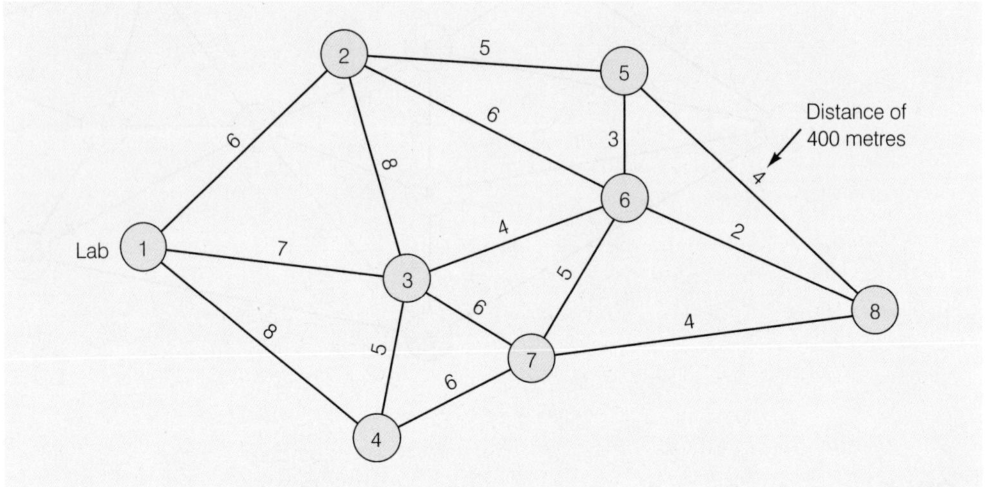

9 North Yorkshire University is installing a secure electronic mail system. The following network shows the possible electronic connections among the offices. Distances between offices are shown in km. Develop a design for the office communication system that will enable all offices to have access to the electronic mail service. Provide the design that minimizes the total length of connection among the eight offices.

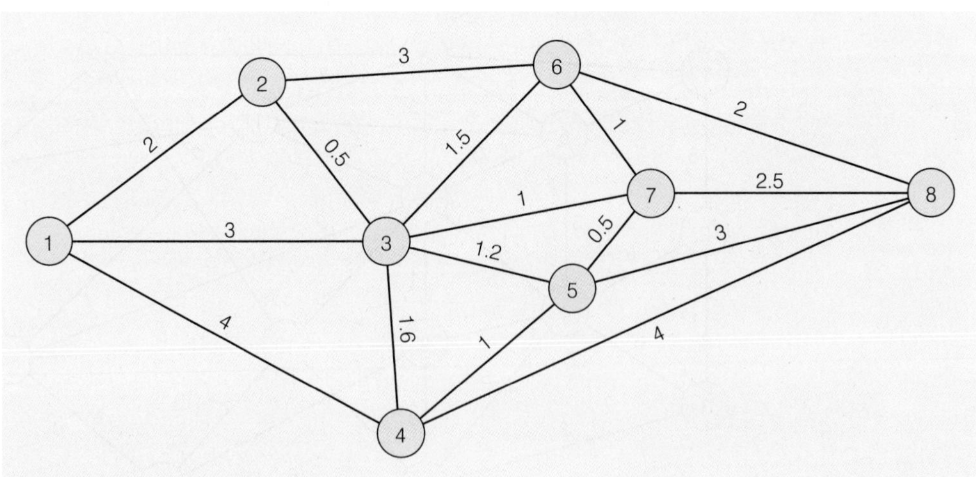

SELF *test*

10 The Metrovision Cable Company just received approval to begin providing cable television service to a suburb of a large city. The nodes of the following network show the distribution points that must be reached by the company's primary cable lines. The arcs of the network show the number of km between the distribution points. Determine the solution that will enable the company to reach all distribution points with the minimum length of primary cable line.

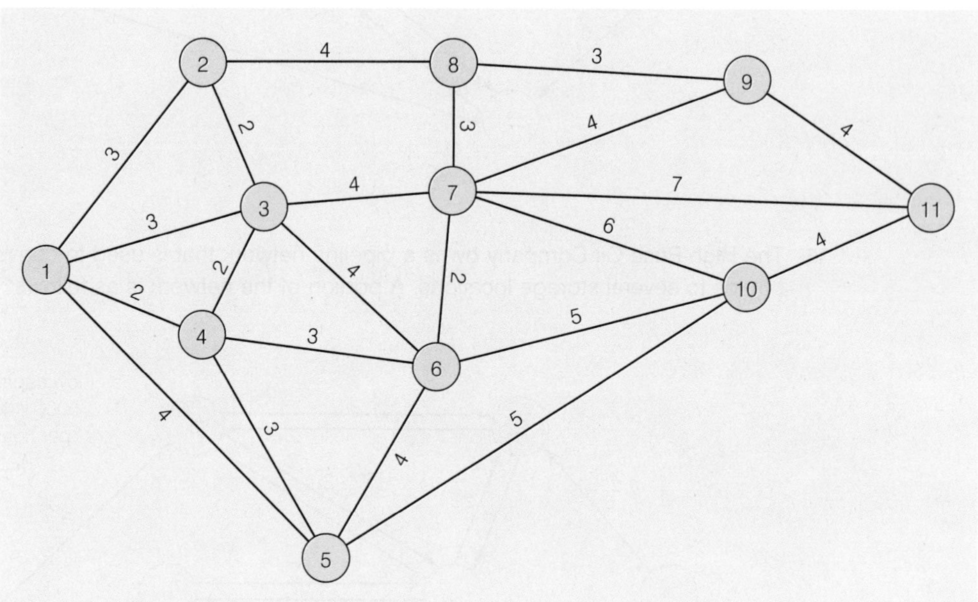

SELF *test*

11 The north–south highway system passing through Frankfurt, Germany, can accommodate the capacities shown.

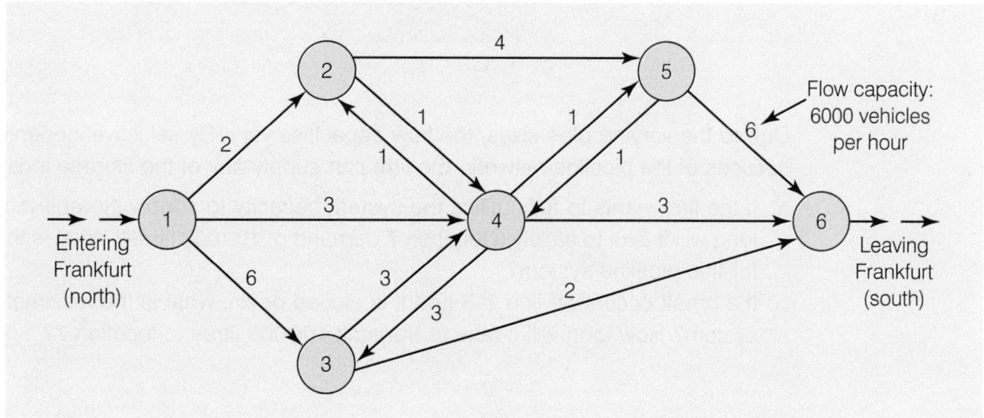

Can the highway system accommodate a north–south flow of 10 000 vehicles per hour?

SELF *test*

12 If the Frankfurt highway system described in Problem 11 has revised flow capacities as shown in the following network, what is the maximal flow in vehicles per hour through the system? How many vehicles per hour must travel over each road (arc) to obtain this maximal flow?

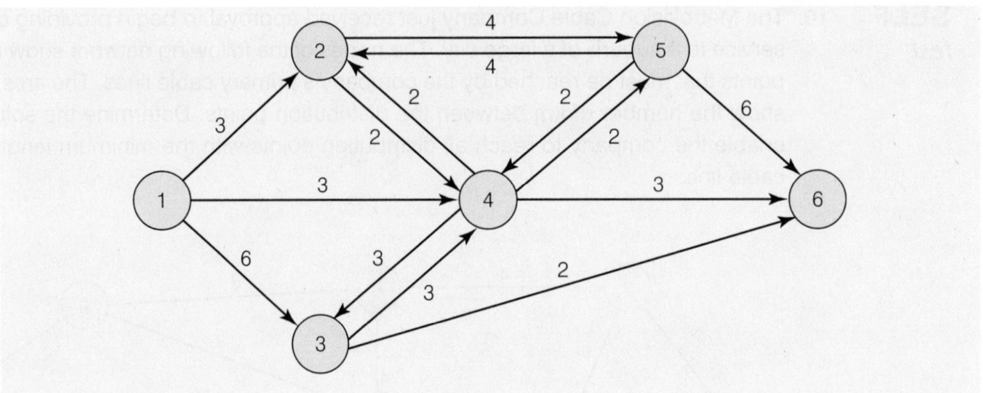

13 The High-Price Oil Company owns a pipeline network that is used to convey oil from its source to several storage locations. A portion of the network is as follows:

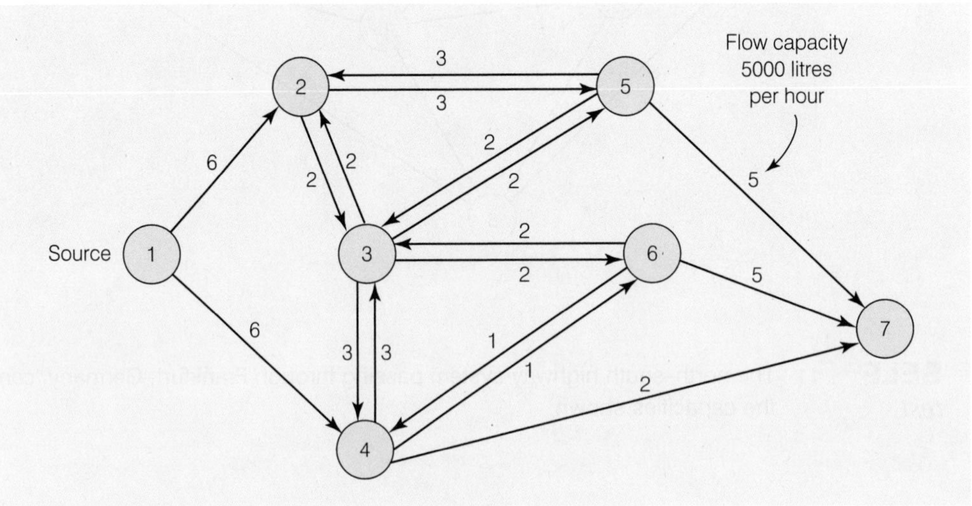

Due to the varying pipe sizes, the flow capacities vary. By selectively opening and closing sections of the pipeline network, the firm can supply any of the storage locations.

a. If the firm wants to fully utilize the system capacity to supply storage location 7, how long will it take to satisfy a location 7 demand of 100 000 litres? What is the maximal flow for this pipeline system?

b. If a break occurs on line 2–3 and it is closed down, what is the maximal flow for the system? How long will it take to transmit 100 000 litres to location 7?

CASE PROBLEM Ambulance Routing

The city of Binghamton is served by two major hospitals: Western Medical and Binghamton General. Western Medical is located in the southwest part of the city, and Binghamton General is in the northeast.

Bob Jones, the hospital administrator at Western Medical, has been discussing the problem of scheduling and routing ambulances with Margaret Johnson, the hospital administrator at Binghamton General. Both administrators feel that some type of system needs to be developed to better coordinate the use of the ambulance services at the two hospitals so that together they can provide the fastest possible emergency service for the city.

A proposal being considered is for all ambulance service calls to be handled through a central dispatcher, who would assign a call to the hospital capable of providing the fastest service. In studying this proposal, a project team consisting of employees from both hospitals met and decided that the best approach would be to divide the city into 20 service zones. In the proposed configuration, Western Medical would be located in zone 1 and Binghamton General in zone 20. A map showing the placement of the 20 zones and the travel time (in minutes) between adjacent zones is provided in Figure 8.20.

According to the proposed operating procedure, incoming emergency calls would be identified by zone number, and an ambulance from the hospital closest to that zone would be assigned the service call. However, if all ambulances from the closest hospital were occupied with other emergencies, the service call would be assigned to the other hospital. Regardless of which hospital responded to the service call, the individual or individuals requiring the emergency service would be taken to the closest hospital.

To make the coordinated service as efficient as possible, the ambulance drivers must know in advance the quickest route to take to each zone, which hospital the individual or individuals in that zone should be taken to, and the quickest route to that hospital.

Figure 8.20 Network for Proposed Ambulance Service

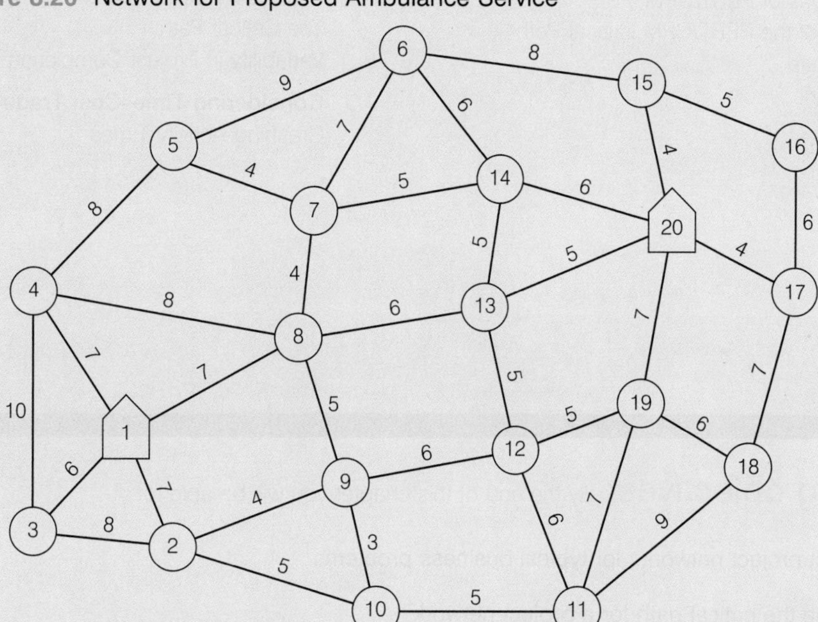

Managerial Report

Prepare a report for the two hospital administrators describing your analysis of the problem. Include in your report recommendations regarding the following items:

1 A chart for the dispatcher that identifies the primary hospital ambulance service for every zone in the city.

2 A chart for the Western Medical ambulance drivers that provides the minimum time routes from Western Medical to every zone in the city, including Binghamton General. Include a chart that tells Western Medical drivers which hospital the individuals should be taken to and the route that should be followed.

3 A chart for the Binghamton General ambulance drivers that provides the minimum time routes from Binghamton General to every zone in the city, including Western Medical. Include a chart that tells Binghamton General drivers which hospital the individuals should be taken to and the route that should be followed.

4 Include recommendations regarding how the system could be modified to take into account varying traffic conditions that occur throughout the day and changes in driving conditions resulting from temporary road construction projects.

Chapter 9

Project Scheduling: PERT/CPM

Learning objectives

By the end of this chapter you will be able to:

- Construct project networks for typical business problems
- Determine the critical path for a project network
- Undertake project scheduling with uncertain activity times

Most managers at some time are responsible for managing business projects. These may vary from relatively small, short-term projects – completing a business report – to large, complex and long-term projects such as multi-national construction projects which may last several years and cost millions of euros. Effective management of projects is critical – ensuring projects are completed on time, within budget and to agreed standards. In these situations the **programme evaluation and review technique (PERT)** and the **critical path method (CPM)** have proven to be extremely valuable.

PERT and CPM can be used to plan, schedule and control a wide variety of projects:

1 research and development of new products and processes;
2 construction of plants, buildings and highways;
3 maintenance of large and complex equipment;
4 design and installation of new systems.

In these types of projects, project managers must schedule and coordinate the various jobs or **activities** so that the entire project is completed on time. A complicating factor in carrying out this task is the interdependence of the activities; for example, some activities depend on the completion of other activities before they can be started. Because projects may have as many as several thousand activities, project managers look for procedures that will help them answer questions such as the following.

The UK Operational Research Society funded a study to identify factors that influenced the success and survival of internal MS consultancy groups. The study found that to be effective an MS group needs good consulting skills and expert project management.

1 How long will it take to complete the project?
2 What are the scheduled start and finish dates for each specific activity?
3 Which activities are 'critical' and must be completed *exactly* as scheduled to keep the project on schedule?
4 How long can 'noncritical' activities be delayed before they cause an increase in the total project completion time?

PERT and CPM can help answer these questions.

Although PERT and CPM have the same general purpose and utilize much of the same terminology, the techniques were developed independently.

MANAGEMENT SCIENCE IN ACTION

Nokia Networks

Nokia Networks is part of the Nokia telecoms company and provides network infrastructure, communications and networks service platforms, as well as professional services to operators and service providers with around 150 mobile network customers in more than 60 countries and with Nokia Network systems serving over 400 million subscribers. Planning and installing cellular networks is, by definition, project oriented with an average sized network typically including several thousand base station sites and with timely installation of the network critical to the client. Nokia Networks has developed an Integrated Project Management (IPM) programme to ensure a client-focused delivery process across its business by better management of the supply chain and is supported by an integrated IT platform, Nokia IPM Suite. The Suite enables integrated management of the different project activities and allows for effective monitoring of activities across different suppliers and clients.

Based on J. Collin and D. Lorenzin, 'Plan for supply chain agility at Nokia: Lessons from the mobile infrastructure industry', *International Journal of Physical Distribution and Logistics Management*, 36/16, (2006): 418–430.

PERT (Navy) and CPM (Du Pont and Remington Rand) differ because they were developed by different people working on different projects. Today, the best aspects of each have been combined to provide a valuable project scheduling technique.

PERT was developed in the late 1950s specifically for the Polaris missile project in the USA. Many activities associated with this project had never been attempted previously, so PERT was developed to handle uncertain activity times. CPM was developed primarily for industrial projects for which activity times were known. CPM offered the option of reducing activity times by adding more workers and/or resources, usually at an increased cost. So, a distinguishing feature of CPM was that it identified trade-offs between time and cost for various project activities.

Today's computerized versions of PERT and CPM combine the best features of both approaches. So, the distinction between the two techniques is no longer necessary. As a result, we refer to the project scheduling procedures covered in this chapter as PERT/CPM.

9.1 Project Scheduling With Known Activity Times

The effort that goes into identifying activities, determining interrelationships among activities and estimating activity times is crucial to the success of PERT/CPM. A significant amount of time may be needed to complete this initial phase of the project scheduling process.

The owner of the Souk al Bustan (SaB) Shopping Centre in Dubai is planning to modernize and expand the current 32-business shopping centre complex. The project is expected to provide room for eight to ten new retail businesses. Financing has been arranged through a private investor. All that remains is for the owner of the shopping centre to plan, schedule and complete the expansion project. Let us show how PERT/CPM can help.

The first step in the PERT/CPM scheduling process is to develop a list of the activities that make up the project. Table 9.1 shows the list of activities for the Shopping Centre expansion project. Nine activities are described and denoted A through I for later reference. Table 9.1 also shows the immediate predecessor(s) and the activity time (in weeks) for each activity. For a given activity, the immediate predecessor column identifies the activities that must be completed *immediately prior* to the start of that activity. Activities A and B do not have immediate predecessors and can be started as soon as the project begins; so, a dash is written in the immediate predecessor column for these activities. The other entries in the immediate predecessor column show that activities C, D and E cannot be started until activity A has been completed; activity F cannot be started until activity E has been completed; activity G cannot be started until both activities D and F have been completed; activity H cannot be started until both activities B and C have been completed; and, finally, activity I cannot be started until both activities G and H have been completed. The project is finished when activity I is completed.

Immediate predecessor information determines whether activities can be completed in parallel (worked on simultaneously) or in series (one completed before another begins). Generally, the more series relationships present in a project, the more time will be required to complete the project.

The last column in Table 9.1 shows the number of weeks required to complete each activity. For example, activity A takes five weeks, activity B takes six weeks and so on. The sum of activity times is 51. As a result, you may think that the total time required to complete the project is 51 weeks. However, as we show, two or more activities may often be scheduled concurrently, so shortening the completion time for the project. Ultimately, PERT/CPM will provide a detailed activity schedule for completing the project in the shortest time possible.

A project network is extremely helpful in visualizing the interrelationships among the activities. No rules guide the conversion of a list of activities and immediate predecessor information into a project network. The process of constructing a project network generally improves with practise and experience.

Using the immediate predecessor information in Table 9.1, we can construct a graphical representation of the project, or the **project network**. Figure 9.1 depicts the project network for the Shopping Centre. The activities correspond to the *nodes* of the network (drawn as rectangles) and the arrows show the precedence relationships among the activities. In addition, nodes have been added to the network to denote the start and the finish of the project. A project network will help a manager visualize the activity relationships and provide a basis for carrying out the PERT/CPM calculations.

Table 9.1 List of Activities for the Souk Al Bustan Shopping Centre Project

Activity	Activity Description	Immediate Predecessor	Activity Time (weeks)
A	Prepare architectural drawings	—	5
B	Identify potential new tenants	—	6
C	Develop prospectus for tenants	A	4
D	Select contractor	A	3
E	Prepare building permits	A	1
F	Obtain approval for building permits	E	4
G	Perform construction	D, F	14
H	Finalize contracts with tenants	B, C	12
I	Tenants move in	G, H	2
			Total 51

There are a few things to note about the diagram. The first is that when you are drawing the diagram manually it will usually take several attempts before it is right, particularly with more complex projects. You should always check your diagram to make sure that the sequencing of activities is correct and that the precedence structure is correct. Secondly, the length of the arrows does not necessarily correspond to the actual time taken. The length of arrows is determined by how we need to show the diagram in terms of logical precedence of activities. Thirdly, this type of diagram is referred to as an activity-on-node diagram (or precedence diagram). An alternative approach is the activity-on-arrow diagram which is described in Appendix 9.1. In this chapter we focus on the activity-on-node approach primarily because this is the approach typically adopted by project management software such as Microsoft Project.

The Concept of a Critical Path

To facilitate the PERT/CPM calculations, we have modified the project network as shown in Figure 9.2. Note that the upper left-hand corner of each node contains the corresponding activity letter. The activity time appears immediately below the letter.

Figure 9.1 Project Network for the Souk al Bustan Shopping Centre

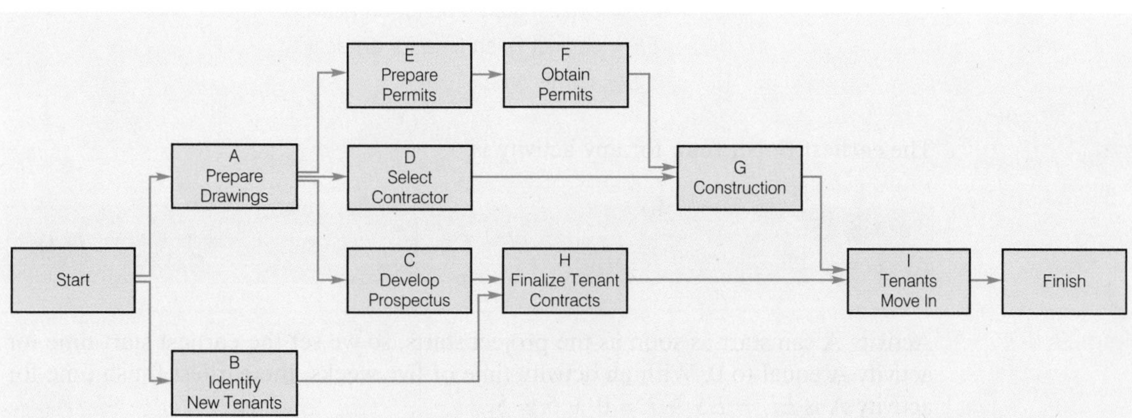

Figure 9.2 Souk al Bustan Shopping Centre Project Network with Activity Times

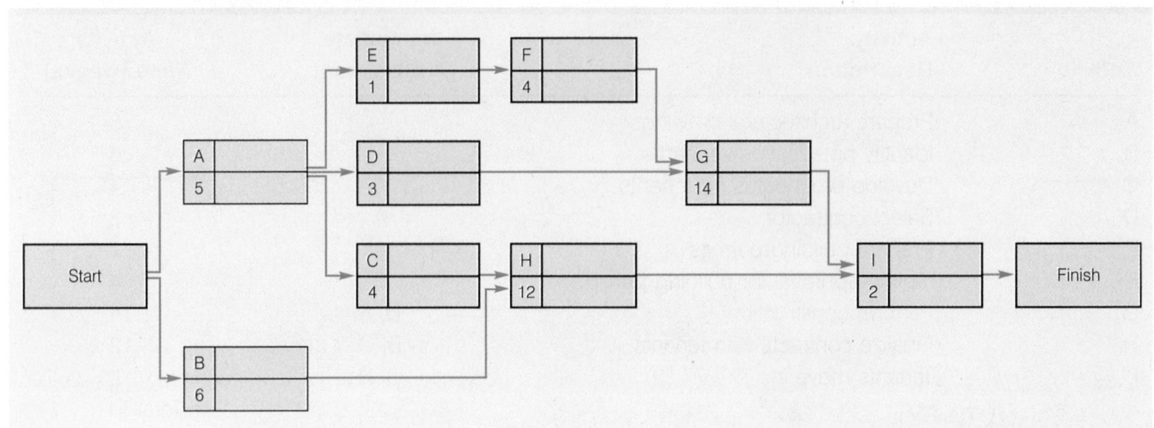

Problem 3 provides the immediate predecessor information for a project with seven activities and asks you to develop the project network.

For convenience, we use the convention of referencing activities with letters. Generally, we assign the letters in approximate order as we move from left to right through the project network.

To determine the project completion time, we have to analyze the network and identify what is called the **critical path** for the network. The critical path is the longest path through the network and shows the minimum time in which the project can be completed. A path is a sequence of connected nodes that leads from the Start node to the Finish node. For instance, one path for the network in Figure 9.2 is defined by the sequence of nodes A-E-F-G-I. By inspection, we see that other paths are possible, such as A-D-G-I, A-C-H-I and B-H-I. All paths in the network must be traversed in order to complete the project, so we will look for the path that requires the most time. Because all other paths are shorter in duration, this *longest* path determines the total time required to complete the project. If activities on the longest path are delayed, the entire project will be delayed. So, the longest path is the *critical path.* Activities on the critical path are referred to as the **critical activities** for the project. The following discussion presents a step-by-step algorithm for finding the critical path in a project network.

Determining the Critical Path

We begin by finding the **earliest start time** and a **latest start time** for all activities in the network. The earliest start time is the earliest time that activity can start (it may be dependent on other activities being completed first). Let:

$$\begin{aligned} ES &= \text{earliest start time for an activity} \\ EF &= \text{earliest finish time for an activity} \\ t &= \text{activity time} \end{aligned}$$

The **earliest finish time** for any activity is:

$$EF = ES + t \qquad \textbf{(9.1)}$$

Activity A can start as soon as the project starts, so we set the earliest start time for activity A equal to 0. With an activity time of five weeks, the earliest finish time for activity A is $EF = ES + t = 0 + 5 = 5$.

We will write the earliest start and earliest finish times in the node to the right of the activity letter. Using activity A as an example, we have:

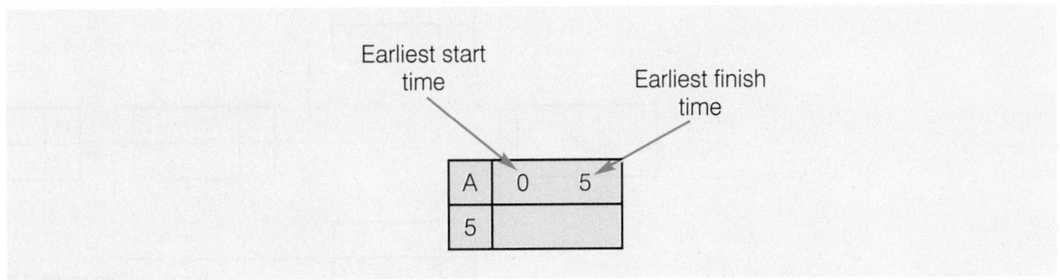

Because an activity cannot be started until *all* immediately preceding activities have been finished, the following rule can be used to determine the earliest start time for each activity.

> The earliest start time for an activity is equal to the *largest* of the earliest finish times for all its immediate predecessors.

Let us apply the earliest start time rule to the portion of the network involving nodes A, B, C and H, as shown in Figure 9.3. With an earliest start time of 0 and an activity time of 6 for activity B, we show $ES = 0$ and $EF = ES + t = 0 + 6 = 6$ in the node for activity B. Looking at node C, we note that activity A is the only immediate predecessor for activity C. The earliest finish time for activity A is 5, so the earliest start time for activity C must be $ES = 5$. So, with an activity time of 4, the earliest finish time for activity C is $EF = ES + t = 5 + 4 = 9$. Both the earliest start time and the earliest finish time can be shown in the node for activity C (see Figure 9.4).

Continuing with Figure 9.4, we move on to activity H and apply the earliest start time rule for this activity. With both activities B and C as immediate predecessors, the earliest start time for activity H must be equal to the largest of the earliest finish times for activities B and C. So, with $EF = 6$ for activity B and $EF = 9$ for activity C, we select the largest value, 9, as the earliest start time for activity H ($ES = 9$). With

Figure 9.3 A Portion of the Souk al Bustan Shopping Centre Project Network, Showing Activities A, B, C and H

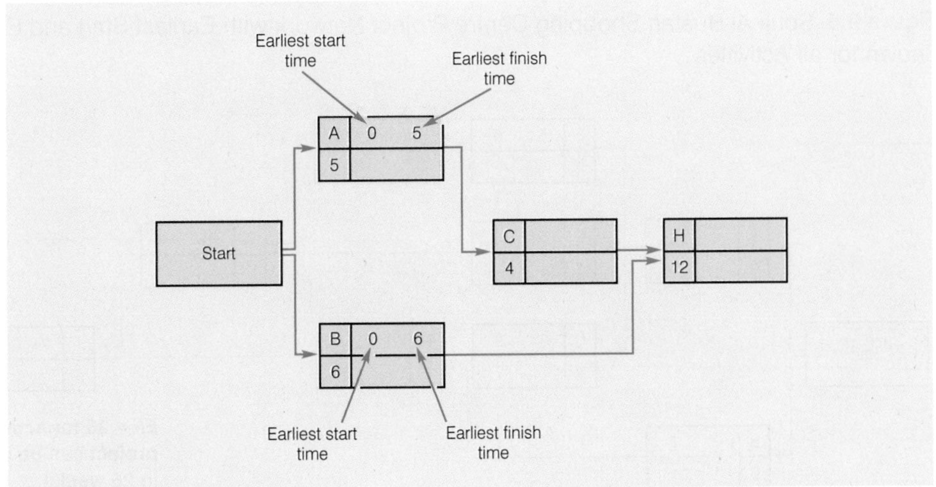

Figure 9.4 Determining the Earliest Start Time for Activity H

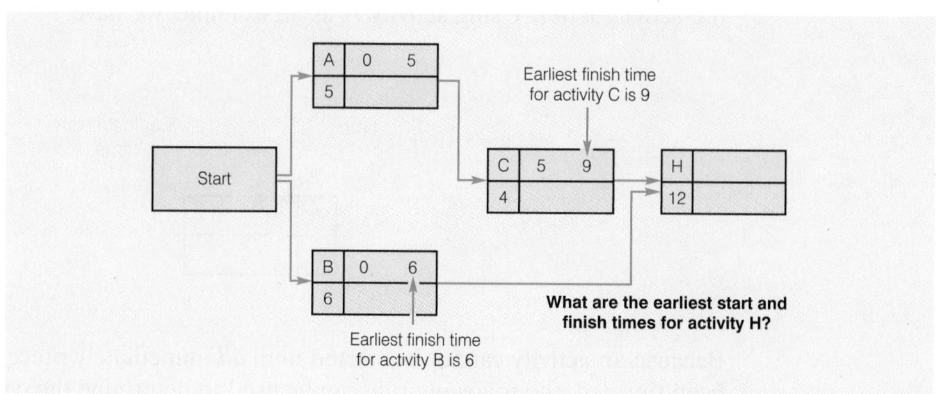

an activity time of 12 as shown in the node for activity H, the earliest finish time is $EF = ES + t = 9 + 12 = 21$. The $ES = 9$ and $EF = 21$ values can now be entered in the node for activity H in Figure 9.4.

Continuing with this **forward pass** through the network, we can establish the earliest start times and the earliest finish times for all activities in the network. Figure 9.5 shows the Shopping Centre project network with the *ES* and *EF* values for each activity. Note that the earliest finish time for activity I, the last activity in the project, is 26 weeks. Therefore, we now know that the total completion time for the project is 26 weeks.

We now continue the algorithm for finding the critical path by making a **backward pass** through the network. Because the total completion time for the project is 26 weeks, we begin the backward pass with a **latest finish time** of 26 for activity I. The latest finish time for an activity shows the latest time by which that activity must be finished if it is not to delay completion of the whole project. Once the latest finish time for an activity is known, the *latest start time* for an activity can be computed as follows. Let:

$$LS = \text{latest start time for an activity}$$
$$LF = \text{latest finish time for an activity}$$

Figure 9.5 Souk Al Bustan Shopping Centre Project Network with Earliest Start and Earliest Finish Times Shown for all Activities

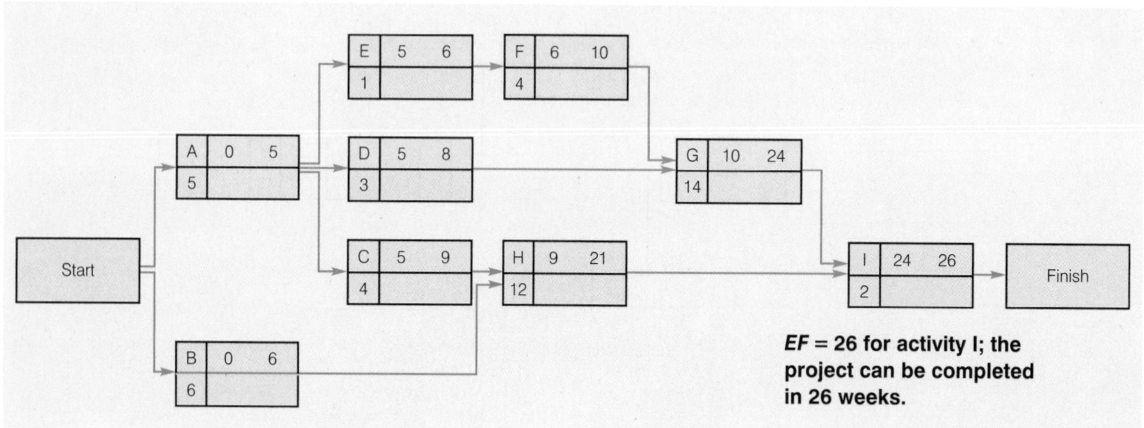

then

$$LS = LF - t \quad \textbf{(9.2)}$$

Beginning the backward pass with activity I, we know that the latest finish time is $LF = 26$ and that the activity time is $t = 2$. Thus, the latest start time for activity I is $LS = LF - t = 26 - 2 = 24$. We will write the LS and LF values in the node directly below the earliest start (ES) and earliest finish (EF) times. So, for node I, we have:

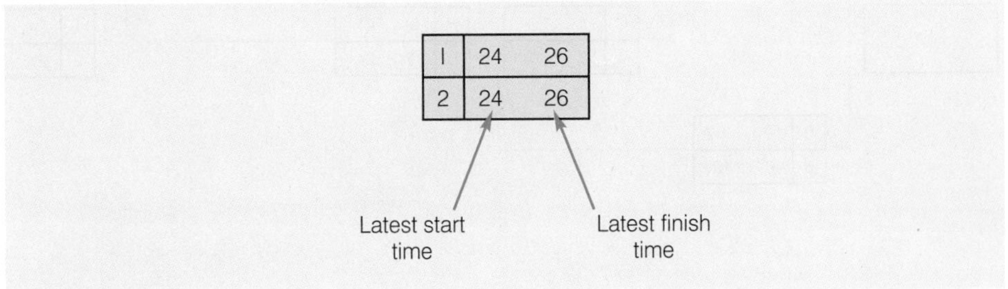

The following rule can be used to determine the latest finish time for each activity in the network.

> The latest finish time for an activity is the smallest of the latest start times for all activities that immediately follow the activity.

Logically, this rule states that the latest time an activity can be finished equals the earliest (smallest) value for the latest start time of following activities. Figure 9.6 shows the complete project network with the LS and LF backward pass results. We can use the latest finish time rule to verify the LS and LF values shown for activity H. The latest finish time for activity H must be the latest start time for activity I. Thus, we set $LF = 24$ for activity H. Using Equation (9.2), we find that $LS = LF - t = 24 - 12 = 12$ as the latest start time for activity H. These values are shown in the node for activity H in Figure 9.6.

Activity A requires a more involved application of the latest start time rule. First, note that three activities (C, D and E) immediately follow activity A. Figure 9.6 shows that the latest start times for activities C, D and E are $LS = 8$, $LS = 7$ and $LS = 5$, respectively. The latest finish time rule for activity A states that the LF for activity A is the smallest of the latest start times for activities C, D and E. With the smallest value being 5 for activity E, we set the latest finish time for activity A to $LF = 5$. Verify this result and the other latest start times and latest finish times shown in the nodes in Figure 9.6.

After we complete the forward and backward passes, we can determine the amount of slack associated with each activity. Slack is the length of time an activity can be delayed without increasing the project completion time (it is also referred to as Float time). The amount of slack for an activity is calculated as follows:

$$\text{Slack} = LS - ES = LF - EF \quad \textbf{(9.3)}$$

The slack for each activity indicates the length of time the activity can be delayed without increasing the overall project completion time.

For example, the slack associated with activity C is $LS - ES = 8 - 5 = 3$ weeks. So, activity C can be delayed up to three weeks, and the entire project can still be completed in 26 weeks. In this sense, activity C is not critical to the completion of the entire project in 26 weeks. Next, we consider activity E. Using the information in Figure 9.6, we find that the slack is $LS - ES = 5 - 5 = 0$. So, activity E has zero,

Figure 9.6 Souk Al Bustan Shopping Centre Project Network with Latest Start and Latest Finish Times Shown in Each Node

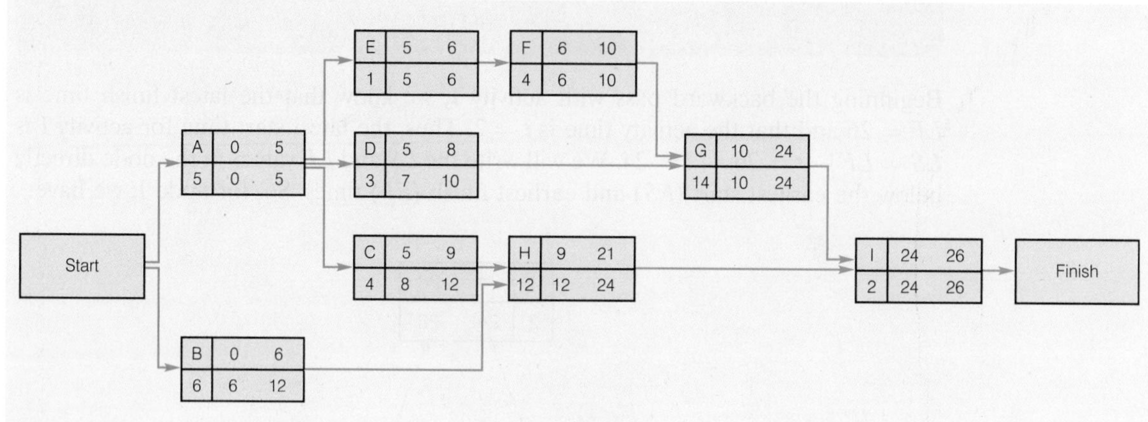

One of the primary contributions of PERT/CPM is the identification of the critical activities. The project manager will want to monitor critical activities closely because a delay in any one of these activities will lengthen the project completion time.

or no, slack. This activity cannot be delayed without increasing the completion time for the entire project. In other words, completing activity E exactly as scheduled is critical in terms of keeping the project on schedule. So, activity E is a critical activity. In general, the *critical activities* are the activities with zero slack.

The start and finish times shown in Figure 9.6 can be used to develop a detailed start time and finish time schedule for all activities. Putting this information in tabular form provides the activity schedule shown in Table 9.2. Note that the slack column shows that activities A, E, F, G and I have zero slack. Hence, these activities are the critical activities for the project. The path formed by nodes A–E–F–G–I is the *critical path* in the Shopping Centre project network. The detailed schedule shown in Table 9.2 indicates the slack or delay that can be tolerated for the noncritical activities before these activities will increase project completion time.

The critical path algorithm is essentially a longest path algorithm. From the start node to the finish node, the critical path identifies the path that requires the most time.

Contributions of PERT/CPM

Previously, we stated that project managers look for procedures that will help answer important questions regarding the planning, scheduling and controlling of projects. Let us reconsider these questions in light of the information that the critical path calculations have given us.

1 How long will the project take to complete?
Answer: The project can be completed in 26 weeks if each activity is completed on schedule.

2 What are the scheduled start and completion times for each activity?
Answer: The activity schedule (see Table 9.2) shows the earliest start, latest start, earliest finish and latest finish times for each activity.

If the total time required to complete the project is too long, judgement about where and how to shorten the time of critical activities must be exercised. If any activity times are altered, the critical path calculations should be repeated to determine the impact on the activity schedule and the impact on total project completion time.

3 Which activities are critical and must be completed *exactly* as scheduled to keep the project on schedule?
Answer: A, E, F, G and I are the critical activities.

4 How long can noncritical activities be delayed before they cause an increase in the completion time for the project?
Answer: The activity schedule (see Table 9.2) shows the slack associated with each activity. So for example Activity H could take up to three weeks longer than planned before delaying completion of the whole project.

Table 9.2 Activity Schedule for the Souk Al Bustan Shopping Centre Project

Activity	Earliest Start (*ES*)	Latest Start (*LS*)	Earliest Finish (*EF*)	Latest Finish (*LF*)	Float (*LS* − *ES*)	Critical Path?
A	0	0	5	5	0	Yes
B	0	6	6	12	6	
C	5	8	9	12	3	
D	5	7	8	10	2	
E	5	5	6	6	0	Yes
F	6	6	10	10	0	Yes
G	10	10	24	24	0	Yes
H	9	12	21	24	3	
I	24	24	26	26	0	Yes

Such information is valuable in managing any project. Although larger projects usually increase the effort required to develop the immediate predecessor relationships and the activity time estimates, the procedure and contribution of PERT/CPM to larger projects are identical to those shown for the shopping centre expansion project.

Software packages such as The Management Scientist perform the critical path calculations quickly and efficiently. The project manager can modify any aspect of the project and quickly determine how the modification affects the activity schedule and the total time required to complete the project.

Finally, computer packages may be used to carry out the steps of the PERT/CPM procedure. Figure 9.7 shows the activity schedule for the shopping centre expansion project developed by The Management Scientist software package. Input to the program included the activities, their immediate predecessors and the expected activity times. Only a few minutes were required to input the information and generate the critical path and activity schedule.

Summary of the PERT/CPM Critical Path Procedure

Before leaving this section, let us summarize the PERT/CPM critical path procedure.

Step 1. Develop a list of the activities that make up the project.

Step 2. Determine the immediate predecessor(s) for each activity in the project.

Step 3. Estimate the completion time for each activity.

Step 4. Draw a project network depicting the activities and immediate predecessors listed in steps 1 and 2.

Step 5. Use the project network and the activity time estimates to determine the earliest start and the earliest finish time for each activity by making a forward pass through the network. The earliest finish time for the last activity in the project identifies the total time required to complete the project.

Step 6. Use the project completion time identified in step 5 as the latest finish time for the last activity and make a backward pass through the network to identify the latest start and latest finish time for each activity.

Step 7. Use the difference between the latest start time and the earliest start time for each activity to determine the slack for each activity.

Step 8. Find the activities with zero slack; these are the critical activities.

Step 9. Use the information from steps 5 and 6 to develop the activity schedule for the project.

Figure 9.7 The Management Scientist Activity Schedule for the Souk Al Bustan Shopping Centre Project

EXCEL *file*

SAB

*** ACTIVITY SCHEDULE ***

ACTIVITY	EARLIEST START	LATEST START	EARLIEST FINISH	LATEST FINISH	SLACK	CRITICAL ACTIVITY
A	0	0	5	5	0	YES
B	0	6	6	12	6	
C	5	8	9	12	3	
D	5	7	8	10	2	
E	5	5	6	6	0	YES
F	6	6	10	10	0	YES
G	10	10	24	24	0	YES
H	9	12	21	24	3	
I	24	24	26	26	0	YES

CRITICAL PATH: A-E-F-G-I

PROJECT COMPLETION TIME = 26

Gantt Charts

One particularly effective way of showing the key information from a project network is the Gannt chart. A Gantt chart is a visual presentation of some of the information from Table 9.2. The Gantt chart for the Souk al Bustan Shopping Centre project is shown in Figure 9.8. The chart shows the project activities on the vertical axis and the project duration on the horizontal timescale. A bar is used for each individual activity with the bar starting at that activity's ES time and ending at the activity's EF time. If there is slack time associated with that activity, this is shown

Figure 9.8 Gantt Chart for the Souk Shopping Centre project

Activity	Time																										
	Project start	1	2	3	4	5	6	7	8	9	10	11	12	13	14	15	16	17	18	19	20	21	22	23	24	25	26
A																											
B																											
C																											
D																											
E																											
F																											
G																											
H																											
I																											

MANAGEMENT SCIENCE IN ACTION

Hospital Revenue Bond at Seasongood & Mayer

Seasongood & Mayer is an investment securities firm located in Cincinnati, Ohio. The firm engages in municipal financing including the underwriting of new issues of municipal bonds, acting as a market maker for previously issued bonds and performing other investment banking services.

Seasongood & Mayer provided the underwriting for a $31 million issue of hospital facilities revenue bonds for Providence Hospital in Hamilton County, Ohio. The project of underwriting this municipal bond issue began with activities such as drafting the legal documents, drafting a description of the existing hospital facilities and completing a feasibility study. A total of 23 activities defined the project that would be completed when the hospital signed the construction contract and then made the bond proceeds available. The immediate predecessor relationships for the activities and the activity times were developed by a project management team.

PERT/CPM analysis of the project network identified the ten critical path activities. The analysis also provided the expected completion time of 29 weeks, or approximately seven months. The activity schedule showed the start time and finish time for each activity and provided the information necessary to monitor the project and keep it on schedule. PERT/CPM was instrumental in helping Seasongood & Mayer obtain the financing for the project within the time specified in the construction bid.

Henry L. Gantt developed the Gantt chart as graphical aid to scheduling jobs on machines in 1918. This application was the first of what has become know as project scheduling techniques.

at the right-hand side of the bar, usually with a different shading. The chart makes it easy to understand the sequencing of the various activities, the critical path activities (with zero slack) and allows a manager to monitor the project's progress over time. We see, for example, that Activity B is non-critical (it has slack time) and can start at the beginning of the project, could finish as early as the end of Week 6 but could take as long as the end of Week 12 without delaying the overall project.

NOTES AND COMMENTS

Suppose that, after analyzing a PERT/CPM network, the project manager finds that the project completion time is unacceptable (i.e., the project is going to take too long). In this case, the manager must take one or both of the following steps. First, review the original PERT/CPM network to see whether any immediate predecessor relationships can be modified so that at least some of the critical path activities can be done simultaneously. Second, consider adding resources to critical path activities in an attempt to shorten the critical path; we discuss this alternative, referred to as *crashing,* in Section 9.3.

9.2 Project Scheduling With Uncertain Activity Times

Clearly, in the example we have just worked through, we have treated the activity times as certain. That is, for example, we have assumed Activity A will take exactly five weeks. In practice, project activities may not be known for certain. Sometimes it may be possible to complete some activities earlier than usual or later than usual. Sometimes, with new projects we may have only a best-estimate of the likely activity time. In such situations we need to be able to deal with uncertainty in activity completion times. We shall show how we do this with the following example.

The Daugherty Porta-Vac Project

Accurate activity time estimates are important in the development of an activity schedule. When activity times are uncertain, the three time estimates – optimistic, most probable and pessimistic – allow the project manager to take uncertainty into consideration in determining the critical path and the activity schedule. This approach was developed by the designers of PERT.

The H.S. Daugherty Company in Ireland has manufactured industrial vacuum cleaning systems for many years. Recently, a member of the company's new-product research team submitted a report suggesting that the company consider manufacturing a cordless vacuum cleaner. The new product, referred to as Porta-Vac, could contribute to Daugherty's expansion into the household market. Management hopes that it can be manufactured at a reasonable cost and that its portability and no-cord convenience will make it extremely attractive.

Daugherty's management wants to study the feasibility of manufacturing the Porta-Vac product. The feasibility study will recommend the action to be taken. To complete this study, information must be obtained from the firm's research and development (R&D), product testing, manufacturing, cost estimating and market research groups. How long will this feasibility study take? In the following discussion, we show how to answer this question and provide an activity schedule for the project.

Again, the first step in the project scheduling process is to identify all activities that make up the project and then determine the immediate predecessor(s) for each activity. Table 9.3 shows these data for the Porta-Vac project.

The Porta-Vac project network is shown in Figures 9.9 and 9.10. Verify that the network does in fact maintain the immediate predecessor relationships shown in Table 9.3.

Uncertain Activity Times

However, suppose that the manager in charge of this project has now been informed that some of the activity times are not guaranteed but are best estimates. After all, this is quite likely in the real world. Unpredictable factors may affect the completion of a particular activity: it may take longer than we thought or sometimes we may be able to complete it earlier than expected. How will this affect the project network, the current critical path and overall project completion? If we consider Activity A, for example, which is currently on the critical path, we may now be informed that the most likely activity time is five weeks but that it could take as long as 12 weeks or, if everything goes well, we might finish this activity in four weeks. In fact, in many cases, activity times are uncertain and are best described by a range of possible

Table 9.3 Activity List for the Porta-Vac Project

Activity	Description	Immediate Predecessor	Activity Time (weeks)
A	Develop product design	—	5
B	Plan market research	—	1.5
C	Prepare routing (manufacturing engineering)	A	3
D	Build prototype model	A	4
E	Prepare marketing brochure	A	3
F	Prepare cost estimates (industrial engineering)	C	2
G	Do preliminary product testing	D	3
H	Complete market survey	B, E	3.5
I	Prepare pricing and forecast report	H	2
J	Prepare final report	F, G, I	2

Figure 9.9 Porta-Vac Cordless Vacuum Cleaner Project Network

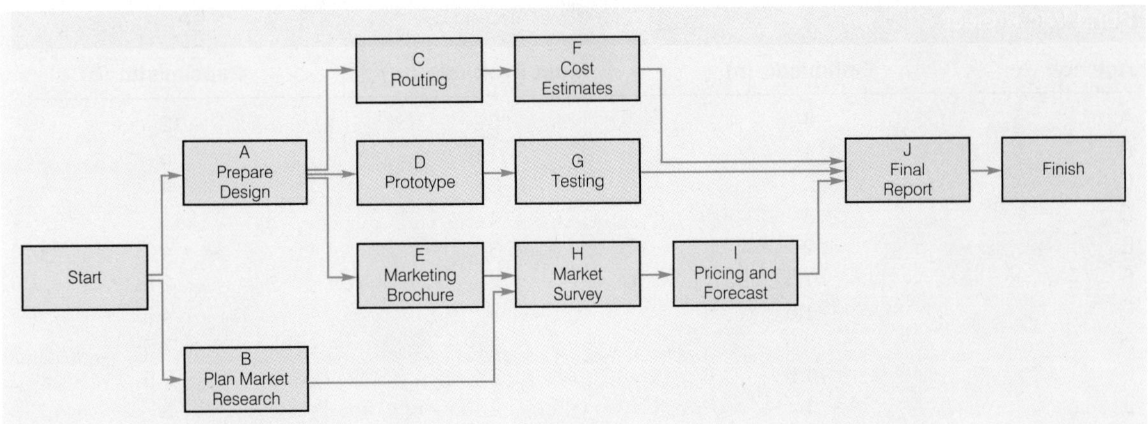

Figure 9.10 Porta-Vac Project Network with Activity Times

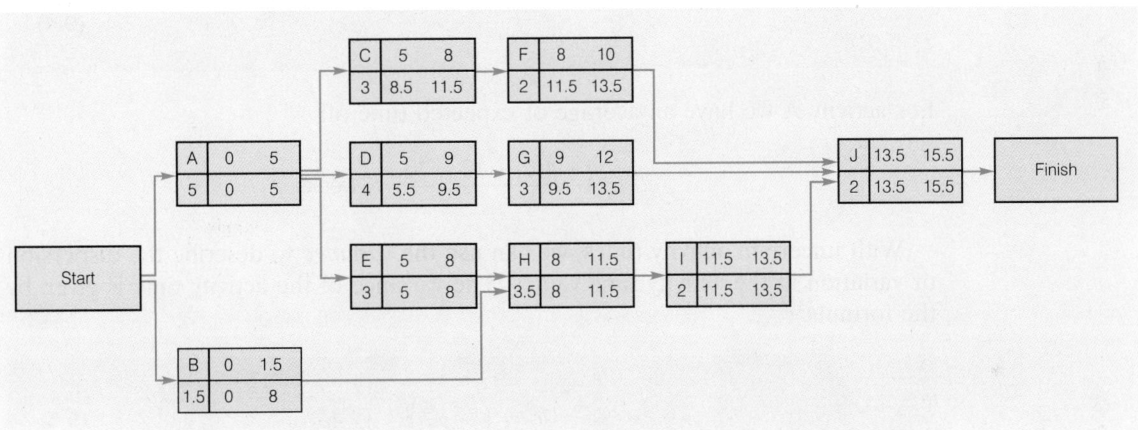

values rather than by one specific time estimate. In these instances, the uncertain activity times are treated as random variables with associated probability distributions. As a result, probability statements will be provided about the ability to meet a specific project completion date.

To incorporate uncertain activity times into the analysis, we need to obtain three time estimates for each activity:

Optimistic time a = the minimum activity time if everything progresses ideally

Most probable time m = the most probable activity time under normal conditions

Pessimistic time b = the maximum activity time if significant delays are encountered

To illustrate the PERT/CPM procedure with uncertain activity times, let us consider the optimistic, most probable and pessimistic time estimates for the Porta-Vac activities as presented in Table 9.4. Using activity A as an example, we see that the most probable time is five weeks with a range from four weeks (optimistic) to 12 weeks (pessimistic). If the activity could be repeated a large number of times, what is the average time for the activity? This average or **expected time** (t) is as follows:

Table 9.4 Optimistic, Most Probable and Pessimistic Activity Time Estimates (In Weeks) for the Porta-Vac Project

Activity	Optimistic (*a*)	Most Probable (*m*)	Pessimistic (*b*)
A	4	5	12
B	1	1.5	5
C	2	3	4
D	3	4	11
E	2	3	4
F	1.5	2	2.5
G	1.5	3	4.5
H	2.5	3.5	7.5
I	1.5	2	2.5
J	1	2	3

$$t = \frac{a + 4m + b}{6} \tag{9.4}$$

For activity A we have an average or expected time of:

$$t_A = \frac{4 + 4(5) + 12}{6} = \frac{36}{6} = 6 \text{ weeks}$$

With uncertain activity times, we can use the *variance* to describe the dispersion or variation in the activity time values. The variance of the activity time is given by the formula[1]:

$$\sigma^2 = \left(\frac{b - a}{6}\right)^2 \tag{9.5}$$

The difference between the pessimistic (b) and optimistic (a) time estimates greatly affects the value of the variance. Large differences in these two values reflect a high degree of uncertainty in the activity time. Using Equation (9.5), we obtain the measure of uncertainty – that is, the variance – of activity A, denoted σ_A^2:

$$\sigma_A^2 = \left(\frac{12 - 4}{6}\right)^2 = \left(\frac{8}{6}\right)^2 = 1.78$$

Equations (9.4) and (9.5) are based on the assumption that the activity time distribution can be described by a **beta probability distribution.**[2] With this assumption, the probability distribution for the time to complete activity A is as shown in Figure 9.11. Using Equations (9.4) and (9.5) and the data in Table 9.4, we calculated the expected times and variances for all Porta-Vac activities; the results are summarized in Table 9.5.

[1]The variance equation is based on the notion that a standard deviation is approximately $\frac{1}{6}$ of the difference between the extreme values of the distribution: $(b - a)/6$. The variance is the square of the standard deviation.

[2]The equations for t and σ^2 require additional assumptions about the parameters of the beta probability distribution. However, even when these additional assumptions are not made, the equations still provide good approximations of t and σ^2.

Figure 9.11 Activity Time Distribution for Product Design (Activity A) for the Porta-Vac Project

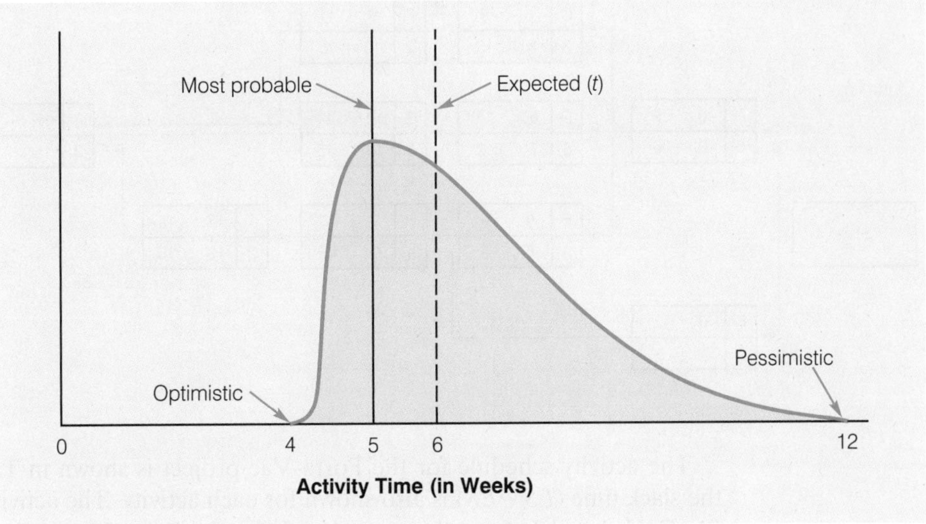

When uncertain activity times are used, the critical path calculations will determine only the expected or average time to complete the project. The actual time required to complete the project may differ. However, for planning purposes, the expected time should be valuable information for the project manager.

Activities that have larger variances show a greater degree of uncertainty. The project manager should monitor the progress of any activity with a large variance even if the expected time does not identify the activity as a critical activity.

The Critical Path

When we have the project network and the expected activity times, we are ready to proceed with the critical path calculations necessary to determine the expected time required to complete the project and determine the activity schedule. In these calculations, we treat the expected activity times (Table 9.5) as the fixed length or known duration of each activity. As a result, we can use the critical path procedure introduced in Section 9.1 to find the critical path for the Porta-Vac project. After the critical activities and the expected time to complete the project have been determined, we analyze the effect of the activity time variability.

Proceeding with a forward pass through the network shown in Figure 9.10, we can establish the earliest start (*ES*) and earliest finish (*EF*) times for each activity. Next, we make a backward pass through the network. The backward pass provides the latest start (*LS*) and latest finish (*LF*) times shown in Figure 9.12. The project is now expected to take 17 weeks to complete.

Table 9.5 Expected Times and Variances for the Porta-Vac Project Activities

Activity	Expected Time (weeks)	Variance
A	6	1.78
B	2	0.44
C	3	0.11
D	5	1.78
E	3	0.11
F	2	0.03
G	3	0.25
H	4	0.69
I	2	0.03
J	2	0.11
	Total 32	

Figure 9.12 Porta-Vac Project Network with Latest Start and Latest Finish Times

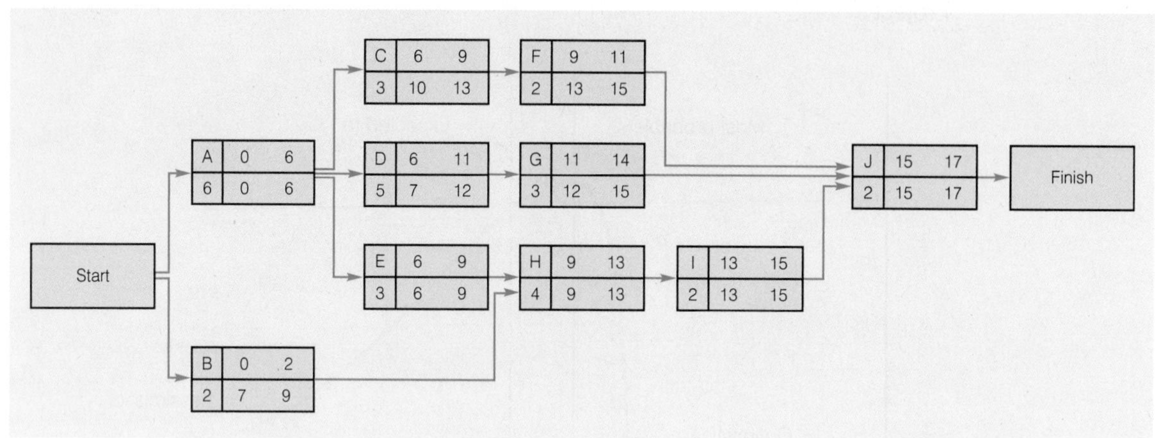

The activity schedule for the Porta-Vac project is shown in Table 9.6. Note that the slack time ($LS - ES$) is also shown for each activity. The activities with zero slack (A, E, H, I and J) form the critical path for the Porta-Vac project network.

Variability in Project Completion Time

We know that for the Porta-Vac project the critical path of A–E–H–I–J resulted in an expected total project completion time of 17 weeks. However, variation in critical activities can cause variation in the project completion time. Variation in noncritical activities ordinarily has no effect on the project completion time because of the slack time associated with these activities. However, if a noncritical activity is delayed long enough to expend its slack time, it becomes part of a new critical path and may affect the project completion time. Variability leading to a longer-than-expected total time for the critical activities will always extend the project completion time, and conversely, variability that results in a shorter-than-expected total time for the critical activities will reduce the project completion time, unless other activities become critical. Let us now use the variance in the critical activities to determine the variance in the project completion time.

Let T denote the total time required to complete the project. The expected value of T, which is the sum of the expected times for the critical activities is:

$$\begin{aligned} E(T) &= t_A + t_E + t_H + t_I + t_J \\ &= 6 + 3 + 4 + 2 + 2 = 17 \text{ weeks} \end{aligned}$$

The variance in the project completion time is the sum of the variances of the critical path activities. Thus, the variance for the Porta-Vac project completion time is:

$$\begin{aligned} \sigma^2 &= \sigma_A^2 + \sigma_E^2 + \sigma_H^2 + \sigma_I^2 + \sigma_J^2 \\ &= 1.78 + 0.11 + 0.69 + 0.03 + 0.11 = 2.72 \end{aligned}$$

Problem 10 involves a project with uncertain activity times and asks you to calculate the expected completion time and the variance for the project.

where $\sigma_A^2, \sigma_E^2, \sigma_H^2, \sigma_I^2$ and σ_J^2 are the variances of the critical activities.

The formula for σ^2 is based on the assumption that the activity times are independent. If two or more activities are dependent, the formula provides only an approximation of the variance of the project completion time. The closer the activities are to being independent, the better the approximation.

Knowing that the standard deviation is the square root of the variance, we compute the standard deviation σ for the Porta-Vac project completion time as:

$$\sigma = \sqrt{\sigma^2} = \sqrt{2.72} = 1.65$$

Table 9.6 Activity Schedule for the Porta-Vac Project

Activity	Earliest Start (*ES*)	Latest Start (*LS*)	Earliest Finish (*EF*)	Latest Finish (*LF*)	Slack (*LS* − *ES*)	Critical Path?
A	0	0	6	6	0	Yes
B	0	7	2	9	7	
C	6	10	9	13	4	
D	6	7	11	12	1	
E	6	6	9	9	0	Yes
F	9	13	11	15	4	
G	11	12	14	15	1	
H	9	9	13	13	0	Yes
I	13	13	15	15	0	Yes
J	15	15	17	17	0	Yes

Assuming that the distribution of the project completion time T follows a normal or bell-shaped distribution[3] allows us to draw the distribution shown in Figure 9.13. With this distribution, we can calculate the probability of meeting a specified project completion date. For example, suppose that management allotted 20 weeks for the Porta-Vac project. What is the probability that we will meet the 20-week deadline? Using the normal probability distribution shown in Figure 9.14, we are asking for the probability that $T \leq 20$; this probability is shown graphically as the shaded area in the figure. The z value for the normal probability distribution at $T = 20$ is:

$$z = \frac{20 - 17}{1.65} = 1.82$$

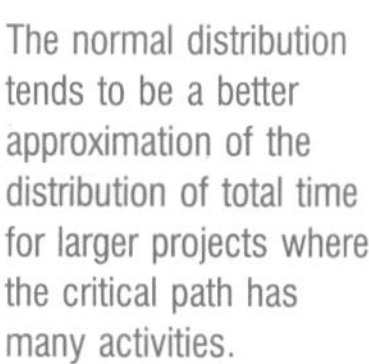
The normal distribution tends to be a better approximation of the distribution of total time for larger projects where the critical path has many activities.

Figure 9.13 Normal Distribution of the Project Completion Time for the Porta-Vac Project

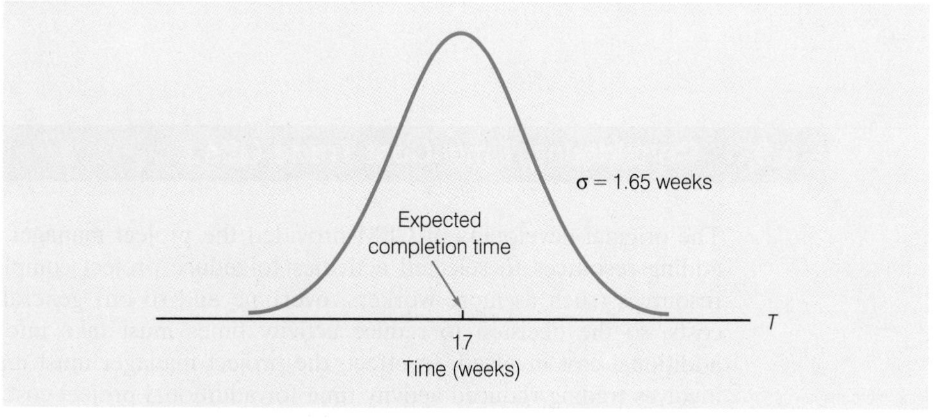

[3]Use of the normal distribution as an approximation is based on the central limit theorem, which indicates that the sum of independent random variables (activity times) follows a normal distribution as the number of random variables becomes large.

Figure 9.14 Probability the Porta-Vac Project Will Meet the 20-Week Deadline

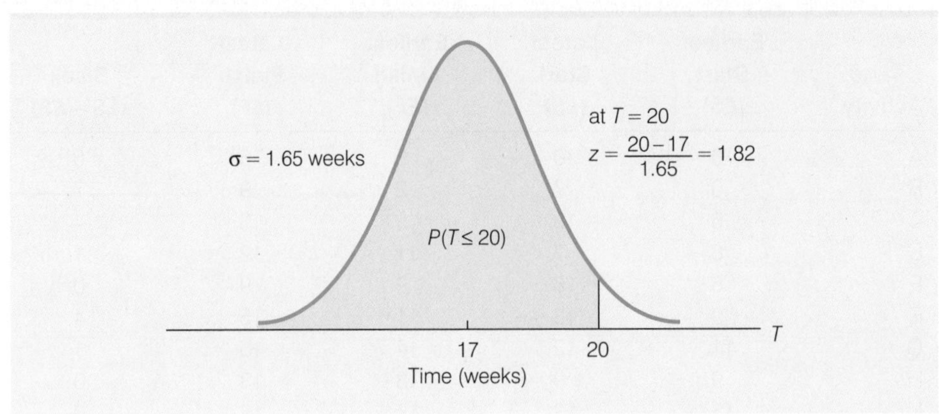

Using $z = 1.82$ and the table for the normal distribution (see Appendix A), we find that the probability of the project meeting the 20-week deadline is $0.4656 + 0.5000 = 0.9656$. Thus, even though activity time variability may cause the completion time to exceed 17 weeks, calculations indicate a high probability that the project will be completed before the 20-week deadline. Similar probability calculations can be made for other project deadline alternatives.

NOTES AND COMMENTS

For projects involving uncertain activity times, the probability that the project can be completed within a specified amount of time is helpful managerial information. However, remember that this probability estimate is based *only* on the critical activities. When uncertain activity times exist, longer-than-expected completion times for one or more noncritical activities may cause an original noncritical activity to become critical and hence increase the time required to complete the project. By frequently monitoring the progress of the project to make sure all activities are on schedule, the project manager will be better prepared to take corrective action if a noncritical activity begins to lengthen the duration of the project.

9.3 Considering Time–Cost Trade-Offs

The original developers of CPM provided the project manager with the option of adding resources to selected activities to reduce project completion time. Added resources (such as more workers, overtime and so on) generally increase project costs, so the decision to reduce activity times must take into consideration the additional cost involved. In effect, the project manager must make a decision that involves trading reduced activity time for additional project cost.

Using more resources to reduce activity times was proposed by the developers of CPM. The shortening of activity times is referred to as crashing.

Consider a scenario in a hospital. In one of the surgical clinics, two specialist machines periodically have to undergo routine maintenance. While this is being done, medical operations are halted and clearly the hospital manager is keen for the time needed for maintenance to be as short as possible. Table 9.7 summarizes the key activities involved in this project. Because management has had substantial

Table 9.7 Activity List for the Two-Machine Maintenance Project

Activity	Description	Immediate Predecessor	Expected Time (days)
A	Overhaul machine I	—	7
B	Calibrate machine I	A	3
C	Overhaul machine II	—	6
D	Calibrate machine II	C	3
E	Test system	B, D	2

experience with similar projects, the times for maintenance activities are considered to be known; hence, a single time estimate is given for each activity. The project network is shown in Figure 9.15.

The procedure for making critical path calculations for the maintenance project network is the same one used to find the critical path in the networks for both the Souk al Bustan Shopping Centre expansion project and the Porta-Vac project. Making the forward pass and backward pass calculations for the network in Figure 9.15, we obtained the activity schedule shown in Table 9.8. The zero slack times, and also the critical path, are associated with activities A–B–E. The length of the critical path, and thus the total time required to complete the project, is 12 days.

Crashing Activity Times

Suppose now the hospital manager insists that the maintenance must be completed within ten days, given the effect on patient treatment. By looking at the length of the critical path of the network (12 days), we realize that meeting the desired project completion time is impossible unless we can shorten some activity times. This shortening of activity times, which usually can be achieved by adding resources, is referred to as **crashing**. However, the added resources associated with crashing activity times usually result in added project costs, so we will want to identify the activities that cost the least to crash and then crash those activities only the amount necessary to meet the desired project completion time.

For example, we know that Activity A, on the critical path, is expected to take seven days. However, suppose that by paying the staff involved a bonus of €300 we could reduce this to four days. Given that Activity A is critical we know that a reduction in activity time, other things being equal, will lead to a reduction in overall

Figure 9.15 Two-Machine Maintenance Project Network

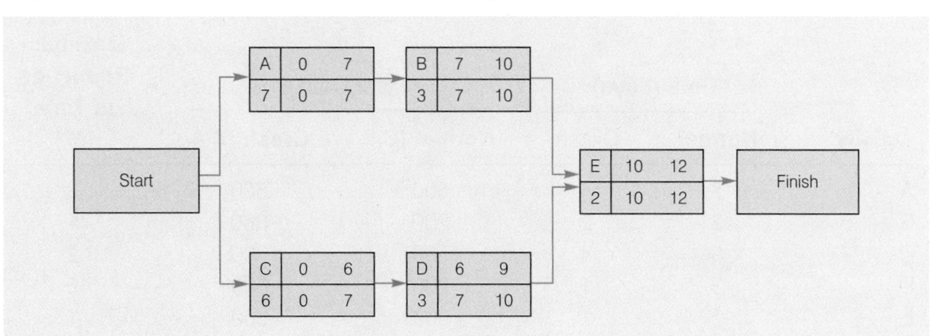

Table 9.8 Activity Schedule for the Two-Machine Maintenance Project

Activity	Earliest Start (*ES*)	Latest Start (*LS*)	Earliest Finish (*EF*)	Latest Finish (*LF*)	Slack (*LS* – *ES*)	Critical Path?
A	0	0	7	7	0	Yes
B	7	7	10	10	0	Yes
C	0	1	6	7	1	
D	6	7	9	10	1	
E	10	10	12	12	0	Yes

completion time. However, it is also evident that as we crash one activity, the slack time associated with other activities may change and therefore the critical path may change. Because of this we adopt an incremental approach to crashing by crashing one activity at a time and crashing by one day at a time. The overall purpose of crashing is to reduce the project duration while minimizing the extra costs. The first step is to pull together relevant information for each activity. This is shown in Table 9.9.

For each activity, we show the normal activity time and the crash time. So, for example, we see that Activity A takes seven days to complete but it is possible to reduce this to four days. Similarly, Activity B takes three days but could be reduced to two. Next we show the normal cost of completing each activity and the crash cost, with the difference between the two being the extra costs incurred by crashing that activity. Activity A, for example, normally costs €500 to complete but could be done more quickly for a total cost of €800. The next column shows the maximum possible reduction in activity time (the Normal time minus the Crash time). Finally we show the crash cost per day calculated as the extra costs incurred by crashing divided by the maximum reduction in time possible through crashing. So, again for Activity A, the extra crash cost is €300 divided by three days or €100 per day. We make the simplifying assumption that there is a linear relationship between crash costs and crash time. Now we have the information we need, we can proceed to crash the project. To reduce overall project duration we only need to consider those activities that are currently critical: A,B,E. Of these, Activity A has the lowest crash cost per day so is to be preferred given that we want to reduce project completion time while minimizing any extra cost.

Table 9.9 Normal and Crash Activity Data for the Two-Machine Maintenance Project

	Time (days)		Total Cost €		Maximum Reduction in Time	Crash Cost per Day
Activity	Normal	Crash	Normal (C_i)	Crash (C'_i)	(M_i)	$\left(K_i = \frac{C'_i - C_i}{M_i}\right)$
A	7	4	500	800	3	€100
B	3	2	200	350	1	150
C	6	4	500	900	2	200
D	3	1	200	500	2	150
E	2	1	300	500	1	200

MANAGEMENT SCIENCE IN ACTION

Kimberly-Clark Europe

Kimberly-Clark are a leading global health and hygiene company employing almost 60 000 staff worldwide and with sales of nearly $16 billion in 2005. It has operations in 37 countries and sells in more than 150 countries. However, in the late 1990s its European business was facing difficulties. Although its UK business was strong, the company were keen to expand market share across the rest of Europe, but a number of critical projects had not been completed successfully and were affecting the company's results to the extent that a profits warning was issued. An independent review concluded that there were major problems relating to: project management lacking standards and discipline; roles and responsibilities being unclear; unrealistic timescales being set. The company decided on an initiative to establish common project management approaches across Kimberly-Clark Europe supported by extensive staff training. As a result the company is now confident that the selection of projects is improved and that those projects are being managed effectively with significant cost savings being achieved.

Based on M. Palmer, 'How an effective project culture can help to achieve business success: Establishing a project culture in Kimberly-Clark Europe', *Industrial and Commercial Training*, 34/3 (2002): 101–105.

So we crash Activity A by one day at a cost of €100. This will reduce the overall completion time from the current 12 days to 11 days. However, we can crash Activity A still further given that there are a further two crash days available. However, crashing Activity A by one day may have affected the slack times of other activities and may have altered the critical path so we need to check the network. On inspection of Figure 9.14 we can see that the A–B part of the network will now have a duration of nine days (six+three) and that of the C–D part of the network will also have a total duration of nine days (six+three). We now have a situation whereby, through crashing Activity A, all activities are now critical. Clearly crashing Activity A by a further day will not reduce the overall project duration time since the path C–D will still take nine days. Clearly, if we were to crash part of the A–B path by one day we would simultaneously have to crash part of the C–D path by one day. The net effect on total project duration, however, would only be one day. In fact we can summarize the crashing options we now have:

Activities to be crashed	Total crash costs
A and C	€300 (€100 + €200)
A and D	€250 (€100 + €150)
B and C	€350 (€150 + €200)
B and D	€300 (€150 + €150)
E	€200

The Project Management Institute (PMI) was formed in 1969 to provide a forum for the project management community.

We now see that the lowest cost option is to crash Activity E next. This will reduce total project duration by a further day, to ten days, at an extra cost of €200. We have now met the hospital manager's target of completing the maintenance in ten days but we should inform her that this will cost an extra €300. If any further reductions are needed, we could simply continue crashing activities using the information above. In this example, crashing can be conducted with some basic calculations and careful inspection of the project network. For more complex projects, crashing would normally be done as part of the computer software solution.

Summary

In this chapter we have introduced techniques for managing projects:

- Developing a project network diagram is an effective way of planning and managing complex projects.
- The diagram is used to show the sequencing and inter-connection between the various project activities.
- By calculating start and finish times we can determine the critical path for the project showing the minimum completion time. The diagram also identifies activities where there is slack time.
- We can incorporate uncertain or variable activity times and calculate the probability that the project is completed by a certain time.
- We can also undertake crashing to assess the cost and feasibility of reducing the project completion time.

WORKED EXAMPLE

The Kellerwirt Gasthaus in Austria is a small, family-run hotel catering for tourists. The hotel is planning to replace its small swimming pool with a heated outdoor pool. However, it is critical that the project is completed in time for the start of the coming summer season, otherwise the hotel risks upsetting guests expecting to use the new facilities and also risks construction work causing noise and disruption. The summer season starts in nine weeks' time. The local company contracted to build the pool have provided the following information and also indicated that they work five days each week.

Activity	Preceding activities	Likely duration (days)	Best case duration (days)	Worst case duration (days)
A Remove existing pool	-	5	3	6
B Transport rubble off site	A	4	2	6
C Excavate new site	B	6	5	7
D Install new pool	C	9	7	10
E Install solar heating system	C	4	2	6
F Test pool for heating and leakage	D, E	2	1	3
G Construction and tiling around pool area	D	8	5	10
H Plant shrubbery around pool	G	8	6	10
I Final clean up	F, H	4	3	5

What advice can we give the hotel?

First we can calculate the Expected duration times and the variances:

Activity	Worst case duration	Likely duration	Best case duration	Expected duration	Variance
A	6	5	3	4.833333	0.25
B	6	4	2	4	0.444444
C	7	6	5	6	0.111111
D	10	9	7	8.833333	0.25
E	6	4	2	4	0.444444
F	3	2	1	2	0.111111
G	10	8	5	7.833333	0.694444
H	10	8	6	8	0.444444
I	5	4	3	4	0.111111

We can then construct the network diagram using the Expected durations to identify the critical path. This is shown below. From the diagram we see that the Expected completion time is 43.5 days with all activities critical except for E and F. However, we can go one stage further. The contractor works five days each week so the hotel's summer season effectively starts in 45 working days' time (nine weeks x five). We can calculate the variance of the critical activities at 2.31 and the standard deviation at 1.51.We can then calculate the probability that the project will be completed within 45 working days:

$$Z = \frac{43.5 - 45}{1.51} = 0.99$$

From the Normal probability table we see this has a probability associated with it of 0.3389. Therefore the probability that the project will be completed within 45 days is 0.84 (0.5+0.3389) or 84 per cent. So we can tell the hotel that, based on the information given, there is an 84 per cent chance the project will be finished before the summer season starts. If this is seen as unacceptable, we can advise the hotel to consider paying a bonus to the contractor for crashing critical activities. We have no information on this at present but it would not be difficult to obtain from the contractor any extra costs incurred in speeding up parts of the project. Clearly, the hotel would then have to assess whether these extra crash costs were worthwhile.

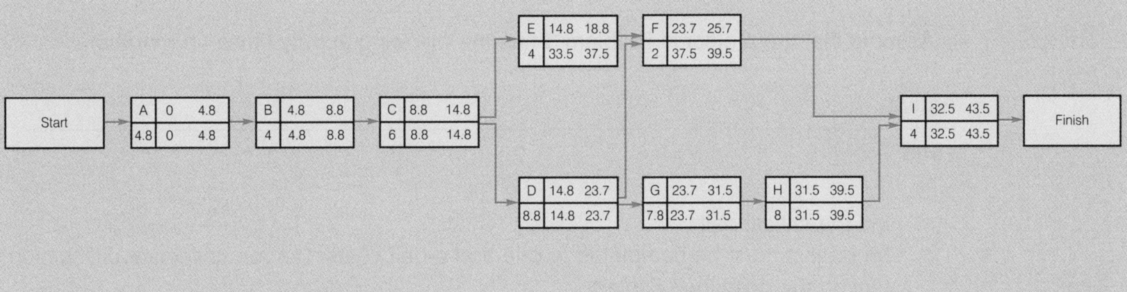

Problems

1 The Mohawk Discount Store is designing a management training programme for staff at its corporate headquarters. The company wants to design the programme so that trainees can complete it as quickly as possible. Important precedence relationships must be maintained between assignments or activities in the programme. For example, a trainee cannot serve as an assistant to the store manager until the trainee has obtained experience in the credit department and at least one sales department. The following activities are the assignments that must be completed by each trainee in the programme. Construct a project network for this problem. Do not perform any further analysis.

Activity	A	B	C	D	E	F	G	H
Immediate Predecessor	—	—	A	A, B	A, B	C	D, F	E, G

SELF *test*

2 Bridge City Developers is coordinating the construction of an office complex. As part of the planning process, the company generated the following activity list. Draw a project network that can be used to assist in the scheduling of the project activities.

Activity	A	B	C	D	E	F	G	H	I	J
Immediate Predecessor	—	—	—	A, B	A, B	D	E	C	C	F, G, H, I

SELF *test*

3 Construct a project network for the following project. The project is completed when activities F and G are both complete.

Activity	A	B	C	D	E	F	G
Immediate Predecessor	—	—	A	A	C, B	C, B	D, E

SELF *test*

4 Assume that the project in Problem 3 has the following activity times (in months).

Activity	A	B	C	D	E	F	G
Time	4	6	2	6	3	3	5

a. Find the critical path.

b. The project must be completed in one-and-a-half years. Do you anticipate difficulty in meeting the deadline? Explain.

5 Management Decision Systems (MDS) is a consulting company that specializes in the development of decision support systems. MDS obtained a contract to develop a computer system to assist the management of a large company in formulating its capital expenditure plan. The project leader developed the following list of activities and immediate predecessors. Construct a project network for this problem.

Activity	A	B	C	D	E	F	G	H	I	J
Immediate Predecessor	—	—	—	B	A	B	C, D	B, E	F, G	H

SELF *test*

6 Consider the following project network and activity times (in weeks).

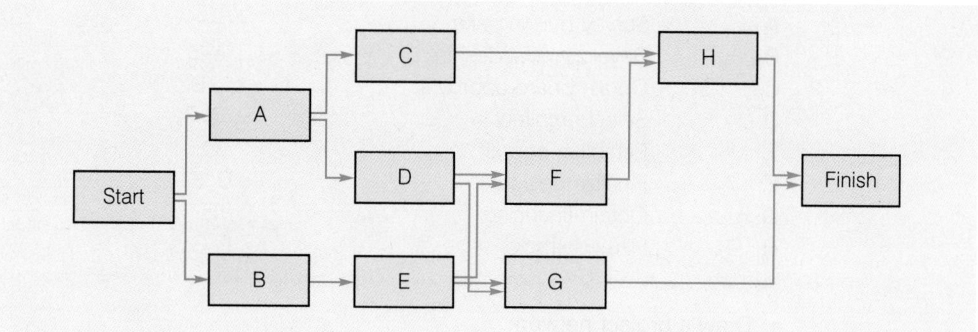

Activity	A	B	C	D	E	F	G	H
Time	5	3	7	6	7	3	10	8

a. Identify the critical path.
b. How much time will be needed to complete this project?
c. Can activity D be delayed without delaying the entire project? If so, by how many weeks?
d. Can activity C be delayed without delaying the entire project? If so, by how many weeks?
e. What is the schedule for activity E?

7 A project involving the installation of a computer system comprises eight activities. The following table lists immediate predecessors and activity times (in weeks).

Activity	Immediate Predecessor	Time
A	—	3
B	—	6
C	A	2
D	B, C	5
E	D	4
F	E	3
G	B, C	9
H	F, G	3

a. Draw a project network.
b. What are the critical activities?
c. What is the expected project completion time?

SELF *test*

8 Khobar Technical College is considering building a new multipurpose athletic complex on campus. The complex would provide a new gymnasium for intercollegiate basketball games, expanded office space, classrooms and intramural facilities. The following activities would have to be undertaken before construction can begin.

Activity	Description	Immediate Predecessor	Time (weeks)
A	Survey building site	—	6
B	Develop initial design	—	8
C	Obtain board approval	A, B	12
D	Select architect	C	4
E	Establish budget	C	6
F	Finalize design	D, E	15
G	Obtain financing	E	12
H	Hire contractor	F, G	8

a. Draw a project network.
b. Identify the critical path.
c. Develop the activity schedule for the project.
d. Does it appear reasonable that construction of the athletic complex could begin one year after the decision to begin the project with the site survey and initial design plans? What is the expected completion time for the project?

9 Hamilton County Parks is planning to develop a new park and recreational area. Project development activities include clearing playground and picnic areas, constructing roads, constructing a shelter house, purchasing picnic equipment and so on. The following network and activity times (in weeks) are being used in the planning, scheduling and controlling of this project.

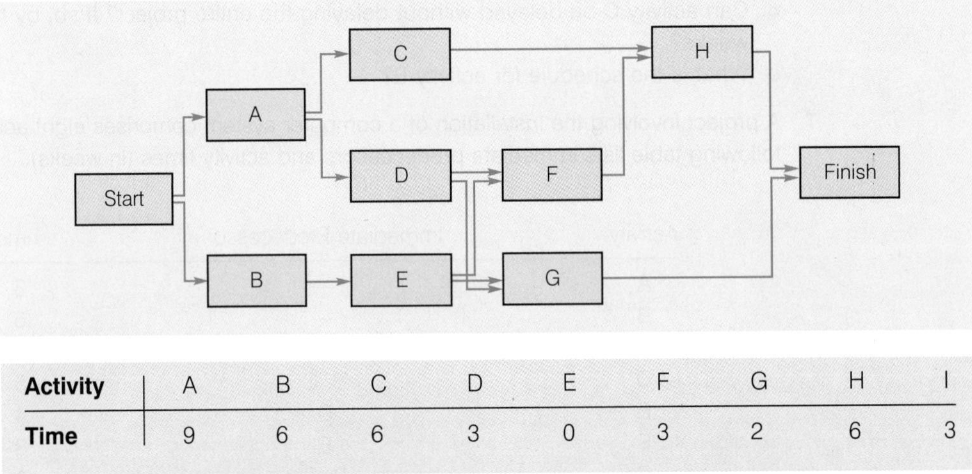

Activity	A	B	C	D	E	F	G	H	I
Time	9	6	6	3	0	3	2	6	3

a. What is the critical path for this network?
b. Show the activity schedule for this project.
c. The park commissioner would like to open the park to the public within six months from the time the work on the project is started. Does this opening date appear to be feasible? Explain.

SELF *test*

10 The following estimates of activity times (in days) are available for a small project.

Activity	Optimistic	Most Probable	Pessimistic
A	4	5.0	6
B	8	9.0	10
C	7	7.5	11
D	7	9.0	10
E	6	7.0	9
F	5	6.0	7

a. Calculate the expected activity completion times and the variance for each activity.
b. An analyst determined that the critical path consists of activities B–D–F. Calculate the expected project completion time and the variance.

SELF *test* 11 Suppose that the following estimates of activity times (in weeks) were provided for the network shown in Problem 6.

Activity	Optimistic	Most Probable	Pessimistic
A	4.0	5.0	6.0
B	2.5	3.0	3.5
C	6.0	7.0	8.0
D	5.0	5.5	9.0
E	5.0	7.0	9.0
F	2.0	3.0	4.0
G	8.0	10.0	12.0
H	6.0	7.0	14.0

What is the probability that the project will be completed
a. Within 21 weeks?
b. Within 22 weeks?
c. Within 25 weeks?

SELF *test* 12 Andreas Bierhoff is in charge of planning and coordinating next spring's sales management training programme for his company. Andreas listed the following activity information for this project.

Activity	Description	Immediate Predecessor	Time (weeks) Optimistic	Most Probable	Pessimistic
A	Plan topic	—	1.5	2.0	2.5
B	Obtain speakers	A	2.0	2.5	6.0
C	List meeting locations	—	1.0	2.0	3.0
D	Select location	C	1.5	2.0	2.5
E	Finalize speaker travel plans	B, D	0.5	1.0	1.5
F	Make final check with speakers	E	1.0	2.0	3.0
G	Prepare and mail brochure	B, D	3.0	3.5	7.0
H	Take reservations	G	3.0	4.0	5.0
I	Handle last-minute details	F, H	1.5	2.0	2.5

a. Draw a project network.
b. Prepare an activity schedule.
c. What are the critical activities and what is the expected project completion time?
d. If Andreas wants a 0.99 probability of completing the project on time, how far ahead of the scheduled meeting date should he begin working on the project?

13 The Daugherty Porta-Vac project discussed in Section 9.2 has an expected project completion time of 17 weeks. The probability that the project could be completed in 20 weeks or less is 0.9656. The noncritical paths in the Porta-Vac project network are:

A–D–G–J
A–C–F–J
B–H–I–J

a. Use the information in Table 9.5 to compute the expected time and variance for each path shown.

b. Calculate the probability that each path will be completed in the desired 20-week period.

c. Why is the calculation of the probability of completing a project on time based on the analysis of the critical path? In what case, if any, would making the probability computation for a noncritical path be desirable?

SELF *test*

14 The manager of the Oak Hills Swimming Club is planning the club's swimming team programme. The first team practice is scheduled for May 1. The activities, their immediate predecessors, and the activity time estimates (in weeks) are as follows.

Activity	Description	Immediate Predecessor	Time (weeks) Optimistic	Most Probable	Pessimistic
A	Meet with board	—	1	1	2
B	Hire coaches	A	4	6	8
C	Reserve pool	A	2	4	6
D	Announce programme	B, C	1	2	3
E	Meet with coaches	B	2	3	4
F	Order team suits	A	1	2	3
G	Register swimmers	D	1	2	3
H	Collect fees	G	1	2	3
I	Plan first practice	E, H, F	1	1	1

a. Draw a project network.

b. Develop an activity schedule.

c. What are the critical activities, and what is the expected project completion time?

d. If the club manager plans to start the project on February 1, what is the probability the swimming programme will be ready by the scheduled May 1 date (13 weeks)? Should the manager begin planning the swimming programme before February 1?

15 The product development group at Landon Corporation has been working on a new computer software product that has the potential to capture a large market share. Through outside sources, Landon's management learned that a competitor is working to introduce a similar product. As a result, Landon's top management increased its pressure on the product development group. The group's leader turned to PERT/CPM as an aid to scheduling the activities remaining before the new product can be brought to the market. The project network is as follows.

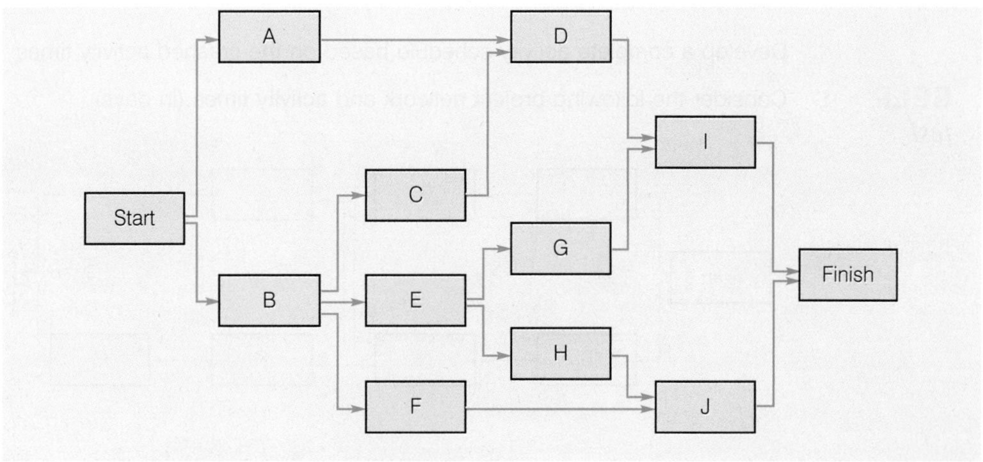

The activity time estimates (in weeks) are:

Activity	Optimistic	Most Probable	Pessimistic
A	3.0	4.0	5.0
B	3.0	3.5	7.0
C	4.0	5.0	6.0
D	2.0	3.0	4.0
E	6.0	10.0	14.0
F	7.5	8.5	12.5
G	4.5	6.0	7.5
H	5.0	6.0	13.0
I	2.0	2.5	6.0
J	4.0	5.0	6.0

a. Develop an activity schedule for this project and identify the critical path activities.

b. What is the probability that the project will be completed so that Landon Corporation may introduce the new product within 25 weeks? Within 30 weeks?

SELF *test*

16 Return to the computer installation project in Problem 7 and assume that the project has to be completed in 16 weeks. Crashing of the project is necessary. Use the following relevant information.

	Time (weeks)		Cost (€)	
Activity	Normal	Crash	Normal	Crash
A	3	1	900	1 700
B	6	3	2 000	4 000
C	2	1	500	1 000
D	5	3	1 800	2 400
E	4	3	1 500	1 850
F	3	1	3 000	3 900
G	9	4	8 000	9 800
H	3	2	1 000	2 000

Develop a complete activity schedule based on the crashed activity times.

SELF *test* 17 Consider the following project network and activity times (in days).

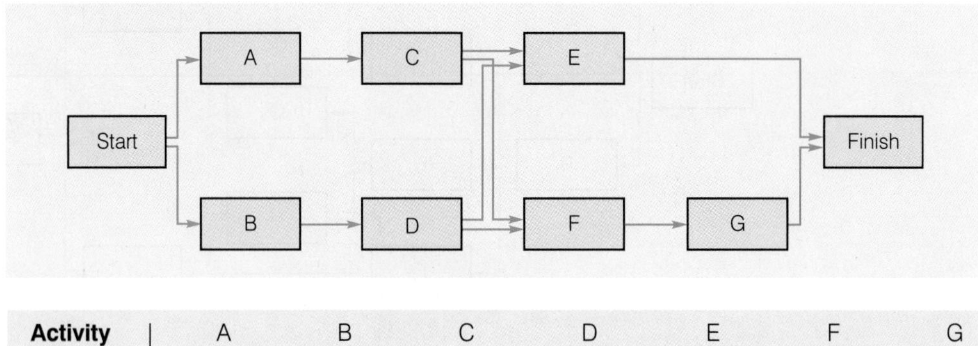

Activity	A	B	C	D	E	F	G
Time	3	2	5	5	6	2	2

The crashing data for this project are as follows.

	Time (days)		Cost (€)	
Activity	**Normal**	**Crash**	**Normal**	**Crash**
A	3	2	800	1 400
B	2	1	1 200	1 900
C	5	3	2 000	2 800
D	5	3	1 500	2 300
E	6	4	1 800	2 800
F	2	1	600	1 000
G	2	1	500	1 000

a. Find the critical path and the expected project completion time.
b. What is the total project cost using the normal times?
c. What is the expected project completion time and cost with crashing?

SELF *test* 18 Office Automation developed a proposal for introducing a new computerized office system that will improve word processing and interoffice communications for a particular company. Contained in the proposal is a list of activities that must be accomplished to complete the new office system project. Use the following relevant information about the activities.

			Time (weeks)		Cost (€1000s)	
Activity	**Description**	**Immediate Predecessor**	**Normal**	**Crash**	**Normal**	**Crash**
A	Plan needs	—	10	8	30	70
B	Order equipment	A	8	6	120	150
C	Install equipment	B	10	7	100	160
D	Set up training lab	A	7	6	40	50
E	Conduct training course	D	10	8	50	75
F	Test system	C, E	3	3	60	—

a. Develop a project network.
b. Develop an activity schedule.
c. What are the critical activities, and what is the expected project completion time?
d. Assume that the company wants to complete the project in six months or 26 weeks. What crashing decisions do you recommend to meet the desired completion time at the least possible cost? Work through the network and attempt to make the crashing decisions by inspection.
e. Develop an activity schedule for the crashed project.
f. What added project cost is required to meet the six-month completion time?

CASE PROBLEM R.C. Coleman

R.C. Coleman distributes a variety of food products that are sold through grocery store and supermarket outlets. The company receives orders directly from the individual outlets, with a typical order requesting the delivery of several cases of anywhere from 20 to 50 different products. Under the company's current warehouse operation, warehouse clerks dispatch order-picking personnel to fill each order and have the goods moved to the warehouse shipping area. Because of the high labour costs and relatively low productivity of hand order-picking, management has decided to automate the warehouse operation by installing a computer-controlled order-picking system, along with a conveyor system for moving goods from storage to the warehouse shipping area.

R.C. Coleman's director of material management has been named the project manager in charge of the automated warehouse system. After consulting with members of the engineering staff and warehouse management personnel, the director compiled a list of activities associated with the project. The optimistic, most probable and pessimistic times (in weeks) have also been provided for each activity.

Activity	Description	Immediate Predecessor
A	Determine equipment needs	—
B	Obtain vendor proposals	—
C	Select vendor	A, B
D	Order system	C
E	Design new warehouse layout	C
F	Design warehouse	E
G	Design computer interface	C
H	Interface computer	D, F, G
I	Install system	D, F
J	Train system operators	H
K	Test system	I, J

Activity	Optimistic	Time Most Probable	Pessimistic
A	4	6	8
B	6	8	16
C	2	4	6
D	8	10	24
E	7	10	13
F	4	6	8
G	4	6	20
H	4	6	8
I	4	6	14
J	3	4	5
K	2	4	6

Managerial Report

Develop a report that presents the activity schedule and expected project completion time for the warehouse expansion project. Include a project network in the report. In addition, take into consideration the following issues.

1 R.C. Coleman's top management established a required 40-week completion time for the project. Can this completion time be achieved? Include probability information in your discussion. What recommendations do you have if the 40-week completion time is required?

2 Suppose that management requests that activity times be shortened to provide an 80 per cent chance of meeting the 40-week completion time. If the variance in the project completion time is the same as you found in part (1), by how much should the expected project completion time be shortened to achieve the goal of an 80 per cent chance of completion within 40 weeks?

3 Using the expected activity times as the normal times and the following crashing information, determine the activity crashing decisions and revised activity schedule for the warehouse expansion project.

		Cost (€)	
Activity	**Crashed Activity Time (weeks)**	**Normal**	**Crashed**
A	4	1 000	1 900
B	7	1 000	1 800
C	2	1 500	2 700
D	8	2 000	3 200
E	7	5 000	8 000
F	4	3 000	4 100
G	5	8 000	10 250
H	4	5 000	6 400
I	4	10 000	12 400
J	3	4 000	4 400
K	3	5 000	5 500

Appendix 9.1 Activity on Arrow Networks

In this chapter we have used the activity on node (AON) approach to project networks. As mentioned, an alternative approach is to construct an activity-on-arrow (AOA) network diagram. In this appendix we briefly explain this type of network diagram. We will use the Shopping Centre example that we introduced in Section 9.1. We show Table 9.1 again with the relevant information.

With AON network diagrams the activities are shown at the nodes and the arrows show the dependencies between activities. In an AOA diagram we use the arrows to show activities being undertaken and the nodes represent moments in time when an activity starts or finishes. To illustrate look at Figure 9.16. This shows part of an AOA diagram for Activity A. Node 1 represents the start of Activity A and Node 2 represents the time Activity A is completed. The arrow itself shows Activity A being undertaken with the time needed shown underneath, five weeks.

Construction of an AOA network diagram follows much the same idea as for an AON diagram. We start at the left with the start of the project and construct the

Table 9.1 List of Activities for the Souk Al Bustan Shopping Centre Project

Activity	Activity Description	Immediate Predecessor	Activity Time (weeks)
A	Prepare architectural drawings	—	5
B	Identify potential new tenants	—	6
C	Develop prospectus for tenants	A	4
D	Select contractor	A	3
E	Prepare building permits	A	1
F	Obtain approval for building permits	E	4
G	Perform construction	D, F	14
H	Finalize contracts with tenants	B, C	12
I	Tenants move in	G, H	2
			Total 51

Figure 9.16 Activity A

diagram activity by activity as we move to the right checking that the precedences in the diagram are consistent with the project information. Figure 9.17 shows the first part of the AOA diagram up to activity C. Activities A and B both start from Node 1 (the start of the project). Activity C starts after Activity A. You should be able to see why we have shown the B and C arrows going into Node 3. Eventually Activity H will be shown on the arrow coming out of Node 3 since H is dependent on both B and C.

The complete AOA diagram for this project is shown in Figure 9.18. You should check the diagram carefully to see that all the dependencies are consistent with the project information given. Note also that some of the arrows have been highlighted to show the critical path through the network. In addition, we have added time information into each node as is usual with the AOA diagram. So, Node 3 for example shows that at this time Activities A,B,C are complete and will take 9 weeks to complete (the first of the two times shown). This is the earliest finish time, EFT, for this part of the network. The second figure of 12 shows the latest finish time, LFT. These times are obtained from the completed network diagram with the usual forward pass to obtain the EFTs for each node and then a backward pass to obtain the LFTs. We see again from Node 7 that the project will take 26 weeks to complete.

Figure 9.17 Activities A,B,C

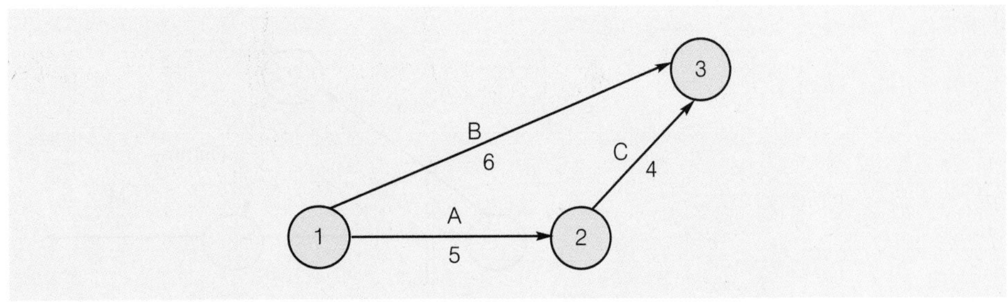

Figure 9.18 Completed AOA Diagram

There is one further aspect of AOA diagrams that is not illustrated with this example. One of the rules of AOA diagrams is that two or more activities are not allowed to share the same start and end node. For example consider a simple network:

Activity	Immediate predecessor
K	—
L	—
M	K, L
N	M

Activities K and L would both Start from node 1 and would both end at node 2 (which would also be the start of Activity M). To get round this, AOA diagrams make use of *dummy* activities. A dummy activity is used to prevent violation of the rule and keep the precedence structure of the project. It is not a real activity and takes zero time. Figure 9.19 shows how we would construct this AOA network usually showing the dummy activity with a dotted line to distinguish it from real activities.

Overall AOA and AON diagrams accomplish the same thing – they both provide a means of planning and managing projects and both contain much the same information. The AON diagram has tended to become more popular as it relates more closely to what project management software produces as output.

Figure 9.19 Dummy Activity

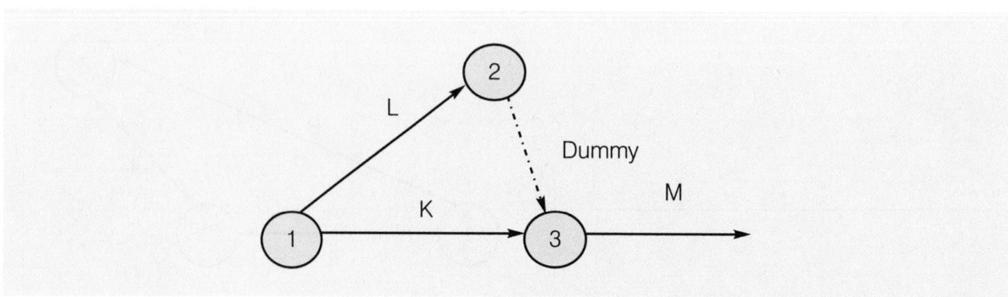

Chapter 10

Inventory Models

Learning Objectives

By the end of this chapter you will be able to:

- Explain the principles of inventory management
- Calculate and interpret the common inventory models
- Incorporate probability into inventory decisions

MANAGEMENT SCIENCE IN ACTION

Ford-Otasan

Ford-Otasan, based in Turkey, produces commercial motor vehicles for the home and European markets. The company was established in 1998 as a joint venture between Ford Motors and the Turkish company, Koc Holdings. Initially production was aimed at the local domestic market but, over time, production increased and the number of models increased. Export markets were targeted. Partly as a result, finished-vehicle stocks increased also. Finished-vehicle stocks comprise vehicles ready for shipment. The company's management set a target for finished-vehicle stock levels equivalent to 2½ days' production (around 900 vehicles). This was a challenging target given that stock levels were typically at least three days' production at over 1000 vehicles. The improvement team tasked with delivering the reduced stock level target initiated a project to improve the existing processes and also developed an integer programming model for production. Finished-vehicle stocks reduced considerably from an average daily level of 1070 down to 550 and there was also improved consistency in monthly stock levels. Using the average vehicle price and the monthly interest rate to calculate holding cost, the average monthly holding cost is estimated to have been cut by around $150 000.

Based on M. Denizel, U. Ekinci, G. Ozyurt and D. Turhan, 'Ford-Otosan optimizes its stocks using a six-sigma framework', *Interfaces* 37 2 (2007): 97–107.

Inventory, or stock, is held by just about every type of organization from the local corner shop which has extra supplies in the back room through to the large multinational. Inventory refers to goods or materials held by an organization for future use and might include raw materials, parts from suppliers and semi-finished products as well as finished goods awaiting sale or shipment. Keeping inventory can be very expensive for organizations but, on the other hand, running out of stock can be just as problematic so there is little surprise that inventory models are an important area for management science.

10.1 Principles of Inventory Management

Every organization holds inventory in one form or another: this may range from boxes of paperclips kept in the office through to replacement engine parts for a jumbojet airliner. Managing this inventory effectively has attracted considerable attention from management scientists and in this section we outline some of the key principles involved.

The Role of Inventory

Organizations hold inventory for a number of reasons, one of the most important being to meet customer demand for a product or service where that demand has a degree of uncertainty. If a large retail organization such as Gap knew for certain that an item in its new fashion range would sell exactly 40 000 units then it would know exactly how many units to orders from its suppliers. However, because demand will not be known for certain, no matter how good our forecasting, the company will hold additional amounts of inventory known as buffer or **safety stocks** in case customer demand is higher than expected. If it doesn't hold such buffer stocks then the company may well lose sales if demand is higher than expected as customers may not be prepared to wait until new stock arrives in the stores.

A second role of inventory is to help organizations cope with seasonal or cyclical demand for items. Demand for many products follows such a pattern: sales of toys increase at Christmas; sales of the latest Xbox from Microsoft will follow a typical product life cycle; sales of garden products will increase in the Spring; sales of fuel will increase at holiday time as motorists go on holiday. The companies producing such products are unlikely to have the production capacity to meet maximum seasonal demand so they will need to schedule their production over the year in order to increase stocks of an item during periods of low demand and then, using this buffer stock, to meet demand when it exceeds production capacity. (We looked at how to do this in Chapters 2 and 4 where LP was used to determine an optimum production schedule over time.)

A third role of inventory is to help organizations reduce, or manage, risk. An organization might anticipate a risk of disruption to its supplies of some item and may therefore decide to increase its buffer stocks now. For example, a high street retailer considers that one of its key suppliers may face the prospect of industrial action from its workforce so it increases its buffer stocks now in anticipation of such a situation. Alternatively, an organization might anticipate the risk of an imminent price increase for some product that it buys for its suppliers so increases buffer stocks now to minimize the future effect of this. An airline, for example, might anticipate a rise in the global price of aviation fuel, or even fuel shortages, in the near future because of increased military conflict in the Middle East so buys buffer stocks of fuel now. Similarly, a manufacturing company might keep buffer stocks of work-in-progress inventory as part of a multi-stage manufacturing process.

A fourth important role of inventory is to take advantage of price discounts. A supplier may be willing to offer a large discount if we purchase in bulk, allowing us to pass low prices on to customers and increase market share and customer loyalty.

Inventory Costs

There are typically three critical costs involved in inventory management. The first of these, **holding costs**, refers to the costs associated with holding or carrying a given level of inventory. Effectively, the more stock you hold the bigger the holding cost incurred by the organization. Holding costs are made up of a mixture of other costs. The cost of financing the inventory is one of these. If the organization has borrowed the money to buy the stock it is holding then it will incur interest charges. If the organization uses its own money, there is an opportunity cost involved since, by definition, the money tied up in stock could have been invested elsewhere to generate income. So, in both cases there is a cost of capital incurred usually expressed as a percentage of the amount tied up in the stock cost. Other costs that contribute to the holding cost include storage costs (perhaps warehouse rent, heating/refrigeration, security, insurance); depreciation; obsolescence as stock becomes out of date; product deterioration; pilferage. Holding costs are normally calculated in one of two ways. The first is to calculate the total holding costs incurred by the organization over a given period of time, normally a year, and then average these per unit of stock. This would be shown as, for example, €10 per unit per year. Alternatively, the holding cost may be shown as a percentage of the value of the stock item – for example holding cost is 10 per cent of the stock value.

Calculating inventory costs accurately can be a major task in many organizations as the component costs may not be readily visible.

The second type of cost involved in inventory management is **ordering cost**. Ordering costs are those costs involved in actually placing an order for more inventory. Such costs are usually fixed regardless of the actual amount ordered and are usually expressed as a cost per order placed, €30 per order for example. The order cost itself is typically made up of staff costs of those involved in raising the order, receiving and checking the order, paying invoices; postage and phone costs; transportation and shipping costs.

The third type of cost is known as the **stockout cost**. This is the cost involved when customer demand cannot be met because of insufficient inventory. The immediate cost may be that involved in obtaining additional inventory as a matter of urgency to meet demand. In the medium to long term such costs may also involve loss of customer goodwill, loss of future sales and loss of future profit – although these are notoriously difficult to quantify accurately. As a result, stockout costs are often an educated 'best guess'.

The prime purpose of effective inventory management is to minimize these costs by determining the optimum amount of inventory that should be held and ordered and when inventory should be ordered. In the next section we introduce the most common model used in inventory management.

10.2 Economic Order Quantity (EOQ) Model

The cost associated with developing and maintaining inventory is larger than many people think. Models such as the ones presented in this chapter can be used to develop cost-effective inventory management decisions.

The **economic order quantity (EOQ)** model is applicable when the demand for an item shows a constant, or nearly constant, rate and when the entire quantity ordered arrives in inventory at one time. The constant demand rate assumption means that the same number of units is taken from inventory each period of time such as five units every day, 25 units every week, 100 units every four-week period and so on.

To illustrate the EOQ model, let us consider the situation faced by the Capetown Beverage Company (CBC) in South Africa. CBC is a distributor of soft drink products. From a main warehouse CBC supplies nearly 1000 small retail stores with beverage products.

The warehouse manager has decided to conduct a detailed study of the inventory costs associated with Cape Cola, the number-one-selling CBC soft drink. The purpose of the study is to establish the how-much-to-order and the when-to-order decisions for Cape Cola that will result in the lowest possible total inventory cost. As the first step in the study, the warehouse manager obtained the following demand data for the past ten weeks:

Week	Demand (cases)
1	2000
2	2025
3	1950
4	2000
5	2100
6	2050
7	2000
8	1975
9	1900
10	2000
Total cases	20000
Average cases per week	2000

One of the most criticized assumptions of the EOQ model is the constant demand rate. Obviously, the model would be inappropriate for items with widely fluctuating and variable demand rates. However, as this example shows, the EOQ model can provide a realistic approximation of the optimal order quantity when demand is relatively stable and occurs at a nearly constant rate.

Strictly speaking, these weekly demand figures do not show a constant demand rate. However, given the relatively low variability exhibited by the weekly demand, inventory planning with a constant demand rate of 2000 cases per week appears acceptable. In practice, you will find that the actual inventory situation seldom, if ever, satisfies the assumptions of the model exactly. So, in any particular application, the manager must determine whether the model assumptions are close enough to reality for the model to be useful. In this situation, because demand varies from a low of 1900 cases to a high of 2100 cases, the assumption of constant demand of 2000 cases per week appears to be a reasonable approximation.

The how-much-to-order decision involves selecting an order quantity that draws a compromise between (1) keeping small inventories and ordering frequently, and (2) keeping large inventories and ordering infrequently. The first alternative can result in undesirably high ordering costs, while the second alternative can result in undesirably high inventory holding costs. To find an optimal compromise between these conflicting alternatives, let us consider a mathematical model that shows the total cost as the sum of the holding cost and the ordering cost.[1]

As with other quantitative models, accurate estimates of cost parameters are critical. In the EOQ model, estimates of both the inventory holding cost and the ordering cost are needed. Also see footnote 1, which refers to relevant costs.

To estimate the holding cost of its inventory, CBC uses its cost of capital at an annual rate of 18 per cent. Other holding costs incurred involve insurance, breakage and pilfering and these are estimated at an additional 7 per cent of inventory. So, for CBC, the total holding cost is 18% + 7% = 25% of the value of the inventory. Each case of Cape Cola has a cost of €8 so the holding cost per year for each case is €2 (0.25×8).

The next step in the inventory analysis is to determine the **ordering cost**. For CBC, the largest portion of the ordering cost involves the salaries of the staff in CBC's purchasing department. An analysis of the purchasing process showed that a purchaser spends approximately 45 minutes preparing and processing an order for Cape Cola. With a wage rate and fringe benefit cost for purchasers of €20 per hour, the labour portion of the ordering cost is €15. Making allowances for paper, postage, telephone, transportation and receiving costs at €17 per order, the manager estimates that the ordering cost is €32 per order. That is, CBC is paying €32 per order regardless of the quantity requested in the order.

Most inventory cost models use an annual cost. Thus, demand should be expressed in units per year and inventory holding cost should be based on an annual rate.

The holding cost, ordering cost and demand information are the three data items that must be known prior to the use of the EOQ model. After developing these data for the CBC problem, we can look at how they are used to develop a total cost model. We begin by defining Q as the order quantity. So, the how-much-to-order decision involves finding the value of Q that will minimize the sum of holding and ordering costs.

The inventory for Cape Cola will have a maximum value of Q units when an order of size Q is received from the supplier. CBC will then satisfy customer demand from inventory until the inventory is depleted, at which time another shipment of Q units will be received. So, assuming a constant demand, the graph of the inventory for Cape Cola is as shown in Figure 10.1. Note that the graph indicates an average inventory of $\frac{1}{2}Q$ for the period in question. This level should appear reasonable because the maximum inventory is Q, the minimum is zero, and the inventory declines at a constant rate over the period.

Figure 10.1 shows the inventory pattern during one order cycle of length T. As time goes on, this pattern will repeat. The complete inventory pattern is shown in Figure 10.2. If the average inventory during each cycle is $\frac{1}{2}Q$, the average inventory over any number of cycles is also $\frac{1}{2}Q$.

[1]Even though analysts typically refer to 'total cost' models for inventory systems, often these models describe only the total variable or total relevant costs for the decision being considered. Costs that are not affected by the how-much-to-order decision are considered fixed or constant and are not included in the model.

Figure 10.1 Inventory for Cape Cola

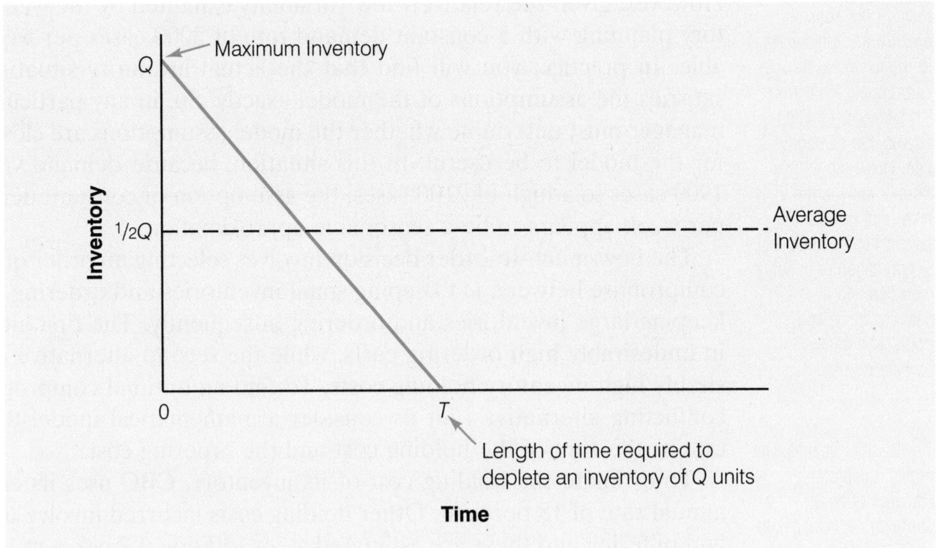

Figure 10.2 Inventory Pattern for the EOQ Inventory Model

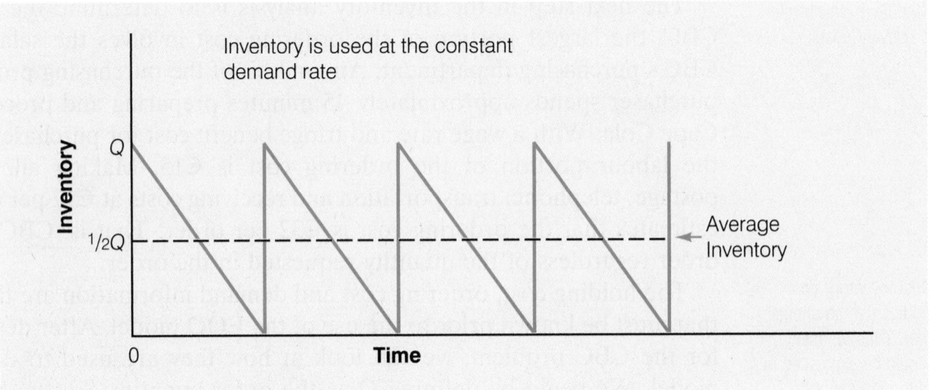

The holding cost can be calculated using the average inventory. That is, we can calculate the holding cost by multiplying the average inventory by the cost of carrying one unit in inventory for the stated period. The period selected for the model is up to you; it could be one week, one month, one year or more. However, because the holding cost for many industries and businesses is expressed as an *annual* percentage, most inventory models are developed on an *annual* cost basis.

Let:

I = annual holding cost rate

C = unit cost of the inventory item

C_h = annual cost of holding one unit in inventory

The annual cost of holding one unit in inventory is:

$$C_h = IC \tag{10.1}$$

C_h is the cost of holding one unit in inventory for one year. Because smaller order quantities Q will result in lower inventory, total annual holding cost can be reduced by using smaller order quantities.

The general equation for the annual holding cost for the average inventory of ½Q units is as follows:

$$\begin{aligned}\text{Annual holding cost} &= \begin{pmatrix}\text{Average}\\\text{inventory}\end{pmatrix}\begin{pmatrix}\text{Annual holding}\\\text{cost}\\\text{per unit}\end{pmatrix}\\&= \frac{1}{2}QC_h\end{aligned} \quad \textbf{(10.2)}$$

To complete the total cost model, we must now include the annual ordering cost. The goal is to express the annual ordering cost in terms of the order quantity Q. The first question is: How many orders will be placed during the year? Let D denote the annual demand for the product. For CBC, D = (52 weeks)(2000 cases per week) = 104 000 cases per year. We know that by ordering Q units every time we order, we will have to place D/Q orders per year. If C_o is the cost of placing one order, the general equation for the annual ordering cost is as follows:

C_o, the fixed cost per order, is independent of the amount ordered. For a given annual demand of D units, the total annual ordering cost can be reduced by using larger order quantities.

$$\begin{aligned}\text{Annual ordering cost} &= \begin{pmatrix}\text{Number of}\\\text{orders}\\\text{per year}\end{pmatrix}\begin{pmatrix}\text{cost}\\\text{per}\\\text{order}\end{pmatrix}\\&= \left(\frac{D}{Q}\right)C_o\end{aligned} \quad \textbf{(10.3)}$$

So, the total annual cost, denoted TC, can be expressed as follows:

$$\begin{aligned}\text{Total annual cost} &= \text{Annual holding cost} + \text{Annual ordering cost}\\TC &= \frac{1}{2}QC_h + \frac{D}{Q}C_o\end{aligned} \quad \textbf{(10.4)}$$

Using the Cape Cola data [$C_h = IC = (0.25)(€8) = €2$, $C_o = €32$ and $D = 104\,000$], the total annual cost model is:

$$TC = {}^1/_2Q(€2) + \frac{104\,000}{Q}(€32) = Q + \frac{3\,328\,000}{Q}$$

The development of the total cost model goes a long way toward solving the inventory problem. We now are able to express the total annual cost as a function of *how much* should be ordered. The development of a realistic total cost model is perhaps the most important part of the application of quantitative methods to inventory management. Equation (10.4) is the general total cost equation for inventory situations in which the assumptions of the economic order quantity model are valid.

The How-Much-to-Order Decision

The next step is to find the order quantity Q that will minimize the total annual cost for Cape Cola. Using a trial-and-error approach, we can calculate the total annual cost for several possible order quantities. As a starting point, let us consider $Q = 8000$. The total annual cost is:

$$TC = Q + \frac{3\,328\,000}{Q}$$
$$= 8\,000 + \frac{3\,328\,000}{8\,000} = €8\,416$$

A trial order quantity of 5000 gives:

$$TC = 5\,000 + \frac{3\,328\,000}{5\,000} = €5\,666$$

The results of several other trial order quantities are shown in Table 10.1. It shows the lowest cost solution to be about 2000 cases. Graphs of the annual holding and ordering costs and total annual costs are shown in Figure 10.3.

Table 10.1 Annual Holding, Ordering, and Total Costs for Various Order Quantities of Cape Cola

	Annual Cost		
Order Quantity	**Holding, €**	**Ordering, €**	**Total €**
5 000	5 000	666	5 666
4 000	4 000	832	4 832
3 000	3 000	1 109	4 109
2 000	2 000	1 664	3 664
1 000	1 000	3 328	4 328

Figure 10.3 Annual Holding, Ordering and Total Costs for Cape Cola

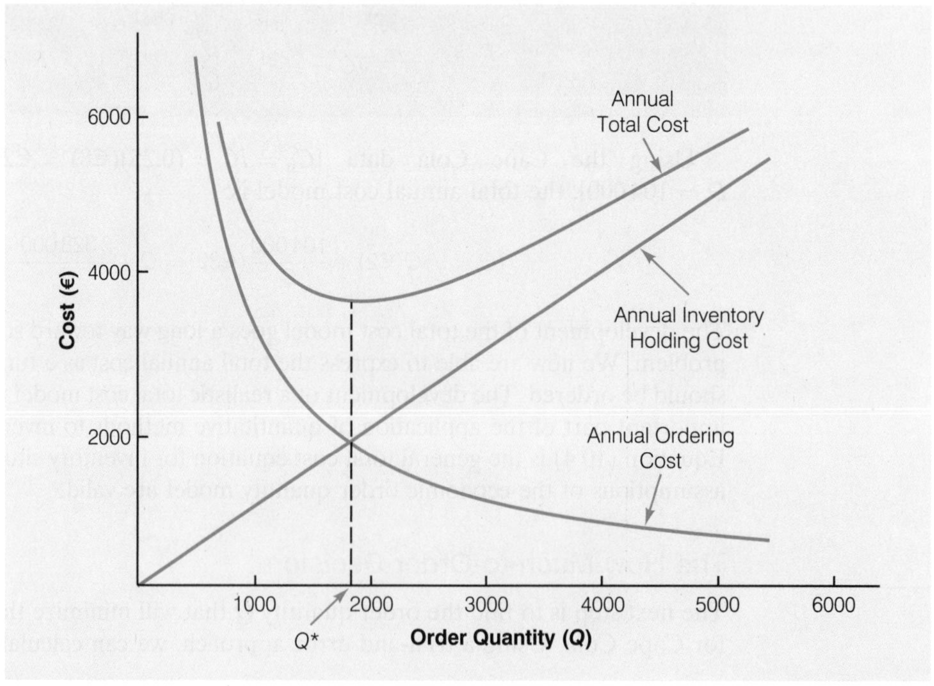

The advantage of the trial-and-error approach is that it is rather easy to do and provides the total annual cost for a number of possible order quantity decisions. In this case, the minimum cost order quantity appears to be approximately 2000 cases. The disadvantage of this approach, however, is that it does not provide the exact minimum cost order quantity.

The EOQ formula determines the optimal order quantity by balancing the annual holding cost and the annual ordering cost.

Refer to Figure 10.3. The minimum total cost order quantity is denoted by an order size of Q^*. By using differential calculus, it can be shown (see Appendix 10.1) that the value of Q^* that minimizes the total annual cost is given by the formula:

$$Q^* = \sqrt{\frac{2DC_o}{C_h}} \tag{10.5}$$

In 1915 F.W. Harris derived the mathematical formula for the economic order quantity. It was the first application of quantitative methods to the area of inventory management.

This formula is referred to as the *economic order quantity (EOQ) formula* and can be applied to any combination of D, C_h and C_o.

Using equation (10.5), the minimum total annual cost order quantity for Cape Cola is:

$$Q^* = \sqrt{\frac{2(104,000)32}{2}} = 1824 \text{ cases}$$

Problem 2 at the end of the chapter asks you to show that equal holding and ordering costs is a property of the EOQ model.

The use of an order quantity of 1824 in Equation (10.4) shows that the minimum cost inventory policy for Cape Cola has a total annual cost of €3649. Note that $Q^* = 1824$ balances the holding and ordering costs. Check for yourself to see that these costs are equal.[2]

The When-to-Order Decision

Now that we know how much to order, we want to address the question of *when* to order. To answer this question, we need to introduce the concept of inventory position. The **inventory position** is defined as the amount of inventory on hand plus the amount of inventory on order. The when-to-order decision is expressed in terms of a **reorder point** – the inventory position at which a new order should be placed.

The reorder point is expressed in terms of inventory position, the amount of inventory on hand plus the amount on order. Some people think that the reorder point is expressed in terms of inventory on hand. With short lead times, inventory position is usually the same as the inventory on hand. However, with long lead times, inventory position may be larger than inventory on hand.

The manufacturer of Cape Cola guarantees a two-day delivery on any order placed by CBC. If we assume that CBC operates 250 days per year, the annual demand of 104 000 cases implies a daily demand of 104 000/250 = 416 cases. So, we expect (two days)(416 cases per day) = 832 cases of Cape Cola to be sold during the two days it takes a new order to reach the CBC warehouse. In inventory terminology, the two-day delivery period is referred to as the **lead time** for a new order, and the 832-case demand anticipated during this period is referred to as the lead-time demand. So CBC should order a new shipment of Cape Cola from the manufacturer when the inventory reaches 832 cases. For inventory systems using the constant demand rate assumption and a fixed lead time, the reorder point is the same as the lead-time demand. For these systems, the general expression for the reorder point is as follows:

$$r = dm \tag{10.6}$$

[2]Actually, Q^* from equation (10.5) is 1824.28, but because we cannot order fractional cases of cola, a Q^* of 1824 is shown. This value of Q^* may cause a few cents deviation between the two costs. If Q^* is used at its exact value, the holding and ordering costs will be exactly the same.

where

$$r = \text{reorder point}$$
$$d = \text{demand per day}$$
$$m = \text{lead time for a new order in days}$$

The question of how frequently the order will be placed can now be answered. The period between orders is referred to as the cycle time. Previously in equation (10.2), we defined D/Q as the number of orders that will be placed in a year. Thus, $D/Q^* = 104\,000/1824 = 57$ is the number of orders CBC will place for Cape Cola each year. If CBC places 57 orders over 250 working days, it will order approximately every $250/57 = 4.39$ working days. So, the cycle time is 4.39 working days. The general expression for a cycle time[3] of T days is given by:

$$T = \frac{250}{D/Q^*} = \frac{250Q^*}{D} \tag{10.7}$$

Sensitivity Analysis for the EOQ Model

Even though substantial time may have been spent in arriving at the cost per order (€32) and the holding cost rate (25 per cent), we should realize that these figures are at best good estimates. So, we may want to consider how much the recommended order quantity would change with different estimated ordering and holding costs. To determine the effects of various cost scenarios, we can calculate the recommended order quantity under several different cost conditions. Table 10.2 shows the minimum total cost order quantity for several cost possibilities. As you can see from the table, the value of Q^* appears relatively stable, even with some variations in the cost estimates. Based on these results, the best order quantity for Cape Cola is in the range of 1700–1950 cases. If operated properly, the total cost for the Cape Cola inventory system should be close to €3400–€3800 per year. We also note that little risk is associated with implementing the calculated order quantity of 1824. For example, if holding cost rate = 24 per cent, C_o = €34, and the true optimal order quantity $Q^* = 1919$, CBC experiences only a €5 increase in the total annual cost; that is, €3690 − €3685 = €5, with $Q = 1824$.

From the preceding analysis, we would say that this EOQ model is insensitive to small variations or errors in the cost estimates. This insensitivity is a property of

Table 10.2 Optimal Order Quantities for Several Cost Possibilities

			Projected Total Annual Cost, €	
Possible Inventory Holding Cost (%)	Possible Cost per Order, €	Optimal Order Quantity (Q^*)	Using Q^*	Using Q = 1 824
24	30	1 803	3 461	3 462
24	34	1 919	3 685	3 690
26	30	1 732	3 603	3 607
26	34	1 844	3 835	3 836

[3]This general expression for cycle time is based on 250 working days per year. If the firm operated 300 working days per year and wanted to express cycle time in terms of working days, the cycle time would be given by $T = 300Q^*/D$.

Figure 10.4 Worksheet for the Cape Cola EOQ Inventory Model

EXCEL *file*

EOQ

	A	B	C
1	**Economic Order Quantity**		
2			
3	Annual Demand	104,000	
4	Ordering Cost	€32.00	
5	Annual Inventory Holding Rate %	25	
6	Cost per Unit	€8.00	
7	Working Days per Year	250	
8	Lead Time (Days)	2	
9			
10			
11	**Optimal Inventory Policy**		
12			
13	Economic Order Quanity	=SQRT(2*B3*B4/(B5/100*B6))	
14	Annual Inventory Holding Cost	=(1/2)*B13*(B5/100*B6)	
15	Annual Ordering Cost	=(B3/B13)*B4	
16	Total Annual Cost	=B14+B15	
17	Maximum Inventory Level	=B13	
18	Average Inventory Level	=B17/2	
19	Reorder Point	=(B3/B7)*B8	
20	Number of Orders per Year	=B3/B13	
21	Cycle Time (Days)	=B7/B20	
22			

	A	B
1	**Economic Order Quantity**	
2		
3	Annual Demand	104,000
4	Ordering Cost	€32.00
5	Annual Inventory Holding Rate %	25
6	Cost per Unit	€8.00
7	Working Days per Year	250
8	Lead Time (Days)	2
9		
10		
11	**Optimal Inventory Policy**	
12		
13	Economic Order Quanity	1824.28
14	Annual Inventory Holding Cost	€1,824.28
15	Annual Ordering Cost	€1,824.28
16	Total Annual Cost	€3,648.56
17	Maximum Inventory Level	1824.28
18	Average Inventory Level	912.14
19	Reorder Point	832.00
20	Number of Orders per Year	57.01
21	Cycle Time (Days)	4.39
22		

EOQ models in general, which indicates that if we have at least reasonable estimates of ordering cost and holding cost, we can expect to obtain a good approximation of the true minimum cost order quantity.

Excel Solution of the EOQ Model

Inventory models such as the EOQ model are easily implemented with the aid of worksheets. The Excel EOQ worksheet for Cape Cola is shown in Figure 10.4. The formula worksheet is in the background; the value worksheet is in the foreground. Data on annual demand, ordering cost, annual inventory holding cost rate, cost per unit, working days per year and lead time in days are input in cells B3 to B8. The appropriate EOQ model formulas, which determine the optimal inventory policy, are placed in cells B13 to B21. The value worksheet in the foreground shows the optimal economic order quantity 1824.28, the total annual cost €3 648.56 and a variety of additional information. If sensitivity analysis is desired, one or more of the input data values can be modified. The impact of any change or changes on the optimal inventory policy will then appear in the worksheet.

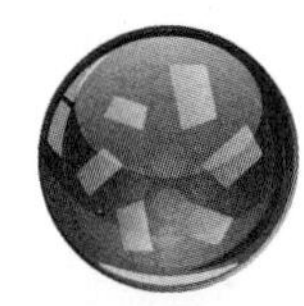

The Management Scientist software has an inventory module that can also be used to solve the inventory problems in this chapter.

The Excel worksheet in Figure 10.4 is a template that can be used for the EOQ model. This worksheet and similar Excel worksheets for the other inventory models presented in this chapter are available on the online platform that accompanies this text.

Summary of the EOQ Model Assumptions

To use the optimal order quantity and reorder point model described in this section, an analyst must make assumptions about how the inventory system operates. The EOQ model with its economic order quantity formula is based on some specific assumptions about the CBC inventory system. A summary of the assumptions for

Table 10.3 The EOQ Model Assumptions

1. Demand D is deterministic and occurs at a constant rate.
2. The order quantity Q is the same for each order. The inventory level increases by Q units each time an order is received.
3. The cost per order, C_o, is constant and does not depend on the quantity ordered.
4. The purchase cost per unit, C, is constant and does not depend on the quantity ordered.
5. The inventory holding cost per unit per time period, C_h, is constant. The total inventory holding cost depends on both C_h and the size of the inventory.
6. Shortages such as stock-outs or backorders are not permitted.
7. The lead time for an order is constant.
8. The inventory position is reviewed continuously. As a result, an order is placed as soon as the inventory position reaches the reorder point.

You should carefully review the assumptions of the inventory model before applying it in an actual situation. Several inventory models discussed later in this chapter alter one or more of the assumptions of the EOQ model.

this model is provided in Table 10.3. Before using the EOQ formula, carefully review these assumptions to ensure that they are applicable to the inventory system being analyzed. If the assumptions are not reasonable, seek a different inventory model.

Various types of inventory systems are used in practice, and the inventory models presented in the following sections alter one or more of the EOQ model assumptions shown in Table 10.3. When the assumptions change, a different inventory model with different optimal operating policies becomes necessary.

NOTES AND COMMENTS

With relatively long lead times, the lead-time demand and the resulting reorder point r, determined by equation (10.6), may exceed Q^*. If this condition occurs, at least one order will be outstanding when a new order is placed. For example, assume that Cape Cola has a lead time of $m = 6$ days. With a daily demand of $d = 432$ cases, equation (10.6) shows that the reorder point would be $r = dm = 6 \times 432 = 2592$ cases. So, a new order for Cape Cola should be placed whenever the inventory position (the amount of inventory on hand plus the amount of inventory on order) reaches 2592. With an order quantity of $Q = 2000$ cases, the inventory position of 2592 cases occurs when one order of 2000 cases is outstanding and $2592 - 2000 = 592$ cases are on hand.

10.3 Economic Production Lot Size Model

The inventory model in this section alters assumption 2 of the EOQ model (see Table 10.3). The assumption concerning the arrival of Q units each time an order is received is changed to a constant production supply rate.

The inventory model presented in this section is similar to the EOQ model in that we are attempting to determine *how much* we should order and *when* the order should be placed. We again assume a constant demand rate. However, instead of assuming that the order arrives in a shipment of size Q^*, as in the EOQ model, we assume that units are supplied to inventory at a constant rate over several days or several weeks. The constant supply rate assumption implies that the same number of units is supplied to inventory each period of time (e.g., ten units every day or 50 units every week). This model is designed for production situations in which, once an order is placed, production begins and a constant number of units is added to inventory each day until the production run has been completed.

To illustrate we shall use the following example. EnviroHealth, a large pharmaceutical company, manufactures a special type of anti-bacterial soap used in local health clinics. The soap is sold in one litre bottles and because of the specialist nature of the product and the strict hygiene controls that are enforced during production, the soap is produced only at limited times and not continuously. The company estimates that its current maximum annual production capacity is 60 000 litres. Current annual demand is 26 000 litres and is fairly constant through the year. Given that the company will not be producing the product continuously through the year it needs to know how often to produce the product and how much of the product to produce each time.

For example, if we have a production system that produces 50 units per day and we decide to schedule ten days of production, we have a 50(10) = 500-unit production lot size. The **lot size** is the number of units in an order. In general, if we let Q indicate the production lot size, the approach to the inventory decisions is similar to the EOQ model; that is, we build a holding and ordering cost model that expresses the total cost as a function of the production lot size. Then we attempt to find the production lot size that minimizes the total cost.

One other condition that should be mentioned at this time is that the model only applies to situations where the production rate is greater than the demand rate; the production system must be able to satisfy demand. For instance, if the constant demand rate is 400 units per day, the production rate must be at least 400 units per day to satisfy demand. For EnviroHealth, this requirement is satisfied: annual production capacity is 60 000 litres whilst annual demand is only 26 000.

During the production run, demand reduces the inventory while production adds to inventory. Because we assume that the production rate exceeds the demand rate, each day during a production run we produce more units than are demanded. So, the excess production causes a gradual inventory buildup during the production period. When the production run is completed, the continuing demand causes the inventory to gradually decline until a new production run is started. The inventory pattern for this system is shown in Figure 10.5.

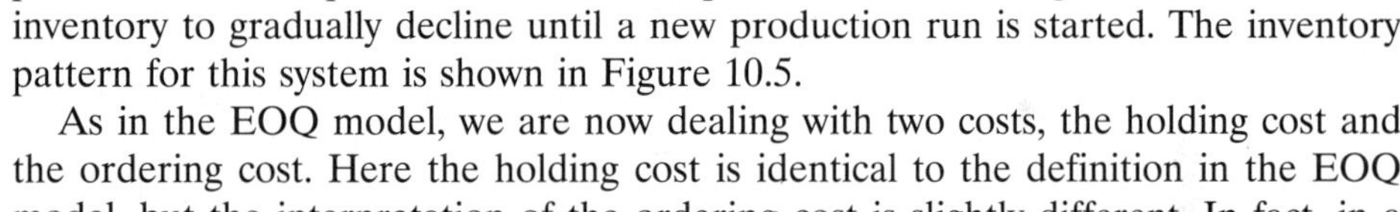

This model differs from the EOQ model in that a setup cost replaces the ordering cost and the saw-tooth inventory pattern shown in Figure 10.5 differs from the inventory pattern shown in Figure 10.2.

As in the EOQ model, we are now dealing with two costs, the holding cost and the ordering cost. Here the holding cost is identical to the definition in the EOQ model, but the interpretation of the ordering cost is slightly different. In fact, in a

Figure 10.5 Inventory Pattern for the Production Lot Size Inventory Model

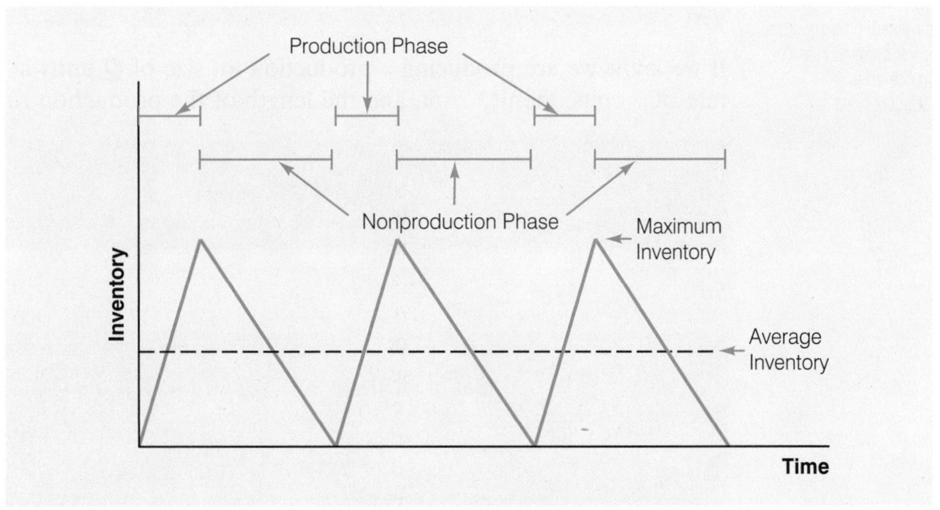

production situation the ordering cost is more correctly referred to as the production **setup cost**. This cost, which includes labour, material and lost production costs incurred while preparing the production system for operation, is a fixed cost that occurs for every production run regardless of the production lot size. EnviroHealth estimates the setup cost to be €135 largely made up of cleaning, preparation and disinfecting. This cost is incurred every time a batch of the product is produced. In order to schedule the setup for this product, the company must have at least six working days notification that production is to be scheduled. The company also knows that it costs €4.50 per litre to produce the product and the annual holding cost is 24 per cent of the inventory value.

Total Cost Model

Let us begin building the production lot size model by showing the holding cost in terms of the production lot size Q. Again, the approach is to develop an expression for average inventory and then establish the holding costs associated with the average inventory. We use a one-year time period and an annual cost for the model.

In the EOQ model the average inventory is one-half the maximum inventory or $\frac{1}{2}Q$. Figure 10.5 shows that for a production lot size model a constant inventory buildup rate occurs during the production run and a constant inventory depletion rate occurs during the nonproduction period; thus, the average inventory will be one-half the maximum inventory. However, in this inventory system the production lot size Q does not go into inventory at one point in time, and so the inventory never reaches a level of Q units.

To show how we can calculate the maximum inventory, let:

$$d = \text{daily demand rate}$$
$$p = \text{daily production rate}$$
$$t = \text{number of days for a production run}$$

At this point, the logic of the production lot size model is easier to follow using a daily demand rate D and a daily production rate P. However, when the total annual cost model is eventually developed, we recommend that inputs to the model be expressed in terms of the annual demand rate D and the annual production rate P.

Because we are assuming that p will be larger than d, the daily inventory buildup rate during the production phase is $p - d$. If we run production for t days and place $p - d$ units in inventory each day, the inventory at the end of the production run will be $(p - d)t$. From Figure 10.5 we can see that the inventory at the end of the production run is also the maximum inventory. Thus:

$$\text{Maximum inventory} = (p - d)t \qquad \textbf{(10.8)}$$

If we know we are producing a production lot size of Q units at a daily production rate of p units, then $Q = pt$, and the length of the production run t must be:

$$t = \frac{Q}{p} \text{ days} \qquad \textbf{(10.9)}$$

So

$$\begin{aligned} \text{Maximum inventory} &= (p - d)t = (p - d)\left(\frac{Q}{p}\right) \\ &= \left(1 - \frac{d}{p}\right)Q \end{aligned} \qquad \textbf{(10.10)}$$

The average inventory, which is one-half the maximum inventory, is given by:

$$\text{Average inventory} = \frac{1}{2}\left(1 - \frac{d}{p}\right)Q \tag{10.11}$$

With an annual per unit holding cost of C_h, the general equation for annual holding cost is as follows:

$$\begin{aligned}\text{Annual holding cost} &= \begin{pmatrix}\text{Average} \\ \text{inventory}\end{pmatrix}\begin{pmatrix}\text{Annual} \\ \text{cost} \\ \text{per unit}\end{pmatrix} \\ &= \frac{1}{2}\left(1 - \frac{d}{p}\right)QC_h\end{aligned} \tag{10.12}$$

If D is the annual demand for the product and C_o is the setup cost for a production run, then the annual setup cost, which takes the place of the annual ordering cost in the EOQ model, is as follows:

$$\begin{aligned}\text{Annual setup cost} &= \begin{pmatrix}\text{Number of production} \\ \text{runs per year}\end{pmatrix}\begin{pmatrix}\text{Setup cost} \\ \text{per run}\end{pmatrix} \\ &= \frac{D}{Q}C_o\end{aligned} \tag{10.13}$$

So, the total annual cost (TC) model is:

$$TC = \frac{1}{2}\left(1 - \frac{d}{p}\right)QC_h + \frac{D}{Q}C_o \tag{10.14}$$

Suppose that a production facility operates 250 days per year. Then we can write daily demand d in terms of annual demand D as follows:

$$d = \frac{D}{250}$$

Now let P denote the annual production for the product if the product were produced every day. Then:

$$P = 250p \quad \text{and} \quad p = \frac{P}{250}$$

Thus[4]

$$\frac{d}{p} = \frac{D/250}{P/250} = \frac{D}{P}$$

[4]The ratio $d/p = D/P$ holds regardless of the number of days of operation; 250 days is used here merely as an illustration.

Therefore, we can write the total annual cost model as follows:

$$TC = \frac{1}{2}\left(1 - \frac{D}{P}\right)QC_h + \frac{D}{Q}C_o \qquad \textbf{(10.15)}$$

Equations (10.14) and (10.15) are equivalent. However, Equation (10.15) may be used more frequently because an *annual* cost model tends to make the analyst think in terms of collecting *annual* demand data (*D*) and *annual* production data (*P*) rather than daily data.

Economic Production Lot Size

Given estimates of the holding cost (C_h), setup cost (C_o), annual demand rate (*D*) and annual production rate (*P*), we could use a trial-and-error approach to compute the total annual cost for various production lot sizes (*Q*). However, trial and error is not necessary; we can use the minimum cost formula for Q^* that has been developed using differential calculus (see Appendix 10.2). The equation is as follows:

As the production rate p approaches infinity, D/P approaches zero. In this case, Equation (10.16) is equivalent to the EOQ model in Equation (10.5).

$$Q^* = \sqrt{\frac{2DC_o}{(1 - D/P)C_h}} \qquad \textbf{(10.16)}$$

We are now in a position to advise EnviroHealth. Recollect that its annual production capacity was 60 000 litres with annual demand at 26 000 and a constant rate of demand through the year. Setup costs were €135 whilst holding cost was 24 per cent of inventory value which, given the product cost of €4.50 per litre, gives an annual holding cost of 0.24 × €4.50 or €1.08 per litre.

EXCEL *file*

LOT SIZE

Using equation (10.16), we have:

$$Q^* = \sqrt{\frac{2(26\,000)(135)}{(1 - 26\,000/60\,000)(1.08)}} = 3387$$

So, we have an optimum production lot size of 3387 litres. That is we should produce 3387 litres during each production run. This lot size minimizes annual inventory costs at €2073 (using Equation (10.15)). We also know that it takes six working days to schedule and set up a production run. Let us also assume that the company works 300 days a year. The lead time demand is then:

$$(26{,}000/300)(6) = 520 \text{ litres}$$

That is, during the six days it takes to schedule and set up a production run, inventory will need to be 520 litres to cope with demand. 520 litres is then the reorder point for EnviroHealth. The cycle time is the time between each production run. Using Equation (10.7) we can calculate the cycle time as:

$$T = 300Q^*/D = [(300)(3387)]/(26000) = 39 \text{ days}$$

So, EnviroHealth should plan for production runs of 3387 litres every 39 working days. For practical convenience, the company might schedule this as 3400 litres every six-and-a-half working weeks.

10.4 Inventory Model with Planned Shortages

A **shortage** or **stock-out** is a demand that cannot be supplied. In many situations, shortages are undesirable and should be avoided if at all possible. However, in other cases it may be desirable – from an economic point of view – to plan for and allow shortages. In practice, these types of situations are most commonly found where the value of the inventory per unit is high and hence the holding cost is high. An example of this type of situation is a new car dealer's inventory. Often the specific car that a customer wants is not in stock. However, if the customer is willing to wait a few weeks, the dealer is usually able to order the car for delivery at some stage in the future.

The assumptions of the EOQ model in Table 10.3 apply to this inventory model with the exception that shortages, referred to as backorders, are now permitted.

The model developed in this section takes into account a type of shortage known as a **backorder**. In a backorder situation, we assume that when a customer places an order and discovers that the supplier is out of stock, the customer waits until the new shipment arrives, and then the order is filled. Frequently, the waiting period in backordering situations is relatively short. So, by promising the customer top priority and immediate delivery when the goods become available, companies may be able to convince the customer to wait until the order arrives. In these cases, the backorder assumption is valid.

The backorder model that we develop is an extension of the EOQ model presented in Section 10.2. We use the EOQ model in which all goods arrive in inventory at one time and are subject to a constant demand rate. If we let S indicate the number of backorders that are accumulated when a new shipment of size Q is received, then the inventory system for the backorder case has the following characteristics:

- If S backorders exist when a new shipment of size Q arrives, then S backorders are shipped to the appropriate customers and the remaining $Q - S$ units are placed in inventory. Therefore, $Q - S$ is the maximum inventory.
- The inventory cycle of T days is divided into two distinct phases: t_1 days when inventory is available and orders are filled as they occur, and t_2 days when stock-outs occur and all new orders are placed on backorder.

The inventory pattern for the inventory model with backorders, where negative inventory represents the number of backorders, is shown in Figure 10.6.

With the inventory pattern now defined, we can proceed with the basic step of all inventory models – namely, the development of a total cost model. For

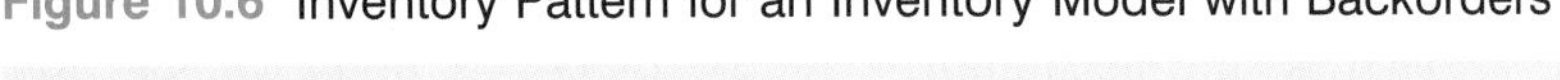
Figure 10.6 Inventory Pattern for an Inventory Model with Backorders

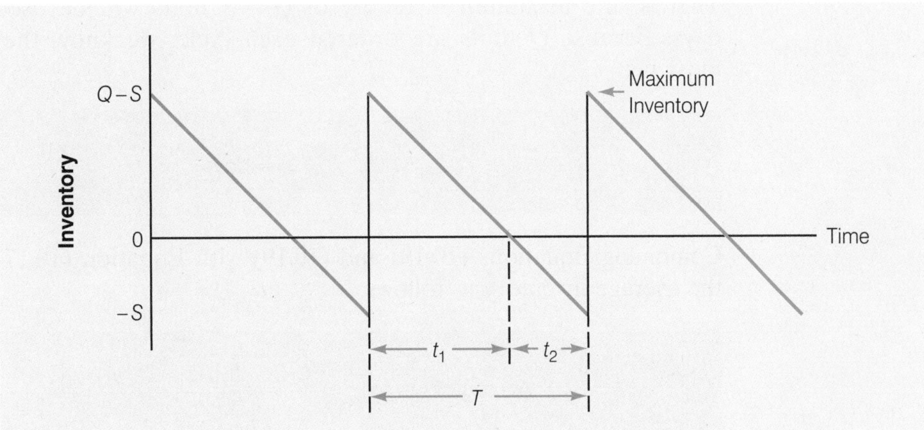

the inventory model with backorders, we encounter the usual holding costs and ordering costs. We also incur a backorder cost in terms of the labour and special delivery costs directly associated with the handling of the backorders. Another element of the backorder cost accounts for the loss of goodwill because some customers will have to wait for their orders. Because the **goodwill cost** depends on how long a customer has to wait, it is customary to adopt the convention of expressing backorder cost in terms of the cost of having a unit on backorder for a stated period of time. This method of costing backorders on a time basis is similar to the method used to calculate the inventory holding cost, and we can use it to calculate a total annual cost of backorders once the average backorder level and the backorder cost per unit per period are known.

Let us begin the development of a total cost model by calculating the average inventory for a hypothetical problem. If we have an average inventory of two units for three days and no inventory on the fourth day, the average inventory over the four-day period is:

$$\frac{2 \text{ units (3 days)} + 0 \text{ units (1 day)}}{4 \text{ days}} = \frac{6}{4} = 1.5 \text{ units}$$

Refer to Figure 10.6. You can see that this situation is what happens in the backorder model. With a maximum inventory of $Q - S$ units, the t_1 days we have inventory on hand will have an average inventory of $(Q - S)/2$. No inventory is carried for the t_2 days in which we experience backorders. So, over the total cycle time of $T = t_1 + t_2$ days, we can calculate the average inventory as follows:

$$\text{Average inventory} = \frac{\frac{1}{2}(Q - S)t_1 + 0t_2}{t_1 + t_2} = \frac{\frac{1}{2}(Q - S)t_1}{T} \qquad \textbf{(10.17)}$$

Can we find other ways of expressing t_1 and T? Because we know that the maximum inventory is $Q - S$ and that d represents the constant daily demand, we have:

$$t_1 = \frac{Q - S}{d} \text{ days} \qquad \textbf{(10.18)}$$

That is, the maximum inventory of $Q - S$ units will be used up in $(Q - S)/d$ days. Because Q units are ordered each cycle, we know the length of a cycle must be:

$$T = \frac{Q}{d} \text{ days} \qquad \textbf{(10.19)}$$

Combining Equations (10.18) and (10.19) with Equation (10.17), we can calculate the average inventory as follows:

$$\text{Average inventory} = \frac{\frac{1}{2}(Q - S)[(Q - S)/d]}{Q/d} = \frac{(Q - S)^2}{2Q} \qquad \textbf{(10.20)}$$

So, the average inventory is expressed in terms of two inventory decisions: how much we will order (Q) and the maximum number of backorders (S).

The formula for the annual number of orders placed using this model is identical to that for the EOQ model. With D representing the annual demand, we have:

$$\text{Annual number of orders} = \frac{D}{Q} \tag{10.21}$$

The next step is to develop an expression for the average backorder level. Because we know the maximum for backorders is S, we can use the same logic we used to establish average inventory in finding the average number of backorders. We have an average number of backorders during the period t_2 of ½ the maximum number of backorders or ½S. We do not have any backorders during the t_1 days we have inventory, therefore we can calculate the average backorders in a manner similar to Equation (10.17). Using this approach, we have:

$$\text{Average backorders} = \frac{0t_1 + (S/2)t_2}{T} = \frac{(S/2)t_2}{T} \tag{10.22}$$

When we let the maximum number of backorders reach an amount S at a daily rate of d, the length of the backorder portion of the inventory cycle is:

$$t_2 = \frac{S}{d} \tag{10.23}$$

Using Equations (10.23) and (10.19) in Equation (10.22), we have:

$$\text{Average backorders} = \frac{(S/2)(S/d)}{Q/d} = \frac{S^2}{2Q} \tag{10.24}$$

Let

C_h = cost to hold one unit in inventory for one year

C_o = cost per order

C_b = cost to maintain one unit on backorder for one year

The total annual cost (TC) for the inventory model with backorders becomes:

$$TC = \frac{(Q-S)^2}{2Q}C_h + \frac{D}{Q}C_o + \frac{S^2}{2Q}C_b \tag{10.25}$$

Given C_h, C_o and C_b and the annual demand D, differential calculus can be used to show that the minimum cost values for the order quantity Q^* and the planned backorders S^* are as follows:

$$Q^* = \sqrt{\frac{2DC_o}{C_h}\left(\frac{C_h + C_b}{C_b}\right)} \tag{10.26}$$

$$S^* = Q^*\left(\frac{C_h}{C_h + C_b}\right) \tag{10.27}$$

EXCEL *file*

SHORTAGE

Higley Electronic Components supplies high-cost electronic parts to companies in the area. One particular component part costs the company €50 and annual demand is 2000 units per year, order cost is €25 per order. The company uses a cost of capital of 20 per cent per annum giving a holding cost of €10 per item per year. The company currently uses the basic EOQ model giving:

$$Q^* = \frac{\sqrt{2(2000)(25)}}{10} = \sqrt{10\,000} = 100$$

An inventory situation that incorporates backorder costs is considered in Problem 9.

The backorder cost C_b is one of the most difficult costs to estimate in inventory models. The reason is that it attempts to measure the cost associated with the loss of goodwill when a customer must wait for an order. Expressing this cost on an annual basis adds to the difficulty.

as the number of units to be ordered each time and with 20 orders placed through the year. Annual order cost is €500, so annual holding cost must also be €500, giving a total annual inventory cost of €1000. The company is considering moving to a backorder policy and wonders if this will reduce annual inventory costs. The annual backorder cost is estimated to be €30 per unit per year. Using Equations (10.26) and (10.27), we have:

$$Q^* = \sqrt{\frac{2(2000)(25)}{10}\left(\frac{10+30}{30}\right)} = 115.47$$

and

$$S^* = 115\left(\frac{10}{10+30}\right) = 28.87$$

That is, the optimum order quantity has now risen to 115.47 units with the planned backorders at 28.87.

If this solution is implemented, the system will operate with the following properties:

$$\text{Maximum inventory} = Q - S = 115.47 - 28.87 = 86.6$$

$$\text{Cycle time} = T = \frac{Q}{D}(250) = \frac{115.47}{2000}(250) = 14.43 \text{ working days}$$

The total annual cost is:

If backorders can be tolerated, the total cost including the back-ordering cost will be less than the total cost of the EOQ model. Some people think the model with backorders will have a greater cost because it includes a back-ordering cost in addition to the usual inventory holding and ordering costs. You can point out the fallacy in this thinking by noting that the backorder model leads to lower inventory and hence lower inventory holding costs.

$$\text{Holding cost} = \frac{(86.6)^2}{2(115.47)}(10) = €325$$

$$\text{Ordering cost} = \frac{2000}{115.47}(25) = €433$$

$$\text{Backorder order} = \frac{(28.87)^2}{2(115.47)}(30) = €108$$

$$\text{Giving Total cost} = €866$$

So, in this problem, allowing backorders is projecting a €1000 – €866 = €134 or 13.4 per cent savings in cost from the no-stock-out EOQ model. The preceding comparison and conclusion are based on the assumption that the backorder model with an annual cost per back-ordered unit of €30 is a valid model for the actual inventory situation. However, if the company is concerned that stock-outs might lead to lost sales, then the savings might not be enough to warrant switching to an inventory policy that allowed for planned shortages.

NOTES AND COMMENTS

Equation (10.27) shows that the optimal number of planned backorders S^* is proportional to the ratio $C_h/(C_h + C_b)$, where C_h is the annual holding cost per unit and C_b is the annual backorder cost per unit. Whenever C_h increases, this ratio becomes larger, and the number of planned backorders increases. This relationship explains why items that have a high per-unit cost and a correspondingly high annual holding cost are more economically handled on a backorder basis. On the other hand, whenever the backorder cost C_b increases, the ratio becomes smaller, and the number of planned backorders decreases. So, the model provides the intuitive result that items with high back-ordering costs will be handled with few backorders. In fact, with high back-order costs, the backorder model and the EOQ model with no back-ordering allowed provide similar inventory policies.

10.5 Quantity Discounts for the EOQ Model

In the quantity discount model, assumption 4 of the EOQ model in Table 10.3 is altered. The cost per unit varies depending on the quantity ordered.

Quantity discounts occur in numerous situations in which suppliers provide an incentive for large order quantities by offering a lower purchase cost when items are ordered in larger quantities. In this section we show how the EOQ model can be used when quantity discounts are available.

A group of local schools operate a common purchasing system to help minimize costs and maximize value for money. They currently purchase boxes of USB sticks for use by pupils. Instead of a fixed unit cost, the supplier quotes the following discount schedule.

Discount Category	Order Size	Discount (%)	Unit Cost, €
1	0 to 999	0	5.00
2	1 000 to 2 499	3	4.85
3	2 500 and over	5	4.75

The 5 per cent discount for the 2500-unit minimum order quantity looks tempting. However, realizing that higher order quantities result in higher inventory holding costs, we should prepare a thorough cost analysis before making a final ordering and inventory policy recommendation.

Suppose that the data and cost analyses show an annual holding cost rate of 20 per cent, an ordering cost of €49 per order, and an annual demand of 5000 units; what order quantity should we select? The following three-step procedure shows the calculations necessary to make this decision. In the preliminary calculations, we use Q_1 to indicate the order quantity for discount category 1, Q_2 for discount category 2 and Q_3 for discount category 3.

Step 1. For each discount category, compute a Q^* using the EOQ formula based on the unit cost associated with the discount category.

Recall that the EOQ model provides $Q^* = \sqrt{2DC_o/C_h}$, where $C_h = IC = (0.20)$ C. With three discount categories providing three different unit costs C, we obtain:

EXCEL *file*

DISCOUNT

$$Q_1^* = \sqrt{\frac{2(5000)49}{(0.20)(5.00)}} = 700$$

$$Q_2^* = \sqrt{\frac{2(5000)49}{(0.20)(4.85)}} = 711$$

$$Q_3^* = \sqrt{\frac{2(5000)49}{(0.20)(4.75)}} = 718$$

Because the only differences in the EOQ formulas come from slight differences in the holding cost, the economic order quantities resulting from this step will be approximately the same. However, these order quantities will usually not all be of the size necessary to qualify for the discount price assumed. In the preceding case, both Q_2^* and Q_3^* are insufficient order quantities to obtain their discounted costs of €4.85 and €4.75, respectively. For those order quantities for which the assumed price cannot be obtained, the following procedure must be used.

Step 2. For the Q^* that is too small to qualify for the assumed discount price, adjust the order quantity upward to the nearest order quantity that will allow the product to be purchased at the assumed price.

In our example, this adjustment causes us to set:

$$Q_2^* = 1000$$

and

$$Q_3^* = 2500$$

Problem 14 at the end of the chapter asks you to show that this property is true.

If a calculated Q^* for a given discount price is large enough to qualify for a bigger discount, that value of Q^* cannot lead to an optimal solution. Although the reason may not be obvious, it does turn out to be a property of the EOQ quantity discount model.

In the previous inventory models considered, the annual purchase cost of the item was not included because it was constant and never affected by the inventory order policy decision. However, in the quantity discount model, the annual purchase cost depends on the order quantity and the associated unit cost. So, annual purchase cost (annual demand $D \times$ unit cost C) is included in the equation for total cost as shown here.

In the EOQ model with quantity discounts, the annual purchase cost must be included because purchase cost depends on the order quantity. So, it is a relevant cost.

$$TC = \frac{Q}{2}C_h + \frac{D}{Q}C_o + DC \qquad \textbf{(10.28)}$$

Using this total cost equation, we can determine the optimal order quantity for the EOQ discount model in step 3.

Step 3. For each order quantity resulting from steps 1 and 2, calculate the total annual cost using the unit price from the appropriate discount category and equation (10.28). The order quantity yielding the minimum total annual cost is the optimal order quantity.

The step 3 calculations for the example problem are summarized in Table 10.4. As you can see, a decision to order 1000 units at the 3 per cent discount rate yields the minimum cost solution. Even though the 2500-unit order quantity would result in a 5 per cent discount, its excessive holding cost makes it the second-best solution. Figure 10.7 shows the total cost curve for each of the three discount categories. Note that $Q^* = 1000$ provides the minimum cost order quantity.

Problem 13 will give you practise in applying the EOQ model to situations with quantity discounts.

Table 10.4 Total Annual Cost Calculations for the EOQ Model with Quantity Discounts

Discount Category	Unit Cost, €	Order Quantity	Annual Cost, € Holding	Annual Cost, € Ordering	Annual Cost, € Purchase	Total
1	5.00	700	350	350	25 000	25 700
2	4.85	1 000	485	245	24 250	24 980
3	4.75	2 500	1 188	98	23 750	25 036

Figure 10.7 Total Cost Curves for the Three Discount Categories

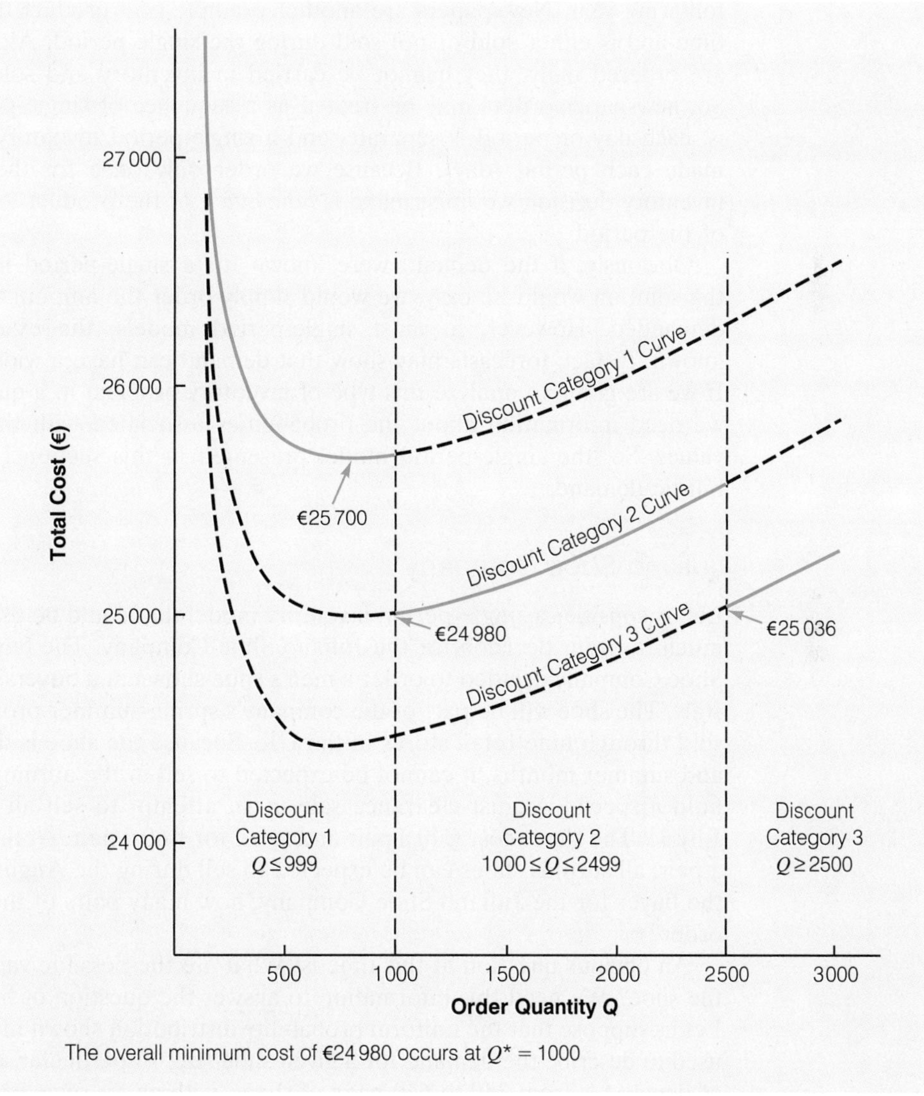

The overall minimum cost of €24 980 occurs at $Q^* = 1000$

10.6 Single-Period Inventory Model with Probabilistic Demand

The inventory models discussed so far were based on the assumption that the demand rate is constant and **deterministic** throughout the year. We developed minimum cost order quantity and reorder point policies based on this assumption.

This inventory model is the first in the chapter that explicitly treats probabilistic demand. Unlike the EOQ model, it is for a single period with unused inventory not carried over to future periods.

In situations in which the demand rate is not deterministic, other models treat demand as probabilistic and best described by a probability distribution. In this section we consider a single-period inventory model with probabilistic demand.

The single-period inventory model refers to inventory situations in which *one* order is placed for the product; at the end of the period, the product has either sold out, or a surplus of unsold items will be sold for a salvage value. The single-period inventory model is applicable in situations involving seasonal or perishable items that cannot be carried in inventory and sold in future periods. Seasonal clothing (such as bathing suits and winter coats) are typically handled in a single-period manner. In these situations, a buyer places one pre-season order for each item and then experiences a stock-out or holds a clearance sale on the surplus stock at the end of the season. No items are carried in inventory and sold the following year. Newspapers are another example of a product that is ordered one time and is either sold or not sold during the single period. Although newspapers are ordered daily, they cannot be carried in inventory and sold in later periods. So, newspaper orders may be treated as a sequence of single-period models; that is, each day or period is separate, and a single-period inventory decision must be made each period (day). Because we order only once for the period, the only inventory decision we must make is *how much* of the product to order at the start of the period.

Obviously, if the demand were known for a single-period inventory situation, the solution would be easy; we would simply order the amount we knew would be demanded. However, in most single-period models, the exact demand is not known. In fact, forecasts may show that demand can have a wide variety of values. If we are going to analyze this type of inventory problem in a quantitative manner, we need information about the probabilities associated with the various demand values. So, the single-period model presented in this section is based on probabilistic demand.

Juliano Shoe Company

Let us consider a single-period inventory model that could be used to make a how-much-to-order decision for the Juliano Shoe Company. The buyer for the Juliano Shoe Company decided to order a men's shoe shown at a buyers' meeting in Milan, Italy. The shoe will be part of the company's spring-summer promotion and will be sold through nine retail stores in the UK. Because the shoe is designed for spring and summer months, it cannot be expected to sell in the autumn. Juliano plans to hold a special August clearance sale in an attempt to sell all shoes not sold by July 31. The shoes cost €40 a pair and retail for €60 a pair. At the sale price of €30 a pair, all surplus shoes can be expected to sell during the August sale. If you were the buyer for the Juliano Shoe Company, how many pairs of the shoes would you order?

An obvious question at this time is: What are the possible values of demand for the shoe? We need this information to answer the question of how much to order. Let us suppose that the uniform probability distribution shown in Figure 10.8 can be used to describe the demand for a given shoe size. In particular, note that the range of demand is from 350 to 650 pairs of shoes, with an average, or expected, demand of 500 pairs of shoes.

Incremental analysis is a method that can be used to determine the optimal order quantity for a single-period inventory model. Incremental analysis addresses the how-much-to-order question by comparing the cost or loss of *ordering one additional unit* with the cost or loss of *not ordering one additional unit*. The costs involved are defined as follows:

Figure 10.8 Uniform Probability Distribution of Demand for the Juliano Shoe Company Problem

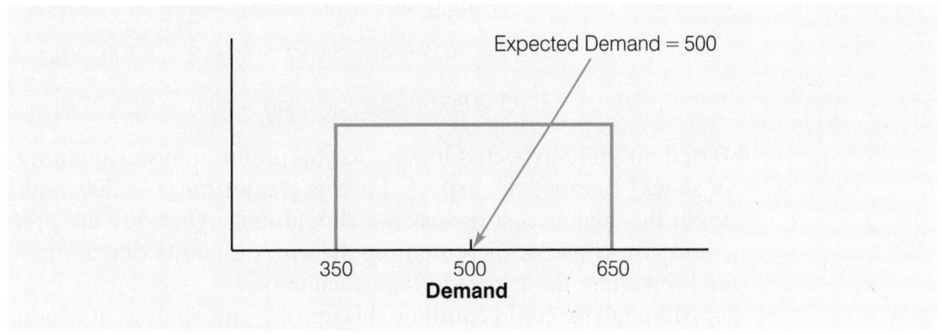

c_o = cost per unit of *overestimating* demand. This cost represents the loss of ordering one additional unit and finding that it cannot be sold.

c_u = cost per unit of *underestimating* demand. This cost represents the opportunity loss of not ordering one additional unit and finding that it could have been sold.

The cost of underestimating demand is usually harder to determine than the cost of overestimating demand. The reason is that the cost of underestimating demand includes a lost profit and may include a customer goodwill cost because the customer is unable to purchase the item when desired.

In the Juliano Shoe Company problem, the company will incur the cost of overestimating demand whenever it orders too much and has to sell the extra shoes during the August sale. Thus, the cost per unit of overestimating demand is equal to the purchase cost per unit minus the August sales price per unit; that is, c_o = €40 – €30 = €10. Therefore, Juliano will lose €10 for each pair of shoes that it orders over the quantity demanded. The cost of underestimating demand is the lost profit because a pair of shoes that could have been sold was not available in inventory. Thus, the per-unit cost of underestimating demand is the difference between the regular selling price per unit and the purchase cost per unit; that is, c_u = €60 – €40 = €20.

Because the exact level of demand is unknown, we have to consider the probability of demand and therefore the probability of obtaining the associated costs or losses. For example, let us assume that Juliano Shoe Company management wishes to consider an order quantity equal to the average or expected demand for 500 pairs of shoes. In incremental analysis, we consider the possible losses associated with an order quantity of 501 (ordering one additional unit) and an order quantity of 500 (not ordering one additional unit). The order quantity alternatives and the possible losses are summarized here.

Order Quantity Alternatives	Loss Occurs if	Possible Loss	Probability Loss Occurs
$Q = 501$	Demand overestimated; the additional unit *cannot* be sold	c_o = €10	$P(\text{demand} \leq 500)$
$Q = 500$	Demand underestimated; an additional unit *could have* been sold	c_u = €20	$P(\text{demand} > 500)$

By looking at the demand probability distribution in Figure 10.8, we see that $P(\text{demand} \leq 500) = 0.50$ and that $P(\text{demand} > 500) = 0.50$. By multiplying the possible losses, $c_o = €10$ and $c_u = €20$, by the probability of obtaining the loss, we can compute the expected value of the loss, or simply the *expected loss* (EL), associated with the order quantity alternatives. So:

$$\text{EL}(Q = 501) = c_o P(\text{demand} \leq 500) = €10(0.50) = €5$$

$$\text{EL}(Q = 500) = c_u P(\text{demand} > 500) = €20(0.50) = €10$$

Based on these expected losses, do you prefer an order quantity of 501 or 500 pairs of shoes? Because the expected loss is greater for $Q = 500$, and because we want to avoid this higher cost or loss, we should make $Q = 501$ the preferred decision. We could now consider incrementing the order quantity one additional unit to $Q = 502$ and repeating the expected loss calculations.

Although we could continue this unit-by-unit analysis, it would be time-consuming and cumbersome. We would have to evaluate $Q = 502$, $Q = 503$, $Q = 504$ and so on, until we found the value of Q where the expected loss of ordering one incremental unit is equal to the expected loss of not ordering one incremental unit; that is, the optimal order quantity Q^* occurs when the incremental analysis shows that:

$$\text{EL}(Q^* + 1) = \text{EL}(Q^*) \qquad \textbf{(10.29)}$$

When this relationship holds, increasing the order quantity by one additional unit has no economic advantage. Using the logic with which we computed the expected losses for the order quantities of 501 and 500, the general expressions for $\text{EL}(Q^* + 1)$ and $\text{EL}(Q^*)$ can be written:

$$\text{EL}(Q^* + 1) = c_o P(\text{demand} \leq Q^*) \qquad \textbf{(10.30)}$$

$$\text{EL}(Q^*) = c_u P(\text{demand} > Q^*) \qquad \textbf{(10.31)}$$

Because we know from basic probability that:

$$P(\text{demand} \leq Q^*) + P(\text{demand} > Q^*) = 1 \qquad \textbf{(10.32)}$$

we can write:

$$P(\text{demand} > Q^*) = 1 - P(\text{demand} \leq Q^*) \qquad \textbf{(10.33)}$$

Using this expression, Equation (10.31) can be rewritten as:

$$\text{EL}(Q^*) = c_u[1 - P(\text{demand} \leq Q^*)] \qquad \textbf{(10.34)}$$

Equations (10.30) and (10.34) can be used to show that $\text{EL}(Q^* + 1) = \text{EL}(Q^*)$ whenever:

$$c_o P(\text{demand} \leq Q*) = c_u[1 - P(\text{demand} \leq Q^*)] \qquad \textbf{(10.35)}$$

Solving for $P(\text{demand} \leq Q^*)$, we have:

$$P(\text{demand} \leq Q^*) = \frac{c_u}{c_u + c_o} \tag{10.36}$$

This expression provides the general condition for the optimal order quantity Q^*in the single-period inventory model.

In the Juliano Shoe Company problem $c_o = €10$ and $c_u = €20$. Thus, equation (10.36) shows that the optimal order size for Juliano shoes must satisfy the following condition:

$$P(\text{demand} \leq Q^*) = \frac{c_u}{c_u + c_o} = \frac{20}{20 + 10} = \frac{20}{30} = \frac{2}{3}$$

We can find the optimal order quantity Q^* by referring to the probability distribution shown in Figure 10.8 and finding the value of Q that will provide $P(\text{demand} \leq Q^*) = {}^2\!/_3$. To find this solution, we note that in the uniform distribution the probability is evenly distributed over the entire range of 350–650 pairs of shoes. So, we can satisfy the expression for Q^* by moving two-thirds of the way from 350 to 650. Because this range is 650 – 350 = 300, we move 200 units from 350 toward 650. Doing so provides the optimal order quantity of 550 pairs of shoes.

In summary, the key to establishing an optimal order quantity for single-period inventory models is to identify the probability distribution that describes the demand for the item and the costs of overestimation and underestimation. Then, using the information for the costs of overestimation and underestimation, Equation (10.36) can be used to find the location of Q^* in the probability distribution.

Arabian Car Rental

As another example of a single period inventory model with probabilistic demand, let us consider the situation faced by the Arabian Car Rental company (ACR), based in Saudi Arabia. ACR operates through the Middle East and must decide how many cars to have available at each car rental location at specific points in time through the year. We shall illustrate using its car rental depot in Dubai as an example. Analysis has shown that one of its more lucrative markets consists of tourists and expatriate workers who rent four-wheel drive cars for a long weekend. Typically, customer demand for this type of vehicle follows a normal distribution with a mean of 150 vehicles demanded and a standard deviation of 14 vehicles.

The ACR situation can benefit from use of a single-period inventory model. The company must establish the number of four-wheel drive cars (4WD) to have available prior to the weekend. Customer demand over the weekend will then result in either a stockout or a surplus. Let us denote the number of 4WD available by Q. If Q is greater than customer demand, ACR will have a surplus of cars. The cost of a surplus is the cost of overestimating demand. This cost is set at €80 per car, which reflects, in part, the opportunity cost of not having the car available for rent elsewhere.

If Q is less than customer demand, ACR will rent all available cars and experience a stock-out or shortage. A shortage results in an underestimation cost of €200 per car. This figure reflects the cost due to lost profit and the lost goodwill of not having a car available for a customer. Given this information, how many 4WDs should ACR make available for the weekend?

Using the cost of underestimation, $c_u = €200$, and the cost of overestimation, $c_o = €80$, equation (10.36) indicates that the optimal order quantity must satisfy the following condition:

Figure 10.9 Probability Distribution of Demand for the ACR Problem Showing the Location of Q^*

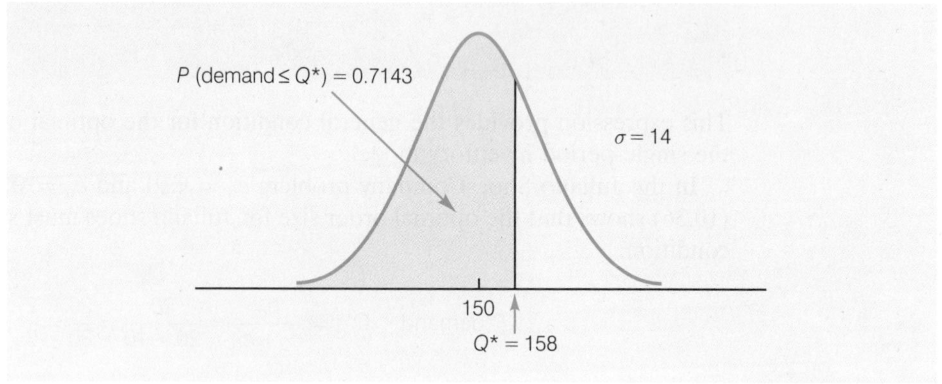

$$P(\text{demand} \leq Q^*) = \frac{c_u}{(c_u + c_o)} = \frac{200}{200 + 80} = 0.7143$$

We can use the normal probability distribution for demand as shown in Figure 10.9 to find the order quantity that satisfies the condition that $P(\text{demand} \leq Q^*) = 0.7143$. From Appendix A, we see that 0.7143 of the area in the left tail of the normal probability distribution occurs at $z = 0.57$ standard deviations *above* the mean. With a mean demand of $\mu = 150$ automobiles and a standard deviation of $\sigma = 14$ automobiles, we have:

EXCEL *file*

SINGLE-PERIOD

$$\begin{aligned} Q^* &= \mu + 0.57\sigma \\ &= 150 + 0.57(14) = 158 \end{aligned}$$

An example of a single-period inventory model with probabilistic demand described by a normal probability distribution is considered in Problem 15.

So, ACR should plan to have 158 4WDs available for the weekend. Note that in this case the cost of overestimation is less than the cost of underestimation. So ACR is willing to risk a higher probability of overestimating demand and hence a higher probability of a surplus. In fact, ACR's optimal order quantity has a 0.7143 probability of a surplus and a $1 - 0.7143 = 0.2857$ probability of a stock-out. As a result, the probability is 0.2857 that all 158 4WDs will be rented during the weekend.

NOTES AND COMMENTS

1 In any probabilistic inventory model, the assumption about the probability distribution for demand is critical and can affect the recommended inventory decision. In the problems presented in this section, we used the uniform and the normal probability distributions to describe demand. In some situations, other probability distributions may be more appropriate. In using probabilistic inventory models, we must exercise care in selecting the probability distribution that most realistically describes demand.

2 In the single-period inventory model, the value of $c_u/(c_u + c_o)$ plays a critical role in selecting the order quantity [see Equation (10.36)]. Whenever $c_u = c_o$, $c_u/(c_u + c_o)$ equals 0.50; in this case, we should select an order quantity corresponding to the median demand. With this choice, a stock-out is just as likely as a surplus because the two costs are equal. However, whenever $c_u < c_o$, a smaller order quantity will be recommended. In this case, the smaller order quantity will provide a higher probability of a stock-out; however, the more

expensive cost of overestimating demand and having a surplus will tend to be avoided. Finally, whenever $c_u > c_o$, a larger order quantity will be recommended. In this case, the larger order quantity provides a lower probability of a stock-out in an attempt to avoid the more expensive cost of underestimating demand and experiencing a stock-out.

10.7 Order-Quantity, Reorder Point Model with Probabilistic Demand

In the previous section we considered a single-period inventory model with probabilistic demand. In this section we extend our discussion to a multiperiod order-quantity, reorder point inventory model with probabilistic demand. In the multiperiod model, the inventory system operates continuously with many repeating periods or cycles; inventory can be carried from one period to the next. Whenever the inventory position reaches the reorder point, an order for Q units is placed. Because demand is probabilistic, the time the reorder point will be reached, the time between orders and the time the order of Q units will arrive in inventory cannot be determined in advance.

The inventory model in this section is based on the assumptions of the EOQ model shown in Table 10.3 with the exception that demand is probabilistic rather than deterministic. With probabilistic demand, occasional shortages may occur.

The inventory pattern for the order-quantity, reorder point model with probabilistic demand will have the general appearance shown in Figure 10.10. Note that the increases or jumps in the inventory occur whenever an order of Q units arrives. The inventory decreases at a nonconstant rate based on the probabilistic demand. A new order is placed whenever the reorder point is reached. At times, the order quantity of Q units will arrive before inventory reaches zero. However, at other times, higher demand will cause a stock-out before a new order is received. As with other order-quantity, reorder point models, the manager must determine the order quantity Q and the reorder point r for the inventory system.

The exact mathematical formulation of an order-quantity, reorder point inventory model with probabilistic demand is beyond the scope of this text. However, we present a procedure that can be used to obtain good, workable order quantity and

Figure 10.10 Inventory Pattern for an Order-Quantity, Reorder Point Model with Probabilistic Demand

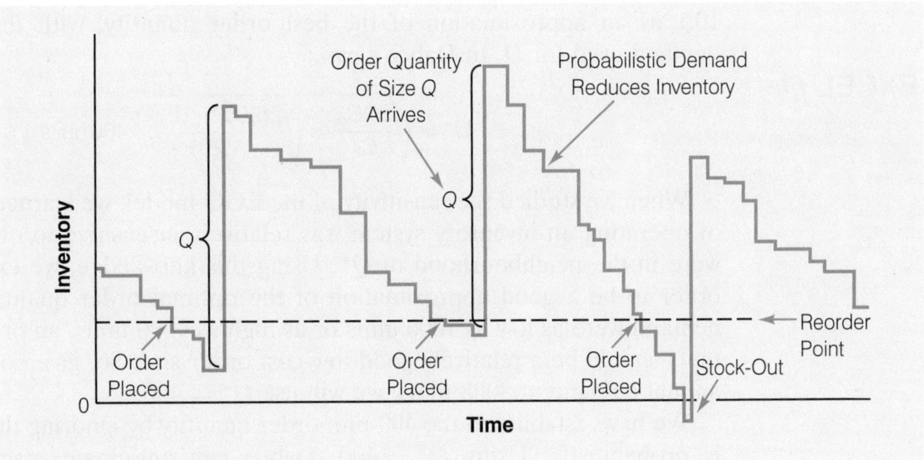

Figure 10.11 Lead-Time Demand Probability Distribution for Dabco Lightbulbs

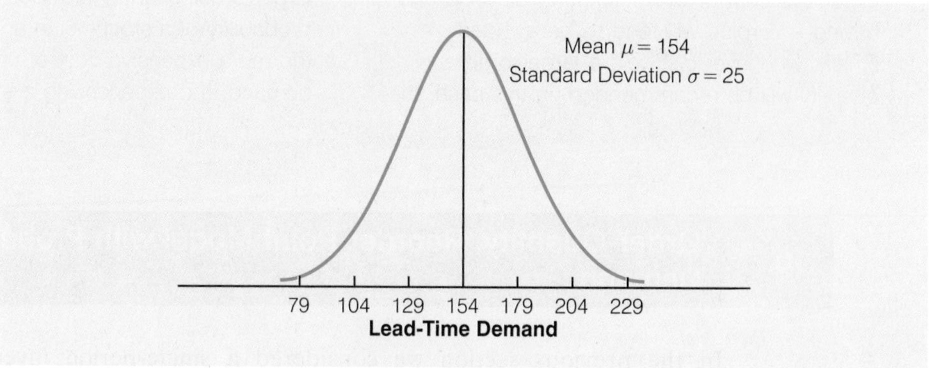

reorder point inventory policies. The solution procedure can be expected to provide only an approximation of the optimal solution, but it can yield good solutions in many practical situations.

Let us consider the inventory problem of Dabco Industrial Lighting Distributors. Dabco purchases a special high-intensity lightbulb for industrial lighting systems from a well-known lightbulb manufacturer. Dabco would like a recommendation on how much to order and when to order so that a low-cost inventory policy can be maintained. Pertinent facts are that the ordering cost is €12 per order, each bulb costs €6 and Dabco uses a 20 per cent annual holding cost rate for its inventory ($C_h = IC = 0.20 \times €6 = €1.20$). Dabco, which has more than 1000 customers, experiences a probabilistic demand; in fact, the number of units demanded varies considerably from day to day and from week to week. The lead time for a new order of lightbulbs is one week. Historical sales data indicate that demand during a one-week lead time can be described by a normal probability distribution with a mean of 154 lightbulbs and a standard deviation of 25 lightbulbs. The normal distribution of demand during the lead time is shown in Figure 10.11. Because the mean demand during one week is 154 units, Dabco can anticipate a mean or expected annual demand of 154 units per week $\times$ 52 weeks per year = 8008 units per year.

The How-Much-to-Order Decision

Although we are in a probabilistic demand situation, we have an estimate of the expected annual demand of 8008 units. We can apply the EOQ model from Section 10.1 as an approximation of the best order quantity, with the expected annual demand used for D. In Dabco's case:

EXCEL *file*
Q PROB

$$Q^* = \sqrt{\frac{2DC_o}{C_h}} = \sqrt{\frac{2(8008)(12)}{(1.20)}} = 400 \text{ units}$$

When we studied the sensitivity of the EOQ model, we learned that the total cost of operating an inventory system was relatively insensitive to order quantities that were in the neighbourhood of Q^*. Using this knowledge, we expect 400 units per order to be a good approximation of the optimal order quantity. Even if annual demand were as low as 7000 units or as high as 9000 units, an order quantity of 400 units should be a relatively good low-cost order size. So, given our best estimate of annual demand at 8008 units, we will use $Q^* = 400$.

We have established the 400-unit order quantity by ignoring the fact that demand is probabilistic. Using $Q^* = 400$, Dabco can anticipate placing approximately

$D/Q^* = 8008/400 = 20$ orders per year with an average of approximately $250/20 = 12.5$ working days between orders.

The When-to-Order Decision

We now want to establish a when-to-order decision rule or reorder point that will trigger the ordering process. With a mean lead-time demand of 154 units, you might first suggest a 154-unit reorder point. However, considering the probability of demand now becomes extremely important. If 154 is the mean lead-time demand, and if demand is normally distributed about 154, then the lead-time demand will be more than 154 units roughly 50 per cent of the time. When the demand during the one-week lead time exceeds 154 units, Dabco will experience a shortage or stock-out. Thus, using a reorder point of 154 units, approximately 50 per cent of the time (ten of the 20 orders a year) Dabco will be short of bulbs before the new supply arrives. This shortage rate would most likely be viewed as unacceptable.

The probability of a stock-out during any one inventory cycle is easiest to estimate by first determining the number of orders that are expected during the year. The inventory manager can usually state a willingness to allow perhaps one, two or three stock-outs during the year. The allowable stock-outs per year divided by the number of orders per year will provide the desired probability of a stock-out.

Refer to the lead-time demand distribution shown in Figure 10.11. Given this distribution, we can now determine how the reorder point r affects the probability of a stock-out. Because stock-outs occur whenever the demand during the lead time exceeds the reorder point, we can find the probability of a stock-out by using the lead-time demand distribution to compute the probability that demand will exceed r.

We could now approach the when-to-order problem by defining a cost per stock-out and then attempting to include this cost in a total cost equation. Alternatively, we can ask management to specify the average number of stock-outs that can be tolerated per year. If demand for a product is probabilistic, a manager who will never tolerate a stock-out is being somewhat unrealistic because attempting to avoid stock-outs completely will require high reorder points, high inventory and an associated high holding cost.

Suppose in this case that Dabco management is willing to tolerate an average of one stock-out per year. Because Dabco places 20 orders per year, this decision implies that management is willing to allow demand during lead time to exceed the reorder point one time in 20, or 5 per cent of the time. The reorder point r can be found by using the lead-time demand distribution to find the value of r with a 5 per cent chance of having a lead-time demand that will exceed it. This situation is shown graphically in Figure 10.12.

From the standard normal probability distribution table in Appendix A, we see that the r value is 1.645 standard deviations above the mean. Therefore, for the

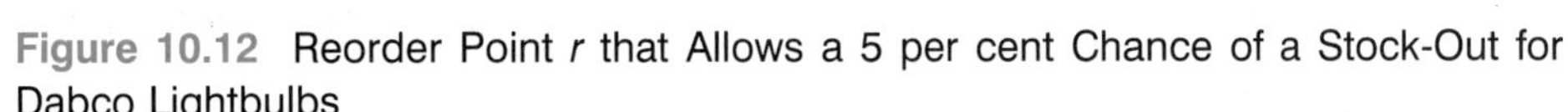

Figure 10.12 Reorder Point r that Allows a 5 per cent Chance of a Stock-Out for Dabco Lightbulbs

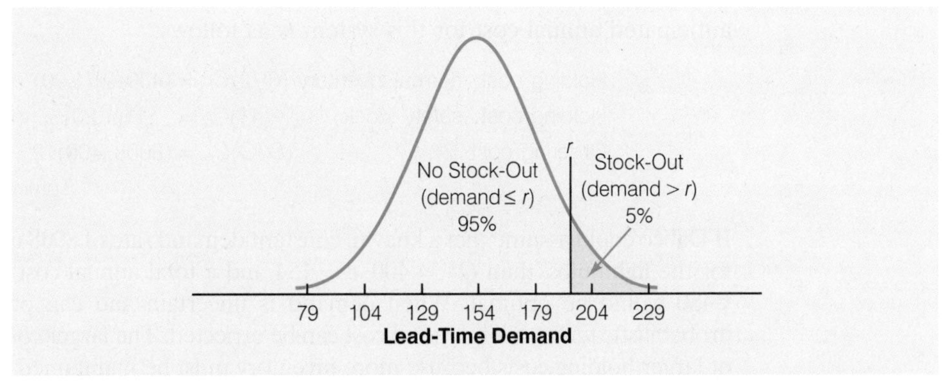

MANAGEMENT SCIENCE IN ACTION

Lowering Inventory Cost at Dutch Companies

In the Netherlands, companies such as Philips, Rank Xerox and Fokker have followed the trend of developing closer relations between the firm and its suppliers. As teamwork, coordination and information sharing improve, opportunities are available for better cost control in the operation of inventory systems.

One Dutch public warehouser has a contract with its supplier under which the supplier routinely provides information regarding the status and schedule of upcoming production runs. The warehouser's inventory system operates as an order-quantity, reorder point system with probabilistic demand. When the order quantity Q has been determined, the warehouser selects the desired reorder point for the product. The distribution of the lead-time demand is essential in determining the reorder point. Usually, the lead-time demand distribution is approximated directly, taking into account both the probabilistic demand and the probabilistic length of the lead-time period.

The supplier's information concerning scheduled production runs provides the warehouser with a better understanding of the lead time involved for a product and the resulting lead-time demand distribution. With this information, the warehouse can modify the reorder point accordingly. Information sharing by the supplier thus enables the order-quantity, reorder point system to operate with a lower inventory holding cost.

Based on F.A. van der Duyn Schouten, M.J.G. van Eijs and R.M.J. Heuts, 'The Value of Supplier Information to Improve Management of a Retailer's Inventory', *Decision Sciences* 25, no. 1 (January/February 1994): 1–14.

assumed normal distribution for lead-time demand with $\mu = 154$ and $\sigma = 25$, the reorder point r is:

$$r = 154 + 1.645(25) = 195$$

If a normal distribution is used for lead-time demand, the general equation for r is:

$$r = \mu + z\sigma \tag{10.37}$$

where z is the number of standard deviations necessary to obtain the acceptable stock-out probability.

So, the recommended inventory decision is to order 400 units whenever the inventory reaches the reorder point of 195. Because the mean or expected demand during the lead time is 154 units, the $195 - 154 = 41$ units serve as a **safety stock**, which absorbs higher-than-usual demand during the lead time. Roughly 95 per cent of the time, the 195 units will be able to satisfy demand during the lead time. The anticipated annual cost for this system is as follows:

Holding cost, normal inventory	$(Q/2)C_h = (400/2)(1.20)$	=	€240
Holding cost, safety stock	$(41)C_h = 41(1.20)$	=	€ 49
Ordering cost	$(D/Q)C_o = (8008/400)12$	=	€240
	Total		€529

If Dabco could assume that a known, constant demand rate of 8008 units per year existed for the lightbulbs, then $Q^* = 400$, $r = 154$ and a total annual cost of €240 + €240 = €480 would be optimal. When demand is uncertain and can only be expressed in probabilistic terms, a larger total cost can be expected. The larger cost occurs in the form of larger holding costs because more inventory must be maintained to limit the number

Try Problem 17 as an example of an order-quantity, reorder point model with probabilistic demand.

of stock-outs. For Dabco, this additional inventory or safety stock was 41 units, with an additional annual holding cost of €49. The *Management Science in Action*, Lowering Inventory Cost at Dutch Companies, describes how a warehouser in the Netherlands implemented an order-quantity, reorder point system with probabilistic demand.

NOTES AND COMMENTS

The Dabco reorder point was based on a 5 per cent probability of a stock-out during the lead-time period. So, on 95 per cent of all order cycles Dabco will be able to satisfy customer demand without experiencing a stock-out. Defining *service level* as the percentage of all order cycles that do not experience a stockout, we would say that Dabco has a 95 per cent service level. However, other definitions of service level may include the percentage of all customer demand that can be satisfied from inventory. Thus, when an inventory manager expresses a desired service level, it is a good idea to clarify exactly what the manager means by the term *service level*.

10.8 Periodic Review Model with Probabilistic Demand

The order-quantity, reorder point inventory models previously discussed require a continuous review inventory system. In such a system, the inventory position is monitored continuously so that an order can be placed whenever the reorder point is reached. Computerized inventory systems can easily provide the continuous review required by the order-quantity, reorder point models.

Up to this point, we have assumed that the inventory position is reviewed continuously so that an order can be placed as soon as the inventory position reaches the reorder point. The inventory model in this section assumes probabilistic demand and a periodic review of the inventory position.

An alternative to the continuous review system is the periodic review inventory system. With a periodic review system, the inventory is checked and reordering is done only at specified points in time. For example, inventory may be checked and orders placed on a weekly, biweekly, monthly or some other periodic basis. When a firm or business handles multiple products, the periodic review system offers the advantage of requiring that orders for several items be placed at the same preset periodic review time. With this type of inventory system, the shipping and receiving of orders for multiple products are easily coordinated. Under the previously discussed order-quantity, reorder point systems, the reorder points for various products can be encountered at substantially different points in time, making the coordination of orders for multiple products more difficult.

To illustrate this system, let us consider Dollar Discounts, a firm with several retail stores that carry a wide variety of products for household use. The company operates its inventory system with a two-week periodic review. Under this system, a retail store manager may order any number of units of any product from the Dollar Discounts central warehouse every two weeks. Orders for all products going to a particular store are combined into one shipment. When making the order quantity decision for each product at a given review period, the store manager knows that a reorder for the product cannot be made until the next review period.

Assuming that the lead time is less than the length of the review period, an order placed at a review period will be received prior to the next review period. In this case, the how-much-to-order decision at any review period is determined using the following:

$$Q = M - H \qquad \textbf{(10.38)}$$

where

Q = the order quantity
M = the replenishment level
H = the inventory on hand at the review period

Because the demand is probabilistic, the inventory on hand at the review period, H, will vary. Thus, the order quantity that must be sufficient to bring the inventory position back to its maximum or replenishment level M can be expected to vary each period. For example, if the replenishment level for a particular product is 50 units, and the inventory on hand at the review period is $H = 12$ units, an order of $Q = M - H = 50 - 12 = 38$ units should be made. Thus, under the periodic review model, enough units are ordered each review period to bring the inventory position back up to the replenishment level.

A typical inventory pattern for a periodic review system with probabilistic demand is shown in Figure 10.13. Note that the time between periodic reviews is predetermined and fixed. The order quantity Q at each review period can vary and is shown to be the difference between the replenishment level and the inventory on hand. Finally, as with other probabilistic models, an unusually high demand can result in an occasional stock-out.

The decision variable in the periodic review model is the replenishment level M. To determine M, we could begin by developing a total cost model, including holding, ordering and stock-out costs. Instead, we describe an approach that is often used in practice. In this approach, the objective is to determine a replenishment level that will meet a desired performance level, such as a reasonably low probability of stock-out or a reasonably low number of stock-outs per year.

In the Dollar Discounts problem, we assume that management's objective is to determine the replenishment level with only a 1 per cent chance of a stock-out.

Figure 10.13 Inventory Pattern for Periodic Review Model with Probabilistic Demand

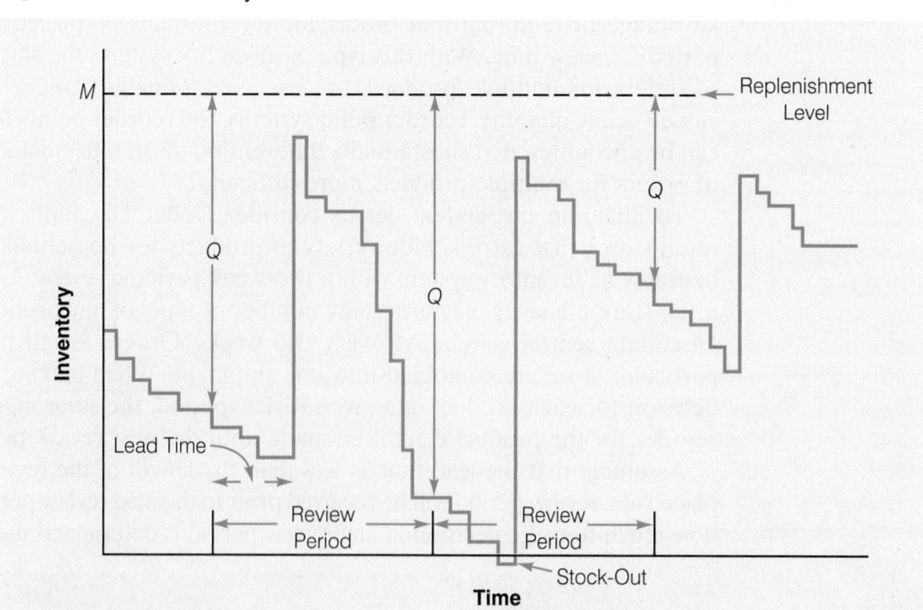

Figure 10.14 Probability Distribution of Demand During the Review Period and Lead Time for the Dollar Discounts Problem

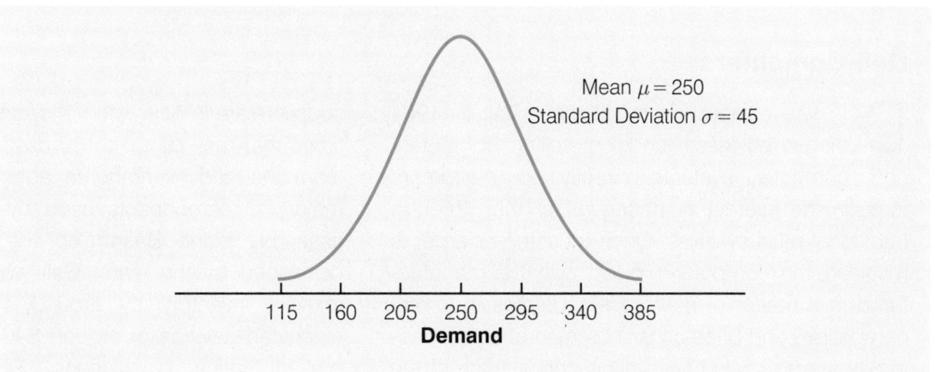

In the periodic review model, the order quantity at each review period must be sufficient to cover demand for the *review period plus the demand for the following lead time*. That is, the order quantity that brings the inventory position up to the replenishment level M must last until the order made at the next review period is received in inventory. The length of this time is equal to the review period plus the lead time. Figure 10.14 shows the normal probability distribution of demand during the review period plus the lead-time period for one of the Dollar Discounts products. The mean demand is 250 units, and the standard deviation of demand is 45 units. Given this situation, the logic used to establish M is similar to the logic used to establish the reorder point in Section 10.7. Figure 10.15 shows the replenishment level M with a 1 per cent chance that demand will exceed that replenishment level. In other words, Figure 10.15 shows the replenishment level that allows a 1 per cent chance of a stock-out associated with the replenishment decision. Using the normal probability distribution table in Appendix A, we see that a value of M that is 2.33 standard deviations above the mean will allow stock-outs with a 1 per cent probability. Therefore, for the assumed normal probability distribution with $\mu = 250$ and $\sigma = 45$, the replenishment level is determined by:

EXCEL *file*

PERIODIC

$$M = 250 + 2.33(45) = 355$$

Figure 10.15 Replenishment Level M that Allows a 1 per cent Chance of a Stock-Out for the Dollar Discounts Problem

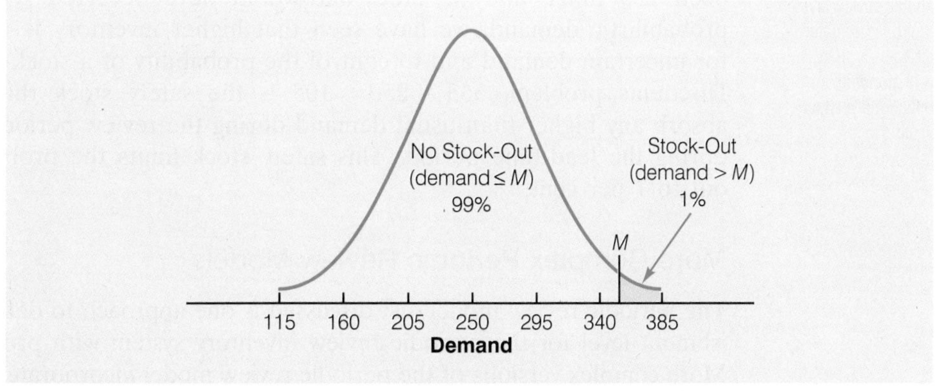

MANAGEMENT SCIENCE IN ACTION

Dell Computers

Dell was established by Michael Dell in 1984 using a business model of selling computers and computer systems directly to customers through the Internet or phone rather than through traditional retail systems. Once a customer order is received the computer product can be manufactured in a matter of hours. Dell operates in a very competitive and price-conscious market so managing its supply chain effectively is critical. One of the key elements is that Dell carries the minimum inventory itself, relying on, and managing, its suppliers to ensure an optimal flow of inventory supplies. Keeping inventory to a minimum clearly enables Dell to keep its costs low and this can then feed through into its pricing strategy. Minimizing inventory also brings benefits in terms of reducing risk from obsolescence and rapidly changing technology developments. However, holding minimum inventory at Dell creates risks of its own given that many of Dell's suppliers are in Asia with transportation and delivery times that may be up to 30 days. In one project a team analyzed inventory management for one of the major PC components used by Dell in its Texas assembly plant. Based on the inventory model developed by the team, Dell was able to reduce relevant inventory by around 40 per cent with estimated savings of around $40 million using net present value calculations. Dick Hunter, Vice President, Americas Manufacturing Operations, Dell Inc., commented 'This model and corresponding logic changed our thinking by directing us to focus on the drivers of variation in our supply chain as a key method to reduce inventory and improve velocity'.

Based on R. Kapuscinski, R. Q. Zhang, P. Carbonneau, R. Moore and B. Reeves, 'Inventory Decisions in Dell's Supply Chain', *Interfaces* 34/3 (May–June 2004): 191–205.

Problem 19 gives you practise in calculating the replenishment level for a periodic review model with probabilistic demand.

Although other probability distributions can be used to express the demand during the review period plus the lead-time period, if the normal probability distribution is used, the general expression for M is:

$$M = \mu + z\sigma \qquad \textbf{(10.39)}$$

where z is the number of standard deviations necessary to obtain the acceptable stock-out probability.

Periodic review systems provide advantages of coordinated orders for multiple items. However, periodic review systems require larger safety stock levels than corresponding continuous review systems.

If demand had been deterministic rather than probabilistic, the replenishment level would have been the demand during the review period plus the demand during the lead-time period. In this case, the replenishment level would have been 250 units, and no stock-out would have occurred. However, with the probabilistic demand, we have seen that higher inventory is necessary to allow for uncertain demand and to control the probability of a stock-out. In the Dollar Discounts problem, $355 - 250 = 105$ is the safety stock that is necessary to absorb any higher-than-usual demand during the review period plus the demand during the lead-time period. This safety stock limits the probability of a stock-out to 1 per cent.

More Complex Periodic Review Models

The periodic review model just discussed is one approach to determining a replenishment level for the periodic review inventory system with probabilistic demand. More complex versions of the periodic review model incorporate a reorder point as another decision variable; that is, instead of ordering at every periodic review, a reorder point is established. If the inventory on hand at the periodic review is at or below the reorder point, a decision is made to order up to the replenishment level. However, if the inventory on hand at the periodic review is greater than the reorder level, such an order is not placed, and the system continues until the next periodic review. In this case, the cost of ordering is a relevant cost and can be included in a cost model along with holding and stock-out costs. Optimal policies can be reached based on minimizing the expected total cost. Situations with lead times longer than the review period add to the complexity of the model. The mathematical level required to treat these more extensive periodic review models is beyond the scope of this text.

NOTES AND COMMENTS

1 The periodic review model presented in this section is based on the assumption that the lead time for an order is less than the periodic review period. Most periodic review systems operate under this condition. However, the case in which the lead time is longer than the review period can be handled by defining H in Equation (10.38) as the inventory position, where H includes the inventory on hand plus the inventory on order. In this case, the order quantity at any review period is the amount needed for the inventory on hand plus *all* outstanding orders needed to reach the replenishment level.

2 In the order-quantity, reorder point model discussed in Section 10.7, a continuous review was used to initiate an order whenever the reorder point was reached. The safety stock for this model was based on the probabilistic demand during the lead time. The periodic review model presented in this section also determined a recommended safety stock. However, because the inventory review was only periodic, the safety stock was based on the probabilistic demand during the *review period plus the lead-time period*. This longer period for the safety stock computation means that periodic review systems tend to require a larger safety stock than continuous review systems.

Summary

In this chapter we introduced a number of inventory models:

- The basic inventory problem for an organization is to balance the need for having enough inventory to meet expected demand but to keep the associated inventory costs at a minimum.
- The key costs involved in inventory are ordering costs, holdings costs and, in some situations, backorder costs. In practice it can be difficult to calculate costs accurately.
- The basic economic order quantity (EOQ) model determines the quantity of inventory to order each time that will minimize total inventory costs. The model also provides details on the re-order time.
- The EOQ model can be adapted to determine the economic production lot size and also to deal with quantity discounts.
- Inventory models can be developed for situations where demand is probabilistic and not deterministic and for multiperiod situations.

MANAGEMENT SCIENCE IN ACTION

Multistage Inventory Planning at Deere & Company

Deere & Company's Commercial & Consumer Equipment (C&CE) Division, located in Raleigh, North Carolina, produces seasonal products such as lawn mowers and snow blowers. The seasonal aspect of demand requires the products to be built in advance. Because many of the products involve impulse purchases, the products must be available at dealerships when the customers walk in. Historically high inventory levels resulted in high inventory costs and an unacceptable return on assets. As a result, management concluded that C&CE needed an inventory planning system that would reduce the average finished goods inventory levels in company warehouses and dealer locations, and at the same time would ensure that stock-outs would not cause a negative impact on sales.

In order to optimize inventory levels, Deere moved from an aggregate inventory planning model to a series of individual product inventory models. This approach enabled Deere to determine optimal inventory levels for each product at each dealer, as well as optimal levels for each product at each plant and warehouse. The computerized system developed, known as Smart Ops Multistage Inventory Planning and Optimization (MIPO), manages inventory for four C&CE Division plants, 21 dealers and 150 products. Easily updated, MIPO provides target inventory levels for each product on a weekly basis. In addition, the system provides information about how optimal inventory levels are affected by lead times, forecast errors and target service levels.

The inventory optimization system enabled the C&CE Division to meet its inventory reduction goals. C&CE management estimates that the company will continue to achieve annual cost savings from lower inventory carrying costs. Meanwhile, the dealers also benefit from lower warehouse expenses, as well as lower interest and insurance costs.

Based on 'Deere's New Software Achieves Inventory Reduction Goals', *Inventory Management Report* (March 2003): 2.

WORKED EXAMPLE

A small women's cooperative based in Edinburgh, Scotland produces hand-printed, eco-friendly t-shirts for the local tourist shops. The cooperative has decided that it is economic only to produce t-shirts in batches through the year rather than continuously. Historically, demand for the t-shirts has been around 6000 a year although the cooperative has the capacity to produce 2000 a month, typically working 20 days each month. The t-shirts cost €10 to produce and there is a setup cost each time a batch of t-shirts is produced of €150. The cooperative estimates a holding cost of 1 per cent per month. The cooperative is trying to plan its t-shirt production for the coming tourist season. What advice can we give them?

Solution

We have a production lot problem where the cooperative is trying to determine how much to produce and how often. Equation (10.16) is appropriate:

$$Q^* = \sqrt{\frac{2DC_o}{(1 - D/P)C_h}}$$

The key variables are:

C_h holding cost
C_o set up cost
D annual demand
P annual production

Here we have:

$$\begin{aligned} C_h &= €1.20\ (12\% \times €10) \\ C_o &= €150 \\ D &= 6\,000 \\ P &= 24\,000 \end{aligned}$$

Substituting into Equation (10.16) we obtain a value of $Q = 1414$. To minimize costs the cooperative should produce batches of 1414 t-shirts at a time.

The cycle time between production batches is given by Equation (10.7):

$$T = \frac{240Q^*}{D} = \frac{240 \times 1414}{6000} = 56.6 \text{ days}$$

In other words the t-shirts should be produced in batches of 1414 every 56.6 working days. In practical terms it will probably be easier to schedule production every three months (60 working days) and, assuming a constant demand of 500 t-shirts per month, to produce batches of 1500. Although technically this is not the minimum cost solution, in practical terms it will be easier for the cooperative to plan and manage.

Problems

SELF *test*

1 Suppose that the CBC has a soft drink product that shows a constant annual demand rate of 3600 cases. A case of the soft drink costs CBC €3. Ordering costs are €20 per order and holding costs are 25 per cent of the value of the inventory. CBC has 250 working days per year, and the lead time is five days. Identify the following aspects of the inventory policy.

a. Economic order quantity.
b. Reorder point.
c. Cycle time.
d. Total annual cost.

SELF *test*

2 A general property of the EOQ inventory model is that total inventory holding and total ordering costs are equal at the optimal solution. Use the data in Problem 1 to show that this result is true. Use Equations (10.1), (10.2) and (10.3) to show that, in general, total holding costs and total ordering costs are equal whenever Q^* is used.

3 The reorder point [see Equation (10.6)] is defined as the lead-time demand for an item. In cases of long lead times, the lead-time demand and thus the reorder point may exceed the economic order quantity Q^*. In such cases, the inventory position will not equal the inventory on hand when an order is placed, and the reorder point may be expressed in terms of either the inventory position or the inventory on hand. Consider the economic order quantity model with $D = 5000$, $C_o = €32$, $C_h = €2$ and 250 working days per year. Identify the reorder point in terms of the inventory position and in terms of the inventory on hand for each of the following lead times.

a. 5 days.
b. 15 days.
c. 25 days.
d. 45 days.

SELF *test*

4 Suyuti Auto purchases a component used in the manufacture of automobile generators directly from the supplier. Suyuti's generator production operation, which is operated at a constant rate, will require 1000 components per month throughout the year (12 000 units annually). Assume that the ordering costs are €25 per order, the unit cost is €2.50 per component and annual holding costs are 20 per cent of the value of the inventory. Suyuti has 250 working days per year and a lead time of five days. Answer the following inventory policy questions.

a. What is the EOQ for this component?
b. What is the reorder point?
c. What is the cycle time?
d. What are the total annual holding and ordering costs associated with your recommended EOQ?

5 Suppose that Suyuti's management in Problem 4 likes the operational efficiency of ordering once each month and in quantities of 1000 units. How much more expensive would this policy be than your EOQ recommendation? Would you recommend in favour of the 1000-unit order quantity? Explain. What would the reorder point be if the 1000-unit quantity were acceptable?

SELF *test*

6 Assume that a production line operates such that the production lot size model of Section 10.3 is applicable. Given $D = 6400$ units per year, $C_o = €100$ and $C_h = €2$ per unit per year, compute the minimum cost production lot size for each of the following production rates:

a. 8 000 units per year.
b. 10 000 units per year.
c. 32 000 units per year.
d. 100 000 units per year.

Compute the EOQ recommended lot size using Equation (10.5). What two observations can you make about the relationship between the EOQ model and the production lot size model?

SELF *test*

7 Groebler Publishing Company produces books for the retail market. Demand for a current book is expected to occur at a constant annual rate of 7200 copies. The cost of one copy of the book is €14.50. The holding cost is based on an 18 per cent annual rate and production setup costs are €150 per setup. The equipment on which the book is produced has an annual production volume of 25 000 copies. Groebler has 250 working days per year, and the lead time for a production run is 15 days. Use the production lot size model to compute the following values:

a. Minimum cost production lot size.
b. Number of production runs per year.
c. Cycle time.
d. Length of a production run.
e. Maximum inventory.
f. Total annual cost.
g. Reorder point.

SELF *test*

8 A well-known manufacturer of several brands of toothpaste uses the production lot size model to determine production quantities for its various products. The product known as Extra White is currently being produced in production lot sizes of 5000 units. The length of the production run for this quantity is ten days. Because of a recent shortage of a particular raw material, the supplier of the material announced that a cost increase will be passed along to the manufacturer of Extra White. Current estimates are that the new raw material cost will increase the manufacturing cost of the toothpaste products by 23 per cent per unit. What will be the effect of this price increase on the production lot sizes for Extra White?

SELF *test*

9 Suppose that Suyuti Auto of Problem 4, with $D = 12\,000$ units per year, $C_h = (2.50)(0.20) = €0.50$ and $C_o = €25$, decided to operate with a backorder inventory policy. Backorder costs are estimated to be €5 per unit per year. Identify the following:

a. Minimum cost order quantity.
b. Maximum number of backorders.
c. Maximum inventory.
d. Cycle time.
e. Total annual cost.

SELF *test* 10 Assuming 250 days of operation per year and a lead time of five days, what is the reorder point for Suyuti Auto in Problem 9? Show the general formula for the reorder point for the EOQ model with backorders. In general, is the reorder point when backorders are allowed greater than or less than the reorder point when backorders are not allowed? Explain.

11 A manager of an inventory system believes that inventory models are important decision-making aids. Even though often using an EOQ policy, the manager never considered a backorder model because of the assumption that backorders were 'bad' and should be avoided. However, with upper management's continued pressure for cost reduction, you have been asked to analyze the economics of a back-ordering policy for some products that can possibly be back ordered. For a specific product with $D = 800$ units per year, $C_o = €150$, $C_h = €3$ and $C_b = €20$, what is the difference in total annual cost between the EOQ model and the planned shortage or backorder model? If the manager adds constraints that no more than 25 per cent of the units can be back ordered and that no customer will have to wait more than 15 days for an order, should the backorder inventory policy be adopted? Assume 250 working days per year.

SELF *test* 12 Assume that the following quantity discount schedule is appropriate. If annual demand is 120 units, ordering costs are €20 per order, and the annual holding cost rate is 25 per cent, what order quantity would you recommend?

Order Size	Discount (%)	Unit Cost €
0 to 49	0	30.00
50 to 99	5	28.50
100 or more	10	27.00

SELF *test* 13 Apply the EOQ model to the following quantity discount situation in which $D = 500$ units per year, $C_o = €40$ and the annual holding cost rate is 20 per cent. What order quantity do you recommend?

Discount Category	Order Size	Discount (%)	Unit Cost €
1	0 to 99	0	10.00
2	100 or more	3	9.70

SELF *test* 14 In the EOQ model with quantity discounts, we stated that if the Q^* for a price category is larger than necessary to qualify for the category price, the category cannot be optimal. Use the two discount categories in Problem 13 to show that this statement is true. That is, plot total cost curves for the two categories and show that if the category 2 minimum cost Q is an acceptable solution, we do not have to consider category 1.

SELF *test* 15 The Gunnarsson Air-Conditioning Company is considering the purchase of a special shipment of portable air conditioners manufactured in Japan. Each unit will cost Gunnarsson €80, and it will be sold for €125. Gunnarsson does not want to carry surplus air conditioners over to the following year. Thus, all surplus air conditioners will be sold to a wholesaler for €50 per unit. Assume that the air conditioner demand follows a normal probability distribution with $\mu = 20$ and $\sigma = 8$.

a. What is the recommended order quantity?
b. What is the probability that Gunnarsson will sell all the units it orders?

16 A retail outlet sells a seasonal product for €10 per unit. The cost of the product is €8 per unit. All units not sold during the regular season are sold for half the retail price in an end-of-season clearance sale. Assume that demand for the product is uniformly distributed between 200 and 800.

a. What is the recommended order quantity?
b. What is the probability that at least some customers will ask to purchase the product after the outlet is sold out? That is, what is the probability of a stock-out, using your order quantity in part (a)?
c. To keep customers happy and returning to the store later, the owner feels that stock-outs should be avoided if at all possible. What is your recommended order quantity if the owner is willing to tolerate a 0.15 probability of a stock-out?
d. Using your answer to part (c), what is the goodwill cost you are assigning to a stock-out?

SELF *test*

17 Isa Distributors, Inc., provides a variety of auto parts to small local garages. Isa purchases parts from manufacturers according to the EOQ model and then ships the parts from a regional warehouse direct to its customers. For a particular type of exhaust, Isa's EOQ analysis recommends orders with $Q^* = 25$ to satisfy an annual demand of 200 exhausts. Isa has 250 working days per year, and the lead time averages 15 days.

a. What is the reorder point if Isa assumes a constant demand rate?
b. Suppose that an analysis of Isa's exhaust demand shows that the lead-time demand follows a normal probability distribution with $\mu = 12$ and $\sigma = 2.5$. If Isa's management can tolerate one stock-out per year, what is the revised reorder point?
c. What is the safety stock for part (b)? If C_h = €5/unit/year, what is the extra cost due to the uncertainty of demand?

18 For Isa Distributors in Problem 17, we were given $Q^* = 25$, $D = 200$, C_h = €5 and a normal lead-time demand distribution with $\mu = 12$ and $\sigma = 2.5$.

a. What is Isa's reorder point if the firm is willing to tolerate two stock-outs during the year?
b. What is Isa's reorder point if the firm wants to restrict the probability of a stock-out on any one cycle to at most 1 per cent?
c. What are the safety stock levels and the annual safety stock costs for the reorder points found in parts (a) and (b)?

SELF *test*

19 A firm uses a one-week periodic review inventory system. A two-day lead time is needed for any order, and the firm is willing to tolerate an average of one stock-out per year.

a. Using the firm's service guideline, what is the probability of a stock-out associated with each replenishment decision?
b. What is the replenishment level if demand during the review period plus lead-time period is normally distributed with a mean of 60 units and a standard deviation of 12 units?
c. What is the replenishment level if demand during the review period plus lead-time period is uniformly distributed between 35 and 85 units?

SELF *test*

20 The pharmacy department in the local hospital is responsible for ensuring the supply of drugs and medicines but is also under pressure to control costs. One particular drug costs €2.95 per unit. The annual holding cost rate is 20 per cent. An order-quantity, reorder point inventory model currently recommends an order quantity of 300 units per order.

a. Lead time is one week and the lead-time demand is normally distributed with a mean of 150 units and a standard deviation of 40 units. What is the reorder point if the pharmacy is willing to tolerate a 1 per cent chance of stock-out on any one cycle?
b. What safety stock and annual safety stock costs are associated with your recommendation in part (a)?
c. The order-quantity, reorder point model requires a continuous review system. Management is considering making a transition to a periodic review system in an attempt to coordinate ordering for many of its products. The demand during the proposed two-week review period and the one-week lead-time period is normally distributed with a mean of 450 units and a standard deviation of 70 units. What is the recommended replenishment level for this periodic review system if the pharmacy is willing to tolerate the same 1 per cent chance of stock-out associated with any replenishment decision?
d. What safety stock and annual safety stock costs are associated with your recommendation in part (c)?
e. Compare your answers to parts (b) and (d). The pharmacy is seriously considering the periodic review system. Would you support this decision? Explain.
f. Would you tend to favour the continuous review system for more expensive items? For example, assume that the drug in the preceding example cost €295 per unit. Explain.

CASE PROBLEM 1 Wagner Fabricating Company

Managers at Wagner Fabricating Company in Germany are reviewing the economic feasibility of manufacturing a part that it currently purchases from a supplier. Forecasted annual demand for the part is 3200 units. Wagner operates 250 days per year.

Wagner's financial analysts established a cost of capital of 14 per cent for the use of funds for investments within the company. In addition, over the past year €600 000 was the average investment in the company's inventory. Accounting information shows that a total of €24 000 was spent on taxes and insurance related to the company's inventory. In addition, an estimated €9000 was lost due to inventory shrinkage, which included damaged goods as well as pilferage. A remaining €15 000 was spent on warehouse overhead, including utility expenses for heating and lighting.

An analysis of the purchasing operation shows that approximately two hours are required to process and coordinate an order for the part regardless of the quantity ordered. Purchasing salaries average €28 per hour, including employee benefits. In addition, a detailed analysis of 125 orders showed that €2375 was spent on telephone, paper and postage directly related to the ordering process.

A one-week lead time is required to obtain the part from the supplier. An analysis of demand during the lead time shows it is approximately normally distributed with a mean of 64 units and a standard deviation of ten units. Service level guidelines indicate that one stock-out per year is acceptable.

Currently, the company has a contract to purchase the part from a supplier at a cost of €18 per unit. However, over the past few months, the company's production capacity has been expanded. As a result, excess capacity is now available in certain production departments, and the company is considering the alternative of producing the parts itself.

Forecasted utilization of equipment shows that production capacity will be available for the part being considered. The production capacity is available at the rate of 1000 units per month, with up to five months of production time available. Management believes that with a two-week lead time, schedules can be arranged so that the part can be produced whenever needed. The demand during the two-week lead time is approximately normally distributed, with a mean of 128 units and a standard deviation of 20 units. Production costs are expected to be €17 per part.

A concern of management is that setup costs will be significant. The total cost of labour and lost production time is estimated to be €50 per hour, and a full eight-hour shift will be needed to set up the equipment for producing the part.

Managerial Report

Develop a report for management of Wagner Fabricating that will address the question of whether the company should continue to purchase the part from the supplier or begin to produce the part itself. Include the following factors in your report:

1. An analysis of the holding costs, including the appropriate annual holding cost rate.
2. An analysis of ordering costs, including the appropriate cost per order from the supplier.
3. An analysis of setup costs for the production operation.
4. A development of the inventory policy for the following two alternatives:
   a. ordering a fixed quantity Q from the supplier.
   b. ordering a fixed quantity Q from in-plant production.
5. Include the following in the policies of parts 4(a) and 4(b):
   a. optimal quantity Q.*
   b. number of order or production runs per year.
   c. cycle time.
   d. reorder point.
   e. amount of safety stock.
   f. expected maximum inventory.
   g. average inventory.
   h. annual holding cost.
   i. annual ordering cost.
   j. annual cost of the units purchased or manufactured.
   k. total annual cost of the purchase policy and the total annual cost of the production policy.
6. Make a recommendation as to whether the company should purchase or manufacture the part. What savings are associated with your recommendation compared with the other alternative?

CASE PROBLEM 2 River City Fire Department

The River City Fire Department (RCFD) fights fires and provides a variety of rescue operations in the River City metropolitan area. The RCFD staffs 13 ladder companies, 26 pumper companies and several rescue units. Normal staffing requires 186 firefighters to be on duty every day.

RCFD is organized with three firefighting units. Each unit works a full 24-hour day and then has two days (48 hours) off. For example, Unit 1 covers Monday, Unit 2 covers Tuesday and Unit 3 covers Wednesday. Then Unit 1 returns on Thursday and so on. Over a three-week (21-day) scheduling period, each unit will be scheduled for seven days. On a rotational basis, firefighters within each unit are given one of the seven regularly scheduled days off. This day off is referred to as a Kelley day. Thus, over a three-week scheduling period, each firefighter in a unit works six of the seven scheduled unit days and gets one Kelley day off.

Determining the number of firefighters to be assigned to each unit includes the 186 firefighters who must be on duty plus the number of firefighters in the unit who are off for a Kelley day. Furthermore, each unit needs additional staffing to cover firefighter absences due to injury, sick leave, vacations or personal time. This additional staffing involves finding the best mix of adding full-time firefighters to each unit and the selective use of overtime. If the number of absences on a particular day brings the number of available firefighters below the required 186, firefighters who are currently off (e.g., on a Kelley day) must be scheduled to work overtime. Overtime is compensated at 1.55 times the regular pay rate.

Analysis of the records maintained over the last several years concerning the number of daily absences shows a normal probability distribution. A mean of 20 and a standard deviation of 5 provides a good approximation of the probability distribution for the number of daily absences.

Managerial Report

Develop a report that will enable the Fire Chief to determine the necessary numbers for the Fire Department. Include, at a minimum, the following items in your report.

1 Assuming no daily absences and taking into account the need to staff Kelley days, determine the base number of firefighters needed by each unit.
2 Using a minimum cost criterion, how many additional firefighters should be added to each unit in order to cover the daily absences? These extra daily needs will be filled by the additional firefighters and, when necessary, the more expensive use of overtime by off-duty firefighters.
3 On a given day, what is the probability that Kelley-day firefighters will be called in to work overtime?
4 Based on the three-unit organization, how many firefighters should be assigned to each unit? What is the total number of full-time firefighters required for the River City Fire Department?

Appendix 10.1 Development of the Optimal Order Quantity (Q) Formula for the EOQ Model

You will need to be familiar with differential calculus for this Appendix 10.1 and 10.2. Given Equation (10.4) as the total annual cost for the EOQ model,

$$TC = \frac{1}{2}QC_h + \frac{D}{Q}C_o \tag{10.4}$$

we can find the order quantity Q that minimizes the total cost by setting the derivative, dTC/dQ, equal to zero and solving for Q^*.

$$\frac{dTC}{dQ} = \frac{1}{2}C_h - \frac{D}{Q^2}C_o = 0$$

$$\frac{1}{2}C_h = \frac{D}{Q^2}C_o$$

$$C_hQ^2 = 2DC_o$$

$$Q^2 = \frac{2DC_o}{C_h}$$

Hence,

$$Q^* = \sqrt{\frac{2DC_o}{C_h}} \tag{10.5}$$

The second derivative is:

$$\frac{d^2TC}{dQ^2} = \frac{2D}{Q^3}C_o$$

Because the value of the second derivative is greater than zero, $Q^*$from equation (10.5) is the minimum cost solution.

Appendix 10.2 Development of the Optimal Lot Size (Q^*) Formula for the Production Lot Size Model

Given Equation (10.15) as the total annual cost for the production lot size model,

$$TC = \frac{1}{2}\left(1 - \frac{D}{P}\right)QC_h + \frac{D}{Q}C_o \tag{10.15}$$

we can find the order quantity Q that minimizes the total cost by setting the derivative, dTC/dQ, equal to zero and solving for Q^*.

$$\frac{dTC}{dQ} = \frac{1}{2}\left(1 - \frac{D}{P}\right)C_h + \frac{D}{Q^2}C_o = 0$$

Solving for Q^*, we have:

$$\frac{1}{2}\left(1 - \frac{D}{P}\right)C_h = \frac{D}{Q^2}C_o$$

$$\left(1 - \frac{D}{P}\right)C_hQ^2 = 2DC_o$$

$$Q^2 = \frac{2DC_o}{(1 - D/P)C_h}$$

Hence,

$$Q^* = \sqrt{\frac{2DC_o}{(1 - D/P)C_h}} \tag{10.16}$$

The second derivative is:

$$\frac{d^2TC}{dQ^2} = \frac{2DC_o}{Q^3}$$

Because the value of the second derivative is greater than zero, $Q^*$from equation (10.16) is a minimum cost solution.

Chapter 11

Queuing Models

Learning Objectives

By the end of this chapter you will be able to:

- Explain the principles of queuing
- Apply the more common queuing models

MANAGEMENT SCIENCE IN ACTION

ATM Waiting Times at Citibank

The New York City franchise of US Citibanking operates approximately 250 banking centres. Each centre provides one or more automatic teller machines (ATMs) capable of performing a variety of banking transactions. At each centre, a queue is formed by randomly arriving customers who seek service at one of the ATMs.

In order to make decisions on the number of ATMs to have at selected banking centre locations, management needed information about potential waiting times and general customer service. Queue operating characteristics such as average number of customers in the queue, average time a customer spends queuing and the probability that an arriving customer has to queue would help management determine the number of ATMs to recommend at each banking centre.

For example, one busy Midtown Manhattan centre had a peak arrival rate of 172 customers per hour. A multiple-channel queuing model with six ATMs showed that 88 per cent of the customers would have to wait, with an average wait time between six and seven minutes. This level of service was judged unacceptable. Expansion to seven ATMs was recommended for this location based on the model's projection of acceptable waiting times. Use of the model provided guidelines for making incremental ATM decisions at each banking centre location.

Based on information provided by Stacey Karter of Citibank.

The queuing model used at Citibank is discussed in Section 11.3.

Queues. We've all experienced them: Queuing at the checkout in a supermarket or shop. Queuing for your turn for a teller at your local bank. Phoning a call centre and being told you're in a queue. Queuing in traffic waiting for the traffic lights to change. From the customer perspective, time spent waiting in a queue is a waste of time and businesses are aware of this. They know that having to wait too long for service irritates customers and may lead to customer dissatisfaction and reduced sales and market share. So why don't they add more checkout staff at the local supermarket? Put more staff on the bank counter? Employ more staff in the call centre? Obviously the answer is not that simple. Adding more staff may reduce queues but clearly it also adds to costs so organizations need to be able to manage the trade-off between longer queues, improved service quality and increased costs. Clearly, we would expect management science models to be used to help managers make decisions about queuing situations (also referred to as waiting time situations) and this chapter introduces the principles of queuing models and the more common types of queuing models used by managers. The principles of queuing theory were developed by A. K. Erlang, a Danish telephone engineer, in the early 1990s. He looked at the congestion and waiting times in making telephone calls. Since then queuing theory has become much more sophisticated with applications in a wide variety of situations.

11.1 Structure of a Queuing System

Like other management science models, queuing models have their own terminology and we shall introduce some of it here and then move on to see how we can build and use a simple queuing model.

The **operating characteristics** of a queuing system describe how the system performs in relation to key requirements: typically these relate to the average number of customers in the queue at any one time and the average time a customer spends in the queue. The major determinants of the operating characteristics for a specific queuing situation include: the arrival rate; the service rate; the queue discipline; the calling population.

The **arrival rate** is the rate at which customers arrive for service during a specified period of time (per hour, per minute, etc.). This is typically taken as an average over the time period. In general arrivals are assumed to be independent of each other and to vary randomly over time. The arrival rate may be derived from empirical observation although it is more usual to assume that the arrival rate can be estimated using a theoretical probability distribution of which the Poisson distribution is most common.

The **service rate** is the average rate at which customers can be served during a specified period of time. As with the arrival rate, the service rate is assumed to be random.

The **queue discipline** refers to the order in which customers in a queue are served and is typically an important feature in a queuing model. In many situations we would expect this to be first-come, first served; that is, the person at the front of the queue who has waited longest is served first; then the second person in the queue and so on. However, other queue disciplines may be used in different situations. An alternative discipline is last-in, first-out where the latest arrival in the queue is served, or dealt with first. This might happen with an office clerk dealing with incoming correspondence placed in the inbox. The item of correspondence at the top of the pile (which came in last) may be picked up first and dealt with. You may also operate this disciple when checking your emails – reading the most recent item first and working down the list. A third discipline is random selection. This may happen in an assembly line situation where an operator is assembling a piece of equipment. The operator reaches into a box of components and selects one at random to be used in the next assembly. Periodically the box is re-filled with more components. Another queue discipline is scheduled service: this occurs where customers are given a pre-determined and time-scheduled appointment for service – as in a doctor's or dentist's surgery, or in a restaurant or when having your car serviced. In this discipline customers are seen in the scheduled order regardless of how long they have been in the queue. The final queue discipline is that where a priority or predetermined discipline is applied. This may be appropriate, for example, in a hospital emergency room where the most medically urgent patients are seen first. Or in an airport check-in where first-class and business-class customers receive priority treatment. Or where there is a pre-determined order to service, perhaps in alphabetical order.

The **calling population** is the source of customers for the queuing system. Some systems have a finite calling population; there may be 15 aircraft waiting to land at a busy airport during the next 100 minutes for example. Other systems may have an infinite calling population; an international retailer's call centre for example can reasonably be assumed to have an infinite number of potential callers over the next hour.

Now we have an understanding of the basic terminology used in queuing theory, let us examine the basic features of a queuing model with an example. The Dome is a small cafeteria based in the local hospital which serves hospital visitors and hospital staff with drinks, refreshments and light meals. The Dome operates as a profit centre within the hospital so has to provide good food and good service to attract customers and remain financially viable.

The Dome is concerned that the methods currently used to serve customers are resulting in excessive waiting times. Management wants to conduct a queuing study to help determine the best approach to reduce waiting times and improve service.

Figure 11.1 The Dome Single-Channel Waiting Line

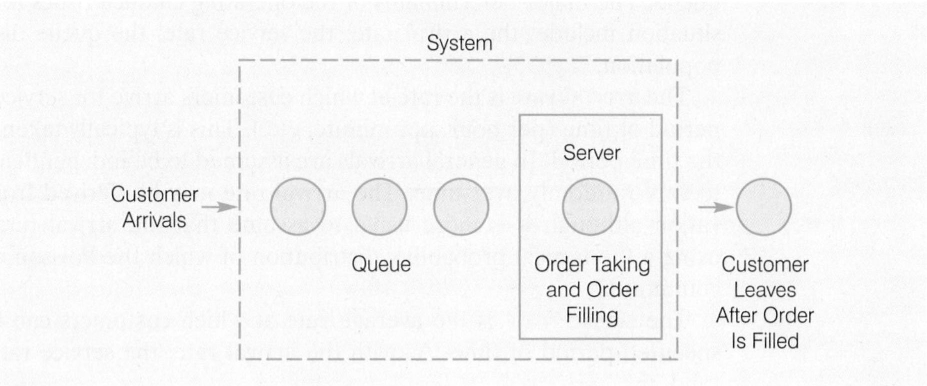

System
Server
Customer Arrivals
Queue
Order Taking and Order Filling
Customer Leaves After Order Is Filled

Single-Channel Queue

In the current Dome operation, a server takes a customer's order, determines the total cost of the order, takes the money from the customer and then fills the order. Once the first customer's order is filled, the server takes the order of the next customer waiting for service. This operation is an example of a **single-channel queuing system**. Each customer entering the Dome restaurant must pass through the *one* channel – one order-taking and order-filling station – to place an order, pay the bill and receive the food. When more customers arrive than can be served immediately, they form a queue and wait for the order-taking and order-filling station to become available. A diagram of the Dome single-channel system is shown in Figure 11.1.

Distribution of Arrivals

Defining the arrival process for a waiting line involves determining the probability distribution for the number of arrivals in a given period of time. For many queuing situations, the arrivals occur *randomly and independently* of other arrivals, and we cannot predict exactly when an arrival will occur. In such cases, quantitative analysts have found that the **Poisson probability distribution** provides a good description of the arrival pattern.

The Poisson probability function provides the probability of x arrivals in a specific time period. The probability function is as follows.[1]

$$P(x) = \frac{\lambda^x e^{-\lambda}}{x!} \quad \text{for } x = 0, 1, 2, \ldots \qquad \textbf{(11.1)}$$

where

x = the number of arrivals in the time period

λ = the mean number of arrivals per time period (pronounced 'lambda')

e = 2.71828

Values of $e^{-\lambda}$ can be found using a spreadsheet, a calculator or by using Appendix B.

[1]The term $x!$, *x factorial*, is defined as $x! = x(x-1)(x-2)\ldots(2)(1)$. For example $4! = (4)(3)(2)(1) = 24$. For the special case of $x = 0$, $0! = 1$ by definition.

Suppose that the Dome has analyzed data on customer arrivals and concluded that the mean arrival rate is 45 customers per hour. For a one-minute period, the mean arrival rate would be $\lambda = 45$ customers/60 minutes $= 0.75$ customers per minute. We can use the following Poisson probability function to calculate the probability of a given number of customer arrivals, x, during a one-minute period:

$$P(x) = \frac{\lambda^x e^{-\lambda}}{x!} = \frac{0.75^x e^{-0.75}}{x!} \quad \textbf{(11.2)}$$

The probabilities of 0, 1 and 2 customer arrivals during a one-minute period are then calculated as:

$$P(0) = \frac{(0.75)^0 e^{-0.75}}{0!} = e^{-0.75} = 0.4724$$

$$P(1) = \frac{(0.75)^1 e^{-0.75}}{1!} = 0.75e^{-0.75} = 0.75(0.4724) = 0.3543$$

$$P(2) = \frac{(0.75)^2 e^{-0.75}}{2!} = \frac{(0.75)^2 e^{-0.75}}{2!} = \frac{(0.5625)(0.4724)}{2} = 0.1329$$

The probability of no customers arriving in a one-minute period is 0.4724, the probability of one customer arriving in a one-minute period is 0.3543, and the probability of two customers arriving in a one-minute period is 0.1329. Table 11.1 shows the Poisson probabilities for several customer arrivals during a one-minute period.

The queuing models that will be developed in Sections 11.2 and 11.3 use the Poisson probability distribution to describe the customer arrivals at the Dome. In practice, you could record the actual number of arrivals per time period for several days or weeks and compare the frequency distribution of the observed number of arrivals to the Poisson probability distribution to determine whether the Poisson probability distribution provides a reasonable approximation of the arrival distribution.

Distribution of Service Times

The service time is the time a customer spends at the service facility once the service has started. At the Dome, the service time starts when a customer begins to place the order with the food server and continues until the customer receives the order. Service times are rarely constant. At the Dome, the number of items ordered and the mix of items ordered vary considerably from one customer to the next. Small orders can be handled in a matter of seconds, but large orders may require more than two minutes.

Table 11.1 Poisson Probabilities for the Number of Customer Arrivals at the Dome Restaurant During a One-Minute Period ($\lambda = 0.75$)

Number of Arrivals	Probability
0	0.4724
1	0.3543
2	0.1329
3	0.0332
4	0.0062
5 or more	0.0010

Management scientists have found that if the probability distribution for the service time can be assumed to follow an **exponential probability distribution**, using an exponential probability distribution, the probability that the service time will be less than or equal to a time of length t is given by:

$$P(\text{service time} \leq t) = 1 - e^{-\mu t} \quad \textbf{(11.3)}$$

where

μ = the mean number of units that can be served per time period

$e = 2.71828$

A property of the exponential probability distribution is that there is a 0.6321 probability that the random variable takes on a value less than its mean. In queuing applications, the exponential probability distribution indicates that approximately 63 per cent of the service times are less than the mean service time and approximately 37 per cent of the service times are greater than the mean service time.

Suppose that the Dome studied the order-taking and order-filling process and found that the single food server can process an average of 60 customer orders per hour. On a one-minute basis, the mean service rate would be $\mu = 60$ customers/60 minutes = one customer per minute. For example, with $\mu = 1$, we can use equation (11.3) to calculate probabilities such as the probability an order can be processed in ½ minute or less, one minute or less and two minutes or less. These calculations are:

$$P(\text{service time} \leq 0.5\,\text{min.}) = 1 - e^{-1(0.5)} = 1 - 0.6065 = 0.3935$$
$$P(\text{service time} \leq 1.0\,\text{min.}) = 1 - e^{-1(1.0)} = 1 - 0.3679 = 0.6321$$
$$P(\text{service time} \leq 2.0\,\text{min.}) = 1 - e^{-1(2.0)} = 1 - 0.1353 = 0.8647$$

So we would conclude that there is a 0.3935 probability that an order can be processed in ½ minute or less, a 0.6321 probability that it can be processed in one minute or less and a 0.8647 probability that it can be processed in two minutes or less.

In several waiting line models presented in this chapter, we assume that the probability distribution for the service time follows an exponential probability distribution. In practice, you should collect data on actual service times to determine whether the exponential probability distribution is a reasonable approximation of the service times for your application.

Steady-State Operation

When the Dome restaurant opens in the morning, no customers are in the restaurant. Gradually, activity builds up to a normal or steady state. The beginning or start-up period is referred to as the **transient period**. The transient period ends when the system reaches the normal or **steady-state operation**. Waiting line models describe the steady-state operating characteristics of a waiting line.

11.2 Single-Channel Queuing Model with Poisson Arrivals and Exponential Service Times

Queuing models are often based on assumptions such as Poisson arrivals and exponential service times. When applying any waiting line model, data should be collected on the actual system to ensure that the assumptions of the model are reasonable.

In this section we present formulas that can be used to determine the steady-state operating characteristics for a single-channel queuing system. The formulas are applicable if the arrivals follow a Poisson probability distribution and the service times follow an exponential probability distribution. As these assumptions apply to the Dome problem introduced in Section 11.1, we show how formulas can be used to determine the Dome's operating characteristics and thus provide management with helpful decision-making information.

The mathematical methodology used to derive the formulas for the operating characteristics of queues is rather complex. However, our purpose in this chapter is not to provide the theoretical development of queuing models, but rather to show how the formulas that have been developed can provide information about operating characteristics of the queue. Readers interested in the mathematical development of the formulas can consult the specialized texts listed in Appendix C at the end of the text.

Operating Characteristics

The following formulas can be used to calculate the steady-state operating characteristics for a single-channel queuing system with Poisson arrivals and exponential service times, where:

λ = the mean number of arrivals per time period (the mean arrival rate)

μ = the mean number of services per time period (the mean service rate)

Equations (11.4) through (11.10) do not provide formulae for optimal conditions. Rather, these equations provide information about the steady-state operating characteristics of a waiting line.

1 The probability that no units are in the system:

$$P_0 = 1 - \frac{\lambda}{\mu} \tag{11.4}$$

2 The average number of units in the queue:

$$L_q = \frac{\lambda^2}{\mu(\mu - \lambda)} \tag{11.5}$$

3 The average number of units in the system:

$$L = L_q + \frac{\lambda}{\mu} \tag{11.6}$$

4 The average time a unit spends in the queue:

$$W_q = \frac{L_q}{\lambda} \tag{11.7}$$

5 The average time a unit spends in the system:

$$W = W_q + \frac{1}{\mu} \tag{11.8}$$

6 The probability that an arriving unit has to wait for service:

$$P_w = \frac{\lambda}{\mu} \tag{11.9}$$

7 The probability of n units in the system:

$$P_n = \left(\frac{\lambda}{\mu}\right)^n P_0 \qquad \textbf{(11.10)}$$

The values of the mean arrival rate λ and the mean service rate μ are clearly important components in determining the operating characteristics. Equation (11.9) shows that the ratio of the mean arrival rate to the mean service rate, λ/μ, provides the probability that an arriving unit has to wait because the service facility is in use. Hence, λ/μ is often referred to as the *utilization factor* for the service facility.

The operating characteristics presented in Equations (11.4) through (11.10) are applicable only when the mean service rate μ is *greater than* the mean arrival rate λ – in other words, when $\lambda/\mu < 1$. If this condition does not exist, the queue will continue to grow without limit because the service facility does not have sufficient capacity to handle the arriving units. Thus, in using Equations (11.4) through (11.10), we must have $\mu > \lambda$.

Operating Characteristics for the Dome Problem

Recall that for the Dome problem we had a mean arrival rate of $\lambda = 0.75$ customers per minute and a mean service rate of $\mu =$ one customer per minute. So, with $\mu > \lambda$, Equations (11.4) through (11.10) can be used to provide operating characteristics for the Dome's single-channel queuing system:

$$P_0 = 1 - \frac{\lambda}{\mu} = 1 - \frac{0.75}{1} = 0.25$$

$$L_q = \frac{\lambda^2}{\mu(\mu - \lambda)} = \frac{0.75^2}{1(1 - 0.75)} = 2.25 \text{ customers}$$

$$L = L_q = \frac{\lambda}{\mu} + 2.25 + \frac{0.75}{1} = 3 \text{ customers}$$

$$W_q = \frac{L_q}{\lambda} = \frac{2.25}{0.75} = 3 \text{ minutes}$$

$$W = W_q + \frac{1}{\mu} = 3 + \frac{1}{1} = 4 \text{ minutes}$$

$$P_w = \frac{\lambda}{\mu} = \frac{0.75}{1} = 0.75$$

Problem 5 asks you to calculate the operating characteristics for a single-channel queuing system application.

Equation (11.10) can be used to determine the probability of any number of customers in the system. Applying it provides the probability information in Table 11.2.

Managers' Use of Queuing Models

The results of the single-channel queue for the Dome show several important things about the operation of the queue. In particular, customers wait an average of three minutes before beginning to place an order. In addition, the facts that the average number of customers waiting is 2.25 and that 75 per cent of the arriving customers have to wait for service are indicators that something should be done to improve the queuing operation. Table 11.2 shows a 0.1335 probability that seven or more customers are in the Dome system at one time. This condition indicates a fairly high probability that the Dome will experience some long queues if it continues to use the single-channel operation.

MANAGEMENT SCIENCE IN ACTION

Ensuring Phone Access to Emergency Services

Imagine a situation where you have to call the emergency services – maybe an emergency ambulance for someone having a heart attack, maybe the police for a road traffic accident, maybe the fire and rescue service to evacuate a burning building. You pick up the phone to call and can not get a dialling tone. Obviously at the best of times this will be a nuisance but in emergencies it could actually be life threatening. In 2001 AT&T, one the world's largest telecoms companies, found itself in a situation where an increasing number of complaints were being received from customers about the lack of a dialling tone at certain times of the day. Although not restricted to emergency situations, it was estimated that this could affect up to 90 life-threatening situations per day. Initial research indicated that the problem was occurring mostly during the evening when residential phone demand peaks, suggesting congestion and queuing in the phone network. The team investigating the problem collected call data and ran computer simulations using queuing theory. However, they quickly realized that the standard use of the exponential distribution was not appropriate. Having analyzed some 4.5 million residential calls and found a mean call length of around five minutes they concluded that the exponential distribution of call times estimated from the mean did not fit the empirical data well. The prime reason for this was that a small number of total calls, around 6 per cent of the total, were customers using dial-up facilities to connect to the Internet. These calls had a mean call length of around 30 minutes. Using sophisticated techniques, the team obtained a better fitting distribution that more accurately modelled call length. The results of their modelling allowed AT&T to improve service quality to customers and reduce costs by better routing of calls over the network.

Based on V. Ramaswami, D.Poole, S. Ahn, S. Byers and A. Kaplan, 'Ensuring Access to Emergency Services in the Presence of Long Internet Dial-up Calls', *Interfaces*, 35 5 (Sept–Oct 2005): 411–422.

If the operating characteristics are unsatisfactory in terms of meeting standards for service, the Dome's management should consider alternative designs or plans for improving the queuing operation.

Improving the Queuing Operation

Queuing models often indicate where improvements in operating characteristics are desirable. However, the decision of how to modify the queuing system configuration to improve the operating characteristics must be based on the insights and creativity of the analyst.

Table 11.2 The Probability of *n* Customers in the System for the Dome Queuing Problem

Number of Customers	Probability
0	0.2500
1	0.1875
2	0.1406
3	0.1055
4	0.0791
5	0.0593
6	0.0445
7 or more	0.1335

Table 11.3 Operating Characteristics for the Dome System with the Mean Service Rate Increased to $\mu = 1.25$ Customers Per Minute

Probability of no customers in the system	0.400
Average number of customers in the queue	0.900
Average number of customers in the system	1.500
Average time in the queue	1.200 minutes
Average time in the system	2.000 minutes
Probability that an arriving customer has to wait	0.600
Probability that seven or more customers are in the system	0.028

After reviewing the operating characteristics provided by the waiting line model, Dome's management concluded that improvements designed to reduce waiting times are desirable. To make improvements in the queuing operation, analysts often focus on ways to improve the service rate. Generally, service rate improvements are obtained by making either or both the following changes:

1 Increase the mean service rate μ by making a creative design change or by using new technology.

2 Add service channels so that more customers can be served simultaneously.

Assume that in considering alternative 1, Dome's management decides to employ an order filler who will assist the order taker at the cash register. The customer begins the service process by placing the order with the order taker. As the order is placed, the order taker announces the order over an intercom system, and the order filler begins filling the order. When the order is completed, the order taker handles the money, while the order filler continues to fill the order. With this design, the Dome's management estimates the mean service rate can be increased from the current service rate of 60 customers per hour to 75 customers per hour. Thus, the mean service rate for the revised system is $\mu = 75$ customers/60 minutes $= 1.25$ customers per minute. For $\lambda = 0.75$ customers per minute and $\mu = 1.25$ customers per minute, Equations (11.4) through (11.10) can be used to provide the new operating characteristics for the Dome queue. These operating characteristics are summarized in Table 11.3.

The information in Table 11.3 indicates that all operating characteristics have improved because of the increased service rate. In particular, the average time a customer spends in the queue has been reduced from three to 1.2 minutes and the average time a customer spends in the system has been reduced from four to two minutes. Are any other alternatives available that the Dome can use to increase the service rate? If so, and if the mean service rate μ can be identified for each alternative, Equations (11.4) through (11.10) can be used to determine the revised operating characteristics and any improvements in the queuing system. The added cost of any proposed change can be compared to the corresponding service improvements to help the manager determine whether the proposed service improvements are worthwhile.

Problem 7 asks you to determine whether a change in the mean service rate will meet the company's service guideline for its customers.

As mentioned previously, another option often available is to provide one or more additional service channels so that more than one customer may be served at the same time. The extension of the single-channel queuing model to the multiple-channel queuing model is the topic of the next section.

Figure 11.2 Worksheet For The Dome Single-Channel Queuing System

	A	B	C
1	**Single-Channel Waiting Line Model**		
2			
3	**Assumptions**		
4	**Poisson Arrivals**		
5	**Exponential Service Times**		
6			
7	Mean Arrival Rate	0.75	
8	Mean Service Rate	1	
9			
10			
11	**Operating Characteristics**		
12			
13	Probability that no customers are in the system, Po		=1-B7/B8
14	Average number of customers in the waiting line, Lq		=B7^2/(B8*(B8-B7))
15	Average number of customers in the system, L		=C14+B7/B8
16	Average time a customer spends in the waiting line, Wq		=C14/B7
17	Average time a customer spends in the system, W		=C16+1/B8
18	Probability an arriving customer has to wait, Pw		=B7/B8
19			

	A	B	C
1	**Single-Channel Waiting Line Model**		
2			
3	**Assumptions**		
4	**Poisson Arrivals**		
5	**Exponential Service Times**		
6			
7	Mean Arrival Rate	0.75	
8	Mean Service Rate	1	
9			
10			
11	**Operating Characteristics**		
12			
13	Probability that no customers are in the system, Po		0.2500
14	Average number of customers in the waiting line, Lq		2.2500
15	Average number of customers in the system, L		3.0000
16	Average time a customer spends in the waiting line, Wq		3.0000
17	Average time a customer spends in the system, W		4.0000
18	Probability an arriving customer has to wait, Pw		0.7500
19			

EXCEL *file*

DOME SINGLE-CHANNEL

Excel Solution of the Queuing Model

Queuing models are easily implemented with the aid of spreadsheets. The Excel spreadsheet for the Dome single-channel queuing system is shown in Figure 11.2. The formula worksheet is in the background; the value worksheet is in the foreground. The mean arrival rate and the mean service rate are entered in cells B7 and B8. The formulas for the operating characteristics are placed in cells C13 to C18. The worksheet shows the same values for the operating characteristics that we obtained earlier. Modifications in the queuing design can be evaluated by entering different mean arrival rates and/or mean service rates into cells B7 and B8. The new operating characteristics of the queue will be shown immediately.

The Management Scientist software also has a queuing module that can be used to solve the problems in this chapter.

The Excel worksheet in Figure 11.2 is a template that can be used with any single-channel queuing model with Poisson arrivals and exponential service times. This worksheet and similar Excel worksheets for the other queuing models presented in this chapter are available on the online platform that accompanies this text.

NOTES AND COMMENTS

1 The assumption that arrivals follow a Poisson probability distribution is equivalent to the assumption that the time between arrivals has an exponential probability distribution. For example, if the arrivals for a waiting line follow a Poisson probability distribution with a mean of 20 arrivals per hour, the time between arrivals will follow an exponential probability distribution, with a mean time between arrivals of $^1/_{20}$ or 0.05 hours.

2 Many individuals believe that whenever the mean service rate μ is greater than the mean arrival rate λ, the system should be able to handle or serve all arrivals. However, as the Dome example shows, the variability of arrival times and service times may result in long waiting times even when the mean service rate exceeds the mean arrival rate. A contribution of queuing system models is that they can point out undesirable operating characteristics even when the μ / λ condition appears satisfactory.

11.3 Multiple-Channel Queuing Model with Poisson Arrivals and Exponential Service Times

You may be familiar with multiple-channel systems that also have multiple queues. The queuing model in this section has multiple channels, but only a single queue. Operating characteristics for a multiple-channel system are better when a single queue, rather than multiple queues, is used.

A multiple-channel queuing system consists of two or more service channels that are assumed to be identical in terms of service capability. In the multiple-channel system, arriving units wait in a single queue and then move to the first available channel to be served. The single-channel Dome operation can be expanded to a two-channel system by opening a second service channel. Figure 11.3 shows a diagram of the Dome two-channel queuing system.

In this section we present formulas that can be used to determine the steady-state operating characteristics for a multiple-channel queuing system. These formulas are applicable if the following conditions exist.

1 The arrivals follow a Poisson probability distribution.
2 The service time for each channel follows an exponential probability distribution.
3 The mean service rate μ is the same for each channel.
4 The arrivals wait in a single queue and then move to the first open channel for service.

Operating Characteristics

The following formulas can be used to compute the steady-state operating characteristics for multiple-channel queueing systems, where:

λ = the mean arrivals rate for the system
μ = the mean service rate for *each* channel
k = the number of channels

1 The probability that no units are in the system:

$$P_0 = \frac{1}{\sum_{n=0}^{k-1} \frac{(\lambda/\mu)^n}{n!} + \frac{(\lambda/\mu)^k}{k!}\left(\frac{k\mu}{k\mu - \lambda}\right)} \tag{11.11}$$

Figure 11.3 The Dome Two-Channel Waiting Line

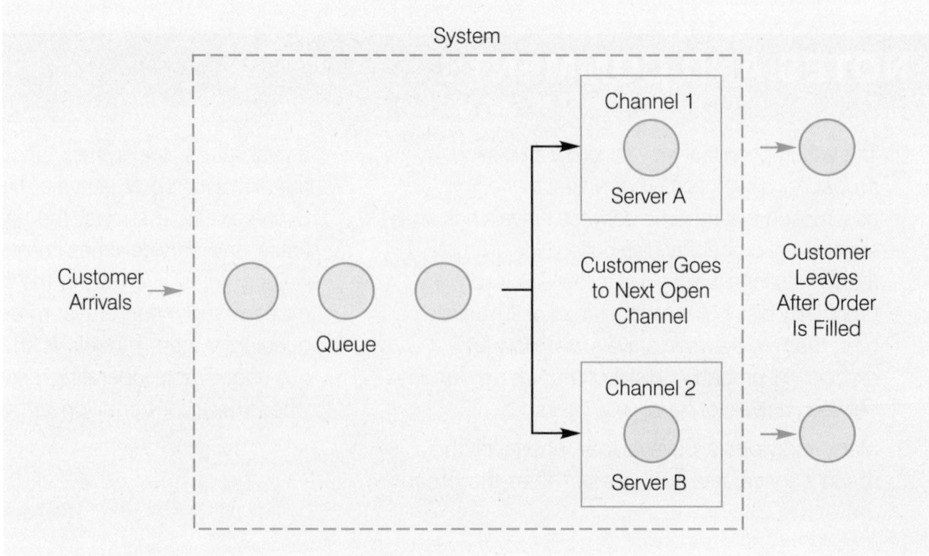

2 The average number of units in the queue:

$$L_q = \frac{(\lambda/\mu)^k \lambda\mu}{(k-1)!(k\mu - \lambda)^2} P_0 \tag{11.12}$$

3 The average number of units in the system:

$$L = L_q + \frac{\lambda}{\mu} \tag{11.13}$$

4 The average time a unit spends in the queue:

$$W_q = \frac{L_q}{\lambda} \tag{11.14}$$

5 The average time a unit spends in the system:

$$W = W_q + \frac{1}{\mu} \tag{11.15}$$

6 The probability that an arriving unit has to wait for service:

$$P_w = \frac{1}{k!}\left(\frac{\lambda}{\mu}\right)^k \left(\frac{k\mu}{k\mu - \lambda}\right) P_0 \tag{11.16}$$

7 The probability of n units in the system:

$$P_n = \frac{(\lambda/\mu)^n}{n!} P_0 \quad \text{for } n \leq k \tag{11.17}$$

$$P_n = \frac{(\lambda/\mu)^n}{k!k^{(n-k)}} P_0 \quad \text{for } n > k \tag{11.18}$$

Because μ is the mean service rate for each channel, $k\mu$ is the mean service rate for the multiple-channel system. As was true for the single-channel queues model, the formulas for the operating characteristics of multiple-channel queues can be applied only in situations where the mean service rate for the system is greater than the mean arrival rate for the system; in other words, the formulas are applicable only if $k\mu$ is greater than λ.

Some expressions for the operating characteristics of multiple-channel queues are more complex than their single-channel counterparts. However, Equations (11.11) through (11.18) provide the same information as provided by the single-channel model. To help simplify the use of the multiple-channel equations, Table 11.4

contains values of P_0 for selected values of λ/μ and k. The values provided in the table correspond to cases where $k\mu > \lambda$, and hence the service rate is sufficient to process all arrivals.

Operating Characteristics for the Dome Problem

To illustrate the multiple-channel queuing model, we return to the Dome restaurant queuing problem. Suppose that management wants to evaluate the desirability of

Table 11.4 Values of P_0 for Multiple-Channel Queues with Poisson Arrivals and Exponential Service Times

	Number of Channels (k)			
Ratio λ/μ	2	3	4	5
0.15	0.8605	0.8607	0.8607	0.8607
0.20	0.8182	0.8187	0.8187	0.8187
0.25	0.7778	0.7788	0.7788	0.7788
0.30	0.7391	0.7407	0.7408	0.7408
0.35	0.7021	0.7046	0.7047	0.7047
0.40	0.6667	0.6701	0.6703	0.6703
0.45	0.6327	0.6373	0.6376	0.6376
0.50	0.6000	0.6061	0.6065	0.6065
0.55	0.5686	0.5763	0.5769	0.5769
0.60	0.5385	0.5479	0.5487	0.5488
0.65	0.5094	0.5209	0.5219	0.5220
0.70	0.4815	0.4952	0.4965	0.4966
0.75	0.4545	0.4706	0.4722	0.4724
0.80	0.4286	0.4472	0.4491	0.4493
0.85	0.4035	0.4248	0.4271	0.4274
0.90	0.3793	0.4035	0.4062	0.4065
0.95	0.3559	0.3831	0.3863	0.3867
1.00	0.3333	0.3636	0.3673	0.3678
1.20	0.2500	0.2941	0.3002	0.3011
1.40	0.1765	0.2360	0.2449	0.2463
1.60	0.1111	0.1872	0.1993	0.2014
1.80	0.0526	0.1460	0.1616	0.1646
2.00		0.1111	0.1304	0.1343
2.20		0.0815	0.1046	0.1094
2.40		0.0562	0.0831	0.0889
2.60		0.0345	0.0651	0.0721
2.80		0.0160	0.0521	0.0581
3.00			0.0377	0.0466
3.20			0.0273	0.0372
3.40			0.0186	0.0293
3.60			0.0113	0.0228
3.80			0.0051	0.0174
4.00				0.0130
4.20				0.0093
4.40				0.0063
4.60				0.0038
4.80				0.0017

opening a second order-processing station so that two customers can be served simultaneously. Assume a single queue with the first customer in line moving to the first available server. Let us evaluate the operating characteristics for this two-channel system.

We use Equations (11.12) through (11.18) for the $k = 2$ channel system. For a mean arrival rate of $\lambda = 0.75$ customers per minute and mean service rate of $\mu =$ one customer per minute for each channel, we obtain the operating characteristics:

EXCEL *file*

MULTIPLE

$$P_0 = 0.4545 \quad \text{(from Table 11.4 with } \lambda/\mu = 0.75\text{)}$$

$$L_q = \frac{(0.75/1)^2(0.75)(1)}{(2-1)![2(1)-0.75]^2}(0.4545) = 0.1227 \text{ customers}$$

$$L = L_q + \frac{\lambda}{\mu} = 0.1227 + \frac{0.75}{1} = 0.8727 \text{ customers}$$

$$W_q = \frac{L_q}{\lambda} = \frac{0.1227}{0.75} = 0.1636 \text{ minute}$$

$$W = W_q + \frac{1}{\mu} = 0.1636 + \frac{1}{1} = 1.1636 \text{ minutes}$$

$$P_w = \frac{1}{2!}\left(\frac{0.75}{1}\right)^2\left[\frac{2(1)}{2(1)-0.75}\right](0.4545) = 0.2045$$

Try Problem 9 for practise in determining the operating characteristics for a two-channel queue.

Using Equations (11.17) and (11.18), we can calculate the probabilities of n customers in the system. The results from these calculations are summarized in Table 11.5.

We can now compare the steady-state operating characteristics of the two-channel system to the operating characteristics of the original single-channel system discussed in Section 11.2.

1 The average time a customer spends in the system (queuing time plus service time) is reduced from $W =$ four minutes to $W = 1.1636$ minutes.
2 The average number of customers in the queue is reduced from $L_q = 2.25$ customers to $L_q = 0.1227$ customers.
3 The average time a customer spends in the queue is reduced from $W_q = 3$ minutes to $W_q = 0.1636$ minutes.
4 The probability that a customer has to wait for service is reduced from $P_w = 0.75$ to $P_w = 0.2045$.

Clearly the two-channel system will significantly improve the operating characteristics of the queuing system. However, adding an order filler at each service station would further increase the mean service rate and improve the operating characteristics. The

Table 11.5 The Probability of *n* Customers in the System for the Dome Two-Channel Queuing System

Number of Customers	Probability
0	0.4545
1	0.3409
2	0.1278
3	0.0479
4	0.0180
5 or more	0.0109

final decision regarding the staffing policy at the Dome rests with the Dome management. The analysis simply provides the operating characteristics that can be anticipated under three configurations: a single-channel system with one employee, a single-channel system with two employees and a two-channel system with an employee for each channel. After considering these results, what action would you recommend? In this case, the Dome adopted the following policy statement: For periods when customer arrivals are expected to average 45 customers per hour, the Dome will open two order-processing channels with one employee assigned to each.

By changing the mean arrival rate λ to reflect arrival rates at different times of the day, and then calculating the operating characteristics, the Dome's management can establish guidelines and policies that tell managers when they should schedule service operations with a single channel, two channels or perhaps even three or more channels.

NOTES AND COMMENTS

The multiple-channel queuing model is based on a single queue. You may also have encountered situations where each of the k channels has its own queue. Management scientists have shown that the operating characteristics of multiple-channel systems are better if a single queue is used. People prefer them also; no one who comes in after you can be served ahead of you. So, when possible, banks, airline reservation counters, food-service establishments and other businesses frequently use a single queue for a multiple-channel system.

11.4 Some General Relationships for Queuing Models

In Sections 11.2 and 11.3 we presented formulas for calculating the operating characteristics for single-channel and multiple-channel queuing systems with Poisson arrivals and exponential service times. The operating characteristics of interest included:

L_q = the average number of units in the queue

L = the average number of units in the system

W_q = the average time a unit spends in the queue

W = the average time a unit spends in the system

John D.C. Little showed that several relationships exist among these four characteristics and that these relationships apply to a variety of different queuing systems. Two of the relationships, referred to as *Little's flow equations*, are:

Little's Law, published in 1961, provided the first proof of these key queuing equations.

$$L = \lambda W \qquad \textbf{(11.19)}$$

$$L_q = \lambda W_q \qquad \textbf{(11.20)}$$

Equation (11.19) shows that the average number of units in the system, L, can be found by multiplying the mean arrival rate, λ, by the average time a unit spends in the system, W. Equation (11.20) shows that the same relationship holds between the average number of units in the queue, L_q, and the average time a unit spends in the queue, W_q.

Using equation (11.20) and solving for W_q, we obtain:

$$W_q = \frac{L_q}{\lambda} \quad \textbf{(11.21)}$$

Equation (11.21) follows directly from Little's second flow equation. We used it for the single-channel queuing model in Section 11.2 and the multiple-channel queuing model in Section 11.3 [see Equations (11.7) and (11.14)]. Once L_q is calculated for either of these models, Equation (11.21) can then be used to calculate W_q.

Another general expression that applies to queuing models is that the average time in the system, W, is equal to the average time in the queue, W_q, plus the average service time. For a system with a mean service rate μ, the mean service time is $1/\mu$. Thus, we have the general relationship:

$$W = W_q + \frac{1}{\mu} \quad \textbf{(11.22)}$$

Recall that we used Equation (11.22) to provide the average time in the system for both the single-and multiple-channel queuing models [see Equations (11.8) and (11.15)].

The advantage of Little's flow equations is that they show how operating characteristics L, L_q, W and W_q are related in any queuing system. Arrivals and service times do not have to follow specific probability distributions for the flow equations to be applicable.

The importance of Little's flow equations is that they apply to *any queuing model* regardless of whether arrivals follow the Poisson probability distribution and regardless of whether service times follow the exponential probability distribution. For example, in a study of the grocery checkout counters at one supermarket, an analyst concluded that arrivals follow the Poisson probability distribution with the mean arrival rate of 24 customers per hour or $\lambda = 24/60 = 0.40$ customers per minute. However, the analyst found that service times follow a normal probability distribution rather than an exponential probability distribution. The mean service rate was found to be 30 customers per hour or $\mu = 30/60 = 0.50$ customers per minute. A time study of actual customer waiting times showed that, on average, a customer spends 4.5 minutes in the system (queuing time plus checkout time); that is, $W = 4.5$. Using the queuing relationships discussed in this section, we can now calculate other operating characteristics for this queue.

First, using Equation (11.22) and solving for W_q, we have:

$$W_q = W - \frac{1}{\mu} = 4.5 - \frac{1}{0.50} = 2.5 \text{ minutes}$$

The application of Little's flow equations is demonstrated in Problem 14.

With both W and W_q known, we can use Little's flow equations, (11.19) and (11.20), to compute:

$$L = \lambda W = 0.40(4.5) = 1.8 \text{ customers}$$
$$L_q = \lambda W_q = 0.40(2.5) = 1 \text{ customer}$$

The manager of the supermarket can now review these operating characteristics to see whether action should be taken to improve the service and to reduce the waiting time and the length of the queue.

NOTES AND COMMENTS

In queuing systems where the length of the queue is limited (e.g., a small waiting area), some arriving units will be blocked from joining the queue and will be lost. In this case, the blocked or lost arrivals will make the mean number of units entering the system something less than the mean arrival rate. By defining λ as the mean number of units *joining the system*, rather than the mean arrival rate, the relationships discussed in this section can be used to determine W, L, W_q and L_q.

11.5 Economic Analysis of Queues

Frequently, decisions involving the design of queuing systems will be based on a subjective evaluation of the operating characteristics of the queue. For example, a manager may decide that an average waiting time of one minute or less and an average of two customers or fewer in the system is reasonable. The models presented in the preceding sections can be used to determine the number of channels that will meet the manager's performance goals.

On the other hand, a manager may want to identify the cost of operating the queuing system and then base the decision regarding system design on a minimum hourly or daily operating cost. Before an economic analysis of a queuing system can be conducted, a total cost model, which includes the cost of waiting and the cost of service, must be developed.

To develop a total cost model for a queuing system, we begin by defining the notation to be used:

Waiting cost is based on average number of units in the system. It includes the time spent queuing plus the time spent being served.

C_W = the waiting cost per time period for each unit
L = the average number of units in the system
C_s = the service cost per time period for each channel
K = the number of channels
TC = the total cost per time period

The total cost is the sum of the waiting cost and the service cost; that is,

$$TC = C_w L + C_s K \tag{11.23}$$

Adding more channels always improves the operating characteristics of the queue and reduces the waiting cost. However, additional channels increase the service cost. An economic analysis of waiting lines attempts to find the number of channels that will minimize total cost by balancing the waiting cost and the service cost.

To conduct an economic analysis of a queue, we must obtain reasonable estimates of the waiting cost and the service cost. Of these two costs, the waiting cost is usually the more difficult to evaluate. In the Dome restaurant problem, the waiting cost would be the cost per minute for a customer waiting for service. This cost is not a direct cost to the Dome. However, if the Dome ignores this cost and allows long waiting lines, customers will ultimately take their business elsewhere. Thus, the Dome will experience lost sales and, in effect, incur a cost.

The service cost is generally easier to determine. This cost is the relevant cost associated with operating each service channel. In the Dome problem, this cost would include the server's wages, benefits and any other direct costs associated with operating the service channel. At the Dome, this cost is estimated to be €7 per hour.

To demonstrate the use of Equation (11.23), we assume that Dome is willing to assign a cost of €10 per hour for customer waiting time. We use the average number

Figure 11.4 The General Shape of Waiting Cost, Service Cost, and Total Cost Curves in Queuing Models

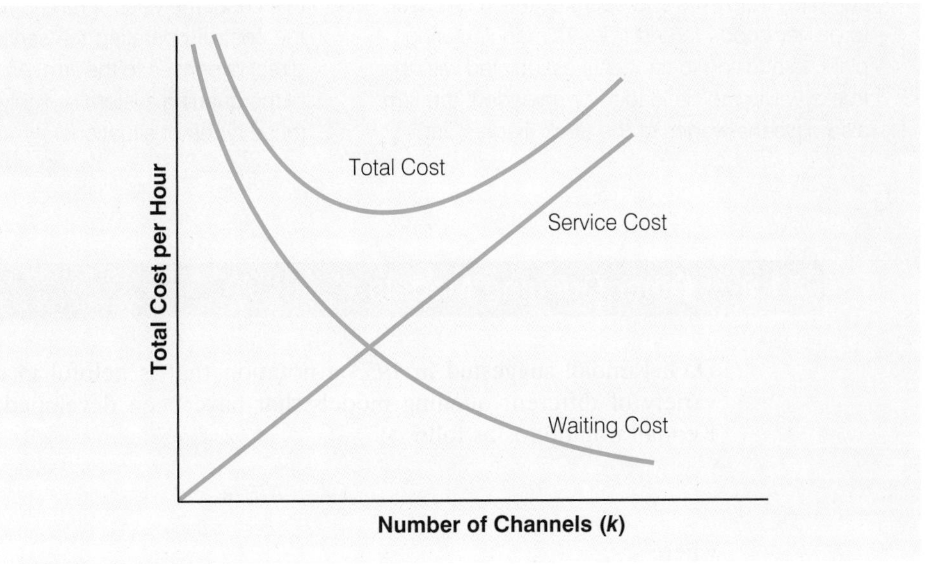

of units in the system, L, as computed in Sections 11.2 and 11.3 to obtain the total hourly cost for the single-channel and two-channel systems:

Single-channel system (L = three customers):

$$TC = C_wL + C_sK$$
$$= 10(3) + 7(1) = €37.00 \text{ per hour}$$

Two-channel system (L = 0.8727 customer):

$$TC = C_wL + C_sK$$
$$= 10(0.8727) + 7(2) = €22.73 \text{ per hour}$$

Thus, based on the cost data provided by the Dome, the two-channel system provides the most economical operation.

Problem 10 tests your ability to conduct an economic analysis of proposed single-channel and two-channel waiting line systems.

Figure 11.4 shows the general shape of the cost curves in the economic analysis of queues. The service cost increases as the number of channels is increased. However, with more channels, the service is better. As a result, waiting time and cost decrease as the number of channels is increased. The number of channels that will provide a good approximation of the minimum total cost design can be found by evaluating the total cost for several design alternatives.

NOTES AND COMMENTS

1 In dealing with government agencies and utility companies, customers may not be able to take their business elsewhere. In these situations, no lost business occurs when long waiting times are encountered. This condition is one reason that service in such organizations may be poor and that customers in such situations may experience long waiting times.

2 In some instances, the organization providing the service also employs the units waiting for the

service. For example, consider the case of a company that owns and operates the trucks used to deliver goods to and from its manufacturing plant. In addition to the costs associated with the trucks waiting to be loaded or unloaded, the firm also pays the wages of the truck loaders and unloaders who operate the service channel. In this case, the cost of having the trucks wait and the cost of operating the service channel are direct expenses to the firm. An economic analysis of the queuing system is highly recommended for these types of situations.

11.6 Other Queuing Models

D.G. Kendall suggested in 1953 a notation that is helpful in classifying the wide variety of different queuing models that have been developed. The three-symbol Kendall notation is as follows:

$$A/B/k$$

where

- A denotes the probability distribution for the arrivals
- B denotes the probability distribution for the service time
- k denotes the number of channels

Depending on the letter appearing in the A or B position, a variety of waiting line systems can be described. The letters that are commonly used are as follows:

- M designates a Poisson probability distribution for the arrivals or an exponential probability distribution for service time
- D designates that the arrivals or the service time is deterministic or constant
- G designates that the arrivals or the service time has a general probability distribution with a known mean and variance

Using the Kendall notation, the single-channel waiting line model with Poisson arrivals and exponential service times is classified as an $M/M/1$ model. The two-channel waiting line model with Poisson arrivals and exponential service times presented in Section 11.3 would be classified as an $M/M/2$ model.

NOTES AND COMMENTS

In some cases, the Kendall notation is extended to five symbols. The fourth symbol indicates the largest number of units that can be in the system, and the fifth symbol indicates the size of the population. The fourth symbol is used in situations where the queue can hold a finite or maximum number of units and the fifth symbol is necessary when the population of arriving units or customers is finite. When the fourth and fifth symbols of the Kendall notation are omitted, the waiting line system is assumed to have infinite capacity, and the population is assumed to be infinite.

11.7 Single-Channel Queuing Model with Poisson Arrivals and Arbitrary Service Times

When providing input to the M/G/1 model, be consistent in terms of the time period. For example, if λ and μ are expressed in terms of the number of units per hour, the standard deviation of the service time should be expressed in hours. The example that follows uses minutes as the time period for the arrival and service data.

Let us return to the single-channel model where arrivals are described by a Poisson probability distribution. However, we now assume that the probability distribution for the service times is not an exponential probability distribution. Thus, using the Kendall notation, the queuing model that is appropriate is an *M*/*G*/1 model, where *G* denotes a general or unspecified probability distribution.

Operating Characteristics for the *M*/*G*/1 Model

The notation used to describe the operating characteristics for the *M*/*G*/1 model is:

λ = the mean arrival rate

μ = the mean service rate

σ = the standard deviation of the service time

Some of the steady-state operating characteristics of the *M*/*G*/1 waiting line model are as follows:

1 The probability that no units are in the system:

$$P_0 = 1 - \frac{\lambda}{\mu} \quad \textbf{(11.24)}$$

2 The average number of units in the waiting line:

$$L_q = \frac{\lambda^2\sigma^2 + (\lambda/\mu)^2}{2(1 - \lambda/\mu)} \quad \textbf{(11.25)}$$

3 The average number of units in the system:

$$L = L_q + \frac{\lambda}{\mu} \quad \textbf{(11.26)}$$

4 The average time a unit spends in the queue:

$$W_q = \frac{L_q}{\lambda} \quad \textbf{(11.27)}$$

5 The average time a unit spends in the system:

$$W = W_q + \frac{1}{\mu} \quad \textbf{(11.28)}$$

6 The probability that an arriving unit has to wait for service:

$$P_w = \frac{\lambda}{\mu} \tag{11.29}$$

Note that the relationships for L, W_q and W are the same as the relationships used for the models in Sections 11.2 and 11.3. They are given by Little's flow equations.

Problem 15 provides another application of a single-channel waiting line with Poisson arrivals and arbitrary service times.

An Example Retail sales at Hartlage's Seafood Supply are handled by one clerk. Customer arrivals are random, and the average arrival rate is 21 customers per hour or $\lambda = 21/60 = 0.35$ customers per minute. A study of the service process shows that the average or mean service time is two minutes per customer, with a standard deviation of $\sigma = 1.2$ minutes. The mean time of two minutes per customer shows that the clerk has a mean service rate of $\mu = ½ = 0.50$ customers per minute. The operating characteristics of this $M/G/1$ waiting line system are:

EXCEL *file*

HARTLAGE

$$P_0 = 1 - \frac{\lambda}{\mu} = 1 - \frac{0.35}{0.50} = 0.30$$

$$L_q = \frac{(0.35)^2(1.2)^2 + (0.35/0.50)^2}{2(1 - 0.35/0.50)} = 1.1107 \text{ customers}$$

$$L = L_q + \frac{\lambda}{\mu} = 1.1107 + \frac{0.35}{0.50} = 1.8107 \text{ customers}$$

$$W_q = \frac{L_q}{\lambda} = \frac{1.1107}{0.35} = 3.1733 \text{ minutes}$$

$$W = W_q + \frac{1}{\mu} = 3.1733 + \frac{1}{0.50} = 5.1733 \text{ minutes}$$

$$P_w = \frac{\lambda}{\mu} = \frac{0.35}{0.50} = 0.70$$

From the analysis we see that there is a 70 per cent chance that a customer will have to wait for service, that on average a customer will have to wait just over three minutes in the queue and will spend just over five minutes in the system.

Hartlage's manager can review these operating characteristics to determine whether scheduling a second clerk appears to be worthwhile.

Constant Service Times

We want to comment briefly on the single-channel model that assumes random arrivals but constant service times. Such a queuing system can occur in production and manufacturing environments where machine-controlled service times are constant. This queue is described by the $M/D/1$ model, with the D referring to the deterministic service times. With the $M/D/1$ model, the average number of units in the queue, L_q, can be found by using Equation (11.25) with the condition that the standard deviation of the constant service time is $\sigma = 0$. Thus, the expression for the average number of units in the queue for the $M/D/1$ model becomes:

$$L_q = \frac{(\lambda/\mu)^2}{2(1 - \lambda/\mu)} \tag{11.30}$$

The other expressions presented earlier in this section can be used to determine additional operating characteristics of the $M/D/1$ system.

NOTES AND COMMENTS

Whenever the operating characteristics of a queuing system are unacceptable, managers often try to improve service by increasing the mean service rate μ. This approach is good, but Equation (11.25) shows that the variation in the service times also affects the operating characteristics of the queue. Because the standard deviation of service times, σ, appears in the numerator of Equation (11.25), a larger variation in service times results in a larger average number of units in the queue. Hence, another alternative for improving the service capabilities of a queue is to reduce the variation in the service times. Thus, even when the mean service rate of the service facility cannot be increased, a reduction in σ will reduce the average number of units in the queue and improve the other operating characteristics of the system.

11.8 Multiple-Channel Model with Poisson Arrivals, Arbitrary Service Times and No Queue

An interesting variation of the queuing models discussed so far involves a system in which no waiting is allowed. Arriving units or customers seek service from one of several service channels. If all channels are busy, arriving units are denied access to the system. In queuing terminology, arrivals occurring when the system is full are blocked and are cleared from the system. Such customers may be lost or may attempt a return to the system later.

A primary application of this model involves the design of telephone and other communication systems where the arrivals are the calls and the channels are the number of telephone or communication lines available. In such a system, the calls are made to one telephone number, with each call automatically switched to an open channel if possible. When all channels are busy, additional calls receive a busy signal and are denied access to the system.

The specific model considered in this section is based on the following assumptions.

1 The system has k channels.
2 The arrivals follow a Poisson probability distribution, with mean arrival rate λ.
3 The service times for each channel may have any probability distribution.
4 The mean service rate μ is the same for each channel.
5 An arrival enters the system only if at least one channel is available. An arrival occurring when all channels are busy is blocked – that is, denied service and not allowed to enter the system.

With G denoting a general or unspecified probability distribution for service times, the appropriate model for this situation is referred to as an $M/G/k$ model with 'blocked customers cleared'. The question addressed in this type of situation is, How many channels or servers should be used?

Operating Characteristics for the *M/G/k* Model with Blocked Customers Cleared

We approach the problem of selecting the best number of channels by calculating the steady-state probabilities that j of the k channels will be busy. These probabilities are:

$$P_j = \frac{(\lambda/\mu)^j/j!}{\sum_{i=0}^{k}(\lambda/\mu)^i/i!} \qquad \textbf{(11.31)}$$

where

λ = the mean arrival rate
μ = the mean service rate for each channel
k = the number of channels
P_j = the probability that j of the k channels are busy for $j = 0, 1, 2, ..., k$

With no waiting allowed, operating characteristics L_q and W_q considered in previous models are automatically zero regardless of the number of service channels. In this situation, the more important design consideration involves determining how the percentage of blocked customers is affected by the number of service channels.

The most important probability value is P_k, which is the probability that all k channels are busy. On a percentage basis, P_k indicates the percentage of arrivals that are blocked and denied access to the system.

Another operating characteristic of interest is the average number of units in the system; note that this number is equivalent to the average number of channels in use. Letting L denote the average number of units in the system, we have:

$$L = \frac{\lambda}{\mu}(1 - P_k) \qquad \textbf{(11.32)}$$

An Example Microdata Software, uses a telephone ordering system for its computer software products. Callers place orders with Microdata by using the company's freephone telephone number. Assume that calls to this telephone number arrive at an average rate of $\lambda = 12$ calls per hour. The time required to process a telephone order varies considerably from order to order. However, each Microdata sales representative can be expected to handle an average of μ = six calls per hour. Currently, the Microdata freephone number has three internal lines or channels, each operated by a separate sales representative. Calls received on the freephone number are automatically transferred to an open line or channel if available.

Whenever all three lines are busy, callers receive a busy signal. In the past, Microdata's management assumed that callers receiving a busy signal would call back later. However, recent research on telephone ordering showed that a substantial number of callers who are denied access do not call back later. These lost calls represent lost revenues for the firm, so Microdata's management requested an analysis of the telephone ordering system. Specifically, management wanted to know the percentage of callers who get busy signals and are blocked from the system. If management's goal is to provide sufficient capacity to handle 90 per cent of the callers, how many telephone lines and sales representatives should Microdata use?

We can demonstrate the use of Equation (11.31) by calculating P_3, the probability that all three of the currently available telephone lines will be in use and additional callers will be blocked:

EXCEL *file*

MICRODATA

$$P_3 = \frac{(^{12}/_6)^3/3!}{(^{12}/_6)^0/0! + (^{12}/_6)^1/1! + (^{12}/_6)^2/2! + (^{12}/_6)^3/3!} = \frac{1.3333}{6.3333} = 0.2105$$

With $P_3 = 0.2105$, approximately 21 per cent of the calls, or slightly more than one in five calls, are being blocked. Only 79 per cent of the calls are being handled immediately by the three-line system.

Table 11.6 Probabilities of Busy Lines for the Microdata Four-Line System

Number of Busy Lines	Probability
0	0.1429
1	0.2857
2	0.2857
3	0.1905
4	0.0952

Let us assume that Microdata expands to a four-line system. Then, the probability that all four channels will be in use and that callers will be blocked is:

$$P_4 = \frac{(^{12}/_6)^4/4!}{(^{12}/_6)^0/0! + (^{12}/_6)^1/1! + (^{12}/_6)^2/2! + (^{12}/_6)^3/3! + (^{12}/_6)^4/4!} = \frac{0.667}{7} = 0.0952$$

Problem 18 provides practise in calculating probabilities for multiple-channel systems with no waiting lines.

With only 9.52 per cent of the callers blocked, 90.48 per cent of the callers will reach the Microdata sales representatives. Thus, Microdata could expand its order-processing operation to four lines to meet management's goal of providing sufficient capacity to handle at least 90 per cent of the callers. The average number of calls in the four-line system and thus the average number of lines and sales representatives that will be busy is:

$$L = \frac{\lambda}{\mu}(1 - P_4) = \frac{12}{6}(1 - 0.0952) = 1.8095$$

Although an average of fewer than two lines will be busy, the four-line system is necessary to provide the capacity to handle at least 90 per cent of the callers. We used Equation (11.31) to calculate the probability that zero, one, two, three or four lines will be busy. These probabilities are summarized in Table 11.6.

As we discussed in Section 11.5, an economic analysis of queues can be used to guide system design decisions. In the Microdata system, the cost of the additional line and additional sales representative should be relatively easy to establish. This cost can be balanced against the cost of the blocked calls. With 9.52 per cent of the calls blocked and $\lambda = 12$ calls per hour, an eight-hour day will have an average of $8(12)(0.0952) = 9.1$ blocked calls. If Microdata can estimate the cost of possible lost sales, the cost of these blocked calls can be established. The economic analysis based on the service cost and the blocked-call cost can assist in determining the optimal number of lines for the system.

NOTES AND COMMENTS

Many of the operating characteristics considered in previous sections are not relevant for the *M/G/k* model with blocked customers cleared. In particular, the average time in the queue, W_q, and the average number of units in the queue, L_q, are no longer considered because waiting is not permitted in this type of system.

11.9 Queuing Models with Finite Calling Populations

For the queuing models introduced so far, the population of units or customers arriving for service has been considered to be unlimited. In technical terms, when no limit is placed on how many units may seek service, the model is said to have an infinite calling population. Under this assumption, the mean arrival rate λ remains constant regardless of how many units are in the queuing system. This assumption of an infinite calling population is made in most queuing models.

In other cases, the maximum number of units or customers that may seek service is assumed to be finite. In this situation, the mean arrival rate for the system changes, depending on the number of units in the waiting line, and the waiting line model is said to have a finite calling population. The formulas for the operating characteristics of the previous waiting line models must be modified to account for the effect of the finite calling population.

In previous models, the arrival rate was constant and independent of the number of units in the system. With a finite calling population, the arrival rate decreases as the number of units in the system increases because, with more units in the system, fewer units are available for arrivals.

The mean arrival rate λ is defined differently for the finite calling population model. Specifically, λ is defined in terms of the mean arrival rate for each unit.

The finite calling population model discussed in this section is based on the following assumptions.

1 The arrivals for *each unit* follow a Poisson probability distribution, with mean arrival rate λ.

2 The service times follow an exponential probability distribution, with mean service rate μ.

3 The population of units that may seek service is finite.

With a single channel, the queuing model is referred to as an *M*/*M*/1 model with a finite calling population.

The mean arrival rate for the *M*/*M*/1 model with a finite calling population is defined in terms of how often *each unit* arrives or seeks service. This situation differs from that for previous queuing models in which λ denoted the mean arrival rate for the system. With a finite calling population, the mean arrival rate for the system varies, depending on the number of units in the system. Instead of adjusting for the changing system arrival rate, in the finite calling population model λ indicates the mean arrival rate for each unit.

Operating Characteristics for the *M*/*M*/1 Model with a Finite Calling Population

The following formulas are used to determine the steady-state operating characteristics for an *M*/*M*/1 model with a finite calling population, where:

λ = the mean arrival rate for each unit

μ = the mean service rate

N = the size of the population

1 The probability that no units are in the system:

$$P_0 = \frac{1}{\sum_{n=0}^{N} \frac{N!}{(N-n)!}\left(\frac{\lambda}{\mu}\right)^n} \tag{11.33}$$

2 The average number of units in the waiting line:

$$L_q = N - \frac{\lambda + \mu}{\lambda}(1 - P_0) \tag{11.34}$$

3 The average number of units in the system:

$$L = L_q + (1 - P_0) \quad \textbf{(11.35)}$$

4 The average time a unit spends in the queue:

$$W_q = \frac{L_q}{(N - L)\lambda} \quad \textbf{(11.36)}$$

5 The average time a unit spends in the system:

$$W = W_q + \frac{1}{\mu} \quad \textbf{(11.37)}$$

6 The probability an arriving unit has to wait for service:

$$P_W = 1 - P_0 \quad \textbf{(11.38)}$$

7 The probability of n units in the system:

$$P_n = \frac{N!}{(N - n)!}\left(\frac{\lambda}{\mu}\right)^n P_0 \quad \text{for } n = 0, 1, \ldots, N \quad \textbf{(11.39)}$$

One of the primary applications of the *M*/*M*/1 model with a finite calling population is referred to as the *machine repair problem*. In this problem, a group of machines is considered to be the finite population of 'customers' that may request repair service. Whenever a machine breaks down, an arrival occurs in the sense that a new repair request is initiated. If another machine breaks down before the repair work has been completed on the first machine, the second machine begins to form a 'queue' for repair service. Additional breakdowns by other machines will add to the length of the waiting line. The assumption of first-come, first-served indicates that machines are repaired in the order they break down. The *M*/*M*/1 model shows that one person or one channel is available to perform the repair service. To return the machine to operation, each machine with a breakdown must be repaired by the single-channel operation.

An Example The Kolkmeyer Manufacturing Company uses a group of six identical machines; each machine operates an average of 20 hours between breakdowns. Thus, the mean arrival rate or request for repair service for each machine is $\lambda = {}^1\!/_{20} = 0.05$ per hour. With randomly occurring breakdowns, the Poisson probability distribution is used to describe the machine breakdown arrival process. One person from the maintenance department provides the single-channel repair service for the six machines. The exponentially distributed service times have a mean of two hours per machine or a mean service rate of $\mu = ½ = 0.50$ machines per hour.

With $\lambda = 0.05$ and $\mu = 0.50$, we use Equations (11.33) through (11.38) to calculate the operating characteristics for this system. Note that the use of Equation

Figure 11.5 Worksheet for the Kolkmeyer Two-Channel Machine Repair Problem

	A	B	C	D
1	**Waiting Line Model with a Finite Calling Population**			
2				
3	**Assumptions**			
4	**Poisson Arrivals**			
5	**Exponential Service Times**			
6	**Finite Calling Population**			
7				
8	Number of Channels	2		
9	Mean Arrival Rate	0.05		
10	Mean Service Rate	0.5		
11	Population Size	6		
12				
13				
14	**Operating Characteristics**			
15				
16	Probability that no machines are in the system, Po		0.5602	
17	Average number of machines in the waiting line, Lq		0.0227	
18	Average number of machines in the system, L		0.5661	
19	Average time a machine spends in the waiting line, Wq		0.0834	
20	Average time a machine spends in the system, W		2.0834	
21	Probability an arriving machine has to wait, Pw		0.1036	
22				

EXCEL *file*

KOLKMEYER

(11.33) makes the computations involved somewhat cumbersome. Confirm for yourself that Equation (11.33) provides the value of $P_0 = 0.4845$. The calculations for the other operating characteristics are:

$$L_q = 6 - \left(\frac{0.05 + 0.50}{0.05}\right)(1 - 0.4845) = 0.3297 \text{ machine}$$

$$L = 0.3295 + (1 - 0.4845) = 0.8451 \text{ machine}$$

$$W_q = \frac{0.3295}{(6 - 0.845)0.50} = 1.279 \text{ hours}$$

$$W = 1.279 + \frac{1}{0.50} = 3.279 \text{ hours}$$

$$P_w = 1 - P_0 = 1 - 0.4845 = 0.5155$$

Operating characteristics of an M/M/1 waiting line with a finite calling population are considered in Problem 20.

Finally, Equation (11.39) can be used to calculate the probabilities of any number of machines being in the repair system.

As with other waiting line models, the operating characteristics provide the manager with information about the operation of the waiting line. In this case, the fact that a machine breakdown waits an average of $W_q = 1.279$ hours before maintenance begins and the fact that more than 50 per cent of the machine breakdowns must wait for service, $P_w = 0.5155$, indicates a two-channel system may be needed to improve the machine repair service.

An Excel worksheet template on the online platform that accompanies this text or The Management Scientist software may be used to analyze the two-channel finite calling population model.

Calculations of the operating characteristics of a multiple-channel finite calling population queuing system are more complex than those for the single-channel model. A computer solution is virtually mandatory in this case. The Excel worksheet for the Kolkmeyer two-channel machine repair system is shown in Figure 11.5. With two repair personnel, the average machine breakdown waiting time is reduced to $W_q = 0.0834$ hours or five minutes and only 10 per cent, $P_w = 0.1036$, of the machine breakdowns wait for service. Thus, the two-channel system significantly improves the machine repair service operation. Ultimately, by considering the cost of machine downtime and the cost of the repair personnel, management can determine whether the improved service of the two-channel system is cost effective.

Summary

In this chapter we have developed a number of queuing models:

- The two key factors in a queuing situation are the arrival rate and the service rate.
- The Poisson probability distribution is often used to describe the arrival pattern.
- The exponential probability distribution is often used to describe the service rate pattern.
- Empirical probability distributions may be needed for more complex queuing situations.
- The operating characteristics describe the performance of the queuing system and include time spent in the system, time spent waiting and probability of queuing.
- An economic analysis of a queuing system can be undertaken by developing a suitable total costs model.

WORKED EXAMPLE

Rural post offices in Scotland have a major role to play in their communities, not simply in terms of the obvious postal services but also providing a wide range of other services – banking and financial services, retail services and often providing a gateway to other public agency services. The post office manager in a large rural town has asked for your help. The post office faces a seasonal demand pattern with a large influx of visitors and tourists to the area in the summer months. The post office is keen to provide a quality service to its customers by providing a prompt service so that customers do not have to wait too long. The post office has three service counters and you have collected some initial data. You have found through observation that the service rate of a postal clerk is an average of 0.75 customers per minute and that the average arrival rate in the summer is 1.2 customers per minute. In addition, this summer additional tourist events are planned in the area leading to an anticipated increase in business. This is expected to increase the average arrival rate to 1.35 customers per minute. Market research has shown that customers are prepared to spend up to five minutes in the post office before customer satisfaction and loyalty falls considerably.

What advice can we give the post office manager?

Solution

Clearly, the key decision facing the manager is how many service counters to open. This is a multiple channel queuing situation so Equations (11.11–11.18) are appropriate if we assume that the Poisson distribution is appropriate for arrivals and the exponential for service rate. We have no specific information on this but it is a fairly standard assumption in this type of analysis. So, we can calculate the operating characteristics of the various alternatives. To begin with, we know that the option of having only one service counter open is a non-starter as the service rate is less than the arrival rate, so a queue will quickly build up and never be cleared. However, if we look at the two-service counter option we can analyze the existing situation with an arrival rate of 1.2 and a service rate for each counter of 0.75. Using Table 11.4 we have $\lambda/\mu = 1.6$ giving $P_o = 0.1111$. We can then proceed to calculate the other operating characteristics:

1 Average number of customers in the queue:

$$Lq = \frac{(1.2/0.75)^2(1.2)(0.75)\,(0.1111)}{(2\text{-}1)!(2(0.75) - 1.2)^2} = 2.84$$

2 Average number of customers in the system:

$$L = 2.84 + 1.2/0.75 = 4.44$$

3 Average time a customer spends in the queue:

$$W_q = 2.84/1.2 = 2.37 \text{ minutes}$$

4 Average time a customer spends in the system:

$$W = 2.37 + 1/0.75 = 3.70 \text{ minutes}$$

5 Probability that a customer arriving has to wait for service:

$$P_w = (1/2!)(1.2/0.75)^2(2(0.75)/(2(0.75) - 1.2))(.1111) = 0.71$$

We can repeat the calculation for three service counters open and then again for the expected increase in the arrival rate to 1.35. The results are summarized below:

	two service counters; arrival rate 1.2	**three service counters, arrival rate 1.2**	**two service counters, arrival rate 1.35**	**three service counters, arrival rate 1.35**
Probability of no customers in the system	0.1111	0.19	0.0526	0.146
Average number of customers in the queue:	2.84	0.31	7.67	0.53
Average number of customers in the system:	4.44	1.91	9.47	2.33
Average time a customer spends in the queue:	2.37	0.26	5.68	0.39
Average time a customer spends in the system:	3.70	1.59	7.02	1.73
Probability that a customer arriving has to wait for service:	0.71	0.27	0.85	0.35

We see that in the current situation having two service counters open will provide an acceptable level of service in that the average time a customer spends in the post office is 2.77 minutes. However, if the arrival rate increases as predicted, two service counters will not be able to cope. We see that on average customers will spend around seven minutes in the post office with 85 per cent of customers having to wait and around seven or eight customers in the queue system at any one time. Opening a third service counter has a marked effect on performance with the average time spent in the system dropping to 1.7 minutes. Clearly we cannot recommend the third service counter be opened as we have no cost information. However, we can provide the manager with this information on predicted performance.

MANAGEMENT SCIENCE IN ACTION

Improving Productivity at the New Haven Fire Department

The New Haven, Connecticut, Fire Department implemented a reorganization plan with cross-trained fire and medical personnel responding to both fire and medical emergencies. A queuing model provided the basis for the reorganization by demonstrating that substantial improvements in emergency medical response time could be achieved with only a small reduction in fire protection. Annual savings were reported to be $1.4 million.

The model was based on Poisson arrivals and exponential service times for both fire and medical emergencies. It was used to estimate the average time that a person placing a call would have to wait for the appropriate emergency unit to arrive at the location. Waiting times were estimated by the model's prediction of the average travel time to reach each of the city's 28 census tracts.

The model was first applied to the original system of 16 fire units and four emergency medical units that operated independently. It was then applied to the proposed reorganization plan that involved cross-trained department personnel qualified to respond to both fire and medical emergencies. Results from the model demonstrated that average travel times could be reduced under the reorganization plan. Various facility location alternatives were also evaluated. When implemented, the reorganization plan reduced operating cost and improved public safety services.

Based on A.J. Swersey, L. Goldring, and E.D. Geyer, 'Improving Fire Department Productivity: Merging Fire and Emergency Medical Units in New Haven', *Interfaces* 23, no. 1 (January/February 1993): 109–129.

The complexity and diversity of waiting line systems found in practice often prevent an analyst from finding an existing waiting line model that fits the specific application being studied. Simulation, the topic discussed in Chapter 12, provides an approach to determining the operating characteristics of such waiting line systems.

Problems

1 Stad National Bank operates a drive-up teller window that allows customers to complete bank transactions without getting out of their cars. On weekday mornings, arrivals to the drive-up teller window occur at random, with a mean arrival rate of 24 customers per hour or 0.4 customer per minute.

a. What is the mean or expected number of customers that will arrive in a five-minute period?

b. Assume that the Poisson probability distribution can be used to describe the arrival process. Use the mean arrival rate in part (a) and compute the probabilities that exactly zero, one, two and three customers will arrive during a five-minute period.

c. Delays are expected if more than three customers arrive during any five-minute period. What is the probability that delays will occur?

SELF *test*

2 In the Stad National Bank waiting line system (see Problem 1), assume that the service times for the drive-up teller follow an exponential probability distribution with a mean service rate of 36 customers per hour or 0.6 customer per minute. Use the exponential probability distribution to answer the following questions.

a. What is the probability the service time is one minute or less?
b. What is the probability the service time is two minutes or less?
c. What is the probability the service time is more than two minutes?

3 Use the single-channel drive-up bank teller operation referred to in Problems 1 and 2 to determine the following operating characteristics for the system.

a. The probability that no customers are in the system.
b. The average number of customers waiting.
c. The average number of customers in the system.
d. The average time a customer spends waiting.
e. The average time a customer spends in the system.
f. The probability that arriving customers will have to wait for service.

SELF *test*

4 Use the single-channel drive-up bank teller operation referred to in Problems 1–3 to determine the probabilities of zero, one, two and three customers in the system. What is the probability that more than three customers will be in the drive-up teller system at the same time?

SELF *test*

5 The reference desk of a university library receives requests for assistance. Assume that a Poisson probability distribution with a mean rate of ten requests per hour can be used to describe the arrival pattern and that service times follow an exponential probability distribution with a mean service rate of 12 requests per hour.

a. What is the probability that no requests for assistance are in the system?
b. What is the average number of requests that will be waiting for service?
c. What is the average waiting time in minutes before service begins?
d. What is the average time at the reference desk in minutes (waiting time plus service time)?
e. What is the probability that a new arrival has to wait for service?

SELF *test*

6 Films Tonight is a typical DVD movie rental outlet for home viewing customers. During the weeknight evenings, customers arrive at Films Tonight at the average rate of 1.25 customers per minute. The cashier can serve an average of two customers per minute. Assume Poisson arrivals and exponential service times.

a. What is the probability that no customers are in the system?
b. What is the average number of customers waiting for service?
c. What is the average time a customer waits for service to begin?
d. What is the probability that an arriving customer will have to wait for service?
e. Do the operating characteristics indicate that the one-cashier checkout system provides an acceptable level of service?

SELF *test*

7 For the Dome single-channel queuing system in Section 11.2, assume that the arrival rate is increased to one customer per minute and that the mean service rate is increased to 1.25 customers per minute. Calculate the following operating characteristics for the new system: P_0, L_q, L, W_q, W and P_w. Does this system provide better or poorer service compared to the original system? Discuss any differences and the reason for these differences.

SELF *test*

8 Agan Interior Design provides home and office decorating assistance to its customers. In normal operation, an average of 2.5 customers arrive each hour. One design consultant is available to answer customer questions and make product recommendations. The consultant averages ten minutes with each customer.

a. Calculate the operating characteristics of the customer waiting line, assuming Poisson arrivals and exponential service times.
b. Service goals dictate that an arriving customer should not wait for service more than an average of five minutes. Is this goal being met? If not, what action do you recommend?
c. If the consultant can reduce the average time spent per customer to eight minutes, what is the mean service rate? Will the service goal be met?

SELF *test*

9 Consider a two-channel waiting line with Poisson arrivals and exponential service times. The mean arrival rate is 14 units per hour, and the mean service rate is ten units per hour for each channel.

a. What is the probability that no units are in the system?
b. What is the average number of units in the system?
c. What is the average time a unit waits for service?
d. What is the average time a unit is in the system?
e. What is the probability of having to wait for service?

SELF *test*

10 Refer to the Agan Interior Design situation in Problem 8. Agan's management would like to evaluate two alternatives:

- Use one consultant with an average service time of eight minutes per customer.
- Expand to two consultants, each of whom has an average service time of ten minutes per customer.

If the consultants are paid $16 per hour and the customer waiting time is valued at $25 per hour for waiting time prior to service, should Agan expand to the two-consultant system? Explain.

11 A fast-food franchise is considering operating a drive-up window food-service operation. Assume that customer arrivals follow a Poisson probability distribution, with a mean arrival rate of 24 cars per hour, and that service times follow an exponential probability distribution. Arriving customers place orders at an intercom station at the back of the parking area and then drive to the service window to pay for and receive their orders. The following three service alternatives are being considered.

- A single-channel operation in which one employee fills the order and takes the money from the customer. The average service time for this alternative is two minutes.
- A single-channel operation in which one employee fills the order while a second employee takes the money from the customer. The average service time for this alternative is 1.25 minutes.
- A two-channel operation with two service windows and two employees. The employee stationed at each window fills the order and takes the money for customers arriving at the window. The average service time for this alternative is two minutes for each channel.

Answer the following questions and recommend an alternative design for the fast-food franchise.

a. What is the probability that no cars are in the system?
b. What is the average number of cars waiting for service?
c. What is the average number of cars in the system?
d. What is the average time a car waits for service?
e. What is the average time in the system?
f. What is the probability that an arriving car will have to wait for service?

12 The following cost information is available for the fast-food franchise in Problem 11.

- Customer waiting time is valued at €25 per hour to reflect the fact that waiting time is costly to the fast-food business.
- The cost of each employee is €6.50 per hour.
- To account for equipment and space, an additional cost of €20 per hour is attributable to each channel.

What is the lowest-cost design for the fast-food business?

13 Patients arrive at a dentist's office at a mean rate of 2.8 patients per hour. The dentist can treat patients at the mean rate of three patients per hour. A study of patient waiting times shows that, on average, a patient waits 30 minutes before seeing the dentist.

a. What are the mean arrival and treatment rates in terms of patients per minute?
b. What is the average number of patients in the waiting room?
c. If a patient arrives at 10:10 A.M., at what time is the patient expected to leave the office?

SELF *test* 14 A study of a multiple-channel food-service operation shows that the average time between the arrival of a customer at the food-service counter and his or her departure with a filled order is ten minutes. Customers arrive at the average rate of four per minute. The food-service operation requires an average of two minutes per customer order.

a. What is the mean service rate per channel in terms of customers per minute?
b. What is the average waiting time in the line prior to placing an order?
c. On average, how many customers are in the food-service system ?

SELF *test* 15 Gubser Welding, Inc., operates a welding service for construction and automotive repair jobs. Assume that the arrival of jobs at the company's office can be described by a Poisson probability distribution with a mean arrival rate of two jobs per eight-hour day. The time required to complete the jobs follows a normal probability distribution with a mean time of 3.2 hours and a standard deviation of two hours. Answer the following questions, assuming that Gubser uses one welder to complete all jobs.

a. What is the mean arrival rate in jobs per hour?
b. What is the mean service rate in jobs per hour?
c. What is the average number of jobs waiting for service?
d. What is the average time a job waits before the welder can begin working on it?
e. What is the average number of hours between when a job is received and when it is completed?
f. What percentage of the time is Gubser's welder busy?

16 Jobs arrive randomly at a particular assembly plant; assume that the mean arrival rate is five jobs per hour. Service times (in minutes per job) do not follow the exponential probability distribution. Two proposed designs for the plant's assembly operation are shown.

	Service Time	
Design	**Mean**	**Standard Deviation**
A	6.0	3.0
B	6.25	0.6

a. What is the mean service rate in jobs per hour for each design?
b. For the mean service rates in part (a), what design appears to provide the best or fastest service rate?
c. What are the standard deviations of the service times in hours?
d. Use the *M*/*G*/1 model to compute the operating characteristics for each design.
e. Which design provides the best operating characteristics? Why?

SELF *test* 17 The Robotics Manufacturing Company operates an equipment repair business where emergency jobs arrive randomly at the rate of three jobs per eight-hour day. The company's repair facility is a single-channel system operated by a repair technician. The service time varies with a mean repair time of two hours and a standard deviation of 1.5 hours. The company's cost of the repair operation is €28 per hour. In the economic analysis of the queuing system, Robotics uses €35 per hour cost for customers waiting during the repair process.

a. What are the arrival rate and service rate in jobs per hour?
b. Show the operating characteristics including the total cost per hour.

c. The company is considering purchasing a computer-based equipment repair system that would enable a constant repair time of two hours. For practical purposes, the standard deviation is zero. Because of the computer-based system, the company's cost of the new operation would be €32 per hour. The firm's director of operations said no to the request for the new system because the hourly cost is €4 higher and the mean repair time is the same. Do you agree? What effect will the new system have on the queuing characteristics of the repair service?

d. Does paying for the computer-based system to reduce the variation in service time make economic sense? How much will the new system save the company during a 40-hour work week?

SELF *test*

18 A large insurance company maintains a central computing system that contains a variety of information about customer accounts. Insurance agents in a six-state area use telephone lines to access the customer information database. Currently, the company's central computer system allows three users to access the central computer simultaneously. Agents who attempt to use the system when it is full are denied access; no waiting is allowed. Management realizes that with its expanding business, more requests will be made to the central information system. Being denied access to the system is inefficient as well as annoying for agents. Access requests follow a Poisson probability distribution, with a mean of 42 calls per hour. The mean service rate per line is 20 calls per hour.

a. What is the probability that zero, one, two and three access lines will be in use?

b. What is the probability that an agent will be denied access to the system?

c. What is the average number of access lines in use?

d. In planning for the future, management wants to be able to handle $\lambda = 50$ calls per hour; in addition, the probability that an agent will be denied access to the system should be no greater than the value computed in part (b). How many access lines should this system have?

SELF *test*

19 Cairo Cab, Inc., uses two dispatchers to handle requests for service and to dispatch the cabs. The telephone calls that are made to Cairo Cab use a common telephone number. When both dispatchers are busy, the caller hears a busy signal; no waiting is allowed. Callers who receive a busy signal can call back later or call another cab service. Assume that the arrival of calls follows a Poisson probability distribution, with a mean of 40 calls per hour, and that each dispatcher can handle a mean of 30 calls per hour.

a. What percentage of time are both dispatchers idle?

b. What percentage of time are both dispatchers busy?

c. What is the probability callers will receive a busy signal if two, three or four dispatchers are used?

d. If management wants no more than 12 per cent of the callers to receive a busy signal, how many dispatchers should be used?

SELF *test*

20 Five administrative assistants use an office copier. The average time between arrivals for each assistant is 40 minutes, which is equivalent to a mean arrival rate of $^1/_{40} = 0.025$ arrival per minute. The mean time each assistant spends at the copier is five minutes, which is equivalent to a mean service rate of $^1/_5 = 0.20$ user per minute. Use the *M*/*M*/1 model with a finite calling population to determine the following:

a. The probability that the copier is idle.

b. The average number of administrative assistants in the queue.

c. The average number of administrative assistants at the copier.

d. The average time an assistant spends waiting for the copier.

e. The average time an assistant spends at the copier.

f. During an eight-hour day, how many minutes does an assistant spend at the copier? How much of this time is waiting time?

g. Should management consider purchasing a second copier? Explain.

CASE PROBLEM 1 Regional Airlines

Regional Airlines is establishing a new telephone system for handling flight reservations. During the 10:00 A.M. to 11:00 A.M.. time period, calls to the reservation agent occur randomly at an average of one call every 3.75 minutes. Historical service time data show that a reservation agent spends an average of three minutes with each customer. The waiting line model assumptions of Poisson arrivals and exponential service times appear reasonable for the telephone reservation system.

Regional Airlines' management believes that offering an efficient telephone reservation system is an important part of establishing an image as a service-oriented airline. If the system is properly implemented, Regional Airlines will establish good customer relations, which in the long run will increase business. However, if the telephone reservation system is frequently overloaded and customers have difficulty contacting an agent, a negative customer reaction may lead to an eventual loss of business. The cost of a ticket reservation agent is €20 per hour. Thus, management wants to provide good service, but it does not want to incur the cost of overstaffing the telephone reservation operation by using more agents than necessary.

At a planning meeting, Regional's management team agreed that an acceptable customer service goal is to answer at least 85 per cent of the incoming calls immediately. During the planning meeting, Regional's vice president of administration pointed out that the data show that the average service rate for an agent is faster than the average arrival rate of the telephone calls. The vice president's conclusion was that personnel costs could be minimized by using one agent and that the single agent should be able to handle the telephone reservations and still have some idle time. The vice president of marketing restated the importance of customer service and expressed support for at least two reservation agents.

The current telephone reservation system design does not allow callers to wait. Callers who attempt to reach a reservation agent when all agents are occupied receive a busy signal and are blocked from the system. A representative from the telephone company suggested that Regional Airlines consider an expanded system that accommodates waiting. In the expanded system, when a customer calls and all agents are busy, a recorded message tells the customer that the call is being held in the order received and that an agent will be available shortly. The customer can stay on the line and listen to background music while waiting for an agent. Regional's management will need more information before switching to the expanded system.

Managerial Report

Prepare a managerial report for Regional Airlines analyzing the telephone reservation system. Evaluate both the system that does not allow waiting and the expanded system that allows waiting. Include the following information in your report.

1 A detailed analysis of the operating characteristics of the reservation system with one agent as proposed by the vice president of administration. What is your recommendation concerning a single-agent system?

2 A detailed analysis of the operating characteristics of the reservation system based on your recommendation regarding the number of agents Regional should use.

3 What appear to be the advantages or disadvantages of the expanded system? Discuss the number of waiting callers the expanded system would need to accommodate.

4 The telephone arrival data presented are for the 10:00 A.M. to 11:00 A.M. time period; however, the arrival rate of incoming calls is expected to change from hour to hour. Describe how your waiting line analysis could be used to develop a ticket agent staffing plan that would enable the company to provide different levels of staffing for the ticket reservation system at different times during the day. Indicate the information that you would need to develop this staffing plan.

CASE PROBLEM 2 Office Equipment, Inc

Office Equipment, Inc. (OEI) leases automatic mailing machines to business customers. The company built its success on a reputation of providing timely maintenance and repair service. Each OEI service contract states that a service technician will arrive at a customer's business site within an average of three hours from the time that the customer notifies OEI of an equipment problem.

Currently, OEI has ten customers with service contracts. One service technician is responsible for handling all service calls. A statistical analysis of historical service records indicates that a customer requests a service call at an average rate of one call per 50 hours of operation. If the service technician is available when a customer calls for service, it takes the technician an average of one hour of travel time to reach the customer's office and an average of 1.5 hours to complete the repair service. However, if the service technician is busy with another customer when a new customer calls for service, the technician completes the current service call and any other waiting service calls before responding to the new service call. In such cases, once the technician is free from all existing service commitments, the technician takes an average of one hour of travel time to reach the new customer's office and an average of 1.5 hours to complete the repair service. The cost of the service technician is €80 per hour. The downtime cost (wait time and service time) for customers is €100 per hour.

OEI is planning to expand its business. Within one year, OEI projects that it will have 20 customers, and within two years, OEI projects that it will have 30 customers. Although OEI is satisfied that one service technician can handle the ten existing customers, management is concerned about the ability of one technician to meet the average three-hour service call guarantee when the OEI customer base expands. In a recent planning meeting, the marketing manager made a proposal to add a second service technician when OEI reaches 20 customers and to add a third service technician when OEI reaches 30 customers. Before making a final decision, management would like an analysis of OEI service capabilities. OEI is particularly interested in meeting the average three-hour waiting time guarantee at the lowest possible total cost.

Managerial Report

Develop a managerial report summarizing your analysis of the OEI service capabilities. Make recommendations regarding the number of technicians to be used when OEI reaches 20 customers and when OEI reaches 30 customers. Include a discussion of the following in your report.

1. What is the mean arrival rate for each customer per hour?
2. What is the mean service rate in terms of the number of customers per hour? Note that the average travel time of one hour becomes part of the service time because the time that the service technician is busy handling a service call includes the travel time plus the time required to complete the repair.
3. Queuing system models generally assume that the arriving customers are in the same location as the service facility. Discuss the OEI situation in light of the fact that a service technician travels an average of one hour to reach each customer. How should the travel time and the waiting time predicted by the model be combined to determine the total customer waiting time?
4. OEI is satisfied that one service technician can handle the ten existing customers. Use a queuing system model to determine the following information:
   - Probability that no customers are in the system.
   - Average number of customers queuing.
   - Average number of customers in the system.
   - Average time a customer waits until the service technician arrives.
   - Average time a customer waits until the machine is back in operation.
   - Probability that a customer will have to wait more than one hour for the service technician to arrive.
   - The number of hours a week the technician is not making service calls.
   - The total cost per hour for the service operation.

Do you agree with OEI management that one technician can meet the average three-hour service call guarantee? Explain.

5 What is your recommendation for the number of service technicians to hire when OEI expands to 20 customers? Use the information that you developed in part (4) to justify your answer.

6 What is your recommendation for the number of service technicians to hire when OEI expands to 30 customers? Use the information that you developed in part (4) to justify your answer.

7 What are the annual savings of your recommendation in part (6) compared to the planning committee's proposal that 30 customers will require three service technicians? Assume 250 days of operation per year.

Chapter 12

Simulation

Learning Objectives

By the end of this chapter you will be able to:

- Explain the principles of simulation modelling
- Build a simulation model

Simulation is probably one of the most widely used quantitative approaches to business decision making. Simulation is typically applied in decision-making situations where it may not be possible or desirable to search for an optimum solution. Instead, a simulation model provides the decision maker with the opportunity to experiment with certain parts of a decision problem and analyze the likely consequences of alternative decisions. Consider the following situation. You are the manager of a local supermarket. Customers have recently been complaining that they have had to wait too long at the checkouts for service and you are concerned that this will affect customer satisfaction and loyalty and future sales and profitability. So, you have decided to try to identify the appropriate number of checkouts to open at specific times of the day to prevent large queues forming. Clearly, given the appropriate information you could try to develop an appropriate queuing model (Chapter 11). However, as manager you have concerns that simply using an average for the service rate and an average for the arrival rate is too simplistic for the situation you face. You know that service rates and arrival rates are highly variable and to some extent unpredictable and that you need to take this complexity into account in terms of trying to decide how many checkouts to open. With simulation, we build an appropriate mathematical model to represent the situation and specifically incorporate the variability and uncertainty we face. The model then allows us to assess *what ifs*. What if we add an extra checkout? How will this affect queuing times? What about two extra checkouts? What if service times at the checkout are slower than usual? What if we have more arrivals than usual? The what-if capability of simulation modelling is one of the features that has made it so popular and successful.

Simulation is commonly applied in a variety of business situations with the following examples being typical.

New product development An organization is trying to decide whether to develop a new product or service and typically may simulate the probability that the new product/service will be profitable or successful. Typical aspects of the problem that will be uncertain include: levels of demand for the new product/service; precise production costs; competitor response. A simulation model allows for different levels of these variables to be factored into the model.

Reservation systems Airlines are faced with a typical situation in their passenger reservation systems. They know that a particular flight has a given passenger capacity. They also know that typically not all passengers booked on to a flight will show up. So, they have the opportunity to overbook a flight – selling more tickets than they have seats. The problem they face is: how many extra tickets to sell given that the number of no-show passengers is uncertain? Too many and they run the risk of an overbooked flight. Too few and they lose potential revenue. A simulation model allows the airline to try out different overbooking strategies to assess the likely consequences. Clearly, the same situation faces any organization that has a reservation system: hotels; car rental companies; service and repair companies; healthcare providers.

Inventory systems As we saw in Chapter 10, having the right inventory strategy in place is critical both for customer service and for cost control. Simulation allows the decision maker to assess the effects of changing elements of the existing inventory system on costs and service levels.

MANAGEMENT SCIENCE IN ACTION

Call Centre Design

A call centre is a place where large volumes of calls are made to or received from current or potential customers. More than 60 000 call centres operate in the United States. Saltzman and Mehrotra describe how a simulation model helped make a strategic change in the design of the technical support call centre for a major software company. The application used a queuing simulation model to balance the service to customers calling for assistance with the cost of agents providing the service.

Historically, the software company provided free phone-in technical support, but over time service requests grew to the point where 80 per cent of the callers were waiting between five and ten minutes and abandonment rates were too high. On some days 40 per cent of the callers hung up before receiving service. This service level was unacceptable. As a result, management considered instituting a Rapid Programme in which customers would pay a fee for service, but would be guaranteed to receive service within one minute, or the service would be free. Nonpaying customers would continue receiving service but without a guarantee of short service times.

A simulation model was developed to help understand the impact of this new programme on the queuing characteristics of the call centre. Available data were used to develop the arrival distribution, the service time distribution and the probability distribution for abandonment. The key design variables considered were the number of agents (channels) and the percentage of callers subscribing to the Rapid Programme. The model was developed using the Arena simulation package.

The simulation results helped the company decide to go ahead with the Rapid Programme. Under most of the scenarios considered, the simulation model showed that 95 per cent of the callers in the Rapid Programme would receive service within one minute and that free service to the remaining customers could be maintained within acceptable limits. Within nine months, 10 per cent of the software company's customers subscribed to the Rapid Programme, generating $2 million in incremental revenue. The company viewed the simulation model as a vehicle for mitigating risk. The model helped evaluate the likely impact of the Rapid Programme without experimenting with actual customers.

Based on Robert M. Saltzman and Vijay Mehrotra, 'A Call Centre Uses Simulation to Drive Strategic Change', *Interfaces* (May/June 2001): 87–101.

Queuing systems As we saw in Chapter 11, in a queuing system we are able to alter the number of service channels in a queuing system. Simulation modelling allows the decision maker to assess the impact of this given uncertainties over customer arrival rates and service times.

Flows Simulation is often used to model flows through a network. This might be traffic flows through a road network; information flows through a computer network; flows of materials and components through an assembly network. Simulation allows the decision maker to assess the effect of changes in parts of the network on flows through the network.

In this chapter we begin by showing how simulation can be used to study the financial risks associated with the development of a new product. We continue with illustrations showing how simulation can be used to establish an effective inventory policy and how simulation can be used to design queuing systems. Other issues, such as verifying the simulation programme, validating the model and selecting a simulation software package, are discussed in Section 12.4.

12.1 Risk Analysis

Risk analysis is the process of predicting the outcome of a decision in the face of uncertainty. In this section, we describe a problem that involves considerable uncertainty: the development of a new product. We first show how risk analysis can be conducted without using simulation; then we show how a more comprehensive risk analysis can be conducted with the aid of simulation.

PortaCom Project

PortaCom manufactures laptop computers and related equipment. PortaCom's product design group developed a prototype for a new portable printer. The new printer features an innovative design and has the potential to capture a significant share of the portable printer market. Preliminary marketing and financial analyses provided the following selling price, first-year administrative cost and first-year advertising cost:

$$\text{Selling price} = €249 \text{ per unit}$$
$$\text{Administrative cost} = €400\,000$$
$$\text{Advertising cost} = €600\,000$$

In the simulation model for the PortaCom problem, the preceding values are constants and are referred to as the **parameters** of the model.

The cost of direct labour, the cost of parts and the first-year demand for the printer are not known with certainty. At this stage of the planning process, PortaCom's best estimates of these inputs are €45 per unit for the direct labour cost,€90 per unit for the parts cost and 15 000 units for the first-year demand. PortaCom would like an analysis of the first-year profit potential for the printer. Because of PortaCom's tight cash flow situation, management is particularly concerned about the potential for a financial loss.

What-If Analysis

One approach to risk analysis is called what-if analysis. With a selling price of €249 per unit and administrative plus advertising costs equal to €400 000 + €600 000 = €1 000 000, the PortaCom profit model is:

$$\text{Profit} = (€249 - \text{Direct labour cost per unit} - \text{Parts cost per unit})(\text{Demand}) - €1\,000\,000$$

Letting

$$c_1 = \text{direct labour cost per unit}$$
$$c_2 = \text{parts cost per unit}$$
$$x = \text{first-year demand}$$

the profit model for the first year can be written as follows:

$$\text{Profit} = (249 - c_1 - c_2)x - 1\,000\,000 \qquad \textbf{(12.1)}$$

Recall that PortaCom's best estimates of the direct labour cost per unit, the parts cost per unit and first-year demand are €45, €90 and 15 000 units, respectively. These values constitute the base-case scenario for PortaCom. Substituting these values into Equation (12.1) yields the following profit projection:

$$\text{Profit} = (249 - 45 - 90)(15\,000) - 1\,000\,000 = 710\,000$$

Thus, the base-case scenario leads to an anticipated profit of €710 000.

In risk analysis we are concerned with both the probability of a loss and the magnitude of a loss. Although the base-case scenario looks appealing, PortaCom might be interested in what happens if the estimates of the direct labour cost per unit, parts cost per unit and first-year demand do not turn out to be as expected under the base-case scenario. For instance, suppose that PortaCom believes that direct labour costs could range from €43 to €47 per unit, parts cost could range from €80 to €100 per unit and first-year demand could range from 1500 to 28 500 units. Using these ranges, what-if analysis can be used to evaluate a worst-case scenario and a best-case scenario.

The worst-case value for the direct labour cost is €47 (the highest value), the worst-case value for the parts cost is €100 (the highest value) and the worst-case value for demand is 1500 units (the lowest value). Thus, in the worst-case scenario, $c_1=47$, $c_2=100$ and $x=1500$. Substituting these values into equation (12.1) leads to the following profit projection:

$$\text{Profit} = (249 - 47 - 100)(1500) - 1\,000\,000 = -847\,000$$

So, the worst-case scenario leads to a projected loss of €847 000.

The best-case value for the direct labour cost is €43 (the lowest value), the best-case value for the parts cost is €80 (the lowest value) and the best-case value for demand is 28 500 units (the highest value). Substituting these values into equation (12.1) leads to the following profit projection:

$$\text{Profit} = (249 - 43 - 80)(28\,500) - 1\,000\,000 = 2\,591\,000$$

Problem 2 will give you practise using what-if analysis.

So, the best-case scenario leads to a projected profit of €2 591 000.

At this point the what-if analysis provides the conclusion that profits could range from a loss of €847 000 to a profit of €2 591 000 with a base-case scenario value of €710 000. Although the base-case profit of €710 000 is possible, the what-if analysis indicates that either a substantial loss or a substantial profit is also possible. Other scenarios that PortaCom might want to consider can also be evaluated. However, the difficulty with what-if analysis is that it does not indicate the likelihood of the various profit or loss values. In particular, we do not know anything about the *probability* of a loss.

Simulation

Using simulation to perform risk analysis for the PortaCom problem is like playing out many what-if scenarios by randomly generating values for the probabilistic inputs. The advantage of simulation is that it allows us to assess the probability of a profit and the probability of a loss.

Using the what-if approach to risk analysis, we selected values for direct labour cost per unit (c_1), parts cost per unit (c_2) and first-year demand (x), and then calculated the resulting profit. Applying simulation to the PortaCom problem requires generating values for these variables that are representative of what we might observe in practice. To generate such values, we must know the probability distribution for each variable. Let's assume that further analysis by PortaCom led to the following probability distributions for the direct labour cost per unit, the parts cost per unit and first-year demand:

One advantage of simulation is the ability to use probability distributions that are unique to the system being studied.

Direct Labour Cost PortaCom believes that the direct labour cost will range from €43 to €47 per unit and is described by the discrete probability distribution shown in Table 12.1. Thus, we see a 0.1 probability that the direct labour cost will be €43 per unit, a 0.2 probability that the direct labour cost will be €44 per unit and so on. The highest probability of 0.4 is associated with a direct labour cost of €45 per unit.

Table 12.1 Probability Distribution for Direct Labour Cost per Unit

Direct Labour Cost per Unit	Probability
€43	0.1
€44	0.2
€45	0.4
€46	0.2
€47	0.1

Figure 12.1 Uniform Probability Distribution for the Parts Cost Per Unit

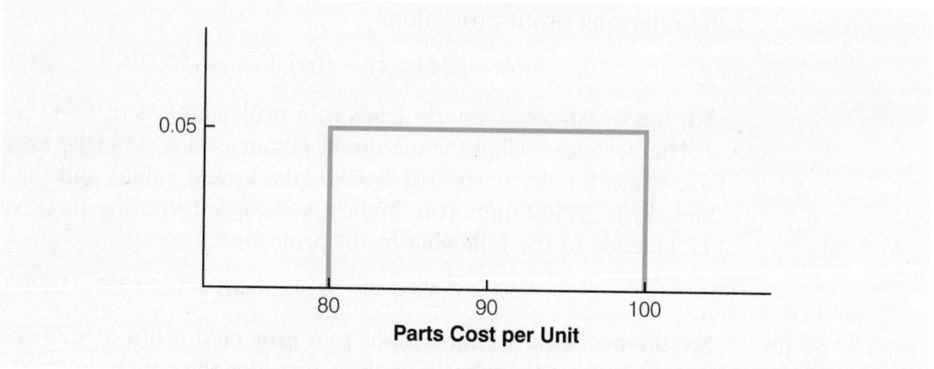

Parts Cost This cost depends upon the general economy, the overall demand for parts, and the pricing policy of PortaCom's parts suppliers. PortaCom believes that the parts cost will range from €80 to €100 per unit and is described by the uniform probability distribution shown in Figure 12.1. Costs per unit between €80 and €100 are equally likely.

First-Year Demand PortaCom believes that first-year demand is described by the normal probability distribution shown in Figure 12.2. The mean or expected value of first-year demand is 15 000 units. The standard deviation of 4500 units describes the variability in the first-year demand.

Figure 12.2 Normal Probability Distribution of First-Year Demand

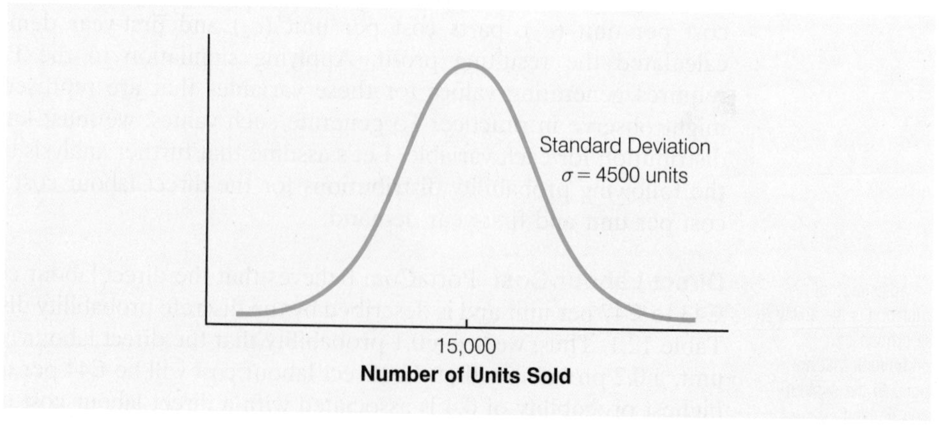

To simulate the PortaCom problem, we must generate values for the three variables and calculate the resulting profit. Then, we generate another set of values for the variables, calculate a second value for profit and so on. We continue this process until we are satisfied that enough trials have been conducted to describe the probability distribution for profit. This process is called *simulation*. In effect we are simulating what could happen in real life by using the information we have about the problem, selecting likely values for the three variables and assessing the effect on profit. If we do this a large number of times (by conducting simulation trials) then we should get a good approximation of what might happen if we were to do this for real. The sequence of logical and mathematical operations required to conduct a simulation can be depicted with a flowchart. A flowchart for the PortaCom simulation is shown in Figure 12.3.

A flowchart provides a graphical representation that helps describe the logic of the simulation model.

Following the logic described by the flowchart we see that the model parameters – selling price, administrative cost and advertising cost – are €249, €400 000 and €600 000, respectively. These values will remain fixed throughout the simulation.

The next three blocks depict the generation of values for the three variables. For each variable in turn we will use its probability distribution to calculate a probabilistic value for that variable. First, a value for the direct labour cost (c_1) is generated. Then a value for the parts cost (c_2) is generated, followed by a value for the first-year demand (x). These probabilistic values are combined using the profit model given by Equation (12.1).

$$\text{Profit} = (249 - c_1 - c_2)x - 1\,000\,000$$

The calculation of profit completes one trial of the simulation. We then return to the flowchart where we generated the direct labour cost and begin another trial. This process is repeated until a satisfactory number of trials has been generated.

At the end of the simulation, key results can be calculated. For example, we will be interested in calculating the average profit and the probability of a loss. For the measures to be meaningful, the probabilistic values must be representative of what is likely to happen when the PortaCom printer is introduced into the market. An essential part of the simulation procedure is the ability to generate representative values for the probabilistic values. We now discuss how to generate these values.

Figure 12.3 Flowchart for the PortaCom Simulation

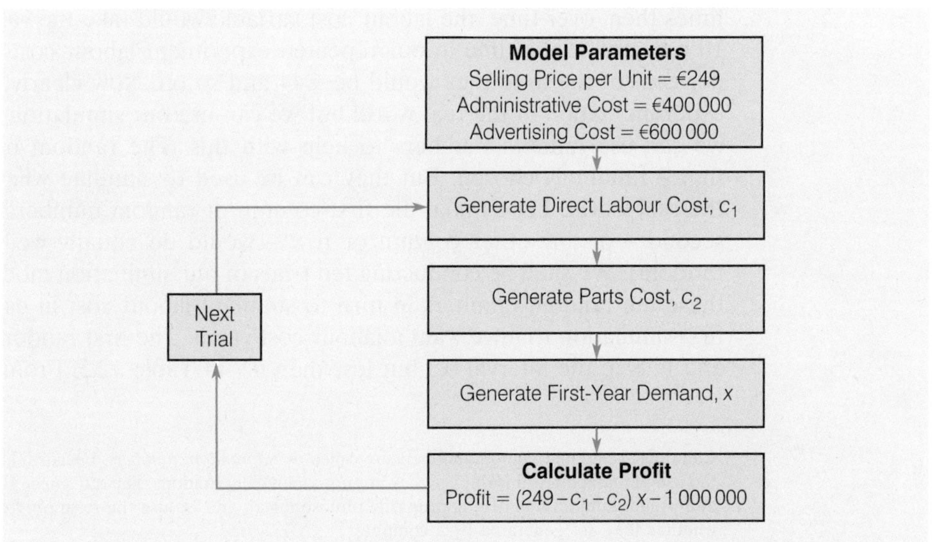

Random numbers were first systematically produced by L. H. C. Tippett in 1925, a statistician in the UK.

Because random numbers are equally likely, quantitative analysts can assign ranges of random numbers to corresponding values of probabilistic inputs so that the probability of any input value to the simulation model is identical to the probability of its occurrence in the real system.

Random Numbers and Generating Probabilistic Values In the PortaCom simulation, representative values must be generated for the direct labour cost per unit (c_1), the parts cost per unit (c_2) and the first-year demand (x). Random numbers and the probability distributions associated with each variable are used to generate representative values. To illustrate how to generate these values, we need to introduce the concept of *computer-generated random numbers*.

Computer-generated random numbers[1] are randomly selected decimal numbers from 0 up to, but not including, 1. The computer-generated random numbers are all equally likely and are uniformly distributed over the interval from 0 to 1. Computer-generated random numbers can be obtained using built-in functions available in computer simulation packages and spreadsheets. For instance, placing =RAND() in a cell of an Excel worksheet will result in a random number between 0 and 1 being placed into that cell.

Table 12.2 contains 500 random numbers generated using Excel. These numbers can be viewed as a random sample of 500 values from a uniform probability distribution over the interval from 0 to 1. Let us show how random numbers can be used to generate values for the PortaCom probability distributions. We begin by showing how to generate a value for the direct labour cost per unit. The approach described is applicable for generating values from any discrete probability distribution.

An interval of random numbers is assigned to each possible value of the direct labour cost in such a fashion that the probability of generating a random number in the interval is equal to the probability of the corresponding direct labour cost shown in Table 12.1 shows how this process is done. The interval of random numbers 0.0 but less than 0.1 is associated with a direct labour cost of €43, the interval of random numbers 0.1 but less than 0.3 is associated with a direct labour cost of €44 and so on. With this assignment of random number intervals to the possible values of the direct labour cost, the probability of generating a random number in any interval is equal to the probability of obtaining the corresponding value for the direct labour cost. So, to select a value for the direct labour cost, we generate a random number between 0 and 1. If the random number is 0.0 but less than 0.1, we set the direct labour cost equal to €43. If the random number is 0.1 but less than 0.3, we set the direct labour cost equal to €44, and so on.

Try Problem 5 for an opportunity to establish intervals of random numbers and simulate demand from a discrete probability distribution.

Let us see how simulation works by looking at the labour cost variable. We know that this follows the probability distribution shown in Table 12.3 – that is, it could vary from €43 to €47. Using what we know about probability we could say that, if we were able to experiment with this problem in the real world, a very large number of times then, over time, the labour cost variable would take the values shown: that is, 10 per cent of the time in our repeated experiment labour costs would be €43, 20 per cent of the time they would be €44 and so on. Now clearly, we cannot do this experimentation in the real world but we can use our simulation model instead and we can use random numbers to help with this. The random numbers are simply that – randomly chosen. But they can be used to simulate what would happen in the real world. Let us take the first column of random numbers in Table 12.2 (the second – or any other column or row – would do equally well since they are all random). We shall be conducting ten trials of our simulation model and we shall use these ten random numbers in turn to simulate labour cost in each trial. So, in our first simulation trial we want a labour cost value. The first random number is 0.6953 and falls in the interval 0.3 but less than 0.7 in Table 12.3. From Table 12.3 we see

[1]Computer-generated random numbers are called *pseudorandom numbers*. Because they are generated through the use of mathematical formulas, they are not technically random. The difference between random numbers and pseudorandom numbers is primarily philosophical, and we use the term *random numbers* regardless of whether they are generated by a computer.

Table 12.2 500 Computer-Generated Random Numbers

0.6953	0.5247	0.1368	0.9850	0.7467	0.3813	0.5827	0.7893	0.7169	0.8166
0.0082	0.9925	0.6874	0.2122	0.6885	0.2159	0.4299	0.3467	0.2186	0.1033
0.6799	0.1241	0.3056	0.5590	0.0423	0.6515	0.2750	0.8156	0.2871	0.4680
0.8898	0.1514	0.1826	0.0004	0.5259	0.2425	0.8421	0.9248	0.9155	0.9518
0.6515	0.5027	0.9290	0.5177	0.3134	0.9177	0.2605	0.6668	0.1167	0.7870
0.3976	0.7790	0.0035	0.0064	0.0441	0.3437	0.1248	0.5442	0.9800	0.1857
0.0642	0.4086	0.6078	0.2044	0.0484	0.4691	0.7058	0.8552	0.5029	0.3288
0.0377	0.5250	0.7774	0.2390	0.9121	0.5345	0.8178	0.8443	0.4154	0.2526
0.5739	0.5181	0.0234	0.7305	0.0376	0.5169	0.5679	0.5495	0.7872	0.5321
0.5827	0.0341	0.7482	0.6351	0.9146	0.4700	0.7869	0.1337	0.0702	0.4219
0.0508	0.7905	0.2932	0.4971	0.0225	0.4466	0.5118	0.1200	0.0200	0.5445
0.4757	0.1399	0.5668	0.9569	0.7255	0.4650	0.4084	0.3701	0.9446	0.8064
0.6805	0.9931	0.4166	0.1091	0.7730	0.0691	0.9411	0.3468	0.0014	0.7379
0.2603	0.7507	0.6414	0.9907	0.2699	0.4571	0.9254	0.2371	0.8664	0.9553
0.8143	0.7625	0.1708	0.1900	0.2781	0.2830	0.6877	0.0488	0.8635	0.3155
0.5681	0.7854	0.5016	0.9403	0.1078	0.5255	0.8727	0.3815	0.5541	0.9833
0.1501	0.9363	0.3858	0.3545	0.5448	0.0643	0.3167	0.6732	0.6283	0.2631
0.8806	0.7989	0.7484	0.8083	0.2701	0.5039	0.9439	0.1027	0.9677	0.4597
0.4582	0.7590	0.4393	0.4704	0.6903	0.3732	0.6587	0.8675	0.2905	0.3058
0.0785	0.1467	0.3880	0.5274	0.8723	0.7517	0.9905	0.8904	0.8177	0.6660
0.1158	0.6635	0.4992	0.9070	0.2975	0.5686	0.8495	0.1652	0.2039	0.2553
0.2762	0.7018	0.6782	0.4013	0.2224	0.4672	0.5753	0.6219	0.6871	0.9255
0.9382	0.6411	0.7984	0.0608	0.5945	0.3977	0.4570	0.9924	0.8398	0.8361
0.5102	0.7021	0.4353	0.3398	0.8038	0.2260	0.1250	0.1884	0.3432	0.1192
0.2354	0.7410	0.7089	0.2579	0.1358	0.8446	0.1648	0.3889	0.5620	0.6555
0.9082	0.7906	0.7589	0.8870	0.1189	0.7125	0.6324	0.1096	0.5155	0.3449
0.6936	0.0702	0.9716	0.0374	0.0683	0.2397	0.7753	0.2029	0.1464	0.8000
0.4042	0.8158	0.3623	0.6614	0.7954	0.7516	0.6518	0.3638	0.3107	0.2718
0.9410	0.2201	0.6348	0.0367	0.0311	0.0688	0.2346	0.3927	0.7327	0.9994
0.0917	0.2504	0.2878	0.1735	0.3872	0.6816	0.2731	0.3846	0.6621	0.8983
0.8532	0.4869	0.2685	0.6349	0.9364	0.3451	0.4998	0.2842	0.0643	0.6656
0.8980	0.0455	0.8314	0.8189	0.6783	0.8086	0.1386	0.4442	0.9941	0.6812
0.8412	0.8792	0.2025	0.9320	0.7656	0.3815	0.5302	0.8744	0.4584	0.3585
0.5688	0.8633	0.5818	0.0692	0.2543	0.5453	0.9955	0.1237	0.7535	0.5993
0.5006	0.1215	0.8102	0.1026	0.9251	0.6851	0.1559	0.1214	0.2628	0.9374
0.5748	0.4164	0.3427	0.2809	0.8064	0.5855	0.2229	0.2805	0.9139	0.9013
0.1100	0.0873	0.9407	0.8747	0.0496	0.4380	0.5847	0.4183	0.5929	0.4863
0.5802	0.7747	0.1285	0.0074	0.6252	0.7747	0.0112	0.3958	0.3285	0.5389
0.1019	0.6628	0.8998	0.1334	0.2798	0.7351	0.7330	0.6723	0.6924	0.3963
0.9909	0.8991	0.2298	0.2603	0.6921	0.5573	0.8191	0.0384	0.2954	0.0636
0.6292	0.4923	0.0276	0.6734	0.6562	0.4231	0.1980	0.6551	0.3716	0.0507
0.9430	0.2579	0.7933	0.0945	0.3192	0.3195	0.7772	0.4672	0.7070	0.5925
0.9938	0.7098	0.7964	0.7952	0.8947	0.1214	0.8454	0.8294	0.5394	0.9413
0.4690	0.1395	0.0930	0.3189	0.6972	0.7291	0.8513	0.9256	0.7478	0.8124
0.2028	0.3774	0.0485	0.7718	0.9656	0.2444	0.0304	0.1395	0.1577	0.8625
0.6141	0.4131	0.2006	0.2329	0.6182	0.5151	0.6300	0.9311	0.3837	0.7828
0.2757	0.8479	0.7880	0.8492	0.6859	0.8947	0.6246	0.1574	0.4936	0.8077
0.0561	0.0126	0.6531	0.0378	0.4975	0.1133	0.3572	0.0071	0.4555	0.7563
0.1419	0.4308	0.8073	0.4681	0.0481	0.2918	0.2975	0.0685	0.6384	0.0812
0.3125	0.0053	0.9209	0.9768	0.3584	0.0390	0.2161	0.6333	0.4391	0.6991

Table 12.3 Random Number Intervals for Generating Values of Direct Labour Cost per Unit

Direct Labour Cost per Unit	Probability	Interval of Random Numbers
€43	0.1	0.0 but less than 0.1
€44	0.2	0.1 but less than 0.3
€45	0.4	0.3 but less than 0.7
€46	0.2	0.7 but less than 0.9
€47	0.1	0.9 but less than 1.0

that the simulated labour cost is then €45. For our second trial the simulated, labour cost is €43 and so on. Table 12.4 shows the results for labour cost for the first ten trials. Clearly with only ten trials we cannot simulate the labour cost probability distribution accurately. But if we were to repeat these trials a sufficiently large number of times then we would be able to accurately simulate this distribution.

Let us now turn to the issue of generating values for the parts cost. The probability distribution for the parts cost per unit is the uniform distribution shown in Figure 12.1. Because this random variable has a different probability distribution than direct labour cost, we use random numbers in a slightly different way to generate values for parts cost. With a uniform probability distribution, the following relationship between the random number and the associated value of the parts cost is used.

$$\text{Parts cost} = a + r(b - a) \qquad \textbf{(12.2)}$$

The use of random numbers in simulation was proposed in a paper published in 1947 by Stanislaw Ulam and John von Neumann, two mathematicians working on atomic bomb research at Los Alamos in the USA during and after World War II.

where

r = random number between 0 and 1
a = smallest value for parts cost
b = largest value for parts cost

For PortaCom, the smallest value for the parts cost is €80, and the largest value is €100. Applying Equation (12.2) with a=80 and b=100 leads to the following formula for generating the parts cost given a random number, r.

$$\text{Parts cost} = 80 + r(100 - 80) = 80 + r20 \qquad \textbf{(12.3)}$$

Table 12.4 Random Generation of 10 Values for the Direct Labour Cost per Unit

Trial	Random Number	Direct Labour Cost (€)
1	0.6953	45
2	0.0082	43
3	0.6799	45
4	0.8898	46
5	0.6515	45
6	0.3976	45
7	0.0642	43
8	0.0377	43
9	0.5739	45
10	0.5827	45

Table 12.5 Random Generation of Ten Values for the Parts Cost per Unit

Trial	Random Number	Parts Cost (€)
1	0.3125	86.25
2	0.0053	80.11
3	0.9209	98.42
4	0.9768	99.54
5	0.3584	87.17
6	0.0390	80.78
7	0.2161	84.32
8	0.6333	92.67
9	0.4391	88.78
10	0.6991	93.98

Equation (12.3) generates a value for the parts cost. Let us use the bottom row of random numbers of Table 12.2 to simulate parts cost (once again it doesn't matter which part of the table we use). With the first random number of 0.3125 we then have:

$$\text{Parts cost} = 80 + 0.3125(20) = 86.25$$

On the second trial we have a random number of 0.0082 simulating a parts cost of €80.11 and so on. Table 12.5 shows the generation of 10 values for the parts cost.

Spreadsheet packages such as Excel have built-in functions that make simulations based on probability distributions such as the normal probability distribution relatively easy.

With appropriate choices of *a* and *b,* Equation (12.2) can be used to generate values for any uniform probability distribution.

Finally, we need a random number procedure for generating the first-year demand. Because first-year demand is normally distributed with a mean of 15 000 units and a standard deviation of 4500 units (see Figure 12.2), we need a procedure for generating random values from a normal probability distribution. Computer simulation packages and spreadsheets include a built-in function that provides randomly generated values from a normal probability distribution. In most cases the user only needs to provide the mean and standard deviation of the normal distribution. For example, using Excel the following formula can be placed into a cell to obtain a value for a probabilistic input that is normally distributed:

= NORMINV(RAND(), Mean, Standard Deviation)

Because the mean for the first-year demand in the PortaCom problem is 15 000 and the standard deviation is 4500, the Excel statement:

= NORMINV(RAND(),15 000,4500) **(12.4)**

will provide a normally distributed value for first-year demand. For example, if Excel's RAND() function generates the random number 0.7005, the Excel function shown in equation (12.4) will provide a first-year demand of 17 366 units. If RAND() generates the random number 0.3204, equation (12.4) will provide a first-year demand of 12 900. Table 12.6 shows the results for the first ten randomly generated

Table 12.6 Random Generation of Ten Values for First-Year Demand

Trial	Random Number	Demand
1	0.7005	17,366
2	0.3204	12,900
3	0.8968	20,686
4	0.1804	10,888
5	0.4346	14,259
6	0.9605	22,904
7	0.5646	15,732
8	0.7334	17,804
9	0.0216	5,902
10	0.3218	12,918

values for demand. Note that random numbers less than 0.5 generate first-year demand values below the mean and that random numbers greater than 0.5 generate first-year demand values greater than the mean.

Running the Simulation Model Running the simulation model means implementing the sequence of logical and mathematical operations described in the flowchart in Figure 12.3. The model parameters are €249 per unit for the selling price, €400 000 for the administrative cost and €600 000 for the advertising cost. Each trial in the simulation involves randomly generating values for direct labour cost, parts cost and first-year demand and for calculating profit. The simulation is complete when a satisfactory number of trials have been conducted.

Using the simulated results in Tables 12.4, 12.5 and 12.6, the results for the first trial will be:

$$\begin{aligned} &\text{Direct labour cost}: c_1 = 45 \\ &\text{Parts cost}: \quad c_2 = 86.25 \\ &\text{First-year demand}: x = 17,366 \end{aligned}$$

And with the profit equation:

$$\text{Profit} = (249 - c_1 - c_2)x - 1\,000\,000$$

we obtain:

$$\text{Profit} = (249 - 45 - 86.25)17\,366 - 1\,000\,000 = 1\,044\,847$$

Table 12.7 shows the simulated profit over the first ten trials. We see that profit could be as high as €1 822 231, although we also note that in one trial we made a loss of €319 972. We note also that the average values for labour cost, parts cost and first-year demand are fairly close to their means of €45, €90 and 15 000, respectively. Clearly with only ten trials, we cannot expect to replicate the decision problem accurately. A much larger number of trials is needed to allow the results to better approximate to the probability distributions we have used. To do this we need to use computer-based simulation.

Table 12.7 Portacom Simulation Results for ten Trials

Trial	Direct Labour Cost per Unit (€)	Parts Cost per Unit (€)	Units Sold	Profit (€)
1	45	86.25	17 366	1 044 847
2	43	80.11	12 900	623 981
3	45	98.42	20 686	1 184 028
4	46	99.54	10 888	126 472
5	45	87.17	14 259	665 879
6	45	80.78	22 904	1 822 231
7	43	84.32	15 732	914 270
8	43	92.67	17 804	1 017 727
9	45	88.78	5 902	−319 972
10	45	93.98	12 918	421 238
Total	445	892.02	151 359	7 500 702
Average	44.5	89.20	15 136	750 070

Simulation of the PortaCom Problem

Using an Excel worksheet, we simulated the PortaCom project 500 times. The worksheet used to carry out the simulation is shown in Figure 12.4. Note that the simulation results for trials 6 through 495 have been hidden so that the results can be shown in a reasonably sized figure. If desired, the rows for these trials can be shown and the simulation results displayed for all 500 trials. The details of the Excel worksheet that provided the PortaCom simulation are described in Appendix 12.1.

Excel worksheets for all simulations presented in this chapter are available on the online platform that accompanies this text.

The simulation summary statistics in Figure 12.4 provide information about the risk associated with PortaCom's new printer. The worst result obtained in a simulation of 500 trials is a loss of €785 234, and the best result is a profit of €2 367 058. The mean profit is €698 457. Fifty-one of the trials resulted in a loss; thus, the estimated probability of a loss is 51/500 = 0.1020.

A histogram of simulated profit values is shown in Figure 12.5. We note that the distribution of profit values is fairly symmetric with a large number of values in the range of €250 000 to €1 250 000. The probability of a large loss or a large gain is small. Only three trials resulted in a loss more than €500 000, and only three trials resulted in a profit greater than €2 000 000. However, the probability of a loss is significant. Forty-eight of the 500 trials resulted in a loss in the €0 to €500 000 range – almost 10 per cent. The modal category, the one with the largest number of values, is the range of profits between €750 000 and €1 000 000.

Simulation studies enable an objective estimate of the probability of a loss, which is an important aspect of risk analysis.

In comparing the simulation approach to risk analysis to the what-if approach, we see that much more information is obtained by using simulation. With the what-if analysis, we learned that the base-case scenario projected a profit of €710 000. The worst-case scenario projected a loss of €847 000, and the best-case scenario projected a profit of €2 591 000. From the 500 trials of the simulation run, we see that the worst-and best-case scenarios, although possible, are unlikely. None of the 500 trials provided a loss as low as the worst-case or a profit as high as the best-case. Indeed, the advantage of simulation for risk analysis is the information it provides on the likely values of the output. We now know the probability of a loss,

Figure 12.4 Excel Worksheet for the PortaCom Problem

EXCEL *file*

PORTACOM

	A	B	C	D	E	F
1	**PortaCom Risk Analysis**					
2						
3	Selling Price per Unit		€249			
4	Administrative Cost		€400,000			
5	Advertising Cost		€600,000			
6						
7	**Direct Labour Cost**			**Parts Cost (Uniform Distribution)**		
8	Lower	Upper		Smallest Value	€80	
9	Random No.	Random No.	Cost per Unit	Largest Value	€100	
10	0.0	0.1	€43			
11	0.1	0.3	€44			
12	0.3	0.7	€45	**Demand (Normal Distribution)**		
13	0.7	0.9	€46	Mean	15000	
14	0.9	1.0	€47	Std Deviation	4500	
15						
16						
17	**Simulation Trials**					
18						
19		Direct Labour	Parts	First-Year		
20	Trial	Cost Per Unit	Cost Per Unit	Demand	Profit	
21	1	47	€85.36	17,366	€1,025,570	
22	2	44	€91.68	12,900	€461,828	
23	3	45	€93.35	20,686	€1,288,906	
24	4	43	€98.56	10,888	€169,807	
25	5	45	€88.36	14,259	€648,911	
516	496	44	€98.67	8,730	(€71,739)	
517	497	45	€94.38	19,257	€1,110,952	
518	498	44	€90.85	14,920	€703,118	
519	499	43	€90.37	13,471	€557,652	
520	500	46	€92.50	18,614	€1,056,847	
521						
522			**Summary Statistics**			
523			Mean Profit		€698,457	
524			Standard Deviation		€520,485	
525			Minimum Profit		(€785,234)	
526			Maximum Profit		€2,367,058	
527			Number of Losses		51	
528			Probabilitiy of Loss		0.1020	
529						

how the profit values are distributed over their range and what profit values are most likely.

For practise working through a simulation problem, try Problems 7 and 9.

The simulation results help PortaCom's management better understand the profit/loss potential of the PortaCom portable printer. The 0.1020 probability of a loss may be acceptable to management given a probability of almost 0.80 (see Figure 12.5) that profit will exceed €250 000. On the other hand, PortaCom might want to conduct further market research before deciding whether to introduce the product. In any case, the simulation results should be helpful in reaching an appropriate decision. The *Management Science in Action*, Meeting Demand Levels at Pfizer, describes how a simulation model helped find ways to meet increasing demand for a product.

Figure 12.5 Histogram of Simulated Profit for 500 Trials of the PortaCom Simulation

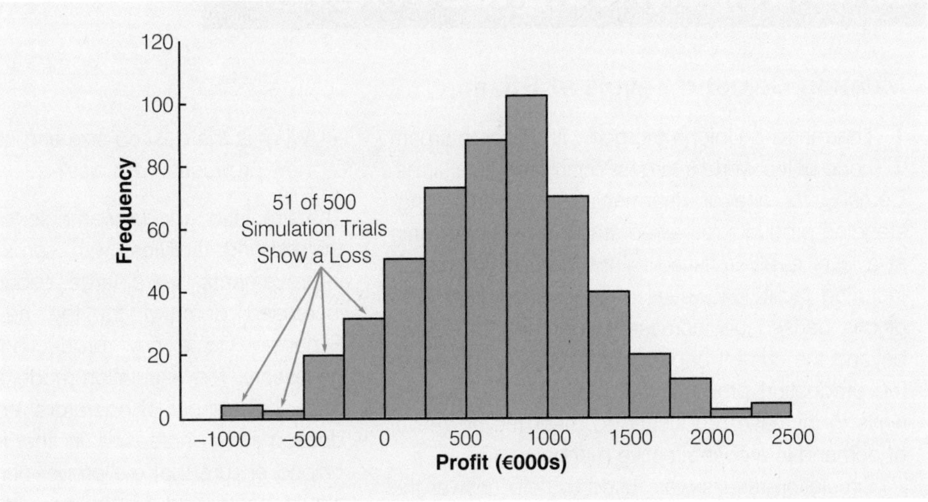

The phrase *Monte Carlo simulation* was proposed by Nicolas Metropolis and Stanislaw Ulam in 1949.

NOTES AND COMMENTS

1 The PortaCom simulation model is based on independent trials in which the results for one trial do not affect what happens in subsequent trials. Historically, this type of simulation study was referred to as a *Monte Carlo simulation*. The term was used because early practitioners of simulation saw similarities between the models they were developing and the gambling games played in the casinos of Monte Carlo. Today, many individuals interpret the term *Monte Carlo simulation* more broadly to mean any simulation that involves randomly generating values for the probabilistic inputs.

2 The probability distribution used to generate values for probabilistic inputs in a simulation model is often developed using historical data. For instance, suppose that an analysis of daily sales at a new car dealership for the past 50 days showed that on two days no cars were sold, on five days one car was sold, on nine days two cars were sold, on 24 days three cars were sold, on seven days four cars were sold and on three days five cars were sold. We can estimate the probability distribution of daily demand using the relative frequencies for the observed data. An estimate of the probability that no cars are sold on a given day is 2/50 = 0.04, an estimate of the probability that one car is sold is 5/50 = 0.10, and so on. The estimated probability distribution of daily demand is as follows:

Daily Sales	0	1	2	3	4	5
Probability	0.04	0.10	0.18	0.48	0.14	0.06

3 Spreadsheet add-in packages such as @RISK® and Crystal Ball® have been developed to make spreadsheet simulation easier. For instance, using Crystal Ball we could simulate the PortaCom new product introduction by first entering the formulae showing the relationships between the probabilistic inputs and the output measure, profit. Then, a probability distribution type is selected for each probabilistic input from among a number of available choices. Crystal Ball will generate random values for each probabilistic input, compute the profit and repeat the simulation for as many trials as specified. Graphical displays and a variety of descriptive statistics can be easily obtained.

MANAGEMENT SCIENCE IN ACTION

Meeting Demand Levels at Pfizer

Pharmacia & Upjohn merged with Pfizer to create one of the world's largest pharmaceutical firms. Demand for one of Pharmacia & Upjohn's long-standing products remained stable for several years at a level easily satisfied by the company's manufacturing facility. However, changes in market conditions caused an increase in demand to a level beyond the current capacity. A simulation model of the production process was developed to explore ways to increase production to meet the new level of demand in a cost-effective manner.

Simulation results were used to help answer the following questions:

- What is the maximum throughput of the existing facility?
- How can the existing production process be modified to increase throughput?
- How much equipment must be added to the existing facility to meet the increased demand?
- What is the desired size and configuration of the new production process?

The simulation model was able to demonstrate that the existing facilities, with some operating policy improvements, were large enough to satisfy the increased demand for the next several years. Expansion to a new production facility was not necessary. The simulation model also helped determine the number of operators required as the production level increased in the future. This result helped ensure that the proper number of operators would be trained by the time they were needed. The simulation model also provided a way reprocessed material could be used to replace fresh raw materials, resulting in a savings of approximately $3 million per year.

Based on information provided by David B. Magerlein, James M. Magerlein and Michael J. Goodrich.

12.2 Inventory Simulation

In this section we describe how simulation can be used to establish an inventory policy for a product that has an uncertain demand. The product is a home ventilation fan distributed by the Butler Electrical Supply Company. Each fan costs Butler €75 and sells for €125. Thus Butler realizes a gross profit of €125 − €75 = €50 for each fan sold. Monthly demand for the fan is described by a normal probability distribution with a mean of 100 units and a standard deviation of 20 units.

Butler receives monthly deliveries from its supplier and replenishes its inventory to a level of Q at the beginning of each month. This beginning inventory level is referred to as the replenishment level. If monthly demand is less than the replenishment level, an inventory holding cost of €15 is charged for each unit that is not sold. However, if monthly demand is greater than the replenishment level, a stock-out occurs and a shortage cost is incurred. Because Butler assigns a goodwill cost of €30 for each customer turned away, a shortage cost of €30 is charged for each unit of demand that cannot be satisfied. Management would like to use a simulation model to determine the average monthly net profit resulting from using a particular replenishment level. Management would also like information on the percentage of total demand that will be satisfied. This percentage is referred to as the *service level*.

The controllable input to the Butler simulation model is the replenishment level, Q. The probabilistic input is the monthly demand, D. The two key measures are the average monthly net profit and the service level. Calculation of the service level requires that we keep track of the number of fans sold each month and the total demand for fans for each month. The service level will be calculated at the end of the simulation run as the ratio of total units sold to total demand.

When demand is less than or equal to the replenishment level ($D \leq Q$), D units are sold, and an inventory holding cost of €15 is incurred for each of the $Q - D$ units that remain in inventory. Net profit for this case is calculated as follows:

Case 1: $D \leq Q$

$$\begin{aligned} \text{Gross profit} &= €50D \\ \text{Holding cost} &= €15(Q - D) \\ \text{Net profit} &= \text{Gross profit} - \text{Holding cost} = €50D - €15(Q - D) \end{aligned} \quad \textbf{(12.5)}$$

When demand is greater than the replenishment level ($D > Q$), Q fans are sold, and a shortage cost of €30 is imposed for each of the $D - Q$ units of demand not satisfied. Net profit for this case is calculated as follows:

Case 2: $D > Q$

$$\begin{aligned} \text{Gross profit} &= €50Q \\ \text{Shortage cost} &= €30(D - Q) \\ \text{Net profit} &= \text{Gross profit} - \text{Shortage cost} = €50Q - €30(D - Q) \end{aligned} \quad \textbf{(12.6)}$$

Figure 12.6 shows a flowchart that defines the sequence of logical and mathematical operations required to simulate the Butler inventory system. Each trial in the simulation represents one month of operation. The simulation is run for 300 months using a given replenishment level, Q. Then, the average profit and service level output measures are calculated. Let us describe the steps involved in the simulation by illustrating the results for the first two months of a simulation run using a replenishment level of $Q = 100$.

The first block of the flowchart in Figure 12.6 sets the values of the model parameters: gross profit = €50 per unit, holding cost = €15 per unit and shortage cost = €30 per unit. The next block shows that a replenishment level of Q is selected; in our illustration, $Q = 100$. Then, a value for monthly demand is generated. Because monthly demand is normally distributed with a mean of 100 units and a standard deviation of 20 units, we can use the Excel function = NORMINV(RAND(),100,20), as described in Section 12.1, to generate a value for monthly demand. Suppose that a value of $D = 79$ is generated on the first trial. This value of demand is then compared with the replenishment level, Q. With the replenishment level set at $Q = 100$, demand is less than the replenishment level, and the left branch of the flowchart is followed. Sales are set equal to demand (79), and gross profit, holding cost and net profit are computed as follows:

$$\begin{aligned} \text{Gross profit} &= 50D = 50(79) = 3950 \\ \text{Holding cost} &= 15(Q - D) = 15(100 - 79) = 315 \\ \text{Net profit} &= \text{Gross profit} - \text{Holding cost} = 3950 - 315 = 3635 \end{aligned}$$

The values of demand, sales, gross profit, holding cost and net profit are recorded for the first month. The first row of Table 12.8 summarizes the information for this first trial.

Figure 12.6 Flowchart for the Butler Inventory Simulation

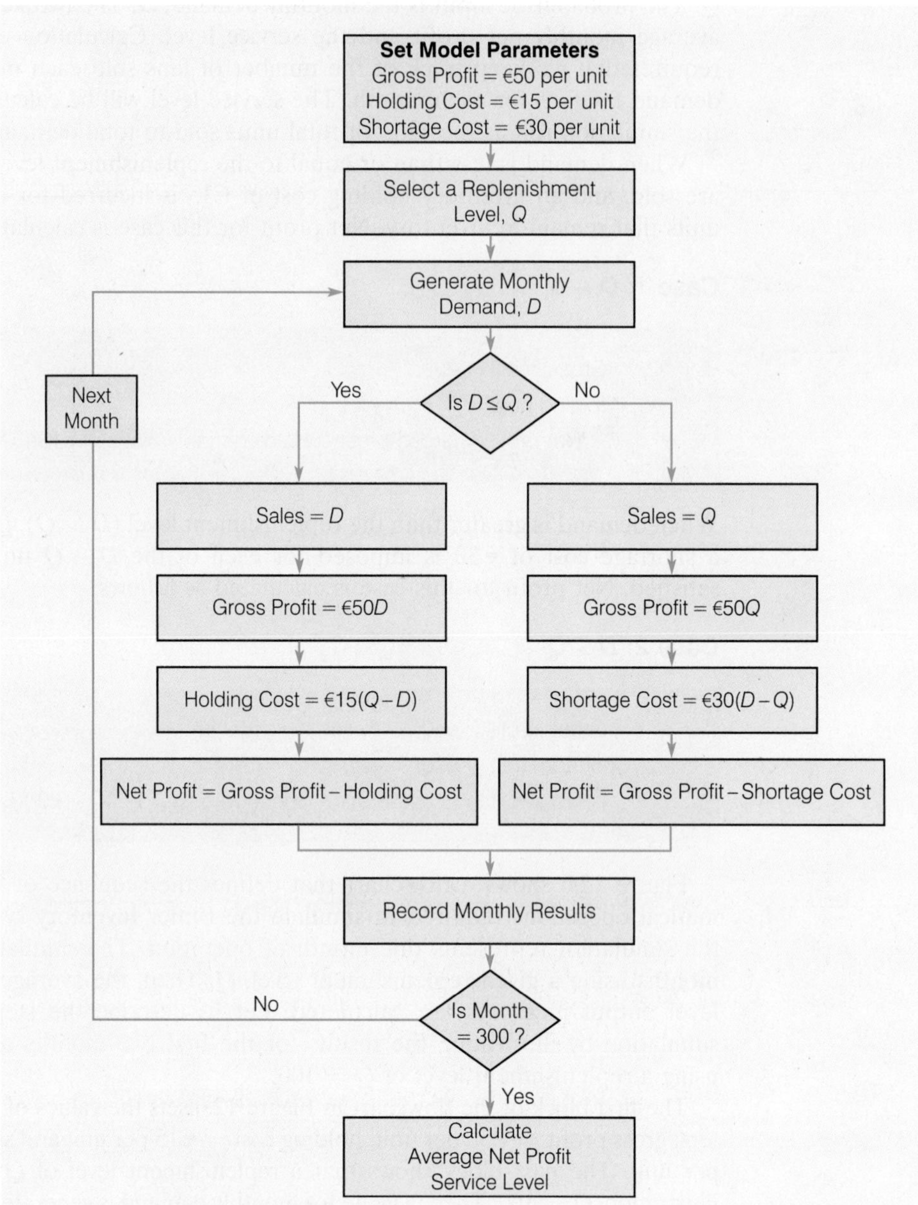

For the second month, suppose that a value of 111 is generated for monthly demand. Because demand is greater than the replenishment level, the right branch of the flowchart is followed. Sales are set equal to the replenishment level (100), and gross profit, shortage cost and net profit are calculated as follows:

$$\text{Gross profit} = 50Q = 50(100) = 5000$$

$$\text{Shortage cost} = 30(D - Q) = 30(111 - 100) = 330$$

$$\text{Net profit} = \text{Gross profit} - \text{Shortage cost} = 5000 - 330 = 4670$$

The values of demand, sales, gross profit, holding cost, shortage cost and net profit are recorded for the second month. The second row of Table 12.8 summarizes the information generated in the second trial.

Table 12.8 Butler Inventory Simulation Results for Five Trials with $Q = 100$

Month	Demand	Sales	Gross Profit (€)	Holding Cost (€)	Shortage Cost (€)	Net Profit (€)
1	79	79	3 950	315	0	3 635
2	111	100	5 000	0	330	4 670
3	93	93	4 650	105	0	4 545
4	100	100	5 000	0	0	5 000
5	118	100	5 000	0	540	4 460
Totals	501	472	23 600	420	870	22 310
Average	100	94	€4 720	€84	€174	€4 462

Results for the first five months of the simulation are shown in Table 12.8. The totals show an accumulated total net profit of €22 310, which is an average monthly net profit of €22 310/5 = €4462. Total unit sales are 472, and total demand is 501. Thus, the service level is 472/501 = 0.942, or 94.2 per cent, indicating Butler has been able to satisfy 94.2 per cent of demand during the five-month period.

Simulation of the Butler Inventory Problem

Using Excel, we simulated the Butler inventory operation for 300 months. The worksheet used to carry out the simulation is shown in Figure 12.7. Note that the simulation results for months 6 through 295 have been hidden so that the results can be shown in a reasonably sized figure. If desired, the rows for these months can be shown and the simulation results displayed for all 300 months.

The summary statistics in Figure 12.7 show what can be anticipated over 300 months if Butler operates its inventory system using a replenishment level of 100. The average net profit is €4293 per month. Because 27 917 units of the total demand of 30 181 units were satisfied, the service level is 27 917/30 181 = 92.5 per cent. We are now ready to use the simulation model to consider other replenishment levels that may improve the net profit and the service level.

Simulation allows the user to consider different operating policies and changes to model parameters and then to observe the impact of the changes on output measures such as profit or service level.

At this point, we conducted a series of simulation experiments by repeating the Butler inventory simulation with replenishment levels of 110, 120, 130 and 140 units. The average monthly net profits and the service levels are shown in Table 12.9. The highest monthly net profit of €4575 occurs with a replenishment level of $Q = 120$. The associated service level is 98.6 per cent. On the basis of these results, Butler selected a replenishment level of $Q = 120$.

Experimental simulation studies, such as this one for Butler's inventory policy, can help identify good operating policies and decisions. Butler's management used simulation to choose a replenishment level of 120 for its home ventilation fan. With the simulation model in place, management can also explore the sensitivity of this decision to some of the model parameters. For instance, we assigned a shortage cost of €30 for any customer demand not met. With this shortage cost, the replenishment level was $Q = 120$ and the service level was 98.6 per cent. If management felt a more appropriate shortage cost was €10 per unit, running the simulation again using €10 as the shortage cost would be a simple matter.

Problem 10 gives you a chance to develop a different simulation model.

We mentioned earlier that simulation is not an optimization technique. Even though we used simulation to choose a replenishment level, it does not guarantee that this choice is optimal. All possible replenishment levels were not tested. Perhaps a manager

Figure 12.7 Excel Worksheet for the Butler Inventory Problem

EXCEL *file*

BUTLER

	A	B	C	D	E	F	G	H
1	**Butler Inventory**							
2								
3	Gross Profit per Unit		€50					
4	Holding Cost per Unit		€15					
5	Shortage Cost per Unit		€30					
6								
7	**Replenishment Level**		100					
8								
9	**Demand (Normal Distribution)**							
10	Mean	100						
11	Std Deviation	20						
12								
13								
14	**Simulation**							
15								
16	Month	Demand	Sales	Gross Profit	Holding Cost	Shortage Cost	Net Profit	
17	1	79	79	€3,950	€315	€0	€3,635	
18	2	111	100	€5,000	€0	€330	€4,670	
19	3	93	93	€4,650	€105	€0	€4,545	
20	4	100	100	€5,000	€0	€0	€5,000	
21	5	118	100	€5,000	€0	€540	€4,460	
312	296	89	89	€4,450	€165	€0	€4,285	
313	297	91	91	€4,550	€135	€0	€4,415	
314	298	122	100	€5,000	€0	€660	€4,340	
315	299	93	93	€4,650	€105	€0	€4,545	
316	300	126	100	€5,000	€0	€780	€4,220	
317								
318	**Totals**	30,181	27,917		**Summary Statistics**			
319					Mean Profit		€4,293	
320					Standard Deviation		€658	
321					Minimum Profit		(€206)	
322					Maximum Profit		€5,000	
323					Service Level		92.5%	
324								

would like to consider additional simulation runs with replenishment levels of $Q = 115$ and $Q = 125$ to search for an even better inventory policy. Also, we have no guarantee that with another set of 300 randomly generated demand values that the replenishment level with the highest profit would not change. However, with a large number of simulation trials, we should find a good and, at least, near optimal solution. The *Management Science in Action*, Petroleum Distribution in the Gulf of Mexico, describes a simulation application for 15 petroleum companies in the state of Florida.

Table 12.9 Butler Inventory Simulation Results for 300 Trials

Replenishment Level	Average Net Profit (€)	Service Level (%)
100	4293	92.5
110	4524	96.5
120	4575	98.6
130	4519	99.6
140	4399	99.9

MANAGEMENT SCIENCE IN ACTION

Petroleum Distribution in the Gulf Of Mexico

Domestic suppliers who operate oil refineries along the Gulf Coast are helping to satisfy Florida's increasing demand for refined petroleum products. Barge fleets, operated either by independent shipping companies or by the petroleum companies themselves, are used to transport more than 20 different petroleum products to 15 Florida petroleum companies. The petroleum products are loaded at refineries in Texas, Louisiana and Mississippi and are discharged at tank terminals concentrated in Tampa, Port Everglades and Jacksonville.

Barges operate under three types of contracts between the fleet operator and the client petroleum company:

- The client assumes total control of a barge and uses it for trips between its own refinery and one or more discharging ports.
- The client is guaranteed a certain volume will be moved during the contract period. Schedules vary considerably depending upon the customer's needs and the fleet operator's capabilities.
- The client hires a barge for a single trip.

A simulation model was developed to analyze the complex process of operating barge fleets in the Gulf of Mexico. An appropriate probability distribution was used to simulate requests for shipments by the petroleum companies. Additional probability distributions were used to simulate the travel times depending upon the size and type of barge. Using this information, the simulation model was used to track barge loading times, barge discharge times, barge utilization and total cost.

Analysts used simulation runs with a variety of what-if scenarios to answer questions about the petroleum distribution system and to make recommendations for improving the efficiency of the operation. Simulation helped determine the following:

- The optimal trade-off between fleet utilization and on-time delivery.
- The recommended fleet size.
- The recommended barge capacities.
- The best service contract structure to balance the trade-off between customer service and delivery cost.

Implementation of the simulation-based recommendations demonstrated a significant improvement in the operation and a significant lowering of petroleum distribution costs.

Based on E.D. Chajakis, 'Sophisticated Crude Transportation', *OR/MS Today* (December 1997): 30–34.

12.3 Queuing Simulation

The simulation models discussed thus far have been based on independent trials in which the results for one trial do not affect what happens in subsequent trials. In this sense, the system being modelled does not change or evolve over time. Simulation models such as these are referred to as **static simulation models**. In this section, we develop a simulation model of a queuing system where the state of the system, including the number of customers in the queue and whether the service facility is busy or idle, changes or evolves over time. To incorporate time into the simulation model, we use a simulation clock to record the time that each customer arrives for service as well as the time that each customer completes service. Simulation models that must take into account how the system changes or evolves over time are referred to as **dynamic simulation models**. In situations where the arrivals and departures of customers are events that occur at *discrete* points in time, the simulation model is also referred to as a **discrete-event simulation model**.

In Chapter 11, we presented formulas that could be used to compute the steady-state operating characteristics of a queue, including the average waiting time, the average number of units in the queue, the probability of queuing and so on. In most cases, the queuing formulas were based on specific assumptions about the probability distribution for arrivals, the probability distribution for service times, the queue discipline and so on. Simulation, as an alternative for studying queue, is more flexible. In applications where the assumptions required by the queuing formulas are not reasonable, simulation may be the only feasible approach to studying the queuing system. In this section we discuss the simulation of the waiting line for the Hong Kong Savings Bank automated teller machine (ATM).

Hong Kong Savings Bank ATM Queuing System

Suppose that Hong Kong Savings Bank (HKSB) will open several new branch banks during the coming year. Each new branch is designed to have one automated teller machine (ATM). A concern is that during busy periods several customers may have to wait to use the ATM. This concern prompted the bank to undertake a study of the ATM queuing system. The bank's vice president wants to determine whether one ATM at each branch will be sufficient. The bank established service guidelines for its ATM system stating that the average customer waiting time for an ATM should be one minute or less. Let us show how a simulation model can be used to study the ATM queue at a particular branch.

Customer Arrival Times

One probabilistic input to the ATM simulation model is the arrival times of customers who use the ATM. In queuing simulations, arrival times are determined by randomly generating the time between two successive arrivals, referred to as the *interarrival time*. For the branch bank being studied, the customer interarrival times are assumed to be uniformly distributed between zero and five minutes as shown in Figure 12.8. With r denoting a random number between zero and one, an interarrival time for two successive customers can be simulated by using the formula for generating values from a uniform probability distribution.

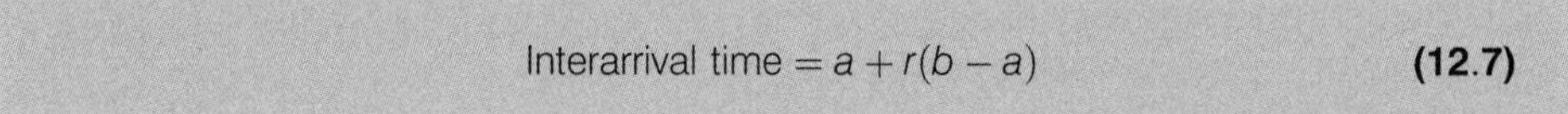

$$\text{Interarrival time} = a + r(b - a) \qquad \textbf{(12.7)}$$

Figure 12.8 Uniform Probability Distribution of Interarrival Times for the ATM Queuing System

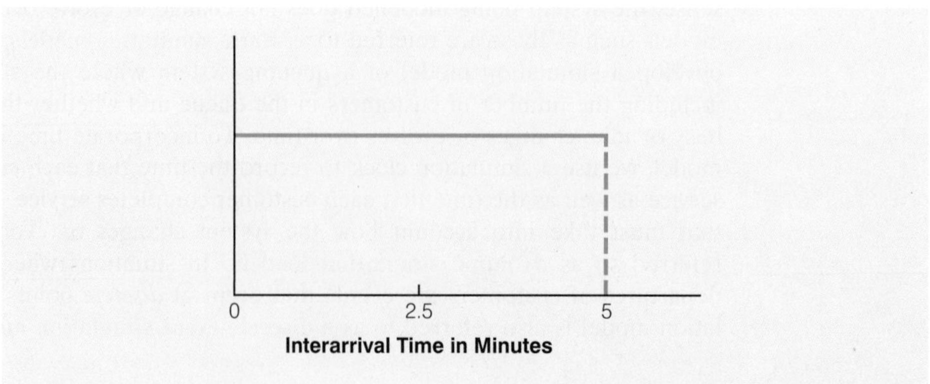

where

r = random number between 0 and 1
a = minimum interarrival time
b = maximum interarrival time

A uniform probability distribution of interarrival times is used here to illustrate the simulation computations. Actually, any interarrival time probability distribution can be assumed, and the logic of the waiting line simulation model will not change.

For the HKSB ATM system, the minimum interarrival time is a = zero minutes, and the maximum interarrival time is b = five minutes; therefore, the formula for generating an interarrival time is:

$$\text{Interarrival time} = 0 + r(5 - 0) = 5r \quad \textbf{(12.8)}$$

Assume that the simulation run begins at time = 0 and the first random number of $r = 0.2804$ generates an interarrival time of 5(0.2804) = 1.4 minutes for customer 1. Thus, customer 1 arrives 1.4 minutes after the simulation run begins. A second random number of $r = 0.2598$ generates an interarrival time of 5(0.2598) = 1.3 minutes, indicating that customer 2 arrives 1.3 minutes after customer 1. Thus, customer 2 arrives 1.4 + 1.3 = 2.7 minutes after the simulation begins. Continuing, a third random number of $r = 0.9802$ indicates that customer 3 arrives 4.9 minutes after customer 2, which is 7.6 minutes after the simulation begins.

Customer Service Times

Another probabilistic input in the ATM simulation model is the service time, which is the time a customer spends using the ATM machine. Past data from similar ATMs indicate that a normal probability distribution with a mean of two minutes and a standard deviation of 0.5 minutes, as shown in Figure 12.9, can be used to describe service times. As discussed in Sections 12.1 and 12.2, values from a normal probability distribution with mean 2 and standard deviation 0.5 can be generated using the Excel function = NORMINV(RAND(),2,0.5). For example, the random number of 0.7257 generates a customer service time of 2.3 minutes.

Simulation Model

The probabilistic inputs to the ATM simulation model are the interarrival time and the service time. The controllable input is the number of ATMs available. The key results will consist of various operating characteristics such as the probability of waiting, the average waiting time, the maximum waiting time and so on.

Figure 12.9 Normal Probability Distribution of Service Times for the ATM Queuing System

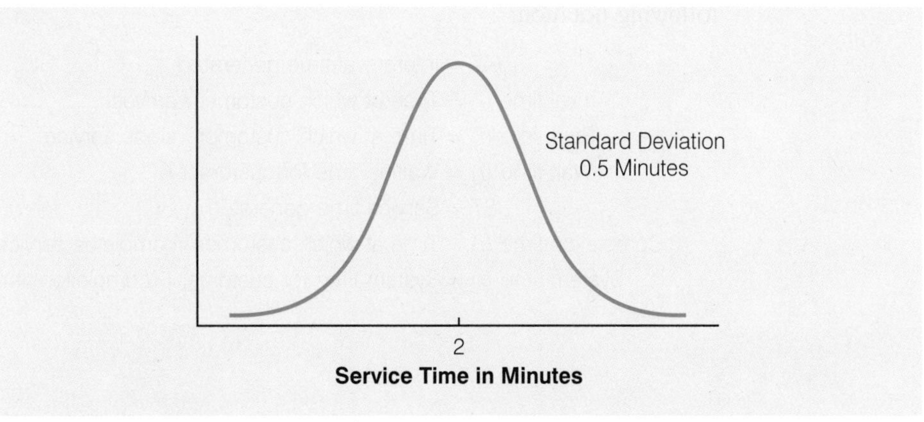

Figure 12.10 Flowchart of the HKSB ATM Waiting Line Simulation

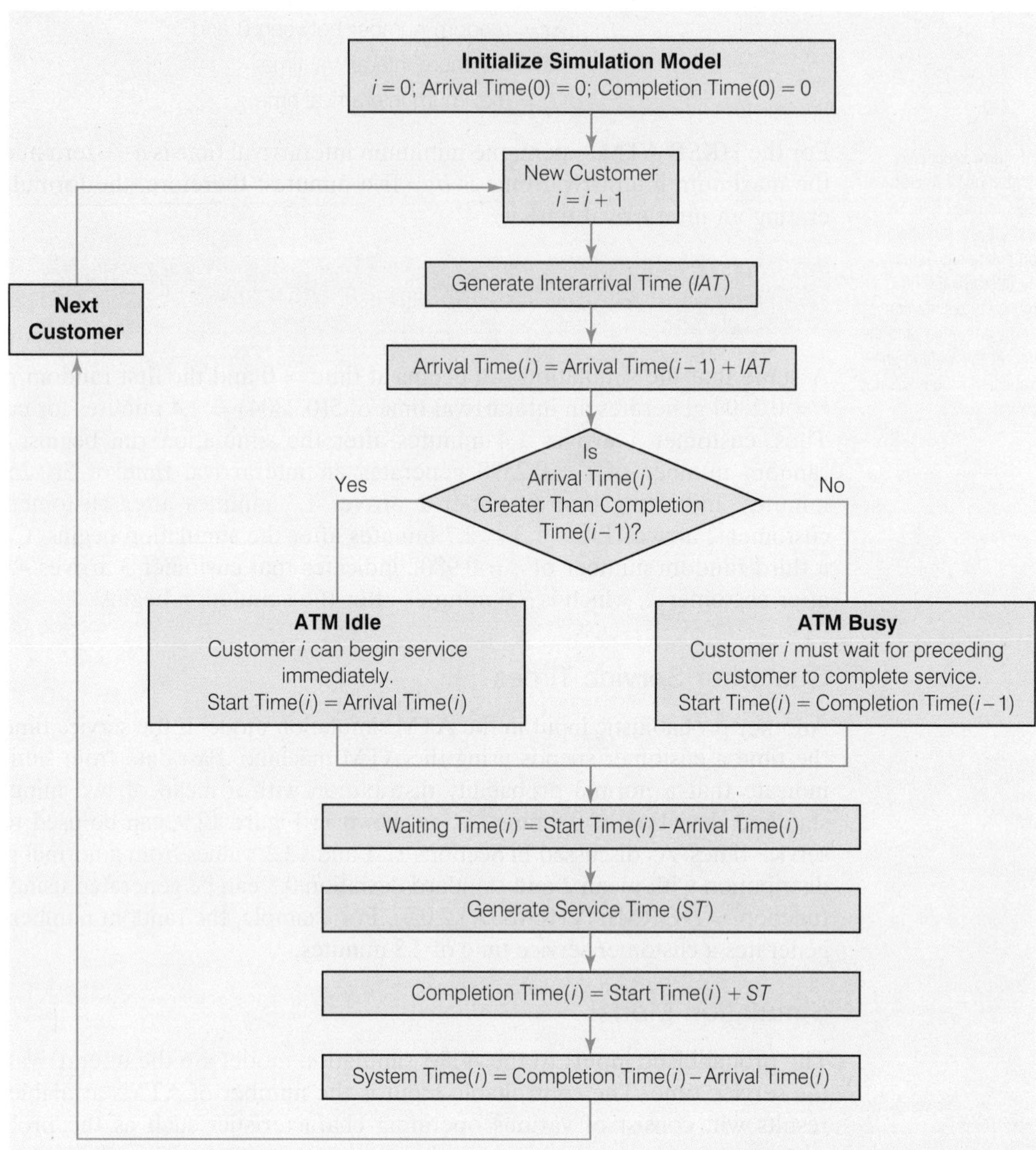

Figure 12.10 shows a flowchart that defines the sequence of logical and mathematical operations required to simulate the ATM system. The flowchart uses the following notation:

IAT = Interarrival time generated
Arrival time (*i*) = Time at which customer *i* arrives
Start time (*i*) = Time at which customer *i* starts service
Wait time (*i*) = Waiting time for customer *i*
ST = Service time generated
Completion time (*i*) = Time at which customer *i* completes service
System time (*i*) = System time for customer *i* (completion time – arrival time)

Referring to Figure 12.10, we see that the simulation is initialized in the first block of the flowchart. Then a new customer arriving is simulated. An interarrival time is generated to determine the time since the preceding customer arrived.[2] The arrival time for the new customer is then calculated by adding the interarrival time to the arrival time of the preceding customer.

The decision rule for deciding whether the ATM is idle or busy is the most difficult aspect of the logic in a queuing simulation model.

The arrival time for the new customer must be compared to the completion time of the preceding customer to determine whether the ATM is idle or busy. If the arrival time of the new customer is greater than the completion time of the preceding customer, the preceding customer will have finished service prior to the arrival of the new customer. In this case, the ATM will be idle, and the new customer can begin service immediately. The service start time for the new customer is equal to the arrival time of the new customer. However, if the arrival time for the new customer is not greater than the completion time of the preceding customer, the new customer arrived before the preceding customer finished service. In this case, the ATM is busy; the new customer must wait to use the ATM until the preceding customer completes service. The service start time for the new customer is equal to the completion time of the preceding customer.

Note that the time the new customer has to wait to use the ATM is the difference between the customer's service start time and the customer's arrival time. At this point, the customer is ready to use the ATM, and the simulation run continues with the generation of the customer's service time. The time at which the customer begins service plus the service time generated determine the customer's completion time. Finally, the total time the customer spends in the system is the difference between the customer's service completion time and the customer's arrival time. At this point, the computations are complete for the current customer, and the simulation continues with the next customer. The simulation is continued until a specified number of customers have been served by the ATM.

Simulation results for the first ten customers are shown in Table 12.10. We discuss the computations for the first three customers to illustrate the logic of the simulation model and to show how the information in Table 12.10 was developed.

Table 12.10 Simulation Results for Ten ATM Customers

Customer	Interarrival Time	Arrival Time	Service Start Time	Waiting Time	Service Time	Completion Time	Time in System
1	1.4	1.4	1.4	0.0	2.3	3.7	2.3
2	1.3	2.7	3.7	1.0	1.5	5.2	2.5
3	4.9	7.6	7.6	0.0	2.2	9.8	2.2
4	3.5	11.1	11.1	0.0	2.5	12.6	2.5
5	0.7	11.8	12.6	1.8	1.8	15.4	3.6
6	2.8	14.6	15.4	0.8	2.4	17.8	3.2
7	2.1	16.7	17.8	1.1	2.1	19.9	3.2
8	0.6	17.3	19.9	2.6	1.8	21.7	4.4
9	2.5	19.8	21.7	1.9	2.0	23.7	3.9
10	1.9	21.7	23.7	2.0	2.3	26.0	4.3
Totals	21.7			11.2	20.9		32.1
Averages	2.17			1.12	2.09		3.21

[2]For the first customer, the interarrival time determines the time since the simulation started. Thus, the first interarrival time determines the time the first customer arrives.

Customer 1

- An interarrival time of $IAT = 1.4$ minutes is generated.
- Because the simulation run begins at time 0, the arrival time for customer 1 is $0 + 1.4 = 1.4$ minutes.
- Customer 1 may begin service immediately with a start time of 1.4 minutes.
- The waiting time for customer 1 is the start time minus the arrival time: $1.4 - 1.4 = 0$ minutes.
- A service time of $ST = 2.3$ minutes is generated for customer 1.
- The completion time for customer 1 is the start time plus the service time: $1.4 + 2.3 = 3.7$ minutes.
- The time in the system for customer 1 is the completion time minus the arrival time: $3.7 - 1.4 = 2.3$ minutes.

Customer 2

- An interarrival time of $IAT = 1.3$ minutes is generated.
- Because the arrival time of customer 1 is 1.4, the arrival time for customer 2 is $1.4 + 1.3 = 2.7$ minutes.
- Because the completion time of customer 1 is 3.7 minutes, the arrival time of customer 2 is not greater than the completion time of customer 1; so, the ATM is busy when customer 2 arrives.
- Customer 2 must wait for customer 1 to complete service before beginning service. Customer 1 completes service at 3.7 minutes, which becomes the start time for customer 2.
- The waiting time for customer 2 is the start time minus the arrival time: $3.7 - 2.7 = 1$ minute.
- A service time of $ST = 1.5$ minutes is generated for customer 2.
- The completion time for customer 2 is the start time plus the service time: $3.7 + 1.5 = 5.2$ minutes.
- The time in the system for customer 2 is the completion time minus the arrival time: $5.2 - 2.7 = 2.5$ minutes.

Customer 3

- An interarrival time of $IAT = 4.9$ minutes is generated.
- Because the arrival time of customer 2 was 2.7 minutes, the arrival time for customer 3 is $2.7 + 4.9 = 7.6$ minutes.
- The completion time of customer 2 is 5.2 minutes, so the arrival time for customer 3 is greater than the completion time of customer 2. Thus, the ATM is idle when customer 3 arrives.
- Customer 3 begins service immediately with a start time of 7.6 minutes.
- The waiting time for customer 3 is the start time minus the arrival time: $7.6 - 7.6 = 0$ minutes.
- A service time of ST=2.2 minutes is generated for customer 3.
- The completion time for customer 3 is the start time plus the service time: $7.6 + 2.2 = 9.8$ minutes.
- The time in the system for customer 3 is the completion time minus the arrival time: $9.8 - 7.6 = 2.2$ minutes.

Using the totals in Table 12.10, we can calculate an average waiting time for the ten customers of 11.2/10 = 1.12 minutes, and an average time in the system of 32.1/10 = 3.21 minutes. Table 12.10 shows that seven of the ten customers had to wait. The total time for the ten-customer simulation is given by the completion time of the tenth customer: 26.0 minutes. However, we realize that a simulation for ten customers is much too short a period to draw any firm conclusions about the operation of the waiting line.

Simulation of the ATM Problem

Using an Excel worksheet, we simulated the operation of the ATM system for 1000 customers. The worksheet used to carry out the simulation is shown in Figure 12.11. Note that the simulation results for customers 6 through 995 have been hidden so that the results can be shown in a reasonably sized figure. If desired, the rows for these customers can be shown and the simulation results displayed for all 1000 customers.

Ultimately, summary statistics will be collected in order to describe the results of 1000 customers. Before collecting the summary statistics, let us point out that most

Figure 12.11 Excel Worksheet for the HKSB with One ATM

EXCEL *file*

HKSB1

	A	B	C	D	E	F	G	H
1	**Hong Kong Savings Bank with One ATM**							
2								
3	**Interarrival Times (Uniform Distribution)**							
4	Smallest Value	0						
5	Largest Value	5						
6								
7	**Service Times (Normal Distribution)**							
8	Mean	2						
9	Std Deviation	0.5						
10								
11								
12	**Simulation**							
13								
14		Interarrival	Arrival	Service	Waiting	Service	Completion	Time
15	Customer	Time	Time	Start Time	Time	Time	Time	in System
16	1	1.4	1.4	1.4	0.0	2.3	3.7	2.3
17	2	1.3	2.7	3.7	1.0	1.5	5.2	2.5
18	3	4.9	7.6	7.6	0.0	2.2	9.8	2.2
19	4	3.5	11.1	11.1	0.0	2.5	13.6	2.5
20	5	0.7	11.8	13.6	1.8	1.8	15.4	3.6
1011	996	0.5	2496.8	2498.1	1.3	0.6	2498.7	1.9
1012	997	0.2	2497.0	2498.7	1.7	2.0	2500.7	3.7
1013	998	2.7	2499.7	2500.7	1.0	1.8	2502.5	2.8
1014	999	3.7	2503.4	2503.4	0.0	2.4	2505.8	2.4
1015	1000	4.0	2507.4	2507.4	0.0	1.9	2509.3	1.9
1016								
1017		**Summary Statistics**						
1018		Number Waiting			549			
1019		Probability of Waiting			0.6100			
1020		Average Waiting Time			1.59			
1021		Maximum Waiting Time			13.5			
1022		Utilization of ATM			0.7860			
1023		Number Waiting > 1 Min			393			
1024		Probability of Waiting > 1 Min			0.4367			
1025								

Figure 12.12 Histogram Showing the Waiting Time for 900 ATM Customers

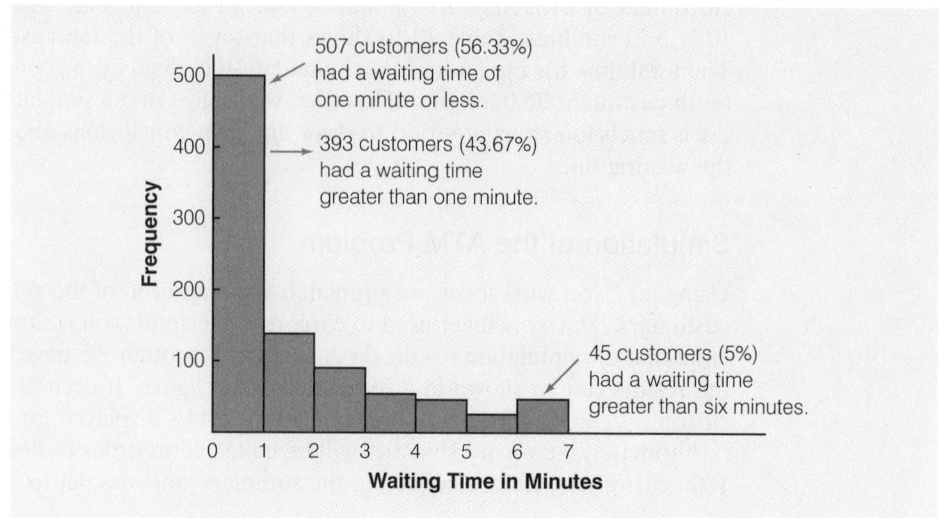

simulation studies of dynamic systems focus on the operation of the system during its long-run or steady-state operation. To ensure that the effect of start-up conditions are not included in the steady-state calculations, a dynamic simulation model is usually run for a specified period without collecting any data about the operation of the system. The length of the start-up period can vary depending on the application. For the ATM simulation, we treated the results for the first 100 customers as the start-up period. Thus, the summary statistics shown in Figure 12.11 are for the 900 customers arriving during the steady-state period.

The summary statistics show that 549 of the 900 ATM customers had to wait. This result provides a 549/900 = 0.61 probability that a customer will have to wait for service. In other words, approximately 61 per cent of the customers will have to wait because the ATM is in use. The average waiting time is 1.59 minutes per customer with at least one customer waiting the maximum time of 12.5 minutes. The utilization rate of 0.7860 indicates that the ATM is in use 78.6 per cent of the time. Finally, 393 of the 900 customers had to wait more than 1 minute (43.67 per cent of all customers). A histogram of waiting times for the 900 customers is shown in Figure 12.12. This figure shows that 45 customers (5 per cent) had a waiting time greater than 6 minutes.

The simulation supports the conclusion that the branch will have a busy ATM system. With an average customer wait time of 1.59 minutes, the branch does not satisfy the bank's customer service guideline. This branch is a good candidate for installation of a second ATM.

Simulation with Two ATMs

We extended the simulation model to the case of two ATMs. For the second ATM we also assume that the service time is normally distributed with a mean of two minutes and a standard deviation of 0.5 minutes. Table 12.11 shows the simulation results for the first ten customers. In comparing the two-ATM system results in Table 12.11 with the single ATM simulation results shown in Table 12.10, we see that two additional columns are needed. These two columns show when each ATM becomes available for customer service. We assume that, when a new customer arrives, the customer will be served by the ATM that frees up first. When the simulation begins, the first customer is assigned to ATM 1.

Table 12.11 Simulation Results for Ten Customers for a Two-ATM System

Customer	Interarrival Time	Arrival Time	Service Start Time	Waiting Time	Service Time	Completion Time in System	Time in System	Time Available ATM 1	Time Available ATM 2
1	1.7	1.7	1.7	0.0	2.1	3.8	2.1	3.8	0.0
2	0.7	2.4	2.4	0.0	2.0	4.4	2.0	3.8	4.4
3	2.0	4.4	4.4	0.0	1.4	5.8	1.4	5.8	4.4
4	0.1	4.5	4.5	0.0	0.9	5.4	0.9	5.8	5.4
5	4.6	9.1	9.1	0.0	2.2	11.3	2.2	5.8	11.3
6	1.3	10.4	10.4	0.0	1.6	12.0	1.6	12.0	11.3
7	0.6	11.0	11.3	0.3	1.7	12.0	2.0	12.0	12.0
8	0.3	11.3	12.0	0.7	2.2	14.2	2.9	14.2	12.0
9	3.4	14.7	14.7	0.0	2.9	17.6	2.9	14.2	17.6
10	0.1	14.8	14.8	0.0	2.8	17.6	2.8	17.6	17.6
Totals	14.8			1.0	19.8		20.8		
Averages	1.48			0.1	1.98		2.08		

Table 12.11 shows that customer 7 is the first customer who has to wait to use an ATM. We describe how customers 6, 7 and 8 are processed to show how the logic of the simulation run for two ATMs differs from that with a single ATM.

Customer 6

- An interarrival time of 1.3 minutes is generated, and customer 6 arrives $9.1 + 1.3 = 10.4$ minutes into the simulation.
- From the customer 5 row, we see that ATM 1 frees up at 5.8 minutes, and ATM 2 will free up at 11.3 minutes into the simulation. Because ATM 1 is free, customer 6 does not wait and begins service on ATM 1 at the arrival time of 10.4 minutes.
- A service time of 1.6 minutes is generated for customer 6. So customer 6 has a completion time of $10.4 + 1.6 = 12.0$ minutes.
- The time ATM 1 will next become available is set at 12.0 minutes; the time available for ATM 2 remains 11.3 minutes.

Customer 7

- An interarrival time of 0.6 minute is generated, and customer 7 arrives $10.4 + 0.6 = 11.0$ minutes into the simulation.
- From the previous row, we see that ATM 1 will not be available until 12.0 minutes, and ATM 2 will not be available until 11.3 minutes. So customer 7 must wait to use an ATM. Because ATM 2 will free up first, customer 7 begins service on that machine at a start time of 11.3 minutes. With an arrival time of 11.0 and a service start time of 11.3, customer 7 experiences a waiting time of $11.3 - 11.0 = 0.3$ minute.
- A service time of 1.7 minutes is generated leading to a completion time of $11.3 + 1.7 = 12.0$ minutes.
- The time available for ATM 2 is updated to 12.0 minutes, and the time available for ATM 1 remains at 12.0 minutes.

Customer 8

- An interarrival time of 0.3 minute is generated, and customer 8 arrives $11.0 + 0.3 = 11.3$ minutes into the simulation.
- From the previous row, we see that ATM 1 will be the first available. So customer 8 starts service on ATM 1 at 12.0 minutes resulting in a waiting time of $12.0 - 11.3 = 0.7$ minute.
- A service time of 2.2 minutes is generated resulting in a completion time of $12.0 + 2.2 = 14.2$ minutes and a system time of $0.7 + 2.2 = 2.9$ minutes.
- The time available for ATM 1 is updated to 14.2 minutes, and the time available for ATM 2 remains at 12.0 minutes.

Worksheets for the one-ATM and two-ATM systems are available on the online platform that accompanies this text.

From the totals in Table 12.11, we see that the average waiting time for these ten customers is only $1.0/10 = 0.1$ minute. Of course, a much longer simulation will be necessary before any conclusions can be drawn.

Simulation Results with Two ATMs

The Excel worksheet that we used to conduct a simulation for 1000 customers using two ATMs is shown in Figure 12.13. Results for the first 100 customers were discarded to account for the start-up period. With two ATMs, the number of customers who had to wait was reduced from 549 to 78. This reduction provides a $78/900 = 0.0867$ probability that a customer will have to wait for service when two

Figure 12.13 Excel Worksheet for the Hong Kong Savings Bank with Two ATMs

EXCEL *file*

HKSB2

	A	B	C	D	E	F	G	H	I	J	K
1	**Hong Kong Savings Bank with Two ATMs**										
2											
3	**Interarrival Times (Uniform Distribution)**										
4	Smallest Value	0									
5	Largest Value	5									
6											
7	**Service Times (Normal Distribution)**										
8	Mean	2									
9	Std Deviation	0.5									
10											
11											
12	**Simulation**										
13											
14		Interarrival	Arrival	Service	Waiting	Service	Completion	Time	Time Available		
15	Customer	Time	Time	Start Time	Time	Time	Time	in System	ATM 1	ATM 2	
16	1	1.7	1.7	1.7	0.0	2.1	3.8	2.1	3.8	0.0	
17	2	0.7	2.4	2.4	0.0	2.0	4.4	2.0	3.8	4.4	
18	3	2.0	4.4	4.4	0.0	1.4	5.8	1.4	5.8	4.4	
19	4	0.1	4.5	4.5	0.0	0.9	5.4	0.9	5.8	5.4	
20	5	4.6	9.1	9.1	0.0	2.2	11.3	2.2	5.8	11.3	
1011	996	3.3	2483.2	2483.2	0.0	2.2	2485.4	2.2	2485.4	2482.1	
1012	997	4.5	2487.7	2487.7	0.0	1.9	2489.6	1.9	2485.4	2489.6	
1013	998	3.8	2491.5	2491.5	0.0	3.2	2494.7	3.2	2494.7	2489.6	
1014	999	0.0	2491.5	2491.5	0.0	2.4	2493.9	2.4	2494.7	2493.9	
1015	1000	2.6	2494.1	2494.1	0.0	2.8	2496.9	2.8	2494.7	2496.9	
1016											
1017		**Summary Statistics**									
1018		Number Waiting			78						
1019		Probability of Waiting			0.0867						
1020		Average Waiting Time			0.07						
1021		Maximum Waiting Time			2.9						
1022		Utilization of ATMs			0.4084						
1023		Number Waiting > 1 Min			23						
1024		Probability of Waiting > 1 Min			0.0256						
1025											

ATMs are used. The two-ATM system also reduced the average waiting time to 0.07 minutes (4.2 seconds) per customer. The maximum waiting time was reduced from 12.5 to 2.9 minutes, and each ATM was in use 40.84 percent of the time. Finally, only 23 of the 900 customers had to wait more than one minute for an ATM to become available. Thus, only 2.56 per cent of customers had to wait more than one minute. The simulation results provide evidence that Hong Kong Savings Bank needs to expand to the two-ATM system.

The simulation models that we developed can now be used to study the ATM operation at other branch banks. In each case, assumptions must be made about the appropriate interarrival time and service time probability distributions. However, once appropriate assumptions have been made, the same simulation models can be used to determine the operating characteristics of the ATM queuing system. The *Management Science in Action*, Preboard Screening at Vancouver International Airport, describes another use of simulation for a queueing system.

NOTES AND COMMENTS

1 The ATM waiting line model was based on uniformly distributed interarrival times and normally distributed service times. One advantage of simulation is its flexibility in accommodating a variety of different probability distributions. For instance, if we believe an exponential distribution is more appropriate for interarrival times, the ATM simulation could be repeated by simply changing the way the interarrival times are generated.

2 At the beginning of this section, we defined *discrete-event simulation* as involving a dynamic system that evolves over time. The simulation computations focus on the sequence of events as they occur at discrete points in time. In the ATM queuing example, customer arrivals and the customer service completions were the discrete events. Referring to the arrival times and completion times in Table 12.10, we see that the first five discrete events for the ATM waiting line simulation were as follows:

Event	Time
Customer 1 arrives	1.4
Customer 2 arrives	2.7
Customer 1 finished	3.7
Customer 2 finished	5.2
Customer 3 arrives	7.6

3 We did not keep track of the number of customers in the ATM waiting line as we carried out the ATM simulation computations on a customer-by-customer basis. However, we can determine the average number of customers in the waiting line from other information in the simulation output. The following relationship is valid for any waiting line system:

$$\text{Average number in waiting line} = \frac{\text{Total waiting time}}{\text{Total time of simulation}}$$

For the system with one ATM, the 100th customer completed service at 247.8 minutes into the simulation. Thus, the total time of the simulation for the next 900 customers was $2509.3 - 247.8 = 2261.5$ minutes. The average waiting time was 1.59 minutes. During the simulation, the 900 customers had a total waiting time of $900(1.59) = 1431$ minutes. Therefore, the average number of customers in the waiting line is

$$\begin{aligned}\text{Average number in waiting line} &= 1431/2261.5 \\ &= 0.63 \text{ customer}\end{aligned}$$

MANAGEMENT SCIENCE IN ACTION

Preboard Screening at Vancouver International Airport

Following the September 11, 2001 terrorist attacks in the United States, long lines at airport security checkpoints have become commonplace. In order to reduce passenger waiting time, the Vancouver International Airport Authority teamed up with students and faculty at the University of British Columbia's Centre for Operations Excellence (COE) to build a simulation model of the airport's preboard screening security checkpoints. The goal was to use the simulation model to help achieve acceptable service standards.

Prior to building the simulation model, students from the COE observed the flow of passengers through the screening process and collected data on the service time at each process step. In addition to service time data, passenger demand data provided input to the simulation model. Two triangular probability distributions were used to simulate passenger arrivals at the preboarding facilities. For flights to Canadian destinations a 90–40–20 triangle was used. This distribution assumes that, for each flight, the first passenger will arrive at the screening checkpoint 90 minutes before departure, the last passenger will arrive 20 minutes before departure, and the most likely arrival time is 40 minutes before departure. For international flights a 150–80–20 triangle was used.

Output statistics from the simulation model provided information concerning resource utilization, waiting line lengths and the time passengers spend in the system. The simulation model provided information concerning the number of personnel needed to process 90 per cent of the passengers with a waiting time of ten minutes or less. Ultimately the airport authority was able to design and staff the preboarding checkpoints in such a fashion that waiting times for 90 per cent of the passengers were a maximum of ten minutes.

Based on Derek Atkins *et al.*, 'Right on Queue', *OR/MS Today* (April 2003): 26–29.

12.4 Other Simulation Issues

Because simulation is one of the most widely used quantitative analysis techniques, various software tools have been developed to help analysts implement a simulation model on a computer. In this section we comment on the software available and discuss some issues involved in verifying and validating a simulation model. We close the section with a discussion of some of the advantages and disadvantages of using simulation to study a real system.

Computer Implementation

The use of spreadsheets for simulation has grown rapidly in recent years, and third-party software vendors have developed spreadsheet add-ins that make building simulation models on a spreadsheet much easier. These add-in packages provide an easy facility for generating random values from a variety of probability distributions and provide a rich array of statistics describing the simulation output. Two popular spreadsheet add-ins are Crystal Ball from Decisioneering and @RISK from Palisade Corporation. Although spreadsheets can be a valuable tool for some simulation studies, they are generally limited to smaller, less complex systems.

With the growth of simulation applications, both users of simulation and software developers began to realize that computer simulations have many common features: model development, generating values from probability distributions, maintaining a record of what happens during the simulation and recording and summarizing the simulation output. A variety of special-purpose simulation packages are available, including GPSS®, SIMSCRIPT®, SLAM® and Arena®. These packages have built-in simulation clocks, simplified methods for generating probabilistic inputs and procedures for collecting and summarizing the simulation output. Special-purpose simulation packages enable quantitative analysts to simplify the process of developing and implementing the simulation model. Indeed, Arena 6.0 was used to develop the simulation model described in the *Management Science in Action*, Preboard Screening at Vancouver International Airport.

Simulation models can also be developed using general-purpose computer programming languages such as BASIC, FORTRAN, PASCAL, C and C++. The disadvantage of using these languages is that special simulation procedures are not built in. One command in a special-purpose simulation package often performs the computations and record-keeping tasks that would require several BASIC, FORTRAN, PASCAL, C or C++ statements to duplicate. The advantage of using a general-purpose programming language is that they offer greater flexibility in terms of being able to model more complex systems.

The computational and record-keeping aspects of simulation models are assisted by special simulation software packages. The packages ease the tasks of developing a computer simulation model.

To decide which software to use, an analyst will have to consider the relative merits of a spreadsheet, a special-purpose simulation package and a general-purpose computer programming language. The goal is to select the method that is easy to use while still providing an adequate representation of the system being studied.

Verification and Validation

An important aspect of any simulation study involves confirming that the simulation model accurately describes the real system. Inaccurate simulation models cannot be expected to provide worthwhile information. So, before using simulation results to draw conclusions about a real system, we have to take steps to verify and validate the simulation model.

Verification is the process of determining that the computer procedure that performs the simulation calculations is logically correct. Verification is largely a debugging task to make sure that no errors are in the computer procedure that implements the simulation. In some cases, an analyst may compare computer results for a limited number of events with independent hand calculations. In other cases, tests may be performed to verify that the probabilistic inputs are being generated correctly and that the output from the simulation model seems reasonable. The verification step is not complete until the user develops a high degree of confidence that the computer procedure is error free.

Validation is the process of ensuring that the simulation model provides an accurate representation of a real system. Validation requires an agreement among analysts and managers that the logic and the assumptions used in the design of the simulation model accurately reflect how the real system operates. The first phase of the validation process is done prior to, or in conjunction with, the development of the computer procedure for the simulation process. Validation continues after the computer program has been developed with the analyst reviewing the simulation output to see whether the simulation results closely approximate the performance of the real system. If possible, the output of the simulation model is compared to the output of an existing real system to make sure that the simulation output closely approximates the performance of the real system. If this form of validation is not possible, an analyst can experiment with the simulation model and have one or more individuals experienced with the operation of the real system review the simulation output to determine whether it is a reasonable approximation of what would be obtained with the real system under similar conditions.

Verification and validation are not tasks to be taken lightly. They are key steps in any simulation study and are necessary to ensure that decisions and conclusions based on the simulation results are appropriate for the real system.

Advantages and Disadvantages of Using Simulation

The primary advantages of simulation are that it is easy to understand and that the methodology can be used to model and learn about the behaviour of complex systems that would be difficult, if not impossible, to deal with analytically. Simulation models are flexible; they can be used to describe systems without requiring the assumptions that are often required by mathematical models. In general, the larger the number of probabilistic inputs a system has, the more likely that a simulation model will provide the best approach for studying the system. Another advantage of simulation is that a simulation model provides a convenient experimental laboratory for the real system. Changing assumptions or operating policies in the simulation model and rerunning it can provide results that help predict how such changes will affect the operation of the real system. Experimenting directly with a real system is often not feasible.

Using simulation, we can ask what-if questions and project how the real system will behave. Although simulation does not guarantee optimality, it will usually provide near-optimal solutions. In addition, simulation models often warn against poor decision strategies by projecting disastrous outcomes such as system failures, large financial losses and so on.

Simulation is not without some disadvantages. For complex systems, the process of developing, verifying and validating a simulation model can be time-consuming and expensive. In addition, each simulation run provides only a sample of how the real system will operate. As such, the summary of the simulation data provides only estimates or approximations about the real system. Consequently, simulation does not guarantee an optimal solution. Nonetheless, the danger of obtaining poor solutions is slight if the analyst exercises good judgement in developing the simulation model and if the simulation process is run long enough under a wide variety of conditions so that the analyst has sufficient data to predict how the real system will operate.

Summary

In this chapter we have introduced simulation modelling:

- Simulation is a popular business technique since it allows for experimenting with a decision situation.
- Simulation does not result in an optimal solution but allows for analysis of alternative decisions and scenarios.
- In practice simulation modelling is computer-based, either through spreadsheet modelling or using dedicated simulation software.
- The development of a simulation model can be complex and time-consuming.

WORKED EXAMPLE

The Government in Malaysia established a network of small regional health clinics which provide basic healthcare services to the local population. Each clinic has been equipped with a variety of medical equipment such as X-ray machines, blood testing equipment and so on. Inevitably given the number of clinics and the level of activity, the medical equipment occasionally malfunctions or requires maintenance and repair. When this happens, a repair technician is called on to carry out a repair and travels out to the clinic affected and repairs the equipment that has malfunctioned. The time taken to repair equipment varies depending on where the clinic is located, the type of equipment that needs repair, the repair required and the availability of spare parts. Some data have been collected. The elapsed time between repairs being needed varies between one and four weeks and the distribution of repair callouts is shown below. So, 50 per cent of callouts for a repair happen one week after the last callout; 30 per cent happen two weeks after the last callout; 10 per cent happen three weeks after the last callout; 10 per cent happen four weeks after the last callout.

Time between repairs (weeks)	% of repair callouts
1	50
2	30
3	10
4	10

The time taken to repair equipment is shown below. 40 per cent of repairs take one day to repair, 40 per cent take two days and 20 per cent take three days.

Time taken to repair equipment (Days)	% of repair callouts
1	40
2	40
3	20

The Health Minister has been receiving complaints from community representatives about the fact that local health care at these clinics is often disrupted or delayed because medical equipment required is waiting for repair. Initial investigations have revealed that one of the factors affecting the time taken to repair equipment is that the repair technician may not carry the necessary spare parts or may not be able to carry out a repair at the clinic because of the lack of the necessary electronic testing equipment to assess exactly what repair is needed. In both cases, the repair technician has to travel back to a central repair depot which adds to the time taken. One option under consideration is equipping the repair technician with a small van that can carry additional spare parts and also carry some of the necessary testing equipment. This would reduce the time taken to carry out some repairs as shown below:

Van option

Time taken to repair equipment (Days)	% of repair callouts
1	80
2	10
3	10

The Health Minister has asked for any advice we can give.

Solution

Clearly, we could do some simple analysis and calculate the effect of the Van option on reducing average repair time. However, this would be quite simplistic and might not give a full picture of the effect. It is probably more useful to build a simple simulation model and simulate the effects of introducing the Van option. We have built an Excel model for the problem which shown is in Figure 12.14.

Figure 12.14 Simulation Model for the Repair Problem

	A	B	C	D	E	F	G	H	I	J	K	L	M	N
1	**Time between repair callouts**					**Repair Time**	**Existing**				**Repair Time Van option**			
2	Probability	Random number range		Weeks		Probability	Random number range		Days		Probability	Random number range		Days
3	0.5	0	0.5	1		0.4	0	0.4	1		0.8	0	0.8	1
4	0.3	0.5	0.8	2		0.4	0.4	0.8	2		0.1	0.8	0.9	2
5	0.1	0.8	0.9	3		0.2	0.8	1	3		0.1	0.9	1	3
6	0.1	0.9	1	4										
7														
8														
9	**Simulation Results**	**Time between callouts**				**Repair Time Existing**				**Repair Time Van option**				
10	Weeks	Actual	%			Days		%		Days		%		
11	1	492	0.49			1	415	0.42		1	804	0.80		
12	2	309	0.31			2	409	0.41		2	91	0.09		
13	3	106	0.11			3	176	0.18		3	105	0.11		
14	4	93	0.09				1000				1000			
15		1000	1											
16						**Total days lost**	1761			**Total days lost**	1301			
17	**Total elapsed time (weeks)**		1800											
18														
19		**Breakdown**	**Time between callouts**		**Repair Time Existing**		**Repair Time New**							
20		1	1		2		1							
21		2	1		1		3							
22		3	2		2		1							
23		4	2		1		1							
24		5	1		1		1							
25		6	3		2		1							
26		7	1		2		1							
1011		992	1		1		1							
1012		993	1		1		1							
1013		994	1		2		1							
1014		995	3		1		1							
1015		996	1		1		1							
1016		997	1		2		1							
1017		998	2		2		1							
1018		999	1		1		1							
1019		1000	2		2		2							

The top part of the spreadsheet shows the data for the problem. First we have the time between repair callouts shown in Cells A1:D6. Note that we have included the random number range for reach of the callout time (Cells B3:C6). Next we show the Existing repair time distribution (Cells F1:I5) and then the repair times with the Van option (Cells K1:N5). The Simulation results are shown from Row 19 onwards. Note that we have simulated 1000 breakdowns and that breakdowns from 8 to 991 are hidden from view to show the first few and last few only. So, the first repair callout is simulated to occur one week after the last callout, will take two days to repair under the existing repair system and one day to repair under the Van option. The second repair callout occurs one week after the first callout, takes one day to repair under the existing system and is simulated to take three days under the Van option. The simulated results have been summarized in Rows 9 to 17. First (Cells A10:C14) we show the aggregated results for the repair callouts. From C11:C14 we see that over the whole simulation of 1000 callouts, 49 per cent of callouts occurred one week after the previous callout, 31 per cent after two weeks, 11 per cent after three weeks and 9 per cent after four weeks. This simulated distribution is pretty close to the actual distribution (Cells A3:A6) and give us confidence that the model is simulating properly. The same can be said for the Existing Repair Time simulation results (Cells F10:F13) and the Van option results (Cells J10:L13).

In Cell G16 we show the total number of days that clinic equipment took to repair under the existing repair system. That is, 1761 days of equipment time was lost due to equipment waiting for repair or being repaired. Under the Van option (Cell K16) we see that this lost time falls to 1301 days. In other words, 460 days of clinic equipment time are made available because of improved repair performance. This is over a period totalling 1800 weeks (Cell C17) which is calculated by summing the simulated Time between callouts. In other words, the Van option would typically save one day of clinic equipment time over a four week period. Clearly using simulation does not allow us to make a specific recommendation. However, we can advise that the Van option would save one day of clinic equipment time over every four week period which presumably would allow the clinics to provide an improved service to their communities. However, the Health Minister will need to weigh up this improvement against the extra cost of providing the van. We can also advise the Minister that the simulation model can easily be adapted to help evaluate other improvement options that may be being considered.

MANAGEMENT SCIENCE IN ACTION

Designing Manufacturing Systems at Mexico's Vilpac

In increasing numbers, US firms are joining diverse geographical and cultural partners in Western Europe, Asia and Mexico to capitalize on each other's advantages and remain competitive in world markets. Mexico, the United States' third largest trading partner, offers a unique opportunity for integrating manufacturing operations. For example, Mexican and US firms have been working together to turn the Mexican truck company, Vilpac, into a world-class manufacturing firm.

The selection of manufacturing configurations and the design of new plants at Vilpac are being guided by a simulation model of the firm's manufacturing operations. A network simulation language, SIMNET II®, has been used to model the manufacturing system that comprises some 95 machines and 1900 parts. Various simulation runs were used to validate the model. When applied to a plant that was producing 20 trucks per day, the simulation model accurately predicted production at 19.8 trucks per day.

The three interrelated modules of the simulation model include operations, corrective maintenance and preventive maintenance. Various components of the model include capabilities for handling changes in customer demand, manufacturing cost, capacity and work-in-process and inventory levels. Experimentation with the model investigated capacity requirements, product-mix effects, new products, inventory policies, product flow, setup times, production planning and control strategies, plant expansion and new plant design. Tangible benefits include an increase in production of 260 per cent, a reduction in work-in-process of 70 per cent and an increase in market share.

Based on J.P. Nuno, D.L. Shunk, J.M. Padillo, and B. Beltran, 'Mexico's Vilpac Truck Company Uses a CIM Implementation to Become a World Class Manufacturer', *Interfaces*, no. 1 (January/February 1993): 59–75.

Problems

Note: Problems 1–8 are designed to give you practise in setting up a simulation model and demonstrating how random numbers can be used to generate values for the probabilistic inputs. These problems, which ask you to provide a small number of simulation trials, can be done with hand calculations. This approach should give you a good understanding of the simulation process, but the simulation results will not be sufficient for you to draw final conclusions or make decisions about the situation. Problems 9–14 are more realistic in that they ask you to generate simulation output(s) for a large number of trials and use the results to draw conclusions about the behaviour of the system being studied. These problems require the use of a computer to carry out the simulation computations. The ability to use Excel or some other spreadsheet package will be necessary when you attempt Problems 9–14.

1 Consider the PortaCom project discussed in Section 12.1

a. An engineer on the product development team believes that first-year sales for the new printer will be 20 000 units. Using estimates of €45 per unit for the direct labour cost and €90 per unit for the parts cost, what is the first-year profit using the engineer's sales estimate?

b. The financial analyst on the product development team is more conservative, indicating that parts cost may well be €100 per unit. In addition, the analyst suggests that a sales volume of 10 000 units is more realistic. Using the most likely value of €45 per unit for the direct labour cost, what is the first-year profit using the financial analyst's estimates?

c. Why is the simulation approach to risk analysis preferable to generating a variety of what-if scenarios such as those suggested by the engineer and the financial analyst?

SELF *test*

2 The management of Madeira Manufacturing Company is considering the introduction of a new product. The fixed cost to begin the production of the product is €30 000. The variable cost for the product is expected to be between €16 and €24 with a most likely value of €20 per unit. The product will sell for €50 per unit. Demand for the product is expected to range from 300 to 2100 units, with 1200 units the most likely demand.

a. Develop the profit model for this product.

b. Provide the base-case, worst-case and best-case analyses.

c. Discuss why simulation would be desirable.

3 Use the random numbers 0.3753, 0.9218, 0.0336, 0.5145 and 0.7000 to generate five simulated values for the PortaCom direct labour cost per unit.

SELF *test*

4 A retail store experiences the following probability distribution for sales of a product.

Sales (units)	0	1	2	3	4	5	6
Probability	0.08	0.12	0.28	0.24	0.14	0.10	0.04

a. Set up intervals of random numbers that can be used to simulate sales.
b. Random numbers generated for the first ten days of a simulation are as follows: 0.4627, 0.8745, 0.4479, 0.6712, 0.4557, 0.8435, 0.2162, 0.1699, 0.1338, 0.2278. What is the sales value generated for each day?
c. What are the total sales over the ten-day period?

SELF *test*

5 The price of a share of a particular stock listed on the Frankfurt Stock Exchange is currently €39. The following probability distribution shows how the price per share is expected to change over a three-month period.

Stock Price Change (€)	Probability
−2	0.05
−1	0.10
0	0.25
+1	0.20
+2	0.20
+3	0.10
+4	0.10

a. Set up intervals of random numbers that can be used to generate the change in stock price over a three-month period.
b. With the current price of €39 per share and the random numbers 0.1091, 0.9407, 0.1941 and 0.8083, simulate the price per share for the next four three-month periods. What is the ending simulated price per share?

SELF *test*

6 A variety of routine maintenance checks are made on commercial aeroplanes prior to each takeoff. One particular maintenance check of an aeroplane's landing gear requires between ten and 18 minutes of a maintenance engineer's time. In fact, the exact time required is uniformly distributed over this interval. As part of a larger simulation model designed to determine total on-ground maintenance time for an aeroplane we will need to simulate the actual time required to perform this maintenance check on the aeroplane's landing gear. Using random numbers of 0.1567, 0.9823, 0.3419, 0.5572 and 0.7758, compute the time required for each of five simulated maintenance checks of the aeroplane's landing gear.

SELF *test*

7 A project has four activities (A, B, C and D) that must be performed sequentially. The probability distributions for the time required to complete each of the activities are as follows:

Activity	Activity Time (weeks)	Probability
A	5	0.25
	6	0.35
	7	0.25
	8	0.15
B	3	0.20
	5	0.55
	7	0.25

C	10	0.10
	12	0.25
	14	0.40
	16	0.20
	18	0.05
D	8	0.60
	10	0.40

a. Provide the base-case, worst-case and best-case calculations for the time to complete the project.
b. Use the random numbers 0.1778, 0.9617, 0.6849 and 0.4503 to simulate the completion time of the project in weeks.
c. Discuss how simulation could be used to estimate the probability the project can be completed in 35 weeks or less.

SELF *test*

8 The management of Jacobsen Corporation is interested in using simulation to estimate the profit per unit for a new product. Probability distributions for the purchase cost, the labour cost and the transportation cost are as follows:

Purchase Cost (€)	Probability	Labour Cost (€)	Probability	Transportation Cost (€)	Probability
10	0.25	20	0.10	3	0.75
11	0.45	22	0.25	5	0.25
12	0.30	24	0.35		
		25	0.30		

Assume that these are the only costs and that the selling price for the product will be €45 per unit.

a. Provide the base-case, worst-case and best-case calculations for the profit per unit.
b. Set up intervals of random numbers that can be used to randomly generate the three cost components.
c. Using the random numbers 0.3726, 0.5839 and 0.8275, calculate the profit per unit.
d. Using the random numbers 0.1862, 0.7466 and 0.6171, calculate the profit per unit.
e. Management believes the project may not be profitable if the profit per unit is less than €5. Explain how simulation can be used to estimate the probability the profit per unit will be less than €5.

SELF *test*

9 Develop a worksheet simulation for the following problem. The management of Madeira Manufacturing Company is considering the introduction of a new product. The fixed cost to begin the production of the product is €30 000. The variable cost for the product is uniformly distributed between €16 and €24 per unit. The product will sell for €50 per unit. Demand for the product is best described by a normal probability distribution with a mean of 1200 units and a standard deviation of 300 units. Develop a spreadsheet simulation similar to Figure 12.4. Use 500 simulation trials to answer the following questions.

a. What is the mean profit for the simulation?
b. What is the probability the project will result in a loss?
c. What is your recommendation concerning the introduction of the product?

SELF *test*

10 A building contractor is preparing a bid on a new construction project. Two other contractors will be submitting bids for the same project. Based on past bidding practices, bids from the other contractors can be described by the following probability distributions:

Contractor	Probability Distribution of Bid
A	Uniform probability distribution between €600 000 and €800 000
B	Normal probability distribution with a mean bid of €700 000 and a standard deviation of €50 000

a. If the building contractor submits a bid of €750 000, what is the probability the building contractor will obtain the bid? Use a worksheet to simulate 1000 trials of the contract bidding process.
b. The building contractor is also considering bids of €775 000 and €785 000. If the building contractor would like to bid such that the probability of winning the bid is about 0.80, what bid would you recommend? Repeat the simulation process with bids of €775 000 and €785 000 to justify your recommendation.

11 In preparing for the upcoming holiday season, Baba Toy Company designated a new doll called Nora. The fixed cost to produce the doll is €100 000. The variable cost, which includes material, labour and shipping costs, is €34 per doll. During the holiday selling season, Baba will sell the dolls for €42 each. If Baba overproduces the dolls, the excess dolls will be sold in January through a distributor who has agreed to pay Baba €10 per doll. Demand for new toys during the holiday selling season is extremely uncertain. Forecasts are for expected sales of 60 000 dolls with a standard deviation of 15 000. The normal probability distribution is assumed to be a good description of the demand.

a. Create a worksheet similar to the inventory worksheet in Figure 12.7. Include columns showing demand, sales, revenue from sales, amount of surplus, revenue from sales of surplus, total cost and net profit. Use your worksheet to simulate the sales of the Nora doll using a production quantity of 60 000 units. Using 500 simulation trials, what is the estimate of the mean profit associated with the production quantity of 60 000 dolls?
b. Before making a final decision on the production quantity, management wants an analysis of a more aggressive 70 000 unit production quantity and a more conservative 50 000 unit production quantity. Run your simulation with these two production quantities. What is the mean profit associated with each? What is your recommendation on the production of the Nora doll?
c. Assuming that Baba's management adopts your recommendation, what is the probability of a stock-out and a shortage of the Nora dolls during the holiday season?

SELF *test*

12 South Central Airlines operates a commuter flight between Munich and Innsbruck. The plane holds 30 passengers, and the airline makes a €100 profit on each passenger on the flight. When South Central takes 30 reservations for the flight, experience has shown that on average, two passengers do not show up. As a result, with 30 reservations, South Central is averaging 28 passengers with a profit of

28(100) = €2800 per flight. The airline operations office has asked for an evaluation of an overbooking strategy where they would accept 32 reservations even though the aeroplane holds only 30 passengers. The probability distribution for the number of passengers showing up when 32 reservations are accepted is as follows.

Passengers Showing Up	Probability
28	0.05
29	0.25
30	0.50
31	0.15
32	0.05

The airline will receive a profit of €100 for each passenger on the flight up to the capacity of 30 passengers. The airline will incur a cost for any passenger denied seating on the flight. This cost covers added expenses of rescheduling the passenger as well as loss of goodwill, estimated to be €150 per passenger. Develop a worksheet model that will simulate the performance of the overbooking system. Simulate the number of passengers showing up for each of 500 flights by using the VLOOKUP function. Use the results to compute the profit for each flight.

a. Does your simulation recommend the overbooking strategy? What is the mean profit per flight if overbooking is implemented?
b. Explain how your simulation model could be used to evaluate other overbooking levels such as 31, 33, 34 and for recommending a best overbooking strategy.

13 The Dome queuing model in Section 11.1 studies the waiting time of customers at its restaurant. Dome's single-channel queuing system has a mean of 0.75 arrivals per minute and a service rate of one customer per minute.

a. Use a worksheet based on Figure 12.11 to simulate the operation of this waiting line. Assuming that customer arrivals follow a Poisson probability distribution, the interarrival times can be simulated with the cell formula $-(1/\lambda)$*LN(RAND()), where $\lambda = 0.75$. Assuming that the service time follows an exponential probability distribution, the service times can be simulated with the cell formula $-\mu$*LN(RAND()), where $\mu = 1$. Run the Dome simulation for 500 customers. The analytical model in Chapter 11 indicates an average waiting time of three minutes per customer. What average waiting time does your simulation model show?
b. One advantage of using simulation is that a simulation model can be altered easily to reflect other assumptions about the probabilistic inputs. Assume that the service time is more accurately described by a normal probability distribution with a mean of one minute and a standard deviation of 0.2 minute. This distribution has less service time variability than the exponential probability distribution used in part (a). What is the impact of this change on the average waiting time?

SELF *test*

14 Telephone calls come into an airline reservations office randomly at the mean rate of 15 calls per hour. The time between calls follows an exponential distribution with a mean of four minutes. When the two reservation agents are busy, a telephone message tells the caller that the call is important and to please wait on the line until the next reservation agent becomes available. The service time for each reservation

agent is normally distributed with a mean of four minutes and a standard deviation of one minute. Use a two-channel queuing simulation model to evaluate this queuing system. Use the worksheet design shown in Figure 12.13. The cell formula =−4*LN(RAND()) can be used to generate the interarrival times. Simulate the operation of the telephone reservation system for 600 customers. Discard the first 100 customers, and collect data over the next 500 customers.

a. Calculate the mean interarrival time and the mean service time. If your simulation model is operating correctly, both of these should have means of approximately four minutes.
b. What is the mean customer waiting time for this system?
c. Use the =COUNTIF function to determine the number of customers who have to wait for a reservation agent. What percentage of the customers have to wait?

CASE PROBLEM 1 Dunes Golf Course

Dunes Golf Course is one of the top golf courses in the Scottish Highlands. The course offers some of the best views available. Dunes targets the upper end of the golf market and in the peak spring golfing season, charges green fees of £160 per person and golf cart fees of £20 per person.

Dunes takes reservations for tee times for groups of four players (foursome) starting at 7:30 each morning. Foursomes start at the same time on both the front nine and the back nine of the course, with a new group teeing off every nine minutes. The process continues with new foursomes starting play on both the front and back nine at noon. To enable all players to complete 18 holes before darkness, the last two afternoon foursomes start their rounds at 1:21 P.M. Under this plan, Dunes can sell a maximum of 20 afternoon tee times.

Last year Dunes was able to sell every morning tee time available for every day of the spring golf season. The same result is anticipated for the coming year. Afternoon tee times, however, are generally more difficult to sell. An analysis of the sales data for last year enabled Dunes to develop the probability distribution of sales for the afternoon tee times as shown in Table 12.12. For the

Table 12.12 Probability Distribution of Sales for the Afternoon Tee Times

Number of Tee Times Sold	Probability
8	0.01
9	0.04
10	0.06
11	0.08
12	0.10
13	0.11
14	0.12
15	0.15
16	0.10
17	0.09
18	0.07
19	0.05
20	0.02

season, Dunes averaged selling approximately 14 of the 20 available afternoon tee times. The average income from afternoon green fees and cart fees has been £10 240. However, the average of six unused tee times per day resulted in lost revenue.

In an effort to increase the sale of afternoon tee times, Dunes is considering an idea popular at other golf courses. These courses offer foursomes that play in the morning the option to play another round of golf in the afternoon by paying a reduced fee for the afternoon round. Dunes is considering two replay options: (1) a green fee of £25 per player plus a cart fee of £20 per player; (2) a green fee of £50 per player plus a cart fee of £20 per player. For option 1, each foursome will generate additional revenues of £180; for option 2, each foursome will generate additional revenues of £280. The key in making a decision as to what option is best depends upon the number of groups that find the option attractive enough to take the replay offer. Working with a consultant who has expertise in statistics and the golf industry, Dunes developed probability distributions for the number of foursomes requesting a replay for each of the two options. These probability distributions are shown in Table 12.13.

In offering these replay options, Dunes' first priority will be to sell full-price afternoon advance reservations. If the demand for replay tee times exceeds the number of afternoon tee times available, Dunes will post a notice that the course is full. In this case, any excess replay requests will not be accepted.

Managerial Report

Develop simulation models for both replay options. Run each simulation for 5000 trials. Prepare a report that will help the management of Dunes Golf Course decide which replay option to implement for the upcoming spring golf season. In preparing your report be sure to include the following:

1. Statistical summaries of the revenue expected under each replay option.
2. Your recommendation as to the best replay option.
3. Assuming a 90-day spring golf season, what is the estimate of the added revenue using your recommendation?
4. Discuss any other recommendations you have that might improve the income for Dunes.

Table 12.13 Probability Distributions for the Number of Groups Requesting a Replay

Option 1: £25 per person + Cart Fee		Option 2: £50 per person + Cart Fee	
Number of Foursomes Requesting a Replay	Probability	Number of Foursomes Requesting a Replay	Probability
0	0.01	0	0.06
1	0.03	1	0.09
2	0.05	2	0.12
3	0.05	3	0.17
4	0.11	4	0.20
5	0.15	5	0.13
6	0.17	6	0.11
7	0.15	7	0.07
8	0.13	8	0.05
9	0.09		
10	0.06		

CASE PROBLEM 2 Effortless Events

Effortless Events, operates a chain of beverage supply stores in Europe. Each store has a single service lane; cars enter at one end of the store and exit at the other end. Customers pick up soft drinks, beer, snacks and party supplies without getting out of their cars. When a new customer arrives at the store, the customer waits until the preceding customer's order is complete and then drives into the store for service.

Typically, three employees operate each store during peak periods; two clerks take and fill orders, and a third clerk serves as cashier and store supervisor. Effortless Events is considering a revised store design in which computerized order-taking and payment are integrated with specialized warehousing equipment. Management hopes that the new design will permit operating each store with one clerk. To determine whether the new design is beneficial, management decided to build a new store using the revised design.

Effortless Events' new store will be located near a major shopping centre. Based on experience at other locations, management believes that during the peak late afternoon and evening hours, the time between arrivals follows an exponential probability distribution with a mean of six minutes. These peak hours are the most critical time period for the company; most of their profit is generated during these peak hours.

An extensive study of times required to fill orders with a single clerk led to the following probability distribution of service times.

Service Time (minutes)	Probability
2	0.24
3	0.20
4	0.15
5	0.14
6	0.12
7	0.08
8	0.05
9	0.02
Total	1.00

In case customer waiting times prove too long with just a single clerk, Effortless Events's management is considering two alternatives: add a second clerk to help with bagging, taking orders and related tasks, or enlarge the drive-thru area so that two cars can be served at once (a two-channel system). With either of these options, two clerks will be needed. With the two-channel option, service times are expected to be the same for each channel. With the second clerk helping with a single channel, service times will be reduced. The following probability distribution describes service times given that option.

Service Time (minutes)	Probability
1	0.20
2	0.35
3	0.30
4	0.10
5	0.05
Total	1.00

Effortless Events's management would like you to develop a spreadsheet simulation model of the new system and use it to compare the operation of the system using the following three designs:

Design	
A	One channel, one clerk
B	One channel, two clerks
C	Two channels, each with one clerk

Management is especially concerned with how long customers have to wait for service. Research has shown that 30 per cent of the customers will wait no longer than six minutes and that 90 per cent will wait no longer than ten minutes. As a guideline, management requires the average waiting time to be less than 1.5 minutes.

Managerial Report

Prepare a report that discusses the general development of the spreadsheet simulation model, and make any recommendations that you have regarding the best store design and staffing plan for Effortless Events. One additional consideration is that the design allowing for a two-channel system will cost an additional €10 000 to build.

1 List the information the spreadsheet simulation model should generate so that a decision can be made on the store design and the desired number of clerks.

2 Run the simulation for 1000 customers for each alternative considered. You may want to consider making more than one run with each alternative. [*Note:* Values from an exponential probability distribution with mean μ can be generated in Excel using the following function: $=-\mu$*LN(RAND()).]

3 Be sure to note the number of customers Effortless Events is likely to lose due to long customer waiting times with each design alternative.

Appendix 12.1 Simulation with Excel

Excel enables small and moderate-sized simulation models to be implemented relatively easily and quickly. In this appendix we show the Excel worksheets for the three simulation models presented in the chapter.

The PortaCom Simulation Model

We simulated the PortaCom problem 500 times. The worksheet used to carry out the simulation is shown again in Figure 12.15. Note that the simulation results for trials 6 through 495 have been hidden so that the results can be shown in a reasonably sized figure. If desired, the rows for these trials can be shown and the

EXCEL *file*

PORTACOM

Figure 12.15 Worksheet for the Portacom Problem

	A	B	C	D	E	F
1	**PortaCom Risk Analysis**					
2						
3	Selling Price per Unit		€249			
4	Administrative Cost		€400,000			
5	Advertising Cost		€600,000			
6						
7	**Direct Labor Cost**			**Parts Cost (Uniform Distribution)**		
8	Lower	Upper		Smallest Value	€80	
9	Random No.	Random No.	Cost per Unit	Largest Value	€100	
10	0.0	0.1	€43			
11	0.1	0.3	€44			
12	0.3	0.7	€45	**Demand (Normal Distribution)**		
13	0.7	0.9	€46	Mean	15000	
14	0.9	1.0	€47	Std Deviation	4500	
15						
16						
17	**Simulation Trials**					
18						
19		Direct Labor	Parts	First-Year		
20	Trial	Cost Per Unit	Cost Per Unit	Demand	Profit	
21	1	47	€85.36	17,366	€1,025,570	
22	2	44	€91.68	12,900	€461,828	
23	3	45	€93.35	20,686	€1,288,906	
24	4	43	€98.56	10,888	€169,807	
25	5	45	€88.36	14,259	€648,911	
516	496	44	€98.67	8,730	(€71,739)	
517	497	45	€94.38	19,257	€1,110,952	
518	498	44	€90.85	14,920	€703,118	
519	499	43	€90.37	13,471	€557,652	
520	500	46	€92.50	18,614	€1,056,847	
521						
522			**Summary Statistics**			
523			Mean Profit		€698,457	
524			Standard Deviation		€520,485	
525			Minimum Profit		(€785,234)	
526			Maximum Profit		€2,367,058	
527			Number of Losses		51	
528			Probabilitiy of Loss		0.1020	
529						

simulation results displayed for all 500 trials. Let us describe the details of the Excel worksheet that provided the PortaCom simulation.

First, the PortaCom data are presented in the first 14 rows of the worksheet. The selling price per unit, administrative cost, and advertising cost parameters are entered directly into cells C3, C4 and C5. The discrete probability distribution for the direct labour cost per unit is shown in a tabular format. Note that the random number intervals are entered first followed by the corresponding cost per unit. For example, 0.0 in cell A10 and 0.1 in cell B10 show that a cost of $43 per unit will be assigned if the random number is in the interval 0.0 but less than 0.1. Thus, approximately 10 per cent of the simulated direct labour costs will be $43 per unit. The uniform probability distribution with a smallest value of €80 in cell E8 and a largest value of €100 in cell E9 describes the parts cost per unit. Finally, a normal probability distribution with a mean of 15 000 units in cell E13 and a standard deviation of 4500 units in cell E14 describes the first-year demand distribution for the product. At this point we are ready to insert the Excel formulas that will carry out each simulation trial.

Simulation information for the first trial appears in row 21 of the worksheet. The cell formulas for row 21 are as follows:

Cell A21	Enter 1 for the first simulation trial
Cell B21	Simulate the direct labour cost per unit* =VLOOKUP(RAND(),$A$10:$C$14,3)
Cell C21	Simulate the parts cost per unit (uniform distribution) =$E$8+($E$9–$E$8)*RAND()
Cell D21	Simulate the first-year demand (normal distribution) =NORMINV(RAND(),$E$13,$E$14)
Cell E21	The profit obtained for the first trial =($C$3–B21–C21)*D21–$C$4–$C$5

Cells A21:E21 can be copied to A520:E520 in order to provide the 500 simulation trials.

Ultimately, summary statistics will be collected in order to describe the results of the 500 simulated trials. Using the standard Excel functions, the following summary statistics are computed for the 500 simulated profits appearing in cells E21 to E520.

Cell E523	The mean profit per trial = AVERAGE(E21:E520)
Cell E524	The standard deviation of profit = STDEV(E21:E520)
Cell E525	The minimum profit = MIN(E21:E520)
Cell E526	The maximum profit = MAX(E21:E520)
Cell E527	The count of the number of trials where a loss occurred (i.e., profit < €0) = COUNTIF(E21:E520,"<0")
Cell E528	The percentage or probability of a loss based on the 500 trials = E527/500

The F9 key can be used to perform another complete simulation of PortaCom. In this case, the entire worksheet will be recalculated and a set of new simulation results will be provided. Any data summaries, measures, or functions that have been built into the worksheet earlier will be updated automatically.

*The VLOOKUP function generates a random number using the RAND() function. Then, using the table defined by the region from cells $A$10 to $C$14, the function identifies the row containing the RAND() random number and assigns the corresponding direct labour cost per unit shown in column C.

The Butler Inventory Simulation Model

We simulated the Butler inventory operation for 300 months. The worksheet used to carry out the simulation is shown again in Figure 12.16. Note that the simulation results for months 6 through 295 have been hidden so that the results can be shown in a reasonably sized figure. If desired, the rows for these months can be shown and the simulation results displayed for all 300 months. Let us describe the details of the Excel worksheet that provided the Butler inventory simulation.

First, the Butler inventory data are presented in the first 11 rows of the worksheet. The gross profit per unit, holding cost per unit and shortage cost per unit data are entered directly into cells C3, C4 and C5. The replenishment level is entered into cell C7, and the mean and standard deviation of the normal probability distribution for demand are entered into cells B10 and B11. At this point we are ready to insert Excel formulas that will carry out each simulation month or trial.

EXCEL *file*
BUTLER

Simulation information for the first month or trial appears in row 17 of the worksheet. The cell formulas for row 17 are as follows:

Figure 12.16 Worksheet for the Butler Inventory Problem

	A	B	C	D	E	F	G	H
1	**Butler Inventory**							
2								
3	Gross Profit per Unit		€50					
4	Holding Cost per Unit		€15					
5	Shortage Cost per Unit		€30					
6								
7	**Replenishment Level**		100					
8								
9	**Demand (Normal Distribution)**							
10	Mean	100						
11	Std Deviation	20						
12								
13								
14	**Simulation**							
15								
16	Month	Demand	Sales	Gross Profit	Holding Cost	Shortage Cost	Net Profit	
17	1	79	79	€3,950	€315	€0	€3,635	
18	2	111	100	€5,000	€0	€330	€4,670	
19	3	93	93	€4,650	€105	€0	€4,545	
20	4	100	100	€5,000	€0	€0	€5,000	
21	5	118	100	€5,000	€0	€540	€4,460	
312	296	89	89	€4,450	€165	€0	€4,285	
313	297	91	91	€4,550	€135	€0	€4,415	
314	298	122	100	€5,000	€0	€660	€4,340	
315	299	93	93	€4,650	€105	€0	€4,545	
316	300	126	100	€5,000	€0	€780	€4,220	
317								
318	**Totals**	30,181	27,917		**Summary Statistics**			
319					Mean Profit		€4,293	
320					Standard Deviation		€658	
321					Minimum Profit		(€206)	
322					Maximum Profit		€5,000	
323					Service Level		92.5%	
324								

Cell A17 Enter 1 for the first simulation month

Cell B17 Simulate demand (normal distribution)
=NORMINV(RAND(),$B$10,$B$11)

Next compute the sales, which is equal to demand (cell B17) if demand is less than or equal to the replenishment level, or is equal to the replenishment level (cell C7) if demand is greater than the replenishment level.

Cell C17 Calculate sales = IF(B17<=$C$7,B17,$C$7)

Cell D17 Calculate gross profit = $C$3*C17

Cell E17 Calculate the holding cost if demand is less than or equal to the replenishment level
= IF(B17<=$C$7,$C$4*($C$7–B17),0)

Cell F17 Calculate the shortage cost if demand is greater than the replenishment level
= IF(B17<$C$7,$C$5*(B17–$C$7),0)

Cell G17 Calculate net profit = D17 – E17 – F17

Cells A17:G17 can be copied to cells A316:G316 in order to provide the 300 simulation months.

Finally, summary statistics will be collected in order to describe the results of the 300 simulated trials. Using the standard Excel functions, the following totals and summary statistics are computed for the 300 months.

Cell B318 Total demand = SUM(B17:B316)

Cell C319 Total sales = SUM(C17:C316)

Cell G319 The mean profit per month = AVERAGE(G17:G316)

Cell G320 The standard deviation of net profit = STDEV(G17:G316)

Cell G321 The minimum net profit = MIN(G17:G316)

Cell G322 The maximum net profit = MAX(G17:G316)

Cell G323 The service level = C318/B318

The ATM Simulation Model

We simulated the operation of the ATM queuing system for 1000 customers. The worksheet used to carry out the simulation is shown again in Figure 12.17. Note that the simulation results for customers 6 through 995 have been hidden so that the results can be shown in a reasonably-sized figure. If desired, the rows for these customers can be shown and the simulation results displayed for all 1000 customers. Let us describe the details of the Excel worksheet that provided the ATM simulation.

The data are presented in the first nine rows of the worksheet. The interarrival times are described by a uniform distribution with a smallest time of zero minutes (cell B4) and a largest time of five minutes (cell B5). A normal probability distribution with a mean of two minutes (cell B8) and a standard deviation of 0.5 minute (cell B9) describes the service time distribution.

Simulation information for the first customer appears in row 16 of the worksheet. The cell formulas for row 16 are as follows:

Cell A16 Enter 1 for the first customer

Cell B16 Simulate the interarrival time for customer 1 (uniform distribution) = $B$4 + RAND()*($B$5 – $B$4)

Cell C16 Compute the arrival time for customer 1 = B16

Figure 12.17 Worksheet for the Hong Kong Savings Bank with One ATM

	A	B	C	D	E	F	G	H	I
1	**Hong Kong Savings Bank with One ATM**								
2									
3	**Interarrival Times (Uniform Distribution)**								
4	Smallest Value	0							
5	Largest Value	5							
6									
7	**Service Times (Normal Distribution)**								
8	Mean	2							
9	Std Deviation	0.5							
10									
11									
12	**Simulation**								
13									
14		Interarrival	Arrival	Service	Waiting	Service	Completion	Time	
15	Customer	Time	Time	Start Time	Time	Time	Time	in System	
16	1	1.4	1.4	1.4	0.0	2.3	3.7	2.3	
17	2	1.3	2.7	3.7	1.0	1.5	5.2	2.5	
18	3	4.9	7.6	7.6	0.0	2.2	9.8	2.2	
19	4	3.5	11.1	11.1	0.0	2.5	13.6	2.5	
20	5	0.7	11.8	13.6	1.8	1.8	15.4	3.6	
1011	996	0.5	2496.8	2498.1	1.3	0.6	2498.7	1.9	
1012	997	0.2	2497.0	2498.7	1.7	2.0	2500.7	3.7	
1013	998	2.7	2499.7	2500.7	1.0	1.8	2502.5	2.8	
1014	999	3.7	2503.4	2503.4	0.0	2.4	2505.8	2.4	
1015	1000	4.0	2507.4	2507.4	0.0	1.9	2509.3	1.9	
1016									
1017		**Summary Statistics**							
1018		Number Waiting			549				
1019		Probability of Waiting			0.6100				
1020		Average Waiting Time			1.59				
1021		Maximum Waiting Time			13.5				
1022		Utilization of ATM			0.7860				
1023		Number Waiting > 1 Min			393				
1024		Probability of Waiting > 1 Min			0.4367				
1025									

EXCEL *file*

HKATM

Cell D16 Calculate the start time for customer 1 = C16

Cell E16 Calculate the waiting time for customer 1 = D1–C16

Cell F16 Simulate the service time for customer 1 (normal distribution) = NORMINV(RAND(),$B$8,$B$9)

Cell G16 Calculate the completion time for customer 1 = D16+F16

Cell H16 Calculate the time in the system for customer 1 = G16–C16

Simulation information for the second customer appears in row 17 of the worksheet. The cell formulas for row 17 are as follows:

Cell A17 Enter 2 for the second customer

Cell B17 Simulate the interarrival time for customer 2 (uniform distribution) =$B$4+RAND()*($B$5–$B$4)

Cell C17 Calculate the arrival time for customer 2 = C16+B17

Cell D17 Calculate the start time for customer 2 = IF(C17>G16,C17,G16)

Cell E17 Calculate the waiting time for customer 2 = D17–C17

Cell F17 Simulate the service time for customer 2 (normal distribution) =NORMINV(RAND(),$B$8,$B$9)

Cell G17 Calculate the completion time for customer 2 = D17 + F17

Cell H17 Calculate the time in the system for customer 2 = G17 – C17

Cells A17:H17 can be copied to cells A1015:H1015 in order to provide the 1000-customer simulation.

Ultimately, summary statistics will be collected in order to describe the results of 1000 customers. Before collecting the summary statistics, let us point out that most simulation studies of dynamic systems focus on the operation of the system during its long-run or steady-state operation. To ensure that the effect of start-up conditions are not included in the steady-state calculations, a dynamic simulation model is usually run for a specified period without collecting any data about the operation of the system. The length of the start-up period can vary depending on the application. For the Hong Kong Savings Bank ATM simulation, we treated the results for the first 100 customers as the start-up period. The simulation information for customer 100 appears in row 115 of the spreadsheet. Cell G115 shows that the completion time for the 100th customer is 247.8. Thus the length of the start-up period is 247.8 minutes.

Summary statistics are collected for the next 900 customers corresponding to rows 116 to 1015 of the spreadsheet. The following Excel formulas provided the summary statistics:

Cell E1018 Number of customers who had to wait (i.e., waiting time > 0) =COUNTIF(E116:E1015,">0")

Cell E1019 Probability of waiting = E1018/900

Cell E1020 The average waiting time = AVERAGE(E116:E1015)

Cell E1021 The maximum waiting time = MAX(E116:E1015)

Cell E1022 The utilization of the ATM* = SUM(F116:F1015)/(G1015–G115)

Cell E1023 The number of customers who had to wait more than one minute =COUNTIF(E116:E1015,">1")

Cell E1024 Probability of waiting more than one minute = E1023/900

*The proportion of time the ATM is in use is equal to the sum of the 900 customer service times in column F divided by the total elapsed time required for the 900 customers to complete service. This total elapsed time is the difference between the completion time of customer 1000 and the completion time of customer 100.

Chapter 13

Decision Analysis

Learning Objectives

By the end of this chapter you will be able to:

- Calculate and explain expected value
- Construct and explain a decision tree
- Evaluate the value of perfect information

MANAGEMENT SCIENCE IN ACTION

Decision Analysis at Eastman Kodak

Clemen and Kwit conducted a study to determine the value of decision analysis at the Eastman Kodak company. The study involved an analysis of 178 decision analysis projects over the ten-year period from 1990 to 1999. The projects involved a variety of applications including strategy development, vendor selection, process analysis, new-product brainstorming, product-portfolio selection and emission-reduction analysis. These projects required 14 372 hours of analyst time and the involvement of many other individuals at Kodak over the ten-year period. The shortest projects took less than 20 hours, and the longest projects took almost a year to complete.

Most decision analysis projects are one-time activities, which makes it difficult to measure the value added to the corporation. Clemen and Kwit used detailed records that were available and some innovative approaches to develop estimates of the incremental dollar value generated by the decision analysis projects. Their conservative estimate of the average value per project was \$6.65 million and their optimistic estimate of the average value per project was \$16.35 million. Their analysis led to the conclusion that all projects taken together added more than \$1 billion in value to Eastman Kodak. Using these estimates, Clemen and Kwit concluded that decision analysis returned substantial value to the company. Indeed, they concluded that the value added by the projects was at least 185 times the cost of the analysts' time.

In addition to the monetary benefits, the authors point out that decision analysis adds value by facilitating discussion among stakeholders, promoting careful thinking about strategies, providing a common language for discussing the elements of a decision problem and speeding implementation by helping to build consensus among decision makers. In commenting on the value of decision analysis at Eastman Kodak, Nancy L. S. Sousa said, 'As General Manager, New Businesses, VP Health Imaging, Eastman Kodak, I encourage all of the business planners to use the decision and risk principles and processes as part of evaluating new business opportunities. The processes have clearly led to better decisions about entry and exit of businesses'.

Although measuring the value of a particular decision analysis project can be difficult, it would be difficult to dispute the success that decision analysis had at Kodak.

Based on Robert T. Clemen and Robert C. Kwit, 'The Value of Decision Analysis at Eastman Kodak Company, 1990–1999', *Interfaces* (September/October 2001): 74–92.

As we have seen in other chapters, managers are typically faced with uncertainty about the consequences of their decisions. Typically, a manager will be faced with several decision alternatives – the different decisions they can make in some situation. The difficulty arises because the outcomes from these alternative decisions will to some extent be uncertain. We could decide to launch a new product but future sales will be uncertain. We could decide to invest in the latest production equipment to boost productivity but the financial benefits will be uncertain. A hospital could decide to introduce the latest medical scanning facilities but the exact effect on patients and patient throughput will be uncertain. In such situations, a good analysis will include risk assessment where the risk associated with some decision is the direct result of the uncertainty surrounding the outcome from that decision. Decision analysis is a technique that can be used to help a manager determine a suitable decision under such uncertain conditions.

We begin the study of decision analysis by considering problems having reasonably few decision alternatives and reasonably few possible future events. Payoff tables are introduced to provide a structure for the decision problem and to illustrate the fundamentals of decision analysis. We then introduce decision trees to show the sequential nature of decision problems. Decision trees are used to analyze more complex problems and to identify an optimal sequence of decisions, referred to as an optimal decision strategy. Sensitivity analysis shows how changes in various aspects of the problem affect the recommended decision alternative.

13.1 Problem Formulation

The first step in the decision analysis process is problem formulation. We begin with a verbal statement of the problem. We then identify the decision alternatives, the uncertain future events, referred to as **chance events** and the **consequences** associated with each decision alternative and each chance event outcome. Let us begin by considering a construction project of the Planning and Development Council (PDC) in Oman.

The PDC is a government agency tasked with supporting the development of the Oman economy. One of PDC's key strategies is to support the diversification of the economy away from a reliance on oil. One of the initiatives under consideration is the construction of a new business complex. The complex will be located near the international airport and will consist of a number of purpose-built business units. Each unit will be equipped to the highest standards in terms of facilities, telecoms, parking, etc. It is expected that local businesses wishing to expand will be attracted to the complex as will overseas companies who wish to establish a base in Oman. The business units will be available on a first-come-first-served basis either on a long-term lease arrangement or for outright purchase.

Whilst the main purpose of the new complex is to attract new businesses, PDC is also expected to maximize the financial return on the project (through the income generated from leases or from sales). However, PDC is facing some uncertainty particularly in relation to the expected demand for units in the complex. When asked about the possible demand for the units, PDC's president acknowledged a wide range of possibilities, but decided that it would be adequate to consider two possible chance event outcomes: a strong demand and a weak demand.

In decision analysis, the possible outcomes for a chance event are referred to as the **states of nature**. The states of nature are defined so that one and only one of the possible states of nature will occur. For the PDC problem, the chance event concerning the demand for the units has two states of nature:

s_1 = strong demand for the units

s_2 = weak demand for the units

As a result of this uncertainty, PDC has commissioned three alternative plans for the complex:

d_1 = to build a small complex of 30 business units

d_2 = to build a medium-sized complex of 60 units

d_3 = to build a large complex of 90 units

These are the decision alternatives for PDC and the situation facing PDC is typical. It must first choose between these decision alternatives (size of the complex), then it must wait to see which state of nature occurs (demand for the units) and then it will see the consequence occurring (the financial return made from the decision given the state of nature).

Table 13.1 Payoff Table for the PDC Project (Payoffs in Million Rials)

	State of Nature	
Decision Alternative	**Strong Demand s_1**	**Weak Demand s_2**
Small complex, d_1	8	7
Medium complex, d_2	14	5
Large complex, d_3	20	−9

Payoff Tables

Given the three decision alternatives and the two states of nature, which complex size should PDC choose? To answer this question, PDC will need to know the consequence associated with each decision alternative and each state of nature. In decision analysis, we refer to the consequence resulting from a specific combination of a decision alternative and a state of nature as a **payoff**. A table showing payoffs for all combinations of decision alternatives and states of nature is a **payoff table**.

Payoffs can be expressed in terms of profit, cost, time, distance or any other measure appropriate for the decision problem being analyzed.

Because PDC wants to select the complex size that provides the largest return, return is used as the consequence. The payoff table with return expressed in millions of Rials is shown in Table 13.1. Note, for example, that if a medium complex is built and demand turns out to be strong, a return of R14 million will be realized. We will use the notation V_{ij} to denote the payoff associated with decision alternative i and state of nature j. Using Table 13.1, $V_{31} = 20$ indicates a payoff of R20 million occurs if the decision is to build a large complex (d_3) and the strong demand state of nature (s_1) occurs. Similarly, $V_{32} = -9$ indicates a loss of R9 million if the decision is to build a large complex (d_3) and the weak demand state of nature (s_2) occurs.

Decision Trees

If you have a payoff table, you can develop a decision tree. Try Problem 1(a).

A **decision tree** provides a graphical representation of the decision-making process. Figure 13.1 presents a decision tree for the PDC problem. Note that the decision tree shows the natural or logical progression that will occur over time. The decision

Figure 13.1 Decision Tree for the PDC Project (Payoffs in R Million)

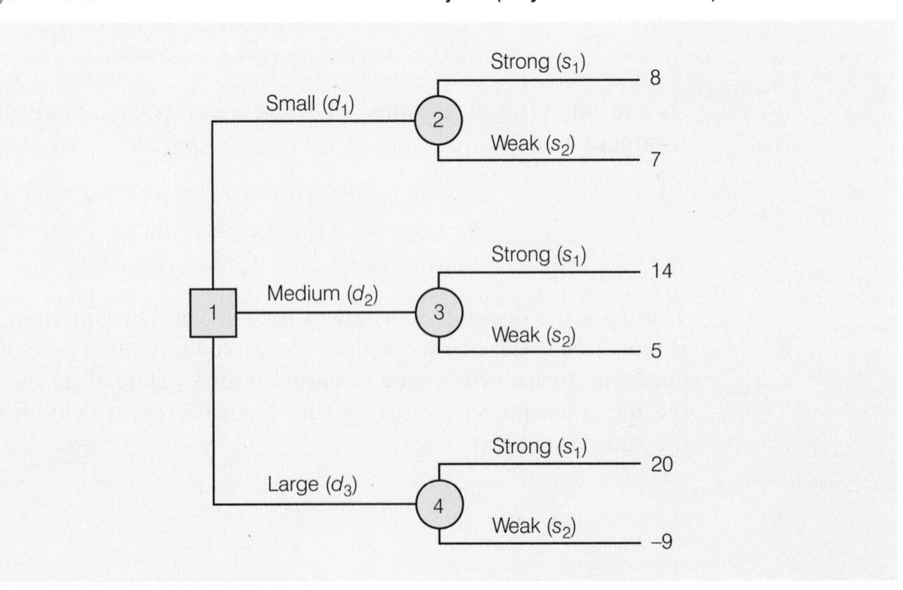

tree is built from left to right. First, PDC must make a decision regarding the size of the complex (d_1, d_2 or d_3). Then, after the decision is implemented, either state of nature s_1 or s_2 will occur. The number at each end point of the tree indicates the payoff associated with a particular sequence. For example the topmost payoff of 8 indicates that an R8 million return is anticipated if PDC constructs a small complex (d_1) and demand turns out to be strong (s_1). The next payoff of 7 indicates an anticipated profit of R7 million if PDC constructs a small complex (d_1) and demand turns out to be weak (s_2). Thus, the decision tree shows graphically the sequences of decision alternatives and states of nature that provide the six possible payoffs for PDC.

The decision tree in Figure 13.1 has four nodes, numbered 1–4. Squares are used to depict decision nodes and circles are used to depict chance nodes. Thus, node 1 is a decision node, and nodes 2, 3 and 4 are chance nodes. The **branches**, which connect the nodes, leaving the decision node correspond to the decision alternatives. The branches leaving each chance node correspond to the states of nature. The payoffs are shown at the end of the states-of-nature branches. We now turn to the question: How can the decision maker use the information in the payoff table or the decision tree to select the best decision alternative? Several approaches may be used.

NOTES AND COMMENTS

1 Experts in problem solving agree that the first step in solving a complex problem is to decompose it into a series of smaller subproblems. Decision trees provide a useful way to show how a problem can be decomposed and the sequential nature of the decision process.

2 People often view the same problem from different perspectives. Thus, the discussion regarding the development of a decision tree may provide additional insight about the problem.

13.2 Decision Making without Probabilities

Many people think of a good decision as one in which the consequence is good. However, in some instances, a good, well-thought-out decision may still lead to a bad or undesirable consequence.

In this section we consider approaches to decision making that do not require knowledge of the probabilities of the states of nature. These approaches are appropriate in situations in which the decision maker has little confidence in his or her ability to assess the probabilities, or in which a simple best-case and worst-case analysis is desirable. Because different approaches sometimes lead to different decision recommendations, the decision maker needs to understand the approaches available and then select the specific approach that, according to the decision maker's judgement, is the most appropriate.

Optimistic Approach

The **optimistic approach** evaluates each decision alternative in terms of the *best* payoff that can occur. The decision alternative that is recommended is the one that provides the best possible payoff. For a problem in which maximum return is desired, as in the PDC problem, the optimistic approach would lead the decision

Table 13.2 Maximum Payoff for Each PDC Decision Alternative

Decision Alternative	Maximum Payoff	
Small complex, d_1	8	
Medium complex, d_2	14	
Large complex, d_3	20	← Maximum of the maximum payoff values

maker to choose the alternative corresponding to the largest return. For problems involving minimization, this approach leads to choosing the alternative with the smallest payoff.

For a maximization problem, the optimistic approach often is referred to as the maximax approach; for a minimization problem, the corresponding terminology is minimin.

To illustrate the optimistic approach, we use it to develop a recommendation for the PDC problem. First, we determine the maximum payoff for each decision alternative; then we select the decision alternative that provides the overall maximum payoff. These steps systematically identify the decision alternative that provides the largest possible profit. Table 13.2 illustrates these steps.

Because 20, corresponding to d_3, is the largest payoff, the decision to construct the large complex is the recommended decision alternative using the optimistic approach.

Conservative Approach

The **conservative approach** evaluates each decision alternative in terms of the *worst* payoff that can occur. The decision alternative recommended is the one that provides the best of the worst possible payoffs. For a problem in which the output measure is return, as in the PDC problem, the conservative approach would lead the decision maker to choose the alternative that maximizes the minimum possible return that could be obtained. For problems involving minimization, this approach identifies the alternative that will minimize the maximum payoff.

For a maximization problem, the conservative approach is often referred to as the maximin approach; for a minimization problem, the corresponding terminology is minimax.

To illustrate the conservative approach, we use it to develop a recommendation for the PDC problem. First, we identify the minimum payoff for each of the decision alternatives; then we select the decision alternative that maximizes the minimum payoff. Table 13.3 illustrates these steps for the PDC problem.

Because 7, corresponding to d_1, yields the maximum of the minimum payoffs, the decision alternative of a small complex is recommended. This decision approach is considered conservative because it identifies the worst possible payoffs and then recommends the decision alternative that avoids the possibility of extremely 'bad' payoffs. In the conservative approach, PDC is guaranteed a return of at least R7 million. Although PDC may make more, it *cannot* make less than R7 million.

Table 13.3 Minimum Payoff for each PDC Decision Alternative

Decision Alternative	Minimum Payoff	
Small complex, d_1	7	← Maximum of the minimum payoff values
Medium complex, d_2	5	
Large complex, d_3	−9	

Minimax Regret Approach

The **minimax regret approach** to decision making is neither purely optimistic nor purely conservative. Let us illustrate the minimax regret approach by showing how it can be used to select a decision alternative for the PDC problem.

Suppose that PDC constructs a small complex (d_1) and demand turns out to be strong (s_1). Table 13.1 showed that the resulting profit for PDC would be R8 million. However, given that the strong demand state of nature (s_1) has occurred, we realize that the decision to construct a large condominium complex (d_3), yielding a profit of R20 million, would have been the best decision. The difference between the payoff for the best decision alternative (R20 million) and the payoff for the decision to construct a small complex (R8 million) is the **opportunity loss**, or **regret**, associated with decision alternative d_1 when state of nature s_1 occurs; so, for this case, the opportunity loss or regret is R20 million − R8 million = R12 million. Similarly, if PDC makes the decision to construct a medium complex (d_2) and the strong demand state of nature (s_1) occurs, the opportunity loss, or regret, associated with d_2 would be R20 million − R14 million = R6 million.

In general the following expression represents the opportunity loss, or regret.

$$R_{ij} = |V_j^* - V_{ij}| \tag{13.1}$$

where

R_{ij} = the regret associated with decision alternative s_j

V_j^* = the payoff value[1] corresponding to the best decision for the state of nature s_j

V_{ij} = the payoff corresponding to decision alternative d_i and state of nature s_j

Note the role of the absolute value in Equation (13.1) shown by the symbol | |. For minimization problems, the best payoff, V_j^*, is the smallest entry in column j. Because this value always is less than or equal to V_{ij}, the absolute value of the difference between V_j^* and V_{ij} ensures that the regret is always the magnitude of the difference.

Using Equation (13.1) and the payoffs in Table 13.1, we can calculate the regret associated with each combination of decision alternative d_i and state of nature s_j. Because the PDC problem is a maximization problem, V_j^* will be the largest entry in column j of the payoff table. Thus, to calculate the regret, we simply subtract each entry in a column from the largest entry in the column. Table 13.4 shows the opportunity loss, or regret, table for the PDC problem.

Table 13.4 Opportunity Loss, or Regret, Table for the PDC Project (R Million)

	State of Nature	
Decision Alternative	**Strong Demand s_1**	**Weak Demand s_2**
Small complex, d_1	12	0
Medium complex, d_2	6	2
Large complex, d_3	0	16

[1] In maximization problems, V_j^* will be the largest entry in column j of the payoff table. In minimization problems, V_j^* will be the smallest entry in column j of the payoff table.

Table 13.5 Maximum Regret for each PDC Decision Alternative

Decision Alternative	Maximum Regret	
Small complex, d_1	12	
Medium complex, d_2	6	← Minimum of the maximum regret
Large complex, d_3	16	

The next step in applying the minimax regret approach is to list the maximum regret for each decision alternative; Table 13.5 shows the results for the PDC problem. Selecting the decision alternative with the *minimum* of the *maximum* regret values – hence, the name *minimax regret* – yields the minimax regret decision. For the PDC problem, the alternative to construct the medium complex, with a corresponding maximum regret of R6 million, is the recommended minimax regret decision.

For practise in developing a decision recommendation using the optimistic, conservative and minimax regret approaches, try Problem 1(b).

Note that the three approaches discussed in this section provide different recommendations, which in itself isn't bad. It simply reflects the difference in decision-making philosophies that underlie the various approaches. Ultimately, the decision maker will have to choose the most appropriate approach and then make the final decision accordingly. The main criticism of the approaches discussed in this section is that they do not consider any information about the probabilities of the various states of nature. In the next section we discuss an approach that utilizes probability information in selecting a decision alternative.

13.3 Decision Making with Probabilities

In many decision-making situations, we can obtain probability assessments for the states of nature. When such probabilities are available, we can use the **expected value approach** to identify the best decision alternative. Let us first define the expected value of a decision alternative and then apply it to the PDC problem.

Let

$$N = \text{the number of states of nature}$$
$$P(s_j) = \text{the probability of state of nature } s_j$$

Because one and only one of the N states of nature can occur, the probabilities must satisfy two conditions:

$$P(s_j) \geq 0 \quad \text{for all states of nature} \tag{13.2}$$

$$\sum_{j=1}^{N} P(s_j) = P(s_1) + P(s_2) + \cdots + P(s_N) = 1 \tag{13.3}$$

Equation (13.2) states that the probability for each state of nature must be greater than, or equal to, zero. Equation (13.3) states that the sum of all the probabilities must equal 1.

The **expected value (EV)** of decision alternative d_i is defined as follows:

$$\text{EV}(d_i) = \sum_{j=1}^{N} P(s_j)V_{ij} \qquad \textbf{(13.4)}$$

In words, the expected value of a decision alternative is the sum of weighted payoffs for the decision alternative. The weight for a payoff is the probability of the associated state of nature and therefore the probability that the payoff will occur. Let us return to the PDC problem to see how the expected value approach can be applied.

PDC is optimistic about the potential for the complex. Suppose that this optimism leads to an initial subjective probability assessment of 0.8 that demand will be strong (s_1) and a corresponding probability of 0.2 that demand will be weak (s_2). Thus, $P(s_1) = 0.8$ and $P(s_2) = 0.2$. Using the payoff values in Table 13.1 and equation (13.4), we calculate the expected value for each of the three decision alternatives as follows:

$$\begin{aligned}\text{EV}(d_1) &= 0.8(8) + 0.2(7) &&= 7.8\\ \text{EV}(d_2) &= 0.8(14) + 0.2(5) &&= 12.2\\ \text{EV}(d_3) &= 0.8(20) + 0.2(-9) &&= 14.2\end{aligned}$$

Thus, using the expected value approach, we find that the large complex, with an expected value of R14.2 million, is the recommended decision.

Can you now use the expected value approach to develop a decision recommendation? Try Problem 4.

The calculations required to identify the decision alternative with the best expected value can be conveniently carried out on a decision tree. Figure 13.2 shows the decision tree for the PDC problem with state-of-nature branch probabilities. Working backward through the decision tree, we first calculate the expected value at each chance node. That is, at each chance node, we weight each possible payoff by its probability of occurrence. By doing so, we obtain the expected values for nodes 2, 3 and 4, as shown in Figure 13.3.

Figure 13.2 PDC Decision Tree with State-of-Nature Branch Probabilities

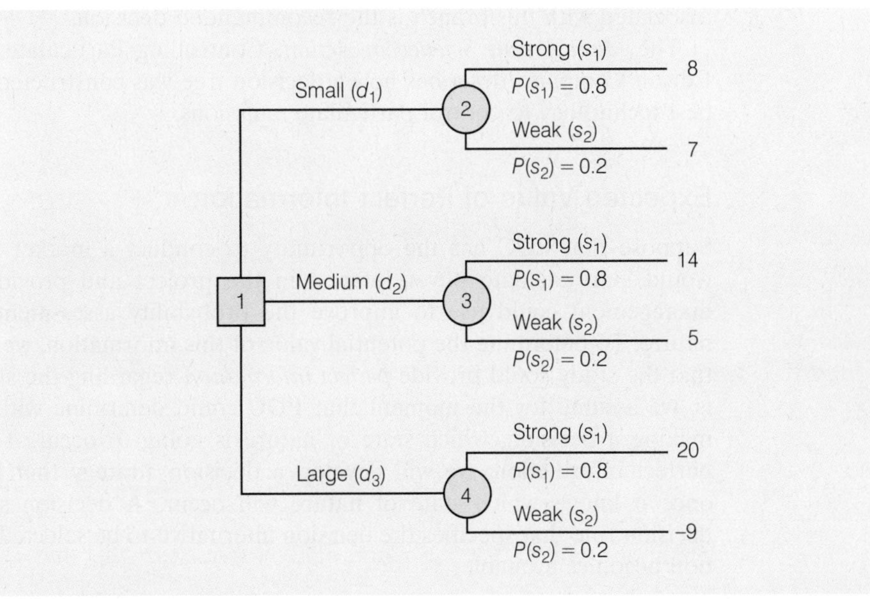

Figure 13.3 Applying the Expected Value Approach Using a Decision Tree

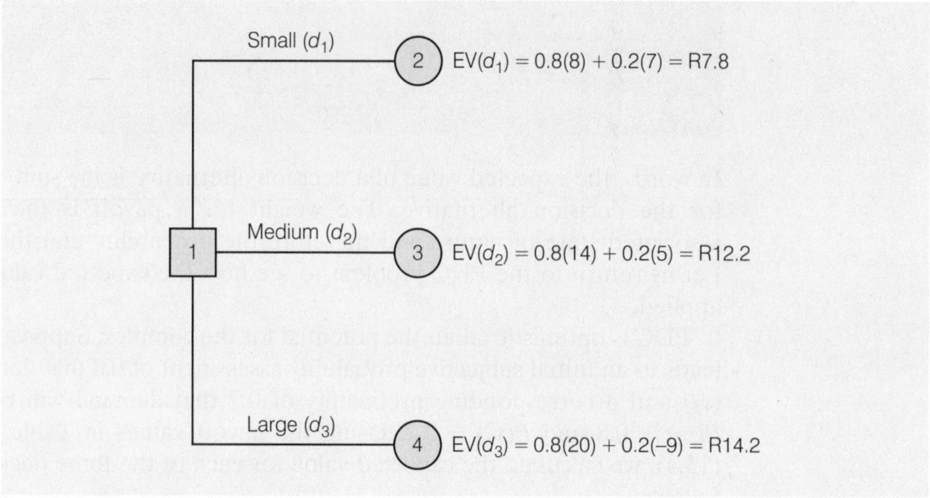

Computer software packages are available to help in constructing more complex decision trees. See Appendix 13.1.

Because the decision maker controls the branch leaving decision node 1 and because we are trying to maximize the expected return, the best decision alternative at node 1 is d_3. Thus, the decision tree analysis leads to a recommendation of d_3 with an expected value of R14.2 million. Note that this recommendation is also obtained with the expected value approach in conjunction with the payoff table.

Other decision problems may be substantially more complex than the PDC problem, but if a reasonable number of decision alternatives and states of nature are present, you can use the decision tree approach outlined here. First, draw a decision tree consisting of decision nodes, chance nodes and branches that describe the sequential nature of the problem. If you use the expected value approach, the next step is to determine the probabilities for each of the states of nature and compute the expected value at each chance node. Then select the decision branch leading to the chance node with the best expected value. The decision alternative associated with this branch is the recommended decision.

The *Management Science in Action*, Controlling Particulate Emissions at Ohio Edison Company, describes how a decision tree was constructed to help choose the best technology to control particulate emissions.

Expected Value of Perfect Information

Suppose that PDC has the opportunity to conduct a market research study that would help evaluate buyer interest in the project and provide information that management could use to improve the probability assessments for the states of nature. To determine the potential value of this information, we begin by supposing that the study could provide *perfect information* regarding the states of nature; that is, we assume for the moment that PDC could determine with certainty, prior to making a decision, which state of nature is going to occur. To make use of this perfect information, we will develop a decision strategy that PDC should follow once it knows which state of nature will occur. A decision strategy is simply a decision rule that specifies the decision alternative to be selected after new information becomes available.

Table 13.6 Payoff Table for the PDC Project (R Million)

	State of Nature	
Decision Alternative	**Strong Demand s_1**	**Weak Demand s_2**
Small complex, d_1	8	7
Medium complex, d_2	14	5
Large complex, d_3	20	−9

To help determine the decision strategy for PDC, we reproduced PDC's payoff table as Table 13.6. Note that, if PDC knew for sure that state of nature s_1 would occur, the best decision alternative would be d_3, with a payoff of R20 million. Similarly, if PDC knew for sure that state of nature s_2 would occur, the best decision alternative would be d_1, with a payoff of R7 million. Thus, we can state PDC's optimal decision strategy when the perfect information becomes available as follows:

If s_1, select d_3 and receive a payoff of R20 million.
If s_2, select d_1 and receive a payoff of R7 million.

What is the expected value for this decision strategy? To calculate the expected value with perfect information, we return to the original probabilities for the states of nature: $P(s_1) = 0.8$, and $P(s_2) = 0.2$. Thus, there is a 0.8 probability that the perfect information will indicate state of nature s_1 and the resulting decision alternative d_3 will provide a R20 million profit. Similarly, with a 0.2 probability for state of nature s_2, the optimal decision alternative d_1 will provide a R7 million profit. Thus, from equation (13.4), the expected value of the decision strategy that uses perfect information is:

$$0.8(20) + 0.2(7) + 17.4$$

We refer to the expected value of R17.4 million as the *expected value with perfect information* (EVwPI).

Earlier in this section we showed that the recommended decision using the expected value approach is decision alternative d_3, with an expected value of R14.2 million. Because this decision recommendation and expected value calculation were made without the benefit of perfect information, R14.2 million is referred to as the *expected value without perfect information* (EVwoPI).

The expected value with perfect information is R17.4 million, and the expected value without perfect information is R14.2; therefore, the expected value of the perfect information (EVPI) is R17.4 − R14.2 = R3.2 million. In other words, R3.2 million represents the additional expected value that can be obtained if perfect information were available about the states of nature.

It would be worth R3.2 million for PDC to learn the level of market acceptance before selecting a decision alternative.

Generally speaking, a market research study will not provide 'perfect' information; however, if the market research study is a good one, the information gathered might be worth a sizeable portion of the R3.2 million. Given the EVPI of R3.2 million, PDC might seriously consider a market survey as a way to obtain more information about the states of nature.

In general, the **expected value of perfect information (EVPI)** is calculated as follows:

$$\text{EVPI} = |\text{EVwPI} - \text{EVwoPI}| \qquad \textbf{(13.5)}$$

MANAGEMENT SCIENCE IN ACTION

Controlling Particulate Emissions at Ohio Edison Company

Ohio Edison Company is an operating company of FirstEnergy Corporation. Ohio Edison and its subsidiary, Pennsylvania Power Company, provide electrical service to more than one million customers in central and northeastern Ohio and western Pennsylvania. Most of this electricity is generated by coal-fired power plants. To meet evolving air quality standards, Ohio Edison conducted a decision analysis to help them select the best particulate control equipment for three of its coal-fired generating units.

Preliminary studies narrowed the particulate control equipment choice to a decision between fabric filters and electrostatic precipitators. The decision was affected by a number of uncertainties: the uncertainty concerning the way air quality regulations might be interpreted, the uncertainty concerning sulfur content requirements for the coal to be burned and the uncertainty concerning construction costs, among others. Because of the complexity of the problem, the uncertain events involved and the importance of the choice, a comprehensive decision analysis was conducted.

The choice was based on minimizing the annual revenue requirements for the three large generating units over their remaining lifetime. These revenue requirements represented the monies that would have to be collected from the utility's customers to recover costs resulting from the choice made. A decision tree was constructed to represent the particulate control decision and its uncertainties and costs. A decision node was used to represent the two choices possible: fabric filters or electrostatic precipitators. Chance nodes were used to represent the uncertainties involved. Costs associated with the decision model were obtained from engineering calculations or estimates. Probabilities for the chance nodes were obtained from existing data or the subjective assessments of knowledgeable persons.

The result of the decision analysis led Ohio Edison to select the electrostatic precipitator technology for the three generating units. Had the decision analysis not been performed, the particulate control decision would have favoured the fabric filter equipment. Decision analysis offered a means for effectively analyzing the uncertainties involved in the decision and led to a decision that yielded both lower expected revenue requirements and lower risk.

Based on information provided by Thomas J. Madden and M.S. Hyrnick of Ohio Edison Company, Akron, Ohio.

where

EVPI = expected value of perfect information

EVwPI = expected value *with* perfect information about the states of nature

EVwoPI = expected value *without* perfect information about the states of nature

For practise in determining the expected value of perfect information, try Problem 9.

Note the role of the absolute value in Equation (13.5). For minimization problems the expected value with perfect information is always less than or equal to the expected value without perfect information. In this case, EVPI is the magnitude of the difference between EVwPI and EVwoPI, or the absolute value of the difference as shown in Equation (13.5).

NOTES AND COMMENTS

We restate the *opportunity loss*, or *regret*, table for the PDC problem (see Table 13.4) as follows.

	State of Nature	
	Strong Demand	Weak Demand
Decision Alternative	s_1	s_2
Small complex, d_1	12	0
Medium complex, d_2	6	2
Large complex, d_3	0	16

Using $P(s_1)$, $P(s_2)$, and the opportunity loss values, we can calculate the *expected opportunity loss* (EOL) for each decision alternative. With $P(s_1) = 0.8$ and $P(s_2) = 0.2$, the expected opportunity loss for each of the three decision alternatives is:

$$\text{EOL}(d_1) = 0.8(12) + 0.2(0) = 9.6$$
$$\text{EOL}(d_2) = 0.8(6) + 0.2(2) = 5.2$$
$$\text{EOL}(d_3) = 0.8(0) + 0.2(16) = 3.2$$

Regardless of whether the decision analysis involves maximization or minimization, the *minimum* expected opportunity loss always provides the best decision alternative. Thus, with $\text{EOL}(d_3) = 3.2$, d_3 is the recommended decision. In addition, the minimum expected opportunity loss always is *equal to the expected value of perfect information*. That is, EOL(best decision) = EVPI; for the PDC problem, this value is R3.2 million.

13.4 Risk Analysis and Sensitivity Analysis

Risk analysis helps the decision maker recognize the difference between the expected value of a decision alternative and the payoff that may actually occur. **Sensitivity analysis** also helps the decision maker by describing how changes in the state-of-nature probabilities and/or changes in the payoffs affect the recommended decision alternative.

Risk Analysis

A decision alternative and a state of nature combine to generate the payoff associated with a decision. The risk profile for a decision alternative shows the possible payoffs along with their associated probabilities.

Let us demonstrate risk analysis and the construction of a risk profile by returning to the PDC project. Using the expected value approach, we identified the large complex (d_3) as the best decision alternative. The expected value of R14.2 million for d_3 is based on a 0.8 probability of obtaining a R20 million profit and a 0.2 probability of obtaining a R9 million loss. The 0.8 probability for the R20 million payoff and the 0.2 probability for the −R9 million payoff provide the risk profile for the large complex decision alternative. This risk profile is shown graphically in Figure 13.4.

Sometimes a review of the risk profile associated with an optimal decision alternative may cause the decision maker to choose another decision alternative even though the expected value of the other decision alternative is not as good. For example, the risk profile for the medium complex decision alternative (d_2) shows a 0.8 probability for a R14 million payoff and 0.2 probability for a R5 million payoff. Because no probability of a loss is associated with decision alternative d_2, the medium complex decision alternative would be judged less risky than the large complex decision alternative. As a result, a decision maker might prefer the less-risky medium complex decision alternative even though it has an expected value of R2 million less than the large complex decision alternative.

Figure 13.4 Risk Profile for the Large Complex Decision Alternative for the PDC Project

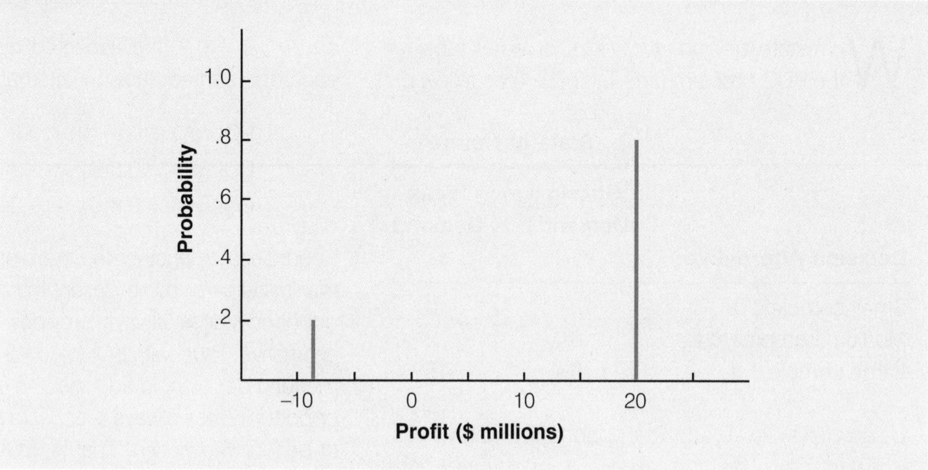

Sensitivity Analysis

Sensitivity analysis can be used to determine how changes in the probabilities for the states of nature or changes in the payoffs affect the recommended decision alternative. In many cases, the probabilities for the states of nature and the payoffs are based on subjective assessments. Sensitivity analysis helps the decision maker understand which of these inputs are critical to the choice of the best decision alternative. If a small change in the value of one of the inputs causes a change in the recommended decision alternative, the solution to the decision analysis problem is sensitive to that particular input. Extra effort and care should be taken to make sure the input value is as accurate as possible. On the other hand, if a modest to large change in the value of one of the inputs does not cause a change in the recommended decision alternative, the solution to the decision analysis problem is not sensitive to that particular input. No extra time or effort would be needed to refine the estimated input value.

One approach to sensitivity analysis is to select different values for the probabilities of the states of nature and the payoffs and then solve the decision analysis problem again. If the recommended decision alternative changes, we know that the solution is sensitive to the changes made. For example, suppose that in the PDC problem the probability for a strong demand is revised to 0.2 and the probability for a weak demand is revised to 0.8. Would the recommended decision alternative change? Using $P(s_1) = 0.2$, $P(s_2) = 0.8$, and Equation (13.4), the revised expected values for the three decision alternatives are:

$$\begin{aligned} \text{EV}(d_1) &= 0.2(8) + 0.8(7) = 7.2 \\ \text{EV}(d_2) &= 0.2(14) + 0.8(5) = 6.8 \\ \text{EV}(d_3) &= 0.2(20) + 0.8(-9) = -3.2 \end{aligned}$$

With these probability assessments the recommended decision alternative is to construct a small complex (d_1), with an expected value of R7.2 million. The probability of strong demand is only 0.2, so constructing the large complex (d_3) is the least preferred alternative, with an expected value of −R3.2 million (a loss).

Thus, when the probability of strong demand is large, PDC should build the large complex; when the probability of strong demand is small, PDC should build the small complex. Obviously, we could continue to modify the probabilities of the states

Computer software packages for decision analysis make it easy to calculate these revised scenarios.

of nature and learn even more about how changes in the probabilities affect the recommended decision alternative. The drawback to this approach is the numerous calculations required to evaluate the effect of several possible changes in the state-of-nature probabilities.

For the special case of two states of nature, a graphical procedure can be used to determine how changes for the probabilities of the states of nature affect the recommended decision alternative. To demonstrate this procedure, we let p denote the probability of state of nature s_1; that is, $P(s_1) = p$. With only two states of nature in the PDC problem, the probability of state of nature s_2 is:

$$P(s_2) = 1 - P(s_1) = 1 - P$$

Using Equation (13.4) and the payoff values in Table 13.1, we determine the expected value for decision alternative d_1 as follows:

$$\begin{aligned} \mathrm{EV}(d_1) &= P(s_1)(8) + P(s_2)(7) \\ &= p(8) + (1-p)(7) \\ &= 8p + 7 - 7p = p + 7 \end{aligned} \tag{13.6}$$

Repeating the expected value computations for decision alternatives d_2 and d_3, we obtain expressions for the expected value of each decision alternative as a function of p:

$$\mathrm{EV}(d_2) = 9p + 5 \tag{13.7}$$

$$\mathrm{EV}(d_3) = 29p - 9 \tag{13.8}$$

Thus, we have developed three equations that show the expected value of the three decision alternatives as a function of the probability of state of nature s_1.

We continue by developing a graph with values of p on the horizontal axis and the associated EVs on the vertical axis. Because Equations (13.6), (13.7) and (13.8) are linear equations, the graph of each equation is a straight line. For each equation, then, we can obtain the line by identifying two points that satisfy the equation and drawing a line through the points. For instance, if we let $p = 0$ in Equation (13.6), $\mathrm{EV}(d_1) = 7$. Then, letting $p = 1$, $\mathrm{EV}(d_1) = 8$. Connecting these two points, (0,7) and (1,8), provides the line labelled $\mathrm{EV}(d_1)$ in Figure 13.5. Similarly, we obtain the lines labelled $\mathrm{EV}(d_2)$ and $\mathrm{EV}(d_3)$; these lines are the graphs of Equations (13.7) and (13.8), respectively.

Figure 13.5 shows how the recommended decision changes as p, the probability of the strong demand state of nature (s_1), changes. Note that for small values of p, decision alternative d_1 (small complex) provides the largest expected value and is thus the recommended decision. When the value of p increases to a certain point, decision alternative d_2 (medium complex) provides the largest expected value and is the recommended decision. Finally, for large values of p, decision alternative d_3 (large complex) becomes the recommended decision.

The value of p for which the expected values of d_1 and d_2 are equal is the value of p corresponding to the intersection of the $\mathrm{EV}(d_1)$ and the $\mathrm{EV}(d_2)$ lines. To determine this value, we set $\mathrm{EV}(d_1) = \mathrm{EV}(d_2)$ and solve for the value of p:

$$\begin{aligned} p + 7 &= 9p + 5 \\ 8p &= 2 \\ p &= \frac{2}{8} = 0.25 \end{aligned}$$

Figure 13.5 Expected Value for the PDC Decision Alternatives as a Function of p

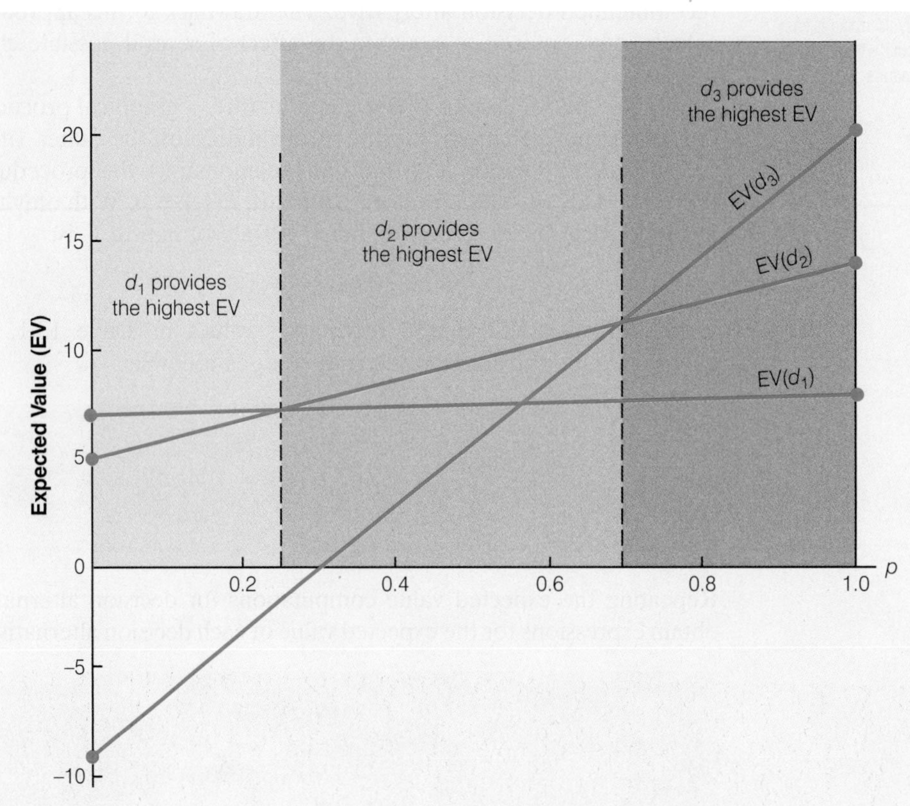

Graphical sensitivity analysis shows how changes in the probabilities for the states of nature affect the recommended decision alternative. Try Problem 6.

Hence, when $p = 0.25$, decision alternatives d_1 and d_2 provide the same expected value. Repeating this calculation for the value of p corresponding to the intersection of the EV(d_2) and EV(d_3) lines, we obtain $p = 0.70$.

Using Figure 13.5, we can conclude that decision alternative d_1 provides the largest expected value for $p \leq 0.25$, decision alternative d_2 provides the largest expected value for $0.25 \leq p \leq 0.70$, and decision alternative d_3 provides the largest expected value for $p \geq 0.70$. Because p is the probability of state of nature s_1 and $(1 - p)$ is the probability of state of nature s_2, we now have the sensitivity analysis information that tells us how changes in the state-of-nature probabilities affect the recommended decision alternative.

Sensitivity analysis calculations can also be made for the values of the payoffs. In the original PDC problem, the expected values for the three decision alternatives were as follows: EV(d_1) = 7.8, EV(d_2) = 12.2 and EV(d_3) = 14.2. Decision alternative d_3 (large complex) was recommended. Note that decision alternative d_2 with EV(d_2) = 12.2 was the second best decision alternative. Decision alternative d_3 will remain the optimal decision alternative as long as EV(d_3) is greater than or equal to the expected value of the second best decision alternative. Thus, decision alternative d_3 will remain the optimal decision alternative as long as:

$$\text{EV}(d_3) \geq 12.2 \tag{13.9}$$

Let

S = the payoff of decision alternative d_3 when demand is strong
W = the payoff of decision alternative d_3 when demand is weak

Using $P(s_1) = 0.8$ and $P(s_2) = 0.2$, the general expression for EV(d_3) is:

$$\text{EV}(d_3) = 0.8S + 0.2W \tag{13.10}$$

Assuming that the payoff for d_3 stays at its original value of −R9 million when demand is weak, the large complex decision alternative will remain optimal as long as:

$$\text{EV}(d_3) = 0.8S + 0.2(-9) \leq 12.2 \tag{13.11}$$

Solving for S, we have:

$$\begin{aligned} 0.8S - 1.8 &\geq 12.2 \\ 0.8S &\geq 14 \\ S &\geq 17.5 \end{aligned}$$

Recall that when demand is strong, decision alternative d_3 has an estimated payoff of R20 million. The preceding calculation shows that decision alternative d_3 will remain optimal as long as the payoff for d_3 when demand is strong is at least R17.5 million.

Assuming that the payoff for d_3 when demand is strong stays at its original value of R20 million, we can make a similar calculation to learn how sensitive the optimal solution is with regard to the payoff for d_3 when demand is weak. Returning to the expected value calculation of Equation (13.10), we know that the large complex decision alternative will remain optimal as long as:

$$\text{EV}(d_3) = 0.8(20) + 0.2W \geq 12.2 \tag{13.12}$$

Solving for W, we have:

$$\begin{aligned} 16 + 0.2W &\geq 12.2 \\ 0.2W &\geq -3.8 \\ W &\geq -19 \end{aligned}$$

Sensitivity analysis can assist management in deciding whether more time and effort should be spent obtaining better estimates of payoffs and probabilities.

Recall that when demand is weak, decision alternative d_3 has an estimated payoff of −R9 million. The preceding calculation shows that decision alternative d_3 will remain optimal as long as the payoff for d_3 when demand is weak is at least −R19 million.

Based on this sensitivity analysis, we conclude that the payoffs for the large complex decision alternative (d_3) could vary considerably and d_3 would remain the recommended decision alternative. Thus, we conclude that the optimal solution for the PDC decision problem is not particularly sensitive to the payoffs for the large complex decision alternative. We note, however, that this sensitivity analysis has been conducted based on only one change at a time. That is, only one payoff was changed and the probabilities for the states of nature remained $P(s_1) = 0.8$ and $P(s_2) = 0.2$. Note that similar sensitivity analysis calculations can be made for the payoffs associated with the small complex decision alternative d_1 and the medium complex decision alternative d_2. However, in these cases, decision alternative d_3 remains optimal only if the changes in the payoffs for decision alternatives d_1 and d_2 meet the requirements that EV(d_1) ≤ 14.2 and EV(d_2) ≤ 14.2.

NOTES AND COMMENTS

1 Some decision analysis software automatically provides the risk profiles for the optimal decision alternative. These packages also allow the user to obtain the risk profiles for other decision alternatives. After comparing the risk profiles, a decision maker may decide to select a decision alternative with a good risk profile even though the expected value of the decision alternative is not as good as the optimal decision alternative.

2 A *tornado diagram*, a graphical display, is particularly helpful when several inputs combine to determine the value of the optimal solution. By varying each input over its range of values, we obtain information about how each input affects the value of the optimal solution. To display this information, a bar is constructed for the input with the width of the bar showing how the input affects the value of the optimal solution. The widest bar corresponds to the input that is most sensitive. The bars are arranged in a graph with the widest bar at the top, resulting in a graph that has the appearance of a tornado.

13.5 Decision Analysis with Sample Information

In applying the expected value approach, we showed how probability information about the states of nature affects the expected value calculations and thus the decision recommendation. Frequently, decision makers have preliminary or **prior probability** assessments for the states of nature that are the best probability values available at that time. However, to make the best possible decision, the decision maker may want to seek additional information about the states of nature. This new information can be used to revise or update the prior probabilities so that the final decision is based on more accurate probabilities for the states of nature. Most often, additional information is obtained through experiments designed to provide sample information about the states of nature. Raw material sampling, product testing and market research studies are examples of experiments (or studies) that may enable management to revise or update the state-of-nature probabilities. These revised probabilities are called **posterior probabilities**.

Let us return to the PDC problem and assume that management is considering a six-month market research study designed to learn more about potential market acceptance of the PDC project. Management anticipates that the market research study will provide one of the following two results:

1 Favourable report: A significant number of the individuals contacted express interest in purchasing or leasing a PDC unit.
2 Unfavourable report: Very few of the individuals contacted express interest in purchasing or leasing a PDC unit.

Decision Tree

The decision tree for the PDC problem with sample information shows the logical sequence for the decisions and the chance events in Figure 13.6.

First, PDC's management must decide whether the market research should be conducted. If it is conducted, PDC's management must be prepared to make a decision about the size of the project if the market research report is favourable and, possibly, a different decision about the size of the project if the market research report is unfavourable. In Figure 13.6, the squares are decision nodes and the circles

Figure 13.6 The PDC Decision Tree Including the Market Research Study

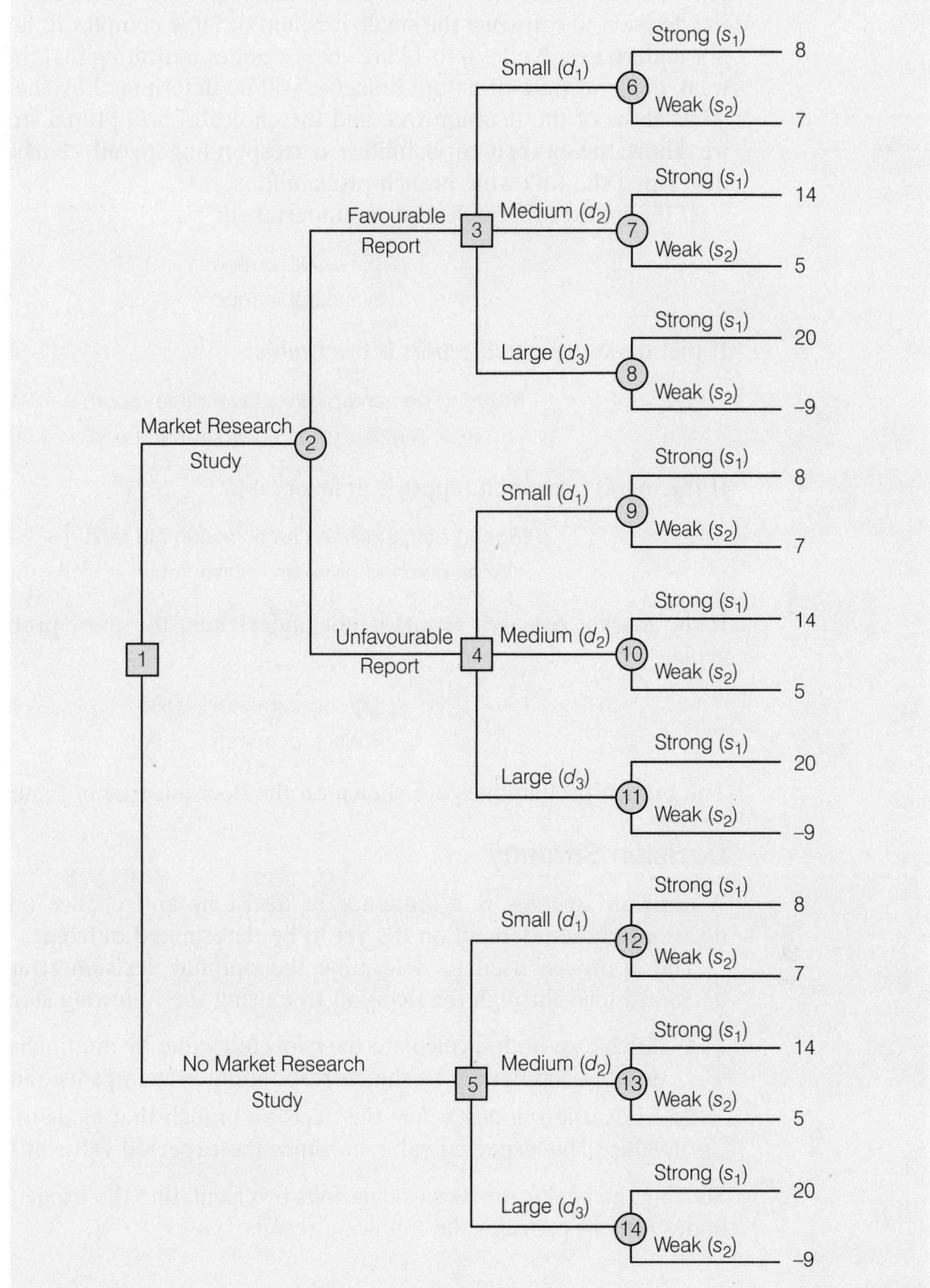

are chance nodes. At each decision node, the branch of the tree that is taken is based on the decision made. At each chance node, the branch of the tree that is taken is based on probability or chance. For example, decision node 1 shows that PDC must first make the decision of whether to conduct the market research study. If the market research study is undertaken, chance node 2 indicates that both the favourable report branch and the unfavourable report branch are not under PDC's control and will be determined by chance. Node 3 is a decision node, indicating that PDC must make the decision to construct the small, medium or large complex if the market research report is favourable. Node 4 is a decision node showing that PDC must make the decision to construct the small, medium or large complex if the market research report is unfavourable. Node 5 is a decision node indicating that PDC must make the decision to construct the small, medium or large complex if the market research is not undertaken. Nodes 6 to 14 are chance nodes indicating that the strong demand or weak demand state-of-nature branches will be determined by chance.

We explain in Section 13.6 how these probabilities can be developed.

Analysis of the decision tree and the choice of an optimal strategy requires that we know the branch probabilities corresponding to all chance nodes. PDC has developed the following branch probabilities.

If the market research study is undertaken:

$$P(\text{Favourable report}) = 0.77$$
$$P(\text{Unfavourable report}) = 0.23$$

If the market research report is favourable:

$$P(\text{Strong demand given a favourable report}) = 0.94$$
$$P(\text{Weak demand given a favourable report}) = 1.06$$

If the market research report is unfavourable:

$$P(\text{Strong demand given an unfavourable report}) = 0.35$$
$$P(\text{Weak demand given an unfavourable report}) = 1.65$$

If the market research report is not undertaken, the prior probabilities are applicable:

$$P(\text{Strong demand}) = 0.80$$
$$P(\text{Weak demand}) = 1.20$$

The branch probabilities are shown on the decision tree in Figure 13.7.

Decision Strategy

A **decision strategy** is a sequence of decisions and chance outcomes where the decisions chosen depend on the yet to be determined outcomes of chance events.

The approach used to determine the optimal decision strategy is based on a backward pass through the decision tree using the following steps:

1. At chance nodes, calculate the expected value by multiplying the payoff at the end of each branch by the corresponding branch probabilities.
2. At decision nodes, select the decision branch that leads to the best expected value. This expected value becomes the expected value at the decision node.

Starting the backward pass calculations by calculating the expected values at chance nodes 6 to 14 provides the following results:

$$\begin{aligned}
\text{EV(Node6)} &= 0.94(8) + 0.06(7) = 7.94\\
\text{EV(Node7)} &= 0.94(14) + 0.06(5) = 13.46\\
\text{EV(Node8)} &= 0.94(20) + 0.06(-9) = 18.26\\
\text{EV(Node9)} &= 0.35(8) + 0.65(7) = 7.35\\
\text{EV(Node10)} &= 0.35(14) + 0.65(5) = 8.15\\
\text{EV(Node11)} &= 0.35(20) + 0.65(-9) = 1.15\\
\text{EV(Node12)} &= 0.80(8) + 0.20(7) = 7.80\\
\text{EV(Node13)} &= 0.80(14) + 0.20(5) = 12.20\\
\text{EV(Node14)} &= 0.80(20) + 0.20(-9) = 14.20
\end{aligned}$$

Figure 13.7 The PDC Decision Tree with Branch Probabilities

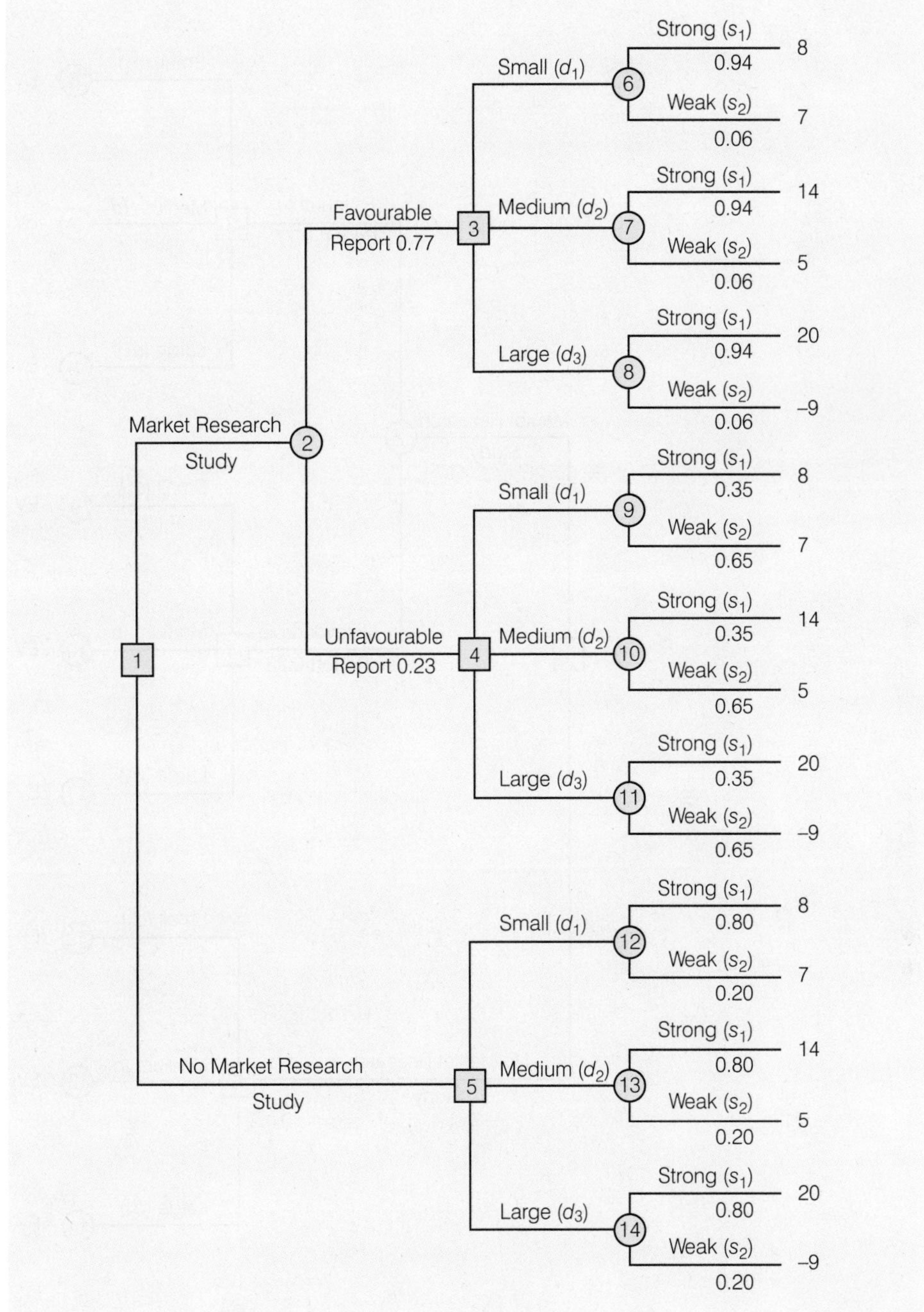

Figure 13.8 shows the reduced decision tree after computing expected values at these chance nodes.

Next, move to decision nodes 3, 4 and 5. For each of these nodes, we select the decision alternative branch that leads to the best expected value. For example, at node 3 we have the choice of the small complex branch with EV(Node 6) = 7.94, the medium complex branch with EV(Node 7) = 13.46 and the large complex branch with EV(Node 8) = 18.26. Thus, we select the large complex decision alternative branch and the expected value at node 3 becomes EV(Node 3) = 18.26.

Figure 13.8 PDC Decision Tree After Calculating Expected Values at Chance Nodes 6 to 14

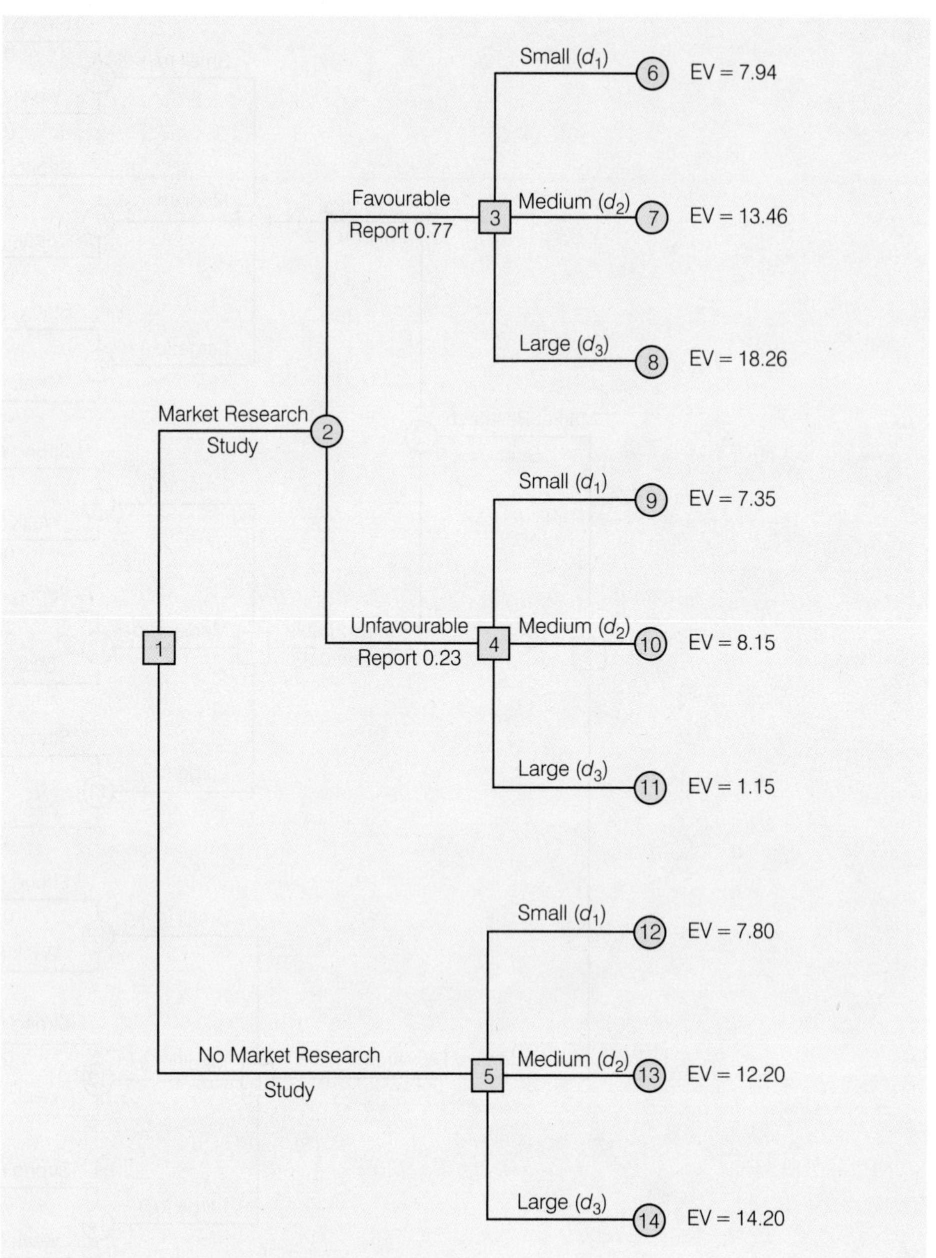

For node 4, we select the best expected value from nodes 9, 10 and 11. The best decision alternative is the medium complex branch that provides EV(Node 4) = 8.15. For node 5, we select the best expected value from nodes 12, 13 and 14. The best decision alternative is the large complex branch that provides EV(Node 5) = 14.20. Figure 13.9 shows the reduced decision tree after choosing the best decisions at nodes 3, 4 and 5.

The expected value at chance node 2 can now be calculated as follows:

$$\begin{aligned} \text{EV(Node2)} &= 0.77\text{EV(Node3)} + 0.23\text{EV(Node4)} \\ &= 0.77(18.26) + 0.23(8.15) = 15.93 \end{aligned}$$

Figure 13.9 PDC Decision Tree After Choosing Best Decisions at Nodes 3, 4 and 5

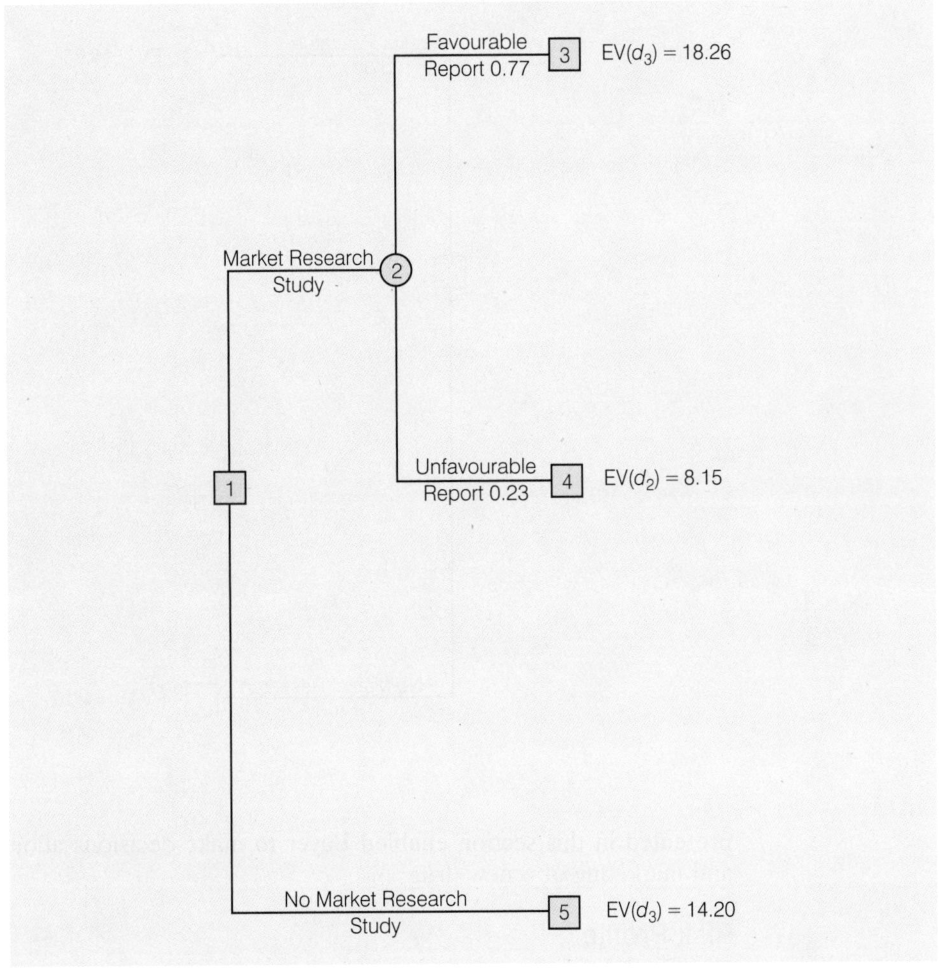

This calculation reduces the decision tree to one involving only the two decision branches from node 1 (see Figure 13.10).

Finally, the decision can be made at decision node 1 by selecting the best expected values from nodes 2 and 5. This action leads to the decision alternative to conduct the market research study, which provides an overall expected value of 15.93.

The optimal decision for PDC is to conduct the market research study and then carry out the following decision strategy:

If the market research is favourable, construct the large complex.

If the market research is unfavourable, construct the medium complex.

Problem 10 will test your ability to develop an optimal decision strategy.

The analysis of the PDC decision tree describes the methods that can be used to analyze more complex sequential decision problems. First, draw a decision tree consisting of decision and chance nodes and branches that describe the sequential nature of the problem. Determine the probabilities for all chance outcomes. Then, by working backward through the tree, calculate expected values at all chance nodes and select the best decision branch at all decision nodes. The sequence of optimal decision branches determines the optimal decision strategy for the problem.

The *Management Science in Action*, New Drug Decision Analysis at Bayer Pharmaceuticals, describes how an extension of the decision analysis principles

Figure 13.10 PDC Decision Tree Reduced to Two Decision Branches

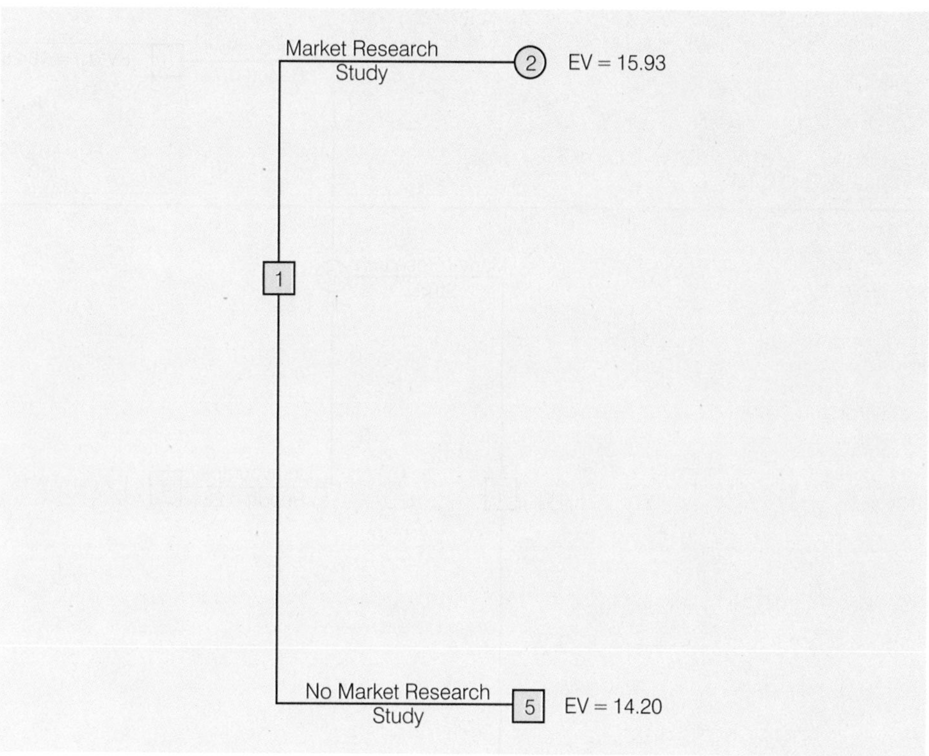

presented in this section enabled Bayer to make decisions about the development and marketing of a new drug.

Risk Profile

Figure 13.11 provides a reduced decision tree showing only the sequence of decision alternatives and chance events for the PDC optimal decision strategy. By implementing the optimal decision strategy, PDC will obtain one of the four payoffs shown at the terminal branches of the decision tree. Recall that a risk profile shows the possible payoffs with their associated probabilities. Thus, in order to construct a risk profile for the optimal decision strategy we will need to calculate the probability for each of the four payoffs.

Note that each payoff results from a sequence of branches leading from node 1 to the payoff. For instance, the payoff of R20 million is obtained by following the upper branch from node 1, the upper branch from node 2, the lower branch from node 3 and the upper branch from node 8. The probability of following that sequence of branches can be found by multiplying the probabilities for the branches from the chance nodes in the sequence. Thus, the probability of the R20 million payoff is (0.77)(0.94) = 0.72. Similarly, the probabilities for each of the other payoffs are obtained by multiplying the probabilities for the branches from the chance nodes leading to the payoffs. Doing so, we find the probability of the −R9 million payoff is (0.77)(0.06) = 0.05; the probability of the R14 million payoff is (0.23)(0.35) = 0.08; and the probability of the R5 million payoff is (0.23)(0.65) = 0.15. The following table showing the probability distribution for the payoffs for the PDC optimal decision strategy is the tabular representation of the risk profile for the optimal decision strategy.

MANAGEMENT SCIENCE IN ACTION

New Drug Decision Analysis at Bayer Pharmaceuticals

Drug development requires substantial investment and is very risky. It can take 15 years to research and develop a new drug. The Bayer Biological Products (BP) group used decision analysis to evaluate the potential for a new blood-clot-busting drug. Six key yes-or-no decision nodes were identified: (1) begin preclinical development, (2) begin testing in humans, (3) continue development into phase 3, (4) continue development into phase 4, (5) file a licence application with the FDA and (6) launch the new drug into the marketplace. More than 50 chance nodes appeared in the influence diagram. The chance nodes showed how uncertainties – related to factors such as direct labour costs, process development costs, market share, tax rate and pricing – affected the outcome. Net present value provided the consequence and the decision-making criterion.

Probability assessments were made concerning both the technical risk and market risk at each stage of the process. The resulting sequential decision tree had 1955 possible paths that led to different net present value outcomes. Cost inputs, judgements of potential outcomes and the assignment of probabilities helped evaluate the project's potential contribution. Sensitivity analysis was used to identify key variables that would require special attention by the project team and management during the drug development process. Application of decision analysis principles allowed Bayer to make good decisions about how to develop and market the new drug.

Based on Jeffrey S. Stonebraker, 'How Bayer Makes Decisions to Develop New Drugs', *Interfaces*, no. 6 (November/December 2002): 77–90.

Payoff (R Million)	Probability
−9	0.05
5	0.15
14	0.08
20	0.72
	1.00

Figure 13.11 PDC Decision Tree Showing Only Branches Associated with Optimal Decision Strategy

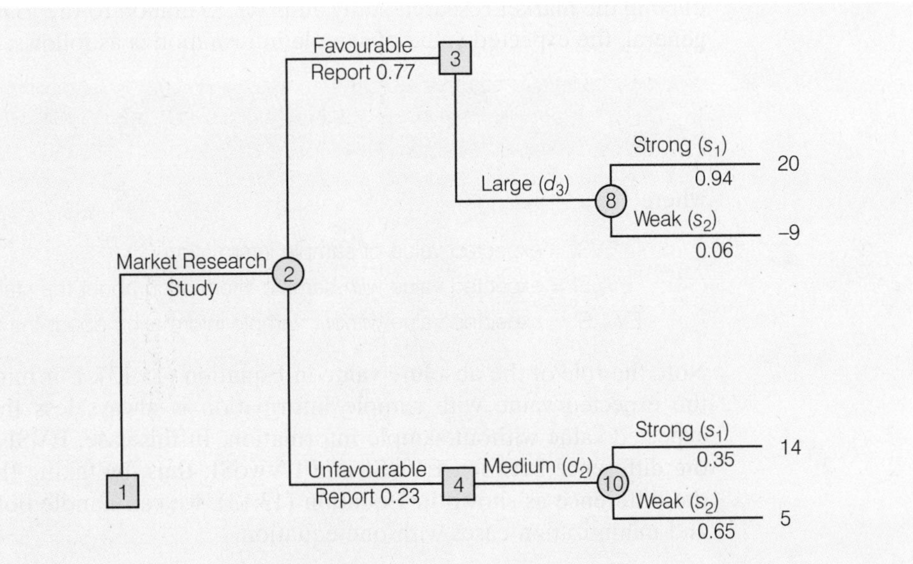

Figure 13.12 Risk Profile for PDC Project with Sample Information Showing Payoffs Associated with Optimal Decision Strategy

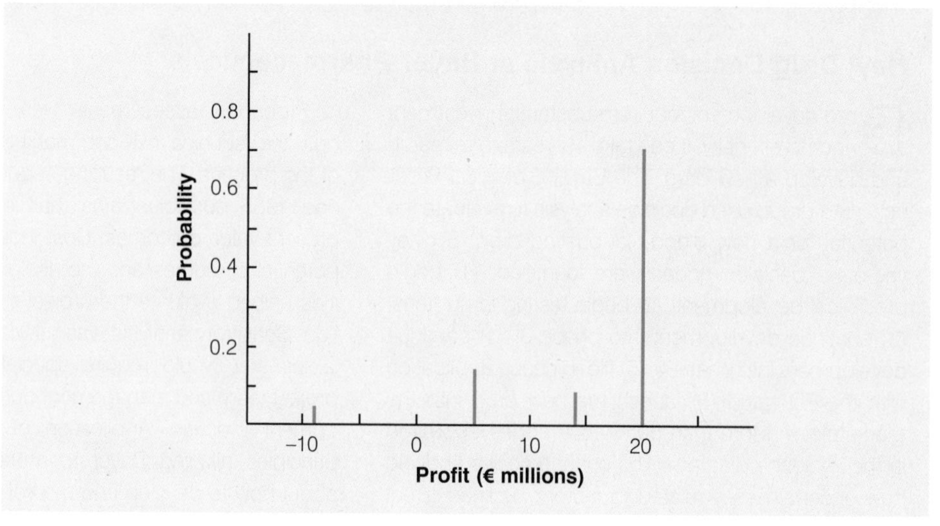

Figure 13.12 provides a graphical representation of the risk profile. Comparing Figures 13.3 and 13.12, we see that the PDC risk profile is changed by the strategy to conduct the market research study. In fact, the use of the market research study has lowered the probability of the R9 million loss from 0.20 to 0.05. PDC's management would most likely view that change as a significant reduction in the risk associated with the project.

Expected Value of Sample Information

The EVSI = R1.73 million suggests PDC should be willing to pay up to R1.73 million to conduct the market research study.

In the PDC problem, the market research study is the sample information used to determine the optimal decision strategy. The expected value associated with the market research study is R15.93 million. In Section 13.3 we showed that the best expected value if the market research study is *not* undertaken is R14.20 million. Thus, we can conclude that the difference, R15.93 million − R14.20 million = R1.73 million, is the expected value of sample information (EVSI). In other words, conducting the market research study adds R1.73 million to the PDC expected value. In general, the expected value of sample information is as follows:

$$EVSI = |EV_{W}SI - EV_{Wo}SI| \quad \textbf{(13.13)}$$

where

$EVSI$ = expected value of sample information

$EV_{W}SI$ = expected value *with* sample information about the states of nature

$EV_{Wo}SI$ = expected value *without* sample information about the states of nature

Note the role of the absolute value in Equation (13.13). For minimization problems the expected value with sample information is always less than or equal to the expected value without sample information. In this case, EVSI is the magnitude of the difference between EVwSI and EVwoSI; thus, by taking the absolute value of the difference as shown in Equation (13.13), we can handle both the maximization and minimization cases with one equation.

Figure 13.13 The PDC Decision Tree

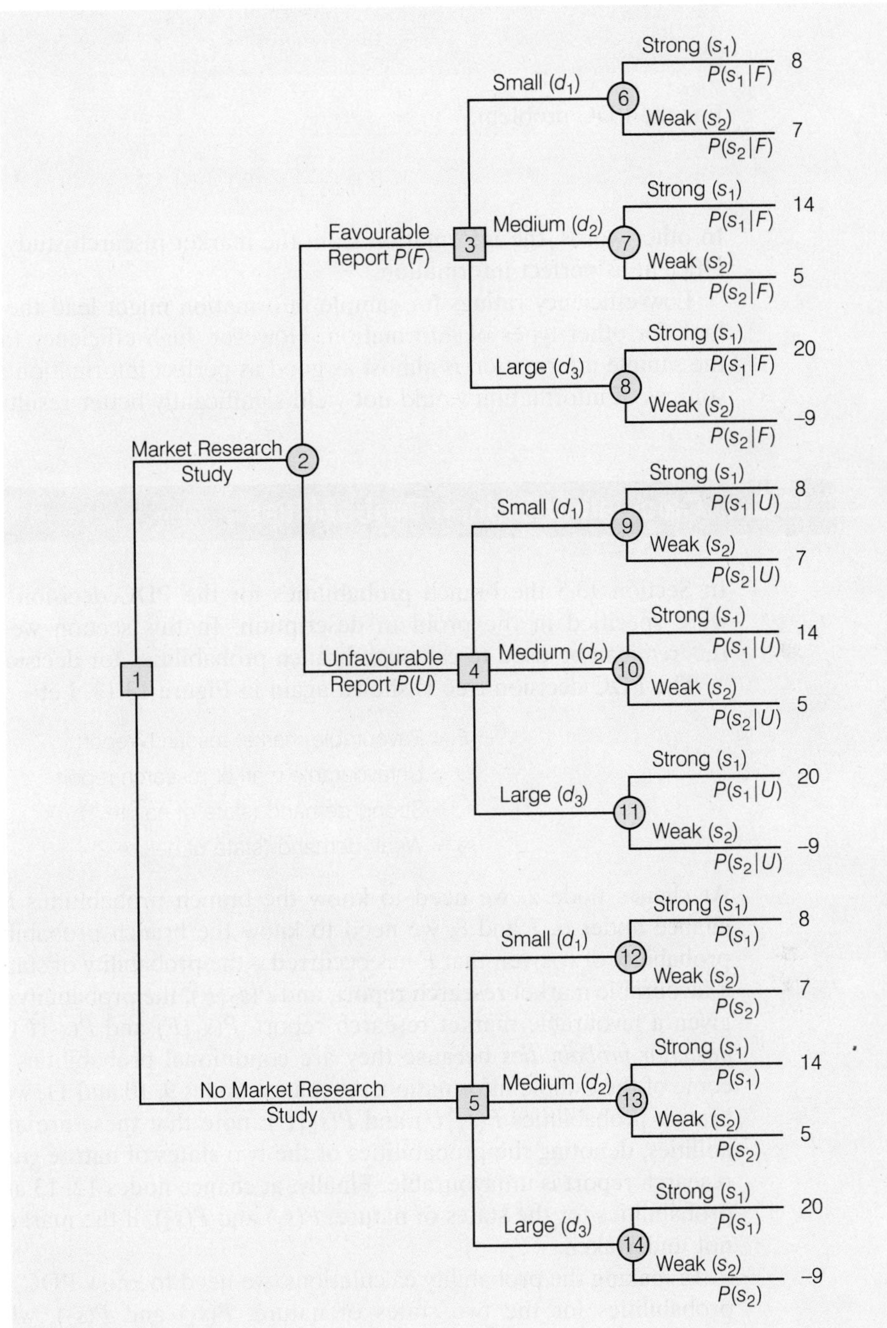

Efficiency of Sample Information

In Section 13.3 we showed that the expected value of perfect information (EVPI) for the PDC problem is R3.2 million. We never anticipated that the market research report would obtain perfect information, but we can use an efficiency measure to express the value of the market research information. With perfect information having an efficiency rating of 100 per cent, the efficiency rating E for sample information is computed as follows.

$$E = \frac{EVSI}{EVPI} \times 100 \qquad (13.14)$$

For the PDC problem,

$$E = \frac{1.73}{3.2} \times 100 = 54.1\%$$

In other words, the information from the market research study is 54.1 per cent as efficient as perfect information.

Low efficiency ratings for sample information might lead the decision maker to look for other types of information. However, high efficiency ratings indicate that the sample information is almost as good as perfect information and that additional sources of information would not yield significantly better results.

13.6 Calculating Branch Probabilities

In Section 13.5 the branch probabilities for the PDC decision tree chance nodes were specified in the problem description. In this section we show how **Bayes' theorem** can be used to calculate branch probabilities for decision trees.

The PDC decision tree is shown again in Figure 13.13. Let:

F = Favourable market research report
U = Unfavourable market research report
s_1 = Strong demand (state of nature 1)
s_2 = Weak demand (state of nature 2)

At chance node 2, we need to know the branch probabilities $P(F)$ and $P(U)$. At chance nodes 6, 7 and 8, we need to know the branch probabilities $P(s_1|F)$ – the probability of s_1 given that F has occurred – the probability of state of nature 1 given a favourable market research report, and $P(s_2|F)$, the probability of state of nature 2 given a favourable market research report. $P(s_1|F)$ and $P(s_2|F)$ are referred to as *posterior probabilities* because they are conditional probabilities based on the outcome of the sample information. At chance nodes 9, 10 and 11, we need to know the branch probabilities $P(s_1|U)$ and $P(s_2|U)$; note that these are also posterior probabilities, denoting the probabilities of the two states of nature *given* that the market research report is unfavourable. Finally, at chance nodes 12, 13 and 14, we need the probabilities for the states of nature, $P(s_1)$ and $P(s_2)$, if the market research study is not undertaken.

In making the probability calculations, we need to know PDC's assessment of the probabilities for the two states of nature, $P(s_1)$ and $P(s_2)$, which are the prior probabilities as discussed earlier. In addition, we must know the **conditional probability** of the market research outcomes (the sample information) *given* each state of nature. For example, we need to know the conditional probability of a favourable market research report given that the state of nature is strong demand for the PDC project; note that this conditional probability of F given state of nature s_1 is written $P(F|s_1)$. To carry out the probability calculations, we will need conditional probabilities for all sample outcomes given all states of nature, that is, $P(F|s_1)$, $P(F|s_2)$, $P(U|s_1)$ and $P(U|s_2)$. In the PDC problem, we assume that the following assessments are available for these conditional probabilities.

State of Nature	Market Research: Favourable, F	Market Research: Unfavourable, U
Strong demand, s_1	$P(F \mid s_1) = 0.90$	$P(U \mid s_1) = 0.10$
Weak demand, s_2	$P(F \mid s_2) = 0.25$	$P(U \mid s_2) = 0.75$

Note that the preceding probability assessments provide a reasonable degree of confidence in the market research study. If the true state of nature is s_1, the probability of a favourable market research report is 0.90 and the probability of an unfavourable market research report is 0.10. If the true state of nature is s_2, the probability of a favourable market research report is 0.25 and the probability of an unfavourable market research report is 0.75.

The reason for a 0.25 probability of a potentially misleading favourable market research report for state of nature s_2 is that when some potential buyers first hear about the new project, their enthusiasm may lead them to overstate their real interest in it. A potential buyer's initial favourable response can change quickly to a 'no thank you' when later faced with the reality of signing a purchase contract and making a down payment.

In the following discussion, we present a tabular approach as a convenient method for carrying out the probability calculations. The calculations for the PDC problem based on a favourable market research report (F) are summarized in Table 13.7. The steps used to develop this table are as follows:

Step 1. In column 1 enter the states of nature. In column 2 enter the *prior probabilities* for the states of nature. In column 3 enter the *conditional probabilities* of a favourable market research report (F) given each state of nature.

Step 2. In column 4 calculate the **joint probabilities** by multiplying the prior probability values in column 2 by the corresponding conditional probability values in column 3.

Step 3. Sum the joint probabilities in column 4 to obtain the probability of a favourable market research report, $P(F)$.

Step 4. Divide each joint probability in column 4 by $P(F) = 0.77$ to obtain the revised or *posterior probabilities*, $P(s_1 \mid F)$ and $P(s_2 \mid F)$.

Table 13.7 shows that the probability of obtaining a favourable market research report is $P(F) = 0.77$. In addition, $P(s_1 \mid F) = 0.94$ and $P(s_2 \mid F) = 0.06$. In particular, note that a favourable market research report will prompt a revised or posterior probability of 0.94 that the market demand will be strong, s_1.

Table 13.7 Branch Probabilities for the PDC Project Based on a Favourable Market Research Report

States of Nature s_j	Prior Probabilities $P(s_j)$	Conditional Probabilities $P(F \mid s_j)$	Joint Probabilities $P(F \cap s_j)$	Posterior Probabilities $P(s_j \mid F)$
s_1	0.8	0.90	0.72	0.94
s_2	0.2	0.25	0.05	0.06
	1.0		$P(F) = 0.77$	1.00

Table 13.8 Branch Probabilities for the PDC Project Based on an Unfavourable Market Research Report

States of Nature s_j	Prior Probabilities $P(s_j)$	Conditional Probabilities $P(U \mid s_j)$	Joint Probabilities $P(U \cap s_j)$	Posterior Probabilities $P(s_j \mid U)$
s_1	0.8	0.10	0.08	0.35
s_2	0.2	0.75	0.15	0.65
	1.0		$P(U) = 0.23$	1.00

The tabular probability calculation procedure must be repeated for each possible sample information outcome. Thus, Table 13.8 shows the calculations of the branch probabilities of the PDC problem based on an unfavourable market research report. Note that the probability of obtaining an unfavourable market research report is $P(U) = 0.23$. If an unfavourable report is obtained, the posterior probability of a strong market demand, s_1, is 0.35 and of a weak market demand, s_2, is 0.65. The branch probabilities from Tables 13.7 and 13.8 were shown on the PDC decision tree in Figure 13.7.

Problem 14 asks you to calculate the posterior probabilities.

The discussion in this section shows an underlying relationship between the probabilities on the various branches in a decision tree. To assume different prior probabilities, $P(s_1)$ and $P(s_2)$, without determining how these changes would alter $P(F)$ and $P(U)$, as well as the posterior probabilities $P(s_1 \mid F)$, $P(s_2 \mid F)$, $P(s_1 \mid U)$ and $P(s_2 \mid U)$, would be inappropriate.

The *Management Science in Action*, Medical Screening Test at Duke University Medical Center, shows how posterior probability information and decision analysis helped management understand the risks and costs associated with a new screening procedure.

13.7 Utility and Decision Making

In the preceding sections of this chapter we expressed the payoffs in terms of monetary values. When probability information was available about the states of nature, we recommended selecting the decision alternative with the best expected monetary value. However, in some situations the decision alternative with the best expected monetary value may not be the most desirable decision.

By the most desirable decision we mean the one that is preferred by the decision maker after taking into account not only monetary value, but also other factors such as the risk associated with the outcomes. Examples of situations in which selecting the decision alternative with the best expected monetary value may not lead to the selection of the most preferred decision are numerous. One such example is the decision to buy house insurance. Clearly, buying insurance for a house does not provide a higher expected monetary value than not buying such insurance. Otherwise, insurance companies could not pay expenses and make a profit. Similarly, many people buy tickets for state lotteries even though the expected monetary value of such a decision is negative.

Should we conclude that persons or businesses that buy insurance or participate in lotteries do so because they are unable to determine which decision alternative leads to the best expected monetary value? On the contrary, we take the view that in these cases monetary value is not the sole measure of the true worth of the outcome to the decision maker.

MANAGEMENT SCIENCE IN ACTION

Medical Screening Test at Duke University Medical Center

A new medical screening test developed at the Duke University Medical Center (USA) involved using blood samples from newborns to screen for metabolic disorders. A positive test result indicated that a deficiency was present, while a negative test result indicated that a deficiency was not present. However, it was understood that the screening test was not a perfect predictor; that is, false-positive test results as well as false-negative test results were possible. A false-positive test result meant that the test detected a deficiency when in fact no deficiency was present. This case resulted in unnecessary further testing as well as unnecessary worry for the parents of the newborn. A false-negative test result meant that the test did not detect the presence of an existing deficiency. Using probability and decision analysis, a research team analyzed the role and value of the screening test.

A decision tree with six nodes, 13 branches and eight outcomes was used to model the screening test procedure. A decision node with the decision branches Test and No Test was placed at the start of the decision tree. Chance nodes and branches were used to describe the possible sequences of a positive test result, a negative test result, a deficiency present and a deficiency not present.

The particular deficiency in question was rare, occurring at a rate of one case for every 250 000 newborns. Thus, the prior probability of a deficiency was 1/250 000 = 0.000004. Based on judgements about the probabilities of false-positive and false-negative test results, Bayes' theorem was used to calculate the posterior probability that a newborn with a positive test result actually had a deficiency. This posterior probability was 0.074. Thus, while a positive test result increased the probability the newborn had a deficiency from 0.000004 to 0.074, the probability that the newborn had a deficiency was still relatively low (0.074). The probability information was helpful to doctors in reassuring worried parents that even though further testing was recommended, the chances were greater than 90 per cent that a deficiency was not present. After the assignment of costs to the eight possible outcomes, decision analysis showed that the decision alternative to conduct the test provided the optimal decision strategy. The expected cost criterion established the expected cost to be approximately $6 per test.

Decision analysis helped provide a realistic understanding of the risks and costs associated with the screening test. In 1998, the test was given to every child born in the state of North Carolina.

Based on James E. Smith and Robert L. Winkler, 'Casey's Problem: Interpreting and Evaluating a New Test', *Interfaces* 29, no. 3 (May/June 1999): 63–76.

We will see that in cases where expected monetary value does not lead to the most preferred decision alternative, expressing the value (or worth) of an outcome in terms of its *utility* will permit the use of *expected utility* to identify the most desirable decision.

The Meaning of Utility

Utility is a measure of the total worth of a particular outcome; it reflects the decision maker's attitude toward a collection of factors such as profit, loss and risk. As an example of a case where utility can help in selecting the best decision alternative, let us consider the problem faced by Swofford, a relatively small real estate investment firm. Swofford currently has two investment opportunities that require approximately the same cash outlay. The cash requirements necessary prohibit Swofford from making more than one investment at this time. Consequently, three possible decision alternatives may be considered.

The three decision alternatives, denoted by d_1, d_2 and d_3, are as follows:

$$d_1 = \text{make investment A}$$
$$d_2 = \text{make investment B}$$
$$d_3 = \text{do not invest}$$

The monetary payoffs associated with the investment opportunities depend largely on what happens to the real estate market during the next six months. Real estate prices could go up, remain stable or go down. Thus, the states of nature, denoted by s_1, s_2 and s_3, are as follows:

$$s_1 = \text{real estate prices go up}$$
$$s_2 = \text{real estate prices remain stable}$$
$$s_3 = \text{real estate prices go down}$$

Using the best information available, Swofford estimated the profits or payoffs associated with each decision alternative and state-of-nature combination. The resulting payoff table is shown in Table 13.9.

The best estimate of the probability that prices will go up is 0.3, the best estimate of the probability that prices will remain stable is 0.5 and the best estimate of the probability that real estate prices will go down is 0.2. Thus, the expected values for the three decision alternatives are:

$$EV(d_1) = 0.3(€30\,000) + 0.5(€20\,000) + 0.2(-€50\,000) = €9\,000$$
$$EV(d_2) = 0.3(€50\,000) + 0.5(-€20\,000) + 0.2(-€30\,000) = -€1\,000$$
$$EV(d_3) = 0.3(€0) + 0.5(€0) + 0.2(€0) = €0$$

Using the expected value approach, the optimal decision is to select investment A, with an expected monetary value of €9000. Is this really the best decision alternative? Let us consider some other relevant factors that relate to Swofford's capability for absorbing the €50 000 loss if investment A is made and real estate prices go down.

It turns out that Swofford's financial position is weak. This fact was partly reflected in Swofford's ability to undertake, at most, one investment at the current time. More important, however, the firm's president feels that if the next investment results in substantial losses, Swofford's future will be in jeopardy. Although the expected value approach leads to a recommendation for d_1, do you think it is the decision the firm's president would prefer? We suspect that d_2 or d_3 would be selected to avoid the possibility of incurring a €50 000 loss. In fact, it is reasonable to believe that if a loss as great as even €30 000 could drive Swofford out of business, the president would select d_3, feeling that both investment A and investment B are too risky for Swofford's current financial position.

The way we resolve Swofford's dilemma is first to determine Swofford's utility for the various monetary outcomes. Recall that the utility of any outcome is the total worth of that outcome, taking into account the risks and payoffs involved. If the

Table 13.9 Payoff Table for Swofford (Profit in €)

	State of Nature		
	Prices Up	Prices Stable	Prices Down
Decision Alternative	s_1	s_2	s_3
Investment A, d_1	30 000	20 000	−50 000
Investment B, d_2	50 000	−20 000	−30 000
Do not invest, d_3	0	0	0

utilities for the various outcomes are assessed correctly, then the decision alternative with the highest expected utility is the most preferred or best alternative.

Developing Utilities for Payoffs

The procedure we use to establish utility values for the payoffs requires that we first assign a utility value to the best and worst possible payoffs in the decision situation. Any values work as long as the utility assigned to the best payoff is greater than the utility assigned to the worst payoff. In Swofford's case, Table 13.9 shows that €50 000 is the best payoff and −€50 000 is the worst payoff. Suppose, then, that we arbitrarily make the following assignments of these two payoffs:

$$\text{Utility of } -€50\,000 = U(-€50\,000) = 0$$
$$\text{Utility of } €50\,000 = U(€50\,000) = 10$$

Now let us see how we can determine the utility associated with every other payoff.

Consider the process of establishing the utility of a payoff of €30 000. First, we ask Swofford's president to state a preference between a guaranteed €30 000 payoff and the opportunity to engage in the following lottery, or bet:

Lottery: Swofford obtains a payoff of €50 000 with probability p and a payoff of −€50 000 with probability $(1 - p)$.

If p is very close to 1, Swofford's president would prefer the lottery to the certain payoff of €30 000 because the firm would virtually guarantee itself a payoff of €50 000. On the other hand, if p is very close to 0, the president would clearly prefer the guarantee of €30 000. In any event, as p changes continuously from 0 to 1, the preference for the guaranteed payoff of €30 000 will change at some point into a preference for the lottery. At the change point, the president is indifferent between the guaranteed payoff of €30 000 and the lottery. For example, let us assume that when $p = 0.95$, the president is indifferent between the certain payoff of €30 000 and the lottery. Given this value of p, we can calculate the utility of a €30 000 payoff as follows:

$$\begin{aligned} U(€30\,000) &= pU(€50\,000) + (1 - p)U(-€50\,000) \\ &= 0.95(10) + (0.5)(0) \\ &= 9.5 \end{aligned}$$

Obviously, if we started with a different assignment of utilities for payoffs of €50 000 and −€50 000, we would end up with a different utility for €30 000. Hence, we must conclude that the utility assigned to each payoff is not unique, but is relative to the initial choice of utilities for the best and worst payoffs. We discuss this factor further at the end of this section. For now, however, we continue to use a value of 10 for the utility of €50 000 and a value of 0 for the utility of −€50 000.

Before calculating the utility for the other payoffs, let us consider the significance of assigning a utility of 9.5 to a payoff of €30 000. Clearly, when $p = 0.95$, the expected value of the lottery is:

$$\begin{aligned} \text{EV(Lottery)} &= 0.95(€50\,000) + 0.05(-€50\,000) \\ &= €47\,500 - €2\,500 \\ &= €45\,000 \end{aligned}$$

We see that although the expected value of the lottery when $p = 0.95$ is €45 000, Swofford's president would just as soon take a guaranteed payoff of €30 000 and thus take a conservative, or risk-avoiding, viewpoint. That is, the president would rather have €30 000 for certain than risk anything greater than a 5 per cent chance of incurring a loss of €50 000. One can view the difference between the EV of €45 000 for the lottery and the €30 000 guaranteed payoff as the risk premium that the president would be willing to pay to avoid the 5 per cent chance of losing €50 000.

To calculate the utility associated with a payoff of −€20 000, we must ask Swofford's president to state a preference between a guaranteed −€20 000 payoff and the opportunity to engage in the following lottery.

Lottery: Swofford obtains a payoff of €50 000 with probability p and a payoff of −€50 000 with probability $(1 - p)$.

Note that it is exactly the same lottery we used to establish the utility of a payoff of €30 000. In fact, this lottery will be used to establish the utility for any monetary value in the Swofford payoff table. Using this lottery, then, we must ask the president to state the value of p that provides an indifference between a guaranteed payoff of −€20 000 and the lottery. For example, we might begin by asking the president to choose between a certain loss of €20 000 and the lottery with a payoff of €50 000 with probability $p = 0.90$ and a payoff of −€50 000 with probability $(1 - p) = 0.10$. What answer do you think we would get? Surely, with this high probability of obtaining a payoff of €50 000, the president would select the lottery. Next, we might ask if $p = 0.85$ would result in indifference between the loss of €20 000 for certain and the lottery. Again, the president might tell us that the lottery would be preferred. Suppose that we continue in this fashion until we get to $p = 0.55$, where we find that with this value of p, the president is indifferent between the payoff of −€20 000 and the lottery. That is, for any value of p less than 0.55, the president would rather take a loss of €20 000 for certain than risk the potential loss of €50 000 with the lottery; for any value of p above 0.55, the president would select the lottery. Thus, the utility assigned to a payoff of −€20 000 is:

$$\begin{aligned} U(-€20\,000) &= pU(€50\,000) + (1 - p)U(-€50\,000) \\ &= 0.55(10) + 0.45(0) \\ &= 5.5 \end{aligned}$$

Again, let us examine the significance of this assignment as compared with the expected value approach. When $p = 0.55$, the expected value of the lottery is:

$$\begin{aligned} \text{EV(Lottery)} &= 0.55(€50\,000) + 0.45(-€50\,000) \\ &= €27\,500 - €22\,500 \\ &= €5\,000 \end{aligned}$$

Thus, the president would just as soon absorb a loss of €20 000 for certain as take the lottery, even though the expected value of the lottery is €5000. Once again we see the conservative, or risk-avoiding, point of view of Swofford's president.

In the two preceding examples where we calculated the utility for a specific monetary payoff, M, we first found the probability p where the decision maker was indifferent between a guaranteed payoff of M and a lottery with a payoff of €50 000 with probability p and −€50 000 with probability $(1 - p)$. The utility of M was then calculated as:

$$\begin{aligned} U(M) &= pU(€50\,000) + (1 - p)U(-€50\,000) \\ &= p(10) + (1 - p)0 \\ &= 10p \end{aligned}$$

Using this procedure, utility values for the rest of the payoffs in Swofford's problem were developed. The results are presented in Table 13.10.

After we determine the utility value of each of the possible monetary values, we can write the original payoff table in terms of utility values. Table 13.11 shows the utility for the various outcomes in the Swofford problem. The notation we use for

Table 13.10 Utility Of Monetary Payoffs for the Swofford Problem

Monetary Value	Indifference Value of *p*	Utility Value
€50 000	Does not apply	10.0
30 000	0.95	9.5
20 000	0.90	9.0
0	0.75	7.5
−20 000	0.55	5.5
−30 000	0.40	4.0
−50 000	Does not apply	0.0

Table 13.11 Utility Table for Swofford Problem

	State of Nature		
Decision Alternative	Prices Up s_1	Prices Stable s_2	Prices Down s_3
Investment A, d_1	9.5	9.0	0.0
Investment B, d_2	10.0	5.5	4.0
Do not invest, d_3	7.5	7.5	7.5

the entries in the utility table is U_{ij}, which denotes the utility associated with decision alternative d_i and state of nature s_j. Using this notation, we see that $U_{23} = 4.0$.

Expected Utility Approach

We can now apply the expected value computations introduced in Section 13.3 to the payoffs in Table 13.11 in order to select an optimal decision alternative for Swofford, However, because utility values represent such a special case of expected value, we refer to the expected value when applied to utility values as the *expected utility* (EU). In this way, we avoid any possible confusion between the expected value for the original payoff table and the expected value for the payoff table consisting of *utility values*. Thus, the **expected utility approach** requires the analyst to compute the expected utility for each decision alternative and then select the alternative yielding the best expected utility. If there are N possible states of nature, the expected utility of a decision alternative d_i is given by:

$$\text{EU}(d_i) = \sum_{j=1}^{N} P(s_j)U_{ij} \tag{13.15}$$

The expected utility for each of the decision alternatives in the Swofford problem is computed as follows:

$$\text{EU}(d_1) = 0.3(9.5) + 0.5(9.0) + 0.2(0) \quad = 7.35$$
$$\text{EU}(d_2) = 0.3(10) \ + 0.5(9.0) + 0.2(4.0) \ = 6.55$$
$$\text{EU}(d_3) = 0.3(7.5) + 0.5(7.5) + 0.2(7.5) \ = 7.50$$

Problem 16 asks you to use the expected utility approach to determine the optimal decision.

We see that the optimal decision using the expected utility approach is d_3, do not invest. The ranking of alternatives according to the president's utility assignments and the associated monetary value is as follows:

Ranking of Decision Alternatives	Expected Utility	Expected Monetary Value
Do not invest	7.50	€ 0
Investment A	7.35	9 000
Investment B	6.55	−1 000

Note that whereas investment A had the highest expected monetary value of €9000, the analysis indicates that Swofford should decline this investment. The rationale behind not selecting Investment A is that the 0.2 probability of a €50 000 loss was considered by Swofford's president to involve a serious risk. The seriousness of this risk and its associated impact on the company were not adequately reflected by the expected monetary value of investment A. It was necessary to assess the utility for each payoff to adequately take this risk into account.

The determination of the appropriate utilities is not a trivial task. As we have seen, measuring utility requires a degree of subjectivity on the part of the decision maker, and different decision makers will have different utility functions. This aspect of utility often causes decision makers to feel uncomfortable about using the expected utility approach. However, if we encounter a decision situation in which we are convinced monetary value is not the only relevant measure of performance, utility analysis should be considered.

NOTES AND COMMENTS

1 In the Swofford problem, we used a utility of 10 for the largest possible payoff and 0 for the smallest. Had we chosen 1 for the utility of the largest payoff and 0 for the utility of the smallest, the utility for any monetary value *M* would have been the value of *p* at which the decision maker was indifferent between a certain payoff of *M* and a lottery in which the best payoff is obtained with probability of *p* and the worst payoff is obtained with probability of $(1 - p)$. Thus, the utility for any monetary value would have been equal to the probability of earning the highest payoff. Often, this choice is made because of the ease in calculation. We chose not to do so to emphasize the distinction between the utility values and the indifference probabilities for the lottery.

2 Generally, when the payoffs for a particular decision-making problem fall into a reasonable range – the best is not too good and the worst is not too bad – decision makers tend to express preferences in agreement with the expected monetary value approach. Thus, as a guideline we suggest asking the decision maker to consider the best and worst possible payoffs for a problem and assess their reasonableness. If the decision maker believes they are in the reasonable range, the expected monetary value criterion can be used. However, if the payoffs appear unreasonably large or unreasonably small and if the decision maker feels monetary values do not adequately reflect the true preferences for the payoffs, a utility analysis of the problem should be considered.

Summary

- Decision analysis is used to evaluate alternative decisions where the outcomes are uncertain.
- A payoff table shows the payoffs or outcomes for a decision problem.
- A decision tree shows the decision problem graphically.
- For decision problems without probability information, three alternative approaches can be used: the optimistic, or maximax approach; the conservative or maximin approach; the minimax regret approach.
- When probability information is available the expected value approach can be used.
- Decision analysis can be used to assess the value of additional information about the decision problem.
- A risk profile provides a probability distribution for the possible payoffs and can help in assessing the risks associated with different decision alternatives.
- The expected utility approach can be used in situations where monetary value is not the only measure of performance.

WORKED EXAMPLE

The Development Team of Potsdam City Council in Germany have a remit to support economic development in the city. The city has a small airport and AirXpress, a German budget airline, has indicated to the Team that if the airport is upgraded and refurbished the airline would seriously consider establishing the airport as one of its regional centres. This would bring income and further investment into the city with an estimated value of €3.5 million. However, the cost to the city council of upgrading the airport would be around €2 million. AirXpress will not consider using the airport unless it is upgraded. In addition, a medical equipment manufacturer, Diagnostic Research International (DRI) is considering building a manufacturing plant in the city which again would increase the city's prosperity by an estimated €4.5 million. The Development Team are of the view that upgrading the airport would increase the chance of DRI locating to Potsdam. However, the city council is under severe financial pressure and €2 million would put considerable pressure on its budget. The following information has been obtained. What advice can we offer the Development Team?

Upgrade the airport

Outcomes	Probability
AirXpress establish a regional centre	0.1
DRI builds manufacturing plant	0.4
AirXpress establish a regional centre and DRI builds manufacturing plant	0.3
Neither AirXpress or DRI locate to the city	0.2

No upgrade of the airport

Outcomes	Probability
DRI does not build manufacturing plant	0.4
DRI builds manufacturing plant	0.6

Solution

We have a decision problem with probability information. The decision facing the city is whether to upgrade the airport or not. If the decision is taken to upgrade the airport then there are four possible outcomes with differing financial consequences for the city (Exhibit 13.2).

Upgrade the airport

Outcomes	Probability	Net financial impact for the city (millions)
AirXpress establish a regional centre	0.1	€1.5
DRI builds manufacturing plant	0.4	€2.5
AirXpress establish a regional centre and DRI builds manufacturing plant	0.3	€6
Neither AirXpress or DRI locate to the city	0.2	−€2

If AirXpress locate to the airport this will bring an estimated €3.5 million into the city but will have cost €2 million giving a net financial impact of €1.5 million. Similarly, if DRI builds a manufacturing plant this will bring €4.5 million into the city but cost €2 million. If both companies decide to relocate to the city the combined benefit will be €8 million but again at a cost of €2 million to the city giving a net benefit of €6 million. However, if neither company locates to the city the cost of upgrading the airport will have been for nothing so the net effect will be −€2 million. On the other hand if the city decides not to upgrade the airport, there are only two outcomes as AirXpress will definitely not create a regional centre at the airport. Again, the financial consequences can be determined. If DRI does not build the plan the net effect is zero. If DRI does build the plant this will bring €4.5 million but without any cost to the city (Exhibit 13.3).

No upgrade of the airport

Outcomes	Probability	Net financial impact for the city (millions)
DRI does not build manufacturing plant	0.4	0
DRI builds manufacturing plant	0.6	€4.5

We can summarize the decision situation with a decision tree and calculate the relevant expected values. Using TreePlan we have the decision tree shown below in Exhibit 13.4. This shows that the decision to upgrade

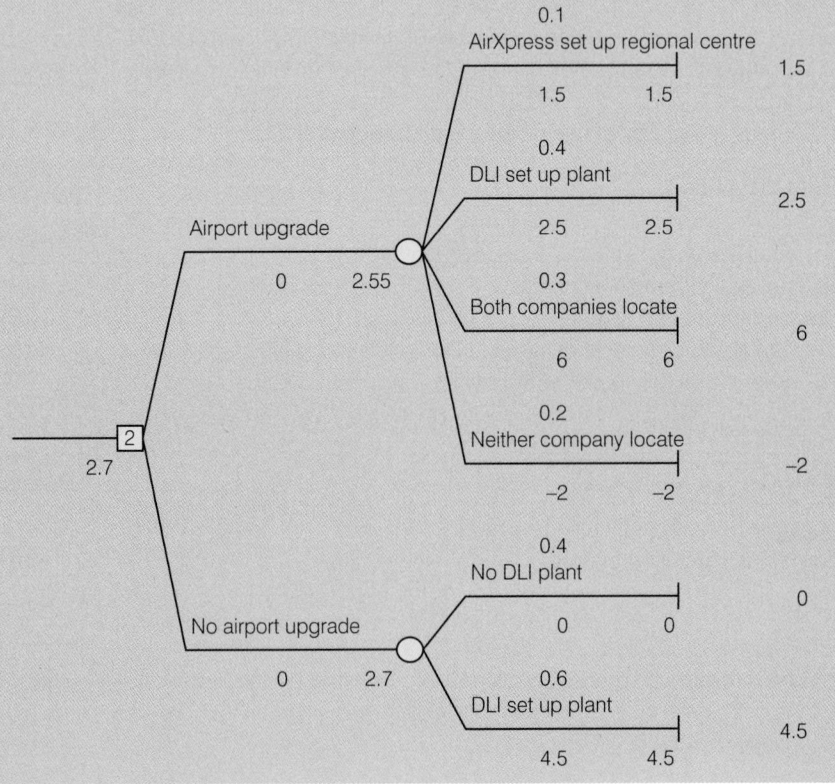

the airport has an expected value of €2.55 million – this is the net return to the city. However, the decision not to upgrade the airport has a slightly higher expected value of €2.7 million and, based on the information available, would be the preferred decision. We can also point out to the Development Team that the decision model allows them to undertake sensitivity analysis and assess the impact that different values would have on the recommended decision.

MANAGEMENT SCIENCE IN ACTION

Investing in a Transmission System at Oglethorpe Power

Oglethorpe Power Corporation (OPC) provides wholesale electrical power to consumer-owned cooperatives in the state of Georgia. Florida Power Corporation proposed that OPC join in the building of a major transmission line from Georgia to Florida. Deciding whether to become involved in the building of the transmission line was a major decision for OPC because it would involve the commitment of substantial OPC resources. OPC worked with Applied Decision Analysis, Inc., to conduct a comprehensive decision analysis of the problem.

In the problem formulation step, three decisions were identified: (1) build a transmission line from Georgia to Florida; (2) upgrade existing transmission facilities; and (3) who would control the new facilities. Oglethorpe was faced with five chance events: (1) construction costs; (2) competition; (3) demand in Florida; (4) OPC's share of the operation; and (5) pricing. The consequence or payoff was measured in terms of dollars saved. The diagram for the problem had three decision nodes, five chance nodes, a consequence node and several intermediate nodes that described intermediate calculations. The decision tree for the problem had more than 8000 paths from the starting node to the terminal branches.

An expected value analysis of the decision tree provided an optimal decision strategy for OPC. However, the risk profile for the optimal decision strategy showed that the recommended strategy was very risky and had a significant probability of increasing OPC's cost rather than providing savings. The risk analysis led to the conclusion that more information about the competition was needed in order to reduce OPC's risk. Sensitivity analysis involving various probabilities and payoffs showed that the value of the optimal decision strategy was stable over a reasonable range of input values. The final recommendation from the decision analysis was that OPC should begin negotiations with Florida Power Corporation concerning the building of the new transmission line.

Based on Adam Borison, 'Oglethorpe Power Corporation Decides about Investing in a Major Transmission System', *Interfaces* (March/April 1995): 25–36.

Problems

SELF *test*

1 The following payoff table shows profit for a decision analysis problem with two decision alternatives and three states of nature.

	State of Nature		
Decision Alternative	s_1	s_2	s_3
d_1	250	100	25
d_2	100	100	75

a. Construct a decision tree for this problem.
b. If the decision maker knows nothing about the probabilities of the three states of nature, what is the recommended decision using the optimistic, conservative and minimax regret approaches?

SELF *test*

2 Suppose that a decision maker faced with four decision alternatives and four states of nature develops the following profit payoff table.

Decision Alternative	State of Nature			
	s_1	s_2	s_3	s_4
d_1	14	9	10	5
d_2	11	10	8	7
d_3	9	10	10	11
d_4	8	10	11	13

a. If the decision maker knows nothing about the probabilities of the four states of nature, what is the recommended decision using the optimistic, conservative and minimax regret approaches?
b. Which approach do you prefer? Explain. Is establishing the most appropriate approach before analyzing the problem important for the decision maker? Explain.
c. Assume that the payoff table provides *cost* rather than profit payoffs. What is the recommended decision using the optimistic, conservative and minimax regret approaches?

SELF *test*

3 Khobar Corporation's decision to produce a new line of recreational products resulted in the need to construct either a small plant or a large plant. The best selection of plant size depends on how the marketplace reacts to the new product line. To conduct an analysis, marketing management has decided to view the possible long-run demand as either low, medium or high. The following payoff table shows the projected profit in millions of euros:

Plant Size	Long-Run Demand		
	Low	Medium	High
Small	150	200	200
Large	50	200	500

a. What is the decision to be made, and what is the chance event for Southland's problem?
b. Construct a decision tree.
c. Recommend a decision based on the use of the optimistic, conservative and minimax regret approaches.

SELF *test*

4 The following profit payoff table was presented in Problem 1. Suppose that the decision maker obtained the probability assessments $P(s_1) = 0.65$, $P(s_2) = 0.15$, and $P(s_3) = 0.20$. Use the expected value approach to determine the optimal decision.

Decision Alternative	State of Nature		
	s_1	s_2	s_3
d_1	250	100	25
d_2	100	100	75

SELF *test*

5 Khan Corporation is considering three options for managing its data processing operation: continuing with its own staff, hiring an outside vendor to do the managing (referred to as *outsourcing*), or using a combination of its own staff and an outside vendor. The cost of the operation depends on future demand. The annual cost of each option (in thousands of euros) depends on demand as follows.

	Demand		
Staffing Options	**High**	**Medium**	**Low**
Own staff	650	650	600
Outside vendor	900	600	300
Combination	800	650	500

a. If the demand probabilities are 0.2, 0.5 and 0.3, which decision alternative will mini-mize the expected cost of the data processing operation? What is the expected annual cost associated with that recommendation?

b. Construct a risk profile for the optimal decision in part (a). What is the probability of the cost exceeding €700 000?

SELF *test*

6 The following payoff table shows the profit for a decision problem with two states of nature and two decision alternatives.

	State of Nature	
Decision Alternative	s_1	s_2
d_1	10	1
d_2	4	3

a. Use graphical sensitivity analysis to determine the range of probabilities of state of nature s_1 for which each of the decision alternatives has the largest expected value.

b. Suppose $P(s_1) = 0.2$ and $P(s_2) = 0.8$. What is the best decision using the expected value approach?

c. Perform sensitivity analysis on the payoffs for decision alternative d_1. Assume the probabilities are as given in part (b) and find the range of payoffs under states of nature s_1 and s_2 that will keep the solution found in part (b) optimal. Is the solution more sensitive to the payoff under state of nature s_1 or s_2?

7 Scot Air Express decided to offer direct service from Edinburgh to Manchester. Management must decide between a full-price service using the company's new fleet of jet aircraft and a discount service using smaller capacity commuter planes. It is clear that the best choice depends on the market reaction to the service Scot Air offers. Management developed estimates of the contribution to profit for each type of service based upon two possible levels of demand for service to Manchester: strong and weak. The following table shows the estimated quarterly profits (in thousands of £).

	Demand for Service	
Service	**Strong**	**Weak**
Full price	£960	−£490
Discount	£670	£320

a. What is the decision to be made, what is the chance event, and what is the consequence for this problem? How many decision alternatives are there? How many outcomes are there for the chance event?
b. If nothing is known about the probabilities of the chance outcomes, what is the recommended decision using the optimistic, conservative and minimax regret approaches?
c. Suppose that management of Scot Air Express believes that the probability of strong demand is 0.7 and the probability of weak demand is 0.3. Use the expected value approach to determine an optimal decision.
d. Suppose that the probability of strong demand is 0.8 and the probability of weak demand is 0.2. What is the optimal decision using the expected value approach?
e. Use graphical sensitivity analysis to determine the range of demand probabilities for which each of the decision alternatives has the largest expected value.

8 For the PDC problem in Section 13.3, the decision alternative to build the large complex was found to be optimal using the expected value approach. In Section 13.4 we conducted a sensitivity analysis for the payoffs associated with this decision alternative. We found that the large complex remained optimal as long as the payoff for the strong demand was greater than or equal to R17.5 million and as long as the payoff for the weak demand was greater than or equal to −R19 million.

a. Consider the medium complex decision. How much could the payoff under strong demand increase and still keep decision alternative d_3 the optimal solution?
b. Consider the small complex decision. How much could the payoff under strong demand increase and still keep decision alternative d_3 the optimal solution?

SELF *test*

9 The following profit payoff table was presented in Problems 1 and 4.

	State of Nature		
Decision Alternative	s_1	s_2	s_3
d_1	250	100	25
d_2	100	100	75

The probabilities for the states of nature are $P(s_1) = 0.65$, $P(s_2) = 0.15$, and $P(s_3) = 0.20$.

a. What is the optimal decision strategy if perfect information is available?
b. What is the expected value for the decision strategy developed in part (a)?
c. Using the expected value approach, what is the recommended decision without perfect information? What is its expected value?
d. What is the expected value of perfect information?

SELF *test*

10 Consider a variation of the PDC decision tree shown in Figure 13.7. The company must first decide whether to undertake the market research study. If the market research study is conducted, the outcome will either be favourable (F) or unfavourable (U). Assume there are only two decision alternatives d_1 and d_2 and two states of nature s_1 and s_2. The payoff table showing profit is as follows:

	State of Nature	
Decision Alternative	s_1	s_2
d_1	100	300
d_2	400	200

a. Show the decision tree.
b. Using the following probabilities, what is the optimal decision strategy?

$$P(F) = 0.56 \quad P(s_1|F) = 0.57 \quad P(s_1|U) = 0.18 \quad P(s_1) = 0.40$$
$$P(F) = 0.44 \quad P(s_2|F) = 0.43 \quad P(s_2|U) = 0.82 \quad P(s_2) = 0.60$$

SELF *test*

11 Dante Development Corporation is considering bidding on a contract for a new office building complex. Figure 13.14 shows the decision tree prepared by one of Dante's analysts. At node 1, the company must decide whether to bid on the contract. The cost of preparing the bid is €200 000. The upper branch from node 2 shows that the company has a 0.8 probability of winning the contract if it submits a bid. If the company wins the bid, it will have to pay €2 000 000 to become a partner in the project. Node 3 shows that the company will then consider doing a market research study to forecast demand for the office units prior to beginning construction. The cost of this study is €150 000. Node 4 is a chance node showing the possible outcomes of the market research study.

Nodes 5, 6 and 7 are similar in that they are the decision nodes for Dante to either build the office complex or sell the rights in the project to another developer. The decision to build the complex will result in an income of €5 000 000 if demand is high and €3 000 000 if demand is moderate. If Dante chooses to sell its rights in the project to another developer, income from the sale is estimated to be €3 500 000. The probabilities shown at nodes 4, 8 and 9 are based on the projected outcomes of the market research study.

a. Verify Dante's profit projections shown at the ending branches of the decision tree by calculating the payoffs of €2 650 000 and €650 000 for the first two outcomes.
b. What is the optimal decision strategy for Dante, and what is the expected profit for this project?
c. What would the cost of the market research study have to be before Dante would change its decision about the market research study?
d. Develop a risk profile for Dante.

Figure 13.14 Decision Tree for the Dante Development Corporation

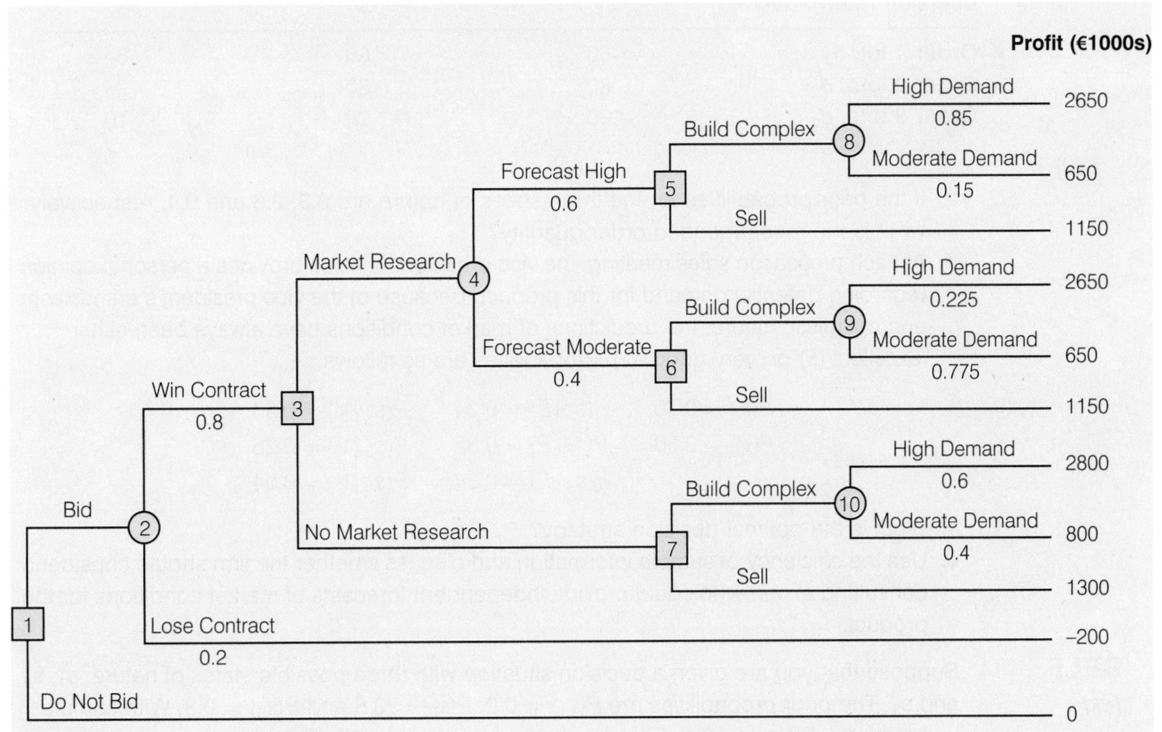

SELF *test*

12 Kotze Publishing Company received a six-chapter manuscript for a new college textbook. The editor of the college division is familiar with the manuscript and estimated a 0.65 probability that the textbook will be successful. If successful, a profit of €750 000 will be realized. If the company decides to publish the textbook and it is unsuccessful, a loss of €250 000 will occur.

Before making the decision to accept or reject the manuscript, the editor is considering sending the manuscript out for review. A review process provides either a favourable (*F*) or unfavourable (*U*) evaluation of the manuscript. Past experience with the review process suggests probabilities $P(F) = 0.7$ and $P(U) = 0.3$ apply. Let s_1 = the textbook is successful, and s_2 = the textbook is unsuccessful. The editor's initial probabilities of s_1 and s_2 will be revised based on whether the review is favourable or unfavourable. The revised probabilities are as follows.

$$P(s_1|F) = 0.75 \qquad P(s_1|U) = 0.417$$
$$P(s_2|F) = 0.25 \qquad P(s_2|U) = 0.583$$

a. Construct a decision tree assuming that the company will first make the decision of whether to send the manuscript out for review and then make the decision to accept or reject the manuscript.

b. Analyze the decision tree to determine the optimal decision strategy for the publishing company.

c. If the manuscript review costs €5000, what is your recommendation?

d. What is the expected value of perfect information? What does this EVPI suggest for the company?

13 Romero's Department Store faces a buying decision for a seasonal product for which demand can be high, medium or low. The purchaser for Romero's can order 1, 2 or 3 lots of the product before the season begins but cannot reorder later. Profit projections (in thousands of euros) are shown.

	State of Nature		
	High Demand	Medium Demand	Low Demand
Decision Alternative	s_1	s_2	s_3
Order 1 lot, d_1	60	60	50
Order 2 lots, d_2	80	80	30
Order 3 lots, d_3	100	70	10

a. If the prior probabilities for the three states of nature are 0.3, 0.3 and 0.4, respectively, what is the recommended order quantity?

b. At each preseason sales meeting, the vice president of sales provides a personal opinion regarding potential demand for this product. Because of the vice president's enthusiasm and optimistic nature, the predictions of market conditions have always been either 'excellent'(*E*) or 'very good' (*V*). Probabilities are as follows.

$$P(E) = 0.70 \qquad P(s_1 | E) = 0.34 \qquad P(s_1 | V) = 0.20$$
$$P(V) = 0.30 \qquad P(s_2 | E) = 0.32 \qquad P(s_2 | V) = 0.26$$
$$P(s_3 | E) = 0.34 \qquad P(s_3 | V) = 0.54$$

What is the optimal decision strategy?

c. Use the efficiency of sample information and discuss whether the firm should consider a consulting expert who could provide independent forecasts of market conditions for the product.

SELF *test*

14 Suppose that you are given a decision situation with three possible states of nature: s_1, s_2 and s_3. The prior probabilities are $P(s_1) = 0.2$, $P(s_2) = 0.5$ and $P(s_3) = 0.3$. With sample information *I*, $P(I|s_1) = 0.1$, $P(I|s_2) = 0.05$ and $P(I|s_3) = 0.2$. Calculate the revised or posterior probabilities: $P(s_1|I)$, $P(s_2|I)$, and $P(s_3|I)$.

15 The Russo Manufacturing Company must decide whether to manufacture a component part at its Milan plant or purchase the component part from a supplier. The resulting profit is dependent upon the demand for the product. The following payoff table shows the projected profit (in thousands of euros).

	State of Nature		
	Low Demand	Medium Demand	High Demand
Decision Alternative	s_1	s_2	s_3
Manufacture, d_1	−20	40	100
Purchase, d_2	10	45	70

The state-of-nature probabilities are $P(s_1) = 0.35$, $P(s_2) = 0.35$ and $P(s_3) = 0.30$.

a. Use a decision tree to recommend a decision.
b. Use EVPI to determine whether Russo should attempt to obtain a better estimate of demand.
c. A test market study of the potential demand for the product is expected to report either a favourable (F) or unfavourable (U) condition. The relevant conditional probabilities are as follows:

$$P(F \mid s_1) = 0.10 \quad P(U \mid s_1) = 0.90$$
$$P(F \mid s_2) = 0.40 \quad P(U \mid s_2) = 0.60$$
$$P(F \mid s_3) = 0.60 \quad P(U \mid s_3) = 0.40$$

What is the probability that the market research report will be favourable?
d. What is Russo's optimal decision strategy?
e. What is the expected value of the market research information?
f. What is the efficiency of the information?

SELF *test* 16 Three decision makers have assessed utilities for the following decision problem (payoff in euros).

	State of Nature		
Decision Alternative	s_1	s_2	s_3
d_1	20	50	−20
d_2	80	100	−100

The indifference probabilities are as follows.

	Indifference Probability (p)		
Payoff	**Risk Avoider**	**Risk Taker**	**Risk Neutral**
100	1.00	1.00	1.00
80	0.95	0.70	0.90
50	0.90	0.60	0.75
20	0.70	0.45	0.60
−20	0.50	0.25	0.40
−100	0.00	0.00	0.00

For the payoff of 20, what is the premium that the risk avoider will pay to avoid risk? What is the premium that the risk taker will pay to have the opportunity of the high payoff?

17 In Problem 16, if $P(s_1) = 0.25$, $P(s_2) = 0.50$ and $P(s_3) = 0.25$, find a recommended decision for each of the three decision makers. Note that for the same decision problem, different utilities can lead to different decisions.

SELF *test*

18 A firm has three investment alternatives. The payoff table (in thousands of euros) and associated probabilities are as follows:

	Economic Condition		
Investment	**Up**	**Stable**	**Down**
d_1	100	25	0
d_2	75	50	25
d_3	50	50	50
Probabilities	0.40	0.30	0.30

a. Using the expected value approach, which decision is preferred?

b. For the lottery having a payoff of €100 000 with probability p and €0 with probability $(1 - p)$, two decision makers expressed the following indifference probabilities:

	Indifference Probability (p)	
Profit	**Decision Maker A**	**Decision Maker B**
€75,000	0.80	0.60
50,000	0.60	0.30
25,000	0.30	0.15

Find the most preferred decision for each decision maker using the expected utility approach.

c. Why don't decision makers A and B select the same decision alternative?

19 Zondo Industries is considering purchasing an insurance policy for its new office building in Port Elizabeth. The policy has an annual cost of €10 000. If Zondo Industries does not purchase the insurance and minor fire damage occurs to the office building, a cost of €100 000 is anticipated; the cost if major or total destruction occurs is €200 000. The payoff table in (€), including the state-of-nature probabilities, is as follows:

	Damage		
	None	**Minor**	**Major**
Decision Alternative	s_1	s_2	s_3
Purchase insurance, d_1	10 000	10 000	10 000
Do not purchase insurance, d_2	0	100 000	200 000
Probabilities	0.96	0.03	0.01

a. Using the expected value approach, what decision do you recommend?

b. What lottery would you use to assess utilities? (*Note*: The data are costs, which makes the best payoff €0.)

c. Assume we found the following indifference probabilities for the lottery defined in part (b):

cost	Indifference Probability (p)
€10 000	0.99
100 000	0.60

What decision would you recommend?

d. Do you favour using expected value or expected utility for this decision problem? Why?

SELF *test*

20 A new product has the following profit projections and associated probabilities:

Profit	Probability
150 000	0.10
100 000	0.25
50 000	0.20
0	0.15
−50 000	0.20
−100 000	0.10

a. Use the expected value approach to make the decision of whether to market the new product.

b. Because of the high euro values involved, especially the possibility of a €100 000 loss, the marketing vice president expressed some concern about the use of the expected value approach. As a consequence, if a utility analysis is performed, what is the appropriate lottery? Assume the following indifference probabilities are assigned:

Profit	Indifference Probability (p)
€100 000	0.95
50 000	0.70
0	0.50
−50 000	0.25

c. Use expected utility to recommend a decision.

d. Should the decision maker feel comfortable with the final decision recommended by the analysis?

CASE PROBLEM 1 Property Purchase Strategy

Glenn Foreman, president of Oceanview Development Corporation based in Portugal, is considering submitting a bid to purchase property that will be sold by sealed bid. Glenn's initial judgement is to submit a bid of €5 million. Based on his experience, Glenn estimates that a bid of €5 million will have a 0.2 probability of being the highest bid and securing the property for Oceanview. The current date is 1 June. Sealed bids for the property must be submitted by 15 August. The winning bid will be announced on 1 September.

If Oceanview submits the highest bid and obtains the property, the firm plans to build and sell a complex of luxury apartments. However, a complicating factor is that the property is currently zoned for single-family residences only. Glenn believes that a referendum could be placed on the voting ballot in time for the November election. Passage of the referendum would change the zoning of the property and permit construction of the apartments.

The sealed-bid procedure requires the bid to be submitted with 10 per cent of the amount bid. If the bid is rejected, the deposit is refunded. If the bid is accepted, the deposit is the down payment for the property. However, if the bid is accepted and the bidder does not follow through with the purchase and meet the remainder of the financial obligation within six months, the deposit will be forfeited. In this case, the county will offer the property to the next highest bidder.

To determine whether Oceanview should submit the €5 million bid, Glenn conducted some preliminary analysis. This preliminary work provided an assessment of 0.3 for the probability that the referendum for a zoning change will be approved and resulted in the following estimates of the costs and revenues that will be incurred if the apartments are built.

Cost and Revenue Estimates

Revenue from apartment sales	€15 000 000
Cost	
Property	€5 000 000
Construction expenses	€8 000 000

If Oceanview obtains the property and the zoning change is rejected in November, Glenn believes that the best option would be for the firm not to complete the purchase of the property. In this case, Oceanview would forfeit the 10 per cent deposit that accompanied the bid.

Because the likelihood that the zoning referendum will be approved is such an important factor in the decision process, Glenn suggested that the firm hire a market research service to conduct a survey of voters. The survey would provide a better estimate of the likelihood that the referendum for a zoning change would be approved. The market research firm that Oceanview Development has worked with in the past has agreed to do the study for €15 000. The results of the study will be available 1 August, so that Oceanview will have this information before the 15 August bid deadline. The results of the survey will be either a prediction that the zoning change will be approved or a prediction that the zoning change will be rejected. After considering the record of the market research service in previous studies conducted for Oceanview, Glenn developed the following probability estimates concerning the accuracy of the market research information.

$$P(A \mid s_1) = 0.9 \qquad P(N \mid s_1) = 0.1$$
$$P(A \mid s_2) = 0.2 \qquad P(N \mid s_2) = 0.8$$

where

A = prediction of zoning change approval

N = prediction that zoning change will not be approved

s_1 = the zoning change is approved by the voters

s_2 = the zoning change is rejected by the voters

Managerial Report

Perform an analysis of the problem facing the Oceanview Development Corporation, and prepare a report that summarizes your findings and recommendations. Include the following items in your report:

1. A decision tree that shows the logical sequence of the decision problem.
2. A recommendation regarding what Oceanview should do if the market research information is not available.
3. A decision strategy that Oceanview should follow if the market research is conducted.
4. A recommendation as to whether Oceanview should employ the market research firm, along with the value of the information provided by the market research firm.

Include the details of your analysis as an appendix to your report.

CASE PROBLEM 2 Lawsuit Defence Strategy

Erik Jansson, an employee of Stockholm Construction Company, claims to have injured his back as a result of a fall while repairing the roof at one of the LakeView apartment buildings. He filed a lawsuit against Linus Olsson the owner of LakeView Apartments, asking for damages of €1 500 000. Erik claims that the roof had rotten sections and that his fall could have been prevented if Mr Olsson had told Stockholm Construction about the problem. Mr Olsson notified his insurance company, Allied Insurance, of the lawsuit. Allied must defend Mr Olsson and decide what action to take regarding the lawsuit.

Some depositions and a series of discussions took place between both sides. As a result, Erik Jansson offered to accept a settlement of €750 000. Thus, one option is for Allied to pay Erik €750 000 to settle the claim. Allied is also considering making Erik a counter offer of €400 000 in the hope that he will accept a lesser amount to avoid the time and cost of going to trial. Allied's preliminary investigation shows that Erik's case is strong; Allied is concerned that Erik may reject their counteroffer and request a jury trial. Allied's lawyers spent some time exploring Erik's likely reaction if they make a counter offer of €400 000.

The lawyers concluded that it is adequate to consider three possible outcomes to represent Erik's possible reaction to a counteroffer of €400 000: (1) Erik will accept the counteroffer and the case will be closed; (2) Erik will reject the counteroffer and elect to have a jury decide the settlement amount; or (3) Erik will make a counteroffer to Allied of €600 000. If Erik does make a counteroffer, Allied decided that they will not make additional counteroffers. They will either accept Erik's counteroffer of €600 000 or go to trial.

If the case goes to a jury trial, Allied considers three outcomes possible: (1) the jury may reject Erik's claim and Allied will not be required to pay any damages; (2) the jury will find in favour of Erik and award him €750 000 in damages; or (3) the jury will conclude that Erik has a strong case and award him the full amount of €1 500 000.

Key considerations as Allied develops its strategy for disposing of the case are the probabilities associated with Erik's response to an Allied counteroffer of €400 000 and the probabilities associated with the three possible trial outcomes. Allied's lawyers believe the probability that Erik will accept a counteroffer of €400 000 is 0.10, the probability that Erik will reject a counteroffer of €400 000 is 0.40 and the probability that Erik will, himself, make a counteroffer to Allied of €600 000 is 0.50. If the case goes to court, they believe that the probability the jury will award Erik damages of €1 500 000 is 0.30, the probability that the jury will award Erik damages of €750 000 is 0.50 and the probability that the jury will award Erik nothing is 0.20.

Managerial Report

Perform an analysis of the problem facing Allied Insurance and prepare a report that summarizes your findings and recommendations. Be sure to include the following items:

1. A decision tree.
2. A recommendation regarding whether Allied should accept Erik's initial offer to settle the claim for €750 000.
3. A decision strategy that Allied should follow if they decide to make Erik a counteroffer of €400 000.
4. A risk profile for your recommended strategy.

Appendix 13.1 Decision Analysis with Treeplan

TreePlan[2] is an Excel add-in that can be used to develop decision trees for decision analysis problems. In this appendix, we show how to use TreePlan to build a decision tree and solve the PDC problem presented in Section 13.3. The decision tree for the PDC problem is shown in Figure 13.15.

[2]TreePlan was developed by Professor Michael R. Middleton at the University of San Francisco and modified for use by Professor James E. Smith at Duke University. The TreePlan Website is located at http://www.treeplan.com.

Figure 13.15 PDC Decision Tree

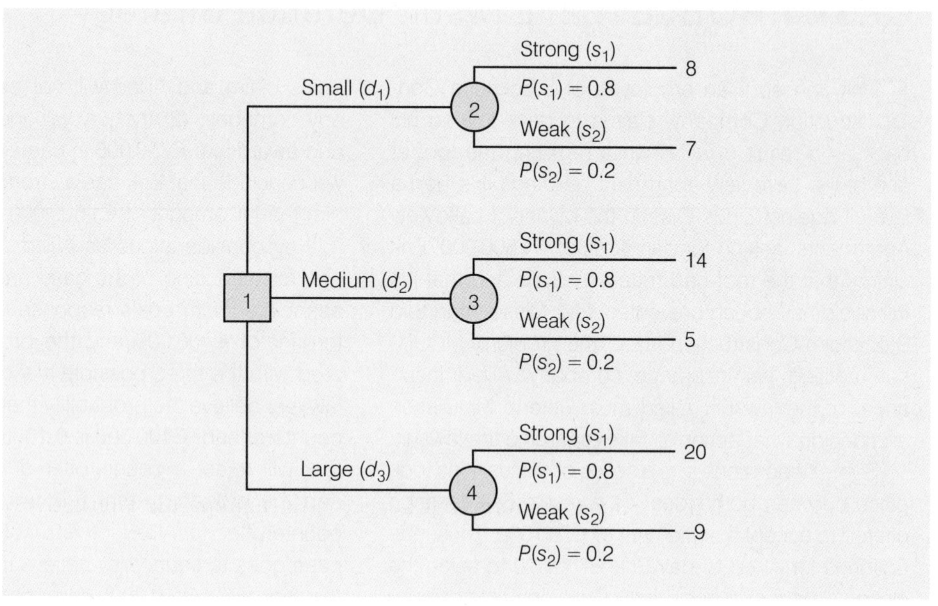

Getting Started: An Initial Decision Tree

We begin by assuming that TreePlan has been installed and an Excel workbook is open. To build a TreePlan version of the PDC decision tree proceed as follows:

Step 1. Select cell A1

Step 2. Select the **Tools** menu and choose **Decision Tree**

Step 3. When the **TreePlan New** dialog box appears:
Click **New Tree**

A decision tree with one decision node and two branches appears as follows:

	A	B	C	D	E	F	G
1							
2				Decision 1			
3							0
4				0	0		
5		1					
6	0						
7				Decision 2			
8							0
9				0	0		

Adding a Branch

The PDC problem has three decision alternatives (small, medium and large complexes), so we must add another decision branch to the tree.

Step 1. Select cell B5

Step 2. Select the **Tools** menu and choose **Decision Tree**

Step 3. When the **TreePlan Decision** dialog box appears:
Select **Add branch**
Click **OK**

A revised tree with three decision branches now appears in the Excel worksheet.

Naming the Decision Alternatives

The decision alternatives can be named by selecting the cells containing the labels Decision 1, Decision 2 and Decision 3, and then entering the corresponding PDC names Small, Medium and Large. After naming the alternatives, the PDC tree with three decision branches appears as follows:

	A	B	C	D	E	F	G
1							
2				Small			
3							0
4				0	0		
5							
6							
7				Medium			
8		1					0
9	0			0	0		
10							
11							
12				Large			
13							0
14				0	0		

Adding Chance Nodes

The chance event for the PDC problem is the demand for the units, which may be either strong or weak. Thus, a chance node with two branches must be added at the end of each decision alternative branch.

Step 1. Select cell F3

Step 2. Select the **Tools** menu and choose **Decision Tree**

Step 3. When the **TreePlan Terminal** dialog box appears:
Select **Change to event node**
Select **Two** in the **Branches** section
Click **OK**

The tree now appears as follows:

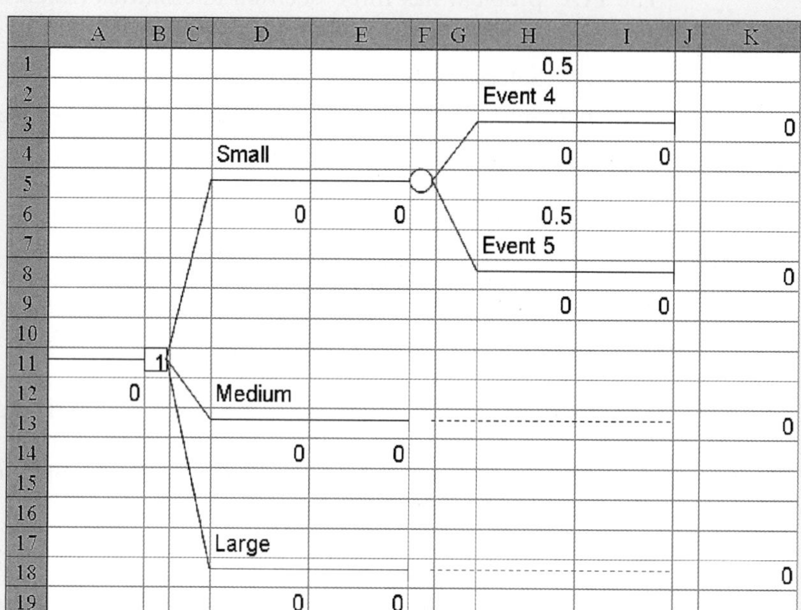

We next select the cells containing Event 4 and Event 5 and rename them Strong and Weak to provide the proper names for the PDC states of nature. After doing so we can copy the subtree for the chance node in cell F5 to the other two decision branches to complete the structure of the PDC decision tree.

Step 1. Select cell F5

Step 2. Select the **Tools** menu and choose **Decision Tree**

Step 3. When the **TreePlan Event** dialog box appears:
Select **Copy subtree**
Click **OK**

Step 4. Select cell F13

Step 5. Select the **Tools** menu and choose **Decision Tree**

Step 6. When the **TreePlan Terminal** dialog box appears
Select **Paste subtree**
Click **OK**

This copy/paste procedure places a chance node at the end of the Medium decision branch. Repeating the same copy/paste procedure for the Large decision branch completes the structure of the PDC decision tree as shown in Figure 13.16.

Inserting Probabilities and Payoffs

TreePlan provides the capability of inserting probabilities and payoffs into the decision tree. In Figure 13.16, we see that TreePlan automatically assigned an equal probability 0.5 to each of the chance outcomes. For PDC, the probability of strong demand is 0.8 and the probability of weak demand is 0.2. We can select cells H1, H6, H11, H16, H21 and H26 and insert the appropriate probabilities. The payoffs for the chance outcomes are inserted in cells H4, H9, H14, H19, H24 and H29. After inserting the PDC probabilities and payoffs, the PDC decision tree appears as shown in Figure 13.17.

Figure 13.16 PDC Decision Tree Developed by Treeplan

	A	B	C	D	E	F	G	H	I	J	K
1								0.5			
2								Strong			
3											0
4				Small				0	0		
5											
6				0	0			0.5			
7								Weak			
8											0
9								0	0		
10											
11								0.5			
12								Strong			
13											0
14				Medium				0	0		
15		1									
16	0			0	0			0.5			
17								Weak			
18											0
19								0	0		
20											
21								0.5			
22								Strong			
23											0
24				Large				0	0		
25											
26				0	0			0.5			
27								Weak			
28											0
29								0	0		

Note that the payoffs also appear in the right-hand margin of the decision tree. The payoffs in the right margin are computed by a formula that adds the payoffs on all of the branches leading to the associated terminal node. For the PDC problem, no payoffs are associated with the decision alternatives branches so we leave the default values of zero in cells D6, D16 and D24. The PDC decision tree is now complete.

Interpreting the Result

When probabilities and payoffs are inserted, TreePlan automatically makes the backward pass computations necessary to determine the optimal solution. Optimal decisions are identified by the number in the corresponding decision node. In the PDC decision tree in Figure 13.17, cell B15 contains the decision node. Note that a 3 appears in this node, which tells us that decision alternative branch 3 provides the optimal decision. Thus, decision analysis recommends PDC construct the Large complex. The expected value of this decision appears at the beginning of the tree in cell A16. Thus, we see the optimal expected value is 14.2 million. The expected values of the other decision alternatives are displayed at the end of the corresponding decision branch. Thus, referring to cells E6 and E16, we see that the expected value of the Small complex is 7.8 million and the expected value of the Medium complex is 12.2 million.

Figure 13.17 PDC Decision Tree With Branch Probabilities and Payoffs

	A	B	C	D	E	F	G	H	I	J	K
1								0.8			
2								Strong			
3											8
4				Small				8	8		
5											
6				0	7.8			0.2			
7								Weak			
8											7
9								7	7		
10											
11								0.8			
12								Strong			
13											14
14				Medium				14	14		
15		3									
16	14.2			0	12.2			0.2			
17								Weak			
18											5
19								5	5		
20											
21								0.8			
22								Strong			
23											20
24				Large				20	20		
25											
26				0	14.2			0.2			
27								Weak			
28											-9
29								-9	-9		

Other Options

TreePlan defaults to a maximization objective. If you would like a minimization objective, follow these steps:

Step 1. Select the **Tools** menu and choose **Decision Tree**

Step 2. Select **Options**

Step 3. Choose **Minimize (costs)**
Click **OK**

In using a TreePlan decision tree, we can modify probabilities and payoffs and quickly observe the impact of the changes on the optimal solution. Using this 'what-if' type of sensitivity analysis, we can identify changes in probabilities and payoffs that would change the optimal decision. Also, because TreePlan is an Excel add-in, most of Excel's capabilities are available. For instance, we could use boldface to highlight the name of the optimal decision alternative on the final decision tree solution. Computer software packages such as TreePlan make it easier to do a thorough analysis of a decision problem.

Chapter 14

Multicriteria Decisions

Learning Objectives

By the end of this chapter you will be able to:

- Formulate and solve a goal programme
- Develop and solve a scoring model
- Use the analytical hierarchy process

In previous chapters we have introduced a variety of models to help managers find the optimal solution to a problem for some defined objective, such as profit, cost, distance, time. In these cases we have used a single criterion which we seek to minimize/maximize. However, it is not uncommon for managers to seek the solution to some problem where there is not one single criterion but rather multiple criteria. For example, consider a government agency that is planning to build a new hospital. It has several possible sites under consideration and is trying to determine the optimal site to choose. Up to now, we have assumed that the agency would use a single criterion – perhaps minimizing total cost – to choose between the alternatives (subject of course to any appropriate constraints). However, the agency may be trying to determine the optimal site using several different criteria. It may want a site that minimizes total cost. But it also wants the site chosen to be easily accessible for public transport for patients using the hospital. Another additional criterion might be that the site has to be close to a major city so as to make staff recruitment easier. In such cases, we are looking for the optimal solution taking into account all the decision criteria that are relevant. This makes the solution process more complex as it is likely that these criteria will conflict – that is, one site might have the lowest total cost but may not be close to a major city. Another site is close to a major city but has poor public transport facilities for patients. This type of situation is referred to as **multicriteria decision making**. In this chapter we shall be looking at a variety of approaches to help the decision maker in such situations.

To introduce the topic of multicriteria decision making, we consider a technique referred to as **goal programming**. This technique has been developed to handle multiple-criteria situations within the general framework of linear programming. We next consider a scoring model as a relatively easy way to identify the best decision alternative for a multicriteria problem. Finally, we introduce a method known as the analytical hierarchy process (AHP), which allows the user to make pairwise comparisons among the criteria and a series of pairwise comparisons among the decision alternatives in order to arrive at a prioritized ranking of the decision alternatives.

14.1 Goal Programming: Formulation and Graphical Solution

To illustrate the goal programming approach to multicriteria decision problems, let us consider a problem facing Nicolo Investment Advisors based in Edinburgh. A client has £80 000 to invest and, as an initial strategy, would like the investment portfolio restricted to two stocks:

Goal programming was first used by Charnes, Cooper and Ferguson in 1955, although the name itself first appeared in a 1961 text by Charnes and Cooper.

Stock	Price/Share	Estimated Annual Return/Share	Risk Index/Share
UK Oil	£25	£3	0.50
Hub Properties	£50	£5	0.25

UK Oil, which has a return of £3 on a £25 share price, provides an annual rate of return of 12 per cent, whereas Hub Properties provides an annual rate of return of 10 per cent. The risk index per share, 0.50 for UK Oil and 0.25 for Hub Properties, is a rating Nicolo assigned to measure the relative risk of the two investments. Higher risk index values imply greater risk; hence, Nicolo judged UK Oil to be the riskier investment. By specifying a maximum portfolio risk index, Nicolo will avoid placing too much of the portfolio in high-risk investments.

To illustrate how to use the risk index per share to measure the total portfolio risk, suppose that Nicolo chooses a portfolio that invests all £80 000 in UK Oil, the higher risk, but higher return, investment. Nicolo could purchase £80 000/£25 = 3200 shares of UK Oil, and the portfolio would have a risk index of 3200(0.50) = 1600. Conversely, if Nicolo purchases no shares of either stock, the portfolio will have no risk, but also no return. Thus, the portfolio risk index will vary from 0 (least risk) to 1600 (most risk).

Nicolo's client would like to avoid a high-risk portfolio; thus, investing all funds in UK Oil would not be desirable. However, the client agreed that an acceptable level of risk would correspond to portfolios with a maximum total risk index of 700. Thus, considering only risk, one *goal* is to find a portfolio with a risk index of 700 or less.

Another goal of the client is to obtain an annual return of at least £9000. This goal can be achieved with a portfolio consisting of 2000 shares of UK Oil [at a cost of 2000(£25) = £50 000] and 600 shares of Hub Properties [at a cost of 600(£50) = £30 000]; the annual return in this case would be 2000(£3) + 600(£5) = £9000. Note, however, that the portfolio risk index for this investment strategy would be 2000(0.50) + 600(0.25) = 1150; thus, this portfolio achieves the annual return goal but does not satisfy the portfolio risk index goal.

So, the portfolio selection problem is a multicriteria decision problem involving two goals: one dealing with risk and one dealing with annual return. The goal programming approach was developed precisely for this kind of problem. Goal programming can be used to identify a solution that comes closest to achieving both goals. Before applying the methodology, the client must determine which, if either, goal is more important.

Suppose that the client's top priority goal is to restrict the risk; that is, keeping the portfolio risk index at 700 or less is so important that the client is not willing to trade the achievement of this goal for any amount of an increase in annual return. As long as the portfolio risk index does not exceed 700, the client seeks the best possible return. Based on this statement of priorities, the goals for the problem are as follows:

Primary Goal (Priority Level 1) **Goal 1:** Find a portfolio that has a risk index of 700 or less.

Secondary Goal (Priority Level 2) **Goal 2:** Find a portfolio that will provide an annual return of at least £9000.

In goal programming with preemptive priorities, we never permit trade-offs between higher and lower level goals.

The primary goal is called a *priority level 1 goal,* and the secondary goal is called a *priority level 2 goal.* In goal programming terminology, these are called **preemptive priorities** because the decision maker is not willing to sacrifice any amount of achievement of the priority level 1 goal for the lower priority goal. The portfolio risk index of 700 is the target value for the priority level 1 (primary) goal, and the annual return of £9000 is the target value for the priority level 2 (secondary) goal. The difficulty in finding a solution that will achieve these goals is that only £80 000 is available for investment.

Developing the Constraints and the Goal Equations

We begin by defining the decision variables:

U = number of shares of UK Oil purchased

H = number of shares of Hub Properties purchased

Constraints for goal programming problems are handled in the same way as in an ordinary linear programming problem. In the Nicolo Investment Advisors problem, one constraint corresponds to the funds available. Because each share of UK Oil costs £25 and each share of Hub Properties costs £50, the constraint representing the funds available is:

$$25U + 50H \leq 80\,000$$

To complete the formulation of the model, we must develop a goal equation for each goal. Let us begin by writing the goal equation for the primary goal. Each share of UK Oil has a risk index of 0.50 and each share of Hub Properties has a risk index of 0.25; therefore, the portfolio risk index is $0.50U + 0.25H$. Depending on the values of U and H, the portfolio risk index may be less than, equal to, or greater than the target value of 700. To represent these possibilities mathematically, we create the goal equation:

$$0.50U + 0.25H = 700 + d_1^+ - d_1^-$$

where

d_1^+ = the amount by which the portfolio risk index exceeds the target value of 700
d_1^- = the amount by which the portfolio risk index is less than the target value of 700

To achieve a goal exactly, the two deviation variables must both equal zero.

In goal programming, d_1^+ and d_1^- are called **deviation variables**. The purpose of deviation variables is to allow for the possibility of not meeting the target value exactly. Consider, for example, a portfolio that consists of $U = 2000$ shares of UK Oil and $H = 0$ shares of Hub Properties. The portfolio risk index is $0.50(2000) + 0.25(0) = 1000$. In this case, $d_1^+ = 300$ reflects the fact that the portfolio risk index exceeds the target value by 300 units; note also that since d_1^+ is greater than zero, the value of d_1^- must be zero. For a portfolio consisting of $U = 0$ shares of UK Oil and $H = 1000$ shares of Hub Properties, the portfolio risk index would be $0.50(0) + 0.25(1000) = 250$. In this case, $d_1^- = 450$ and $d_1^+ = 0$, indicating that the solution provides a portfolio risk index of 450 less than the target value of 700.

In general, the letter d is used for deviation variables in a goal programming model. A superscript of plus (+) or minus (−) is used to indicate whether the variable corresponds to a positive or negative deviation from the target value. If we bring the deviation variables to the left-hand side, we can rewrite the goal equation for the primary goal as:

$$0.50U + 0.25H - d_1^+ + d_1^- = 700$$

Note that the value on the right-hand side of the goal equation is the target value for the goal. The left-hand side of the goal equation consists of two parts:

1 A function that defines the amount of goal achievement in terms of the decision variables (e.g., $0.50U + 0.25H$).
2 Deviation variables representing the difference between the target value for the goal and the level achieved.

To develop a goal equation for the secondary goal, we begin by writing a function representing the annual return for the investment:

$$\text{Annual return} = 3U + 5H$$

Then we define two deviation variables that represent the amount of over- or underachievement of the goal. Doing so, we obtain:

d_2^+ = the amount by which the annual return for the portfolio is greater than the target value of £9000

d_2^- = the amount by which the annual return for the portfolio is less than the target value of £9000

Using these two deviation variables, we write the goal equation for goal 2 as:

$$3U + 5H = 9000 + d_2^+ - d_2^-$$

or

$$3U + 5H - d_2^+ + d_2^- = 9000$$

This step completes the development of the goal equations and the constraints for the Nicolo portfolio problem. We are now ready to develop an appropriate objective function for the problem.

Developing an Objective Function with Preemptive Priorities

The objective function in a goal programming model calls for minimizing a function of the deviation variables. In the portfolio selection problem, the most important goal, denoted P_1, is to find a portfolio with a risk index of 700 or less. This problem has only two goals, and the client is unwilling to accept a portfolio risk index greater than 700 to achieve the secondary annual return goal. Therefore, the secondary goal is denoted P_2. As we stated previously, these goal priorities are referred to as preemptive priorities because the satisfaction of a higher level goal cannot be traded for the satisfaction of a lower level goal.

Goal programming problems with preemptive priorities are solved by treating priority level 1 goals (P_1) first in an objective function. The idea is to start by finding a solution that comes closest to satisfying the priority level 1 goals. This solution is then modified by solving a problem with an objective function involving only priority level 2 goals (P_2); however, revisions in the solution are permitted only if they do not hinder achievement of the P_1 goals. In general, solving a goal programming problem with preemptive priorities involves solving a sequence of linear programmes with different objective functions; P_1 goals are considered first, P_2 goals second, P_3 goals third and so on. At each stage of the procedure, a revision in the solution is permitted only if it causes no reduction in the achievement of a higher priority goal.

We must solve one linear programme for each priority level.

The number of linear programmes that we must solve in sequence to develop the solution to a goal programming problem is determined by the number of priority levels. One linear programme must be solved for each priority level. We will call the first linear programme solved the priority level 1 problem, the second linear programme solved the priority level 2 problem and so on. Each linear programme is obtained from the one at the next higher level by changing the objective function and adding a constraint.

We first formulate the objective function for the priority level 1 problem. The client stated that the portfolio risk index should not exceed 700. Is underachieving the target value of 700 a concern? Clearly, the answer is no because portfolio risk index values of less than 700 correspond to less risk. Is overachieving the target value of 700 a concern? The answer is yes because portfolios with a risk index greater than 700 correspond to unacceptable levels of risk. Thus, the objective function corresponding to the priority level 1 linear programme should minimize the value of d_1^+.

The goal equations and the funds available constraint have already been developed. Thus, the priority level 1 linear programme can now be stated.

P_1 Problem

$$
\begin{aligned}
&\text{Min} \quad d_1^+ \\
&\text{s.t.} \\
&\quad 25U + 50H && \leq 80\,000 && \text{Funds available} \\
&\quad 0.50U + 0.25H - d_1^+ + d_1^- && = 700 && P_1 \text{ goal} \\
&\quad 3U + 5H \qquad - d_2^+ + d_2^- && = 9000 && P_2 \text{ goal} \\
&\quad U, H, d_1^+, d_1^-, d_2^+, d_2^- \geq 0
\end{aligned}
$$

Graphical Solution Procedure

One approach that can often be used to solve a difficult problem is to break the problem into two or more smaller or easier problems. The linear programming procedure we use to solve the goal programming problem is based on this approach.

The graphical solution procedure for goal programming is similar to that for linear programming presented in Chapter 2. The only difference is that the procedure for goal programming involves a separate solution for each priority level. Recall that the linear programming graphical solution procedure uses a graph to display the values for the decision variables. Because the decision variables are nonnegative, we consider only that portion of the graph where $U \geq 0$ and $H \geq 0$. Recall also that every point on the graph is called a *solution point*.

We begin the graphical solution procedure for the Nicolo Investment problem by identifying all solution points that satisfy the available funds constraint:

$$25U + 50H \leq 80\,000$$

The shaded region in Figure 14.1, feasible portfolios, consists of all points that satisfy this constraint – that is, values of U and H for which $25U + 50H \leq 80\,000$.

The objective for the priority level 1 linear programme is to minimize d_1^+, the amount by which the portfolio index exceeds the target value of 700. Recall that the P_1 goal equation is:

$$0.50U + 0.25H - d_1^+ + d_1^- = 700$$

When the P_1 goal is met exactly, $d_1^+ = 0$ and $d_1^- = 0$; the goal equation then reduces to $0.50U + 0.25H = 700$. Figure 14.2 shows the graph of this equation; the shaded region identifies all solution points that satisfy the available funds constraint and

Figure 14.1 Portfolios that Satisfy the Available Funds Constraint

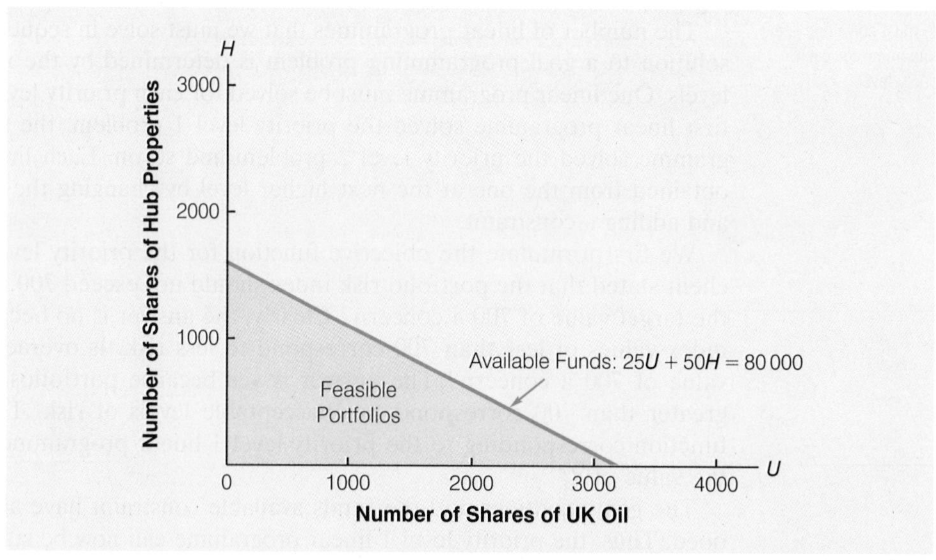

Figure 14.2 Portfolios that Satisfy the P_1 Goal

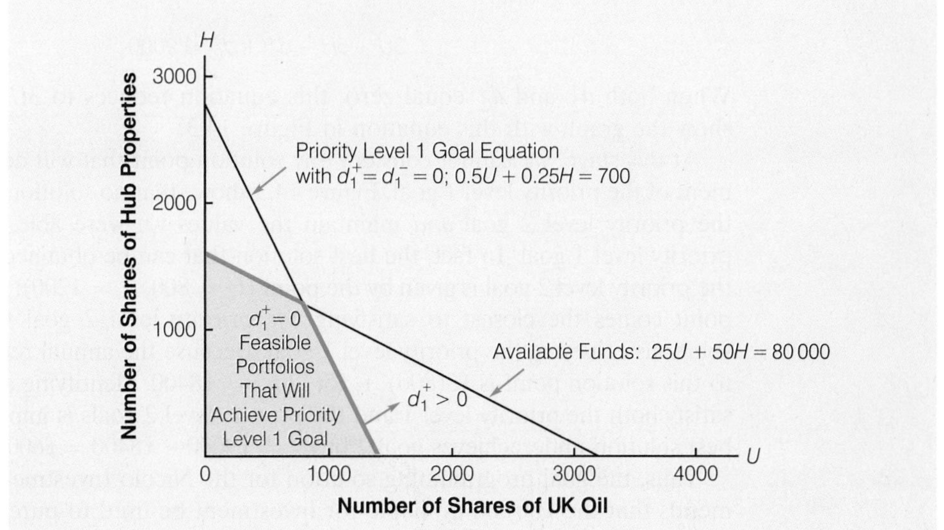

also result in the value of $d_1^+ = 0$. Thus, the shaded region contains all the feasible solution points that achieve the priority level 1 goal.

At this point, we have solved the priority level 1 problem. Note that alternative optimal solutions are possible; in fact, all solution points in the shaded region in Figure 14.2 maintain a portfolio risk index of 700 or less, and hence $d_1^+ = 0$.

The priority level 2 goal for the Nicolo Investment problem is to find a portfolio that will provide an annual return of at least £9000. Is overachieving the target value of £9000 a concern? Clearly, the answer is no because portfolios with an annual return of more than £9000 correspond to higher returns. Is underachieving the target value of £9000 a concern? The answer is yes because portfolios with an annual return of less than £9000 are not acceptable to the client. Thus, the objective function corresponding to the priority level 2 linear programme should minimize the value of d_2^-. However, because goal 2 is a secondary goal, the solution to the priority level 2 linear programme must not degrade the optimal solution to the priority level 1 problem. Thus, the priority level 2 linear programme can now be stated.

P_2 Problem

$$
\begin{aligned}
\text{Min} \quad & d_2^- \\
\text{s.t.} \quad & \\
& 25U + 50H \leq 80\,000 && \text{Funds available} \\
& 0.50U + 0.25H - d_1^+ + d_1^- = 700 && P_1 \text{ goal} \\
& 3U + 5H - d_2^+ + d_2^- = 9\,000 && P_2 \text{ goal} \\
& d_1^+ = 0 && \text{Maintain achievement of } P_1 \text{ goal} \\
& U, H, d_1^+, d_1^-, d_2^+, d_2^- \geq 0
\end{aligned}
$$

Note that the priority level 2 linear programme differs from the priority level 1 linear programme in two ways. The objective function involves minimizing the amount by which the portfolio annual return underachieves the level 2 goal, and another constraint has been added to ensure that no amount of achievement of the priority level 1 goal is sacrificed.

Let us now continue the graphical solution procedure. The goal equation for the priority level 2 goal is:

$$3U + 5H - d_2^+ + d_2^- = 9000$$

When both d_2^+ and d_2^- equal zero, this equation reduces to $3U + 5H = 9000$; we show the graph with this equation in Figure 14.3.

At this stage, we cannot consider any solution point that will degrade the achievement of the priority level 1 goal. Figure 14.3 shows that no solution points will achieve the priority level 2 goal *and* maintain the values we were able to achieve for the priority level 1 goal. In fact, the best solution that can be obtained when considering the priority level 2 goal is given by the point ($U = 800, H = 1200$); in other words, this point comes the closest to satisfying the priority level 2 goal from among those solutions satisfying the priority level 1 goal. Because the annual return corresponding to this solution point is £3(800) + £5(1200) = £8400, identifying a portfolio that will satisfy both the priority level 1 and the priority level 2 goals is impossible. In fact, the best solution underachieves goal 2 by $d_2^- =$ £9000 – £8400 = £600.

Thus, the goal programming solution for the Nicolo Investment problem recommends that the £80 000 available for investment be used to purchase 800 shares of UK Oil and 1200 shares of Hub Properties. Note that the priority level 1 goal of a portfolio risk index of 700 or less has been achieved. However, the priority level 2 goal of at least a £9000 annual return is not achievable. The annual return for the recommended portfolio is £8400.

In summary, the graphical solution procedure for goal programming involves the following steps:

Step 1. Identify the feasible solution points that satisfy the problem constraints.

Step 2. Identify all feasible solutions that achieve the highest-priority goal; if no feasible solutions will achieve the highest-priority goal, identify the solution(s) that comes closest to achieving it.

Step 3. Move down one priority level, and determine the 'best' solution possible without sacrificing any achievement of higher priority goals.

Step 4. Repeat step 3 until all priority levels have been considered.

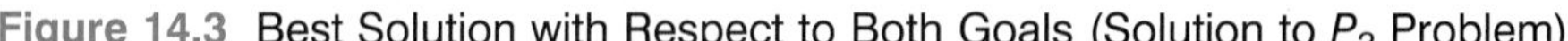

Figure 14.3 Best Solution with Respect to Both Goals (Solution to P_2 Problem)

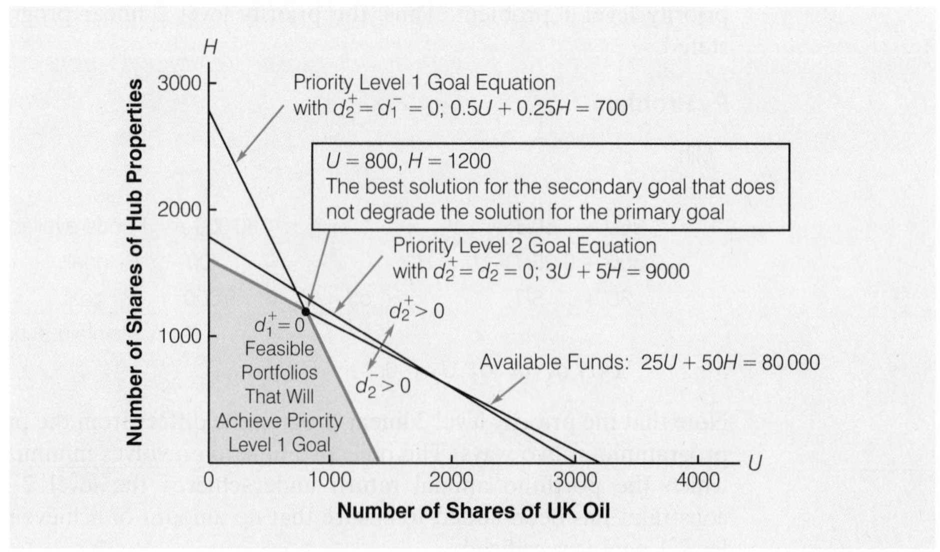

Problem 2 will test your ability to formulate a goal programming model and use the graphical solution procedure to obtain a solution.

Although the graphical solution procedure is a convenient method for solving goal programming problems involving two decision variables, the solution of larger problems requires a computer-aided approach. In Section 14.2 we illustrate how to use a computer software package to solve more complex goal programming problems.

Goal Programming Model

As we stated, preemptive goal programming problems are solved as a sequence of linear programmes: one linear programme for each priority level. However, notation that permits writing a goal programming problem in one concise statement is helpful.

In writing the overall objective for the portfolio selection problem, we must write the objective function in a way that reminds us of the preemptive priorities. We can do so by writing the objective function as:

$$\text{Min} \quad P_1(d_1^+) + P_2(d_2^-)$$

The priority levels P_1 and P_2 are not numerical weights on the deviation variables, but simply labels that remind us of the priority levels for the goals.

We now write the complete goal programming model as:

$$\begin{array}{lllllll}
\text{Min} & P_1(d_1^+) + P_2(d_2^-) & & & & \\
\text{s.t.} & & & & & \\
 & 25U + \ \ 50H & & \leq & 80\,000 & \text{Funds available} \\
 & 0.50U + 0.25H - d_1^+ + d_1^- & & = & 700 & P_1 \text{ goal} \\
 & 3U + \ \ 5H & - d_2^+ + d_2^- & = & 9\,000 & P_2 \text{ goal} \\
 & U, H, d_1^+, d_1^-, d_2^+, d_2^-, \geq 0 & & & &
\end{array}$$

With the exception of the P_1 and P_2 priority levels in the objective function, this model is a linear programming model. The solution of this linear programme involves solving a sequence of linear programmes involving goals at decreasing priority levels.

We now summarize the procedure used to develop a goal programming model.

Step 1. Identify the goals and any constraints that reflect resource capacities or other restrictions that may prevent achievement of the goals.

Step 2. Determine the priority level of each goal; goals with priority level P_1 are most important, those with priority level P_2 are next most important and so on.

Step 3. Define the decision variables.

Step 4. Formulate the constraints in the usual linear programming fashion.

Step 5. For each goal, develop a goal equation, with the right-hand side specifying the target value for the goal. Deviation variables d_1^+ and d_1^- are included in each goal equation to reflect the possible deviations above or below the target value.

Step 6. Write the objective function in terms of minimizing a prioritized function of the deviation variables.

NOTES AND COMMENTS

1 The constraints in the general goal programming model are of two types: goal equations and ordinary linear programming constraints. Some analysts call the goal equations *goal constraints* and the ordinary linear programming constraints *system constraints*.

2 You might think of the general goal programming model as having 'hard' and 'soft' constraints. The hard constraints are the ordinary linear programming constraints that cannot be violated. The soft constraints are the ones resulting from the goal equations. Soft constraints can be violated but with a penalty for doing so. The penalty is reflected by the coefficient of the deviation variable in the objective function. In Section 14.2 we illustrate this point with a problem that has a coefficient of 2 for one of the deviation variables.

3 Note that the constraint added in moving from the linear programming problem at one priority level to the linear programming problem at the next lower priority level becomes a hard constraint. No amount of achievement of a higher priority goal may be sacrificed to achieve a lower priority goal.

14.2 Goal Programming: Solving More Complex Problems

In Section 14.1 we formulated and solved a goal programming model that involved one priority level 1 goal and one priority level 2 goal. In this section we show how to formulate and solve goal programming models that involve multiple goals within the same priority level. Although specially developed computer programs can solve goal programming models, these programs are not as readily available as general purpose linear programming software packages. Thus, the computer solution procedure outlined in this section develops a solution to a goal programming model by solving a sequence of linear programming models with a general purpose linear programming software package.

Suncoast Office Supplies Problem

Suncoast Office Supplies is based in Seville, Spain, and provides office supplies to local companies in Southern Spain. The management of Suncoast Office Supplies establishes monthly goals, or quotas, for the types of customers contacted. For the next four weeks, Suncoast's customer contact strategy calls for the salesforce, which consists of four salespeople, to make 200 contacts with established customers who have previously purchased supplies from the firm. In addition, the strategy calls for 120 contacts of new customers. The purpose of this latter goal is to ensure that the salesforce is continuing to investigate new sources of sales.

After making allowances for travel and waiting time, as well as for demonstration and direct sales time, Suncoast allocated two hours of salesforce effort to each contact of an established customer. New customer contacts tend to take longer and require three hours per contact. Normally, each salesperson works 40 hours per week, or 160 hours over the four-week planning horizon; under a normal work schedule, the four salespeople will have $4(160) = 640$ hours of salesforce time available for customer contacts.

Management is willing to use some overtime, if needed, but is also willing to accept a solution that uses less than the scheduled 640 hours available. However, management wants both overtime and underutilization of the workforce limited to no more than 40 hours over the four-week period. Thus, in terms of overtime, management's goal is to use no more than $640 + 40 = 680$ hours of salesforce time; and in terms of labour utilization, management's goal is to use at least $640 - 40 = 600$ hours of salesforce time.

In addition to the customer contact goals, Suncoast established a goal regarding sales volume. Based on its experience, Suncoast estimates that each established customer contacted will generate €250 of sales and that each new customer contacted will generate €125 of sales. Management wants to generate sales revenue of at least €70 000 for the next month.

Given Suncoast's small salesforce and the short time frame involved, management decided that the overtime goal and the labour utilization goal are both priority level 1 goals. Management also concluded that the €70 000 sales revenue goal should be a priority level 2 goal and that the two customer contact goals should be priority level 3 goals. Based on these priorities, we can now summarize the goals.

Priority Level 1 Goals

Goal 1: Do not use any more than 680 hours of salesforce time.

Goal 2: Do not use any less than 600 hours of salesforce time.

Priority Level 2 Goal

Goal 3: Generate sales revenue of at least €70 000.

Priority Level 3 Goals

Goal 4: Call on at least 200 established customers.

Goal 5: Call on at least 120 new customers.

Formulating the Goal Equations

Next, we must define the decision variables whose values will be used to determine whether we are able to achieve the goals. Let:

E = the number of established customers contacted
N = the number of new customers contacted

Using these decision variables and appropriate deviation variables, we can develop a goal equation for each goal. The procedure used parallels the approach introduced in the preceding section. A summary of the results obtained is shown for each goal.

Goal 1

$$2E + 3N - d_1^+ + d_1^- = 680$$

where

d_1^+ = the amount by which the number of hours used by the salesforce is greater than the target value of 680 hours
d_1^- = the amount by which the number of hours used by the salesforce is less than the target value of 680 hours

Goal 2

$$2E + 3N - d_2^+ + d_2^- = 600$$

where

d_2^+ = the amount by which the number of hours used by the salesforce is greater than the target value of 600 hours
d_2^- = the amount by which the number of hours used by the salesforce is less than the target value of 600 hours

Goal 3

$$250E + 125N - d_3^+ + d_3^- = 70\,000$$

where

d_3^+ = the amount by which the sales revenue is greater than the target value of €70 000

d_3^- = the amount by which the sales revenue is less than the target value of €70 000

Goal 4

$$E - d_4^+ + d_4^- = 200$$

where

d_4^+ = the amount by which the number of established customer contacts is greater than the target value of 200 established customer contacts

d_4^- = the amount by which the number of established customer contacts is less than the target value of 200 established customer contacts

Goal 5

$$N - d_5^+ + d_5^- = 120$$

where

d_5^+ = the amount by which the number of new customer contacts is greater than the target value of 120 new customer contacts

d_5^- = the amount by which the number of new customer contacts is less than the target value of 120 new customer contacts

Formulating the Objective Function

To develop the objective function for the Suncoast Office Supplies problem, we begin by considering the priority level 1 goals. When considering goal 1, if $d_1^+ = 0$, we will have found a solution that uses no more than 680 hours of salesforce time. Because solutions for which d_1^+ is greater than zero represent overtime beyond the desired level, the objective function should minimize the value of d_1^+. When considering goal 2, if $d_2^- = 0$, we will have found a solution that uses *at least* 600 hours of salesforce time. If d_2^- is greater than zero, however, labour utilization will not have reached the acceptable level. Thus, the objective function for the priority level 1 goals should minimize the value of d_2^-. Because both priority level 1 goals are equally important, the objective function for the priority level 1 problem is:

$$\text{Min} \quad d_1^+ + d_2^-$$

In considering the priority level 2 goal, we note that management wants to achieve sales revenues of at least €70 000. If $d_3^- = 0$, Suncoast will achieve revenues of *at least* €70 000, and if $d_3^- > 0$, revenues of less than €70 000 will be obtained. Thus, the objective function for the priority level 2 problem is:

$$\text{Min} \quad d_3^-$$

Next, we consider what the objective function must be for the priority level 3 problem. When considering goal 4, if $d_4^- = 0$, we will have found a solution with *at least* 200 established customer contacts; however, if $d_4^- > 0$, we will have underachieved the goal of contacting at least 200 established customers. Thus, for goal 4 the objective is to minimize d_4^-. When considering goal 5, if $d_5^- = 0$, we will have found a solution with *at least* 120 new customer contacts; however, if $d_5^- > 0$, we will have underachieved the goal of contacting at least 120 new customers. Thus, for goal 5 the objective is to minimize d_5^-. If both goals 4 and 5 are equal in importance, the objective function for the priority level 3 problem would be:

$$\text{Min} \quad d_4^- + d_5^-$$

However, suppose that management believes that generating new customers is vital to the long-run success of the firm and that goal 5 should be weighted more than goal 4. If management believes that goal 5 is twice as important as goal 4, the objective function for the priority level 3 problem would be:

$$\text{Min} \quad d_4^- + 2d_5^-$$

Combining the objective functions for all three priority levels, we obtain the overall objective function for the Suncoast Office Supplies problem:

$$\text{Min} \quad P_1(d_1^+) + P_1(d_2^-) + P_2(d_3^-) + P_3(d_4^-) + P_3(2d_5^-)$$

As we indicated previously, P_1, P_2 and P_3 are simply labels that remind us that goals 1 and 2 are the priority level 1 goals, goal 3 is the priority level 2 goal and goals 4 and 5 are the priority level 3 goals. We can now write the complete goal programming model for the Suncoast Office Supplies problem as follows:

$$\begin{aligned}
\text{Min} \quad & P_1(d_1^+) + P_1(d_2^-) + P_2(d_3^-) + P_3(d_4^-) + P_3(2d_5^-) \\
& \text{s.t.} \\
& 2E + 3N - d_1^+ + d_1^- = 680 \quad \text{Goal 1} \\
& 2E + 3N - d_2^+ + d_2^- = 600 \quad \text{Goal 2} \\
& 250E + 125N - d_3^+ + d_3^- = 70\,000 \quad \text{Goal 3} \\
& E - d_4^+ + d_4^- = 200 \quad \text{Goal 4} \\
& N - d_5^+ + d_5^- = 120 \quad \text{Goal 5} \\
& E, N, d_1^+, d_1^-, d_2^+, d_2^-, d_3^+, d_3^-, d_4^+, d_4^-, d_5^+, d_5^- \geq 0
\end{aligned}$$

Computer Solution

The following computer procedure develops a solution to a goal programming model by solving a sequence of linear programming problems. The first problem comprises all the constraints and all the goal equations for the complete goal programming model; however, the objective function for this problem involves only the P_1 priority level goals. Again, we refer to this problem as the P_1 problem.

Whatever the solution to the P_1 problem, a P_2 problem is formed by adding a constraint to the P_1 model that ensures that subsequent problems will not degrade the solution obtained for the P_1 problem. The objective function for the priority level 2 problem takes into consideration only the P_2 goals. We continue the process until we have considered all priority levels.

To solve the Suncoast Office Supplies problem, we begin by solving the P_1 problem:

$$\begin{aligned}
\text{Min} \quad & d_1^+ + d_2^- \\
\text{s.t.} \quad & \\
& 2E + 3N - d_1^+ + d_1^- = 680 \quad \text{Goal 1} \\
& 2E + 3N - d_2^+ + d_2^- = 600 \quad \text{Goal 2} \\
& 250E + 125N - d_3^+ + d_3^- = 70\,000 \quad \text{Goal 3} \\
& E - d_4^+ + d_4^- = 200 \quad \text{Goal 4} \\
& N - d_5^+ + d_5^- = 120 \quad \text{Goal 5} \\
& E, N, d_1^+, d_1^-, d_2^+, d_2^-, d_3^+, d_3^-, d_4^+, d_4^-, d_5^+, d_5^- \geq 0
\end{aligned}$$

In Figure 14.4 we show the computer solution for this linear programme. Note that D1PLUS refers to d_1^+, D2MINUS refers to d_2^-, D1MINUS refers to d_1^- and so on. The solution shows $E = 250$ established customer contacts and $N = 60$ new customer contacts. Because D1PLUS = 0 and D2MINUS = 0, we see that the solution achieves both goals 1 and 2. Alternatively, the value of the objective function is 0, confirming that both priority level 1 goals have been achieved. Next, we consider goal 3, the priority level 2 goal, which is to minimize D3MINUS. The solution in Figure 14.4 shows that D3MINUS = 0. Thus, the solution of $E = 250$ established customer contacts and $N = 60$ new customer contacts also achieves goal 3, the priority level 2 goal, which is to generate a sales revenue of at least €70 000. The fact that D3PLUS = 0 indicates that the current solution satisfies goal 3 exactly at €70 000. Finally, the solution in Figure 14.4 shows D4PLUS = 50 and D5MINUS = 60. These values tell us that goal 4 of the priority level 3 goals is overachieved by 50 established customers, but that goal 5 is underachieved by 60 new customers. At this point, both the priority level 1 and 2 goals have been achieved, but we need to solve another linear programme to determine whether a solution can be identified that will satisfy both of the priority level 3 goals. Therefore, we go directly to the P_3 problem.

The linear programming model for the P_3 problem is a modification of the linear programming model for the P_1 problem. The objective function must now be expressed in terms of the priority level 3 goal and we seek to minimize $d_4^- + 2d_5^-$. The original five constraints of the P_1 problem remain but we must add two

Figure 14.4 The Computer Solution of the P_1 Problem

```
Objective Function Value = 0.000

  Variable                 Value               Reduced Costs
--------------       ---------------        -----------------
   D1PLUS                  0.000                    1.000
   D2MINUS                 0.000                    1.000
   E                     250.000                    0.000
   N                      60.000                    0.000
   D1MINUS                 0.000                    0.000
   D2PLUS                 80.000                    0.000
   D3PLUS                  0.000                    0.000
   D3MINUS                 0.000                    0.000
   D4PLUS                 50.000                    0.000
   D4MINUS                 0.000                    0.000
   D5PLUS                  0.000                    0.000
   D5MINUS                60.000                    0.000
```

additional constraints. One is to ensure that the solution to the P_3 problem continues to satisfy the priority level 1 goal and the second that the solution continues to satisfy the priority level 2 goal. The new formulation is then:

$$
\begin{array}{llcrl}
\text{Min} & d_4^+ + 2d_5^- & & & \\
\text{s.t.} & & & & \\
& 2E + 3N - d_1^+ + d_1^- & = & 680 & \text{Goal 1} \\
& 2E + 3N \quad - d_2^+ + d_2^- & = & 600 & \text{Goal 2} \\
& 250E + 125N \quad - d_3^+ + d_3^- & = & 70\,000 & \text{Goal 3} \\
& E \quad - d_4^+ + d_4^- & = & 200 & \text{Goal 4} \\
& N \quad - d_5^+ + d_5^- & = & 120 & \text{Goal 5} \\
& d_1^+ + d_2^- & = & 0 & \text{Priority level 1} \\
& d_3^- & = & 0 & \text{Priority level 1} \\
& E, N, d_1^+, d_1^-, d_2^+, d_2^-, d_3^+, d_3^-, d_4^+, d_4^-, d_5^+, d_5^- \geq 0 & & &
\end{array}
$$

Making these modifications to the P_1 problem, we obtain the solution to the P_3 problem shown in Figure 14.5.

Referring to Figure 14.5, we see the objective function value of 120 indicates that the priority level 3 goals cannot be achieved. Since D5MINUS = 60, the optimal solution of $E = 250$ and $N = 60$ results in 60 fewer new customer contacts than desired. However, the fact that we solved the P_3 problem tells us the goal programming solution comes as close as possible to satisfying priority level 3 goals given the achievement of both the priority level 1 and 2 goals. Because all priority levels have been considered, the solution procedure is finished. The optimal solution for Suncoast is to contact 250 established customers and 60 new customers. Although this solution will not achieve management's goal of contacting at least 120 new customers, it does achieve each of the other goals specified. If management isn't happy with this solution, a different set of priorities could be considered. Management must keep in mind, however, that in any situation involving multiple goals at different priority levels, rarely will all the goals be achieved with existing resources.

Figure 14.5 The Computer Solution of the P_3 Problem

```
Objective Function Value = 120.000

   Variable              Value               Reduced Costs
 --------------     ---------------        -----------------
   D1PLUS                 0.000                    0.000
   D2MINUS                0.000                    1.000
   E                    250.000                    0.000
   N                     60.000                    0.000
   D1MINUS                0.000                    1.000
   D2PLUS                80.000                    0.000
   D3PLUS                 0.000                    0.008
   D3MINUS                0.000                    0.000
   D4PLUS                50.000                    0.000
   D4MINUS                0.000                    1.000
   D5PLUS                 0.000                    2.000
   D5MINUS               60.000                    0.000
```

MANAGEMENT SCIENCE IN ACTION

Vehicle Fleet Management in Quebec

At the time of this project the Transport Ministry in Quebec had established a unit (CGER) that was responsible for the management of the Ministry's fleet of vehicles and motorized equipment used for maintenance of the roads network in Quebec, with the fleet consisting of over 2000 vehicles and trucks and around 1000 items of motorized equipment. The management of the vehicle fleet was not an easy task. CGER had to maintain, repair and deploy its fleet efficiently and effectively, it had to meet the needs of its internal customers, over 50 service centres within the Ministry, and it had to operate within budget. To compound the problems, the government had imposed a financial target of CGER to reduce the vehicle fleet by 20 per cent. A goal programming model was developed to help CGER's management decide how to meet these multiple, and conflicting, goals. The first priority was to determine a vehicle fleet combination that would meet the government's goal of a 20 per cent reduction in fleet size. The deviation variables indicated the extent to which CGER exceeded or fell short of this target. The second priority was that of operating within the existing budget. The deviation variables indicated budget underspend or overspend. The underspend deviation was removed from the model given that an underspend in one year was likely to have adverse consequences on budget allocations in future years. The third priority related to the extent to which internal customer needs were met with the new fleet combination. The deviation variables represented the extent to which the service provided fell short of customer requirements or exceeded customer requirements. One of the key findings emerging from the model was a threshold budget which revealed that once the budget fell to this level there would be a negative impact on CGER's ability to provide a satisfactory service to its customers. The model allowed CGER's management the opportunity to examine different potential scenarios and assess their impact on the service and this flexibility was seen as a key feature of the model.

Based on H. Gighrod, J.M. Martel and B. Aouni, 'Vehicle Park Management Through the Goal Programming Model', *INFOR* 41/1 (2003): 93–104.

NOTES AND COMMENTS

1 Not all goal programming problems involve multiple priority levels. For problems with one priority level, only one linear programme needs to be solved to obtain the goal programming solution. The analyst simply minimizes the weighted deviations from the goals. Trade-offs are permitted among the goals because they are all at the same priority level.

2 The goal programming approach can be used when the analyst is confronted with an infeasible solution to an ordinary linear programme. Reformulating some constraints as goal equations with deviation variables allows a solution that minimizes the weighted sum of the deviation variables. Often, this approach will suggest a reasonable solution.

3 The approach that we used to solve goal programming problems with multiple priority levels is to solve a sequence of linear programmes. These linear programmes are closely related so that complete reformulation and solution are not necessary. By changing the objective function and adding a constraint, we can go from one linear programme to the next.

14.3 Scoring Models

The second approach we shall introduce to help with multicriteria decision problems is a scoring model. A scoring model is a relatively quick and easy way to identify the best decision alternative for a multicriteria decision problem. We will demonstrate the use of a scoring model for a job selection application.

As an example, we will use a recently graduated management science student who has received job offers for three positions:

- working in Frankfurt as a financial analyst in an investment company;
- working in London as a policy advisor in a government agency;
- working in demand forecasting in a multinational oil company in Amsterdam.

When asked about which job is preferred, the student made the following comments: 'The financial analyst position in Frankfurt provides the best opportunity for my long-run career advancement. However, I would prefer living in London rather than in Frankfurt or Amsterdam. On the other hand, I liked the management style and philosophy at the Amsterdam firm the best'. The student's statement points out that this example is clearly a multicriteria decision problem. Considering only the *long-run career advancement* criterion, the financial analyst position in Frankfurt is the preferred decision alternative. Considering only the *location* criterion, the best decision alternative is the policy advisor position in London. Finally, considering only the *management style* criterion, the best alternative is the forecasting position with the oil firm in Amsterdam. For most individuals, a multicriteria decision problem that requires a trade-off among the several criteria is difficult to solve. In this section, we describe how a **scoring model** can assist in analyzing a multicriteria decision problem and help identify the preferred decision alternative.

A scoring model enables a decision maker to identify the criteria and indicate the weight or importance of each criterion.

The steps required to develop a scoring model are as follows:

Step 1. Develop a list of the criteria to be considered. The criteria are the factors that the decision maker considers relevant for evaluating each decision alternative.

Step 2. Assign a weight to each criterion that describes the criterion's relative importance. Let:

$$w_i = \text{the weight for criterion } i$$

Step 3. Assign a rating for each criterion that shows how well each decision alternative satisfies the criterion. Let:

$$r_{ij} = \text{the rating for criterion } i \text{ and decision alternative } j$$

Step 4. Calculate the score for each decision alternative. Let:

$$S_j = \text{score for decision alternative } j$$

The equation used to calculate S_j is as follows:

$$S_j = \sum_i w_i r_{ij} \qquad \textbf{(14.1)}$$

Step 5. Order the decision alternatives from the highest score to the lowest score to provide the scoring model's ranking of the decision alternatives. The decision alternative with the highest score is the recommended decision alternative.

Let us return to the multicriteria job selection problem the graduating student was facing and illustrate the use of a scoring model to assist in the decision-making process. In carrying out step 1 of the scoring model procedure, the student listed seven criteria as important factors in the decision-making process. These criteria are as follows:

- Career advancement.
- Location.
- Management style.
- Salary.
- Prestige.
- Job security.
- Enjoyment of the work.

In step 2, a weight is assigned to each criterion to indicate the criterion's relative importance in the decision-making process. For example, using a five-point scale, the question used to assign a weight to the career advancement criterion would be as follows:

Relative to the other criteria you are considering, how important is career advancement?

Importance	Weight
Very important	5
Somewhat important	4
Average importance	3
Somewhat unimportant	2
Very unimportant	1

By repeating this question for each of the seven criteria, the student provided the criterion weights shown in Table 14.1. Using this table, we see that career advancement and enjoyment of the work are the two most important criteria, each receiving a weight of 5. The management style and job security criteria are both considered somewhat important, and thus each received a weight of 4. Location and salary are considered average in importance, each receive a weight of 3. Finally, because prestige is considered to be somewhat unimportant, it received a weight of 2.

Table 14.1 Weights for the Seven Job Selection Criteria

Criterion	Importance	Weight (w_i)
Career advancement	Very important	5
Location	Average importance	3
Management style	Somewhat important	4
Salary	Average importance	3
Prestige	Somewhat unimportant	2
Job security	Somewhat important	4
Enjoyment of the work	Very important	5

The weights shown in Table 14.1 are subjective values provided by the student. A different student would most likely choose to weight the criteria differently. One of the key advantages of a scoring model is that it uses the subjective weights that most closely reflect the preferences of the individual decision maker.

In step 3, each decision alternative is rated in terms of how well it satisfies each criterion. For example, using a nine-point scale, the question used to assign a rating for the 'financial analyst in Frankfurt' alternative and the career advancement criterion would be as follows:

To what extent does the financial analyst position in Frankfurt satisfy your career advancement criterion?

Level of Satisfaction	Rating
Extremely high	9
Very high	8
High	7
Slightly high	6
Average	5
Slightly low	4
Low	3
Very low	2
Extremely low	1

A score of 8 on this question would indicate that the student believes the financial analyst position would be rated 'very high' in terms of satisfying the career advancement criterion.

This scoring process must be completed for each combination of decision alternative and decision criterion. Because seven decision criteria and three decision alternatives need to be considered, $7 \times 3 = 21$ ratings must be provided. Table 14.2 summarizes the student's responses. Scanning this table provides some insights about how the student rates each decision criterion and decision alternative combination. For example, a rating of 9, corresponding to an extremely high level of satisfaction, only appears for the management style criterion and the position in Amsterdam. Thus, considering all combinations, the student rates the position in Amsterdam as the very best in terms of satisfying the management style criterion.

Table 14.2 Ratings for Each Decision Criterion and Each Decision Alternative Combination

	Decision Alternative		
Criterion	Financial Analyst Frankfurt	Policy advisor London	Forecaster Amsterdam
Career advancement	8	6	4
Location	3	8	7
Management style	5	6	9
Salary	6	7	5
Prestige	7	5	4
Job security	4	7	6
Enjoyment of the work	8	6	5

Table 14.3 Computation of Scores for the Three Decision Alternatives

		Decision Alternative					
		Financial Analyst Frankfurt		Policy advisor London		Forecaster Amsterdam	
Criterion	Weight w_i	Rating r_{i1}	Score w_ir_{i1}	Rating r_{i2}	Score w_ir_{i2}	Rating r_{i3}	Score w_ir_{i3}
Career advancement	5	8	40	6	30	4	20
Location	3	3	9	8	24	7	21
Management style	4	5	20	6	24	9	36
Salary	3	6	18	7	21	5	15
Prestige	2	7	14	5	10	4	8
Job security	4	4	16	7	28	6	24
Enjoyment of the work	5	8	40	6	30	5	25
Score			157		167		149

The lowest rating in the table is a 3 that appears for the location criterion of the financial analyst position in Frankfurt. This rating indicates that Frankfurt is rated 'low' in terms of satisfying the student's location criterion. Other insights and interpretations are possible, but the question at this point is how a scoring model uses the data in Tables 14.1 and 14.2 to identify the best overall decision alternative.

Step 4 of the procedure shows that Equation (14.1) is used to calculate the score for each decision alternative. The data in Table 14.1 provide the weight for each criterion (w_i) and the data in Table 14.2 provide the ratings of each decision alternative for each criterion (r_{ij}). Thus, for decision alternative 1, the score for the financial analyst position in Frankfurt is:

$$S_1 = \sum_i w_i r_{i1} = 5(8) + 3(3) + 4(5) + 3(6) + 2(7) + 4(4) + 5(8) = 157$$

The scores for the other decision alternatives are calculated in the same manner. The calculations are summarized in Table 14.3.

By comparing the scores for each criterion, a decision maker can learn why a particular decision alternative has the highest score.

From Table 14.3, we see that the highest score of 167 corresponds to the position in London. Thus, the position in London is the recommended decision alternative. The financial analyst position in Frankfurt, with a score of 157, is ranked second, and the position in Amsterdam, with a score of 149, is ranked third.

The job selection example that illustrates the use of a scoring model involved seven criteria, each of which was assigned a weight from 1 to 5. In other applications the weights assigned to the criteria may be percentages that reflect the importance of each of the criteria. In addition, multicriteria problems often involve additional subcriteria that enable the decision maker to incorporate additional detail into the decision process. For instance, consider the location criterion in the job selection example. This criterion might be further subdivided into the following three subcriteria:

- Affordability of housing.
- Recreational opportunities.
- Climate.

MANAGEMENT SCIENCE IN ACTION

Scoring Model at Ford Motor Company

Ford Motor Company needed benchmark data in order to set performance targets for future and current model automobiles. A detailed proposal was developed and sent to five suppliers. Three suppliers were considered acceptable for the project.

Because the three suppliers had different capabilities in terms of teardown analysis and testing, Ford developed three project alternatives:

Alternative 1: Supplier C does the entire project alone.

Alternative 2: Supplier A does the testing portion of the project and works with Supplier B to complete the remaining parts of the project.

Alternative 3: Supplier A does the testing portion of the project and works with Supplier C to complete the remaining parts of the project.

For routine projects, selecting the lowest cost alternative might be appropriate. However, because this project involved many nonroutine tasks, Ford incorporated four criteria into the decision process.

The four criteria selected by Ford are as follows:

1. Skill level (effective project leader and a skilled team).
2. Cost containment (ability to stay within approved budget).
3. Timing containment (ability to meet programme timing requirements).
4. Hardware display (location and functionality of teardown centre and user friendliness).

Using team consensus, a weight of 25 per cent was assigned to each of these criteria; note that these weights indicate that members of the Ford project team considered each criterion to be equally important in the decision process.

Each of the four criteria was further subdivided into subcriteria. For example, the skill-level criterion had four subcriteria: project manager leadership; team structure organization; team players' communication; and past Ford experience. In total, 17 subcriteria were considered. A team-consensus weighting process was used to develop percentage weights for the subcriteria. The weights assigned to the skill-level subcriteria were 40 per cent for project manager leadership; 20 per cent for team structure organization; 20 per cent for team players' communication; and 20 per cent for past Ford experience.

Team members visited all the suppliers and individually rated them for each subcriterion using a 1–10 scale (1-worst, 10-best). Then, in a team meeting, consensus ratings were developed. For Alternative 1, the consensus ratings developed for the skill-level subcriteria were 8 for project manager leadership; 8 for team structure organization; 7 for team players' communication; and 8 for past Ford experience. Because the weights assigned to the skill-level subcriteria are 40 per cent, 20 per cent, 20 per cent and 20 per cent, the rating for Alternative 1 corresponding to the skill-level criterion is:

$$\text{Rating} = .4(8) + .2(8) + .2(7) + .2(8) = 7.8$$

In a similar fashion, ratings for Alternative 1 corresponding to each of the other criteria were developed. The results obtained were a rating of 6.8 for cost containment, 6.65 for timing containment and 8 for hardware display. Using the initial weights of 25 per cent assigned to each criterion, the final rating for Alternative 1 = .25(7.8) + .25(6.8) + .25(6.65) + .25(8) = 7.3. In a similar fashion, a final rating of 7.4 was developed for Alternative 2, and a final rating of 7.5 was developed for Alternative 3. Thus, Alternative 3 was the recommended decision. Subsequent sensitivity analysis on the weights assigned to the criteria showed that Alternative 3 still received equal or higher ratings than Alternative 1 or Alternative 2. These results increased the team's confidence that Alternative 3 was the best choice.

Based on Senthil A. Gurusami, 'Ford's Wrenching Decision', *OR/MS Today* (December 1998): 36–39.

In this case, the three subcriteria would have to be assigned weights, and a score for each decision alternative would have to be calculated for each subcriterion. The *Management Science in Action*, Scoring Model at Ford Motor Company, illustrates how scoring models can be applied for a problem involving four criteria, each of which has several subcriteria. This example also demonstrates the use of percentage weights for the criteria and the wide applicability of scoring models in more complex problem situations.

14.4 Analytic Hierarchy Process

The third approach to dealing with multicriteria decision problems is the analytical hierarchy process. The **analytic hierarchy process (AHP)**, developed by Thomas L. Saaty,[1] is designed to help with complex multicriteria decision problems. AHP requires the decision maker to provide judgements about the relative importance of each criterion and then specify a preference for each decision alternative using each criterion. The output of AHP is a prioritized ranking of the decision alternatives based on the overall preferences expressed by the decision maker.

To introduce AHP, we consider a car purchasing decision problem faced by Diane Payne. Diane is responsible for deciding which vehicle the company should use for its salesforce. After a preliminary analysis of the makes and models of several cars, Diane narrowed her list of decision alternatives to three cars: an Accord, a Saturn and a Cavalier. Table 14.4 summarizes the information Diane collected about these cars. Diane decided that the following criteria were relevant for her car selection decision process:

- Price.
- Miles per gallon (MPG).
- Comfort.
- Style.

Data regarding the Price and MPG are provided in Table 14.4. However, measures of the Comfort and Style cannot be specified so directly. Diane will need to consider factors such as the car's interior, type of audio system, ease of entry, seat adjustments and driver visibility in order to determine the comfort level of each car. The style criterion will have to be based on Diane's subjective evaluation of the colour and the general appearance of each car.

Even when a criterion such as price can be easily measured, subjectivity becomes an issue whenever a decision maker indicates his or her personal preference for the decision alternatives based on price. For instance, the price of the Accord (£13 100)

Table 14.4 Information for the Car Selection Problem

	Decision Alternative		
Characteristics	**Accord**	**Saturn**	**Cavalier**
Price	£13 100	£11 200	£9 500
Colour	Black	Red	Blue
Miles per gallon	29	33	38
Interior	Deluxe	Above Average	Standard
Body type	four-door midsize	two-door sport	two-door compact
Sound and Navigation System	CD + GPS	CD + GPS	CD

[1]T. Saaty, *Decision Making for Leaders: The Analytic Hierarchy Process for Decisions in a Complex World,* 3d. ed., RWS, 1999.

Figure 14.6 Hierarchy for the Car Selection Problem

Overall Goal:	Select the Best Car			
Criteria:	Price	MPG	Comfort	Style
Decision Alternatives:	Accord Saturn Cavalier	Accord Saturn Cavalier	Accord Saturn Cavalier	Accord Saturn Cavalier

is £3600 more than the price of the Cavalier (£9500). The £3600 difference might represent a great deal of money to one person, but not much of a difference to another person. Thus, whether the Accord is considered 'extremely more expensive' than the Cavalier or perhaps only 'moderately more expensive' than the Cavalier depends upon the financial status and the subjective opinion of the person making the comparison. An advantage of AHP is that it can handle situations in which the unique subjective judgements of the individual decision maker constitute an important part of the decision-making process.

AHP allows a decision maker to express personal preferences and subjective judgements about the various aspects of a multicriteria problem.

Developing the Hierarchy

The first step in AHP is to develop a diagrammatic representation of the problem in terms of the overall goal, the criteria to be used, and the decision alternatives. Such a diagram depicts the hierarchy for the problem. Figure 14.6 shows the hierarchy for the car selection problem. Note that the first level of the hierarchy shows that the overall goal is to select the best car. At the second level, the four criteria (Price, MPG, Comfort and Style) each contribute to the achievement of the overall goal. Finally, at the third level, each decision alternative – Accord, Saturn and Cavalier – contributes to each criterion in a unique way.

Using AHP, the decision maker specifies judgements about the relative importance of each of the four criteria in terms of its contribution to the achievement of the overall goal. At the next level, the decision maker indicates a preference for each decision alternative based on each criterion. A mathematical process is used to synthesize the information on the relative importance of the criteria and the preferences for the decision alternatives to provide an overall priority ranking of the decision alternatives. In the car selection problem, AHP will use Diane's personal preferences to provide a priority ranking of the three cars in terms of how well each car meets the overall goal of being the *best* car.

14.5 Establishing Priorities Using AHP

In this section we show how AHP uses pairwise comparisons expressed by the decision maker to establish priorities for the criteria and priorities for the decision alternatives based on each criterion. Using the car selection example, we show how AHP determines priorities for each of the following:

1 How the four criteria contribute to the overall goal of selecting the best car.
2 How the three cars compare using the Price criterion.
3 How the three cars compare using the MPG criterion.
4 How the three cars compare using the Comfort criterion.
5 How the three cars compare using the Style criterion.

In the following discussion, we demonstrate how to establish priorities for the four criteria in terms of how each contributes to the overall goal of selecting the best car. The priorities of the three cars using each criterion can be determined similarly.

Pairwise Comparisons

Pairwise comparisons form the fundamental building blocks of AHP. In establishing the priorities for the four criteria, AHP will require Diane to state how important each criterion is relative to each other criterion when the criteria are compared two at a time (pairwise). That is, with the four criteria (Price, MPG, Comfort and Style) Diane must make the following pairwise comparisons:

Price compared to MPG.
Price compared to Comfort.
Price compared to Style.
MPG compared to Comfort.
MPG compared to Style.
Comfort compared to Style.

In each comparison, Diane must select the more important criterion and then express a judgement of how much more important the selected criterion is.

For example, in the Price–MPG pairwise comparison, assume that Diane indicates that Price is more important than MPG. To measure how much more important Price is compared to MPG, AHP uses a scale with values from 1 to 9. Table 14.5 shows how the decision maker's verbal description of the relative importance between the two criteria are converted into a numerical rating. In the car selection example, suppose that Diane states that Price is 'moderately more important' than MPG. In this case, a numerical rating of 3 is assigned to the Price–MPG pairwise comparison. From Table 14.5, we see 'strongly more important' receives a numerical rating of 5, while 'very strongly more important' receives a numerical rating of 7. Intermediate judgements such as 'strongly to very strongly more important' are possible and would receive a numerical rating of 6.

Table 14.5 Comparison Scale for the Importance of Criteria Using AHP

Verbal Judgement	Numerical Rating
Extremely more important	9
	8
Very strongly more important	7
	6
Strongly more important	5
	4
Moderately more important	3
	2
Equally important	1

Table 14.6 Summary Of Diane Payne's Pairwise Comparisons of the Four Criteria for the Car Selection Problem

Pairwise Comparison	More Important Criterion	How Much More Important	Numerical Rating
Price–MPG	Price	Moderately	3
Price–Comfort	Price	Equally to moderately	2
Price–Style	Price	Equally to moderately	2
MPG–Comfort	Comfort	Moderately to strongly	4
MPG–Style	Style	Moderately to strongly	4
Comfort–Style	Style	Equally to moderately	2

Table 14.6 provides a summary of the six pairwise comparisons that Diane provided for the car selection problem. Using the information in this table, Diane has specified that:

Price is moderately more important than MPG.

Price is equally to moderately more important than Comfort.

Price is equally to moderately more important than Style.

Comfort is moderately to strongly more important than MPG.

Style is moderately to strongly more important than MPG.

Style is equally to moderately more important than Comfort.

AHP uses the numerical ratings from the pairwise comparisons to establish a priority or importance measure for each criterion.

As shown, the flexibility of AHP can accommodate the unique preferences of each individual decision maker. First, the choice of the criteria that are considered can vary depending upon the decision maker. Not everyone would agree that Price, MPG, Comfort and Style are the only criteria to be considered in a car selection problem. Perhaps you would want to add safety, resale value and/or other criteria if you were making the car selection decision. AHP can accommodate any set of criteria specified by the decision maker. Of course, if additional criteria are added, more pairwise comparisons will be necessary. In addition, if you agree with Diane that Price, MPG, Comfort and Style are the four criteria to use, you would probably disagree with her as to the relative importance of the criteria. Using the format of Table 14.6, you could provide your own assessment of the importance of each pairwise comparison, and AHP would adjust the numerical ratings to reflect your personal preferences.

Pairwise Comparison Matrix

To determine the priorities for the four criteria, we now need to construct a matrix of the pairwise comparison ratings provided in Table 14.6. Using the four criteria, the **pairwise comparison matrix** will consist of four rows and four columns as shown here:

	Price	MPG	Comfort	Style
Price				
MPG				
Comfort				
Style				

Each of the numerical ratings in Table 14.6 must be entered into the pairwise comparison matrix. As an illustration of this process consider the numerical rating of 3 for the Price–MPG pairwise comparison. Table 14.6 shows that for this pairwise comparison Price is the most important criterion. Thus, we must enter a 3 into the row labelled Price and the column labelled MPG in the pairwise comparison matrix. In general, the entries in the column labelled Most Important Criterion in Table 14.6 indicate which row of the pairwise comparison matrix the numerical rating must be placed in. As another illustration, consider the MPG–Comfort pairwise comparison. Table 14.6 shows that Comfort is the most important criterion for this pairwise comparison and that the numerical rating is 4. Thus, we enter a 4 into the row labelled Comfort and into the column labelled MPG. Following this procedure for the other pairwise comparisons shown in Table 14.6, we obtain the following pairwise comparison matrix.

	Price	MPG	Comfort	Style
Price		3	2	2
MPG				
Comfort		4		
Style		4	2	

Because the diagonal elements are comparing each criterion to itself, the diagonal elements of the pairwise comparison matrix are always equal to 1. For example, if Price is compared to Price, the verbal judgement would be 'equally important' with a rating of 1; so, a 1 would be placed into the row labelled Price and into the column labelled Price in the pairwise comparison matrix. At this point, the pairwise comparison matrix appears as follows:

	Price	MPG	Comfort	Style
Price	1	3	2	2
MPG		1		
Comfort		4	1	
Style		4	2	1

All that remains is to complete the entries for the remaining cells of the matrix. To illustrate how these values are obtained, consider the numerical rating of 3 for the Price–MPG pairwise comparison. This rating implies that the MPG–Price pairwise comparison should have a rating of ⅓. That is, because Diane already indicated Price is moderately more important than MPG (a rating of 3), we can infer that a pairwise comparison of MPG relative to Price should be ⅓. Similarly, because the Comfort–MPG pairwise comparison has a rating of 4, the MPG–Comfort pairwise comparison would be ¼. Thus, the complete pairwise comparison matrix for the car selection criteria is as follows:

	Price	MPG	Comfort	Style
Price	1	3	2	2
MPG	$^1/_3$	1	$^1/_4$	$^1/_4$
Comfort	$^1/_2$	4	1	$^1/_2$
Style	$^1/_2$	4	2	1

Synthesization

Using the pairwise comparison matrix, we can now calculate the priority of each criterion in terms of its contribution to the overall goal of selecting the best car. This aspect of AHP is referred to as synthesization. The exact mathematical procedure required to perform synthesization is beyond the scope of this text. However, the following three-step procedure provides a good approximation of the synthesization results.

1. Sum the values in each column of the pairwise comparison matrix.
2. Divide each element in the pairwise comparison matrix by its column total; the resulting matrix is referred to as the normalized pairwise comparison matrix.
3. Calculate the average of the elements in each row of the normalized pairwise comparison matrix; these averages provide the priorities for the criteria.

To show how the synthesization process works, we carry out this three-step procedure for the criteria pairwise comparison matrix.

Step 1. Sum the values in each column.

	Price	MPG	Comfort	Style
Price	1	3	2	2
MPG	$^1/_3$	1	$^1/_4$	$^1/_4$
Comfort	$^1/_2$	4	1	$^1/_2$
Style	$^1/_2$	4	2	1
Sum	2.333	12.000	5.250	3.750

Step 2. Divide each element of the matrix by its column total.

	Price	MPG	Comfort	Style
Price	0.429	0.250	0.381	0.533
MPG	0.143	0.083	0.048	0.067
Comfort	0.214	0.333	0.190	0.133
Style	0.214	0.333	0.381	0.267

Step 3. Average the elements in each row to determine the priority of each criterion.

	Price	MPG	Comfort	Style	Priority
Price	0.429	0.250	0.381	0.533	0.398
MPG	0.143	0.083	0.048	0.067	0.085
Comfort	0.214	0.333	0.190	0.133	0.218
Style	0.214	0.333	0.381	0.267	0.299

The AHP synthesization procedure provides the priority of each criterion in terms of its contribution to the overall goal of selecting the best car. Thus, using Diane's pairwise comparisons provided in Table 14.6, AHP determines that Price with a priority of 0.398 is the most important criterion in the car selection process. Style with a priority of 0.299 ranks second in importance and is closely followed by Comfort with a priority of 0.218. MPG is the least important criterion with a priority of 0.085.

Consistency

A key step in AHP is the making of several pairwise comparisons as previously described. An important consideration in this process is the consistency of the pairwise judgements provided by the decision maker. For example, if criterion A compared to criterion B has a numerical rating of 3 and if criterion B compared to criterion C has a numerical rating of 2, perfect consistency of criterion A compared to criterion C would have a numerical rating of $3 \times 2 = 6$. If the A to C numerical rating assigned by the decision maker was 4 or 5, some inconsistency would exist among the pairwise comparison.

With numerous pairwise comparisons, perfect consistency is difficult to achieve. In fact, some degree of inconsistency can be expected to exist in almost any set of pairwise comparisons. To handle the consistency issue, AHP provides a method for measuring the degree of consistency among the pairwise comparisons provided by the decision maker. If the degree of consistency is unacceptable, the decision maker should review and revise the pairwise comparisons before proceeding with the AHP analysis.

A consistency ratio greater than 0.10 indicates inconsistency in the pairwise comparisons. In such cases, the decision maker should review the pairwise comparisons before proceeding.

AHP provides a measure of the consistency for the pairwise comparisons by calculating a consistency ratio. This ratio is designed in such a way that a value *greater than* 0.10 indicates an inconsistency in the pairwise judgements. So, if the consistency ratio is 0.10 or less, the consistency of the pairwise comparisons is considered reasonable and the AHP process can continue.

Although the exact mathematical calculation of the consistency ratio is beyond the scope of this text, an approximation of the ratio can be obtained with little difficulty. The step-by-step procedure for estimating the consistency ratio for the criteria of the car selection problem follows.

Step 1. Multiply each value in the first column of the pairwise comparison matrix by the priority of the first item; multiply each value in the second column of the pairwise comparison matrix by the priority of the second item; continue this process for all columns of the pairwise comparison matrix. Sum the values across the rows to obtain a vector of values labelled 'weighted sum'. This calculation for the car selection problem is as follows:

$$0.398\begin{bmatrix}1\\ 1/3\\ 1/2\\ 1/2\end{bmatrix} + 0.085\begin{bmatrix}3\\ 1\\ 4\\ 4\end{bmatrix} + 0.218\begin{bmatrix}2\\ 1/2\\ 1\\ 2\end{bmatrix} + 0.299\begin{bmatrix}2\\ 1/4\\ 1/2\\ 1\end{bmatrix}$$

$$\begin{bmatrix}0.398\\ 0.133\\ 0.199\\ 0.199\end{bmatrix} + \begin{bmatrix}0.255\\ 0.085\\ 0.340\\ 0.340\end{bmatrix} + \begin{bmatrix}0.436\\ 0.054\\ 0.218\\ 0.436\end{bmatrix} + \begin{bmatrix}0.598\\ 0.075\\ 0.149\\ 0.299\end{bmatrix} = \begin{bmatrix}1.687\\ 0.347\\ 0.907\\ 1.274\end{bmatrix}$$

Step 2. Divide the elements of the weighted sum vector obtained in step 1 by the corresponding priority for each criterion.

$$\text{Price} \quad \frac{1.687}{0.398} = 4.236$$

$$\text{MPG} \quad \frac{0.347}{0.085} = 4.077$$

$$\text{Comfort} \quad \frac{0.907}{0.218} = 4.163$$

$$\text{Style} \quad \frac{1.274}{0.299} = 4.264$$

Step 3. Calculate the average of the values found in step 2; this average is denoted λ_{max}.

$$\lambda_{max} = \frac{(4.236 + 4.077 + 4.163 + 4.264)}{4} = 4.185$$

Step 4. Calculate the consistency index (CI) as follows:

$$CI = \frac{\lambda_{max} - n}{n - 1}$$

where n is the number of items (criteria) being compared. Thus, we have:

$$CI = \frac{4.185 - 4}{4 - 1} = 0.0616$$

Step 5. Compute the consistency ratio, which is defined as:

$$CR = \frac{CI}{RI}$$

where RI is the consistency index of a *randomly* generated pairwise comparison matrix. The value of RI depends on the number of items being compared and is given as follows:

n	3	4	5	6	7	8
RI	0.58	0.90	1.12	1.24	1.32	1.41

Thus, for the car selection problem with $n = 4$ criteria, we have RI = 0.90 and a consistency ratio:

$$\text{CR} = \frac{0.0616}{0.90} = 0.068$$

Problem 10 will give you practise with the synthesization calculations and determining the consistency ratio.

As mentioned previously, a consistency ratio of 0.10 or less is considered acceptable. Because the pairwise comparisons for the car selection criteria show CR = 0.068, we can conclude that the degree of consistency in the pairwise comparisons is acceptable.

Other Pairwise Comparisons for the Car Selection Problem

Continuing with the AHP analysis of the car selection problem, we need to use the pairwise comparison procedure to determine the priorities for the three cars using each of the criteria: Price, MPG, Comfort and Style. Determining these priorities requires Diane to express pairwise comparison preferences for the cars using each criterion one at a time. For example, using the Price criterion, Diane must make the following pairwise comparisons:

The Accord compared to the Saturn.

The Accord compared to the Cavalier.

THE Saturn compared to the Cavalier.

In each comparison, Diane must select the more preferred car and then express a judgement of how much more preferred the selected car is.

For example, using Price as the basis for comparison, assume that Diane considers the Accord–Saturn pairwise comparison and indicates that the less expensive Saturn is preferred. Table 14.7 shows how AHP uses Diane's verbal description of the preference between the Accord and Saturn to determine a numerical rating of the preference. For example, suppose that Diane states that based on Price, the Saturn is 'moderately more preferred' to the Accord. Thus, using the Price criterion, a numerical rating of 3 is assigned to the Saturn row and Accord column of the pairwise comparison matrix.

Table 14.8 shows the summary of the car pairwise comparisons that Diane provided for each criterion of the car selection problem. Using this table and referring to selected pairwise comparison entries, we see that Diane stated the following preferences:

In terms of Price, the Cavalier is moderately to strongly more preferred than the Accord.

Table 14.7 Pairwise Comparison Scale for the Preference of Decision Alternatives Using AHP

Verbal Judgement	Numerical Rating
Extremely preferred	9
	8
Very strongly preferred	7
	6
Strongly preferred	5
	4
Moderately preferred	3
	2
Equally preferred	1

Table 14.8 Pairwise Comparison Matrixes Showing Preferences for the Cars Using Each Criterion

Price

	Accord	Saturn	Cavalier
Accord	1	1/3	1/4
Saturn	3	1	1/2
Cavalier	4	2	1

MPG

	Accord	Saturn	Cavalier
Accord	1	1/4	1/6
Saturn	4	1	1/3
Cavalier	6	3	1

Comfort

	Accord	Saturn	Cavalier
Accord	1	2	8
Saturn	1/2	1	6
Cavalier	1/8	1/6	1

Style

	Accord	Saturn	Cavalier
Accord	1	1/3	4
Saturn	3	1	7
Cavalier	1/4	1/7	1

Table 14.9 Priorities for Each Car Using Each Criterion

	Criterion			
	Price	**MPG**	**Comfort**	**Style**
Accord	0.123	0.087	0.593	0.265
Saturn	0.320	0.274	0.341	0.656
Cavalier	0.557	0.639	0.065	0.080

In terms of MPG, the Cavalier is moderately more preferred than the Saturn.

In terms of Comfort, the Accord is very strongly to extremely more preferred than the Cavalier.

In terms of Style, the Saturn is moderately more preferred than the Accord.

Practise setting up a pairwise comparison matrix and determine whether judgements are consistent by working Problem 12.

Using the pairwise comparison matrixes in Table 14.8, many other insights may be gained about the preferences Diana expressed for the cars. However, at this point, AHP continues by synthesizing each of the four pairwise comparison matrixes in Table 14.8 in order to determine the priority of each car using each criterion. A synthesization is conducted for each pairwise comparison matrix using the three-step procedure described previously for the criteria pairwise comparison matrix. Four synthesization computations provide the four sets of priorities shown in Table 14.9. Using this table, we see that the Cavalier is the preferred alternative based on Price (0.557), the Cavalier is the preferred alternative based on MPG (0.639), the Accord is the preferred alternative based on Comfort (0.593) and the Saturn is the preferred alternative based on Style (0.656). At this point, no car is the clear, overall best. The next section shows how to combine the priorities for the criteria and the priorities in Table 14.9 to develop an overall priority ranking for the three cars.

14.6 Using AHP to Develop an Overall Priority Ranking

In Section 14.5, we used Diane's pairwise comparisons of the four criteria to develop the priorities of 0.398 for Price, 0.085 for MPG, 0.218 for Comfort and 0.299 for Style. We now want to use these priorities and the priorities shown in Table 14.9 to develop an overall priority ranking for the three cars.

The procedure used to calculate the overall priority is to weight each car's priority shown in Table 14.9 by the corresponding criterion priority. For example, the Price criterion has a priority of 0.398, and the Accord has a priority of 0.123 in terms of the Price criterion. So, $0.398 \times 0.123 = 0.049$ is the priority value of the Accord based on the Price criterion. To obtain the overall priority of the Accord, we need to make similar calculations for the MPG, Comfort and Style criteria and then add the values to obtain the overall priority. This calculation is as follows:

Overall Priority of the Accord:

$$0.398(0.123) + 0.085(0.087) + 0.218(0.593) + 0.299(0.265) = 0.265$$

Repeating this calculation for the Saturn and the Cavalier, we obtain the following results:

Overall Priority of the Saturn:

$$0.398(0.320) + 0.085(0.274) + 0.218(0.341) + 0.299(0.656) = 0.421$$

Overall Priority of the Cavalier:

$$0.398(0.557) + 0.085(0.639) + 0.218(0.065) + 0.299(0.080) = 0.314$$

Ranking these priorities, we have the AHP ranking of the decision alternatives:

Car	Priority
1. Saturn	0.421
2. Cavalier	0.314
3. Accord	0.265

These results provide a basis for Diane to make a decision regarding the purchase of a car. As long as Diane believes that her judgements regarding the importance of the criteria and her preferences for the cars using each criterion are valid, the AHP priorities show that the Saturn is preferred. In addition to the recommendation of the Saturn as the best car, the AHP analysis helped Diane gain a better understanding of the trade-offs in the decision-making process and a clearer understanding of why the Saturn is the AHP recommended alternative.

NOTES AND COMMENTS

1 The scoring model in Section 14.3 used the following equation to compute the overall score of a decision alternative.

$$S_j = \sum_i w_i r_{ij}$$

where

w_i = the weight for criterion i

r_{ij} = the rating for criterion i and decision alternative j

In Section 14.5 AHP used the same calculation to determine the overall priority of each decision alternative. The difference between the two approaches is that the scoring model required the decision maker to estimate the values of w_i and r_{ij} directly. AHP used synthesization to compute the criterion priorities w_i and the decision alternative priorities r_{ij} based on the pairwise comparison information provided by the decision maker.

MANAGEMENT SCIENCE IN ACTION

Muticriteria Decision Making at NASA

NASA's space shuttle project engineering office at the Kennedy Space Center is faced with many complex decisions. One area relates to evaluating proposals for funding and developing advanced-technology projects relating to the space shuttle programme submitted by contractors or by other divisions within the Center. Between 30 and 50 such projects are received each year and are assessed by five senior staff who have to consider the different criteria involved such as safety, engineering, cost implications, reliability and implementation. Historically, the decision makers gave a numerical score to each proposal, the individual scores were then averaged and used to decide which projects should be funded. However, management expressed concern about the subjectivity of the existing decision-making process and its potential for lack of consistency. Accordingly a group decision-making model based on multicriteria approaches was developed: CROSS – consensus-ranking organizational-support system – incorporating the analytic hierarchy process (AHP). AHP is used to weight the importance of the different Center departments which will be affected by a particular project. AHP is also used to weight the importance of the various criteria being used to evaluate the differing projects. The intention behind CROSS is to help those making decisions think systematically about the decision problem and to help improve the quality and consistency of decision making.

Based on M. Tavara, 'CROSS: A Multicriteria Group-Decision-Making Model for Evaluating and Prioritizing Advanced-Technology Projects at NASA', *Interfaces* 33/3 (2003): 4–56.

Summary

In this chapter we have introduced three approaches to dealing with multicriteria decision problems.

- Multicriteria decision problems occur where the decision maker must take more than one criteria into account when making a decision.
- Goal programming can be used to solve problems with multiple goals within the linear programming framework.
- Scoring models help identify the most appropriate decision alternative by using subjective weights for the importance of each criterion and then by getting the decision maker to assess how well each decision alternative satisfies each criterion.
- The analytic hierarchy process is a method for ranking the different decision alternatives using a series of pairwise comparisons for the different elements in the hierarchy.

WORKED EXAMPLE

The regional health service in Scotland is trying to encourage males over the age of 50 to visit their family doctor for a health checkup. This will help identify potential health problems at an early stage. The initiative is an experimental one and if successful the scheme will be extended to cover the whole country. The health service intends to mailshot a letter and an explanatory leaflet to a sample of male patients on the health service database. The cost of mailing out each letter and leaflet will be £1 and the budget is £3000. Similar initiatives have found that for patients who have visited their family doctor within the last year, 50 per cent will arrange a checkup if invited to do so. For patients who have not visited their family doctor in the last year, the takeup rate drops to 40 per cent. The health service wants to get at least 500 male patients who have visited their family doctor in the last year booking a checkup. For those who have not visited their family doctor in the last year the target is 1000. The health service thinks getting patients who *have not* visited their doctor in the last year to get a checkup is twice as important as getting those who *have* seen their doctor to get a checkup. Staying within budget is seen as a secondary priority.

What advice can we give the health service?

Solution

The decision problem relates to deciding how many males in each of the two categories to mailshot to meet the targets for those taking up the checkup but also to remain within budget. So we have a goal programming problem. The priority one goal for the health service is to meet the checkup targets. Staying within the budget is priority two. We will use x_1 for males who have been to see their doctor in the last year and x_2 for those males who have not. To get at least 500 males who have been to see their family doctor in the last 12 months taking up a checkup we will need to mail out a minimum of 1000 letters (given the 50 per cent takeup rate). For the second group of males we will need a minimum of 2500 letters. Using appropriate deviation variables we then have:

$$
\begin{aligned}
x_1 \quad - d_1^+ + d_1^- \quad &= 1000 \quad \text{Goal 1}\\
x_2 \quad - d_2^+ + d_2^- \quad &= 2500 \quad \text{Goal 2}\\
x_1 + x_2 \quad - d_3^+ + d_3^- &= 3000 \quad \text{Goal 3}
\end{aligned}
$$

The deviational variables indicate the extent to which we exceed the relevant target or fall short of it. Goals 1 and 2 are priority 1 with goal 3 being priority 2. For the priority 1 goals we want to minimize any shortfall in meeting the relevant targets but with Goal 2 being twice as important as Goal 1. For the priority 2 goal we want to minimize any budget overspend. The full formulation then becomes:

$$
\begin{aligned}
&\text{Min. } P_1(d_1^-) + P_1(2d_2^-) + P_2(d_3^+)\\
&\text{s.t.}\\
&x_1 \quad - d_1^+ + d_1^- \quad = 1000 \quad \text{Goal 1}\\
&x_2 \quad - d_2^+ + d_2^- \quad = 2500 \quad \text{Goal 2}\\
&x_1 + x_2 \quad - d_3^+ + d_3^- = 3000 \quad \text{Goal 3}\\
&x_1, x_2, d_1^+, d_1^-, d_2^+, d_2^-, d_3^+, d_3^- \geq 0
\end{aligned}
$$

The initial formulation for priority 1 is then:

$$
\begin{aligned}
&\text{Min.}(d_1^-) + (2d_2^-)\\
&\text{s.t.}\\
&x_1 \quad - d_1^+ + d_1^- \quad = 1000 \quad \text{Goal 1}\\
&x_2 \quad - d_2^+ + d_2^- \quad = 2500 \quad \text{Goal 2}\\
&x_1 + x_2 \quad - d_3^+ + d_3^- \quad = 3000 \quad \text{Goal 3}\\
&x_1, x_2, d_1^+, d_1^-, d_2^+, d_2^-, d_3^+, d_3^- \geq 0
\end{aligned}
$$

The computer solution is shown below. To meet the Priority 1 goals we must mailshot the required numbers of 1000 and 2500 letters to each of the two groups of males. However, this will result in a budget overspend of £500.

Objective function value: 0.000

Variable	Value
X1	1000.000
X2	2500.000
D1PLUS	0.000
D1MINUS	0.000
D2PLUS	0.000
D2MINUS	0.000
D3PLUS	500.00
D3MINUS	0.000

We now introduce the Priority 2 goal into the problem and our new formulation becomes:

$$
\begin{array}{llll}
\text{Min.}(d_3^+) & & & \\
\text{s.t.} & & & \\
x_1 - d_1^+ + d_1^- & = 1000 & \text{Goal 1} \\
x_2 - d_2^+ + d_2^- & = 2500 & \text{Goal 2} \\
x_1 + x_2 - d_3^+ + d_3^- & = 3000 & \text{Goal 3} \\
d_1^- & = 0 & \text{Priority level 1} \\
d_2^- & = 0 & \text{Priority level 1} \\
x_1, x_2, d_1^+, d_1^-, d_2^+, d_2^-, d_3^+, d_3^- \geq 0 & &
\end{array}
$$

We have added the necessary two constraints to ensure that any new solution continues to satisfy the Priority level 1 goals. The solution to this formulation is then:

Objective function value: 250.000

Variable	Value
X1	1000.000
X2	2500.000
D1PLUS	0.000
D1MINUS	0.000
D2PLUS	0.000
D2MINUS	0.000
D3PLUS	500.00
D3MINUS	0.000

In fact the new solution is the same as the previous except for the value of the objective function. We are effectively being told that we cannot achieve both priorities. In order to achieve the Priority 1 goals we must accept a budget overspend.

Problems

1 The RMC Corporation blends three raw materials to produce two products: a fuel additive and a solvent base. Each ton of fuel additive is a mixture of 0.4 ton of material 1 and 0.6 ton of material 3. A ton of solvent base is a mixture of 0.5 ton of material 1, 0.2 ton of material 2 and 0.3 ton of material 3. RMC's production is constrained by a limited availability of the three raw materials. For the current production period, RMC has the following quantities of each raw material: material 1, 20 tons; material 2, 5 tons; material 3, 21 tons. Management wants to achieve the following P_1 priority level goals.

Goal 1: Produce at least 30 tons of fuel additive.

Goal 2: Produce at least 15 tons of solvent base.

Assume there are no other goals.

a. Is it possible for management to achieve both P_1 level goals given the constraints on the amounts of each material available? Explain.
b. Treating the amounts of each material available as constraints, formulate a goal programming model to determine the optimal product mix. Assume that both P_1 priority level goals are equally important to management.
c. Use the graphical goal programming procedure to solve the model formulated in part (b).
d. If goal 1 is twice as important as goal 2, what is the optimal product mix?

SELF *test*

2 DJS Investment Services must develop an investment portfolio for a new client. As an initial investment strategy, the new client would like to restrict the portfolio to a mix of two stocks:

Stock	Price/Share (€)	Estimated Annual Return (%)
AGA Products	50	6
Key Oil	100	10

The client wants to invest €50 000 and established the following two investment goals.

Priority Level 1 Goal

Goal 1: Obtain an annual return of at least 9 per cent.

Priority Level 2 Goal

Goal 2: Limit the investment in Key Oil, the riskier investment, to no more than 60 per cent of the total investment.

a. Formulate a goal programming model for the DJS Investment problem.
b. Use the graphical goal programming procedure to obtain a solution.

3 The Ruiters' Manufacturing Company produces two products, which have the following profit and resource requirement characteristics.

Characteristic	Product 1	Product 2
Profit/unit	€4	€2
Dept. A hours/unit	1	1
Dept. B hours/unit	2	5

Last month's production schedule used 350 hours of labour in department A and 1000 hours of labour in department B.

Ruiters' management has been experiencing workforce morale and labour union problems during the past six months because of monthly departmental workload fluctuations. New hiring, layoffs and interdepartmental transfers have been common because the firm has not attempted to stabilize workload requirements.

Management would like to develop a production schedule for the coming month that will achieve the following goals.

Goal 1: Use 350 hours of labour in department A.

Goal 2: Use 1000 hours of labour in department B.

Goal 3: Earn a profit of at least €1300.

a. Formulate a goal programming model for this problem, assuming that goals 1 and 2 are P_1 level goals and goal 3 is a P_2 level goal; assume that goals 1 and 2 are equally important.
b. Solve the model formulated in part (a) using the graphical goal programming procedure.
c. Suppose that the firm ignores the workload fluctuations and considers the 350 hours in department A and the 1000 hours in department B as the maximum available. Formulate and solve a linear programming problem to maximize profit subject to these constraints.
d. Compare the solutions obtained in parts (b) and (c). Discuss which approach you favour, and why.
e. Reconsider part (a) assuming that the priority level 1 goal is goal 3 and the priority level 2 goals are goals 1 and 2; as before, assume that goals 1 and 2 are equally important. Solve this revised problem using the graphical goal programming procedure and compare your solution to the one obtained for the original problem.

SELF *test*

4 Industrial Chemicals produces two adhesives used in the manufacturing process for aeroplanes. The two adhesives, which have different bonding strengths, require different amounts of production time: the IC-100 adhesive requires 20 minutes of production time per gallon of finished product, and the IC-200 adhesive uses 30 minutes of production time per gallon. Both products use one kilo of a highly perishable resin for each litre of finished product. Inventory currently holds 300 kilos of the resin, and more can be obtained if necessary. However, because of the shelf life of the material, any amount not used in the next two weeks will be discarded.

The firm has existing orders for 100 litres of IC-100 and 120 litres of IC-200. Under normal conditions, the production process operates eight hours per day, five days per week. Management wants to schedule production for the next two weeks to achieve the following goals.

Priority Level 1 Goals

Goal 1: Avoid underutilization of the production process.
Goal 2: Avoid overtime in excess of 20 hours for the two weeks.

Priority Level 2 Goals

Goal 3: Satisfy existing orders for the IC-100 adhesive; that is, produce at least 100 litres of IC-100.
Goal 4: Satisfy existing orders for the IC-200 adhesive; that is, produce at least 120 litres of IC-200.

Priority Level 3 Goal

Goal 5: Use all the available resin.

a. Formulate a goal programming model for the Industrial Chemicals problem. Assume that both priority level 1 goals and that both priority level 2 goals are equally important.
b. Use the graphical goal programming procedure to develop a solution for the model formulated in part (a).

5 A committee in charge of promoting a Ladies' Professional Golf Association tournament is trying to determine how best to advertise the event during the two weeks prior to the tournament. The committee obtained the following information about the three advertising media they are considering using.

Category	Audience Reached per Advertisement	Cost per Advertisement, €	Maximum Number of Advertisements
TV	200 000	2 500	10
Radio	50 000	400	15
Newspaper	100 000	500	20

The last column in this table shows the maximum number of advertisements that can be run during the next two weeks; these values should be treated as constraints. The committee established the following goals for the campaign.

Priority Level 1 Goal

Goal 1: Reach at least four million people.

Priority Level 2 Goal

Goal 2: The number of television advertisements should be at least 30 per cent of the total number of advertisements.

Priority Level 3 Goal

Goal 3: The number of radio advertisements should not exceed 20 per cent of the total number of advertisements.

Priority Level 4 Goal

Goal 4: Limit the total amount spent for advertising to €20 000.

a. Formulate a goal programming model for this problem.
b. Use the goal programming computer procedure illustrated in Section 14.2 to solve the model formulated in part (a).

SELF *test*

6 One advantage of using the multicriteria decision-making methods presented in this chapter is that the criteria weights and the decision alternative ratings may be modified to reflect the unique interests and preferences of each individual decision maker. For example, assume that another graduating college student had the same three job offers described in Section 14.3. This student provided the following scoring model information. Rank the overall preference for the three positions. Which position is recommended?

		Ratings		
Criteria	**Weight**	**Analyst Frankfurt**	**Policy advisor London**	**Forecaster Amsterdam**
Career advancement	5	7	4	4
Location	2	5	6	4
Management style	5	6	5	7
Salary	4	7	8	4
Prestige	4	8	5	6
Job security	2	4	5	8
Enjoyment of the work	4	7	5	5

7 The Davis family of Bristol, England is planning its annual summer holiday. Three vacation locations along with criteria weights and location ratings follow. What is the recommended holiday location?

Criteria	Weight	Ratings		
		Scottish Highlands, Scotland	Nice, France	Cardiff, Wales
Travel distance	2	5	7	3
Holiday cost	5	5	6	4
Entertainment available	3	7	4	8
Outdoor activities	2	9	6	5
Unique experience	4	6	7	8
Family fun	5	8	7	7

SELF *test*

8 Mr and Mrs Msibi are interested in purchasing a holiday property. The three most preferred are listed along with criteria weights and rating information. Which property is preferred?

Criteria	Weight	Ratings		
		Park Shore	The Terrace	Gulf View
Cost	5	5	6	5
Location	4	7	4	9
Appearance	5	7	4	7
Parking	2	5	8	5
Floor plan	4	8	7	5
Swimming pool	1	7	2	3
View	3	5	4	9
Kitchen	4	8	7	6
Closet space	3	6	8	4

9 Use the pairwise comparison matrix for the price criterion shown in Table 14.8 to verify that the priorities after synthesization are 0.123, 0.320 and 0.557. Calculate the consistency ratio and comment on its acceptability.

SELF *test*

10 Use the pairwise comparison matrix for the style criterion as shown in Table 14.8 to verify that the priorities after synthesization are 0.265, 0.656 and 0.080. Compute the consistency ratio and comment on its acceptability.

11 An organization is investigating relocating its corporate headquarters to one of three possible cities. The following pairwise comparison matrix shows the president's judgements regarding the desirability for the three cities.

	City 1	City 2	City 3
City 1	1	5	7
City 2	$1/5$	1	3
City 3	$1/7$	$1/3$	1

a. Determine the priorities for the three cities.
b. Is the president consistent in terms of the judgements provided? Explain.

SELF *test* 12 Asked to compare three soft drinks with respect to flavour, an individual stated that:

A is moderately more preferable than B.
A is equally to moderately more preferable than C.
A is strongly more preferable than C.

a. Set up the pairwise comparison matrix for this problem.
b. Determine the priorities for the soft drinks with respect to the flavour criterion.
c. Compute the consistency ratio. Are the individual's judgements consistent? Explain.

13 Refer to Problem 12. Suppose that the individual had stated the following judgements instead of those given in Problem 12.

A is strongly more preferable than C.
B is equally to moderately more preferable than A.
B is strongly more preferable than C.

Answer parts (a), (b) and (c) as stated in Problem 12.

SELF *test* 14 A study comparing four laptop computers resulted in the following pairwise comparison matrix for the performance criterion.

	1	2	3	4
1	1	3	7	$\frac{1}{3}$
2	$\frac{1}{3}$	1	4	$\frac{1}{4}$
3	$\frac{1}{4}$	$\frac{1}{4}$	1	$\frac{1}{6}$
4	3	4	6	1

a. Determine the priorities for the four computers relative to the performance criterion.
b. Calculate the consistency ratio. Are the judgements regarding performance consistent? Explain.

SELF *test* 15 An individual was interested in determining which of two stocks to invest in, Central Computing Company (CCC) or Software Research, Inc. (SRI). The criteria thought to be most relevant in making the decision are the potential yield of the stock and the risk associated with the investment. The pairwise comparison matrixes for this problem are:

	Criterion			Yield			Risk	
	Yield	Risk		CCC	SRI		CCC	SRI
Yield	1	2	**CCC**	1	3	**CCC**	1	½
Risk	½	1	**SRI**	$\frac{1}{3}$	1	**SRI**	2	1

a. Calculate the priorities for each pairwise comparison matrix.
b. Determine the overall priority for the two investments, CCC and SRI. Which investment is preferred based on yield and risk?

SELF *test* 16 The vice president of Harling Equipment needs to select a new director of marketing. The two possible candidates are Sara Bowers and Kiara Fakier, and the criteria thought to be most relevant in the selection are leadership ability (L), personal skills (P) and administrative skills (A). The following pairwise comparison matrixes were obtained.

	Criterion				Leadership	
	L	P	A		Jacobs	Martin
L	1	$\frac{1}{3}$	$\frac{1}{4}$	**Bowers**	1	4
P	3	1	2	**Fakier**	$\frac{1}{4}$	1
A	4	$\frac{1}{2}$	1			

	Personal			Administrative	
	Jacobs	Martin		Jacobs	Martin
Bowers	1	$\frac{1}{3}$	**Bowers**	1	2
Fakier	3	1	**Fakier**	$\frac{1}{2}$	1

a. Calculate the priorities for each pairwise comparison matrix.
b. Determine an overall priority for each candidate. Which candidate is preferred?

CASE PROBLEM EZ Trailers

EZ Trailers located in Southampton, England manufactures a variety of general purpose trailers, including a complete line of boat trailers. Two of their best-selling boat trailers are the EZ-190 and the EZ-250. The EZ-190 is designed for boats up to 19 feet in length, and the EZ-250 can be used for boats up to 25 feet in length.

EZ Trailers would like to schedule production for the next two months for these two models. Each unit of the EZ-190 requires four hours of production time, and each unit of the EZ-250 uses six hours of production time. The following orders have been received for March and April.

Model	March	April
EZ-190	800	600
EZ-250	1 100	1 200

The ending inventory from February was 200 units of the EZ-190 and 300 units of the EZ-250. The total number of hours of production time used in February was 6300 hours.

The management of EZ Trailers is concerned about being able to satisfy existing orders for the EZ-250 for both March and April. In fact, it believes that this goal is the most important one that a production schedule should meet. Next in importance is satisfying existing orders for the EZ-190. In addition, management doesn't want to implement any production schedule that would involve significant labour fluctuations from month to month. In this regard, its goal is to develop a production schedule that would limit fluctuations in labour hours used to a maximum of 1000 hours from one month to the next.

Managerial Report

Perform an analysis of EZ Trailers's production scheduling problem, and prepare a report for EZ's president that summarizes your findings. Include a discussion and analysis of the following items in your report.

1 The production schedule that best achieves the goals as specified by management.

2 Suppose that EZ Trailers' storage facilities would accommodate only a maximum of 300 trailers in any one month. What effect would this have on the production schedule?

3 Suppose that EZ Trailers can store only a maximum of 300 trailers in any one month. In addition, suppose management would like to have an ending inventory in April of at least 100 units of each model. What effect would both changes have on the production schedule?

4 What changes would occur in the production schedule if the labour fluctuation goal was the highest priority goal?

Appendix 14.1 Scoring Models with Excel

Excel provides an efficient way to analyze a multicriteria decision problem that can be described by a scoring model. We will use the job selection application from Section 14.3 to demonstrate this procedure.

A worksheet for the job selection scoring model is shown in Figure 14.7. The criteria weights are placed into cells B6 to B12. The ratings for each criterion and decision alternative are entered into cells C6 to E12.

The calculations used to compute the score for each decision alternative are shown in the bottom portion of the worksheet. The calculation for cell C18 is provided by the cell formula:

$$= \$B6 * C6$$

This cell formula can be copied from cell C18 to cells C18:E24 to provide the results shown in rows 18 to 24. The score for the financial analyst position in Frankfurt is found by placing the following formula in cell C26:

$$= \text{SUM}(C18 : C24)$$

Copying cell C26 to cells D26:E26 provides the scores for the policy advisor in London and the forecaster in Amsterdam positions.

EXCEL *file*

SCORING

Figure 14.7 Worksheet for the Job Selection Scoring Model

	A	B	C	D	E	F
1	**Job Selection Scoring Model**					
2						
3				**Ratings**		
4			**Analyst**	**Policy advisor**	**Forecoster**	
5	**Criteria**	**Weight**	**Frankfort**	**London**	**Amsterdam**	
6	Career Advancement	5	8	6	4	
7	Location	3	3	8	7	
8	Management	4	5	6	9	
9	Salary	3	6	7	5	
10	Prestige	2	7	5	4	
11	Job Security	4	4	7	6	
12	Enjoy the Work	5	8	6	5	
13						
14						
15	**Scoring Calculations**					
16			**Analyst**	**Policy advisor**	**Forecoster**	
17	**Criteria**		**Frankfort**	**London**	**Amsterdam**	
18	Career Advancement		40	30	20	
19	Location		9	24	21	
20	Management		20	24	36	
21	Salary		18	21	15	
22	Prestige		14	10	8	
23	Job Security		16	28	24	
24	Enjoy the Work		40	30	25	
25						
26	**Score**		157	167	149	

Conclusion: Management Science in Practice

Throughout the text we have introduced a number of quantitative management science techniques and shown how they can be used to help decision making. As we have illustrated with case studies and the *Management Science in Action* cases, management science potentially has a role to play in almost any decision situation in any organization. Without doubt, many organizations round the world routinely use management science and many others apply management science to major decision situations. Equally, computer software such as Excel and decision support software used in organizations often has management science techniques and algorithms built in. However, as any management science practitioner will tell you, a good academic understanding of management science does not guarantee successful application in practice and there are many managers and organizations who do not use management science and in this conclusion we will briefly discuss some of the issues involved in applying management science successfully.

The complexity of management science

As we have seen, many of the quantitative management science techniques and models are particularly complex and technical, frequently involving some detailed mathematics. This can be a major deterrent to the manager who is the ultimate decision maker. As the client, their own knowledge of management science may be non-existent or very limited and their ability to understand the detail of the analysis and modelling being conducted may consequently also be very limited. This means that the decision maker has to trust in the findings and recommendations being made by the management scientist. Clearly the trust and the client–consultant relationship then becomes a critical issue and much will depend on exact circumstances: whether the management scientist is part of the organization or an outside consultant; the history of previous management science projects within the organization; the interpersonal skills of the management scientist. This can be a major barrier to the adoption of management science by an organization.

Effective model building

As we have seen throughout the text, models and model building are critical to management science and the management scientist, almost by definition, has an intrinsic interest in developing and applying complex, sophisticated models. The client/decision maker, however, probably has no real interest in the model at all but wants a solution to a problem or information they can use as part of the decision-making process. Clearly there are tensions and conflicts to be managed here. The model used needs to be good enough to represent the real-life situation sufficiently accurately but should not be overly-sophisticated for the decision situation.

Data requirements

Many of the management science models we have looked at can be classed as 'data hungry'. That is, they require large amounts of data that has to be accurate, reliable and timely. Without this, many of the models we have looked at simply cannot be applied. It is convenient to assume that an organization will have the data required by a particular model. Determining the precise cost of shipping an item from point A to point B, for example, can be very problematic. Knowing exactly how long a customer waits in a queue for service may be information that is not currently collected or available. In practice, however, this can be a major problem, adding both to the time needed and the costs involved in developing a suitable model.

The need for an optimal solution

As we have seen, many management science models are built around the principle of optimality – finding the best solution to some decision problem. Whilst this seems perfectly sensible and rational, many managers may take a different approach, known as *satisficing*. A satisficing approach to decision making is where the decision maker selects a decision option that meets a given need or that seems to address most needs rather than spending valuable time and resources searching for the optimal solution. Satisficing can also occur in group decision making when the group agrees on a solution everyone can agree on even if it may not be the best. Consider a situation where a company is considering a new delivery network to transport its products to its customers. A delivery route network is agreed by the production manager, the customer service managers and the finance manager that has an acceptable level of cost, even though it may not be the optimal network from a management science perspective. It's an OK solution rather than the optimal solution. It may be acceptable to some managers but this then diminishes the value added by management science.

Client versus decision maker

Clearly, the prime purpose of the management science techniques we have looked at is to help the decision maker make better decisions. There are situations, however, where the decision maker and the client may be different people. For example, we may be working with the stock control manager as the client, modelling inventory systems in an organization and looking for ways to reduce some of the cost involved by changing stock control policy. However, it may well be that the recommendations coming out of the analysis and modelling require a decision by someone else in the organization. This may be the Finance Director if there are major financial implications; it may be the Production Director if the recommendations would affect production. The ultimate decision maker may be several steps removed from the actual client and the problem. If the decision maker has not been involved up to that point, we may have a difficult time persuading them to act on the analysis and modelling information.

The changing business environment

Anyone with real-world business experience will tell you that virtually all organizations – public and private sector, large and small, industrial and service sector – are facing an increasingly turbulent and changing business environment in which they have to operate successfully. Increased competition, increased uncertainty, ever-changing demands all add to the difficulty of decision-making. All of this may seem to add to the need for management science input into decision making – and many organizations appreciate this and take advantage of using management science to help. However, it also brings problems. As we have seen from some of the *Management Science in Action* cases, some management science models can take considerable time to develop – often several months, sometimes several years. In that time, the business environment can change considerably with the risk that the analysis and modelling work that has been done becomes redundant and worthless. Equally, managers may consider that they do not have time to wait for better information before taking a decision – the business faces a crisis and decisions are needed now not in several months' time. Of course, if they had been using management science in the first place maybe they would not have a crisis now.

Managing change

It is also important for the management scientist to appreciate that – almost by definition – decisions taken on the basis of the application of management science models will lead to change in the organization. The change may be relatively low level or operational or it may be major and strategic. The application of a queuing simulation model may lead to recommendations for reorganizing a call centre within an organization; the application of linear programming may lead to major changes in the production mix of a chemicals company. Whilst such changes may be perfectly rational from an analytical perspective, it may be that the level of change required is judged to be unacceptable at that time by the decision maker. In the call centre, for example, delicate negotiations may be underway with the workforce about future salary levels. In the chemicals company, a major change in production schedules may bring short-term cash flow problems which would be a major concern to the banks which have loaned the company funding. It may be very difficult, or impossible, to factor such issues directly into the modelling, but such issues may be a major reason for not acting upon the analysis.

The business benefits of management science

Finally, although every management scientist is convinced of the relevance and benefits of applying management science to business decision problems, it can be difficult to quantify the business benefits achieved. Applying management science costs money – staff or consultants have to be hired, computer hardware and specialist software is frequently needed, there may be additional data collection costs. Clearly, any organization will ask the question: what are we getting for the costs involved? With some management science applications, it may be possible to answer the question directly. With a linear programming application, for example, we may be able to show the cost savings we have achieved for the organization by identifying the optimal solution to some problem compared with the existing solution. However, with other management science applications – simulation modelling for example, or the application of project management techniques – it may be impossible to quantify the financial effects. This can make organizations wary of using management science – particularly those with little or no previous experience of it, or SMEs (small to medium-sized enterprises) where management time and money are scarce resources, or public sector organizations that are concerned about being criticized for 'wasting' public money.

Clearly the issues and potential problems in successfully applying management science are not insurmountable and many organizations successfully use the models and techniques we have introduced in this text. However, in practice, these issues do arise and can prevent management science being used effectively. Which brings us back full circle to where we started in Chapter 1 where we discussed, amongst other things, the Management Science Approach, the Modelling Process and the need to use both hard and soft management science – a combination of both quantitative and qualitative methods. A good understanding of the MS approach or methodology is critical in practice, providing an insight into the wider context of the decision problem and not simply focusing in on the technique. The approach (shown again in Figure 1.1) emphasizes the need for an iterative and integrated process of problem recognition; problem structuring; modelling and analysis; solutions and recommendations; implementation. Even though the management scientist may not be actively involved in all parts of this approach – implementation for example is likely to involve management rather than the analyst – it is necessary for the management scientist to be aware of the potential implementation issues to avoid developing a model or providing a solution that is simply unrealistic from an implementation perspective. Similarly, a combination of both hard and soft MS is likely to be needed to provide a robust problem structure that takes into account some of the softer issues likely to be involved such as the change management issues raised earlier. Equally, the approach stresses the importance of a robust approach to model building to help avoid some of the issues raised earlier and on the involvement of the client in the process wherever possible. A 'good' management scientist is not someone who is simply technically proficient in a particular management science technique, important though that proficiency is. To be effective, a management scientist not only needs the technical knowledge we have tried to develop in this text but also the interpersonal skills needed to work effectively with managers and decision makers. Good luck!

Figure 1.1 The MS approach

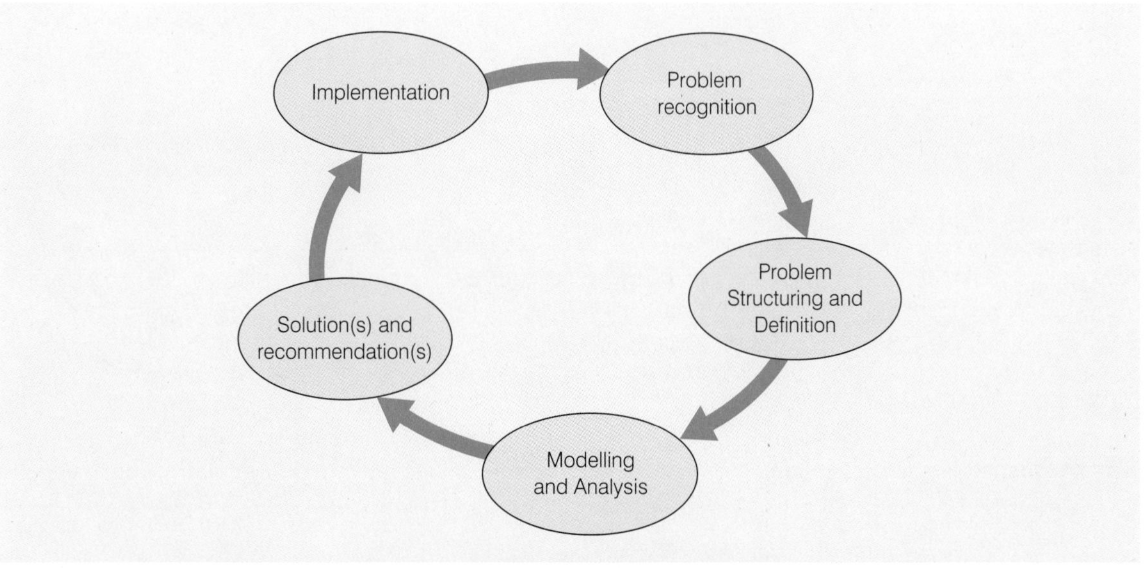

Appendices

Appendix A Areas for the Standard Normal Distribution

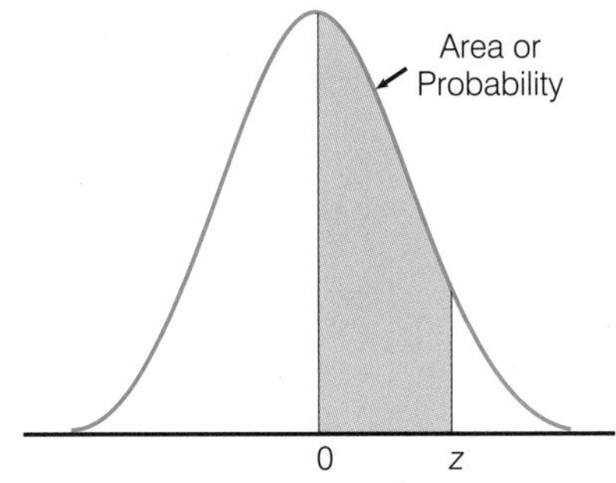

Entries in the following table give the area under the curve between the mean and z standard deviations above the mean. For example, for $z = 1.25$ the area under the curve between the mean and z is 0.3944.

z	0.00	0.01	0.02	0.03	0.04	0.05	0.06	0.07	0.08	0.09
0.0	0.0000	0.0040	0.0080	0.0120	0.0160	0.0199	0.0239	0.0279	0.0319	0.0359
0.1	0.0398	0.0438	0.0478	0.0517	0.0557	0.0596	0.0636	0.0675	0.0714	0.0753
0.2	0.0793	0.0832	0.0871	0.0910	0.0948	0.0987	0.1026	0.1064	0.1103	0.1141
0.3	0.1179	0.1217	0.1255	0.1293	0.1331	0.1368	0.1406	0.1443	0.1480	0.1517
0.4	0.1554	0.1591	0.1628	0.1664	0.1700	0.1736	0.1772	0.1808	0.1844	0.1879
0.5	0.1915	0.1950	0.1985	0.2019	0.2054	0.2088	0.2123	0.2157	0.2190	0.2224
0.6	0.2257	0.2291	0.2324	0.2357	0.2389	0.2422	0.2454	0.2486	0.2517	0.2549
0.7	0.2580	0.2611	0.2642	0.2673	0.2704	0.2734	0.2764	0.2794	0.2823	0.2852
0.8	0.2881	0.2910	0.2939	0.2967	0.2995	0.3023	0.3051	0.3078	0.3106	0.3133
0.9	0.3159	0.3186	0.3212	0.3238	0.3264	0.3289	0.3315	0.3340	0.3365	0.3389
1.0	0.3413	0.3438	0.3461	0.3485	0.3508	0.3531	0.3554	0.3577	0.3599	0.3621
1.1	0.3643	0.3665	0.3686	0.3708	0.3729	0.3749	0.3770	0.3790	0.3810	0.3830
1.2	0.3849	0.3869	0.3888	0.3907	0.3925	0.3944	0.3962	0.3980	0.3997	0.4015
1.3	0.4032	0.4049	0.4066	0.4082	0.4099	0.4115	0.4131	0.4147	0.4162	0.4177
1.4	0.4192	0.4207	0.4222	0.4236	0.4251	0.4265	0.4279	0.4292	0.4306	0.4319
1.5	0.4332	0.4345	0.4357	0.4370	0.4382	0.4394	0.4406	0.4418	0.4429	0.4441
1.6	0.4452	0.4463	0.4474	0.4484	0.4495	0.4505	0.4515	0.4525	0.4535	0.4545
1.7	0.4554	0.4564	0.4573	0.4582	0.4591	0.4599	0.4608	0.4616	0.4625	0.4633
1.8	0.4641	0.4649	0.4656	0.4664	0.4671	0.4678	0.4686	0.4693	0.4699	0.4706
1.9	0.4713	0.4719	0.4726	0.4732	0.4738	0.4744	0.4750	0.4756	0.4761	0.4767
2.0	0.4772	0.4778	0.4783	0.4788	0.4793	0.4798	0.4803	0.4808	0.4812	0.4817
2.1	0.4821	0.4826	0.4830	0.4834	0.4838	0.4842	0.4846	0.4850	0.4854	0.4857
2.2	0.4861	0.4864	0.4868	0.4871	0.4875	0.4878	0.4881	0.4884	0.4887	0.4890
2.3	0.4893	0.4896	0.4898	0.4901	0.4904	0.4906	0.4909	0.4911	0.4913	0.4916
2.4	0.4918	0.4920	0.4922	0.4925	0.4927	0.4929	0.4931	0.4932	0.4934	0.4936
2.5	0.4938	0.4940	0.4941	0.4943	0.4945	0.4946	0.4948	0.4949	0.4951	0.4952
2.6	0.4953	0.4955	0.4956	0.4957	0.4959	0.4960	0.4961	0.4962	0.4963	0.4964
2.7	0.4965	0.4966	0.4967	0.4968	0.4969	0.4970	0.4971	0.4972	0.4973	0.4974
2.8	0.4974	0.4975	0.4976	0.4977	0.4977	0.4978	0.4979	0.4979	0.4980	0.4981
2.9	0.4981	0.4982	0.4982	0.4983	0.4984	0.4984	0.4985	0.4985	0.4986	0.4986
3.0	0.4987	0.4987	0.4987	0.4988	0.4988	0.4989	0.4989	0.4989	0.4990	0.4990

Appendix B Values of $e^{-\lambda}$

λ	$e^{-\lambda}$	λ	$e^{-\lambda}$	λ	$e^{-\lambda}$
0.05	0.9512	2.05	0.1287	4.05	0.0174
0.10	0.9048	2.10	0.1225	4.10	0.0166
0.15	0.8607	2.15	0.1165	4.15	0.0158
0.20	0.8187	2.20	0.1108	4.20	0.0150
0.25	0.7788	2.25	0.1054	4.25	0.0143
0.30	0.7408	2.30	0.1003	4.30	0.0136
0.35	0.7047	2.35	0.0954	4.35	0.0129
0.40	0.6703	2.40	0.0907	4.40	0.0123
0.45	0.6376	2.45	0.0863	4.45	0.0117
0.50	0.6065	2.50	0.0821	4.50	0.0111
0.55	0.5769	2.55	0.0781	4.55	0.0106
0.60	0.5488	2.60	0.0743	4.60	0.0101
0.65	0.5220	2.65	0.0707	4.65	0.0096
0.70	0.4966	2.70	0.0672	4.70	0.0091
0.75	0.4724	2.75	0.0639	4.75	0.0087
0.80	0.4493	2.80	0.0608	4.80	0.0082
0.85	0.4274	2.85	0.0578	4.85	0.0078
0.90	0.4066	2.90	0.0550	4.90	0.0074
0.95	0.3867	2.95	0.0523	4.95	0.0071
1.00	0.3679	3.00	0.0498	5.00	0.0067
1.05	0.3499	3.05	0.0474	5.05	0.0064
1.10	0.3329	3.10	0.0450	5.10	0.0061
1.15	0.3166	3.15	0.0429	5.15	0.0058
1.20	0.3012	3.20	0.0408	5.20	0.0055
1.25	0.2865	3.25	0.0388	5.25	0.0052
1.30	0.2725	3.30	0.0369	5.30	0.0050
1.35	0.2592	3.35	0.0351	5.35	0.0047
1.40	0.2466	3.40	0.0334	5.40	0.0045
1.45	0.2346	3.45	0.0317	5.45	0.0043
1.50	0.2231	3.50	0.0302	5.50	0.0041
1.55	0.2122	3.55	0.0287	5.55	0.0039
1.60	0.2019	3.60	0.0273	5.60	0.0037
1.65	0.1920	3.65	0.0260	5.65	0.0035
1.70	0.1827	3.70	0.0247	5.70	0.0033
1.75	0.1738	3.75	0.0235	5.75	0.0032
1.80	0.1653	3.80	0.0224	5.80	0.0030
1.85	0.1572	3.85	0.0213	5.85	0.0029
1.90	0.1496	3.90	0.0202	5.90	0.0027
1.95	0.1423	3.95	0.0193	5.95	0.0026
2.00	0.1353	4.00	0.0183	6.00	0.0025
				7.00	0.0009
				8.00	0.000335
				9.00	0.000123
				10.00	0.000045

Appendix C Bibliography and References

Chapter 1 Introduction

Churchman, C. W., Ackoff, R. L. and Arnoff, E. L. *Introduction to Operations Research*. Wiley, 1957.

Horner, P. 'The Sabre Story', *OR/MS Today* (June 2000).

Leon, L., Przasnyski, Z. and Seal, K.C. 'Spreadsheets and OR/MS Models: An End-User Perspective', *Interfaces* (March/April 1996).

Powell, S. G. 'Innovative Approaches to Management Science', *OR/MS Today* (October 1996).

Savage, S. 'Weighing the Pros and Cons of Decision Technology and Spreadsheets', *OR/MS Today* (February 1997).

Winston, W. L. 'The Teachers' Forum: Management Science with Spreadsheets for MBAs at Indiana University', *Interfaces* (March/April 1996).

Chapters 2 to 7 Linear Programming, Transportation, Assignment and Transshipment and Problems

Bazarra, M. S., Jarvis, J. J. and Sherali, H. D. *Linear Programming and Network Flows*, 3rd ed. Wiley Blackwell, 2005.

Carino, H. F. and Le Noir, C. H. Jr. 'Optimizing Wood Procurement in Cabinet Manufacturing', *Interfaces* (March/April 1988): 10–19.

Dantzig, G. B. *Linear Programming and Extensions*. Princeton University Press, 1963.

Geoffrion, A. and Graves, G. 'Better Distribution Planning with Computer Models', *Harvard Business Review* (July/ August 1976).

Greenberg, H. J. 'How to Analyze the Results of Linear Programs – Part 1: Preliminaries', *Interfaces* 23, no. 4 (July/August 1993): 56–67.

Greenberg, H. J. 'How to Analyze the Results of Linear Programs – Part 2: Price Interpretation', *Interfaces* 23, no. 5 (September/October 1993): 97–114.

Greenberg, H. J. 'How to Analyze the Results of Linear Programs – Part 3: Infeasibility Diagnosis', *Interfaces* 23, no. 6 (November/December 1993): 120–139.

Lillien, G. and Rangaswamy, A. *Marketing Engineering: Computer-Assisted Marketing Analysis and Planning*, 2nd edition. Trafford Publishing, 2004.

Nemhauser, G. L. and Wolsey, L. A. *Integer and Combinatorial Optimization*. Wiley, 1999.

Schrage, L. *Optimization Modeling with LINDO*, 4th ed. LINDO Systems Inc., 2000.

Sherman, H. D. 'Hospital Efficiency Measurement and Evaluation', *Medical Care* 22, no. 10 (October 1984): 922–938.

Winston, W. L. and Albright, S. C. *Practical Management Science*, 3rd ed. Cengage South Western, 2007.

Chapter 8 Network Models

Bazarra, M. S., J. J. Jarvis and Sherali, H. D. *Linear Programming and Network Flows*, 3rd ed. Wiley Blackwell, 2005.

Evans, J. R. and Minieka, E. *Optimization Algorithms for Networks and Graphs*, 2nd ed. Marcel Dekker, 1992.

Ford, L. R. and Fulkerson, D. R. *Flows and Networks*. Princeton University Press, 1962.

Glover, F. and Klingman, D. 'Network Applications in Industry and Government', *AIIE Transactions* (December 1977).

Jensen, P. A. and Barnes, W. J. *Network Flow Programming*. Krieger, 1987.

Chapter 9 Project Scheduling: PERT/CPM

Moder, J. J., Phillips, C. R. and Davis, E. W. *Project Management with CPM, PERT and Precedence Diagramming*, 3d ed. Blitz, 1995.

Wasil, E. A. and Assad, A. A. 'Project Management on the PC: Software, Applications, and Trends', *Interfaces* 18, no. 2 (March/April 1988): 75–84.

Wiest, J. and F. Levy, F. *Management Guide to PERT-CPM*, 2nd ed. Prentice Hall, 1977.

Chapter 10 Inventory Models

Fogarty, D.W., Blackstone, J. H. and Hoffman, T. R. *Production and Inventory Management*, 2nd ed. South-Western, 1990.

Hillier, F. and Lieberman, G. J. *Introduction to Operations Research*, 8th ed. McGraw-Hill, 2005.

Narasimhan, S. L., McLeavey, D. W. and Lington, P. B. *Production Planning and Inventory Control*, 2nd ed. Prentice Hall, 1995.

Orlicky, J. and Plossi, G. W. *Orlicky's Material Requirements Planning*, 2nd ed. McGraw-Hill, 1994.

Vollmann, T. E., Berry, W. L. and Whybark, D. C. *Manufacturing Planning and Control Systems*, 5th ed. McGraw-Hill, 2004.

Chapter 11 Queuing Models

Bunday, B. D. *An Introduction to Queueing Theory*. Wiley, 1996.

Gross, D. and Harris, C. M. *Fundamentals of Queueing Theory*, 3rd ed. Wiley, 1997.

Hall, R. W. *Queueing Methods: For Services and Manufacturing*. Prentice Hall, 1997.

Hillier, F. and Lieberman, G. J. *Introduction to Operations Research*, 8th ed. McGraw-Hill, 2005.

Kao, E. P. C. *An Introduction to Stochastic Processes*. Duxbury, 1996.

Chapter 12 Simulation

Banks, J., Carson, J. S. Nelson, B. L. and Nicol. D. *Discrete-Event System Simulation*, 4th ed. Prentice Hall, 2004.

Fishwick, P. A. *Simulation Model Design and Execution: Building Digital Worlds*. Prentice Hall, 1995.

Harrell, C. R. and K. Tumau, K. *Simulation Made Easy: A Manager's Guide*. Institute of Industrial Engineers, 1996.

Kelton, W. D., Sadowski, R. P. and Sadowski, D. A. *Simulation with Arena*, 3rd ed. McGraw-Hill, 2003.

Law, A. M. and Kelton, W. D. *Simulation Modeling and Analysis*, 3rd ed. McGraw-Hill, 1999.

Pidd, M. *Computer Simulation in Management Science*, 5th ed. Wiley, 2004.

Thesen, A. and Travis, L. E. *Simulation for Decision Making*. Wadsworth, 1992.

Chapter 13 Decision Analysis

Berger, J. O. *Statistical Decision Theory and Bayesian Analysis*, 2nd ed. Springer-Verlag, 1985.

Chernoff, H. and L. E. Moses, L. E. *Elementary Decision Theory*. Dover, 1987.

Clemen, R. T. and Reilly, T. *Making Hard Decisions with Decision Tools*. Duxbury, 2001.

Goodwin, P. and Wright, G. *Decision Analysis for Management Judgment*, 3rd ed. Wiley, 2003.

Gregory, G. *Decision Analysis*. Plenum, 1988.

Pratt, J. W., Raiffa, H. and Schlaifer, R. *Introduction to Statistical Decision Theory*. MIT Press, 1995.

Raiffa, H. *Decision Analysis*. McGraw-Hill, 1997.

Schlaifer, R. *Analysis of Decisions Under Uncertainty*. Krieger, 1978.

Chapter 14 Multicriteria Decisions

Dyer, J. S. 'A Clarification of Remarks on the Analytic Hierarchy Process', *Management Science* 36, no. 3 (March 1990): 274–275.

Dyer, J. S. 'Remarks on the Analytic Hierarchy Process', *Management Science* 36, no. 3 (March 1990): 249–258.

Harker, P. T. and Vargas, L. G. 'Reply to Remarks on the Analytic Hierarchy Process by J. S. Dyer', *Management Science* 36, no. 3 (March 1990): 269–273.

Harker, P. T. and Vargas, L. G. 'The Theory of Ratio Scale Estimation: Saaty's Analytic Hierarchy Process', *Management Science* 33, no. 11 (November 1987): 1383–1403.

Ignizio, J. *Introduction to Linear Goal Programming*. Sage, 1986.

Keeney, R. L. and Raiffa, H. *Decisions with Multiple Objectives: Preferences and Value Tradeoffs*. Cambridge, 1993.

Saaty, T. *Decision Making for Leaders: The Analytic Hierarchy Process for Decisions in a Complex World*, 3rd ed. RWS, 1999.

Saaty, T. *Multicriteria Decision Making*, 2nd ed. RWS, 1996.

Saaty, T. L. 'An Exposition of the AHP in Reply to the Paper Remarks on the Analytic Hierarchy Process', *Management Science* 36, no. 3 (March 1990): 259–268.

Saaty, T. L. 'Rank Generation, Preservation, and Reversal in the Analytic Hierarchy Decision Process', *Decision Sciences* 18 (1987): 157–177.

Winkler, R. L. 'Decision Modelling and Rational Choice: AHP and Utility Theory', *Management Science* 36, no. 3 (March 1990): 247–248.

Appendix D Self-Test Solutions

Chapter 1

2 Define the problem
Identify the alternatives
Determine the criteria
Evaluate the alternatives
Choose an alternative
For further discussion see section 1.3

4 Models usually have time, cost and risk advantages over experimenting with actual situations.

6 Let d = distance
k = kilometres per litre
c = cost per litre,

$$\therefore \text{Total Cost} = \left(\frac{2d}{k}\right)c$$

We must be willing to treat m and c as known and not subject to variation.

8 a. at €20 $d = 800 - 10(20) = 600$
at €70 $d = 800 - 10(70) = 100$

b. $TR = dp = (800 - 10p)p = 800p - 10p^2$

c. at €30 $TR = 800(30) - 10(30)^2 = 15{,}000$
at €40 $TR = 800(40) - 10(40)^2 = 16{,}000$
at €50 $TR = 800(50) - 10(50)^2 = 15{,}000$
Total Revenue is maximized at the €40 price.

d. $d = 800 - 10(40) = 400$ units
$TR =$ €16,000

10 a. Total cost $= 4800 + 60x$

b. Total profit = total revenue – total cost
$= 300x - (4800 + 60x)$
$= 240x - 4800$

c. Total profit $= 240(30) - 4800 = 2400$

d. $240x - 4800 = 0$
$x = 4800/240 = 20$
The breakeven point is approximately 20 participants.

12 a. Profit $= 100\,000x$

$$-(1\,500\,000 + 50\,000x) = 0$$

$$50\,000x = 1\,500\,000$$

$$x = 30$$

b. Build the luxury boxes.

$$\text{Profit} = 100\,000(50) - (1\,500\,000 + 50\,000(50))$$

$$= €1\,000\,000$$

Chapter 2

1 a, b and e, are acceptable linear programming relationships.
c is not acceptable because of $-2x_2^{\,2}$
d is not acceptable because of $\sqrt[3]{x_1}$
f is not acceptable because of $1x_1x_2$
c, d and f could not be found in a linear programming model because they have the above nonlinear terms.

2 a.

b.

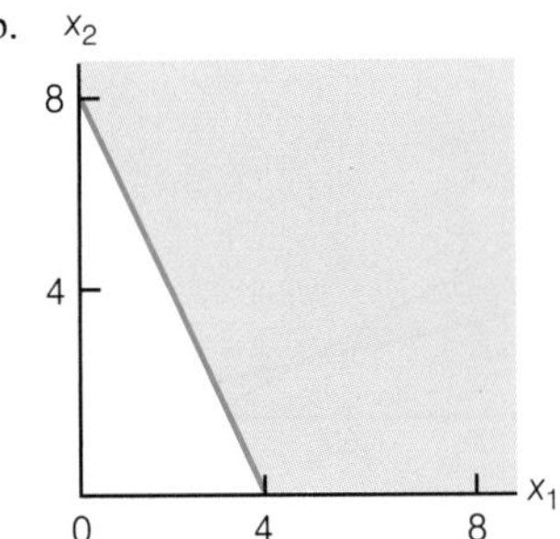

c.

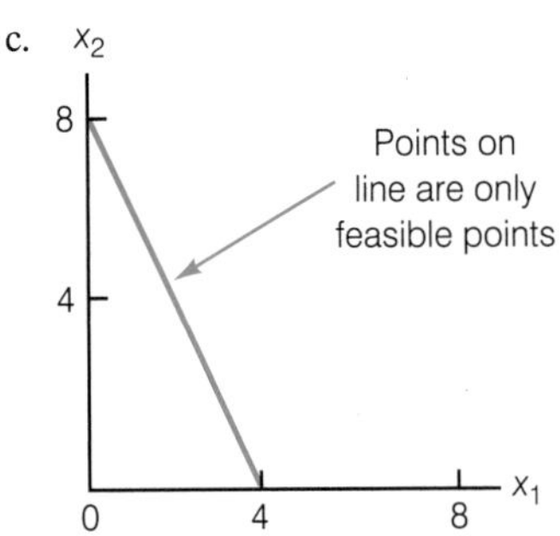

4

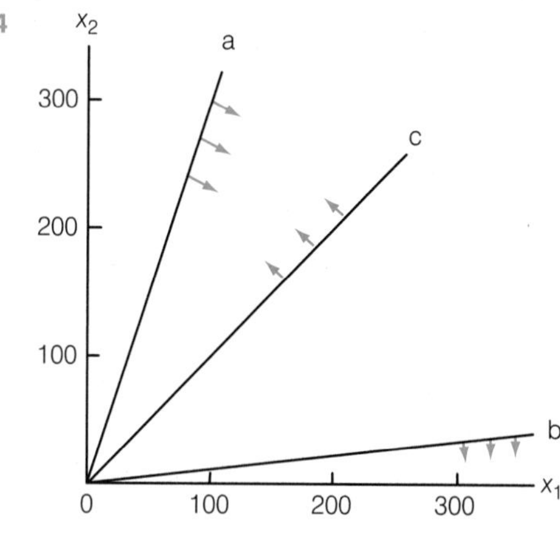

5 For $7x_1 + 10x_2$, slope $= -7/10$

For $6x_1 + 4x_2$, slope $= -6/4 = -3/2$

For $z = -4x_1 + 7x_2$, slope $= 4/7$

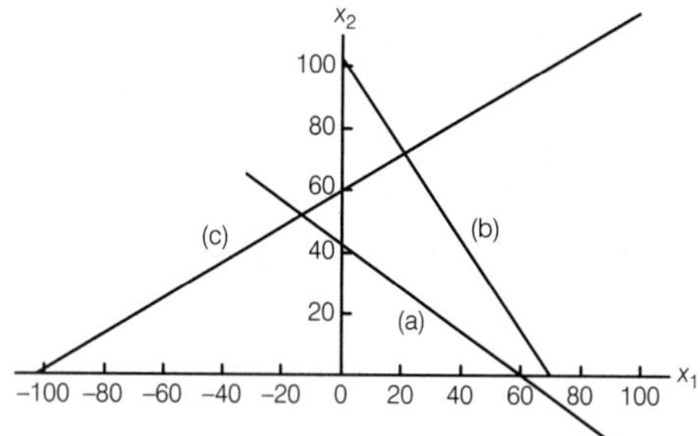

6

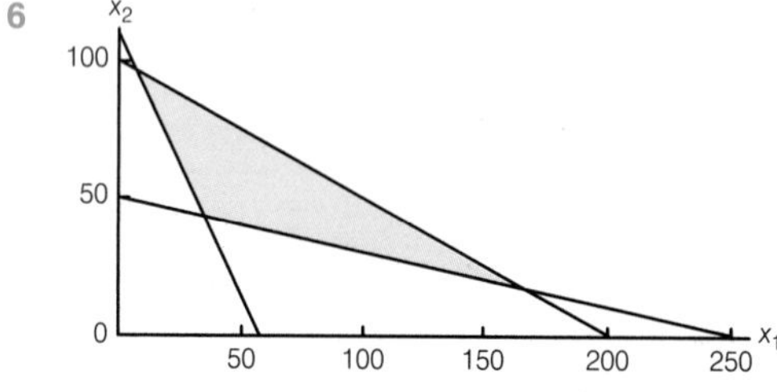

7

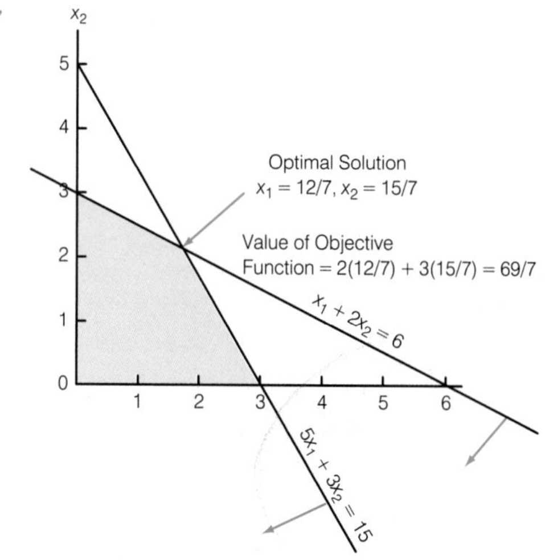

$$
\begin{array}{lrcrcrl}
 & x_1 & + & 2x_2 & = & 6 & (1) \\
 & 5x_1 & + & 3x_2 & = & 15 & (2) \\
(1) \times 5 & 5x_1 & + & 10x_2 & = & 30 & (3) \\
(2) - (3) & & - & 7x_2 & = & -15 & \\
 & & & x_2 & = & 15/7 &
\end{array}
$$

From (1), $x_1 = 6 - 2(15/7) = 6 - 30/7 = 12/7$

8

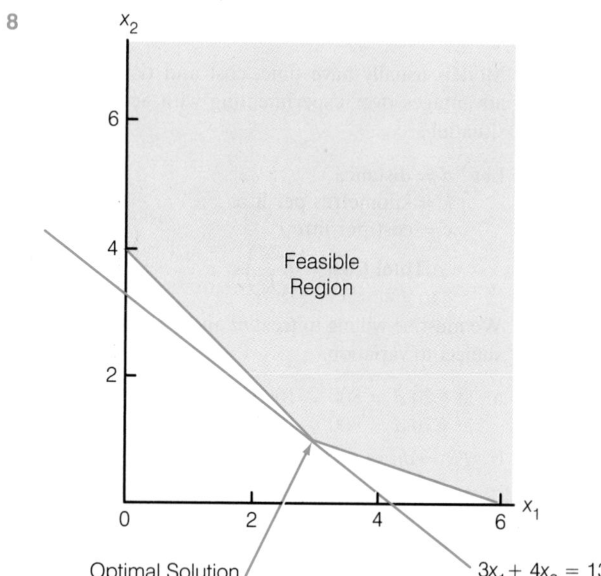

Objective Function Value = 13

9 a.

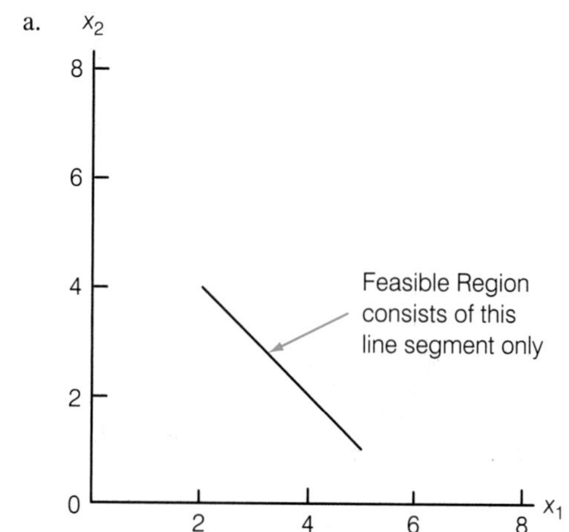

b. The extreme points are (5, 1) and (2, 4).

c.

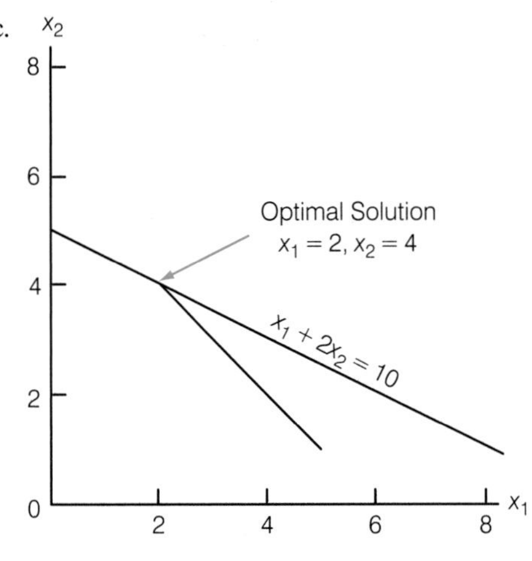

11 Max $5x_1 + 2x_2 + 8x_3 + 0s_1 + 0s_2 + 0s_3$
s.t.

$$\begin{aligned}
1x_1 - 2x_2 + 1/2x_3 + 1s_1 \quad\quad\quad\quad &= 420\\
2x_1 + 3x_2 - 1x_3 \quad\quad + 1s_2 \quad\quad &= 610\\
6x_1 - 1x_2 + 3x_3 \quad\quad\quad\quad + 1s_3 &= 125\\
x_1, x_2, x_3, s_1, s_2, s_3 &\geq 0
\end{aligned}$$

12 a. Let F = number of kilos of fuel additive
S = number of kilos of solvent base

Max $40F + 30S$
s.t.

$$\begin{aligned}
2/5F + 1/2S &\leq 200 \quad \text{Material 1}\\
1/5S &\leq 5 \quad \text{Material 2}\\
3/5F + 3/10S &\leq 21 \quad \text{Material 3}\\
F, S &\geq 0
\end{aligned}$$

b. $F = 25$, $S = 20$, profit = 1600

c. Material 2: four tons are used, one ton is unused.

d. No redundant constraints.

13 a. Let
R = number of units of regular model.
P = number of units of professional model.

Max $5R + 8P$
s.t.

$$\begin{aligned}
1R + 3/2P &\leq 900 \quad \text{Cutting and sewing}\\
1/2R + 1/3P &\leq 300 \quad \text{Finishing}\\
1/8R + 1/4P &\leq 100 \quad \text{Packing and Shipping}\\
R, P &\geq 0
\end{aligned}$$

b.

c. $5(500) + 8(150) = \$3\,700$

d. C & S $1(500) + 3/2(150) = 725$
F $1/2(500) + 1/3(150) = 300$
P & S $1/8(500) + 1/4(150) = 100$

e.

Department	Capacity	Usage	Slack
C & S	900	725	175 hours
F	300	300	0 hours
P & S	100	100	0 hours

15 a. Max $1W + 1.25M$
s.t.

$$\begin{aligned}
140W + 196M &\leq 280\,000\\
84W + 28M &\leq 130\,000\\
56W + 56M &\leq 100\,000\\
W, M &\geq 0
\end{aligned}$$

b. Optimal solution: $W = 1250$, $M = 535$
Value of optimal solution is 1919

16 a. Min $10\,000T + 8\,000P$
s.t.

$$\begin{aligned}
T &\geq 8\\
P &\geq 10\\
T + P &\geq 25\\
3T + 2P &\leq 84\\
T, P &\geq 0
\end{aligned}$$

b.

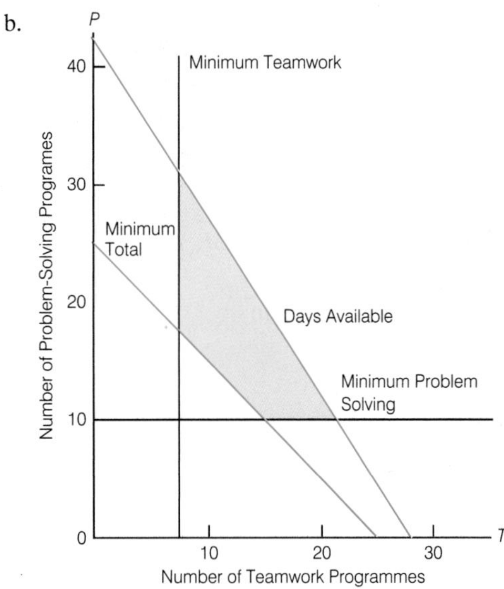

c. There are four extreme points: (15,10); (21.33,10); (8,30); (8,17)

d. The minimum cost solution is $T = 8$, $P = 17$
Total cost = €216 000

17 Infeasibility

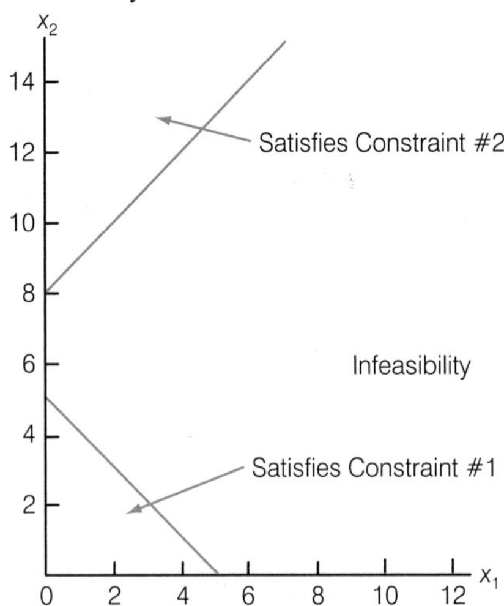

18 Unbounded

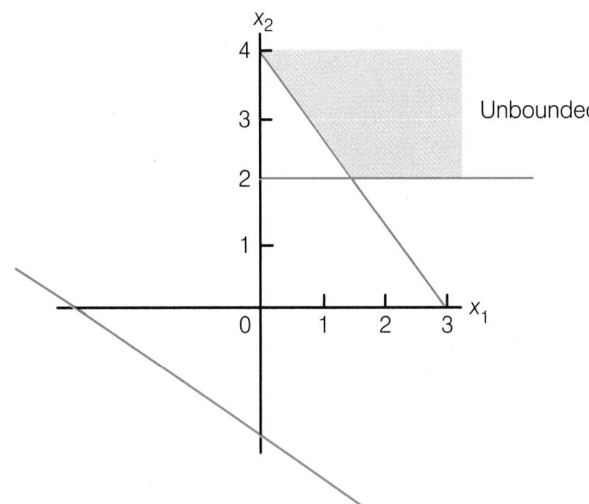

20 a. Max $160M_1 + 345M_2$

s.t.

$$\begin{aligned} M_1 & & \leq 15 \\ & M_2 & \leq 10 \\ M_1 & & \geq 5 \\ & M_2 & \geq 5 \\ 40M_1 + & 50M_2 & \leq 1000 \\ M_1, M_2 \geq 0 & & \end{aligned}$$

b. $M_1 = 12.5, M_2 = 10$

21 a.

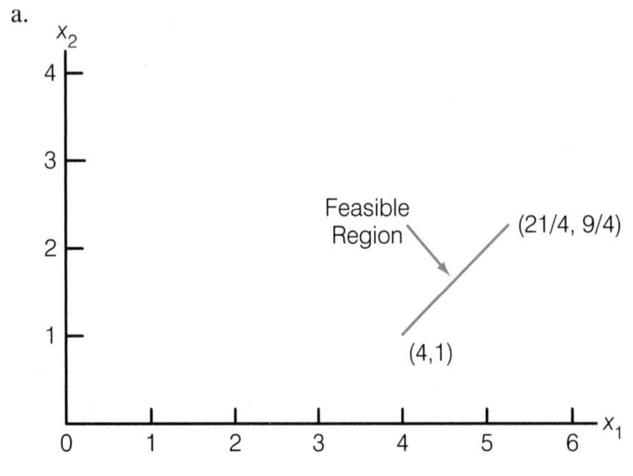

b. There are two extreme points: ($x_1 = 4,\ x_2 = 1$) and ($x_1 = 21/4,\ x_2 = 9/4$)

c. The optimal solution is $x_1 = 4,\ x_2 = 1$

Chapter 3

2 New optimal solution is $F = 100/3$ and $S = 40/3$. Dual price for material 3 constraint is 44.44.

3 a.

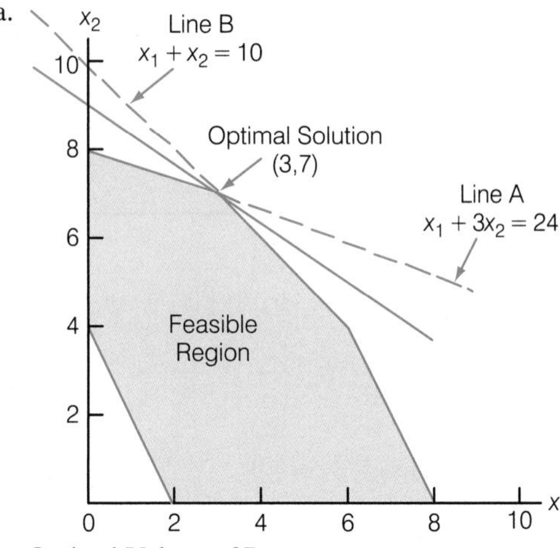

Optimal Value = 27

b. Slope of Line B = −1

Slope of Line A = −1/3

Let C_1 = objective function coefficient of x_1

C_2 = objective function coefficient of x_2

$$-1 \leq -C_1/3 \leq -1/3$$
$$1 \geq C_1/3 \qquad C_1/3 \geq 1/3$$
$$C_1 \leq 3 \qquad C_1 \geq 1$$

Range: $1 \leq C_1 \leq 3$

c. $-1 \leq -2/C_2 \leq -1/3$

$$1 \geq 2/C_2 \qquad 2/C_2 \geq 1/3$$
$$C_2 \geq 2 \qquad C_2 \leq 6$$

Range: $2 \leq C_2 \leq 6$

d. Since this change leaves C_1 in its range of optimality, the same solution ($x_1 = 3, x_2 = 7$) is optimal.

e. This change moves C_2 outside its range of optimality. The new optimal solution is shown below.

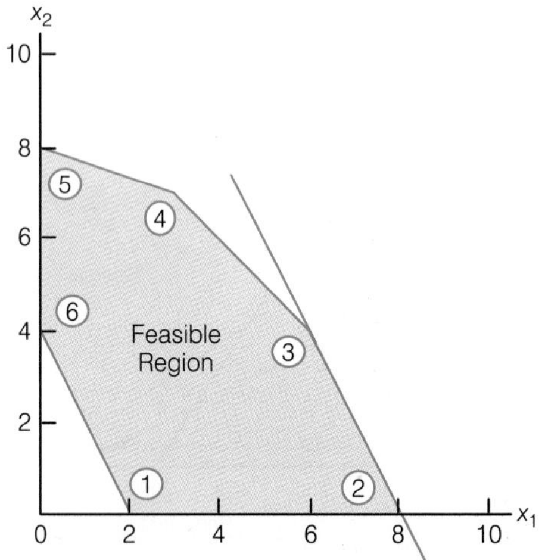

Alternative optimal solutions exist. Extreme points 2 and 3 and all points on the line segment between them are optimal.

4 By making a small increase in the right-hand side of constraint one and re-solving we find a dual price of 1.5 for the constraint. Thus the objective function will increase at the rate of 1.5 per unit increase in the right-hand side.
Since constraint two is not binding, its dual price is zero.

6 −0.333, −0.333, 0

8 a. Regular Glove = 500
Professional glove = 150
Value = 3700

b. The finishing and packaging and shipping constraints are binding.

c. Cutting and Sewing = 0
Finishing = 3
Packaging and Shipping = 28
Additional finishing time is worth \$3 per unit and additional packaging and shipping time is worth \$28 per unit.

d. In the packaging and shipping department. Each additional hour is worth \$28.

10 a. $U = 800$
$H = 1200$
Estimated Annual Return = €8400

b. Constraints 1 and 2. All funds available are being utilized and the maximum permissible risk is being incurred.

c. 0.09, 1.33, 0

d. No, the optimal solution does not call for investing the maximum amount in United Oil.

11 a. By more than €7.00 per share.

b. By more than €3.50 per share.

c. None. This is only a reduction of 100 shares and the allowable decrease is 200. Management may want to address.

12 a. 1250, 535.714, \$1919.64

b. 0.893 to 1.25 and 1.0 to 1.4

c. 0.004, 0, 0.07. The change in profit for each extra gram of resource

d. 270 000 to 350 000, 120 000 to infinity, 80 000 to 102 500

14 a. Range of optimality:

E	47.5 to 75
S	87 to 126
D	No lower limit to 159.

b.

Model	Profit	Change	Allowable Increase/ Decrease	%
E	€63	Increase €6	€75 − €63 = €12	6/12 = 0.50
S	€95	Decrease €2	€95 − €87 = €8	2/8 = 0.25
D	€135	Increase €4	€159 − €135 = €24	4/24 = 0.17
				0.92

Since changes are 92 per cent of allowable changes, the optimal solution of $E = 80$, $S = 120$, $D = 0$ will not change.
The change in total profit will be:

E 80 unit @ + €6 = €480
S 120 unit @ − €2 = −240
€240

∴ Profit = €16 440 + 240 = 16 680.

c. Range of feasibility:

Constraint 1	160 to 180
Constraint 2	200 to 400
Constraint 3	2080 to No Upper Limit

d. Yes, fan motors = 200 + 100 = 300 is outside the range of feasibility.
The dual price will change.

16 a.

Decision Variable	Ranges of Optimality
AM	No lower limit to 11.75
BM	3.667 to 9
AP	12.25 to No Upper Limit
BP	6 to 11.333

Provided a single change of an objective function coefficient is within its above range, the optimal solution AM = 100, BM = 60, AP = 0 and BP = 90 will not change.

b. This change is within the range of optimality. The optimal solution remains AM = 100, BM = 60, AP = 0, and BP = 90. The €11.20 − €10.00 = €1.20 per unit cost increase will increase the total cost to €2170 = €1.20(100) = €2290.

c.

Variable	Cost	Change	Allowable Increase/ Decrease	Percentage Change
AM	10	Increase 1.20	11.75 − 10 = 1.75	(1.20/1.75) 100 = 68.57
BM	6	Decrease 1	6.0 − 3.667 = 2.333	(1/2.333)100 = 42.86
				111.43

111.43 per cent exceeds 100 per cent; therefore, we must re-solve the problem.

20 a. Optimal Solution: $L = 3, N = 7, W = 5, S = 5$
Total cost = €3 300

b. Each additional minute of broadcast time increases cost by €100; conversely, each minute reduced will decrease cost by €100. These interpretations are valid for increases up to ten minutes and decreases up to two minutes from the current level of 20 minutes.

c. If local coverage is increased by one minute, total cost will increase by €100.

d. If the time devoted to local and national news is increased by one minute, total cost will increase by €100.

e. Increasing the sports by one minute will have no effect for this constraint since the dual price is 0.

Chapter 4

1 a. Let T = number of television spot advertisements
R = number of Internet advertisements
N = number of newspaper advertisements

Max $100000T + 18000I + 40000N$

s.t.

$$
\begin{aligned}
2000T + 300I + 600N &\leq 18200 \quad \text{Budget} \\
T &\leq 10 \quad \text{Max TV} \\
I &\leq 20 \quad \text{Max Internet} \\
N &\leq 10 \quad \text{Max News} \\
-0.5T + 0.5I - 0.5N &\leq 0 \quad \text{Max 50\% Internet} \\
0.9T - 0.1I - 0.1N &\geq 0 \quad \text{Min 10\% TV} \\
T, I, N &\geq 0
\end{aligned}
$$

		Budget €	
Solution:	$T = 4$	€8 000	
	$I = 14$	4 200	
	$N = 10$	6 000	
		€18 200	Audience = 1 052 000.

b. The dual price for the budget constraint is 51.30. Thus, a €100 increase in budget should provide an increase in audience coverage of approximately 5 130. The right-hand-side range for the budget constraint will show this interpretation is correct.

2 a. Solution: $x_1 = 77.89, x_2 = 63.16$ Profit = 3284.21

b. Dept. A €15.79, Dept. B €47.37.

c. $x_1 = 87.21, x_2 = 65.12$, €3341.34.
Department A ten hours.
Department B 3.2 hours

4 Solution: $x_1 = 4, x_2 = 4, x_3 = 2$ Cost = €0.70 per litre.

6 Schedule 19 officers as follows:
three begin at 8:00 a.m.; three begin at noon; seven begin at 4:00 p.m.; zero begin at 8:00 p.m.; four begin at midnight; two begin at 4:00 a.m.

7 a. Let each decision variable, A, P, M, H and G, represent the fraction or proportion of the total investment placed in each investment alternative.

Max .073A + .103P + .064M + .075H + .045G

s.t.

$$
\begin{aligned}
A + P + M + H + G &= 1 \\
.5A + .5P - .5M - .5H &\leq 0 \\
-.5A - .5P + .5M + .5H &\leq 0 \\
- .25M - .25H + G &\geq 0 \\
-.6A + .4P &\leq 0 \\
A, P, M, H, G &\geq 0
\end{aligned}
$$

Solution: Objective function = 0.079 with

A = 0.178
P = 0.267
M = 0.000
H = 0.444
G = 0.111

b. For a total investment of €100 000, we show:

A = €17 800
P = 26 700
M = 0.000
H = 44 400
G = 11 100
Total €100 000

c. Total earnings = €100 000 (.079) = €7 900

d. Marginal rate of return is .079

8 Solution:

	Supplier		
	1	2	3
Drug A	600	400	0
Drug B	0	0	800
	Purchase Cost = €20 400		

10 The complete linear programme is:

Max 2.033BR + 2.583BD + 1.868CR + 2.418CD

s.t.

$$\begin{aligned} 0.25BR \quad - 0.75CR \quad &= 0 \\ 0.60BD \quad - 0.40CD &= 0 \\ BR + CR &= 1000 \\ BD + CD &= 500 \\ BR, BD, CR, CD &\geq 0 \end{aligned}$$

The optimal solution is BR = 750, BD = 200, CR = 250 and CD = 300.
The value of the optimal solution is €3233.75.

11 Let x_{11} = litres of crude 1 used to produce regular
x_{12} = litres of crude 1 used to produce high-octane
x_{21} = litres of crude 2 used to produce regular
x_{22} = litres of crude 2 used to produce high-octane

$$\text{Min } 0.10x_{11} + 0.10x_{12} + 0.15x_{21} + 0.15x_{22}$$

s.t.
Each litre of regular must have at least 40 per cent A.

$x_{11} + x_{21}$ = amount of regular produced
$0.4(x_{11} + x_{21})$ = amount of A required for regular
$0.2x_{11} + 0.50x_{21}$ = amount of A in $(x_{11} + x_{21})$ litres of regular gas

$$\therefore\ 0.2x_{11} + 0.50x_{21} \geq 0.4x_{11} + 0.40x_{21} \quad \textbf{(1)}$$
$$\therefore -0.2x_{11} + 0.10x_{21} \geq 0$$

Each litre of high octane can have at most 50 per cent B.

$x_{12} + x_{22}$ = amount high-octane
$0.5(x_{12} + x_{22})$ = amount of B required for high octane
$0.60x_{12} + 0.30x_{22}$ = amount of B in $(x_{12} + x_{22})$ litres of high octane.

$$\therefore\ 0.60x_{12} + 0.30x_{22} \leq 0.5x_{12} + 0.5x_{22}$$
$$\therefore\ 0.1x_{12} - 0.2x_{22} \leq 0 \quad \textbf{(2)}$$
$$x_{11} + x_{21} \geq 800\,000 \quad \textbf{(3)}$$
$$x_{12} + x_{22} \geq 500\,000 \quad \textbf{(4)}$$
$$x_{11},\ x_{12},\ x_{21},\ x_{22} \geq 0$$

Optimal Solution: $x_{11} = 266\,667$, $x_{12} = 333\,333$, $x_{21} = 533\,333$, $x_{22} = 166\,667$
Cost = €165 000

14 a. Let x_{11} = amount of men's model in month 1
x_{21} = amount of women's model in month 1
x_{12} = amount of men's model in month 2
x_{22} = amount of women's model in month 2
s_{11} = inventory of men's model at end of month 1
s_{21} = inventory of women's model at end of month 1
s_{12} = inventory of men's model at end of month 2
s_{22} = inventory of women's model at end of month

The model formulation for part (a) is given.

$$\text{Min } 120x_{11} + 90x_{21} + 120x_{12} + 90x_{22} + 2.4s_{11} + 1.8s_{21} + 2.4s_{12} + 1.8s_{22}$$

s.t.

$x_{11} - s_{11} = 130$	Satisfy Demand
$x_{21} - s_{21} = 95$	Satisfy Demand
$s_{11} + x_{12} - s_{12} = 200$	Satisfy Demand
$s_{21} + x_{22} - s_{22} = 150$	Satisfy Demand
$s_{12} \geq 25$	Ending Inventory
$s_{22} \geq 25$	Ending Inventory

Labour Hours: Men's = 2.0 + 1.5 = 3.5
Women's = 1.6 + 1.0 = 2.6

$3.5x_{11} + 2.6x_{21} \geq 900$	Labour Smoothing for
$3.5x_{11} + 2.6x_{21} \leq 1100$	Month 1
$3.5x_{11} + 2.6x_{21} - 3.5x_{12} - 2.6x_{22} \leq 100$	Labour Smoothing for
$-3.5x_{11} - 2.6x_{21} + 3.5x_{12} + 2.6x_{22} \leq 100$	Month 2

$$x_{11},\ x_{12},\ x_{21},\ x_{22},\ s_{11},\ s_{12},\ s_{21},\ s_{22} \geq 0$$

The optimal solution is to produce 193 of the men's model in month 1, 162 of the men's model in month 2, 95 units of the women's model in month 1 and 175 of the women's model in month 2. Total Cost = INR 67,156
Inventory levels: $s_{11} = 63, s_{12} = 25, s_{21} = 0, s_{22} = 25$

Labour Levels	
Previous month	1 000.00 hours
Month 1	922.25 hours
Month 2	1 022.25 hours

b. To accommodate this new policy the right-hand sides of constraints [7] to [10] must be changed to 950, 1050, 50 and 50 respectively. The revised cost is INR 67,175.

16 Decision variables: Regular

Model	Month 1	Month 2
Bookshelf	2 100	1 200
Floor	930	1 560

Decision variables: Overtime

Model	Month 1	Month 2
Bookshelf	0	0
Floor	610	1 000

18 a. The optimal schedule calls for:
eight starting at 11:00 a.m.
two starting at 3:00 p.m.
four starting at 5:00 p.m.
six starting at 6:00 p.m.

b. Total daily salary cost = €608
There are seven surplus employees scheduled from 2:00–3:00 p.m. and four from 8:00–9:00 p.m. suggesting the desirability of rotating employees off sooner.

c. Considering three-hour shifts
Optimal schedule for part-time employees:

three-Hour Shifts	four-Hour Shifts
eight start at 11.00 a.m.	six start at 6.00 p.m.
one starts at 1.00 p.m.	
one starts at 3.00 p.m.	
four start at 5.00 p.m.	

Total cost reduced to €501.60. Still have 20 part-time shifts, but 14 are three-hour shifts. The surplus has been reduced by a total of 14 hours.

20 a. Edinburgh

b. Using a larger plane based in Edinburgh, the optimal allocations are:

GAQ = 33	**GSQ** = 23	**GVQ** = 43
GAY = 16	GSY = 6	GVY = 11
EAQ = 26	**ESQ** = 56	EVQ = 39
EAY = 15	ESY = 7	EVY = 9
ASQ = 32	ASY = 8	
AVY = 46	AVQ = 10	

The differences between the new allocations above and the allocations for the original Leisure Air problem involve the five ODIFs that are boldfaced in the solution shown above.

c. Using a larger plane based in Pittsburgh and a larger plane based in Edinburgh, the optimal allocations are:

GAQ = 33	**GSQ** = 44	**GVQ** = 45
GAY = 16	GSY = 6	GVY = 11
EAQ = 26	**ESQ** = 56	EVQ = 39
EAY = 15	ESY = 7	EVY = 9
ASQ = 37	ASY = 8	
AVY = 44	AVQ = 10	

The differences between the new allocations above and the allocations for the original Leisure Air problem involve the four ODIFs that are boldfaced in the solution shown above. The total revenue associated with the new optimal solution is €115 073, which is a difference of €11 970.

d. AVY, The bid price tells us that if one more Y class seat were available from Amsterdam to Geneva that revenue would increase by €443.

Chapter 5

1 a. With $x_1 = 0$, we have:

$$x_2 = 6 \quad \textbf{(1)}$$
$$4x_2 + x_3 = 12 \quad \textbf{(2)}$$

From (1), we have $x_2 = 6$. Substituting for x_2 in (2) yields:

$$4(6) + x_3 = 12$$
$$x_3 = 12 - 24 = -12$$

Basic Solution: $x_1 = 0, x_2 = 6, x_3 = -12$

b. With $x_2 = 0$, we have:

$$3x_1 = 6 \quad \textbf{(3)}$$
$$2x_1 + x_3 = 12 \quad \textbf{(4)}$$

From (3), we find $x_1 = 2$. Substituting for x_1 in (4) yields:

$$2(2) + x_3 = 12$$
$$x_3 = 12 - 4 = 8$$

Basic Solution: $x_1 = 2, x_2 = 0, x_3 = 8$

c. With $x_3 = 0$, we have:

$$3x_1 + x_2 = 6 \quad \textbf{(5)}$$
$$2x_1 + 4x_2 = 12 \quad \textbf{(6)}$$

Multiplying (6) by 3/2 and Subtracting from (5) yields:

$$3x_1 + x_2 = 6$$
$$\underline{-(3x_1 + 6x_2) = -18}$$
$$-5x_2 = -12$$
$$x_2 = 12/5$$

Substituting $x_2 = 12/5$ into (5) yields:

$$3x_1 + 12/5 = 6$$
$$3x_1 = 18/5$$
$$x_1 = 6/5$$

Basic Solution: $x_1 = 6/5, x_2 = 12/5, x_3 = 0$

d. The basic solutions found in (b) and (c) are basic feasible solutions. The one in (a) is not because $x_3 = -12$.

2 a. Standard Form:

$$\begin{aligned} \text{Max} \quad & x_1 + 2x_2 \\ \text{s.t.} \quad & \\ & x_1 + 5x_2 + s_1 = 10 \\ & 2x_1 + 6x_2 + s_2 = 16 \\ & x_1, x_2, s_1, s_2 \geq 0 \end{aligned}$$

b/c. $x_1 = 0,\ x_2 = 0,\ s_1 = 10,\ s_2 = 16$ Feasible
$x_1 = 0,\ x_2 = 2,\ s_1 = 0,\ s_2 = 4$ Feasible
$x_1 = 0,\ x_2 = 8/3,\ s_1 = -10/3,\ s_2 = 0$ Not feasible
$x_1 = 10,\ x_2 = 0,\ s_1 = 0,\ s_2 = -4$ Not feasible
$x_1 = 8,\ x_2 = 0,\ s_1 = 2,\ s_2 = 0$ Feasible
$x_1 = 5,\ x_2 = 1,\ s_1 = 0,\ s_2 = 0$ Feasible

d. The optimal solution is $x_1 = 8, x_2 = 0$ with value $= 8$.

4 a. Standard Form:

$$\begin{aligned} \text{Max} \quad & 60x_1 + 90x_2 \\ \text{s.t.} \quad & \\ & 15x_1 + 45x_2 + s_1 = 90 \\ & 5x_1 + 5x_2 + s_2 = 20 \\ & x_1, x_2, s_1, s_2 \geq 0 \end{aligned}$$

b. Partial initial simplex tableau:

x_1	x_2	s_1	s_2	
60	90	0	0	
15	45	1	0	90
5	5	0	1	20

5 a. Initial tableau:

		x_1	x_2	s_1	s_2	
Basis	c_B	5	9	0	0	
s_1	0	10	9	1	0	90
s_2	0	−5	3	0	1	15
	z_j	0	0	0	0	0
	$c_j - z_j$	5	9	0	0	

b. We would introduce x_2 at the first iteration.

c.
$$\begin{aligned} \text{Max} \quad & 5x_1 + 9x_2 \\ \text{s.t.} \quad & \\ & 10x_1 + 9x_2 \leq 90 \\ & -5x_1 + 3x_2 \leq 15 \\ & x_1, x_2 \geq 0 \end{aligned}$$

6 a.

		x_1	x_2	x_3	s_1	s_2	s_3	
Basis	C_B	5	20	25	0	0	0	
s_1	0	2	1	0	1	0	0	40
s_2	0	0	2	1	0	1	0	30
s_3	0	3	0	−0.5	0	0	1	15
	z_j	0	0	0	0	0	0	0
	$c_j - z_j$	5	20	25	0	0	0	

b.
$$\begin{aligned} \text{Max} \quad & 5x_1 + 20x_2 + 25x_3 + 0s_1 + 0s_2 + 0s_3 \\ \text{s.t.} \quad & \\ & 2x_1 + 1x_2 + 1s_1 = 40 \\ & 2x_2 + 1x_3 + 1s_2 = 30 \\ & 3x_1 - 1/2x_3 + 1s_3 = 15 \\ & x_1, x_2, x_3, s_1, s_2, s_3 \geq 0. \end{aligned}$$

c. s_1, s_2 and s_3. It is the origin

d. 0.

e. x_3 enters and s_2 will leave.

f. 30; 750.

g. $x_1 = 10 \quad s_1 = 20$
$x_2 = 0 \quad s_2 = 0$
$x_3 = 30 \quad s_3 = 0$
$z = 800.$

8 a. $x_1 = 540$ standard bags
$x_2 = 252$ deluxe bags

b. $7668

c. & d.

Slack	Production Time
$s_1 = 0$	Cutting and dyeing time = 630 hours
$s_2 = 120$	Sewing time = 600 − 120 = 480 hours
$s_3 = 0$	Finishing time = 708 hours
$s_4 = 18$	Inspection and Packaging time = 135 − 18 = 117 hours

10 Optimal Solution: A = 0, B = 0, C = 33 1/3
Profit = 500.

12
$$\begin{aligned} \text{Max} \quad & 4x_1 + 2x_2 - 3x_3 + 5x_4 + 0s_1 - Ma_1 + 0s_2 - Ma_3 \\ \text{s.t.} \quad & \\ & 2x_1 - 1x_2 + 1x_3 + 2x_4 - 1s_1 + 1a_1 = 50 \\ & 3x_1 - 1x_3 + 2x_4 + 1s_2 = 80 \\ & 1x_1 + 1x_2 + 1x_4 + 1a_3 = 60 \\ & x_1, x_2, x_3, x_4, s_1, s_2, a_1, a_3 \geq 0 \end{aligned}$$

14 $x_1 = 1, x_2 = 4, z = 19$

16 $x_1 = 480, x_4 = 480\ x_2 = 0, x_5 = 0\ x_3 = 0, x_6 = 800$
Objective Function maximized at 46,400.

17 Final simplex tableau:

Basis	C_B	x_1	x_2	s_1	s_2	a_2	
		4	8	0	0	$-M$	
x_2	8	1	1	1/2	0	0	5
a_2	$-M$	-2	0	$-1/2$	-1	1	3
	z_j	$8 + 2M$	8	$4 + M/2$	$+M$	$-M$	$40 - 3M$
	$c_j - z_j$	$-4 - 2M$	0	$-4 - M/2$	$-M$	0	

Infeasible; optimal solution condition is reached with the artificial variable a_2 still in the solution.

18 Alternative Optimal Solutions:

Basis	C_B	x_1	x_2	s_1	s_2	s_3	
		-3	-3	0	0	0	
s_2	0	0	0	$-4/3$	1	1/6	4
x_1	-3	1	0	$-2/3$	0	1/12	4
x_2	-3	0	1	2/3	0	$-1/3$	4
	z_j	-3	-3	0	0	3/4	-24
	$c_j - z_j$	0	0	0	0	$-3/4$	

↑ indicates alternative optimal solutions exist

$x_1 = 4, x_2 = 4, z = 24$

$x_1 = 8, x_2 = 0, z = 24$

19 Unbounded Solution:

Basis	C_B	x_1	x_2	s_1	s_2	s_3	
		1	1	0	0	0	
s_3	0	8/3	0	$-1/3$	0	1	4
s_2	0	4	0	-1	1	0	36
x_2	1	4/3	1	$-1/6$	0	0	4
	z_j	4/3	1	$-1/6$	0	0	4
	$c_j - z_j$	$-1/3$	0	1/6	0	0	

↑ Incoming Column

20 Alternative Optimal Solutions:

Basis	C_B	x_1	x_2	x_3	s_1	s_2	s_3	
		2	1	1	0	0	0	
x_1	2	1	2	1/2	0	0	1/4	4
s_2	0	0	0	-1	0	1	$-1/2$	12
s_1	0	0	6	0	1	0	1	12
	z_j	2	4	1	0	0	1/4	8
	$c_j - z_j$	0	-3	0	0	0	$-1/4$	

Two possible solutions:

$$x_1 = 4,\ x_2 = 0,\ x_3 = 0 \text{ or } x_1 = 0,\ x_2 = 0,\ x_3 = 8$$

Chapter 6

1 a. Recalculating the $c_j - z_j$ values for the nonbasic variables with c_1 as the coefficient of x_1 leads to the following inequalities that must be satisfied. For x_2, we get no inequality since there is a zero in the x_2 column for the row x_1 is a basic variable For s_1, we get:

$$0 + 4 - c_1 \leq 0$$

For s_2, we get: $c_1 \geq 4$

$$0 - 12 + 2c_1 \leq 0$$
$$2c_1 \leq 12$$
$$c_1 \leq 6$$

Range $4 \leq c_1 \leq 6$

b. Since x_2 is nonbasic we have:

$$\mathbf{c_2 \leq 8}$$

c. Since s_1 is nonbasic we have:

$$\mathbf{c_{s_1} \leq 1}$$

2 a. $31.25 \leq \mathbf{c_2} \leq 83.33$

b. $-43.33 \leq \mathbf{c_{s_2}} \leq 8.75$

c. $\mathbf{c_{s_3}} \leq 26/5$

d. No change in optimal solution since $c_2 = 35$ is within range of optimality. Value of solution decreases to €1920.

3 a. It is the z_j value for s_1. Dual Price = 1.

b. It is the z_j value for s_2. Dual Price = 2.

c. It is the z_j value for s_3. Dual Price = 0.

d.
$$s_3 = 80 + 5(-2) = 70$$
$$x_3 = 30 + 5(-1) = 25$$
$$x_1 = 20 + 5(1) = 25$$
$$\text{Value} = 220 + 5(1) = 225$$

e.
$$s_3 = 80 - 10(-2) = 100$$
$$x_3 = 30 - 10(-1) = 40$$
$$x_1 = 20 - 10(1) = 10$$
$$\text{Value} = 220 - 10(1) = 210$$

4 a. $80 + \Delta b_1(-2) \geq 0 \rightarrow \Delta b_1 \leq 40$

$$30 + \Delta b_1(-1) \geq 0 \rightarrow \Delta b_1 \leq 30$$
$$20 + \Delta b_1(1) \geq 0 \rightarrow \Delta b_1 \geq -20$$
$$-20 \leq \Delta b_1 \leq 30$$
$$100 \leq b_1 \leq 150$$

b.
$$\begin{aligned} 80 + \Delta b_2(7) \geq 0 &\rightarrow \Delta b_2 \geq -80/7 \\ 30 + \Delta b_2(3) \geq 0 &\rightarrow \Delta b_2 \geq -10 \\ 20 + \Delta b_2(-2) \geq 0 &\rightarrow \Delta b_2 \geq \ \ 10 \\ -10 \leq \Delta b_2 &\leq 10 \\ 40 \leq \mathbf{b_2} &\leq 60 \end{aligned}$$

c.
$$\begin{aligned} 80 - \Delta b_3(1) &\geq \ 0 \rightarrow \Delta b_3 \leq 80 \\ 30 - \Delta b_3(0) &\geq \ 0 \\ 20 - \Delta b_3(0) &\geq \ 0 \\ \Delta b_3 &\leq \ 80 \\ b_3 &\leq 110 \end{aligned}$$

6 a. $6.3 \leq \mathbf{c_1} \leq 13.5$

b. $6.667 \leq \mathbf{c_2} \leq 14.286$

c. There would be no change in product mix, but profit will drop to 7164.

d. It would have to drop below €6.667 or increase above €14.286.

e. $x_1 = 300,\ x_2 = 420$
Optimal Value: $9300

8 a.

		x_1	x_2	s_1	s_2	s_3	s_4	
Basis	C_B	10	9	0	0	0	0	
x_2	9	0	1	30/16	0	−21/16	3852/11	0
x_2	0	0	0	−15/16	1	5/32	0	780/11
x_1	10	1	0	−20/16	0	(30/16)	0	5220/11
s_4	0	0	0	−11/32	0	9/64	1	0
	z_j	10	9	70/16	0	111/16	0	86,868/ 11=7897$^1/_{11}$
	$c_j - z_j$	5	9	0	0			

b. No, s_4 would become nonbasic and s_1 would become a basic variable.

10 a. The value of the objective function would go up since the first constraint is binding. When there is no idle time, increased efficiency results in increased profits.

b. No. This would just increase the number of idle hours in the sewing department.

12 a. The dual is given by:

$$\begin{aligned} \text{Min} \quad & 550u_1 + 700u_2 + 200u_3 \\ \text{s.t.} \quad & \\ & 1.5u_1 + 4u_2 + 2u_3 \geq 4 \\ & 2u_1 + 1u_2 + 3u_3 \geq 6 \\ & 4u_1 + 2u_2 + 1u_3 \geq 3 \\ & 3u_1 + 1u_2 + 2u_3 \geq 1 \\ & u_1,\ u_2,\ u_3, \geq 0 \end{aligned}$$

b. Optimal solution: $u_1 = 0.3,\ u_2 = 0,\ u_3 = 1.8$
The z_j values for the four surplus variables of the dual show $x_1 = 0, x_2 = 25, x_3 = 125$ and $x_4 = 0$.

c. Since $u_1 = 0.3$, $u_2 = 0$, and $u_3 = 1.8$, machines A and C ($u_j > 0$) are operating at capacity. Machine C is the priority machine since each hour is worth 1.8.

13 The dual is given by:

$$\begin{aligned} \text{Max} \quad & 5u_1 + 5u_2 + 24u_3 \\ \text{s.t.} \quad & \\ & 15u_1 + 4u_2 + 12u_3 \leq 2800 \\ & 15u_1 + 8u_2 \leq 6000 \\ & u_1 + 8u_3 \leq 1200 \\ & u_1,\ u_2,\ u_3 \geq 0 \end{aligned}$$

14 The canonical form is:

$$\begin{aligned} \text{Max} \quad & 3x_1 + x_2 + 5x_3 + 3x_4 \\ \text{s.t.} \quad & \\ & 3x_1 + 1x_2 + 2x_3 \leq 30 \\ & -3x_1 - 1x_2 - 2x_3 \leq -30 \\ & -2x_1 - 1x_2 - 3x_3 - x_4 \leq -15 \\ & 2x_2 + 3x_4 \leq 25 \\ & x_1,\ x_2,\ x_3,\ x_4, \geq 0. \end{aligned}$$

The dual is:

$$\begin{aligned} \text{Max} \quad & 30u_1' - 30u_1'' - 15u_2 + 25u_3 \\ \text{s.t.} \quad & \\ & 3u_1' - 3u_1'' - 2u_2 \geq 3 \\ & u_1' - u_1'' - u_2 + 2u_3 \geq 1 \\ & 2u_1' - 20u_1'' - 3u_2 \geq 5 \\ & - u_2 + 3u_3 \geq 3 \\ & u_1', u_1'',\ u_2,\ u_3 \geq 0 \end{aligned}$$

16 a. Extreme point 1 : $x_1 = 0,\ x_2 = 0$ value $= 0$
Extreme point 2 : $x_1 = 5,\ x_2 = 0$ value $= 15$
Extreme point 3 : $x_1 = 4,\ x_2 = 2$ value $= 16$

b. Dual problem:

$$\begin{aligned} \text{Min} \quad & 8u_1 + 10u_2 \\ \text{s.t.} \quad & u_1 + 2u_2 \geq 3 \\ & 2u_1 + u_2 \geq 2 \\ & u_1,\ u_2, \geq 0 \end{aligned}$$

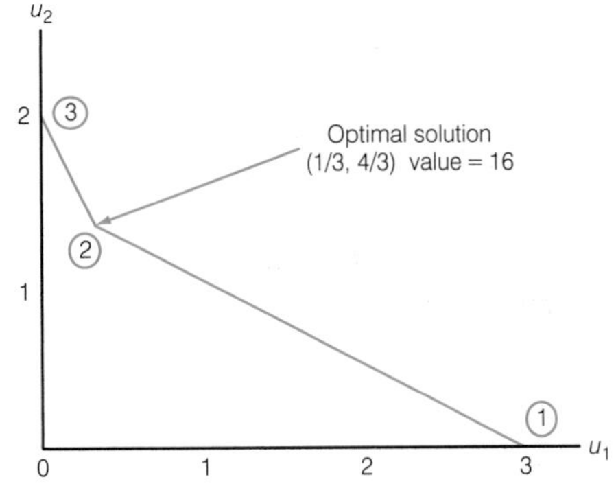

c. Extreme Point 1 : $u_1 = 3,\ u_2 = 0$ value $= 24$
Extreme Point 2 : $u_1 = 1/3,\ u_2 = 4/3$ value $= 16$
Extreme Point 3 : $u_1 = 0,\ u_2 = 2$ value $= 20$

d. Each dual extreme point solution yields a value greater-than-or-equal-to each primal extreme point solution.

e. No. The value of any feasible solution to the dual problem provides an upper bound on the value of any feasible primal solution.

Chapter 7

1 The network model is shown.

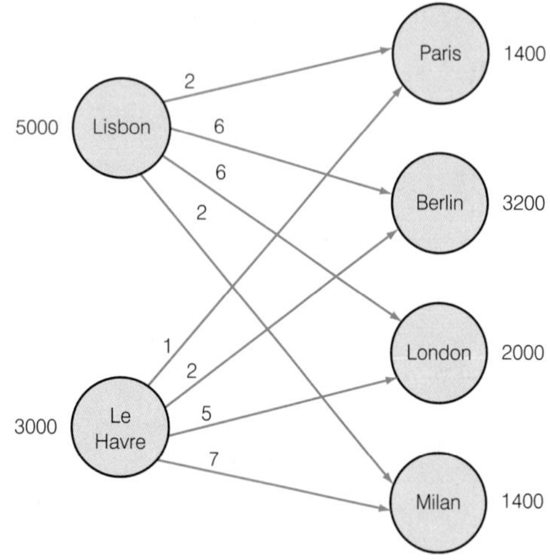

2 a.

Let x_{11} : Amount shipped from Jefferson City to Des Moines
x_{12} : Amount shipped from Jefferson City to Kansas City

.
.
.

x_{23} : Amount shipped from Omaha to St. Louis

Min $14x_{11} + 9x_{12} + 7x_{13} + 8x_{21} + 10x_{22} + 5x_{23}$

s.t.

$$\begin{aligned}
x_{11} + x_{12} + x_{13} &\le 30\\
x_{21} + x_{22} + x_{23} &\le 20\\
x_{11} + x_{21} &= 25\\
x_{12} + x_{22} &= 15\\
x_{13} + x_{23} &= 10\\
x_{11}, x_{12}, x_{13}, x_{21}, x_{22}, x_{23}, &\ge 0
\end{aligned}$$

b. Optimal Solution:

	Amount	Cost
Jefferson City – Des Moines	5	70
Jefferson City – Kansas City	15	135
Jefferson City – St. Louis	10	70
Omaha – Des Moines	20	160
Total		435

4 a.

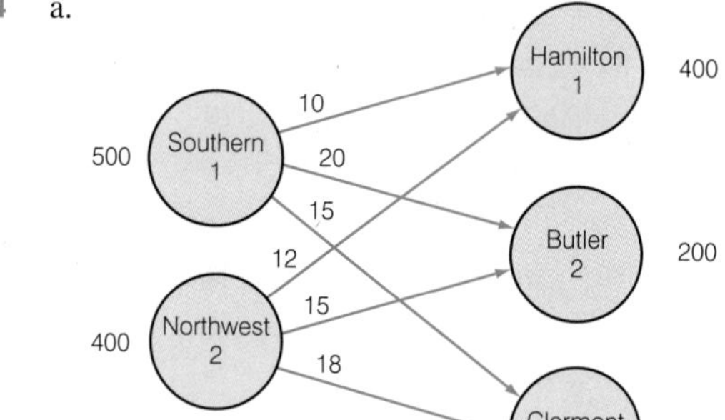

b. Let x_{ij} = amount shipped from supply node i to demand node j.

Min $10x_{11} + 20x_{12} + 15x_{13} + 12x_{21} + 15x_{22} + 18x_{23}$

s.t.

$$\begin{aligned}
x_{11} + x_{12} + x_{13} &\le 500\\
x_{21} + x_{22} + x_{23} &\le 400\\
x_{11} + x_{21} &= 400\\
x_{12} + x_{22} &= 200\\
x_{13} + x_{23} &= 300\\
x_{ij} \ge 0 \text{ for all } i, j
\end{aligned}$$

c. Optimal Solution:

	Amount	Cost
Southern – Hamilton	200	$ 2 000
Southern – Clermont	300	4 500
Northwest – Hamilton	200	2 400
Northwest – Butler	200	3 000
Total Cost		$11 900

d. To answer this question the simplest approach is to increase the Butler County demand to 300 and to increase the supply by 100 at both Southern Gas and Northwest Gas.
The new optimal solution is:

	Amount	Cost
Southern – Hamilton	300	$ 3 000
Southern – Clermont	300	4 500
Northwest – Hamilton	100	1 200
Northwest – Butler	300	4 500
Total Cost		$13 200

From the new solution we see that Tri-County should contract with Southern Gas for the additional 100 units.

6 a.

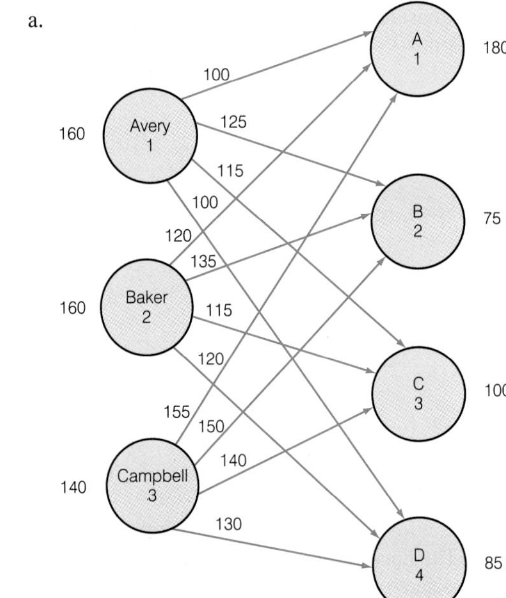

b. Let x_{ij} = number of hours from consultant i assigned to client j.

$$
\begin{aligned}
\text{Max } & 100x_{11} + 125x_{12} + 115x_{13} + 100x_{14} + 120x_{21} + 135x_{22} + 115x_{23} \\
\text{s.t.} \quad & + 120x_{24} + 155x_{31} + 150x_{32} + 140x_{33} + 130x_{34} \\
& x_{11} + x_{12} + x_{13} + x_{14} \leq 160 \\
& x_{21} + x_{22} + x_{23} + x_{24} \leq 160 \\
& x_{31} + x_{32} + x_{33} + x_{34} \leq 140 \\
& x_{11} + x_{21} + x_{31} = 180 \\
& x_{12} + x_{22} + x_{32} = 75 \\
& x_{13} + x_{23} + x_{33} = 100 \\
& x_{14} + x_{24} + x_{34} = 85 \\
& x_{ij} \geq 0 \text{ for all } i, j
\end{aligned}
$$

Optimal Solution:

	Hours Assigned	Billing
Avery – Client B	40	\$ 5 000
Avery – Client C	100	11 500
Baker – Client A	40	4 800
Baker – Client B	35	4 725
Baker – Client D	85	10 200
Campbell – Client A	140	21 700
	Total Billing:	\$57 925

c. New Optimal Solution:

	Hours Assigned	Billing
Avery – Client A	40	\$ 4 000
Avery – Client C	100	11 500
Baker – Client B	75	10 125
Baker – Client D	85	10 200
Campbell – Client A	140	21 700
	Total Billing:	\$57 525

7 The network model, the linear programming formulation and the optimal solution are shown. Note that the third constraint corresponds to the dummy origin. The variables x_{31}, x_{32}, x_{33} and x_{34} are the amounts shipped out of the dummy origin; they do not appear in the objective function since they are given a coefficient of zero.

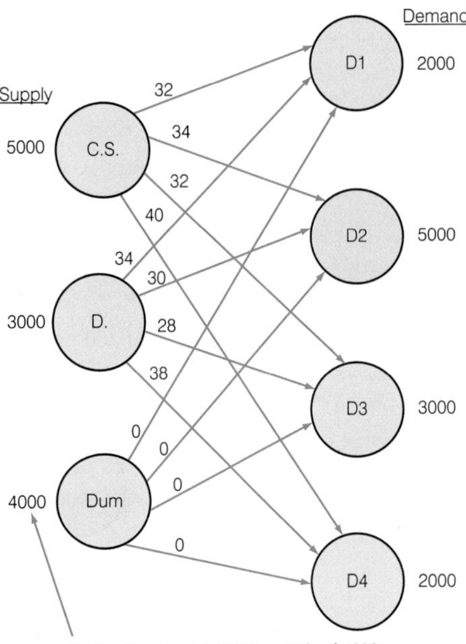

$$
\begin{aligned}
\text{Max } & 32x_{11} + 34x_{12} + 32x_{13} + 40x_{14} + 34x_{21} + 30x_{22} + 28x_{23} + 38x_{24} \\
\text{s.t.} \quad & \\
& x_{11} + x_{12} + x_{13} + x_{14} \leq 5000 \\
& x_{21} + x_{22} + x_{23} + x_{24} \leq 3000 \\
& x_{31} + x_{32} + x_{33} + x_{34} \leq 4000 \text{ Dummy} \\
& x_{11} + x_{21} + x_{31} = 2000 \\
& x_{12} + x_{22} + x_{32} = 5000 \\
& x_{13} + x_{23} + x_{33} = 3000 \\
& x_{14} + x_{24} + x_{34} = 2000 \\
& x_{ij} \geq 0 \text{ for all } i, j
\end{aligned}
$$

Optimal Solution	Units	Cost
Clifton Springs - D2	4 000	€136 000
Clifton Springs - D4	1 000	40 000
Danville - D1	2 000	68 000
Danville - D4	1 000	38 000
	Total Cost:	€282 000

Customer 2 demand has a shortfall of 1000
Customer 3 demand of 3000 is not satisfied.

8 The linear programming formulation and optimal solution are shown.

$$\text{Max}\, x_{1A} + 1.2x_{1B} + 0.9x_{1C} + 1.3x_{2A} + 1.4x_{2B} + 1.2x_{2C} + 1.1x_{3A} + x_{3B} + 1.2x_{3C}$$

s.t.

$$\begin{array}{llllllllll}
x_{1A} + x_{1B} + x_{1C} & & & & & & & & & \le 1500 \\
& & & x_{2A} + x_{2B} + x_{2C} & & & & & & \le 1500 \\
& & & & & & x_{3A} + x_{3B} + x_{3C} & & & \le 1000 \\
x_{1A} & & & + x_{2A} & & & + x_{3A} & & & = 2000 \\
& x_{1B} & & & + x_{2B} & & & + x_{3B} & & = 500 \\
& & x_{1C} & & & + x_{2C} & & & + x_{3C} & = 1200 \\
\end{array}$$

$$x_{ij} \ge 0 \text{ for all } i, j$$

Optimal Solution	Units	Cost
1 - A	300	$ 300
1 - C	1 200	1 080
2 - A	1 200	1 560
3 - A	500	550
3 - B	500	500
	Total:	$3 990

Note: There is an unused capacity of 300 units on machine 2.

9 a.

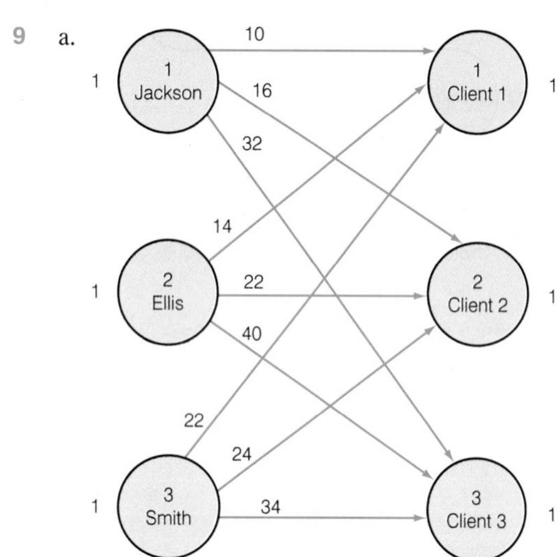

b.

$$\text{Min}\, 10x_{11} + 16x_{12} + 32x_{13} + 14x_{21} + 22x_{22} + 40x_{23} + 22x_{31} + 24x_{32} + 34x_{33}$$

s.t.

$$\begin{array}{llllllllll}
x_{11} + x_{12} + x_{13} & & & & & & & & & \le 1 \\
& & & x_{21} + x_{22} + x_{23} & & & & & & \le 1 \\
& & & & & & x_{31} + x_{32} + x_{33} & & & \le 1 \\
x_{11} & & & + x_{21} & & & + x_{31} & & & = 1 \\
& x_{12} & & & + x_{22} & & & + x_{32} & & = 1 \\
& & x_{13} & & & + x_{23} & & & + x_{33} & = 1 \\
\end{array}$$

$$x_{ij} \ge 0 \text{ for all } i, j$$

Solution $x_{12} = 1, x_{21} = 1, x_{33} = 1$
Total completion time $= 64$

10 a. Optimal assignment: Jackson to 1, Smith to 3, and Burton to 2. Time requirement is 62 days.

b. Considering Burton has saved two days.

c. Ellis.

11 a. Network Model

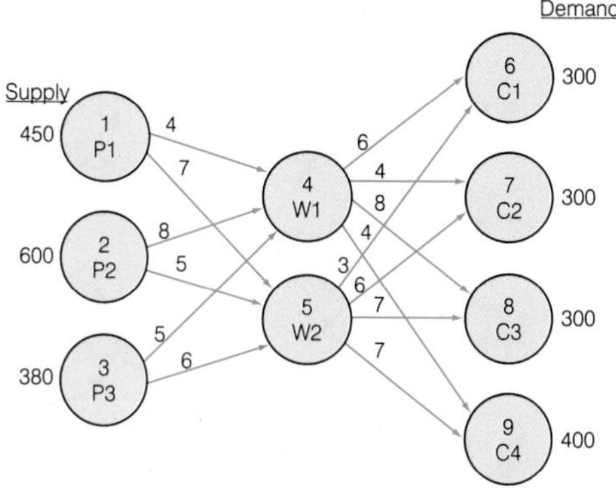

b. The linear programming formulation and solution is shown.

```
MIN 4X14+7X15+8X24+5X25+5X34+6X35+6X46
    +4X47+8X48+4X49+3X56+6X57+7X58+7X59
    S.T.
      1) X14+X15<450
      2) X24+X25<600
      3) X34+X35<380
      4) X46+X47+X48+X49-X14-X24-X34=0
      5) X56+X57+X58+X59-X15-X25-X35=0
      6) X46+X56=300
      7) X47+X57=300
      8) X48+X58=300
      9) X49+X59=400
```

```
OPTIMAL SOLUTION
Objective Function Value = 11850.000
Variable        Value        Reduced Costs
----------   ---------   ----------------
X14           450.000              0.000
X15             0.000              3.000
X24             0.000              3.000
X25           600.000              0.000
X34           250.000              0.000
X35             0.000              1.000
X46             0.000              3.000
X47           300.000              0.000
X48             0.000              1.000
X49           400.000              0.000
X56           300.000              0.000
X57             0.000              2.000
X58           300.000              0.000
X59             0.000              3.000
```

There is an excess capacity of 130 units at plant 3.

c. The linear programming formulation and optimal solution as printed by The Management Scientist follow:

```
LINEAR PROGRAMMING PROBLEM
MIN 4X14 + 7X15 + 8X24 + 5X25 + 5X34 + 6X35
+ 6X46 + 4X47 + 8X48 + 4X49 + 3X56 + 6X57
+ 7X58 + 7X59 + 7X39 + 2X45 + 2X54
S.T.
 1)  X14 + X15 < 450
 2)  X24 + X25 < 600
 3)  X34 + X35 + X39< 380
 4)  X45 + X46 + X47 + X48 + X49 - X14 - X24 - X34 - X54 = 0
 5)  X54 + X56 + X57 + X58 + X59 - X15 - X25 - X35 - X45 = 0
 6)  X46 + X56 = 300
 7)  X47 + X57 = 300
 8)  X48 + X58 = 300
 9)  X39 + X49 + X59= 400

OPTIMAL SOLUTION
Objective Function Value = 11220.000
Variable          Value        Reduced Costs
----------      --------      --------------
X14              320.000               0.000
X15                0.000               2.000
X24                0.000               4.000
X25              600.000               0.000
X34                0.000               2.000
X35                0.000               2.000
X46                0.000               2.000
X47              300.000               0.000
X48                0.000               0.000
X49               20.000               0.000
X56              300.000               0.000
X57                0.000               3.000
X58              300.000               0.000
X59                0.000               4.000
X39              380.000               0.000
X45                0.000               1.000
X54                0.000               3.000
```

The value of the solution here is €630 less than the value of the solution for problem 23. The new shipping route from plant 3 to customer 4 has helped ($x_{39} = 380$). There is now excess capacity of 130 units at plant 1.

12 a.

$$\text{Min } 20x_{12}+25x_{15}+30x_{25}+45x_{27}+20x_{31}+35x_{36} +30x_{42}+25x_{53}+15x_{54}+28x_{56}+12x_{67}+27x_{74}$$

s.t.

$$x_{31}- x_{12}- x_{15} = 8$$
$$x_{25}+ x_{27}- x_{12}- x_{42} = 5$$
$$x_{31}+ x_{36}- x_{53} = 3$$
$$x_{54}+ x_{74}- x_{42} = 3$$
$$x_{53}+ x_{54}+ x_{56}- x_{15}- x_{25} = 2$$
$$x_{36}+ x_{56}- x_{67} = 5$$
$$x_{74}- x_{27}- x_{67} = 6$$
$$x_{ij} \geq 0 \text{ for all } i, j$$

b.

$x_{12} = 0$	$x_{42} = 3$
$x_{15} = 0$	$x_{53} = 5$
$x_{25} = 8$	$x_{54} = 0$
$x_{27} = 0$	$x_{56} = 5$
$x_{31} = 8$	$x_{67} = 0$
$x_{36} = 0$	$x_{74} = 6$

Total cost of redistributing cars = \$917

14 a. Solution:

Shipping Route (Arc)	Units	Unit Cost	Arc Shipping Cost
O1 – D1	25	5	125
O1 – D3	50	10	500
O2 – D3	100	8	800
O2 – D4	75	2	150
O3 – D1	100	6	600
O4 – D2	100	5	500
O4 – D4	50	4	200
Total Transportation Cost:			2875

b. Yes, $e_{32} = 0$. This indicates that we can ship over route O3 – D2 without increasing the cost.

u_i \ v_j	5	5	10	4	Supply
0	[5] 75	[7] (2)	[10] (0)	[5] (1)	75
–2	[6] (3)	[5] (2)	[8] 150	[2] 25	175
1	[6] 50	[6] 50	[12] (1)	[7] (2)	100
0	[8] (3)	[5] 50	[14] (4)	[4] 100	150
Demand	125	100	150	125	

Note that all $e_{ij} \geq 0$ indicating that this solution is also optimal. Also note that $e_{13} = 0$ indicating there is an alternative optimal solution with cell (1, 3) in solution. This is the solution we found in part (a).

18 a.

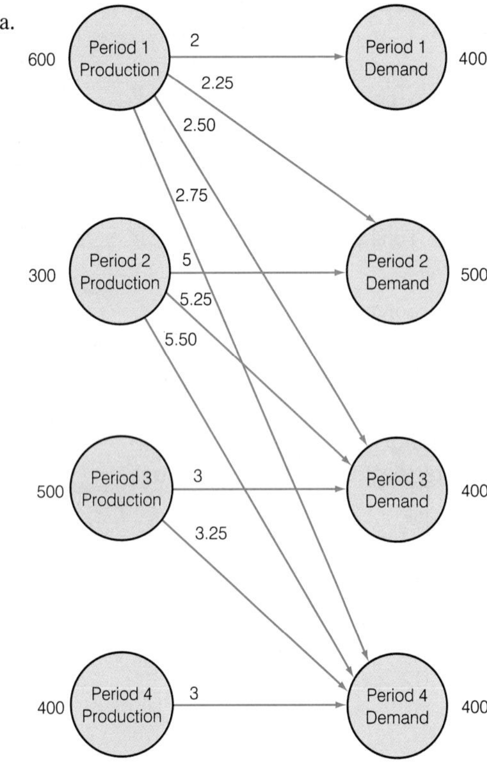

b. All of the cells corresponding to production in one period being used to satisfy demand in a previous period are assigned a 'big M' cost. The initial solution found using the minimum cost method is optimal.

	[2] 400	[2.25] 200	[2.50]	[2.75]	600
	[M]	[5] 300	[5.25]	[5.50]	300
	[M]	[M]	[3] 400	[3.25]	500
	[M]	[M]	[M]	[3] 400	400
	400	500	400	400	

19 Subtract 10 from row 1, 14 from row 2, and 22 from row 3 to obtain:

	1	2	3
Jackson	0	6	22
Ellis	0	8	26
Smith	0	2	12

Subtract 0 from column 1, 2 from column 2, and 12 from column 3 to obtain:

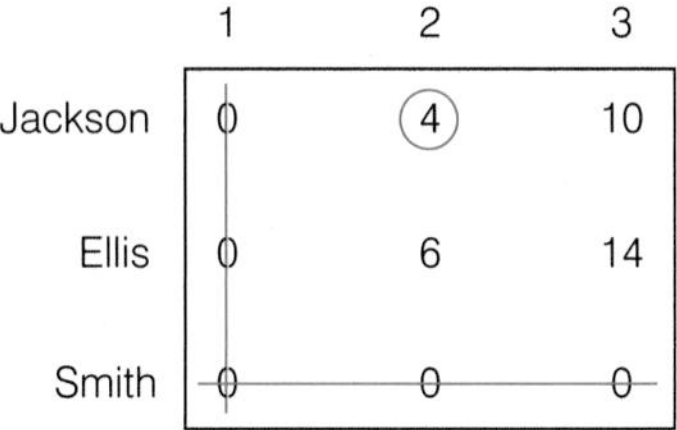

	1	2	3
Jackson	0	(4)	10
Ellis	0	6	14
Smith	0	0	0

Two lines cover the zeros. The minimum unlined element is 4. Step 3 yields:

	1	2	3
Jackson	0	[0]	6
Ellis	[0]	2	10
Smith	0	0	[0]

Optimal Solution:

Jackson -2
Ellis -1
Smith -3

Time requirement is 64 days.

20 We start with the opportunity loss matrix.

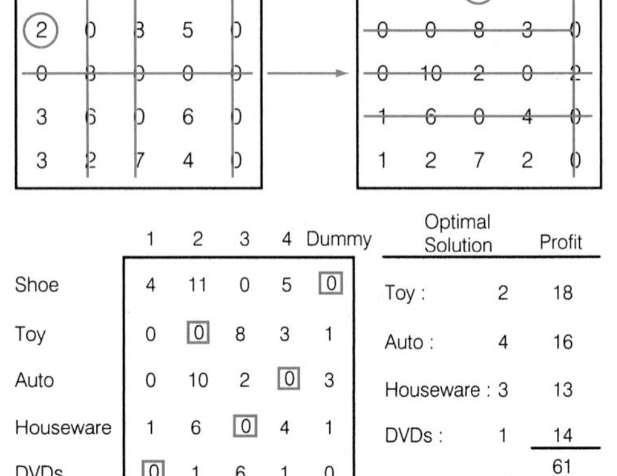

7	12	1	8	0
(2)	0	3	5	0
0	3	0	0	0
3	6	0	6	0
3	2	7	4	0

5	12	(1)	6	0
0	0	8	3	0
0	10	2	0	2
1	6	0	4	0
1	2	7	2	0

	1	2	3	4	Dummy
Shoe	4	11	0	5	[0]
Toy	0	[0]	8	3	1
Auto	0	10	2	[0]	3
Houseware	1	6	[0]	4	1
DVDs	[0]	1	6	1	0

	Optimal Solution	Profit
Toy :	2	18
Auto :	4	16
Houseware :	3	13
DVDs :	1	14
		61

Chapter 8

1

Node	Shortest Route From Node 1	Distance
2	1–2	7
3	1–3	9
4	1–2–5–64	17
5	1–2–5	12
6	1–2–5–6	14
7	1–2–5–67	17

2

Node	Shortest Route From Node 7	Distance
1	7–6–5–21	17
2	7–6–5–2	10
3	7–6–5–3	9
4	7–6–4	6
5	7–6–5	5
6	7–6	3

4 Shortest route: 1–3–5–8–10
Total Distance: 19.

6 Shortest route: 1–5–4–6–7–10
Time = 10 + 4 + 3 + 4 + 4 = 25 minutes

7

Start Node	End Node	Distance
1	6	2
6	7	3
7	8	1
7	10	2
10	9	3
9	4	2
9	3	3
3	2	1
4	5	3
7	11	4
8	13	4
14	15	2
15	12	3
14	13	4
		Total length = 37

8

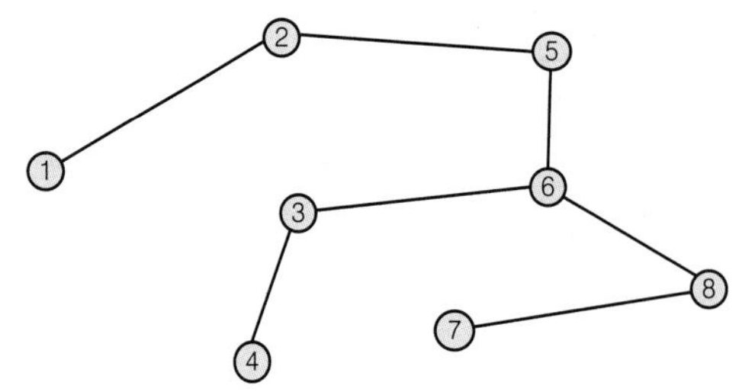

1–2	6
2–5	5
5–6	3
6–3	4
6–8	2
3–4	5
8–7	4
	29

10

Minimum length of cable lines = 2 + 2 + 2 + 3 + 3 + 2 + 3 + 3 + 4 + 4 = 28km

11/12 The capacitated transshipment problem to solve is given:

Max x_{61}

s.t.

$$x_{12} + x_{13} + x_{14} - x_{61} = 0$$
$$x_{24} + x_{25} - x_{12} - x_{42} = 0$$
$$x_{34} + x_{36} - x_{13} - x_{43} = 0$$
$$x_{42} + x_{43} + x_{45} + x_{46} - x_{14} - x_{24} - x_{34} - x_{54} = 0$$
$$x_{54} + x_{56} - x_{25} - x_{45} = 0$$
$$x_{61} - x_{36} + x_{46} - x_{56} = 0$$
$$x_{12} \leq 2 \quad x_{13} \leq 6 \quad x_{14} \leq 3$$
$$x_{24} \leq 1 \quad x_{25} \leq 4$$
$$x_{34} \leq 3 \quad x_{36} \leq 2$$
$$x_{42} \leq 1 \quad x_{43} \leq 3 \quad x_{45} \leq 1 \quad x_{46} \leq 3$$
$$x_{54} \leq 1 \quad x_{56} \leq 6$$
$$x_{ij} \geq 0 \text{ for all } i, j$$

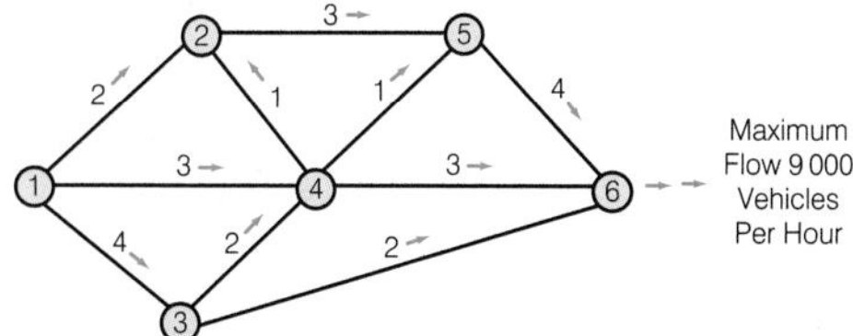

The system cannot accommodate a flow of 10 000 vehicles per hour.

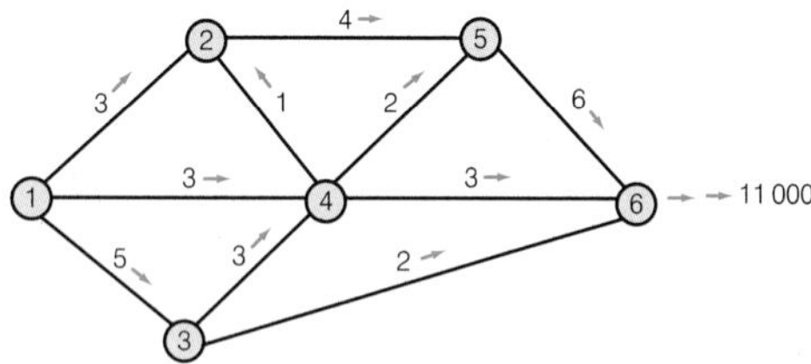

Chapter 9

2

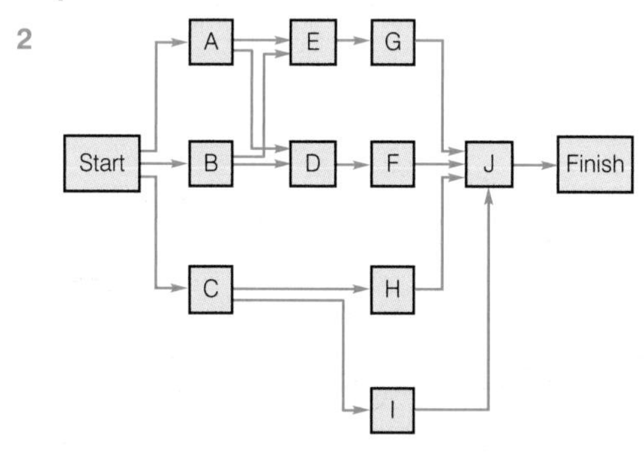

3

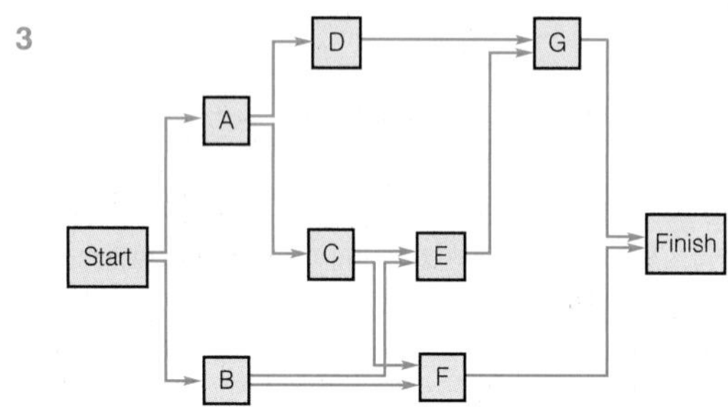

4 a. Critical Path: A–D–G

b. The critical path activities require 15 months to complete. Thus the project should be completed in 1 to 2 years.

6 a. Critical path: A–D–F–H

b. 22 weeks

c. No, it is a critical activity

d. Yes, two weeks

e. Schedule for activity E:

Earliest start	3
Latest start	4
Earliest Finish	10
Latest Finish	11

8 a.

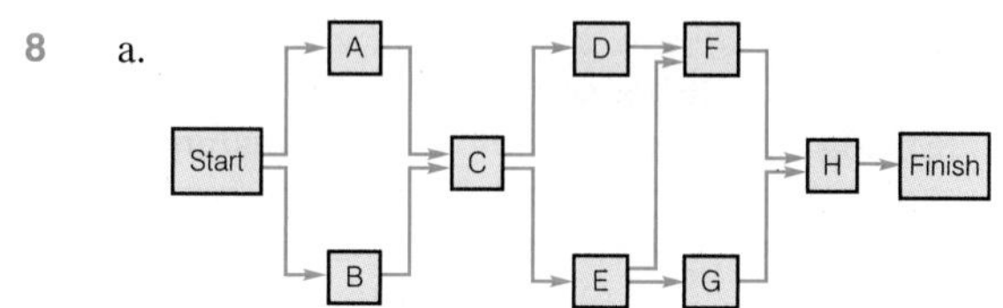

b. B–C–E–F–H

c.

Activity	Earliest Start	Latest Start	Earliest Finish	Latest Finish	Slack	Critical Activity
A	0	2	6	8	2	
B	0	0	8	8	0	Yes
C	8	8	20	20	0	Yes
D	20	22	24	26	2	
E	20	20	26	26	0	Yes
F	26	26	41	41	0	Yes
G	26	29	38	41	3	
H	41	41	49	49	0	Yes

d. Yes. Project Completion Time 49 weeks.

10 a.

Activity	Optimistic	Most Probable	Pessimistic	Expected Times	Variance
A	4	5	6	5.00	0.11
B	8	9	10	9.00	0.11
C	7	7.5	11	8.00	0.44
D	6	9	10	8.83	0.25
E	6	7	9	7.17	0.25
F	5	6	7	6.00	0.11

b. Critical activities: B–D–F
Expected project completion time:
$9.00 + 8.83 + 6.00 = 23.83$.
Variance of projection completion time:
$0.11 + 0.25 + 0.11 = 0.47$

11

Activity	Expected Time	Variance
A	5	0.11
B	3	0.03
C	7	0.11
D	6	0.44
E	7	0.44
F	3	0.11
G	10	0.44
H	8	1.78

From problem 6, A–D–F–H is the critical path.

$$E(T) = 5 + 6 + 3 + 8 = 22$$

$$\sigma^2 = 0.11 + 0.44 + 0.11 + 1.78 = 2.44$$

$$z = \frac{\text{Time} - E(T)}{\sigma} = \frac{\text{Time} - 22}{\sqrt{2.44}}$$

a. $P(21 \text{ weeks}) = 0.2611$
b. $P(22 \text{ weeks}) = 0.5000$
c. $P(25 \text{ weeks}) = 0.9726$

12 a.

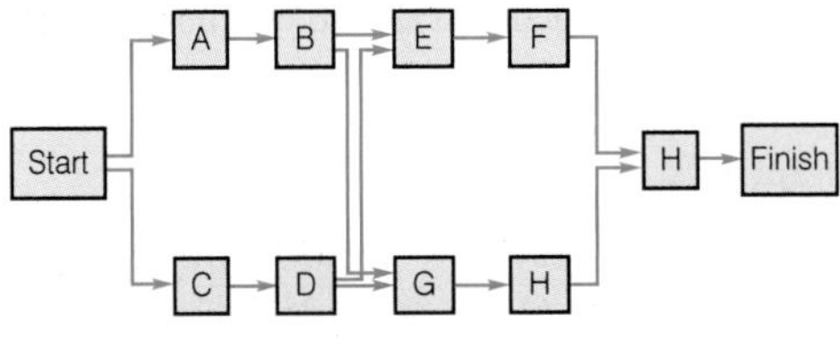

b.

Activity	Expected Time	Variance
A	2	0.03
B	3	0.44
C	2	0.11
D	2	0.03
E	1	0.03
F	2	0.11
G	4	0.44
H	4	0.11
I	2	0.03

Activity	Earliest Start	Latest Start	Earliest Finish	Latest Finish	Slack	Critical Activity
A	0	0	2	2	0	Yes
B	2	2	5	5	0	Yes
C	0	1	2	3	1	
D	2	3	4	5	1	
E	5	10	6	11	5	
F	6	11	8	13	5	
G	5	5	9	9	0	Yes
H	9	9	13	13	0	Yes
I	13	13	15	15	0	Yes

c. Critical Path: A–B–G–H–I
$E(T) = 2 + 3 + 4 + 4 + 2 = 15$ weeks

d. Variance on critical path
$\sigma^2 = 0.03 + 0.44 + 0.44 + 0.11 + 0.03 = 1.05$
From Appendix, we find 0.99 probability occurs at $z = +2.33$. Thus:

$$z = \frac{T - E(T)}{\sigma} = \frac{T - 15}{\sqrt{1.05}} = 2.33$$

or

$$T = 15 + 2.33\sqrt{1.05} = 17.4 \text{ weeks}$$

14 a.

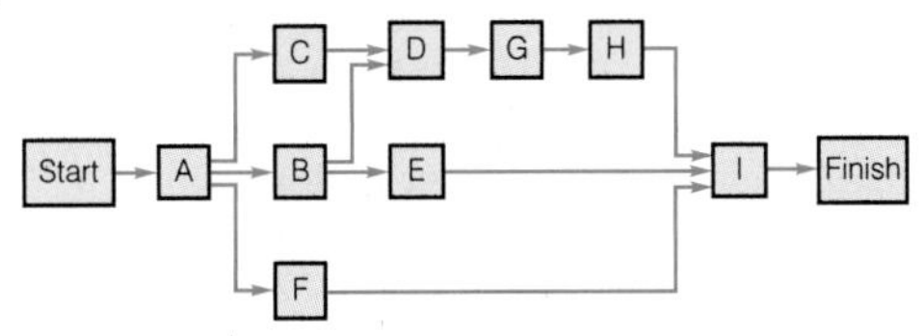

b.

Activity	Expected Time	Variance
A	1.17	0.03
B	6.00	0.44
C	4.00	0.44
D	2.00	0.11
E	3.00	0.11
F	2.00	0.11
G	2.00	0.11
H	2.00	0.11
I	1.00	0.00

Activity	Earliest Start	Latest Start	Earliest Finish	Latest Finish	Slack	Critical Activity
A	0.00	0.00	1.17	1.17	0.00	Yes
B	1.17	1.17	7.17	7.17	0.00	Yes
C	1.17	3.17	5.17	7.17	2.00	
D	7.17	7.17	9.17	9.17	0.00	Yes
E	7.17	10.17	10.17	13.17	3.00	
F	1.17	11.17	3.17	13.17	10.00	
G	9.17	9.17	11.17	11.17	0.00	Yes
H	11.17	11.17	13.17	13.17	0.00	Yes
I	13.17	13.17	14.17	14.17	0.00	Yes

c. Critical Path: A–B–D–G–H–I
Expected Project Completion
Time = 1.17 + 6 + 2 + 2 + 2 + 1 = 14.17 weeks

d. Compute the probability of project completion in 13 weeks or less.

$$\sigma^2 = \sigma_A^2 + \sigma_B^2 + \sigma_D^2 + \sigma_G^2 + \sigma_H^2 + \sigma_I^2$$

$$= 0.03 + 0.44 + 0.11 + 0.11 + 0.11 + 0.00 = 0.80$$

$$z = \frac{13 - E(T)}{\sigma} = \frac{13 - 14.17}{\sqrt{0.80}} = -1.31$$

Area
0.4049$P(13 \text{ weeks}) = 0.5000 - 0.4049 = 0.0951$
With this low probability, the manager should start prior to February 1.

16

Activity	Earliest Start	Latest Start	Earliest Finish	Latest Finish	Slack	Critical Activity
A	0	0	3	3	0	Yes
B	0	0	5	5	0	Yes
C	3	3	5	5	0	Yes
D	5	5	8	8	0	Yes
E	8	8	11	11	0	Yes
F	11	11	13	13	0	Yes
G	5	5	13	13	0	Yes
H	13	13	16	16	0	Yes

All activities are critical.

17 a.

Activity	Earliest Start	Latest Start	Earliest Finish	Latest Finish	Slack	Critical Activity
A	0	0	3	3	0	Yes
B	0	1	2	3	1	
C	3	3	8	8	0	Yes
D	2	3	7	8	1	
E	8	8	14	14	0	Yes
F	8	10	10	12	2	
G	10	12	12	14	2	

Critical Path: A–C–E
Project Completion
Time $= t_A + t_C + t_E = 3 + 5 + 6 = 14$ days

b & c. Total Cost = €8 400

18 a.

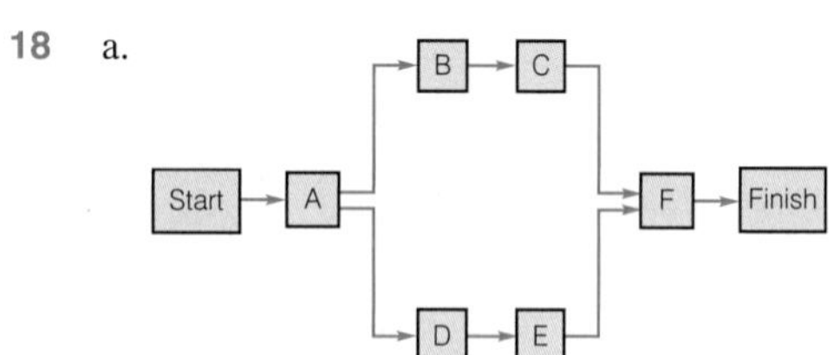

b.

Activity	Earliest Start	Latest Start	Earliest Finish	Latest Finish	Slack
A	0	0	10	10	0
B	10	10	18	18	0
C	18	18	28	28	0
D	10	11	17	18	1
E	17	18	27	28	1
F	28	28	31	31	0

c. Activities A, B, C and F are critical. The expected project completion time is 31 weeks.

d.

Crash Activities	Number of Weeks	Cost
A	2	€40
B	2	30
C	1	20
D	1	10
E	1	12.5
		€112.5

e.

Activity	Earliest Start	Latest Start	Earliest Finish	Latest Finish	Slack
A	0	0	8	8	0
B	8	8	14	14	0
C	14	14	23	23	0
D	8	8	14	14	0
E	14	14	23	23	0
F	23	23	26	26	0

All activities are critical.

f. Total added cost due to crashing €112 500 (see part d.)

Chapter 10

1 a. $Q^* = \sqrt{\dfrac{2DC_o}{C_h}} = \sqrt{\dfrac{2(3600)(20)}{0.25(3)}} = 438.18$

b. $r = dm = \dfrac{3600}{250}(5) = 72$

c. $T = \dfrac{250Q^*}{D} = \dfrac{250(438.18)}{3600} = 30.43$ days

d. $TC = \dfrac{1}{2}QC_h + \dfrac{D}{Q}C_o = \dfrac{1}{2}(438.18)(0.25)(3)$

$+\dfrac{3600}{438.18}(20) = €328.63$

2 Annual Holding Cost:

$\dfrac{1}{2}QC_h = \dfrac{1}{2}(438.18)(0.25)(3) = €164.32$

Annual Ordering Cost:

$\dfrac{D}{Q}C_o = \dfrac{3600}{438.18}(20) = 164.32$

Total Cost = €328.64.

4 a. 1095.45

b. 240

c. 22.82

d. Holding = €278.86
Ordering = €273.86
Total Cost = €547.72

6 a. 1789

b. 1333

c. 894

d. 827

$Q^* = 800$

Production Lot Size Q^* is always greater than the EOQ Q^* with the same D, C_0 and C_h values. As the production rate P increases, the recommended Q^* decreases, but always remains greater than the EOQ Q^*.

7 a. $Q^* = \sqrt{\dfrac{2DC_o}{(1 - D/P)C_h}} = \sqrt{\dfrac{2(7200)(150)}{(1 - \frac{7200}{25000})(0.18)(14.50)}}$

$= 1078.12$

b. Number of production runs $= D/Q^* = 7200/1078.12 = 6.68$

c. $T = \dfrac{250Q}{D} = \dfrac{250(1078.12)}{7200} = 37.43$ days

d. Production run length $= \dfrac{Q}{P/250} = \dfrac{1078.12}{25000/250}$

$= 10.78$ days

e. Maximum Inventory

$$\left(1 - \frac{D}{P}\right)Q = \left(1 - \frac{7200}{25000}\right)(1078.12) = 767.62$$

f. Holding Cost:

$$\frac{1}{2}\left(1 - \frac{D}{P}\right)QC_h = \frac{1}{2}\left(1 - \frac{7200}{25000}\right) \times (1078.12)(0.18)(14.50) = €1001.74$$

Ordering cost $= \dfrac{D}{Q}C_o = \dfrac{7200}{1078.12}(150) = €1001.74$

Total Cost $= €2,003.48$

g. $r = dm = \left(\dfrac{D}{250}\right)m = \dfrac{7200}{250}(15) = 432$

8 New $Q^* = 4509$

9 a. $Q^* = \sqrt{\dfrac{2DC_o}{C_h}\left(\dfrac{C_h + C_b}{C_b}\right)}$

$= \sqrt{\dfrac{2(1200)(25)}{0.50}\left(\dfrac{0.50 + 5}{0.50}\right)} = 1148.91$

b. $S^* = Q^*\left(\dfrac{C_h}{C_h + C_b}\right) = 1148.91\left(\dfrac{0.50}{0.50 + 5}\right)$

$= 104.45$

c. Max inventory $= Q^* - S^* = 1044.46$

d. $T = \dfrac{250Q^*}{D} = \dfrac{250(1148.91)}{12000} = 23.94$

e. Holding: $\dfrac{(Q - S)^2}{2Q}C_h = €237.38$

Ordering: $\dfrac{D}{Q}C_o = 261.12$

Backorder: $\dfrac{S^2}{2Q}C_b = 23.74$

Total Cost: €522.24

The total cost for the EOQ model in problem 4 was €547.72. Allowing backorders reduces the total cost.

10 240

With backorder allowed the reorder point should be revised to:

$$r = dm - S = 240 - 104.45 = 135.55$$

The reorder point will be smaller when backorders are allowed.

12 The 10 per cent discount is worthwhile.

13 $Q = \sqrt{\dfrac{2DC_o}{C_h}}$

$Q_1 = \sqrt{\dfrac{2(500)(40)}{0.20(10)}} = 141.42$

$Q_2 = \sqrt{\dfrac{2(500)(40)}{0.20(9.7)}} = 143.59$

Since Q_1 is over its limit of 99 units, Q_1 cannot be optimal. Use $Q_2 = 143.59$ as the optimal order quantity.

$$\text{Total Cost}: = \frac{1}{2}QC_h + \frac{D}{Q}C_o + DC = 139.28 + 139.28 + 4,850.00 = €5,128.56$$

14 $TC = \dfrac{1}{2}QIC + \dfrac{D}{Q}C_o + DC$

At a specific Q (and given I, D, and C_0), since C of category 2 is less than C of category 1, the TC for 2 is less than TC for 1.

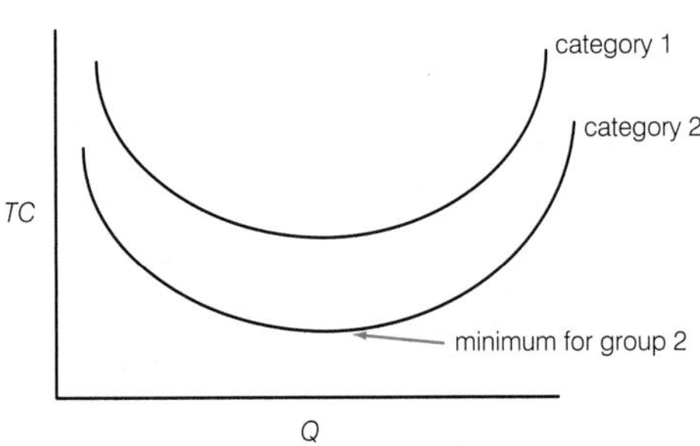

Thus, if the minimum cost solution for category 2 is feasible, there is no need to search category 1. From the graph we can see that all TC values of category 1 exceed the minimum cost solution of category 2.

15 a. $c_o = 80 - 50 = 30$

$c_u = 125 - 80 = 45$

$$P(D \le Q^*) = \frac{c_u}{c_u + c_o} = \frac{45}{45 + 30} = 0.60$$

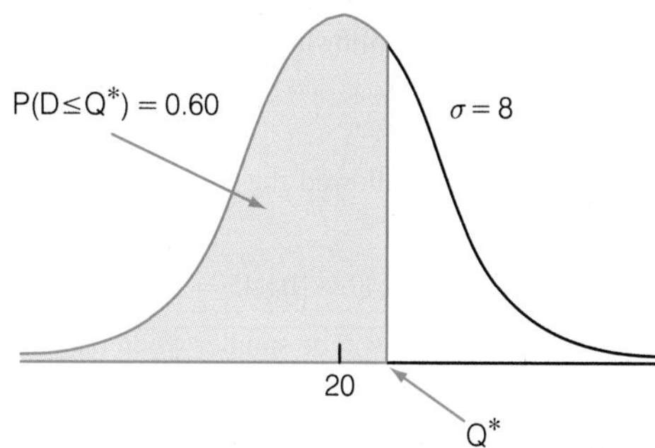

For an area of 0.60 below Q^*, $z = 0.25$

$Q^* = 20 + 0.25(8) = 22$

b. $P(\text{Sell All}) = P(D \geq Q^*) = 1 - 0.60 = 0.40$

17 a. $r = dm = (200/250)15 = 12$

b. $D/Q = 200/25$ = eight orders/year
The limit of one stockout per year means that $P(\text{Stockout/cycle}) = 1/8 = 0.125$

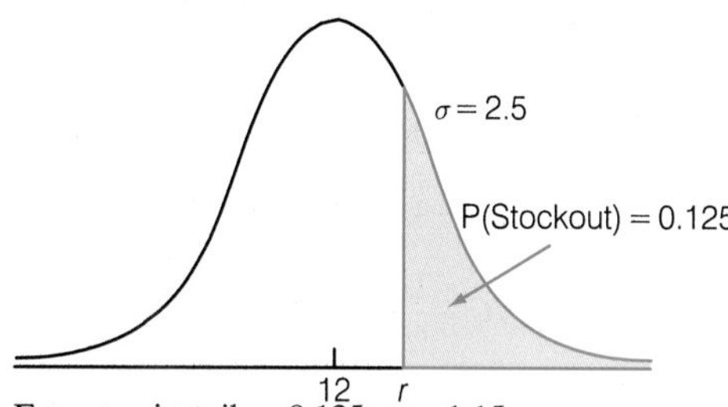

For area in tail = 0.125, $z = 1.15$

$$z = \frac{r - 12}{2.5} = 0.15$$

or

$r = 12 + 1.15(2.5) = 14.875$ Use 15

c. Safety Stock = three units
Added Cost = 3(€5) = €15/year

19 a. $1/52 = 0.0192$

b. $M = \mu + z\sigma = 60 + 2.07(12) = 85$

c. $M = 35 + (0.9808)(85 - 35) = 84$

20 a. 243

b. Safety Stock = 93 units
Annual Cost = €54.87

c. 613 units

d. Safety Stock = 163 units
Annual Cost = €96.17

e. The periodic review model is more expensive (€96.17 – €54.87) = €41.30 per year. However, this added cost may be worth the advantage of coordinating orders for multi products. Go with the periodic review system.

f. Unit Cost = €295 Annual Difference = €4 130
Use continuous review for the more expensive items.

Chapter 11

2 a. 0.4512
b. 0.6988
c. 0.3012

4 0.3333, 0.2222, 0.1481, 0.0988, 0.1976

5 a. $P_0 = 1 - \frac{\lambda}{\mu} = 1 - \frac{10}{12} = 0.1667$

b. $L_q = \frac{\lambda^2}{\mu(\mu - \lambda)} = \frac{10^2}{12\ (12 - 10)} = 4.1667$

c. $W_q = \frac{L_q}{\lambda} = 0.4167$ hours (25 minutes)

d. $W = W_q + \frac{1}{\mu} = .5$ hours (30 minutes)

e. $P_w = \frac{\lambda}{\mu} = \frac{10}{12} = 0.8333$

6 a. 0.375
b. 1.0417
c. 0.8333 minutes (50 seconds)
d. 0.625
e. Average one customer in line with a 50 second average wait appears reasonable.

7 0.20, 3.2, 4, 3.2, 4, 0.80
Even though the services rate is increased to $\mu = 1.25$, this system provides slightly poorer service due to the fact that arrivals are occurring at a higher rate. The average waiting times are identical, but there is a higher probability of waiting and the number waiting increases with the new system.

8 a. $\lambda = 2.5$ $\mu = 60/10$ = six customers per hour

$$L_q = \frac{\lambda^2}{\mu\ (\mu - \lambda)} = \frac{(2.5)^2}{6\ (6 - 2.5)} = 0.2976$$

$$L = L_q + \frac{\lambda}{\mu} = 0.7143$$

$$W_q = \frac{L_q}{\lambda} = 0.1190 \text{ hours (7.14 minutes)}$$

$$W = W_q + \frac{1}{\mu} = 0.2857 \text{ hours}$$

$$P_w = \frac{\lambda}{\mu} = \frac{2.5}{6} = 0.4167$$

b. No; $W_q = 7.14$ minutes. Firm should increase the mean service rate (μ) for the consultant or hire a second consultant.

c. $\mu = 60/8 = 7.5$ customers per hour

$$L_q = \frac{\lambda^2}{\mu\ (\mu - \lambda)} = \frac{(2.5)^2}{7.5\ (7.5 - 2.5)} = 0.1667$$

$$W_q = \frac{L_q}{\lambda} = 0.0667 \text{ hours (four minutes)}$$

The service goal is being met.

9 a. $k = 2\ \lambda/\mu = 14/10 = 1.4$
$P_0 = 0.1765$

b. $L_q = \dfrac{b\lambda/\mu^2 g\lambda_\mu}{1!(2\mu-\lambda)^2}P_0 = \dfrac{(1.4)^2(14)(10)}{(20-14)^2}(0.1765) = 1.3451$

$L = L_q + \dfrac{\lambda}{\mu} = 1.3451 + \dfrac{14}{10} = 2.7451$

c. $W_q = \dfrac{L_q}{\lambda} = \dfrac{1.3453}{14} = 0.0961$ hours (5.77 minutes)

d. $W = W_q + \dfrac{1}{\mu} = 0.0961 + \dfrac{1}{10} = 0.196$ hours (11.77 minutes)

e. $P_0 = 0.1765$

$P_1 = 1 - \dfrac{(\lambda/\mu)^1}{1!}P_0 = \dfrac{14}{10}(0.1765) = 0.2470$

$P(\text{wait}) = P(n \geq 2) = 1 - P(n \leq 1)$

$= 1 - 0.4235 = 0.5765$

10 A service time of eight minutes has $\mu = 60/8 = 7.5$

$L_q = \dfrac{\lambda^2}{\mu\,(\mu-\lambda)} = \dfrac{(2.5)^2}{7.5\,(7.5-2.5)} = 0.1667$

$L = L_q + \dfrac{\lambda}{\mu} = 0.50$

Total Cost $= \$25L + \$16$

$= 25(0.50) + 16 = \$28.50$

Two channels: $\lambda = 2.5$ $\mu = 60/10 = 6$
Using equation, $P_0 = 0.6552$

$L_q = \dfrac{(\lambda/\mu)^2\lambda\mu}{1!\,(2\,\mu-\lambda)^2}P_0 = 0.0189$

$L = L_q + \dfrac{\lambda}{\mu} = 0.4356$

Total Cost $= 25(0.4356) + 2(16) = \$42.89$
Use the one consultant with an eight minute service time.

14 $\lambda = 4$, $W =$ ten minutes

a. $\mu = 1/2 = 0.5$

b. $W_q = W - 1/\mu = 10 - 1/0.5 =$ eight minutes

c. $L = \lambda W = 4(10) = 40$

15 a. 2/8 hours = 0.25 per hour

b. 1/3.2 hours = 0.3125 per hour

c. $L_q = \dfrac{\lambda^2\sigma^2 + (\lambda/\mu)^2}{2(1-\lambda/\mu)} = \dfrac{(0.25)^2(2)^2 + (0.25/0.3125)^2}{2(1-0.25/0.3125)} = 2.225$

d. $W_q = \dfrac{L_q}{\lambda} = \dfrac{2.225}{0.25} = 8.9$ hours

e. $W = W_q + \dfrac{1}{\mu} = 8.9 + \dfrac{1}{1.3125} = 12.1$ hours

f. Same at $P_W = \dfrac{\lambda}{\mu} = \dfrac{0.25}{0.3125} = 0.80$

80% of the time the welder is busy.

17 a. .375, 0.5

b. 1.7578, 2.5078, €115.71

c.

Current System (σ = 1.5)	New System (σ = 0)
$L_q = 1.7578$	$L_q = 1.125$
$L = 2.5078$	$L = 1.875$
$W_q = 4.6875$	$W_q = 3.00$
$W = 6.6875$	$W = 5.00$
$TC =$ €115.77	

$TC =$ €97.63

d. Yes; Savings = €725.60

18 a. $\lambda = 42$ $\mu = 20$

i	$(\lambda/\mu)^i/i!$
0	1.0000
1	2.1000
2	2.2050
3	1.5435
	6.8485

j	P_j		
0	1/6.8485	=	0.1460
1	2.1/6.8485	=	0.3066
2	2.2050/6.8485	=	0.3220
3	1.5435/6.8485	=	0.2254
			1.0000

b. 0.2254

c. $L = \lambda/\mu(1 - P_k) = 42/20\,(1 - 0.2254) = 1.6267$

d. Four lines will be necessary. The probability of denied access is 0.1499.

19 a. 31.04 per cent

b. 27.58 per cent

c. 0.2758, 0.1092, 0.0357

d. 3, 10.92 per cent

20 a. $N = 5$ $\lambda = 0.025$ $\mu = 0.20$ $\lambda/\mu = 0.125$

n	$\dfrac{N!}{(N-n)!}\left(\dfrac{\lambda}{\mu}\right)^n$
0	1.0000
1	0.6250
2	0.3125
3	0.1172
4	0.0293
5	0.0037
	2.0877

$P_0 = 1/2.0877 = 0.4790$

b. $L_q = N - \left(\frac{\lambda+\mu}{\lambda}\right)(1-P_0) = 5 - \left(\frac{0.225}{0.025}\right)(1-0.4790) = 0.3110$

c. $L = L_q + (1 - P_0) = 0.3110 + (1 - 0.4790)$
$= 0.8321$

d. $W_q = \frac{L_q}{(N-L)\lambda} = \frac{0.3110}{(5-0.8321)(0.025)} = 2.9854 \text{ min}$

e. $W = W_q + \frac{1}{\mu} = 2.9854 + \frac{1}{0.20} = 7.9854 \text{ min}$

f. Trips/Days = (eight hours)(60 min /hour)(λ)
= (8)(60)(0.025) = 12 trips

Time at Copier: 12 × 7.9854 = 95.8 minutes/day
Wait Time at Copier: 12 × 2.9854 = 35.8 minutes/day

g. Yes. Five administrative assistants × 35.8 = 179 min. (three hours/day) three hours per day are lost to waiting. (35.8/480)(100) = 7.5 per cent of each administrative assistant's day is spent waiting for the copier.

Chapter 12

2 a. Let c = variable cost per unit
x = demand

Profit = $(50 - c)\,x - 30\,000$

b. Base case : Profit = (50 – 20) 1200 – 30 000 = 6 000
Worst case : Profit = (50 – 24) 300 – 30 000 = –22 200
Best case : Profit = (50 – 16) 2100 – 30 000 = 41 400

c. The possibility of a €41 400 profit is interesting, but the worst case loss of €22 200 is risky. Risk analysis would be helpful in evaluating the probability of a loss.

4 a.

Sales	Interval
0	.00 but less than .08
1	.08 but less than .20
2	.20 but less than .48
3	.48 but less than .72
4	.72 but less than .86
5	.86 but less than .96
6	.96 but less than 1.00

b. 2, 5, 2, 3, 2, 4, 2, 1, 1, 2

c. Total Sales = 24 units

5 a.

Stock Price Change	Probability	Interval
−2	.05	.00 but less than .05
−1	.10	.05 but less than .15
0	.25	.15 but less than .40
+1	.20	.40 but less than .60
+2	.20	.60 but less than .80
+3	.10	.80 but less than .90
+4	.10	.90 but less than 1.00

b.

Random Number	Price Change	Ending Price Per Share
0.1091	−1	$38
0.9407	+4	$42
0.1941	0	$42
0.8083	+3	$45

Ending price per share = $45

6

r	Time
0.1567	11.25 minutes
0.9823	17.86 minutes
0.3419	12.74 minutes
0.5572	14.46 minutes
0.7758	16.21 minutes

7 a. Base case using most likely completion times.

A	6
B	5
C	14
D	8
	33 weeks

Worst case: 8 + 7 + 18 + 10 = 43 weeks
Best case: 5 + 3 + 10 + 8 = 26 weeks

b.

Activity	Random Number	Completion Time
A	0.1778	5
B	0.9617	7
C	0.6849	14
D	0.4503	8
		Total: 34 Weeks

c. Simulation will provide a distribution of project completion time values. Calculating the percentage of simulation trials with completion times of 35 weeks or less can be used to estimate the probability of meeting the completion time target of 35 weeks.

8 a. €7, €3, €12

b.

Purchase Cost	Interval	Labour Cost	Interval	Transportation Cost	Interval
€10	.00 but less than .25	€20	.00 but less than .10	€3	.00 but less than .75
11	.25 but less than .70	22	.10 but less than .35	5	.75 but less than 1.00
12	.70 but less than 1.00	24	.35 but less than .70		
		25	.70 but less than 1.00		

c. Profit = €5/unit

d. Profit = €7/unit

e. Simulation will provide a distribution of the profit per unit values. Calculating the percentage of simulation trials providing a profit less than €5 per unit would provide an estimate of the probability that the profit per unit will be unacceptably low.

9 The spreadsheet for this problem is shown in Figure F13.9 Selected cell formulas are as follows:

Cell	Formula
B13	=$C$7 + RAND()*($C$8 – $C$7)
C13	=NORMINV(RAND(),$G$7,$G$8)
D13	=($C$3 – B13)*C13 – $C$4

a. The mean profit should be approximately €6 000. Simulation results will vary with most simulations having a mean profit between €5 500 and €6 500.

b. 120 to 150 of the 500 simulation trials should show a loss. Thus, the probability of a loss should be between 0.24 and 0.30.

c. This project appears too risky. The relatively high probability of a loss and only roughly €6000 as a mean profit indicate that the potential gain is not worth the risk of a loss. More precise estimates of the variable cost per unit and the demand could help determine a more precise profit estimate.

10 The spreadsheet with data in thousands of euros is shown in Figure F13.10.
Selected cell formulas are as follows:

Cell	Formula
B11	=$C$4 + RAND()*($C$5 – $C$4)
C11	=NORMINV(RAND(),$H$4,$H$5)
D11	=MAX(B11:C11)
G11	=COUNTIF(D11:D1010," <750")
H11	=G11/COUNT(D11:D1010)

Figure F13.9 Worksheet for the Madeira Manufacturing Company

	A	B	C	D	E	F	G
1	**Madeira Manufacturing Company**						
2							
3	Selling Price per Unit		€50				
4	Fixed Cost		€30 000				
5							
6	**Variable Cost (Uniform Distribution)**				**Demand (Normal distribution)**		
7	Smallest Value		€16		Mean		1200
8	Largest Value		€24		Standard Deviation		300
9							
10	**Simulation Trials**						
11		Variable					
12	Trial	Cost per Unit	Demand	Profit			
13	1	€23.41	1179	€1 338			
14	2	€19.95	1022	€722			
15							
16	**Note: To reconstruct the complete speadsheet:**						
17	1. **Block** rows 21 to 509						
18	2. On the **Insert** menu, click**Rows**						
19	3. **Copy** row 14 (Trial 2) to fill rows 15 to 510.						
20	Trial 500 will appear in row 512 of the spreadsheet.						
21							
22	499	€16.36	1044	€5 117			
23	500	€19.93	924	(€2 209)			
24							
25		**Summary Statistics**					
26		Mean Profit		€5 198			
27		Standard Deviation		€9934			
28		Minimum Profit		–€24 310			
29		Maximum Profit		€34 455			
30		Number of Losses		129			
31		Probability of Loss		0.2580			

Figure F13.10 Worksheet for the Contractor Bidding

	A	B	C	D	E	F	G	H
1	**Contractor Bidding**							
2								
3	**Contractor A (Uniform Distribution)**					**Contractor B (Normal Distribution)**		
4	Smallest Value		€600			Mean		€700
5	Largest Value		€800			Standard Deviation		€50
6								
7								
8	**Simulation**					**Results**		
9		Contractor	Contractor	Highest		Contractor's	Number	Probability
10	Trial	A's Bid	B's Bid	Bid		Bid	of Wins	of Winning
11	1	€739.2	€628.2	€739.2		750	629	0.629
12	2	€705.9	€729.6	€729.6		775	824	0.824
13	3	€795.2	€771.1	€795.2		785	887	0.887
14	4	€630.4	€690.8	€690.8				
15								
16	**Note: To reconstruct the complete speadsheet:**							
17	1. **Block** rows 21 to 1007							
18	2. On the **Insert** menu, click**Rows**							
19	3. **Copy** row 14 (Trial 4) to fill rows 15 to 1008.							
20	Trial 1000 will appear in row 1010 of the spreadsheet.							
21								
22	999	€660.0	€709.2	€709.2				
23	1000	€751.7	€586.4	€751.7				

a. Cell G11 provides the number of times the contractor's bid of €750 000 will beat the highest competitive bid shown in column D. Simulation results will vary but the bid of €750 000 should win roughly 600 to 650 of the 1000 times. The probability of winning the bid should be between 0.60 and 0.65.

b. Cells G12 and G13 provide the number of times the bids of €775 000 and €785 000 win. Again, simulation results vary but the probability of €750 000 winning should be roughly 0.82 and the probability of €785 000 winning should be roughly 0.88. Given these results, a contractor's bid of €775 000 is recommended.

12 a. Without overbooking, the problem states that South Central has a mean profit of €2 800 per flight. The overbooking simulation model with a total of 32 reservations (two overbookings) projects a mean profit of approximately €2925. This is an increase in profit of €125 per flight (4.5 per cent). The overbooking strategy appears worthwhile. The simulation spreadsheet indicates a service level of approximately 99.2 per cent for all passenger demand. This indicates that only 0.8 per cent of the passengers would encounter an overbooking problem. The overbooking strategy up to a total of 32 reservations is recommended.

b. The same spreadsheet design can be used to simulate other overbooking strategies including accepting 31, 33 and 34 passenger reservations. In each case, South Central would need to obtain data on the passenger demand probabilities. Changing the passenger demand table and rerunning the simulation model would enable South Central to evaluate the other overbooking alternatives and arrive at the most beneficial overbooking policy.

14 a. Both the mean interarrival time and the mean service time should be approximately four minutes.

b. Simulation results should provide a mean waiting time of approximately .8 minutes (48 seconds).

c. Simulation results should predict approximately 150 to 170 customers had to wait. Generally, the percentage should be 30 to 35 per cent.

Chapter 13

1 a.

d_1: s_1 250; s_2 100; s_3 25

d_2: s_1 100; s_2 100; s_3 75

b.

Decision	Maximum Profit	Minimum Profit
d_1	250	25
d_2	100	75

Optimistic approach: select d_1
Conservative approach: select d_2

Regret or opportunity loss table:

	s_1	s_2	s_3
d_1	0	0	50
d_2	150	0	0

Maximum Regret: 50 for d_1 and 150 for d_2; select d_1

2 a. Optimistic approach: select d_1
Conservative approach: select d_3
Minimax regret approach: select d_3

b. The choice of which approach to use is up to the decision maker. Since different approaches can result in different recommendations, the most appropriate approach should be selected before analysing the problem.

c. Optimistic approach: select d_1
Conservative approach: select d_2 or d_3
Minimax regret approach: select d_2

3 a. The decision to be made is to choose the best plant size. There are two alternatives to choose from: a small plant or a large plant.
The chance event is the market demand for the new product line. It is viewed as having three possible outcomes (states of nature): low, medium and high.

b.

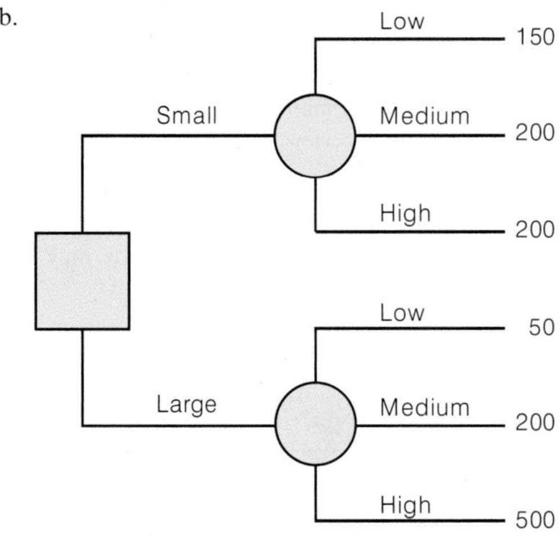

c.

Decision	Maximum Profit	Minimum Profit	Maximum Regret
Small	200	150	300
Large	500	50	100

Optimistic approach: select Large plant
Conservative approach: select Small plant
Minimax regret approach: select Large plant

4 $\text{EV}(d_1) = .65(250) + .15(100) + .20(25) = 182.5$
$\text{EV}(d_2) = .65(100) + .15(100) + .20(75) = 95$
The optimal decision is d_1

5 a. $\text{EV(own staff)} = 0.2(650) + 0.5(650) + 0.3(600) = 635$
$\text{EV(outside vendor)} = 0.2(900) + 0.5(600) + 0.3(300) = 570$
$\text{EV(combination)} = 0.2(800) + 0.5(650) + 0.3(500) = 635$

The optimal decision is to hire an outside vendor with an expected annual cost of €570 000.

b. The risk profile in tabular form is shown.

Cost	Probability
300	0.3
600	0.5
900	0.2
	1.0

A graphical representation of the risk profile is also shown:

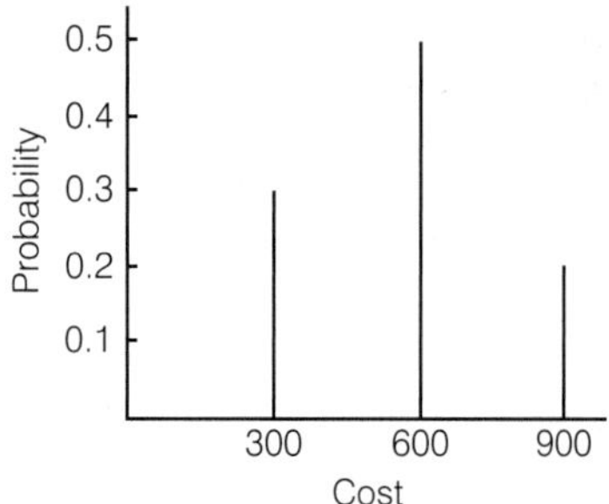

6 a. $\text{EV}(d_1) = p(10) + (1-p)(1) = 9p + 1$
$\text{EV}(d_2) = p(4) + (1-p)(3) = 1p + 3$

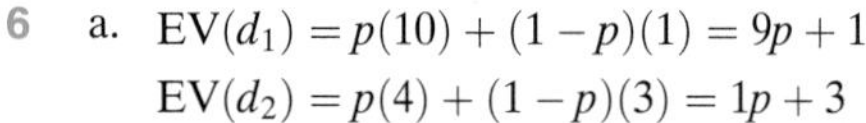

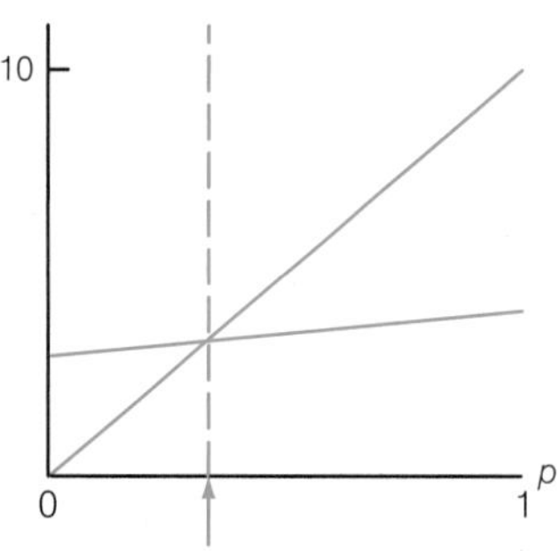

$9p + 1 = 1p + 3$ and hence $p = .25$
d_2 is optimal for $p \le 0.25$; d_1 is optimal for $p \ge 0.25$.

b. d_2

c. As long as the payoff for s_1 is ≥ 2, then d_2 will be optimal.

9 a. If s_1 then d_1; if s_2 then d_1 or d_2; if s_3 then d_2

b. $\text{EVwPI} = .65(250) + .15(100) + .20(75) = 192.5$

c. $\text{EVwoPI} = 182.5$.

d. $\text{EVPI} = 10$

10 a.

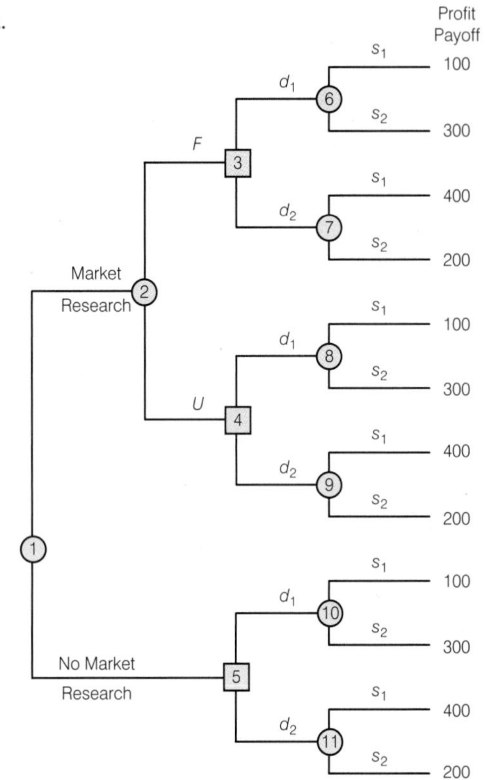

b. Conduct Market Research

If Favourable, decision d_2
If Unfavourable, decision d_1

11 a. Outcome 1 (€ in 000s):

Bid	−€200
Contract	−2 000
Market Research	−150
High Demand	+5 000
	€2 650

Outcome 2 (€ in 000s):

Bid	−€200
Contract	−2 000
Market Research	−150
Moderate Demand	+3 000
	€650

b. Decision Strategy:

Bid on the Contract
Do not do the Market Research
Build the Complex
Expected Value is €1 560 000

c. Market research cost would have to be lowered €130 000 to €20 000 or less to make undertaking the research desirable.

d.

Payoff (€million)	Probability
−200	=.20
800	=.32
2800	=.48

12 a.

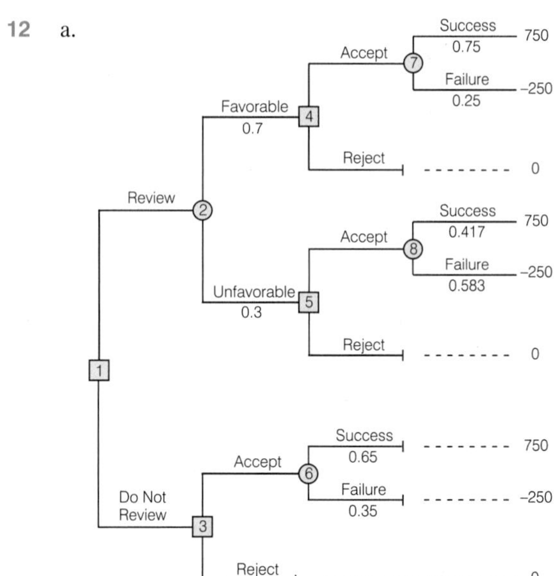

b. The company should accept the manuscript.

c. The manuscript review cannot alter the decision to accept the manuscript. Do not do the manuscript review.

d. EVPI = €87 500.
A better procedure for assessing the market potential for the textbook may be worthwhile.

14

State of Nature	$P(s_j)$	$P(I\|s_j)$	$P(I \cap s_j)$	$P(s_j\|I)$
s_1	0.2	0.10	0.020	0.1905
s_2	0.5	0.05	0.025	0.2381
s_3	0.3	0.20	0.060	0.5714
	1.0	$P(I)$ =	0.105	1.0000

16 Risk avoider, at €20 payoff $p = 0.70$

$\therefore$ EV(Lottery) = 0.70(100) + 0.30(−100) = €40

$\therefore$ Will Pay 40 − 20 = €20
Risk taker B, at €20 payoff $p = 0.45$

$\therefore$ EV(Lottery) = 0.45(100) + 0.55(−100) = −€10

$\therefore$ Will Pay 20 − (−10) = €30

18 a. $EV(d_1) = 0.40(100) + 0.30(25) + 0.30(0) = 47.5$
$EV(d_2) = 0.40(75) + 0.30(50) + 0.30(25) = 52.5$
$EV(d_3) = 0.40(50) + 0.30(50) + 0.30(50) = 50.0$

b. Using Utilities

Decision Maker A		Decision Maker B	
$EU(d_1) = 4.9$		$EU(d_1) = 4.45$	
$EU(d_2) = 5.9$	d_3	$EU(d_2) = 3.75$	d_1
$EU(d_3) = 6.0$		$EU(d_3) = 3.00$	

c. Difference in attitude toward risk. Decision maker A tends to avoid risk, while decision maker B tends to take a risk for the opportunity of a large payoff.

20 a. Market the new product.

b. Lottery

$$p = \text{probability of } €150\,000$$
$$(1-p) = \text{probability of } -€100\,000$$

$EU(€0) = 5.0$

c. Market the new product.

d. Yes - Both EV and EU recommend marketing the product.

Chapter 14

2 a. Let

x_1 = number of shares of AGA Products purchased
x_2 = number of shares of Key Oil purchased

To obtain an annual return of exactly 9 per cent

$$0.06(50)x_1 + 0.10(100)x_2 = 0.09(50\,000)$$
$$3x_1 + 10x_2 = 4500$$

To have exactly 60 per cent of the total investment in Key Oil

$$100x_2 = 0.60(50\,000)$$
$$x_2 = 300$$

Therefore, we can write the goal programming model as follows:

$$\text{Min } P_1(d_1^-) + P_2(d_2^+)$$
s.t.
$$\begin{aligned} 50x_1 + 100x_2 & & \leq 50\,000 & \text{ Funds Available} \\ 3x_1 + 10x_2 - d_1^+ + d_1^- & & = 4\,500 & \ P_1 \text{ Goal} \\ x_2 - d_2^+ + d_2^- & & = 300 & \ P_2 \text{ Goal} \end{aligned}$$
$$x_1, x_2, d_1^+, d_1^-, d_2^+, d_2^- \geq 0$$

b. In the graphical solution shown below, $x_1 = 250$ and $x_2 = 375$.

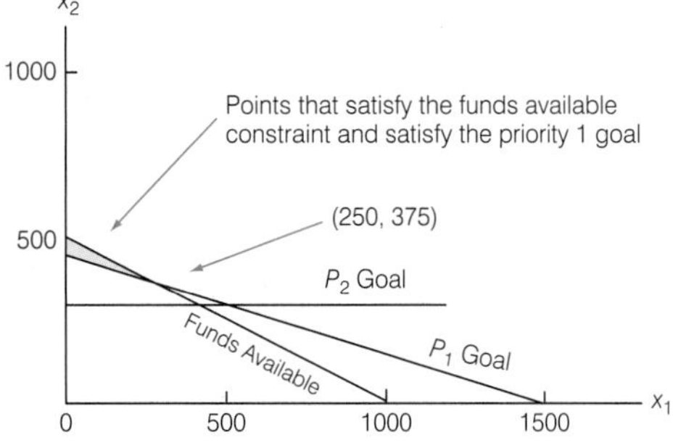

4 a.

$$\text{Min} P_1(d_1^-) + P_1(d_2^+) + P_2(d_3^-) + P_2(d_4^-) + P_3(d_5^-)$$
s.t.
$$\begin{aligned} 20x_1 + 30x_2 - d_1^+ + d_1^- &= 4800 \text{ Goal1} \\ 20x_1 + 30x_2 - d_2^+ + d_2^- &= 6000 \text{ Goal2} \\ x_1 - d_3^+ + d_3^- &= 100 \text{ Goal3} \\ x_2 - d_4^+ + d_4^- &= 120 \text{ Goal4} \\ x_1 + x_2 - d_5^+ + d_5^- &= 300 \text{ Goal5} \end{aligned}$$
x_1, x_2, all deviation variables ≥ 0

$x_1 = 120$ and $x_2 = 120$

b. Objective function becomes:

$$\text{Min } P_1(d_1^-) + P_1(2d_2^-) + P_2(d_3^+)$$

Optimal solution does not change since it is possible to achieve both goals 1 and 2 in the original problem.

6

Scoring Calculations				
		Analyst	Policy advisor	Forecaster
Criteria		Frankfurt	London	Amsterdam
Career Advancement		35	20	20
Location		10	12	8
Management		30	25	35
Salary		28	32	16
Prestige		32	20	24
Job Security		8	10	16
Enjoy the Work		28	20	20
Score		171	139	139

The analyst position in Frankfurt is recommended.

8 Park Shore is the preferred property.

10 Synthesization
Step 1: Column totals are 17/4, 31/21, and 12
Step 2:

Style	Accord	Saturn	Cavalier
Accord	4/17	7/31	4/12
Saturn	12/17	21/31	7/12
Cavalier	1/17	3/31	1/12

Step 3:

Style	Accord	Saturn	Cavalier	Row Average
Accord	0.235	0.226	0.333	0.265
Saturn	0.706	0.677	0.583	0.656
Cavalier	0.059	0.097	0.083	0.080

Consistency Ratio
Step 1:

$$0.265\begin{bmatrix}1\\3\\1/4\end{bmatrix}+0.656\begin{bmatrix}1/3\\1\\1/7\end{bmatrix}+0.080\begin{bmatrix}4\\7\\1\end{bmatrix}$$

$$\begin{bmatrix}0.265\\0.795\\0.066\end{bmatrix}+\begin{bmatrix}0.219\\0.656\\0.094\end{bmatrix}+\begin{bmatrix}0.320\\0.560\\0.080\end{bmatrix}=\begin{bmatrix}0.802\\2.007\\0.239\end{bmatrix}$$

Step 2:

$$0.802/0.265 = 3.028$$
$$2.007/0.656 = 3.062$$
$$0.239/0.080 = 3.007$$

Step 3: $\lambda_{max} = (3.028 + 3.062 + 3.007)/3 = 3.032$
Step 4: CI = (3.032 − 3)/2 = 0.016
Step 5: CR = 0.016/0.58 = 0.028
Since CR = 0.028 is less than 0.10, the degree of consistency exhibited in the pairwise comparison matrix for style is acceptable.

12 a.

Flavour	A	B	C
A	1	3	2
B	1/3	1	5
C	1/2	1/5	1

b. Step 1: Column totals are 11/6, 21/5, and 8
Step 2:

Flavour	A	B	C
A	6/11	15/21	2/8
B	2/11	5/21	5/8
C	3/11	1/21	1/8

Step 3:

Flavour	A	B	C	Row Average
A	0.545	0.714	0.250	0.503
B	0.182	0.238	0.625	0.348
C	0.273	0.048	0.125	0.148

c. Step 1:

$$0.503\begin{bmatrix}1\\1/3\\1/2\end{bmatrix}+0.348\begin{bmatrix}3\\1\\1/5\end{bmatrix}+0.148\begin{bmatrix}2\\5\\1\end{bmatrix}$$

Weighted Sum:

$$\begin{bmatrix}0.503\\0.168\\0.252\end{bmatrix}+\begin{bmatrix}1.044\\0.348\\0.070\end{bmatrix}+\begin{bmatrix}0.296\\0.740\\0.148\end{bmatrix}=\begin{bmatrix}1.845\\1.258\\0.470\end{bmatrix}$$

Step 2: $1.845/0.503 = 3.668$
$1.258/0.348 = 3.615$
$0.470/0.148 = 3.123$

Step 3: $\lambda_{max} = (3.668 + 3.615 + 3.123)/3 = 3.469$
Step 4: CI = (3.469 − 3)/2 = 0.235
Step 5: CR = 0.235/0.58 = 0.415
Since CR = 0.415 is greater than 0.10, the individual's judgements are not consistent.

14 a. Laptops in order: 4, 1, 2, 3
b. Since CR = 0.083 is less than 0.10, the judgements are consistent.

15 a. Criteria: Yield and Risk
Step 1: Column totals are 1.5 and 3
Step 2:

Criterion	Yield	Risk	Priority
Yield	0.667	0.667	0.667
Risk	0.333	0.333	0.333

With only two criteria, CR = 0 and no computation of CR is made.
The same calculations for the Yield and the Risk pairwise comparison matrices provide the following:

Stocks	Yield Priority	Risk Priority
CCC	0.750	0.333
SRI	0.250	0.667

b. Overall Priorities:

CCC 0.667(0.750) + 0.333(0.333) = 0.611
SRI 0.667(0.250) + 0.333(0.667) = 0.389

CCC is preferred.

16 a.

Candidate	Leadership Priority	Personal Priority	Administrative Priority
Jacobs	0.800	0.250	0.667
Martin	0.200	0.750	0.333

b. Overall Priorities:

Jacobs $0.128(0.800) + 0.512(0.250) + 0.360(0.667) = 0.470$
Martin $0.128(0.200) + 0.512(0.250) + 0.360(0.333) = 0.530$

Martin is preferred.

Glossary

100 per cent rule A rule indicating when simultaneous changes in two or more objective function coefficients will not cause a change in the optimal solution. It can also be applied to indicate when two or more right-hand-side changes will not cause a change in any of the dual prices.

Activities Specific jobs or tasks that are parts of a project.

AHP See Analytic Hierarchy Process.

Alternative optimal solution The case in which more than one solution provides the optimal value for the objective function.

All-integer linear programme An integer linear programme in which all variables are required to be integer.

Analytic hierarchy process (AHP) An approach to multicriteria decision making based on pairwise comparisons for elements in a hierarchy.

Arcs The lines connecting the nodes in a network.

Arrival rate In a queuing system the number of arrivals within a given time period.

Artificial variable In linear programming, a variable that is added to a constraint taking the form $\geq$ or $=$ to enable a basic feasible solution to be created for starting the simplex method.

Assignment model A type of mathematical programming model where agents are assigned to tasks

Assignment problem A class of optimization problems where agents are to be assigned to tasks to optimize a given objective function.

Backorder In stock control models, the receipt of an order for a product when no units are in inventory. These backorders become shortages, which are eventually satisfied when a new supply of the product becomes available.

Backward pass Part of the PERT/CPM project planning procedure that involves moving backward through the network to determine the latest start and latest finish times for each activity.

Basic feasible solution In mathematical programming, a basic solution that is also feasible; that is, it satisfies the nonnegativity constraints. A basic feasible solution corresponds to an extreme point.

Basic solution Given a linear programme in standard form, with n variables and m constraints, a basic solution is obtained by setting n-m of the variables equal to zero and solving the constraint equations for the values of the other m variables. If a unique solution exists, it is a basic solution.

Basic variable One of the m variables not required to equal zero in a basic solution. In mathematical programming, the set of variables that are not restricted to equal zero in the current basic solution. The variables that make up the basis are termed basic variables, and the remaining variables are called nonbasic variables.

Bayes' theorem A theorem that enables the use of sample information to revise prior probabilities.

Beta probability distribution A probability distribution used to describe project activity times.

Binary integer programme An all-integer or mixed-integer linear programme in which the integer variables are only permitted to assume the values 0 or 1. Also called 0-1 integer programme.

Binding constraint In mathematical programming a binding constraint is one that passes through the optimal solution and therefore binds, or restricts, the solution from improving further.

Branch Lines showing the alternatives from decision nodes and the outcomes from chance nodes.

Branch and bound In integer programming a solution method for finding the optimal solution by keeping the best solution found so far. If a partial solution cannot improve on the best, it is abandoned.

Breakeven point The volume at which total revenue equals total cost.

Calling population The population of customers or units that may seek service in a queueing situation.

Canonical form for a maximization problem A maximization problem with all less-than- or-equal-to constraints and nonnegativity requirements for the decision variables.

Canonical form for a minimization problem A minimization problem with all greater-than- or-equal-to constraints and nonnegativity requirements for the decision variables.

Capacitated transportation problem A variation of the basic transportation problem in which some or all of the arcs are subject to capacity constraints.

Chance event An uncertain future event affecting the consequence, or payoff, associated with a decision.

Chance nodes Nodes indicating points where an uncertain event will occur.

Coefficient of determination A statistical measure of the strength of the relationship between variables in a regression equation.

Conditional probabilities The probability of one event given the known outcome of a (possibly) related event.

Consequence The result obtained when a decision alternative is chosen and a chance event occurs. A measure of the consequence is often called a payoff.

Conservative approach An approach to choosing a decision alternative without using probabilities. For a maximization problem, it leads to choosing the decision alternative that maximizes the minimum payoff; for a minimization problem, it leads to choosing the decision alternative that minimizes the maximum payoff.

Constraint A restriction or limitation imposed on a problem. In a mathematical programming model a mathematical relationship that imposes a restriction on possible solutions to the problem.

Correlation A statistical measure of the strength of a relationship between two variables in regression analysis.

CPM Critical Path Method.

Crashing The shortening of project activity times by adding resources and hence usually increasing cost.

Critical activities The activities on the critical path of a project network.

Critical path The longest path in a project network.

Critical path method (CPM) A network-based project scheduling procedure.

Data envelopment analysis (DEA) A linear programming application used to measure the relative efficiency of operating units with the same goals and objectives.

Decision nodes Nodes indicating points where a decision is made.

Decision strategy A strategy involving a sequence of decisions and chance outcomes to provide the optimal solution to a decision problem.

Decision tree A graphical representation of the decision problem that shows the sequential nature of the decision-making process.

Decision variable A controllable value for a linear programming model.

Degeneracy In mathematical programming, when one or more of the basic variables has a value of zero.

Deterministic A decision situation where there is no uncertainty.

Deterministic inventory model A model where demand is considered known and not subject to uncertainty.

Deviation variables Variables that are added to the goal equation to allow the solution to deviate from the goal's target value.

Discrete-event simulation model A simulation model that describes how a system evolves over time by using events that occur at discrete points in time.

Dual price The change in the value of the objective function per unit increase in the right-hand side of a constraint.

Dual problem A linear programming problem related to the primal problem. Solution of the dual also provides the solution to the primal.

Dual value At the optimal solution point, the change in the value of the objective function for a unit change in the right hand side of the constraint.

Dual variable The variable in a dual linear programming problem. Its optimal value provides the dual price for the associated primal resource.

Dummy activity A branch that is required to construct the CPM network but that takes zero time to complete.

Dummy destination A destination added to a transportation problem to make the total supply equal to the total demand. The demand assigned to the dummy destination is the difference between the total supply and the total demand.

Dummy origin An origin added to a transportation problem in order to make the total supply equal to the total demand. The supply assigned to the dummy origin is the difference between the total demand and the total supply.

Dynamic simulation model A simulation model used in situations where the state of the system affects how the system changes or evolves over time.

Earliest finish time The earliest time a project activity may be completed.

Earliest start time The earliest time a project activity may begin.

Economic order quantity (EOQ) The order quantity that minimizes the annual holding cost plus the annual ordering cost.

Expected time The average time a project activity is expected to take.

Expected utility approach An approach that considers the expected utility for each decision alternative and then selects the decision alternative yielding the highest expected utility

Expected value (EV) For a chance node, it is the weighted average of the payoffs. The weights are the state-of-nature probabilities.

Expected value approach An approach to choosing a decision alternative based on the expected value of each decision alternative. The recommended decision alternative is the one that provides the best expected value.

Expected value of perfect information (EVPI) The expected value of information that would tell the decision maker exactly which state of nature is going to occur (i.e., perfect information).

Exponential probability distribution A probability distribution used to describe the service time for some waiting line models.

Extreme point Graphically speaking, extreme points are the feasible solution points occurring at the vertices or 'corners' of the feasible region. With two-variable problems, extreme points are determined by the intersection of the constraint lines.

Feasible region The set of all feasible solutions.

Feasible solution A solution that satisfies all the constraints.

First-come, first-served (FCFS) The queue discipline that serves waiting units on a first come, first-served basis.

Float The length of time an activity can be delayed without affecting the project completion time.

Flow capacity The maximum flow for an arc of the network. The flow capacity in one direction may not equal the flow capacity in the reverse direction.

Forward pass Part of the PERT/CPM procedure that involves moving forward through the project network to determine the earliest start and earliest finish times for each activity.

Gantt chart A graph showing time information for each activity in a project.

Goal programming A linear programming approach to multicriteria decision problems whereby the objective function is designed to minimize the deviations from goals.

Goodwill cost A cost associated with a backorder, a lost sale or any form of stock-out or unsatisfied demand. This cost may be used to reflect the loss of future profits because a customer experienced an unsatisfied demand.

Hard MS Quantitative analysis and modelling approaches used in management science.

Heuristic A common-sense procedure for quickly finding a solution to a problem. Heuristics are used to find initial feasible solutions for the transportation simplex method and in other applications.

Holding cost The cost associated with maintaining an inventory investment, including the cost of the capital investment in the inventory, insurance, taxes, warehouse overhead and so on. This cost may be stated as a percentage of the inventory investment or as a cost per unit.

Hungarian method A special-purpose solution procedure for solving an assignment problem.

Iconic model A physical replica or prototype, often scaled down, of a real object that may be impractical or expensive to build full scale (such as a vehicle or aeroplane).

Infeasibility The situation in which no solution to the problem satisfies all the constraints.

Interpretation The stage at which findings from the problem solution are translated into usable information.

Inventory The stock of an item kept on hand to meet customer demand.

Inventory position The amount of inventory on hand plus the amount of inventory on order.

Iteration The process of moving from one basic feasible solution to another.

Joint probability The probability of several events occurring simultaneously.

Latest finish time The latest time an activity may be completed without increasing the project completion time.

Latest start time The latest time an activity may begin without increasing the project completion time.

Lead time The time between the placing of an order and its receipt in the inventory system.

Linear functions Mathematical expressions in which the variables appear in separate terms and are raised to the first power.

Linear programme Another term for linear programming models.

Linear programming model A mathematical model with a linear objective function, a set of linear constraints and nonnegative variables.

Linear regression A method for determining the linear equation that represents the relationship between two or more variables.

Lot size The order quantity in the production inventory model.

MAD Mean absolute deviation.

Mathematical model A representation of a problem where the objective and all constraint conditions are described by mathematical expressions.

Maximal flow The maximum amount of flow that can enter and exit a network system during a given period of time.

Minimal spanning tree The spanning tree with the minimum length.

Minimax regret approach An approach to choosing a decision alternative without using probabilities. For each alternative, the maximum regret is calculated, which leads to choosing the decision alternative that minimizes the maximum regret.

Minimum cost method A heuristic used to find an initial feasible solution to a transportation problem; it is easy to use and usually provides a good (but not optimal) solution.

Model An abstract representation of a real object or situation.

Modelling The process of translating the verbal statement of a problem into a mathematical statement.

MODI method A procedure in which a modified distribution method determines the incoming arc in the transportation simplex method.

Monte Carlo process The random selection of values from a distribution.

Most probable time The most probable activity time under normal conditions.

MSE Mean squared error.

Multicriteria decision making A situation in which there are several distinct decision criteria that must be considered in the decision making process.

Multiple-channel waiting line A queuing system with two or more parallel service facilities.

Multiple regression A regression equation between three or more variables.

Network A graphical representation of a problem consisting of numbered circles (nodes) interconnected by a series of lines (arcs); arrowheads on the arcs show the direction of flow.

Network flow model A model that shows the flows through a system.

Nodes The intersection or junction points of a network.

Nonbasic variable One of n-m variables set equal to zero in a basic solution.

Non-binding constraint In mathematical programming a non-binding constraint is one that does pass through the optimal solution and therefore does not bind, or restrict, the solution from improving further.

Nonnegativity constraints A set of constraints that requires all variables to be nonnegative.

Objective function A mathematical statement of the required objective for a decision problem.

Operating characteristics The performance measures for a queuing system including the probability that no units are in the system, the average number of units in the waiting line, the average waiting time and so on.

Opportunity cost At the optimal solution point, the change in the value of the objective function for a unit change in the right hand side of the constraint.

Opportunity loss, or regret The amount of loss (lower profit or higher cost) from not making the best decision for each state of nature.

Optimal solution The best solution to a given problem.

Optimistic approach An approach to choosing a decision alternative without using probabilities. For a maximization problem, it leads to choosing the decision alternative corresponding to the largest payoff; for a minimization problem, it leads to choosing the decision alternative corresponding to the smallest payoff.

Optimistic time The minimum activity time if everything progresses ideally.

Ordering cost The fixed cost (salaries, paper, transportation, etc.) associated with placing an order for an item.

Parameters Numerical values that appear in the mathematical relationships of a model.

PERT Programme Evaluation and Review Technique.

Payoff A measure of the consequence of a decision such as profit, cost or time. Each combination of a decision alternative and a state of nature has an associated payoff (consequence).

Payoff table A tabular representation of the payoffs for a decision problem.

Pessimistic time The maximum activity time if significant delays are encountered.

Phase I When artificial variables are present in the initial simplex tableau, phase I refers to the iterations of the simplex method that are required to eliminate the artificial variables. At the end of phase I, the basic feasible solution in the simplex tableau is also feasible for the real problem.

Pivot column The column in the simplex tableau corresponding to the nonbasic variable that is about to be introduced into solution.

Pivot element The element of the simplex tableau that is in both the pivot row and the pivot column.

Pivot row The row in the simplex tableau corresponding to the basic variable that will leave the solution.

Poisson probability distribution A probability distribution used to describe the arrival pattern for some waiting line models.

Posterior (revised) probabilities The probabilities of the states of nature after revising the prior probabilities based on sample information.

Preemptive priorities Priorities assigned to goals that ensure that the satisfaction of a higher level goal cannot be traded for the satisfaction of a lower level goal.

Primal problem The original formulation of a linear programming problem.

Prior probabilities The probabilities of the states of nature prior to obtaining sample information.

Probabilistic inventory model A model where demand is not known exactly; probabilities must be associated with the possible values for demand.

Problem formulation The process of translating the verbal statement of a problem into a mathematical statement called the mathematical model.

Problem solution The stage at which an answer to the specific decision problem is found.

Programme evaluation and review technique (PERT) A network-based project scheduling procedure.

Project network A graphical representation of a project that depicts the activities and shows the predecessor relationships among the activities.

Qualitative forecasting Non-quantitative subjective forecasting methods.

Quantity discounts Discounts or lower unit costs offered by the manufacturer when a customer purchases larger quantities of the product.

Queue discipline The order in which customers waiting in a queue are served.

Range of feasibility The range of values over which the dual price is applicable.

Range of optimality The range of values over which an objective function coefficient may vary without causing any change in the values of the decision variables in the optimal solution.

Reduced cost The amount by which an objective function coefficient would have to improve (increase for a maximization problem, decrease for a minimization problem) before it would be possible for the corresponding variable to assume a positive value in the optimal solution.

Redundant constraint A constraint that does not affect the feasible region. If a constraint is redundant, it can be removed from the problem without affecting the feasible region.

Relevant cost A cost that depends on the decision made. The amount will vary depending on the values of the decision variables.

Reorder point The inventory position at which a new order should be placed.

Risk analysis The process of predicting the outcome of a decision in the face of uncertainty.

Safety stock Inventory maintained in order to reduce the number of stock-outs resulting from higher-than-expected demand.

Scoring model An approach to multicriteria decision making that requires the user to assign weights to each criterion that describes the criterion's relative importance and to assign a rating that shows how well each decision alternative satisfies each criterion. The output is a score for each decision alternative.

Sensitivity analysis The study of how changes in the coefficients of problems affect the optimal solution.

Service rate The average number of customers or units that can be served by one service facility in a given period of time.

Setup cost The fixed cost (labour, materials, lost production) associated with preparing for a new production run.

Shadow price At the optimal solution point, the change in the value of the objective function for a unit change in the right hand side of the constraint.

Shortage or stock-out Demand that cannot be supplied from inventory.

Shortest route Shortest path between two nodes in a network.

Simplex method A common algebraic procedure for solving linear programming problems.

Simplex tableau A table used to keep track of the calculations required by the simplex method.

Simulation A method for learning about a real system by experimenting with a model that represents the system.

Single-channel queuing system A queuing system with only one service facility.

Slack variable A variable added to the left-hand side of a less-than-or-equal-to constraint to convert the constraint into an equality. The value of this variable can usually be interpreted as the amount of unused resource.

Soft MS Qualitative analysis and modelling approaches used in management science.

Spanning tree A set of N - 1 arcs that connects every node in the network with all other nodes where N is the number of nodes.

Standard form A linear programme in which all the constraints are written as equalities. The optimal solution of the standard form of a linear programme is the same as the optimal solution of the original formulation of the linear programme.

States of nature The possible outcomes for chance events that affect the payoff associated with a decision alternative.

Static simulation model A simulation model used in situations where the state of the system at one point in time does not affect the state of the system at future points in time. Each trial of the simulation is independent.

Steady-state operation The normal operation of a queuing system after it has gone through a start-up or transient period. The operating characteristics of queues are calculated for steady-state conditions.

Stepping-stone method Using a sequence or path of occupied cells to identify flow adjustments necessary when flow is assigned to an unused arc in the transportation simplex method. This identifies the outgoing arc.

Stochastic (probabilistic) A model in which at least one uncontrollable input is uncertain and subject to variation; stochastic models are also referred to as probabilistic models.

Stockout cost The cost involved when customer demand cannot be met because of insufficient inventory.

Sunk cost A cost that is not affected by the decision made. It will be incurred no matter what values the decision variables assume.

Surplus variable A variable subtracted from the left-hand side of a greater-than-or equal-to constraint to convert the constraint into an equality. The value of this variable can usually be interpreted as the amount over and above some required minimum level.

Tableau form The form in which a linear programme must be written before setting up the initial simplex tableau. When a linear programme is written in tableau form, its A matrix contains m unit columns corresponding to the basic variables, and the values of these basic variables are given by the values in the b column. A further requirement is that the entries in the b column be greater than or equal to zero.

Transient period The start-up period for a queuing system, occurring before the queue reaches a normal or steady-state operation.

Transportation problem A network flow problem that often involves minimizing the cost of shipping goods from a set of origins to a set of destinations; it can be formulated and solved as a linear programme by including a variable for each arc and a constraint for each node or solved using a specialized algorithm.

Transportation tableau A table representing a transportation problem in which each cell corresponds to a variable, or arc.

Transshipment problem An extension of the transportation problem to distribution problems involving transfer points and possible shipments between any pair of nodes.

Unbounded If the value of the solution may be made infinitely large in a maximization linear programming problem or infinitely small in a minimization problem without violating any of the constraints, the problem is said to be unbounded.

Unit column or unit vector A vector or column of a matrix that has a zero in every position except one. In the nonzero position there is a 1. There is a unit column in the simplex tableau for each basic variable.

Utility A measure of the total worth of an outcome reflecting a decision maker's attitude toward considerations such as profit and loss and intangibles such as risk.

Index